W9-AHE-280

ACCOUNTING CONCEPTS (Chapters 2–4)

Characteristics	Assumptions	Principles	Constraints
Relevance	Monetary unit	Cost	Materiality
Reliability	Economic entity	Full disclosure	Conservatism
Comparability	Time period	Revenue recognition	
Consistency	Going concern	Matching	

INVENTORY (Chapters 5 and 6)

Ownership

Freight Terms	Ownership of goods on public carrier resides with:
FOB Shipping point	Buyer
FOB Destination	Seller

BASIC ACCOUNTING EQUATION (Chapter 3)

Basic Equation	Assets = Liabilities + Stockholders' Equity

Expanded Basic Equation	Assets	=	Liabilities	+	Common Stock	+	Retained Earnings	−	Dividends	+	Revenues	−	Expenses
Debit / Credit Rules	Dr. + / Cr. −		Dr. − / Cr. +		Dr. − / Cr. +		Dr. − / Cr. +		Dr. + / Cr. −		Dr. − / Cr. +		Dr. + / Cr. −

ADJUSTING ENTRIES (Chapter 4)

	Type	Adjusting Entry	
Deferrals	1. Prepaid expenses	Dr. Expenses	Cr. Assets
	2. Unearned revenues	Dr. Liabilities	Cr. Revenues
Accruals	1. Accrued revenues	Dr. Assets	Cr. Revenues
	2. Accrued expenses	Dr. Expenses	Cr. Liabilities

Note: Each adjusting entry will affect one or more income statement accounts and one or more balance sheet accounts.

Interest Computation

Interest = Face value of note × Annual interest rate × Time in terms of one year

CLOSING ENTRIES (Chapter 4)

Purpose

1. Update the Retained Earnings account in the ledger by transferring net income (loss) and dividends to retained earnings.
2. Prepare the temporary accounts (revenue, expense, dividends) for the next period's postings by reducing their balances to zero.

ACCOUNTING CYCLE (Chapter 4)

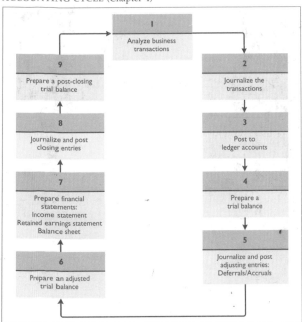

Perpetual vs. Periodic Journal Entries

Event	Perpetual	Periodic
Purchase of goods	Inventory Cash (A/P)	Purchases Cash (A/P)
Freight (shipping point)	Inventory Cash	Freight In Cash
Return of goods	Cash (or A/P) Inventory	Cash (or A/P) Purchase Returns and Allowances
Sale of goods	Cash (or A/R) Sales Cost of Goods Sold Inventory	Cash (or A/R) Sales No entry
End of period	No entry	Closing or adjusting entry required

FRAUD, INTERNAL CONTROL, AND CASH (Chapter 7)

Principles of Internal Control

Establishment of responsibility
Segregation of duties
Documentation procedures
Physical controls
Independent internal verification
Human resource controls

The Fraud Triangle

Opportunity

Financial pressure — Rationalization

Bank Reconciliation

Bank	Books
Balance per bank statement Add: Deposits in transit	Balance per books Add: Unrecorded credit memoranda from bank statement
Deduct: Outstanding checks	Deduct: Unrecorded debit memoranda from bank statement
Adjusted cash balance	Adjusted cash balance

Note: 1. Errors should be offset (added or deducted) on the side that made the error.
2. Adjusting journal entries should only be made for items affecting books.

STOP AND CHECK: Does the adjusted cash balance in the Cash account equal the reconciled balance?

Chapter Content

RECEIVABLES (Chapter 8)

Two Methods to Account for Uncollectible Accounts

Direct write-off method	Record bad debts expense when the company determines a particular account to be uncollectible.
Allowance method	At the end of each period estimate the amount of uncollectible receivables. Debit Bad Debts Expense and credit Allowance for Doubtful Accounts in an amount that results in a balance in the allowance account equal to the estimate of uncollectibles. As specific accounts become uncollectible, debit Allowance for Doubtful Accounts and credit Accounts Receivable.

Steps to Manage Accounts Receivable

1. Determine to whom to extend credit.
2. Establish a payment period.
3. Monitor collections.
4. Evaluate the receivables balance.
5. Accelerate cash receipts from receivables when necessary.

PLANT ASSETS (Chapter 9)

Computation of Annual Depreciation Expense

Straight-line	$\dfrac{\text{Cost} - \text{Salvage value}}{\text{Useful life (in years)}}$
*Declining-balance	Book value at beginning of year $\times$ Declining balance rate* *Declining-balance rate = 1 $\div$ Useful life (in years)
*Units-of-activity	$\dfrac{\text{Depreciable cost}}{\text{Useful life (in units)}} \times$ Units of activity during year

Note: If depreciation is calculated for partial periods, the straight-line and declining-balance methods must be adjusted for the relevant proportion of the year. Multiply the annual depreciation expense by the number of months expired in the year divided by 12 months.

BONDS (Chapter 10)

Premium	Market interest rate < Contractual interest rate
Face Value	Market interest rate = Contractual interest rate
Discount	Market interest rate > Contractual interest rate

Computation of Annual Bond Interest Expense

Interest expense = Interest paid (payable) + Amortization of discount
(OR − Amortization of premium)

*Straight-line amortization	$\dfrac{\text{Bond discount (premium)}}{\text{Number of interest periods}}$	
*Effective-interest amortization (preferred method)	Bond interest expense	Bond interest paid
	Carrying value of bonds at beginning of period $\times$ Effective interest rate	Face amount of bonds $\times$ Contractual interest rate

STOCKHOLDERS' EQUITY (Chapter 11)

No-Par Value vs. Par Value Stock Journal Entries

No-Par Value	Par Value

Cash
    Common Stock
	Cash
	    Common Stock (par value)
	    Paid-in Capital in Excess of Par Value

Comparison of Dividend Effects

	Cash	Common Stock	Retained Earnings
Cash dividend	↓	No effect	↓
Stock dividend	No effect	↑	↓
Stock split	No effect	No effect	No effect

STATEMENT OF CASH FLOWS (Chapter 12)

Cash flows from operating activities (**indirect method**)

Net income		
Add:	Amortization and depreciation	$ X
	Losses on disposals of assets	X
	Decreases in current assets	X
	Increases in current liabilities	X
Deduct:	Increases in current assets	(X)
	Decreases in current liabilities	(X)
	Gains on disposals of assets	(X)
Cash provided (used) by operating activities		$ X

Cash flows from operating activities (**direct method**)

Cash receipts
(Examples: from sales of goods and services to customers, from receipts of interest and dividends) $ X
Cash payments
(Examples: to suppliers, for operating expenses, for interest, for taxes)   (X)
Cash provided (used) by operating activities $ X

FINANCIAL STATEMENT ANALYSIS (Chapter 13)

Discontinued operations	Income statement (presented separately after "Income from continuing operations")
Extraordinary items	Income statement (presented separately after "Discontinued operations")
Changes in accounting principle	In most instances, use the new method in current period and restate previous years results using new method. For changes in depreciation and amortization methods, use the new method in the current period, but do not restate previous periods.

Income Statement and Comprehensive Income

Sales	$ XX
Cost of goods sold	XX
Gross profit	XX
Operating expenses	XX
Income from operations	XX
Other revenues (expenses) and gains (losses)	XX
Income before income taxes	XX
Income tax expense	XX
Income before irregular items	XX
Irregular items (net of tax)	**XX**
Net income	**XX**
Other comprehensive income items (net of tax)	**XX**
Comprehensive income	**$ XX**

INVESTMENTS (Appendix D)

Comparison of Long-Term Bond Investment and Liability Journal Entries

Event	Investor	Investee

Purchase / issue of bonds	Debt Investments
	    Cash
		Cash
		    Bonds Payable

Interest receipt / payment	Cash
	    Interest Revenue
		Interest Expense
		    Cash

Comparison of Cost and Equity Methods of Accounting for Long-Term Stock Investments

Event	Cost	Equity

Acquisition	Stock Investments
	    Cash
		Stock Investments
		    Cash

Investee reports earnings	No entry	Stock Investments Investment Revenue

Investee pays dividends	Cash
	    Dividend Revenue
		Cash
		    Stock Investments

*Items with asterisk are covered in appendix.

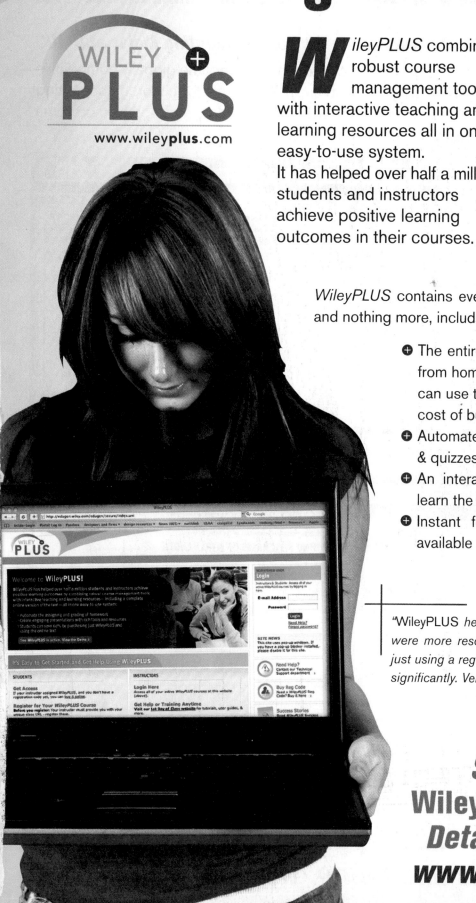

Why WileyPLUS for Accounting?

WileyPLUS helps today's students succeed in the classroom and become globally competitive with step-by-step instruction, instant feedback, and support material to reinforce accounting concepts. Instructors can easily monitor progress by student or by class, and spend more time teaching and less time grading homework.

➕ **WileyPLUS** *links students directly from homework problems to specific sections of their online text to read about specific topics.*

➕ *Students can also link to contextual help such as interactive tutorials, chapter reviews, and demonstration problems; simulations; and video for visual review or help when they need it most.*

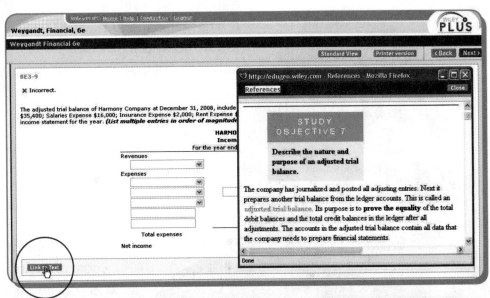

WILEY PLUS
www.wileyplus.com

See and try WileyPLUS in action!
Details and Demo: www.wileyplus.com

WileyPLUS combines robust course management tools with the complete online text and all of the interactive teaching and learning resources you and your students need in one easy to use system.

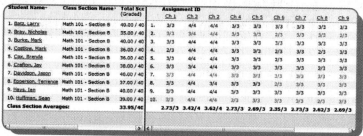

ABE3-3

Windsor Advertising Company's trial balance at December 31 shows Advertising Supplies $6,200 and Advertising Supplies Expense $0. On December 31, there are $3,000 of supplies on hand.

Prepare the adjusting entry at December 31.

Date	Account / Description	Debit	Credit
Dec. 31		$	
			$

Using T accounts, enter the balances in the accounts, post the adjusting entry, and indicate the adjusted balance in each account.
(If an amount should be blank enter a 0 all boxes must be filled to be correct.)

Advertising Supplies

| 12/31 | | 12/31 | |
| 12/31 Bal. | | 12/31 Bal. | |

Advertising Supplies Expense

| 12/31 | | 12/31 | |

Show Solution   Show Answer

Link to Text

Question Attempts: 0 of 3 used   Save for later   Submit Answer

BE3-3

Windsor Advertising Company's trial balance at December 31 shows Advertising Supplies $6,700 and Advertising Supplies Expense $0. On December 31, there are $2,700 of supplies on hand.

Prepare the adjusting entry at December 31.

Date	Account /Description	Debit	Credit
Dec. 31		$	
			$

Using T accounts, enter the balances in the accounts, post the adjusting entry, and indicate the adjusted balance in each account.
(If an amount should be blank enter a 0 all boxes must be filled to be correct.)

Advertising Supplies

| 12/31 | | 12/31 | |
| 12/31 Bal. | | 12/31 Bal. | |

Advertising Supplies Expense

| 12/31 | | 12/31 | |

Show Solution   Show Answer

Link to Text

Question Attempts: 0 of 3 used   Save for later   Submit Answer

➕ *Algorithmically generated, end-of-chapter exercises and problems allow a number of students to take the same assignment with differing variables.*

Student Name	Class Section Name	Total Sce (Graded)	Assignment ID Ch 1	Ch 2	Ch 3	Ch 4	Ch 5	Ch 6	Ch 7	Ch 8	Ch 9
1. Batz, Larry	Math 101 - Section B	40.00 / 40	1. 3/3	4/4	4/4	3/3	3/3	3/3	3/3	3/3	3/3
2. Bray, Nicholas	Math 101 - Section B	35.00 / 40	2. 3/3	3/4	4/4	3/3	3/3	2/3	3/3	3/3	2/3
3. Burke, Mark	Math 101 - Section B	40.00 / 40	3. 3/3	4/4	4/4	3/3	3/3	3/3	3/3	3/3	3/3
4. Costlow, Mark	Math 101 - Section B	36.00 / 40	4. 2/3	4/4	4/4	3/3	3/3	2/3	3/3	2/3	3/3
5. Cox, Brenda	Math 101 - Section B	36.00 / 40	5. 3/3	4/4	4/4	3/3	3/3	2/3	3/3	3/3	3/3
6. Crafton, Jay	Math 101 - Section B	38.00 / 40	6. 3/3	4/4	4/4	3/3	3/3	3/3	3/3	2/3	3/3
7. Davidson, Jason	Math 101 - Section B	40.00 / 40	7. 3/3	4/4	4/4	3/3	3/3	3/3	3/3	3/3	3/3
8. Epperson, Terrence	Math 101 - Section B	37.00 / 40	8. 3/3	4/4	3/4	3/3	3/3	2/3	3/3	3/3	3/3
9. Hays, Ian	Math 101 - Section B	40.00 / 40	9. 3/3	4/4	4/4	3/3	3/3	3/3	3/3	3/3	3/3
10. Huffman, Sean	Math 101 - Section B	39.00 / 40	10. 4/4	4/4	4/4	3/3	3/3	3/3	3/3	2/3	2/3
Class Section Averages:		**33.95/40**	2.73/3	3.42/4	3.62/4	2.73/3	2.69/3	2.35/3	2.73/3	2.62/3	2.69/3

Gradebook >> **Results of Terrence Epperson**

Math 101 - Section B

ID	Assignment Name	Assignment Type	Progress	Score	Details	Student Accessibility	Saved to Gradebook
Ch 1	Ch 1: Welcome to WileyPLUS	Questions	-	3/3	Attempted; Due Date Reached	Yes	12 04 2006, 05:50 AM
Ch 3	Ch 3: WileyPLUS Performance Metrics	Questions	-	4/4	Attempted; Due Date Reached	Yes	12 05 2006, 08:57 AM
Ch 2	Ch 2: The History of WileyPLUS	Questions	-	3/4	Attempted; Due Date Reached	Yes	12 04 2006, 10:11 AM
Ch 4	Ch 4: Why WileyPLUS Matters	Questions	-	3/3	Attempted; Due Date Reached	Yes	12 05 2006, 09:27 AM
Ch 5	Ch 5: Developing a WileyPLUS Course	Questions	-	3/3	Attempted; Due Date Reached	Yes	12 05 2006, 09:31 AM
Ch 6	Ch 6: Adopting & Registering for WileyPLUS	Questions	-	2/3	Attempted After Due Date	Yes	12 30 2006, 07:59 AM
Ch 7	Ch 7: Help & Support for WileyPLUS	Questions	-	3/3	Attempted After Due Date	Yes	12 30 2006, 08:05 AM
Ch 8	Ch 8: Read, Study & Practice	Questions	-	3/3	Attempted After Due Date	Yes	12 30 2006, 08:14 AM
Ch 9	Ch 9: Assignments - Part I	Questions	-	3/3	Attempted After Due Date	Yes	12 30 2006, 08:35 AM
Ch 10	Ch 10: Assignments - Part II	Questions	-	4/4	Attempted After Due Date	Yes	12 30 2006, 09:21 AM
Ch 11	Ch 11: Prepare & Present	Questions	-	2/3	Attempted; Due Date Reached	Yes	12 30 2006, 09:26 AM
Ch 12	Ch 12: Gradebook	Questions	-	4/4	Attempted; Due Date Reached	Yes	12 30 2006, 09:32 AM
		Total	**0%**	**37.00/40**			

➕ *Assessment and Homework Management tools help instructors monitor students' progress individually—or by class.*

"I received an A in accounting because WileyPLUS helped me understand the material by practicing."
— Student Crista Dixon, University of Nevada, Reno

WILEY PLUS

www.wileyplus.com

www.wileyplus.com

Wiley is committed to making your entire *WileyPLUS* experience productive & enjoyable by providing the help, resources, and personal support you & your students need, when you need it. It's all here: www.wileyplus.com –

TECHNICAL SUPPORT:

- ➕ A fully searchable knowledge base of FAQs and help documentation, available 24/7
- ➕ Live chat with a trained member of our support staff during business hours
- ➕ A form to fill out and submit online to ask any question and get a quick response
- ➕ **Instructor-only** phone line during business hours: 1.877.586.0192

FACULTY-LED TRAINING THROUGH THE WILEY FACULTY NETWORK:
Register online: www.wherefacultyconnect.com
Connect with your colleagues in a complimentary virtual seminar, with a personal mentor in your field, or at a live workshop to share best practices for teaching with technology.

1ST DAY OF CLASS...AND BEYOND!
Resources You & Your Students Need to Get Started & Use *WileyPLUS* from the first day forward.

- ➕ 2-Minute Tutorials on how to set up & maintain your *WileyPLUS* course
- ➕ User guides, links to technical support & training options
- ➕ *WileyPLUS for Dummies*: Instructors' quick reference guide to using *WileyPLUS*
- ➕ Student tutorials & instruction on how to register, buy, and use *WileyPLUS*

YOUR *WileyPLUS* ACCOUNT MANAGER:
Your personal *WileyPLUS* connection for any assistance you need!

SET UP YOUR *WileyPLUS* COURSE IN MINUTES!
Selected *WileyPLUS* courses with QuickStart contain pre-loaded assignments & presentations created by subject matter experts who are also experienced *WileyPLUS* users.

Interested? See and try WileyPLUS in action!
Details and Demo: www.wileyplus.com

Financial Accounting

Tools for Business Decision Making

PAUL D. KIMMEL PhD, CPA
University of Wisconsin—Milwaukee

JERRY J. WEYGANDT PhD, CPA
University of Wisconsin

DONALD E. KIESO PhD, CPA
Northern Illinois University

WILEY

John Wiley & Sons, Inc.

Dedicated to our wives,
Merlynn, Enid, and Donna,
and to our children,
Croix, Marais, and Kale; Matt, Erin, and Lia;
and Douglas and Debra

Publisher   George Hoffman
Associate Publisher   Christopher DeJohn
Associate Editor   Brian Kamins
Senior Marketing Manager   Julia Flohr
Senior Media Editor   Allie K. Morris
Project Editor   Ed Brislin
Assistant Marketing Manager   Carly DeCandia
Production Services Manager   Dorothy Sinclair
Senior Production Editor   Trish McFadden
Production Management   Ingrao Associates
Creative Director   Harry Nolan
Senior Designer   Madelyn Lesure
Senior Photo Editor   Elle Wagner
Cover Designer   Madelyn Lesure
Editorial Assistant   Kara Taylor
Marketing Assistant   Alana Filipovich

This book was set by Aptara®, Inc. and printed and bound by RRD. The cover was printed by RR Donnelley.

This book is printed on acid free paper. ∞

To order books or for customer service please, call 1-800-CALL WILEY (225-5945).

ISBN-13: 9780470239803

Printed in the United States of America

10 9 8 7 6 5 4 3 2 1

Dear Student,

Why This Course?
Remember your biology course in high school? Did you have one of those "invisible man" models (or maybe something more high-tech than that) that gave you the opportunity to look "inside" the human body? This accounting course offers something similar: To understand a business, you have to understand the financial insides of a business organization. An accounting course will help you understand the essential financial components of businesses. Whether you are looking at a large multinational company like Microsoft or Starbucks or a single-owner software consulting business or coffee shop, knowing the fundamentals of accounting will help you understand what is happening. As an employee, a manager, an investor, a business owner, or a manager of your own personal finances—any of which roles you will have at some point in your life—you will be much the wiser for having taken this course.

Why This Book?
Hundreds of thousands of students have used this textbook. Your instructor has chosen it for you because of its trusted reputation. The authors have worked hard to keep the book fresh, timely, and accurate.

The book contains features to help you learn best, whatever your learning style. To understand what your learning style is, spend about ten minutes to take the learning style quiz at the book's companion site, **www.wiley.com/college/kimmel**, and then look at pages xxiii to xxv for how you can apply an understanding of your learning style to this course. Then, when you know more about your own learning style, browse through the Student Owner's Manual online at the book's companion website (www.wiley.com/college/kimmel). It shows you the main features you will find in this textbook and explains their purpose.

How To Succeed?
We've asked many students and many instructors whether there is a secret for success in this course. The nearly unanimous answer turns out to be not much of a secret: "Do the homework." This is one course where doing is learning, and the more time you spend on the homework assignments—using the various tools that this book provides—the more likely you are to learn the essential concepts, techniques, and methods of accounting. Besides the textbook itself, the companion website offers various support resources.

Good luck in this course. We hope you enjoy the experience and that you put to good use throughout a lifetime of success the lessons you learn about accounting and about business! We are sure you will not be disappointed.

Paul D. Kimmel

Jerry J. Weygandt

Donald E. Kieso

about the authors

Paul D. Kimmel, PhD, CPA, received his bachelor's degree from the University of Minnesota and his doctorate in accounting from the University of Wisconsin. He is an Associate Professor at the University of Wisconsin—Milwaukee, and has public accounting experience with Deloitte & Touche (Minneapolis). He was the recipient of the UWM School of Business Advisory Council Teaching Award, the Reggie Taite Excellence in Teaching Award, and a three-time winner of the Outstanding Teaching Assistant Award at the University of Wisconsin. He is also a recipient of the Elijah Watts Sells Award for Honorary Distinction for his results on the CPA exam. He is a member of the American Accounting Association and the Institute of Management Accountants and has published articles in *Accounting Review, Accounting Horizons, Advances in Management Accounting, Managerial Finance, Issues in Accounting Education, Journal of Accounting Education*, as well as other journals. His research interests include accounting for financial instruments and innovation in accounting education. He has published papers and given numerous talks on incorporating critical thinking into accounting education, and helped prepare a catalog of critical thinking resources for the Federated Schools of Accountancy.

Jerry J. Weygandt, PhD, CPA, is Arthur Andersen Alumni Emeritus Professor of Accounting at the University of Wisconsin—Madison. He holds a Ph.D. in accounting from the University of Illinois. Articles by Professor Weygandt have appeared in the *Accounting Review, Journal of Accounting Research, Accounting Horizons, Journal of Accountancy*, and other academic and professional journals. These articles have examined such financial reporting issues as accounting for price-level adjustments, pensions, convertible securities, stock option contracts, and interim reports. Professor Weygandt is author of other accounting and financial reporting books and is a member of the American Accounting Association, the American Institute of Certified Public Accountants, and the Wisconsin Society of Certified Public Accountants. He has served on numerous committees of the American Accounting Association and as a member of the editorial board of the *Accounting Review*; he also has served as President and Secretary-Treasurer of the American Accounting Association. In addition, he has been actively involved with the American Institute of Certified Public Accountants and has been a member of the Accounting Standards Executive Committee (AcSEC) of that organization. He has served on the FASB task force that examined the reporting issues related to accounting for income taxes and served as a trustee of the Financial Accounting Foundation. Professor Weygandt has received the Chancellor's Award for Excellence in Teaching and the Beta Gamma Sigma Dean's Teaching Award. He is on the board of directors of M & I Bank of Southern Wisconsin. He is the recipient of the Wisconsin Institute of CPA's Outstanding Educator's Award and the Lifetime Achievement Award. In 2001 he received the American Accounting Association's Outstanding Accounting Educator Award.

Donald E. Kieso, PhD, CPA, received his bachelor's degree from Aurora University and his doctorate in accounting from the University of Illinois. He has served as chairman of the Department of Accountancy and is currently the KPMG Emeritus Professor of Accountancy at Northern Illinois University. He has public accounting experience with Price Waterhouse & Co. (San Francisco and Chicago) and Arthur Andersen & Co. (Chicago) and research experience with the Research Division of the American Institute of Certified Public Accountants (New York). He has done postdoctorate work as a Visiting Scholar at the University of California at Berkeley and is a recipient of NIU's Teaching Excellence Award and four Golden Apple Teaching Awards. Professor Kieso is the author of other accounting and business books and is a member of the American Accounting Association, the American Institute of Certified Public Accountants, and the Illinois CPA Society. He has served as a member of the Board of Directors of the Illinois CPA Society, the AACSB's Accounting Accreditation Committees, the State of Illinois Comptroller's Commission, as Secretary-Treasurer of the Federation of Schools of Accountancy, and as Secretary-Treasurer of the American Accounting Association. Professor Kieso is currently serving on the Board of Trustees and Executive Committee of Aurora University, as a member of the Board of Directors of Kishwaukee Community Hospital, and as Treasurer and Director of Valley West Community Hospital. From 1989 to 1993 he served as a charter member of the national Accounting Education Change Commission. He is the recipient of the Outstanding Accounting Educator Award from the Illinois CPA Society, the FSA's Joseph A. Silvoso Award of Merit, the NIU Foundation's Humanitarian Award for Service to Higher Education, a Distinguished Service Award from the Illinois CPA Society, and in 2003 an honorary doctorate from Aurora University.

preface

The goal of this text is to introduce students to accounting in a way that demonstrates the importance of accounting to society and the relevance of accounting to their future careers. We strive to teach the students those things that they really need to know and to do it in a way that maximizes their opportunities for successful completion of the course. To accomplish these goals, the foundation of this text relies on a few key beliefs.

"It really matters" The collapse of Enron, WorldCom, Arthur Andersen, and others had devastating consequences. A number of the book's features are designed to reveal accounting's critical role to society: Some of the *Feature Stories*, the *Ethics Insight* boxes, end-of-chapter *Ethics Cases* and *Research Cases*, and the new *Anatomy of a Fraud* boxes introduce students to the important effects of accounting on business and society. In short, it has never been more apparent that accounting really matters.

"Less is more" Our instructional objective is to provide students with an understanding of those core concepts that are fundamental to the use of accounting. Most students will forget procedural details within a short period of time. On the other hand, students should remember well-taught concepts for a lifetime. Concepts are especially important in a world where the details are constantly changing.

"Don't just sit there—do something" The overriding pedagogical objective of this book is to provide students with continual opportunities for active learning. One of the best tools for active learning is strategically placed questions and activities. Our discussions are framed by questions, often beginning with rhetorical questions and ending with review questions. Our analytical devices, called *Decision Toolkits*, use key questions to demonstrate the purpose of each. Also, the "Do It" exercises, considerably expanded in this edition, invite students to practice concepts and techniques just covered in the text.

"Get real" Students will be most willing to commit time and energy to a topic when they believe that it is relevant to their future careers. There is no better way to demonstrate relevance than to ground discussion in the real world. We do this in several ways: First, we use high-profile companies such as Nike, Microsoft, and Intel to frame our discussion of accounting issues. Second, the book employs a "macro" approach in its first two chapters teaching students how to understand and use the real financial statements of Tootsie Roll, Hershey, and Best Buy, before teaching how to record transactions. Many students determine their opinion of a course during the initial weeks, and this macro approach clearly demonstrates the relevance of accounting while students are forming their impression of the course. Finally, *Accounting Across the Organization* boxes specifically connect accounting to business functions such as finance, marketing, and management and show uses of accounting for students with business majors other than accounting.

"Make a decision" All business people must make decisions. Decision making involves critical evaluation and analysis of the information at hand, and this takes practice. We have integrated important analytical tools throughout the book. After each new decision tool is presented, we summarize the key features of that tool in a *Decision Toolkit*. At the end of each chapter we provide a comprehensive demonstration of an analysis of a real company using the decision tools presented in the chapter. This sequence of decision tools culminates in a capstone analysis chapter at the end of the book.

"It's a small world" To heighten student awareness of international issues, we have many references to international companies and issues. Also, many *Interpreting Financial Statements* problems have an international focus. In addition, through our *International Notes*, and a comprehensive summary discussion and table at the back of the text, we provide insight into how U.S. accounting standards may change in the near future as U.S. GAAP converges with international accounting standards.

Financial Accounting, 5th Edition, provides many proven pedagogical tools to help students learn accounting concepts and apply them to decision making in the business world. The **Student Owner's Manual** at the book's companion site describes all the learning tools of the book in detail. Here are a few key features.

Learning How to Use the Text

- Students who take the new online **Learning Styles Quiz** will identify their learning style. Pages xxiii and xxiv list learning strategies and tips for the seven learning styles, and page xxv shows resources in WileyPLUS and the textbook that relate to those learning styles.

- **The Navigator** guides students through each chapter by pulling all the learning tools together into a learning system. Throughout the chapter, **The Navigator** prompts students to use the learning aids and to set priorities as they study.

- Marginal notes in blue in Chapter 1 explain how to use the text's learning tools to help achieve success in the course.

Understanding the Context

- **Study Objectives**, listed at the beginning of each chapter, reappear in the margins and again in the **Summary of Study Objectives**.

- A **Feature Story** helps students understand how the chapter topic relates to the real world of accounting and business and illustrates the necessity of sound accounting as the basis of informed decisions.

- A **Chapter Preview** links the Feature Story to the major topics of the chapter and provides a road map to the chapter.

---

preview of chapter 2

If you are thinking of purchasing Best Buy stock, or any stock, how can you decide what the stock is worth? If you manage J. Crew's credit department, how should you determine whether to extend credit to a new customer? If you are a financial executive of IBM, how do you decide whether your company is generating adequate cash to expand operations without borrowing? Your decision in each of these situations will be influenced by a variety of considerations. One of them should be your careful analysis of a company's financial statements. The reason: Financial statements offer relevant and reliable information, which will help you in your decision making.

In this chapter we take a closer look at the balance sheet and introduce some useful ways for evaluating the information provided by the financial statements. We also examine the financial reporting concepts underlying the financial statements.

A Further Look At Financial Statements

The Classified Balance Sheet	Using the Financial Statements	Financial Reporting Concepts
• Current assets • Long-term investments • Property, plant, and equipment • Intangible assets • Current liabilities • Long-term liabilities • Stockholders' equity	• Ratio analysis • Using the income statement • Using the statement of stockholders' equity • Using a classified balance sheet • Using the statement of cash flows	• The standard-setting environment • Characteristics of useful information • Assumptions and principles • Constraints

Learning the Material

- Emphasis on accounting experiences of **real companies and business situations throughout**.

- Three types of **Insight** boxes highlight ethics, investor, and international perspectives. These stories provide glimpses into how real companies make decisions using accounting information. In addition, **Accounting Across the Organization** boxes provide glimpses of how individuals in non-accounting functions use accounting information in their decision making.

- The **Insight** boxes and the **Accounting Across the Organization** boxes end with a question, which tests students' understanding of the real-world application in the box. Guideline answers for these questions appear at the end of the **Broadening Your Perspective** section at the end of the chapter.

- **Color illustrations**, including **infographics**, create "visual anchors" that help students visualize and apply accounting concepts.

- **Do It! exercises** appear at key breaks in the chapter narrative. These mini demonstration problems invite students to test their understanding of the just-completed section before they proceed to the next one.

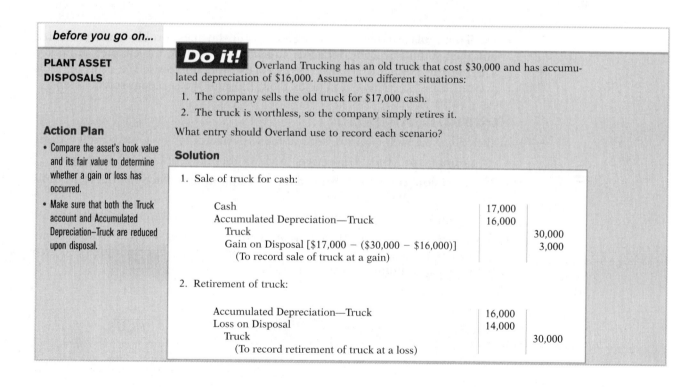

before you go on...

PLANT ASSET DISPOSALS

Do it! Overland Trucking has an old truck that cost $30,000 and has accumulated depreciation of $16,000. Assume two different situations:

1. The company sells the old truck for $17,000 cash.
2. The truck is worthless, so the company simply retires it.

What entry should Overland use to record each scenario?

Action Plan

- Compare the asset's book value and its fair value to determine whether a gain or loss has occurred.
- Make sure that both the Truck account and Accumulated Depreciation–Truck are reduced upon disposal.

Solution

1. Sale of truck for cash:

Cash	17,000	
Accumulated Depreciation—Truck	16,000	
Truck		30,000
Gain on Disposal [$17,000 − ($30,000 − $16,000)]		3,000
(To record sale of truck at a gain)		

2. Retirement of truck:

Accumulated Depreciation—Truck	16,000	
Loss on Disposal	14,000	
Truck		30,000
(To record retirement of truck at a loss)		

- **Accounting equation analyses** in the margin next to key journal entries reinforce understanding of the impact of an accounting transaction on the financial statements. They also report the **cash effect** of each transaction to reinforce understanding of the difference between cash effects and accrual accounting.

- **Helpful Hints, Alternative Terminology**, and blue-highlighted **key terms and concepts** help focus students on key concepts as they study the material.

- In the margins, **International Notes** and **Ethics Notes** provide a convenient way to expose students to international and ethics issues. The Fifth Edition greatly expands the number of these notes.

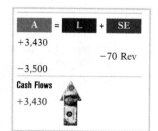

A	=	L	+	SE
+3,430				
				−70 Rev
−3,500				

Cash Flows
+3,430

- New in this edition, text sections titled **"Keeping an Eye on Cash"** highlight differences between accrual accounting and cash accounting while increasing the student's understanding of the statement of cash flows. This feature aids the student's ability to evaluate accrual accounting and to use cash-basis numbers as tools of analysis when appropriate.

| KEEPING AN EYE ON CASH | Free cash flow is closely monitored by analysts and investors for many reasons and in a variety of ways. One measure that is gaining increased attention is "price to free cash flow." This is a variant of the price to earnings (P-E) ratio, which has been a staple of analysts for a long time. The difference is that rather than divide the company's stock price by its earnings per share (an accrual-accounting–based number), the price to free cash flow ratio divides the company's stock price by its free cash flow per share. A high measure suggests that the stock price is high relative to the company's ability to generate cash. A low measure indicates that the company's stock might be a bargain.

The average price to free cash flow ratio for companies in the Standard and Poor's 500-stock index was recently 22. At the same time, the following companies reported measures way below the average. While you should not use this measure as the sole factor in choosing a stock, it can serve as a useful screen by which to identify companies that merit further investigation. |
| --- | --- |

- **Decision tools** useful for analyzing and solving business problems are presented and then summarized in **Decision Toolkits**. Just before the chapter summary, a **Using the Decision Toolkit** exercise asks students to use the decision tools presented in the chapter and takes them through the problem-solving steps.

Putting It Together

At the end of each chapter are several features useful for review and reference.

- A **Summary of Study Objectives** reviews the main points of the chapter.
- The **Decision Toolkit—A Summary** presents in one place the decision tools used throughout the chapter.
- A **Glossary** of key terms gives definitions with page references to the text.
- A **Comprehensive Do It problem**, with an **Action Plan**, gives students another opportunity to study a detailed solution to a representative problem before they do homework assignments.

Comprehensive

DuPage Company purchased a factory machine at a cost of $18,000 on January 1, 2010. DuPage expected the machine to have a salvage value of $2,000 at the end of its 4-year useful life.

Instructions

Prepare a depreciation schedule using the straight-line method.

Action Plan

- Under the straight-line method, apply the depreciation rate to depreciable cost.

Solution to Comprehensive Do it!

DUPAGE COMPANY
Depreciation Schedule—Straight-Line Method

	Computation			Annual	End of Year	
Year	Depreciable Cost (a)	×	Depreciation Rate (b)	= Depreciation Expense	Accumulated Depreciation	Book Value (c)
2010	$16,000		25%	$4,000	$ 4,000	$14,000
2011	16,000		25	4,000	8,000	10,000

Developing Skills Through Practice

Each chapter is supported by a full complement of homework material. **Self-Study Questions, Questions, Brief Exercises, Do It! Review exercises, Exercises**, and three sets of **Problems** (one of which is at the book's website) are all keyed to the Study Objectives. In addition:

- Questions marked with the **Tootsie Roll** send students to find information in Tootsie Roll's 2007 annual report printed in the book.

- Certain Questions, Exercises, and Problems make use of the decision tools presented in the chapter. These are marked with the icon ⊶⊷. Also, certain Questions, Exercises, and Problems show applications of accounting issues for business functions across the organization. These are marked with the icon ◀ .

- A **Comprehensive Problem** (in Chapters 5-11) combines material of the current chapter with previous chapters so that students understand how "it all fits together." Each of these problems requires the recording of transaction and adjusting entries, and culminates in the preparation of financial statements.

Comprehensive Problem

CP9 Pinkerton Corporation's trial balance at December 31, 2010, is presented on page xxx. All 2010 transactions have been recorded except for the items described after the trial balance.

- A **Continuing Cookie Chronicle** problem in every chapter traces the growth of an entrepreneurial venture. Each week students apply their newly acquired accounting skills to solve the financial reporting issues faced by this small business.

- Certain Exercises and Problems can be solved using the Excel supplement that is available to accompany the text and are identified by these icons.

- Other Exercises and Problems can be solved with the **General Ledger Software** available with the text and are marked with this icon. **GLS**

Expanding and Applying Knowledge

Broadening Your Perspective at the end of each chapter offers a wealth of resources for those instructors who want to broaden the learning experience by bringing in more real-world decision making, analysis, and critical thinking activities.

---

broadening your perspective

Financial Reporting and Analysis

FINANCIAL REPORTING PROBLEM: *Tootsie Roll Industries, Inc.*

BYP4-1 The financial statements of Tootsie Roll are presented in Appendix A at the end of this book.

Instructions
(a) Using the consolidated income statement and balance sheet, identify items that may result in adjusting entries for prepayments.

- A **Financial Reporting Problem** directs students to study various aspects of the 2007 financial statements of Tootsie Roll Industries, Inc., which are printed in Chapter 1 (in simplified form) and in Appendix A (in full)

- A **Comparative Analysis Problem** offers the opportunity to compare and contrast the financial reporting of Tootsie Roll Industries, Inc., with a competitor Hershey Foods Corporation.

- **Research Cases** direct students to the *Wall Street Journal* and other business periodicals and references for further study and analysis of key topics. All Research Cases in this edition are *new*.

- **Interpreting Financial Statements** problems offer mini-cases that ask students to read parts of financial statements of actual companies and use the decision tools of the chapter to interpret them. Some of these cases, indicated by a globe icon, focus on specific situations faced by actual international companies.

- **Financial Analysis on the Web** problems guide students to websites from which they can mine and analyze information related to the chapter topic.

- **Decision Making Across the Organization** cases help promote group collaboration and build decision-making and business communication skills by requiring teams of students to consider business problems from various functional perspectives.

- **Communication Activities** provide practice in written communication, a skill much in demand among employers.

- **Ethics Cases** ask students to analyze situations, identify the ethical issues involved, and decide on an appropriate course of action.

- A new **"All About You" Activity** offers students an opportunity to link the accounting concepts learned in the chapter to some aspect of personal finance such as applying for a student loan, protecting themselves from identity theft, and the use of credit cards. These topics provide great opportunities for classroom discussion.

"ALL ABOUT YOU" ACTIVITY

BYP2-10 Every company needs to plan in order to move forward. Its top management must consider where it wants the company to be in three to five years. Like a company, you need to think about where you want to be three to five years from now, and you need to start taking steps now in order to get there.

Instructions
Provide responses to each of the following items.
(a) Where would you like to be working in three to five years? Describe your plan for

---

Major Changes and Key Features of Each Chapter

The fourth edition was a tremendous success. In the spirit of continuous improvement, we have made numerous changes in this edition. These changes come in response to suggestions made by reviewers, focus group participants, instructors, and students. We sincerely appreciate your input.

Major Changes in the Fifth Edition

The "focus companies" are again Tootsie Roll Industries and Hershey Foods. We chose them because they have high name recognition with students, they operate primarily in a single industry, and they have relatively simple financial statements.

In addition, we made the following major changes in the Fifth Edition:

- In response to the rapidly evolving environment for international accounting standards, we used a three-pronged approach to develop students' understanding of these issues. First, we significantly increased the number of International Notes and International Insights integrated throughout the text to highlight key differences between U.S. GAAP and IFRS. Second, at the back of the text, we provide a summary discussion of IFRS, as well as a table that provides a comprehensive listing of key similarities and differences as well as anticipated developments that are relevant to introductory financial accounting. Finally, as they arise, additional international accounting developments that relate to introductory financial accounting will be provided at the student portion of the book's companion site.

- To address the increased importance of internal controls to business managers, we significantly revised Chapter 7 related to fraud and internal control. We added a new discussion of fraud, which is framed by a discussion of the fraud triangle. We expanded the discussion of internal controls to incorporate elements emphasized by COSO. And, most significantly, we added a new feature, **Anatomy of a Fraud**, which is used to illustrate how the lack of specific internal controls resulted in real-world frauds. We believe these stories will be especially effective in demonstrating the importance of internal controls to nonaccounting majors.

- In nearly every chapter we added a section titled "Keeping an Eye on Cash." This section highlights differences between accrual accounting and cash accounting and increases students' understanding of the statement of cash flows. This feature aids student' ability to evaluate accrual accounting and to use cash basis-numbers as tools of analysis.

- In Chapter 3 we revised all tabular analyses to use the expanded accounting equation rather than the basic equation.

Other Changes in the Fifth Edition

- We added 27 new **Do It** activities within the book, doubling the total to 54. These exercises give students an opportunity to stop and actively test their understanding of the material as they read the chapter.

- In the end-of-chapter materials, placed between Brief Exercises and Exercises, is a new section of exercises titled **Do It! Review**. Similar to the idea of B Exercises and C Problems, this new section contains parallel versions of the in-chapter Do Its. This new section provides an opportunity for homework assignments related directly to the in-chapter Do Its. We added 50 new multiple-choice **Self-Study Questions** (about three to five new items per chapter), so that each chapter has approximately 15 self-study questions. Additional self-test quiz questions are available to students online, at the book's companion site.

- We added a new set of **B Exercises**, which parallel the A Exercises. Like the C Problems, the B Exercises are available on the book's companion site.

- Over 350 **new questions** are included in this edition of the Test Bank. Instructors can now tailor examinations by different learning outcomes—by study objectives, Bloom's taxonomy, level of difficulty, time on task, AACSB and AICPA professional standards.

- New **PowerPoint** presentations.

- New **QuickBooks Templates**.

- In addition, the Fifth Edition includes 26 new Brief Exercises or Exercises.

- We discuss the financial reporting implications of the Sarbanes–Oxley Act at numerous points throughout the text.

Key Features of Each Chapter

Chapter 1 Introduction to Financial Statements

- Explains the purpose of each financial statement.
- Uses financial statements of a hypothetical company (to keep it simple), followed by those for a

real company, **Tootsie Roll Industries** (to make it relevant).

- *Changes:* Added International Note; 2 Ethics Notes; an International Insight box on accounting of tsunami-relief funds; and 2 Do It exercises. New end-of-chapter materials: 5 Self-Study Questions, 1 Question, 4 Do It Review exercises, 1 Exercise, Research Case, and "All About You" Activity.

Chapter 2 A Further Look at Financial Statements

- Discusses revenue, expenses, assets, and liabilities.
- Presents the classified balance sheet.
- Applies ratio analysis (current ratio, debt to total assets, earnings per share, and free cash flow) to real companies—Best Buy and Circuit City.
- *Changes:* Revised the discussion of the cost principle to include discussion of fair value. Added an International Insight box on accounting for South Korean companies; discussion of PCAOB in text and as glossary term; cash flow section; 3 International Notes; 2 Ethics Notes; and 3 Do It exercises. New end-of-chapter materials: 3 Self-Study Questions, 1 Question, 4 Do It Review exercises, 1 Exercise, Research Case, and "All About You" Activity.

Chapter 3 The Accounting Information System

- Covers transaction analysis—emphasizes fundamentals while avoiding unnecessary detail.
- *Changes:* Revised all tabular analyses to use the expanded accounting equation. Added an illustration to show expansion of the stockholders' equity part of the accounting equation; cash flow section, with related learning objective; 2 Ethics Notes; International Note. New end-of-chapter materials: 3 Self-Study Questions, 1 Question, 4 Do It Review exercises, 2 Exercises, Research Case, Ethics Case, and "All About You" Activity.

Chapter 4 Accrual Accounting Concepts

- Emphasizes difference between cash and accrual accounting.
- Discusses how some companies manage earnings through accrual practices.
- Presents minimal discussion of closing and work sheets; provides additional detail on work sheets in an appendix.
- *Changes:* Added new journal entries to illustrate revenue recognition principles; 4 new illustrations that summarize types of adjusting entries; new cash flow section, with related learning objective; 2 Ethics Notes; 2 Do It exercises. New end-of-chapter materials: 2 Self-Study Questions, 1 Question, 1 Brief Exercise, 4 Do It

Review exercises, 1 Exercise, Research Case, and "All About You" Activity.

Chapter 5 Merchandising Operations and the Multiple-Step Income Statement

- Introduces merchandising concepts using the perpetual inventory approach.
- Presents the multiple-step income statement.
- Applies ratio analysis (gross profit rate and profit margin ratio) to real companies—**Target** and **Wal-Mart**.
- *Changes:* Revised section on flow of inventory costs, with related illustration, and section on freight costs. Added T accounts to show effects of sales discounts, returns and allowances; Accounting Across the Organization box on return policy at Costco; cash flow section, with related learning objective; International Note; 2 Do It exercises; income tax expense consideration to Problems 4A and 4B. New end-of-chapter materials: 3 Self-Study Questions, 2 Questions, 2 Brief Exercises, 4 Do It Review exercises, 1 Exercise, Research Case, and "All About You" Activity.

Chapter 6 Reporting and Analyzing Inventory

- Covers cost flow assumptions and their implications for financial reporting, emphasizing the periodic approach (for simplicity).
- Applies ratio analysis (inventory turnover) to real companies—**Target** and **Wal-Mart**.
- Discusses implication of LIFO reserve for real company—**Caterpillar Inc**.
- End-of-chapter appendix covers inventory cost flow assumptions under perpetual inventory systems.
- *Changes:* Updated the Feature Story; revised and expanded the introductory discussion of cost flow assumptions. Added cash flow section; Ethics Note; International Note; 3 Do It exercises. New end-of-chapter materials: 4 Self-Study Questions, 2 Questions, 1 Brief Exercise, 4 Do It Review exercises, 1 Exercise, Research Case, and "All About You" Activity.

Chapter 7 Fraud, Internal Control, and Cash

- Begins with a *new* section on fraud. Seven case vignettes highlight specific real-world frauds and explain how use of internal control activities might have prevented or detected the fraud.
- Covers internal control concepts and implications of control failures.
- Presents bank reconciliation as a control device.
- Discusses cash management, including operating cycle and cash budgeting.

- *Changes:* Chapter begins with new section on fraud, including illustration of the fraud triangle and seven "Anatomy of a Fraud" vignettes. Added Feature Story; cash flow section; and Ethics Note. Moved electronic funds transfer into "Use of a Bank" section; made changes to P6A, 7a, and 7B. New end-of-chapter materials: 4 Self-Study Questions, 4 Questions, 2 Brief Exercises, 4 Do It Review exercises, 1 Exercise, Research Case, Interpreting Financial Statements, and "All About You" Activity.

Chapter 8 Reporting and Analyzing Receivables

- Presents the basics of account and notes receivable, bad debt estimation, and interest calculations.

- Discusses receivables management, including determining to whom to extend credit, establishing the payment period; monitoring collections; evaluating the receivables balance; and accelerating receipts.

- Applies ratio analysis (receivables turnover) to a real company—**McKesson.**

- *Changes:* Added explanation of retailers' credit cards; section on determining the maturity date; timeline showing accrual of interest receivable; several in-text references to experiences of real companies; Accounting Across the Organization on Countrywide's mortgage loans; cash flow section; International Note; 2 Ethics Notes, and Do It exercise. New end-of-chapter materials: 3 Self-Study Questions, 3 Questions, one Brief Exercise, 4 Do It Review exercises, 1 Exercise, Research Case, and "All About You" Activity.

Chapter 9 Reporting and Analyzing Long-Lived Assets

- Covers the basics of plant assets and intangible assets.

- Discusses the basics of the buy or lease decision.

- Covers the implications of depreciation method choice; shows details of accelerated methods in an appendix.

- Applies ratio analysis (asset turnover and return on assets) to real companies—**Southwest Airlines** and **AirTran.**

- Demonstrates implications of estimated useful life for amortization of intangibles.

- Discusses the statement of cash flows presentation of fixed-asset transactions.

- *Changes:* Added International Insight about Softbank Company; 2 International Notes; 2 Ethics Notes; Do it exercise; cash flow section. New end-of-chapter materials: 4 Self-Study Questions,

2 Questions, 3 Brief Exercises, 4 Do It Review exercises, 3 Exercises, Research Case, and "All About You" Activity.

Chapter 10 Reporting and Analyzing Liabilities

- Covers current liabilities: notes payable, sales taxes, payroll, unearned revenues, and current maturities of long-term debt.

- Covers long-term liabilities, bond pricing, and various types of bonds.

- Presents straight-line amortization and the effective-interest method in a chapter-end appendix.

- Includes present value discussion in an appendix at the back of the book.

- Discusses the basics of contingent liabilities, lease obligations, and off-balance-sheet financing.

- Applies ratio analysis (current ratio, debt to total assets ratio, and times interest earned) to real companies—**Ford** and **General Motors.**

- Discusses the statement of cash flows presentation of debt transactions.

- *Changes:* Reorganized heading levels for greater clarity of presentation; moved payroll liabilities to end of current liabilities section. In Appendix 10B, changed example to show effective-interest amortization for *same company* as used in body of chapter. Added Investor Insight on debt covenants; 2 International Notes; 2 Ethics Notes; cash flow section. New end-of-chapter materials: 5 Self-Study Questions, 1 Question, 5 Do It Review exercises, Research Case, and "All About You" Activity.

Chapter 11 Reporting and Analyzing Stockholders' Equity

- Presents pros and cons of the corporate form of organization.

- Covers issues related to common and preferred stock, and reasons companies purchase treasury stock.

- Explains reasons for cash dividends, stock dividends, and stock splits, and implications for analysis.

- Discusses debt versus equity choice.

- Applies ratio analysis (return on common stockholders' equity and payout ratio) to real companies—**Nike** and **Reebok.**

- Discusses the statement of cash flows presentation of equity transactions.

- *Changes:* Added illustration on effects of stock dividend; International Note; 2 Ethics Notes, 3 Do It Exercises, cash flow section. New end-of-chapter materials: 5 Self-Study Questions, one

Question, 6 Do It Review exercises, 2 Exercises, Research Case, and "All About You" Activity.

Chapter 12 Statement of Cash Flows

- Explains the purpose and usefulness of the statement of cash flows.

- Presents the indirect method in the body of the chapter and the direct method in a chapter-end appendix.

- Applies ratio analysis (free cash flow, current cash debt coverage ratio, and cash debt coverage ratio) to real companies—**Microsoft**, **Oracle**, **AMD**, and **Intel**.

- *Changes:* Added marginal T accounts to show changes in noncash accounts; Ethics Note; Do It exercise, cash flow section. In chapter appendix, change explanation of the direct method to use the *same company* used for the indirect method in the body of the chapter. International Note; New end-of-chapter materials: 4 Self-Study Questions, 1 Question, 2 Brief Exercises, 3 Do It Review exercises, Research Case, and "All About You" Activity.

Chapter 13 Financial Analysis: The Big Picture

- Capstone chapter—presents some new analytical tools, and reinforces previous analytical tools and demonstrates their interrelationships.

- Demonstrates horizontal and vertical analysis of **Kellogg**.

- Discusses "sustainable income" and implications of discontinued operations, extraordinary items,

accounting changes, nonrecurring charges, and comprehensive earnings.

- Discusses factors that affect the quality of earnings.

- In an appendix, applies comprehensive ratio analysis to real companies—**Kellogg** and **General Mills**.

- *Changes:* Added Ethics Note, International Note, 4 Do It exercises, and cash flow section. New end-of-chapter materials: 5 Self-Study Questions, 1 Question, 4 Do It Review exercises, Research Case, and "All About You" Activity.

Appendix A Specimen Financial Statements: Tootsie Roll Industries, Inc.

Appendix B Specimen Financial Statements: Hershey Food Corportation

Appendix C Time Value of Money

- Provides coverage of present value and future value of single sums and annuities.

- *Changes:* Added section on using financial calculators to solve time value of money problems.

Appendix D Reporting and Analyzing Investments

- Provides a comprehensive discussion of reporting and analyzing investments.

- Discusses statement of cash flows presentation of investments.

- *Changes:* Added International Note and Ethics Note.

ACTIVE TEACHING AND LEARNING SUPPLEMENTARY MATERIAL

Financial Accounting, 5th Edition, features a full line of teaching and learning resources. Driven by the same basic beliefs as the textbook, these supplements provide a consistent and well-integrated learning system. This hands-on, real-world package guides *instructors* through the process of active learning and gives them the tools to create an interactive learning environment. With its emphasis on activities, exercises, and the Internet, the package encourages *students* to take an active role in the course and prepares them for decision making in a real-world context.

Wiley's Integrated Technology Solutions: Helping Teachers Teach and Students Learn

The *Financial Accounting, 5th Edition*, book companion site, at ***www.wiley.com/college/kimmel***,

provides a seamless integration of text and media and keeps all of the book's online resources in one easily accessible location.

FOR INSTRUCTORS

On the book's website, instructors will find electronic versions of the Solutions Manual, Test Bank, Instructor's Manual, Algorithmic Computerized Test Bank, Set B Exercises, Set C Problems and solutions, and other resources.

Also available is *WileyPLUS*, an online suite of resources, including a complete online version of the text, that helps students come to class better prepared for lectures, gives immediate feedback and help on assignments, and allows instructors to track student progress throughout the course. Students can take advantage of tools such as self-assessment quizzes, tutorials, and animations to help them study more effectively and receive instant feedback when they practice on their own. Instructors, in turn, can use their gradebook to create assignments and automate the assigning and grading of homework or quizzes. They can also create class presentations using PowerPoint slides, image galleries, and interactive simulations. Key components of WileyPLUS for instructors are the following:

- **Course Administration** tools help instructors manage their course and integrate Wiley website resources with WebCT or Angel Learning, thereby helping instructors keep all class materials in one location.

- A **"Prepare and Present"** tool contains all of the Wiley-provided resources, such as PowerPoint slides, Chapter Reviews, and Lecture Outlines, making your preparation time more efficient. You may easily adapt, customize, and add to Wiley content to meet the needs of your course. Instructors can quickly access content via traditional chapter files or quickly retrieve files with a new "sort by study objective" functionality.

- An **"Assignment"** area is one of the most powerful features of WileyPLUS. This area of the website allows professors to assign homework and quizzes comprised of textbook Brief Exercises, Exercises, Problems, and Test Bank materials. Instructors save time as results are automatically graded and recorded in an instructor gradebook. Students benefit by the option to receive immediate feedback on their work, allowing them to determine right away how well they understand the course material.

- An **Instructors Gradebook** keeps track of student progress and allows instructors to analyze individual and overall class results to determine their progress and level of understanding.

FOR STUDENTS

On the student portion of the book's companion site, students will find Exercise Set B, Problem Set C, and the full version of the Continuing Cookie Chronicle. Also available there are the Accounting Cycle Tutorial, an online Excel workbook and templates, PowerPoint slides, web quizzes, annual reports, and more.

In addition, **WileyPLUS** provides a wealth of support materials that will help students develop their conceptual understanding of class material and increase their ability to solve problems. Here, students will find interactive tutorials, Excel Templates, and PowerPoint Presentations. WileyPLUS is built around student activity:

- **"Read, Study and Practice"** In addition to the complete online textbook, students can access Interactive Chapter Reviews, Guided Online

Demonstration Problem Tutorials, Student Quizzes, Flash Cards, Audio Review Files, and other problem-solving resources.

- An **"Assignment"** area that helps students stay "on task" by containing all homework assignments in one location. Many homework problems contain a link to the relevant sections of the ebook, providing students with context-sensitive help that allows them to conquer problem-solving obstacles. General Ledger Software problems for select problems are identified. You can also further track student progress using the new "Time on Task" and "Timed Assignment" features.

- A **Personal Gradebook** for each student will allow students to view their results from past assignments at any time.

Active Teaching Aids for Instructors

Solutions Manual. The Solutions Manual contains detailed solutions to all brief exercises, exercises, and problems in the textbook and suggested answers to the questions and cases. Print is large and bold for easy readability in lecture settings. The Solutions Manual has been carefully verified by a team of independent accuracy checkers. *All solutions are now classified by the following learning outcomes: study objectives, Bloom's taxonomy, level of difficulty, time on task, and AASCB and AICPA professional standards.*

Solutions Transparencies. The solutions transparencies contain detailed solutions to all brief exercises, exercises, and problems in the textbook. They feature large, bold type for better projection and easy readability in large classroom settings. Solutions transparencies are printed on-demand via the Kimmel *Financial Accounting, 5th Edition*, instructor website at *www.wiley.com/college/kimmel*.

Teaching Transparencies. Text images are printed on-demand via the Kimmel *Financial Accounting, 5th Edition*, instructor website at *www.wiley.com/college/kimmel*.

Instructor's Manual. The Instructor's Manual features a comprehensive chapter outline, chapter review quizzes, activities, and sample syllabi.

PowerPoint Presentations. The new PowerPoint presentations contain a combination of key concepts, images, and problems from the textbook for use in the classroom. Designed to follow the organization of content in the textbook, they visually reinforce financial accounting principles.

Test Bank. The Test Bank is a comprehensive testing package that allows instructors to tailor examinations according to study objectives, learning skills, and content. Over **350 new questions** are included in this edition of the Test Bank. Achievement tests, comprehensive exams, and a final exam are include. All questions are now identified with the following learning outcomes: study objective, Bloom's taxonomy, level of difficulty, time on task, and AACSB and AICPA professional standards.

New! **Algorithmic Computerized Test Bank.** The new algorithmic computerized test bank allows instructors to assign printed test bank questions or, alternatively, the same questions that are populated with randomly generated names and data. The software can also generate a report detailing the learning outcomes addressed in an assigned test.

Instructor's Resource CD-ROM. The Instructor's Resource CD (IRCD) provides all instructor support material in an electronic format that is easy to navigate and use. The IRCD gives you the flexibility to access and prepare instructional material based on your individual needs.

WebCT or Angel Learning. WebCT or Angel Learning offer an integrated set of course-management tools that enable instructors to easily design, develop, and manage web-based and web-enhanced courses.

Active Learning Aids for Students

Student Guide. The Study Guide is a helpful tool for review and exam preparation. Each chapter contains a detailed review of all text study objectives. Multiple-choice, matching, and comprehensive problems are also provided with detailed solutions.

Working Papers. Working Papers are accounting templates for all end-of-chapter brief exercises, exercises, problems, and cases. A convenient resource for organizing and completing homework assignments, they demonstrate how to correctly present homework solutions.

Excel Working Papers. An electronic version of the print working papers, these Excel-formatted templates help students properly format solutions to end-of-chapter exercises, problems, and cases. Available through WileyPLUS.

General Ledger Software. The General Ledger Software program allows students to solve select end-of-chapter text problems or customized problems using a computerized accounting system. Easy to use, GLS demonstrates the immediate effects of each transaction and enables students to enter and post journal entries, generate trial balances, and income statements. The application is available on CD-ROM, or instructors can assign selected end-of-chapter problems from the textbook in the GLS software. The report is fed to the Gradebook, where the instructor can assign a grade after reviewing the student's work.

Peachtree Complete Accounting Software Templates and Workbook. This new workbook teaches students how to effectively use Peachtree Complete® Accounting software, a valuable accounting tool. Accompanying the workbook are software and templates, available on a CD.

Online Excel Workbook and Templates. An online workbook and accompanying Excel templates allow students to complete select end-of-chapter exercises and problems identified by a spreadsheet icon in the margin of the main textbook. A useful introduction to Excel, these electronic spreadsheets also enhance students' accounting skills.

New QuickBooks Templates are available for download on the student companion site and within WileyPLUS.

Acknowledgments

Financial Accounting has benefited greatly from the input of focus group participants, manuscript reviewers, those who have sent comments by letter or e-mail, ancillary authors, and proofers. We greatly appreciate the constructive suggestions and innovative ideas of reviewers and the creativity and accuracy of the ancillary authors and checkers.

PRIOR EDITIONS

Thanks to the following reviewers and focus group participants of prior editions of Financial Accounting:

Dawn Addington, *Central New Mexico Community College;* Solochidi Ahiarah, *Buffalo State College;* Sheila Ammons, *Austin Community College;* Thomas G. Amyot, *College of Santa Rose;* Cheryl Bartlett, *Central New Mexico Community College;* Victoria Beard, *University of North Dakota;* Angela H. Bell, *Jacksonville State University;* John A. Booker, *Tennessee Technological University;* Robert L. Braun, *Southeastern Louisiana University;* Daniel Brickner, *Eastern Michigan University;* Sarah Ruth Brown, *University of North Alabama;* and James Byrne, *Oregon State University.*

Judy Cadle, *Tarleton State University*; David Carr, *Austin Community College*; Jack Cathey, *University of North Carolina–Charlotte*; Andy Chen, *Northeast Illinois University*; Jim Christianson, *Austin Community College*; Laura Claus, *Louisiana State University*; Leslie A. Cohen, *University of Arizona*; Teresa L. Conover, *University of North Texas*; Janet Courts, *San Bernadino Valley College*; Helen Davis, *Johnson and Wales University*; Cheryl Dickerson, *Western Washington University*; George M. Dow, *Valencia Community College–West*; Kathy J. Dow, *Salem State College*; and Lola Dudley, *Eastern Illinois University*.

Mary Emery, *St. Olaf College*; Martin L. Epstein, *Central New Mexico Community College*; Larry R. Falcetto, *Emporia State University*; Scott Fargason, *Louisiana State University*; Janet Farler, *Pima Community College*; Sheila D. Foster, *The Citadel*; Jessica J. Frazier, *Eastern Kentucky University*; Norman H. Godwin, *Auburn University*; David Gotlob, *Indiana University-Purdue University–Fort Wayne*; Emmett Griner, *Georgia State University*; Leon J. Hanouille, *Syracuse University*; Kenneth M. Hiltebeitel, *Villanova University*; Harry Hooper, *Santa Fe Community College*; Judith A. Hora, *University of San Diego*; and Carol Olson Houston, *San Diego State University*.

Norma Jacobs, *Austin Community College*; Marianne L. James, *California State University–Los Angeles*; Stanley Jenne, *University of Montana*; Christopher Jones, *George Washington University*; Jane Kaplan, *Drexel University*; John E. Karayan, *California State University–Pomona*; Susan Kattelus, *Eastern Michigan University*; Dawn Kelly, *Texas Tech University*; Cindi Khanlarian, *University of North Carolina–Greensboro*; Robert Kiddoo, *California State University–Northridge*; Robert J. Kirsch, *Southern Connecticut State University*; Frank Korman, *Mountain View College*; and Jerry G. Kreuze, *Western Michigan University*.

John Lacey, *California State University–Long Beach*; Doug Laufer, *Metropolitan State College of Denver*; Keith Leeseberg, *Manatee Community College*; Glenda Levendowski, *Arizona State University*; Seth Levine, *DeVry University*; James Lukawitz, *University of Memphis*; Noel McKeon, *Florida Community College*; P. Merle Maddocks, *University of Alabama–Huntsville*; Janice Mardon, *Green River Community College*; John Marts, *University of North Carolina–Wilmington*; Alan Mayer-Sommer, *Georgetown University*; Barbara Merino, *University of North Texas*; Jeanne Miller, *Cypress College*; Robert Miller, *California State University–Fullerton*; Elizabeth Minbiole, *Northwood University*; and Marguerite Muise, *Santa Ana College*; James Neurath, *Central Michigan University*; and Gale E. Newell, *Western Michigan University*.

Suzanne Ogilby, *Sacramento State University*; Sarah N. Palmer, *University of North Carolina–Charlotte*; Patricia Parker, *Columbus State Community College*; Charles Pier, *Appalachian State University*; Meg Pollard, *American River College*; Franklin J. Plewa, *Idaho State University*; John Purisky, *Salem State College*; Donald J. Raux, *Siena College*; Judith Resnick, *Borough of Manhattan Community College*; Mary Ann Reynolds, *Western Washington University*; Carla Rich, *Pensacola Junior College*; Ray Rigoli, *Ramapo College of New Jersey*; Jeff Ritter, *St. Norbert College*; Brandi Roberts, *Southeastern Louisiana University*; Patricia A. Robinson, *Johnson and Wales University*; Nancy Rochman, *University of Arizona*; and Marc A. Rubin, *Miami University*.

Alfredo Salas, *El Paso Community College*; Christine Schalow, *California State University–San Bernadino*; Michael Schoderbek, *Rutgers University*; Richard Schroeder, *University of North Carolina–Charlotte*; Jerry Searfoss, *University of Utah*; Cindy Seipel, *New Mexico State University*; Anne E. Selk, *University of Wisconsin–Green Bay*; William Seltz, *University of Massachusetts*; Suzanne Sevalstad, *University of Nevada*; Mary Alice Seville, *Oregon State University*; Donald Smillie, *Southwest Missouri State University*; Aileen Smith, *Stephen F. Austin State University*; Talitha Smith, *Auburn University*; William E. Smith, *Xavier University*; Will Snyder, *San Diego State University*; Teresa A. Speck, *St. Mary's University of Minnesota*; Charles Stanley, *Baylor University*; Ron Stone, *California State University–Northridge*; Gary Stout, *California State University–Northridge*; and Ellen L. Sweatt, *Georgia Perimeter College*.

Pamadda Tantral, *Fairleigh Dickinson University*; Andrea B. Weickgenannt, *Northern Kentucky University*; David P. Weiner, *University of San Francisco*; Frederick Weis, *Claremont McKenna College*; T. Sterling Wetzel, *Oklahoma State University*; Allan Young, *DeVry University*; Michael F. van Breda, *Texas Christian University*; Linda G. Wade, *Tarleton State University*; Stuart K. Webster, *University of Wyoming*; V. Joyce Yearley, *New Mexico State University*.

FIFTH EDITION

Thanks to the following reviewers, focus group participants, and others who provided suggestions for the Fifth Edition:

Gilda Agacer, *Monmouth University*
C. Richard Aldridge, *Western Kentucky University*
Joseph Antenucci, *Youngstown State University*
Brian Baick, *Montgomery College*
Timothy Baker, *California State University—Fresno*
Benjamin Bean, *Utah Valley State College*
Charles Bokemeier, *Michigan State University*

Charles Bunn, *Wake Technical Community College*
Thane Butt, *Champlain College*
Sandra Byrd, *Missouri State University*
Julia Camp, *University of Massachusetts—Boston*
Jack Cathey, *University of North Carolina—Charlotte*
Patrick Christensen, *Butte College*
Leslie Cohen, *University of Arizona*
Samantha Cox, *Wake Technical Community College*
Dori Danko, *Grand Valley State University*
Lisa Gillespie, *Loyola University—Chicago*
Sam Isley, *Wake Technical Community College*
Doulas Larson, *Salem State College*
Sara Melendy, *Gonzaga University*
Sherry Mirbod, *Montgomery College*
Andrew Morgret, *University of Memphis*
Michelle Moshier, *SUNY Albany*
Jim Neurath, *Central Michigan University*
Garth Novack, *Utah State University*
John A. Rude, *Bloomsburg University*
Bill N. Schwartz, *Stevens Institute of Technology*
Pam Smith, *Northern Illinois University*
Chris Solomon, *Trident Technical College*
Gracelyn Stuart, *Palm Beach Community College*
William Talbot, *Montgomery College*
Diane Tanner, *University of North Florida*
Steve Teeter, *Utah Valley State College*
Joan Van Hise, *Fairfield University*

ANCILLARY AUTHORS, CONTRIBUTORS, AND PROOFERS

We sincerely thank the following individuals for their hard work in preparing the content that accompanies this textbook:

LuAnn Bean, *Florida Institute of Technology*
Richard Campbell, *University of Rio Grande*
James M. Emig, *Villanova University*
Larry R. Falcetto, *Emporia Sate University*
Anthony Falgiani, *Western Illinois University*
Janet Farler, *Pima Community College*
Cecelia M. Fewox, *College of Charleston*
Coby Harmon, *University of California, Santa Barbara*
Harry Howe, *State University of New York—Geneseo*
Rick Lillie, *California State University—San Bernardino*
Laura McNally
Yvonne Phang, *Borough of Manhattan Community College*
Rex Schildhouse, *San Diego Community College*
Ellen L. Sweatt, *Georgia Perimeter College*
Dick D. Wasson, *Southwestern College*
Bernie Weinrich, *Lindenwood University*

We also greatly appreciate the expert assistance provided by the following individuals in checking the accuracy of the content that accompanies this textbook:

Terry Elliott, *Morehead State University*
Jill Misuraca, *Central Connecticut State University*

John Plouffe, *California State University—Los Angeles*
Ed Schell, *University of Hawaii at Manoa*
Alice Sineath, *Forsyth Technical Community College*
Teresa Speck, *Saint Mary's University of Minnesota*
Lynn Stallworth, *Appalachian State University*
Sheila Viel, *University of Wisconsin—Milwaukee*

We appreciate the exemplary support and professional commitment given us by Wiley's editorial and marketing personnel: Chris DeJohn, associate publisher; Julia Flohr, senior marketing manager; Carly DeCandia, assistant marketing manager; Allie Morris, senior media editor; Brian Kamins, associate editor; Ed Brislin, project editor; Alana Filopovich, marketing assistant; Ann Torbert and Terry Ann Kremer, development editors; Karyn Morrison, permissions editor; and Jen Battista, media assistant. Thanks also to the talented people who turned the material into the physical textbook: Ann Berlin, vice-president of higher education production and manufacturing; Harry Nolan, creative director; Pam Kennedy, director of production and manufacturing; Dorothy Sinclair, production services manager; Trish McFadden, senior production editor; Madelyn Lesure, senior designer; Sandra Rigby, senior illustration editor; Elle Wagner, senior photo editor; Suzanne Ingrao of Ingrao Associates, project editor; Jane Shifflet, product manager at Aptara; and Amanda Grant, project manager at Elm Street Publishing Services.

Finally, our thanks for the support provided by the management of John Wiley & Sons, Inc.—especially Joe Heider, Vice President of Product and e-Business Development; Bonnie Lieberman, Senior Vice President of the College Division; and Will Pesce, President and Chief Executive Officer.

We thank Tootsie Roll Industries and Hershey Foods Corporation for permitting us the use of their 2007 Annual Reports for our specimen financial statements and accompanying notes.

We appreciate and encourage suggestions and comments from users. Please feel free to email any one of us at *AccountingAuthors@yahoo.com*.

Paul D. Kimmel
Milwaukee, Wisconsin

Jerry J. Weygandt
Madison, Wisconsin

Donald E. Kieso
DeKalb, Illinois

what are learning styles?

Have you ever repeated something to yourself over and over to help remember it? Or does your best friend ask you to draw a map to someplace where the two of you are planning to meet, rather than just *tell* her the directions? If so, then you already have an intuitive sense that people learn in different ways.

Researchers in learning theory have developed various categories of learning styles. Some people, for example, learn best by reading or writing. Others learn best by using various senses—seeing, hearing, feeling, tasting, or even smelling.

When you understand how you learn best, you can make use of learning strategies that will optimize the time you spend studying. To find out what your particular learning style is, go to the book's companion site at **www.wiley.com/college/ kimmel** and take the learning styles quiz you find there. The quiz will help you determine which is your primary learning style:

Visual learner	**Auditory learner**	**Haptic learner**	**Olfactory learner**
Print learner	**Interactive learner**	**Kinesthetic learner**	

Then, consult the information below and on the following pages for study tips for each learning style. This information will help you better understand your learning style and how to apply it to the study of accounting.

✓ Study Tips for Visual Learners

If you are a **Visual Learner** you prefer to work with images and diagrams. It is important that you *see* information.

Visual Learning:

- Draw charts/diagrams during lecture.
- Examine textbook figures and graphs.
- Look at images and videos on WileyPLUS and other websites.
- Pay close attention to charts, drawings, and handouts your instructors use.
- Underline; use different colors
- Use symbols, flow charts, graphs, different arrangements on the page, white spaces.

Visual Reinforcement:

- Make flashcards by drawing tables/charts on one side and definition or description on the other side
- Use art-based worksheets. Cover labels on images in text and then rewrite the labels.
- Use colored pencils/markers and colored paper to organize information into types.
- Convert your lecture notes into "page pictures." To do this:
  - Use the visual learning strategies outlined above.
  - Reconstruct images in different ways.
  - Redraw pages from memory.
  - Replace words with symbols and initials.
  - Draw diagrams where appropriate.
  - Practice turning your visuals back into words.

If visual learning is your weakness: If you are **not** a Visual Learner but want to improve your visual learning, try re-keying tables/charts from the textbook.

✓ Study Tips for Print Learners

If you are **Print Learner**, reading will be important but writing will be much more important.

Print Learning:

- Write text lecture notes during lecture.
- Read relevant topics in textbook, especially textbook tables.
- Look at text descriptions in animations and websites.
- Use lists and headings.
- Use dictionaries, glossaries, and definitions.

- Read handouts, textbooks, and supplementary library readings.
- Use lecture notes.

Print Reinforcement:

- Rewrite your notes from class and copy classroom handouts in your own handwriting.
- Make your own flashcards.
- Write out essays summarizing lecture notes or textbook topics.
- Develop mnemonics.
- Identify word relationships.
- Create tables with information extracted from textbook or lecture notes.
- Use text-based worksheets or crossword puzzles.
- Write out words again and again.
- Reread notes silently.
- Rewrite ideas and principles into other words.
- Turn charts, diagrams, and other illustrations into statements.
- Practice writing exam answers.
- Practice with multiple-choice questions.
- Write paragraphs, especially beginnings and endings.
- Write your lists in outline form.
- Arrange your words into hierarchies and points.

If print learning is your weakness: If you are **not** a Print Learner but want to improve your print learning, try covering labels of figures from the textbook and writing in the labels.

✓ Study Tips for Auditory Learners

If you are an **Auditory Learner**, then you prefer listening as a way to learn information. Hearing will be very important, and sound helps you focus.

Auditory Learning:

- Make audio recordings during lecture.
- Do not skip class. Hearing the lecture is essential to understanding.
- Play audio files provided by instructor and textbook.
- Listen to narration of animations.
- Attend lecture and tutorials.
- Discuss topics with students and instructors.
- Explain new ideas to other people.

- Leave spaces in your lecture notes for later recall.
- Describe overheads, pictures, and visuals to somebody who was not in class.

Auditory Reinforcement:

- Record yourself reading the notes and listen to the recording.
- Write out transcripts of the audio files.
- Summarize information that you have read, speaking out loud.
- Use a recorder to create self-tests.
- Compose "songs" about information.
- Play music during studying to help focus.
- Expand your notes by talking with others and with information from your textbook
- Read summarized notes out loud.
- Explain your notes to another auditory learner.
- Talk with the instructor.
- Spend time in quiet places recalling the ideas.
- Say your answers out loud.

If auditory learning is your weakness: If you are **not** an Auditory Learner but want to improve your auditory learning, try writing out the scripts from pre-recorded lectures.

✔ Study Tips for Interactive Learners

If you are an **Interactive Learner**, you will want to share your information. A study group will be important.

Interactive Learning:

- Ask a lot of questions during lecture or laboratory meetings.
- Contact other students, via email or discussion forums, and ask them to explain what they learned.

Interactive Reinforcement:

- "Teach" the content to a group of other students.
- Talking to an empty room may seem odd, but it will be effective for you.
- Discuss information with others, making sure that you both ask and answer questions.
- Work in small group discussions, making a verbal and written summary of what others say.

If interactive learning is your weakness: If you are **not** an Interactive Learner but want to improve your interactive learning, try asking your study partner questions and then repeating them to the instructor.

✔ Study Tips for Haptic Learners

If you are a **Haptic Learner**, you prefer to work with your hands. It is important to physically manipulate material.

Haptic Learning:

- Take blank paper to lecture to draw charts/tables/diagrams.
- Using the textbook, run your fingers along the figures and graphs to get a "feel" for shapes and relationships.

Haptic Reinforcement:

- Trace words and pictures on flash cards.
- Perform electronic exercises that involve drag-and-drop activities.
- Alternate between speaking and writing information.

- Observe someone performing a task that you would like to learn.
- Make sure you have freedom of movement while studying.

If haptic learning is your weakness: If you are **not** a Haptic Learner but want to improve your haptic learning, try spending more time in class working with formulas, financial statements, and tables while speaking or writing down information.

✔ Study Tips for Kinesthetic Learners

If you are a **Kinesthetic Learner** it will be important that you involve your body during studying.

Kinesthetic Learning:

- Ask permission to get up and move during lecture.
- Participate in role playing activities, in the classroom.
- Use all your senses
- Go to labs, take field trips
- Listen to real-life examples
- Pay attention to applications
- Use hands-on approaches
- Use trial-and-error methods

Kinesthetic Reinforcement:

- Make flash cards, place them on the floor and move your body around them.
- Move while you are "teaching" the material to others.
- Put examples in your summaries.
- Use case studies and applications to help with principles and abstract concepts.
- Talk about your notes with another Kinesthetic person.
- Use pictures and photographs that illustrate an idea.
- Write practice answers.
- Role-play the exam situation.

If kinesthetic learning is your weakness: If you are **not** a Kinesthetic Learner but want to improve your kinesthetic learning, try using flash cards to reconstruct balance sheets, income statements, cash flow statements, etc.

✔ Study Tips for Olfactory Learners

If you are an **Olfactory Learner**, then you will prefer to use the senses of smell and test to reinforce learning. This is a rare learning modality.

Olfactory Learning:

- During lecture, use different scented markers to identify different types of information.

Olfactory Reinforcement:

- Rewrite notes with scented markers.
- If possible, go back to the computer lab to do your studying.
- Burn aromatic candles while studying.
- Try to associate the material that you're studying with a pleasant taste or smell.

If olfactory learning is your weakness: If you are **not** an **Olfactory Learner**, but want to improve your olfactory learning, try burning an aromatic candle or incense while you study or eating cookies during study sessions.

WileyPLUS and Textbook Resources for Various Learning Styles

RESOURCES	Visual	Print	Auditory	Interactive	Haptic	Kinesthetic	Olfactory*
Content of textbook		✓					
The Navigator/Feature Story/Preview	✓	✓					
Study Objectives		✓					
Infographics/Illustrations	✓	✓					
Accounting Equation Analyses	✓	✓	✓	✓	✓	✓	
Decision Toolkits/Decision Toolkit Summaries	✓	✓		✓			
Do It! Exercises/Comprehensive Do It! Problem/Action Plan	✓	✓		✓	✓	✓	
Summary of Study Objectives		✓					
Glossary/Self-study questions		✓		✓	✓	✓	
Questions/Exercises/Problems	✓	✓		✓			
Alternate versions of exercises & problems (B exercises; Problem sets B & C)	✓	✓		✓			
Financial Reporting/Comparative Analysis Problems	✓	✓		✓	✓	✓	
Writing activities—Exercises and Problems marked with a pencil icon	✓	✓		✓	✓	✓	
Exploring the Web activity	✓	✓	✓	✓	✓	✓	
Communication Activity		✓		✓	✓	✓	
AAY Activity		✓		✓	✓	✓	
Practice quizzes		✓		✓	✓	✓	
Flash cards	✓	✓	✓	✓	✓	✓	
Audio Reviews/Video Clips/Clicker Content			✓	✓	✓	✓	
Flash Tutorial Reviews (Comprehensive Do It!/Accounting Cycle/Annual Report)	✓	✓	✓	✓	✓	✓	
Crossword Puzzles	✓	✓		✓	✓	✓	
Excel Templates/Excel Working Papers	✓	✓		✓	✓	✓	
Checklist of Key Figures	✓	✓					
Peachtree/Quickbooks/GLS	✓	✓		✓	✓	✓	
Self-study/Self-test web quizzes	✓	✓		✓	✓	✓	

*To improve your learning using your olfactory modality, look at the resources recommended for your other most preferred learning styles. Then, pair olfactory study techniques with other resources, to enhance your learning. For example, you can burn aromatic candles while working on Flash tutorial reviews or Excel templates in WileyPLUS, or you can use scented markers to create flashcards.

brief contents

contents

Introduction to Financial Statements

✓ the navigator

- Scan **Study Objectives** ○
- Read **Feature Story** ○
- Scan **Preview** ○
- Read **Text and Answer** **Do it!**
  p. 5 ○   p. 11 ○   p. 18 ○   p. 23 ○
- Work **Using the Decision Toolkit** ○
- Review **Summary of Study Objectives** ○
- Work **Comprehensive** **Do it!** p. 26 ○
- Answer **Self-Study Questions** ○
- Complete **Assignments** ○

study objectives

After studying this chapter, you should be able to:

1 Describe the primary forms of business organization.

2 Identify the users and uses of accounting information.

3 Explain the three principal types of business activity.

4 Describe the content and purpose of each of the financial statements.

5 Explain the meaning of assets, liabilities, and stockholders' equity, and state the basic accounting equation.

6 Describe the components that supplement the financial statements in an annual report.

✓ the navigator

The Navigator is a learning system designed to prompt you to use the learning aids in the chapter and to set priorities as you study.

Knowing the Numbers

Many students who take this course do not plan to be accountants. If you are in that group, you might be thinking, "If I'm not going to be an accountant, why do I need to know accounting?" In response, consider this quote from Harold Geneen, the former chairman of IT&T: "To be good at your business, you have to know the numbers—cold." Success in any business comes back to the numbers. You will rely on them to make decisions, and managers will use them to evaluate your performance. That is true whether your job involves marketing, production, management, or information systems.

In business, accounting and financial statements are the means for communicating the numbers. If you don't know how to read financial statements, you can't really know your business.

Many companies spend significant resources teaching their employees basic accounting so that they can read financial statements and understand how their actions affect the company's financial results. One such company is Springfield ReManufacturing Corporation (SRC). When Jack Stack and 11 other managers purchased SRC for 10 cents a share, it was a failing division of International Harvester. Jack's 119 employees were counting on him for their livelihood. He decided that for the company to survive, every employee needed to think like a businessperson and to act like an owner. To accomplish this, all employees at SRC took basic accounting courses and participated in weekly reviews of the company's financial statements. SRC survived, and eventually thrived. To this day, every employee (now numbering more than 1,000) undergoes this same training.

Many other companies have adopted this approach, which is called "open-book management." Even in companies that do not practice open-book management, employers generally assume that managers in all areas of the company are "financially literate."

Taking this course will go a long way to making you financially literate. In this book you will learn how to read and prepare financial statements, and how to use basic tools to evaluate financial results. In this first chapter we will introduce you to the financial statements of a real company whose products you are probably familiar with—Tootsie Roll. Tootsie Roll's presentation of its financial results is complete, yet also relatively easy to understand.

Tootsie Roll started off humbly in 1896 in a small New York City candy shop owned by an Austrian immigrant, Leo Hirshfield. The candy's name came from his five-year-old daughter's nickname—"Tootsie." Today the Chicago-based company produces more than 49 million Tootsie Rolls and 16 million Tootsie Pops *each day*. In fact, Tootsie Pops are at the center of one of science's most challenging questions: How many licks does it take to get to the Tootsie Roll center of a Tootsie Pop? The answer varies: Licking machines created at Purdue University and the University of Michigan report an average of 364 and 411 licks, respectively. In studies using human lickers, the answer ranges from 144 to 252. We recommend that you take a few minutes today away from your studies to determine your own results.

Source: Tootsie Roll information adapted from *www.tootsie.com*.

On the World Wide Web
Springfield ReManufacturing Corporation:
www.srcreman.com
Tootsie Roll Industries:
www.tootsie.com

How do you start a business? How do you determine whether your business is making or losing money? How should you finance expansion—should you borrow, should you issue stock, should you use your own funds? How do you convince lenders to lend you money or investors to buy your stock? Success in business requires making countless decisions, and decisions require financial information.

The purpose of this chapter is to show you what role accounting plays in providing financial information. The content and organization of the chapter are as follows.

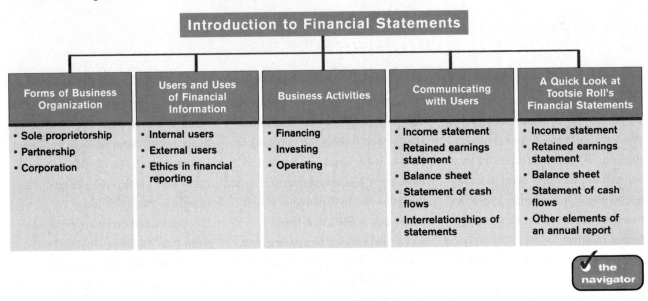

Forms of Business Organization

study objective **1**

Describe the primary forms of business organization.

Essential terms are printed in blue. They are defined again in the **glossary** at the end of the chapter.

Alternative Terminology notes present synonymous terms that you may come across in practice.

Alternative Terminology
Stockholders are sometimes called *shareholders.*

Suppose you graduate with a marketing degree and open your own marketing agency. One of your initial decisions is what organizational form your business will have. You have three choices—sole proprietorship, partnership, or corporation.

You will probably choose the sole proprietorship form for your marketing agency. A business owned by one person is a sole proprietorship. It is **simple to set up** and **gives you control** over the business. Small owner-operated businesses such as barber shops, law offices, and auto repair shops are often sole proprietorships, as are farms and small retail stores.

Another possibility is for you to join forces with other individuals to form a partnership. A business owned by two or more persons associated as partners is a partnership. Partnerships often are formed because one individual does not have **enough economic resources** to initiate or expand the business. Sometimes **partners bring unique skills or resources** to the partnership. You and your partners should formalize your duties and contributions in a written partnership agreement. Retail and service-type businesses, including professional practices (lawyers, doctors, architects, and certified public accountants), often organize as partnerships.

As a third alternative, you might organize as a corporation. A business organized as a separate legal entity owned by stockholders is a corporation. As an investor in a corporation you receive shares of stock to indicate your ownership claim. Buying stock in a corporation is often more attractive than investing in a partnership because shares of stock are **easy to sell** (transfer ownership). Selling a proprietorship or partnership interest is much more involved. Also, individuals can become **stockholders** by investing relatively small amounts of money. Therefore, it is **easier for corporations to raise funds**. Successful corporations often have thousands of stockholders, and their stock is traded on organized stock exchanges like the New York Stock Exchange. Many businesses start as sole proprietorships or partnerships and eventually incorporate. For example, in 1896 Leo Hirshfield started Tootsie Roll as a sole proprietorship, and by 1919 the company had incorporated.

Other factors to consider in deciding which organizational form to choose are **taxes and legal liability**. If you choose a sole proprietorship or partnership, you generally receive more favorable tax treatment than a corporation. However, proprietors and partners are personally liable for all debts of the business; corporate stockholders are not. In other words, corporate stockholders generally pay higher taxes but have no personal liability. We will discuss these issues in more depth in a later chapter. Illustration 1-1 highlights the three types of organizations and the advantages of each.

Illustrations like this one convey information in pictorial form to help you visualize and apply the ideas as you study.

Illustration 1-1 Forms of business organization

Sole Proprietorship

-Simple to establish
-Owner controlled
-Tax advantages

Partnership

-Simple to establish
-Shared control
-Broader skills and resources
-Tax advantages

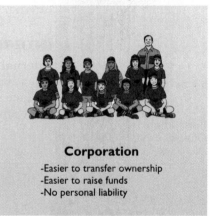

Corporation

-Easier to transfer ownership
-Easier to raise funds
-No personal liability

The combined number of proprietorships and partnerships in the United States is more than five times the number of corporations. However, the revenue produced by corporations is eight times greater. Most of the largest enterprises in the United States—for example, Coca-Cola, ExxonMobil, General Motors, Citigroup, and Microsoft—are corporations. Because the majority of U.S. business is transacted by corporations, the emphasis in this book is on the corporate form of organization.

Before You Go On...
Do it! exercises prompt you to stop and review the key points you have just studied.

before you go on...

Do it! Identify each of the following organizational characteristics with the organizational form or forms with which it is associated.

BUSINESS ORGANIZATION FORMS

1. Easier to raise funds
2. Simple to establish
3. No personal legal liability
4. Tax advantages
5. Easier to transfer ownership

Action Plan

• Know which organizational form best matches the business type, size, and preferences of the owner(s).

Action Plans give you tips about how to approach the problem.

Solution

1. Easier to raise funds: Corporation.
2. Simple to establish: Sole proprietorship and partnership.
3. No personal legal liability: Corporation.
4. Tax advantages: Sole proprietorship and partnership.
5. Easier to transfer ownership: Corporation.

Users and Uses of Financial Information

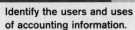 **study objective** 2

Identify the users and uses of accounting information.

The purpose of financial information is to provide inputs for decision making. **Accounting** is the information system that identifies, records, and communicates the economic events of an organization to interested users. **Users** of accounting information can be divided broadly into two groups: internal users and external users.

INTERNAL USERS

Internal users of accounting information are managers who plan, organize, and run a business. These include **marketing managers**, **production supervisors**, **finance directors**, **and company officers**. In running a business, managers must answer many important questions, as shown in Illustration 1-2.

Illustration 1-2
Questions that internal users ask

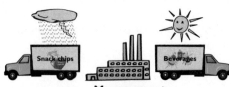

Questions Asked by Internal Users

Finance
Is cash sufficient to pay dividends to Microsoft stockholders?

Marketing
What price for an Apple iPod will maximize the company's net income?

Human Resources
Can we afford to give General Motors employees pay raises this year?

Management
Which PepsiCo product line is the most profitable? Should any product lines be eliminated?

To answer these and other questions, you need detailed information on a timely basis. For internal users, accounting provides internal reports, such as financial comparisons of operating alternatives, projections of income from new sales campaigns, and forecasts of cash needs for the next year. In addition, companies present summarized financial information in the form of financial statements.

Accounting Across the Organization

Accounting can serve as a useful recruiting tool even for the human resources department. Rhino Foods, located in Burlington, Vermont, is a manufacturer of specialty ice cream. Its corporate website includes the following:

> "Wouldn't it be great to work where you were part of a team? Where your input and hard work made a difference? Where you weren't kept in the dark about what management was thinking? . . . Well—it's not a dream! It's the way we do business . . . Rhino Foods believes in family, honesty and open communication—we really care about and appreciate our employees—and it shows. Operating results are posted and monthly group meetings inform all employees about what's happening in the Company. Employees also share in the Company's profits, in addition to having an excellent comprehensive *benefits* package."

Source: www.rhinofoods.com/workforus/workforus.html.

? What are the benefits to the company and to the employees of making the financial statements available to all employees? **Answers to questions appear on the last page of the chapter (p. 44).**

Accounting Across the Organization stories show applications of accounting information in various business functions.

EXTERNAL USERS

There are several types of **external users** of accounting information. **Investors** (owners) use accounting information to make decisions to buy, hold, or sell stock. **Creditors** such as suppliers and bankers use accounting information to evaluate the risks of selling on credit or lending money. Some questions that investors and creditors may ask about a company are shown in Illustration 1-3.

Illustration 1-3
Questions that external users ask

Questions Asked by External Users

Investors
Is General Electric earning satisfactory income?

Investors
How does Disney compare in size and profitability with Time Warner?

Creditors
Will United Airlines be able to pay its debts as they come due?

The information needs and questions of other external users vary considerably. **Taxing authorities**, such as the Internal Revenue Service, want to know whether the company complies with the tax laws. **Customers** are interested in whether a company like General Motors will continue to honor product warranties and otherwise support its product lines. **Labor unions** such as the Major League Baseball Players Association want to know whether the owners have the ability to pay increased wages and benefits. **Regulatory agencies**, such as the Securities and Exchange Commission or the Federal Trade Commission, want to know whether the company is operating within prescribed rules. For example, Enron, Dynegy, Duke Energy, and other big energy-trading companies reported record profits at the same time as California was paying extremely high prices for energy and suffering from blackouts. This disparity caused regulators to investigate the energy traders to make sure that the profits were earned by legitimate and fair practices.

Accounting Across the Organization

One question that accounting students frequently ask is, "How will the study of accounting help me?" It should help you a great deal, because a working knowledge of accounting is desirable for virtually every field of endeavor. Some examples of how accounting is used in business careers include:

General management: Imagine running Ford Motors, Massachusetts General Hospital, California State University–Fullerton, a McDonald's franchise, a Trek bike shop. All general managers need to understand accounting data in order to make wise business decisions.

Marketing: A marketing specialist at a company like Procter & Gamble develops strategies to help the sales force be successful. But making a sale is meaningless unless it is a profitable sale. Marketing people must be sensitive to costs and benefits, which accounting helps them quantify and understand.

Finance: Do you want to be a banker for Citicorp, an investment analyst for Goldman Sachs, a stock broker for Merrill Lynch? These fields rely heavily on accounting. In all of them you will regularly examine and analyze financial statements. In fact, it is difficult to get a good job in a finance function without two or three courses in accounting.

Real estate: Are you interested in being a real estate broker for Prudential Real Estate? Because a third party–the bank–is almost always involved in financing a real estate transaction, brokers must understand the numbers involved: Can the buyer afford to make the payments to the bank? Does the cash flow from an industrial property justify the purchase price? What are the tax benefits of the purchase?

? How might accounting help you?

ETHICS IN FINANCIAL REPORTING

People won't gamble in a casino if they think it is "rigged." Similarly, people won't "play" the stock market if they think stock prices are rigged. In recent years the financial press has been full of articles about financial scandals at Enron, WorldCom, HealthSouth, and AIG. As more scandals came to light, a mistrust of financial reporting in general seemed to be developing. One article in the *Wall Street Journal* noted that "repeated disclosures about questionable accounting practices have bruised investors' faith in the reliability of earnings reports, which in turn has sent stock prices tumbling."[1] Imagine trying to carry on a business or invest money if you could not depend on the financial statements to be honestly prepared. Information would have no credibility. There is no doubt that a sound, well-functioning economy depends on accurate and dependable financial reporting.

---

[1]"U.S. Share Prices Slump," *Wall Street Journal* (February 21, 2002).

United States regulators and lawmakers were very concerned that the economy would suffer if investors lost confidence in corporate accounting because of unethical financial reporting. In 2002 Congress passed the Sarbanes-Oxley Act (SOX) to reduce unethical corporate behavior and decrease the likelihood of future corporate scandals. As a result of SOX, top management must now certify the accuracy of financial information. In addition, penalties for fraudulent financial activity are much more severe. Also, SOX increased the independence of the outside auditors who review the accuracy of corporate financial statements, and increased the oversight role of boards of directors.

Effective financial reporting depends on sound ethical behavior. To sensitize you to ethical situations and to give you practice at solving ethical dilemmas, we address ethics in a number of ways in this book: (1) A number of the *Feature Stories* and other parts of the text discuss the central importance of ethical behavior to financial reporting. (2) *Business Insight boxes* with an ethics perspective highlight ethics situations and issues in actual business settings. (3) At the end of the chapter, an *Ethics Case* simulates a business situation and asks you to put yourself in the position of a decision maker in that case.

When analyzing these various ethics cases and your own ethical experiences, you should apply the three steps outlined in Illustration 1-4.

Ethics Note Circus-founder P.T. Barnum is alleged to have said, "Trust everyone, but cut the deck." What Sarbanes-Oxley does is to provide measures that (like cutting the deck of playing cards) help ensure that fraud will not occur.

Illustration 1-4 Steps in analyzing ethics cases

Solving an Ethical Dilemma

1. Recognize an ethical situation and the ethical issues involved.

Use your personal ethics to identify ethical situations and issues. Some businesses and professional organizations provide written codes of ethics for guidance in some business situations.

2. Identify and analyze the principal elements in the situation.

Identify the *stakeholders*— persons or groups who may be harmed or benefited. Ask the question: What are the responsibilities and obligations of the parties involved?

3. Identify the alternatives, and weigh the impact of each alternative on various stakeholders.

Select the most ethical alternative, considering all the consequences. Sometimes there will be one right answer. Other situations involve more than one right solution; these situations require you to evaluate each alternative and select the best one.

 ### International Insight

Accounting plays an important role for a wide range of business organizations worldwide. Just as the integrity of the numbers matters for business, it matters at least as much for not-for-profit organizations. Proper control and reporting help ensure that money is used the way donors intended. Donors are less inclined to give to an organization if they think the organization is subject to waste or theft. The accounting challenges of some large international not-for-profits rival those of the world's largest businesses. For example, billions of dollars were donated for relief of the tsunami victims of India and Sri Lanka. To assist in that effort, one international accounting firm volunteered to help create a system that would investigate allegations of fraud or waste. Another accounting system proposed by the United Nations would enable donors to track donations via the Web. In addition, the United Nations created rules to protect employees who report possible fraudulent activity.

Business Insights provide examples of business situations from various perspectives— ethics, investor, and international.

 What benefits does a sound accounting system provide to a not-for-profit organization?

Business Activities

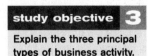

All businesses are involved in three types of activity—financing, investing, and operating. For example, Leo Hirshfield the founder of Tootsie Roll, obtained cash through financing to start and grow his business. Some of this **financing** came from personal savings, and some likely came from outside sources like banks. Hirshfield then **invested** the cash in equipment to run the business, such as mixing equipment and delivery vehicles. Once this equipment was in place, he could begin the **operating** activities of making and selling candy.

The **accounting information system** keeps track of the results of each of the various business activities—financing, investing, and operating. Let's look in more detail at each type of business activity.

FINANCING ACTIVITIES

Financing

It takes money to make money. The two primary sources of outside funds for corporations are borrowing money and issuing (selling) shares of stock in exchange for cash.

Tootsie Roll Industries may borrow money in a variety of ways. For example, it can take out a loan at a bank or borrow directly from investors by issuing debt securities called bonds. Persons or entities to whom Tootsie Roll owes money are its **creditors**. Amounts owed to creditors—in the form of debt and other obligations—are called liabilities. Specific names are given to different types of liabilities, depending on their source. Tootsie Roll may have a **note payable** to a bank for the money borrowed to purchase delivery trucks. Debt securities sold to investors that must be repaid at a particular date some years in the future are **bonds payable**.

A corporation may also obtain funds by selling shares of stock to investors. Common stock is the term used to describe the total amount paid in by stockholders for the shares they purchase.

The claims of creditors differ from those of stockholders. If you loan money to a company, you are one of its creditors. In lending money, you specify a payment schedule (e.g., payment at the end of three months). As a creditor, you have a legal right to be paid at the agreed time. In the event of nonpayment, you may legally force the company to sell property to pay its debts. In the case of financial difficulty, creditor claims must be paid before stockholders' claims.

Stockholders, on the other hand, have no claim to corporate cash until the claims of creditors are satisfied. If you buy a company's stock instead of loaning it money, you have no legal right to expect any payments until all of its creditors are paid. However, many corporations make payments to stockholders on a regular basis as long as there is sufficient cash to cover required payments to creditors. These payments to stockholders are called dividends.

INVESTING ACTIVITIES

Investing

Alternative Terminology
Property, plant, and equipment is sometimes called *fixed assets.*

Once the company has raised cash through financing activities, it will then use that cash in investing activities. Investing activities involve the purchase of the resources a company needs in order to operate. A growing company purchases many resources, such as computers, delivery trucks, furniture, and buildings. Resources owned by a business are called assets. Different types of assets are given different names. Tootsie Roll's mixing equipment is a type of asset referred to as **property**, **plant**, **and equipment**.

Cash is one of the more important assets owned by Tootsie Roll or any other business. If a company has excess cash that it does not need for a while, it might choose to invest in securities (stocks or bonds) of other corporations. **Investments** are another example of an investing activity.

OPERATING ACTIVITIES

Once a business has the assets it needs to get started, it can begin its operations. Tootsie Roll is in the business of selling all things that taste, look, or smell like candy. It sells Tootsie Rolls, Tootsie Pops, Blow Pops, Caramel Apple Pops, Mason Dots, Mason Crows, Sugar Daddy, and Sugar Babies. We call amounts earned on the sale of these products *revenues*. Revenue is the increase in assets resulting from the sale of a product or service in the normal course of business. For example, Tootsie Roll records revenue when it sells a candy product.

Operating

Revenues arise from different sources and are identified by various names depending on the nature of the business. For instance, Tootsie Roll's primary source of revenue is the sale of candy products. However, it also generates interest revenue on debt securities held as investments. Sources of revenue common to many businesses are **sales revenue**, **service revenue**, and **interest revenue**.

The company purchases its longer-lived assets through investing activities as described earlier. Other assets with shorter lives, however, result from operating activities. For example, supplies are assets used in day-to-day operations. Goods available for future sales to customers are assets called **inventory**. Also, if Tootsie Roll sells goods to a customer and does not receive cash immediately, then the company has a right to expect payment from that customer in the near future. This right to receive money in the future is called an **account receivable**.

Before Tootsie Roll can sell a single Tootsie Roll, Tootsie Pop, or Blow Pop, it must purchase sugar, corn syrup, and other ingredients, mix these ingredients, process the mix, and wrap and ship the finished product. It also incurs costs like salaries, rents, and utilities. All of these costs, referred to as *expenses*, are necessary to produce and sell the product. In accounting language, expenses are the cost of assets consumed or services used in the process of generating revenues.

Expenses take many forms and are identified by various names depending on the type of asset consumed or service used. For example, Tootsie Roll keeps track of these types of expenses: **cost of goods sold** (such as the cost of ingredients); **selling expenses** (such as the cost of salespersons' salaries); **marketing expenses** (such as the cost of advertising); **administrative expenses** (such as the salaries of administrative staff, and telephone and heat costs incurred at the corporate office); **interest expense** (amounts of interest paid on various debts); and **income taxes** (corporate taxes paid to government).

Tootsie Roll may also have liabilities arising from these expenses. For example, it may purchase goods on credit from suppliers; the obligations to pay for these goods are called **accounts payable**. Additionally, Tootsie Roll may have **interest payable** on the outstanding amounts owed to the bank. It may also have **wages payable** to its employees and **sales taxes payable**, **property taxes payable**, and **income taxes payable** to the government.

Tootsie Roll compares the revenues of a period with the expenses of that period to determine whether it earned a profit. When revenues exceed expenses, net income results. When expenses exceed revenues, a net loss results.

before you go on...

Do it! Classify each item as an asset, liability, common stock, revenue, or expense.

BUSINESS ACTIVITIES

1. Cost of renting property
2. Truck purchased
3. Notes payable
4. Issuance of ownership shares
5. Amount earned from providing service
6. Amounts owed to suppliers

Action Plan

• Classify each item based on its economic characteristics. Proper classification of items is critical if accounting is to provide useful information.

Solution

1. Cost of renting property: Expense.
2. Truck purchased: Asset.
3. Notes payable: Liabilities.
4. Issuance of ownership shares: Common stock.
5. Amount earned from providing service: Revenue.
6. Amounts owed to suppliers: Liabilities.

Communicating with Users

study objective 4

Describe the content and purpose of each of the financial statements.

Assets, liabilities, expenses, and revenues are of interest to users of accounting information. This information is arranged in the format of four different **financial statements**, which form the backbone of financial accounting:

• To present a picture at a point in time of what your business owns (its assets) and what it owes (its liabilities), you prepare a **balance sheet**.

• To show how successfully your business performed during a period of time, you report its revenues and expenses in an **income statement**.

International Note The primary types of financial statements required by international accounting standards (IFRS) and U.S. accounting standards (GAAP) are the same. Neither IFRS nor GAAP is very specific regarding format requirements for the primary financial statements. However, in practice, some format differences do exist in presentations commonly employed by IFRS companies compared to GAAP companies.

• To indicate how much of previous income was distributed to you and the other owners of your business in the form of dividends, and how much was retained in the business to allow for future growth, you present a **retained earnings statement**.

• To show where your business obtained cash during a period of time and how that cash was used, you present a **statement of cash flows**.

To introduce you to these statements, we have prepared the financial statements for a marketing agency, Sierra Corporation.

INCOME STATEMENT

The income statement reports the success or failure of the company's operations for a period of time. To indicate that its income statement reports the results of operations for a **period of time**, Sierra dates the income statement "For the Month Ended October 31, 2010." The income statement lists the company's revenues followed by its expenses. Finally, Sierra determines the net income (or net loss) by deducting expenses from revenues. Sierra Corporation's income statement is shown in Illustration 1-5.

Illustration 1-5 Sierra Corporation's income statement

Helpful Hint The heading identifies the company, the type of statement, and the time period covered. Sometimes another line indicates the unit of measure—e.g., "in thousands" or "in millions."

SIERRA CORPORATION Income Statement For the Month Ended October 31, 2010		
Revenues		
Service revenue		$10,600
Expenses		
Salaries expense	$5,200	
Supplies expense	1,500	
Rent expense	900	
Insurance expense	50	
Interest expense	50	
Depreciation expense	40	
Total expenses		7,740
Net income		$ 2,860

Why are financial statement users interested in net income? Investors are interested in Sierra's past net income because it provides useful information for predicting future net income. Investors buy and sell stock based on their beliefs about Sierra's future performance. If you believe that Sierra will be successful in the future and that this will result in a higher stock price, you should buy its stock. Creditors also use the income statement to predict future earnings. When a bank loans money to a company, it believes that it will be repaid in the future. If it didn't think it would be repaid, it wouldn't loan the money. Therefore, prior to making the loan the bank loan officer uses the income statement as a source of information to predict whether the company will be profitable enough to repay its loan.

Amounts received from issuing stock are not revenues, and amounts paid out as dividends are not expenses. As a result, they are not reported on the income statement. For example, Sierra Corporation does not treat as revenue the $10,000 of cash received from issuing new stock, nor does it regard as a business expense the $500 of dividends paid.

Ethics Note When companies find errors in previously released income statements, they restate those numbers. Perhaps because of the increased scrutiny caused by Sarbanes-Oxley, in a recent year companies filed a record 1,195 restatements.

Decision Toolkits summarize the financial decision-making process.

DECISION TOOLKIT

DECISION CHECKPOINTS	INFO NEEDED FOR DECISION	TOOL TO USE FOR DECISION	HOW TO EVALUATE RESULTS
Are the company's operations profitable?	Income statement	The income statement reports on the success or failure of the company's operations by reporting its revenues and expenses.	If the company's revenue exceeds its expenses, it will report net income; otherwise it will report a net loss.

RETAINED EARNINGS STATEMENT

If Sierra is profitable, at the end of each period it must decide what portion of profits to pay to shareholders in dividends. In theory it could pay all of its current-period profits, but few companies do this. Why? Because they want to retain part of the profits to allow for further expansion. High-growth companies, such as Google and Cisco Systems, often pay no dividends. Retained earnings is the net income retained in the corporation.

The retained earnings statement shows the amounts and causes of changes in retained earnings during the period. The time period is the same as that covered by the income statement. The beginning retained earnings amount appears on the first line of the statement. Then the company adds net income and deducts dividends to determine the retained earnings at the end of the period. If a company has a net loss, it deducts (rather than adds) that amount in the retained earnings statement. Illustration 1-6 presents Sierra Corporation's retained earnings statement.

SIERRA CORPORATION Retained Earnings Statement For the Month Ended October 31, 2010	
Retained earnings, October 1	$ 0
Add: Net income	2,860
	2,860
Less: Dividends	500
Retained earnings, October 31	$2,360

Illustration 1-6 Sierra Corporation's retained earnings statement

Helpful Hint The heading of this statement identifies the company, the type of statement, and the time period covered by the statement.

By monitoring the retained earnings statement, financial statement users can evaluate dividend payment practices. Some investors seek companies, such as Dow Chemical, that have a history of paying high dividends. Other investors seek companies, such as Amazon.com, that reinvest earnings to increase the company's growth instead of paying dividends. Lenders monitor their corporate customers' dividend payments because any money paid in dividends reduces a company's ability to repay its debts.

DECISION TOOLKIT

DECISION CHECKPOINTS	INFO NEEDED FOR DECISION	TOOL TO USE FOR DECISION	HOW TO EVALUATE RESULTS
What is the company's policy toward dividends and growth?	Retained earnings statement	How much of this year's income did the company pay out in dividends to shareholders?	A company striving for rapid growth will pay a low (or no) dividend.

BALANCE SHEET

study objective 5

Explain the meaning of assets, liabilities, and stockholders' equity, and state the basic accounting equation.

The **balance sheet** reports assets and claims to assets at a specific **point** in time. Claims to assets are subdivided into two categories: claims of creditors and claims of owners. As noted earlier, claims of creditors are called **liabilities**. Claims of owners are called stockholders' equity.

Illustration 1-7 shows the relationship among the categories on the balance sheet in equation form. This equation is referred to as the **basic accounting equation**.

Illustration 1-7 Basic accounting equation

Assets = Liabilities + Stockholders' Equity

This relationship is where the name "balance sheet" comes from. Assets must balance with the claims to assets.

As you can see from looking at Sierra's balance sheet in Illustration 1-8, the balance sheet presents the company's financial position as of a specific date—in this case, October 31, 2010. It lists assets first, followed by liabilities and stockholders' equity. Stockholders' equity is comprised of two parts: (1) common stock

Illustration 1-8 Sierra Corporation's balance sheet

Helpful Hint The heading of a balance sheet must identify the company, the statement, and the date.

SIERRA CORPORATION
Balance Sheet
October 31, 2010

Assets

Cash		$15,200
Accounts receivable		200
Advertising supplies		1,000
Prepaid insurance		550
Office equipment, net		4,960
Total assets		$21,910

Liabilities and Stockholders' Equity

Liabilities		
Notes payable	$ 5,000	
Accounts payable	2,500	
Salaries payable	1,200	
Unearned revenue	800	
Interest payable	50	
Total liabilities		$ 9,550
Stockholders' equity		
Common stock	10,000	
Retained earnings	2,360	
Total stockholders' equity		12,360
Total liabilities and stockholders' equity		$21,910

and (2) retained earnings. As noted earlier, common stock results when the company sells new shares of stock; retained earnings is the net income retained in the corporation. Sierra has common stock of $10,000 and retained earnings of $2,360, for total stockholders' equity of $12,360.

Creditors analyze a company's balance sheet to determine the likelihood that they will be repaid. They carefully evaluate the nature of the company's assets and liabilities. For example, does Sierra have assets that could be easily sold to repay its debts? Sierra's managers use the balance sheet to determine whether cash on hand is sufficient for immediate cash needs. They also look at the relationship between debt and stockholders' equity to determine whether the company has a satisfactory proportion of debt and common stock financing.

DECISION TOOLKIT

DECISION CHECKPOINTS	INFO NEEDED FOR DECISION	TOOL TO USE FOR DECISION	HOW TO EVALUATE RESULTS
Does the company rely primarily on debt or stockholders' equity to finance its assets?	Balance sheet	The balance sheet reports the company's resources and claims to those resources. There are two types of claims: liabilities and stockholders' equity.	Compare the amount of debt versus the amount of stockholders' equity to determine whether the company relies more on creditors or owners for its financing.

Ethics Insight

What topic has performers such as Tom Waits, Clint Black, Sheryl Crow, and Madonna so concerned that they are pushing for new laws regarding its use? Accounting. Recording-company accounting to be more precise. Musicians receive royalty payments based on the accounting done by their recording companies. Many performers say that the recording companies—either intentionally or unintentionally—have very poor accounting systems, which, the performers say, has resulted in many inaccurate royalty payments. They would like to see laws created that would hit the recording companies with stiff fines for accounting errors.

? What is one way that some of these disputes might be resolved?

STATEMENT OF CASH FLOWS

The primary purpose of a statement of cash flows is to provide financial information about the cash receipts and cash payments of a business for a specific period of time. To help investors, creditors, and others in their analysis of a company's cash position, the statement of cash flows reports the cash effects of a company's **operating**, **investing**, and **financing** activities. In addition, the statement shows the net increase or decrease in cash during the period, and the amount of cash at the end of the period.

Users are interested in the statement of cash flows because they want to know what is happening to a company's most important resource. The statement of cash flows provides answers to these simple but important questions:

• Where did cash come from during the period?
• How was cash used during the period?
• What was the change in the cash balance during the period?

The statement of cash flows for Sierra, in Illustration 1-9, shows that cash increased $15,200 during the month. This increase resulted because operating activities (services to clients) increased cash $5,700, and financing activities increased cash $14,500. Investing activities used $5,000 of cash for the purchase of equipment.

Illustration 1-9 Sierra Corporation's statement of cash flows

SIERRA CORPORATION Statement of Cash Flows For the Month Ended October 31, 2010		
Cash flows from **operating** activities		
Cash receipts from operating activities	$11,200	
Cash payments for operating activities	(5,500)	
Net cash provided by operating activities		$ 5,700
Cash flows from **investing** activities		
Purchased office equipment	(5,000)	
Net cash used by investing activities		(5,000)
Cash flows from **financing** activities		
Issuance of common stock	10,000	
Issued note payable	5,000	
Payment of dividend	(500)	
Net cash provided by financing activities		14,500
Net increase in cash		15,200
Cash at beginning of period		0
Cash at end of period		$15,200

Helpful Hint The heading of this statement identifies the company, the type of statement, and the time period covered by the statement. Negative numbers are shown in parentheses.

DECISION TOOLKIT

DECISION CHECKPOINTS	INFO NEEDED FOR DECISION	TOOL TO USE FOR DECISION	HOW TO EVALUATE RESULTS
Does the company generate sufficient cash from operations to fund its investing activities?	Statement of cash flows	The statement of cash flows shows the amount of cash provided or used by operating activities, investing activities, and financing activities.	Compare the amount of cash provided by operating activities with the amount of cash used by investing activities. Any deficiency in cash from operating activities must be made up with cash from financing activities.

INTERRELATIONSHIPS OF STATEMENTS

Because the results on some financial statements become inputs to other statements, the statements are interrelated. Illustration 1-10 shows the interrelationships for Sierra's financial statements, which we describe below.

1. The retained earnings statement depends on the results of the income statement. Sierra reported net income of $2,860 for the period. It adds the net income amount to the beginning amount of retained earnings in order to determine ending retained earnings.

2. The balance sheet and retained earnings statement also are interrelated: Sierra reports the ending amount of $2,360 on the retained earnings statement as the retained earnings amount on the balance sheet.

3. Finally, the statement of cash flows relates to information on the balance sheet. The statement of cash flows shows how the cash account changed during the period. It shows the amount of cash at the beginning of the period, the sources and uses of cash during the period, and the $15,200 of cash at the end of the period. The ending amount of cash shown on the statement of cash flows must agree with the amount of cash on the balance sheet.

Study these interrelationships carefully. To prepare financial statements you must understand the sequence in which these amounts are determined, and how each statement impacts the next.

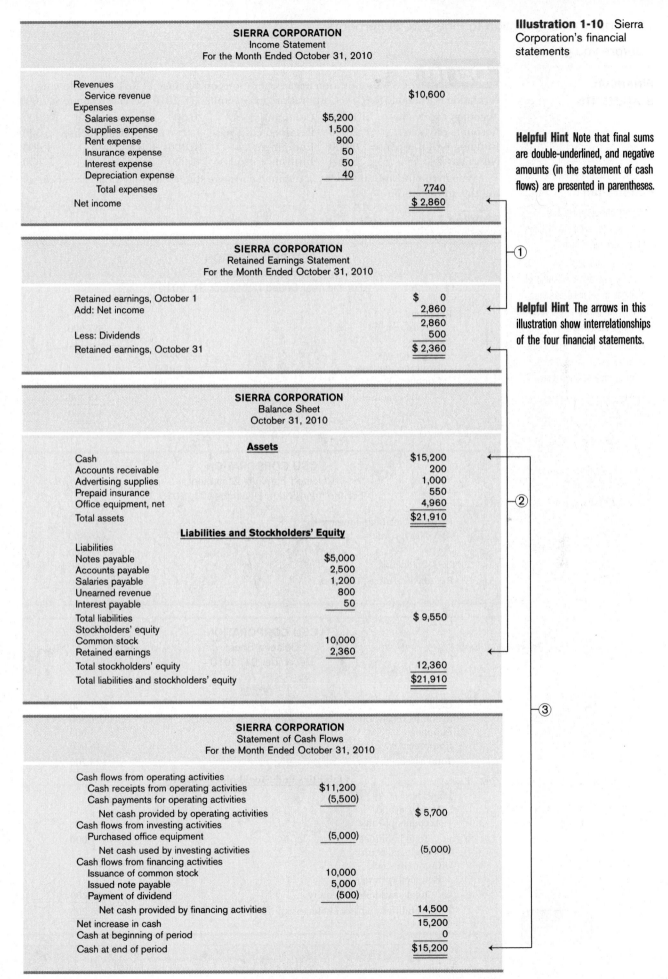

SIERRA CORPORATION
Income Statement
For the Month Ended October 31, 2010

Revenues		
Service revenue		$10,600
Expenses		
Salaries expense	$5,200	
Supplies expense	1,500	
Rent expense	900	
Insurance expense	50	
Interest expense	50	
Depreciation expense	40	
Total expenses		7,740
Net income		$ 2,860

Helpful Hint Note that final sums are double-underlined, and negative amounts (in the statement of cash flows) are presented in parentheses.

①

SIERRA CORPORATION
Retained Earnings Statement
For the Month Ended October 31, 2010

Retained earnings, October 1	$ 0
Add: Net income	2,860
	2,860
Less: Dividends	500
Retained earnings, October 31	$ 2,360

Helpful Hint The arrows in this illustration show interrelationships of the four financial statements.

SIERRA CORPORATION
Balance Sheet
October 31, 2010

Assets

Cash		$15,200
Accounts receivable		200
Advertising supplies		1,000
Prepaid insurance		550
Office equipment, net		4,960
Total assets		$21,910

Liabilities and Stockholders' Equity

Liabilities		
Notes payable	$5,000	
Accounts payable	2,500	
Salaries payable	1,200	
Unearned revenue	800	
Interest payable	50	
Total liabilities		$ 9,550
Stockholders' equity		
Common stock	10,000	
Retained earnings	2,360	
Total stockholders' equity		12,360
Total liabilities and stockholders' equity		$21,910

②

③

SIERRA CORPORATION
Statement of Cash Flows
For the Month Ended October 31, 2010

Cash flows from operating activities		
Cash receipts from operating activities	$11,200	
Cash payments for operating activities	(5,500)	
Net cash provided by operating activities		$ 5,700
Cash flows from investing activities		
Purchased office equipment	(5,000)	
Net cash used by investing activities		(5,000)
Cash flows from financing activities		
Issuance of common stock	10,000	
Issued note payable	5,000	
Payment of dividend	(500)	
Net cash provided by financing activities		14,500
Net increase in cash		15,200
Cash at beginning of period		0
Cash at end of period		$15,200

Illustration 1-10 Sierra Corporation's financial statements

before you go on...

**FINANCIAL
STATEMENTS**

Do it! CSU Corporation began operations on January 1, 2010. The following information is available for CSU Corporation on December 31, 2010: Service revenue $17,000

Accounts receivable	1,800	Common stock	10,000	Supplies	4,000
Accounts payable	2,000	Retained earnings	?	Supplies expense	200
Building rental expense	9,000	Equipment	16,000	Cash	1,400
Notes payable	5,000	Insurance expense	1,000	Dividends	600

Prepare an income statement, a retained earnings statement, and a balance sheet using this information.

Action Plan

- Report the revenues and expenses for a period of time in an income statement.
- Show the amounts and causes (net income and dividends) of changes in retained earnings during the period in the retained earnings statement.
- Present the assets and claims to those assets at a specific point in time in the balance sheet.

Solution

CSU CORPORATION
Income Statement
For the Year Ended December 31, 2010

Revenues		
Service revenue		$17,000
Expenses		
Rent expense	$9,000	
Insurance expense	1,000	
Supplies expense	200	
Total expenses		10,200
Net income		$ 6,800

CSU CORPORATION
Retained Earnings Statement
For the Year Ended December 31, 2010

Retained earnings, January 1	$ 0
Add: Net income	6,800
	6,800
Less: Dividends	600
Retained earnings, December 31	$6,200

CSU CORPORATION
Balance Sheet
December 31, 2010

Assets

Cash	$ 1,400
Accounts receivable	1,800
Supplies	4,000
Equipment	16,000
Total assets	$23,200

Liabilities and Stockholders' Equity

Liabilities		
Notes payable	$ 5,000	
Accounts payable	2,000	
Total liabilities		$ 7,000
Stockholders' equity		
Common stock	10,000	
Retained earnings	6,200	
Total stockholders' equity		16,200
Total liabilities and stockholders' equity		$23,200

the
navigator

A Quick Look at Tootsie Roll's Financial Statements

The same relationships that you observed among the financial statements of Sierra Corporation are evident in the 2007 financial statements of Tootsie Roll Industries, Inc., which are presented in Illustrations 1-11 through 1-14. We have simplified the financial statements to assist your learning. Tootsie Roll's **actual financial statements** are presented in **Appendix A** at the end of the book.

Before we dive in, we need to explain two points:

Tootsie Roll Annual Report Walkthrough

1. Note that numbers are reported in thousands on Tootsie Roll's financial statements—that is, the last three 000s are omitted. Thus, Tootsie Roll's net income in 2007 is $51,625,000, not $51,625.

2. Tootsie Roll, like most companies, presents its financial statements for more than one year. Financial statements that report information for more than one period are called comparative statements. Comparative statements allow users to compare the financial results of the business from one accounting period with those of previous periods.

Helpful Hint The percentage change in any amount from one year to the next is calculated as follows:

$$\frac{\text{Change during period}}{\text{Previous value}}$$

Thus, the percentage change in income is:

$$\frac{\text{Change in income}}{\text{Previous year's income}}$$

INCOME STATEMENT

Tootsie Roll's income statement is presented in Illustration 1-11. It reports total revenues in 2007 of $497,717,000. It then subtracts three types of expenses—cost of goods sold; selling, marketing, and administrative expenses; and income tax expense—to arrive at net income of $51,625,000. This is a 21.7% decrease from income for the previous year.

Illustration 1-11 Tootsie Roll's income statement

TOOTSIE ROLL INDUSTRIES, INC.
Income Statements
For the Years Ended December 31, 2007, and December 31, 2006
(in thousands)

	2007	2006
Revenues		
Sales revenue	$492,742	$495,990
Other revenues	4,975	5,150
Total revenues	497,717	501,140
Expenses		
Cost of goods sold	327,695	311,267
Selling, marketing, and administrative expenses, and other	92,855	95,158
Income tax expense	25,542	28,796
Total expenses	446,092	435,221
Net income	$ 51,625	$ 65,919

RETAINED EARNINGS STATEMENT

Illustration 1-12 (next page) presents Tootsie Roll's retained earnings statement. (Many companies present changes in retained earnings in a broader report called the Statement of Stockholders' Equity.) Find the line "Retained earnings, December 31, 2006." This number, $169,233,000, agrees with the retained earnings balance from the December 31, 2006, balance sheet.

As you proceed down the retained earnings statement, the next figure is net income of $51,625,000. Tootsie Roll distributed dividends of $64,106,000. The ending balance of retained earnings is $156,752,000 on December 31, 2007. Find

Illustration 1-12 Tootsie Roll's retained earnings statement

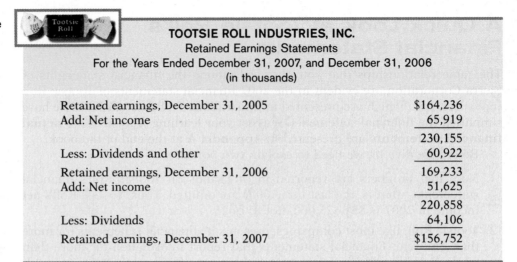

TOOTSIE ROLL INDUSTRIES, INC.
Retained Earnings Statements
For the Years Ended December 31, 2007, and December 31, 2006
(in thousands)

Retained earnings, December 31, 2005	$164,236
Add: Net income	65,919
	230,155
Less: Dividends and other	60,922
Retained earnings, December 31, 2006	169,233
Add: Net income	51,625
	220,858
Less: Dividends	64,106
Retained earnings, December 31, 2007	$156,752

this amount of retained earnings near the bottom of Tootsie Roll's balance sheet for December 31, 2007 (Illustration 1-13).

BALANCE SHEET

As shown in its balance sheet in Illustration 1-13, Tootsie Roll's assets include the kinds previously mentioned in our discussion of Sierra Corporation. These

Illustration 1-13 Tootsie Roll's balance sheet

TOOTSIE ROLL INDUSTRIES, INC.
Balance Sheets
December 31, 2007, and December 31, 2006
(in thousands)

Assets	**2007**	**2006**
Cash	$ 57,606	$ 55,729
Investments	41,307	23,531
Accounts receivable	35,284	39,007
Inventories	57,402	63,957
Prepaid expenses	6,551	6,489
Property, plant, and equipment, net	201,401	202,898
Other assets	413,174	400,028
Total assets	$812,725	$791,639
Liabilities and Stockholders' Equity		
Liabilities		
Accounts payable	$ 11,572	$ 13,102
Dividends payable	4,344	4,300
Accrued liabilities	42,056	43,802
Income taxes payable	0	1,007
Bonds payable	7,500	7,500
Employee benefits payable	53,027	50,383
Other liabilities	55,996	40,864
Total liabilities	174,495	160,958
Stockholders' equity		
Common stock	481,478	461,448
Retained earnings	156,752	169,233
Total stockholders' equity	638,230	630,681
Total liabilities and stockholders' equity	$812,725	$791,639

are cash, inventories, and property, plant, and equipment, plus other types of assets that we will discuss in later chapters, such as prepaid expenses. Tootsie Roll's total assets increased from $791,639,000 on December 31, 2006, to $812,725,000 on December 31, 2007. Its liabilities include accounts payable as well as items not yet discussed, such as employee benefits payable.

You can see that Tootsie Roll relies far more on equity financing than on debt—it has more than three times as much stockholders' equity as it has liabilities. As you learn more about financial statements we will discuss how to interpret the relationships and changes in financial statement items.

STATEMENT OF CASH FLOWS

Tootsie Roll's balance sheet shows that cash was $55,729,000 at December 31, 2006, and $57,606,000 at December 31, 2007. Thus, Tootsie Roll's cash increased $1,877,000 during 2007. The reasons for this increase can be determined by examining the statement of cash flows in Illustration 1-14. Tootsie Roll generated $90,064,000 from its operating activities during 2007. Its investing activities included capital expenditures (purchases of property, plant, and equipment) as well as purchases and sales of investment securities. The net effect of its investment activities is an outflow of cash of $43,345,000. Its financing activities involve the repurchase of its own common stock and the payment of cash dividends. In all, the net effect of the cash generated from its operating and financing activities, less the cash used in its investing activities, was a increase in cash of $1,877,000.

Illustration 1-14 Tootsie Roll's statement of cash flows

TOOTSIE ROLL INDUSTRIES, INC.
Statements of Cash Flows
For the Years Ended December 31, 2007, and December 31, 2006
(in thousands)

	2007	2006
Cash flows from operating activities		
Cash receipts from operating activities	$500,315	$455,647
Cash payments for operating activities	(410,251)	(399,991)
Net cash provided by operating activities	90,064	55,656
Cash flows from investing activities		
Capital expenditures and acquisitions	(14,767)	(39,207)
Purchase of investment securities	(59,132)	(35,663)
Sales of investment securities and other	30,554	85,896
Net cash provided (used) in investing activities	(43,345)	11,026
Cash flows from financing activities		
Repayment of bank loan	—	(32,001)
Repurchase of common stock	(27,300)	(30,694)
Dividends paid in cash	(17,542)	(17,264)
Net cash (used) by financing activities	(44,842)	(79,959)
Net increase (decrease) in cash	1,877	(13,277)
Cash at beginning of year	55,729	69,006
Cash at end of year	$57,606	$55,729

study objective 6

Describe the components that supplement the financial statements in an annual report.

OTHER ELEMENTS OF AN ANNUAL REPORT

U.S. companies that are publicly traded must provide shareholders with an annual report. The annual report always includes the financial statements introduced in this chapter. The annual report also includes other important information such as a management discussion and analysis section, notes to the financial statements, and an independent auditor's report. No analysis of a company's financial situation and prospects is complete without a review of these items.

Management Discussion and Analysis

The **management discussion and analysis (MD&A)** section covers various financial aspects of a company, including **its ability to pay near-term obligations, its ability to fund operations and expansion, and its results of operations**. Management must highlight favorable or unfavorable trends and identify significant events and uncertainties that affect these three factors. This discussion obviously involves a number of subjective estimates and opinions. A brief excerpt from the MD&A section of Tootsie Roll's annual report is presented in Illustration 1-15.

Illustration 1-15 Tootsie Roll's management discussion and analysis

TOOTSIE ROLL INDUSTRIES, INC.
Management's Discussion and Analysis of
Financial Condition and Results of Operations

The Company has a relatively straight-forward financial structure and has historically maintained a conservative financial position. Except for an immaterial amount of operating leases, the Company has no special financing arrangements or "off-balance sheet" special purpose entities. Cash flows from operations plus maturities of short term investments are expected to be adequate to meet the Company's overall financing needs, including capital expenditures, in 2008.

Notes to the Financial Statements

Explanatory notes and supporting schedules accompany every set of financial statements and are an integral part of the statements. The **notes to the financial statements** clarify the financial statements, and provide additional detail. Information in the notes does not have to be quantifiable (numeric). Examples of notes are descriptions of the significant accounting policies and methods used in preparing the statements, explanations of uncertainties and contingencies, and various statistics and details too voluminous to be included in the statements. The notes are essential to understanding a company's operating performance and financial position.

Illustration 1-16 is an excerpt from the notes to Tootsie Roll's financial statements. It describes the methods that Tootsie Roll uses to account for revenues.

Illustration 1-16 Notes to Tootsie Roll's financial statements

TOOTSIE ROLL INDUSTRIES, INC.
Notes to Financial Statements

Revenue recognition
Revenue, net of applicable provisions for discounts, returns, allowances, and certain advertising and promotional costs, is recognized when products are delivered to customers based on a customer purchase order, and collectibility is reasonably assured.

Auditor's Report

An **auditor's report** is prepared by an independent outside auditor. It states the auditor's opinion as to the fairness of the presentation of the financial position and results of operations and their conformance with generally accepted accounting standards.

An **auditor** is an accounting professional who conducts an independent examination of a company's financial statements. Only accountants who meet certain criteria and thereby attain the designation Certified Public Accountant (CPA) may perform audits. If the auditor is satisfied that the financial statements provide a fair representation of the company's financial position and results of operations in accordance with generally accepted accounting principles, then the auditor expresses an **unqualified opinion**. If the auditor expresses anything other than an unqualified opinion, then readers should only use the financial statements with caution. That is, without an unqualified opinion, we cannot have complete confidence that the financial statements give an accurate picture of the company's financial health.

Illustration 1-17 is an excerpt from the auditor's report from Tootsie Roll's 2007 annual report. Tootsie Roll received an unqualified opinion from its auditor, PricewaterhouseCoopers.

TOOTSIE ROLL INDUSTRIES, INC.
Excerpt from Auditor's Report

To the Board of Directors and Shareholders of Tootsie Roll Industries, Inc.

In our opinion, the accompanying consolidated balance sheets and the related consolidated statements of earnings, comprehensive earnings, retained earnings, and cash flows present fairly, in all material respects, the financial position of Tootsie Roll Industries, Inc. and its subsidiaries at December 31, 2007 and 2006, and the results of their operations and their cash flows for each of the three years in the period ended December 31, 2007, in conformity with accounting principles generally accepted in the United States of America.

Illustration 1-17 Excerpt from auditor's report on Tootsie Roll's financial statements

before you go on...

Do it!

State whether each of the following items is most closely associated with the management discussion and analysis (MD&A), the notes to the financial statements, or the auditor's report.

1. Descriptions of significant accounting policies
2. Unqualified opinion
3. Explanations of uncertainties and contingencies
4. Description of ability to fund operations and expansion
5. Description of results of operations
6. Certified Public Accountant (CPA)

Solution

1. Descriptions of significant accounting policies: Notes.
2. Unqualified opinion: Auditor's report.
3. Explanations of uncertainties and contingencies: Notes.
4. Description of ability to fund operations and expansion: MD&A.
5. Description of results of operations: MD&A.
6. Certified Public Accountant (CPA): Auditor's report.

COMPONENTS OF ANNUAL REPORTS

Action Plan

• Realize that financial statements provide information about a company's performance and financial position.

• Be familar with the other elements of the annual report in order to gain a fuller understanding of a company.

USING THE *DECISION TOOLKIT*

Hershey Foods Corporation, located in Hershey, Pennsylvania, is the leading North American manufacturer of chocolate—for example, Hershey's Kisses, Reese's Peanut Butter Cups, Kit Kat, and Take 5 bars. Imagine that you are considering the purchase of shares of Hershey's common stock.

Instructions

Answer these questions related to your decision whether to invest.
(a) What financial statements should you request from the company?
(b) What should these financial statements tell you?
(c) Should you request audited financial statements? Explain.
(d) Appendix B at the end of this book contains financial statements for Hershey Foods. What comparisons can you make between Tootsie Roll and Hershey in terms of their respective results from operations and financial position?

Solution

(a) Before you invest, you should investigate the income statement, retained earnings statement, statement of cash flows, and balance sheet.
(b) You would probably be most interested in the income statement because it tells about past performance and thus gives an indication of future performance. The retained earnings statement provides a record of the company's dividend history. The statement of cash flows reveals where the company is getting and spending its cash. This is especially important for a company that wants to grow. Finally, the balance sheet reveals the relationship between assets and liabilities.
(c) You would want audited financial statements. These statements indicate that a CPA (certified public accountant) has examined and expressed an opinion that the statements present fairly the financial position and results of operations of the company. Investors and creditors should not make decisions without studying audited financial statements.
(d) Many interesting comparisons can be made between the two companies. Tootsie Roll is smaller, with total assets of $812,725,000 versus $4,247,113,000 for Hershey, and it has lower revenue—$497,717,000 versus $4,946,716,000 for Hershey. In addition, Tootsie Roll's cash provided by operating activities of $90,064,000 is less than Hershey's $778,836,000.

While useful, these basic measures are not enough to determine whether one company is a better investment than the other. In later chapters you will learn of tools that will allow you to compare the relative profitability and financial health of these and other companies.

Summary of Study Objectives

1 Describe the primary forms of business organization. A sole proprietorship is a business owned by one person. A partnership is a business owned by two or more people associated as partners. A corporation is a separate legal entity for which evidence of ownership is provided by shares of stock.

2 Identify the users and uses of accounting information. Internal users are managers who need accounting information to plan, organize, and run business operations. The primary external users are investors and creditors. Investors (stockholders) use accounting information to help them decide whether to buy, hold, or sell shares of a company's stock. Creditors (suppliers and bankers) use accounting information to assess the risk of granting credit or loaning money to a business. Other groups who have an indirect interest in a business are taxing authorities, customers, labor unions, and regulatory agencies.

3 Explain the three principal types of business activity. Financing activities involve collecting the necessary funds to support the business. Investing activities involve acquiring the resources necessary to run the business. Operating activities involve putting the resources of the business into action to generate a profit.

4 **Describe the content and purpose of each of the financial statements.** An income statement presents the revenues and expenses of a company for a specific period of time. A retained earnings statement summarizes the changes in retained earnings that have occurred for a specific period of time. A balance sheet reports the assets, liabilities, and stockholders' equity of a business at a specific date. A statement of cash flows summarizes information concerning the cash inflows (receipts) and outflows (payments) for a specific period of time.

5 **Explain the meaning of assets, liabilities, and stockholders' equity, and state the basic accounting equation.** Assets are resources owned by a business. Liabilities are the debts and obligations of the business. Liabilities represent claims of creditors on the assets of the business. Stockholders' equity represents the claims of

owners on the assets of the business. Stockholders' equity is subdivided into two parts: common stock and retained earnings. The basic accounting equation is: Assets = Liabilities + Stockholders' Equity.

6 **Describe the components that supplement the financial statements in an annual report.** The management discussion and analysis provides management's interpretation of the company's results and financial position as well as a discussion of plans for the future. Notes to the financial statements provide additional explanation or detail to make the financial statements more informative. The auditor's report expresses an opinion as to whether the financial statements present fairly the company's results of operations and financial position.

DECISION TOOLKIT   A SUMMARY

DECISION CHECKPOINTS	INFO NEEDED FOR DECISION	TOOL TO USE FOR DECISION	HOW TO EVALUATE RESULTS
Are the company's operations profitable?	Income statement	The income statement reports on the success or failure of the company's operations by reporting its revenues and expenses.	If the company's revenue exceeds its expenses, it will report net income; otherwise it will report a net loss.
What is the company's policy toward dividends and growth?	Retained earnings statement	How much of this year's income did the company pay out in dividends to shareholders?	A company striving for rapid growth will pay a low (or no) dividend.
Does the company rely primarily on debt or stockholders' equity to finance its assets?	Balance sheet	The balance sheet reports the company's resources and claims to those resources. There are two types of claims: liabilities and stockholders' equity.	Compare the amount of debt versus the amount of stockholders' equity to determine whether the company relies more on creditors or owners for its financing.
Does the company generate sufficient cash from operations to fund its investing activities?	Statement of cash flows	The statement of cash flows shows the amount of cash provided or used by operating activities, investing activities, and financing activities.	Compare the amount of cash provided by operating activities with the amount of cash used by investing activities. Any deficiency in cash from operating activities must be made up with cash from financing activities.

Glossary

Accounting *(p. 6)* The information system that identifies, records, and communicates the economic events of an organization to interested users.

Annual report *(p. 21)* A report prepared by corporate management that presents financial information including financial statements, notes, a management discus-

sion and analysis section, and an independent auditor's report.

Assets *(p. 10)* Resources owned by a business.

Auditor's report *(p. 22)* A report prepared by an independent outside auditor stating the auditor's opinion as to the fairness of the presentation of the financial position and results of operations and their conformance with generally accepted accounting standards.

Balance sheet *(p. 14)* A financial statement that reports the assets and claims to those assets at a specific point in time.

Basic accounting equation *(p. 14)* Assets = Liabilities + Stockholders' Equity.

Certified Public Accountant (CPA) *(p. 23)* An individual who has met certain criteria and is thus allowed to perform audits of corporations.

Common stock *(p. 10)* Term used to describe the total amount paid in by stockholders for the shares they purchase.

Comparative statements *(p. 19)* A presentation of the financial statements of a company for more than one year.

Corporation *(p. 4)* A business organized as a separate legal entity having ownership divided into transferable shares of stock.

Dividends *(p. 10)* Payments of cash from a corporation to its stockholders.

Expenses *(p. 11)* The cost of assets consumed or services used in the process of generating revenues.

Income statement *(p. 12)* A financial statement that presents the revenues and expenses and resulting net income or net loss of a company for a specific period of time.

Liabilities *(p. 10)* The debts and obligations of a business. Liabilities represent the amounts owed to creditors.

Management discussion and analysis (MD&A) *(p. 22)* A section of the annual report that presents management's views on the company's ability to pay near-term obligations, its ability to fund operations and expansion, and its results of operations.

Net income *(p. 11)* The amount by which revenues exceed expenses.

Net loss *(p. 11)* The amount by which expenses exceed revenues.

Notes to the financial statements *(p. 22)* Notes that clarify information presented in the financial statements, as well as expand upon it where additional detail is needed.

Partnership *(p. 4)* A business owned by two or more persons associated as partners.

Retained earnings *(p. 13)* The amount of net income retained in the corporation.

Retained earnings statement *(p. 13)* A financial statement that summarizes the amounts and causes of changes in retained earnings for a specific period of time.

Revenue *(p. 11)* The increase in assets that result from the sale of a product or service in the normal course of business.

Sarbanes-Oxley Act *(p. 9)* Regulations passed by Congress in 2002 to try to reduce unethical corporate behavior.

Sole proprietorship *(p. 4)* A business owned by one person.

Statement of cash flows *(p. 15)* A financial statement that provides financial information about the cash receipts and cash payments of a business for a specific period of time.

Stockholders' equity *(p. 14)* The owners' claim on total assets.

Comprehensive **Do it!**

The Comprehensive Do It! is a final review before you begin homework.

Jeff Andringa, a former college hockey player, quit his job and started Ice Camp, a hockey camp for kids ages 8 to 18. Eventually he would like to open hockey camps nationwide. Jeff has asked you to help him prepare financial statements at the end of his first year of operations. He relates the following facts about his business activities.

In order to get the business off the ground, he decided to incorporate. He sold shares of common stock to a few close friends, as well as buying some of the shares himself. He initially raised $25,000 through the sale of these shares. In addition, the company took out a $10,000 loan at a local bank.

Ice Camp purchased, for $12,000 cash, a bus for transporting kids. The company also bought hockey goals and other miscellaneous equipment with $1,500 cash. The company earned camp tuition during the year of $100,000 but had collected only $80,000 of this amount. Thus, at the end of the year its customers still owed $20,000. The company rents time at a local rink for $50 per hour. Total rink rental costs during the year were $8,000, insurance was $10,000, salary expense was $20,000, and administrative expenses totaled $9,000, all of which were paid in cash. The company incurred $800 in interest expense on the bank loan, which it still owed at the end of the year.

The company paid dividends during the year of $5,000 cash. The balance in the corporate bank account at December 31, 2010, was $49,500.

Instructions

Using the format of the Sierra Corporation statements in this chapter, prepare an income statement, retained earnings statement, balance sheet, and statement of cash flows. (*Hint:* Prepare the statements in the order stated to take advantage of the flow of information from one statement to the next, as shown in Illustration 1-10 on page 17.)

Solution to Comprehensive Do it!

ICE CAMP

Income Statement
For the Year Ended December 31, 2010

Revenues		
Camp tuition revenue		$100,000
Expenses		
Salaries expense	$20,000	
Insurance expense	10,000	
Administrative expense	9,000	
Rink rental expense	8,000	
Interest expense	800	
Total expenses		47,800
Net income		$ 52,200

ICE CAMP

Retained Earnings Statement
For the Year Ended December 31, 2010

Retained earnings, January 1, 2010	$ 0
Add: Net income	52,200
	52,200
Less: Dividends	5,000
Retained earnings, December 31, 2010	$47,200

ICE CAMP

Balance Sheet
December 31, 2010

Assets

Cash	$49,500
Accounts receivable	20,000
Bus	12,000
Equipment	1,500
Total assets	$83,000

Liabilities and Stockholders' Equity

Liabilities		
Bank loan payable	$10,000	
Interest payable	800	
Total liabilities		$10,800
Stockholders' equity		
Common stock	25,000	
Retained earnings	47,200	
Total stockholders' equity		72,200
Total liabilities and stockholders' equity		$83,000

Action Plan

- On the income statement: Show revenues and expenses for a period of time.
- On the retained earnings statement: Show the changes in retained earnings for a period of time.
- On the balance sheet: Report assets, liabilities, and stockholders' equity at a specific date.
- On the statement of cash flows: Report sources and uses of cash from operating, investing, and financing activities for a period of time.

Solution continues on next page.

ICE CAMP

Statement of Cash Flows

For the Year Ended December 31, 2010

Cash flows from operating activities		
Cash receipts from operating activities	$80,000	
Cash payments for operating activities	(47,000)	
Net cash provided by operating activities		$33,000
Cash flows from investing activities		
Purchase of bus	(12,000)	
Purchase of equipment	(1,500)	
Net cash used by investing activities		(13,500)
Cash flows from financing activities		
Issuance of bank loan payable	10,000	
Issuance of common stock	25,000	
Dividends paid	(5,000)	
Net cash provided by financing activities		30,000
Net increase in cash		49,500
Cash at beginning of period		0
Cash at end of period		$49,500

the navigator

This would be a good time to look at the **Student Owner's Manual** at the beginning of the book. Knowing the purpose of the different types of homework will help you understand what each contributes to your accounting skills and competencies.

The tool icon ⚙ indicates that an activity employs one of the decision tools presented in the chapter. The ◀ indicates that an activity relates to a business function beyond accounting. The pencil icon ✏ indicates that an activity requires written communication.

Self-Study Questions

WILEY PLUS

Answers are at the end of the chapter.

(SO 1) **1.** Which is not one of the three forms of business organization?
  (a) Sole proprietorship.   (c) Partnership.
  (b) Creditorship.   (d) Corporation.

(SO 1) **2.** Which is an advantage of corporations relative to partnerships and sole proprietorships?
  (a) Lower taxes.
  (b) Harder to transfer ownership.
  (c) Reduced legal liability for investors.
  (d) Most common form of organization.

(SO 2) **3.** Which statement about users of accounting information is *incorrect*?
  (a) Management is considered an internal user.
  (b) Taxing authorities are considered external users.
  (c) Present creditors are considered external users.
  (d) Regulatory authorities are considered internal users.

(SO 2) **4.** Which of the following did *not* result from the Sarbanes-Oxley Act?

  (a) Top management must now certify the accuracy of financial information.
  (b) Penalties for fraudulent activity increased.
  (c) Independence of auditors increased.
  (d) Tax rates on corporations increased.

5. Which is not one of the three primary business (SO 3) activities?
  (a) Financing.   (c) Advertising.
  (b) Operating.   (d) Investing.

6. Which of the following is an example of a financing (SO 3) activity?
  (a) Issuing shares of common stock.
  (b) Selling goods on account.
  (c) Buying delivery equipment.
  (d) Buying inventory.

7. Net income will result during a time period when: (SO 4)
  (a) assets exceed liabilities.
  (b) assets exceed revenues.
  (c) expenses exceed revenues.
  (d) revenues exceed expenses.

(SO 4) **8.** The financial statements for Harold Corporation contained the following information.

Accounts receivable	$ 5,000
Sales revenue	75,000
Cash	15,000
Salaries expense	20,000
Rent expense	10,000

What was Harold's net income?
(a) $60,000.   (c) $65,000.
(b) $15,000.   (d) $45,000.

(SO 4, 5) **9.** What section of a cash flow statement indicates the cash spent on new equipment during the past accounting period?
(a) The investing section.
(b) The operating section.
(c) The financing section.
(d) The cash flow statement does not give this information.

(SO 4, 5) **10.** Which statement presents information as of a specific point in time?
(a) Income statement.
(b) Balance sheet.
(c) Statement of cash flows.
(d) Retained earnings statement.

(SO 5) **11.** Which financial statement reports assets, liabilities, and stockholders' equity?
(a) Income statement.
(b) Retained earnings statement.
(c) Balance sheet.
(d) Statement of cash flows.

(SO 5) **12.** Stockholders' equity represents:
(a) claims of creditors.
(b) claims of employees.
(c) the difference between revenues and expenses.
(d) claims of owners.

(SO 5) **13.** As of December 31, 2007, Stoneland Corporation has assets of $3,500 and stockholders' equity of $2,000. What are the liabilities for Stoneland Corporation as of December 31, 2007?
(a) $1,500.   (c) $2,500.
(b) $1,000.   (d) $2,000.

(SO 6) **14.** The element of a corporation's annual report that describes the corporation's accounting methods is the:
(a) notes to the financial statements.
(b) management discussion and analysis.
(c) auditor's report.
(d) income statement.

(SO 6) **15.** The element of the annual report that presents an opinion regarding the fairness of the presentation of the financial position and results of operations is/are the:
(a) income statement.
(b) auditor's opinion.
(c) balance sheet.
(d) comparative statements.

Go to the book's companion website, **www.wiley.com/college/kimmel**, to access additional Self-Study Questions.

Questions

1. What are the three basic forms of business organizations?

2. What are the advantages to a business of being formed as a corporation? What are the disadvantages?

3. What are the advantages to a business of being formed as a partnership or sole proprietorship? What are the disadvantages?

4. "Accounting is ingrained in our society and is vital to our economic system." Do you agree? Explain.

5. Who are the internal users of accounting data? How does accounting provide relevant data to the internal users?

6. Who are the external users of accounting data? Give examples.

7. What are the three main types of business activity? Give examples of each activity.

8. Listed here are some items found in the financial statements of Ellyn Toth, Inc. Indicate in which financial statement(s) each item would appear.
(a) Service revenue.   (d) Accounts receivable.
(b) Equipment.   (e) Common stock.
(c) Advertising expense.   (f) Wages payable.

9. Why would a bank want to monitor the dividend payment practices of the corporations it lends money to?

10. "A company's net income appears directly on the income statement and the retained earnings statement, and it is included indirectly in the company's balance sheet." Do you agree? Explain.

11. What is the primary purpose of the statement of cash flows?

12. What are the three main categories of the statement of cash flows? Why do you think these categories were chosen?

13. What is retained earnings? What items increase the balance in retained earnings? What items decrease the balance in retained earnings?

14. What is the basic accounting equation?

15. (a) Define the terms *assets*, *liabilities*, and *stockholders' equity*.
(b) What items affect stockholders' equity?

16. Which of these items are liabilities of White Glove Cleaning Service?
(a) Cash.   (c) Dividends.
(b) Accounts payable.   (d) Accounts receivable.

(e) Supplies.
(f) Equipment.
(g) Salaries payable.

(h) Service revenue.
(i) Rent expense.

17. How are each of the following financial statements interrelated? (a) Retained earnings statement and income statement. (b) Retained earnings statement and balance sheet. (c) Balance sheet and statement of cash flows.

18. What is the purpose of the management discussion and analysis section (MD&A)?

19. Why is it important for financial statements to receive an unqualified auditor's opinion?

20. What types of information are presented in the notes to the financial statements?

21. The accounting equation is: Assets = Liabilities + Stockholders' Equity. Appendix A, at the end of this book, reproduces Tootsie Roll's financial statements. Replacing words in the equation with dollar amounts, what is Tootsie Roll's accounting equation at December 31, 2007?

the navigator

Brief Exercises

WILEY
PLUS

Describe forms of business organization.
(SO 1)

BE1-1 Match each of the following forms of business organization with a set of characteristics: sole proprietorship (SP), partnership (P), corporation (C).
(a) _____ Shared control, tax advantages, increased skills and resources.
(b) _____ Simple to set up and maintains control with founder.
(c) _____ Easier to transfer ownership and raise funds, no personal liability.

Identify users of accounting information.
(SO 2)

BE1-2 Match each of the following types of evaluation with one of the listed users of accounting information.

1. Trying to determine whether the company complied with tax laws.
2. Trying to determine whether the company can pay its obligations.
3. Trying to determine whether a marketing proposal will be cost effective.
4. Trying to determine whether the company's net income will result in a stock price increase.
5. Trying to determine whether the company should employ debt or equity financing.
(a) _____ Investors in common stock.
(b) _____ Marketing managers.
(c) _____ Creditors.
(d) _____ Chief Financial Officer.
(e) _____ Internal Revenue Service.

Classify items by activity.
(SO 3, 4)

BE1-3 Indicate in which part of the statement of cash flows each item would appear: operating activities (O), investing activities (I), or financing activities (F).
(a) _____ Cash received from customers.
(b) _____ Cash paid to stockholders (dividends).
(c) _____ Cash received from issuing new common stock.
(d) _____ Cash paid to suppliers.
(e) _____ Cash paid to purchase a new office building.

Determine effect of transactions on stockholders' equity.
(SO 4)

BE1-4 Presented below are a number of transactions. Determine whether each transaction affects common stock (C), dividends (D), revenue (R), expense (E), or does not affect stockholders' equity (NSE). Provide titles for the revenues and expenses.
(a) Costs incurred for advertising.
(b) Assets received for services performed.
(c) Costs incurred for insurance.
(d) Amounts paid to employees.
(e) Cash distributed to stockholders.
(f) Assets received in exchange for allowing the use of the company's building.
(g) Costs incurred for utilities used.
(h) Cash purchase of equipment.
(i) Issued common stock for cash.

Prepare a balance sheet.
(SO 4, 5)

BE1-5 In alphabetical order below are balance sheet items for Mantle Company at December 31, 2010. Prepare a balance sheet following the format of Illustration 1-8.

Accounts payable	$75,000
Accounts receivable	81,000
Cash	22,000
Common stock	28,000

BE1-6   Eskimo Pie Corporation markets a broad range of frozen treats, including its famous Eskimo Pie ice cream bars. The following items were taken from a recent income statement and balance sheet. In each case identify whether the item would appear on the balance sheet (BS) or income statement (IS).

Determine where items appear on financial statements.
(SO 4, 5)

(a) _____ Income tax expense.
(b) _____ Inventories.
(c) _____ Accounts payable.
(d) _____ Retained earnings.
(e) _____ Property, plant, and equipment.

(f) _____ Net sales.
(g) _____ Cost of goods sold.
(h) _____ Common stock.
(i) _____ Receivables.
(j) _____ Interest expense.

BE1-7   Indicate which statement you would examine to find each of the following items: income statement (I), balance sheet (B), retained earnings statement (R), or statement of cash flows (C).

Determine proper financial statement.
(SO 4)

(a) Revenue during the period.
(b) Supplies on hand at the end of the year.
(c) Cash received from issuing new bonds during the period.
(d) Total debts outstanding at the end of the period.

BE1-8   Use the basic accounting equation to answer these questions.

Use basic accounting equation.
(SO 5)

(a) The liabilities of Cummings Company are $90,000 and the stockholders' equity is $230,000. What is the amount of Cummings Company's total assets?
(b) The total assets of Haldeman Company are $170,000 and its stockholders' equity is $90,000. What is the amount of its total liabilities?
(c) The total assets of Dain Co. are $800,000 and its liabilities are equal to one-fourth of its total assets. What is the amount of Dain Co.'s stockholders' equity?

BE1-9   At the beginning of the year, Fuqua Company had total assets of $800,000 and total liabilities of $500,000.

Use basic accounting equation.
(SO 5)

(a) If total assets increased $150,000 during the year and total liabilities decreased $80,000, what is the amount of stockholders' equity at the end of the year?
(b) During the year, total liabilities increased $100,000 and stockholders' equity decreased $70,000. What is the amount of total assets at the end of the year?
(c) If total assets decreased $90,000 and stockholders' equity increased $110,000 during the year, what is the amount of total liabilities at the end of the year?

BE1-10   Indicate whether each of these items is an asset (A), a liability (L), or part of stockholders' equity (SE).

Identify assets, liabilities, and stockholders' equity.
(SO 5)

(a) Accounts receivable.
(b) Salaries payable.
(c) Equipment.

(d) Office supplies.
(e) Common stock.
(f) Notes payable.

BE1-11   Which is *not* a required part of an annual report of a publicly traded company?
(a) Statement of cash flows.
(b) Notes to the financial statements.
(c) Management discussion and analysis.
(d) All of these are required.

Determine required parts of annual report.
(SO 6)

Do it! Review

Do it! **1-1**   Identify each of the following organizational characteristics with the organizational form or forms with which it is associated.

Identify benefits of business organization forms.
(SO 1)

1. Easier to transfer ownership
2. Easier to raise funds
3. More owner control
4. Tax advantages
5. No personal legal liability

Do it! **1-2**   Classify each item as an asset, liability, common stock, revenue, or expense.

Classify business activities.
(SO 3)

1. Issuance of ownership shares
2. Land purchased
3. Amounts owed to suppliers
4. Bonds payable
5. Amount earned from selling a product
6. Cost of advertising

Prepare financial statements.
(SO 4)

Do it! **1-3** Cougar Corporation began operations on January 1, 2010. The following information is available for Cougar Corporation on December 31, 2010.

Accounts payable	$ 5,000	Notes payable	$ 7,000
Accounts receivable	3,000	Rent expense	10,000
Advertising expense	2,000	Retained earnings	?
Cash	3,100	Service revenue	25,000
Common stock	15,000	Supplies	1,900
Dividends	2,500	Supplies expense	1,700
Equipment	27,800		

Prepare an income statement, a retained earnings statement, and a balance sheet for Cougar Corporation.

Identify components of
annual reports.
(SO 6)

Do it! **1-4** Indicate whether each of the following items is most closely associated with the management discussion and analysis (MD&A), the notes to the financial statements, or the auditor's report.

1. Description of ability to pay near-term obligations
2. Unqualified opinion
3. Details concerning liabilities, too voluminous to be included in the statements
4. Description of favorable and unfavorable trends
5. Certified Public Accountant (CPA)
6. Descriptions of significant accounting policies

Exercises

Match items with
descriptions.
(SO 1, 2, 4, 6)

E1-1 Here is a list of words or phrases discussed in this chapter:

1. Corporation	4. Partnership	7. Accounts payable
2. Creditor	5. Stockholder	8. Auditor's opinion
3. Accounts receivable	6. Common stock	

Instructions
Match each word or phrase with the best description of it.

_____ (a) An expression about whether financial statements are presented in conformance with generally accepted accounting principles.
_____ (b) A business enterprise that raises money by issuing shares of stock.
_____ (c) The portion of stockholders' equity that results from receiving cash from investors.
_____ (d) Obligations to suppliers of goods.
_____ (e) Amounts due from customers.
_____ (f) A party to whom a business owes money.
_____ (g) A party that invests in common stock.
_____ (h) A business that is owned jointly by two or more individuals but does not issue stock.

Identify business activities.
(SO 3)

E1-2 All businesses are involved in three types of activities—financing, investing, and operating. Listed below are the names and descriptions of companies in several different industries.

Abitibi Consolidated Inc.—manufacturer and marketer of newsprint
Cal State–Northridge Stdt Union—university student union
Oracle Corporation—computer software developer and retailer
Sportsco Investments—owner of the Vancouver Canucks hockey club
Grant Thornton LLP—professional accounting and business advisory firm
Southwest Airlines—discount airline

Instructions
(a) For each of the above companies, provide examples of (1) a financing activity, (2) an investing activity, and (3) an operating activity that the company likely engages in.
(b) Which of the activities that you identified in (a) are common to most businesses? Which activities are not?

E1-3 The Long Run Golf & Country Club details the following accounts in its financial statements.

Classify accounts.
(SO 3, 4)

	(a)	(b)
Accounts payable and accrued liabilities	___	___
Accounts receivable	___	___
Property, plant, and equipment	___	___
Food and beverage operations revenue	___	___
Golf course operations revenue	___	___
Inventory	___	___
Long-term debt	___	___
Office and general expense	___	___
Professional fees expense	___	___
Wages and benefits expense	___	___

Instructions
(a) Classify each of the above accounts as an asset (A), liability (L), stockholders' equity (SE), revenue (R), or expense (E) item.
(b) Classify each of the above accounts as a financing activity (F), investing activity (I), or operating activity (O). If you believe a particular account doesn't fit in any of these activities, explain why.

E1-4 This information relates to Denson Co. for the year 2010.

Prepare income statement and retained earnings statement.
(SO 4)

Retained earnings, January 1, 2010	$64,000
Advertising expense	1,800
Dividends paid during 2010	6,000
Rent expense	10,400
Service revenue	53,000
Utilities expense	2,400
Salaries expense	30,000

Instructions
After analyzing the data, prepare an income statement and a retained earnings statement for the year ending December 31, 2010.

E1-5 The following information was taken from the 2006 financial statements of pharmaceutical giant Merck and Co. All dollar amounts are in millions.

Prepare income statement and retained earnings statement.
(SO 4)

Retained earnings, January 1, 2006	$37,980.0
Materials and production expense	6,001.1
Marketing and administrative expense	8,165.4
Dividends	3,318.7
Sales revenue	22,636.0
Research and development expense	4,782.9
Tax expense	1,787.6
Other revenue	2,677.1

Instructions
(a) After analyzing the data, prepare an income statement and a retained earnings statement for the year ending December 31, 2006.
(b) Suppose that Merck decided to reduce its research and development expense by 50%. What would be the short-term implications? What would be the long-term implications? How do you think the stock market would react?

E1-6 Presented here is information for Willingham Inc. for 2010.

Prepare a retained earnings statement.
(SO 4)

Retained earnings, January 1	$130,000
Revenue from legal services	400,000
Total expenses	170,000
Dividends	82,000

Instructions
Prepare the 2010 retained earnings statement for Willingham Inc.

E1-7 Consider each of the following independent situations.
(a) The retained earnings statement of Hollis Corporation shows dividends of $68,000, while net income for the year was $75,000.

Interpret financial facts.
(SO 4)

(b) The statement of cash flows for Zhiang Corporation shows that cash provided by operating activities was $10,000, cash used in investing activities was $110,000, and cash provided by financing activities was $130,000.

Instructions

For each company provide a brief discussion interpreting these financial facts. For example, you might discuss the company's financial health or its apparent growth philosophy.

Identify financial statement components and prepare income statement.
(SO 4)

E1-8 The following items and amounts were taken from Wayside Inc.'s 2010 income statement and balance sheet.

_____ Cash and short-term		_____ Receivables	88,419
investments	$ 84,700	_____ Sales revenue	584,951
_____ Retained earnings	123,192	_____ Income taxes payable	6,499
_____ Cost of goods sold	438,458	_____ Accounts payable	49,384
_____ Selling, general, and		_____ Franchising revenues	4,786
administrative expenses	115,131	_____ Interest expense	1,994
_____ Prepaid expenses	7,818		
_____ Inventories	$ 64,618		

Instructions

(a) In each, case, identify on the blank line whether the item is an asset (A), liability (L), stockholder's equity (SE), revenue (R), or expense (E) item.
(b) Prepare an income statement for Wayside Inc. for the year ended December 31, 2010.

Calculate missing amounts.
(SO 4, 5)

E1-9 Here are incomplete financial statements for Garrett, Inc.

GARRETT, INC.
Balance Sheet

Assets		Liabilities and Stockholders' Equity	
Cash	$ 5,000	Liabilities	
Inventory	10,000	Accounts payable	$ 5,000
Building	45,000	Stockholders' equity	
		Common stock	(a)
Total assets	$60,000	Retained earnings	(b)
		Total liabilities and	
		stockholders' equity	$60,000

Income Statement

Revenues	$85,000
Cost of goods sold	(c)
Administrative expenses	10,000
Net income	$ (d)

Retained Earnings Statement

Beginning retained earnings	$10,000
Add: Net income	(e)
Less: Dividends	5,000
Ending retained earnings	$25,000

Instructions

Calculate the missing amounts.

Compute net income and prepare a balance sheet.
(SO 4, 5)

E1-10 Forest Park is a private camping ground near the Lathom Peak Recreation Area. It has compiled the following financial information as of December 31, 2010.

Revenues during 2010: camping fees	$132,000	Dividends	$ 9,000
Revenues during 2010: general store	25,000	Notes payable	50,000
Accounts payable	11,000	Expenses during 2010	129,000
Cash	8,500	Supplies	2,500
Equipment	114,000	Common stock	40,000
		Retained earnings (1/1/2010)	5,000

Instructions
(a) Determine Forest Park's net income for 2010.
(b) Prepare a retained earnings statement and a balance sheet for Forest Park as of December 31, 2010.
(c) Upon seeing this income statement, Steve Shatner, the campground manager immediately concluded, "The general store is more trouble than it is worth—let's get rid of it." The marketing director isn't so sure this is a good idea. What do you think?

E1-11 Kellogg Company is the world's leading producer of ready-to-eat cereal and a leading producer of grain-based convenience foods such as frozen waffles and cereal bars. The following items were taken from its 2006 income statement and balance sheet. All dollars are in millions.

Identify financial statement components and prepare an income statement.
(SO 4, 5)

____ Retained earnings	$3,630.4	____ Long-term debt	$ 3,053.0
____ Cost of goods sold	6,081.5	____ Inventories	823.9
____ Selling and		____ Net sales	10,906.7
administrative expenses	3,059.4	____ Accounts payable	910.4
____ Cash	410.6	____ Common stock	104.6
____ Notes payable	1,268.0	____ Income tax expense	466.5
____ Interest expense	307.4	____ Other revenue	13.2

Instructions
Perform each of the following.
(a) In each case identify whether the item is an asset (A), liability (L), stockholders' equity (SE), revenue (R), or expense (E).
(b) Prepare an income statement for Kellogg Company for the year ended December 31, 2006.

E1-12 This information is for Damon Corporation for the year ended December 31, 2010.

Prepare a statement of cash flows.
(SO 5)

Cash received from lenders	$20,000
Cash received from customers	60,000
Cash paid for new equipment	35,000
Cash dividends paid	8,000
Cash paid to suppliers	18,000
Cash balance 1/1/10	12,000

Instructions
(a) Prepare the 2010 statement of cash flows for Damon Corporation.
(b) Suppose you are one of Damon's creditors. Referring to the statement of cash flows, evaluate Damon's ability to repay its creditors.

E1-13 The following data are derived from the 2006 financial statements of Southwest Airlines. All dollars are in millions. Southwest has a December 31 year-end.

Prepare a statement of cash flows.
(SO 5)

Cash balance, January 1, 2006	$2,280
Cash paid for repayment of debt	607
Cash received from issuance of common stock	260
Cash received from issuance of long-term debt	300
Cash received from customers	9,081
Cash paid for property and equipment	1,399
Cash paid for dividends	14
Cash paid for repurchase of common stock	800
Cash paid for goods and services	7,583

Instructions
(a) After analyzing the data, prepare a statement of cash flows for Southwest Airlines for the year ended December 31, 2006.
(b) Discuss whether the company's cash from operations was sufficient to finance its investing activities. If it was not, how did the company finance its investing activities?

E1-14 Mike Paul is the bookkeeper for Benelli Company. Mike has been trying to get the balance sheet of Benelli Company to balance. It finally balanced, but now he's not sure it is correct.

Correct an incorrectly prepared balance sheet.
(SO 5)

BENELLI COMPANY
Balance Sheet
December 31, 2010

Assets		Liabilities and Stockholders' Equity	
Cash	$20,500	Accounts payable	$16,000
Supplies	9,500	Accounts receivable	(12,000)
Equipment	40,000	Common stock	40,000
Dividends	8,000	Retained earnings	34,000
Total assets	$78,000	Total liabilities and stockholders' equity	$78,000

Instructions
Prepare a correct balance sheet.

Classify items as assets, liabilities, and stockholders' equity and prepare accounting equation.
(SO 5)

E1-15   The following items were taken from the balance sheet of Nike, Inc.

1.	Cash	$ 828.0	7.	Inventories	$1,633.6
2.	Accounts receivable	2,120.2	8.	Income taxes payable	118.2
3.	Common stock	890.6	9.	Property, plant, and equipment	1,586.9
4.	Notes payable	146.0	10.	Retained earnings	3,891.1
5.	Other assets	1,722.9	11.	Accounts payable	763.8
6.	Other liabilities	2,081.9			

Instructions
Perform each of the following.
(a) Classify each of these items as an asset, liability, or stockholders' equity and determine the total dollar amount for each classification. (All dollars are in millions.)
(b) Determine Nike's accounting equation by calculating the value of total assets, total liabilities, and total stockholders' equity.
(c) To what extent does Nike rely on debt versus equity financing?

Use financial statement relationships to determine missing amounts.
(SO 5)

E1-16   The summaries of data from the balance sheet, income statement, and retained earnings statement for two corporations, Elder Corporation and Holden Enterprises, are presented below for 2010.

	Elder Corporation	Holden Enterprises
Beginning of year		
Total assets	$110,000	$130,000
Total liabilities	70,000	(d)
Total stockholders' equity	(a)	70,000
End of year		
Total assets	(b)	180,000
Total liabilities	120,000	55,000
Total stockholders' equity	50,000	(e)
Changes during year in retained earnings		
Dividends	(c)	5,000
Total revenues	215,000	(f)
Total expenses	165,000	80,000

Instructions
Determine the missing amounts. Assume all changes in stockholders' equity are due to changes in retained earnings.

Classify various items in an annual report.
(SO 6)

E1-17   The annual report provides financial information in a variety of formats including the following.

   Management discussion and analysis (MD&A)
   Financial statements
   Notes to the financial statements
   Auditor's opinion

Instructions
For each of the following, state in what area of the annual report the item would be presented. If the item would probably not be found in an annual report, state "Not disclosed."

(a) The total cumulative amount received from stockholders in exchange for common stock.
(b) An independent assessment concerning whether the financial statements present a fair depiction of the company's results and financial position.
(c) The interest rate that the company is being charged on all outstanding debts.
(d) Total revenue from operating activities.
(e) Management's assessment of the company's results.
(f) The names and positions of all employees hired in the last year.

Exercises: Set B

Visit the book's companion website, at **www.wiley.com/college/kimmel**, and choose the Student Companion site, to access Exercise Set B.

Problems: Set A

P1-1A Presented below are five independent situations.

(a) Three physics professors at MIT have formed a business to improve the speed of information transfer over the Internet for stock exchange transactions. Each has contributed an equal amount of cash and knowledge to the venture. Although their approach looks promising, they are concerned about the legal liabilities that their business might confront.
(b) Daniel Remington, a college student looking for summer employment, opened a bait shop in a small shed at a local marina.
(c) Terry Hill and Bill Mayo each owned separate shoe manufacturing businesses. They have decided to combine their businesses. They expect that within the coming year they will need significant funds to expand their operations.
(d) Alexis, Danny, and Robert recently graduated with marketing degrees. They have been friends since childhood. They have decided to start a consulting business focused on marketing sporting goods over the Internet.
(e) Stan McGlone wants to rent CD players and CDs in airports across the country. His idea is that customers will be able to rent equipment and CDs at one airport, listen to the CDs on their flights, and return the equipment and CDs at their destination airport. Of course, this will require a substantial investment in equipment and CDs, as well as employees and locations in each airport. Stan has no savings or personal assets. He wants to maintain control over the business.

Instructions
In each case explain what form of organization the business is likely to take—sole proprietorship, partnership, or corporation. Give reasons for your choice.

Determine forms of business organization.
(SO 1)

P1-2A Financial decisions often place heavier emphasis on one type of financial statement over the others. Consider each of the following hypothetical situations independently.

(a) The North Face, Inc. is considering extending credit to a new customer. The terms of the credit would require the customer to pay within 30 days of receipt of goods.
(b) An investor is considering purchasing common stock of Amazon.com. The investor plans to hold the investment for at least 5 years.
(c) Chase Manhattan is considering extending a loan to a small company. The company would be required to make interest payments at the end of each year for 5 years, and to repay the loan at the end of the fifth year.
(d) The president of Campbell Soup is trying to determine whether the company is generating enough cash to increase the amount of dividends paid to investors in this and future years, and still have enough cash to buy equipment as it is needed.

Identify users and uses of financial statements.
(SO 2, 4, 5)

Instructions
In each situation, state whether the decision maker would be most likely to place primary emphasis on information provided by the income statement, balance sheet, or statement of cash flows. In each case provide a brief justification for your choice. Choose only one financial statement in each case.

Prepare an income statement, retained earnings statement, and balance sheet; discuss results.

(SO 4, 5)

Marginal check figures (in blue) provide a key number to let you know you are on the right track.
(a) Net income $3,300
      Ret. earnings $1,300
      Tot. assets $40,000

Determine items included in a statement of cash flows, prepare the statement, and comment.

(SO 4, 5)

(a) Net increase $27,000

Comment on proper accounting treatment and prepare a corrected balance sheet.

(SO 4, 5)

P1-3A On June 1 Eckersley Service Co. was started with an initial investment in the company of $26,200 cash. Here are the assets and liabilities of the company at June 30, and the revenues and expenses for the month of June, its first month of operations:

Cash	$ 4,600	Notes payable	$12,000
Accounts receivable	4,000	Accounts payable	500
Revenue	7,000	Supplies expense	1,000
Supplies	2,400	Gas and oil expense	600
Advertising expense	400	Utilities expense	300
Equipment	29,000	Wage expense	1,400

In June, the company issued no additional stock, but paid dividends of $2,000.

Instructions

(a) Prepare an income statement and a retained earnings statement for the month of June and a balance sheet at June 30, 2010.
(b) Briefly discuss whether the company's first month of operations was a success.
(c) Discuss the company's decision to distribute a dividend.

P1-4A Presented below is selected financial information for Maris Corporation for December 31, 2010.

Inventory	$ 25,000	Cash paid to purchase equipment	$ 10,000
Cash paid to suppliers	108,000	Equipment	40,000
Building	200,000	Revenues	100,000
Common stock	50,000	Cash received from customers	132,000
Cash dividends paid	9,000	Cash received from issuing common stock	22,000

Instructions

(a) Determine which items should be included in a statement of cash flows and then prepare the statement for Maris Corporation.
(b) Comment on the adequacy of net cash provided by operating activities to fund the company's investing activities and dividend payments.

P1-5A Penington Corporation was formed on January 1, 2010. At December 31, 2010, Trent Radinsky, the president and sole stockholder, decided to prepare a balance sheet, which appeared as follows.

PENINGTON CORPORATION
Balance Sheet
December 31, 2010

Assets		Liabilities and Stockholders' Equity	
Cash	$20,000	Accounts payable	$30,000
Accounts receivable	50,000	Notes payable	15,000
Inventory	33,000	Boat loan	18,000
Boat	24,000	Stockholders' equity	64,000

Trent willingly admits that he is not an accountant by training. He is concerned that his balance sheet might not be correct. He has provided you with the following additional information.

1. The boat actually belongs to Radinsky, not to Penington Corporation. However, because he thinks he might take customers out on the boat occasionally, he decided to list it as an asset of the company. To be consistent he also listed as a liability of the corporation his personal loan that he took out at the bank to buy the boat.
2. The inventory was originally purchased for $21,000, but due to a surge in demand Trent now thinks he could sell it for $33,000. He thought it would be best to record it at $33,000.
3. Included in the accounts receivable balance is $12,000 that Trent loaned to his brother 5 years ago. Trent included this in the receivables of Penington Corporation so he wouldn't forget that his brother owes him money.

Instructions

(a) Comment on the proper accounting treatment of the three items above.
Tot. assets $79,000
(b) Provide a corrected balance sheet for Penington Corporation. (*Hint:* To get the balance sheet to balance, adjust stockholders' equity.)

Problems: Set B

P1-1B Presented below are five independent situations.

(a) Sally Quayle, a college student looking for summer employment, opened a vegetable stand along a busy local highway. Each morning she buys produce from local farmers, then sells it in the afternoon as people return home from work.

(b) Jack Nabb and Kevin Klein each owned separate swing-set manufacturing businesses. They have decided to combine their businesses and try to expand their reach beyond their local market. They expect that within the coming year they will need significant funds to expand their operations.

(c) Three chemistry professors at FIU have formed a business to employ bacteria to clean up toxic waste sites. Each has contributed an equal amount of cash and knowledge to the venture. The use of bacteria in this situation is experimental, and legal obligations could result.

(d) Lois Shore has run a successful, but small cooperative health food store for over 20 years. The increased sales of her store have made her believe that the time is right to open a national chain of health food stores across the country. Of course, this will require a substantial investment in stores, inventory, and employees in each store. Lois has no savings or personal assets. She wants to maintain control over the business.

(e) Megan Piper and Brett Tanner recently graduated with masters degrees in economics. They have decided to start a consulting business focused on teaching the basics of international economics to small business owners interested in international trade.

Determine forms of business organization.
(SO 1)

Instructions

In each case explain what form of organization the business is likely to take—sole proprietorship, partnership, or corporation. Give reasons for your choice.

P1-2B Financial decisions often place heavier emphasis on one type of financial statement over the others. Consider each of the following hypothetical situations independently.

(a) An investor is considering purchasing common stock of the Bally Total Fitness company. The investor plans to hold the investment for at least 3 years.

(b) Boeing is considering extending credit to a new customer. The terms of the credit would require the customer to pay within 60 days of receipt of goods.

(c) The president of Northwest Airlines is trying to determine whether the company is generating enough cash to increase the amount of dividends paid to investors in this and future years, and still have enough cash to buy new flight equipment as it is needed.

(d) Bank of America is considering extending a loan to a small company. The company would be required to make interest payments at the end of each year for 5 years, and to repay the loan at the end of the fifth year.

Identify users and uses of financial statements.
(SO 2, 4, 5)

Instructions

In each of the situations above, state whether the decision maker would be most likely to place primary emphasis on information provided by the income statement, balance sheet, or statement of cash flows. In each case provide a brief justification for your choice. Choose only one financial statement in each case.

P1-3B Labette Delivery was started on May 1 with an investment of $45,000 cash. To "jump start" its sales, the company spent significant money on advertising. Following are the assets and liabilities of the company on May 31, 2010, and the revenues and expenses for the month of May, its first month of operations.

Prepare an income statement, retained earnings statement, and balance sheet; discuss results.
(SO 4, 5)

Accounts receivable	$ 6,200	Notes payable	$28,000
Service revenue	9,800	Wage expense	2,200
Advertising expense	800	Equipment	57,300
Accounts payable	2,400	Repair expense	500
Cash	13,700	Fuel expense	2,400
		Insurance expense	400

(a) Net income $3,500
Ret. earnings $1,800
Tot. assets $77,200

No additional common stock was issued in May, but a dividend of $1,700 in cash was paid.

Instructions

(a) Prepare an income statement and a retained earnings statement for the month of May and a balance sheet at May 31, 2010.

(b) Briefly discuss whether the company's first month of operations was a success.

(c) Discuss the company's decision to distribute a dividend.

Determine items included in a statement of cash flows, prepare the statement, and comment.

(SO 4, 5)

P1-4B Presented below are selected financial statement items for Eaton Corporation for December 31, 2010.

Inventory	$ 55,000	Cash paid to purchase equipment	$ 34,000
Cash paid to suppliers	154,000	Equipment	40,000
Building	400,000	Revenues	200,000
Common stock	20,000	Cash received from customers	178,000
Cash dividends paid	9,000	Cash received from issuing bonds payable	35,000

Instructions

(a) Net increase $16,000

(a) Determine which items should be included in a statement of cash flows, and then prepare the statement for Eaton Corporation.

(b) Comment on the adequacy of net cash provided by operating activities to fund the company's investing activities and dividend payments.

Comment on proper accounting treatment and prepare a corrected income statement.

(SO 4, 5)

P1-5B Houston Corporation was formed during 2009 by Glenda Lee. Glenda is the president and sole stockholder. At December 31, 2010, Glenda prepared an income statement for Houston Corporation. Glenda is not an accountant, but she thinks she did a reasonable job preparing the income statement by looking at the financial statements of other companies. She has asked you for advice. Glenda's income statement appears as follows.

HOUSTON CORPORATION
Income Statement
For the Year Ended December 31, 2010

Accounts receivable	$17,000
Revenue	50,000
Rent expense	12,000
Insurance expense	7,000
Vacation expense	2,000
Net income	58,000

Glenda has also provided you with these facts.

1. Included in the revenue account is $3,000 of revenue that the company earned and received payment for in 2009. She forgot to include it in the 2009 income statement, so she put it in this year's statement.

2. Glenda operates her business out of the basement of her parents' home. They do not charge her anything, but she thinks that if she paid rent it would cost her about $12,000 per year. She, therefore, included $12,000 of rent expense in the income statement.

3. To reward herself for a year of hard work, Glenda went to Greece. She did not use company funds to pay for the trip, but she reported it as an expense on the income statement since it was her job that made her need the vacation.

Instructions

(a) Net income $40,000

(a) Comment on the proper accounting treatment of the three items above.

(b) Prepare a corrected income statement for Houston Corporation.

Problems: Set C

Visit the book's companion website at **www.wiley.com/college/kimmel** and choose the Student Companion site to access Problem Set C.

Continuing Cookie Chronicle

CCC1 Natalie Koebel spent much of her childhood learning the art of cookie-making from her grandmother. They spent many happy hours mastering every type of cookie imaginable and later devised new recipes that were both healthy and delicious. Now at the start of her second year in college, Natalie is investigating possibilities for starting her own business as part of the entrepreneurship program in which she is enrolled.

A long-time friend insists that Natalie has to include cookies in her business plan. After a series of brainstorming sessions, Natalie settles on the idea of operating a cookie-making school. She will start on a part-time basis and offer her services in people's homes. Now that she has started thinking about it, the possibilities seem endless. During the fall, she will concentrate on holiday cookies. She will offer group sessions (which will probably be more entertainment than education) and individual lessons. Natalie also decides to include children in her target market. The first difficult decision is coming up with the perfect name for her business. She settles on "Cookie Creations," and then moves on to more important issues.

This serial problem starts in Chapter 1 and continues in every chapter. You can also find this problem at the book's companion website, **www.wiley.com/ college/kimmel**.

Instructions

(a) What form of business organization—proprietorship, partnership, or corporation—do you recommend that Natalie use for her business? Discuss the benefits and weaknesses of each form that Natalie might consider.

(b) Will Natalie need accounting information? If yes, what information will she need and why? How often will she need this information?

(c) Identify specific asset, liability, revenue, and expense accounts that Cookie Creations will likely use to record its business transactions.

(d) Should Natalie open a separate bank account for the business? Why or why not?

(e) Natalie expects she will have to use her car to drive to people's homes and to pick up supplies, but she also needs to use her car for personal reasons. She recalls from her first-year accounting course something about keeping business and personal assets separate. She wonders what she should do for accounting purposes. What do you recommend?

broadening your perspective

Financial Reporting and Analysis

FINANCIAL REPORTING PROBLEM: *Tootsie Roll Industries Inc.*

BYP1-1   Simplified 2007 financial statements of Tootsie Roll Industries, Inc. are given in Illustrations 1-11 through 1-14.

Instructions

Refer to Tootsie Roll's financial statements to answer the following questions.

(a) What were Tootsie Roll's total assets at December 31, 2007? At December 31, 2006?

(b) How much cash did Tootsie Roll have on December 31, 2007?

(c) What amount of accounts payable did Tootsie Roll report on December 31, 2007? On December 31, 2006?

(d) What were Tootsie Roll's sales revenue in 2007? In 2006?

(e) What is the amount of the change in Tootsie Roll's net income from 2006 to 2007?

COMPARATIVE ANALYSIS PROBLEM: *Tootsie Roll vs. Hershey Foods*

BYP1-2   Financial statements of Hershey Foods Corporation are presented in Appendix B, and Tootsie Roll's simplified financial statements are presented in Illustrations 1-11 through 1-14.

Instructions

(a) Based on the information in these financial statements, determine the following for each company.

(1) Total assets at December 31, 2007.

(2) Net property, plant, and equipment at December 31, 2007.

(3) Sales revenue for 2007.

(4) Net income for 2007.

(b) What conclusions concerning the two companies can you draw from these data?

RESEARCH CASE

BYP1-3 The September 24, 2007, issue of *BusinessWeek* includes an article by Lindsey Gerdes titled "The Best Places to Launch a Career." It provides interesting information regarding the job opportunities for accounting students.

Instructions
Read the article and answer the following questions.
(a) What position did each of the "Big Four" (the four largest international accounting firms) receive in the survey?
(b) To what did the article attribute the accounting firms' success?
(c) What did Deloitte and Touche name as its most desirable trait for a new employee?
(d) What was the starting salary for a new employee at Deloitte and Touche?
(e) At the time the article was written in 2007, how much had the number of students graduating with accounting degrees increased relative to 2002?

INTERPRETING FINANCIAL STATEMENTS

BYP1-4 Xerox was not having a particularly pleasant year. The company's stock price had already fallen in the previous year from $60 per share to $30. Just when it seemed things couldn't get worse, Xerox's stock fell to $4 per share. The data below were taken from the statement of cash flows of Xerox. All dollars are in millions.

Cash used in operating activities		$ (663)
Cash used in investing activities		(644)
Financing activities		
Dividends paid	$ (587)	
Net cash received from issuing debt	3,498	
Cash provided by financing activities		2,911

Instructions
Analyze the information above, and then answer the following questions.
(a) If you were a creditor of Xerox, what reaction might you have to the above information?
(b) If you were an investor in Xerox, what reaction might you have to the above information?
(c) If you were evaluating the company as either a creditor or a stockholder, what other information would you be interested in seeing?
(d) Xerox decided to pay a cash dividend. This dividend was approximately equal to the amount paid in the previous year. Discuss the issues that were probably considered in making this decision.

FINANCIAL ANALYSIS ON THE WEB

BYP1-5 *Purpose:* Identify summary information about companies. This information includes basic descriptions of the company's location, activities, industry, financial health, and financial performance.

Address: **http://biz.yahoo.com/i**, or go to **www.wiley.com/college/kimmel**

Steps
1. Type in a company name, or use the index to find company name.
2. Choose **Quote**, then choose **Profile**, then choose **Income Statement**. Perform instructions (a) and (b) below.
3. Choose **Industry** to identify others in this industry. Perform instructions (c)–(e) below.

Instructions
Answer the following questions.
(a) What was the company's net income? Over what period was this measured?
(b) What was the company's total sales? Over what period was this measured?
(c) What is the company's industry?
(d) What are the names of four companies in this industry?
(e) Choose one of the competitors. What is this competitor's name? What were its sales? What was its net income?

Critical Thinking

DECISION MAKING ACROSS THE ORGANIZATION

BYP1-6   Kim Walters recently accepted a job in the production department at Tootsie Roll. Before she starts work, she decides to review the company's annual report to better understand its operations.

Instructions
Use the annual report provided in Appendix A to answer the following questions.
(a) What CPA firm performed the audit of Tootsie Roll's financial statements?
(b) What was the amount of Tootsie Roll's earnings per share in 2007?
(c) What are the company's net sales in foreign countries in 2007?
(d) What did management suggest as the cause of the decrease in the sales in 2007?
(e) What were net sales in 2003?
(f) How many shares of Class B common stock have been authorized?
(g) How much cash was spent on capital expenditures in 2007?
(h) Over what life does the company depreciate its buildings?
(i) What was the value of raw material and supplies inventory in 2006?

COMMUNICATION ACTIVITY

BYP1-7   Diane Wynne is the bookkeeper for Bates Company, Inc. Diane has been trying to get the company's balance sheet to balance. She finally got it to balance, but she still isn't sure that it is correct.

BATES COMPANY, INC.
Balance Sheet
For the Month Ended December 31, 2010

Assets		Liabilities and Stockholders' Equity	
Equipment	$20,500	Common stock	$12,000
Cash	10,500	Accounts receivable	(6,000)
Supplies	2,000	Dividends	(2,000)
Accounts payable	(5,000)	Notes payable	14,000
Total assets	$28,000	Retained earnings	10,000
		Total liabilities and stockholders' equity	$28,000

Instructions
Explain to Diane Wynne in a memo (a) the purpose of a balance sheet, and (b) why this balance sheet is incorrect and what she should do to correct it.

ETHICS CASE

BYP1-8   Rules governing the investment practices of individual certified public accountants prohibit them from investing in the stock of a company that their firm audits. The Securities and Exchange Commission became concerned that some accountants were violating this rule. In response to an SEC investigation, PricewaterhouseCoopers fired 10 people and spent $25 million educating employees about the investment rules and installing an investment tracking system.

Instructions
Answer the following questions.
(a) Why do you think rules exist that restrict auditors from investing in companies that are audited by their firms?
(b) Some accountants argue that they should be allowed to invest in a company's stock as long as they themselves aren't involved in working on the company's audit or consulting. What do you think of this idea?
(c) Today a very high percentage of publicly traded companies are audited by only four very large public accounting firms. These firms also do a high percentage of the consulting work that is done for publicly traded companies. How does this fact complicate the decision regarding whether CPAs should be allowed to invest in companies audited by their firm?

(d) Suppose you were a CPA and you had invested in IBM when IBM was not one of your firm's clients. Two years later, after IBM's stock price had fallen considerably, your firm won the IBM audit contract. You will not in any way be involved in working with the IBM audit, which will be done by one of your firm's other offices in a different state. You know that your firm's rules, as well as U.S. law, require that you sell your shares immediately. If you do sell immediately, you will sustain a large loss. Do you think this is fair? What would you do?

(e) Why do you think PricewaterhouseCoopers took such extreme steps in response to the SEC investigation?

"ALL ABOUT YOU" ACTIVITY

BYP1-9 Some people are tempted to make their finances look worse to get financial aid. Companies sometimes also manage their financial numbers in order to accomplish certain goals. Earnings management is the planned timing of revenues, expenses, gains, and losses to smooth out bumps in net income. In managing earnings, companies' actions vary from being within the range of ethical activity, to being both unethical and illegal attempts to mislead investors and creditors.

Instructions
Provide responses for each of the following questions.
(a) Discuss whether you think each of the following actions (adapted from *www.finaid. org/fafsa/maximize.phtml*) to increase the chances of receiving financial aid is ethical.
  (i) Spend down the student's assets and income first, before spending parents' assets and income.
  (ii) Accelerate necessary expenses to reduce available cash. For example, if you need a new car, buy it before applying for financial aid.
  (iii) State that a truly financially dependent child is independent.
  (iv) Have a parent take an unpaid leave of absence for long enough to get below the "threshold" level of income.
(b) What are some reasons why a *company* might want to overstate its earnings?
(c) What are some reasons why a *company* might want to understate its earnings?
(d) Under what circumstances might an otherwise ethical person decide to illegally overstate or understate earnings?

❓ *Answers to Insight and Accounting Across the Organization Questions*

p. 7
Q: What are the benefits to the company and to the employees of making the financial statements available to all employees?
A: If employees can read and use financial reports, a company will benefit in the following ways. The *marketing department* will make better decisions about products to offer and prices to charge. The *finance department* will make better decisions about debt and equity financing and how much to distribute in dividends. The *production department* will make better decisions about when to buy new equipment and how much inventory to produce. The *human resources department* will be better able to determine whether employees can be given raises. Finally, *all employees* will be better informed about the basis on which they are evaluated, which will increase employee morale.

p. 8
Q: How might accounting help you?
A: You will need to understand financial reports in any enterprise with which you are associated. Whether you become a manager, a doctor, a lawyer, a social worker, a teacher, an engineer, an architect, or an entrepreneur, a working knowledge of accounting is relevant.

p. 9
Q: What benefits does a sound accounting system provide to a not-for-profit organization?
A: Accounting provides at least two benefits to not-for-profit organizations. First, it helps to ensure that money is used in the way that donors intended. Second, it assures donors that their money is not going to waste, and thus increases the likelihood of future donations.

p. 15

Q: What is one way that some of these disputes might be resolved?

A: Frequently, when contractual payments depend on accounting-based financial results, interested parties employ outside auditors to evaluate whether the financial information has been prepared fairly and accurately. The musicians would like auditors to have easy access to inventory and manufacturing information of the recording companies.

Answers to Self-Study Questions

1. b 2. c 3. d 4. d 5. c 6. a 7. d 8. d 9. a 10. b 11. c 12. d 13. a 14. a 5. b

✔ Remember to go back to the navigator box on the chapter-opening page and check off your completed work.

chapter 2

A Further Look at Financial Statements

✓ the navigator

- Scan Study Objectives ○
- Read Feature Story ○
- Scan Preview ○
- Read Text and answer **Do it!**
  p. 52 ○   p. 53 ○   p. 63 ○   p. 70 ○
- Work Using the Decision Toolkit ○
- Review Summary of Study Objectives ○
- Work Comprehensive **Do it!** p. 75 ○
- Answer Self-Study Questions ○
- Complete Assignments ○

study objectives

After studying this chapter, you should be able to:

1 Identify the sections of a classified balance sheet.

2 Identify and compute ratios for analyzing a company's profitability.

3 Explain the relationship between a retained earnings statement and a statement of stockholders' equity.

4 Identify and compute ratios for analyzing a company's liquidity and solvency using a balance sheet.

5 Use the statement of cash flows to evaluate solvency.

6 Explain the meaning of generally accepted accounting principles.

7 Discuss financial reporting concepts.

✓ the navigator

Just Fooling Around?

Few people could have predicted how dramatically the Internet would change the investment world. One of the most interesting results is how it has changed the way ordinary people invest their savings. More and more people are striking out on their own, making their own investment decisions.

Two early pioneers in providing investment information to the masses were Tom and David Gardner, brothers who created an online investor bulletin board called The Motley Fool. The name comes from Shakespeare's *As You Like It*. The fool in Shakespeare's plays was the only one who could speak unpleasant truths to kings and queens without being killed. Tom and David view themselves as 21st-century "fools," revealing the "truths" of Wall Street to the small investor, who they feel has been taken advantage of by Wall Street insiders. Their online bulletin board enables investors to exchange information and insights about companies.

Critics of these bulletin boards contend that they are high-tech rumor mills. They suggest that the fervor created by bulletin board chatter causes investors to bid up stock prices to unreasonable levels. Because bulletin board participants typically use aliases, there is little to stop people from putting misinformation on the board to influence a stock's price. For example, the stock of PairGain Technologies jumped 32 percent in a single day as a result of a bogus takeover rumor on an investment bulletin board. Some observers are concerned that small investors—ironically, the very people the Gardner brothers are trying to help—will be hurt the most by misinformation and intentional scams.

To show how these bulletin boards work, suppose that in a recent year you had $10,000 to invest. You were considering Best Buy Company, the largest seller of electronics equipment in the United States. You scanned the Internet investment bulletin boards and found messages posted by two different investors. Here are excerpts from actual postings during the same recent year.

From: "TMPVenus": "Where are the prospects for positive movement for this company? Poor margins, poor management, astronomical P/E!"

From "broachman": "I believe that this is a LONG TERM winner, and presently at a good price."

One says sell, and one says buy. Whom should you believe? If you had taken "broachman's" advice and purchased the stock, the $10,000 you invested would have been worth over $300,000 five years later. Best Buy was one of America's best-performing stocks during that period of time.

Deciding what information to rely on is becoming increasingly complex. For example, shortly before its share price completely collapsed, nearly every professional analyst who followed Enron was recommending its stock as a "buy."

Rather than getting swept away by rumors, investors must sort out the good information from the bad. One thing is certain—as information services such as The Motley Fool increase in number, gathering information will become even easier. Evaluating it will be the harder task.

On the World Wide Web
The Motley Fool: www.fool.com.
Best Buy Company: www.bestbuy.com

If you are thinking of purchasing Best Buy stock, or any stock, how can you decide what the stock is worth? If you manage J. Crew's credit department, how should you determine whether to extend credit to a new customer? If you are a financial executive of IBM, how do you decide whether your company is generating adequate cash to expand operations without borrowing? Your decision in each of these situations will be influenced by a variety of considerations. One of them should be your careful analysis of a company's financial statements. The reason: Financial statements offer relevant and reliable information, which will help you in your decision making.

In this chapter we take a closer look at the balance sheet and introduce some useful ways for evaluating the information provided by the financial statements. We also examine the financial reporting concepts underlying the financial statements.

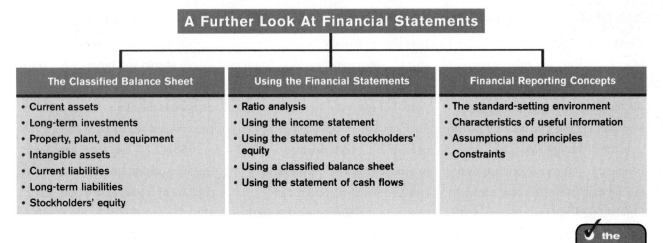

In Chapter 1 we introduced the four financial statements. In this section we review the financial statements and present tools that are useful for evaluating them. We begin by introducing the classified balance sheet.

The Classified Balance Sheet

study objective 1

Identify the sections of a classified balance sheet.

In Chapter 1 you learned that a balance sheet presents a snapshot of a company's financial position at a point in time. The balance sheet in Chapter 1 listed individual asset, liability and stockholders' equity items in no particular order. To improve users' understanding of a company's financial position, companies often use a classified balance sheet. A **classified balance sheet** groups together similar assets and similar liabilities, using a number of standard classifications and sections. This is useful because items within a group have similar economic characteristics. A classified balance sheet generally contains the standard classifications listed in Illustration 2-1.

Illustration 2-1 Standard balance sheet classifications

Assets	Liabilities and Stockholders' Equity
Current assets	Current liabilities
Long-term investments	Long-term liabilities
Property, plant, and equipment	Stockholders' equity
Intangible assets	

These groupings help readers determine such things as (1) whether the company has enough assets to pay its debts as they come due, and (2) the claims of short- and long-term creditors on the company's total assets. Many of these groupings can be seen in the balance sheet of Franklin Corporation shown in Illustration 2-2. In the sections that follow, we explain each of these groupings.

CURRENT ASSETS

Current assets are assets that a company expects to convert to cash or use up within one year or its operating cycle, whichever is longer. In Illustration 2-2, Franklin Corporation had current assets of $22,100. For most businesses the cut-off for classification as current assets is one year from the balance sheet date. For example, accounts receivable are current assets because the company will

Illustration 2-2 Classified balance sheet

FRANKLIN CORPORATION
Balance Sheet
October 31, 2010

Assets

Current assets
Cash	$ 6,600	
Short-term investments	2,000	
Accounts receivable	7,000	
Notes receivable	1,000	
Inventories	3,000	
Supplies	2,100	
Prepaid insurance	400	
Total current assets		$22,100

Long-term investments
Investment in stock of Walters Corp.	5,200	
Investment in real estate	2,000	7,200

Property, plant, and equipment
Land		10,000	
Office equipment	$24,000		
Less: Accumulated depreciation	5,000	19,000	29,000

Intangible assets
Patents		3,100
Total assets		$61,400

Liabilities and Stockholders' Equity

Current liabilities
Notes payable	$11,000	
Accounts payable	2,100	
Salaries payable	1,600	
Unearned revenue	900	
Interest payable	450	
Total current liabilities		$16,050

Long-term liabilities
Mortgage payable	10,000	
Notes payable	1,300	
Total long-term liabilities		11,300
Total liabilities		27,350

Stockholders' equity
Common stock	14,000	
Retained earnings	20,050	
Total stockholders' equity		34,050
Total liabilities and stockholders' equity		$61,400

Helpful Hint Recall that the accounting equation is Assets = Liabilities + Stockholders' Equity.

collect them and convert them to cash within one year. Supplies is a current asset because the company expects to use them up in operations within one year.

Some companies use a period longer than one year to classify assets and liabilities as current because they have an operating cycle longer than one year. The **operating cycle** of a company is the average time that it takes to go from cash to cash in producing revenue—to purchase inventory, sell it on account, and then collect cash from customers. For most businesses this cycle takes less than a year, so they use a one-year cutoff. But, for some businesses, such as vineyards or airplane manufacturers, this period may be longer than a year. **Except where noted, we will assume that companies use one year to determine whether an asset or liability is current or long-term.**

Common types of current assets are (1) cash, (2) short-term investments (such as short-term U.S. government securities), (3) receivables (notes receivable, accounts receivable, and interest receivable), (4) inventories, and (5) prepaid expenses (insurance and supplies). **Companies list current assets in the order in which they expect to convert them into cash.** *Follow this rule when doing your homework.*

Illustration 2-3 presents the current assets of Southwest Airlines Co.

Illustration 2-3 Current assets section

SOUTHWEST AIRLINES CO.
Balance Sheet (partial)
(in millions)

Current assets	
Cash and cash equivalents	$1,390
Short-term investments	369
Accounts receivable	241
Inventories	181
Prepaid expenses and other current assets	420
Total current assets	$2,601

As explained later in the chapter, a company's current assets are important in assessing its short-term debt-paying ability.

LONG-TERM INVESTMENTS

Alternative Terminology Long-term investments are often referred to simply as *investments*.

Long-term investments are generally: (1) investments in stocks and bonds of other corporations that are held for more than one year, and (2) long-term assets such as land or buildings that a company is not currently using in its operating activities. In Illustration 2-2 Franklin Corporation reported total long-term investments of $7,200 on its balance sheet.

Yahoo! Inc. reported long-term investments on its balance sheet as shown in Illustration 2-4.

Illustration 2-4 Long-term investments section

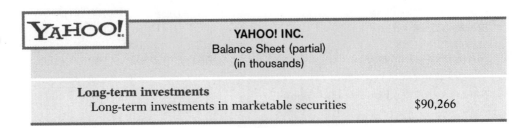

YAHOO! INC.
Balance Sheet (partial)
(in thousands)

Long-term investments	
Long-term investments in marketable securities	$90,266

PROPERTY, PLANT, AND EQUIPMENT

Property, plant, and equipment are assets with relatively long useful lives that a company is currently using in operating the business. This category includes land, buildings, machinery and equipment, delivery equipment, and furniture. In Illustration 2-2 Franklin Corporation reported property, plant, and equipment of $29,000.

Depreciation is the practice of allocating the cost of assets to a number of years. Companies do this by systematically assigning a portion of an asset's cost as an expense each year (rather than expensing the full purchase price in the year of purchase). The assets that the company depreciates are reported on the balance sheet at cost less accumulated depreciation. The **accumulated depreciation** account shows the total amount of depreciation that the company has expensed thus far in the asset's life. In Illustration 2-2 Franklin Corporation reported accumulated depreciation of $5,000.

Illustration 2-5 presents the property, plant, and equipment of Cooper Tire & Rubber Company.

Alternative Terminology
Property, plant, and equipment is sometimes called *fixed assets* or *plant assets.*

International Note In 2007 China adopted international financial reporting standards. This was done in an effort to reduce fraud and increase investor confidence in financial reports. Under these standards, many items, such as property, plant, and equipment, may be reported at current market values, rather than historical cost.

Illustration 2-5 Property, plant, and equipment section

COOPER TIRE & RUBBER COMPANY Balance Sheet (partial) (in thousands)		
Property, plant, and equipment		
Land and land improvements	$ 41,553	
Buildings	298,706	
Machinery and equipment	1,636,091	
Molds, cores, and rings	268,158	$2,244,508
Less: Accumulated depreciation		1,252,692
		$ 991,816

INTANGIBLE ASSETS

Many companies have assets that do not have physical substance yet often are very valuable. We call these assets intangible assets. One common intangible is goodwill. Others include patents, copyrights, and trademarks or trade names that give the company **exclusive right** of use for a specified period of time. Franklin Corporation reported intangible assets of $3,100.

Illustration 2-6 shows the intangible assets of media giant Time Warner, Inc.

Helpful Hint Sometimes intangible assets are reported under a broader heading called *"Other assets."*

Illustration 2-6 Intangible assets section

TIME WARNER, INC. Balance Sheet (partial) (in millions)	
Intangible assets	
Goodwill	$40,953
Film library	2,690
Customer lists	2,540
Cable television franchises	38,048
Sports franchises	262
Brands, trademarks, and other intangible assets	8,313
	$92,806

before you go on...

ASSETS SECTION OF BALANCE SHEET

Do it! Baxter Hoffman recently received the following information related to Hoffman Corporation's December 31, 2010, balance sheet.

Prepaid expenses	$ 2,300	Inventory	$3,400
Cash	800	Accumulated depreciation	2,700
Property, plant, and equipment	10,700	Accounts receivable	1,100

Prepare the assets section of Hoffman Corporation's balance sheet.

Action Plan

- Present current assets first. Current assets are cash and other resources that the company expects to convert to cash or use up within one year.
- Present current assets in the order in which the company expects to convert them into cash.
- Subtract accumulated depreciation from property, plant, and equipment to determine net property, plant, and equipment.

Solution

HOFFMAN CORPORATION
Balance Sheet (partial)
December 31, 2010

Assets

Current assets		
Cash	$ 800	
Accounts receivable	1,100	
Inventory	3,400	
Prepaid expenses	2,300	
Total current assets		$ 7,600
Property, plant, and equipment	10,700	
Less: Accumulated depreciation	2,700	8,000
Total assets		$15,600

CURRENT LIABILITIES

In the liabilities and stockholders' equity section of the balance sheet, the first grouping is current liabilities. Current liabilities are obligations that the company is to pay within the coming year or operating cycle, whichever is longer. Common examples are accounts payable, wages payable, bank loans payable, interest payable, and taxes payable. Also included as current liabilities are current maturities of long-term obligations—payments to be made within the next year on long-term obligations. In Illustration 2-2 Franklin Corporation reported five different types of current liabilities, for a total of $16,050.

Within the current liabilities section, companies usually list notes payable first, followed by accounts payable. Other items then follow in the order of their magnitude. In your homework, you should present notes payable first, followed by accounts payable, and then other liabilities in order of magnitude.

Illustration 2-7 shows the current liabilities section adapted from the balance sheet of Marcus Corporation.

Illustration 2-7 Current liabilities section

MARCUS CORPORATION
Balance Sheet (partial)
(in thousands)

Current liabilities	
Notes payable	$ 239
Accounts payable	24,242
Current maturities of long-term debt	57,250
Other current liabilities	27,477
Taxes payable	11,215
Accrued compensation payable	6,720
Total current liabilities	$127,143

LONG-TERM LIABILITIES

Long-term liabilities are obligations that a company expects to pay **after** one year. Liabilities in this category include bonds payable, mortgages payable, long-term notes payable, lease liabilities, and pension liabilities. Many companies report long-term debt maturing after one year as a single amount in the balance sheet and show the details of the debt in notes that accompany the financial statements. Others list the various types of long-term liabilities. In Illustration 2-2 Franklin Corporation reported long-term liabilities of $11,300. In your homework, list long-term liabilities in the order of their magnitude.

Illustration 2-8 shows the long-term liabilities that Procter & Gamble Company reported in its balance sheet.

Illustration 2-8 Long-term liabilities section

THE PROCTER & GAMBLE COMPANY
Balance Sheet (partial)
(in millions)

Long-term liabilities	
Long-term debt	$23,375
Deferred income taxes	12,015
Other noncurrent liabilities	5,147
Total long-term liabilities	$40,537

STOCKHOLDERS' EQUITY

Stockholders' equity consists of two parts: common stock and retained earnings. Companies record as **common stock** the investments of assets into the business by the stockholders. They record as **retained earnings** the income retained for use in the business. These two parts, combined, make up **stockholders' equity** on the balance sheet. In Illustration 2-2 Franklin reported common stock of $14,000 and retained earnings of $20,050.

Alternative Terminology
Common stock is sometimes called *capital stock*.

before you go on...

Do it!

The following financial statement items were taken from the financial statements of Callahan Corp.

_____ Salaries payable
_____ Service revenue
_____ Dividends payable
_____ Goodwill
_____ Short-term investments
_____ Mortgage note payable due in 3 years
_____ Investment in real estate
_____ Delivery truck
_____ Accumulated depreciation
_____ Depreciation expense
_____ Retained earnings
_____ Unearned revenue

Match each of the items to its proper balance sheet classification, shown below. If the item would not appear on a balance sheet, use "NA."

Current assets (CA)
Long-term investments (LTI)
Property, plant, and equipment (PPE)
Intangible assets (IA)

Current liabilities (CL)
Long-term liabilities (LTL)
Stockholders' equity (SE)

BALANCE SHEET CLASSIFICATIONS

Action Plan
• Analyze whether each financial statement item is an asset, liability, or stockholders' equity item.
• Determine if asset and liability items are current or long-term.

Solution

CL	Salaries payable	LTI	Investment in real estate
NA	Service revenue	PPE	Delivery truck
CL	Dividends payable	PPE	Accumulated depreciation
IA	Goodwill	NA	Depreciation expense
CA	Short-term investments	SE	Retained earnings
LTL	Mortgage note payable due in 3 years	CL	Unearned revenue

the navigator

Using the Financial Statements

In Chapter 1 we introduced the four financial statements. We discussed how these statements provide information about a company's performance and financial position. In this chapter we extend this discussion by showing you specific tools that you can use to analyze financial statements in order to make a more meaningful evaluation of a company.

RATIO ANALYSIS

Ratio analysis expresses the relationship among selected items of financial statement data. A ratio expresses the mathematical relationship between one quantity and another. The relationship is expressed in terms of either a percentage, a rate, or a simple proportion.

To illustrate, Best Buy has current assets of $9,081 million and current liabilities of $6,301 million. We can determine a relationship between these accounts by dividing current assets by current liabilities, to get 1.44. The alternative means of expression are:

Percentage: Current assets are 144% of current liabilities.

Rate: Current assets are 1.44 times as great as current liabilities.

Proportion: The relationship of current assets to current liabilities is 1.44:1.

For analysis of the primary financial statements, we classify ratios as follows.

Illustration 2-9 Financial ratio classifications

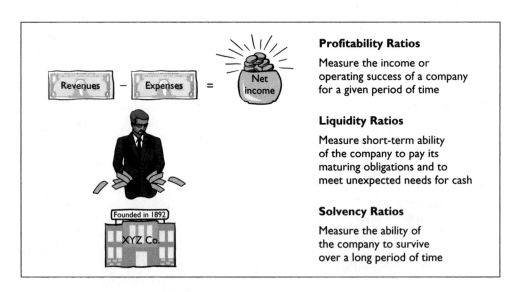

Profitability Ratios

Measure the income or operating success of a company for a given period of time

Liquidity Ratios

Measure short-term ability of the company to pay its maturing obligations and to meet unexpected needs for cash

Solvency Ratios

Measure the ability of the company to survive over a long period of time

Ratios can provide clues to underlying conditions that may not be apparent from examination of the individual items on the financial statements. However, a single ratio by itself is not very meaningful. Accordingly, in this and the following chapters we will use various comparisons to shed light on company performance:

1. **Intracompany comparisons** covering two years for the same company.
2. **Industry-average comparisons** based on average ratios for particular industries.
3. **Intercompany comparisons** based on comparisons with a competitor in the same industry.

USING THE INCOME STATEMENT

Best Buy Company generates profits for its stockholders by selling electronics. The income statement reports how successful it is at generating a profit from its sales. The income statement reports the amount earned during the period (revenues) and the costs incurred during the period (expenses). Illustration 2-10 shows a simplified income statement for Best Buy.

Illustration 2-10 Best Buy's income statement

BEST BUY CO., INC.
Income Statements
For the Years Ended March 3, 2007,
and February 25, 2006 (in millions)

	2007	2006
Revenues		
Net sales and other revenue	$35,934	$30,848
Expenses		
Cost of goods sold	27,165	23,122
Selling, general, and administrative expenses	6,640	6,005
Income tax expense	752	581
Total expenses	34,557	29,708
Net income	$ 1,377	$ 1,140

From this income statement we can see that Best Buy's sales and net income both increased during the period. Net income increased from $1,140 million to $1,377 million. Best Buy's primary competitor is Circuit City. Circuit City reported a net loss of $10.2 million for the year ended February 28, 2007.

To evaluate the profitability of Best Buy, we will use ratio analysis. Profitability ratios measure the operating success of a company for a given period of time.

EARNINGS PER SHARE. Earnings per share (EPS) measures the net income earned on each share of common stock. We compute EPS by dividing **net income** by the **average number of common shares outstanding during the year**. Stockholders usually think in terms of the number of shares they own or plan to buy or sell, so stating net income earned as a per share amount provides a useful perspective for determining the investment return. Advanced accounting courses present more refined techniques for calculating earnings per share.

For now, a basic approach for calculating earnings per share is to divide earnings available to common stockholders by average common shares outstanding during the year. What is "earnings available to common stockholders"? It is an earnings amount calculated as net income less dividends paid on another type of stock, called preferred stock (Net income − Preferred stock dividends).

By comparing earnings per share of **a single company over time**, one can evaluate its relative earnings performance from the perspective of a stockholder—that is, on a per share basis. It is very important to note that comparisons of earnings per share across companies are **not meaningful** because of the wide variations in the numbers of shares of outstanding stock among companies.

Illustration 2-11 shows the earnings per share calculation for Best Buy in 2007 and 2006, based on the information presented below. (Note that to simplify our calculations, we assumed that any change in the number of shares for Best Buy occurred in the middle of the year.)

(in millions)	2007	2006
Net income	$1,377	$1,140
Preferred stock dividends	–0–	–0–
Shares outstanding at beginning of year	485	493
Shares outstanding at end of year	481	485

Illustration 2-11 Best Buy earnings per share

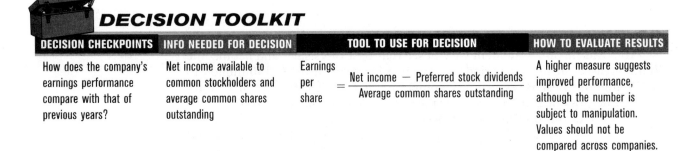

$$\text{Earnings per Share} = \frac{\text{Net Income} - \text{Preferred Stock Dividends}}{\text{Average Common Shares Outstanding}}$$		
($ and shares in millions)	2007	2006
Earnings per share	$\dfrac{\$1,377 - \$0}{(481 + 485)/2} = \$2.85$	$\dfrac{\$1,140 - \$0}{(485 + 493)/2} = \$2.33$

DECISION TOOLKIT

DECISION CHECKPOINTS	INFO NEEDED FOR DECISION	TOOL TO USE FOR DECISION	HOW TO EVALUATE RESULTS
How does the company's earnings performance compare with that of previous years?	Net income available to common stockholders and average common shares outstanding	$\text{Earnings per share} = \dfrac{\text{Net income} - \text{Preferred stock dividends}}{\text{Average common shares outstanding}}$	A higher measure suggests improved performance, although the number is subject to manipulation. Values should not be compared across companies.

USING THE STATEMENT OF STOCKHOLDERS' EQUITY

study objective 3

Explain the relationship between a retained earnings statement and a statement of stockholders' equity.

As discussed in Chapter 1, the retained earnings statement describes the changes in retained earnings during the year. This statement adds net income and then subtracts dividends from the beginning retained earnings to arrive at ending retained earnings.

Stockholders' equity is comprised of two parts: retained earnings and common stock. Therefore, the stockholders' equity of most companies is affected by factors other than just changes in retained earnings. For example, the company may issue or retire shares of common stock. Most companies, therefore, use what is called a statement of stockholders' equity, rather than a retained earnings statement, so that they can report **all changes** in stockholders' equity accounts. Illustration 2-12 is a simplified statement of stockholders' equity for Best Buy.

BEST BUY CO., INC.
Statement of Stockholders' Equity
(in millions)

	Common Stock	Retained Earnings
Balances at February 28, 2004	$ 868	$2,554
Issuance of common stock	117	
Net income		984
Dividends		(137)
Other adjustments		63
Balances at February 26, 2005	985	3,464
Repurchase of common stock	(293)	
Net income		1,140
Dividends		(151)
Other adjustments		112
Balances at February 25, 2006	692	4,565
Repurchase of common stock	(214)	
Net income		1,377
Dividends		(174)
Other adjustments		(45)
Balances at March 3, 2007	$ 478	$5,723

Illustration 2-12 Best Buy's statement of stockholders' equity

We can observe from this financial statement that Best Buy's common stock increased during the first year as the result of issuance of common stock. It declined in the second and third years as the result of repurchasing shares of stock. Another observation from this financial statement is that Best Buy paid an increasing amount of dividends each year. This is a recent practice for Best Buy. Prior to 2003, it did not pay dividends, even though it was profitable and could do so. You might wonder why Best Buy paid no dividends during prior years when it was profitable. In fact, in a prior year, two Best Buy stockholders discussed this question about the company's dividend policy on an investor bulletin board. Here are excerpts:

From "Katwoman": "Best Buy has a nice price increase. Earnings are on the way up. But why no dividends?"

From "AngryCandy": "I guess they feel they can make better use of the money by investing back in the business. They still view Best Buy as a rapidly growing company and would prefer to invest in expanding the infrastructure (building new stores, advertising, etc.) than in paying out dividends . . . . If Best Buy gets to the stage of 'stable, big company' with little room for expansion, then I'm sure you'll see them elect to pay out a dividend."

AngryCandy's response is an excellent explanation of the thought process that management goes through in deciding whether to pay a dividend. Management must evaluate what its cash needs are. If it has uses for cash that will increase the value of the company (for example, building a new, centralized warehouse), then it should retain cash in the company. However, if it has more cash than it has valuable opportunities, it should distribute its excess cash as a dividend.

USING A CLASSIFIED BALANCE SHEET

You can learn a lot about a company's financial health by also evaluating the relationship between its various assets and liabilities. Illustration 2-13 provides a simplified balance sheet for Best Buy.

Illustration 2-13 Best Buy's balance sheet

BEST BUY CO., INC.
Balance Sheets
(in millions)

Assets	March 3, 2007	February 25, 2006
Current assets		
Cash and cash equivalents	$ 1,205	$ 748
Receivables	548	449
Merchandise inventories	4,028	3,338
Other current assets	3,300	3,450
Total current assets	9,081	7,985
Property and equipment	4,904	4,836
Less: Accumulated depreciation	1,966	2,124
Net property and equipment	2,938	2,712
Other assets	1,551	1,167
Total assets	$13,570	$11,864
Liabilities and Stockholders' Equity		
Current liabilities		
Accounts payable	$ 3,934	$ 3,234
Accrued liabilities	1,486	1,347
Accrued income taxes	489	703
Other current liabilities	60	418
Accrued compensation payable	332	354
Total current liabilities	6,301	6,056
Long-term liabilities		
Long-term debt	590	178
Other long-term liabilities	478	373
Total long-term liabilities	1,068	551
Total liabilities	7,369	6,607
Stockholders' equity		
Common stock	478	692
Retained earnings	5,723	4,565
Total stockholders' equity	6,201	5,257
Total liabilities and stockholders' equity	$13,570	$11,864

Liquidity

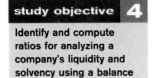

study objective **4**

Identify and compute ratios for analyzing a company's liquidity and solvency using a balance sheet.

Suppose you are a banker at CitiGroup considering lending money to Best Buy, or you are a sales manager at Hewlett-Packard interested in selling computers to Best Buy on credit. You would be concerned about Best Buy's **liquidity**—its ability to pay obligations expected to become due within the next year or operating cycle. You would look closely at the relationship of its current assets to current liabilities.

WORKING CAPITAL. One measure of liquidity is working capital, which is the difference between the amounts of current assets and current liabilities:

Illustration 2-14 Working capital

$$\text{Working Capital} = \text{Current Assets} - \text{Current Liabilities}$$

When current assets exceed current liabilities, working capital is positive. When this occurs, there is greater likelihood that the company will pay its liabilities. When working capital is negative, a company might not be able to pay short-term creditors, and the company might ultimately be forced into bankruptcy. Best Buy had working capital in 2007 of $2,780 million ($9,081 million − $6,301 million).

CURRENT RATIO. Liquidity ratios measure the short-term ability of the company to pay its maturing obligations and to meet unexpected needs for cash. One liquidity ratio is the current ratio, computed as current assets divided by current liabilities.

The current ratio is a more dependable indicator of liquidity than working capital. Two companies with the same amount of working capital may have significantly different current ratios. Illustration 2-15 shows the 2007 and 2006 current ratios for Best Buy and for Circuit City, along with the 2007 industry average.

Illustration 2-15 Current ratio

$$\text{Current Ratio} = \frac{\text{Current Assets}}{\text{Current Liabilities}}$$

	2007	2006
Best Buy ($ in millions)	$\dfrac{\$9,081}{\$6,301} = 1.44{:}1$	$\dfrac{\$7,985}{\$6,056} = 1.32{:}1$
Circuit City	1.68:1	1.75:1
Industry average	1.21:1	

What does the ratio actually mean? Best Buy's 2007 current ratio of 1.44:1 means that for every dollar of current liabilities, Best Buy has $1.44 of current assets. Best Buy's current ratio increased in 2007. When compared to the industry average of 1.21:1, Best Buy's liquidity seems adequate, although it is less than that of Circuit City.

One potential weakness of the current ratio is that it does not take into account the **composition** of the current assets. For example, a satisfactory current ratio does not disclose whether a portion of the current assets is tied up in slow-moving inventory. The composition of the current assets matters because a dollar of cash is more readily available to pay the bills than is a dollar of inventory. For example, suppose a company's cash balance declined while its merchandise inventory increased substantially. If inventory increased because the company is having difficulty selling its products, then the current ratio might not fully reflect the reduction in the company's liquidity.

Ethics Note A company that has more current assets than current liabilities can increase the ratio of current assets to current liabilities by using cash to pay off some current liabilities. This gives the appearance of being more liquid. Do you think this move is ethical?

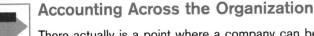

Accounting Across the Organization

There actually is a point where a company can be too liquid—that is, it can have too much working capital. While it is important to be liquid enough to be able to pay short-term bills as they come due, a company does not want to tie up its cash in extra inventory or receivables that are not earning the company money.

By one estimate from the REL Consultancy Group, the thousand largest U.S. companies have on their books cumulative excess working capital of $764 billion. Based on this figure, companies could have reduced debt by 36% or increased net income by 9%. Given that managers throughout a company are interested in improving profitability, it is clear that they should have an eye toward managing working capital. They need to aim for a "Goldilocks solution"—not too much, not too little, but just right.

Source: K. Richardson, "Companies Fall Behind in Cash Management," *Wall Street Journal,* June 19, 2007.

 What can various company managers do to ensure that working capital is managed efficiently to maximize net income?

Solvency

Now suppose that instead of being a short-term creditor, you are interested in either buying Best Buy's stock or extending the company a long-term loan. Long-term creditors and stockholders are interested in a company's solvency—its ability to pay interest as it comes due and to repay the balance of a debt due at its maturity. Solvency ratios measure the ability of the company to survive over a long period of time.

DEBT TO TOTAL ASSETS RATIO. The debt to total assets ratio is one source of information about long-term debt-paying ability. It measures the percentage of total financing provided by creditors rather than stockholders. Debt financing is more risky than equity financing because debt must be repaid at specific points in time, whether the company is performing well or not. Thus, the higher the percentage of debt financing, the riskier the company.

We compute the debt to total assets ratio as total debt (both current and long-term liabilities) divided by total assets. The higher the percentage of total liabilities (debt) to total assets, the greater the risk that the company may be unable to pay its debts as they come due. Illustration 2-16 shows the debt to total assets ratios for Best Buy and Circuit City, along with the 2007 industry average.

Helpful Hint Some users evaluate solvency using a ratio of liabilities divided by stockholders' equity. The higher this "debt to equity" ratio, the lower is a company's solvency.

Illustration 2-16 Debt to total assets ratio

Debt to Total Assets Ratio $= \dfrac{\text{Total Liabilities}}{\text{Total Assets}}$		
	2007	2006
Best Buy ($ in millions)	$\dfrac{\$7,369}{\$13,570} = 54\%$	$\dfrac{\$6,607}{\$11,864} = 56\%$
Circuit City	55%	52%
Industry average	21%	

The 2007 ratio of 54% means that every dollar of assets was financed by 54 cents of debt. Best Buy's ratio exceeds the industry average of 21%, and is approximately the same as Circuit City's ratio of 55%. The higher the ratio, the lower the equity "buffer" available to creditors if the company becomes insolvent. Thus, from the creditors' point of view, a high ratio of debt to total assets is undesirable. Best Buy's solvency appears roughly the same as that of Circuit City but significantly lower than the average company in the industry.

The adequacy of this ratio is often judged in the light of the company's earnings. Generally, companies with relatively stable earnings, such as public utilities, can support higher debt to total assets ratios than can cyclical companies with widely fluctuating earnings, such as many high-tech companies. In later chapters you will learn additional ways to evaluate solvency.

 Investor Insight

Debt financing differs greatly across industries and companies. Here are some debt to total assets ratios for selected companies:

	Debt to Total Assets Ratio
American Pharmaceutical Partners	19%
Callaway Golf Company	20%
Microsoft	21%
Sears Holdings Corporation	73%
Eastman Kodak Company	78%
General Motors Corporation	94%

 Discuss the difference in the debt to total assets ratio of Microsoft and General Motors.

DECISION TOOLKIT

DECISION CHECKPOINTS	INFO NEEDED FOR DECISION	TOOL TO USE FOR DECISION	HOW TO EVALUATE RESULTS
Can the company meet its near-term obligations?	Current assets and current liabilities	$Current\ ratio = \dfrac{Current\ assets}{Current\ liabilities}$	Higher ratio suggests favorable liquidity.
Can the company meet its long-term obligations?	Total debt and total assets	$\dfrac{Debt\ to\ total}{assets\ ratio} = \dfrac{Total\ liabilities}{Total\ assets}$	Lower value suggests favorable solvency.

USING THE STATEMENT OF CASH FLOWS

Investors, creditors, and others want to know what is happening to a company's most liquid resource—its cash. In fact, people often say that "cash is king" because if a company cannot generate cash, it will not survive. Neither the income statement nor the balance sheet is prepared using a "cash basis" of accounting (explained in Chapter 4). Consequently, they do not answer many important questions about a company's cash. Instead, the **statement of cash flows** provides financial information about the sources and uses of a company's cash.

To aid in the analysis of cash, the statement of cash flows reports the cash effects of (1) a company's **operating activities**, (2) its **investing activities**, and (3) its **financing activities**. Sources of cash matter. For example, you would feel much better about a company's health if you knew that most of its cash was generated by operating its business rather than by borrowing cash from lenders. Illustrates 2-17 (page 62) shows a simplified statement of cash flows for Best Buy.

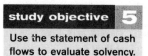

study objective 5
Use the statement of cash flows to evaluate solvency.

Illustration 2-17 Best Buy's statement of cash flows

BEST BUY CO., INC.
Statement of Cash Flows
(in millions)

	For fiscal year ending	
	March 3, 2007	February 25, 2006
Cash flows provided by operating activities		
Cash receipts from operating activities	$35,864	$30,805
Cash payments for operating activities	34,102	29,065
Net cash provided (used) by operations	1,762	1,740
Cash flows provided by investing activities		
(Increase) decrease in property and plant	(733)	(648)
Other cash inflow (outflow)	(59)	(79)
Net cash provided (used) by investing	(792)	(727)
Cash flows provided by financing activities		
Issue of equity securities	248	337
Increase (decrease) in borrowing	12	(33)
Dividends	(174)	(151)
Repurchase of common stock	(599)	(772)
Net cash provided (used) by financing	(513)	(619)
Net increase (decrease) in cash and equivalents	457	394
Cash and equivalents at start of year	748	354
Cash and equivalents at year-end	$ 1,205	$ 748

If you were a creditor of Best Buy, you would want to know where it would get cash to pay you. If you have a long-term interest in Best Buy as a stockholder, you would want information regarding the company's ability to generate cash over the long run to meet its cash needs for growth.

Companies generally get cash from two sources: operating activities and financing activities. In the early years of a company's life it typically does not generate enough cash from operating activities to meet its investing needs, so it issues stock or borrows money. Established companies, however, often meet most cash needs with cash from operations. Best Buy's cash provided by operating activities was sufficient to meet its needs for acquisitions of property, plant, and equipment. For example, in 2007 cash provided by operating activities was $1,762 million, whereas cash spent on property, plant, and equipment was $733 million.

KEEPING AN EYE ON CASH

In the statement of cash flows, cash provided by operating activities is intended to indicate the cash-generating capability of the company. Analysts have noted, however, that **cash provided by operating activities fails to take into account that a company must invest in new property, plant, and equipment** (capital expenditures) just to maintain its current level of operations. Companies also must at least **maintain dividends at current levels** to satisfy investors. A measurement to provide additional insight regarding a company's cash-generating ability is free cash flow. Free cash flow describes the cash remaining from operating activities after adjusting for capital expenditures and dividends paid.

Consider the following example: Suppose that MPC produced and sold 10,000 personal computers this year. It reported $100,000 cash provided by operating activities. In order to maintain production at 10,000 computers, MPC invested $15,000 in equipment. It chose to pay $5,000 in dividends. Its free cash flow was $80,000 ($100,000 − $15,000 − $5,000). The company could use this $80,000 to purchase new assets to expand the business, to pay off debts, or to increase its dividend distribution. In practice, analysts often calculate free cash flow with the formula shown below. (Alternative definitions also exist.)

$$\text{Free Cash Flow} = \text{Cash Provided by Operations} - \text{Capital Expenditures} - \text{Cash Dividends}$$

We can calculate Best Buy's free cash flow as follows (dollars in millions).

Cash provided by operating activities	$1,762
Less: Expenditures on property, plant, and equipment	733
Dividends paid	174
Free cash flow	$ 855

Best Buy generated free cash flow of $855 million which is available for the acquisition of new assets, the retirement of stock or debt, or the payment of additional dividends. Long-term creditors consider a high free cash flow amount an indication of solvency. Circuit City's free cash flow for 2007 is $10.5 million. This lack of free cash flow calls into question Circuit City's ability to repay its long-term obligations as they come due.

DECISION TOOLKIT

DECISION CHECKPOINTS	INFO NEEDED FOR DECISION	TOOL TO USE FOR DECISION	HOW TO EVALUATE RESULTS
How much cash did the company generate to expand operations, pay off debts, or distribute dividends?	Cash provided by operating activities, cash spent on fixed assets, and cash dividends	$\text{Free cash flow} = \text{Cash provided by operations} - \text{Capital expenditures} - \text{Cash dividends}$	Significant free cash flow indicates greater potential to finance new investment and pay additional dividends.

before you go on...

Do it! The following information is available for Ozone Inc.

RATIO ANALYSIS

	2010	2009
Current assets	$ 88,000	$ 60,800
Total assets	400,000	341,000
Current liabilities	40,000	38,000
Total liabilities	120,000	150,000
Net income	100,000	50,000
Cash provided by operating activities	110,000	70,000
Preferred stock dividends	10,000	10,000
Common stock dividends	5,000	2,500
Expenditures on property, plant, and equipment	45,000	20,000
Shares outstanding at beginning of year	60,000	40,000
Shares outstanding at end of year	120,000	60,000

(a) Compute earnings per share for 2010 and 2009 for Ozone, and comment on the change. Ozone's primary competitor, Frost Corporation, had earnings per share of $2 in 2010. Comment on the difference in the ratios of the two companies.

(b) Compute the current ratio and debt to total assets ratio for each year, and comment on the changes.

(c) Compute free cash flow for each year, and comment on the changes.

Action Plan

- Use the formula for earnings per share (EPS): (Net income − Preferred stock dividends) ÷ (Average common shares outstanding).
- Use the formula for the current ratio: Current assets ÷ Current liabilities.
- Use the formula for the debt to total assets ratio: Total liabilities ÷ Total assets.
- Use the formula for free cash flow: Cash provided by operating activities − Capital expenditures − Cash dividends.

Solution

(a) Earnings per share

2010	**2009**
$\dfrac{(\$100{,}000 - \$10{,}000)}{(120{,}000 + 60{,}000)/2} = \$1.00$	$\dfrac{(\$50{,}000 - \$10{,}000)}{(60{,}000 + 40{,}000)/2} = \$0.80$

Ozone's profitability, as measured by the amount of income available to each share of common stock, increased by 25% [($1.00 − $0.80) ÷ $0.80] during 2010. Earnings per share should not be compared across companies because the number of shares issued by companies varies widely. Thus, we cannot conclude that Frost Corporation is more profitable than Ozone based on its higher EPS.

(b)

	2010	**2009**
Current ratio	$\dfrac{\$88{,}000}{\$40{,}000} = 2.20{:}1$	$\dfrac{\$60{,}800}{\$38{,}000} = 1.60{:}1$
Debt to total assets ratio	$\dfrac{\$120{,}000}{\$400{,}000} = 30\%$	$\dfrac{\$150{,}000}{\$341{,}000} = 44\%$

The company's liquidity, as measured by the current ratio, improved from 1:60:1 to 2.20:1. Its solvency also improved, as measured by the debt to total assets ratio, which declined from 44% to 30%.

(c) Free cash flow

2010:	$110,000 − $45,000 − ($10,000 + $5,000) = $50,000
2009:	$70,000 − $20,000 − ($10,000 + $2,500) = $37,500

The amount of cash generated by the company above its needs for dividends and capital expenditures increased from $37,500 to $50,000.

the navigator

Financial Reporting Concepts

In Chapter 1 you learned about the four financial statements, and in this chapter we introduced you to some basic ways to interpret those statements. In this last section we will discuss concepts that underly these financial statements. It would be unwise to make business decisions based on financial statements without understanding the implications of these concepts.

THE STANDARD-SETTING ENVIRONMENT

study objective 6

Explain the meaning of generally accepted accounting principles.

How does Best Buy decide on the type of financial information to disclose? What format should it use? How should it measure assets, liabilities, revenues, and expenses? The answers are found in a set of rules and practices having substantial authoritative support, referred to as **generally accepted accounting principles (GAAP)**. Various standard-setting bodies, in consultation with the accounting profession and the business community, determine these guidelines:

The **Securities and Exchange Commission (SEC)** is the agency of the U.S. government that oversees U.S. financial markets and accounting standard-setting bodies.

The **Public Company Accounting Oversight Board (PCAOB)** determines auditing standards and reviews auditing firms.

The **Financial Accounting Standards Board (FASB)** is the primary accounting standard-setting body in the United States.

The **International Accounting Standards Board (IASB)** issues standards (IFRS) that have been adopted by many countries outside of the United States.

The FASB and IASB have worked closely to try to minimize the differences in their standards. Recently the SEC announced that foreign companies that wish to have their shares traded on U.S. stock exchanges will no longer have to prepare reports that conform with U.S. accounting standards, as long as their reports conform with international accounting standards. Also, the SEC proposed that it will allow some U.S companies to adopt IFRS as early as 2009. The SEC also laid out a roadmap by which all U.S. companies will be required to switch to IFRS by 2016. The adoption of IFRS by U.S. companies would make it easier for investors to compare U.S. and foreign companies, as well as for U.S. companies to raise capital in international markets.

International Note Over 100 countries use international standards (called IFRS). For example, all companies in the European Union follow international standards. The differences between U.S. and international standards are not generally significant. In this book, we highlight any major differences using International Notes like this one.

International Insight

If you think that accounting standards don't matter, consider recent events in South Korea. For many years, international investors complained that the financial reports of South Korean companies were inadequate and inaccurate. Accounting practices there often resulted in huge differences between stated revenues and actual revenues. Because investors did not have faith in the accuracy of the numbers, they were unwilling to pay as much for the shares of these companies relative to shares of comparable companies in different countries. This difference in share price was often referred to as the "Korean discount."

In response, Korean regulators decided that, beginning in 2011, companies will have to comply with international accounting standards. This change was motivated by a desire to "make the country's businesses more transparent" in order to build investor confidence and spur economic growth. Many other Asian countries, including China, India, Japan, and Hong Kong, have also decided either to adopt international standards or to create standards that are based on the international standards.

Source: Evan Ramstad, "End to 'Korea Discount'?" *Wall Street Journal*, March 16, 2007.

? What is meant by the phrase "make the country's businesses more transparent"? Why would increasing transparency spur economic growth?

CHARACTERISTICS OF USEFUL INFORMATION

In establishing guidelines for reporting financial information, the FASB believes that the overriding consideration should be the generation of financial information **useful** for making business decisions. To be useful, information should possess these characteristics: relevance, reliability, comparability, and consistency.

Relevance

Accounting information is considered relevant if it would make a difference in a business decision. For example, the information in Best Buy's financial statements is considered relevant because it provides a basis for forecasting Best Buy's future earnings. Accounting information is also relevant to business decisions because it confirms or corrects prior expectations. Financial statements provide

study objective **7**
Discuss financial reporting concepts.

relevant information that helps **predict** future events and **provide feedback** about prior expectations for the financial health of the company.

For accounting information to be relevant it must be **timely**. That is, it must be available to decision makers before it loses its capacity to influence decisions. The SEC requires that public companies provide their annual reports to investors within 60 days of their year-end.

Reliability

Reliability of information means that the information can be depended on. To be reliable, accounting information must be **verifiable**—we must be able to prove that it is free of error. Also, the information must be a **faithful representation** of what it purports to be—it must be factual. If Best Buy's income statement reports sales of $20 billion when it actually had sales of $10 billion, then the statement is not a faithful representation of Best Buy's financial performance. Finally, accounting information must be **neutral**—it cannot be selected, prepared, or presented to favor one set of interested users over another. As noted in Chapter 1, to ensure reliability, certified public accountants audit financial statements.

Comparability

In accounting, comparability results when different companies use the same accounting principles. U.S. accounting standards are relatively comparable because they are based on certain basic principles and assumptions. However, these principles and assumptions allow for some variation in methods. For example, there are a variety of ways to report inventory. Often these different methods result in different amounts of net income. To make comparison across companies easier, each company **must disclose** the accounting methods used.

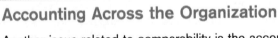

Accounting Across the Organization

Another issue related to comparability is the accounting time period. An accounting period that is one-year long is called a **fiscal year**. But a fiscal year need not match the calendar year. For example, a company could end its fiscal year on April 30, rather than December 31.

Why do companies choose the particular year-ends that they do? For example, why doesn't every company use December 31 as the accounting year-end? Many companies choose to end their accounting year when inventory or operations are at a low. This is advantageous because compiling accounting information requires much time and effort by managers, so they would rather do it when they aren't as busy operating the business. Also, inventory is easier and less costly to count when its volume is low.

Some companies whose year-ends differ from December 31 are Delta Air Lines, June 30; Walt Disney Productions, September 30; and Dunkin' Donuts, Inc., October 31. In the notes to its financial statements, Best Buy states that its accounting year-end is the Saturday nearest the end of February.

 What problems might Best Buy's year-end create for analysts?

Consistency

To compare Best Buy's net income over several years, you would need to know that it used the same accounting principles from year to year. Consistency means that a company uses the same accounting principles and methods from year to year. Thus, if a company selects one inventory accounting method in the first year of operations, it is expected to continue to use that same method in succeeding years.

A company *may* change to a new method of accounting if management can justify that the new method produces more useful financial information. In the year in which the change occurs, the change must be disclosed in the notes to the financial statements so that users of the statements are aware of the lack of consistency.

Illustration 2-18 summarizes the characteristics that make accounting information useful.

Illustration 2-18
Characteristics of useful information

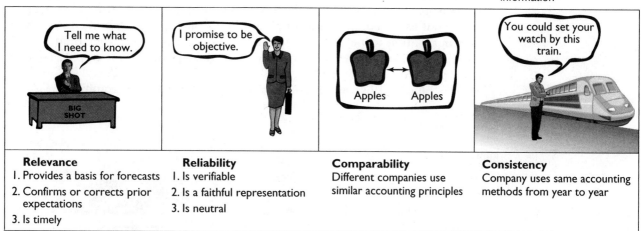

Relevance	**Reliability**	**Comparability**	**Consistency**
1. Provides a basis for forecasts	1. Is verifiable	Different companies use similar accounting principles	Company uses same accounting methods from year to year
2. Confirms or corrects prior expectations	2. Is a faithful representation		
3. Is timely	3. Is neutral		

ASSUMPTIONS AND PRINCIPLES IN FINANCIAL REPORTING

To develop accounting standards, the FASB relies on some key assumptions and principles.

Monetary Unit Assumption

The **monetary unit assumption** requires that only those things that can be expressed in money are included in the accounting records. Because the exchange of money is fundamental to business transactions, it makes sense that we measure a business in terms of money.

However, the monetary unit assumption also means that certain important information needed by investors, creditors, and managers is not reported in the financial statements. For example, customer satisfaction is important to every business, but it is not easily quantified in dollar terms; thus it is not reported in the financial statements.

Economic Entity Assumption

The **economic entity assumption** states that every economic entity can be separately identified and accounted for. For example, suppose you are a stockholder of Best Buy. The amount of cash you have in your personal bank account and the balance owed on your personal car loan are not reported in Best Buy's balance sheet. In order to accurately assess Best Buy's performance and financial position, it is important that we not blur it with your personal transactions, or the transactions of any other person (especially its managers) or other company.

Time Period Assumption

Next, notice that the income statement, retained earnings statement, and statement of cash flows all cover periods of one year, and the balance sheet is prepared

Ethics Note The importance of the economic entity assumption is illustrated by scandals involving Adelphia. In this case, senior company employees entered into transactions that blurred the line between the employees' financial interests and those of the company. For example, Adelphia guaranteed over $2 billion of loans to the founding family.

at the end of each year. The time period assumption states that the life of a business can be divided into artificial time periods and that useful reports covering those periods can be prepared for the business. All companies report financial results at least annually. Many also report every three months (quarterly) to stockholders, and many prepare monthly statements for internal purposes.

Going Concern Assumption

The going concern assumption states that the business will remain in operation for the foreseeable future. Of course many businesses do fail, but in general, it is reasonable to assume that the business will continue operating. If going concern is not assumed, then the company should state property and equipment at their liquidation value (selling price less cost of disposal), rather than at their cost. Only when liquidation of the business appears likely is the going concern assumption inappropriate.

Illustration 2-19 shows these four accounting assumptions graphically.

Illustration 2-19
Accounting assumptions

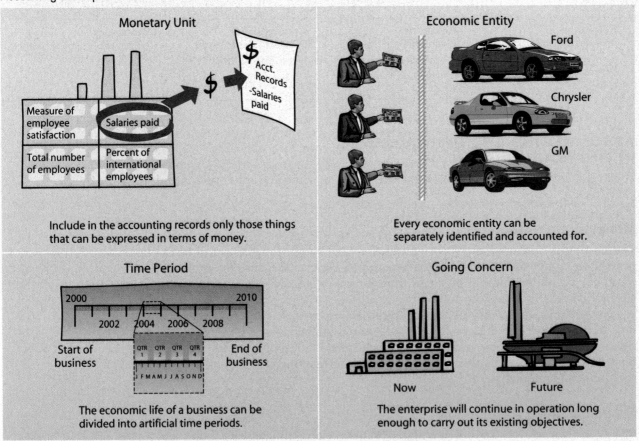

Cost Principle

The cost principle dictates that assets be recorded at their cost. This is true not only at the time the asset is purchased, but also over the time the asset is held. For example, if Best Buy were to purchase some land for $30,000, the company would initially report it on the balance sheet at $30,000. But what would Best Buy do if, by the end of the next year, the land had increased in value to $40,000? Under the cost principle the company would continue to report the land at $30,000.

Proponents of the cost principle state that cost is the best measure because it can be easily verified from transactions between two parties, whereas market value is often subjective. However, the cost principle is often criticized as being irrelevant. Critics contend that market value would be more useful to financial decision makers. The FASB now requires that certain investment securities be recorded at their market value. In choosing between cost and market value, the FASB weighed the reliability of cost figures against the relevance of market value.

In addition, to encourage broader use of market values in the financial statements, a new accounting standard gives companies the option to use market value to account for a wide range of items. This change makes U.S. standards more similar to international standards, which already gave foreign companies this option.

International Note The results of a recent survey by Deloitte & Touche LLP (USA) show that approximately 20% of CFOs and senior finance professionals (representing about 300 U.S. companies) would consider adopting International Financial Reporting Standards, if given a choice by the U.S. Securities and Exchange Commission.

Full Disclosure Principle

The **full disclosure principle** requires that companies disclose all circumstances and events that would make a difference to financial statement users. Some important financial information is not easily reported on the face of the statements. For example, Best Buy has debt outstanding. Investors and creditors would like to know the terms of the debt; that is, when does it mature, what is its interest rate, and is it renewable? Also, Best Buy might be sued by one of its customers. Investors and creditors might not know about this lawsuit. If an important item cannot reasonably be reported directly in one of the four types of financial statements, then it should be discussed in notes that accompany the statements. Some investors who lost money in Enron, WorldCom, and Global Crossing complained that the lack of full disclosure regarding some of the companies' transactions caused the financial statements to be misleading.

Illustration 2-20 depicts these two accounting principles.

Illustration 2-20
Accounting principles

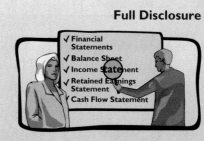

CONSTRAINTS IN ACCOUNTING

Efforts to provide useful financial information can be costly to a company. Therefore, the profession has agreed upon **constraints** to ensure that companies apply accounting rules in a reasonable fashion, from the perspectives of both the company and the user. The constraints are materiality and conservatism.

Materiality

Materiality relates to a financial statement item's impact on a company's overall financial condition and operations. An item is **material** when its **size** makes it likely to influence the decision of an investor or creditor. It is **immaterial** if it is too small to impact a decision maker. In short, if the item does not make a difference, the company does not have to follow GAAP in reporting it. To determine the materiality of an amount—that is, to determine its financial significance—the company compares the item with such items as total assets, sales revenue, and net income.

To illustrate, assume that Best Buy made a $100 error in recording revenue. Best Buy's total revenue is almost $36 billion; thus a $100 error is not material.

Conservatism

Conservatism in accounting means that when preparing financial statements, a company should choose the accounting method that will be least likely to overstate assets or income. It does not mean, however, that a company should intentionally understate assets or income.

A common application of the conservatism constraint is in valuing inventories. Companies normally record inventories at their cost. Conservatism, however, requires that companies write down inventories to market value if market value is below cost. Conservatism also requires that when the market value of inventory exceeds cost, the company should not increase the value of the inventory on the books, but instead keep it at cost. This practice results in lower net income on the income statement and a lower amount reported for inventory on the balance sheet.

Illustration 2-21 graphically depicts the two constraints.

Illustration 2-21
Accounting constraints

Materiality	Conservatism
Companies do not have to follow GAAP for small amounts.	When in doubt, choose the solution that will be least likely to overstate assets and income.

---

before you go on...

FINANCIAL ACCOUNTING CONCEPTS AND PRINCIPLES

Do it!   The following are characteristics, assumptions, principles, or constraints that guide the FASB when it creates accounting standards.

Relevance	Time period assumption
Reliability	Going concern assumption
Comparability	Cost principle
Consistency	Full disclosure principle
Monetary unit assumption	Materiality
Economic entity assumption	Conservatism

Match each item above with a description below.

1. _____ Ability to easily evaluate one company's results relative to another's.

2. _____ Belief that a company will continue to operate for the foreseeable future.

3. _____ The judgment concerning whether an item is large enough to matter to decision makers.

4. _____ The reporting of all information that would make a difference to financial statement users.

5. _____ The practice of preparing financial statements at regular intervals.

6. _____ The quality of information that indicates the information makes a difference in a decision.

7. _____ A belief that items should be reported on the balance sheet at the price that was paid to acquire the item.

8. _____ A company's use of the same accounting principles and methods from year to year.

9. _____ The use of accounting methods that do not overstate assets or income.

10. _____ Tracing accounting events to particular companies.

11. _____ The desire to minimize errors and bias in financial statements.

12. _____ Reporting only those things that can be measured in dollars.

Action Plan

- Understand the need for conceptual guidelines in accounting.
- List the characteristics of useful financial information.
- Review the assumptions, principles, and constraints that comprise the guidelines in accounting.

Solution

1. Comparability	7. Cost principle
2. Going concern assumption	8. Consistency
3. Materiality	9. Conservatism
4. Full disclosure principle	10. Economic entity assumption
5. Time period assumption	11. Reliability
6. Relevance	12. Monetary unit assumption

USING THE DECISION TOOLKIT

In this chapter we evaluated a home electronics giant, Best Buy. Tweeter Home Entertainment sold consumer electronics products from 154 stores on the East Coast under various names. It specialized in products with high-end features. Tweeter filed for bankruptcy in June 2007 and was acquired by another company in July 2007. Financial data for Tweeter, prior to its bankruptcy, are provided below.

	September 30	
(amounts in millions)	**2006**	**2005**
Current assets	$146.4	$158.2
Total assets	258.6	284.0
Current liabilities	107.1	119.0
Total liabilities	190.4	201.1
Total common stockholders' equity	68.2	82.9
Net income (loss)	(16.5)	(74.4)
Cash provided (used) by operating activities	15.6	(26.7)
Capital expenditures (net)	17.4	22.2
Dividends paid	0	0
Average shares of common stock (millions)	25.2	24.6

Instructions

Using the data provided, answer the following questions and discuss how these results might have provided an indication of Tweeter's financial troubles.

1. Calculate the current ratio for Tweeter for 2006 and 2005 and discuss its liquidity position.

2. Calculate the debt to total assets ratio and free cash flow for Tweeter for 2006 and 2005 and discuss its solvency.

3. Calculate the earnings per share for Tweeter for 2006 and 2005, and discuss its change in profitability.

4. Best Buy's accounting year-end was February 28, 2007; Tweeter's was September 30, 2006. How does this difference affect your ability to compare their profitability?

Solution

1. Current ratio:

   2006: $146.4 ÷ $107.1 = 1.37:1   *2005:* $158.2 ÷ $119.0 = 1.33:1

   Tweeter's liquidity improved slightly from 2005 to 2006, but in both years it would most likely have been considered inadequate. In 2006 Tweeter had only $1.37 in current assets for every dollar of current liabilities. Sometimes larger companies, such as Best Buy and Circuit City, can function with lower current ratios because they have alternative sources of working capital. But a company of Tweeter's size would normally want a higher ratio.

2. Debt to total assets:

   2006: $190.4 ÷ $258.6 = 73.6%   *2005:* $201.1 ÷ $284.0 = 70.8%

   Tweeter's solvency, as measured by its debt to total assets ratio, declined from 2005 to 2006. Its ratio of 73.6% meant that every dollar of assets was financed by 73.6 cents of debt. For a retailer, this is extremely high reliance on debt. This low solvency suggests Tweeter's ability to meet its debt payments was questionable.

   Free cash flow:

   2006: $15.6 − $17.4 − $0 = −$1.8 million
   2005: −$26.7 − $22.2 − $0 = −$48.9 million

   Tweeter's free cash flow was negative in both years. The company did not generate enough cash from operations even to cover its capital expenditures, and it was not paying a dividend. While this is not unusual for new companies in their early years, it is also not sustainable for very long. Part of the reason that its debt to assets ratio, discussed above, was so high was that it had to borrow money to make up for its deficient free cash flow.

3. Loss per share:

   2006: −$16.5 ÷ 25.2 = −$0.65 per share
   2005: −$74.4 ÷ 24.6 = −$3.02 per share

   Tweeter's loss per share declined substantially. However, this was little consolation for its shareholders, who experienced losses in previous years as well. The company's lack of profitability, combined with its poor liquidity and solvency, increased the likelihood that it would eventually file for bankruptcy.

4. Tweeter's income statement covers 7 months not covered by Best Buy's. Suppose that the economy changed dramatically during this 7-month period, either improving or declining. This change in the economy would be reflected in Tweeter's income statement but would not be reflected in Best Buy's income statement until the following March, thus reducing the usefulness of a comparison of the income statements of the two companies.

Summary of Study Objectives

1 Identify the sections of a classified balance sheet. In a classified balance sheet, companies classify assets as current assets; long-term investments; property, plant, and equipment; and intangibles. They classify liabilities as either current or long-term. A stockholders'

equity section shows common stock and retained earnings.

2 Identify and compute ratios for analyzing a company's profitability. Profitability ratios, such as earnings per share (EPS), measure aspects of the operating success of a company for a given period of time.

3 **Explain the relationship between a retained earnings statement and a statement of stockholders' equity.** The retained earnings statement presents the factors that changed the retained earnings balance during the period. A statement of stockholders' equity presents the factors that changed stockholders' equity during the period, including those that changed retained earnings. Thus, a statement of stockholders' equity is more inclusive.

4 **Identify and compute ratios for analyzing a company's liquidity and solvency using a balance sheet.** Liquidity ratios, such as the current ratio, measure the short-term ability of a company to pay its maturing obligations and to meet unexpected needs for cash. Solvency ratios, such as the debt to total assets ratio, measure the ability of an enterprise to survive over a long period.

5 **Use the statement of cash flows to evaluate solvency.** Free cash flow indicates a company's ability to generate cash from operations that is sufficient to pay debts, acquire assets, and distribute dividends.

6 **Explain the meaning of generally accepted accounting principles.** Generally accepted accounting principles are a set of rules and practices recognized as a general guide for financial reporting purposes. The basic objective of financial reporting is to provide information that is useful for decision making.

7 **Discuss financial reporting concepts.** To be judged useful, information should have relevance, reliability, comparability, and consistency.

The *monetary unit assumption* requires that companies include in the accounting records only transaction data that can be expressed in terms of money. The *economic entity assumption* states that economic events can be identified with a particular unit of accountability. The *time period assumption* states that the economic life of a business can be divided into artificial time periods and that meaningful accounting reports can be prepared for each period. The *going concern assumption* states that the enterprise will continue in operation long enough to carry out its existing objectives and commitments.

The *cost principle* states that companies should record assets at their cost. The *full disclosure principle* dictates that companies disclose circumstances and events that matter to financial statement users.

The major constraints are materiality and conservatism.

DECISION TOOLKIT   A SUMMARY

DECISION CHECKPOINTS	INFO NEEDED FOR DECISION	TOOL TO USE FOR DECISION	HOW TO EVALUATE RESULTS
How does the company's earnings performance compare with that of previous years?	Net income available to common stockholders and average common shares outstanding	Earnings per share $= \dfrac{\text{Net income} - \text{Preferred stock dividends}}{\text{Average common shares outstanding}}$	A higher measure suggests improved performance, although the number is subject to manipulation. Values should not be compared across companies.
Can the company meet its near-term obligations?	Current assets and current liabilities	Current ratio $= \dfrac{\text{Current assets}}{\text{Current liabilities}}$	Higher ratio suggests favorable liquidity.
Can the company meet its long-term obligations?	Total debt and total assets	Debt to total assets ratio $= \dfrac{\text{Total liabilities}}{\text{Total assets}}$	Lower value suggests favorable solvency.
How much cash did the company generate to expand operations, pay off debts, or distribute dividends?	Cash provided by operating activities, cash spent on fixed assets, and cash dividends	Free cash flow $=$ Cash provided by operations $-$ Capital expenditures $-$ Cash dividends	Significant free cash flow indicates greater potential to finance new investment and pay additional dividends.

Glossary

Classified balance sheet *(p. 48)* A balance sheet that contains a number of standard classifications and sections.

Comparability *(p. 66)* Ability to compare the accounting information of different companies because they use the same accounting principles.

Conservatism *(p. 70)* The approach of choosing an accounting method, when alternatives exist, that will least likely overstate assets and net income.

Consistency *(p. 66)* Use of the same accounting principles and methods from year to year within a company.

Cost principle *(p. 68)* An accounting principle that states that companies should record assets at their cost.

Current assets *(p. 49)* Cash and other resources that companies reasonably expect to convert to cash or use up within one year or the operating cycle, whichever is longer.

Current liabilities *(p. 52)* Obligations that a company reasonably expects to pay within the next year or operating cycle, whichever is longer.

Current ratio *(p. 59)* A measure used to evaluate a company's liquidity and short-term debt-paying ability; computed as current assets divided by current liabilities.

Debt to total assets ratio *(p. 60)* Measures the percentage of total financing provided by creditors; computed as total debt divided by total assets.

Earnings per share (EPS) *(p. 55)* A measure of the net income earned on each share of common stock; computed as net income minus preferred stock dividends divided by the average number of common shares outstanding during the year.

Economic entity assumption *(p. 67)* An assumption that every economic entity can be separately identified and accounted for.

Financial Accounting Standards Board (FASB) *(p. 65)* The primary accounting standard-setting body in the United States.

Free cash flow *(p. 62)* Cash remaining from operating activities after adjusting for capital expenditures and dividends paid.

Full disclosure principle *(p. 69)* Accounting principle that dictates that companies disclose circumstances and events that make a difference to financial statement users.

Generally accepted accounting principles (GAAP) *(p. 64)* A set of rules and practices, having substantial authoritative support, that the accounting profession recognizes as a general guide for financial reporting purposes.

Going concern assumption *(p. 68)* The assumption that the company will continue in operation for the foreseeable future.

Intangible assets *(p. 51)* Assets that do not have physical substance.

International Accounting Standards Board (IASB) *(p. 65)* An accounting standard-setting body that issues standards adopted by many countries outside of the United States.

Liquidity *(p. 58)* The ability of a company to pay obligations that are expected to become due within the next year or operating cycle.

Liquidity ratios *(p. 59)* Measures of the short-term ability of the company to pay its maturing obligations and to meet unexpected needs for cash.

Long-term investments *(p. 50)* Generally, (1) investments in stocks and bonds of other corporations that companies hold for more than one year, and (2) long-term assets, such as land and buildings, not currently being used in the company's operations.

Long-term liabilities (Long-term debt) *(p. 53)* Obligations that a company expects to pay after one year.

Materiality *(p. 69)* The constraint of determining whether an item is large enough to likely influence the decision of an investor or creditor.

Monetary unit assumption *(p. 67)* An assumption that requires that only those things that can be expressed in money are included in the accounting records.

Operating cycle *(p. 50)* The average time required to go from cash to cash in producing revenues.

Profitability ratios *(p. 55)* Measures of the operating success of a company for a given period of time.

Property, plant, and equipment *(p. 51)* Assets with relatively long useful lives that companies use in operating the business and are not intended for resale.

Public Company Accounting Oversight Board (PCAOB) *(p. 65)* The group charged with determining auditing standards and reviewing the performance of auditing firms.

Ratio *(p. 54)* An expression of the mathematical relationship between one quantity and another; may be expressed as a percentage, a rate, or a proportion.

Ratio analysis *(p. 54)* A technique for evaluating financial statements that expresses the relationship among selected items of financial statement data.

Relevance *(p. 65)* The quality of information that indicates the information makes a difference in a decision.

Reliability *(p. 66)* The quality of information that gives assurance that it is free of error, is factual, and is neutral.

Securities and Exchange Commission (SEC) *(p. 64)* The agency of the U.S. government that oversees U.S. financial markets and accounting standard-setting bodies.

Solvency *(p. 60)* The ability of a company to pay interest as it comes due and to repay the balance of debt at its maturity.

Solvency ratios *(p. 60)* Measures of the ability of the company to survive over a long period of time.

Statement of stockholders' equity *(p. 56)* A financial statement that presents the factors that caused stockholders' equity to change during the period, including those that caused retained earnings to change.

Time period assumption *(p. 68)* An assumption that the life of a business can be divided into artificial time periods and that useful reports covering those periods can be prepared for the business.

Working capital *(p. 59)* The difference between the amounts of current assets and current liabilities.

Comprehensive Do it!

Listed here are items taken from the income statement and balance sheet of Circuit City Stores, Inc. for the year ended February 28, 2007. Certain items have been combined for simplification. Amounts are given in millions.

Long-term debt, excluding current installments	$ 50.5
Cash and cash equivalents	141.1
Selling, general, and administrative expenses	2,933.6
Common stock	454.9
Accounts payable	922.2
Prepaid expenses and other current assets	723.3
Property and equipment, net	921.0
Cost of goods sold	9,501.4
Current portion of long-term debt	7.2
Interest expense	1.5
Other long-term liabilities	451.5
Retained earnings	1,336.3
Merchandise inventory	1,636.5
Net sales and operating revenues	12,456.9
Accounts receivable, net	382.6
Income tax expense	30.5
Other assets	202.7
Accrued expenses and other current liabilities	784.6

Instructions

Prepare an income statement and a classified balance sheet using the items listed. Do not use any item more than once.

Solution to Comprehensive Do it!

Action Plan

- In preparing the income statement, list revenues, then expenses.
- In preparing a classified balance sheet, list current assets in order of liquidity.

CIRCUIT CITY STORES, INC.
Income Statement
For the Year Ended February 28, 2007
(in millions)

Net sales and operating revenues		$12,456.9
Cost of goods sold	$9,501.4	
Selling, general, and administrative expenses	2,933.6	
Interest expense	1.5	
Income tax expense	30.5	
Total expenses		12,467.0
Net loss		$ (10.1)

CIRCUIT CITY STORES, INC.
Balance Sheet
February 28, 2007
(in millions)

Assets

Current assets		
Cash and cash equivalents	$ 141.1	
Accounts receivable, net	382.6	
Merchandise inventory	1,636.5	
Prepaid expenses and other current assets	723.3	
Total current assets		$2,883.5
Property and equipment, net		921.0
Other assets		202.7
Total assets		$4,007.2

Liabilities and Stockholders' Equity

Current liabilities		
Accounts payable	$ 922.2	
Accrued expenses and other current liabilities	784.6	
Current portion of long-term debt	7.2	
Total current liabilities		$1,714.0
Long-term liabilities		
Other long-term liabilities	451.5	
Long-term debt, excluding current installments	50.5	502.0
Total liabilities		2,216.0
Stockholders' equity		
Common stock	454.9	
Retained earnings	1,336.3	
Total stockholders' equity		1,791.2
Total liabilities and stockholders' equity		$4,007.2

Self-Study Questions

Answers are at the end of the chapter.

(SO 1) **1.** In a classified balance sheet, assets are usually classified as:
   (a) current assets; long-term assets; property, plant, and equipment; and intangible assets.
   (b) current assets; long-term investments; property, plant, and equipment; and common stock.
   (c) current assets; long-term investments; tangible assets; and intangible assets.
   (d) current assets; long-term investments; property, plant, and equipment; and intangible assets.

2. Current assets are listed: (SO 1)
   (a) by order of expected conversion to cash.
   (b) by importance.
   (c) by longevity.
   (d) alphabetically.

3. The correct order of presentation in a classified balance sheet for the following current assets is: (SO 1)
   (a) accounts receivable, cash, prepaid insurance, inventories.
   (b) cash, inventories, accounts receivable, prepaid insurance.

(c) cash, accounts receivable, inventories, prepaid insurance.

(d) inventories, cash, accounts receivable, prepaid insurance.

(SO 1) **4.** A company has purchased a tract of land. It expects to build a production plant on the land in approximately 5 years. During the 5 years before construction, the land will be idle. The land should be reported as:

(a) property, plant, and equipment.

(b) land expense.

(c) a long-term investment.

(d) an intangible asset.

(SO 2) **5.** Which is an indicator of profitability?

(a) Current ratio.

(b) Earnings per share.

(c) Debt to total assets ratio.

(d) Free cash flow.

(SO 2) **6.** For 2010 Stoneland Corporation reported net income $26,000; net sales $400,000; and average shares outstanding 6,000. There were preferred stock dividends of $2,000. What was the 2010 earnings per share?

(a) $4.00

(b) $0.06

(c) $16.67

(d) $66.67

(SO 3) **7.** The balance in retained earnings is *not* affected by:

(a) net income.

(b) net loss.

(c) issuance of common stock.

(d) dividends.

(SO 4) **8.** Which of these measures is an evaluation of a company's ability to pay current liabilities?

(a) Earnings per share.

(b) Current ratio.

(c) Both (a) and (b).

(d) None of the above.

(SO 2, 4) **9.** The following ratios are available for Leer Inc. and Stable Inc.

	Current Ratio	Debt to Assets Ratio	Earnings per Share
Leer Inc.	2:1	75%	$3.50
Stable Inc.	1.5:1	40%	$2.75

Compared to Stable Inc., Leer Inc. has:

(a) higher liquidity, higher solvency, and higher profitability.

(b) lower liquidity, higher solvency, and higher profitability.

(c) higher liquidity, lower solvency, and higher profitability.

(d) higher liquidity and lower solvency, but profitability cannot be compared based on information provided.

(SO 5) **10.** Companies can use free cash flow to:

(a) pay additional dividends.

(b) acquire property, plant, and equipment.

(c) pay off debts.

(d) All of the above.

(SO 6) **11.** Generally accepted accounting principles are:

(a) a set of standards and rules that are recognized as a general guide for financial reporting.

(b) usually established by the Internal Revenue Service.

(c) the guidelines used to resolve ethical dilemmas.

(d) fundamental truths that can be derived from the laws of nature.

(SO 6) **12.** What organization issues U.S. accounting standards?

(a) Financial Accounting Standards Board.

(b) International Accounting Standards Committee.

(c) International Auditing Standards Committee.

(d) None of the above.

(SO 7) **13.** What is the primary criterion by which accounting information can be judged?

(a) Consistency.

(b) Predictive value.

(c) Usefulness for decision making.

(d) Comparability.

(SO 7) **14.** Verifiability is an ingredient of:

	Reliability	Relevance
(a)	Yes	Yes
(b)	No	No
(c)	Yes	No
(d)	No	Yes

(SO 7) **15.** What accounting constraint refers to the tendency of accountants to resolve uncertainty in a way least likely to overstate assets and net income?

(a) Comparability.

(b) Materiality.

(c) Conservatism.

(d) Consistency.

Go to the book's companion website, **www.wiley.com/college/kimmel**, to access additional Self-Study Questions.

Questions

1. What is meant by the term *operating cycle?*

2. Define current assets. What basis is used for ordering individual items within the current assets section?

3. Distinguish between long-term investments and property, plant, and equipment.

4. How do current liabilities differ from long-term liabilities?

5. Identify the two parts of stockholders' equity in a corporation and indicate the purpose of each.

6. ⚲━━⚲
   (a) Glenda Rosen believes that the analysis of financial statements is directed at two characteristics of a company: liquidity and profitability. Is Glenda correct? Explain.
   (b) Are short-term creditors, long-term creditors, and stockholders primarily interested in the same characteristics of a company? Explain.

7. ⚲━━⚲ Name ratios useful in assessing (a) liquidity, (b) solvency, and (c) profitability.

8. ⬅ ⚲━━⚲ Jack Pine, the founder of Waterboots Inc., needs to raise $500,000 to expand his company's operations. He has been told that raising the money through debt will increase the riskiness of his company much more than issuing stock. He doesn't understand why this is true. Explain it to him.

9. ⚲━━⚲ What do these classes of ratios measure?
   (a) Liquidity ratios.
   (b) Profitability ratios.
   (c) Solvency ratios.

10. ⬅ ⚲━━⚲ Holding all other factors constant, indicate whether each of the following signals generally good or bad news about a company.
    (a) Increase in earnings per share.
    (b) Increase in the current ratio.
    (c) Increase in the debt to total assets ratio.
    (d) Decrease in free cash flow.

11. ⚲━━⚲ Which ratio or ratios from this chapter do you think should be of greatest interest to:
    (a) a pension fund considering investing in a corporation's 20-year bonds?
    (b) a bank contemplating a short-term loan?
    (c) an investor in common stock?

12. (a) What are generally accepted accounting principles (GAAP)?
    (b) What body provides authoritative support for GAAP?

13. (a) What is the basic objective of financial reporting?
    (b) Identify the characteristics of useful accounting information.

14. Jan Leonard, the president of King Company, is pleased. King substantially increased its net income in 2010 while keeping its unit inventory relatively the same. Joe Morton, chief accountant, cautions Jan, however. Morton says that since King changed its method of inventory valuation, there is a consistency problem and it is difficult to determine whether King is better off. Is Morton correct? Why or why not?

15. What is the distinction between comparability and consistency?

16. Describe the two constraints inherent in the presentation of accounting information.

17. Your roommate believes that international accounting standards are uniform throughout the world. Is your roommate correct? Explain.

18. What purpose does the going concern assumption serve?

19. Laurie Belk is president of Better Books. She has no accounting background. Belk cannot understand why market value is not used as the basis for accounting measurement and reporting. Explain what basis is used and why.

20. What is the economic entity assumption? Give an example of its violation.

21. What was Tootsie Roll's largest current asset, largest current liability, and largest item under "Other assets" at December 31, 2007?

Brief Exercises

WILEY PLUS

Classify accounts on balance sheet.
(SO 1)

BE2-1 The following are the major balance sheet classifications:

Current assets (CA)	Current liabilities (CL)
Long-term investments (LTI)	Long-term liabilities (LTL)
Property, plant, and equipment (PPE)	Common stock (CS)
Intangible assets (IA)	Retained earnings (RE)

Match each of the following accounts to its proper balance sheet classification.

_____ Accounts payable	_____ Income tax payable
_____ Accounts receivable	_____ Investment in long-term bonds
_____ Accumulated depreciation	_____ Land
_____ Building	_____ Merchandise inventory
_____ Cash	_____ Patent
_____ Goodwill	_____ Supplies

Prepare the current assets section of a balance sheet.
(SO 1)

BE2-2 A list of financial statement items for Rondelli Company includes the following: accounts receivable $14,000; prepaid insurance $3,300; cash $10,400; supplies $3,800; and short-term investments $8,200. Prepare the current assets section of the balance sheet listing the items in the proper sequence.

BE2-3 The following information (in millions of dollars) is available for Limited Brands for 2007: Sales revenue $10,671; net income $676; preferred stock dividend $0; average shares outstanding 402 million. Compute the earnings per share for Limited Brands for 2007.

Compute earnings per share.
(SO 2)

BE2-4 For each of the following events affecting the stockholders' equity of Haulmarke, indicate whether the event would: increase retained earnings (IRE), decrease retained earnings (DRE), increase common stock (ICS), or decrease common stock (DCS).

Identify items affecting stockholders' equity.
(SO 3)

_____ (a) Issued new shares of common stock.
_____ (b) Paid a cash dividend.
_____ (c) Reported net income of $75,000.
_____ (d) Reported a net loss of $20,000.

BE2-5 These selected condensed data are taken from a recent balance sheet of Bob Evans Farms (in millions of dollars).

Calculate liquidity ratios.
(SO 4)

Cash	$ 29.3
Accounts receivable	20.5
Inventories	28.7
Other current assets	24.0
Total current assets	$ 102.5
Total current liabilities	$ 201.2

Compute working capital and the current ratio.

BE2-6 Danny's Books & Music Inc. reported the following selected information at March 31.

Calculate liquidity and solvency ratios.
(SO 4, 5)

	2010
Total current assets	$262,787
Total assets	439,832
Total current liabilities	293,625
Total liabilities	376,002
Cash provided by operating activities	55,472

Calculate (a) the current ratio, (b) the debt to total assets ratio, and (c) free cash flow for March 31, 2010. The company paid dividends of $15,000 and spent $24,787 on capital expenditures.

BE2-7 Indicate whether each statement is *true* or *false*.
(a) GAAP is a set of rules and practices established by accounting standard-setting bodies to serve as a general guide for financial reporting purposes.
(b) Substantial authoritative support for GAAP usually comes from two standards-setting bodies: the FASB and the IRS.

Recognize generally accepted accounting principles.
(SO 6)

BE2-8 The accompanying chart shows the qualitative characteristics of accounting information. Fill in the blanks.

Identify characteristics of useful information.
(SO 7)

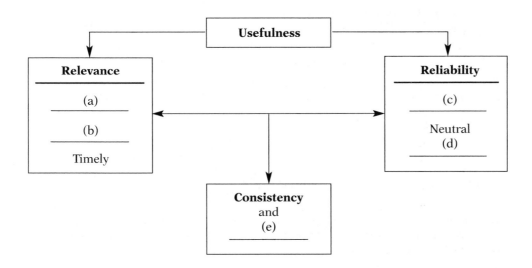

Identify characteristics of useful information.

(SO 7)

BE2-9 Given the *characteristics* of useful accounting information, complete each of the following statements.

(a) For information to be _____, it should have predictive or feedback value, and it must be presented on a timely basis.

(b) _____ is the quality of information that gives assurance that it is free of error and bias; it can be depended on.

(c) _____ means using the same accounting principles and methods from year to year within a company.

Identify characteristics of useful information.

(SO 7)

BE2-10 Here are some qualitative characteristics of accounting information:

1. Predictive value   3. Verifiable
2. Neutral   4. Timely

Match each qualitative characteristic to one of the following statements.

_____ (a) Accounting information should help users make predictions about the outcome of past, present, and future events.

_____ (b) Accounting information cannot be selected, prepared, or presented to favor one set of interested users over another.

_____ (c) Accounting information must be proved to be free of error.

_____ (d) Accounting information must be available to decision makers before it loses its capacity to influence their decisions.

Define full disclosure principle

(SO 7)

BE2-11 The full disclosure principle dictates that:

(a) financial statements should disclose all assets at their cost.

(b) financial statements should disclose only those events that can be measured in dollars.

(c) financial statements should disclose all events and circumstances that would matter to users of financial statements.

(d) financial statements should not be relied on unless an auditor has expressed an unqualified opinion on them.

Identify constraints that have been violated.

(SO 7)

BE2-12 Gantner Company uses these accounting practices:

(a) Inventory is reported at cost when market value is lower.

(b) Small tools are recorded as plant assets and depreciated.

(c) The income statement shows paper clips expense of $10.

Indicate the accounting constraint, if any, that each practice has violated.

Do it! Review

WILEY
PLUS

Prepare assets section of balance sheet.

(SO 1)

Do it! 2-1 Theremin Corporation has collected the following information related to its December 31, 2010, balance sheet.

Accounts receivable	$22,000	Equipment	$180,000
Accumulated depreciation	45,000	Inventory	58,000
Cash	13,000	Supplies	9,000

Prepare the assets section of Theremin Corporation's balance sheet.

Classify financial statement items by balance sheet classification.

(SO 1)

Do it! 2-2 The following financial statement items were taken from the financial statements of de Vries Corp.

_____ Trademarks	_____ Inventories
_____ Current maturities of long-term debt	_____ Accumulated depreciation
_____ Interest revenue	_____ Land improvements
_____ Taxes payable	_____ Common stock
_____ Long-term marketable debt securities	_____ Advertising expense
_____ Unearned consulting fees	_____ Mortgage note payable due in 3 years

Match each of the financial statement items to its proper balance sheet classification. (See E2-1, on page 81, for a list of the balance sheet classifications.) If the item would not appear on a balance sheet, use "NA."

Do it! 2-3 The following information is available for Allotrope Corporation.

Compute ratios and analyze.
(SO 4, 5)

	2010	2009
Current assets	$ 54,000	$ 36,000
Total assets	240,000	205,000
Current liabilities	24,000	33,000
Total liabilities	72,000	100,000
Net income	80,000	40,000
Cash provided by operating activities	90,000	56,000
Preferred stock dividends	6,000	6,000
Common stock dividends	3,000	1,500
Expenditures on property, plant, and equipment	27,000	12,000
Shares outstanding at beginning of year	40,000	30,000
Shares outstanding at end of year	75,000	40,000

(a) Compute earnings per share for 2010 and 2009 for Allotrope, and comment on the change. Allotrope's primary competitor, Triatomic Corporation, had earnings per share of $1 per share in 2010. Comment on the difference in the ratios of the two companies.
(b) Compute the current ratio and debt to total assets ratio for each year, and comment on the changes.
(c) Compute free cash flow for each year, and comment on the changes.

Do it! 2-4 The following are characteristics, assumptions, principles, or constraints that guide the FASB when it creates accounting standards.

Identify financial accounting concepts and principles.
(SO 7)

Relevance	Time period assumption
Reliability	Going concern assumption
Comparability	Cost principle
Consistency	Full disclosure principle
Monetary unit assumption	Materiality
Economic entity assumption	Conservatism

Match each item above with a description below.

1. _____ Items not easily quantified in dollar terms are not reported in the financial statements.
2. _____ Accounting information must be verifiable, neutral, and a faithful representation of what it purports to measure.
3. _____ Personal transactions are not mixed with the company's transactions.
4. _____ Choosing the accounting method least likely to overstate assets or income.
5. _____ A company's use of the same accounting principles from year to year.
6. _____ Assets are recorded and reported at original purchase price.
7. _____ Accounting information should be timely, should help users predict future events, and should provide feedback about prior expectations.
8. _____ The life of a business can be divided into artificial segments of time.
9. _____ The reporting of all information that would make a difference to financial statement users.
10. _____ The judgment concerning whether an item's size makes it likely to influence a decision maker.
11. _____ Assumes a business will remain in operation for the foreseeable future.
12. _____ Different companies use the same accounting principles.

Exercises

E2-1 The following are the major balance sheet classifications.

Classify accounts on balance sheet.
(SO 1)

Current assets (CA)	Current liabilities (CL)
Long-term investments (LTI)	Long-term liabilities (LTL)
Property, plant, and equipment (PPE)	Common stock (CS)
Intangible assets (IA)	Retained earnings (RE)

Instructions

Classify each of the following financial statement items taken from Remington Corporation's balance sheet.

____ Accounts payable and accrued liabilities	____ Income taxes payable
____ Accounts receivable	____ Inventories
____ Accumulated depreciation	____ Investments
____ Buildings	____ Land
____ Cash and short-term investments	____ Long-term debt
____ Dividends payable	____ Materials and supplies
____ Goodwill	____ Office equipment and furniture
	____ Prepaid expenses

Classify financial statement items by balance sheet classification.

(SO 1)

E2-2 The major balance sheet classifications are listed in E2-1, on page 81.

Instructions

Classify each of the following financial statement items based upon the major balance sheet classifications listed in E2-1.

____ Prepaid expenses	____ Land held for future use
____ Machinery and equipment	____ Patents
____ Trademarks	____ Bonds payable
____ Dividends payable	____ Common stock
____ Taxes payable	____ Accumulated depreciation
____ Retained earnings	____ Unearned revenue
____ Accounts receivable	____ Inventory

Classify items as current or noncurrent, and prepare assets section of balance sheet.

(SO 1)

E2-3 The following items were taken from the December 31, 2006, assets section of the Boeing Company balance sheet. (All dollars are in millions.)

Inventories	$ 8,105	Other current assets	$ 2,837
Notes receivable—due after December 31, 2007	12,605	Property, plant, and equipment	19,310
Notes receivable—due before December 31, 2007	370	Cash and cash equivalents	6,118
		Accounts receivable	5,285
Accumulated depreciation	11,635	Other noncurrent assets	3,786
Intangible assets	4,745	Short-term investments	268

Instructions

Prepare the assets section of a classified balance sheet, listing the current assets in order of their liquidity.

Prepare assets section of a classified balance sheet.

(SO 1)

E2-4 The following information (in thousands of dollars) is available for H.J. Heinz Company—famous for ketchup and other fine food products—for the year ended May 2, 2007.

Prepaid expenses	$ 132,561	Inventories	$1,197,957
Land	51,950	Buildings and equipment	4,002,913
Other current assets	38,736	Cash and cash equivalents	652,896
Intangible assets	4,139,872	Accounts receivable	996,852
Other noncurrent assets	875,999	Accumulated depreciation	2,056,710

Instructions

Prepare the assets section of a classified balance sheet, listing the items in proper sequence and including a statement heading.

Prepare a classified balance sheet.

(SO 1)

E2-5 These items are taken from the financial statements of Cleland Co. at December 31, 2010.

Building	$105,800
Accounts receivable	12,600
Prepaid insurance	4,680
Cash	11,840
Equipment	82,400
Land	61,200
Insurance expense	780
Depreciation expense	5,300
Interest expense	2,600
Common stock	62,000

Retained earnings (January 1, 2010)	$40,000
Accumulated depreciation—building	45,600
Accounts payable	9,500
Note payable	~~93,600~~ 80,000
Accumulated depreciation—equipment	18,720
Interest payable	3,600
Bowling revenues	14,180

Instructions

Prepare a classified balance sheet. Assume that $13,600 of the note payable will be paid in 2011. _current_

E2-6 The following items were taken from the 2006 financial statements of Texas Instruments, Inc. (All dollars are in millions.)

Prepare a classified balance sheet.
(SO 1)

Common stock	$2,624	Cash and cash equivalents	$1,183
Prepaid expenses	181	Accumulated depreciation	3,801
Property, plant, and equipment	7,751	Accounts payable	560
Other current assets	745	Other noncurrent assets	1,839
Other current liabilities	1,475	Noncurrent liabilities	492
Long-term investments	287	Retained earnings	8,736
Short-term investments	2,534	Accounts receivable	1,774
Note payable in 2007	43	Inventories	1,437

Instructions

Prepare a classified balance sheet in good form as of December 31, 2006.

E2-7 The following information is available for Callaway Golf Company for the years 2006 and 2005. (Dollars are in thousands, except share information.)

Compute and interpret profitability ratio.
(SO 2)

	2006	2005
Net sales	$1,017,907	$998,093
Net income (loss)	23,290	13,284
Total assets	845,947	764,498
Share information		
Shares outstanding at year-end	67,954,213	70,495,136
Preferred dividends	–0–	–0–

There were 69,111,349 shares outstanding at the end of 2004.

Instructions

(a) What was the company's earnings per share for each year?
(b) Based on your findings above, how did the company's profitability change from 2005 to 2006?
(c) Suppose the company had paid dividends on preferred stock and on common stock during the year. How would this affect your calculation in part (a)?

E2-8 These financial statement items are for Barone Corporation at year-end, July 31, 2010.

Prepare financial statements.
(SO 1, 3, 4)

Salaries payable	$ 2,080
Salaries expense	51,700
Utilities expense	22,600
Equipment	18,500
Accounts payable	4,100
Commission revenue	66,100
Rent revenue	8,500
Long-term note payable	1,800
Common stock	16,000
Cash	29,200
Accounts receivable	9,780
Accumulated depreciation	6,000
Dividends	4,000
Depreciation expense	4,000
Retained earnings (beginning of the year)	35,200

Instructions
(a) Prepare an income statement and a retained earnings statement for the year. Barone Corporation did not issue any new stock during the year.
(b) Prepare a classified balance sheet at July 31.
(c) Compute the current ratio and debt to total assets ratio.
(d) Suppose that you are the president of Allied Equipment. Your sales manager has approached you with a proposal to sell $20,000 of equipment to Barone. He would like to provide a loan to Barone in the form of a 10%, 5-year note payable. Evaluate how this loan would change Barone's current ratio and debt to total assets ratio, and discuss whether you would make the sale.

Compute liquidity ratios and compare results.
(SO 4)

E2-9 Nordstrom, Inc. operates department stores in numerous states. Selected financial statement data (in millions of dollars) for the year ended February 3, 2007, follow.

	End of Year	Beginning of Year
Cash and cash equivalents	$ 403	$ 463
Receivables (net)	684	640
Merchandise inventory	997	956
Other current assets	658	815
Total current assets	$2,742	$2,874
Total current liabilities	$1,433	$1,623

Instructions
(a) Compute working capital and the current ratio at the beginning of the year and at the end of the current year.
(b) Did Nordstrom's liquidity improve or worsen during the year?
(c) Using the data in the chapter, compare Nordstrom's liquidity with Best Buy's.

Compute liquidity measures and discuss findings.
(SO 4)

E2-10 The chief financial officer (CFO) of Greenstem Corporation requested that the accounting department prepare a preliminary balance sheet on December 30, 2010, so that the CFO could get an idea of how the company stood. He knows that certain debt agreements with its creditors require the company to maintain a current ratio of at least 2:1. The preliminary balance sheet is as follows.

GREENSTEM CORP.
Balance Sheet
December 30, 2010

Current assets			Current liabilities		
Cash	$30,000		Accounts payable	$ 25,000	
Accounts receivable	30,000		Salaries payable	15,000	$ 40,000
Prepaid insurance	10,000	$ 70,000	Long-term liabilities		
Property, plant, and			Notes payable		80,000
equipment (net)		190,000	Total liabilities		120,000
Total assets		$260,000	Stockholders' equity		
			Common stock	100,000	
			Retained earnings	40,000	140,000
			Total liabilities and		
			stockholders' equity		$260,000

Instructions
(a) Calculate the current ratio and working capital based on the preliminary balance sheet.
(b) Based on the results in (a), the CFO requested that $25,000 of cash be used to pay off the balance of the accounts payable account on December 31, 2010. Calculate the new current ratio and working capital after the company takes these actions.
(c) Discuss the pros and cons of the current ratio and working capital as measures of liquidity.
(d) Was it unethical for the CFO to take these steps?

E2-11 The following data were taken from the 2007 and 2006 financial statements of American Eagle Outfitters. (All dollars are in thousands.)

Compute and interpret solvency ratios.

(SO 4, 5)

	2007	**2006**
Current assets	$1,198,254	$1,076,781
Total assets	1,987,484	1,605,649
Current liabilities	460,464	351,487
Total liabilities	570,172	450,097
Total stockholders' equity	1,417,312	1,155,552
Cash provided by operating activities	749,268	480,419
Capital expenditures	225,939	81,545
Dividends paid	61,521	42,058

Instructions

Perform each of the following.
(a) Calculate the debt to total assets ratio for each year.
(b) Calculate the free cash flow for each year.
(c) Discuss American Eagle's solvency in 2007 versus 2006.
(d) Discuss American Eagle's ability to finance its investment activities with cash provided by operating activities, and how any deficiency would be met.

E2-12 Presented below are the assumptions and principles discussed in this chapter.

Identify accounting assumptions and principles.

(SO 7)

 1. Full disclosure principle. 4. Time period assumption.

 2. Going concern assumption. 5. Cost principle.

 3. Monetary unit assumption. 6. Economic entity assumption.

Instructions

Identify by number the accounting assumption or principle that is described below. Do not use a number more than once.

_____ (a) Is the rationale for why plant assets are not reported at liquidation value. (*Note:* Do not use the cost principle.)

_____ (b) Indicates that personal and business record-keeping should be separately maintained.

_____ (c) Assumes that the dollar is the "measuring stick" used to report on financial performance.

_____ (d) Separates financial information into time periods for reporting purposes.

_____ (e) Indicates that companies should not record in the accounts market value changes subsequent to purchase.

_____ (f) Dictates that companies should disclose all circumstances and events that make a difference to financial statement users.

E2-13 Ghosh Co. had three major business transactions during 2010.
(a) Reported at its market value of $260,000 merchandise inventory with a cost of $208,000.
(b) The president of Ghosh Co., Dipak Ghosh, purchased a truck for personal use and charged it to his expense account.
(c) Ghosh Co. wanted to make its 2010 income look better, so it added 2 more weeks to the year (a 54-week year). Previous years were 52 weeks.

Identify the assumption or principle that has been violated.

(SO 7)

Instructions

In each situation, identify the assumption or principle that has been violated, if any, and discuss what the company should have done.

Exercises: Set B

Visit the book's companion website, at **www.wiley.com/college/kimmel**, and choose the Student Companion site, to access Exercise Set B.

Problems: Set A

WILEY PLUS

Prepare a classified balance sheet.
(SO 1)

P2-1A The following items are taken from the 2006 balance sheet of Yahoo! Inc. (All dollars are in thousands.)

Intangible assets	$3,374,379
Common stock	5,292,545
Property and equipment, net	1,101,379
Accounts payable	109,130
Other assets	459,988
Long-term investments	2,827,720
Accounts receivable	930,964
Prepaid expenses and other current assets	217,779
Short-term investments	1,031,528
Retained earnings	3,868,065
Cash and cash equivalents	1,569,871
Long-term debt	749,915
Accrued expenses and other current liabilities	1,046,882
Unearned revenue—current	317,982
Other long-term liabilities	129,089

Tot. current assets $3,750,142
Tot. assets $11,513,608

Instructions
Prepare a classified balance sheet for Yahoo! Inc. as of December 31, 2006.

Prepare financial statements.
(SO 1, 3)

P2-2A These items are taken from the financial statements of Finn Corporation for 2010.

Retained earnings (beginning of year)	$31,000
Utilities expense	2,000
Equipment	66,000
Accounts payable	18,300
Cash	12,900
Salaries payable	3,000
Common stock	13,000
Dividends	12,000
Service revenue	72,000
Prepaid insurance	3,500
Repair expense	1,800
Depreciation expense	3,300
Accounts receivable	14,200
Insurance expense	2,200
Salaries expense	37,000
Accumulated depreciation	17,600

Net income $25,700
Tot. assets $79,000

Instructions
Prepare an income statement, a retained earnings statement, and a classified balance sheet as of December 31, 2010.

Prepare financial statements.
(SO 1, 3)

P2-3A You are provided with the following information for Kiley Enterprises, effective as of its April 30, 2010, year-end.

Accounts payable	$ 834
Accounts receivable	810
Building, net of accumulated depreciation	1,537
Cash	1,270
Common stock	900
Cost of goods sold	990
Current portion of long-term debt	450
Depreciation expense	335
Dividends	325
Equipment, net of accumulated depreciation	1,220
Income tax expense	165

Income taxes payable	$ 135
Interest expense	400
Inventories	967
Land	2,100
Long-term debt	3,500
Prepaid expenses	12
Retained earnings, beginning	1,600
Revenues	4,600
Selling expenses	210·
Short-term investments	1,200
Wages expense	700
Wages payable	222

Instructions

(a) Prepare an income statement and a retained earnings statement for Kiley Enterprises for the year ended April 30, 2010.

(b) Prepare a classified balance sheet for Kiley Enterprises as of April 30, 2010.

Net income	$1,800
Tot. current assets	$4,259
Tot. assets	$9,116

P2-4A Comparative financial statement data for Bedene Corporation and Groneman Corporation, two competitors, appear below. All balance sheet data are as of December 31, 2010.

Compute ratios; comment on relative profitability, liquidity, and solvency.

(SO 2, 4, 5)

	Bedene Corporation 2010	Groneman Corporation 2010
Net sales	$1,900,000	$620,000
Cost of goods sold	1,175,000	340,000
Operating expenses	303,000	98,000
Interest expense	9,000	3,800
Income tax expense	85,000	36,000
Current assets	407,200	190,336
Plant assets (net)	532,000	139,728
Current liabilities	66,325	40,348
Long-term liabilities	108,500	29,620
Cash from operating activities	138,000	36,000
Capital expenditures	90,000	20,000
Dividends paid	36,000	15,000
Average number of shares outstanding	100,000	50,000

Instructions

(a) Comment on the relative profitability of the companies by computing the net income and earnings per share for each company for 2010.

(b) Comment on the relative liquidity of the companies by computing working capital and the current ratios for each company for 2010.

(c) Comment on the relative solvency of the companies by computing the debt to total assets ratio and the free cash flow for each company for 2010.

P2-5A Here and on page 88 are financial statements of Edmiston Company.

Compute and interpret liquidity, solvency, and profitability ratios.

(SO 2, 4, 5)

EDMISTON COMPANY
Income Statement
For the Year Ended December 31, 2010

Net sales	$2,218,500
Cost of goods sold	1,012,400
Selling and administrative expenses	906,000
Interest expense	98,000
Income tax expense	69,000
Net income	$ 133,100

EDMISTON COMPANY
Balance Sheet
December 31, 2010

Assets

Current assets
Cash	$ 60,100
Short-term investments	74,000
Accounts receivable (net)	169,800
Inventory	125,000
Total current assets	428,900
Plant assets (net)	625,300
Total assets	$1,054,200

Liabilities and Stockholders' Equity

Current liabilities
Accounts payable	$ 180,000
Income taxes payable	35,500
Total current liabilities	215,500
Bonds payable	200,000
Total liabilities	415,500
Stockholders' equity	
Common stock	350,000
Retained earnings	288,700
Total stockholders' equity	638,700
Total liabilities and stockholders' equity	$1,054,200

Additional information: The cash provided by operating activities for 2010 was $190,800. The cash used for capital expenditures was $92,000. The cash used for dividends was $31,000. The average number of shares outstanding during the year was 50,000.

Instructions

(a) Compute the following values and ratios for 2010. (We provide the results from 2009 for comparative purposes.)
  (i) Working capital. (2009: $160,500)
  (ii) Current ratio. (2009: 1.65:1)
  (iii) Free cash flow. (2009: $48,700)
  (iv) Debt to total assets ratio. (2009: 31%)
  (v) Earnings per share. (2009: $3.15)
(b) Using your calculations from part (a), discuss changes from 2009 in liquidity, solvency, and profitability.

Compute and interpret liquidity, solvency, and profitability ratios.

(SO 2, 4, 5)

P2-6A Condensed balance sheet and income statement data for Lark Corporation are presented here.

LARK CORPORATION
Balance Sheets
December 31

Assets	2010	2009
Cash	$ 25,000	$ 20,000
Receivables (net)	70,000	62,000
Other current assets	80,000	73,000
Long-term investments	75,000	60,000
Plant and equipment (net)	510,000	470,000
Total assets	$760,000	$685,000

Liabilities and Stockholders' Equity		
Current liabilities	$ 75,000	$ 70,000
Long-term debt	80,000	90,000
Common stock	330,000	300,000
Retained earnings	275,000	225,000
Total liabilities and stockholders' equity	$760,000	$685,000

LARK CORPORATION
Income Statements
For the Years Ended December 31

	2010	2009
Sales	$750,000	$670,000
Cost of goods sold	440,000	400,000
Operating expenses (including income taxes)	240,000	220,000
Net income	$ 70,000	$ 50,000

Additional information:

Cash from operating activities	$87,000	$60,000
Cash used for capital expenditures	$45,000	$38,000
Dividends paid	$20,000	$15,000
Average number of shares outstanding	33,000	30,000

Instructions
Compute these values and ratios for 2009 and 2010.
(a) Earnings per share.
(b) Working capital.
(c) Current ratio.
(d) Debt to total assets ratio.
(e) Free cash flow.
(f) Based on the ratios calculated, discuss briefly the improvement or lack thereof in financial position and operating results from 2009 to 2010 of Lark Corporation.

P2-7A Selected financial data of two competitors, Target and Wal-Mart, are presented here. (All dollars are in millions.)

Compute ratios and compare liquidity, solvency, and profitability for two companies.
(SO 2, 4, 5)

	Target (2/3/07)	Wal-Mart (1/31/07)
	Income Statement Data for Year	
Net sales	$59,490	$344,992
Cost of goods sold	39,399	264,152
Selling and administrative expenses	14,315	64,001
Interest expense	572	1,529
Other income (loss)	(707)	3,658
Income taxes	1,710	6,365
Net income	$ 2,787	$ 12,603

	Target	Wal-Mart
	Balance Sheet Data (End of Year)	
Current assets	$14,706	$ 46,588
Noncurrent assets	22,643	104,605
Total assets	$37,349	$151,193
Current liabilities	$11,117	$ 51,754
Long-term debt	10,599	37,866
Total stockholders' equity	15,633	61,573
Total liabilities and stockholders' equity	$37,349	$151,193
Cash from operating activities	$4,862	$20,209
Cash paid for capital expenditures	3,928	15,666
Dividends declared and paid on common stock	380	2,802
Average shares outstanding (millions)	869	4,168

Instructions
For each company, compute these values and ratios.
(a) Working capital.
(b) Current ratio.

(c) Debt to total assets ratio.
(d) Free cash flow.
(e) Earnings per share.
(f) Compare the liquidity, solvency, and profitability of the two companies.

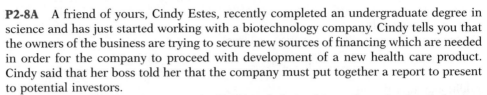

Comment on the objectives and qualitative characteristics of financial reporting.
(SO 6, 7)

P2-8A A friend of yours, Cindy Estes, recently completed an undergraduate degree in science and has just started working with a biotechnology company. Cindy tells you that the owners of the business are trying to secure new sources of financing which are needed in order for the company to proceed with development of a new health care product. Cindy said that her boss told her that the company must put together a report to present to potential investors.

Cindy thought that the company should include in this package the detailed scientific findings related to the Phase I clinical trials for this product. She said, "I know that the biotech industry sometimes has only a 10% success rate with new products, but if we report all the scientific findings, everyone will see what a sure success this is going to be! The president was talking about the importance of following some set of accounting principles. Why do we need to look at some accounting rules? What they need to realize is that we have scientific results that are quite encouraging, some of the most talented employees around, and the start of some really great customer relationships. We haven't made any sales yet, but we will. We just need the funds to get through all the clinical testing and get government approval for our product. Then these investors will be quite happy that they bought in to our company early!"

Instructions
(a) What is financial reporting? Explain to Cindy what is meant by generally accepted accounting principles.
(b) Comment on how Cindy's suggestions for what should be reported to prospective investors conforms to the qualitative characteristics of accounting information. Do you think that the things that Cindy wants to include in the information for investors will conform to financial reporting guidelines?

Problems: Set B

Prepare a classified balance sheet.
(SO 1)

P2-1B The following items are from the 2006 balance sheet of Kellogg Company. (All dollars are in millions.)

Common stock	$ 396.9
Other assets	5,471.4
Notes payable—current	1,268.0
Other current assets	247.7
Current maturities of long-term debt	723.3
Cash and cash equivalents	410.6
Other long-term liabilities	1,571.8
Retained earnings	1,672.1
Accounts payable	910.4
Other current liabilities	1,118.5
Accounts receivable, net	944.8
Property, net	2,815.6
Inventories	823.9
Long-term debt	3,053.0

Tot. current assets $2,427.0
Tot. assets $10,714.0

Instructions
Prepare a classified balance sheet for Kellogg Company as of December 31, 2006.

Prepare financial statements.
(SO 1, 3)

P2-2B These items are taken from the financial statements of Pinson, Inc.

Prepaid insurance	$ 1,800
Equipment	31,000
Salaries expense	36,000
Utilities expense	2,100
Accumulated depreciation	8,600
Accounts payable	10,200
Cash	5,300

Accounts receivable	$ 5,500
Salaries payable	2,000
Common stock	5,900
Depreciation expense	4,300
Retained earnings (beginning)	14,000
Dividends	3,600
Service revenue	53,000
Repair expense	2,900
Insurance expense	1,200

Instructions

Prepare an income statement, a retained earnings statement, and a classified balance sheet as of December 31, 2010.

Net income $6,500
Tot. assets $35,000

P2-3B   You are provided with the following information for Milner Corporation, effective as of its April 30, 2010, year-end.

Prepare financial statements.
(SO 1, 3)

Accounts payable	$ 2,400
Accounts receivable	9,150
Accumulated depreciation	6,600
Depreciation expense	2,200
Cash	21,955
Common stock	20,000
Dividends	2,800
Equipment	25,050
Sales revenue	21,450
Income tax expense	1,100
Income taxes payable	300
Interest expense	350
Interest payable	175
Long-term notes payable	5,700
Prepaid rent	380
Rent expense	760
Retained earnings, beginning	13,960
Salaries expense	6,840

Instructions

(a) Prepare an income statement and a retained earnings statement for Milner Corporation for the year ended April 30, 2010.
(b) Prepare a classified balance sheet for Milner as of April 30, 2010.
(c) Explain how each financial statement interrelates with the others.

Net income $10,200
Tot. current assets $31,485
Tot. assets $49,935

P2-4B   Comparative statement data for Smyth Company and James Company, two competitors, are presented below. All balance sheet data are as of December 31, 2010.

Compute ratios; comment on relative profitability, liquidity, and solvency.
(SO 2, 4, 5)

	Smyth Company	James Company
	2010	**2010**
Net sales	$450,000	$898,000
Cost of goods sold	260,000	620,000
Operating expenses	134,000	55,000
Interest expense	6,000	10,000
Income tax expense	10,000	65,000
Current assets	180,000	700,000
Plant assets (net)	600,000	800,000
Current liabilities	75,000	300,000
Long-term liabilities	190,000	200,000
Cash from operating activities	36,000	180,000
Capital expenditures	20,000	50,000
Dividends paid	4,000	15,000
Average number of shares outstanding	200,000	400,000

Instructions

(a) Comment on the relative profitability of the companies by computing the net income and earnings per share for each company for 2010.

(b) Comment on the relative liquidity of the companies by computing working capital and the current ratios for each company for 2010.

(c) Comment on the relative solvency of the companies by computing the debt to total assets ratio and the free cash flow for each company for 2010.

Compute and interpret liquidity, solvency, and profitability ratios.

(SO 2, 4, 5)

P2-5B The financial statements of Windsor Company are presented here.

WINDSOR COMPANY
Income Statement
For the Year Ended December 31, 2010

Net sales	$700,000
Cost of goods sold	400,000
Selling and administrative expenses	150,000
Interest expense	7,800
Income tax expense	43,000
Net income	$ 99,200

WINDSOR COMPANY
Balance Sheet
December 31, 2010

Assets

Current assets	
Cash	$ 23,100
Short-term investments	34,800
Accounts receivable (net)	106,200
Inventory	155,000
Total current assets	319,100
Plant assets (net)	465,300
Total assets	$784,400

Liabilities and Stockholders' Equity

Current liabilities	
Accounts payable	$120,200
Income taxes payable	29,000
Total current liabilities	149,200
Bonds payable	130,000
Total liabilities	279,200
Stockholders' equity	
Common stock	170,000
Retained earnings	335,200
Total stockholders' equity	505,200
Total liabilities and stockholders' equity	$784,400

Cash from operating activities	$ 71,300
Capital expenditures	$ 42,000
Dividends paid	$ 10,000
Average number of shares outstanding	65,000

Instructions

(a) Compute the following values and ratios for 2010. (We provide the results from 2009 for comparative purposes.)

  (i) Current ratio. (2009: 2.4:1)

  (ii) Working capital. (2009: $178,000)

(iii) Debt to total assets ratio. (2009: 31%)
(iv) Free cash flow. (2009: $13,000)
(v) Earnings per share. (2009: $1.35)
(b) Using your calculations from part (a), discuss changes from 2009 in liquidity, solvency, and profitability.

P2-6B Condensed balance sheet and income statement data for Pratt Corporation are presented below.

Compute and interpret liquidity, solvency, and profitability ratios.

(SO 2, 4, 5)

PRATT CORPORATION
Balance Sheets
December 31

Assets	2010	2009
Cash	$ 40,000	$ 24,000
Receivables (net)	90,000	55,000
Other current assets	74,000	73,000
Long-term investments	78,000	70,000
Plant and equipment (net)	525,000	427,000
Total assets	$807,000	$649,000

Liabilities and Stockholders' Equity	2010	2009
Current liabilities	$ 93,000	$ 75,000
Long-term debt	90,000	70,000
Common stock	370,000	340,000
Retained earnings	254,000	164,000
Total liabilities and stockholders' equity	$807,000	$649,000

PRATT CORPORATION
Income Statements
For the Years Ended December 31

	2010	2009
Sales	$760,000	$800,000
Cost of goods sold	420,000	400,000
Operating expenses (including income taxes)	200,000	237,000
Net income	$140,000	$163,000
Cash from operating activities	$165,000	$178,000
Cash used for capital expenditures	85,000	45,000
Dividends paid	50,000	43,000
Average number of shares outstanding	370,000	320,000

Instructions
Compute the following values and ratios for 2009 and 2010.
(a) Earnings per share.
(b) Working capital.
(c) Current ratio.
(d) Debt to total assets ratio.
(e) Free cash flow.
(f) Based on the ratios calculated, discuss briefly the improvement or lack thereof in the financial position and operating results of Pratt from 2009 to 2010.

Compute ratios and compare liquidity, solvency, and profitability for two companies.

(SO 2, 4, 5)

P2-7B Selected financial data of two competitors, Blockbuster Inc. and Movie Gallery, Inc., in 2006 are presented on page 94. (All dollars are in millions.)

	Blockbuster Inc.	Movie Gallery, Inc.
	Income Statement Data for Year	
Net sales	$ 5,524	$2,542
Cost of goods sold	2,476	1,012
Selling and administrative expenses	2,755	1,431
Interest expense	102	120
Other expense	212	3
Income tax expense (refund)	(76)	2
Net income (loss)	$ 55	$ (26)

	Blockbuster Inc.	Movie Gallery, Inc.
	Balance Sheet Data (End of Year)	
Current assets	$ 1,566	$ 239
Property, plant, and equipment (net)	580	243
Intangible assets	835	297
Other assets	156	374
Total assets	$ 3,137	$1,153
Current liabilities	$ 1,395	$ 268
Long-term debt	851	1,122
Total stockholders' equity	891	(237)
Total liabilities and stockholders' equity	$ 3,137	$1,153
Cash from operating activities	$329	$(10)
Cash used for capital expenditures	79	20
Dividends paid	11	–0–
Average shares outstanding	189.0	31.8

Instructions

For each company, compute these values and ratios.
(a) Working capital.
(b) Current ratio. (Round to two decimal places.)
(c) Debt to total assets ratio.
(d) Free cash flow.
(e) Earnings per share.
(f) Compare the liquidity, profitability, and solvency of the two companies.

Comment on the objectives and qualitative characteristics of accounting information.
(SO 6, 7)

P2-8B Net Nanny Software International Inc., headquartered in Vancouver, specializes in Internet safety and computer security products for both the home and commercial markets. In a recent balance sheet, it reported a deficit (negative retained earnings) of US $5,678,288. It has reported only net losses since its inception. In spite of these losses, Net Nanny's common shares have traded anywhere from a high of $3.70 to a low of $0.32 on the Canadian Venture Exchange.

Net Nanny's financial statements have historically been prepared in Canadian dollars. Recently, the company adopted the U.S. dollar as its reporting currency.

Instructions

(a) What is the objective of financial reporting? How does this objective meet or not meet Net Nanny's investor's needs?
(b) Why would investors want to buy Net Nanny's shares if the company has consistently reported losses over the last few years? Include in your answer an assessment of the relevance of the information reported on Net Nanny's financial statements.
(c) Comment on how the change in reporting information from Canadian dollars to U.S. dollars likely affected the readers of Net Nanny's financial statements. Include in your answer an assessment of the comparability of the information.

Problems: Set C

Visit the book's companion website at **www.wiley.com/college/kimmel** and choose the Student Companion site to access Problem Set C.

Continuing Cookie Chronicle

(*Note:* This is a continuation of the Cookie Chronicle from Chapter 1.)

CCC2   After investigating the different forms of business organization, Natalie Koebel decides to operate her business as a corporation, Cookie Creations Inc., and she begins the process of getting her business running.

Go to the book's companion website, **www.wiley.com/college/kimmel,** to find the completion of this problem.

broadening your perspective

FINANCIAL REPORTING PROBLEM: *Tootsie Roll Industries, Inc.*

BYP2-1   The financial statements of Tootsie Roll Industries, Inc., appear in Appendix A at the end of this book.

Instructions
Answer the following questions using the Consolidated Balance Sheet and the Notes to Consolidated Financial Statements section.
(a) What were Tootsie Roll's total current assets at December 31, 2007, and December 31, 2006?
(b) Are the assets included in current assets listed in the proper order? Explain.
(c) How are Tootsie Roll's assets classified?
(d) What were Tootsie Roll's current liabilities at December 31, 2007, and December 31, 2006?

COMPARATIVE ANALYSIS PROBLEM: *Tootsie Roll vs. Hershey Foods*

BYP2-2   The financial statements of Hershey Foods appear in Appendix B, following the financial statements for Tootsie Roll in Appendix A. Assume Hershey's average number of shares outstanding was 228,652,000, and Tootsie Roll's was 54,980,000.

Instructions
(a) For each company calculate the following values for 2007.
   (1) Working capital.   (4) Free cash flow.
   (2) Current ratio.   (5) Earnings per share.
   (3) Debt to total assets ratio

   (*Hint:* When calculating free cash flow, **do not** consider business acquisitions to be part of capital expenditures.)

(b) Based on your findings above, discuss the relative liquidity, solvency, and profitability of the two companies.

RESEARCH CASE

BYP 2-3   The January 2008 edition of *Strategic Finance* includes an article by Curtis C. Verschoor titled "ERC Says Ethics Risk Landscape Still Treacherous."

Instructions
Read the article and answer the following questions.
(a) In 2007 what percentage of employees in the survey said that they had personally observed violations of company ethics standards, policy, or the law? How did this percentage compare with 2005 and 2003?

(b) What were the three most frequent types of observed misconduct, and what percentage of employees observed each type of behavior?

(c) What percentage of employees who witnessed misconduct did not report it through company channels? What were the two most common reasons given for not reporting?

(d) What are the key elements of an effective ethics and compliance program?

INTERPRETING FINANCIAL STATEMENTS

BYP2-4 The following information was reported by Gap, Inc. in its 2006 annual report.

	2006	2005	2004	2003	2002
Total assets (millions)	$8,544	$8,821	$10,048	$10,713	$10,283
Working capital	$2,757	$3,297	$4,062	$4,156	$2,972
Current ratio	2.21:1	2.70:1	2.81:1	2.63:1	2.08:1
Debt to total assets ratio	.39:1	.38:1	.51:1	.57:1	.66:1
Earnings per share	$0.94	$1.26	$1.29	$1.15	$0.55

(a) Determine the overall percentage decrease in Gap's total assets from 2002 to 2006. What was the average decrease per year?

(b) Comment on the change in Gap's liquidity. Does working capital or the current ratio appear to provide a better indication of Gap's liquidity? What might explain the change in Gap's liquidity during this period?

(c) Comment on the change in Gap's solvency during this period.

(d) Comment on the change in Gap's profitability during this period. How might this affect your prediction about Gap's future profitability?

FINANCIAL ANALYSIS ON THE WEB

BYP2-5 *Purpose:* Identify summary liquidity, solvency, and profitability information about companies, and compare this information across companies in the same industry.

Address: **http://biz.yahoo.com/i**, or go to **www.wiley.com/college/kimmel**

Steps
1. Type in a company name, or use the index to find a company name. Choose **Profile**. Choose **Key Statistics**. Perform instruction (a) below.
2. Go back to **Profile**. Click on the company's particular industry behind the heading "Industry." Perform instructions (b), (c), and (d).

Instructions
Answer the following questions.

(a) What is the company's name? What was the company's current ratio and debt to equity ratio (a variation of the debt to total assets ratio)?

(b) What is the company's industry?

(c) What is the name of a competitor? What is the competitor's current ratio and its debt to equity ratio?

(d) Based on these measures: Which company is more liquid? Which company is more solvent?

BYP2-6 The opening story described the dramatic effect that investment bulletin boards are having on the investment world. This exercise will allow you to evaluate a bulletin board discussing a company of your choice.

Address: **http://biz.yahoo.com/i**, or go to **www.wiley.com/college/kimmel**

Steps
1. Type in a company name, or use the index to find a company name.
2. Choose **Msgs** or **Message Board**. (for messages).
3. Read the ten most recent messages.

Instructions
Answer the following questions.

(a) State the nature of each of these messages (e.g., offering advice, criticizing company, predicting future results, ridiculing other people who have posted messages).

(b) For those messages that expressed an opinion about the company, was evidence provided to support the opinion?

(c) What effect do you think it would have on bulletin board discussions if the participants provided their actual names? Do you think this would be a good policy?

Critical Thinking

DECISION MAKING ACROSS THE ORGANIZATION

BYP2-7   As a financial analyst in the planning department for Steigner Industries, Inc., you have been requested to develop some key ratios from the comparative financial statements. This information is to be used to convince creditors that Steigner Industries, Inc. is liquid, solvent, and profitable, and that it deserves their continued support. Lenders are particularly concerned about the company's ability to continue as a going concern.

Here are the data requested and the computations developed from the financial statements:

	2010	**2009**
Current ratio	3.1	2.1
Working capital	Up 22%	Down 7%
Free cash flow	Up 25%	Up 18%
Debt to total assets ratio	0.60	0.70
Net income	Up 32%	Down 8%
Earnings per share	$2.40	$1.15

Instructions

Steigner Industries, Inc. asks you to prepare brief comments stating how each of these items supports the argument that its financial health is improving. The company wishes to use these comments to support presentation of data to its creditors. With the class divided into groups, prepare the comments as requested, giving the implications and the limitations of each item separately, and then the collective inference that may be drawn from them about Steigner's financial well-being.

COMMUNICATION ACTIVITY

BYP2-8   T. J. Rains is the chief executive officer of Tomorrow's Products. T. J. is an expert engineer but a novice in accounting.

Instructions

Write a letter to T. J. Rains that explains (a) the three main types of ratios; (b) examples of each, how they are calculated, and what they measure; and (c) the bases for comparison in analyzing Tomorrow's Products' financial statements.

ETHICS CASE

BYP2-9   A May 20, 2002, *Business Week* story by Stanley Holmes and Mike France entitled "Boeing's Secret" discusses issues surrounding the timing of the disclosure of information at the giant airplane manufacturer. To summarize, on December 11, 1996, Boeing closed a giant deal to acquire another manufacturer, McDonnell Douglas. Boeing paid for the acquisition by issuing shares of its own stock to the stockholders of McDonnell Douglas. In order for the deal not to be revoked, the value of Boeing's stock could not decline below a certain level for a number of months after the deal.

The article suggests that during the first half of 1997 Boeing suffered significant cost overruns because of severe inefficiencies in its production methods. Had these problems been disclosed in the quarterly financial statements during the first and second quarter of 1997, the company's stock most likely would have plummeted, and the deal would have been revoked. Company managers spent considerable time debating when the bad news should be disclosed. One public relations manager suggested that the company's problems be revealed on the date of either Princess Diana's or Mother Teresa's funeral, in the hope that it would be lost among those big stories that day. Instead, the company waited until October 22 of that year to announce a $2.6 billion write-off due to cost overruns. Within one week the company's stock price had fallen 20%, but by this time the McDonnell Douglas deal could not be reversed.

Instructions

Answer the following questions. Although it is not required in order to answer the questions, you may want to read the *Business Week* article.
(a) Who are the stakeholders in this situation?
(b) What are the ethical issues?

(c) What assumptions or principles of accounting are relevant to this case?

(d) Do you think it is ethical to try to "time" the release of a story so as to diminish its effect?

(e) What would you have done if you were the chief executive officer of Boeing?

(f) Boeing's top management maintains that it did not have an obligation to reveal its problems during the first half of 1997, and that it wouldn't do anything differently today. What implications does this have for investors and analysts who follow Boeing's stock?

"ALL ABOUT YOU" ACTIVITY

BYP2-10 Every company needs to plan in order to move forward. Its top management must consider where it wants the company to be in three to five years. Like a company, you need to think about where you want to be three to five years from now, and you need to start taking steps now in order to get there.

Instructions

Provide responses to each of the following items.

(a) Where would you like to be working in three to five years? Describe your plan for getting there by identifying between five and 10 specific steps that you need to take in order to get there.

(b) In order to get the job you want, you will need a résumé. Your résumé is the equivalent of a company's annual report. It needs to provide relevant and reliable information about your past accomplishments so that employers can decide whether to "invest" in you. Do a search on the Internet to find a good résumé format. What are the basic elements of a résumé?

(c) A company's annual report provides information about a company's accomplishments. In order for investors to use the annual report, the information must be reliable; that is, users must have faith that the information is accurate and believable. How can you provide assurance that the information on your résumé is reliable?

(d) Prepare a résumé assuming that you have accomplished the five to 10 specific steps you identified in part (a). Also, provide evidence that would give assurance that the information is reliable.

Answers to Insight and Accounting Across the Organization Questions

p. 60

Q: What can various company managers do to ensure that working capital is managed efficiently to maximize net income?

A: Marketing and sales managers must understand that by extending generous repayment terms they are expanding the company's receivables balance and slowing the company's cash flow. Production managers must strive to minimize the amount of excess inventory on hand. Managers must coordinate efforts to speed up the collection of receivables, while also ensuring that the company pays its payables on time, but never too early.

p. 61

Q: Discuss the difference in the debt to total assets ratio of Microsoft and General Motors.

A: Microsoft has a very low debt to total assets ratio. The company is in a rapidly changing industry and thus should try to minimize the risk associated with increased debt. Also, because Microsoft generates significant amounts of cash and has minimal needs for large investments in plant assets, it does not need to borrow a lot of cash. General Motors needs to make huge investments in plant assets, and it has a very large credit operation. Thus it has large borrowing needs.

p. 65

Q: What is meant by the phrase "make the country's businesses more transparent"? Why would increasing transparency spur economic growth?

A: Transparency refers to the extent to which outsiders have knowledge regarding a company's financial performance and financial position. If a company lacks transparency, its financial reports do not adequately inform investors of critical information that is needed to make investment decisions. If corporate transparency is increased, investors will be more willing to supply the financial capital that businesses need in order to grow, which would spur the country's economic growth.

p. 66

Q: What problems might Best Buy's year-end create for analysts?

A: First, if Best Buy's competitors use a different year-end, then when you compare their financial results, you are not comparing performance over the same period of time or financial position at the same point in time. Also, by not picking a particular date, the number of weeks in Best Buy's fiscal year will change. For example, fiscal years 2005 and 2006 had 52 weeks, but fiscal year 2007 had 53 weeks.

Answers to Self-Study Questions

1. d   2. a   3. c   4. c   5. b   6. a   7. c   8. b   9. d   10. d   11. a   12. a   13. c   14. c   15. c

✔ Remember to go back to the navigator box on the chapter-opening page and check off your completed work.

chapter 3

The Accounting Information System

✔ the navigator

- Scan **Study Objectives** ○
- Read **Feature Story** ○
- Scan **Preview** ○
- Read **Text and answer** *Do it!*
  p. 110 ○   p. 115 ○   p. 118 ○   p. 128 ○
- Work **Using the Decision Toolkit** ○
- Review **Summary of Study Objectives** ○
- Work **Comprehensive** *Do it!* p. 133 ○
- Answer **Self-Study Questions** ○
- Complete **Assignments** ○

study objectives

After studying this chapter, you should be able to:

1 Analyze the effect of business transactions on the basic accounting equation.
2 Explain what an account is and how it helps in the recording process.
3 Define debits and credits and explain how they are used to record business transactions.
4 Identify the basic steps in the recording process.
5 Explain what a journal is and how it helps in the recording process.
6 Explain what a ledger is and how it helps in the recording process.
7 Explain what posting is and how it helps in the recording process.
8 Explain the purposes of a trial balance.
9 Classify cash activities as operating, investing, or financing.

✔ the navigator

Accidents Happen

How organized are you financially? Take a short quiz. Answer *yes* or *no* to each question:

- Does your wallet contain so many cash machine receipts that you've been declared a walking fire hazard?
- Is your wallet such a mess that it is often faster to fish for money in the crack of your car seat than to dig around in your wallet?
- Was Lebron James playing high school basketball the last time you balanced your bank account?
- Have you ever been tempted to burn down your house so you don't have to try to find all of the receipts and records that you need to fill out your tax returns?

If you think it is hard to keep track of the many transactions that make up *your* life, imagine what it is like for a major corporation like Fidelity Investments. Fidelity is one of the largest mutual fund management firms in the world. If you had your life savings invested at Fidelity Investments, you might be just slightly displeased if, when you called to find out your balance, the representative said, "You know, I kind of remember someone with a name like yours sending us some money— now what did we do with that?"

To ensure the accuracy of your balance and the security of your funds, Fidelity Investments, like all other companies large and small, relies on a sophisticated accounting information system. That's not to say that Fidelity or any other company is error-free. In fact, if you've ever really messed up your checkbook register, you may take some comfort from one accountant's mistake at Fidelity Investments. The accountant failed to include a minus sign while doing a calculation, making what was actually a $1.3 billion loss look like a $1.3 billion gain—yes, *billion!* Fortunately, like most accounting errors, it was detected before any real harm was done.

No one expects that kind of mistake at a company like Fidelity, which has sophisticated computer systems and top investment managers. In explaining the mistake to shareholders, a spokesperson wrote, "Some people have asked how, in this age of technology, such a mistake could be made. While many of our processes are computerized, accounting systems are complex and dictate that some steps must be handled manually by our managers and accountants, and people can make mistakes."

On the World Wide Web
Fidelity Investments: www.fidelity.com

As indicated in the Feature Story, a reliable information system is a necessity for any company. The purpose of this chapter is to explain and illustrate the features of an accounting information system. The organization and content of the chapter are as follows.

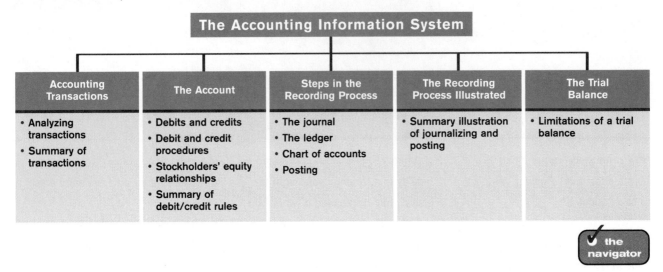

The Accounting Information System

Accounting Transactions	The Account	Steps in the Recording Process	The Recording Process Illustrated	The Trial Balance
• Analyzing transactions • Summary of transactions	• Debits and credits • Debit and credit procedures • Stockholders' equity relationships • Summary of debit/credit rules	• The journal • The ledger • Chart of accounts • Posting	• Summary illustration of journalizing and posting	• Limitations of a trial balance

the navigator

The Accounting Information System

The system of collecting and processing transaction data and communicating financial information to decision makers is known as the accounting information system. Factors that shape these systems include: the nature of the company's business, the types of transactions, the size of the company, the volume of data, and the information demands of management and others.

Most businesses use computerized accounting systems—sometimes referred to as electronic data processing (EDP) systems. These systems handle all the steps involved in the recording process, from initial data entry to preparation of the financial statements. In order to remain competitive, companies continually improve their accounting systems to provide accurate and timely data for decision making. For example, in a recent annual report, Tootsie Roll states, "We also invested in additional processing and data storage hardware during the year. We view information technology as a key strategic tool, and are committed to deploying leading edge technology in this area." In addition, many companies have upgraded their accounting information systems in response to the requirements of Sarbanes-Oxley.

In this chapter we focus on a manual accounting system because the accounting concepts and principles do not change whether a system is computerized or manual, and manual systems are easier to illustrate. However, many of the homework problems in this and subsequent chapters can also be done using the computerized general ledger package that supplements this text.

Accounting Transactions

To use an accounting information system, you need to know which economic events to recognize (record). Not all events are recorded and reported in the financial statements. For example, suppose General Motors hired a new employee or purchased a new computer. Are these events entered in its accounting records? The first event would not be recorded, but the second event would. We call economic events that require recording in the financial statements accounting transactions.

An accounting transaction occurs when assets, liabilities, or stockholders' equity items change as a result of some economic event. The purchase of a computer by General Motors, the payment of rent by Microsoft, and the sale of advertising space by Sierra Corporation are examples of events that change a company's assets, liabilities, or stockholders' equity. Illustration 3-1 summarizes the decision process companies use to decide whether or not to record economic events.

Illustration 3-1
Transaction identification process

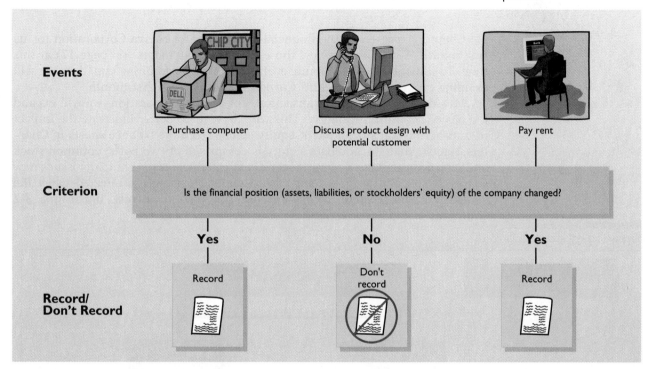

ANALYZING TRANSACTIONS

In Chapter 1 you learned the basic accounting equation:

$$\text{Assets} = \text{Liabilities} + \text{Stockholders' Equity}$$

In this chapter you will learn how to analyze transactions in terms of their effect on assets, liabilities, and stockholders' equity. **Transaction analysis** is the process of identifying the specific effects of economic events on the accounting equation.

The accounting equation must always balance. Each transaction has a dual (double-sided) effect on the equation. For example, if an individual asset is increased, there must be a corresponding:

Decrease in another asset, *or*

Increase in a specific liability, *or*

Increase in stockholders' equity.

Two or more items could be affected when an asset is increased. For example, if a company purchases a computer for $10,000 by paying $6,000 in cash and signing a note for $4,000, one asset (computer) increases $10,000, another asset (cash) decreases $6,000, and a liability (notes payable) increases $4,000.

The result is that the accounting equation remains in balance—assets increased by a net $4,000 and liabilities increased by $4,000, as shown below.

Assets	=	Liabilities	+	Stockholders' Equity
+$10,000		+$4,000		
− 6,000				
$ 4,000	=	$4,000		

Chapter 1 presented the financial statements for Sierra Corporation for its first month. You should review those financial statements (on page 17) at this time. To illustrate how economic events affect the accounting equation, we will examine events affecting Sierra Corporation during its first month.

In order to analyze the transactions for Sierra Corporation, we will expand the basic accounting equation. This will allow us to better illustrate the impact of transactions on stockholders' equity. Recall from the balance sheets in Chapters 1 and 2 that stockholders' equity is comprised of two parts: common stock and retained earnings. Common stock is affected when the company issues new shares of stock in exchange for cash. Retained earnings is affected when the company earns revenue, incurs expenses, or pays dividends. Illustration 3-2 shows the expanded equation.

Illustration 3-2 Expanded accounting equation

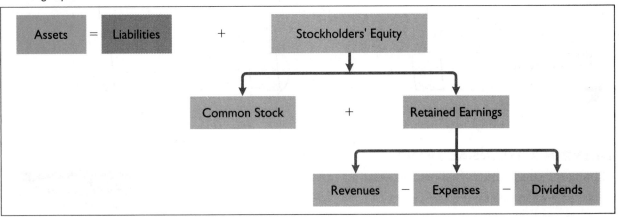

If you are tempted to skip ahead after you've read a few of the following transaction analyses, don't do it. Each has something unique to teach, something you'll need later. (We assure you that we've kept them to the minimum needed!)

EVENT (1). INVESTMENT OF CASH BY STOCKHOLDERS. On October 1 cash of $10,000 is invested in the business by investors in exchange for $10,000 of common stock. This event is an accounting transaction because it results in an increase in both assets and stockholders' equity. There is an increase of $10,000 in the asset Cash and an increase of $10,000 in Common Stock on the books of Sierra Corporation. The effect of this transaction on the accounting equation is:

	Assets	=	Liabilities	+	Stockholders' Equity	
					Common	
	Cash	=			Stock	
(1)	+$10,000	=			+$10,000	Issued stock

The equation is in balance after the issuance of common stock. Keeping track of the source of each change in stockholders' equity is essential for later accounting activities. In particular, items recorded in the revenue and expense columns are used for the calculation of net income.

EVENT (2). NOTE ISSUED IN EXCHANGE FOR CASH. On October 1 Sierra borrowed $5,000 from Castle Bank by signing a 3-month, 12%, $5,000 note payable. This transaction results in an equal increase in assets and liabilities: Cash (an asset) increases $5,000, and Notes Payable (a liability) increases $5,000. The specific effect of this transaction and the cumulative effect of the first two transactions are:

	Assets	=	Liabilities	+	Stockholders' Equity
			Notes		Common
	Cash	=	Payable	+	Stock
	$10,000				$10,000
(2)	+5,000		+$5,000		
	$15,000	=	$5,000	+	$10,000
				$15,000	

Total assets are now $15,000, and stockholders' equity plus the new liability also total $15,000.

EVENT (3). PURCHASE OF OFFICE EQUIPMENT FOR CASH. On October 2 Sierra purchased office equipment by paying $5,000 cash to Superior Equipment Sales Co. This event is a transaction because an equal increase and decrease in Sierra's assets occur: Office Equipment (an asset) increases $5,000, and Cash (an asset) decreases $5,000.

	Assets			=	Liabilities	+	Stockholders' Equity
			Office				Common
	Cash	+	Equipment	=	N/P	+	Stock
	$15,000				$5,000		$10,000
(3)	−5,000		+$5,000				
	$10,000	+	$5,000	=	$5,000	+	$10,000
		$15,000				$15,000	

The total assets are now $15,000, and stockholders' equity plus the liability also total $15,000.

EVENT (4). RECEIPT OF CASH IN ADVANCE FROM CUSTOMER. On October 2 Sierra received a $1,200 cash advance from R. Knox, a client. This event is a transaction because Sierra received cash (an asset) for advertising services that are expected to be completed by Sierra in the future. Although Sierra received cash, **it does not record revenue until it has performed the work**. In some industries, such as the magazine and airline industries, customers are expected to prepay. These companies have a liability to the customer until they deliver the magazines or provide the flight. When the company eventually provides the product or service, it records the revenue.

Since Sierra received cash prior to performance of the service, Sierra has a liability for the work due. Cash increases by $1,200, and a liability, Unearned Service Revenue, increases by an equal amount.

	Assets			=	Liabilities			+	Stockholders' Equity
	Cash	+	Office Equip.	=	N/P	+	Unearned Service Revenue	+	Common Stock
	$10,000		$5,000		$5,000				$10,000
(4)	+1,200						+$1,200		
	$11,200	+	$5,000	=	$5,000	+	$1,200	+	$10,000
		$16,200					$16,200		

EVENT (5). SERVICES PROVIDED FOR CASH. On October 3 Sierra received $10,000 in cash from Copa Company for advertising services performed. This event is a transaction because Sierra received an asset (cash) in exchange for services.

Advertising service is the principal revenue-producing activity of Sierra. **Revenue increases stockholders' equity.** This transaction, then, increases both assets and stockholders' equity. Cash is increased $10,000, and revenues (specifically, Service Revenue) is increased $10,000. The new balances in the equation are:

	Assets			=	Liabilities			+	Stockholders' Equity					
			Office				Unearned		Common		Retained Earnings			
	Cash	+	Equip.	=	N/P	+	Serv. Rev.	+	Stock	+	Rev.	−	Exp.	− Div.
	$11,200		$5,000		$5,000		$1,200		$10,000					
(5)	+10,000										+$10,000			Service Revenue
	$21,200	+	$5,000	=	$5,000	+	$1,200	+	$10,000	+	$10,000			
		$26,200							$26,200					

Often companies provide services "on account." That is, they provide service for which they are paid at a later date. Revenue, however, is earned when services are performed. Therefore, revenues would increase when services are performed, even though cash has not been received. Instead of receiving cash, the company receives a different type of asset, an **account receivable**. Accounts receivable represent the right to receive payment at a later date. Suppose that Sierra had provided these services on account rather than for cash. This event would be reported using the accounting equation as:

Assets	=	Liabilities	+	Stockholders' Equity	
Accounts Receivable	=			Revenues	
+$10,000				+$10,000	Service Revenue

Later, when Sierra collects the $10,000 from the customer, Accounts Receivable declines by $10,000, and Cash increases by $10,000.

Assets		=	Liabilities	+	Stockholders' Equity
Cash	Accounts Receivable				
+$10,000	−$10,000				

Note that in this case, revenues is not affected by the collection of cash. Instead we record an exchange of one asset (Accounts Receivable) for a different asset (Cash).

EVENT (6). PAYMENT OF RENT. On October 3 Sierra Corporation paid its office rent for the month of October in cash, $900. This rent payment is a transaction because it results in a decrease in an asset, cash.

Rent is an expense incurred by Sierra Corporation in its effort to generate revenues. **Expenses decrease stockholders' equity.** Sierra records the rent payment by decreasing cash and increasing expenses to maintain the balance of the accounting equation. To record this transaction, Sierra decreases Cash $900, and increases expense (specifically, Rent Expense) $900. The effect of this payment on the accounting equation is:

		Assets	=	Liabilities			+		Stockholders' Equity			
		Office				Unearned		Common		Retained Earnings		
	Cash	+ Equip.	=	N/P	+	Serv. Rev.	+	Stock	+	Rev.	− Exp.	− Div.
	$21,200	$5,000		$5,000		$1,200		$10,000		$10,000		
(6)	−900										−$900	Rent
	$20,300	+ $5,000	=	$5,000	+	$1,200	+	$10,000	+	$10,000	− $900	Expense
		$25,300								$25,300		

EVENT (7). PURCHASE OF INSURANCE POLICY FOR CASH. On October 4 Sierra paid $600 for a one-year insurance policy that will expire next year on September 30. In this transaction the asset Cash is decreased $600. Payments of expenses that will benefit more than one accounting period are identified as assets called prepaid expenses or prepayments. Therefore the asset Prepaid Insurance is increased $600. The balance in total assets did not change; one asset account decreased by the same amount that another increased.

		Assets			=	Liabilities			+		Stockholders' Equity		
		Prepaid	Office				Unearned		Common		Retained Earnings		
	Cash	+ Insurance	+ Equip.	=	N/P	+	Serv. Rev.	+	Stock	+	Rev.	− Exp.	− Div.
	$20,300		$5,000		$5,000		$1,200		$10,000		$10,000	$900	
(7)	−600	+$600											
	$19,700	+ $600	+ $5,000	=	$5,000	+	$1,200	+	$10,000	+	$10,000	− $900	
		$25,300								$25,300			

EVENT (8). PURCHASE OF SUPPLIES ON ACCOUNT. On October 5 Sierra purchased a three-month supply of advertising materials on account from Aero Supply for $2,500. In this case, "on account" means that the company receives goods or services that it will pay for at a later date. Supplies, an asset, increases $2,500 by this transaction. Accounts Payable, a liability, increases $2,500, to indicate the amount due to Aero Supply. The effect on the equation is:

			Assets			=		Liabilities			+		Stockholders' Equity		
			Prepd.	Office				Accounts	Unearned		Common		Retained Earnings		
	Cash	+ Supplies	+ Insur.	+ Equip.	=	N/P	+	Payable	+ Serv. Rev.	+	Stock	+	Rev.	− Exp.	− Div.
	$19,700		$600	$5,000		$5,000			$1,200		$10,000		$10,000	$900	
(8)		+$2,500						+$2,500							
	$19,700	+ $2,500	+ $600	+ $5,000	=	$5,000	+	$2,500	+ $1,200	+	$10,000	+	$10,000	− $900	
			$27,800								$27,800				

EVENT (9). HIRING OF NEW EMPLOYEES. On October 9 Sierra hired four new employees to begin work on October 15. Each employee will receive a weekly salary of $500 for a five-day work week, payable every two weeks. Employees will receive their first paychecks on October 26. On the date Sierra hires the employees, there is no effect on the accounting equation because the assets, liabilities, and stockholders' equity of the company have not changed. **An accounting transaction has not occurred.** At this point there is only an agreement that the employees will begin work on October 15. [See Event (11) for the first payment.]

EVENT (10). PAYMENT OF DIVIDEND. On October 20 Sierra paid a $500 dividend. **Dividends** are a reduction of stockholders' equity but not an expense. Dividends are not included in the calculation of net income. Instead, a dividend is a distribution of the company's assets to its stockholders. This dividend transaction affects assets (Cash) and stockholders' equity (Dividends) by $500.

	Assets				=	**Liabilities**			+	**Stockholders' Equity**			
			Prepd.	Office				Unearned		Common	Retained Earnings		
	Cash	+ Supp.	+ Insur.	+ Equip.	= N/P	+ A/P	+ Serv. Rev.	+	Stock	+	Rev.	− Exp.	− Div.
	$19,700	$2,500	$600	$5,000	$5,000	$2,500	$1,200		$10,000	$10,000	$900	
(10)	−500												− $500
	$19,200	+ $2,500	+ $600	+ $5,000	= $5,000	+ $2,500	+ $1,200	+	$10,000	+ $10,000	− $900	− $500
		$27,300					$27,300					

EVENT (11). PAYMENT OF CASH FOR EMPLOYEE SALARIES. Employees have worked two weeks, earning $4,000 in salaries, which were paid on October 26. Salaries are an expense which reduce stockholders' equity. This event is a transaction because assets and stockholders' equity are affected. Thus, Cash is decreased $4,000 and expenses (specifically, Salaries Expense) is increased $4,000.

 Investor Insight

While most companies record transactions very carefully, the reality is that mistakes still happen. For example, bank regulators fined Bank One Corporation (now Chase) $1.8 million because they felt that the unreliability of the bank's accounting system caused it to violate regulatory requirements.

Also, in recent years Fannie Mae, the government-chartered mortgage association, announced a series of large accounting errors. These announcements caused alarm among investors, regulators, and politicians because they fear that the errors may suggest larger, undetected problems. This is important because the home-mortgage market depends on Fannie Mae to buy hundreds of billions of dollars of mortgages each year from banks, thus enabling the banks to issue new mortgages.

Finally, before a major overhaul of its accounting system, the financial records of Waste Management Company were in such disarray that of the company's 57,000 employees, 10,000 were receiving pay slips that were in error.

The Sarbanes-Oxley Act of 2002 was created to minimize the occurrence of errors like these by increasing every employee's responsibility for accurate financial reporting.

? In order for these companies to prepare and issue financial statements, their accounting equations (debits and credits) must have been in balance at year-end. How could these errors or misstatements have occurred?

	Assets				=	Liabilities			+	Stockholders' Equity				
			Prepd.	Office				Unearned		Common	Retained Earnings			
	Cash	+ Supp.	+ Insur.	+ Equip.	= N/P	+ A/P	+ Serv. Rev.	+	Stock	+ Rev.	− Exp.	− Div.		
	$19,200	$2,500	$600	$5,000	$5,000	$2,500	$1,200		$10,000	$10,000	$ 900	$500		
(11)	−4,000										− 4,000			Salaries
	$15,200 +	$2,500 +	$600 +	$5,000 =	$5,000 +	$2,500 +	$1,200	+	$10,000 +	$10,000	− $4,900	− $500		Expenses

$23,300 | $23,300

SUMMARY OF TRANSACTIONS

Illustration 3-3 summarizes the transactions of Sierra Corporation to show their cumulative effect on the basic accounting equation. It includes the transaction number in the first column on the left. The right-most column shows the specific effect of any transaction that affects stockholders' equity. Remember that Event (9) did not result in a transaction, so no entry is included for that event. The illustration demonstrates three important points:

1. Each transaction is analyzed in terms of its effect on assets, liabilities, and stockholders' equity.
2. The two sides of the equation must always be equal.
3. The cause of each change in stockholders' equity must be indicated.

Illustration 3-3 Summary of transactions

	Assets				=	Liabilities			+	Stockholders' Equity				
			Prepd.	Office				Unearned		Common	Retained Earnings			
	Cash	+ Supp.	+ Insur.	+ Equip.	= N/P	+ A/P	+ Serv. Rev.	+	Stock	+ Rev.	− Exp.	− Div.		
(1)	+$10,000				=				+$10,000					Issued stock
(2)	+5,000				+$5,000									
(3)	−5,000			+$5,000										
(4)	+1,200						+$1,200							
(5)	+10,000									+$10,000				Service Revenue
(6)	−900										−$ 900			Rent Expense
(7)	−600		+$600											
(8)		+$2,500				+ $2,500								
(10)	−500											−$500		Dividends
(11)	−4,000										−4,000			Salaries Expense
	$15,200 +	$2,500 +	$600 +	$5,000 =	$5,000 +	$2,500 +	$1,200	+	$10,000 +	$10,000	− $4,900	− $500		

$23,300 | $23,300

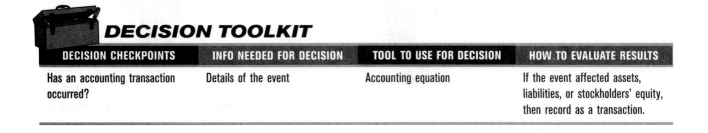

DECISION TOOLKIT

DECISION CHECKPOINTS	INFO NEEDED FOR DECISION	TOOL TO USE FOR DECISION	HOW TO EVALUATE RESULTS
Has an accounting transaction occurred?	Details of the event	Accounting equation	If the event affected assets, liabilities, or stockholders' equity, then record as a transaction.

before you go on...

**TRANSACTION
ANALYSIS**

Do it! A tabular analysis of the transactions made by Roberta Mendez & Co., a certified public accounting firm, for the month of August is shown below. Each increase and decrease in stockholders' equity is explained.

	Assets		=	Liabilities	+		Stockholders' Equity			
		Office		Accounts		Common		Retained Earnings		
	Cash	+	Equipment	=	Payable	+	Stock	+	Revenue	−	Expenses	
1.	+$25,000						+$25,000				Issued Stock
2.			+$7,000	=	+$7,000						
3.	+8,000								+$8,000		Service Revenue
4.	−850									−$850	Rent Expense
	$32,150	+	$7,000	=	$7,000	+	$25,000	+	$8,000	−	$850
		$39,150						$39,150		

Action Plan

• Analyze the tabular analysis to determine the nature and effect of each transaction.

• Keep the accounting equation in balance.

• Remember that a change in an asset will require a change in another asset, a liability, or in stockholders' equity.

Describe each transaction that occurred for the month.

Solution

1. The company issued shares of stock to stockholders for $25,000 cash.
2. The company purchased $7,000 of office equipment on account.
3. The company received $8,000 of cash in exchange for services performed.
4. The company paid $850 for this month's rent.

The Account

study objective 2

Explain what an account is and how it helps in the recording process.

Rather than using a tabular summary like the one in Illustration 3-3 for Sierra Corporation, an accounting information system uses accounts. An **account** is an individual accounting record of increases and decreases in a specific asset, liability, stockholders' equity, revenue, or expense item. For example, Sierra Corporation has separate accounts for Cash, Accounts Receivable, Accounts Payable, Service Revenue, Salaries Expense, and so on. (Note that whenever we are referring to a specific account, we capitalize the name.)

In its simplest form, an account consists of three parts: (1) the title of the account, (2) a left or debit side, and (3) a right or credit side. Because the alignment of these parts of an account resembles the letter T, it is referred to as a **T account**. The basic form of an account is shown in Illustration 3-4.

Illustration 3-4 Basic form of account

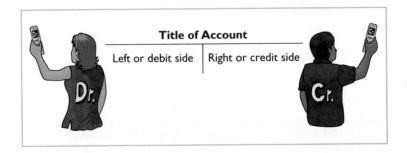

We use this form of account often throughout this book to explain basic accounting relationships.

DEBITS AND CREDITS

The term debit indicates the left side of an account, and credit indicates the right side. They are commonly abbreviated as **Dr.** for debit and **Cr.** for credit. They **do not** mean increase or decrease, as is commonly thought. We use the terms *debit* and *credit* repeatedly in the recording process to describe **where** entries are made in accounts. For example, the act of entering an amount on the left side of an account is called **debiting** the account. Making an entry on the right side is **crediting** the account.

When comparing the totals of the two sides, an account shows a **debit balance** if the total of the debit amounts exceeds the credits. An account shows a **credit balance** if the credit amounts exceed the debits. Note the position of the debit side and credit side in Illustration 3-4.

The procedure of recording debits and credits in an account is shown in Illustration 3-5 for the transactions affecting the Cash account of Sierra Corporation. The data are taken from the Cash column of the tabular summary in Illustration 3-3.

study objective 3
Define debits and credits and explain how they are used to record business transactions.

Tabular Summary		Account Form			
Cash		**Cash**			
$10,000		(Debits)	10,000	(Credits)	5,000
5,000			5,000		900
−5,000			1,200		600
1,200			10,000		500
10,000					4,000
−900		Balance	15,200		
−600		**(Debit)**			
−500					
−4,000					
$15,200					

Illustration 3-5 Tabular summary and account form for Sierra Corporation's Cash account

Every positive item in the tabular summary represents a receipt of cash; every negative amount represents a payment of cash. **Notice that in the account form we record the increases in cash as debits, and the decreases in cash as credits.** For example, the $10,000 receipt of cash (in red) is debited to Cash, and the −$5,000 payment of cash (in blue) is credited to Cash.

Having increases on one side and decreases on the other reduces recording errors and helps in determining the totals of each side of the account as well as the account balance. The balance is determined by netting the two sides (subtracting one amount from the other). The account balance, a debit of $15,200, indicates that Sierra had $15,200 more increases than decreases in cash. That is, since it started with a balance of zero, it has $15,200 in its Cash account.

DEBIT AND CREDIT PROCEDURES

Each transaction must affect two or more accounts to keep the basic accounting equation in balance. In other words, **for each transaction, debits must equal credits**. The equality of debits and credits provides the basis for the double-entry accounting system.

Under the double-entry system, the two-sided effect of each transaction is recorded in appropriate accounts. This system provides a logical method for recording transactions. The double-entry system also helps to ensure the accuracy of the recorded amounts and helps to detect errors such as those at Fidelity Investments as discussed in the Feature Story. If every transaction is recorded with equal debits and credits, then the sum of all the debits to the accounts must

International Note Rules for accounting for specific events sometimes differ across countries. For example, European companies rely less on historical cost and more on fair value than U.S. companies. Despite the differences, the double-entry accounting system is the basis of accounting systems worldwide.

equal the sum of all the credits. The double-entry system for determining the equality of the accounting equation is much more efficient than the plus/minus procedure used earlier.

Dr./Cr. Procedures for Assets and Liabilities

In Illustration 3-5 for Sierra Corporation, increases in Cash—an asset—were entered on the left side, and decreases in Cash were entered on the right side. We know that both sides of the basic equation (Assets = Liabilities + Stockholders' Equity) must be equal. It therefore follows that increases and decreases in liabilities will have to be recorded *opposite from* increases and decreases in assets. Thus, increases in liabilities must be entered on the right or credit side, and decreases in liabilities must be entered on the left or debit side. The effects that debits and credits have on assets and liabilities are summarized in Illustration 3-6.

Illustration 3-6 Debit and credit effects–assets and liabilities

Debits	Credits
Increase assets	Decrease assets
Decrease liabilities	Increase liabilities

Asset accounts normally show debit balances. That is, debits to a specific asset account should exceed credits to that account. Likewise, **liability accounts normally show credit balances**. That is, credits to a liability account should exceed debits to that account. The **normal balances** may be diagrammed as in Illustration 3-7.

Illustration 3-7 Normal balances–assets and liabilities

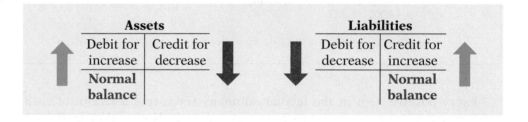

Helpful Hint The normal balance is the side where increases in the account are recorded.

Knowing which is the normal balance in an account may help when you are trying to identify errors. For example, a credit balance in an asset account such as Land or a debit balance in a liability account such as Wages Payable usually indicates errors in recording. Occasionally, however, an abnormal balance may be correct. The Cash account, for example, will have a credit balance when a company has overdrawn its bank balance (written a check that "bounced"). In automated accounting systems, the computer is programmed to flag violations of the normal balance and to print out error or exception reports. In manual systems, careful visual inspection of the accounts is required to detect normal balance problems.

Dr./Cr. Procedures for Stockholders' Equity

In Chapter 1 we indicated that stockholders' equity is comprised of two parts: common stock and retained earnings. In the transaction events earlier in this chapter, you saw that revenues, expenses, and the payment of dividends affect retained earnings. Therefore, the subdivisions of stockholders' equity are: common stock, retained earnings, dividends, revenues, and expenses.

COMMON STOCK. Common stock is issued to investors in exchange for the stockholders' investment. The Common Stock account is increased by credits and decreased by debits. For example, when cash is invested in the business, Cash is debited and Common Stock is credited. The effects of debits and credits on the Common Stock account are shown in Illustration 3-8.

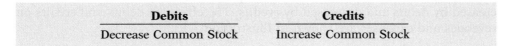

Debits	Credits
Decrease Common Stock	Increase Common Stock

Illustration 3-8 Debit and credit effects—Common Stock

The normal balance in the Common Stock account may be diagrammed as in Illustration 3-9.

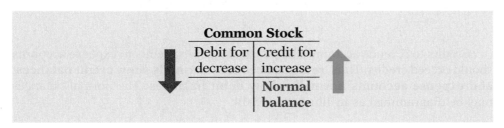

Illustration 3-9 Normal balance—Common Stock

RETAINED EARNINGS. Retained earnings is net income that is retained in the business. It represents the portion of stockholders' equity that has been accumulated through the profitable operation of the company. Retained Earnings is increased by credits (for example, by net income) and decreased by debits (for example, by a net loss), as shown in Illustration 3-10.

Debits	Credits
Decrease Retained Earnings	Increase Retained Earnings

Illustration 3-10 Debit and credit effects—Retained Earnings

The normal balance for Retained Earnings may be diagrammed as in Illustration 3-11.

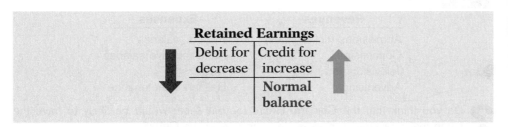

Illustration 3-11 Normal balance—Retained Earnings

DIVIDENDS. A dividend is a distribution by a corporation to its stockholders. The most common form of distribution is a cash dividend. Dividends result in a reduction of the stockholders' claims on retained earnings. Because dividends reduce stockholders' equity, increases in the Dividends account are recorded with debits. As shown in Illustration 3-12, the Dividends account normally has a debit balance.

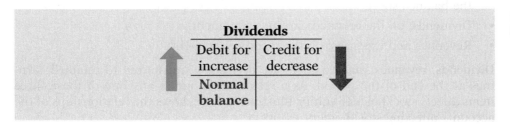

Illustration 3-12 Normal balance—Dividends

REVENUES AND EXPENSES. When a company earns revenues, stockholders' equity is increased. Revenue accounts are increased by credits and decreased by debits.

Expenses decrease stockholders' equity. Thus, expense accounts are increased by debits and decreased by credits. The effects of debits and credits on revenues and expenses are shown in Illustration 3-13.

Illustration 3-13 Debit and credit effects—revenues and expenses

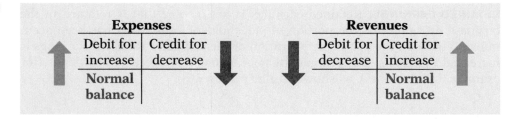

Debits	Credits
Decrease revenue	Increase revenue
Increase expenses	Decrease expenses

Credits to revenue accounts should exceed debits; debits to expense accounts should exceed credits. Thus, **revenue accounts normally show credit balances, and expense accounts normally show debit balances**. The normal balances may be diagrammed as in Illustration 3-14.

Illustration 3-14 Normal balances—revenues and expenses

Expenses		Revenues	
Debit for increase	Credit for decrease	Debit for decrease	Credit for increase
Normal balance			Normal balance

Investor Insight

The Chicago Cubs baseball team has these major revenue and expense accounts:

Revenues	Expenses
Admissions (ticket sales)	Players' salaries
Concessions	Administrative salaries
Television and radio	Travel
Advertising	Ballpark maintenance

 Do you think that the Chicago Bears football team would be likely to have the same major revenue and expense accounts as the Cubs?

STOCKHOLDERS' EQUITY RELATIONSHIPS

Companies report the subdivisions of stockholders' equity in various places in the financial statements:

- Common stock and retained earnings: in the stockholders' equity section of the balance sheet.
- Dividends: on the retained earnings statement.
- Revenues and expenses: on the income statement.

Dividends, revenues, and expenses are eventually transferred to retained earnings at the end of the period. As a result, a change in any one of these three items affects stockholders' equity. Illustration 3-15 shows the relationships of the accounts affecting stockholders' equity.

60   cash
60

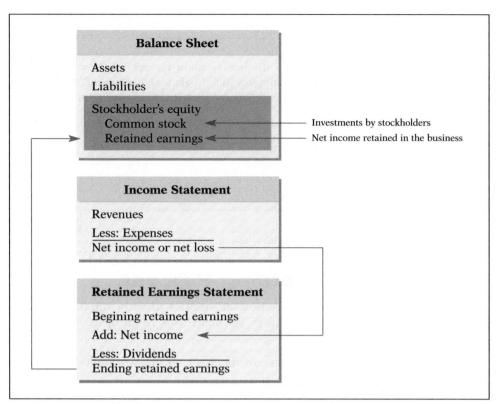

Illustration 3-15
Stockholders' equity
relationships

SUMMARY OF DEBIT/CREDIT RULES

Illustration 3-16 summarizes the debit/credit rules and effects on each type of account. **Study this diagram carefully.** It will help you understand the fundamentals of the double-entry system. No matter what the transaction, total debits must equal total credits in order to keep the accounting equation in balance.

Illustration 3-16 Summary of debit/credit rules

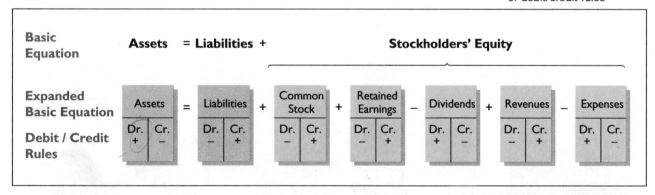

before you go on...

Do it! Kate Browne, president of Hair It Is Inc., has just rented space in a shopping mall for the purpose of opening and operating a beauty salon. Long before opening day and before purchasing equipment, hiring assistants, and remodeling the space, Kate was strongly advised to set up a double-entry set of accounting records in which to record all of her business transactions.

Identify the balance sheet accounts that Hair It Is Inc. will likely need to record the transactions necessary to establish and open for business. Also, indicate whether the normal balance of each account is a debit or a credit.

**DEBITS AND CREDITS
FOR BALANCE SHEET
ACCOUNTS**

Action Plan

• First identify asset accounts for each different type of asset invested in the business.

Action Plan (cont.)

- Then identify liability accounts for debts incurred by the business.
- Remember that Hair It Is Inc. will need only one stockholders' equity account for common stock when it begins the business. The other stockholders' equity accounts will be needed only after the business is operating.

Solution

Hair It Is Inc. would likely need the following accounts in which to record the transactions necessary to establish and ready the beauty salon for opening day: Cash (debit balance); Equipment (debit balance); Supplies (debit balance); Accounts Payable (credit balance); Notes Payable (credit balance), if the business borrows money; and Common Stock (credit balance).

the navigator

---

study objective 4

Identify the basic steps in the recording process.

Ethics Note Business documents provide evidence that transactions actually occurred. International Outsourcing Services, LLC, was accused of submitting fraudulent documents (store coupons) to companies such as Kraft Foods and PepsiCo for reimbursement of as much as $250 million. Ensuring that all recorded transactions are backed up by proper business documents reduces the likelihood of fraudulent activity.

Steps in the Recording Process

Although it is possible to enter transaction information directly into the accounts, few businesses do so. Practically every business uses these basic steps in the recording process:

1. Analyze each transaction in terms of its effect on the accounts.
2. Enter the transaction information in a journal.
3. Transfer the journal information to the appropriate accounts in the ledger (book of accounts).

The actual sequence of events begins with the transaction. Evidence of the transaction comes in the form of a **source document**, such as a sales slip, a check, a bill, or a cash register tape. This evidence is analyzed to determine the effect of the transaction on specific accounts. The transaction is then entered in the **journal**. Finally, the journal entry is transferred to the designated accounts in the **ledger**. The sequence of events in the recording process is shown in Illustration 3-17.

Illustration 3-17 The recording process

The Recording Process

Analyze each transaction | Enter transaction in a journal | Transfer journal information to ledger accounts

---

study objective 5

Explain what a journal is and how it helps in the recording process.

THE JOURNAL

Transactions are initially recorded in chronological order in journals before they are transferred to the accounts. For each transaction the journal shows the debit and credit effects on specific accounts. (In a computerized system, journals are kept as files, and accounts are recorded in computer databases.)

Companies may use various kinds of journals, but every company has at least the most basic form of journal, a general journal. **The journal makes three significant contributions to the recording process:**

1. It discloses in one place the **complete effect of a transaction**.
2. It provides a **chronological record** of transactions.
3. It **helps to prevent or locate errors** because the debit and credit amounts for each entry can be readily compared.

Entering transaction data in the journal is known as journalizing. To illustrate the technique of journalizing, let's look at the first three transactions of Sierra Corporation in equation form.

On October 1, Sierra issued common stock in exchange for $10,000 cash:

Assets	=	Liabilities	+	Stockholders' Equity	
Cash	=			Common Stock	
+$10,000				+$10,000	Issued stock

On October 1, Sierra borrowed $5,000 by signing a note:

Assets	=	Liabilities	+	Stockholders' Equity
Cash	=	Notes Payable		
+$5,000		+$5,000		

On October 2, Sierra purchased office equipment for $5,000:

Assets		=	Liabilities	+	Stockholders' Equity
Cash	Office Equipment				
−$5,000	+$5,000				

Sierra makes separate journal entries for each transaction. A complete entry consists of: (1) the date of the transaction, (2) the accounts and amounts to be debited and credited, and (3) a brief explanation of the transaction. These transactions are journalized in Illustration 3-18 (on page 118).

Note the following features of the journal entries.

1. The date of the transaction is entered in the Date column.
2. The account to be debited is entered first at the left. The account to be credited is then entered on the next line, indented under the line above. The indentation differentiates debits from credits and decreases the possibility of switching the debit and credit amounts.
3. The amounts for the debits are recorded in the Debit (left) column, and the amounts for the credits are recorded in the Credit (right) column.
4. A brief explanation of the transaction is given.

Illustration 3-18
Recording transactions in journal form

		GENERAL JOURNAL		
Date		**Account Titles and Explanation**	**Debit**	**Credit**
2010				
Oct.	1	Cash	10,000	
		Common Stock		10,000
		(Issued stock for cash)		
	1	Cash	5,000	
		Notes Payable		5,000
		(Issued 3-month, 12% note payable for cash)		
	2	Office Equipment	5,000	
		Cash		5,000
		(Purchased office equipment for cash)		

It is important to use correct and specific account titles in journalizing. Erroneous account titles lead to incorrect financial statements. Some flexibility exists initially in selecting account titles. The main criterion is that each title must appropriately describe the content of the account. For example, a company could use any of these account titles for recording the cost of delivery trucks: Delivery Equipment, Delivery Trucks, or Trucks. Once the company chooses the specific title to use, however, it should record under that account title all subsequent transactions involving the account.

Accounting Across the Organization

Bryan Lee is head of finance at Microsoft's Home and Entertainment Division. In recent years the division lost over $4 billion, mostly due to losses on the original Xbox videogame player. With the Xbox 360 videogame player, Mr. Lee hoped the division would become profitable. He set strict goals for sales, revenue, and profit. "A manager seeking to spend more on a feature such as a disk drive has to find allies in the group to cut spending elsewhere, or identify new revenue to offset the increase," he explains.

For example, Microsoft originally designed the new Xbox to have 256 megabytes of memory. But the design department said that amount of memory wouldn't support the best special effects. The purchasing department said that adding more memory would cost $30—which was 10% of the estimated selling price of $300. But the marketing department "determined that adding the memory would let Microsoft reduce marketing costs and attract more game developers, boosting royalty revenue. It would also extend the life of the console, generating more sales." Microsoft doubled the memory to 512 megabytes.

Source: Robert A. Guth, "New Xbox Aim for Microsoft: Profitability," *Wall Street Journal*, May 24, 2005, p. C1.

 In what ways is this Microsoft division using accounting to assist in its effort to become more profitable?

before you go on...

JOURNAL ENTRIES

Do it! The following events occurred during the first month of business of Hair It Is Inc., Kate Browne's beauty salon:

1. Issued common stock to shareholders in exchange for $20,000 cash.
2. Purchased $4,800 of equipment on account (to be paid in 30 days).
3. Interviewed three people for the position of beautician.

In what form (type of record) should the company record these three activities? Prepare the entries to record the transactions.

Solution

Each transaction that is recorded is entered in the general journal. The three activities are recorded as follows.

1. Cash		20,000	
Common Stock			20,000
(Issued stock for cash)			
2. Equipment		4,800	
Accounts Payable			4,800
(Purchased equipment on account)			
3. No entry because no transaction occurred.			

Action Plan

- Record the transactions in a journal, which is a chronological record of the transactions.
- Make sure to provide a complete and accurate representation of the transactions' effects on the assets, liabilities, and stockholders' equity of the business.

THE LEDGER

The entire group of accounts maintained by a company is referred to collectively as the ledger. The ledger keeps in one place all the information about changes in specific account balances.

Companies may use various kinds of ledgers, but every company has a general ledger. A general ledger contains all the assets, liabilities, stockholders' equity, revenue, and expense accounts, as shown in Illustration 3-19. Whenever we use the term *ledger* in this textbook without additional specification, it will mean the general ledger.

study objective **6**

Explain what a ledger is and how it helps in the recording process.

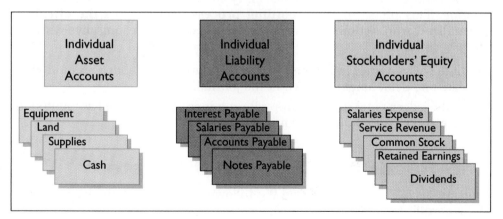

Illustration 3-19 The general ledger

CHART OF ACCOUNTS

The number and type of accounts used differ for each company, depending on the size, complexity, and type of business. For example, the number of accounts depends on the amount of detail desired by management. The management of one company may want one single account for all types of utility expense.

Another may keep separate expense accounts for each type of utility expenditure, such as gas, electricity, and water. A small corporation like Sierra Corporation will not have many accounts compared with a corporate giant like Ford Motor Company. Sierra may be able to manage and report its activities in 20 to 30 accounts, whereas Ford requires thousands of accounts to keep track of its worldwide activities.

Most companies list the accounts in a chart of accounts. They may create new accounts as needed during the life of the business. Illustration 3-20 shows the chart of accounts for Sierra Corporation in the order that they are typically listed (assets, liabilities, stockholders' equity, revenues, and expenses). **Accounts shown in red are used in this chapter**; accounts shown in black are explained in later chapters.

Illustration 3-20 Chart of accounts for Sierra Corporation

SIERRA CORPORATION—CHART OF ACCOUNTS

Assets	Liabilities	Stockholders' Equity	Revenues	Expenses
Cash	Notes Payable	Common Stock	Service Revenue	Salaries Expense
Accounts Receivable	Accounts Payable	Retained Earnings		Supplies Expense
Advertising Supplies	Interest Payable	Dividends		Rent Expense
Prepaid Insurance	Unearned	Income Summary		Insurance Expense
Office Equipment	Service Revenue			Interest Expense
Accumulated Depreciation—	Salaries Payable			Depreciation Expense
Office Equipment				

POSTING

study objective 7

Explain what posting is and how it helps in the recording process.

The procedure of transferring journal entry amounts to ledger accounts is called posting. **This phase of the recording process accumulates the effects of journalized transactions in the individual accounts.** Posting involves these steps:

1. In the ledger, enter in the appropriate columns of the debited account(s) the date and debit amount shown in the journal.

2. In the ledger, enter in the appropriate columns of the credited account(s) the date and credit amount shown in the journal.

The Recording Process Illustrated

Illustrations 3-21 through 3-31 on the following pages show the basic steps in the recording process using the October transactions of Sierra Corporation. Sierra's accounting period is a month. A basic analysis and a debit–credit analysis precede the journalizing and posting of each transaction. Study these transaction analyses carefully. **The purpose of transaction analysis is first to identify the type of account involved and then to determine whether a debit or a credit to the account is required.** You should always perform this type of analysis before preparing a journal entry. Doing so will help you understand the journal entries discussed in this chapter as well as more complex journal entries to be described in later chapters.

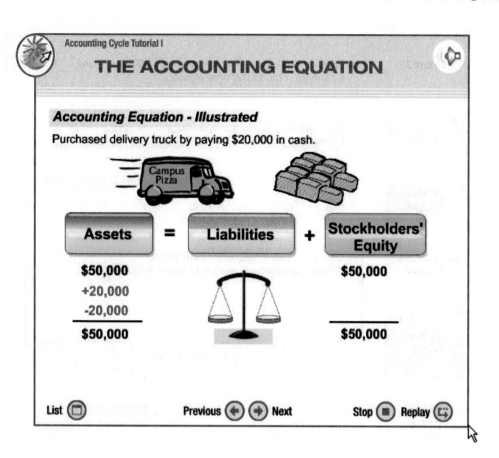

Accounting Cycle Tutorial

The diagrams in Illustrations 3-21 to 3-31 review the accounting cycle. If you would like additional practice, an Accounting Cycle Tutorial is available on WileyPLUS. The illustration to the left is an example of a screen from the tutorial.

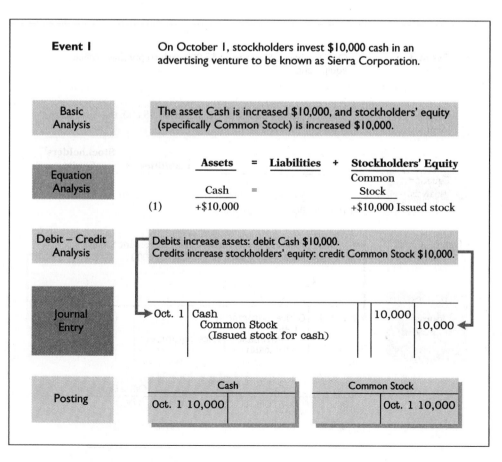

Illustration 3-21
Investment of cash by stockholders

Illustration 3-22 Issue
of note payable

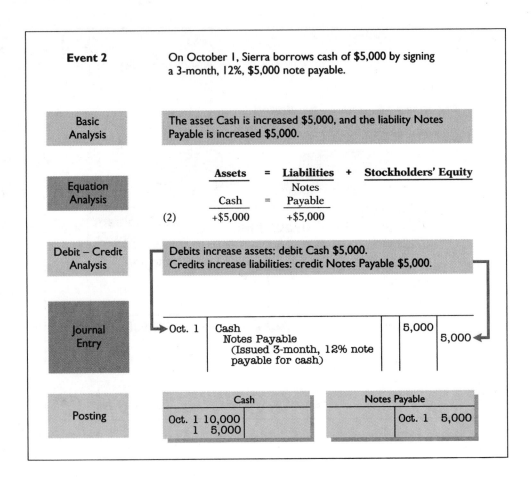

Illustration 3-23
Purchase of office
equipment

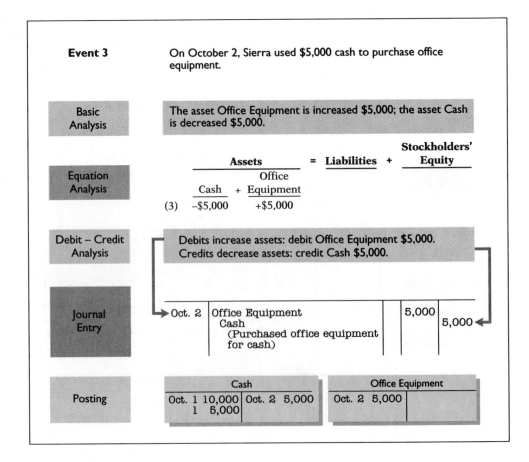

Event 4

On October 2, Sierra received a $1,200 cash advance from R. Knox, a client, for advertising services that are expected to be completed in the future.

Basic Analysis

The asset Cash is increased $1,200; the liability Unearned Service Revenue is increased $1,200 because the service has not been provided yet. That is, when an advance payment is received, an unearned revenue (a liability) should be recorded in order to recognize the obligation that exists.

Equation Analysis

	Assets	=	Liabilities	+	Stockholders' Equity
	Cash	=	Unearned Serv. Rev.		
(4)	+$1,200		+$1,200		

Debit – Credit Analysis

Debits increase assets: debit Cash $1,200.
Credits increase liabilities: credit Unearned Revenue $1,200.

Journal Entry

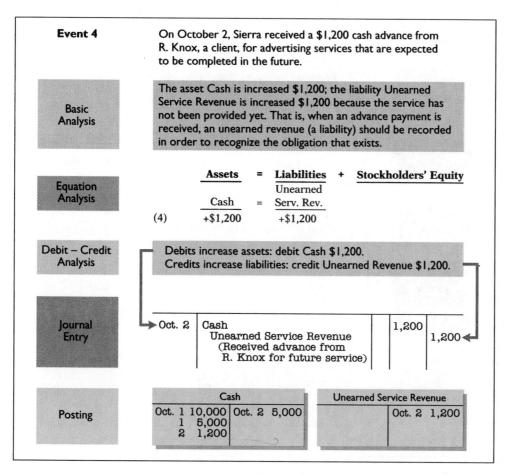

Oct. 2 Cash 1,200
      Unearned Service Revenue 1,200
      (Received advance from
      R. Knox for future service)

Posting

Cash		Unearned Service Revenue
Oct. 1 10,000 Oct. 2 5,000		Oct. 2 1,200
1 5,000		
2 1,200		

Illustration 3-24
Receipt of cash in advance from customer

Helpful Hint Many liabilities have the word "payable" in their title. But note that Unearned Service Revenue is considered a liability even though the word *payable* is not used.

Event 5

On October 3, Sierra received $10,000 in cash from Copa Company for advertising services provided in October.

Basic Analysis

The asset Cash is increased $10,000; the revenue Service Revenue is increased $10,000.

Equation Analysis

	Assets	=	Liabilities	+	Stockholders' Equity
	Cash	=			Revenues
(5)	+$10,000				+$10,000 Service Revenue

Debit – Credit Analysis

Debits increase assets: debit Cash $10,000.
Credits increase revenues: credit Service Revenue $10,000.

Journal Entry

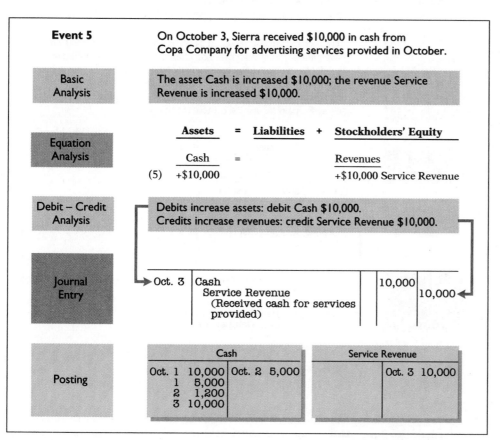

Oct. 3 Cash 10,000
      Service Revenue 10,000
      (Received cash for services
      provided)

Posting

Cash		Service Revenue
Oct. 1 10,000 Oct. 2 5,000		Oct. 3 10,000
1 5,000		
2 1,200		
3 10,000		

Illustration 3-25
Services provided for cash

Illustration 3-26
Payment of rent with cash

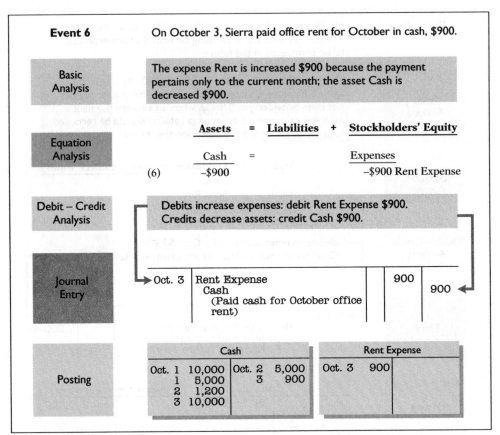

Event 6	On October 3, Sierra paid office rent for October in cash, $900.
Basic Analysis	The expense Rent is increased $900 because the payment pertains only to the current month; the asset Cash is decreased $900.

Equation Analysis

	Assets	=	Liabilities	+	Stockholders' Equity
	Cash	=			Expenses
(6)	–$900				–$900 Rent Expense

Debit – Credit Analysis

Debits increase expenses: debit Rent Expense $900.
Credits decrease assets: credit Cash $900.

Journal Entry

Oct. 3	Rent Expense		900	
	Cash			900
	(Paid cash for October office rent)			

Posting

Cash			
Oct. 1	10,000	Oct. 2	5,000
1	5,000	3	900
2	1,200		
3	10,000		

Rent Expense	
Oct. 3	900

Illustration 3-27
Purchase of insurance policy with cash

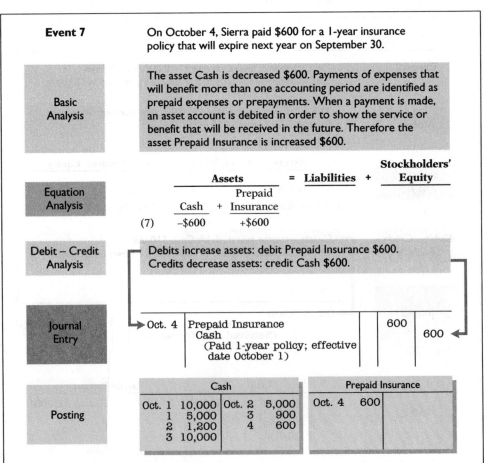

Event 7	On October 4, Sierra paid $600 for a 1-year insurance policy that will expire next year on September 30.
Basic Analysis	The asset Cash is decreased $600. Payments of expenses that will benefit more than one accounting period are identified as prepaid expenses or prepayments. When a payment is made, an asset account is debited in order to show the service or benefit that will be received in the future. Therefore the asset Prepaid Insurance is increased $600.

Equation Analysis

	Assets		=	Liabilities	+	Stockholders' Equity
	Cash	+	Prepaid Insurance			
(7)	–$600		+$600			

Debit – Credit Analysis

Debits increase assets: debit Prepaid Insurance $600.
Credits decrease assets: credit Cash $600.

Journal Entry

Oct. 4	Prepaid Insurance		600	
	Cash			600
	(Paid 1-year policy; effective date October 1)			

Posting

Cash			
Oct. 1	10,000	Oct. 2	5,000
1	5,000	3	900
2	1,200	4	600
3	10,000		

Prepaid Insurance	
Oct. 4	600

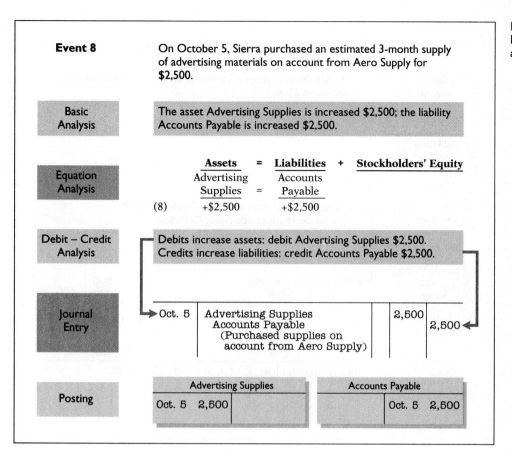

Illustration 3-28
Purchase of supplies on
account

| Event 8 | On October 5, Sierra purchased an estimated 3-month supply of advertising materials on account from Aero Supply for $2,500. |

Basic Analysis

The asset Advertising Supplies is increased $2,500; the liability Accounts Payable is increased $2,500.

Equation Analysis

		Assets	=	Liabilities	+	Stockholders' Equity
		Advertising Supplies	=	Accounts Payable		
(8)		+$2,500		+$2,500		

Debit – Credit Analysis

Debits increase assets: debit Advertising Supplies $2,500.
Credits increase liabilities: credit Accounts Payable $2,500.

Journal Entry

Oct. 5	Advertising Supplies	2,500	
	Accounts Payable		2,500
	(Purchased supplies on account from Aero Supply)		

Posting

Advertising Supplies		Accounts Payable	
Oct. 5 2,500			Oct. 5 2,500

Illustration 3-29 Hiring
of new employees

| Event 9 | On October 9, Sierra hired four employees to begin work on October 15. Each employee is to receive a weekly salary of $500 for a 5-day work week, payable every 2 weeks — first payment made on October 26. |

Basic Analysis

An accounting transaction has not occurred. There is only an agreement that the employees will begin work on October 15. Thus, a debit–credit analysis is not needed because there is no accounting entry. (See transaction of October 26 for first entry.)

Illustration 3-30
Payment of dividend

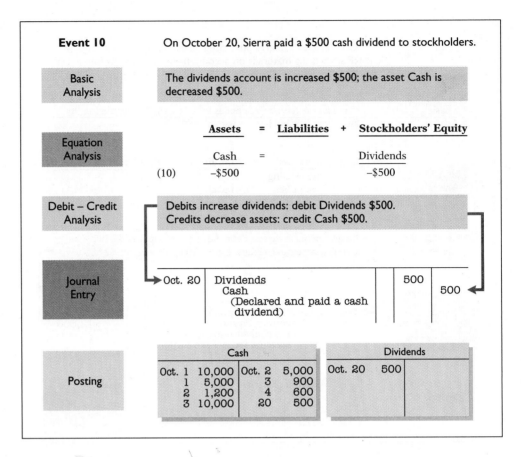

Event 10 On October 20, Sierra paid a $500 cash dividend to stockholders.

Basic Analysis The dividends account is increased $500; the asset Cash is decreased $500.

Equation Analysis

	Assets	=	Liabilities	+	Stockholders' Equity
	Cash	=			Dividends
(10)	−$500				−$500

Debit – Credit Analysis Debits increase dividends: debit Dividends $500.
Credits decrease assets: credit Cash $500.

Journal Entry

Oct. 20	Dividends		500	
	Cash			500
	(Declared and paid a cash dividend)			

Posting

Cash					Dividends	
Oct. 1	10,000	Oct. 2	5,000		Oct. 20	500
1	5,000	3	900			
2	1,200	4	600			
3	10,000	20	500			

Illustration 3-31 Payment of cash for employee salaries

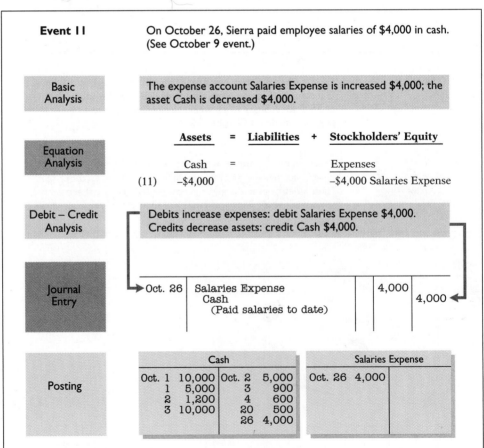

Event 11 On October 26, Sierra paid employee salaries of $4,000 in cash. (See October 9 event.)

Basic Analysis The expense account Salaries Expense is increased $4,000; the asset Cash is decreased $4,000.

Equation Analysis

	Assets	=	Liabilities	+	Stockholders' Equity
	Cash	=			Expenses
(11)	−$4,000				−$4,000 Salaries Expense

Debit – Credit Analysis Debits increase expenses: debit Salaries Expense $4,000.
Credits decrease assets: credit Cash $4,000.

Journal Entry

Oct. 26	Salaries Expense		4,000	
	Cash			4,000
	(Paid salaries to date)			

Posting

Cash					Salaries Expense	
Oct. 1	10,000	Oct. 2	5,000		Oct. 26	4,000
1	5,000	3	900			
2	1,200	4	600			
3	10,000	20	500			
		26	4,000			

SUMMARY ILLUSTRATION OF JOURNALIZING AND POSTING

The journal for Sierra Corporation for the month of October is summarized in Illustration 3-32. The ledger is shown in Illustration 3-33 (on page 128) with all balances highlighted in red.

Date		Account Titles and Explanation	Debit	Credit
GENERAL JOURNAL				
2010				
Oct.	1	Cash	10,000	
		Common Stock		10,000
		(Issued stock for cash)		
	1	Cash	5,000	
		Notes Payable		5,000
		(Issued 3-month, 12% note payable for cash)		
	2	Office Equipment	5,000	
		Cash		5,000
		(Purchased office equipment for cash)		
	2	Cash	1,200	
		Unearned Service Revenue		1,200
		(Received advance from R. Knox for future service)		
	3	Cash	10,000	
		Service Revenue		10,000
		(Received cash for services provided)		
	3	Rent Expense	900	
		Cash		900
		(Paid cash for October office rent)		
	4	Prepaid Insurance	600	
		Cash		600
		(Paid 1-year policy; effective date October 1)		
	5	Advertising Supplies	2,500	
		Accounts Payable		2,500
		(Purchased supplies on account from Aero Supply)		
	20	Dividends	500	
		Cash		500
		(Paid a cash dividend)		
	26	Salaries Expense	4,000	
		Cash		4,000
		(Paid salaries to date)		

Illustration 3-32 General journal for Sierra Corporation

Illustration 3-33 General ledger for Sierra Corporation

GENERAL LEDGER

Cash

Oct.	1	10,000	Oct.	2	5,000
	1	5,000		3	900
	2	1,200		4	600
	3	10,000		20	500
				26	4,000
Bal.		15,200			

Unearned Service Revenue

			Oct.	2	1,200
			Bal.		1,200

Advertising Supplies

Oct.	5	2,500
Bal.		2,500

Common Stock

			Oct.	1	10,000
			Bal.		10,000

Prepaid Insurance

Oct.	4	600
Bal.		600

Dividends

Oct. 20	500
Bal.	500

Office Equipment

Oct.	2	5,000
Bal.		5,000

Service Revenue

			Oct.	3	10,000
			Bal.		10,000

Notes Payable

			Oct.	1	5,000
			Bal.		5,000

Salaries Expense

Oct. 26	4,000
Bal.	4,000

Accounts Payable

			Oct.	5	2,500
			Bal.		2,500

Rent Expense

Oct.	3	900
Bal.		900

---

before you go on...

POSTING

Do it!

Selected transactions from the journal of Faital Inc. during its first month of operations are presented below. Post these transactions to T accounts.

Date		Account Titles	Debit	Credit
July	1	Cash	30,000	
		Common Stock		30,000
	9	Accounts Receivable	6,000	
		Service Revenue		6,000
	24	Cash	4,000	
		Accounts Receivable		4,000

Action Plan

- Journalize transactions to keep track of financial activities (receipts, payments, receivables, payables, etc.).
- To make entries useful, classify and summarize them by posting the entries to specific ledger accounts.

Solution

Cash

July	1	30,000
	24	4,000

Accounts Receivable

July 9	6,000	July 24	4,000

Common Stock

	July 1	30,000

Service Revenue

	July 9	6,000

the navigator

The Trial Balance

A trial balance lists accounts and their balances at a given time. A company usually prepares a trial balance at the end of an accounting period. The accounts are listed in the order in which they appear in the ledger. Debit balances are listed in the left column and credit balances in the right column. The totals of the two columns must be equal.

study objective 8

Explain the purposes of a trial balance.

The trial balance proves the mathematical equality of debits and credits after posting. Under the double-entry system this equality occurs when the sum of the debit account balances equals the sum of the credit account balances. **A trial balance may also uncover errors in journalizing and posting.** For example, a trial balance may well have detected the error at Fidelity Investments discussed in the Feature Story. **In addition, a trial balance is useful in the preparation of financial statements.**

These are the procedures for preparing a trial balance:

1. List the account titles and their balances.
2. Total the debit column and total the credit column.
3. Verify the equality of the two columns.

Illustration 3-34 presents the trial balance prepared from the ledger of Sierra Corporation. Note that the total debits, $28,700, equal the total credits, $28,700.

Illustration 3-34 Sierra Corporation trial balance

SIERRA CORPORATION Trial Balance October 31, 2010		
	Debit	**Credit**
Cash	$15,200	
Advertising Supplies	2,500	
Prepaid Insurance	600	
Office Equipment	5,000	
Notes Payable		$ 5,000
Accounts Payable		2,500
Unearned Service Revenue		1,200
Common Stock		10,000
Dividends	500	
Service Revenue		10,000
Salaries Expense	4,000	
Rent Expense	900	
	$28,700	$28,700

Helpful Hint Note that the order of presentation in the trial balance is:
  Assets
  Liabilities
  Stockholders' equity
  Revenues
  Expenses

LIMITATIONS OF A TRIAL BALANCE

A trial balance does not prove that all transactions have been recorded or that the ledger is correct. Numerous errors may exist even though the trial balance column totals agree. For example, the trial balance may balance even when any of the following occurs: (1) a transaction is not journalized, (2) a correct journal entry is not posted, (3) a journal entry is posted twice, (4) incorrect accounts·are used in journalizing or posting, or (5) offsetting errors are made in recording the amount of a transaction. In other words, as long as equal debits and credits are posted, even to the wrong account or in the wrong amount, the total debits will equal the total credits. Nevertheless, despite these limitations, the trial balance is a useful screen for finding errors and is frequently used in practice.

Ethics Note An *error* is the result of an unintentional mistake; it is neither ethical nor unethical. An *irregularity* is an intentional misstatement, which *is* viewed as unethical.

DECISION TOOLKIT

DECISION CHECKPOINTS	INFO NEEDED FOR DECISION	TOOL TO USE FOR DECISION	HOW TO EVALUATE RESULTS
How do you determine that debits equal credits?	All account balances	Trial balance	List the account titles and their balances; total the debit and credit columns; verify equality.

KEEPING AN EYE ON CASH

The Cash account shown below reflects all of the inflows and outflows of cash that occurred during October. We have also provided a description of each transaction that affected the cash account.

Cash

Oct.	1	10,000	Oct.	2	5,000
	1	5,000		3	900
	2	1,200		4	600
	3	10,000		20	500
				26	4,000
Bal.		15,200			

1. Oct. 1 Issued stock for $10,000 cash.
2. Oct. 1 Issued note payable for $5,000 cash.
3. Oct. 2 Purchased office equipment for $5,000 cash.
4. Oct. 2 Received $1,200 cash in advance from customer.
5. Oct. 3 Received $10,000 cash for services provided.
6. Oct. 3 Paid $900 cash for October rent.
7. Oct. 4 Paid $600 cash for one-year insurance policy.
8. Oct. 20 Paid $500 cash dividend to stockholders.
9. Oct. 26 Paid $4,000 cash salaries.

The cash account and the related cash transactions indicate why cash changed during October. However, to make this information useful for analysis, it is summarized in a statement of cash flows. The statement of cash flows classifies each transaction as an operating activity, an investing activity, or a financing activity. A user of this statement can then determine the amount of cash provided by operations, the amount of cash used for investing purposes, and the amount of cash provided by financing activities.

Operating activities are the types of activities the company performs to generate profits. Sierra Corporation is a marketing agency, so its operating activities involve providing marketing services. Activities 4, 5, 6, 7, and 9 relate to cash received or spent to directly support its marketing services.

Investing activities include the purchase or sale of long-lived assets used in operating the business, or the purchase or sale of investment securities (stocks and bonds of companies other than Sierra). Activity 3, the purchase of office equipment, is an investment activity.

The primary types of *financing activities* are borrowing money, issuing shares of stock, and paying dividends. The financing activities of Sierra Corporation are activities 1, 2, and 8.

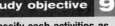

study objective 9

Classify cash activities as operating, investing, or financing.

USING THE DECISION TOOLKIT

The Kansas Farmers' Vertically Integrated Cooperative, Inc. (K-VIC), was formed by over 200 northeast Kansas farmers in the late 1980s. Its purpose is to use raw materials, primarily grain and meat products grown by K-VIC's members, to process this material into end-user food products, and to distribute the products nationally. Profits not needed for expansion or investment are returned to the members annually, on a pro-rata basis, according to the market value of the grain and meat products received from each farmer.

Assume that the following trial balance was prepared for K-VIC.

KANSAS FARMERS' VERTICALLY INTEGRATED COOPERATIVE, INC.
Trial Balance
December 31, 2010
(in thousands)

	Debit	Credit
Accounts Receivable	$ 712,000	
Accounts Payable		$ 37,000
Advertising and Promotion Payable		141,000
Buildings	365,000	
Cash	32,000	
Cost of Goods Sold	2,384,000	
Current Maturity of Long-Term Debt		12,000
Inventories	1,291,000	
Land	110,000	
Long-Term Debt		873,000
Machinery and Equipment	63,000	
Notes Payable to Members		495,000
Retained Earnings		822,000
Sales Revenue		3,741,000
Salaries and Wages Payable		62,000
Selling and Administrative Expense	651,000	
Trucking Expense	500,000	
	$6,108,000	$6,183,000

Because the trial balance is not in balance, you have checked with various people responsible for entering accounting data and have discovered the following.

1. The purchase of 35 new trucks, costing $7 million and paid for with cash, was not recorded.

2. A data entry clerk accidentally deleted the account name for an account with a credit balance of $472 million, so the amount was added to the Long-Term Debt account in the trial balance.

3. December cash sales revenue of $75 million was credited to the Sales Revenue account, but the other half of the entry was not made.

4. $50 million of selling expenses were mistakenly charged to Trucking Expense.

Instructions

Answer these questions.

(a) Which mistake(s) have caused the trial balance to be out of balance?

(b) Should all of the items be corrected? Explain.

(c) What is the name of the account the data entry clerk deleted?

(d) Make the necessary corrections and prepare a correct trial balance with accounts listed in proper order.

(e) On your trial balance, write BAL beside the accounts that go on the balance sheet and INC beside those that go on the income statement.

Solution

(a) Only mistake #3 has caused the trial balance to be out of balance.

(b) All of the items should be corrected. The misclassification error (mistake #4) on the selling expense would not affect bottom-line net income, but it does affect the amounts reported in the two expense accounts.

(c) There is no Common Stock account, so that must be the account that was deleted by the data entry clerk.

(d) and (e):

KANSAS FARMERS' VERTICALLY INTEGRATED COOPERATIVE, INC.
Trial Balance
December 31, 2010
(in thousands)

	Debit	Credit	
Cash ($32,000 − $7,000 + $75,000)	$ 100,000		BAL
Accounts Receivable	712,000		BAL
Inventories	1,291,000		BAL
Land	110,000		BAL
Machinery and Equipment	70,000		BAL
Buildings	365,000		BAL
Notes Payable to Members		$ 495,000	BAL
Accounts Payable		37,000	BAL
Advertising and Promotion Payable		141,000	BAL
Salaries and Wages Payable		62,000	BAL
Current Maturity of Long-Term Debt		12,000	BAL
Long-Term Debt ($873,000 − $472,000)		401,000	BAL
Common Stock		472,000	BAL
Retained Earnings		822,000	BAL
Sales Revenue		3,741,000	INC
Cost of Goods Sold	2,384,000		INC
Selling and Administrative Expense	701,000		INC
Trucking Expense	450,000		INC
	$6,183,000	$6,183,000	

Summary of Study Objectives

1 **Analyze the effect of business transactions on the basic accounting equation.** Each business transaction must have a dual effect on the accounting equation. For example, if an individual asset is increased, there must be a corresponding (a) decrease in another asset, or (b) increase in a specific liability, or (c) increase in stockholders' equity.

2 **Explain what an account is and how it helps in the recording process.** An account is an individual accounting record of increases and decreases in specific asset, liability, and stockholders' equity items.

3 **Define debits and credits and explain how they are used to record business transactions.** The terms *debit* and *credit* are synonymous with *left* and *right*. Assets, dividends, and expenses are increased by debits and decreased by credits. Liabilities, common stock, retained earnings, and revenues are increased by credits and decreased by debits.

4 **Identify the basic steps in the recording process.** The basic steps in the recording process are: (a) analyze each transaction in terms of its effect on the accounts, (b) enter the transaction information in a journal, and (c) transfer the journal information to the appropriate accounts in the ledger.

5 **Explain what a journal is and how it helps in the recording process.** The initial accounting record of a transaction is entered in a journal before the data are entered in the accounts. A journal (a) discloses in one place the complete effect of a transaction, (b) provides a chronological record of transactions, and (c) prevents or locates errors because the debit and credit amounts for each entry can be readily compared.

6 **Explain what a ledger is and how it helps in the recording process.** The entire group of accounts maintained by a company is referred to collectively as a ledger. The ledger keeps in one place all the information about changes in specific account balances.

7 **Explain what posting is and how it helps in the recording process.** Posting is the procedure of transferring journal entries to the ledger accounts. This phase of the recording process accumulates the effects of journalized transactions in the individual accounts.

8 **Explain the purposes of a trial balance.** A trial balance is a list of accounts and their balances at a given time. The primary purpose of the trial balance is to prove the mathematical equality of debits and credits after posting. A trial balance also uncovers errors in journalizing and posting and is useful in preparing financial statements.

9 Classify cash activities as operating, investing, or financing. Operating activities are the types of activities the company uses to generate profits. Investing activities relate to the purchase or sale of long-lived assets used in operating the business, or to the purchase or sale of investment securities (stock and bonds of other companies). Financing activities are borrowing money, issuing shares of stock, and paying dividends.

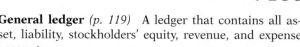

DECISION TOOLKIT   A SUMMARY

DECISION CHECKPOINTS	INFO NEEDED FOR DECISION	TOOL TO USE FOR DECISION	HOW TO EVALUATE RESULTS
Has an accounting transaction occurred?	Details of the event	Accounting equation	If the event affected assets, liabilities, or stockholders' equity, then record as a transaction.
How do you determine that debits equal credits?	All account balances	Trial balance	List the account titles and their balances; total the debit and credit colums; verify equality.

Glossary

Account *(p. 110)* An individual accounting record of increases and decreases in specific asset, liability, stockholders' equity, revenue or expense items.

Accounting information system *(p. 102)* The system of collecting and processing transaction data and communicating financial information to interested parties.

Accounting transactions *(p. 102)* Events that require recording in the financial statements because they affect assets, liabilities, or stockholders' equity.

Chart of accounts *(p. 120)* A list of a company's accounts.

Credit *(p. 111)* The right side of an account.

Debit *(p. 111)* The left side of an account.

Double-entry system *(p. 111)* A system that records the dual effect of each transaction in appropriate accounts.

General journal *(p. 117)* The most basic form of journal.

General ledger *(p. 119)* A ledger that contains all asset, liability, stockholders' equity, revenue, and expense accounts.

Journal *(p. 116)* An accounting record in which transactions are initially recorded in chronological order.

Journalizing *(p. 117)* The procedure of entering transaction data in the journal.

Ledger *(p. 119)* The group of accounts maintained by a company.

Posting *(p. 120)* The procedure of transferring journal entry amounts to the ledger accounts.

T account *(p. 110)* The basic form of an account.

Trial balance *(p. 129)* A list of accounts and their balances at a given time.

Comprehensive Do it!

Bob Sample and other student investors opened Campus Carpet Cleaning, Inc. on September 1, 2010. During the first month of operations the following transactions occurred.

Sept. 1   Stockholders invested $20,000 cash in the business.
   2   Paid $1,000 cash for store rent for the month of September.
   3   Purchased industrial carpet-cleaning equipment for $25,000, paying $10,000 in cash and signing a $15,000 6-month, 12% note payable.
   4   Paid $1,200 for 1-year accident insurance policy.
   10   Received bill from the *Daily News* for advertising the opening of the cleaning service, $200.
   15   Performed services on account for $6,200.
   20   Paid a $700 cash dividend to stockholders.
   30   Received $5,000 from customers billed on September 15.

The chart of accounts for the company is the same as for Sierra Corporation except for the following additional accounts: Cleaning Equipment and Advertising Expense.

Instructions

(a) Journalize the September transactions.
(b) Open ledger accounts and post the September transactions.
(c) Prepare a trial balance at September 30, 2010.

Action Plan

• Proceed through the accounting cycle in the following sequence:

1. Make separate journal entries for each transaction.

2. Note that all debits precede all credit entries.

3. In journalizing, make sure debits equal credits.

4. In journalizing, use specific account titles taken from the chart of accounts.

5. Provide an appropriate explanation of each journal entry.

6. Arrange ledger in statement order, beginning with the balance sheet accounts.

7. Post in chronological order.

8. Prepare a trial balance, which lists accounts in the order in which they appear in the ledger.

9. List debit balances in the left column and credit balances in the right column.

Solution to Comprehensive Do it!

(a)   **GENERAL JOURNAL**

Date	Account Titles and Explanation	Debit	Credit
2010			
Sept. 1	Cash	20,000	
	Common Stock		20,000
	(Issued stock for cash)		
2	Rent Expense	1,000	
	Cash		1,000
	(Paid September rent)		
3	Cleaning Equipment	25,000	
	Cash		10,000
	Notes Payable		15,000
	(Purchased cleaning equipment for cash and 6-month, 12% note payable)		
4	Prepaid Insurance	1,200	
	Cash		1,200
	(Paid 1-year insurance policy)		
10	Advertising Expense	200	
	Accounts Payable		200
	(Received bill from *Daily News* for advertising)		
15	Accounts Receivable	6,200	
	Service Revenue		6,200
	(Services performed on account)		
20	Dividends	700	
	Cash		700
	(Declared and paid a cash dividend)		
30	Cash	5,000	
	Accounts Receivable		5,000
	(Collection of accounts receivable)		

(b)   **GENERAL LEDGER**

Cash					Common Stock	
Sept. 1	20,000	Sept. 2	1,000			Sept. 1	20,000
30	5,000	3	10,000				
		4	1,200			Bal.	20,000
		20	700				
Bal.	12,100					

Accounts Receivable				Dividends	
Sept. 15	6,200	Sept. 30	5,000	Sept. 20	700
Bal.	1,200			Bal.	700

Prepaid Insurance				Service Revenue		
Sept. 4	1,200				Sept. 15	6,200
Bal.	1,200				Bal.	6,200

Cleaning Equipment				Advertising Expense		
Sept. 3	25,000			Sept. 10	200	
Bal.	25,000			Bal.	200	

Notes Payable				Rent Expense		
		Sept. 3	15,000	Sept. 2	1,000	
		Bal.	15,000	Bal.	1,000	

Accounts Payable			
		Sept. 10	200
		Bal.	200

(c)

CAMPUS CARPET CLEANING, INC.
Trial Balance
September 30, 2010

	Debit	Credit
Cash	$12,100	
Accounts Receivable	1,200	
Prepaid Insurance	1,200	
Cleaning Equipment	25,000	
Notes Payable		$15,000
Accounts Payable		200
Common Stock		20,000
Dividends	700	
Service Revenue		6,200
Advertising Expense	200	
Rent Expense	1,000	
	$41,400	$41,400

Self-Study Questions

Answers are at the end of this chapter.

(SO 1) **1.** The effects on the basic accounting equation of performing services for cash are to:
  (a) increase assets and decrease stockholders' equity.
  (b) increase assets and increase stockholders' equity.
  (c) increase assets and increase liabilities.
  (d) increase liabilities and increase stockholders' equity.

2. Genesis Company buys a $900 machine on credit. (SO 1) This transaction will affect the:
  (a) income statement only.
  (b) balance sheet only.
  (c) income statement and retained earnings statement only.
  (d) income statement, retained earnings statement, and balance sheet.

(SO 1) 3. Which of the following events is *not* recorded in the accounting records?
(a) Equipment is purchased on account.
(b) An employee is terminated.
(c) A cash investment is made into the business.
(d) Company pays dividend to stockholders.

(SO 1) 4. During 2010, Gibson Company assets decreased $50,000 and its liabilities decreased $90,000. Its stockholders' equity therefore:
(a) increased $40,000.
(b) decreased $140,000.
(c) decreased $40,000.
(d) increased $140,000.

(SO 2) 5. Which statement about an account is *true*?
(a) In its simplest form, an account consists of two parts.
(b) An account is an individual accounting record of increases and decreases in specific asset, liability, and stockholders' equity items.
(c) There are separate accounts for specific assets and liabilities but only one account for stockholders' equity items.
(d) The left side of an account is the credit or decrease side.

(SO 3) 6. Debits:
(a) increase both assets and liabilities.
(b) decrease both assets and liabilities.
(c) increase assets and decrease liabilities.
(d) decrease assets and increase liabilities.

(SO 3) 7. A revenue account:
(a) is increased by debits.
(b) is decreased by credits.
(c) has a normal balance of a debit.
(d) is increased by credits.

(SO 3) 8. Which accounts normally have debit balances?
(a) Assets, expenses, and revenues.
(b) Assets, expenses, and retained earnings.
(c) Assets, liabilities, and dividends.
(d) Assets, dividends, and expenses.

(SO 3) 9. Paying an account payable with cash affects the components of the accounting equation in the following way.
(a) Decreases stockholders' equity and decreases liabilities.
(b) Increases assets and decreases liabilities.
(c) Decreases assets and increases stockholders' equity.
(d) Decreases assets and decreases liabilities.

10. Which is *not* part of the recording process? (SO 4)
(a) Analyzing transactions.
(b) Preparing a trial balance.
(c) Entering transactions in a journal.
(d) Posting transactions.

11. Which of these statements about a journal is *false*? (SO 5)
(a) It contains only revenue and expense accounts.
(b) It provides a chronological record of transactions.
(c) It helps to locate errors because the debit and credit amounts for each entry can be readily compared.
(d) It discloses in one place the complete effect of a transaction.

12. A ledger: (SO 6)
(a) contains only asset and liability accounts.
(b) should show accounts in alphabetical order.
(c) is a collection of the entire group of accounts maintained by a company.
(d) provides a chronological record of transactions.

13. Posting: (SO 7)
(a) normally occurs before journalizing.
(b) transfers ledger transaction data to the journal.
(c) is an optional step in the recording process.
(d) transfers journal entries to ledger accounts.

14. A trial balance: (SO 8)
(a) is a list of accounts with their balances at a given time.
(b) proves that proper account titles were used.
(c) will not balance if a correct journal entry is posted twice.
(d) proves that all transactions have been recorded.

15. A trial balance will *not* balance if: (SO 8)
(a) a correct journal entry is posted twice.
(b) the purchase of supplies on account is debited to Supplies and credited to Cash.
(c) a $100 cash dividend is debited to Dividends for $1,000 and credited to Cash for $100.
(d) a $450 payment on account is debited to Accounts Payable for $45 and credited to Cash for $45.

Go to the book's companion website, **www.wiley.com/college/kimmel**, to access additional Self-Study Questions.

Questions

1. Describe the accounting information system and the steps in the recording process.

2. Can a business enter into a transaction that affects only the left side of the basic accounting equation? If so, give an example.

3. Are the following events recorded in the accounting records? Explain your answer in each case.

(a) A major stockholder of the company dies.
(b) Supplies are purchased on account.
(c) An employee is fired.
(d) The company pays a cash dividend to its stockholders.

4. Indicate how each business transaction affects the basic accounting equation.
(a) Paid cash for janitorial services.
(b) Purchased equipment for cash.

(c) Issued common stock to investors in exchange for cash.

(d) Paid an account payable in full.

5. Why is an account referred to as a T account?

6. The terms *debit* and *credit* mean "increase" and "decrease," respectively. Do you agree? Explain.

7. Steve Rondelli, a fellow student, contends that the double-entry system means each transaction must be recorded twice. Is Steve correct? Explain.

8. Marie Likert, a beginning accounting student, believes debit balances are favorable and credit balances are unfavorable. Is Marie correct? Discuss.

9. State the rules of debit and credit as applied to (a) asset accounts, (b) liability accounts, and (c) the common stock account.

10. What is the normal balance for each of these accounts?
(a) Accounts Receivable.
(b) Cash.
(c) Dividends.
(d) Accounts Payable.
(e) Service Revenue.
(f) Salaries Expense.
(g) Common Stock.

11. Indicate whether each account is an asset, a liability, or a stockholders' equity account, and whether it would have a normal debit or credit balance.
(a) Accounts Receivable.
(b) Accounts Payable.
(c) Equipment.
(d) Dividends.
(e) Supplies.

12. For the following transactions, indicate the account debited and the account credited.
(a) Supplies are purchased on account.
(b) Cash is received on signing a note payable.
(c) Employees are paid salaries in cash.

13. For each account listed here, indicate whether it generally will have debit entries only, credit entries only, or both debit and credit entries.
(a) Cash.
(b) Accounts Receivable.
(c) Dividends.
(d) Accounts Payable.

(e) Salaries Expense.
(f) Service Revenue.

14. What are the normal balances for the following accounts of Tootsie Roll Industries? (a) Accounts Receivable. (b) Income Taxes Payable. (c) Sales. (d) Selling, Marketing, and Administrative Expenses.

15. What are the basic steps in the recording process?

16. (a) When entering a transaction in the journal, should the debit or credit be written first?
(b) Which should be indented, the debit or the credit?

17. (a) Can accounting transaction debits and credits be recorded directly in the ledger accounts?
(b) What are the advantages of first recording transactions in the journal and then posting to the ledger?

18. Journalize these accounting transactions.
(a) Stockholders invested $12,000 in the business in exchange for common stock.
(b) Insurance of $800 is paid for the year.
(c) Supplies of $1,500 are purchased on account.
(d) Cash of $7,500 is received for services rendered.

19. (a) What is a ledger?
(b) Why is a chart of accounts important?

20. What is a trial balance and what are its purposes?

21. Pete Riser is confused about how accounting information flows through the accounting system. He believes information flows in this order:
(a) Debits and credits are posted to the ledger.
(b) Accounting transaction occurs.
(c) Information is entered in the journal.
(d) Financial statements are prepared.
(e) Trial balance is prepared.
Indicate to Pete the proper flow of the information.

22. Two students are discussing the use of a trial balance. They wonder whether the following errors, each considered separately, would prevent the trial balance from balancing. What would you tell them?
(a) The bookkeeper debited Cash for $600 and credited Wages Expense for $600 for payment of wages.
(b) Cash collected on account was debited to Cash for $800, and Service Revenue was credited for $80.

Brief Exercises

BE3-1 Presented below are three economic events. On a sheet of paper, list the letters (a), (b), and (c) with columns for assets, liabilities, and stockholders' equity. In each column, indicate whether the event increased (+), decreased (−), or had no effect (NE) on assets, liabilities, and stockholders' equity.
(a) Purchased supplies on account.
(b) Received cash for providing a service.
(c) Expenses paid in cash.

Determine effect of transactions on basic accounting equation.
(SO 1)

Determine effect of transactions on basic accounting equation.

(SO 1)

BE3-2 During 2010, Bleeker Corp. entered into the following transactions.
1. Borrowed $60,000 by issuing bonds.
2. Paid $9,000 cash dividend to stockholders.
3. Received $17,000 cash from a previously billed customer for services provided.
4. Purchased supplies on account for $3,100.

Using the following tabular analysis, show the effect of each transaction on the accounting equation. Put explanations for changes to Stockholders' Equity in the right-hand margin. For Retained Earnings, use separate columns for Revenues, Expenses, and Dividends if necessary. Use Illustration 3-3 (page 109) as a model.

		Assets			=		Liabilities		+	Stockholders' Equity	
		Accounts					Accounts	Bonds		Common	Retained
Cash	+	Receivable	+	Supplies	=		Payable	+ Payable	+	Stock	+ Earnings

Determine effect of transactions on basic accounting equation.

(SO 1)

BE3-3 During 2010, Estes company entered into the following transactions.
1. Purchased property, plant, and equipment for $286,176 cash.
2. Issued common stock to investors for $137,590 cash.
3. Purchased inventory of $77,662 on account.

Using the following tabular analysis, show the effect of each transaction on the accounting equation. Put explanations for changes to Stockholders' Equity in the right-hand margin. For Retained Earnings, use separate columns for Revenues, Expenses, and Dividends if necessary. Use Illustration 3-3 (page 109) as a model.

		Assets			=	Liabilities	+	Stockholders' Equity	
			Property, Plant,			Accounts		Common	Retained
Cash	+	Inventory	+	and Equipment	=	Payable	+	Stock	+ Earnings

Indicate debit and credit effects.

(SO 3)

BE3-4 For each of the following accounts indicate the effect of a debit or a credit on the account and the normal balance.
(a) Accounts Payable.   (d) Accounts Receivable.
(b) Advertising Expense.   (e) Retained Earnings.
(c) Service Revenue.   (f) Dividends.

Identify accounts to be debited and credited.

(SO 3)

BE3-5 Transactions for Marquis Company for the month of June are presented next. Identify the accounts to be debited and credited for each transaction.

June 1 Issues common stock to investors in exchange for $5,000 cash.
     2 Buys equipment on account for $1,100.
     3 Pays $500 to landlord for June rent.
    12 Bills Jeff Gore $700 for welding work done.

Journalize transactions.

(SO 5)

BE3-6 Use the data in BE3-5 and journalize the transactions. (You may omit explanations.)

Identify steps in the recording process.

(SO 4)

BE3-7 Terry Rolen, a fellow student, is unclear about the basic steps in the recording process. Identify and briefly explain the steps in the order in which they occur.

Indicate basic debit–credit analysis.

(SO 4)

BE3-8 Ankiel Corporation has the following transactions during August of the current year. Indicate (a) the basic analysis and (b) the debit–credit analysis illustrated on pages 121–126.
Aug. 1 Issues shares of common stock to investors in exchange for $10,000.
     4 Pays insurance in advance for 3 months, $1,500.
    16 Receives $900 from clients for services rendered.
    27 Pays the secretary $500 salary.

Journalize transactions.

(SO 5)

BE3-9 Use the data in BE3-8 and journalize the transactions. (You may omit explanations.)

Post journal entries to T accounts.

(SO 7)

BE3-10 Selected transactions for Martinez Company are presented on page 139 in journal form (without explanations). Post the transactions to T accounts.

Date	Account Title	Debit	Credit
May 5	Accounts Receivable	3,800	
	Service Revenue		3,800
12	Cash	1,900	
	Accounts Receivable		1,900
15	Cash	2,000	
	Service Revenue		2,000

BE3-11   From the ledger balances below, prepare a trial balance for Trowman Company at June 30, 2010. All account balances are normal.

Prepare a trial balance.
(SO 8)

Accounts Payable	$ 3,000	Service Revenue	$8,600
Cash	5,400	Accounts Receivable	3,000
Common Stock	18,000	Salaries Expense	4,000
Dividends	1,200	Rent Expense	1,000
Equipment	15,000		

BE3-12   An inexperienced bookkeeper prepared the following trial balance that does not balance. Prepare a correct trial balance, assuming all account balances are normal.

Prepare a corrected trial balance.
(SO 8)

PETTENGILL COMPANY
Trial Balance
December 31, 2010

	Debit	Credit
Cash	$20,800	
Prepaid Insurance		$ 3,500
Accounts Payable		2,500
Unearned Revenue	1,800	
Common Stock		10,000
Retained Earnings		6,400
Dividends		5,000
Service Revenue		25,600
Salaries Expense	14,600	
Rent Expense		2,400
	$37,200	$55,400

Do it! Review

WILEY
PLUS

Do it! 3-1   Transactions made by Orlando Carbrera Co. for the month of March are shown below. Prepare a tabular analysis which shows the effects of these transactions on the expanded accounting equation, similar to that shown in Illustration 3-3 (page 109).

Prepare tabular analysis.
(SO 1)

1. The company provided $20,000 of services for customers on account.
2. The company received $20,000 in cash from customers who had been billed for services [in transaction (1)].
3. The company received a bill for $2,000 of advertising, but will not pay it until a later date.
4. Orlando Carbrera Co. paid a cash dividend of $5,000.

Do it! 3-2   Josh Borke has just rented space in a strip mall. In this space, he will open a photography studio, to be called "Picture This!" A friend has advised Josh to set up a double-entry set of accounting records in which to record all of his business transactions.

Identify normal balances.
(SO 2, 3)

Identify the balance sheet accounts that Josh will likely need to record the transactions needed to open his business (a corporation). Indicate whether the normal balance of each account is a debit or credit.

Record business activities.
(SO 4, 5)

Do it! **3-3** Josh Borke engaged in the following activities in establishing his photography studio, Picture This!:

1. Opened a bank account in the name of Picture This! and deposited $8,000 of his own money into this account in exchange for common stock.
2. Purchased photography supplies at a total cost of $1,100. The business paid $400 in cash, and the balance is on account.
3. Obtained estimates on the cost of photography equipment from three different manufacturers.

In what form (type of record) should Josh record these three activities? Prepare the entries to record the transactions.

Post transactions.
(SO 6, 7)

Do it! **3-4** Josh Borke recorded the following transactions during the month of April.

Apr. 3	Cash	3,400	
	Photography Revenue		3,400
Apr. 16	Rent Expense	600	
	Cash		600
Apr. 20	Salaries Expense	300	
	Cash		300

Post these entries to the Cash account of the general ledger to determine the ending balance in cash. The beginning balance in cash on April 1 was $1,600.

Exercises

Analyze the effect of transactions.
(SO 1)

E3-1 Selected transactions for Ruiz Advertising Company, Inc., are listed here.

1. Issued common stock to investors in exchange for cash received from investors.
2. Paid monthly rent.
3. Received cash from customers when service was provided.
4. Billed customers for services performed.
5. Paid dividend to stockholders.
6. Incurred advertising expense on account.
7. Received cash from customers billed in (4).
8. Purchased additional equipment for cash.
9. Purchased equipment on account.

Instructions
Describe the effect of each transaction on assets, liabilities, and stockholders' equity. For example, the first answer is: (1) Increase in assets and increase in stockholders' equity.

Analyze the effect of transactions on assets, liabilities, and stockholders' equity.
(SO 1)

E3-2 McBride Company entered into these transactions during May 2010.

1. Purchased computers for office use for $30,000 from Dell on account.
2. Paid $4,000 cash for May rent on storage space.
3. Received $12,000 cash from customers for contracts billed in April.
4. Provided computer services to Brieske Construction Company for $5,000 cash.
5. Paid Southern States Power Co. $11,000 cash for energy usage in May.
6. Stockholders invested an additional $40,000 in the business in exchange for common stock of the company.
7. Paid Dell for the computers purchased in (1).
8. Incurred advertising expense for May of $1,000 on account.

Instructions
Using the following tabular analysis, show the effect of each transaction on the accounting equation. Put explanations for changes to Stockholders' Equity in the right-hand margin. Use Illustration 3-3 (page 109) as a model.

Assets			=	Liabilities	+	Stockholders' Equity			
	Accounts	Office		Accounts		Common		Retained Earnings	
Cash	+ Receivable +	Equipment =		Payable	+	Stock	+ Revenues −	Expenses −	Dividends

E3-3   During 2010, its first year of operations as a delivery service, Lopez Corp. entered into the following transactions.

Determine effect of transactions on basic accounting equation.

(SO 1)

1. Issued shares of common stock to investors in exchange for $100,000 in cash.
2. Borrowed $45,000 by issuing bonds.
3. Purchased delivery trucks for $60,000 cash.
4. Received $16,000 from customers for services provided.
5. Purchased supplies for $4,200 on account.
6. Paid rent of $5,600.
7. Performed services on account for $10,000.
8. Paid salaries of $28,000.
9. Paid a dividend of $11,000 to shareholders.

Instructions
Using the following tabular analysis, show the effect of each transaction on the accounting equation. Put explanations for changes to Stockholders' Equity in the right-hand margin. Use Illustration 3-3 (page 109) as a model. ("P/P/E" refers to Property, Plant, and Equipment.)

Assets				=	**Liabilities**		+		**Stockholders' Equity**			
	Accounts				Accounts	Bonds		Common		Retained Earnings		
Cash +	Receivable +	Supplies +	P/P/E =		Payable +	Payable +		Stock +	Revenues −	Expenses −	Dividends

E3-4   A tabular analysis of the transactions made during August 2010 by Witten Company during its first month of operations is shown below. Each increase and decrease in stockholders' equity is explained.

Analyze transactions and compute net income.

(SO 1)

	Assets					=	**Liabilities**	+		**Stockholders' Equity**				
					Office		Accounts		Common		Retained Earnings			
	Cash	+ A/R	+ Supp.	+	Equip.	=	Payable	+	Stock	+	Rev.	− Exp.	− Div.	
1.	+$20,000								+$20,000					Com. Stock
2.	−1,000				+$5,000		+$4,000							
3.	−750		+$750											
4.	+4,400	+$5,400									+$9,800			Serv. Rev.
5.	−1,500						−1,500							
6.	−2,000												−$2,000	Div.
7.	−800											−$ 800		Rent Exp.
8.	+450	−450												
9.	−3,000											−3,000		Sal. Exp.
10.							+500					−500		Util. Exp.

15,800 + 4950 + 750 + 5000 = 3000 + 20,000 + 9800 − 7800 − 2000

4300

Instructions
(a) Describe each transaction.
(b) Determine how much stockholders' equity increased for the month.
(c) Compute the net income for the month.

E3-5   The tabular analysis of transactions for Witten Company is presented in E3-4.

Prepare an income statement, retained earnings statement, and balance sheet.

(SO 1)

Instructions
Prepare an income statement and a retained earnings statement for August and a classified balance sheet at August 31, 2010.

E3-6   Selected transactions for Loving Home, an interior decorator corporation, in its first month of business, are as follows.

Identify debits, credits, and normal balances and journalize transactions.

(SO 3, 5)

1. Issued stock to investors for $15,000 in cash.
2. Purchased used car for $8,000 cash for use in business.
3. Purchased supplies on account for $300.
4. Billed customers $3,600 for services performed.
5. Paid $200 cash for advertising start of the business.

6. Received $1,100 cash from customers billed in transaction (4).
7. Paid creditor $300 cash on account.
8. Paid dividends of $400 cash to stockholders.

Instructions
(a) For each transaction indicate (a) the basic type of account debited and credited (asset, liability, stockholders' equity); (b) the specific account debited and credited (Cash, Rent Expense, Service Revenue, etc.); (c) whether the specific account is increased or decreased; and (d) the normal balance of the specific account. Use the following format, in which transaction 1 is given as an example.

	Account Debited				Account Credited			
Trans-action	(a) Basic Type	(b) Specific Account	(c) Effect	(d) Normal Balance	(a) Basic Type	(b) Specific Account	(c) Effect	(d) Normal Balance
1	Asset	Cash	Increase	Debit	Stock-holders' equity	Common Stock	Increase	Credit

(b) Journalize the transactions. Do not provide explanations.

Analyze transactions and determine their effect on accounts.
(SO 3)

E3-7 This information relates to Pickert Real Estate Agency.

Oct. 1 Stockholders invest $30,000 in exchange for common stock of the corporation.
2 Hires an administrative assistant at an annual salary of $42,000.
3 Buys office furniture for $4,600, on account.
6 Sells a house and lot for M.E. Petty; commissions due from Petty, $10,800 (not paid by Petty at this time).
10 Receives cash of $140 as commission for acting as rental agent renting an apartment.
27 Pays $700 on account for the office furniture purchased on October 3.
30 Pays the administrative assistant $3,500 in salary for October.

Instructions
Prepare the debit–credit analysis for each transaction as illustrated on pages 121–126.

Journalize transactions.
(SO 5)

E3-8 Transaction data for Pickert Real Estate Agency are presented in E3-7.

Instructions
Journalize the transactions. Do not provide explanations.

Post journal entries and prepare a trial balance.
(SO 7, 8)

E3-9 Transaction data and journal entries for Pickert Real Estate Agency are presented in E3-7 and E3-8.

Instructions
(a) Post the transactions to T accounts.
(b) Prepare a trial balance at October 31, 2010.

Analyze transactions, prepare journal entries, and post transactions to T accounts.
(SO 1, 5, 7)

E3-10 Selected transactions for A. B. Coors Corporation during its first month in business are presented below.

Sept. 1 Issued common stock in exchange for $20,000 cash received from investors.
5 Purchased equipment for $10,000, paying $2,000 in cash and the balance on account.
25 Paid $5,000 cash on balance owed for equipment.
30 Paid $500 cash dividend.

A. B. Coors's chart of accounts shows: Cash, Equipment, Accounts Payable, Common Stock, and Dividends.

Instructions
(a) Prepare a tabular analysis of the September transactions. The column headings should be: Cash + Equipment = Accounts Payable + Stockholders' Equity. For transactions affecting stockholders' equity, provide explanations in the right margin, as shown on page 109.
(b) Journalize the transactions. Do not provide explanations.
(c) Post the transactions to T accounts.

Journalize transactions from T accounts and prepare a trial balance.
(SO 5, 8)

E3-11 The T accounts on page 143 summarize the ledger of Sutton's Gardening Company, Inc. at the end of the first month of operations.

Cash						Unearned Revenue				
Apr.	1	15,000	Apr.	15	900			Apr.	30	600
	12	700		25	3,500					
	29	800								
	30	600								

Accounts Receivable						Common Stock				
Apr.	7	3,400	Apr.	29	800			Apr.	1	15,000

Supplies				Service Revenue				
Apr.	4	5,200				Apr.	7	3,400
							12	700

Accounts Payable						Salaries Expense			
Apr.	25	3,500	Apr.	4	5,200	Apr.	15	900

Instructions

(a) Prepare in the order they occurred the journal entries (including explanations) that resulted in the amounts posted to the accounts.

(b) Prepare a trial balance at April 30, 2010. (*Hint:* Compute ending balances of T accounts first.)

E3-12 Selected transactions from the journal of Gipson Inc. during its first month of operations are presented here.

Post journal entries and prepare a trial balance.
(SO 7, 8)

Date		Account Titles	Debit	Credit
Aug.	1	Cash	5,000	
		Common Stock		5,000
	10	Cash	1,700	
		Service Revenue		1,700
	12	Office Equipment	6,200	
		Cash		1,200
		Notes Payable		5,000
	25	Accounts Receivable	3,100	
		Service Revenue		3,100
	31	Cash	600	
		Accounts Receivable		600

Instructions

(a) Post the transactions to T accounts.

(b) Prepare a trial balance at August 31, 2010.

E3-13 Here is the ledger for Brumbaugh Co.

Journalize transactions from T accounts and prepare a trial balance.
(SO 5, 8)

Cash						Common Stock				
Oct.	1	7,000	Oct.	4	400			Oct.	1	7,000
	10	750		12	1,500				25	2,000
	10	8,000		15	250					
	20	800		30	300					
	25	2,000		31	500					

Accounts Receivable						Dividends			
Oct.	6	800	Oct.	20	800	Oct.	30	300
	20	920						

Supplies						Service Revenue				
Oct.	4	400	Oct.	31	180			Oct.	6	800
									10	750
									20	920

Furniture				Store Wages Expense		
Oct.	3	3,000	Oct.	31	500

Notes Payable				Supplies Expense		
	Oct.	10	8,000	Oct.	31	180

Accounts Payable						Rent Expense		
Oct.	12	1,500	Oct.	3	3,000	Oct.	15	250

Instructions

(a) Reproduce the journal entries for only the transactions that **occurred on October 1, 10, and 20**, and provide explanations for each.

(b) Prepare a trial balance at October 31, 2010. (*Hint:* Compute ending balances of T accounts first.)

Analyze errors and their effects on trial balance.

(SO 8)

E3-14 The bookkeeper for Biggio Corporation made these errors in journalizing and posting.

1. A credit posting of $400 to Accounts Receivable was omitted.
2. A debit posting of $750 for Prepaid Insurance was debited to Insurance Expense.
3. A collection on account of $100 was journalized and posted as a debit to Cash $100 and a credit to Accounts Payable $100.
4. A credit posting of $300 to Property Taxes Payable was made twice.
5. A cash purchase of supplies for $250 was journalized and posted as a debit to Supplies $25 and a credit to Cash $25.
6. A debit of $395 to Advertising Expense was posted as $359.

Instructions

For each error, indicate (a) whether the trial balance will balance; if the trial balance will not balance, indicate (b) the amount of the difference, and (c) the trial balance column that will have the larger total. Consider each error separately. Use the following form, in which error 1 is given as an example.

Error	(a) In Balance	(b) Difference	(c) Larger Column
1	No	$400	Debit

Prepare a trial balance and financial statements.

(SO 8)

E3-15 The accounts in the ledger of Thornton Delivery Service contain the following balances on July 31, 2010.

Accounts Receivable	$13,400	Prepaid Insurance	$ 1,800
Accounts Payable	8,400	Repair Expense	1,200
Cash	?	Service Revenue	15,500
Delivery Equipment	59,360	Dividends	700
Gas and Oil Expense	758	Common Stock	40,000
Insurance Expense	600	Salaries Expense	7,428
Notes Payable, due 2013	28,450	Salaries Payable	900
		Retained Earnings (July 1, 2010)	5,200

Instructions

(a) Prepare a trial balance with the accounts arranged as illustrated in the chapter, and fill in the missing amount for Cash.

(b) Prepare an income statement, a retained earnings statement, and a classified balance sheet for the month of July 2010.

Identify normal account balance and corresponding financial statement.

(SO 3)

E3-16 The following accounts, in alphabetical order, were selected from the 2007 financial statements of Krispy Kreme Doughnuts, Inc.

Accounts payable	Interest income
Accounts receivable	Inventories
Common stock	Prepaid expenses
Depreciation expense	Property and equipment
Interest expense	Revenues

Instructions

For each account, indicate (a) whether the normal balance is a debit or a credit, and (b) the financial statement—balance sheet or income statement—where the account should be presented.

Classify transactions as cash-flow activities.

(SO 9)

E3-17 Review the transactions listed in E3-1 for Ruiz Advertising Company, and classify each transaction as either an operating activity, investing activity, or financing activity, or if no cash is exchanged, as a non-cash event.

Classify transactions as cash-flow activities.

(SO 9)

E3-18 Review the transactions listed in E3-3 for Lopez Corp. and classify each transaction as either an operating activity, investing activity, or financing activity, or if no cash is exchanged, as a non-cash event.

Exercises: Set B

Visit the book's companion website, at **www.wiley.com/college/kimmel,** and choose the Student Companion site, to access Exercise Set B.

Problems: Set A

P3-1A On April 1 Flint Hills Travel Agency Inc. was established. These transactions were completed during the month.

1. Stockholders invested $25,000 cash in the company in exchange for common stock.
2. Paid $900 cash for April office rent.
3. Purchased office equipment for $2,800 cash.
4. Purchased $200 of advertising in the *Chicago Tribune*, on account.
5. Paid $500 cash for office supplies.
6. Earned $10,000 for services provided: Cash of $1,000 is received from customers, and the balance of $9,000 is billed to customers on account.
7. Paid $400 cash dividends.
8. Paid *Chicago Tribune* amount due in transaction (4).
9. Paid employees' salaries $1,200.
10. Received $9,000 in cash from customers billed previously in transaction (6).

Analyze transactions and compute net income.
(SO 1)

Instructions

(a) Prepare a tabular analysis of the transactions using these column headings: Cash, Accounts Receivable, Supplies, Office Equipment, Accounts Payable, Common Stock, and Retained Earnings (with separate columns for Revenues, Expenses, and Dividends). Include margin explanations for any changes in Retained Earnings.
(b) From an analysis of the Retained Earnings columns, compute the net income or net loss for April.

(a) Cash $29,000
    Ret. earnings $ 7,300

P3-2A Diana Kuhlmann started her own consulting firm, Kuhlmann Consulting Inc., on May 1, 2010. The following transactions occurred during the month of May.

Analyze transactions and prepare financial statements.
(SO 1)

May	1	Stockholders invested $15,000 cash in the business in exchange for common stock.
	2	Paid $700 for office rent for the month.
	3	Purchased $500 of supplies on account.
	5	Paid $150 to advertise in the *County News*.
	9	Received $1,000 cash for services provided.
	12	Paid $200 cash dividend.
	15	Performed $4,200 of services on account.
	17	Paid $2,500 for employee salaries.
	20	Paid for the supplies purchased on account on May 3.
	23	Received a cash payment of $1,500 for services provided on account on May 15.
	26	Borrowed $5,000 from the bank on a note payable.
	29	Purchased office equipment for $2,000 paying $200 in cash and the balance on account.
	30	Paid $150 for utilities.

Instructions

(a) Show the effects of the previous transactions on the accounting equation using the following format. Assume the note payable is to be repaid within the year.

(a) Cash $18,100
    Ret. earnings $ 1,500

	Assets			=	Liabilities		+	Stockholders' Equity		
Date	Cash +	Accounts Receivable +	Supplies +	Office Equipment =	Notes Payable +	Accounts Payable +	Common Stock +	Retained Earnings		
								Revenues −	Expenses −	Dividends

Include margin explanations for any changes in Retained Earnings.

(b) Prepare an income statement for the month of May.

(c) Prepare a classified balance sheet at May 31, 2010.

(b) Net income $1,700

Analyze transactions and prepare an income statement, retained earnings statement, and balance sheet.

(SO 1)

P3-3A Dick Reber created a corporation providing legal services, Dick Reber Inc., on July 1, 2010. On July 31 the balance sheet showed: Cash $4,000; Accounts Receivable $2,500; Supplies $500; Office Equipment $5,000; Accounts Payable $4,200; Common Stock $6,200; and Retained Earnings $1,600. During August the following transactions occurred.

1. Collected $1,500 of accounts receivable due from customers.
2. Paid $2,700 cash for accounts payable due.
3. Earned revenue of $5,400, of which $3,000 is collected in cash and the balance is due in September.
4. Purchased additional office equipment for $4,000, paying $400 in cash and the balance on account.
5. Paid salaries $1,400, rent for August $900, and advertising expenses $350.
6. Paid a cash dividend of $700.
7. Received $5,000 from Standard Federal Bank; the money was borrowed on a 4-month note payable.
8. Incurred utility expenses for the month on account $450.

Instructions

(a) Cash $7,050
Ret. earnings $3,200

(a) Prepare a tabular analysis of the August transactions beginning with July 31 balances. The column heading should be: Cash + Accounts Receivable + Supplies + Office Equipment = Notes Payable + Accounts Payable + Common Stock + Retained Earnings. (Use separate Revenue, Expense, and Dividend columns). Include margin explanations for any changes in Retained Earnings.

(b) Net income $2,300

(b) Prepare an income statement for August, a retained earnings statement for August, and a classified balance sheet at August 31.

Journalize a series of transactions.

(SO 3, 5)

P3-4A Four Oaks Miniature Golf and Driving Range Inc. was opened on March 1 by Tiger Woodley. These selected events and transactions occurred during March.

Mar. 1 Stockholders invested $50,000 cash in the business in exchange for common stock of the corporation.

3 Purchased Arnie's Golf Land for $38,000 cash. The price consists of land $23,000, building $9,000, and equipment $6,000. (Record this in a single entry.)

5 Advertised the opening of the driving range and miniature golf course, paying advertising expenses of $1,600 cash.

6 Paid cash $2,400 for a 1-year insurance policy.

10 Purchased golf clubs and other equipment for $4,700 from Golden Bear Company, payable in 30 days.

18 Received golf fees of $1,200 in cash from customers for golf fees earned.

19 Sold 100 coupon books for $25 each in cash. Each book contains ten coupons that enable the holder to play one round of miniature golf or to hit one bucket of golf balls. (*Hint:* The revenue is not earned until the customers use the coupons.)

25 Paid a $500 cash dividend.

30 Paid salaries of $700.

30 Paid Golden Bear Company in full for equipment purchased on March 10.

31 Received $800 in cash from customers for golf fees earned.

The company uses these accounts: Cash, Prepaid Insurance, Land, Buildings, Equipment, Accounts Payable, Unearned Golf Revenue, Common Stock, Retained Earnings, Dividends, Golf Revenue, Advertising Expense, and Salaries Expense.

Instructions

Journalize the March transactions, including explanations.

P3-5A   Sunflower Architects incorporated as licensed architects on April 1, 2010. During the first month of the operation of the business, these events and transactions occurred:

Journalize transactions, post, and prepare a trial balance.
(SO 3, 5, 6, 7, 8)

Apr.	1	Stockholders invested $15,000 cash in exchange for common stock of the corporation.
	1	Hired a secretary-receptionist at a salary of $375 per week, payable monthly.
	2	Paid office rent for the month $900.
	3	Purchased architectural supplies on account from Spring Green Company $1,000.
	10	Completed blueprints on a carport and billed client $1,500 for services.
	11	Received $500 cash advance from J. Madison to design a new home.
	20	Received $2,300 cash for services completed and delivered to M. Svetlana.
	30	Paid secretary-receptionist for the month $1,500.
	30	Paid $300 to Spring Green Company for accounts payable due.

 — Something / cash

The company uses these accounts: Cash, Accounts Receivable, Supplies, Accounts Payable, Unearned Revenue, Common Stock, Service Revenue, Salaries Expense, and Rent Expense.

Instructions
(a) Journalize the transactions, including explanations.
(b) Post to the ledger T accounts.
(c) Prepare a trial balance on April 30, 2010.

(c) Cash $15,100
    Tot. trial
    balance $20,000

P3-6A   This is the trial balance of Slocombe Company on September 30.

Journalize transactions, post, and prepare a trial balance.
(SO 3, 5, 6, 7, 8)

SLOCOMBE COMPANY
Trial Balance
September 30, 2010

	Debit	Credit
Cash	$ 8,300	
Accounts Receivable	2,600	
Supplies	2,100	
Equipment	8,000	
Accounts Payable		$ 5,100
Unearned Revenue		900
Common Stock		15,000
	$21,000	$21,000

The October transactions were as follows.

Oct.	5	Received $1,300 in cash from customers for accounts receivable due.
	10	Billed customers for services performed $5,100.
	15	Paid employee salaries $1,400.
	17	Performed $600 of services for customers who paid in advance in August.
	20	Paid $1,500 to creditors for accounts payable due.
	29	Paid a $300 cash dividend.
	31	Paid utilities $500.

Instructions
(a) Prepare a general ledger using T accounts. Enter the opening balances in the ledger accounts as of October 1. Provision should be made for these additional accounts: Dividends, Service Revenue, Salaries Expense, and Utilities Expense.
(b) Journalize the transactions, including explanations.
(c) Post to the ledger accounts.
(d) Prepare a trial balance on October 31, 2010.

(d) Cash $ 5,900
    Tot. trial
    balance $24,600

Prepare a correct trial balance.

(SO 8)

P3-7A This trial balance of Titus Co. does not balance.

TITUS CO.
Trial Balance
June 30, 2010

	Debit	Credit
Cash		$ 3,090
Accounts Receivable	$ 3,460	
Supplies	800	
Equipment	3,000	
Accounts Payable		3,666
Unearned Revenue	1,200	
Common Stock		9,000
Dividends	800	
Service Revenue		3,480
Salaries Expense	3,600	
Office Expense	910	
	$13,770	$19,236

Each of the listed accounts has a normal balance per the general ledger. An examination of the ledger and journal reveals the following errors:

1. Cash received from a customer on account was debited for $590, and Accounts Receivable was credited for the same amount. The actual collection was for $950.
2. The purchase of a printer on account for $340 was recorded as a debit to Supplies for $340 and a credit to Accounts Payable for $340.
3. Services were performed on account for a client for $800. Accounts Receivable was debited for $80 and Service Revenue was credited for $800.
4. A debit posting to Salaries Expense of $500 was omitted.
5. A payment on account for $206 was credited to Cash for $206 and credited to Accounts Payable for $260.
6. Payment of a $600 cash dividend to Titus's stockholders was debited to Salaries Expense for $600 and credited to Cash for $600.

Instructions

Tot. trial balance $16,880

Prepare the correct trial balance. (*Hint:* All accounts have normal balances.)

Journalize transactions, post, and prepare a trial balance.

(SO 3, 5, 6, 7, 8)

P3-8A The Star-Lite Theater Inc. was recently formed. It began operations in March 2010. The Star-Lite is unique in that it will show only triple features of sequential theme movies. On March 1, the ledger of The Star-Lite showed: Cash $16,000; Land $38,000; Buildings (concession stand, projection room, ticket booth, and screen) $22,000; Equipment $16,000; Accounts Payable $12,000; and Common Stock $80,000. During the month of March the following events and transactions occurred.

Mar.		
	2	Rented the three Star Wars movies (*Star Wars®, The Empire Strikes Back,* and *The Return of the Jedi*) to be shown for the first three weeks of March. The film rental was $10,000; $2,000 was paid in cash and $8,000 will be paid on March 10.
	3	Ordered the first three *Star Trek* movies to be shown the last 10 days of March. It will cost $400 per night.
	9	Received $9,200 cash from admissions.
	10	Paid balance due on *Star Wars* movies rental and $2,600 on March 1 accounts payable.
	11	Hired J. Carne to operate the concession stand. Carne agrees to pay The Star-Lite Theater 15% of gross receipts, payable monthly.
	12	Paid advertising expenses $900.
	20	Received $7,100 cash from customers for admissions.
	20	Received the *Star Trek* movies and paid rental fee of $4,000.
	31	Paid salaries of $3,800.

31   Received statement from J. Carne showing gross receipts from concessions of $10,000 and the balance due to The Star-Lite of $1,500 for March. Carne paid half the balance due and will remit the remainder on April 5.

31   Received $20,000 cash from customers for admissions.

In addition to the accounts identified above, the chart of accounts includes: Accounts Receivable, Admission Revenue, Concession Revenue, Advertising Expense, Film Rental Expense, and Salaries Expense.

Instructions

(a) Using T accounts, enter the beginning balances to the ledger.
(b) Journalize the March transactions, including explanations.
(c) Post the March journal entries to the ledger.
(d) Prepare a trial balance on March 31, 2010.

(d) Cash $ 31,750
     Tot. trial
         balance $127,200

P3-9A   The bookkeeper for Sandy McClain's dance studio made the following errors in journalizing and posting.

Analyze errors and their effects on the trial balance.
(SO 8)

1. A credit to Supplies of $600 was omitted.
2. A debit posting of $300 to Accounts Payable was inadvertently debited to Accounts Receivable.
3. A purchase of supplies on account of $450 was debited to Supplies for $540 and credited to Accounts Payable for $540.
4. A credit posting of $350 to Wages Payable was posted twice.
5. A debit posting to Wages Payable for $250 and a credit posting to Cash for $250 were made twice.
6. A debit posting for $1,200 of Dividends was inadvertently posted to Travel Expense instead.
7. A credit to Service Revenue for $450 was inadvertently posted as a debit to Service Revenue.
8. A credit to Accounts Receivable of $250 was credited to Accounts Payable.

Instructions

For each error, indicate (a) whether the trial balance will balance; (b) the amount of the difference if the trial balance will not balance; and (c) the trial balance column that will have the larger total. Consider each error separately. Use the following form, in which error 1 is given as an example.

Error	(a) In Balance	(b) Difference	(c) Larger Column
1.	No	$600	Debit

Problems: Set B

P3-1B   Hermesch Window Washing Inc. was started on May 1. Here is a summary of the May transactions.

Analyze transactions and compute net income.
(SO 1)

1. Stockholders invested $20,000 cash in the company in exchange for common stock.
2. Purchased equipment for $7,000 cash.
3. Paid $700 cash for May office rent.
4. Paid $400 cash for supplies.
5. Purchased $750 of advertising in the *Beacon News* on account.
6. Received $5,800 in cash from customers for service.
7. Paid a $500 cash dividend.
8. Paid part-time employee salaries $1,700.
9. Paid utility bills $140.
10. Provided service on account to customers $1,000.
11. Collected cash of $240 for services billed in transaction (10).

Instructions

(a) Prepare a tabular analysis of the transactions using these column headings: Cash, Accounts Receivable, Supplies, Equipment, Accounts Payable, Common Stock, and Retained Earnings (with separate columns for Revenues, Expenses, and Dividends). Revenue is called Service Revenue. Include margin explanations for any changes in Retained Earnings.

(b) Net income $3,510

(b) From an analysis of the Retained Earnings columns, compute the net income or net loss for May.

Analyze transactions and prepare financial statements.

(SO 1)

GLS

P3-2B Richard Mordica started his own delivery service, Speedy Service Inc., on June 1, 2010. The following transactions occurred during the month of June.

June	1	Stockholders invested $15,000 cash in the business in exchange for common stock.
	2	Purchased a used van for deliveries for $15,000. Richard paid $2,000 cash and signed a note payable for the remaining balance.
	3	Paid $500 for office rent for the month.
	5	Performed $2,400 of services on account.
	9	Paid $300 in cash dividends.
	12	Purchased supplies for $150 on account.
	15	Received a cash payment of $750 for services provided on June 5.
	17	Purchased gasoline for $200 on account.
	20	Received a cash payment of $1,500 for services provided.
	23	Made a cash payment of $800 on the note payable.
	26	Paid $250 for utilities.
	29	Paid for the supplies purchased on account on June 12.
	30	Paid $750 for employee salaries.

(a) Cash $12,500

Instructions

(a) Show the effects of the previous transactions on the accounting equation using the following format. Assume the note payable is to be repaid within the year.

		Assets			=	Liabilities		+	Stockholders' Equity			
			Accounts			Delivery	Notes	Accounts	Common	Retained Earnings		
Date	Cash	+ Receivable	+ Supplies +	Van	= Payable	+ Payable	+	Stock	+ Revenues −	Expenses −	Dividends

Include margin explanations for any changes in Retained Earnings.

(b) Net income $2,200

(b) Prepare an income statement for the month of June.

(c) Prepare a classified balance sheet at June 30, 2010.

Analyze transactions and prepare an income statement, retained earnings statement, and balance sheet.

(SO 1)

GLS

P3-3B Nancy Grey opened Grey Company, a veterinary business in Neosho, Wisconsin, on August 1, 2010. On August 31 the balance sheet showed: Cash $9,000; Accounts Receivable $1,700; Supplies $600; Office Equipment $5,000; Accounts Payable $3,600; Common Stock $12,000; and Retained Earnings $700. During September the following transactions occurred.

1. Paid $3,400 cash for accounts payable due.
2. Received $1,600 from customers in payment of accounts receivable.
3. Purchased additional office equipment for $5,100, paying $1,000 in cash and the balance on account.
4. Earned revenue of $9,500, of which $2,300 is paid in cash and the balance is due in October.
5. Declared and paid a $600 cash dividend.
6. Paid salaries $900, rent for September $800, and advertising expense $250.
7. Incurred utility expenses for the month on account $170.
8. Received $5,000 from Hilldale Bank on a 6-month note payable.

Instructions

(a) Cash $10,950
Ret. earnings $ 7,480

(a) Prepare a tabular analysis of the September transactions beginning with August 31 balances. The column headings should be: Cash + Accounts Receivable + Supplies + Office Equipment = Notes Payable + Accounts Payable + Common Stock + Retained Earnings. Include margin explanations for any changes in Retained Earnings.

(b) Prepare an income statement for September, a retained earnings statement for September, and a classified balance sheet at September 30, 2010.

P3-4B   RV Haven was started on April 1 by Tom Larkin. These selected events and transactions occurred during April.

Journalize a series of transactions.
(SO 3, 5)

Apr.	1	Stockholders invested $70,000 cash in the business in exchange for common stock.
	4	Purchased land costing $50,000 for cash.
	8	Purchased advertising in local newspaper for $1,200 on account.
	11	Paid salaries to employees $2,700.
	12	Hired park manager at a salary of $3,000 per month, effective May 1.
	13	Paid $6,000 for a 1-year insurance policy.
	17	Paid $600 cash dividends.
	20	Received $5,000 in cash from customers for admission fees.
	25	Sold 100 coupon books for $75 each. Each book contains ten coupons that entitle the holder to one admission to the park. (*Hint*: The revenue is not earned until the coupons are used.)
	30	Received $7,900 in cash from customers for admission fees.
	30	Paid $500 of the balance owed for the advertising purchased on account on April 8.

The company uses the following accounts: Cash, Prepaid Insurance, Land, Accounts Payable, Unearned Admissions, Common Stock, Dividends, Admission Revenue, Advertising Expense, and Salaries Expense.

Instructions
Journalize the April transactions, including explanations.

P3-5B   Sammy Baden incorporated Baden Consulting, an accounting practice, on May 1, 2010. During the first month of operations, these events and transactions occurred.

Journalize transactions, post, and prepare a trial balance.
(SO 3, 5, 6, 7, 8)

May	1	Stockholders invested $50,000 cash in exchange for common stock of the corporation.
	2	Hired a secretary-receptionist at a salary of $2,000 per month.
	3	Purchased $800 of supplies on account from Fleming Supply Company.
	7	Paid office rent of $1,100 for the month.
	11	Completed a tax assignment and billed client $1,000 for services provided.
	12	Received $4,200 advance on a management consulting engagement.
	17	Received cash of $3,600 for services completed for Goodman Co.
	31	Paid secretary-receptionist $2,000 salary for the month.
	31	Paid 50% of balance due Fleming Supply Company.

The company uses the following chart of accounts: Cash, Accounts Receivable, Supplies, Accounts Payable, Unearned Revenue, Common Stock, Service Revenue, Salaries Expense, and Rent Expense.

Instructions
(a) Journalize the transactions, including explanations.
(b) Post to the ledger T accounts.
(c) Prepare a trial balance on May 31, 2010.

(c) Cash $54,300
    Tot. trial
    balance $59,200

P3-6B   The trial balance of Capaldo Dry Cleaners on June 30 is given here.

Journalize transactions, post, and prepare a trial balance.
(SO 3, 5, 6, 7, 8)

CAPALDO DRY CLEANERS
Trial Balance
June 30, 2010

	Debit	Credit
Cash	$12,532	
Accounts Receivable	10,536	
Supplies	3,512	
Equipment	25,950	
Accounts Payable		$15,800
Unearned Revenue		1,730
Common Stock		35,000
	$52,530	$52,530

The July transactions were as follows.

July   8   Received $5,189 in cash on June 30 accounts receivable.
       9   Paid employee salaries $2,100.
       11 Received $6,100 in cash for services provided.
       14 Paid creditors $10,750 of accounts payable.
       17 Purchased supplies on account $720.
       22 Billed customers for services provided $4,700.
       30 Paid employee salaries $3,114, utilities $1,767, and repairs $492.
       31 Paid $400 cash dividend.

Instructions

(a) Prepare a general ledger using T accounts. Enter the opening balances in the ledger accounts as of July 1. Provision should be made for the following additional accounts: Dividends, Dry Cleaning Revenue, Repair Expense, Salaries Expense, and Utilities Expense.

(d) Cash $ 5,198

Tot. trial

   balance $53,300

(b) Journalize the transactions, including explanations.
(c) Post to the ledger accounts.
(d) Prepare a trial balance on July 31, 2010.

Prepare a correct trial balance.

(SO 8)

P3-7B   This trial balance of Schumaker Company does not balance.

SCHUMAKER COMPANY
Trial Balance
May 31, 2010

	Debit	Credit
Cash	$ 6,340	
Accounts Receivable		$ 2,750
Prepaid Insurance	700	
Equipment	8,000	
Accounts Payable		4,100
Property Taxes Payable	750	
Common Stock		5,700
Retained Earnings		6,000
Service Revenue	7,690	
Salaries Expense	4,200	
Advertising Expense		1,100
Property Tax Expense	900	
	$28,580	$19,650

Your review of the ledger reveals that each account has a normal balance. You also discover the following errors.

1. The totals of the debit sides of Prepaid Insurance, Accounts Payable, and Property Tax Expense were each understated $100.
2. Transposition errors were made in Accounts Receivable and Service Revenue. Based on postings made, the correct balances were $2,570 and $7,960, respectively.
3. A debit posting to Salaries Expense of $400 was omitted.
4. An $800 cash dividend was debited to Common Stock for $800 and credited to Cash for $800.
5. A $350 purchase of supplies on account was debited to Equipment for $350 and credited to Cash for $350.
6. A cash payment of $450 for advertising was debited to Advertising Expense for $45 and credited to Cash for $45.
7. A collection from a customer for $240 was debited to Cash for $240 and credited to Accounts Payable for $240.

Instructions

Cash $ 6,285

Tot. trial balance $25,320

Prepare the correct trial balance, assuming all accounts have normal balances. (*Note:* The chart of accounts also includes the following: Dividends and Supplies.)

P3-8B   Granada Theater Inc. was recently formed. All facilities were completed on March 31. On April 1, the ledger showed: Cash $6,300; Land $10,000; Buildings (concession stand, projection room, ticket booth, and screen) $8,000; Equipment $6,000; Accounts Payable $2,300; Mortgage Payable $8,000; and Common Stock $20,000. During April, the following events and transactions occurred.

Journalize transactions, post, and prepare a trial balance.
(SO 3, 5, 6, 7, 8)

Apr.	2	Paid film rental fee of $800 on first movie.
	3	Ordered two additional films at $900 each.
	9	Received $4,900 cash from admissions.
	10	Paid $2,000 of mortgage payable and $1,200 of accounts payable.
	11	Hired M. Gavin to operate the concession stand. Gavin agrees to pay Granada Theater 17% of gross receipts, payable monthly.
	12	Paid advertising expenses $460.
	20	Received one of the films ordered on April 3 and was billed $900. The film will be shown in April.
	25	Received $3,000 cash from customers for admissions.
	29	Paid salaries $1,900.
	30	Received statement from M. Gavin showing gross receipts of $2,000 and the balance due to Granada Theater of $340 for April. Gavin paid half of the balance due and will remit the remainder on May 5.
	30	Prepaid $1,000 rental fee on special film to be run in May.

In addition to the accounts identified above, the chart of accounts shows: Accounts Receivable, Prepaid Rentals, Admission Revenue, Concession Revenue, Advertising Expense, Film Rental Expense, Salaries Expense.

Instructions
(a) Enter the beginning balances in the ledger T accounts as of April 1.
(b) Journalize the April transactions, including explanations.
(c) Post the April journal entries to the ledger T accounts.
(d) Prepare a trial balance on April 30, 2010.

(d) Cash $ 7,010
Tot. trial
balance $36,240

P3-9B   A first year co-op student working for UR Here.com recorded the transactions for the month. He wasn't exactly sure how to journalize and post, but he did the best he could. He had a few questions, however, about the following transactions.

Analyze errors and their effects on the trial balance.
(SO 8)

1. Cash received from a customer on account was recorded as a debit to Cash of $360 and a credit to Accounts Receivable of $630, instead of $360.
2. A service provided for cash was posted as a debit to Cash of $2,000 and a credit to Service Revenue of $2,000.
3. A debit of $880 for services provided on account was neither recorded nor posted. The credit was recorded correctly.
4. The debit to record $1,000 of cash dividends was posted to the Salary Expense account.
5. The purchase, on account, of a computer that cost $2,500 was recorded as a debit to Supplies and a credit to Accounts Payable.
6. A cash payment of $495 for salaries was recorded as a debit to Dividends and a credit to Cash.
7. Payment of month's rent was debited to Rent Expense and credited to Cash, $850.
8. Issue of $7,000 of common shares was credited to the Common Stock account, but no debit was recorded.

Instructions
(a) Indicate which of the above transactions are correct, and which are incorrect.
(b) For each error identified in (a), indicate (1) whether the trial balance will balance; (2) the amount of the difference if the trial balance will not balance; and (3) the trial balance column that will have the larger total. Consider each error separately. Use the following form, in which transaction 1 is given as an example.

Error	**(1)** **In Balance**	**(2)** **Difference**	**(3)** **Larger Column**
1.	No	$270	Credit

Problems: Set C

Visit the book's companion website at **www.wiley.com/college/kimmel** and choose the Student Companion site to access Problem Set C.

Continuing Cookie Chronicle

(*Note:* This is a continuation of the Cookie Chronicle from Chapters 1 and 2.)

CCC3 In November 2009 after having incorporated Cookie Creations Inc., Natalie begins operations. She has decided to not pursue the offer to supply cookies to Biscuits. Instead she will focus on offering cooking classes.

Go to the book's companion website, **www.wiley.com/college/kimmel,** to find the completion of this problem.

---

broadening your perspective

Financial Reporting and Analysis

FINANCIAL REPORTING PROBLEM: *Tootsie Roll Industries*

BYP3-1 The financial statements of Tootsie Roll in Appendix A at the back of this book contain the following selected accounts, all in thousands of dollars.

Common Stock	$ 24,586
Accounts Payable	11,572
Accounts Receivable	32,371
Selling, Marketing, and Administrative Expenses	97,821
Prepaid Expenses	6,551
Property, Plant, and Equipment	201,401
Net Sales	492,742

Instructions
(a) What is the increase and decrease side for each account? What is the normal balance for each account?
(b) Identify the probable other account in the transaction and the effect on that account when:
  (1) Accounts Receivable is decreased.
  (2) Accounts Payable is decreased.
  (3) Prepaid Expenses is increased.
(c) Identify the other account(s) that ordinarily would be involved when:
  (1) Interest Expense is increased.
  (2) Property, Plant, and Equipment is increased.

COMPARATIVE ANALYSIS PROBLEM: *Tootsie Roll vs. Hershey Foods*

BYP3-2 The financial statements of Hershey Foods appear in Appendix B, following the financial statements for Tootsie Roll in Appendix A.

Instructions
(a) Based on the information contained in these financial statements, determine the normal balance for:

Tootsie Roll Industries	**Hershey Foods**
(1) Accounts Receivable	(1) Inventories
(2) Property, Plant, and Equipment	(2) Provision for Income Taxes
(3) Accounts Payable	(3) Accrued Liabilities
(4) Retained Earnings	(4) Common Stock
(5) Net Sales	(5) Interest Expense

(b) Identify the other account ordinarily involved when:
  (1) Accounts Receivable is increased.
  (2) Notes Payable is decreased.
  (3) Machinery is increased.
  (4) Interest Income is increased.

RESEARCH CASE

BYP3-3 Sid Cato provides critiques of corporate annual reports. He maintains a website at **www.sidcato.com** that provides many useful resources for those who are interested in preparing or using annual reports.

Instructions
Go to the website and answer the following questions.
(a) Read the section, "What makes a good annual report?" and choose which three factors you think are most important. Explain why you think each item is important.
(b) For the most recent year, which companies were listed in the section "Producers of the best annuals for (*most recent year*)"?
(c) What potential benefits might a company gain by receiving a high rating from Sid Cato's organization?

INTERPRETING FINANCIAL STATEMENTS

BYP3-4 Chieftain International, Inc., is an oil and natural gas exploration and production company. A recent balance sheet reported $208 million in assets with only $4.6 million in liabilities, all of which were short-term accounts payable.

During the year, Chieftain expanded its holdings of oil and gas rights, drilled 37 new wells, and invested in expensive 3-D seismic technology. The company generated $19 million cash from operating activities and paid no dividends. It had a cash balance of $102 million at the end of the year.

Instructions
(a) Name at least two advantages to Chieftain from having no long-term debt. Can you think of disadvantages?
(b) What are some of the advantages to Chieftain from having this large a cash balance? What is a disadvantage?
(c) Why do you suppose Chieftain has the $4.6 million balance in accounts payable, since it appears that it could have made all its purchases for cash?

BYP3-5 Doman Industries Ltd., whose products are sold in 30 countries worldwide, is an integrated Canadian forest products company.

Doman sells the majority of its lumber products in the United States, and a significant amount of its pulp products in Asia. Doman also has loans from other countries. For example, the Company borrowed US$160 million at an annual interest rate of 12%. Doman must repay this loan, and interest, in U.S. dollars.

One of the challenges global companies face is to make themselves attractive to investors from other countries. This is difficult to do when different accounting rules in different countries blur the real impact of earnings. For example, in a recent year Doman reported a loss of $2.3 million, using Canadian accounting rules. Had it reported under U.S. accounting rules, its loss would have been $12.1 million.

Many companies that want to be more easily compared with U.S. and other global competitors have switched to U.S. accounting principles. Canadian National Railway, Corel, Cott, Inco, and Thomson Corporation are but a few examples of large Canadian companies whose financial statements are now presented in U.S. dollars, adhere to U.S. GAAP, or are reconciled to U.S. GAAP.

Instructions
(a) Identify advantages and disadvantages that companies should consider when switching to U.S. reporting standards.
(b) Suppose you compare Doman Industries to a U.S.-based competitor. Do you believe the use of country-specific accounting policies would hinder your ability to compare the companies? If so, explain how.

(c) Suppose you compare Doman Industries to a Canadian-based competitor. If the companies apply generally acceptable Canadian accounting policies differently, how could this affect your ability to compare their financial results?

(d) Do you see any significant distinction between comparing statements prepared using generally accepted accounting principles of different countries and comparing statements prepared using generally accepted accounting principles of the same country (e.g. U.S.) but that apply the principles differently?

FINANCIAL ANALYSIS ON THE WEB

BYP3-6   *Purpose:* This activity provides information about career opportunities for CPAs.

Address: **www.icpas.org/students.htm**, or go to **www.wiley.com/college/kimmel**

Steps
1. Go to the address shown above.
2. Click on **High School**, then **CPA101** for parts a, b, and c.
3. Click **College** to answer part d.

Instructions
Answer the following questions.
(a) What does CPA stand for? Where do CPAs work?
(b) What is meant by "public accounting"?
(c) What skills does a CPA need?
(d) What is the salary range for a CPA at a large firm during the first three years? What is the salary range for chief financial officers and treasurers at large corporations?

Critical Thinking

DECISION MAKING ACROSS THE ORGANIZATION

BYP3-7   Donna Dye operates Double D Riding Academy, Inc. The academy's primary sources of revenue are riding fees and lesson fees, which are provided on a cash basis. Donna also boards horses for owners, who are billed monthly for boarding fees. In a few cases, boarders pay in advance of expected use. For its revenue transactions, the academy maintains these accounts: Cash, Accounts Receivable, Unearned Revenue, Riding Revenue, Lesson Revenue, and Boarding Revenue.

The academy owns 10 horses, a stable, a riding corral, riding equipment, and office equipment. These assets are accounted for in the following accounts: Horses, Building, Riding Corral, Riding Equipment, and Office Equipment.

The academy employs stable helpers and an office employee, who receive weekly salaries. At the end of each month, the mail usually brings bills for advertising, utilities, and veterinary service. Other expenses include feed for the horses and insurance. For its expenses, the academy maintains the following accounts: Hay and Feed Supplies, Prepaid Insurance, Accounts Payable, Salaries Expense, Advertising Expense, Utilities Expense, Veterinary Expense, Hay and Feed Expense, and Insurance Expense.

Donna Dye's sole source of personal income is dividends from the academy. Thus, the corporation declares and pays periodic dividends. To account for stockholders' equity in the business and dividends, two accounts are maintained: Common Stock and Dividends.

During the first month of operations an inexperienced bookkeeper was employed. Donna Dye asks you to review the following eight entries of the 50 entries made during the month. In each case, the explanation for the entry is correct.

May	1	Cash	15,000	
		Unearned Revenue		15,000
		(Issued common stock in exchange for		
		$15,000 cash)		
	5	Cash	250	
		Lesson Revenue		250
		(Received $250 cash for lesson fees)		

May	7	Cash	500	
		Boarding Revenue		500
		(Received $500 for boarding of horses		
		beginning June 1)		
	9	Hay and Feed Expense	1,500	
		Cash		1,500
		(Purchased estimated 5 months' supply		
		of feed and hay for $1,500 on account)		
	14	Riding Equipment	80	
		Cash		800
		(Purchased desk and other office		
		equipment for $800 cash)		
	15	Salaries Expense	400	
		Cash		400
		(Issued check to Donna Dye for		
		personal use)		
	20	Cash	145	
		Riding Revenue		154
		(Received $154 cash for riding fees)		
	31	Veterinary Expense	75	
		Accounts Receivable		75
		(Received bill of $75 from veterinarian		
		for services provided)		

Instructions

With the class divided into groups, answer the following.

(a) For each journal entry that is correct, so state. For each journal entry that is incorrect, prepare the entry that should have been made by the bookkeeper.

(b) Which of the incorrect entries would prevent the trial balance from balancing?

(c) What was the correct net income for May, assuming the bookkeeper originally reported net income of $4,500 after posting all 50 entries?

(d) What was the correct cash balance at May 31, assuming the bookkeeper reported a balance of $12,475 after posting all 50 entries?

COMMUNICATION ACTIVITY

BYP3-8 Clean Sweep Company offers home cleaning service. Two recurring transactions for the company are billing customers for services provided and paying employee salaries. For example, on March 15 bills totaling $6,000 were sent to customers, and $2,000 was paid in salaries to employees.

Instructions

Write a memorandum to your instructor that explains and illustrates the steps in the recording process for each of the March 15 transactions. Use the format illustrated in the text under the heading "The Recording Process Illustrated" (pp. 120–126).

ETHICS CASES

BYP3-9 Monica Geller is the assistant chief accountant at BIT Company, a manufacturer of computer chips and cellular phones. The company presently has total sales of $20 million. It is the end of the first quarter and Monica is hurriedly trying to prepare a general ledger trial balance so that quarterly financial statements can be prepared and released to management and the regulatory agencies. The total credits on the trial balance exceed the debits by $1,000.

In order to meet the 4 P.M. deadline, Monica decides to force the debits and credits into balance by adding the amount of the difference to the Equipment account. She chose Equipment because it is one of the larger account balances; percentage-wise it will be the least misstated. Monica plugs the difference! She believes that the difference is quite small and will not affect anyone's decisions. She wishes that she had another few days to find the error but realizes that the financial statements are already late.

Instructions

(a) Who are the stakeholders in this situation?
(b) What ethical issues are involved?
(c) What are Monica's alternatives?

BYP3-10   The July 28, 2007, issue of the *Wall Street Journal* includes an article by Kathryn Kranhold titled "GE's Accounting Draws Fresh Focus on News of Improper Sales Bookings."

Instructions
Read the article and answer the following questions.
(a) What improper activity did the employees at GE engage in?
(b) Why might the employees have engaged in this activity?
(c) What were the implications for the employees who engaged in this activity?
(d) What does it mean to "restate" financial results? Why didn't GE restate its results to correct for the improperly reported locomotive sales?

"ALL ABOUT YOU" ACTIVITY

BYP3-11   In their annual reports to stockholders, companies must report or disclose information about all liabilities, including potential liabilities related to environmental clean-up. There are many situations in which you will be asked to provide personal financial information about your assets, liabilities, revenue, and expenses. Sometimes you will face difficult decisions regarding what to disclose and how to disclose it.

Instructions
Suppose that you are putting together a loan application to purchase a home. Based on your income and assets, you qualify for the mortgage loan, but just barely. How would you address each of the following situations in reporting your financial position for the loan application? Provide responses for each of the following questions.

(a) You signed a guarantee for a bank loan that a friend took out for $20,000. If your friend doesn't pay, you will have to pay. Your friend has made all of the payments so far, and it appears he will be able to pay in the future.
(b) You were involved in an auto accident in which you were at fault. There is the possibility that you may have to pay as much as $50,000 as part of a settlement. The issue will not be resolved before the bank processes your mortgage request.
(c) The company at which you work isn't doing very well, and it has recently laid off employees. You are still employed, but it is quite possible that you will lose your job in the next few months.

❓ Answers to Insight and Accounting Across the Organization Questions

p. 108
Q: In order for these companies to prepare and issue financial statements, their accounting equations (debit and credits) must have been in balance at year-end. How could these errors or misstatements have occurred?
A: A company's accounting equation (its books) can be in balance yet its financial statements have errors or misstatements because of the following: entire transactions were not recorded; transactions were recorded at wrong amounts; transactions were recorded in the wrong accounts; transactions were recorded in the wrong accounting period. Audits of financial statements uncover some, but obviously not all, errors or misstatements.
p. 114
Q: Do you think that the Chicago Bears football team would be likely to have the same major revenue and expense accounts as the Cubs?
A: Because their businesses are similar—professional sports—many of the revenue and expense accounts for the baseball and football teams might be similar.
p. 118
Q: In what ways is this Microsoft division using accounting to assist in its effort to become more profitable?

A: The division has used accounting to set very strict sales, revenue, and profit goals. In addition, the managers in this division use accounting to keep a tight reign on product costs. Also, accounting serves as the basis of communication so that the marketing managers and product designers can work with production managers, engineers, and accountants to create an exciting product within specified cost constraints.

Answers to Self-Study Questions

1. b   2. b   3. b   4. a   5. b   6. c   7. d   8. d   9. d   10. b   11. a   12. c   13. d   14. a   15. c

✔ Remember to go back to the navigator box on the chapter-opening page and check off your completed work.

Accrual Accounting Concepts

✔ the navigator

- Scan **Study Objectives** ○
- Read **Feature Story** ○
- Scan **Preview** ○
- Read **Text and answer** *Do it!*
  p. 173 ○   p. 178 ○   p. 183 ○   p. 187 ○
- Work **Using the Decision Toolkit** ○
- Review **Summary of Study Objectives** ○
- Work Comprehensive *Do it!* p. 195 ○
- Answer **Self-Study Questions** ○
- Complete **Assignments** ○

study objectives

After studying this chapter, you should be able to:

1. Explain the revenue recognition principle and the matching principle.
2. Differentiate between the cash basis and the accrual basis of accounting.
3. Explain why adjusting entries are needed, and identify the major types of adjusting entries.
4. Prepare adjusting entries for deferrals.
5. Prepare adjusting entries for accruals.
6. Describe the nature and purpose of the adjusted trial balance.
7. Explain the purpose of closing entries.
8. Describe the required steps in the accounting cycle.
9. Understand the causes of differences between net income and cash provided by operating activities.

✔ the navigator

What Was Your Profit?

The accuracy of the financial reporting system depends on answers to a few fundamental questions. At what point has revenue been earned? At what point is the earnings process complete? When have expenses really been incurred?

During the 1990s the stock prices of dot-com companies boomed. Many dot-com companies earned most of their revenue from selling advertising space on their Web sites. To boost reported revenue, some dot-coms began swapping website ad space. Company A would put an ad for its website on company B's website, and company B would put an ad for its website on company A's website. No money ever changed hands, but each company recorded revenue (for the value of the space that it gave up on its site). This practice did little to boost net income and resulted in no additional cash

flow—but it did boost *reported revenue*. Regulators eventually put an end to the practice.

Another type of transgression results from companies recording revenue or expenses in the wrong year. In fact, shifting revenues and expenses is one of the most common abuses of financial accounting. Xerox recently admitted reporting billions of dollars of lease revenue in periods earlier than it should have been reported. And WorldCom stunned the financial markets with its admission that it had boosted net income by billions of dollars by delaying the recognition of expenses until later years.

Unfortunately, revelations such as these have become all too common in the corporate world. It is no wonder that recently the U.S. Trust Survey of affluent Americans reported that 85 percent of its respondents believed

that there should be tighter regulation of financial disclosures, and 66 percent said they did not trust the management of publicly traded companies.

Why did so many companies violate basic financial reporting rules and sound ethics? Many speculate that as stock prices climbed, executives were under increasing pressure to meet higher and higher earnings expectations. If actual results weren't as good as hoped for, some gave in to temptation and "adjusted" their numbers to meet market expectations.

On the World Wide Web
Xerox: www.xerox.com

As indicated in the Feature Story, making adjustments is necessary to avoid misstatement of revenues and expenses such as those at Xerox and WorldCom. In this chapter we introduce you to the accrual accounting concepts that make such adjustments possible.

The organization and content of the chapter are as follows.

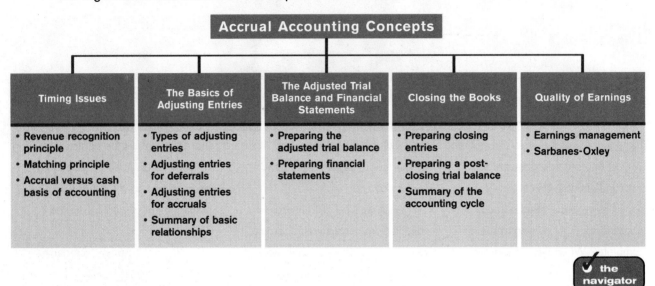

Timing Issues

Helpful Hint An accounting time period that is one year long is called a fiscal year.

Most businesses need immediate feedback about how well they are doing. For example, management usually wants monthly reports on financial results, most large corporations are required to present quarterly and annual financial statements to stockholders, and the Internal Revenue Service requires all businesses to file annual tax returns. **Accounting divides the economic life of a business into artificial time periods.** As indicated in Chapter 2, this is the time period assumption. **Accounting time periods are generally a month, a quarter, or a year.**

Many business transactions affect more than one of these arbitrary time periods. For example, a new building purchased by Citigroup or a new airplane purchased by Delta Air Lines will be used for many years. It doesn't make sense to expense the full cost of the building or the airplane at the time of purchase because each will be used for many subsequent periods. Instead, we determine the impact of each transaction on specific accounting periods.

Determining the amount of revenues and expenses to report in a given accounting period can be difficult. Proper reporting requires an understanding of the nature of the company's business. Two principles are used as guidelines: the revenue recognition principle and the matching principle.

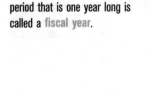

Revenue Recognition

Service performed

Customer requests service — At time cash received

Revenue should be recognized in the accounting period in which it is earned (generally when service is performed).

THE REVENUE RECOGNITION PRINCIPLE

The revenue recognition principle requires that companies recognize revenue in the accounting period **in which it is earned**. In a service company, revenue is considered to be earned at the time the service is performed. To illustrate, assume Conrad Dry Cleaners cleans clothing on June 30, but customers do not claim and pay for their clothes until the first week of July. Under the revenue recognition principle, Conrad earns revenue in June when it performs the service, not in July when it receives the cash. At June 30 Conrad would report a receivable on its balance sheet and revenue in its income statement for the service performed. The journal entries for June and July would be as follows.

June	Accounts Receivable	xxx	
	Service Revenue		xxx
July	Cash	xxx	
	Accounts Receivable		xxx

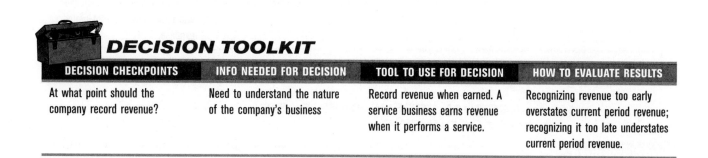

DECISION TOOLKIT

DECISION CHECKPOINTS	INFO NEEDED FOR DECISION	TOOL TO USE FOR DECISION	HOW TO EVALUATE RESULTS
At what point should the company record revenue?	Need to understand the nature of the company's business	Record revenue when earned. A service business earns revenue when it performs a service.	Recognizing revenue too early overstates current period revenue; recognizing it too late understates current period revenue.

THE MATCHING PRINCIPLE

In recognizing expenses, a simple rule is followed: "Let the expenses follow the revenues." Thus, expense recognition is tied to revenue recognition. Applied to the preceding example, this means that the salary expense Conrad incurred in performing the cleaning service on June 30 should be reported in the same period in which it recognizes the service revenue. The critical issue in expense recognition is determining when the expense makes its contribution to revenue. This may or may not be the same period in which the expense is paid. If Conrad does not pay the salary incurred on June 30 until July, it would report salaries payable on its June 30 balance sheet.

The practice of expense recognition is referred to as the **matching principle** because it dictates that efforts (expenses) be matched with accomplishments (revenues). Illustration 4-1 shows these relationships.

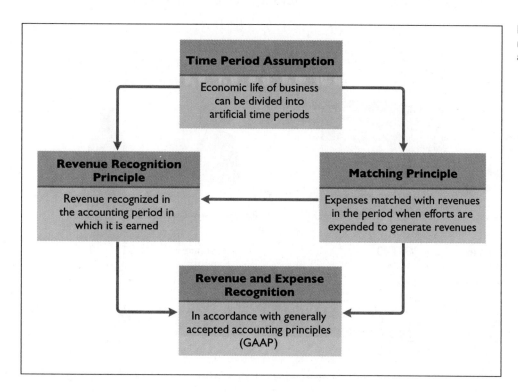

Illustration 4-1 GAAP relationships in revenue and expense recognition

DECISION TOOLKIT

DECISION CHECKPOINTS	INFO NEEDED FOR DECISION	TOOL TO USE FOR DECISION	HOW TO EVALUATE RESULTS
At what point should the company record expenses?	Need to understand the nature of the company's business	Expenses should "follow" revenues—that is, match the effort (expense) with the result (revenue).	Recognizing expenses too early overstates current period expense; recognizing them too late understates current period expense.

ACCRUAL VERSUS CASH BASIS OF ACCOUNTING

Accrual-basis accounting means that transactions that change a company's financial statements are recorded **in the periods in which the events occur**, even if cash was not exchanged. For example, using the accrual basis means that companies recognize revenues **when earned** (the revenue recognition principle), even if cash was not received. **Likewise, under the accrual basis, companies recognize expenses when incurred** (the matching principle), even if cash was not paid.

An alternative to the accrual basis is the cash basis. Under **cash-basis accounting, companies record revenue only when cash is received. They record expense only when cash is paid. The cash basis of accounting is prohibited under generally accepted accounting principles.** Why? Because it does not record revenue when earned, thus violating the revenue recognition principle. Similarly, it does not record expenses when incurred, which violates the matching principle.

International Note Although different accounting standards are often used by companies in other countries, the accrual basis of accounting is central to all of these standards.

Illustration 4-2 compares accrual-based numbers and cash-based numbers. Suppose that Fresh Colors paints a large building in 2009. In 2009 it incurs and pays total expenses (salaries and paint costs) of $50,000. It bills the customer $80,000, but does not receive payment until 2010. On an accrual basis, Fresh Colors reports $80,000 of revenue during 2009 because that is when it is earned.

Illustration 4-2 Accrual versus cash basis accounting

	2009	2010
Activity	Purchased paint, painted building, paid employees	Received payment for work done in 2009
Accrual basis	Revenue $80,000 Expense 50,000 Net income $30,000	Revenue $ 0 Expense 0 Net income $ 0
Cash basis	Revenue $ 0 Expense 50,000 Net loss $(50,000)	Revenue $80,000 Expense 0 Net income $80,000

The company matches expenses of $50,000 to the $80,000 of revenue. Thus, 2009 net income is $30,000 ($80,000 − $50,000). The $30,000 of net income reported for 2009 indicates the profitability of Fresh Colors' efforts during that period.

If, instead, Fresh Colors were to use cash-basis accounting, it would report $50,000 of expenses in 2009 and $80,000 of revenues during 2010. As shown in Illustration 4-2, it would report a loss of $50,000 in 2009 and would report net income of $80,000 in 2010. Clearly, the cash-basis measures are misleading because the financial performance of the company would be misstated for both 2009 and 2010.

Ethics Insight

Allegations of abuse of the revenue recognition principle have become all too common in recent years. For example, it was alleged that Krispy Kreme sometimes doubled the number of doughnuts shipped to wholesale customers at the end of a quarter to boost quarterly results. The customers shipped the unsold doughnuts back after the beginning of the next quarter for a refund. Conversely, Computer Associates International was accused of backdating sales—that is, saying that a sale that occurred at the beginning of one quarter occurred at the end of the previous quarter in order to achieve the previous quarter's sales targets.

 What motivates sales executives and finance and accounting executives to participate in activities that result in inaccurate reporting of revenues?

The Basics of Adjusting Entries

In order for revenues to be recorded in the period in which they are earned, and for expenses to be recognized in the period in which they are incurred, companies make adjusting entries. **Adjusting entries ensure that the revenue recognition and matching principles are followed.**

Adjusting entries are necessary because the **trial balance**—the first pulling together of the transaction data—may not contain up-to-date and complete data. This is true for several reasons:

1. Some events are not recorded daily because it is not efficient to do so. Examples are the use of supplies and the earning of wages by employees.

2. Some costs are not recorded during the accounting period because these costs expire with the passage of time rather than as a result of recurring daily transactions. Examples are charges related to the use of buildings and equipment, rent, and insurance.

3. Some items may be unrecorded. An example is a utility service bill that will not be received until the next accounting period.

Adjusting entries are required every time a company prepares financial statements. The company analyzes each account in the trial balance to determine whether it is complete and up to date for financial statement purposes. **Every adjusting entry will include one income statement account and one balance sheet account.**

> **study objective 3**
>
> Explain why adjusting entries are needed, and identify the major types of adjusting entries.

International Note Recording correct financial information requires good internal control. Internal controls are a system of checks and balances designed to detect and prevent fraud and errors. The Sarbanes-Oxley Act requires U.S. companies to enhance their systems of internal control. However, many foreign companies do not have this requirement, and some U.S. companies believe that not having it gives foreign firms unfair advantage in the capital markets.

TYPES OF ADJUSTING ENTRIES

Adjusting entries are classified as either deferrals or accruals. As Illustration 4-3 (next page) shows, each of these classes has two subcategories.

Illustration 4-3
Categories of adjusting
entries

Deferrals:

1. Prepaid expenses: Expenses paid in cash and recorded as assets before they are used or consumed.
2. Unearned revenues: Cash received and recorded as liabilities before revenue is earned.

Accruals:

1. Accrued revenues: Revenues earned but not yet received in cash or recorded.
2. Accrued expenses: Expenses incurred but not yet paid in cash or recorded.

Subsequent sections give examples of each type of adjustment. Each example is based on the October 31 trial balance of Sierra Corporation, from Chapter 3, reproduced in Illustration 4-4. Note that Retained Earnings, with a zero balance, has been added to this trial balance. We will explain its use later.

Illustration 4-4   Trial balance

| SIERRA CORPORATION | | |
| Trial Balance | | |
October 31, 2010		
	Debit	**Credit**
Cash	$15,200	
Advertising Supplies	2,500	
Prepaid Insurance	600	
Office Equipment	5,000	
Notes Payable		$ 5,000
Accounts Payable		2,500
Unearned Service Revenue		1,200
Common Stock		10,000
Retained Earnings		0
Dividends	500	
Service Revenue		10,000
Salaries Expense	4,000	
Rent Expense	900	
	$28,700	$28,700

We assume that Sierra Corporation uses an accounting period of one month. Thus, monthly adjusting entries are made. The entries are dated October 31.

ADJUSTING ENTRIES FOR DEFERRALS

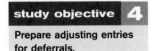

study objective 4

Prepare adjusting entries for deferrals.

To defer means to postpone or delay. Deferrals are costs or revenues that are recognized at a date later than the point when cash was originally exchanged. Companies make adjusting entries for deferrals to record the portion of the deferred item that was incurred as an expense or earned as revenue during the current accounting period. The two types of deferrals are prepaid expenses and unearned revenues.

Prepaid Expenses

Companies record payments of expenses that will benefit more than one accounting period as assets called prepaid expenses or prepayments. When expenses are prepaid, an asset account is increased (debited) to show the service or benefit that the company will receive in the future. Examples of common prepayments are insurance, supplies, advertising, and rent. In addition, companies make prepayments when they purchase buildings and equipment.

Prepaid expenses are costs that expire either with the passage of time (e.g., rent and insurance) **or through use** (e.g., supplies). The expiration of these costs does not require daily entries, which would be impractical and unnecessary. Accordingly, companies postpone the recognition of such cost expirations until they prepare financial statements. At each statement date, they make adjusting entries to record the expenses applicable to the current accounting period and to show the remaining amounts in the asset accounts.

Prior to adjustment, assets are overstated and expenses are understated. Therefore, as shown in Illustration 4-5, **an adjusting entry for prepaid expenses results in an increase (a debit) to an expense account and a decrease (a credit) to an asset account**.

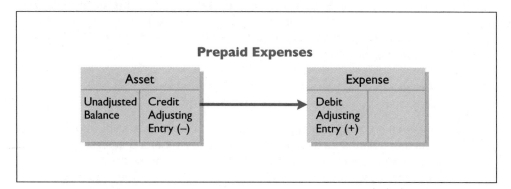

Illustration 4-5 Adjusting entries for prepaid expenses

Let's look in more detail at some specific types of prepaid expenses, beginning with supplies.

SUPPLIES. The purchase of supplies, such as paper and envelopes, results in an increase (a debit) to an asset account. During the accounting period, the company uses supplies. Rather than record supplies expense as the supplies are used, companies recognize supplies expense at the **end** of the accounting period. At the end of the accounting period the company counts the remaining supplies. The difference between the unadjusted balance in the Supplies (asset) account and the actual cost of supplies on hand represents the supplies used (an expense) for that period.

Recall from Chapter 3 that Sierra Corporation purchased advertising supplies costing $2,500 on October 5. Sierra recorded the purchase by increasing (debiting) the asset Advertising Supplies. This account shows a balance of $2,500 in the October 31 trial balance. An inventory count at the close of business on October 31 reveals that $1,000 of supplies are still on hand. Thus, the cost of supplies used is $1,500 ($2,500 − $1,000). This use of supplies decreases an asset, Advertising Supplies. It also decreases stockholders' equity by increasing an expense account, Advertising Supplies Expense. The use of supplies affects the accounting equation in the following way.

Supplies

Oct.5

Supplies purchased;
record asset

Oct.31
Supplies used;
record supplies expense

Assets	=	Liabilities	+	Stockholders' Equity
−$1,500				−$1,500

Thus, Sierra makes the following adjusting entry:

Oct. 31	Advertising Supplies Expense	1,500	
	Advertising Supplies		1,500
	(To record supplies used)		

After the adjusting entry is posted, the accounts, in T account form, appear as in Illustration 4-6.

Illustration 4-6 Supplies accounts after adjustment

Advertising Supplies		Advertising Supplies Expense	
Oct. 5 2,500	Oct. 31 **Adj. 1,500**	Oct. 31 **Adj. 1,500**	
Oct. 31 Bal. 1,000		Oct. 31 Bal. 1,500	

The asset account Advertising Supplies now shows a balance of $1,000, which is equal to the cost of supplies on hand at the statement date. In addition, Advertising Supplies Expense shows a balance of $1,500, which equals the cost of supplies used in October. **If Sierra does not make the adjusting entry, October expenses will be understated and net income overstated by $1,500. Moreover, both assets and stockholders' equity will be overstated by $1,500 on the October 31 balance sheet.**

Accounting Across the Organization

The method of accounting for advertising costs affects sales and marketing executives. In the past, companies sometimes recorded as assets the costs of media advertising for burgers, bleaches, athletic shoes, and such products and expensed those costs in subsequent periods as sales took place. The reasoning behind this treatment was that long ad campaigns provided benefits over multiple accounting periods. Today the accounting profession no longer allows this treatment because it was decided that the benefits were too difficult to measure.

Instead, companies now must expense advertising costs when the advertising takes place. The issue is important because the outlays for advertising can be substantial. Recent big spenders: Coca-Cola spent $2.8 billion, PepsiCo., Inc. $1.9 billion, Nike, Inc. $1.9 billion, and Limited Brands $519 million.

? Why might the new accounting method cause companies sometimes to spend less on advertising?

Insurance

Oct.4

Insurance purchased; record asset

Insurance Policy			
Oct $50	Nov $50	Dec $50	Jan $50
Feb $50	March $50	April $50	May $50
June $50	July $50	Aug $50	Sept $50
1 YEAR $600			

Oct.31
    Insurance expired;
record insurance expense

INSURANCE. Companies purchase insurance to protect themselves from losses due to fire, theft, and unforeseen events. Insurance must be paid in advance, often for more than one year. The cost of insurance (premiums) paid in advance is recorded as an increase (debit) in the asset account Prepaid Insurance. At the financial statement date companies increase (debit) Insurance Expense and decrease (credit) Prepaid Insurance for the cost of insurance that has expired during the period.

On October 4 Sierra Corporation paid $600 for a one-year fire insurance policy. Coverage began on October 1. Sierra recorded the payment by increasing (debiting) Prepaid Insurance. This account shows a balance of $600 in the October 31 trial balance. Insurance of $50 ($600 ÷ 12) expires each month. The expiration of prepaid insurance decreases an asset, Prepaid Insurance. It also decreases stockholders' equity by increasing an expense account, Insurance Expense. The expiration of Prepaid Insurance affects the accounting equation in October (and in each of the next 11 months) in the following way.

Assets	=	Liabilities	+	Stockholders' Equity
−$50				−$50

Thus, the following adjusting entry is made.

Oct. 31	Insurance Expense		50	
	Prepaid Insurance			50
	(To record insurance expired)			

After Sierra posts the adjusting entry, the accounts appear as in Illustration 4-7.

Prepaid Insurance				Insurance Expense		
Oct. 4	600	Oct. 31	Adj. 50	Oct. 31	Adj. 50	
Oct. 31	Bal. 550			Oct. 31	Bal. 50	

Illustration 4-7 Insurance accounts after adjustment

The asset Prepaid Insurance shows a balance of $550, which represents the unexpired cost for the remaining 11 months of coverage. At the same time the balance in Insurance Expense equals the insurance cost that expired in October. If Sierra does not make this adjustment, October expenses are understated by $50 and net income is overstated by $50. Moreover, as the accounting equation shows, both assets and stockholders' equity will be overstated by $50 on the October 31 balance sheet.

DEPRECIATION. A company typically owns a variety of assets that have long lives, such as buildings, equipment, and motor vehicles. The period of service is referred to as the useful life of the asset. Because a building is expected to provide service for many years, it is recorded as an asset, rather than an expense, on the date it is acquired. As explained in Chapter 2, companies record such assets **at cost**, as required by the cost principle. To follow the matching principle, companies allocate a portion of this cost as an expense during each period of the asset's useful life. Depreciation is the process of allocating the cost of an asset to expense over its useful life.

Need for adjustment.   The acquisition of long-lived assets is essentially a long-term prepayment for the use of an asset. An adjusting entry for depreciation is needed to recognize the cost that has been used (an expense) during the period and to report the unused cost (an asset) at the end of the period. One very important point to understand: **Depreciation is an allocation concept, not a valuation concept.** That is, depreciation **allocates an asset's cost to the periods in which it is used. Depreciation does not attempt to report the actual change in the value of the asset.**

For Sierra Corporation, assume that depreciation on the office equipment is $480 a year, or $40 per month. Rather than decrease (credit) the asset account directly, Sierra instead credits Accumulated Depreciation. Accumulated Depreciation is called a contra asset account. Such an account is offset against an asset account on the balance sheet. Thus, the Accumulated Depreciation—Office Equipment account offsets the asset Office Equipment. This account keeps track of the total amount of depreciation expense taken over the life of the asset. To keep the accounting equation in balance, Sierra decreases stockholders' equity by increasing an expense account, Depreciation Expense. Depreciation affects the accounting equation in the following way.

Depreciation

Oct.2

Office equipment purchased; record asset

Office Equipment			
Oct	Nov	Dec	Jan
$40	$40	$40	$40
Feb	March	April	May
$40	$40	$40	$40
June	July	Aug	Sept
$40	$40	$40	$40
Depreciation = $480/year			

Oct.31
Depreciation recognized; record depreciation expense

Assets	=	Liabilities	+	Stockholders' Equity
−$40				−$40

Sierra recognizes depreciation for October by this adjusting entry.

Oct. 31	Depreciation Expense	40	
	Accumulated Depreciation—Office		
	Equipment		40
	(To record monthly depreciation)		

After the company posts the adjusting entry, the accounts appear as in Illustration 4-8.

Illustration 4-8 Accounts after adjustment for depreciation

Office Equipment

Oct. 2	5,000	
Oct. 31	Bal. 5,000	

Accumulated Depreciation— Office Equipment

		Oct. 31	**Adj. 40**
		Oct. 31	**Bal. 40**

Depreciation Expense

Oct. 31	**Adj. 40**	
Oct. 31	**Bal. 40**	

The balance in the Accumulated Depreciation account will increase $40 each month, and the balance in Office Equipment remains $5,000.

Helpful Hint All contra accounts have increases, decreases, and normal balances **opposite to** the account to which they relate.

Statement presentation. As noted above, Accumulated Depreciation—Office Equipment is a contra asset account. It is offset against Office Equipment on the balance sheet. The normal balance of a contra asset account is a credit. A theoretical alternative to using a contra asset account would be to decrease (credit) the asset account by the amount of depreciation each period. But using the contra account is preferable for a simple reason: it discloses *both* the original cost of the equipment *and* the total cost that has expired to date. Thus, in the balance sheet, Sierra deducts Accumulated Depreciation—Office Equipment from the related asset account as shown in Illustration 4-9.

Illustration 4-9 Balance sheet presentation of accumulated depreciation

Office equipment	$ 5,000
Less: Accumulated depreciation—office equipment	40
	$4,960

Alternative Terminology Book value is also referred to as *carrying value.*

Book value is the difference between the cost of any depreciable asset and its related accumulated depreciation. In Illustration 4-9, the book value of the equipment at the balance sheet date is $4,960. The book value and the market value of the asset are generally two different values. As noted earlier, **the purpose of depreciation is not valuation, but a means of cost allocation.**

Depreciation expense identifies the portion of an asset's cost that expired during the period (in this case, in October). The accounting equation shows that without this adjusting entry, total assets, total stockholders' equity, and net income are overstated by $40 and depreciation expense is understated by $40.

Illustration 4-10 summarizes the accounting for prepaid expenses.

ACCOUNTING FOR PREPAID EXPENSES			
Examples	**Reason for Adjustment**	**Accounts Before Adjustment**	**Adjusting Entry**
Insurance, supplies, advertising, rent, depreciation	Prepaid expenses recorded in asset accounts have been used.	Assets overstated. Expenses understated.	Dr. Expenses Cr. Assets

Illustration 4-10
Accounting for prepaid expenses

Unearned Revenues

Companies record cash received before revenue is earned by increasing (crediting) a liability account called **unearned revenues**. Items like rent, magazine subscriptions, and customer deposits for future service may result in unearned revenues. Airlines such as United, American, and Delta, for instance, treat receipts from the sale of tickets as unearned revenue until the flight service is provided.

Unearned revenues are the opposite of prepaid expenses. Indeed, unearned revenue on the books of one company is likely to be a prepayment on the books of the company that has made the advance payment. For example, if identical accounting periods are assumed, a landlord will have unearned rent revenue when a tenant has prepaid rent.

When a company receives payment for services to be provided in a future accounting period, it increases (credits) an unearned revenue (a liability) account to recognize the liability that exists. The company subsequently earns revenues by providing service. During the accounting period it is not practical to make daily entries as the company earns the revenue. Instead, we delay recognition of earned revenue until the adjustment process. Then the company makes an adjusting entry to record the revenue earned during the period and to show the liability that remains at the end of the accounting period. Typically, prior to adjustment, liabilities are overstated and revenues are understated. Therefore, as shown in Illustration 4-11, **the adjusting entry for unearned revenues results in a decrease (a debit) to a liability account and an increase (a credit) to a revenue account.**

Unearned Revenues

Oct.2 Thank you in advance for your work. I will finish by Dec. 31 ~$1,200

Cash is received in advance; liability is recorded

Oct.31 Some service has been provided; some revenue is recorded

Illustration 4-11
Adjusting entries for unearned revenues

Unearned Revenues

Liability — Debit Adjusting Entry (−) | Unadjusted Balance

Revenue — Credit Adjusting Entry (+)

Sierra Corporation received $1,200 on October 2 from R. Knox for advertising services expected to be completed by December 31. Sierra credited the payment to Unearned Service Revenue, and this liability account shows a balance of $1,200 in the October 31 trial balance. From an evaluation of the work Sierra performed for Knox during October, the company determines that it has earned $400 in October. The liability (Unearned Service Revenue) is therefore decreased, and stockholders' equity (Service Revenue) is increased. The accounting equation is affected in the following way.

Assets	=	Liabilities	+	Stockholders' Equity
		−$400		+$400

Thus, Sierra makes the following adjusting entry.

Oct. 31	Unearned Service Revenue	400	
	Service Revenue		400
	(To record revenue earned)		

After the company posts the adjusting entry, the accounts appear as in Illustration 4-12.

Illustration 4-12 Service revenue accounts after adjustment

Unearned Service Revenue				Service Revenue		
Oct. 31 Adj. 400	Oct. 2	1,200			Oct. 3	10,000
					31 Adj.	400
	Oct. 31 Bal. 800				Oct. 31 Bal. 10,400	

The liability Unearned Service Revenue now shows a balance of $800. That amount represents the remaining advertising services expected to be performed in the future. At the same time, Service Revenue shows total revenue earned in October of $10,400. **Without this adjustment, revenues and net income are understated by $400 in the income statement. Moreover, liabilities are overstated and stockholders' equity is understated by $400 on the October 31 balance sheet.**

Illustration 4-13 summarizes the accounting for unearned revenues.

Illustration 4-13 Accounting for unearned revenues

ACCOUNTING FOR UNEARNED REVENUES			
Examples	**Reason for Adjustment**	**Accounts Before Adjustment**	**Adjusting Entry**
Rent, magazine subscriptions, customer deposits for future service	Unearned revenues recorded in liability accounts have been earned.	Liabilities overstated. Revenues understated.	Dr. Liabilities Cr. Revenues

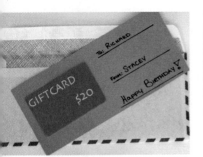

Accounting Across the Organization

Those of you who are marketing majors (and even most of you who are not) know that gift cards are among the hottest marketing tools in merchandising today. Customers purchase gift cards and give them to someone for later use. In a recent year gift-card sales topped $95 billion.

Although these programs are popular with marketing executives, they create accounting questions. Should revenue be recorded at the time the gift card is sold, or when it is exercised? How should expired gift cards be accounted for? In its 2007 balance sheet Best Buy reported unearned revenue related to gift cards of $496 million.

Source: Robert Berner, "Gift Cards: No Gift to Investors," *Business Week* (March 14, 2005), p. 86.

 Suppose that Robert Jones purchases a $100 gift card at Best Buy on December 24, 2009, and gives it to his wife, Mary Jones, on December 25, 2009. On January 3, 2010, Mary uses the card to purchase $100 worth of CDs. When do you think Best Buy should recognize revenue and why?

before you go on...

Do it! The ledger of Hammond, Inc., on March 31, 2010, includes these selected accounts before adjusting entries are prepared.

ADJUSTING ENTRIES FOR DEFERRALS

	Debit	Credit
Prepaid Insurance	$ 3,600	
Office Supplies	2,800	
Office Equipment	25,000	
Accumulated Depreciation—Office Equipment		$5,000
Unearned Service Revenue		9,200

An analysis of the accounts shows the following.

1. Insurance expires at the rate of $100 per month.
2. Supplies on hand total $800.
3. The office equipment depreciates $200 a month.
4. One-half of the unearned service revenue was earned in March.

Prepare the adjusting entries for the month of March.

Solution

1. Insurance Expense	100	
Prepaid Insurance		100
(To record insurance expired)		
2. Office Supplies Expense	2,000	
Office Supplies		2,000
(To record supplies used)		
3. Depreciation Expense	200	
Accumulated Depreciation—Office Equipment		200
(To record monthly depreciation)		
4. Unearned Service Revenue	4,600	
Service Revenue		4,600
(To record revenue earned)		

Action Plan

- Make adjusting entries at the end of the period for revenues earned and expenses incurred in the period.
- Don't forget to make adjusting entries for prepayments. Failure to adjust for prepayments leads to overstatement of the asset or liability and understatement of the related expense or revenue.

ADJUSTING ENTRIES FOR ACCRUALS

The second category of adjusting entries is **accruals**. Prior to an accrual adjustment, the revenue account (and the related asset account) or the expense account (and the related liability account) are understated. Thus, the adjusting entry for accruals will **increase both a balance sheet and an income statement account**.

Accrued Revenues

Revenues earned but not yet recorded at the statement date are accrued revenues. Accrued revenues may accumulate (accrue) with the passing of time, as in the case of interest revenue. These are unrecorded because the earning of interest does not involve daily transactions. Companies do not record interest revenue on a daily basis because it is often impractical to do so. Accrued revenues also may result from services that have been performed but not yet billed nor collected, as in the case of commissions and fees. These may be unrecorded because only a portion of the total service has been provided and the clients won't be billed until the service has been completed.

An adjusting entry records the receivable that exists at the balance sheet date and the revenue earned during the period. Prior to adjustment both assets and

study objective 5
Prepare adjusting entries for accruals.

Accrued Revenues

Oct.31

My fee is $200

Revenue and receivable are recorded for unbilled services

Nov.10

Cash is received; receivable is reduced

revenues are understated. As shown in Illustration 4-14, **an adjusting entry for accrued revenues results in an increase (a debit) to an asset account and an increase (a credit) to a revenue account**.

Helpful Hint For accruals, there may have been no prior entry, and the accounts requiring adjustment may both have zero balances prior to adjustment.

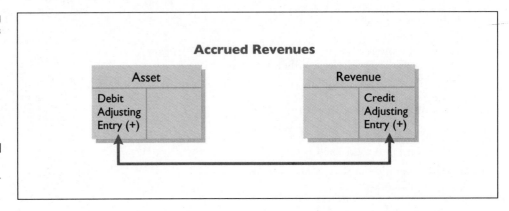

Ethics Note Computer Associates International **was accused of** backdating sales–that is, saying that a sale that occurred at the beginning of one quarter occurred at the end of the previous quarter, in order to achieve the previous quarter's sales targets.

In October Sierra Corporation earned $200 for advertising services that were not billed to clients on or before October 31. Because these services are not billed, they are not recorded. The accrual of unrecorded service revenue increases an asset account, Accounts Receivable. It also increases stockholders' equity by increasing a revenue account, Service Revenue. The accrual of unrecorded service revenue affects the accounting equation in the following way.

Assets	=	Liabilities	+	Stockholders' Equity
+$200				+$200

Thus, Sierra makes the following adjusting entry.

Oct. 31	Accounts Receivable	200	
	Service Revenue		200
	(To record revenue earned)		

After the company posts the adjusting entry, the accounts appear as in Illustration 4-15.

Illustration 4-15
Receivable and revenue accounts after accrual adjustments

Accounts Receivable		Service Revenue	
Oct. 31 Adj. 200		Oct. 3 10,000	
		31 400	
		31 Adj. 200	
Oct. 31 Bal. 200		Oct. 31 Bal. 10,600	

The asset Accounts Receivable shows that clients owe Sierra $200 at the balance sheet date. The balance of $10,600 in Service Revenue represents the total revenue Sierra earned during the month ($10,000 + $400 + $200). **Without the adjusting entry, assets and stockholders' equity on the balance sheet and revenues and net income on the income statement are understated.**

On November 10, Sierra receives cash of $200 for the services performed in October and makes the following entry.

Nov. 10	Cash	200	
	Accounts Receivable		200
	(To record cash collected on account)		

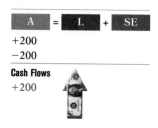

A = L + SE
+200
−200

Cash Flows
+200

Equation analyses summarize the effects of transactions on the three elements of the accounting equation, as well as the effect on cash flows.

The company records the collection of the receivables by a debit (increase) to Cash and a credit (decrease) to Accounts Receivable.

Illustration 4-16 summarizes the accounting for accrued revenues.

ACCOUNTING FOR ACCRUED REVENUES

Examples	Reason for Adjustment	Accounts Before Adjustment	Adjusting Entry
Interest, rent, services performed but not collected	Revenues have been earned but not yet received in cash or recorded.	Assets understated. Revenues understated.	Dr. Assets Cr. Revenues

Illustration 4-16
Accounting for accrued revenues

Accrued Expenses

Expenses incurred but not yet paid or recorded at the statement date are called accrued expenses. Interest, taxes, and salaries are common examples of accrued expenses.

Companies make adjustments for accrued expenses to record the obligations that exist at the balance sheet date and to recognize the expenses that apply to the current accounting period. Prior to adjustment, both liabilities and expenses are understated. Therefore, **an adjusting entry for accrued expenses results in an increase (a debit) to an expense account and an increase (a credit) to a liability account.**

Ethics Note A report released by Fannie Mae's board of directors stated that improper adjusting entries at the mortgage-finance company resulted in delayed recognition of expenses caused by interest-rate changes. The motivation for such accounting apparently was the desire to hit earnings estimates.

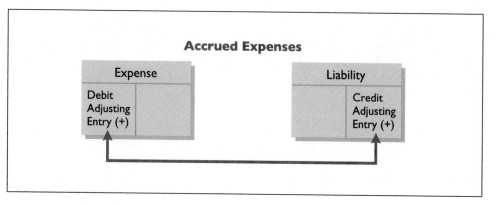

Accrued Expenses

Expense
Debit Adjusting Entry (+)

Liability
Credit Adjusting Entry (+)

Illustration 4-17
Adjusting entries for accrued expenses

Let's look in more detail at some specific types of accrued expenses, beginning with accrued interest.

ACCRUED INTEREST. Sierra Corporation signed a three-month note payable in the amount of $5,000 on October 1. The note requires Sierra to pay interest at an annual rate of 12%.

The amount of the interest recorded is determined by three factors: (1) the face value of the note, (2) the interest rate, which is always expressed as an annual rate, and (3) the length of time the note is outstanding. For Sierra, the total interest due on the $5,000 note at its maturity date three months in the future is $150 ($5,000 × 12% × $\frac{3}{12}$), or $50 for one month. Illustration 4-18 shows the formula for computing interest and its application to Sierra Corporation for the month of October.

Illustration 4-18 Formula for computing interest

Face Value of Note	×	Annual Interest Rate	×	Time in Terms of One Year	=	Interest
$5,000	×	12%	×	$\frac{1}{12}$	=	$50

Helpful Hint In computing interest, we express the time period as a fraction of a year.

The accrual of interest at October 31 increases a liability account, Interest Payable. It also decreases stockholders' equity by increasing an expense account, Interest Expense. The accrual of interest at October 31 affects the accounting equation in the following way.

Assets	=	Liabilities	+	Stockholders' Equity
		+$50		−$50

Thus, Sierra makes an accrued expense adjusting entry at October 31 as follows.

Oct. 31	Interest Expense	50	
	Interest Payable		50
	(To record interest on notes payable)		

After the company posts this adjusting entry, the accounts appear as in Illustration 4-19.

Illustration 4-19 Interest accounts after adjustment

Interest Expense		Interest Payable	
Oct. 31 Adj. 50			Oct. 31 Adj. 50
Oct. 31 Bal. 50			Oct. 31 Bal. 50

Interest Expense shows the interest charges for the month of October. Interest Payable shows the amount of interest the company owes at the statement date. Sierra will not pay the interest until the note comes due at the end of three months. Companies use the Interest Payable account, instead of crediting Notes Payable, to disclose the two different types of obligations—interest and principal—in the accounts and statements. **Without this adjusting entry, liabilities and interest expense are understated, and net income and stockholders' equity are overstated.**

ACCRUED SALARIES. Companies pay for some types of expenses, such as employee salaries and commissions, after the services have been performed. Sierra Corporation last paid salaries on October 26; the next payment of salaries will not occur until November 9. As the calendar in Illustration 4-20 shows, three working days remain in October (October 29–31).

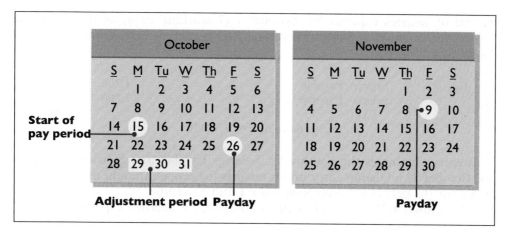

Illustration 4-20 Calendar showing Sierra Corporation's pay periods

At October 31 the salaries for these three days represent an accrued expense and a related liability to Sierra. The employees receive total salaries of $2,000 for a five-day work week, or $400 per day. Thus, accrued salaries at October 31 are $1,200 ($400 × 3). This accrual increases a liability, Salaries Payable. It also decreases stockholders' equity by increasing an expense account, Salaries Expense. The accrual of salaries affects the accounting equation in the following way.

Assets	=	Liabilities	+	Stockholders' Equity
		+$1,200		−$1,200

Thus, Sierra makes the following adjusting entry:

Oct. 31	Salaries Expense	1,200	
	Salaries Payable		1,200
	(To record accrued salaries)		

After the company posts this adjusting entry, the accounts are as shown in Illustration 4-21.

Illustration 4-21 Salary accounts after adjustment

Salaries Expense			Salaries Payable	
Oct. 26	4,000			Oct. 31 Adj. 1,200
31 Adj. 1,200				
Oct. 31 Bal. 5,200				Oct. 31 Bal. 1,200

After this adjustment, the balance in Salaries Expense of $5,200 (13 days × $400) is the actual salary expense for October. The balance in Salaries Payable of $1,200 is the amount of the liability for salaries Sierra owes as of October 31. **Without the $1,200 adjustment for salaries, Sierra's expenses are understated $1,200 and its liabilities are understated $1,200.**

Sierra Corporation pays salaries every two weeks. Consequently, the next payday is November 9, when the company will again pay total salaries of $4,000. The payment consists of $1,200 of salaries payable at October 31 plus

$2,800 of salaries expense for November (7 working days, as shown in the November calendar × $400). Therefore, Sierra makes the following entry on November 9.

Nov. 9	Salaries Payable	1,200	
	Salaries Expense	2,800	
	Cash		4,000
	(To record November 9 payroll)		

This entry eliminates the liability for Salaries Payable that Sierra recorded in the October 31 adjusting entry, and it records the proper amount of Salaries Expense for the period between November 1 and November 9.

Illustration 4-22 summarizes the accounting for accrued expenses.

Illustration 4-22
Accounting for accrued expenses

ACCOUNTING FOR ACCRUED EXPENSES			
Examples	**Reason for Adjustment**	**Accounts Before Adjustment**	**Adjusting Entry**
Interest, rent, salaries	Expenses have been incurred but not yet paid in cash or recorded.	Expenses understated. Liabilities understated.	Dr. Expenses Cr. Liabilities

---

before you go on...

ADJUSTING ENTRIES FOR ACCRUALS

Do it! Micro Computer Services Inc. began operations on August 1, 2010. At the end of August 2010, management attempted to prepare monthly financial statements. The following information relates to August.

1. At August 31 the company owed its employees $800 in salaries that will be paid on September 1.

2. On August 1 the company borrowed $30,000 from a local bank on a 15-year mortgage. The annual interest rate is 10%.

3. Revenue earned but unrecorded for August totaled $1,100.

Prepare the adjusting entries needed at August 31, 2010.

Action Plan

• Make adjusting entries at the end of the period for revenues earned and expenses incurred in the period.

• Don't forget to make adjusting entries for accruals. Adjusting entries for accruals will increase both a balance sheet and an income statement account.

Solution

1. Salaries Expense	800	
Salaries Payable		800
(To record accrued salaries)		
2. Interest Expense	250	
Interest Payable		250
(To record accrued interest:		
$30,000 × 10% × $\frac{1}{12}$ = $250)		
3. Accounts Receivable	1,100	
Service Revenue		1,100
(To record revenue earned)		

SUMMARY OF BASIC RELATIONSHIPS

Illustration 4-23 summarizes the four basic types of adjusting entries. Take some time to study and analyze the adjusting entries. Be sure to note that **each adjusting entry affects one balance sheet account and one income statement account**.

Type of Adjustment	Accounts Before Adjustment	Adjusting Entry
Prepaid expenses	Assets overstated Expenses understated	Dr. Expenses Cr. Assets
Unearned revenues	Liabilities overstated Revenues understated	Dr. Liabilities Cr. Revenues
Accrued revenues	Assets understated Revenues understated	Dr. Assets Cr. Revenues
Accrued expenses	Expenses understated Liabilities understated	Dr. Expenses Cr. Liabilities

Illustration 4-23
Summary of adjusting entries

Illustrations 4-24 and 4-25 (page 180) show the journalizing and posting of adjusting entries for Sierra Corporation on October 31. When reviewing the general ledger in Illustration 4-25, note that for learning purposes, we have highlighted the adjustments in color.

GENERAL JOURNAL

Date	Account Titles and Explanation	Debit	Credit
2010	Adjusting Entries		

Oct. 31	Advertising Supplies Expense
	    Advertising Supplies
	      (To record supplies used)
		1,500	1,500

31	Insurance Expense
	    Prepaid Insurance
	      (To record insurance expired)
		50	50

31	Depreciation Expense
	    Accumulated Depreciation—Office Equipment
	      (To record monthly depreciation)
		40	40

31	Unearned Service Revenue
	    Service Revenue
	      (To record revenue earned)
		400	400

31	Accounts Receivable
	    Service Revenue
	      (To record revenue earned)
		200	200

31	Interest Expense
	    Interest Payable
	      (To record interest on notes payable)
		50	50

31	Salaries Expense
	    Salaries Payable
	      (To record accrued salaries)
		1,200	1,200

Illustration 4-24 General journal showing adjusting entries

Illustration 4-25 General ledger after adjustments

GENERAL LEDGER

Cash

Oct.	1	10,000	Oct.	2	5,000
	1	5,000		3	900
	2	1,200		4	600
	3	10,000		20	500
				26	4,000

Oct. 31 Bal. 15,200

Accounts Receivable

| Oct. 31 | 200 | | |

Oct. 31 Bal. 200

Advertising Supplies

| Oct. 5 | 2,500 | Oct. 31 | 1,500 |

Oct. 31 Bal. 1,000

Prepaid Insurance

| Oct. 4 | 600 | Oct. 31 | 50 |

Oct. 31 Bal. 550

Office Equipment

| Oct. 2 | 5,000 | | |

Oct. 31 Bal. 5,000

Accumulated Depreciation— Office Equipment

		Oct. 31	40
		Oct. 31	Bal. 40

Notes Payable

		Oct. 1	5,000
		Oct. 31	Bal. 5,000

Accounts Payable

		Oct. 5	2,500
		Oct. 31	Bal. 2,500

Interest Payable

		Oct. 31	50
		Oct. 31	Bal. 50

Unearned Service Revenue

Oct. 31	400	Oct. 2	1,200
		Oct. 31	Bal. 800

Salaries Payable

		Oct. 31	1,200
		Oct. 31	Bal. 1,200

Common Stock

		Oct. 1	10,000
		Oct. 31 Bal. 10,000	

Retained Earnings

| | | Oct. 31 | Bal. 0 |

Dividends

| Oct. 20 | 500 | | |

Oct. 31 Bal. 500

Service Revenue

		Oct.	3	10,000
			31	400
			31	200

Oct. 31 Bal. 10,600

Salaries Expense

Oct. 26	4,000		
31	1,200		

Oct. 31 Bal. 5,200

Advertising Supplies Expense

| Oct. 31 | 1,500 | | |

Oct. 31 Bal. 1,500

Rent Expense

| Oct. 3 | 900 | | |

Oct. 31 Bal. 900

Insurance Expense

| Oct. 31 | 50 | | |

Oct. 31 Bal. 50

Interest Expense

| Oct. 31 | 50 | | |

Oct. 31 Bal. 50

Depreciation Expense

| Oct. 31 | 40 | | |

Oct. 31 Bal. 40

The Adjusted Trial Balance and Financial Statements

After a company has journalized and posted all adjusting entries, it prepares another trial balance from the ledger accounts. This trial balance is called an **adjusted trial balance**. It shows the balances of all accounts, including those adjusted, at the end of the accounting period. The purpose of an adjusted trial balance is to **prove the equality** of the total debit balances and the total credit balances in the ledger after all adjustments. Because the accounts contain all data needed for financial statements, the adjusted trial balance is the **primary basis for the preparation of financial statements**.

> **study objective   6**
>
> Describe the nature and purpose of the adjusted trial balance.

PREPARING THE ADJUSTED TRIAL BALANCE

Illustration 4-26 presents the adjusted trial balance for Sierra Corporation prepared from the ledger accounts in Illustration 4-25. The amounts affected by the adjusting entries are highlighted in color.

Illustration 4-26
Adjusted trial balance

SIERRA CORPORATION Adjusted Trial Balance October 31, 2010		
	Dr.	Cr.
Cash	$ 15,200	
Accounts Receivable	200	
Advertising Supplies	1,000	
Prepaid Insurance	550	
Office Equipment	5,000	
Accumulated Depreciation—Office Equipment		$ 40
Notes Payable		5,000
Accounts Payable		2,500
Interest Payable		50
Unearned Service Revenue		800
Salaries Payable		1,200
Common Stock		10,000
Retained Earnings		0
Dividends	500	
Service Revenue		10,600
Salaries Expense	5,200	
Advertising Supplies Expense	1,500	
Rent Expense	900	
Insurance Expense	50	
Interest Expense	50	
Depreciation Expense	40	
	$30,190	$30,190

PREPARING FINANCIAL STATEMENTS

Companies can prepare financial statements directly from an adjusted trial balance. Illustrations 4-27 and 4-28 (next page) present the interrelationships of data in the adjusted trial balance of Sierra Corporation. As Illustration 4-27 shows, companies prepare the income statement from the revenue and expense accounts. Similarly, they derive the retained earnings statement from the retained earnings account, dividends account, and the net income (or net loss) shown in the income statement. As Illustration 4-28 shows, companies then prepare the balance sheet from the asset, liability, and stockholders' equity accounts. They obtain the amount reported for retained earnings on the balance sheet from the ending balance in the retained earnings statement.

Illustration 4-27
Preparation of the income statement and retained earnings statement from the adjusted trial balance

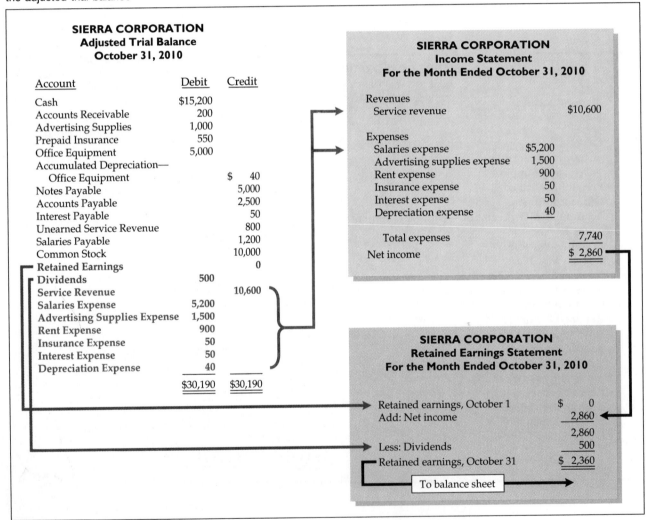

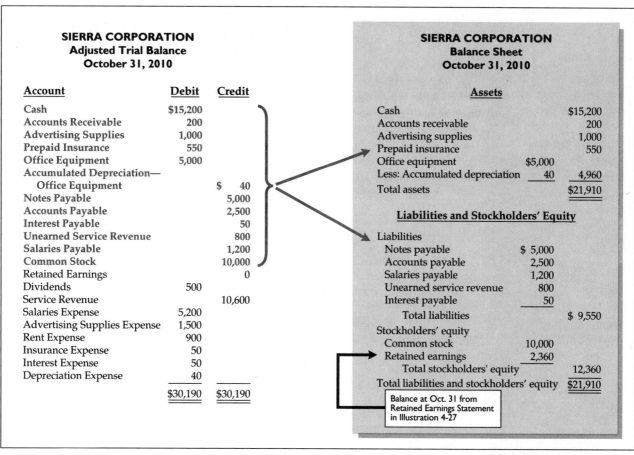

Illustration 4-28
Preparation of the balance
sheet from the adjusted
trial balance

before you go on...

Do it! Skolnick Co. was organized on April 1, 2010. The company prepares **TRIAL BALANCE**
quarterly financial statements. The adjusted trial balance amounts at June 30 are shown
below:

	Debits		Credits
Cash	$ 6,700	Accumulated Depreciation—Equipment	$ 850
Accounts Receivable	600	Notes Payable	5,000
Prepaid Rent	900	Accounts Payable	1,510
Supplies	1,000	Salaries Payable	400
Equipment	15,000	Interest Payable	50
Dividends	600	Unearned Rent	500
Salaries Expense	9,400	Common Stock	14,000
Rent Expense	1,500	Commission Revenue	14,200
Depreciation Expense	850	Rent Revenue	800
Supplies Expense	200		
Utilities Expense	510		
Interest Expense	50		
Total debits	$37,310	Total credits	$37,310

(a) Determine the net income for the quarter April 1 to June 30.

(b) Determine the total assets and total liabilities at June 30, 2010 for Skolnick Co.

(c) Determine the amount that appears for Retained Earnings.

Action Plan

- In an adjusted trial balance, all asset, liability, revenue, and expense accounts are properly stated.
- To determine the ending balance in Retained Earnings, add net income and subtract dividends.

Solution

(a) The net income is determined by adding revenues and subtracting expenses. The net income is computed as follows:

Revenues		
Commission revenue	$14,200	
Rent revenue	800	
Total revenues		$15,000
Expenses		
Salaries expense	$ 9,400	
Rent expense	1,500	
Depreciation expense	850	
Utilities expense	510	
Supplies expense	200	
Interest expense	50	
Total expenses		12,510
Net income		$ 2,490

(b) Total assets and liabilities are computed as follows:

Assets			Liabilities	
Cash		$ 6,700	Notes payable	$5,000
Accounts receivable		600	Accounts payable	1,510
Supplies		1,000	Unearned rent	500
Prepaid rent		900	Salaries payable	400
Equipment	15,000		Interest payable	50
Less: Accumulated depreciation	850	14,150		
Total assets		$23,350	Total liabilities	$7,460

(c)
Retained earnings, April 1	$ 0
Add: Net income	2,490
Less: Dividends	600
Retained earnings, June 30	$1,890

the navigator

Closing the Books

Alternative Terminology
Temporary accounts are sometimes called *nominal accounts*, and permanent accounts are sometimes called *real accounts*.

In previous chapters you learned that revenue and expense accounts and the dividends account are subdivisions of retained earnings, which is reported in the stockholders' equity section of the balance sheet. Because revenues, expenses, and dividends relate to only a given accounting period, they are considered temporary accounts. In contrast, all balance sheet accounts are considered permanent accounts because their balances are carried forward into future accounting periods. Illustration 4-29 (next page) identifies the accounts in each category.

PREPARING CLOSING ENTRIES

study objective 7

Explain the purpose of closing entries.

At the end of the accounting period, companies transfer the temporary account balances to the permanent stockholders' equity account—Retained Earnings— through the preparation of closing entries. Closing entries transfer net income (or net loss) and dividends to Retained Earnings, so the balance in Retained Earnings agrees with the retained earnings statement. For example, notice that

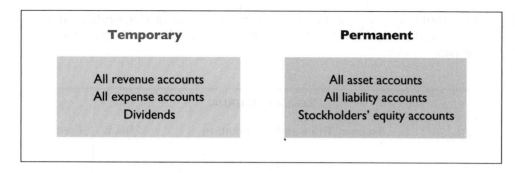

Illustration 4-29
Temporary versus
permanent accounts

in the adjusted trial balance in Illustration 4-24, Retained Earnings has a balance of zero. Prior to the closing entries, the balance in Retained Earnings will be its beginning-of-the-period balance. (For Sierra this is zero because it is Sierra's first month of operations.)

In addition to updating Retained Earnings to its correct ending balance, closing entries produce a **zero balance in each temporary account**. As a result, these accounts are ready to accumulate data about revenues, expenses, and dividends in the next accounting period separate from the data in the prior periods. **Permanent accounts are not closed.**

When companies prepare closing entries, they could close each income statement account directly to Retained Earnings. However, to do so would result in excessive detail in the retained earnings account. Accordingly, companies close the revenue and expense accounts to another temporary account, Income Summary, and they transfer only the resulting net income or net loss from this account to Retained Earnings. Illustration 4-30 depicts the closing process. While it still takes the average large company seven days to close, some companies such as Cisco employ technology that allows them to do a so-called "virtual close" almost instantaneously any time during the year. Besides dramatically reducing the cost of closing, the virtual close provides companies with accurate data for decision making whenever they desire it.

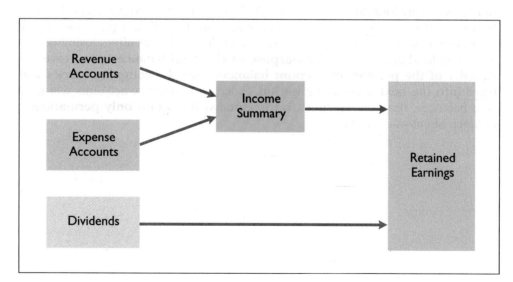

Illustration 4-30 The closing process

Illustration 4-31 shows the closing entries for Sierra Corporation. Illustration 4-32 (next page) diagrams the posting process for Sierra Corporation's closing entries.

Illustration 4-31 Closing entries journalized

Helpful Hint Income Summary is a very descriptive title: Companies close total revenues to Income Summary and total expenses to Income Summary. The balance in the Income Summary is a net income or net loss.

GENERAL JOURNAL			
Date	**Account Titles and Explanation**	**Debit**	**Credit**
	<u>Closing Entries</u>		
2010	(1)		
Oct. 31	Service Revenue	10,600	
	Income Summary		10,600
	(To close revenue account)		
	(2)		
31	Income Summary	7,740	
	Salaries Expense		5,200
	Advertising Supplies Expense		1,500
	Rent Expense		900
	Insurance Expense		50
	Interest Expense		50
	Depreciation Expense		40
	(To close expense accounts)		
	(3)		
31	Income Summary	2,860	
	Retained Earnings		2,860
	(To close net income to retained earnings)		
	(4)		
31	Retained Earnings	500	
	Dividends		500
	(To close dividends to retained earnings)		

PREPARING A POST-CLOSING TRIAL BALANCE

After a company journalizes and posts all closing entries, it prepares another trial balance, called a post-closing trial balance, from the ledger. A post-closing trial balance is a list of all permanent accounts and their balances after closing entries are journalized and posted. **The purpose of this trial balance is to prove the equality of the permanent account balances that the company carries forward into the next accounting period.** Since all temporary accounts will have zero balances, **the post-closing trial balance will contain only permanent—balance sheet—accounts.**

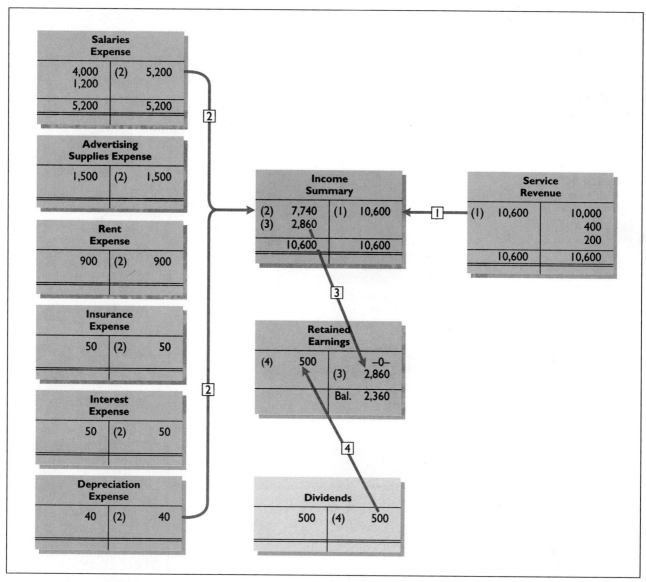

Illustration 4-32 Posting of closing entries

before you go on...

Do it!

After making entries to close its revenue and expense accounts to Income Summary, Hancock Company has the following balances.

CLOSING ENTRIES

Dividends	$15,000
Retained Earnings	$42,000
Income Summary	$18,000 (credit balance)

Prepare the closing entries at December 31 that affect the stockholders' equity accounts.

Solution

Dec. 31	Income Summary	18,000	
	Retained Earnings		18,000
	(To close net income to retained earnings)		
31	Retained Earnings	15,000	
	Dividends		15,000
	(To close dividends to retained earnings)		

Action Plan

• Close Income Summary to Retained Earnings.

• Close Dividends to Retained Earnings.

SUMMARY OF THE ACCOUNTING CYCLE

Illustration 4-33 shows the required steps in the accounting cycle. You can see that the cycle begins with the analysis of business transactions and ends with the preparation of a post-closing trial balance. Companies perform the steps in the cycle in sequence and repeat them in each accounting period.

Illustration 4-33
Required steps in the accounting cycle

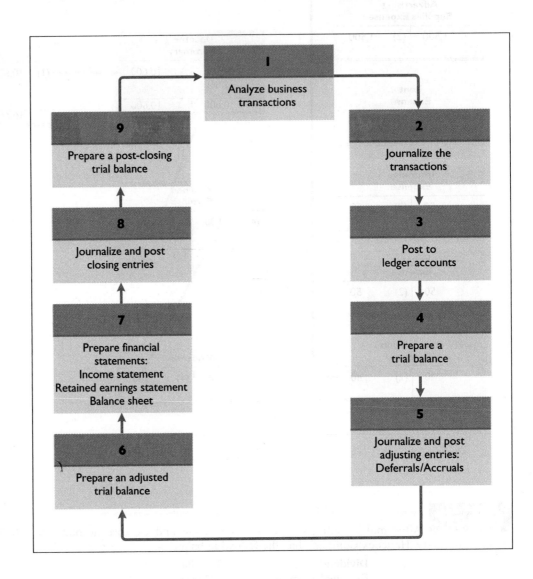

Helpful Hint Some companies prefer to reverse certain adjusting entries at the beginning of a new accounting period. The company makes a *reversing entry* at the beginning of the next accounting period; this entry is the exact opposite of the adjusting entry made in the previous period.

Steps 1–3 may occur daily during the accounting period, as explained in Chapter 3. Companies perform Steps 4–7 on a periodic basis, such as monthly, quarterly, or annually. Steps 8 and 9, closing entries and a post-closing trial balance, usually take place only at the end of a company's **annual** accounting period.

Quality of Earnings

"Did you make your numbers today?" is a question asked often in both large and small businesses. Companies and employees are continually under pressure to "make the numbers"—that is, to have earnings that are in line with expectations. As a consequence it is not surprising that many companies practice earnings management. Earnings management is the planned timing of revenues, expenses, gains, and losses to smooth out bumps in net income. The quality of earnings is greatly affected when a company manages earnings up or down to meet some targeted earnings number. A company that has a high quality of earnings provides full and transparent information that will not confuse or mislead users of the financial statements. A company with questionable quality of earnings may mislead investors and creditors, who believe they are relying on relevant and reliable information. As a consequence, investors and creditors lose confidence in financial reporting, and it becomes difficult for our capital markets to work efficiently.

Companies manage earnings in a variety of ways. One way is through the use of **one-time items** to prop up earnings numbers. For example, ConAgra Foods recorded a nonrecurring gain from the sale of Pilgrim's Pride stock for $186 million to help meet an earnings projection for the quarter.

Another way is to **inflate revenue** numbers in the short-run to the detriment of the long-run. For example, Bristol-Myers Squibb provided sales incentives to its wholesalers to encourage them to buy products at the end of the quarter. As a result Bristol-Myers was able to meet its sales projections. The problem was that the wholesalers could not sell that amount of merchandise and ended up returning it to Bristol-Myers. The result was that Bristol-Myers had to restate its income numbers.

Companies also manage earnings through **improper adjusting entries**. Regulators investigated Xerox for accusations that it was booking too much revenue up-front on multi-year contract sales. Financial executives at Office Max resigned amid accusations that the company was recognizing rebates from its vendors too early and therefore overstating revenue. Finally, WorldCom's abuse of adjusting entries to meet its net income targets is unsurpassed: It used adjusting entries to increase net income by reclassifying liabilities as revenue and reclassifying expenses as assets. Investigations of the company's books after it went bankrupt revealed adjusting entries of more than a billion dollars that had no supporting documentation.

The good news is that, as a result of investor pressure as well as the **Sarbanes-Oxley Act**, many companies are trying to improve the quality of their financial reporting. For example, hotel operator Marriott is now providing detailed information on the write-offs it has on loan guarantees it gives hotels. General Electric has decided to provide more detail on its revenues and operating profits for individual businesses it owns. IBM is attempting to provide a better breakdown of its earnings. At the same time, regulators are taking a tough stand on the issue of quality of earnings. For example, one regulator noted that companies may be required to restate their financials every single time that they account for any transaction that had no legitimate purpose but was done solely for an accounting purpose, such as to smooth net income.

WorldCom Project

KEEPING AN EYE ON CASH

In this chapter you learned that adjusting entries are used to adjust numbers that would otherwise be stated on a cash basis. Sierra Corporation's income statement (Illustration 4-27) shows net income of $2,860. The statement of cash flows reports a form of cash basis income referred to as "Net cash provided by operating activities." For example, Illustration 1-9 (page 16), which shows a statement of cash flows, reports net cash provided by operating activities of $5,700 for Sierra. Net income and net cash provided by operating activities often differ. The difference for Sierra is $2,840 ($5,700 − $2,860). The following summary shows the causes of this difference of $2,840.

Understand the causes of differences between net income and cash provided by operating activities.

SO 9

	Computation of Net Cash Provided by Operating Activities	Computation of Net Income
(1) Cash received in advance from customer	$ 1,200	$ 0
(2) Cash received from customers for services provided	10,000	10,000
(3) Services provided for cash received previously in (1)	0	400
(4) Services provided on account	0	200
(5) Payment of rent	(900)	(900)
(6) Purchase of insurance	(600)	0
(7) Payment of employee salaries	(4,000)	(4,000)
(8) Use of supplies	0	(1,500)
(9) Use of insurance	0	(50)
(10) Depreciation	0	(40)
(11) Interest cost incurred, but not paid	0	(50)
(12) Salaries incurred, but not paid	0	(1,200)
	$ 5,700	$ 2,860

For each item included in the computation of net cash provided by operating activities, you should confirm that cash was either received or paid. For each item in the income statement, the company should confirm that revenue was earned (even when cash was not received) or that an expense was incurred (even when cash was not paid).

USING THE DECISION TOOLKIT

Humana Corporation provides managed health care services to approximately 7 million people. Headquartered in Louisville, Kentucky, it has over 13,700 employees in 15 states and Puerto Rico. A simplified version of Humana's December 31, 2007, adjusted trial balance is shown at the top of the next page.

Instructions

From the trial balance, prepare an income statement, retained earnings statement, and classified balance sheet. **Be sure to prepare them in that order, since each statement depends on information determined in the preceding statement.**

HUMANA CORPORATION
Adjusted Trial Balance
December 31, 2007
(in millions)

Account	Dr.	Cr.
Cash	$ 2,040	
Short-Term Investments	3,635	
Receivables	606	
Other Current Assets	2,451	
Property and Equipment, Net	637	
Long-Term Investments	1,015	
Goodwill	1,664	
Other Long-Term Assets	830	
Benefits Payable		$ 2,697
Accounts Payable		1,269
Other Current Liabilities		1,826
Long-Term Debt		3,059
Common Stock		1,272
Dividends	0	
Retained Earnings		1,922
Revenues		25,290
Medical Cost Expense	20,271	
Selling, General, and Administrative Expense	3,476	
Depreciation Expense	185	
Interest Expense	69	
Income Tax Expense	456	
	$37,335	$37,335

Solution

HUMANA CORPORATION
Income Statement
For the Year Ended December 31, 2007
(in millions)

Revenues		$25,290
Medical cost expense	$20,271	
Selling, general, and administrative expense	3,476	
Depreciation expense	185	
Interest expense	69	
Income tax expense	456	24,457
Net income		$ 833

HUMANA CORPORATION
Retained Earnings Statement
For the Year Ended December 31, 2007
(in millions)

Beginning retained earnings	$1,922
Add: Net income	833
Less: Dividends	0
Ending retained earnings	$2,755

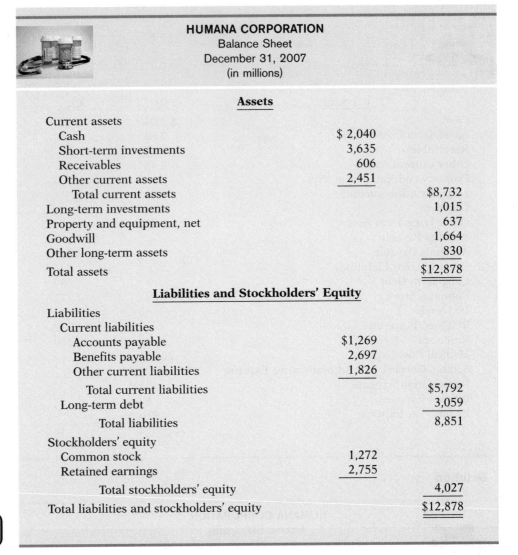

HUMANA CORPORATION
Balance Sheet
December 31, 2007
(in millions)

Assets

Current assets		
Cash	$ 2,040	
Short-term investments	3,635	
Receivables	606	
Other current assets	2,451	
Total current assets		$8,732
Long-term investments		1,015
Property and equipment, net		637
Goodwill		1,664
Other long-term assets		830
Total assets		$12,878

Liabilities and Stockholders' Equity

Liabilities		
Current liabilities		
Accounts payable	$1,269	
Benefits payable	2,697	
Other current liabilities	1,826	
Total current liabilities		$5,792
Long-term debt		3,059
Total liabilities		8,851
Stockholders' equity		
Common stock	1,272	
Retained earnings	2,755	
Total stockholders' equity		4,027
Total liabilities and stockholders' equity		$12,878

Summary of Study Objectives

1 **Explain the revenue recognition principle and the matching principle.** The revenue recognition principle dictates that companies recognize revenue in the accounting period in which it is earned. The matching principle dictates that companies recognize expenses when expenses make their contribution to revenues.

2 **Differentiate between the cash basis and the accrual basis of accounting.** Accrual-based accounting means that companies record, in the periods in which the events occur, events that change a company's financial statements even if cash has not been exchanged. Under the cash basis, companies record events only in the periods in which the company receives or pays cash.

3 **Explain why adjusting entries are needed, and identify the major types of adjusting entries.** Companies make adjusting entries at the end of an accounting period. These entries ensure that companies record revenues in the period in which they are earned and that com-

panies recognize expenses in the period in which they are incurred. The major types of adjusting entries are prepaid expenses, unearned revenues, accrued revenues, and accrued expenses.

4 **Prepare adjusting entries for deferrals.** Deferrals are either prepaid expenses or unearned revenues. Companies make adjusting entries for deferrals at the statement date to record the portion of the deferred item that represents the expense incurred or the revenue earned in the current accounting period.

5 **Prepare adjusting entries for accruals.** Accruals are either accrued revenues or accrued expenses. Adjusting entries for accruals record revenues earned and expenses incurred in the current accounting period that have not been recognized through daily entries.

6 **Describe the nature and purpose of the adjusted trial balance.** An adjusted trial balance is a trial balance that shows the balances of all accounts, including those that have been adjusted, at the end of an accounting period. The purpose of an adjusted trial balance is to show the effects of all financial events that have occurred during the accounting period.

7 Explain the purpose of closing entries. One purpose of closing entries is to transfer net income or net loss for the period to Retained Earnings. A second purpose is to "zero-out" all temporary accounts (revenue accounts, expense accounts, and dividends) so that they start each new period with a zero balance. To accomplish this, companies "close" all temporary accounts at the end of an accounting period. They make separate entries to close revenues and expenses to Income Summary; Income Summary to Retained Earnings; and Dividends to Retained Earnings. Only temporary accounts are closed.

8 Describe the required steps in the accounting cycle. The required steps in the accounting cycle are: (a) analyze business transactions, (b) journalize the transactions, (c) post to ledger accounts, (d) prepare a trial balance, (e) journalize and post adjusting entries, (f) prepare an adjusted trial balance, (g) prepare financial statements, (h) journalize and post closing entries, and (i) prepare a post-closing trial balance.

9 Understand the causes of differences between net income and net cash provided by operating activities. Net income is based on accrual accounting, which relies on the adjustment process. Net cash provided by operating activities is determined by adding cash received from operating the business and subtracting cash expended during operations.

DECISION TOOLKIT   A SUMMARY

DECISION CHECKPOINTS	INFO NEEDED FOR DECISION	TOOL TO USE FOR DECISION	HOW TO EVALUATE RESULTS
At what point should the company record revenue?	Need to understand the nature of the company's business	Record revenue when earned. A service business earns revenue when it performs a service.	Recognizing revenue too early overstates current period revenue; recognizing it too late understates current period revenue.
At what point should the company record expenses?	Need to understand the nature of the company's business	Expenses should "follow" revenues—that is, match the effort (expense) with the result (revenue).	Recognizing expenses too early overstates current period expense; recognizing them too late understates current period expense.

appendix

Adjusting Entries in an Automated World—Using a Worksheet

In the previous discussion we used T accounts and trial balances to arrive at the amounts used to prepare financial statements. Accountants frequently use a device known as a worksheet to determine these amounts. A worksheet is a multiple-column form that may be used in the adjustment process and in preparing financial statements. Accountants can prepare worksheets manually, but today most use computer spreadsheets.

As its name suggests, the worksheet is a working tool for the accountant. **A worksheet is not a permanent accounting record**; it is neither a journal nor a part of the general ledger. The worksheet is merely a supplemental device used to make it easier to prepare adjusting entries and the financial statements. Small companies with relatively few accounts and adjustments may not need a worksheet. In large companies with numerous accounts and many adjustments, a worksheet is almost indispensable.

study objective 10

Describe the purpose and the basic form of a worksheet.

Sierra Corporation.xls

File   Exit   View   Insert   Format   Tools   Data   Window   Help

SIERRA CORPORATION
Worksheet
For the Month Ended October 31, 2010

Account Titles	Trial Balance Dr.	Trial Balance Cr.	Adjustments Dr.	Adjustments Cr.	Adjusted Trial Balance Dr.	Adjusted Trial Balance Cr.	Income Statement Dr.	Income Statement Cr.	Balance Sheet Dr.	Balance Sheet Cr.
Cash	15,200				15,200				15,200	
Advertising Supplies	2,500			(a) 1,500	1,000				1,000	
Prepaid Insurance	600			(b) 50	550				550	
Office Equipment	5,000				5,000				5,000	
Notes Payable		5,000				5,000				5,000
Accounts Payable		2,500				2,500				2,500
Unearned Service Revenue		1,200	(d) 400			800				800
Common Stock		10,000				10,000				10,000
Retained Earnings		–0–				–0–				–0–
Dividends	500				500				500	
Service Revenue		10,000		(d) 400		10,600		10,600		
				(e) 200						
Salaries Expense	4,000		(g) 1,200		5,200		5,200			
Rent Expense	900				900		900			
Totals	28,700	28,700								
Advertising Supplies Expense			(a) 1,500		1,500		1,500			
Insurance Expense			(b) 50		50		50			
Accum. Depreciation—Office										
Equipment				(c) 40		40				40
Depreciation Expense			(c) 40		40		40			
Interest Expense			(f) 50		50		50			
Accounts Receivable			(e) 200		200				200	
Interest Payable				(f) 50		50				50
Salaries Payable				(g) 1,200		1,200				1,200
Totals			3,440	3,440	30,190	30,190	7,740	10,600	22,450	19,590
Net Income							2,860			2,860
Totals							10,600	10,600	22,450	22,450

1. Prepare a trial balance on the worksheet

2. Enter adjustment data

3. Enter adjusted balances

4. Extend adjusted balances to appropriate statement columns

5. Total the statement columns, compute net income (or net loss), and complete worksheet

Illustration 4A-1 Form and procedure for a worksheet

Illustration 4A-1 shows the basic form of a worksheet. Note the headings: The worksheet starts with two columns for the Trial Balance. The next two columns record all Adjustments. Next is the Adjusted Trial Balance. The last two sets of columns correspond to the Income Statement and the Balance Sheet. All items listed in the Adjusted Trial Balance columns are included in either the Income Statement or the Balance Sheet columns.

Summary of Study Objective for Appendix

10 **Describe the purpose and the basic form of a worksheet.** The worksheet is a device to make it easier to prepare adjusting entries and the financial statements. Companies often prepare a worksheet on a computer spreadsheet. The sets of columns of the worksheet are, from left to right, the unadjusted trial balance, adjustments, adjusted trial balance, income statement, and balance sheet.

Glossary

Accrual-basis accounting *(p. 164)* Accounting basis in which companies record, in the periods in which the events occur, transactions that change a company's financial statements, even if cash was not exchanged.

Accrued expenses *(p. 175)* Expenses incurred but not yet paid in cash or recorded.

Accrued revenues *(p. 173)* Revenues earned but not yet received in cash or recorded.

Adjusted trial balance *(p. 181)* A list of accounts and their balances after all adjustments have been made.

Adjusting entries *(p. 165)* Entries made at the end of an accounting period to ensure that the revenue recognition and matching principles are followed.

Book value *(p. 170)* The difference between the cost of a depreciable asset and its related accumulated depreciation.

Cash-basis accounting *(p. 164)* Accounting basis in which a company records revenue only when it receives cash, and an expense only when it pays cash.

Closing entries *(p. 184)* Entries at the end of an accounting period to transfer the balances of temporary accounts to a permanent stockholders' equity account, Retained Earnings.

Contra asset account *(p. 169)* An account that is offset against an asset account on the balance sheet.

Depreciation *(p. 169)* The process of allocating the cost of an asset to expense over its useful life.

Earnings management *(p. 188)* The planned timing of revenues, expenses, gains, and losses to smooth out bumps in net income.

Fiscal year *(p. 162, in margin)* An accounting period that is one year long.

Income Summary *(p. 185)* A temporary account used in closing revenue and expense accounts.

Matching principle *(p. 163)* The principle that dictates that companies match efforts (expenses) with accomplishments (revenues).

Permanent accounts *(p. 184)* Balance sheet accounts whose balances are carried forward to the next accounting period.

Post-closing trial balance *(p. 186)* A list of permanent accounts and their balances after a company has journalized and posted closing entries.

Prepaid expenses (Prepayments) *(p. 166)* Assets that result from the payment of expenses that benefit more than one accounting period.

Quality of earnings *(p. 189)* Indicates the level of full and transparent information that a company provides to users of its financial statements.

Revenue recognition principle *(p. 162)* The principle that companies recognize revenue in the accounting period in which it is earned.

Reversing entry *(p. 188, in margin)* An entry made at the beginning of the next accounting period; the exact opposite of the adjusting entry made in the previous period.

Temporary accounts *(p. 184)* Revenue, expense, and dividend accounts whose balances a company transfers to Retained Earnings at the end of an accounting period.

Time period assumption *(p. 162)* An assumption that the economic life of a business can be divided into artificial time periods.

Unearned revenues *(p. 171)* Cash received before a company earns revenues and recorded as a liability until earned.

Useful life *(p. 169)* The length of service of a productive asset.

Worksheet *(p. 193)* A multiple-column form that companies may use in the adjustment process and in preparing financial statements.

Comprehensive

Terry Thomas and a group of investors incorporate the Green Thumb Lawn Care Corporation on April 1. At April 30 the trial balance shows the following balances for selected accounts.

Prepaid Insurance	$ 3,600
Equipment	28,000
Notes Payable	20,000
Unearned Service Revenue	4,200
Service Revenue	1,800

Analysis reveals the following additional data pertaining to these accounts.

1. Prepaid insurance is the cost of a 2-year insurance policy, effective April 1.

2. Depreciation on the equipment is $500 per month.

3. The note payable is dated April 1. It is a 6-month, 12% note.

4. Seven customers paid for the company's 6-month lawn service package of $600 begin-ning in April. These customers received the first month of services in April.

5. Lawn services performed for other customers but not billed at April 30 totaled $1,500.

Instructions

Prepare the adjusting entries for the month of April. Show computations.

Action Plan

- Note that adjustments are being made for one month.
- Make computations carefully.
- Select account titles carefully.
- Make sure debits are made first and credits are indented.
- Check that debits equal credits for each entry.

Solution to Comprehensive **Do it!**

	GENERAL JOURNAL		
Date	**Account Titles and Explanation**	**Debit**	**Credit**
	Adjusting Entries		
Apr. 30	Insurance Expense	150	
	Prepaid Insurance		150
	(To record insurance expired:		
	$3,600 \div 24 = $150 per month)		
30	Depreciation Expense	500	
	Accumulated Depreciation—Equipment		500
	(To record monthly depreciation)		
30	Interest Expense	200	
	Interest Payable		200
	(To accrue interest on notes payable:		
	$20,000 \times 12\% \times \frac{1}{12} = $200)		
30	Unearned Service Revenue	700	
	Service Revenue		700
	(To record revenue earned: $600 \div 6 = $100;		
	$100 per month \times 7 = $700)		
30	Accounts Receivable	1,500	
	Service Revenue		1,500
	(To accrue revenue earned but not billed		
	or collected)		

Self-Study Questions

Answers are at the end of this chapter.

(SO 1) 1. What is the time period assumption?
(a) Companies should recognize revenue in the accounting period in which it is earned.
(b) Companies should match expenses with revenues.
(c) The economic life of a business can be divided into artificial time periods.
(d) The fiscal year should correspond with the calendar year.

(SO 1) 2. Which principle dictates that efforts (expenses) be recorded with accomplishments (revenues)?
(a) Matching principle.
(b) Cost principle.
(c) Periodicity principle.
(d) Revenue recognition principle.

3. Which one of these statements about the (SO 2) accrual basis of accounting is *false*?
(a) Companies record events that change their financial statements in the period in which events occur, even if cash was not exchanged.
(b) Companies recognize revenue in the period in which it is earned.
(c) This basis is in accord with generally accepted accounting principles.
(d) Companies record revenue only when they receive cash, and record expense only when they pay out cash.

4. Adjusting entries are made to ensure that: (SO 3)
(a) expenses are recognized in the period in which they are incurred.

(b) revenues are recorded in the period in which they are earned.

(c) balance sheet and income statement accounts have correct balances at the end of an accounting period.

(d) All of the above.

(SO 4, 5) **5.** Each of the following is a major type (or category) of adjusting entry *except:*

(a) prepaid expenses.

(b) accrued revenues.

(c) accrued expenses.

(d) earned expenses.

(SO 4) **6.** The trial balance shows Supplies $1,350 and Supplies Expense $0. If $600 of supplies are on hand at the end of the period, the adjusting entry is:

(a) Supplies 600
  Supplies Expense 600

(b) Supplies 750
  Supplies Expense 750

(c) Supplies Expense 750
  Supplies 750

(d) Supplies Expense 600
  Supplies 600

(SO 4) **7.** Adjustments for unearned revenues:

(a) decrease liabilities and increase revenues.

(b) increase liabilities and increase revenues.

(c) increase assets and increase revenues.

(d) decrease revenues and decrease assets.

(SO 4) **8.** Adjustments for prepaid expenses:

(a) decrease assets and increase revenues.

(b) decrease expenses and increase assets.

(c) decrease assets and increase expenses.

(d) decrease revenues and increase assets.

(SO 4) **9.** Queenan Company computes depreciation on delivery equipment at $1,000 for the month of June. The adjusting entry to record this depreciation is as follows:

(a) Depreciation Expense 1,000
  Accumulated Depreciation—
    Queenan Company 1,000

(b) Depreciation Expense 1,000
  Delivery Equipment 1,000

(c) Depreciation Expense 1,000
  Accumulated Depreciation—
    Delivery Equipment 1,000

(d) Delivery Equipment Expense 1,000
  Accumulated Depreciation—
    Delivery Equipment 1,000

(SO 5) **10.** Adjustments for accrued revenues:

(a) increase assets and increase liabilities.

(b) increase assets and increase revenues.

(c) decrease assets and decrease revenues.

(d) decrease liabilities and increase revenues.

(SO 5) **11.** Colleen Mooney earned a salary of $400 for the last week of September. She will be paid on October 1. The adjusting entry for Colleen's employer at September 30 is:

(a) No entry is required.

(b) Salaries Expense 400
    Salaries Payable 400

(c) Salaries Expense 400
    Cash 400

(d) Salaries Payable 400
    Cash 400

(SO 6) **12.** Which statement is *incorrect* concerning the adjusted trial balance?

(a) An adjusted trial balance proves the equality of the total debit balances and the total credit balances in the ledger after all adjustments are made.

(b) The adjusted trial balance provides the primary basis for the preparation of financial statements.

(c) The adjusted trial balance does not list temporary accounts.

(d) The company prepares the adjusted trial balance after it has journalized and posted the adjusting entries.

(SO 7) **13.** Which account will have a zero balance after a company has journalized and posted closing entries?

(a) Service Revenue.

(b) Advertising Supplies.

(c) Prepaid Insurance.

(d) Accumulated Depreciation.

(SO 7) **14.** Which types of accounts will appear in the post-closing trial balance?

(a) Permanent accounts.

(b) Temporary accounts.

(c) Accounts shown in the income statement columns of a work sheet.

(d) None of the above.

(SO 8) **15.** All of the following are required steps in the accounting cycle *except:*

(a) journalizing and posting closing entries.

(b) preparing an adjusted trial balance.

(c) preparing a post-closing trial balance.

(d) preparing a work sheet.

Go to the book's companion website, **www. wiley.com/college/kimmel**, to access additional Self-Study Questions.

Note: All asterisked Questions relate to material in the appendix to the chapter.

Questions

1. (a) How does the time period assumption affect an accountant's analysis of accounting transactions?

(b) Explain the term *fiscal year.*

2. Identify and state two generally accepted accounting principles that relate to adjusting the accounts.

3. 🔧 Tony Carino, a lawyer, accepts a legal engagement in March, performs the work in April, and is paid in May. If Carino's law firm prepares monthly financial statements, when should it recognize revenue from this engagement? Why?

4. 🔧 In completing the engagement in question 3, Carino pays no costs in March, $2,500 in April, and $2,000 in May (incurred in April). How much expense should the firm deduct from revenues in the month when it recognizes the revenue? Why?

5. "The cost principle of accounting requires adjusting entries." Do you agree? Explain.

6. Why may the financial information in a trial balance not be up-to-date and complete?

7. Distinguish between the two categories of adjusting entries, and identify the types of adjustments applicable to each category.

8. What accounts does a company debit and credit in a prepaid expense adjusting entry?

9. "Depreciation is a process of valuation that results in the reporting of the fair market value of the asset." Do you agree? Explain.

10. Explain the differences between depreciation expense and accumulated depreciation.

11. Harding Company purchased equipment for $15,000. By the current balance sheet date, the company had depreciated $9,000. Indicate the balance sheet presentation of the data.

12. What accounts are debited and credited in an unearned revenue adjusting entry?

13. Computer Technologies provides maintenance service for computers and office equipment for companies throughout the Northeast. The sales manager is elated because she closed a $300,000 three-year maintenance contract on December 29, 2009, two days before the company's year-end. "Now we will hit this year's net income target for sure," she crowed. The customer is required to pay $100,000 on December 29 (the day the deal was closed). Two more payments of $100,000 each are also required on December 29, 2010 and 2011. Discuss the effect that this event will have on the company's financial statements.

14. SquareDeal, a large national retail chain, is nearing its fiscal year-end. It appears that the company is not going to hit its revenue and net income targets. The company's marketing manager, Mickey Cox, suggests running a promotion selling $50 gift cards for $40. He believes that this would be very popular and would enable the company to meet its targets for revenue and net income. What do you think of this idea?

15. 🔧 A company fails to recognize revenue earned but not yet received. Which of the following accounts are involved in the adjusting entry: (a) asset, (b) liability, (c) revenue, or (d) expense? For the accounts selected, indicate whether they would be debited or credited in the entry.

16. 🔧 A company fails to recognize an expense incurred but not paid. Indicate which of the following accounts is debited and which is credited in the adjusting entry: (a) asset, (b) liability, (c) revenue, or (d) expense.

17. 🔧 A company makes an accrued revenue adjusting entry for $800 and an accrued expense adjusting entry for $500. How much was net income understated prior to these entries? Explain.

18. On January 9 a company pays $6,000 for salaries, of which $1,100 was reported as Salaries Payable on December 31. Give the entry to record the payment.

19. For each of the following items before adjustment, indicate the type of adjusting entry—prepaid expense, unearned revenue, accrued revenue, and accrued expense—that is needed to correct the misstatement. If an item could result in more than one type of adjusting entry, indicate each of the types.
    (a) Assets are understated.
    (b) Liabilities are overstated.
    (c) Liabilities are understated.
    (d) Expenses are understated.
    (e) Assets are overstated.
    (f) Revenue is understated

20. One-half of the adjusting entry is given below. Indicate the account title for the other half of the entry.
    (a) Salaries Expense is debited.
    (b) Depreciation Expense is debited.
    (c) Interest Payable is credited.
    (d) Supplies is credited.
    (e) Accounts Receivable is debited.
    (f) Unearned Service Revenue is debited.

21. "An adjusting entry may affect more than one balance sheet or income statement account." Do you agree? Why or why not?

22. 🍬 Which balance sheet account provides evidence that Tootsie Roll records sales on an accrual basis rather than a cash basis? Explain.

23. Why is it possible to prepare financial statements directly from an adjusted trial balance?

24. 🔧
    (a) What information do accrual basis financial statements provide that cash basis statements do not?
    (b) What information do cash basis financial statements provide that accrual basis statements do not?

25. What is the relationship, if any, between the amount shown in the adjusted trial balance column for an account and that account's ledger balance?

26. Identify the account(s) debited and credited in each of the four closing entries, assuming the company has net income for the year.

27. ➡️ Some companies employ technologies that allow them to do a so-called "virtual close." This enables them to close their books nearly instantaneously any time during the year. What advantages does a "virtual close" provide?

28. Describe the nature of the Income Summary account, and identify the types of summary data that may be posted to this account.

29. What items are disclosed on a post-closing trial balance, and what is its purpose?

30. Which of these accounts would not appear in the post-closing trial balance? Interest Payable, Equipment, Depreciation Expense, Dividends, Unearned Service Revenue, Accumulated Depreciation—Equipment, and Service Revenue.

31. Indicate, in the sequence in which they are made, the three required steps in the accounting cycle that involve journalizing.

32. Identify, in the sequence in which they are prepared, the three trial balances that are required in the accounting cycle.

33. Explain the terms earnings management and quality of earnings.

34. Give examples of how companies manage earnings.

*35. What is the purpose of a worksheet?

*36. What is the basic form of a worksheet?

Brief Exercises

PLUS

BE4-1 Transactions that affect earnings do not necessarily affect cash.

Instructions
Identify the effect, if any, that each of the following transactions would have upon cash and net income. The first transaction has been completed as an example.

	Cash	Net Income
(a) Purchased $100 of supplies for cash.	−$100	$ 0
(b) Recorded an adjusting entry to record use of $40 of the above supplies.		
(c) Made sales of $1,300, all on account.		
(d) Received $800 from customers in payment of their accounts.		
(e) Purchased equipment for cash, $2,500.		
(f) Recorded depreciation of building for period used, $600.		

Identify impact of transactions on cash and net income.
(SO 2, 9)

BE4-2 The ledger of Greenwood Company includes the following accounts. Explain why each account may require adjustment.
(a) Prepaid Insurance.
(b) Depreciation Expense.
(c) Unearned Service Revenue.
(d) Interest Payable.

Indicate why adjusting entries are needed.
(SO 3)

BE4-3 Bura Company accumulates the following adjustment data at December 31. Indicate (1) the type of adjustment (prepaid expense, accrued revenue, and so on) and (2) the status of the accounts before adjustment (overstated or understated).
(a) Supplies of $400 are on hand. Supplies account shows $1,900 balance.
(b) Service Revenue earned but unbilled total $700.
(c) Interest of $300 has accumulated on a note payable.
(d) Rent collected in advance totaling $1,100 has been earned.

Identify the major types of adjusting entries.
(SO 3)

BE4-4 Dawes Advertising Company's trial balance at December 31 shows Advertising Supplies $8,800 and Advertising Supplies Expense $0. On December 31 there are $1,400 of supplies on hand. Prepare the adjusting entry at December 31 and, using T accounts, enter the balances in the accounts, post the adjusting entry, and indicate the adjusted balance in each account.

Prepare adjusting entry for supplies.
(SO 4)

BE4-5 At the end of its first year, the trial balance of Hinz Company shows Equipment $22,000 and zero balances in Accumulated Depreciation—Equipment and Depreciation Expense. Depreciation for the year is estimated to be $2,200. Prepare the adjusting entry for depreciation at December 31, post the adjustments to T accounts, and indicate the balance sheet presentation of the equipment at December 31.

Prepare adjusting entry for depreciation.
(SO 4)

BE4-6 On July 1, 2010, Noble Co. pays $10,800 to Russo Insurance Co. for a 2-year insurance contract. Both companies have fiscal years ending December 31. For Noble Co. journalize and post the entry on July 1 and the adjusting entry on December 31.

Prepare adjusting entry for prepaid expense.
(SO 4)

BE4-7 Using the data in BE4-6, journalize and post the entry on July 1 and the adjusting entry on December 31 for Russo Insurance Co. Russo uses the accounts Unearned Insurance Revenue and Insurance Revenue.

Prepare adjusting entry for unearned revenue.
(SO 4)

BE4-8 The bookkeeper for Biggs Company asks you to prepare the following accrual adjusting entries at December 31.

Prepare adjusting entries for accruals.
(SO 5)

(a) Interest on notes payable of $300 is accrued.
(b) Service revenue earned but unbilled totals $1,400.
(c) Salaries of $780 earned by employees have not been recorded.
Use these account titles: Service Revenue, Accounts Receivable, Interest Expense, Interest Payable, Salaries Expense, and Salaries Payable.

Analyze accounts in an adjusted trial balance.
(SO 6)

BE4-9 The trial balance of Fink Company includes the following balance sheet accounts. Identify the accounts that might require adjustment. For each account that requires adjustment, indicate (1) the type of adjusting entry (prepaid expenses, unearned revenues, accrued revenues, and accrued expenses) and (2) the related account in the adjusting entry.
(a) Accounts Receivable.
(b) Prepaid Insurance.
(c) Equipment.
(d) Accumulated Depreciation—Equipment.
(e) Notes Payable.
(f) Interest Payable.
(g) Unearned Service Revenue.

Prepare an income statement from an adjusted trial balance.
(SO 6)

BE4-10 The adjusted trial balance of Rose Corporation at December 31, 2010, includes the following accounts: Retained Earnings $17,200; Dividends $6,000; Service Revenue $32,000; Salaries Expense $13,000; Insurance Expense $1,800; Rent Expense $3,500; Supplies Expense $1,200; and Depreciation Expense $1,000. Prepare an income statement for the year.

Prepare a retained earnings statement from an adjusted trial balance.
(SO 6)

BE4-11 Partial adjusted trial balance data for Rose Corporation are presented in BE4-10. The balance in Retained Earnings is the balance as of January 1. Prepare a retained earnings statement for the year assuming net income is $10,000.

Identify financial statement for selected accounts.
(SO 6)

BE4-12 The following selected accounts appear in the adjusted trial balance for Reno Company. Indicate the financial statement on which each account would be reported.
(a) Accumulated Depreciation.
(b) Depreciation Expense.
(c) Retained Earnings.
(d) Dividends.
(e) Service Revenue.
(f) Supplies.
(g) Accounts Payable.

Identify post-closing trial balance accounts.
(SO 7)

BE4-13 Using the data in BE4-12, identify the accounts that would be included in a post-closing trial balance.

Prepare and post closing entries
(SO 7)

BE4-14 The income statement for the Edgebrook Golf Club Inc. for the month ended July 31 shows Green Fees Revenue $16,000; Salaries Expense $8,400; Maintenance Expense $2,500; and Income Tax Expense $1,000. The statement of retained earnings shows an opening balance for Retained Earnings of $20,000 and Dividends $1,000.
(a) Prepare and post the closing journal entries.
(b) What is the ending balance in Retained Earnings?

List required steps in the accounting cycle sequence.
(SO 8)

BE4-15 The required steps in the accounting cycle are listed in random order below. List the steps in proper sequence.
(a) Prepare a post-closing trial balance.
(b) Prepare an adjusted trial balance.
(c) Analyze business transactions.
(d) Prepare a trial balance.
(e) Journalize the transactions.
(f) Journalize and post closing entries.
(g) Prepare financial statements.
(h) Journalize and post adjusting entries.
(i) Post to ledger accounts.

Do it! Review

WILEY PLUS

Prepare adjusting entries for deferrals.
(SO 4)

Do it! 4-1 The ledger of Buerhle, Inc. on March 31, 2010, includes the following selected accounts before adjusting entries.

	Debit	Credit
Prepaid Insurance	2,400	
Office Supplies	2,500	
Office Equipment	30,000	
Unearned Revenue		10,000

An analysis of the accounts shows the following:

1. Insurance expires at the rate of $300 per month.
2. Supplies on hand total $900.
3. The office equipment depreciates $500 per month.
4. 2/5 of the unearned revenue was earned in March.

Prepare the adjusting entries for the month of March.

Do it! **4-2**   Jose Contreras is the new owner of Curveball Computer Services. At the end of July 2010, his first month of ownership, Jose is trying to prepare monthly financial statements. He has the following information for the month.

Prepare adjusting entries for accruals.

(SO 5)

1. At July 31, Contreras owed employees $1,100 in salaries that the company will pay in August.
2. On July 1, Contreras borrowed $20,000 from a local bank on a 10-year note. The annual interest rate is 12%.
3. Service revenue unrecorded in July totaled $1,600.

Prepare the adjusting entries needed at July 31, 2010.

Do it! **4-3**   Explain in which financial statement each of the following adjusted trial balance accounts would be presented.

Prepare financial statements from adjusted trial balance.

(SO 6)

Service Revenue	Accounts Receivable
Notes Payable	Accumulated Depreciation
Common Stock	Utilities Expense

Do it! **4-4**   After closing revenues and expense, Adams Company shows the following account balances.

Prepare closing entries.

(SO 7)

Dividends	$22,000
Retained Earnings	70,000
Income Summary	29,000 (credit balance)

Prepare the remaining closing entries at December 31.

Exercises

E4-1   The following independent situations require professional judgement for determining when to recognize revenue from the transactions.

Identify point of revenue recognition.

(SO 1)

(a) Southwest Airlines sells you an advance-purchase airline ticket in September for your flight home at Christmas.
(b) Ultimate Electronics sells you a home theatre on a "no money down, no interest, and no payments for one year" promotional deal.
(c) The Toronto Blue Jays sell season tickets online to games in the Skydome. Fans can purchase the tickets at any time, although the season doesn't officially begin until April. The major league baseball season runs from April through October.
(d) You borrow money in August from RBC Financial Group. The loan and the interest are repayable in full in November.
(e) In August, you order a sweater from Sears using its online catalog. The sweater arrives in September, and you charge it to your Sears credit card. You receive and pay the Sears bill in October.

Instructions
Identify when revenue should be recognized in each of the above situations.

E4-2   These are the assumptions, principles, and constraints discussed in this and previous chapters.

Identify accounting assumptions, principles, and constraints.

(SO 1)

1. Economic entity assumption.
2. Matching principle.
3. Monetary unit assumption.
4. Time period assumption.
5. Cost principle.
6. Materiality.

7. Full disclosure principle.
8. Going concern assumption.
9. Revenue recognition principle.
10. Conservatism.

Instructions

Identify by number the accounting assumption, principle, or constraint that describes each situation below. Do not use a number more than once.

_____ (a) Is the rationale for why plant assets are not reported at liquidation value. (Do not use the cost principle.)

_____ (b) Indicates that personal and business record-keeping should be separately maintained.

_____ (c) Ensures that all relevant financial information is reported.

_____ (d) Assumes that the dollar is the "measuring stick" used to report on financial performance.

_____ (e) Requires that accounting standards be followed for all *significant* items.

_____ (f) Separates financial information into time periods for reporting purposes.

_____ (g) Requires recognition of expenses in the same period as related revenues.

_____ (h) Indicates that market value changes subsequent to purchase are not recorded in the accounts.

Identify the violated assumption, principle, or constraint.

(SO 1)

E4-3 Here are some accounting reporting situations.

(a) Hansell Company recognizes revenue at the end of the production cycle but before sale. The price of the product, as well as the amount that can be sold, is not certain.

(b) Falk Company is in its fifth year of operation and has yet to issue financial statements. (Do not use the full disclosure principle.)

(c) Tavarez, Inc. is carrying inventory at its original cost of $100,000. Inventory has a market value of $110,000.

(d) Forgetta Hospital Supply Corporation reports only current assets and current liabilities on its balance sheet. Property, plant, and equipment and bonds payable are reported as current assets and current liabilities, respectively. Liquidation of the company is unlikely.

(e) Kile Company has inventory on hand that cost $400,000. Kile reports inventory on its balance sheet at its current market value of $425,000.

(f) Kim Farris, president of Classic Music Company, bought a computer for her personal use. She paid for the computer by using company funds and debited the "Computers" account.

Instructions

For each situation, list the assumption, principle, or constraint that has been violated, if any. Some of these assumptions, principles, and constraints were presented in earlier chapters. List only one answer for each situation.

Convert earnings from cash to accrual basis.

(SO 2, 4, 5, 9)

E4-4 Your examination of the records of a company that follows the cash basis of accounting tells you that the company's reported cash basis earnings in 2010 are $33,640. If this firm had followed accrual basis accounting practices, it would have reported the following year-end balances.

	2010	2009
Accounts receivable	$3,400	$2,800
Supplies on hand	1,300	1,160
Unpaid wages owed	2,000	2,400
Other unpaid amounts	1,400	1,600

Instructions

Determine the company's net earnings on an accrual basis for 2010. Show all your calculations in an orderly fashion.

Determine cash basis and accrual basis earnings.

(SO 2, 9)

E4-5 In its first year of operations Cope Company earned $28,000 in service revenue, $6,000 of which was on account and still outstanding at year-end. The remaining $22,000 was received in cash from customers.

The company incurred operating expenses of $15,500. Of these expenses $13,000 were paid in cash; $2,500 was still owed on account at year-end. In addition, Cope prepaid $2,600 for insurance coverage that would not be used until the second year of operations.

Instructions

(a) Calculate the first year's net earnings under the cash basis of accounting, and calculate the first year's net earnings under the accrual basis of accounting.

(b) Which basis of accounting (cash or accrual) provides more useful information for decision makers?

E4-6 Boulder Company, a ski tuning and repair shop, opened in November 2009. The company carefully kept track of all its cash receipts and cash payments. The following information is available at the end of the ski season, April 30, 2010.

Convert earnings from cash to accrual basis; prepare accrual-based financial statements.

(SO 2, 4, 5, 9)

	Cash Receipts	Cash Payments
Issue of common shares	$20,000	
Payment for repair equipment		$ 9,200
Rent payments		1,225
Newspaper advertising payment		375
Utility bills payments		970
Part-time helper's wages payments		2,600
Income tax payment		10,000
Cash receipts from ski and snowboard repair services	32,150	
Subtotals	52,150	24,370
Cash balance		27,780
Totals	$52,150	$52,150

You learn that the repair equipment has an estimated useful life of 5 years. The company rents space at a cost of $175 per month on a one-year lease. The lease contract requires payment of the first and last months' rent in advance, which was done. The part-time helper is owed $420 at April 30, 2010, for unpaid wages. At April 30, 2010, customers owe Boulder Company $350 for services they have received but have not yet paid for.

Instructions

(a) Prepare an accrual-basis income statement for the 6 months ended April 30, 2010.

(b) Prepare the April 30, 2010, classified balance sheet.

E4-7 FunPlay, a maker of electronic games for kids, has just completed its first year of operations. The company's sales growth was explosive. To encourage large national stores to carry its products FunPlay offered 180-day financing—meaning its largest customers do not pay for nearly 6 months. Because FunPlay is a new company, its components suppliers insist on being paid cash on delivery. Also, it had to pay up front for 2 years of insurance. At the end of the year FunPlay owed employees for one full month of salaries, but due to a cash shortfall, it promised to pay them the first week of next year.

Identify differences between cash and accrual accounting.

(SO 2, 3, 9)

Instructions

(a) Explain how cash and accrual accounting would differ for each of the events listed above and describe the proper accrual accounting.

(b) Assume that at the end of the year FunPlay reported a favorable net income, yet the company's management is concerned because the company is very short of cash. Explain how FunPlay could have positive net income and yet run out of cash.

E4-8 Proctor Company accumulates the following adjustment data at December 31.

(a) Service Revenue earned but unbilled totals $600.

(b) Store supplies of $300 are on hand. Supplies account shows $1,900 balance.

(c) Utility expenses of $275 are unpaid.

(d) Service revenue of $490 collected in advance has been earned.

(e) Salaries of $800 are unpaid.

(f) Prepaid insurance totaling $400 has expired.

Identify types of adjustments and accounts before adjustment.

(SO 3, 4, 5)

Instructions

For each item indicate (1) the type of adjustment (prepaid expense, unearned revenue, accrued revenue, or accrued expense) and (2) the status of the accounts before adjustment (overstated or understated).

E4-9 The ledger of Thurston Rental Agency on March 31 of the current year includes these selected accounts before adjusting entries have been prepared.

Prepare adjusting entries from selected account data.

(SO 4, 5)

	Debits	Credits
Prepaid Insurance	$ 3,600	
Supplies	3,000	
Equipment	25,000	
Accumulated Depreciation—Equipment		$ 8,400
Notes Payable		20,000
Unearned Rent Revenue		10,200
Rent Revenue		60,000
Interest Expense	0	
Wage Expense	14,000	

An analysis of the accounts shows the following.

1. The equipment depreciates $280 per month.
2. Half of the unearned rent revenue was earned during the quarter.
3. Interest of $440 is accrued on the notes payable.
4. Supplies on hand total $850.
5. Insurance expires at the rate of $400 per month.

Instructions
Prepare the adjusting entries at March 31, assuming that adjusting entries are made quarterly. Additional accounts are: Depreciation Expense, Insurance Expense, Interest Payable, and Supplies Expense.

Prepare adjusting entries.
(SO 4, 5)

E4-10 Mark Bennett, D.D.S., opened an incorporated dental practice on January 1, 2010. During the first month of operations the following transactions occurred:

1. Performed services for patients who had dental plan insurance. At January 31, $680 of such services was earned but not yet billed to the insurance companies.
2. Utility expenses incurred but not paid prior to January 31 totaled $520.
3. Purchased dental equipment on January 1 for $80,000, paying $20,000 in cash and signing a $60,000, 3-year note payable (Interest is paid each December 31). The equipment depreciates $400 per month. Interest is $500 per month.
4. Purchased a 1-year malpractice insurance policy on January 1 for $24,000.
5. Purchased $1,750 of dental supplies (recorded as increase to Supplies). On January 31 determined that $550 of supplies were on hand.

Instructions
Prepare the adjusting entries on January 31. Account titles are: Accumulated Depreciation—Dental Equipment, Depreciation Expense, Service Revenue, Accounts Receivable, Insurance Expense, Interest Expense, Interest Payable, Prepaid Insurance, Supplies, Supplies Expense, Utilities Expense, and Utilities Payable.

Prepare adjusting entries.
(SO 4, 5)

E4-11 The unadjusted trial balance for Sierra Corp. is shown in Illustration 4-4 (page 166). In lieu of the adjusting entries shown in the text at October 31, assume the following adjustment data.

1. Advertising supplies on hand at October 31 total $500.
2. Expired insurance for the month is $100.
3. Depreciation for the month is $50.
4. As of October 31, $800 of the previously recorded unearned revenue had been earned.
5. Services provided but unbilled (and no receivable has been recorded) at October 31 are $200.
6. Interest expense accrued at October 31 is $70.
7. Accrued salaries at October 31 are $1,400.

Instructions
Prepare the adjusting entries for the items above.

Prepare a correct income statement.
(SO 1, 4, 5, 6)

E4-12 The income statement of Marx Co. for the month of July shows net income of $1,500 based on Service Revenue $5,500; Wages Expense $2,300; Supplies Expense $900, and Utilities Expense $800. In reviewing the statement, you discover the following:

1. Insurance expired during July of $350 was omitted.
2. Supplies expense includes $200 of supplies that are still on hand at July 31.
3. Depreciation on equipment of $150 was omitted.
4. Accrued but unpaid wages at July 31 of $300 were not included.
5. Revenue earned but unrecorded totaled $700.

Instructions
Prepare a correct income statement for July 2010.

E4-13 This is a partial adjusted trial balance of Orlando Company.

Analyze adjusted data.
(SO 1, 4, 5, 6)

ORLANDO COMPANY
Adjusted Trial Balance
January 31, 2010

	Debit	Credit
Supplies	$ 700	
Prepaid Insurance	1,560	
Salaries Payable		$1,200
Unearned Service Revenue		750
Supplies Expense	950	
Insurance Expense	520	
Salaries Expense	1,800	
Service Revenue		2,000

Instructions
Answer these questions, assuming the year begins January 1.
(a) If the amount in Supplies Expense is the January 31 adjusting entry, and $650 of supplies was purchased in January, what was the balance in Supplies on January 1?
(b) If the amount in Insurance Expense is the January 31 adjusting entry, and the original insurance premium was for 1 year, what was the total premium and when was the policy purchased?
(c) If $2,500 of salaries was paid in January, what was the balance in Salaries Payable at December 31, 2009?
(d) If $1,800 was received in January for services performed in January, what was the balance in Unearned Service Revenue at December 31, 2009?

E4-14 A partial adjusted trial balance for Orlando Company is given in E4-13.

Prepare closing entries.
(SO 7)

Instructions
Prepare the closing entries at January 31, 2010.

E4-15 Selected accounts of Callahan Company are shown here.

*Journalize basic transactions
and adjusting entries.*
(SO 4, 5, 6)

Supplies Expense				Salaries Payable		
July 31	750				July 31	1,200

Salaries Expense				Accounts Receivable		
July 15	1,200			July 31	500	
31	1,200					

Service Revenue				Unearned Service Revenue			
		July 14	4,100	July 31	900	July 1	Bal. 1,500
		31	900			20	600
		31	500				

Supplies			
July 1	Bal. 1,100	July 31	750
10	200		

Instructions
After analyzing the accounts, journalize (a) the July transactions and (b) the adjusting entries that were made on July 31. (*Hint:* July transactions were for cash.)

E4-16 The trial balances shown on page 206 are before and after adjustment for Ivy Company at the end of its fiscal year.

*Prepare adjusting entries
from analysis of trial balance.*
(SO 4, 5, 6)

IVY COMPANY
Trial Balance
August 31, 2010

	Before Adjustment		After Adjustment	
	Dr.	**Cr.**	**Dr.**	**Cr.**
Cash	$10,900		$10,900	
Accounts Receivable	8,800		9,400	
Office Supplies	2,500		500	
Prepaid Insurance	4,000		2,500	
Office Equipment	16,000		16,000	
Accumulated Depreciation—Office Equipment		$ 3,600		$ 4,800
Accounts Payable		5,800		5,800
Salaries Payable		0		1,100
Unearned Rent Revenue		1,800		900
Common Stock		10,000		10,000
Retained Earnings		5,600		5,600
Dividends	2,800		2,800	
Service Revenue		34,000		34,600
Rent Revenue		13,200		14,100
Salaries Expense	17,000		18,100	
Office Supplies Expense	0		2,000	
Rent Expense	12,000		12,000	
Insurance Expense	0		1,500	
Depreciation Expense	0		1,200	
	$74,000	$74,000	$76,900	$76,900

Instructions
Prepare the adjusting entries that were made.

Prepare financial statements from adjusted trial balance.
(SO 6)

E4-17 The adjusted trial balance for Ivy Company is given in E4-16.

Instructions
Prepare the income and retained earnings statements for the year and the classified balance sheet at August 31.

Prepare closing entries.
(SO 7)

E4-18 The adjusted trial balance for Ivy Company is given in E4-16.

Instructions
Prepare the closing entries for the temporary accounts at August 31.

Exercises: Set B

Visit the book's companion website, at **www.wiley.com/college/kimmel**, and choose the Student Companion site, to access Exercise Set B.

Problems: Set A

Record transactions on accrual basis; convert revenue to cash receipts.
(SO 2, 4, 9)

P4-1A The following selected data are taken from the comparative financial statements of Ottawa Curling Club. The Club prepares its financial statements using the accrual basis of accounting.

September 30	2010	2009
Accounts receivable for member dues	$ 18,000	$ 11,000
Unearned ticket revenue	20,000	26,000
Dues revenue	153,000	$135,000

Dues are billed to members based upon their use of the Club's facilities. Unearned ticket revenues arise from the sale of tickets to events such as the Skins Game.

Instructions
(*Hint:* You will find it helpful to use T accounts to analyze the following data. You must analyze these data sequentially, as missing information must first be deduced before moving on. Post your journal entries as you progress, rather than waiting until the end.)
(a) Prepare journal entries for each of the following events that took place during 2010.
  1. Dues receivable from members from 2009 were all collected during 2010.
  2. Unearned ticket revenue at the end of 2009 was all earned during 2010.
  3. Additional tickets were sold for $44,000 cash during 2010; a portion of these were used by the purchasers during the year. The entire balance remaining relates to the upcoming Skins Game in 2010.
  4. Dues for the 2009–2010 fiscal year were billed to members.
  5. Dues receivable for 2010 (i.e., those billed in item (4) above) were partially collected.
(b) Determine the amount of cash received by the Club from the above transactions during the year ended September 30, 2010.

(b) Cash received $190,000

P4-2A   Nick Waege started his own consulting firm, Waegelein Consulting, on June 1, 2010. The trial balance at June 30 is as follows.

Prepare adjusting entries, post to ledger accounts, and prepare adjusted trial balance.
(SO 4, 5, 6)

WAEGELEIN CONSULTING
Trial Balance
June 30, 2010

	Debit	Credit
Cash	$ 6,850	
Accounts Receivable	7,000	
Prepaid Insurance	2,640	
Supplies	2,000	
Office Equipment	15,000	
Accounts Payable		$ 4,540
Unearned Service Revenue		5,200
Common Stock		21,750
Service Revenue		8,000
Salaries Expense	4,000	
Rent Expense	2,000	
	$39,490	$39,490

In addition to those accounts listed on the trial balance, the chart of accounts for Waegelein also contains the following accounts: Accumulated Depreciation—Office Equipment, Utilities Payable, Salaries Payable, Depreciation Expense, Insurance Expense, Utilities Expense, and Supplies Expense.

Other data:

1. Supplies on hand at June 30 total $980.
2. A utility bill for $180 has not been recorded and will not be paid until next month.
3. The insurance policy is for a year.
4. $3,900 of unearned service revenue has been earned at the end of the month.
5. Salaries of $1,250 are accrued at June 30.
6. The office equipment has a 5-year life with no salvage value and is being depreciated at $250 per month for 60 months.
7. Invoices representing $3,500 of services performed during the month have not been recorded as of June 30.

Instructions
(a) Prepare the adjusting entries for the month of June.
(b) Post the adjusting entries to the ledger accounts. Enter the totals from the trial balance as beginning account balances. Use T accounts.
(c) Prepare an adjusted trial balance at June 30, 2010.

(b) Service rev. $15,400
(c) Tot. trial
*   balance $44,670*

*Prepare adjusting entries,
adjusted trial balance, and
financial statements.*
(SO 4, 5, 6, 7)

P4-3A The Olathe Hotel opened for business on May 1, 2010. Here is its trial balance before adjustment on May 31.

OLATHE HOTEL
Trial Balance
May 31, 2010

	Debit	Credit
Cash	$ 2,500	
Prepaid Insurance	1,800	
Supplies	2,600	
Land	15,000	
Lodge	70,000	
Furniture	16,800	
Accounts Payable		$ 4,700
Unearned Rent Revenue		3,300
Mortgage Payable		36,000
Common Stock		60,000
Rent Revenue		9,000
Salaries Expense	3,000	
Utilities Expense	800	
Advertising Expense	500	
	$113,000	$113,000

Other data:

1. Insurance expires at the rate of $300 per month.
2. A count of supplies shows $1,050 of unused supplies on May 31.
3. Annual depreciation is $3,600 on the lodge and $3,000 on furniture.
4. The mortgage interest rate is 7%. (The mortgage was taken out on May 1.)
5. Unearned rent of $2,500 has been earned.
6. Salaries of $750 are accrued and unpaid at May 31.

Instructions
(a) Journalize the adjusting entries on May 31.
(b) Prepare a ledger using T accounts. Enter the trial balance amounts and post the adjusting entries.

(c) Rent revenue $11,500
Tot. adj. trial
balance $114,510
(d) Net income $3,840

(c) Prepare an adjusted trial balance on May 31.
(d) Prepare an income statement and a retained earnings statement for the month of May and a classified balance sheet at May 31.
(e) Identify which accounts should be closed on May 31.

*Prepare adjusting entries and
financial statements; identify
accounts to be closed.*
(SO 4, 5, 6, 7)

P4-4A Four Oaks Golf Inc. was organized on July 1, 2010. Quarterly financial statements are prepared. The trial balance and adjusted trial balance on September 30 are shown here.

FOUR OAKS GOLF INC.
Trial Balance
September 30, 2010

	Unadjusted		Adjusted	
	Dr.	Cr.	Dr.	Cr.
Cash	$ 6,700		$ 6,700	
Accounts Receivable	400		1,000	
Prepaid Rent	1,800		900	
Supplies	1,200		360	
Equipment	15,000		15,000	
Accumulated Depreciation—Equipment				$ 350
Notes Payable		$ 5,000		5,000
Accounts Payable		1,710		1,710
Salaries Payable				600
Interest Payable				50
Unearned Rent Revenue		1,000		800

	Unadjusted		Adjusted	
	Dr.	**Cr.**	**Dr.**	**Cr.**
Common Stock		14,000		14,000
Retained Earnings		0		0
Dividends	600		600	
Dues Revenue		13,800		14,400
Rent Revenue		400		600
Salaries Expense	8,800		9,400	
Rent Expense	900		1,800	
Depreciation Expense			350	
Supplies Expense			840	
Utilities Expense	510		510	
Interest Expense			50	
	$35,910	$35,910	$37,510	$37,510

Instructions

(a) Journalize the adjusting entries that were made.

(b) Prepare an income statement and a retained earnings statement for the 3 months ending September 30 and a classified balance sheet at September 30.

(c) Identify which accounts should be closed on September 30.

(d) If the note bears interest at 12%, how many months has it been outstanding?

(b) Net income $2,050
Tot. assets $23,610

P4-5A   A review of the ledger of Napier Company at December 31, 2010, produces these data pertaining to the preparation of annual adjusting entries.

Prepare adjusting entries.
(SO 4, 5)

1. Prepaid Insurance $15,200. The company has separate insurance policies on its buildings and its motor vehicles. Policy B4564 on the building was purchased on July 1, 2009, for $9,600. The policy has a term of 3 years. Policy A2958 on the vehicles was purchased on January 1, 2010, for $7,200. This policy has a term of 2 years.

2. Unearned Subscription Revenue $29,400: The company began selling magazine subscriptions on October 1, 2010 on an annual basis. The selling price of a subscription is $30. A review of subscription contracts reveals the following.

Subscription Start Date	**Number of Subscriptions**
October 1	280
November 1	300
December 1	400
	980

3. Notes Payable, $40,000: This balance consists of a note for 6 months at an annual interest rate of 7%, dated October 1.

4. Salaries Payable $0: There are eight salaried employees. Salaries are paid every Friday for the current week. Five employees receive a salary of $600 each per week, and three employees earn $700 each per week. Assume December 31 is a Wednesday. Employees do not work weekends. All employees worked the last 3 days of December.

Instructions

Prepare the adjusting entries at December 31, 2010.

P4-6A   Happy Camper Travel Court was organized on July 1, 2009, by Kristen Silas. Kristen is a good manager but a poor accountant. From the trial balance prepared by a part-time bookkeeper, Kristen prepared the following income statement (shown below and on the next page) for her fourth quarter, which ended June 30, 2010.

Prepare adjusting entries and a corrected income statement.
(SO 4, 5)

HAPPY CAMPER TRAVEL COURT
Income Statement
For the Quarter ended June 30, 2010

Revenues		
Travel court rental revenues		$216,000
Operating expenses		
Advertising	$ 3,800	
Wages	80,500	

Utilities	900	
Depreciation	2,700	
Repairs	4,000	
Total operating expenses		91,900
Net income		$124,100

Kristen suspected that something was wrong with the statement because net income had never exceeded $30,000 in any one quarter. Knowing that you are an experienced accountant, she asks you to review the income statement and other data.

You first look at the trial balance. In addition to the account balances reported above in the income statement, the ledger contains the following additional selected balances at June 30, 2010.

Supplies	$ 8,200
Prepaid Insurance	14,400
Note Payable	12,000

You then make inquiries and discover the following.

1. Travel court rental revenues include advanced rental payments received for summer occupancy, in the amount of $55,000.

2. There were $1,800 of supplies on hand at June 30.

3. Prepaid insurance resulted from the payment of a one-year policy on April 1, 2010.

4. The mail in July 2010 brought the following bills: advertising for the week of June 24, $110; repairs made June 18, $4,450; and utilities for the month of June, $215.

5. There are three employees who receive wages that total $300 per day. At June 30, two days' wages have been incurred but not paid.

6. The note payable is a 8% note dated May 1, 2010, and due on July 31, 2010.

7. Income tax of $13,400 for the quarter is due in July but has not yet been recorded.

Instructions
(a) Prepare any adjusting journal entries required at June 30, 2010.
(b) Net income $40,165   (b) Prepare a correct income statement for the quarter ended June 30, 2010.
(c) Explain to Kristen the generally accepted accounting principles that she did not recognize in preparing her income statement and their effect on her results.

Journalize transactions and follow through accounting cycle to preparation of financial statements.
(SO 4, 5, 6)

P4-7A On November 1, 2010, the following were the account balances of Montana Equipment Repair.

	Debits		**Credits**
Cash	$ 2,790	Accumulated Depreciation	$ 500
Accounts Receivable	2,910	Accounts Payable	2,300
Supplies	1,120	Unearned Service Revenue	400
Store Equipment	10,000	Salaries Payable	620
		Common Stock	10,000
		Retained Earnings	3,000
	$16,820		$16,820

During November the following summary transactions were completed.

Nov.	8	Paid $1,220 for salaries due employees, of which $600 is for November and $620 is for October salaries payable.
	10	Received $1,500 cash from customers in payment of account.
	12	Received $1,700 cash for services performed in November.
	15	Purchased store equipment on account $4,000.
	17	Purchased supplies on account $1,300.
	20	Paid creditors $2,500 of accounts payable due.
	22	Paid November rent $450.
	25	Paid salaries $1,000.
	27	Performed services on account and billed customers for services provided $900.
	29	Received $550 from customers for services to be provided in the future.

Adjustment data:

1. Supplies on hand are valued at $1,100.
2. Accrued salaries payable are $480.
3. Depreciation for the month is $250.
4. Unearned service revenue of $300 is earned.

Instructions
(a) Enter the November 1 balances in the ledger accounts. (Use T accounts.)
(b) Journalize the November transactions.
(c) Post to the ledger accounts. Use Service Revenue, Depreciation Expense, Supplies Expense, Salaries Expense, and Rent Expense.
(d) Prepare a trial balance at November 30.
(e) Journalize and post adjusting entries.
(f) Prepare an adjusted trial balance.
(g) Prepare an income statement and a retained earnings statement for November and a classified balance sheet at November 30.

(f) Cash $1,370
Tot. adj. trial
balance $22,880
(g) Net loss $1,200

P4-8A Linda Blye opened Cardinal Window Washing Inc. on July 1, 2010. During July the following transactions were completed.

Complete all steps in accounting cycle.
(SO 4, 5, 6, 7, 8)

GLS

July	1	Issued 11,000 shares of common stock for $11,000 cash.
	1	Purchased used truck for $9,000, paying $2,000 cash and the balance on account.
	3	Purchased cleaning supplies for $900 on account.
	5	Paid $1,800 cash on 1-year insurance policy effective July 1.
	12	Billed customers $3,200 for cleaning services.
	18	Paid $1,000 cash on amount owed on truck and $500 on amount owed on cleaning supplies.
	20	Paid $2,000 cash for employee salaries.
	21	Collected $1,400 cash from customers billed on July 12.
	25	Billed customers $2,500 for cleaning services.
	31	Paid $260 for gas and oil used in the truck during month.
	31	Declared and paid $600 cash dividend.

The chart of accounts for Cardinal Window Washing contains the following accounts: Cash, Accounts Receivable, Cleaning Supplies, Prepaid Insurance, Equipment, Accumulated Depreciation—Equipment, Accounts Payable, Salaries Payable, Common Stock, Retained Earnings, Dividends, Income Summary, Service Revenue, Gas & Oil Expense, Cleaning Supplies Expense, Depreciation Expense, Insurance Expense, Salaries Expense.

Instructions
(a) Journalize the July transactions.
(b) Post to the ledger accounts. (Use T accounts.)
(c) Prepare a trial balance at July 31.
(d) Journalize the following adjustments.
   (1) Services provided but unbilled and uncollected at July 31 were $1,700.
   (2) Depreciation on equipment for the month was $250.
   (3) One-twelfth of the insurance expired.
   (4) An inventory count shows $360 of cleaning supplies on hand at July 31.
   (5) Accrued but unpaid employee salaries were $400.
(e) Post adjusting entries to the T accounts.
(f) Prepare an adjusted trial balance.
(g) Prepare the income statement and a retained earnings statement for July and a classified balance sheet at July 31.
(h) Journalize and post closing entries and complete the closing process.
(i) Prepare a post-closing trial balance at July 31.

(f) Cash $4,240
(g) Tot. assets $21,000

Problems: Set B

Record transactions on accrual basis; convert revenue to cash receipts.
(SO 2, 4, 9)

P4-1B The following data are taken from the comparative balance sheets of Pinebluff Club, which prepares its financial statements using the accrual basis of accounting.

December 31	2010	2009
Accounts receivable for member fees	$20,000	$ 6,000
Unearned fees revenue	17,000	18,000

Fees are billed to members based upon their use of the club's facilities. Unearned fees arise from the sale of gift certificates, which members can apply to their future use of club facilities. The 2010 income statement for the club showed that fee revenue of $162,000 was earned during the year.

Instructions

(*Hint:* You will find it helpful to use T accounts to analyze these data.)

(a) Prepare journal entries for each of the following events that took place during 2010.

1. Fees receivable from 2009 were all collected during 2010.
2. Gift certificates outstanding at the end of 2009 were all redeemed during 2010.
3. An additional $40,000 worth of gift certificates were sold during 2010; a portion of these were used by the recipients during the year; the remainder were still outstanding at the end of 2010.
4. Fees for 2010 were billed to members.
5. Fees receivable for 2010 (i.e., those billed in item (4) above) were partially collected.

(b) Cash received $147,000

(b) Determine the amount of cash received by the club with respect to fees during 2010.

Prepare adjusting entries, post to ledger accounts, and prepare an adjusted trial balance.

(SO 4, 5, 6)

P4-2B Tiffany Goren started her own consulting firm, Goren Consulting, on May 1, 2010. The trial balance at May 31 is as shown below.

GOREN CONSULTING
Trial Balance
May 31, 2010

	Debit	Credit
Cash	$ 7,500	
Accounts Receivable	3,000	
Prepaid Insurance	3,600	
Supplies	2,500	
Office Furniture	12,000	
Accounts Payable		$ 3,500
Unearned Service Revenue		4,000
Common Stock		19,100
Service Revenue		7,500
Salaries Expense	4,000	
Rent Expense	1,500	
	$34,100	$34,100

In addition to those accounts listed on the trial balance, the chart of accounts for Goren Consulting also contains the following accounts: Accumulated Depreciation—Office Furniture, Travel Payable, Salaries Payable, Depreciation Expense, Insurance Expense, Travel Expense, and Supplies Expense.

Other data:

1. $500 of supplies have been used during the month.
2. Travel costs incurred but not paid are $260.
3. The insurance policy is for 3 years.
4. $1,500 of the balance in the Unearned Service Revenue account remains unearned at the end of the month.
5. Assume May 31 is a Wednesday and employees are paid on Fridays. Goren Consulting has two employees that are paid $600 each for a 5-day work week.
6. The office furniture has a 5-year life with no salvage value and is being depreciated at $200 per month for 60 months.
7. Invoices representing $2,400 of services performed during the month have not been recorded as of May 31.

Instructions

(a) Prepare the adjusting entries for the month of May.

(b) Post the adjusting entries to the ledger accounts. Enter the totals from the trial balance as beginning account balances. Use T accounts.

(c) Prepare an adjusted trial balance at May 31, 2010.

(c) Tot. trial
balance $37,680

P4-3B Flint Hills Resort opened for business on June 1 with eight air-conditioned units. Its trial balance before adjustment on August 31 is presented here.

Prepare adjusting entries, adjusted trial balance, and financial statements.

(SO 4, 5, 6, 7)

FLINT HILLS RESORT
Trial Balance
August 31, 2010

	Debit	Credit
Cash	$ 24,600	
Prepaid Insurance	5,400	
Supplies	4,300	
Land	40,000	
Cottages	132,000	
Furniture	36,000	
Accounts Payable		$ 6,500
Unearned Rent Revenue		6,800
Mortgage Payable		120,000
Common Stock		100,000
Dividends	5,000	
Rent Revenue		80,000
Salaries Expense	53,000	
Utilities Expense	9,400	
Repair Expense	3,600	
	$313,300	$313,300

Other data:

1. Insurance expires at the rate of $450 per month.

2. A count of supplies on August 31 shows $700 of supplies on hand.

3. Annual depreciation is $4,400 on cottages and $4,000 on furniture.

4. Unearned rent of $5,000 was earned prior to August 31.

5. Salaries of $600 were unpaid at August 31.

6. Rentals of $1,200 were due from tenants at August 31. (Use Accounts Receivable.)

7. The mortgage interest rate is 8% per year. (The mortgage was taken out August 1.)

Instructions

(a) Journalize the adjusting entries on August 31 for the 3-month period June 1–August 31.

(b) Prepare a ledger using T accounts. Enter the trial balance amounts and post the adjusting entries.

(c) Prepare an adjusted trial balance on August 31.

(d) Prepare an income statement and a retained earnings statement for the 3 months ended August 31 and a classified balance sheet as of August 31.

(e) Identify which accounts should be closed on August 31.

(c) Tot. adj. trial
balance $318,000
(d) Net income $11,750

P4-4B Longly Advertising Agency was founded by Jeff Longly in January 2005. Presented here are both the adjusted and unadjusted trial balances as of December 31, 2010.

Prepare adjusting entries and financial statements; identify accounts to be closed.

(SO 4, 5, 6, 7)

LONGLY ADVERTISING AGENCY
Trial Balance
December 31, 2010

	Unadjusted		Adjusted	
	Dr.	Cr.	Dr.	Cr.
Cash	$ 11,000		$ 11,000	
Accounts Receivable	16,000		19,500	
Art Supplies	8,400		6,500	
Prepaid Insurance	3,350		1,790	
Printing Equipment	60,000		60,000	

Accumulated Depreciation		$ 25,000		$ 30,000
Notes Payable		8,000		8,000
Accounts Payable		2,000		2,000
Interest Payable		0		320
Unearned Advertising Revenue		4,000		3,100
Salaries Payable		0		1,300
Common Stock		20,000		20,000
Retained Earnings		5,500		5,500
Dividends	10,000		10,000	
Advertising Revenue		57,600		62,000
Salaries Expense	9,000		10,300	
Insurance Expense			1,560	
Interest Expense			320	
Depreciation Expense			5,000	
Art Supplies Expense			1,900	
Rent Expense	4,350		4,350	
	$122,100	$122,100	$132,220	$132,220

Instructions

(a) Journalize the annual adjusting entries that were made.

(b) Net income $38,570
Tot. assets $68,790

(b) Prepare an income statement and a retained earnings statement for the year ended December 31, and a classified balance sheet at December 31.

(c) Identify which accounts should be closed on December 31.

(d) If the note has been outstanding 6 months, what is the annual interest rate on that note?

(e) If the company paid $10,500 in salaries in 2010, what was the balance in Salaries Payable on December 31, 2009?

Prepare adjusting entries.
(SO 4, 5)

P4-5B A review of the ledger of Quayle Company at December 31, 2010, produces the following data pertaining to the preparation of annual adjusting entries.

1. Salaries Payable $0: There are eight salaried employees. Salaries are paid every Friday for the current week. Six employees receive a salary of $800 each per week, and two employees earn $600 each per week. Assume December 31 is a Wednesday. Employees do not work weekends. All employees worked the last 3 days of December.

2. Unearned Rent Revenue $300,000: The company began subleasing office space in its new building on November 1. Each tenant is required to make a $5,000 security deposit that is not refundable until occupancy is terminated. At December 31 the company had the following rental contracts that are paid in full for the entire term of the lease.

Date	Term (in months)	Monthly Rent	Number of Leases
Nov. 1	6	$4,000	5
Dec. 1	6	7,500	4

3. Prepaid Advertising $13,200: This balance consists of payments on two advertising contracts. The contracts provide for monthly advertising in two trade magazines. The terms of the contracts are as follows.

Contract	Date	Amount	Number of Magazine Issues
A650	May 1	$6,000	12
B974	Sept. 1	7,200	18

The first advertisement runs in the month in which the contract is signed.

4. Notes Payable $80,000: This balance consists of a note for 1 year at an annual interest rate of 7%, dated October 1, 2010.

Instructions

Prepare the adjusting entries at December 31, 2010. Show all computations.

P4-6B   The Wyandotte Travel Agency was organized on January 1, 2008, by Ron Dexter. Ron is a good manager but a poor accountant. From the trial balance prepared by a part-time bookkeeper, Ron prepared the following income statement for the quarter that ended March 31, 2010.

Prepare adjusting entries and a corrected income statement.
(SO 4, 5)

WYANDOTTE TRAVEL AGENCY
Income Statement
For the Quarter Ended March 31, 2010

Revenues		
Travel service revenue		$50,000
Operating expenses		
Advertising	$2,600	
Depreciation	400	
Income tax	1,500	
Salaries	9,000	
Utilities	400	13,900
Net income		$36,100

Ron knew that something was wrong with the statement because net income had never exceeded $5,000 in any one quarter. Knowing that you are an experienced accountant, he asks you to review the income statement and other data.

You first look at the trial balance. In addition to the account balances reported above in the income statement, the trial balance contains the following additional selected balances at March 31, 2010.

Supplies	$ 2,900
Prepaid insurance	1,200
Note payable	10,000

You then make inquiries and discover the following:

1. Travel service revenue includes advance payments for cruises, $20,000.
2. There were $800 of supplies on hand at March 31.
3. Prepaid insurance resulted from the payment of a one-year policy on March 1, 2010.
4. The mail on April 1, 2010, brought the utility bill for the month of March's heat, light, and power, $210.
5. There are two employees who receive salaries of $75 each per day. At March 31, three days' salaries have been incurred but not paid.
6. The note payable is a 6-month, 8% note dated January 1, 2010.

Instructions
(a) Prepare any adjusting journal entries required at March 31, 2010.
(b) Prepare a correct income statement for the quarter ended March 31, 2010.
(c) Explain to Ron the generally accepted accounting principles that he did not recognize in preparing his income statement and their effect on his results.

(b) Net income $13,040

P4-7B   On September 1, 2010, the following were the account balances of Pittsburg Equipment Repair.

Journalize transactions and follow through accounting cycle to preparation of financial statements.
(SO 4, 5, 6)

`GLS`

Debits		**Credits**	
Cash	$ 4,880	Accumulated Depreciation	$ 1,600
Accounts Receivable	3,820	Accounts Payable	3,100
Supplies	800	Unearned Service Revenue	400
Store Equipment	15,000	Salaries Payable	700
	$24,500	Common Stock	10,000
		Retained Earnings	8,700
			$24,500

During September the following summary transactions were completed.

Sept.	8	Paid $1,100 for salaries due employees, of which $400 is for September and $700 is for August salaries payable.
	10	Received $1,500 cash from customers in payment of account.
	12	Received $3,400 cash for services performed in September.
	15	Purchased store equipment on account $3,000.

Sept. 17 Purchased supplies on account $2,000.
20 Paid creditors $4,500 of accounts payable due.
22 Paid September rent $400.
25 Paid salaries $1,200.
27 Performed services on account and billed customers for services provided $1,850.
29 Received $650 from customers for services to be provided in the future.

Adjustment data:

1. Supplies on hand $1,800.
2. Accrued salaries payable $400.
3. Depreciation $200 per month.
4. Unearned service revenue of $250 earned.

Instructions
(a) Enter the September 1 balances in the ledger T accounts.
(b) Journalize the September transactions.
(c) Post to the ledger T accounts. Use Service Revenue, Depreciation Expense, Supplies Expense, Salaries Expense, and Rent Expense.
(d) Prepare a trial balance at September 30.
(e) Journalize and post adjusting entries.

(f) Tot. adj. trial
  balance $30,800
(g) Tot. assets $25,400

(f) Prepare an adjusted trial balance.
(g) Prepare an income statement and a retained earnings statement for September and a classified balance sheet at September 30.

Complete all steps in accounting cycle.

(SO 4, 5, 6, 7, 8)

GLS

P4-8B Kathy Herman opened Kwick Cleaners on March 1, 2010. During March, the following transactions were completed.

Mar. 1 Issued 10,000 shares of common stock for $15,000 cash.
1 Purchased used truck for $8,000, paying $3,000 cash and the balance on account.
3 Purchased cleaning supplies for $1,200 on account.
5 Paid $2,400 cash on 1-year insurance policy effective March 1.
14 Billed customers $3,700 for cleaning services.
18 Paid $1,500 cash on amount owed on truck and $500 on amount owed on cleaning supplies.
20 Paid $1,750 cash for employee salaries.
21 Collected $1,600 cash from customers billed on March 14.
28 Billed customers $4,200 for cleaning services.
31 Paid $350 for gas and oil used in truck during month.
31 Declared and paid a $900 cash dividend.

The chart of accounts for Kwick Cleaners contains the following accounts: Cash, Accounts Receivable, Cleaning Supplies, Prepaid Insurance, Equipment, Accumulated Depreciation—Equipment, Accounts Payable, Salaries Payable, Common Stock, Retained Earnings, Dividends, Income Summary, Service Revenue, Gas & Oil Expense, Cleaning Supplies Expense, Depreciation Expense, Insurance Expense, Salaries Expense.

Instructions
(a) Journalize the March transactions.
(b) Post to the ledger accounts. (Use T accounts.)
(c) Prepare a trial balance at March 31.
(d) Journalize the following adjustments.
  1. Earned but unbilled revenue at March 31 was $600.
  2. Depreciation on equipment for the month was $250.
  3. One-twelfth of the insurance expired.
  4. An inventory count shows $280 of cleaning supplies on hand at March 31.
  5. Accrued but unpaid employee salaries were $830.
(e) Post adjusting entries to the T accounts.

(f) Tot. adj. trial
  balance $28,780
(g) Tot. assets $23,330

(f) Prepare an adjusted trial balance.
(g) Prepare the income statement and a retained earnings statement for March and a classified balance sheet at March 31.
(h) Journalize and post closing entries and complete the closing process.
(i) Prepare a post-closing trial balance at March 31.

Problems: Set C

Visit the book's companion website at **www.wiley.com/college/kimmel** and choose the Student Companion site to access Problem Set C.

Continuing Cookie Chronicle

(*Note:* This is a continuation of the Cookie Chronicle from Chapters 1 through 3.)

CCC4 Cookie Creations is gearing up the winter holiday season. Natalie has had a busy month of December. She needs to journalize and post the month's transactions and complete the accounting cycle, including preparation of financial statements.

Go to the book's companion website. **www.wiley.com/college/kimmel**, to see the completion of this problem.

broadening your perspective

Financial Reporting and Analysis

FINANCIAL REPORTING PROBLEM: *Tootsie Roll Industries, Inc.*

BYP4-1 The financial statements of Tootsie Roll are presented in Appendix A at the end of this book.

Instructions
(a) Using the consolidated income statement and balance sheet, identify items that may result in adjusting entries for prepayments.
(b) Using the consolidated income statement, identify two items that may result in adjusting entries for accruals.
(c) What was the amount of depreciation expense for 2007 and 2006? (You will need to examine the notes to the financial statements or the statement of cash flows.) Where was accumulated depreciation reported?
(d) What was the cash paid for income taxes during 2007, reported at the bottom of the consolidated statement of cash flows? What was income tax expense (provision for income taxes) for 2007? Where is income tax payable reported?

COMPARATIVE ANALYSIS PROBLEM: *Tootsie Roll vs. Hershey Foods*

BYP4-2 The financial statements of Hershey Foods are presented in Appendix B, following the financial statements for Tootsie Roll in Appendix A.

Instructions
(a) Identify two accounts on Hershey Foods' balance sheet that provide evidence that Hershey uses accrual accounting. In each case, identify the income statement account that would be affected by the adjustment process.
(b) Identify two accounts on Tootsie Roll's balance sheet that provide evidence that Tootsie Roll uses accrual accounting (different from the two you listed for Hershey). In each case, identify the income statement account that would be affected by the adjustment process.

RESEARCH CASE

BYP4-3 The August 16, 2007, issue of the *Wall Street Journal* includes an article by Michael Corkery and David Reilly titled "Beazer's Accounting Woes Extend Roller-Coaster Ride."

Instructions
Read the article and answer the following.
(a) Explain what is meant by *cookie-jar accounting*? Why might a company engage in cookie-jar accounting?
(b) The article says the company released "unaudited" financial statements to investors. What does "unaudited" mean? What are the implications to investors of receiving "unaudited" financial statements?
(c) Because of its accounting problems, Beazer was late in providing its audited financial statements to the SEC. What are the possible ramifications of not submitting an annual report on a timely basis?

INTERPRETING FINANCIAL STATEMENTS

BYP4-4 Laser Recording Systems, founded in 1981, produces disks for use in the home market. The following is an excerpt from Laser Recording Systems' financial statements (all dollars in thousands).

LASER RECORDING SYSTEMS
Management Discussion

Accrued liabilities increased to $1,642 at January 31, from $138 at the end of the previous fiscal year. Compensation and related accruals increased $195 due primarily to increases in accruals for severance, vacation, commissions, and relocation expenses. Accrued professional services increased by $137 primarily as a result of legal expenses related to several outstanding contractual disputes. Other expenses increased $35, of which $18 was for interest payable.

Instructions
(a) Can you tell from the discussion whether Laser Recording Systems has prepaid its legal expenses and is now making an adjustment to the asset account Prepaid Legal Expenses, or whether the company is handling the legal expense via an accrued expense adjustment?
(b) Identify each of the adjustments Laser Recording Systems is discussing as one of the four types of possible adjustments discussed in the chapter. How is net income ultimately affected by each of the adjustments?
(c) What journal entry did Laser Recording make to record the accrued interest?

FINANCIAL ANALYSIS ON THE WEB

BYP4-5 *Purpose:* To learn about the functions of the Securities and Exchange Commission (SEC).

Address: **www.sec.gov/about/whatwedo.shtml,** or go to **www.wiley.com/college/kimmel**

Instructions
Use the information in this site to answer the following questions.
(a) What event spurred the creation of the SEC? Why was the SEC created?
(b) What are the four divisions of the SEC? Briefly describe the purpose of each.
(c) What are the responsibilities of the chief accountant?

Critical Thinking

DECISION MAKING ACROSS THE ORGANIZATION

BYP4-6 Grand Valley Park was organized on April 1, 2009, by Janet Elston. Janet is a good manager but a poor accountant. From the trial balance prepared by a part-time bookkeeper, Janet prepared the following income statement for the quarter that ended March 31, 2010.

GRAND VALLEY PARK

Income Statement

For the Quarter Ended March 31, 2010

Revenues		
Rental revenues		$89,000
Operating expenses		
Advertising	$ 4,200	
Wages	27,600	
Utilities	900	
Depreciation	800	
Repairs	2,800	
Total operating expenses		36,300
Net income		$52,700

Janet knew that something was wrong with the statement because net income had never exceeded $20,000 in any one quarter. Knowing that you are an experienced accountant, she asks you to review the income statement and other data.

You first look at the trial balance. In addition to the account balances reported in the income statement, the ledger contains these selected balances at March 31, 2010.

Supplies	$ 5,200
Prepaid Insurance	7,200
Notes Payable	20,000

You then make inquiries and discover the following.

1. Rental revenues include advanced rentals for summer-month occupancy, $21,000.
2. There were $1,800 of supplies on hand at March 31.
3. Prepaid insurance resulted from the payment of a 1-year policy on January 1, 2010.
4. The mail on April 1, 2010, brought the following bills: advertising for week of March 24, $110; repairs made March 10, $380; and utilities $240.
5. There are four employees who receive wages totaling $290 per day. At March 31, 3 days' wages have been incurred but not paid.
6. The note payable is a 3-month, 8% note dated January 1, 2010.

Instructions

With the class divided into groups, answer the following.

(a) Prepare a correct income statement for the quarter ended March 31, 2010.
(b) Explain to Janet the generally accepted accounting principles that she did not follow in preparing her income statement and their effect on her results.

COMMUNICATION ACTIVITY

BYP4-7 On numerous occasions proposals have surfaced to put the federal government on the accrual basis of accounting. This is no small issue because if this basis were used, it would mean that billions in unrecorded liabilities would have to be booked and the federal deficit would increase substantially.

Instructions

(a) What is the difference between accrual basis accounting and cash basis accounting?
(b) Comment on why politicians prefer a cash basis accounting system over an accrual basis system.
(c) Write a letter to your senators explaining why you think the federal government should adopt the accrual basis of accounting.

ETHICS CASE

BYP4-8 Diamond Company is a pesticide manufacturer. Its sales declined greatly this year due to the passage of legislation outlawing the sale of several of Diamond's chemical pesticides. During the coming year, Diamond will have environmentally safe and competitive replacement chemicals to replace these discontinued products. Sales in the next year are expected to greatly exceed those of any prior year. Therefore, the decline in this year's sales and profits appears to be a one-year aberration.

Even so, the company president believes that a large dip in the current year's profits could cause a significant drop in the market price of Diamond's stock and make it a takeover target. To avoid this possibility, he urges Terry Holton, controller, in making this period's year-end adjusting entries to accrue every possible revenue and to defer as many expenses as possible. The president says to Terry, "We need the revenues this year, and next year we can easily absorb expenses deferred from this year. We can't let our stock price be hammered down!" Terry didn't get around to recording the adjusting entries until January 17, but she dated the entries December 31 as if they were recorded then. Terry also made every effort to comply with the president's request.

Instructions
(a) Who are the stakeholders in this situation?
(b) What are the ethical considerations of the president's request and Terry's dating the adjusting entries December 31?
(c) Can Terry accrue revenues and defer expenses and still be ethical?

"ALL ABOUT YOU" ACTIVITY

BYP4-9 Companies prepare balance sheets in order to know their financial position at a specific point in time. This enables them to make a comparison to their position at previous points in time and gives them a basis for planning for the future. In order to evaluate *your* financial position, you can prepare a personal balance sheet. Assume that you have compiled the following information regarding your finances. (*Hint:* Some of the items might not be used in your personal balance sheet.)

Amount owed on student loan balance (long-term)	$5,000
Balance in checking account	1,200
Certificate of deposit (6-month)	3,000
Annual earnings from part-time job	11,300
Automobile	7,000
Balance on automobile loan (current portion)	1,500
Balance on automobile loan (long-term portion)	4,000
Home computer	800
Amount owed to you by younger brother	300
Balance in money market account	1,800
Annual tuition	6,400
Video and stereo equipment	1,250
Balance owed on credit card (current portion)	150
Balance owed on credit card (long-term portion)	1,650

Instructions
Prepare a personal balance sheet using the format you have learned for a classified balance sheet for a company. For the equity account, use M. Y. Own, Capital.

? Answers to Insight and Accounting Across the Organization Questions

p. 165
Q. What motivates sales executives and finance and accounting executives to participate in activities that result in inaccurate reporting of revenues?
A. Sales executives typically receive bonuses based on their ability to meet quarterly sales targets. In addition, they often face the possibility of losing their jobs if they miss those targets. Executives in accounting and finance are very aware of the earnings targets

of Wall Street analysts and investors. If they fail to meet these targets, the company's stock price will fall. As a result of these pressures, executives sometimes knowingly engage in unethical efforts to misstate revenues. As a result of the Sarbanes-Oxley Act of 2002, the penalties for such behavior are now much more severe.

p. 168

Q. Why might the new accounting method cause companies sometimes to spend less on advertising?

A. Under the old approach companies could delay to future periods the expensing of advertising costs. Under that approach, money spent this period did not necessarily immediately reduce income. Under the new approach, a dollar spent on advertising immediately reduces this year's income. If the company is concerned that it might not hit this year's earnings target, it might decide to reduce its advertising spending.

p. 172

Q. Suppose that Robert Jones purchases a $100 gift card at Best Buy on December 24, 2009, and gives it to his wife Mary Jones on December 25, 2009. On January 3, 2010, Mary uses the card to purchase $100 worth of CDs. When do you think Best Buy should recognize revenue and why?

A. According to the revenue recognition principle, companies should recognize revenue when earned. In this case revenue is not earned until Best Buy provides the goods. Thus, when Best Buy receives cash in exchange for the gift card on December 24, 2009, it should recognize a liability, Unearned Revenue, for $100. On January 3, 2010, when Mary Jones exchanges the card for merchandise, Best Buy should recognize revenue and eliminate $100 from the balance in the Unearned Revenue account.

Answers to Self-Study Questions

1. c 2. a 3. d 4. d 5. d 6. c 7. a 8. c 9. c 10. b 11. b 12. c 13. a 14. a 15. d

Merchandising Operations and the Multiple-Step Income Statement

✔ the navigator

- Scan **Study Objectives** ○
- Read **Feature Story** ○
- Scan **Preview** ○
- Read **Text and answer** *Do it!*
  p. 231 ○   p. 234 ○   p. 239 ○   p. 241 ○
- Work **Using the Decision Toolkit** ○
- Review **Summary of Study Objectives** ○
- Work **Comprehensive** *Do it!* p. 250 ○
- Answer **Self-Study Questions** ○
- Complete **Assignments** ○

study objectives

After studying this chapter, you should be able to:

1 Identify the differences between a service company and a merchandising company.

2 Explain the recording of purchases under a perpetual inventory system.

3 Explain the recording of sales revenues under a perpetual inventory system.

4 Distinguish between a single-step and a multiple-step income statement.

5 Determine cost of goods sold under a periodic system.

6 Explain the factors affecting profitability.

7 Identify a quality of earnings indicator.

Who Doesn't Shop at Wal-Mart?

In his book *The End of Work,* Jeremy Rifkin notes that until the 20th century the word *consumption* evoked negative images; to be labeled a "consumer" was an insult. (In fact, one of the deadliest diseases in history, tuberculosis, was often referred to as "consumption.") Twentieth-century merchants realized, however, that in order to prosper, they had to convince people of the need for things not previously needed. For example, General Motors made annual changes in its cars so that people would be discontented with the cars they already owned. Thus began consumerism.

Today consumption describes the U.S. lifestyle in a nutshell. We consume twice as much today per person as we did at the end of World War II. The amount of U.S. retail space per person is vastly greater than that of any other country. It appears that we live to shop.

The first great retail giant was Sears, Roebuck. It started as a catalog company enabling people in rural areas to buy things by mail. For decades it was the uncontested merchandising leader.

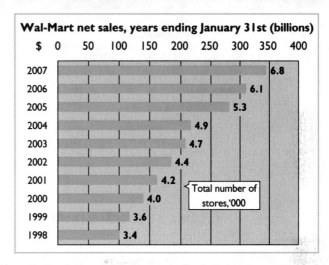

Wal-Mart net sales, years ending January 31st (billions)

Year	Sales	Total number of stores, '000
2007	~350	6.8
2006	~315	6.1
2005	~285	5.3
2004	~255	4.9
2003	~230	4.7
2002	~215	4.4
2001	~190	4.2
2000	~165	4.0
1999	~140	3.6
1998	~120	3.4

Source: "How Big Can It Grow?" *The Economist* (April 17, 2004), pp. 67–69 and *www.walmart.com* (accessed March 17, 2008).

Today Wal-Mart is the undisputed champion provider of basic (and perhaps not-so-basic) human needs. Wal-Mart opened its first store in 1962, and it now has almost 7,000 stores, serving more than 100 million customers every week. A key cause of Wal-Mart's incredible growth is its amazing system of inventory control and distribution. Wal-Mart has a management information system that employs six satellite channels, from which company computers receive 8.4 million updates every minute on what items customers buy and the relationship among items sold to each person.

Measured by sales revenues, Wal-Mart is the largest company in the world. In six years it went from selling almost no groceries to being America's largest grocery retailer.

It would appear that things have never looked better at Wal-Mart. On the other hand, a *Wall Street Journal* article entitled "How to Sell More to Those Who Think It's Cool to Be Frugal" suggests that consumerism as a way of life might be dying. Don't bet your wide-screen TV on it, though.

✔ **the navigator**

On the World Wide Web
Wal-Mart: www.wal-mart.com

Merchandising is one of the largest and most influential industries in the United States. It is likely that a number of you will work for a merchandiser. Therefore, understanding the financial statements of merchandising companies is important. In this chapter you will learn the basics about reporting merchandising transactions. In addition, you will learn how to prepare and analyze a commonly used form of the income statement—the multiple-step income statement. The content and organization of the chapter are as follows.

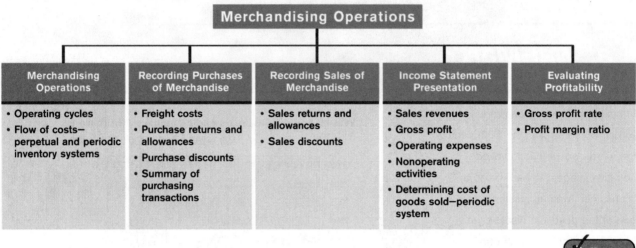

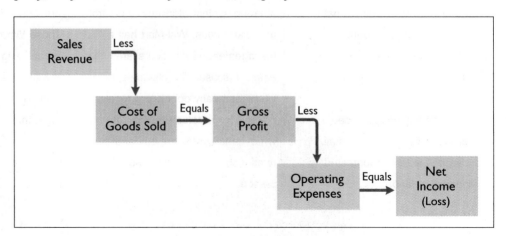

Merchandising Operations

study objective 1

Identify the differences between a service company and a merchandising company.

Wal-Mart, Kmart, and Target are called merchandising companies because they buy and sell merchandise rather than perform services as their primary source of revenue. Merchandising companies that purchase and sell directly to consumers are called **retailers**. Merchandising companies that sell to retailers are known as **wholesalers**. For example, retailer Walgreens might buy goods from wholesaler McKesson; retailer Office Depot might buy office supplies from wholesaler United Stationers. The primary source of revenues for merchandising companies is the sale of merchandise, often referred to simply as sales revenue or **sales**. A merchandising company has two categories of expenses: the cost of goods sold and operating expenses.

The cost of goods sold is the total cost of merchandise sold during the period. This expense is directly related to the revenue recognized from the sale of goods. Illustration 5-1 shows the income measurement process for a merchandising company. The items in the two blue boxes are unique to a merchandising company; they are not used by a service company.

Illustration 5-1 Income measurement process for a merchandising company

OPERATING CYCLES

The operating cycle of a merchandising company ordinarily is longer than that of a service company. The purchase of merchandise inventory and its eventual sale lengthen the cycle. Illustration 5-2 contrasts the operating cycles of service and merchandising companies. Note that the added asset account for a merchandising company is the Merchandise Inventory account.

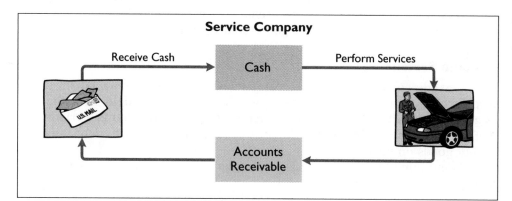

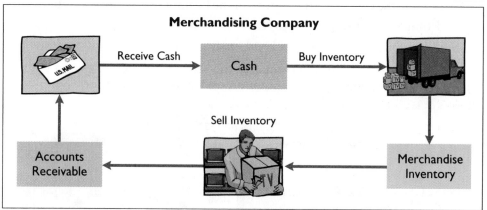

Illustration 5-2
Operating cycles for a service company and a merchandising company

FLOW OF COSTS

The flow of costs for a merchandising company is as follows: Beginning inventory is added to the cost of goods purchased to arrive at cost of goods available for sale. Cost of goods available for sale is assigned to the cost of goods sold (goods sold this period) and ending inventory (goods to be sold in the future). Illustration 5-3 describes these relationships. Companies use one of two systems to account for inventory: a **perpetual inventory system** or a **periodic inventory system**.

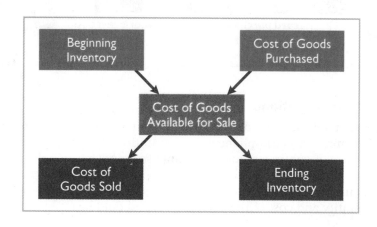

Illustration 5-3 Flow of costs

Perpetual System

In a **perpetual inventory system**, companies maintain detailed records of the cost of each inventory purchase and sale. These records continuously—perpetually—show the inventory that should be on hand for every item. For example, a Ford dealership has separate inventory records for each automobile, truck, and van on its lot and showroom floor. Similarly, a grocery store uses bar codes and optical scanners to keep a daily running record of every box of cereal and every jar of jelly that it buys and sells. Under a perpetual inventory system, a company determines the cost of goods sold **each time a sale occurs**.

Periodic System

In a **periodic inventory system**, companies do not keep detailed inventory records of the goods on hand throughout the period. They determine the cost of goods sold **only at the end of the accounting period**—that is, periodically. At that point, the company takes a physical inventory count to determine the cost of goods on hand.

To determine the cost of goods sold under a periodic inventory system, the following steps are necessary:

1. Determine the cost of goods on hand at the beginning of the accounting period.
2. Add to it the cost of goods purchased.
3. Subtract the cost of goods on hand at the end of the accounting period.

Illustration 5-4 graphically compares the sequence of activities and the timing of the cost of goods sold computation under the two inventory systems.

Illustration 5-4
Comparing perpetual and periodic inventory systems

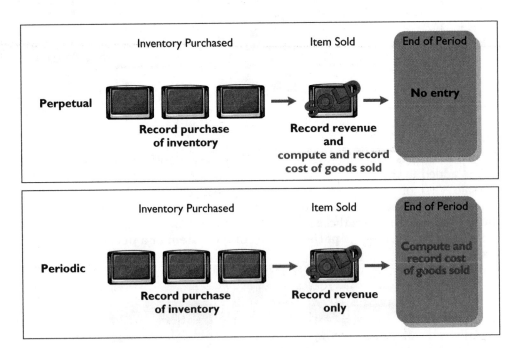

Additional Considerations

Companies that sell merchandise with high unit values, such as automobiles, furniture, and major home appliances, have traditionally used perpetual systems. The growing use of computers and electronic scanners has enabled many more companies to install perpetual inventory systems. The perpetual inventory system is so named because the accounting records continuously—perpetually—show the quantity and cost of the inventory that should be on hand at any time.

A perpetual inventory system provides better control over inventories than a periodic system. Since the inventory records show the quantities that should be on hand, the company can count the goods at any time to see whether the amount of goods actually on hand agrees with the inventory records. If shortages are uncovered, the company can investigate immediately. Although a perpetual inventory system requires additional clerical work and additional cost to maintain inventory records, a computerized system can minimize this cost. As noted in the Feature Story, much of Wal-Mart's success is attributed to its sophisticated inventory system.

Some businesses find it either unnecessary or uneconomical to invest in a computerized perpetual inventory system. Many small merchandising businesses, in particular, find that a perpetual inventory system costs more than it is worth. Managers of these businesses can control their merchandise and manage day-to-day operations using a periodic inventory system.

Because the perpetual inventory system is growing in popularity and use, we illustrate it in this chapter. An appendix to this chapter describes the journal entries for the periodic system.

Investor Insight

Investors are often eager to invest in a company that has a hot new product. However, when snowboard maker Morrow Snowboards, Inc., issued shares of stock to the public for the first time, some investors expressed reluctance to invest in Morrow because of a number of accounting control problems. To reduce investor concerns, Morrow implemented a perpetual inventory system to improve its control over inventory. In addition, it stated that it would perform a physical inventory count every quarter until it felt that the perpetual inventory system was reliable.

? If a perpetual system keeps track of inventory on a daily basis, why do companies ever need to do a physical count?

Recording Purchases of Merchandise

Companies may purchase inventory for cash or on account (credit). They normally record purchases when they receive the goods from the seller. Every purchase should be supported by business documents that provide written evidence of the transaction. Each cash purchase should be supported by a canceled check or a cash register receipt indicating the items purchased and amounts paid. Companies record cash purchases by an increase in Merchandise Inventory and a decrease in Cash.

Each purchase should be supported by a **purchase invoice**, which indicates the total purchase price and other relevant information. However, the purchaser does not prepare a separate purchase invoice. Instead, the purchaser uses as a purchase invoice the copy of the sales invoice sent by the seller. In Illustration 5-5 (page 228), for example, Sauk Stereo (the buyer) uses as a purchase invoice the sales invoice prepared by PW Audio Supply, Inc. (the seller).

The associated entry for Sauk Stereo for the invoice from PW Audio Supply increases Merchandise Inventory and increases Accounts Payable.

May	4	Merchandise Inventory	3,800	
		Accounts Payable		3,800
		(To record goods purchased on account from PW Audio Supply)		

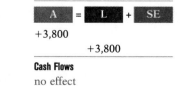

A = L + SE
+3,800
            +3,800

Cash Flows
no effect

Illustration 5-5 Sales invoice used as purchase invoice by Sauk Stereo

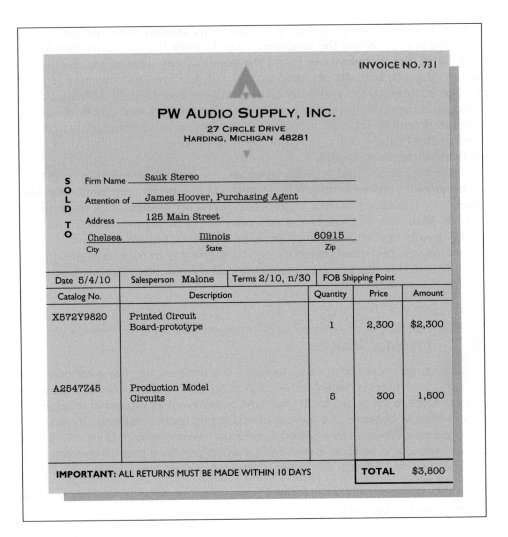

Helpful Hint To better understand the contents of this invoice, identify these items:
1. Seller
2. Invoice date
3. Purchaser
4. Salesperson
5. Credit terms
6. Freight terms
7. Goods sold: catalog number, description, quantity, price per unit
8. Total invoice amount

Under the perpetual inventory system, companies record purchases of merchandise for sale in the Merchandise Inventory account. Thus, Wal-Mart would increase (debit) Merchandise Inventory for clothing, sporting goods, and anything else purchased for resale to customers. Not all purchases are debited to Merchandise Inventory, however. Companies record purchases of assets acquired for use and not for resale, such as supplies, equipment, and similar items, as increases to specific asset accounts rather than to Merchandise Inventory. For example, to record the purchase of materials used to make shelf signs or for cash register receipt paper, Wal-Mart would increase Supplies.

FREIGHT COSTS

The sales agreement should indicate who—the seller or the buyer—is to pay for transporting the goods to the buyer's place of business. When a common carrier such as a railroad, trucking company, or airline transports the goods, the carrier prepares a freight bill in accord with the sales agreement.

Freight terms are expressed as either FOB shipping point or FOB destination. The letters FOB mean **free on board**. Thus, **FOB shipping point** means that the seller places the goods free on board the carrier, and the buyer pays the freight costs. Conversely, **FOB destination** means that the seller places the goods free on board to the buyer's place of business, and the seller pays the freight. For example, the sales invoice in Illustration 5-5 indicates FOB shipping point.

Thus, the buyer (Sauk Stereo) pays the freight charges. Illustration 5-6 illustrates these shipping terms.

Illustration 5-6 Shipping terms

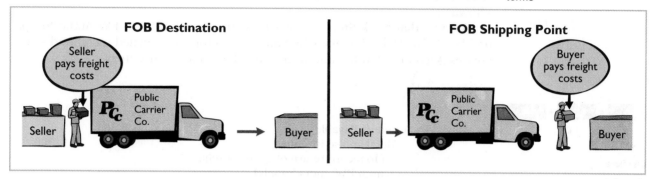

Freight Costs Incurred by Buyer

When the buyer pays the transportation costs, these costs are considered part of the cost of purchasing inventory. As a result, the account **Merchandise Inventory is increased**. For example, if Sauk Stereo (the buyer) pays Haul-It Freight Company $150 for freight charges on May 6, the entry on Sauk's books is:

May	6	Merchandise Inventory	150	
		Cash		150
		(To record payment of freight on goods purchased)		

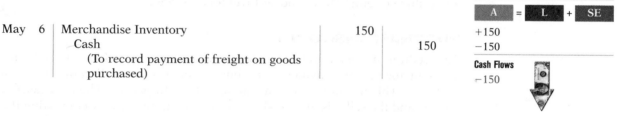

Thus, any freight costs incurred by the buyer are part of the cost of merchandise purchased. The reason: Inventory cost should include any freight charges necessary to deliver the goods to the buyer.

Freight Costs Incurred by Seller

In contrast, **freight costs incurred by the seller on outgoing merchandise are an operating expense to the seller**. These costs increase an expense account titled Freight-out or Delivery Expense. For example, if the freight terms on the invoice in Illustration 5-5 had required that PW Audio Supply (the seller) pay the $150 freight charges, the entry by PW Audio would be:

May	4	Freight-out	150	
		Cash		150
		(To record payment of freight on goods sold)		

When the seller pays the freight charges, the seller will usually establish a higher invoice price for the goods, to cover the expense of shipping.

PURCHASE RETURNS AND ALLOWANCES

A purchaser may be dissatisfied with the merchandise received because the goods are damaged or defective, of inferior quality, or do not meet the purchaser's specifications. In such cases, the purchaser may return the goods to the seller for credit if the sale was made on credit, or for a cash refund if the purchase was for cash. This transaction is known as a **purchase return**. Alternatively, the purchaser may choose to keep the merchandise if the seller is willing to grant a reduction of the purchase price. This transaction is known as a **purchase allowance**.

Assume that Sauk Stereo returned goods costing $300 to PW Audio Supply on May 8. The following entry by Sauk Stereo for the returned merchandise decreases Accounts Payable and decreases Merchandise Inventory.

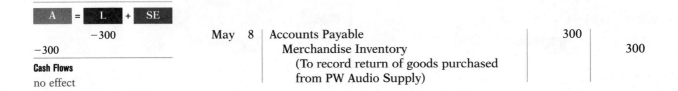

		A = L + SE		
		−300		
−300				

Cash Flows
no effect

May	8	Accounts Payable	300	
		Merchandise Inventory		300
		(To record return of goods purchased from PW Audio Supply)		

Because Sauk Stereo increased Merchandise Inventory when the goods were received, Merchandise Inventory is decreased when Sauk returns the goods.

Suppose instead that Sauk Stereo chose to keep the goods after being granted a $50 allowance (reduction in price). It would reduce (debit) Accounts Payable and reduce (credit) Merchandise Inventory for $50.

PURCHASE DISCOUNTS

The credit terms of a purchase on account may permit the buyer to claim a cash discount for prompt payment. The buyer calls this cash discount a **purchase discount**. This incentive offers advantages to both parties: The purchaser saves money, and the seller is able to shorten the operating cycle by converting the accounts receivable into cash earlier.

Helpful Hint The term *net* in "net 30" means the remaining amount due after subtracting any returns and allowances and partial payments.

The **credit terms** specify the amount of the cash discount and time period during which it is offered. They also indicate the length of time in which the purchaser is expected to pay the full invoice price. In the sales invoice in Illustration 5-5, credit terms are 2/10, n/30, which is read "two-ten, net thirty." This means that a 2% cash discount may be taken on the invoice price less ("net of") any returns or allowances, if payment is made within 10 days of the invoice date (the **discount period**). Otherwise, the invoice price, less any returns or allowances, is due 30 days from the invoice date. Alternatively, the discount period may extend to a specified number of days following the month in which the sale occurs. For example, 1/10 EOM (end of month) means that a 1% discount is available if the invoice is paid within the first 10 days of the next month.

When the seller elects not to offer a cash discount for prompt payment, credit terms will specify only the maximum time period for paying the balance due. For example, the credit terms may state the time period as n/30, n/60, or n/10 EOM. This means, respectively, that the buyer must pay the net amount in 30 days, 60 days, or within the first 10 days of the next month.

When an invoice is paid within the discount period, the amount of the discount decreases Merchandise Inventory. Why? Because the merchandiser records inventory at its cost and, by paying within the discount period, it has reduced that cost. To illustrate, assume Sauk Stereo pays the balance due of $3,500 (gross invoice price of $3,800 less purchase returns and allowances of $300) on May 14, the last day of the discount period. The cash discount is $70 ($3,500 × 2%), and the amount of cash Sauk Stereo paid is $3,430 ($3,500 − $70). The entry Sauk makes to record its May 14 payment decreases Accounts Payable by the amount of the gross invoice price, reduces Merchandise Inventory by the $70 discount, and reduces Cash by the net amount owed.

May 14	Accounts Payable	3,500	
	Cash		3,430
	Merchandise Inventory		70
	(To record payment within discount period)		

If Sauk Stereo failed to take the discount and instead made full payment of $3,500 on June 3, Sauk would debit Accounts Payable and credit Cash for $3,500 each.

June 3	Accounts Payable	3,500	
	Cash		3,500
	(To record payment with no discount taken)		

A merchandising company usually should take all available discounts. Passing up the discount may be viewed as **paying interest** for use of the money. For example, passing up the discount offered by PW Audio would be like Sauk Stereo paying an interest rate of 2% for the use of $3,500 for 20 days. This is the equivalent of an annual interest rate of approximately 36.5% (2% × 365/20). Obviously, it would be better for Sauk Stereo to borrow at prevailing bank interest rates of 6% to 10% than to lose the discount.

SUMMARY OF PURCHASING TRANSACTIONS

The following T account (with transaction descriptions in blue) provides a summary of the effect of the previous transactions on Merchandise Inventory. Sauk originally purchased $3,800 worth of inventory for resale. It then returned $300 of goods. It paid $150 in freight charges, and finally, it received a $70 discount off the balance owed because it paid within the discount period. This results in a balance in Merchandise Inventory of $3,580.

	Merchandise Inventory				
Purchase	May 4	3,800	May 8	300	Purchase return
Freight-in	6	150	14	70	Purchase discount
Balance		3,580			

before you go on...

Do it! On September 5, De La Hoya Company buys merchandise on account from Junot Diaz Company. The selling price of the goods is $1,500. On September 8, De La Hoya returns defective goods with a selling price of $200. Record the transactions on the books of De La Hoya Company.

PURCHASE TRANSACTIONS

Action Plan

- Purchaser records goods at cost.
- When goods are returned, purchaser reduces Merchandise Inventory.

Solution

Sept. 5	Merchandise Inventory		1,500	
	Accounts Payable			1,500
	(To record goods purchased on account)			
8	Accounts Payable		200	
	Merchandise Inventory			200
	(To record return of defective goods)			

Recording Sales of Merchandise

Companies record sales revenues, like service revenues, when earned, in compliance with the revenue recognition principle. Typically, companies earn sales revenues when the goods are transferred from the seller to the buyer. At this point the sales transaction is completed and the sales price is established.

Sales may be made on credit or for cash. Every sales transaction should be supported by a **business document** that provides written evidence of the sale. **Cash register tapes** provide evidence of cash sales. A sales invoice, like the one that was shown in Illustration 5-5 (page 228), provides support for each sale. The original copy of the invoice goes to the customer, and the seller keeps a copy for use in recording the sale. The invoice shows the date of sale, customer name, total sales price, and other relevant information.

The seller makes two entries for each sale: (1) It increases Accounts Receivable or Cash, as well as the Sales account. (2) It increases Cost of Goods Sold and decreases Merchandise Inventory. As a result, the Merchandise Inventory account will show at all times the amount of inventory that should be on hand.

To illustrate a credit sales transaction, PW Audio Supply records the sale of $3,800 on May 4 to Sauk Stereo (see Illustration 5-5) as follows (assume the merchandise cost PW Audio Supply $2,400).

A	=	L	+	SE
+3,800				
				+3,800 Rev.

Cash Flows
no effect

May 4	Accounts Receivable		3,800	
	Sales			3,800
	(To record credit sale to Sauk Stereo			
	per invoice #731)			

A	=	L	+	SE
				−2,400 Exp
−2,400				

Cash Flows
no effect

4	Cost of Goods Sold		2,400	
	Merchandise Inventory			2,400
	(To record cost of merchandise sold on			
	invoice #731 to Sauk Stereo)			

Helpful Hint The merchandiser credits the Sales account only for sales of goods held for resale. Sales of assets not held for resale, such as equipment or land, are credited directly to the asset account.

For internal decision-making purposes, merchandising companies may use more than one sales account. For example, PW Audio Supply may decide to keep separate sales accounts for its sales of TV sets, DVD players, and microwave ovens. Wal-Mart might use separate accounts for sporting goods, children's clothing, and hardware—or it might have even more narrowly defined accounts. By using separate sales accounts for major product lines, rather than a single combined sales account, company management can monitor sales trends more closely and respond more strategically to changes in sales patterns. For example, if TV sales are increasing while microwave oven sales are decreasing, the company might reevaluate both its advertising and pricing policies on each of these items to ensure they are optimal.

On its income statement presented to outside investors a merchandising company would normally provide only a single sales figure—the sum of all of its individual sales accounts. This is done for two reasons. First, providing detail on all of its individual sales accounts would add considerable length to its income statement. Second, companies do not want their competitors to know the details of their operating results. However, Microsoft recently expanded its disclosure of revenue from three to five types. The reason: The additional categories will better enable financial statement users to evaluate the growth of the company's consumer and Internet businesses.

Ethics Note Many companies are trying to improve the quality of their financial reporting. For example, General Electric now provides more detail on its revenues and operating profits.

SALES RETURNS AND ALLOWANCES

We now look at the "flipside" of purchase returns and allowances, which the seller records as sales returns and allowances. These are transactions where the seller either accepts goods back from a purchaser (a return) or grants a reduction in the purchase price (an allowance) so that the buyer will keep the goods. PW Audio Supply's entries to record credit for returned goods involve (1) an increase in Sales Returns and Allowances and a decrease in Accounts Receivable at the $300 selling price, and (2) an increase in Merchandise Inventory (assume a $140 cost) and a decrease in Cost of Goods Sold as shown below. (We have assumed that the goods were not defective. If they were defective, PW Audio would make an adjustment to the inventory account to reflect their decline in value.)

May	8	Sales Returns and Allowances	300	
		Accounts Receivable		300
		(To record credit granted to Sauk Stereo		
		for returned goods)		
	8	Merchandise Inventory	140	
		Cost of Goods Sold		140
		(To record cost of goods returned)		

A = L + SE
−300 Rev
−300
Cash Flows
no effect

A = L + SE
+140
+140 Exp
Cash Flows
no effect

Sales Returns and Allowances is a contra revenue account to Sales. The normal balance of Sales Returns and Allowances is a debit. Companies use a contra account, instead of debiting Sales, to disclose in the accounts and in the income statement the amount of sales returns and allowances. Disclosure of this information is important to management. Excessive returns and allowances suggest problems—inferior merchandise, inefficiencies in filling orders, errors in billing customers, or mistakes in delivery or shipment of goods. Moreover, a decrease (debit) recorded directly to Sales would obscure the relative importance of sales returns and allowances as a percentage of sales. It also could distort comparisons between total sales in different accounting periods.

Accounting Across the Organization

In most industries sales returns are relatively minor. But returns of consumer electronics can really take a bite out of profits. Recently, the marketing executives at Costco Wholesale Corp. faced a difficult decision. Costco has always prided itself on its generous return policy. Most goods have had an unlimited grace period for returns. A new policy will require that certain electronics must be returned within 90 days of their purchase. The reason? The cost of returned products such as flat-panel TVs, computers, and iPods cut an estimated 8 cents per share off Costco's earnings per share, which was $2.30.

Source: Kris Hudson, "Costco Tightens Policy on Returning Electronics," *Wall Street Journal* (February 27, 2007), p. B4.

 If a company expects significant returns, what are the implications for revenue recognition?

SALES DISCOUNTS

As mentioned in our discussion of purchase transactions, the seller may offer the customer a cash discount—called by the seller a sales discount—for the prompt payment of the balance due. Like a purchase discount, a sales discount is based on the invoice price less returns and allowances, if any. The seller increases (debits) the Sales Discounts account for discounts that are taken. The entry by PW Audio Supply to record the cash receipt on May 14 from Sauk Stereo within the discount period is:

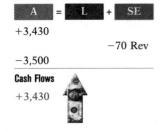

A = L + SE
+3,430
             −70 Rev
−3,500

Cash Flows
+3,430

May 14	Cash	3,430	
	Sales Discounts	70	
	Accounts Receivable		3,500
	(To record collection within 2/10, n/30		
	discount period from Sauk Stereo)		

Like Sales Returns and Allowances, Sales Discounts is a **contra revenue account** to Sales. Its normal balance is a debit. Sellers use this account, instead of debiting sales, to disclose the amount of cash discounts taken by customers. If the customer does not take the discount, PW Audio Supply increases Cash for $3,500 and decreases Accounts Receivable for the same amount at the date of collection.

The following T accounts summarize the three sales-related transactions and show their combined effect on net sales.

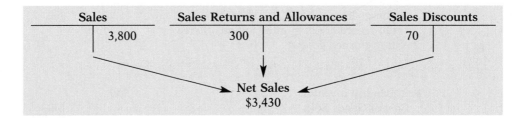

Sales	Sales Returns and Allowances	Sales Discounts
3,800	300	70

Net Sales
$3,430

before you go on...

SALES TRANSACTIONS

Action Plan

- Seller records both the sale and the cost of goods sold at the time of the sale.
- When goods are returned, the seller records the return in a contra account, Sales Returns and Allowances, and reduces Accounts Receivable.
- Any goods returned increase Merchandise Inventory and reduce Cost of Goods Sold. The merchandise inventory should be recorded at its market value (scrap value).

Do it!

On September 5, De La Hoya Company buys merchandise on account from Junot Diaz Company. The selling price of the goods is $1,500, and the cost to Diaz Company was $800. On September 8, De La Hoya returns goods with a selling price of $200 and a cost of $105. Record the transactions on the books of Junot Diaz Company.

Solution

Sept.	5	Accounts Receivable	1,500	
		Sales		1,500
		(To record credit sale)		
	5	Cost of Goods Sold	800	
		Merchandise Inventory		800
		(To record cost of goods sold on		
		account)		
Sept.	8	Sales Returns and Allowances	200	
		Accounts Receivable		200
		(To record credit granted for receipt of		
		returned goods)		
	8	Merchandise Inventory	105	
		Cost of Goods Sold		105
		(To record cost of goods returned)		

the navigator

Income Statement Presentation

Companies widely use two forms of the income statement. One is the **single-step income statement**. The statement is so named because only one step, subtracting total expenses from total revenues, is required in determining net income (or net loss).

study objective **4**
Distinguish between a single-step and a multiple-step income statement.

In a single-step statement, all data are classified into two categories: (1) **revenues**, which include both operating revenues and nonoperating revenues and gains (for example, interest revenue and gain on sale of equipment); and (2) **expenses**, which include cost of goods sold, operating expenses, and nonoperating expenses and losses (for example, interest expense, loss on sale of equipment, or income tax expense). The single-step income statement is the form we have used thus far in the text. Illustration 5-7 shows a single-step statement for Wal-Mart.

Illustration 5-7 Single-step income statements

WAL★MART
ALWAYS LOW PRICES.
Always

WAL-MART STORES, INC.
Income Statements
(in millions)

	For the years ended January 31	
	2007	**2006**
Revenues		
Net sales	$344,992	$308,945
Other revenues, net	3,658	3,156
	348,650	312,101
Expenses		
Cost of goods sold	264,152	237,649
Selling, general, and administrative expenses	64,001	55,739
Interest expense	1,529	1,178
Other expense	1,319	501
Income taxes	6,365	5,803
	337,366	300,870
Net income	$ 11,284	$ 11,231

There are two primary reasons for using the single-step form: (1) A company does not realize any type of profit or income until total revenues exceed total expenses, so it makes sense to divide the statement into these two categories. (2) The form is simple and easy to read.

A second form of the income statement is the **multiple-step income statement**. The multiple-step income statement is often considered more useful because it highlights the components of net income. The Wal-Mart income statement in Illustration 5-8 (page 236) is an example.

The multiple-step income statement has three important line items: gross profit, income from operations, and net income. They are determined as follows.

1. Subtract cost of goods sold from net sales to determine **gross profit**.
2. Deduct operating expenses from gross profit to determine **income from operations**.
3. Add or subtract the results of activities not related to operations to determine **net income**.

International Note The IASB and FASB are involved in a joint project to evaluate the format of financial statements. The first phase of that project involves a focus on how to best present revenues and expenses. One longer-term result of the project may well be an income statement format that better reflects how businesses are run.

Illustration 5-8
Multiple-step income
statements

	WAL-MART STORES, INC. Income Statements (in millions)		
		For the years ended January 31	
		2007	**2006**
Net sales		$344,992	$308,945
Cost of goods sold		264,152	237,649
Gross profit		80,840	71,296
Operating expenses			
Selling, general, and administrative expenses		64,001	55,739
Income from operations		16,839	15,557
Other revenues and gains			
Other revenues, net		3,658	3,156
Other expenses and losses			
Interest expense		1,529	1,178
Other expense		1,319	501
Income before income taxes		17,649	17,034
Income tax expense		6,365	5,803
Net income		$ 11,284	$ 11,231

Note that companies report income tax expense in a separate section of the income statement before net income. The net incomes in Illustrations 5-7 (page 235) and 5-8 are the same. The difference in the two income statements is the amount of detail displayed and the order presented. The following discussion provides additional information about the components of a multiple-step income statement.

SALES REVENUES

The income statement for a merchandising company typically presents gross sales revenues for the period. The company deducts sales returns and allowances and sales discounts (both contra accounts) from sales in the income statement to arrive at net sales. Illustration 5-9 shows the sales revenues section of the income statement for PW Audio Supply.

Illustration 5-9 Statement
presentation of sales
revenues section

PW AUDIO SUPPLY, INC. Income Statement (partial)		
Sales revenues		
Sales		$ 480,000
Less: Sales returns and allowances	$12,000	
Sales discounts	8,000	20,000
Net sales		$460,000

GROSS PROFIT

Alternative Terminology Gross
profit is sometimes referred to as
gross margin.

Companies deduct **cost of goods sold** from sales revenue to determine gross profit. As shown in Illustration 5-8, for example, Wal-Mart had a gross profit of $80.8 billion in fiscal year 2007. Sales revenue used for this computation is **net sales**, which takes into account sales returns and allowances and sales discounts.

On the basis of the PW Audio Supply sales data presented in Illustration 5-9 (net sales of $460,000) and the cost of goods sold (assume a balance of $316,000), PW Audio Supply's gross profit is $144,000, computed as follows.

Net sales	$ 460,000
Cost of goods sold	316,000
Gross profit	**$144,000**

It is important to understand what gross profit is—and what it is not. Gross profit represents the **merchandising profit** of a company. Because operating expenses have not been deducted, it is *not* a measure of the overall profit of a company. Nevertheless, management and other interested parties closely watch the amount and trend of gross profit. Comparisons of current gross profit with past amounts and rates and with those in the industry indicate the effectiveness of a company's purchasing and pricing policies.

OPERATING EXPENSES

Operating expenses are the next component in measuring net income for a merchandising company. At Wal-Mart, for example, operating expenses were $64 billion in fiscal year 2007.

At PW Audio Supply, operating expenses were $114,000. The firm determines its income from operations by subtracting operating expenses from gross profit. Thus, income from operations is $30,000, as shown below.

Gross profit	$144,000
Operating expenses	114,000
Income from operations	$ 30,000

NONOPERATING ACTIVITIES

Nonoperating activities consist of various revenues and expenses and gains and losses that are unrelated to the company's main line of operations. When nonoperating items are included, the label "**Income from operations**" (or "Operating income") precedes them. This label clearly identifies the results of the company's normal operations, an amount determined by subtracting cost of goods sold and operating expenses from net sales. The results of nonoperating activities are shown in the categories "**Other revenues and gains**" and "**Other expenses and losses.**" Illustration 5-10 (page 238) lists examples of each.

Nonoperating income is sometimes very significant. For example, in a recent quarter Sears Holdings earned more than half of its net income from investments in derivative securities.

Illustration 5-10
Examples of nonoperating activities

Other Revenues and Gains
Interest revenue from notes receivable and marketable securities.
Dividend revenue from investments in capital stock.
Rent revenue from subleasing a portion of the store.
Gain from the sale of property, plant, and equipment.
Other Expenses and Losses
Interest expense on notes and loans payable.
Casualty losses from recurring causes, such as vandalism and accidents.
Loss from the sale or abandonment of property, plant, and equipment.
Loss from strikes by employees and suppliers.

Ethics Note Companies manage earnings in various ways. ConAgra Foods recorded a nonrecurring gain for $186 million from the sale of Pilgrim's Pride stock to help meet an earnings projection for the quarter.

The distinction between operating and nonoperating activities is crucial to external users of financial data. These users view operating income as sustainable and many nonoperating activities as nonrecurring. When forecasting next year's income, analysts put the most weight on this year's operating income, and less weight on this year's nonoperating activities.

Ethics Insight

After Enron, increased investor criticism and regulator scrutiny forced many companies to improve the clarity of their financial disclosures. For example, IBM announced that it would begin providing more detail regarding its "Other gains and losses." It had previously included these items in its selling, general, and administrative expenses, with little disclosure.

Disclosing other gains and losses in a separate line item on the income statement will not have any effect on bottom-line income. However, analysts complained that burying these details in the selling, general, and administrative expense line reduced their ability to fully understand how well IBM was performing. For example, previously if IBM sold off one of its buildings at a gain, it would include this gain in the selling, general, and administrative expense line item, thus reducing that expense. This made it appear that the company had done a better job of controlling operating expenses than it actually had.

Other companies that also recently announced changes to increase the informativeness of their income statements included PepsiCo and General Electric.

? Why have investors and analysts demanded more accuracy in isolating "Other gains and losses" from operating items?

The nonoperating activities are reported in the income statement immediately after the operating activities. Included among these activities in Illustration 5-8 for Wal-Mart is net interest expense of $1.5 billion for fiscal year 2007. The amount remaining, after adding the operating and nonoperating sections together, is Wal-Mart's net income of nearly $11.3 billion.

In Illustration 5-11 we have provided the multiple-step income statement of a hypothetical company. This statement provides more detail than that of Wal-Mart and thus is useful as a guide for homework. **(For WileyPLUS homework, individual revenues and expenses are listed in order of magnitude.)**

Illustration 5-11 Multiple step income statement

PW AUDIO SUPPLY, INC.
Income Statement
For the Year Ended December 31, 2010

Sales revenues		
Sales		$480,000
Less: Sales returns and allowances	$12,000	
Sales discounts	8,000	20,000
Net sales		460,000
Cost of goods sold		316,000
Gross profit		144,000
Operating expenses		
Store salaries expense	45,000	
Administrative salaries expense	19,000	
Utilities expense	17,000	
Advertising expense	16,000	
Depreciation expense—store equipment	8,000	
Freight-out	7,000	
Insurance expense	2,000	
Total operating expenses		114,000
Income from operations		30,000
Other revenues and gains		
Interest revenue	3,000	
Gain on sale of equipment	600	
	3,600	
Other expenses and losses		
Interest expense	1,800	
Casualty loss from vandalism	200	
	2,000	
		1,600
Income before income taxes		31,600
Income tax expense		10,100
Net income		$ 21,500

Calculation of gross profit

Calculation of income from operations

Results of activities not related to operations

For homework problems, use the multiple-step form of the income statement unless the requirements state otherwise.

before you go on...

Do it! The following information is available for Art Center Corp. for the year ended December 31, 2010.

MULTIPLE-STEP INCOME STATEMENT

Other revenues and gains	$ 8,000	Net sales	$442,000
Other expenses and losses	3,000	Operating expenses	187,000
Cost of goods sold	147,000		

Prepare a multiple-step income statement for Art Center Corp. The company has a tax rate of 25%.

Action Plan

- Subtract cost of goods sold from net sales to determine gross profit.
- Subtract operating expenses from gross profit to determine income from operations.
- Multiply the tax rate by income before tax to determine tax expense.

Solution

ART CENTER CORP.
Income Statement
For the Year Ended December 31, 2010

Net sales	$442,000
Cost of goods sold	147,000
Gross profit	295,000
Operating expenses	187,000
Income from operations	108,000
Other revenues and gains	8,000
Other expenses and losses	3,000
Income before income taxes	113,000
Income tax expense	28,250
Net income	$ 84,750

DETERMINING COST OF GOODS SOLD UNDER A PERIODIC SYSTEM

study objective 5

Determine cost of goods sold under a periodic system.

Determining cost of goods sold is different when a periodic inventory system is used rather than a perpetual system. As you have seen, a company using a **perpetual system** makes an entry to record cost of goods sold and to reduce inventory *each time a sale is made.* A company using a **periodic system** does not determine cost of goods sold *until the end of the period.* At the end of the period the company performs a count to determine the ending balance of inventory. It then calculates cost of goods sold by subtracting ending inventory from the goods available for sale. Goods available for sale is the sum of beginning inventory plus purchases, as shown in Illustration 5-12.

Illustration 5-12 Basic formula for cost of goods sold using the periodic system

Beginning Inventory
+ Cost of Goods Purchased
Cost of Goods Available for Sale
− Ending Inventory
Cost of Goods Sold

Another difference between the two approaches is that the perpetual system directly adjusts the Merchandise Inventory account for any transaction that affects inventory (such as freight costs, returns, and discounts). The periodic system does not do this. Instead, it creates different accounts for purchases, freight costs, returns, and discounts. These various accounts are shown in Illustration 5-13 (next page), which presents the calculation of cost of goods sold for PW Audio Supply using the periodic approach. Note that the basic elements from Illustration 5-12 are highlighted in Illustration 5-13. You will learn more in Chapter 6 about how to determine cost of goods sold using the periodic system.

The use of the periodic inventory system does not affect the form of presentation in the balance sheet. As under the perpetual system, a company reports merchandise inventory in the current assets section.

The appendix to this chapter provides further detail on the use of the periodic system.

Illustration 5-13 Cost of goods sold for a merchandiser using a periodic inventory system

PW AUDIO SUPPLY, INC.			
Cost of Goods Sold			
For the Year Ended December 31, 2010			
Cost of goods sold			
Inventory, January 1			$ 36,000
Purchases		$325,000	
Less: Purchase returns and			
allowances	$10,400		
Purchase discounts	6,800	17,200	
Net purchases		307,800	
Add: Freight-in		12,200	
Cost of goods purchased			320,000
Cost of goods available for sale			356,000
Inventory, December 31			40,000
Cost of goods sold			$316,000

Helpful Hint The far right column identifies the primary items that make up cost of goods sold of $316,000. The middle column explains cost of goods purchased of $320,000. The left column reports contra purchase items of $17,200.

before you go on...

Do it!

Aerosmith Company's accounting records show the following at the year-end December 31, 2010.

Purchase Discounts	$ 3,400
Freight-in	6,100
Purchases	162,500
Beginning Inventory	18,000
Ending Inventory	20,000
Purchase Returns	5,200

Assuming that Aerosmith Company uses the periodic system, compute (a) cost of goods purchased and (b) cost of goods sold.

Solution

(a) Cost of goods purchased:
  Purchases − Purchase returns − Purchase discounts + Freight-in
  $162,500 − $5,200 − $3,400 + $6,100 = $160,000
(b) Cost of goods sold:
  Beginning inventory + Cost of goods purchased − Ending inventory
  $18,000 + $160,000 − $20,000 = $158,000

COST OF GOODS SOLD–PERIODIC SYSTEM

Action Plan

• To determine cost of goods purchased, adjust purchases for returns, discounts, and freight-in.

• To determine cost of goods sold, add cost of goods purchased to beginning inventory, and subtract ending inventory.

Evaluating Profitability

GROSS PROFIT RATE

A company's gross profit may be expressed as a **percentage** by dividing the amount of gross profit by net sales. This is referred to as the gross profit rate. For PW Audio Supply the gross profit rate is 31.3% ($144,000 ÷ $460,000).

Analysts generally consider the gross profit *rate* to be more informative than the gross profit *amount* because it expresses a more meaningful (qualitative) relationship between gross profit and net sales. For example, a gross profit amount of $1,000,000 may sound impressive. But if it was the result of sales of $100,000,000, the company's gross profit rate was only 1%. A 1% gross profit rate is acceptable in very few industries. Illustration 5-14 presents gross profit rates of a variety of industries.

study objective 6

Explain the factors affecting profitability.

Illustration 5-14 Gross profit rate by industry

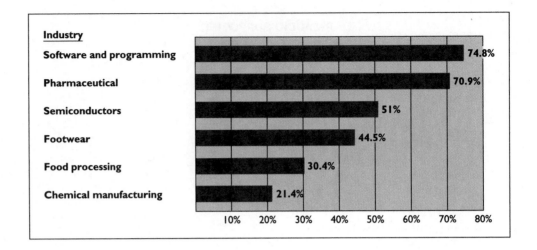

Industry	
Software and programming	74.8%
Pharmaceutical	70.9%
Semiconductors	51%
Footwear	44.5%
Food processing	30.4%
Chemical manufacturing	21.4%

A decline in a company's gross profit rate might have several causes. The company may have begun to sell products with a lower "markup"—for example, budget blue jeans versus designer blue jeans. Increased competition may have resulted in a lower selling price. Or, the company may be forced to pay higher prices to its suppliers without being able to pass these costs on to its customers. The gross profit rates for Wal-Mart and Target, and the industry average, are presented in Illustration 5-15.

Illustration 5-15 Gross profit rate

Gross Profit Rate = $\dfrac{\text{Gross Profit}}{\text{Net Sales}}$		
	2007	2006
Wal-Mart ($ in millions)	$\dfrac{\$80,840}{\$344,992} = 23.4\%$	$\dfrac{\$71,296}{\$308,945} = 23.1\%$
Target	31.9%	31.9%
Industry average	26.7%	

Wal-Mart's gross profit rate increased from 23.1% in 2006 to 23.4% in 2007. In its Management Discussion and Analysis (MD&A), Wal-Mart explained, "Our Wal-Mart Stores and International segment sales yield higher gross margins than our Sam's Club segment. Accordingly, the greater increases in net sales for the Wal-Mart Stores and International segments in fiscal 2007 and 2006 had a favorable impact on the Company's total gross margin."

At first glance it might be surprising that Wal-Mart has a lower gross profit rate than Target and the industry average. It is likely, however, that this can be explained by the fact that grocery products are becoming an increasingly large component of Wal-Mart's sales. In fact, in its MD&A, Wal-Mart once stated, "Because food items carry a lower gross margin than our other merchandise, increasing food sales tends to have an unfavorable impact on our total gross margin." Also, Wal-Mart has substantial warehouse-style sales in its Sam's Club stores, which are a low-margin, high-volume operation. In later chapters we will provide further discussion of the trade-off between sales volume and gross profit.

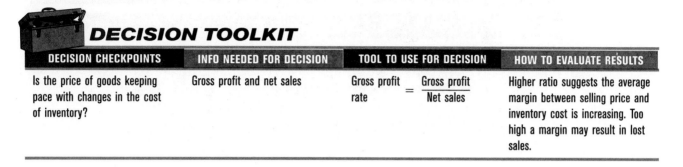

DECISION TOOLKIT

DECISION CHECKPOINTS	INFO NEEDED FOR DECISION	TOOL TO USE FOR DECISION	HOW TO EVALUATE RESULTS
Is the price of goods keeping pace with changes in the cost of inventory?	Gross profit and net sales	$\text{Gross profit rate} = \dfrac{\text{Gross profit}}{\text{Net sales}}$	Higher ratio suggests the average margin between selling price and inventory cost is increasing. Too high a margin may result in lost sales.

PROFIT MARGIN RATIO

The **profit margin ratio** measures the percentage of each dollar of sales that results in net income. We compute this ratio by dividing net income by net sales (revenue) for the period.

How do the gross profit rate and profit margin ratio differ? The gross profit rate measures the margin by which selling price exceeds cost of goods sold. **The profit margin ratio measures the extent by which selling price covers all expenses** (including cost of goods sold). A company can improve its profit margin ratio by either increasing its gross profit rate and/or by controlling its operating expenses and other costs. For example, Radio Shack recently reported increased profit margins which it accomplished by closing stores and slashing costs. While its total sales have been declining, its profitability as measured by its profit margin has increased.

Profit margins vary across industries. Businesses with high turnover, such as grocery stores (Safeway and Kroger) and discount stores (Target and Wal-Mart), generally experience low profit margins. Low-turnover businesses, such as high-end jewelry stores (Tiffany and Co.) or major drug manufacturers (Merck), have high profit margins. Illustration 5-16 shows profit margin ratios from a variety of industries.

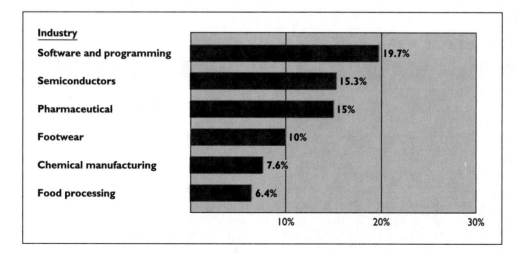

Illustration 5-16 Profit margin ratio by industry

Profit margins for Wal-Mart and Target and the industry average are presented in Illustration 5-17 (page 244).

Illustration 5-17 Profit margin ratio

Profit Margin Ratio = $\dfrac{\text{Net Income}}{\text{Net Sales}}$		
	2007	2006
Wal-Mart ($ in millions)	$\dfrac{\$11,284}{\$344,992}$ = 3.3%	$\dfrac{\$11,231}{\$308,945}$ = 3.6%
Target	4.8%	4.7%
Industry average	3.8%	

Wal-Mart's profit margin declined from 3.6% to 3.3% between 2006 and 2007. This means that the company generated 3.3 cents on each dollar of sales. How does Wal-Mart compare to its competitors? Its profit margin ratio was lower than Target's in both 2006 and 2007 and was less than the industry average. Thus, its profit margin ratio does not suggest exceptional profitability. However, we must again keep in mind that an increasing percentage of Wal-Mart's sales is from low-margin groceries.

Accounting Across the Organization

In its death spiral toward bankruptcy, Kmart appeared to make two very costly strategic errors. First, in an effort to attract customers, it decided to reduce selling prices on over 30,000 items. The problem was that this reduced its gross profit rate—and didn't even have the intended effect of increasing sales because Wal-Mart quickly matched these price cuts. Because Wal-Mart operated much more efficiently than Kmart, Wal-Mart could afford to absorb these price cuts and still operate at a profit. Kmart could not. Its second error was to try to reduce operating costs by cutting its advertising expenditures. This resulted in a reduction in customers—and sales revenue.

 Explain how Wal-Mart's profitability gave it a strategic advantage over Kmart.

DECISION TOOLKIT

DECISION CHECKPOINTS	INFO NEEDED FOR DECISION	TOOL TO USE FOR DECISION	HOW TO EVALUATE RESULTS
Is the company maintaining an adequate margin between sales and expenses?	Net income and net sales	Profit margin ratio $=\dfrac{\text{Net income}}{\text{Net sales}}$	Higher value suggests favorable return on each dollar of sales.

KEEPING AN EYE ON CASH

In Chapter 4 you learned that **earnings have high quality if they provide a full and transparent depiction of how a company performed**. In order to quickly assess earnings quality, analysts sometimes employ the quality of earnings ratio. It is calculated as net cash provided by operating activities divided by net income.

$$\text{Quality of Earnings Ratio} = \frac{\text{Net Cash Provided by Operating Activities}}{\text{Net Income}}$$

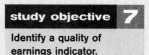

In general, a measure significantly less than 1 suggests that a company may be using more aggressive accounting techniques in order to accelerate income recognition (record income in earlier periods). A measure significantly greater than 1 suggests that a company is using conservative accounting techniques which cause it to delay the recognition of income.

Measures that are significantly less than 1 do not provide definitive evidence of low-quality earnings. Low measures do, however, indicate that analysts should investigate the company's earnings quality by evaluating the causes of the difference between net income and net cash provided by operating activities. Examples of factors that would cause differences are presented in Chapter 4 (p. 190).

Here are the quality of earnings ratios for a number of well-known companies, all of which have measures in excess of 1.

Company Name (dollars in millions)	Net Cash Provided by Operating Activities	÷	Net Income	=	Quality of Earnings Ratio
DuPont	$4,290		$2,988		1.4
Intel	$12,625		$6,976		1.8
Nike	$1,879		$1,492		1.3
Microsoft	$17,796		$14,065		1.3
Wal-Mart	$19,952		$11,284		1.8

 USING THE DECISION TOOLKIT

After having once been as dominant as Wal-Mart, in recent years Sears has struggled to survive. It has enacted many changes trying to turn itself around. In the 1990s, it shocked and disappointed many loyal customers by closing its catalog business. It also closed 113 stores and eliminated 50,000 jobs. None of these changes was enough to make Sears truly competitive, so in March 2005 Sears merged with Kmart to form the third largest U.S. retailer. Here is recent data for Sears Holdings, Inc.

	Year ended	
($ in millions)	01/03/07	12/28/06
Net income	$ 1,490	$ 858
Sales	53,012	48,911
Cost of goods sold	37,820	35,505

Instructions

Using the basic facts in the table, evaluate the following components of Sears's profitability for the years ended January 3, 2007 and December 28, 2006.

Profit margin ratio
Gross profit rate

How do Sears's profit margin ratio and gross profit rate compare to those of Wal-Mart and Target for 2007?

Solution

	Year ended	
($ in millions)	01/03/07	12/28/06
Profit margin ratio	$\frac{\$1,490}{\$53,012}$ = 2.8%	$\frac{\$858}{\$48,911}$ = 1.8%
Gross profit rate	$\frac{\$15,192^*}{\$53,012}$ = 28.7%	$\frac{\$13,406^{**}}{\$48,911}$ = 27.4%

*$53,012 − $37,820   **$48,911 − $35,505

Sears's profit margin ratio (income per dollar of sales) increased from 1.8% to 2.8%. This is well below both Wal-Mart's (3.3%) and Target's (4.8%). Thus, Sears is not as effective at turning its sales into net income as these two competitors.

Sears's gross profit rate improved from 27.4% to 28.7%. This suggests that its ability to maintain its mark-up above its cost of goods sold improved during this period. Sears's gross profit rate of 28.7% is lower than Target's (31.9%) but higher than Wal-Mart's (23.4%). As discussed in the chapter, Wal-Mart's gross profit is depressed by the fact that it sells many grocery products, which are very low-margin. Target is superior to Sears both in its ability to maintain its mark-up above its costs of goods sold (its gross profit rate) and in its ability to control operating costs (its profit margin ratio).

Summary of Study Objectives

1 Identify the differences between a service company and a merchandising company. Because of the presence of inventory, a merchandising company has sales revenue, cost of goods sold, and gross profit. To account for inventory, a merchandising company must choose between a perpetual inventory system and a periodic inventory system.

2 Explain the recording of purchases under a perpetual inventory system. The Merchandise Inventory account is debited for all purchases of merchandise and for freight costs, and it is credited for purchase discounts and purchase returns and allowances.

3 Explain the recording of sales revenues under a perpetual inventory system. When inventory is sold, Accounts Receivable (or Cash) is debited and Sales is credited for the selling price of the merchandise. At the same time, Cost of Goods Sold is debited and Merchandise Inventory is credited for the cost of inventory items sold. Subsequent entries are required for (a) sales returns and allowances and (b) sales discounts.

4 Distinguish between a single-step and a multiple-step income statement. In a single-step income statement, companies classify all data under two categories, revenues or expenses, and net income is determined in one step. A multiple-step income statement shows numerous steps in determining net income, including results of nonoperating activities.

5 Determine cost of goods sold under a periodic system. The periodic system uses multiple accounts to keep track of transactions that affect inventory. To determine cost of goods sold, first calculate cost of goods purchased by adjusting purchases for returns, allowances, discounts, and freight-in. Then calculate cost of goods sold by adding cost of goods purchased to beginning inventory and subtracting ending inventory.

6 Explain the factors affecting profitability. Profitability is affected by gross profit, as measured by the gross profit rate, and by management's ability to control costs, as measured by the profit margin ratio.

7 Identify a quality of earnings indicator. Earnings have high quality if they provide a full and transparent depiction of how a company performed. An indicator of the quality of earnings is the quality of earnings ratio, which is net cash provided by operating activities divided by net income. Measures above 1 suggest the company is employing conservative accounting practices. Measures significantly below 1 might suggest the company is using aggressive accounting to accelerate the recognition of income.

DECISION TOOLKIT   A SUMMARY

DECISION CHECKPOINTS	INFO NEEDED FOR DECISION	TOOL TO USE FOR DECISION	HOW TO EVALUATE RESULTS
Is the price of goods keeping pace with changes in the cost of inventory?	Gross profit and net sales	$\text{Gross profit rate} = \dfrac{\text{Gross profit}}{\text{Net sales}}$	Higher ratio suggests the average margin between selling price and inventory cost is increasing. Too high a margin may result in lost sales.
Is the company maintaining an adequate margin between sales and expenses?	Net income and net sales	$\text{Profit margin ratio} = \dfrac{\text{Net income}}{\text{Net sales}}$	Higher value suggests favorable return on each dollar of sales.

Periodic Inventory System

As described in this chapter, companies may use one of two basic systems of accounting for inventories: (1) the perpetual inventory system or (2) the periodic inventory system. In the chapter we focused on the characteristics of the perpetual inventory system. In this appendix we discuss and illustrate the **periodic inventory system**. One key difference between the two systems is the point at which the company computes cost of goods sold. For a visual reminder of this difference, you may want to refer back to Illustration 5-4 on page 226.

RECORDING MERCHANDISE TRANSACTIONS

In a **periodic inventory system**, companies record revenues from the sale of merchandise when sales are made, just as in a perpetual system. Unlike the perpetual system, however, companies **do not attempt on the date of sale to record the cost of the merchandise sold**. Instead, they take a physical inventory count at the **end of the period** to determine (1) the cost of the merchandise then on hand and (2) the cost of the goods sold during the period. And, **under a periodic system, companies record purchases of merchandise in the Purchases account rather than the Merchandise Inventory account**. Also, in a periodic system, purchase returns and allowances, purchase discounts, and freight costs on purchases are recorded in separate accounts.

> **study objective 8**
>
> Explain the recording of purchases and sales of inventory under a periodic inventory system.

To illustrate the recording of merchandise transactions under a periodic inventory system, we will use purchase/sale transactions between PW Audio Supply, Inc. and Sauk Stereo, as illustrated for the perpetual inventory system in this chapter.

RECORDING PURCHASES OF MERCHANDISE

On the basis of the sales invoice (Illustration 5-5, shown on page 228) and receipt of the merchandise ordered from PW Audio Supply, Sauk Stereo records the $3,800 purchase as follows.

May 4	Purchases	3,800	
	Accounts Payable		3,800
	(To record goods purchased on account from PW Audio Supply)		

Purchases is a temporary account whose normal balance is a debit.

FREIGHT COSTS

When the purchaser directly incurs the freight costs, it debits the account Freight-in (or Transportation-in). For example, if Sauk pays Haul-It Freight Company $150 for freight charges on its purchase from PW Audio Supply on May 6, the entry on Sauk's books is:

May 6	Freight-in (Transportation-in)	150	
	Cash		150
	(To record payment of freight on goods purchased)		

Like Purchases, Freight-in is a temporary account whose normal balance is a debit. **Freight-in is part of cost of goods purchased**. The reason is that cost of goods purchased should include any freight charges necessary to bring the goods to the purchaser. Freight costs are not subject to a purchase discount. Purchase discounts apply on the invoice cost of the merchandise.

Purchase Returns and Allowances

Because $300 of merchandise received from PW Audio Supply is inoperable, Sauk Stereo returns the goods and prepares the following entry to recognize the return.

May	8	Accounts Payable	300	
		Purchase Returns and Allowances		300
		(To record return of goods purchased from PW Audio Supply)		

Purchase Returns and Allowances is a temporary account whose normal balance is a credit.

Purchase Discounts

On May 14 Sauk Stereo pays the balance due on account to PW Audio Supply, taking the 2% cash discount allowed by PW Audio for payment within 10 days. Sauk Stereo records the payment and discount as follows.

May	14	Accounts Payable ($3,800 − $300)	3,500	
		Purchase Discounts ($3,500 ×.02)		70
		Cash		3,430
		(To record payment within the discount period)		

Purchase Discounts is a temporary account whose normal balance is a credit.

RECORDING SALES OF MERCHANDISE

The seller, PW Audio Supply, records the sale of $3,800 of merchandise to Sauk Stereo on May 4 (sales invoice No. 731, Illustration 5-5) as follows.

May	4	Accounts Receivable	3,800	
		Sales		3,800
		(To record credit sales to Sauk Stereo per invoice #731)		

Sales Returns and Allowances

To record the returned goods received from Sauk Stereo on May 8, PW Audio Supply records the $300 sales return as follows.

May	8	Sales Returns and Allowances	300	
		Accounts Receivable		300
		(To record credit granted to Sauk Stereo for returned goods)		

Sales Discounts

On May 14, PW Audio Supply receives payment of $3,430 on account from Sauk Stereo. PW Audio honors the 2% cash discount and records the payment of Sauk's account receivable in full as follows.

May 14	Cash	3,430	
	Sales Discounts ($3,500 ×.02)	70	
	Accounts Receivable ($3,800 − $300)		3,500
	(To record collection within 2/10, n/30		
	discount period from Sauk Stereo)		

COMPARISON OF ENTRIES— PERPETUAL vs. PERIODIC

ENTRIES ON SAUK STEREO'S BOOKS

	Transaction	Perpetual Inventory System		Periodic Inventory System	

May 4	Purchase of merchandise on credit.	Merchandise Inventory
		  Accounts Payable
			3,800
			3,800
				Purchases
				  Accounts Payable
					3,800
					3,800

May 6	Freight costs on purchases.	Merchandise Inventory
		  Cash
			150
			150
				Freight-in
				  Cash
					150
					150

May 8	Purchase returns and allowances.	Accounts Payable
		  Merchandise Inventory
			300
			300
				Accounts Payable
				  Purchase Returns
				  and Allowances
					300
					
					300

May 14	Payment on account with a discount.	Accounts Payable
		  Cash
		  Merchandise Inventory
			3,500
			3,430
			70
				Accounts Payable
				  Cash
				  Purchase Discounts
					3,500
					3,430
					70

ENTRIES ON PW AUDIO SUPPLY'S BOOKS

	Transaction	Perpetual Inventory System		Periodic Inventory System	

May 4	Sale of merchandise on credit.	Accounts Receivable
		  Sales
			3,800
			3,800
				Accounts Receivable
				  Sales
					3,800
					3,800

		Cost of Goods Sold
		  Merchandise Inventory
			2,400
			2,400
				No entry for cost of
				  goods sold	

May 8	Return of merchandise sold.	Sales Returns and Allowances
		  Accounts Receivable
			300
			300
				Sales Returns and Allowances
				  Accounts Receivable
					300
					300

		Merchandise Inventory Cost of Goods Sold	140 140	No entry	

May 14	Cash received on account with a discount.	Cash
		Sales Discounts
		  Accounts Receivable
			3,430
			70
			3,500
				Cash
				Sales Discounts
				  Accounts Receivable
					3,430
					70
					3,500

Summary of Study Objective for Appendix

8 **Explain the recording of purchases and sales of inventory under a periodic inventory system.** To record purchases, entries are required for (a) cash and credit purchases, (b) purchase returns and allowances, (c) purchase discounts, and (d) freight costs. To record sales, entries are required for (a) cash and credit sales, (b) sales returns and allowances, and (c) sales discounts.

Glossary

Contra revenue account *(p. 233)* An account that is offset against a revenue account on the income statement.

Cost of goods sold *(p. 224)* The total cost of merchandise sold during the period.

Gross profit *(p. 236)* The excess of net sales over the cost of goods sold.

Gross profit rate *(p. 241)* Gross profit expressed as a percentage by dividing the amount of gross profit by net sales.

Net sales (p. 236) Sales less sales returns and allowances and sales discounts.

Periodic inventory system (p. 226) An inventory system in which a company does not maintain detailed records of goods on hand and determines the cost of goods sold only at the end of an accounting period.

Perpetual inventory system (p. 226) A detailed inventory system in which a company maintains the cost of each inventory item and the records continuously show the inventory that should be on hand.

Profit margin ratio (p. 243) Measures the percentage of each dollar of sales that results in net income, computed by dividing net income by net sales.

Purchase allowance (p. 230) A deduction made to the selling price of merchandise, granted by the seller so that the buyer will keep the merchandise.

Purchase discount (p. 230) A cash discount claimed by a buyer for prompt payment of a balance due.

Purchase invoice (p. 227) A document that supports each purchase.

Purchase return (p. 230) A return of goods from the buyer to the seller for cash or credit.

Quality of earnings ratio (p. 244) A measure used to indicate the extent to which a company's earnings provide a full and transparent depiction of its performance; computed as net cash provided by operating activities divided by net income.

Sales discount (p. 234) A reduction given by a seller for prompt payment of a credit sale.

Sales invoice (p. 232) A document that provides support for each sale.

Sales returns and allowances (p. 233) Transactions in which the seller either accepts goods back from the purchaser (a return) or grants a reduction in the purchase price (an allowance) so that the buyer will keep the goods.

Sales revenue (p. 224) Primary source of revenue in a merchandising company.

Comprehensive Do it!

The adjusted trial balance for the year ended December 31, 2010, for Dykstra Company is shown below.

DYKSTRA COMPANY
Adjusted Trial Balance
For the Year Ended December 31, 2010

	Dr.	Cr.
Cash	$ 14,500	
Accounts Receivable	11,100	
Merchandise Inventory	29,000	
Prepaid Insurance	2,500	
Store Equipment	95,000	
Accumulated Depreciation		$ 18,000
Notes Payable		25,000
Accounts Payable		10,600
Common Stock		70,000
Retained Earnings		11,000
Dividends	12,000	
Sales		536,800
Sales Returns and Allowances	6,700	
Sales Discounts	5,000	
Cost of Goods Sold	363,400	
Freight-out	7,600	
Advertising Expense	12,000	
Store Salaries Expense	56,000	
Utilities Expense	18,000	
Rent Expense	24,000	
Depreciation Expense	9,000	
Insurance Expense	4,500	
Interest Expense	3,600	
Interest Revenue		2,500
	$673,900	$673,900

Instructions

Prepare a multiple-step income statement for Dykstra Company. Assume a tax rate of 30 percent.

Solution to Comprehensive Do it!

DYKSTRA COMPANY
Income Statement
For the Year Ended December 31, 2010

Sales revenues		
Sales		$536,800
Less: Sales returns and allowances	$ 6,700	
Sales discounts	5,000	11,700
Net sales		525,100
Cost of goods sold		363,400
Gross profit		161,700
Operating expenses		
Store salaries expense	56,000	
Rent expense	24,000	
Utilities expense	18,000	
Advertising expense	12,000	
Depreciation expense	9,000	
Freight-out	7,600	
Insurance expense	4,500	
Total operating expenses		131,100
Income from operations		30,600
Other revenues and gains		
Interest revenue	2,500	
Other expenses and losses		
Interest expense	3,600	1,100
Income before income taxes		29,500
Income tax expense		8,850
Net income		$ 20,650

Action Plan

- In preparing the income statement, remember that the key components are net sales, cost of goods sold, gross profit, total operating expenses, and net income (loss). These components are reported in the right-hand column of the income statement.
- Present nonoperating items after income from operations.

Note: All Questions, Exercises, and Problems marked with an asterisk relate to material in the appendix to the chapter.

Self-Study Questions

Answers are at the end of the chapter.

(SO 1) 1. Which of the following statements about a periodic inventory system is true?
(a) Companies determine cost of goods sold only at the end of the accounting period.
(b) Companies continuously maintain detailed records of the cost of each inventory purchase and sale.
(c) The periodic system provides better control over inventories than a perpetual system.
(d) The increased use of computerized systems has increased the use of the periodic system.

2. Which of the following items does *not* result in an (SO 2) adjustment in the merchandise inventory account under a perpetual system?
(a) A purchase of merchandise.
(b) A return of merchandise inventory to the supplier.
(c) Payment of freight costs for goods shipped to a customer.
(d) Payment of freight costs for goods received from a supplier.

3. Which sales accounts normally have a debit balance? (SO 3)
(a) Sales discounts.
(b) Sales returns and allowances.

(c) Both (a) and (b).
(d) Neither (a) nor (b).

(SO 3) 4. A company makes a credit sale of $750 on June 13, terms 2/10, n/30, on which it grants a return of $50 on June 16. What amount is received as payment in full on June 23?
(a) $700.   (c) $685.
(b) $686.   (d) $650.

(SO 3) 5. To record the sale of goods for cash in a perpetual inventory system:
(a) only one journal entry is necessary to record cost of goods sold and reduction of inventory.
(b) only one journal entry is necessary to record the receipt of cash and the sales revenue.
(c) two journal entries are necessary: one to record the receipt of cash and sales revenue, and one to record the cost of goods sold and reduction of inventory.
(d) two journal entries are necessary: one to record the receipt of cash and reduction of inventory, and one to record the cost of goods sold and sales revenue.

(SO 4) 6. Gross profit will result if:
(a) operating expenses are less than net income.
(b) sales revenues are greater than operating expenses.
(c) sales revenues are greater than cost of goods sold.
(d) operating expenses are greater than cost of goods sold.

(SO 4) 7. If sales revenues are $400,000, cost of goods sold is $310,000, and operating expenses are $60,000, what is the gross profit?
(a) $30,000.   (c) $340,000.
(b) $90,000.   (d) $400,000.

(SO 4) 8. The income statement for a merchandising company shows each of these features *except*:
(a) gross profit.
(b) cost of goods sold.
(c) a sales revenue section.
(d) All of these are present.

(SO 5) 9. If beginning inventory is $60,000, cost of goods purchased is $380,000, and ending inventory is $50,000, what is cost of goods sold under a periodic system?
(a) $390,000.   (c) $330,000.
(b) $370,000.   (d) $420,000.

(SO 5) 10. Arbor Corporation had reported the following amounts at December 31, 2010: Sales $184,000; ending inventory $11,600; beginning inventory $17,200; purchases

$60,400; purchase discounts $3,000; purchase returns and allowances $1,100; freight-in $600; freight-out $900. Calculate the cost of goods available for sale.
(a) $69,400.
(b) $74,100.
(c) $56,900.
(d) $197,700.

11. Which of the following would affect the (SO 6) gross profit rate? (Assume sales remains constant.)
(a) An increase in advertising expense.
(b) A decrease in depreciation expense.
(c) An increase in cost of goods sold.
(d) A decrease in insurance expense.

12. The gross profit *rate* is equal to: (SO 6)
(a) net income divided by sales.
(b) cost of goods sold divided by sales.
(c) net sales minus cost of goods sold, divided by net sales.
(d) sales minus cost of goods sold, divided by cost of goods sold.

13. During the year ended December 31, 2010, State (SO 6) Street Corporation had the following results: Sales $267,000; cost of good sold $107,000; net income $92,400; operating expenses $55,400; net cash provided by operating activities $108,950. What was the company's profit margin ratio?
(a) 40%.   (c) 20.5%.
(b) 60%.   (d) 34.6%.

14. A quality of earnings ratio: (SO 7)
(a) is computed as net income divided by net cash provided by operating activities.
(b) that is less than 1 indicates that a company might be using aggressive accounting tactics.
(c) that is greater than 1 indicates that a company might be using aggressive accounting tactics.
(d) is computed as net cash provided by operating activities divided by total assets.

*15. When goods are purchased for resale by a company (SO 8) using a periodic inventory system:
(a) purchases on account are debited to Merchandise Inventory.
(b) purchases on account are debited to Purchases.
(c) purchase returns are debited to Purchase Returns and Allowances.
(d) freight costs are debited to Purchases.

Go to the book's companion website, **www. wiley.com/college/kimmel**, to access additional Self-Study Questions.

Questions

1. (a) "The steps in the accounting cycle for a merchandising company differ from the steps in the accounting cycle for a service enterprise." Do you agree or disagree?
(b) Is the measurement of net income in a merchandising company conceptually the same as in a service enterprise? Explain.

2. How do the components of revenues and expenses differ between a merchandising company and a service enterprise?

3. Denise Fritz, CEO of Save-A-Lot Discount Stores, is considering a recommendation made by both the company's purchasing manager and director

of finance that the company should invest in a sophisticated new perpetual inventory system to replace its periodic system. Explain the primary difference between the two systems, and discuss the potential benefits of a perpetual inventory system.

4. (a) Explain the income measurement process in a merchandising company.
   (b) How does income measurement differ between a merchandising company and a service company?

5. Keisler Co. has sales revenue of $100,000, cost of goods sold of $65,000, and operating expenses of $20,000. What is its gross profit?

6. Janet Kent believes revenues from credit sales may be earned before they are collected in cash. Do you agree? Explain.

7. (a) What is the primary source document for recording (1) cash sales and (2) credit sales?
   (b) Using XXs for amounts, give the journal entry for each of the transactions in part (a).

8. A credit sale is made on July 10 for $900, terms 2/10, n/30. On July 12, the purchaser returns $100 of goods for credit. Give the journal entry on July 19 to record the receipt of the balance due within the discount period.

9. ◀ As the end of Ray Company's fiscal year-end approached, it became clear that the company had considerable excess inventory. Jefferson Bunker, the head of marketing and sales, ordered salespeople to "add 20% more units to each order that you ship. The customers can always ship the extra back next period if they decide they don't want it. We've got to do it to meet this year's sales goal." Discuss the accounting implications of Jefferson's action.

10. ◀ To encourage bookstores to buy a broader range of book titles, and to discourage price discounting, the publishing industry allows bookstores to return unsold books to the publisher. This results in very significant returns each year. To ensure proper recognition of revenues, how should publishing companies account for these returns?

11. Goods costing $1,900 are purchased on account on July 15 with credit terms of 2/10, n/30. On July 18 the purchaser receives a $200 credit memo from the supplier for damaged goods. Give the journal entry on July 24 to record payment of the balance due within the discount period.

12. ◀ Medina Company reports net sales of $800,000, gross profit of $560,000, and net income of $260,000. What are its operating expenses?

13. ◀ Allison Company has always provided its customers with payment terms of 1/10, n/30. Members of its sale force have commented that competitors are offering customers 2/10, n/45. Explain what these terms mean, and discuss the implications to Allison of switching its payment terms to those of its competitors.

14. ◀ In its year-end earnings announcement press release, Optimistic Corp. announced that its earnings increased by $15 million relative to the previous year. This represented a 20% increase. Inspection of its in-

come statement reveals that the company reported a $20 million gain under "Other revenues and gains" from the sale of one of its factories. Discuss the implications of this gain from the perspective of a potential investor.

15. Identify the distinguishing features of an income statement for a merchandising company.

16. Why is the normal operating cycle for a merchandising company likely to be longer than for a service company?

17. 🍬 What title does Tootsie Roll use for gross profit? How did it present gross profit? By how much did its total gross profit change, and in what direction, in 2007?

18. What merchandising account(s) will appear in the post-closing trial balance?

19. What types of businesses are most likely to use a perpetual inventory system?

20. Identify the accounts that are added to or deducted from purchases to determine the cost of goods purchased under a periodic system. For each account, indicate (a) whether it is added or deducted and (b) its normal balance.

21. In the following cases, use a periodic inventory system to identify the item(s) designated by the letters X and Y.
   (a) Purchases $- X - Y =$ Net purchases.
   (b) Cost of goods purchased $-$ Net purchases $= X$.
   (c) Beginning inventory $+ X =$ Cost of goods available for sale.
   (d) Cost of goods available for sale $-$ Cost of goods sold $= X$.

22. 🔧 What two ratios measure factors that affect profitability?

23. 🔧 What factors affect a company's gross profit rate—that is, what can cause the gross profit rate to increase and what can cause it to decrease?

24. ◀ Tim Messer, director of marketing, wants to reduce the selling price of his company's products by 15% to increase market share. He says, "I know this will reduce our gross profit rate, but the increased number of units sold will make up for the lost margin." Before this action is taken, what other factors does the company need to consider?

25. Benny Kat is considering investing in Stevenson Pet Food Company. Stevenson's net income increased considerably during the most recent year, even though many other companies in the same industry reported disappointing earnings. Benny wants to know whether the company's earnings provide a reasonable depiction of its results. What initial step can Benny take to help determine whether he needs to investigate further?

*26. On July 15 a company purchases on account goods costing $1,900, with credit terms of 2/10, n/30. On July 18 the company receives a $200 credit memo from the supplier for damaged goods. Give the journal entry on July 24 to record payment of the balance due within the discount period assuming a periodic inventory system.

Brief Exercises

Compute missing amounts in determining net income.
(SO 1, 4)

BE5-1 Presented here are the components in Pedersen Company's income statement. Determine the missing amounts.

Sales	Cost of Goods Sold	Gross Profit	Operating Expenses	Net Income
$ 71,200	(b)	$ 30,000	(d)	$10,800
$108,000	$70,000	(c)	(e)	$29,500
(a)	$71,900	$109,600	$46,200	(f)

Journalize perpetual inventory entries.
(SO 2, 3)

BE5-2 Prior Company buys merchandise on account from Wood Company. The selling price of the goods is $900 and the cost of the goods sold is $630. Both companies use perpetual inventory systems. Journalize the transactions on the books of both companies.

Journalize sales transactions.
(SO 3)

BE5-3 Prepare the journal entries to record the following transactions on Ramirez Company's books using a perpetual inventory system.
(a) On March 2 Ramirez Company sold $800,000 of merchandise to Ikerd Company, terms 2/10, n/30. The cost of the merchandise sold was $540,000.
(b) On March 6 Ikerd Company returned $110,000 of the merchandise purchased on March 2. The cost of the merchandise returned was $75,000.
(c) On March 12 Ramirez Company received the balance due from Ikerd Company.

Journalize purchase transactions.
(SO 2)

BE5-4 From the information in BE5-3, prepare the journal entries to record these transactions on Ikerd Company's books under a perpetual inventory system.

Prepare sales revenue section of income statement.
(SO 4)

BE5-5 Carpenter Company provides this information for the month ended October 31, 2010: sales on credit $300,000; cash sales $150,000; sales discounts $5,000; and sales returns and allowances $22,000. Prepare the sales revenues section of the income statement based on this information.

Identify placement of items on a multiple-step income statement.
(SO 4)

BE5-6 Explain where each of these items would appear on a multiple-step income statement: gain on sale of equipment, cost of goods sold, depreciation expense, and sales returns and allowances.

Determine cost of goods sold using basic periodic formula.
(SO 5)

BE5-7 Holmes Company sold goods with a total selling price of $800,000 during the year. It purchased goods for $380,000 and had beginning inventory of $70,000. A count of its ending inventory determined that goods on hand was $50,000. What was its cost of goods sold?

Compute net purchases and cost of goods purchased.
(SO 5)

BE5-8 Assume that Lehman Company uses a periodic inventory system and has these account balances: Purchases $404,000; Purchase Returns and Allowances $11,000; Purchase Discounts $7,000; and Freight-in $16,000. Determine net purchases and cost of goods purchased.

Compute cost of goods sold and gross profit.
(SO 5)

BE5-9 Assume the same information as in BE5-8 and also that Lehman Company has beginning inventory of $60,000, ending inventory of $90,000, and net sales of $620,000. Determine the amounts to be reported for cost of goods sold and gross profit.

Calculate profitability ratios.
(SO 6)

BE5-10 Maxfield Corporation reported net sales of $250,000, cost of goods sold of $150,000, operating expenses of $50,000, net income of $37,500, beginning total assets of $500,000, and ending total assets of $600,000. Calculate each of the following values and explain what they mean.
(a) Profit margin ratio.   (b) Gross profit rate.

Calculate profitability ratios.
(SO 6)

BE5-11 Davenport Corporation reported net sales $800,000; cost of goods sold $520,000; operating expenses $210,000; and net income $70,000. Calculate the following values and explain what they mean.
(a) Profit margin ratio.   (b) Gross profit rate.

Evaluate quality of earnings.
(SO 7)

BE5-12 Watson Corporation reported net income of $352,000, cash of $67,800, and net cash provided by operating activities of $221,200. What does this suggest about the quality of the company's earnings? What further steps should be taken?

Journalize purchase transactions.
(SO 8)

*BE5-13 Prepare the journal entries to record these transactions on Kesler Company's books using a periodic inventory system.
(a) On March 2, Kesler Company purchased $800,000 of merchandise from Rice Company, terms 2/10, n/30.
(b) On March 6 Kesler Company returned $110,000 of the merchandise purchased on March 2.
(c) On March 12 Kesler Company paid the balance due to Rice Company.

Do it! Review

Record transactions of purchasing company.
(SO 2)

Do it! 5-1   On October 5, Lane Company buys merchandise on account from O'Brien Company. The selling price of the goods is $5,000, and the cost to O'Brien Company is $3,000. On October 8, Lane returns defective goods with a selling price of $700 and a scrap value of $250. Record the transactions on the books of Lane Company.

Record transactions of selling company.
(SO 3)

Do it! 5-2   Assume information similar to that in Do It! 5-1. That is: On October 5, Lane Company buys merchandise on account from O'Brien Company. The selling price of the goods is $5,000, and the cost to O'Brien Company is $3,000. On October 8, Lane returns defective goods with a selling price of $700 and a scrap value of $250. Record the transactions on the books of O'Brien Company.

Prepare multiple-step income statement.
(SO 4)

Do it! 5-3   The following information is available for Juneau Corp. for the year ended December 31, 2010:

Other revenues and gains	$ 12,700	Net sales	$552,000
Other expenses and losses	2,300	Operating expenses	186,000
Cost of goods sold	156,000		

Prepare a multiple-step income statement for Juneau Corp. The company has a tax rate of 30%.

Determine cost of goods sold using periodic system.
(SO 5)

Do it! 5-4   Grand Lake Corporation's accounting records show the following at year-end December 31, 2010:

Purchase Discounts	$ 5,700	Beginning Inventory	$31,720
Freight-in	8,400	Ending Inventory	27,950
Freight-out	11,100	Purchase Returns	3,200
Purchases	162,500		

Assuming that Grand Lake Corporation uses the periodic system, compute (a) cost of goods purchased and (b) cost of goods sold.

Exercises

Journalize sales transactions.
(SO 3)

E5-1   The following transactions are for Mack Company.
1. On December 3 Mack Company sold $500,000 of merchandise to Pickert Co., terms 1/10, n/30. The cost of the merchandise sold was $320,000.
2. On December 8 Pickert Co. was granted an allowance of $28,000 for merchandise purchased on December 3.
3. On December 13 Mack Company received the balance due from Pickert Co.

Instructions
(a) Prepare the journal entries to record these transactions on the books of Mack Company. Mack uses a perpetual inventory system.
(b) Assume that Mack Company received the balance due from Pickert Co. on January 2 of the following year instead of December 13. Prepare the journal entry to record the receipt of payment on January 2.

Journalize perpetual inventory entries.
(SO 2, 3)

E5-2   Assume that on September 1 Office Depot had an inventory that included a variety of calculators. The company uses a perpetual inventory system. During September these transactions occurred.

Sept. 6   Purchased calculators from Green Box Co. at a total cost of $1,620, terms n/30.
   9   Paid freight of $50 on calculators purchased from Green Box Co.
   10   Returned calculators to Green Box Co. for $38 credit because they did not meet specifications.
   12   Sold calculators costing $520 for $690 to University Book Store, terms n/30.
   14   Granted credit of $45 to University Book Store for the return of one calculator that was not ordered. The calculator cost $34.
   20   Sold calculators costing $570 for $760 to Campus Card Shop, terms n/30.

Instructions
Journalize the September transactions.

Journalize purchase transactions.
(SO 2)

E5-3 This information relates to Prophet Co.
1. On April 5 purchased merchandise from Lombard Company for $25,000, terms 2/10, n/30.
2. On April 6 paid freight costs of $900 on merchandise purchased from Lombard.
3. On April 7 purchased equipment on account for $30,000.
4. On April 8 returned some of April 5 merchandise to Lombard Company which cost $3,600.
5. On April 15 paid the amount due to Lombard Company in full.

Instructions
(a) Prepare the journal entries to record the transactions listed above on the books of Prophet Co. Prophet Co. uses a perpetual inventory system.
(b) Assume that Prophet Co. paid the balance due to Lombard Company on May 4 instead of April 15. Prepare the journal entry to record this payment.

Journalize perpetual inventory entries.
(SO 2, 3)

E5-4 On June 10 Hopson Company purchased $8,000 of merchandise from Gore Company, terms 3/10, n/30. Hopson pays the freight costs of $400 on June 11. Goods totaling $500 are returned to Gore for credit on June 12. On June 19 Hopson Company pays Gore Company in full, less the purchase discount. Both companies use a perpetual inventory system.

Instructions
(a) Prepare separate entries for each transaction on the books of Hopson Company.
(b) Prepare separate entries for each transaction for Gore Company. The merchandise purchased by Hopson on June 10 cost Gore $5,000, and the goods returned cost Gore $310.

Prepare sales revenues section of income statement.
(SO 4)

E5-5 The adjusted trial balance of Davisen Company shows these data pertaining to sales at the end of its fiscal year, October 31, 2010: Sales $900,000; Freight-out $12,000; Sales Returns and Allowances $18,000; and Sales Discounts $13,500.

Instructions
Prepare the sales revenues section of the income statement.

Prepare an income statement and calculate profitability ratios.
(SO 4, 6)

E5-6 Presented below is information for Yates Co. for the month of January 2010.

Cost of goods sold	$212,000	Rent expense	$32,000
Freight-out	7,000	Sales discounts	8,000
Insurance expense	12,000	Sales returns and allowances	17,000
Salary expense	62,000	Sales	370,000

Instructions
(a) Prepare an income statement using the format presented on page 239. Assume a 25% tax rate.
(b) Calculate the profit margin ratio and the gross profit rate.

Compute missing amounts and calculate profitability ratios.
(SO 4, 6)

E5-7 Financial information is presented here for two companies.

	Iwig Company	Pratt Company
Sales	$90,000	95,000
Sales returns	6000	$ 5,000
Net sales	84,000	100,000
Cost of goods sold	56,700	?
Gross profit	28000	40,000
Operating expenses	14,580	?
Net income	13,420	18,000

Prepare multiple-step income statement and calculate profitability ratios.
(SO 4, 6)

Instructions
(a) Fill in the missing amounts. Show all computations.
(b) Calculate the profit margin ratio and the gross profit rate for each company.
(c) Discuss your findings in part (b).

E5-8 In its income statement for the year ended December 31, 2010, Maris Company reported the following condensed data.

Administrative expenses	$435,000	Selling expenses	$ 490,000
Cost of goods sold	987,000	Loss on sale of equipment	83,500
Interest expense	68,000	Net sales	2,050,000
Interest revenue	65,000	Income tax expense	20,000

Instructions
(a) Prepare a multiple-step income statement.
(b) Calculate the profit margin ratio and gross profit rate.
(c) In 2009 Maris had a profit margin ratio of 5%. Is the decline in 2010 a cause for concern?

E5-9 In its income statement for the year ended June 30, 2007, The Clorox Company reported the following condensed data (dollars in millions).

Prepare multiple-step income statement and calculate profitability ratios.
(SO 4, 6)

Selling and		Research and	
administrative expenses	$ 642	development expense	$ 108
Net sales	4,847	Income tax expense	247
Interest expense	113	Other expense	11
Advertising expense	474	Cost of goods sold	2,756

Instructions
(a) Prepare a multiple-step income statement.
(b) Calculate the gross profit rate and the profit margin ratio and explain what each means.
(c) Assume the marketing department has presented a plan to increase advertising expenses by $340 million. It expects this plan to result in an increase in both net sales and cost of goods sold of 25%. Redo parts (a) and (b) and discuss whether this plan has merit. (Assume a tax rate of 35%, and round all amounts to whole dollars.)

E5-10 The trial balance of Perine Company at the end of its fiscal year, August 31, 2010, includes these accounts: Beginning Merchandise Inventory $19,200; Purchases $154,000; Sales $190,000; Freight-in $8,000; Sales Returns and Allowances $3,000; Freight-out $1,000; and Purchase Returns and Allowances $5,000. The ending merchandise inventory is $22,000.

Prepare cost of goods sold section using periodic system.
(SO 5)

Instructions
Prepare a cost of goods sold section (periodic system) for the year ending August 31.

E5-11 Below is a series of cost of goods sold sections for companies A, F, L, and V.

Prepare cost of goods sold section using periodic system.
(SO 5)

	A	F	L	V
Beginning inventory	$ 250	$ 120	$1,000	$ (j) 800
Purchases	1,500	1,080	(g)	43,590
Purchase returns and allowances	60	(d)	290	(k) 1,300
Net purchases	(a)	1,040	7,410	42,290
Freight-in	130	(e)	(h)	2,240
Cost of goods purchased	(b)	1,230	8,050	(l)
Cost of goods available for sale	1,820	1,350	(i)	49,530
Ending inventory	310	(f)	1,450	6,230
Cost of goods sold	(c)	1,230	7,600	43,300

Instructions
Fill in the lettered blanks to complete the cost of goods sold sections.

E5-12 Powderhorn Corporation reported sales of $257,000, net income of $45,300, cash of $9,300, and net cash provided by operating activities of $21,200. Accounts receivable have increased at three times the rate of sales during the last 3 years.

Evaluate quality of earnings.
(SO 7)

Instructions
(a) Explain what is meant by high quality of earnings.
(b) Evaluate the quality of the company's earnings. Discuss your findings.
(c) What factors might have contributed to the company's quality of earnings?

*E5-13 This information relates to Emley Co.

Journalize purchase transactions.
(SO 8)

1. On April 5 purchased merchandise from Hatcher Company for $25,000, terms 2/10, net/30.
2. On April 6 paid freight costs of $900 on merchandise purchased from Hatcher Company.

3. On April 7 purchased equipment on account for $30,000.
4. On April 8 returned some of the April 5 merchandise to Hatcher Company which cost $3,600.
5. On April 15 paid the amount due to Hatcher Company in full.

Instructions
(a) Prepare the journal entries to record these transactions on the books of Emley Co. using a periodic inventory system.
(b) Assume that Emley Co. paid the balance due to Hatcher Company on May 4 instead of April 15. Prepare the journal entry to record this payment.

Exercises: Set B

Visit the book's companion website, at **www.wiley.com/college/kimmel,** and choose the Student Companion site, to access Exercise Set B.

Problems: Set A

Journalize, post, prepare partial income statement, and calculate ratios.

(SO 2, 3, 4, 6)

GLS

P5-1A Stein Hardware Store completed the following merchandising transactions in the month of May. At the beginning of May, Stein's ledger showed Cash of $8,000 and Common Stock of $8,000.

May 1 Purchased merchandise on account from Hilton Wholesale Supply for $8,000, terms 2/10, n/30.
  2 Sold merchandise on account for $4,400, terms 3/10, n/30. The cost of the merchandise sold was $3,300.
  5 Received credit from Hilton Wholesale Supply for merchandise returned $200.
  9 Received collections in full, less discounts, from customers billed on May 2.
  10 Paid Hilton Wholesale Supply in full, less discount.
  11 Purchased supplies for cash $900.
  12 Purchased merchandise for cash $2,700.
  15 Received $230 refund for return of poor-quality merchandise from supplier on cash purchase.
  17 Purchased merchandise from Northern Distributors for $2,500, terms 2/10, n/30.
  19 Paid freight on May 17 purchase $250.
  24 Sold merchandise for cash $5,400. The cost of the merchandise sold was $4,020.
  25 Purchased merchandise from Toolware Inc. for $800, terms 3/10, n/30.
  27 Paid Northern Distributors in full, less discount.
  29 Made refunds to cash customers for returned merchandise $124. The returned merchandise had cost $90.
  31 Sold merchandise on account for $1,280, terms n/30. The cost of the merchandise sold was $830.

Stein Hardware's chart of accounts includes Cash, Accounts Receivable, Merchandise Inventory, Supplies, Accounts Payable, Common Stock, Sales, Sales Returns and Allowances, Sales Discounts, and Cost of Goods Sold.

Instructions
(a) Journalize the transactions using a perpetual inventory system.
(b) Post the transactions to T accounts. Be sure to enter the beginning cash and common stock balances.
(c) Prepare an income statement through gross profit for the month of May 2010.
(d) Calculate the profit margin ratio and the gross profit rate. (Assume operating expenses were $1,400.)

(c) Gross profit $2,764

Journalize purchase and sale transactions under a perpetual system.

(SO 2, 3)

P5-2A Goldenrod Warehouse distributes hardback books to retail stores and extends credit terms of 2/10, n/30 to all of its customers. During the month of June the following merchandising transactions occurred.

June	1	Purchased books on account for $960 (including freight) from Barnum Publishers, terms 2/10, n/30.
	3	Sold books on account to the Flint Hills bookstore for $1,200. The cost of the merchandise sold was $720.
	6	Received $60 credit for books returned to Barnum Publishers.
	9	Paid Barnum Publishers in full.
	15	Received payment in full from the Flint Hills bookstore.
	17	Sold books on account to Town Crier Bookstore for $1,400. The cost of the merchandise sold was $840.
	20	Purchased books on account for $720 from Good Book Publishers, terms 1/15, n/30.
	24	Received payment in full from Town Crier Bookstore.
	26	Paid Good Book Publishers in full.
	28	Sold books on account to HomeTown Bookstore for $1,300. The cost of the merchandise sold was $780.
	30	Granted HomeTown Bookstore $150 credit for books returned costing $90.

Instructions

Journalize the transactions for the month of June for Goldenrod Warehouse, using a perpetual inventory system.

P5-3A   At the beginning of the current season on April 1, the ledger of Wichita Pro Shop showed Cash $2,500; Merchandise Inventory $3,500; and Common Stock $6,000. The following transactions were completed during April 2010.

Journalize, post, and prepare trial balance and partial income statement.

(SO 2, 3, 4)

Apr.	4	Purchased golf bags, clubs, and balls on account from Roland Co. $1,500, terms 3/10, n/60.
	6	Paid freight on Roland purchase $80.
	8	Received credit from Roland Co. for merchandise returned $200.
	10	Sold merchandise on account to members $910, terms n/30. The merchandise sold had a cost of $620.
	12	Purchased golf shoes, sweaters, and other accessories on account from Eagle Sportswear $830, terms 1/10, n/30.
	14	Paid Roland Co. in full.
	17	Received credit from Eagle Sportswear for merchandise returned $30.
	20	Made sales on account to members $810, terms n/30. The cost of the merchandise sold was $550.
	21	Paid Eagle Sportswear in full.
	27	Granted an allowance to members for clothing that did not fit properly $60.
	30	Received payments on account from members $1,100.

The chart of accounts for the pro shop includes Cash, Accounts Receivable, Merchandise Inventory, Accounts Payable, Common Stock, Sales, Sales Returns and Allowances, and Cost of Goods Sold.

Instructions

(a) Journalize the April transactions using a perpetual inventory system.

(b) Using T accounts, enter the beginning balances in the ledger accounts and post the April transactions.

(c) Prepare a trial balance on April 30, 2010.

(d) Prepare an income statement through gross profit.

(c) Tot. trial balance $7,720
(d) Gross profit $ 490

P5-4A   Lowry Department Store is located in midtown Metropolis. During the past several years, net income has been declining because suburban shopping centers have been attracting business away from city areas. At the end of the company's fiscal year on November 30, 2010, these accounts appeared in its adjusted trial balance.

Prepare financial statements and calculate profitability ratios.

(SO 4, 6)

Accounts Payable	$ 23,300
Accounts Receivable	17,200
Accumulated Depreciation—Delivery Equipment	20,000
Accumulated Depreciation—Store Equipment	38,000
Cash	8,000
Common Stock	35,000
Cost of Goods Sold	633,300
Delivery Expense	6,200

Delivery Equipment	57,000
Depreciation Expense—Delivery Equipment	4,000
Depreciation Expense—Store Equipment	9,500
Dividends	12,000
Gain on Sale of Equipment	2,000
Income Tax Expense	10,000
Insurance Expense	9,000
Interest Expense	5,000
Merchandise Inventory	26,200
Notes Payable	47,500
Prepaid Insurance	6,000
Property Tax Expense	3,500
Property Taxes Payable	3,500
Rent Expense	34,000
Retained Earnings	14,200
Salaries Expense	117,000
Sales	904,000
Salaries Payable	6,000
Sales Returns and Allowances	20,000
Store Equipment	105,000
Utilities Expense	10,600

Additional data: Notes payable are due in 2014.

Instructions

(a) Net income $ 43,900
     Tot. assets $161,400

(a) Prepare a multiple-step income statement, a retained earnings statement, and a classified balance sheet.

(b) Calculate the profit margin ratio and the gross profit rate.

(c) The vice-president of marketing and the director of human resources have developed a proposal whereby the company would compensate the sales force on a strictly commission basis using 20% of net sales. Given the increased incentive, they expect net sales to increase by 15%. As a result, they estimate that gross profit will increase by $37,605 and operating expenses by $62,595. Compute the expected new net income. (*Hint*: You do not need to prepare an income statement). Then compute the revised profit margin ratio and gross profit rate. Comment on the effect that this plan would have on net income and on the ratios, and evaluate the merit of this proposal.

Prepare a correct multiple-step income statement.

(SO 4)

P5-5A An inexperienced accountant prepared this condensed income statement for Hight Company, a retail firm that has been in business for a number of years.

HIGHT COMPANY
Income Statement
For the Year Ended December 31, 2010

Revenues	
Net sales	$850,000
Other revenues	22,000
	872,000
Cost of goods sold	555,000
Gross profit	317,000
Operating expenses	
Selling expenses	109,000
Administrative expenses	103,000
	212,000
Net earnings	$105,000

As an experienced, knowledgeable accountant, you review the statement and determine the following facts.

1. Net sales consist of sales $911,000, less delivery expense on merchandise sold $31,000, and sales returns and allowances $30,000.

2. Other revenues consist of sales discounts $14,000 and rent revenue $8,000.

3. Selling expenses consist of salespersons' salaries $80,000; depreciation on accounting equipment $8,000; advertising $15,000; and sales commissions $6,000. The

commissions represent commissions paid. At December 31, $3,000 of commissions have been earned by salespersons but have not been paid.

4. Administrative expenses consist of office salaries $47,000; dividends $18,000; utilities $12,000; interest expense $2,000; and rent expense $24,000, which includes prepayments totaling $4,000 for the first quarter of 2011.

Instructions

Prepare a correct detailed multiple-step income statement. Assume a 25% tax rate.

Net income $72,000

P5-6A   The trial balance of Save-Mart Wholesale Company contained the accounts shown at December 31, the end of the company's fiscal year.

Journalize, post, and prepare adjusted trial balance and financial statements.

(SO 4)

SAVE-MART WHOLESALE COMPANY
Trial Balance
December 31, 2010

	Debit	Credit
Cash	$ 31,400	
Accounts Receivable	37,600	
Merchandise Inventory	70,000	
Land	92,000	
Buildings	200,000	
Accumulated Depreciation—Buildings		$ 60,000
Equipment	83,500	
Accumulated Depreciation—Equipment		40,500
Notes Payable		54,700
Accounts Payable		17,500
Common Stock		160,000
Retained Earnings		68,200
Dividends	10,000	
Sales		922,100
Sales Discounts	5,000	
Cost of Goods Sold	709,900	
Salaries Expense	51,300	
Utilities Expense	11,400	
Repair Expense	8,900	
Gas and Oil Expense	7,200	
Insurance Expense	4,800	
	$1,323,000	$1,323,000

Adjustment data:
1. Depreciation is $12,000 on buildings and $9,000 on equipment. (Both are operating expenses.)
2. Interest of $4,500 is due and unpaid on notes payable at December 31.
3. Income tax due and unpaid at December 31 is $20,000.

Other data: $15,000 of the notes payable are payable next year.

Instructions
(a) Journalize the adjusting entries.
(b) Create T accounts for all accounts used in part (a). Enter the trial balance amounts into the T accounts and post the adjusting entries.
(c) Prepare an adjusted trial balance.
(d) Prepare a multiple-step income statement and a retained earnings statement for the year, and a classified balance sheet at December 31, 2010.

(c) Tot. trial balance $1,368,500
(d) Net income $78,100
     Tot. assets $393,000

P5-7A   At the end of Kane Department Store's fiscal year on November 30, 2010, these accounts appeared in its adjusted trial balance.

Determine cost of goods sold and gross profit under a periodic system.

(SO 4, 5)

Freight-in	$ 5,060
Merchandise Inventory (beginning)	42,200
Purchases	616,000
Purchase Discounts	7,000
Purchase Returns and Allowances	6,760
Sales	904,000
Sales Returns and Allowances	20,000

Additional facts:
1. Merchandise inventory on November 30, 2010, is $36,200.
2. Note that Kane Department Store uses a periodic system.

Gross profit $270,700

Calculate missing amounts and assess profitability.
(SO 4, 5, 6)

Instructions
Prepare an income statement through gross profit for the year ended November 30, 2010.

P5-8A Pierson Inc. operates a retail operation that purchases and sells snowmobiles, amongst other outdoor products. The company purchases all merchandise inventory on credit and uses a perpetual inventory system. The accounts payable account is used for recording inventory purchases only; all other current liabilities are accrued in separate accounts. You are provided with the following selected information for the fiscal years 2008 through 2011, inclusive.

	2008	**2009**	**2010**	**2011**
Income Statement Data				
Sales		$96,850	$ (e)	$82,220
Cost of goods sold		(a)	25,140	26,490
Gross profit		67,260	59,540	(i)
Operating expenses		63,640	(f)	52,870
Net income		$ (b)	$ 4,570	$ (j)
Balance Sheet Data				
Merchandise inventory	$13,000	$ (c)	$14,700	$ (k)
Accounts payable	5,800	6,500	4,600	(l)
Additional Information				
Purchases of merchandise inventory on account		$25,890	$ (g)	$24,050
Cash payments to suppliers		(d)	(h)	24,650

Instructions
(a) Calculate the missing amounts.
(b) The vice-presidents of sales, marketing, production, and finance are discussing the company's results with the CEO. They note that sales declined over the 3-year fiscal period, 2009–2011. Does that mean that profitability necessarily also declined? Explain, computing the gross profit rate and the profit margin ratio for each fiscal year to help support your answer.

Journalize, post, and prepare trial balance and partial income statement under a periodic system.
(SO 5, 8)

P5-9A At the beginning of the current season on April 1, the ledger of Wichita Pro Shop showed Cash $2,500; Merchandise Inventory $3,500; and Common Stock $6,000. These transactions occured during April 2010.

Apr. 5   Purchased golf bags, clubs, and balls on account from Roland Co. $1,500, terms 3/10, n/60.
7   Paid freight on Roland Co. purchases $80.
9   Received credit from Roland Co. for merchandise returned $200.
10   Sold merchandise on account to members $910, terms n/30.
12   Purchased golf shoes, sweaters, and other accessories on account from Eagle Sportswear $830, terms 1/10, n/30.
14   Paid Roland Co. in full.
17   Received credit from Eagle Sportswear for merchandise returned $30.
20   Made sales on account to members $810, terms n/30.
21   Paid Eagle Sportswear in full.
27   Granted credit to members for clothing that did not fit properly $60.
30   Received payments on account from members $1,100.

The chart of accounts for the pro shop includes Cash, Accounts Receivable, Merchandise Inventory, Accounts Payable, Common Stock, Sales, Sales Returns and Allowances, Purchases, Purchase Returns and Allowances, Purchase Discounts, and Freight-in.

Instructions
(a) Journalize the April transactions using a periodic inventory system.
(b) Using T accounts, enter the beginning balances in the ledger accounts and post the April transactions.

(c) Tot. trial balance $7,997
Gross profit $682

(c) Prepare a trial balance on April 30, 2010.
(d) Prepare an income statement through Gross Profit, assuming merchandise inventory on hand at April 30 is $4,655.

Problems: Set B

P5-1B Cordell Distributing Company completed these merchandising transactions in the month of April. At the beginning of April, the ledger of Cordell showed Cash of $9,000 and Common Stock of $9,000.

Journalize, post, prepare partial income statement, and calculate ratios.
(SO 2, 3, 4, 6)

Apr.	2	Purchased merchandise on account from Lang Supply Co. $8,300, terms 2/10, n/30.

Apr. 2   Purchased merchandise on account from Lang Supply Co. $8,300, terms 2/10, n/30.

4   Sold merchandise on account $6,000, terms 2/10, n/30. The cost of the merchandise sold was $3,700.

5   Paid $200 freight on April 4 sale.

6   Received credit from Lang Supply Co. for merchandise returned $300.

11   Paid Lang Supply Co. in full, less discount.

13   Received collections in full, less discounts, from customers billed on April 4.

14   Purchased merchandise for cash $4,700.

16   Received refund from supplier for returned merchandise on cash purchase of April 14, $500.

18   Purchased merchandise from Great Plains Distributors $5,500, terms 2/10, n/30.

20   Paid freight on April 18 purchase $100.

23   Sold merchandise for cash $8,300. The cost of the merchandise sold was $5,820.

26   Purchased merchandise for cash $2,300.

27   Paid Great Plains Distributors in full, less discount.

29   Made refunds to cash customers for returned merchandise $180. The returned merchandise had a cost of $120.

30   Sold merchandise on account $3,980, terms n/30. The cost of the merchandise sold was $2,500.

Cordell Distributing Company's chart of accounts includes Cash, Accounts Receivable, Merchandise Inventory, Accounts Payable, Common Stock, Sales, Sales Returns and Allowances, Sales Discounts, Cost of Goods Sold, and Freight-out.

Instructions
(a) Journalize the transactions.
(b) Post the transactions to T accounts. Be sure to enter the beginning cash and common stock balances.
(c) Prepare the income statement through gross profit for the month of April 2010.
(d) Calculate the profit margin ratio and the gross profit rate. (Assume operating expenses were $2,050.)

(c) Gross profit $6,080

P5-2B Travelers Warehouse distributes suitcases to retail stores and extends credit terms of 1/10, n/30 to all of its customers. During the month of July the following merchandising transactions occurred.

Journalize purchase and sale transactions under a perpetual system.
(SO 2, 3)

July 1   Purchased suitcases on account for $2,700 from Valise Manufacturers, terms 2/15, n/30.

3   Sold suitcases on account to The Emporium for $2,500. The cost of the merchandise sold was $1,500.

9   Paid Valise Manufacturers in full.

12   Received payment in full from The Emporium.

17   Sold suitcases on account to Bon Voyage for $2,000. The cost of the merchandise sold was $1,200.

18   Purchased suitcases on account for $1,800 (including freight) from Vektek Manufacturers, terms 1/10, n/30.

20   Received $300 credit for suitcases returned to Vektek Manufacturers.

21   Received payment in full from Bon Voyage.

22   Sold suitcases on account to Run Around for $3,120. The cost of the merchandise sold was $1,800.

30   Paid Vektek Manufacturers in full.

31   Granted Run Around $260 credit for suitcases returned costing $150.

Instructions
Journalize the transactions for the month of July for Travelers Warehouse, using a perpetual inventory system.

Journalize, post, and prepare trial balance and partial income statement.
(SO 2, 3, 4)

P5-3B At the beginning of the current season, the ledger of Colorado Tennis Shop showed Cash $2,500; Merchandise Inventory $1,700; and Common Stock $4,200. The following transactions were completed during April.

Apr.	4	Purchased racquets and balls from Helton Co. $980, terms 2/10, n/30.
	6	Paid freight on Helton Co. purchase $60.
	8	Sold merchandise to members $900, terms n/30. The merchandise sold cost $600.
	10	Received credit of $130 from Helton Co. for damaged racquets that were returned.
	11	Purchased tennis shoes from No Fault for cash $300.
	13	Paid Helton Co. in full.
	14	Purchased tennis shirts and shorts from Renfro Sportswear $900, terms 3/10, n/60.
	15	Received cash refund of $50 from No Fault for damaged merchandise that was returned.
	17	Paid freight on Renfro Sportswear purchase $30.
	18	Sold merchandise to members $660, terms n/30. The cost of the merchandise sold was $440.
	20	Received $500 in cash from members in settlement of their accounts.
	21	Paid Renfro Sportswear in full.
	27	Granted an allowance of $30 to members for tennis clothing that did not fit properly.
	30	Received cash payments on account from members $350.

The chart of accounts for the tennis shop includes Cash, Accounts Receivable, Merchandise Inventory, Accounts Payable, Common Stock, Sales, Sales Returns and Allowances, and Cost of Goods Sold.

Instructions
(a) Journalize the April transactions.
(b) Using T accounts, enter the beginning balances in the ledger accounts and post the April transactions.
(c) Prepare a trial balance on April 30, 2010.
(d) Prepare an income statement through gross profit.

(c) Tot. trial balance $5,760
(d) Gross profit $490

Prepare financial statements and calculate profitability ratios.
(SO 4, 6)

P5-4B Flanagin Department Store is located near the Crystal Shopping Mall. At the end of the company's fiscal year on December 31, 2010, the following accounts appeared in its adjusted trial balance.

Accounts Payable	$ 73,300
Accounts Receivable	50,300
Accumulated Depreciation—Building	52,500
Accumulated Depreciation—Equipment	42,600
Building	190,000
Cash	28,000
Common Stock	140,000
Cost of Goods Sold	418,000
Depreciation Expense—Building	10,400
Depreciation Expense—Equipment	13,000
Dividends	15,000
Equipment	100,000
Gain on Sale of Equipment	4,300
Income Tax Expense	15,000
Insurance Expense	8,400
Interest Expense	7,000
Interest Payable	2,000
Merchandise Inventory	53,000
Mortgage Payable	80,000
Office Salaries Expense	37,000
Prepaid Insurance	2,400
Property Taxes Payable	4,800

Property Taxes Expense	6,200
Retained Earnings	19,200
Sales Salaries Expense	75,500
Sales	626,000
Sales Salaries Payable	3,500
Sales Returns and Allowances	8,000
Utilities Expense	11,000

Additional data: $20,000 of the mortgage payable is due for payment next year.

Instructions

(a) Prepare a multiple-step income statement, a retained earnings statement, and a classified balance sheet.

(b) Calculate the profit margin ratio and the gross profit rate.

(c) The vice-president of marketing and the director of human resources have developed a proposal whereby the company would compensate the sales force on a strictly commission basis using 15% of net sales. Given the increased incentive, they expect net sales to increase by 25%. As a result, they estimate that gross profit will increase by $50,500 and operating expenses by $27,800. Compute the expected new net income. (*Hint:* You do not need to prepare an income statement.) Then compute the revised profit margin ratio and gross profit rate. Comment on the effect that this plan would have on net income and the ratios, and evaluate the merit of this proposal.

(a) Net income $20,800
Tot. assets $328,600

P5-5B A part-time bookkeeper prepared this income statement for Chowdhury Company for the year ending December 31, 2010.

Prepare a correct multiple-step income statement.
(SO 4)

CHOWDHURY COMPANY
Income Statement
December 31, 2010

Revenues		
Sales		$712,000
Less: Freight-out	$14,000	
Sales discounts	11,300	25,300
Net sales		686,700
Other revenues (net)		1,300
Total revenues		688,000
Expenses		
Cost of goods sold		460,000
Selling expenses		103,000
Administrative expenses		54,000
Dividends		12,000
Total expenses		629,000
Net income		$ 59,000

As an experienced, knowledgeable accountant, you review the statement and determine the following facts.

1. Sales include $12,000 of deposits from customers for future sales orders.
2. Other revenues contain two items: interest expense $4,000 and interest revenue $5,300.
3. Selling expenses consist of sales salaries $76,000, advertising $13,000, depreciation on store equipment $7,500, and sales commissions expense $6,500.
4. Administrative expenses consist of office salaries $23,000; utilities expense $9,500; rent expense $14,500; and insurance expense $7,000. Insurance expense includes $800 of insurance applicable to 2011.

Operating expenses $170,200
Net income $47,840

Instructions

Prepare a correct detailed multiple-step income statement. Assume a tax rate of 20%.

Journalize, post, and prepare adjusted trial balance and financial statements.
(SO 4)

P5-6B The trial balance of Calhoun Fashion Center contained the following accounts at November 30, the end of the company's fiscal year.

CALHOUN FASHION CENTER
Trial Balance
November 30, 2010

	Debit	Credit
Cash	$ 37,700	
Accounts Receivable	33,700	
Merchandise Inventory	43,000	
Store Supplies	8,800	
Store Equipment	105,000	
Accumulated Depreciation—Store Equipment		$ 35,000
Delivery Equipment	38,000	
Accumulated Depreciation—Delivery Equipment		6,000
Notes Payable		65,000
Accounts Payable		19,800
Common Stock		80,000
Retained Earnings		30,000
Dividends	12,000	
Sales		757,200
Sales Returns and Allowances	6,200	
Cost of Goods Sold	505,400	
Salaries Expense	110,000	
Advertising Expense	26,400	
Utilities Expense	14,000	
Repair Expense	12,100	
Delivery Expense	16,700	
Rent Expense	24,000	
	$993,000	$993,000

Adjustment data:

1. Store supplies on hand total $3,500.
2. Depreciation is $14,000 on the store equipment and $6,000 on the delivery equipment.
3. Interest of $5,000 is accrued on notes payable at November 30.
4. Income tax due and unpaid at November 30 is $3,000.

Other data: $30,000 of notes payable are due for payment next year.

Instructions
(a) Journalize the adjusting entries.
(b) Prepare T accounts for all accounts used in part (a). Enter the trial balance amounts into the T accounts and post the adjusting entries.

(c) Tot. trial balance $1,021,000
(d) Net income $9,100
Tot. assets $199,900

(c) Prepare an adjusted trial balance.
(d) Prepare a multiple-step income statement and a retained earnings statement for the year, and a classified balance sheet at November 30, 2010.

Determine cost of goods sold and gross profit under a periodic system.
(SO 4, 5)

P5-7B At the end of Eisenhaver Department Store's fiscal year on December 31, 2010, these accounts appeared in its adjusted trial balance.

Freight-in	$ 5,600
Merchandise Inventory (beginning)	40,500
Purchases	456,000
Purchase Discounts	12,000
Purchase Returns and Allowances	6,400
Sales	707,000
Sales Returns and Allowances	8,000

Additional facts:

1. Merchandise inventory on December 31, 2010, is $71,000.
2. Note that Eisenhaver Department Store uses a periodic system.

Instructions

Gross profit $286,300

Prepare an income statement through gross profit for the year ended December 31, 2010.

Calculate missing amounts and assess profitability.
(SO 4, 5, 6)

P5-8B Barbara Brislen operates a clothing retail operation. She purchases all merchandise inventory on credit and uses a perpetual inventory system. The accounts payable account is used for recording inventory purchases only; all other current liabilities are accrued in separate accounts. You are provided with the following selected information for the fiscal years 2008, 2009, 2010, and 2011.

	2008	2009	2010	2011
Inventory (ending)	$13,000	$ 11,300	$ 16,400	$ 12,200
Accounts payable (ending)	17,000			
Sales		225,700	227,600	224,000
Purchases of merchandise inventory on account		146,000	155,700	141,000
Cash payments to suppliers		135,000	159,000	127,000

Instructions

(a) Calculate cost of goods sold for each of the 2009, 2010, and 2011 fiscal years.

(b) Calculate the gross profit for each of the 2009, 2010, and 2011 fiscal years.

(c) Calculate the ending balance of accounts payable for each of the 2009, 2010, and 2011 fiscal years.

(d) The vice-presidents of sales, marketing, production, and finance are discussing the company's results with the CEO. They note that sales declined in fiscal 2011. They wonder whether that means that profitability, as measured by the gross profit rate, necessarily also declined. Explain, calculating the gross profit rate for each fiscal year to help support your answer.

(a) 2010 $150,600

(c) 2010 $24,700

*P5-9B At the beginning of the current season, the ledger of Colorado Tennis Shop showed Cash $2,500; Merchandise Inventory $1,700; and Common Stock $4,200. The following transactions were completed during April.

Journalize, post, and prepare trial balance and partial income statement under a periodic system.

(SO 5, 8)

Apr.	4	Purchased racquets and balls from Helton Co. $980, terms 2/10, n/30.
	6	Paid freight on Helton Co. purchase $60.
	8	Sold merchandise to members $900, terms n/30.
	10	Received credit of $130 from Helton Co. for damaged racquets that were returned.
	11	Purchased tennis shoes from No Fault for cash $300.
	13	Paid Helton Co. in full.
	14	Purchased tennis shirts and shorts from Renfro Sportswear $900, terms 3/10, n/60.
	15	Received cash refund of $50 from No Fault for damaged merchandise that was returned.
	17	Paid freight on Renfro Sportswear purchase $30.
	18	Sold merchandise to members $660, terms n/30.
	20	Received $500 in cash from members in settlement of their accounts.
	21	Paid Renfro Sportswear in full.
	27	Granted an allowance of $30 to members for tennis clothing that did not fit properly.
	30	Received cash payments on account from members $350.

The chart of accounts for the tennis shop includes Cash, Accounts Receivable, Merchandise Inventory, Accounts Payable, Common Stock, Sales, Sales Returns and Allowances, Purchases, Purchase Returns and Allowances, Purchase Discounts, and Freight-in.

Instructions

(a) Journalize the April transactions using a periodic inventory system.

(b) Using T accounts, enter the beginning balances in the ledger accounts and post the April transactions.

(c) Prepare a trial balance on April 30, 2010.

(d) Prepare an income statement through Gross Profit, assuming merchandise inventory on hand at April 30 is $2,706.

(c) Tot. trial balance	$5,984
(d) Gross profit	$490

Problems: Set C

Visit the book's companion website at **www.wiley.com/college/kimmel** and choose the Student Companion site to access Problem Set C.

Comprehensive Problem

CP5 On December 1, 2010, Sleezer Distributing Company had the following account balances.

	Debits		**Credits**
Cash	$ 7,300	Accumulated Depreciation	$ 2,200
Accounts Receivable	5,600	Accounts Payable	4,600
Merchandise Inventory	12,000	Salaries Payable	1,000
Supplies	1,200	Common stock	15,000
Equipment	22,000	Retained Earnings	25,300
	$48,100		$48,100

During December the company completed the following summary transactions.

Dec. 6 Paid $1,600 for salaries due employees, of which $600 is for December and $1,000 is for November salaries payable.

8 Received $1,800 cash from customers in payment of account (no discount allowed).

10 Sold merchandise for cash $6,000. The cost of the merchandise sold was $4,000.

13 Purchased merchandise on account from Helm Co. $9,000, terms 2/10, n/30.

15 Purchased supplies for cash $2,000.

18 Sold merchandise on account $12,000, terms 1/10, n/30. The cost of the merchandise sold was $8,000.

20 Paid salaries $1,800.

23 Paid Helm Co. in full, less discount.

27 Received collections in full, less discounts, from customers billed on December 18.

Adjustment data:

1. Accrued salaries payable $600.
2. Depreciation $300 per month.
3. Supplies on hand $1,500.
4. Income tax due and unpaid at December 31 is $200.

Instructions

(a) Journalize the December transactions.

(b) Enter the December 1 balances in the ledger T accounts and post the December transactions. Use Cost of Goods Sold, Depreciation Expense, Salaries Expense, Sales, Sales Discounts, Supplies Expense, Income Tax Expense, and Income Tax Payable.

(c) Journalize and post adjusting entries.

(d) Totals $66,200   (d) Prepare an adjusted trial balance.

(e) Net income $680   (e) Prepare an income statement and a retained earnings statement for December and a classified balance sheet at December 31.

Continuing Cookie Chronicle

(*Note:* This is a continuation of the Cookie Chronicle from Chapters 1 through 4.)

CCC5 Because Natalie has had such a successful first few months, she is considering other opportunities to develop her business. One opportunity is to become the exclusive distributor of a line of fine European mixers. Natalie comes to you for advice on how to account for these mixers.

Go to the book's companion website, **www.wiley.com/college/kimme**l, to find the completion of this problem.

broadening your perspective

Financial Reporting and Analysis

FINANCIAL REPORTING PROBLEM: *Tootsie Roll, Industries Inc.*

BYP5-1   The financial statements for Tootsie Roll Industries appear in Appendix A at the end of this book.

Instructions
Answer these questions using the Consolidated Income Statement.
(a) What was the percentage change in total revenue and in net income from 2006 to 2007?
(b) What was the profit margin ratio in each of the 3 years? Comment on the trend.
(c) What was Tootsie Roll's gross profit rate in each of the 3 years? (Use total gross margin and total revenue.) Comment on the trend.

COMPARATIVE ANALYSIS PROBLEM: *Tootsie Roll vs. Hershey Foods*

BYP5-2   The financial statements of Hershey Foods appear in Appendix B, following the financial statements for Tootsie Roll in Appendix A.

Instructions
(a) Based on the information contained in these financial statements, determine the following values for each company.
　(1) Profit margin ratio for 2007.
　(2) Gross profit for 2007.
　(3) Gross profit rate for 2007.
　(4) Operating income for 2007.
　(5) Percentage change in operating income from 2007 to 2006.
(b) What conclusions concerning the relative profitability of the two companies can be drawn from these data?

RESEARCH CASE

BYP5-3   The July 31, 2006, issue of the *Wall Street Journal* includes an article by Justin Lahart titled "Ahead of the Tape."

Instructions
Read the article and answer the following questions.
(a) During the period discussed in the article, by what percentage did sales increase? By what percentage did profits increase? What explanation is given for the big difference between the increase in sales and increase in profits?
(b) In what direction were analysts expecting margins to move in the future, and why were they expecting this change? What implications does this have for stock prices?

INTERPRETING FINANCIAL STATEMENTS

BYP5-4   Recently it was announced that two giant French retailers, Carrefour SA and Promodes SA, would merge. A headline in the *Wall Street Journal* blared, "French Retailers Create New Wal-Mart Rival." While Wal-Mart's total sales would still exceed those of the combined company, Wal-Mart's international sales are far less than those of the combined company. This is a serious concern for Wal-Mart, since its primary opportunity for future growth lies outside of the United States.

　　Below are basic financial data for the combined corporation (in euros) and Wal-Mart (in U.S. dollars). Even though their results are presented in different currencies, by employing ratios we can make some basic comparisons.

	Carrefour (in millions)	Wal-Mart (in millions)
Sales	euros 70,486	$256,329
Cost of goods sold	54,630	198,747
Net income	1,738	9,054
Total assets	39,063	104,912
Current assets	14,521	34,421
Current liabilities	13,660	37,418
Total liabilities	29,434	61,289

Instructions

Compare the two companies by answering the following.

(a) Calculate the gross profit rate for each of the companies, and discuss their relative abilities to control cost of goods sold.

(b) Calculate the profit margin ratio, and discuss the companies' relative profitability.

(c) Calculate the current ratio and debt to total assets ratios for the two companies, and discuss their relative liquidity and solvency.

(d) What concerns might you have in relying on this comparison?

FINANCIAL ANALYSIS ON THE WEB

BYP5-5 *Purpose*: No financial decision maker should ever rely solely on the financial information reported in the annual report to make decisions. It is important to keep abreast of financial news. This activity demonstrates how to search for financial news on the Web.

Address: **http://biz.yahoo.com/i**, or go to **www.wiley.com/college/kimmel**

Steps

1. Type in either Wal-Mart, Target Corp., or Kmart.
2. Choose **News**.
3. Select an article that sounds interesting to you and that would be relevant to an investor in these companies.

Instructions

(a) What was the source of the article? (For example, Reuters, Businesswire, Prnewswire.)

(b) Assume that you are a personal financial planner and that one of your clients owns stock in the company. Write a brief memo to your client summarizing the article and explaining the implications of the article for their investment.

Critical Thinking

DECISION MAKING ACROSS THE ORGANIZATION

BYP5-6 Three years ago Sue Gilligan and her brother-in-law Dan Laurent opened Mallmart Department Store. For the first 2 years, business was good, but the following condensed income statement results for 2010 were disappointing.

MALLMART DEPARTMENT STORE
Income Statement
For the Year Ended December 31, 2010

Net sales		$700,000
Cost of goods sold		560,000
Gross profit		140,000
Operating expenses		
Selling expenses	$100,000	
Administrative expenses	20,000	
		120,000
Net income		$ 20,000

Sue believes the problem lies in the relatively low gross profit rate of 20%. Dan believes the problem is that operating expenses are too high. Sue thinks the gross profit rate can be improved by making two changes: (1) Increase average selling prices by 15%; this increase is expected to lower sales volume so that total sales dollars will increase only 4%. (2) Buy merchandise in larger quantities and take all purchase discounts; these changes are expected to increase the gross profit rate by 5%. Sue does not anticipate that these changes will have any effect on operating expenses.

Dan thinks expenses can be cut by making these two changes: (1) Cut 2010 sales salaries of $60,000 in half and give sales personnel a commission of 2% of net sales. (2) Reduce store deliveries to one day per week rather than twice a week; this change will reduce 2010 delivery expenses of $40,000 by 40%. Dan feels that these changes will not have any effect on net sales.

Sue and Dan come to you for help in deciding the best way to improve net income.

Instructions

With the class divided into groups, answer the following.

(a) Prepare a condensed income statement for 2011 assuming (1) Sue's changes are implemented and (2) Dan's ideas are adopted.

(b) What is your recommendation to Sue and Dan?

(c) Prepare a condensed income statement for 2011 assuming both sets of proposed changes are made.

(d) Discuss the impact that other factors might have. For example, would increasing the quantity of inventory increase costs? Would a salary cut affect employee morale? Would decreased morale affect sales? Would decreased store deliveries decrease customer satisfaction? What other suggestions might be considered?

COMMUNICATION ACTIVITY

BYP5-7 The following situation is presented in chronological order.

1. Finley decides to buy a surfboard.
2. He calls Surfing USA Co. to inquire about their surfboards.
3. Two days later he requests Surfing USA Co. to make him a surfboard.
4. Three days later Surfing USA Co. sends him a purchase order to fill out.
5. He sends back the purchase order.
6. Surfing USA Co. receives the completed purchase order.
7. Surfing USA Co. completes the surfboard.
8. Finley picks up the surfboard.
9. Surfing USA Co. bills Finley.
10. Surfing USA Co. receives payment from Finley.

Instructions

In a memo to the president of Surfing USA Co., answer the following questions.

(a) When should Surfing USA Co. record the sale?

(b) Suppose that with his purchase order, Finley is required to make a down payment. Would that change your answer to part (a)?

ETHICS CASE

BYP5-8 Angie Oaks was just hired as the assistant treasurer of Yorkshire Stores, a specialty chain store company that has nine retail stores concentrated in one metropolitan area. Among other things, the payment of all invoices is centralized in one of the departments Angie will manage. Her primary responsibility is to maintain the company's high credit rating by paying all bills when due and to take advantage of all cash discounts.

Harvey Mayo, the former assistant treasurer, who has been promoted to treasurer, is training Angie in her new duties. He instructs Angie that she is to continue the practice of preparing all checks "net of discount" and dating the checks the last day of the discount period. "But," Harvey Mayo continues, "we always hold the checks at least 4 days beyond the discount period before mailing them. That way we get another 4 days of interest on our money. Most of our creditors need our business and don't complain. And, if they scream about our missing the discount period, we blame it on the mail room or the post office. We've only lost one discount out of every hundred we take that way. I think everybody does it. By the way, welcome to our team!"

Instructions

(a) What are the ethical considerations in this case?

(b) What stakeholders are harmed or benefited?

(c) Should Angie continue the practice started by Harvey? Does she have any choice?

"ALL ABOUT YOU" ACTIVITY

BYP5-9 There are many situations in business where it is difficult to determine the proper period in which to record revenue. Suppose that after graduation with a degree in finance, you take a job as a manager at a consumer electronics store called Atlantis Electronics. The company has expanded rapidly in order to compete with Best Buy and Circuit City.

Atlantis has also begun selling gift cards. The cards are available in any dollar amount and allow the holder of the card to purchase an item for up to 2 years from the time the card is purchased. If the card is not used during that 2 years, it expires.

Instructions

Answer the following questions.

At what point should the revenue from the gift cards be recognized? Should the revenue be recognized at the time the card is sold, or should it be recorded when the card is redeemed? Explain the reasoning to support your answers.

? Answers to Insight and Accounting Across the Organization Questions

p. 227

Q: If a perpetual system keeps track of inventory on a daily basis, why do companies ever need to do a physical count?

A: A perpetual system keeps track of all sales and purchases on a continuous basis. This provides a constant record of the number of units in the inventory. However, if employees make errors in recording sales or purchases, or if there is theft, the inventory value will not be correct. As a consequence, all companies do a physical count of inventory at least once a year.

p. 233

Q: If a company expects significant returns, what are the implications for revenue recognition?

A: If a company expects significant returns, it should make an adjusting entry at the end of the year reducing sales by the estimated amount of sales returns. This is necessary so as not to overstate the amount of revenue recognized in the period.

p. 238

Q: Why have investors and analysts demanded more accuracy in isolating "Other gains and losses" from operating items?

A: Greater accuracy in the classification of operating versus nonoperating ("Other gains and losses") items permits investors and analysts to judge the real operating margin, the results of continuing operations, and management's ability to control operating expenses.

p. 244

Q: Explain how Wal-Mart's profitability gave it a strategic advantage over Kmart.

A: If two competitors get into a "price war," the company with the lower costs can reduce prices further (thus eroding its gross profit rate), but still operate at a profit. Thus, Wal-Mart's success at minimizing its operating costs has enabled it to drive many competitors out of business.

Answers to Self-Study Questions

1. a   2. c   3. c   4. b   5. c   6. c   7. b   8. d   9. a   10. b   11. c   12. c   13. d   14. b
*15. b

chapter 6

Reporting and Analyzing Inventory

the navigator

- Scan **Study Objectives** ○
- Read **Feature Story** ○
- Scan **Preview** ○
- Read **Text and answer** **Do it!**
  p. 279 ○   p. 285 ○   p. 290 ○   p. 292 ○
- Work **Using the Decision Toolkit** ○
- Review **Summary of Study Objectives** ○
- Work **Comprehensive** **Do it!** p. 301 ○
- Answer **Self-Study Questions** ○
- Complete **Assignments** ○

study objectives

After studying this chapter, you should be able to:

1 Describe the steps in determining inventory quantities.

2 Explain the basis of accounting for inventories and apply the inventory cost flow methods under a periodic inventory system.

3 Explain the financial statement and tax effects of each of the inventory cost flow assumptions.

4 Explain the lower of cost or market basis of accounting for inventories.

5 Compute and interpret the inventory turnover ratio.

6 Describe the LIFO reserve and explain its importance for comparing results of different companies.

"Where Is That Spare Bulldozer Blade?"

Let's talk inventory–big, bulldozer-size inventory. Caterpillar Inc. is the world's largest manufacturer of construction and mining equipment, diesel and natural gas engines, and industrial gas turbines. It sells its products in over 200 countries, making it one of the most successful U.S. exporters. More than 70% of its productive assets are located domestically, and nearly 50% of its sales are foreign.

During the 1980s Caterpillar's profitability suffered, but today it is very successful. A big part of this turnaround can be attributed to effective management of its inventory. Imagine what a bulldozer costs. Now imagine what it costs Caterpillar to have too many bulldozers sitting around in inventory–a situation the company definitely wants to avoid. Conversely, Caterpillar must make sure it has enough inventory to meet demand.

During a recent 7-year period, Caterpillar's sales increased by 100%, while its inventory increased by only 50%. To achieve this dramatic reduction in the amount of resources tied up in inventory, while continuing to meet customers' needs, Caterpillar used a two-pronged approach. First, it completed a factory modernization program, which dramatically increased its production efficiency. The program reduced by 60% the amount of inventory the company processed at any one time. It also reduced by an incredible 75% the time it takes to manufacture a part.

Second, Caterpillar dramatically improved its parts distribution system. It ships more than 100,000 items daily from its 23 distribution centers strategically located around the world (10 *million* square feet of warehouse space–remember, we're talking bulldozers). The company can virtually guarantee that it can get any part to anywhere in the world within 24 hours.

In 2006 Caterpillar had record exports, profits, and revenues. It would have seemed that things couldn't have been better. But industry analysts, as well as the company's managers, thought otherwise. In order to maintain Caterpillar's position as the industry leader, management began another major overhaul of inventory production and inventory management processes. The goal: Within 4 years the company wants to have cut the number of repairs in half, increased productivity by 20%, and increased inventory turnover by 40%. In short, Caterpillar's ability to manage its inventory has been a key reason for its past success, and inventory management will very likely play a huge part in its ability to succeed in the future.

On the World Wide Web
Caterpillar Inc.: www.cat.com

In the previous chapter, we discussed the accounting for merchandise inventory using a perpetual inventory system. In this chapter, we explain the methods used to calculate the cost of inventory on hand at the balance sheet date and the cost of goods sold. We conclude by illustrating methods for analyzing inventory.

The content and organization of this chapter are as follows.

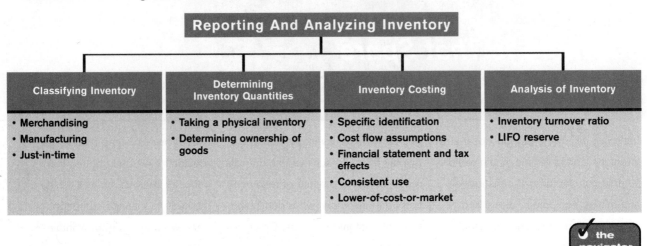

Classifying Inventory

How a company classifies its inventory depends on whether the firm is a merchandiser or a manufacturer. In a **merchandising** company, such as those described in Chapter 5, inventory consists of many different items. For example, in a grocery store, canned goods, dairy products, meats, and produce are just a few of the inventory items on hand. These items have two common characteristics: (1) They are owned by the company, and (2) they are in a form ready for sale to customers in the ordinary course of business. Thus, merchandisers need only one inventory classification, **merchandise inventory**, to describe the many different items that make up the total inventory.

In a **manufacturing** company, some inventory may not yet be ready for sale. As a result, manufacturers usually classify inventory into three categories: finished goods, work in process, and raw materials. Finished goods inventory is manufactured items that are completed and ready for sale. Work in process is that portion of manufactured inventory that has begun the production process but is not yet complete. Raw materials are the basic goods that will be used in production but have not yet been placed into production.

> **Helpful Hint** Regardless of the classification, companies report all inventories under Current Assets on the balance sheet.

For example, Caterpillar classifies earth-moving tractors completed and ready for sale as **finished goods**. It classifies the tractors on the assembly line in various stages of production as **work in process**. The steel, glass, tires, and other components that are on hand waiting to be used in the production of tractors are identified as **raw materials**.

The accounting concepts discussed in this chapter apply to the inventory classifications of both merchandising and manufacturing companies. Our focus throughout most of this chapter is on merchandise inventory.

By observing the levels and changes in the levels of these three inventory types, financial statement users can gain insight into management's production plans. For example, low levels of raw materials and high levels of finished goods suggest that management believes it has enough inventory on hand, and production will be slowing down—perhaps in anticipation of a recession. On the other hand, high levels of raw materials and low levels of finished goods probably indicate that management is planning to step up production.

Many companies have significantly lowered inventory levels and costs using **just-in-time (JIT) inventory** methods. Under a just-in-time method, companies manufacture or purchase goods just in time for use. Dell is famous for having developed a system for making computers in response to individual customer requests. Even though it makes computers to meet a customer's particular specifications, Dell is able to assemble the computer and put it on a truck in less than 48 hours. The success of a JIT system depends on reliable suppliers. By integrating its information systems with those of its suppliers, Dell reduced its inventories to nearly zero. This is a huge advantage in an industry where products become obsolete nearly overnight.

 ## Accounting Across the Organization

A Big Hiccup

JIT can save a company a lot of money, but it isn't without risk. An unexpected disruption in the supply chain can cost a company a lot of money. Japanese automakers experienced just such a disruption when a 6.8-magnitude earthquake caused major damage to the company that produces 50% of their piston rings. The rings themselves cost only $1.50, but without them you cannot make a car. No other supplier could quickly begin producing sufficient quantities of the rings to match the desired specifications. As a result, the automakers were forced to shut down production for a few days—a loss of tens of thousands of cars.

Source: Amy Chozick, "A Key Strategy of Japan's Car Makers Backfires," *Wall Street Journal*, July 20, 2007.

? What steps might the companies take to avoid such a serious disruption in the future?

Determining Inventory Quantities

No matter whether they are using a periodic or perpetual inventory system, all companies need to determine inventory quantities at the end of the accounting period. If using a perpetual system, companies take a physical inventory for two purposes: The first purpose is to check the accuracy of their perpetual inventory records. The second is to determine the amount of inventory lost due to wasted raw materials, shoplifting, or employee theft.

Companies using a periodic inventory system must take a physical inventory for two *different* purposes: to determine the inventory on hand at the balance sheet date, and to determine the cost of goods sold for the period.

Determining inventory quantities involves two steps: (1) taking a physical inventory of goods on hand and (2) determining the ownership of goods.

study objective   1

Describe the steps in determining inventory quantities.

TAKING A PHYSICAL INVENTORY

Companies take the physical inventory at the end of the accounting period. Taking a physical inventory involves actually counting, weighing, or measuring each kind of inventory on hand. In many companies, taking an inventory is a formidable task. Retailers such as Target, True Value Hardware, or Home Depot have thousands of different inventory items. An inventory count is generally more accurate when a limited number of goods are being sold or received during the counting. Consequently, companies often "take inventory" when the business is closed or when business is slow. Many retailers close early on a chosen day in January—after the holiday sales and returns, when inventories are at their lowest level—to count inventory. Recall from Chapter 5 that Wal-Mart had a year-end of January 31.

Ethics Note In a famous fraud, a salad oil company filled its storage tanks mostly with water. The oil rose to the top, so auditors thought the tanks were full of oil. The company also said it had more tanks than it really did: it repainted numbers on the tanks to confuse auditors.

 ## Ethics Insight

Managers at women's apparel maker Leslie Fay were convicted of falsifying inventory records to boost net income—and consequently to boost management bonuses. In another case, executives at Craig Consumer Electronics were accused of defrauding lenders by manipulating inventory records. The indictment said the company classified "defective goods as new or refurbished" and claimed that it owned certain shipments "from overseas suppliers" when, in fact, Craig either did not own the shipments or the shipments did not exist.

? What effect does an overstatement of inventory have on a company's financial statements?

DETERMINING OWNERSHIP OF GOODS

One challenge in determining inventory quantities is making sure a company owns the inventory. To determine ownership of goods, two questions must be answered: Do all of the goods included in the count belong to the company? Does the company own any goods that were not included in the count?

Goods in Transit

A complication in determining ownership is **goods in transit** (on board a truck, train, ship, or plane) at the end of the period. The company may have purchased goods that have not yet been received, or it may have sold goods that have not yet been delivered. To arrive at an accurate count, the company must determine ownership of these goods.

Goods in transit should be included in the inventory of the company that has legal title to the goods. Legal title is determined by the terms of the sale, as shown in Illustration 6-1 and described below.

Illustration 6-1 Terms of sale

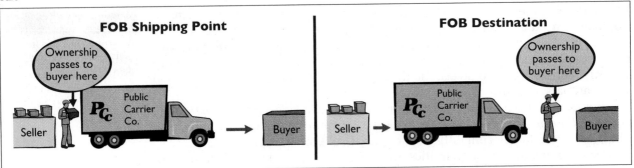

1. When the terms are **FOB (free on board) shipping point**, ownership of the goods passes to the buyer when the public carrier accepts the goods from the seller.
2. When the terms are **FOB destination**, ownership of the goods remains with the seller until the goods reach the buyer.

Consigned Goods

In some lines of business, it is common to hold the goods of other parties and try to sell the goods for them for a fee, but without taking ownership of the goods. These are called **consigned goods**.

For example, you might have a used car that you would like to sell. If you take the item to a dealer, the dealer might be willing to put the car on its lot and charge you a commission if it is sold. Under this agreement the dealer **would not take ownership** of the car, which would still belong to you. If an inventory count were taken, the car would not be included in the dealer's inventory.

Many car, boat, and antique dealers sell goods on consignment to keep their inventory costs down and to avoid the risk of purchasing an item that they won't be able to sell. Today even some manufacturers are making consignment agreements with their suppliers in order to keep their inventory levels low.

before you go on...

Do it!

Hasbeen Company completed its inventory count. It arrived at a total inventory value of $200,000. You have been given the information listed below. Discuss how this information affects the reported cost of inventory.

1. Hasbeen included in the inventory goods held on consignment for Falls Co., costing $15,000.
2. The company did not include in the count purchased goods of $10,000 which were in transit (terms: FOB shipping point).
3. The company did not include in the count sold inventory with a cost of $12,000 which was in transit (terms: FOB shipping point).

Solution

The goods of $15,000 held on consignment should be deducted from the inventory count. The goods of $10,000 purchased FOB shipping point should be added to the inventory count. Sold goods of $12,000 which were in transit FOB shipping point should not be included in the ending inventory. Inventory should be $195,000 ($200,000 − $15,000 + $10,000).

RULES OF OWNERSHIP

Action Plan
• Apply the rules of ownership to goods held on consignment.
• Apply the rules of ownership to goods in transit.

Inventory Costing

Inventory is accounted for at cost. Cost includes all expenditures necessary to acquire goods and place them in a condition ready for sale. After a company has determined the quantity of units of inventory, it applies unit costs to the quantities to determine the total cost of the inventory and the cost of goods sold. This process can be complicated if a company has purchased inventory items at different times and at different prices.

For example, assume that Crivitz TV Company purchases three identical 46-inch TVs on different dates at costs of $700, $750, and $800. During the year Crivitz sold two sets at $1,200 each. These facts are summarized in Illustration 6-2.

study objective 2

Explain the basis of accounting for inventories and apply the inventory cost flow methods under a periodic inventory system.

Purchases			
Feb. 3	1 TV	at	$700
March 5	1 TV	at	$750
May 22	1 TV	at	$800
Sales			
June 1	2 TVs	for	$2,400 ($1,200 × 2)

Illustration 6-2 Data for inventory costing example

Cost of goods sold will differ depending on which two TVs the company sold. For example, it might be $1,450 ($700 + $750), or $1,500 ($700 + $800), or $1,550 ($750 + $800). In this section we discuss alternative costing methods available to Crivitz.

SPECIFIC IDENTIFICATION

If Crivitz can positively identify which particular units it sold and which are still in ending inventory, it can use the **specific identification method** of inventory costing. For example, if Crivitz sold the TVs it purchased on February 3 and May 22, then its cost of goods sold is $1,500 ($700 + $800), and its ending inventory is $750 (see Illustration 6-3). Using this method, companies can accurately determine ending inventory and cost of goods sold.

Illustration 6-3 Specific identification method

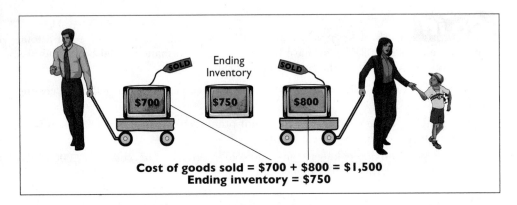

Cost of goods sold = $700 + $800 = $1,500
Ending inventory = $750

Ethics Note A major disadvantage of the specific identification method is that management may be able to manipulate net income. For example, it can boost net income by selling units purchased at a low cost, or reduce net income by selling units purchased at a high cost.

Specific identification requires that companies keep records of the original cost of each individual inventory item. Historically, specific identification was possible only when a company sold a limited variety of high-unit-cost items that could be identified clearly from the time of purchase through the time of sale. Examples of such products are cars, pianos, or expensive antiques.

Today, with bar coding, electronic product codes, and radio frequency identification, it is theoretically possible to do specific identification with nearly any type of product. The reality is, however, that this practice is still relatively rare. Instead, rather than keep track of the cost of each particular item sold, most companies make assumptions, called **cost flow assumptions**, about which units were sold.

COST FLOW ASSUMPTIONS

Because specific identification is often impractical, other cost flow methods are permitted. These differ from specific identification in that they **assume** flows of costs that may be unrelated to the actual physical flow of goods. There are three assumed cost flow methods:

1. First-in, first-out (FIFO)
2. Last-in, first-out (LIFO)
3. Average cost

There is no accounting requirement that the cost flow assumption be consistent with the physical movement of the goods. Company management selects the appropriate cost flow method.

To demonstrate the three cost flow methods we will use a *periodic* inventory system. We assume a periodic system for two main reasons. First, many small companies use periodic rather than perpetual systems. Second, **very few companies use *perpetual* LIFO, FIFO, or average cost** to cost their inventory and related cost of goods sold. Instead, companies that use perpetual systems often use an assumed cost (called a standard cost) to record cost of goods sold at the time of sale. Then, at the end of the period when they count their inventory, they **recalculate cost of goods sold using** *periodic* **FIFO, LIFO or average cost** and adjust cost of goods sold to this recalculated number.[1]

To illustrate the three inventory cost flow methods we will use the data for Houston Electronics' Astro condensers, shown in Illustration 6-4.

Illustration 6-4 Data for Houston Electronics

HOUSTON ELECTRONICS
Astro Condensers

Date	Explanation	Units	Unit Cost	Total Cost
Jan. 1	Beginning inventory	100	$10	$ 1,000
Apr. 15	Purchase	200	11	2,200
Aug. 24	Purchase	300	12	3,600
Nov. 27	Purchase	400	13	5,200
	Total units available for sale	1,000		$12,000
	Units in ending inventory	450		
	Units sold	550		

From Chapter 5, the cost of goods sold formula in a periodic system is:

(Beginning Inventory + Purchases) − Ending Inventory = Cost of Goods Sold

Houston Electronics had a total of 1,000 units available to sell during the period (beginning inventory plus purchases). The total cost of these 1,000 units is $12,000, referred to as *cost of goods available for sale*. A physical inventory taken at December 31 determined that there were 450 units in ending inventory. Therefore, Houston sold 550 units (1,000 − 450) during the period. To determine the cost of the 550 units that were sold (the cost of goods sold), we assign a cost to the ending inventory and subtract that value from the cost of goods available for sale. The value assigned to the ending inventory **will depend on which cost flow method we use**. No matter which cost flow assumption we use, though, the sum of cost of goods sold plus the cost of the ending inventory must equal the cost of goods available for sale—in this case, $12,000.

First-In, First-Out (FIFO)

The FIFO (first-in, first-out) method assumes that the **earliest goods** purchased are the first to be sold. FIFO often parallels the actual physical flow of merchandise because it generally is good business practice to sell the oldest units first. Under the FIFO method, therefore, the **costs** of the earliest goods purchased are the first to be recognized in determining cost of goods sold, regardless which units were actually sold. (Note that this does not mean that the oldest units *are* sold first, but that the costs of the oldest units are *recognized* first. In a bin of picture hangers at the hardware store, for example, no one really knows, nor would it matter, which hangers are sold first.) Illustration 6-5 (page 282) shows the allocation of the cost of goods available for sale at Houston Electronics under FIFO.

Under FIFO, since it is assumed that the first goods purchased were the first goods sold, ending inventory is based on the prices of the most recent units

---

[1]Also, some companies use a perpetual system to keep track of units, but they do not make an entry for perpetual cost of goods sold. In addition, firms that employ LIFO tend to use *dollar-value LIFO*, a method discussed in upper-level courses. FIFO periodic and FIFO perpetual give the same result; therefore firms should not incur the additional cost to use FIFO perpetual. Few firms use perpetual average-cost because of the added cost of record-keeping. Finally, for instructional purposes, we believe it is easier to demonstrate the cost flow assumptions under the periodic system, which makes it more pedagogically appropriate.

Illustration 6-5 Allocation of costs—FIFO method

Helpful Hint Note the sequencing of the allocation: (1) Compute ending inventory, and (2) determine cost of goods sold.

Helpful Hint Another way of thinking about the calculation of FIFO **ending inventory** is the *LISH* assumption—last in still here.

COST OF GOODS AVAILABLE FOR SALE

Date	Explanation	Units	Unit Cost	Total Cost
Jan. 1	Beginning inventory	100	$10	$ 1,000
Apr. 15	Purchase	200	11	2,200
Aug. 24	Purchase	300	12	3,600
Nov. 27	Purchase	400	13	5,200
	Total	1,000		$12,000

STEP 1: ENDING INVENTORY

Date	Units	Unit Cost	Total Cost
Nov. 27	400	$13	$ 5,200
Aug. 24	50	12	600
Total	450		$5,800

STEP 2: COST OF GOODS SOLD

Cost of goods available for sale	$12,000
Less: Ending inventory	5,800
Cost of goods sold	$ 6,200

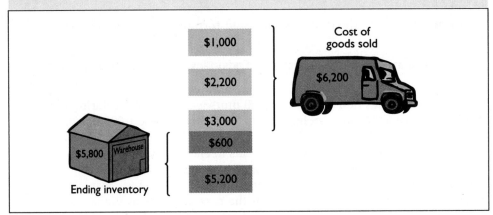

purchased. That is, **under FIFO, companies determine the cost of the ending inventory by taking the unit cost of the most recent purchase and working backward until all units of inventory have been costed.** In this example, Houston Electronics prices the 450 units of ending inventory using the *most recent* prices. The last purchase was 400 units at $13 on November 27. The remaining 50 units are priced using the unit cost of the second most recent purchase, $12, on August 24. Next, Houston Electronics calculates cost of goods sold by subtracting the cost of the units **not sold** (ending inventory) from the cost of all goods available for sale.

Illustration 6-6 demonstrates that companies also can calculate cost of goods sold by pricing the 550 units sold using the prices of the first 550 units acquired. Note that of the 300 units purchased on August 24, only 250 units are assumed sold. This agrees with our calculation of the cost of ending inventory, where 50 of these units were assumed unsold and thus included in ending inventory.

Illustration 6-6 Proof of cost of goods sold

Date	Units	Unit Cost	Total Cost
Jan. 1	100	$10	$ 1,000
Apr. 15	200	11	2,200
Aug. 24	250	12	3,000
Total	550		$6,200

Last-In, First-Out (LIFO)

The **LIFO (last-in, first-out) method** assumes that the **latest goods** purchased are the first to be sold. LIFO seldom coincides with the actual physical flow of inventory. (Exceptions include goods stored in piles, such as coal or hay, where goods are removed from the top of the pile as they are sold.) Under the LIFO method, the **costs** of the latest goods purchased are the first to be recognized in determining cost of goods sold. Illustration 6-7 shows the allocation of the cost of goods available for sale at Houston Electronics under LIFO.

Illustration 6-7 Allocation of costs–LIFO method

COST OF GOODS AVAILABLE FOR SALE

Date	Explanation	Units	Unit Cost	Total Cost
Jan. 1	Beginning inventory	100	$10	$ 1,000
Apr. 15	Purchase	200	11	2,200
Aug. 24	Purchase	300	12	3,600
Nov. 27	Purchase	400	13	5,200
	Total	1,000		$12,000

STEP 1: ENDING INVENTORY

Date	Units	Unit Cost	Total Cost
Jan. 1	100	$10	$ 1,000
Apr. 15	200	11	2,200
Aug. 24	150	12	1,800
Total	450		$5,000

STEP 2: COST OF GOODS SOLD

Cost of goods available for sale	$12,000
Less: Ending inventory	5,000
Cost of goods sold	$ 7,000

Helpful Hint Another way of thinking about the calculation of LIFO **ending inventory** is the *FISH assumption*–first in still here.

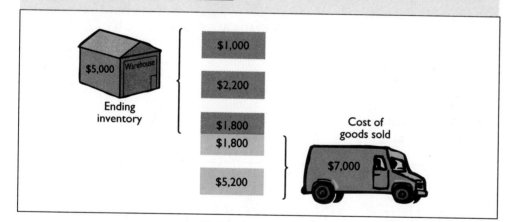

Under LIFO, since it is assumed that the first goods sold were those that were most recently purchased, ending inventory is based on the prices of the oldest units purchased. That is, **under LIFO, companies obtain the cost of the ending inventory by taking the unit cost of the earliest goods available for sale and working forward until all units of inventory have been costed**. In this example, Houston Electronics prices the 450 units of ending inventory using the *earliest* prices. The first purchase was 100 units at $10 in the January 1 beginning inventory. Then 200 units were purchased at $11. The remaining 150 units needed are priced at $12 per unit (August 24 purchase). Next, Houston Electronics calculates cost of goods sold by subtracting the cost of the units **not sold** (ending inventory) from the cost of all goods available for sale.

Illustration 6-8 (page 284) demonstrates that we can also calculate cost of goods sold by pricing the 550 units sold using the prices of the last 550 units acquired. Note that of the 300 units purchased on August 24, only 150 units are assumed sold. This agrees with our calculation of the cost of ending inventory, where 150 of these units were assumed unsold and thus included in ending inventory.

Illustration 6-8 Proof of cost of goods sold

Date	Units	Unit Cost	Total Cost
Nov. 27	400	$13	$ 5,200
Aug. 24	150	12	1,800
Total	550		$7,000

Under a periodic inventory system, which we are using here, **all goods purchased during the period are assumed to be available for the first sale**, regardless of the date of purchase.

Average Cost

The average-cost method allocates the cost of goods available for sale on the basis of the weighted average unit cost incurred. The average-cost method assumes that goods are similar in nature. Illustration 6-9 presents the formula and a sample computation of the weighted-average unit cost.

Illustration 6-9 Formula for weighted average unit cost

Cost of Goods Available for Sale	÷	Total Units Available for Sale	÷	Weighted Average Unit Cost
$12,000	÷	1,000	÷	$12.00

The company then applies the weighted average unit cost to the units on hand to determine the cost of the ending inventory. Illustration 6-10 shows the

Illustration 6-10 Allocation of costs—average-cost method

COST OF GOODS AVAILABLE FOR SALE				
Date	Explanation	Units	Unit Cost	Total Cost
Jan. 1	Beginning inventory	100	$10	$ 1,000
Apr. 15	Purchase	200	11	2,200
Aug. 24	Purchase	300	12	3,600
Nov. 27	Purchase	400	13	5,200
	Total	1,000		$12,000

STEP 1: ENDING INVENTORY

$12,000 ÷ 1,000 = $12.00

Units	Unit Cost	Total Cost
450	$12.00	$5,400

STEP 2: COST OF GOODS SOLD

Cost of goods available for sale	$12,000
Less: Ending inventory	5,400
Cost of goods sold	$ 6,600

$\dfrac{\$12,000}{1{,}000 \text{ units}} = \$12 \text{ per unit}$

Cost per unit

450 units × $12 = $5,400 Warehouse

Ending inventory

$12,000 − $5,400 = $6,600

Cost of goods sold

allocation of the cost of goods available for sale at Houston Electronics using average cost.

We can verify the cost of goods sold under this method by multiplying the units sold times the weighted average unit cost (550 × $12 = $6,600). Note that this method does not use the simple average of the unit costs. That average is $11.50 ($10 + $11 + $12 + $13 = $46; $46 ÷ 4). The average cost method instead uses the average **weighted by** the quantities purchased at each unit cost.

before you go on...

Do it!

The accounting records of Shumway Ag Implement show the following data.

Beginning inventory	4,000 units at $3
Purchases	6,000 units at $4
Sales	7,000 units at $12

Determine (a) the cost of goods available for sale and (b) the cost of goods sold during the period under a periodic system using (i) FIFO, (ii) LIFO, and (iii) average cost.

Solution

(a) Cost of goods available for sale: (4,000 × $3) + (6,000 × $4) = $36,000
(b) Cost of goods sold using:
   (i) FIFO: $36,000 − (3,000 × $4) = $24,000
   (ii) LIFO: $36,000 − (3,000 × $3) = $27,000
   (iii) Average cost: Weighted average price = ($36,000 ÷ 10,000) = $3.60
         $36,000 − (3,000 × $3.60) = $25,200

COST FLOW METHODS

Action Plan

• Understand the periodic inventory system.

• Allocate costs between goods sold and goods on hand (ending inventory) for each cost flow method.

• Compute cost of goods sold for each cost flow method.

FINANCIAL STATEMENT AND TAX EFFECTS OF COST FLOW METHODS

Each of the three assumed cost flow methods is acceptable for use under GAAP. For example, Reebok International Ltd. and Wendy's International currently use the FIFO method of inventory costing. Campbell Soup Company, Krogers, and Walgreens use LIFO for part or all of their inventory. Bristol-Myers Squibb, Starbucks, and Motorola use the average cost method. In fact, a company may also use more than one cost flow method at the same time. Black & Decker Manufacturing Company, for example, uses LIFO for domestic inventories and FIFO for foreign inventories. Illustration 6-11 shows the use of the three cost flow methods in the 600 largest U.S. companies.

The reasons companies adopt different inventory cost flow methods are varied, but they usually involve at least one of the following three factors:

1. Income statement effects
2. Balance sheet effects
3. Tax effects

Income Statement Effects

To understand why companies might choose a particular cost flow method, let's examine the effects of the different cost flow assumptions on the financial statements of Houston Electronics. The condensed income statements in Illustration 6-12 assume that Houston sold its 550 units for $18,500, had operating expenses of $9,000, and is subject to an income tax rate of 30%.

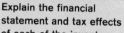 3

Explain the financial statement and tax effects of each of the inventory cost flow assumptions.

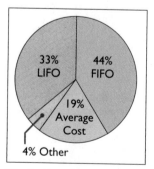

Illustration 6-11 Use of cost flow methods in major U.S. companies

Illustration 6-12
Comparative effects of
cost flow methods

HOUSTON ELECTRONICS Condensed Income Statements			
	FIFO	LIFO	Average Cost
Sales	$18,500	$18,500	$18,500
Beginning inventory	1,000	1,000	1,000
Purchases	11,000	11,000	11,000
Cost of goods available for sale	12,000	12,000	12,000
Ending inventory	**5,800**	**5,000**	**5,400**
Cost of goods sold	6,200	7,000	6,600
Gross profit	12,300	11,500	11,900
Operating expenses	9,000	9,000	9,000
Income before income taxes	3,300	2,500	2,900
Income tax expense (30%)	990	750	870
Net income	**$ 2,310**	**$ 1,750**	**$ 2,030**

Note the cost of goods available for sale ($12,000) is the same under each of the three inventory cost flow methods. However, the ending inventories and the costs of goods sold are different. This difference is due to the unit costs that the company allocated to cost of goods sold and to ending inventory. Each dollar of difference in ending inventory results in a corresponding dollar difference in income before income taxes. For Houston, an $800 difference exists between FIFO and LIFO cost of goods sold.

In periods of changing prices, the cost flow assumption can have a significant impact on income and on evaluations based on income. In most instances, prices are rising (inflation). In a period of inflation, FIFO produces a higher net income because the lower unit costs of the first units purchased are matched against revenues. In a period of rising prices (as is the case in the Houston example), FIFO reports the highest net income ($2,310) and LIFO the lowest ($1,750); average cost falls in the middle ($2,030). If prices are falling, the results from the use of FIFO and LIFO are reversed: FIFO will report the lowest net income and LIFO the highest.

To management, higher net income is an advantage: It causes external users to view the company more favorably. In addition, management bonuses, if based on net income, will be higher. Therefore, when prices are rising (which is usually the case), companies tend to prefer FIFO because it results in higher net income.

Some argue that the use of LIFO in a period of inflation reduces the likelihood that the company will report **paper** (or **phantom**) **profit** as economic gain. To illustrate, assume that Kralik Company buys 200 units of a product at $20 per unit on January 10 and 200 more on December 31 at $24 each. During the year, Kralik sells 200 units at $30 each. Illustration 6-13 shows the results under FIFO and LIFO.

Illustration 6-13 Income statement effects compared

	FIFO		LIFO	
Sales (200 × $30)	$6,000		$6,000	
Cost of goods sold	4,000	(200 × $20)	4,800	(200 × $24)
Gross profit	$2,000		$1,200	

Under LIFO, Kralik Company has recovered the current replacement cost ($4,800) of the units sold. Thus, the gross profit in economic terms is real. However, under FIFO, the company has recovered only the January 10 cost ($4,000).

To replace the units sold, it must reinvest $800 (200 × $4) of the gross profit. Thus, $800 of the gross profit is said to be phantom or illusory. As a result, reported net income is also overstated in real terms.

Balance Sheet Effects

A major advantage of the FIFO method is that in a period of inflation, the costs allocated to ending inventory will approximate their current cost. For example, for Houston Electronics, 400 of the 450 units in the ending inventory are costed under FIFO at the higher November 27 unit cost of $13.

Conversely, a major shortcoming of the LIFO method is that in a period of inflation, the costs allocated to ending inventory may be significantly understated in terms of current cost. The understatement becomes greater over prolonged periods of inflation if the inventory includes goods purchased in one or more prior accounting periods. For example, **Caterpillar** has used LIFO for 50 years. Its balance sheet shows ending inventory of $4,675 million. But the inventory's actual current cost if FIFO had been used is $6,799 million.

Tax Effects

We have seen that both inventory on the balance sheet and net income on the income statement are higher when companies use FIFO in a period of inflation. Yet, many companies use LIFO. Why? The reason is that LIFO results in the lowest income taxes (because of lower net income) during times of rising prices. For example, in Illustration 6-12, income taxes are $750 under LIFO, compared to $990 under FIFO. The tax savings of $240 makes more cash available for use in the business.

Helpful Hint A tax rule, often referred to as the *LIFO conformity rule*, requires that if companies use LIFO for tax purposes they must also use it for financial reporting purposes. This means that if a company chooses the LIFO method to reduce its tax bills, it will also have to report lower net income in its financial statements.

 ## International Insight

Exxon Mobil Corporation, like many U.S. companies, uses LIFO to value its inventory for financial reporting and tax purposes. In one recent year, this resulted in a cost of goods sold figure that was $5.6 billion higher than under FIFO. By increasing cost of goods sold, Exxon Mobil reduces net income, which reduces taxes. Critics say that LIFO provides an unfair "tax dodge." As Congress looks for more sources of tax revenue, some lawmakers favor the elimination of LIFO. Supporters of LIFO argue that the method is conceptually sound because it matches current costs with current revenues. In addition, they point out that this matching provides protection against inflation.

International accounting standards do not allow the use of LIFO. Because of this, the net income of foreign oil companies such as **BP** and **Royal Dutch Shell** are not directly comparable to U.S. companies, which makes analysis difficult.

Source: David Reilly, "Big Oil's Accounting Methods Fuel Criticism," *Wall Street Journal*, August 8, 2006, p. C1.

 What are the arguments for and against the use of LIFO?

You have just seen that when prices are rising the use of LIFO can have a big effect on taxes. The lower taxes paid using LIFO can significantly increase cash flows. To demonstrate the effect of the cost flow assumptions on cash flow, we will calculate net cash provided by operating activities, using the data for Houston Electronics from Illustration 6-12. To simplify our example, we assume that

KEEPING AN EYE ON CASH

Houston's sales and purchases are all cash transactions. We also assume that operating expenses, other than $4,600 of depreciation, are cash transactions.

	FIFO	LIFO	Average Cost
Cash received from customers	$18,500	$18,500	$18,500
Cash purchases of goods	11,000	11,000	11,000
Cash paid for operating expenses ($9,000 − $4,600)	4,400	4,400	4,400
Cash paid for taxes	990	750	870
Net cash provided by operating activities	$ 2,110	$ 2,350	$ 2,230

LIFO has the highest net cash provided by operating activities because it results in the lowest tax payments. Since cash flow is the lifeblood of any organization, the choice of inventory method is very important.

LIFO also impacts the quality of earnings ratio. Recall that the quality of earnings ratio is net cash provided by operating activities divided by net income. Here we calculate the quality earnings ratio under each cost flow assumption.

	FIFO	LIFO	Average Cost
Net income (from Illustration 6-12)	$2,310	$1,750	$2,030
Quality of earnings ratio	0.91	1.34	1.1

LIFO has the highest quality of earnings ratio for two reasons: (1) It has the highest net cash provided by operating activities, which increases the ratio's numerator. (2) It reports a conservative measure of net income, which decreases the ratio's denominator. As discussed earlier, LIFO provides a conservative measure of net income because it does not include the phantom profits reported under FIFO.

DECISION TOOLKIT

DECISION CHECKPOINTS	INFO NEEDED FOR DECISION	TOOL TO USE FOR DECISION	HOW TO EVALUATE RESULTS
Which inventory costing method should be used?	Are prices increasing, or are they decreasing?	Income statement, balance sheet, and tax effects	Depends on objective. In a period of rising prices, income and inventory are higher and cash flow is lower under FIFO. LIFO provides opposite results. Average cost can moderate the impact of changing prices.

USING INVENTORY COST FLOW METHODS CONSISTENTLY

Whatever cost flow method a company chooses, it should use that method consistently from one accounting period to another. Consistent application enhances the ability to analyze a company's financial statements over successive time periods. In contrast, using the FIFO method one year and the LIFO method the next year would make it difficult to compare the net incomes of the two years.

Although consistent application is preferred, it does not mean that a company may *never* change its method of inventory costing. When a company adopts a different method, it should disclose in the financial statements the change and its effects on net income. A typical disclosure is shown in Illustration 6-14, using information from recent financial statements of the Quaker Oats Company.

Helpful Hint As you learned in Chapter 2, consistency and comparability are important characteristics of accounting information.

QUAKER OATS COMPANY
Notes to the Financial Statements

Note 1: Effective July 1, the Company adopted the LIFO cost flow assumption for valuing the majority of U.S. Grocery Products inventories. The Company believes that the use of the LIFO method better matches current costs with current revenues. The effect of this change on the current year was to decrease net income by $16.0 million.

Illustration 6-14
Disclosure of change in cost flow method

LOWER-OF-COST-OR-MARKET

The value of inventory for companies selling high-technology or fashion goods can drop very quickly due to changes in technology or changes in fashions. These circumstances sometimes call for inventory valuation methods other than those presented so far. For example, in a recent year purchasing managers at Ford decided to make a large purchase of palladium, a precious metal used in vehicle emission devices. They made this large purchase because they feared a future shortage. The shortage did not materialize, and by the end of the year the price of palladium had plummeted. Ford's inventory was then worth $1 billion less than its original cost. Do you think Ford's inventory should have been stated at cost, in accordance with the cost principle, or at its lower replacement cost?

As you probably reasoned, this situation requires a departure from the cost basis of accounting. When the value of inventory is lower than its cost, companies write down the inventory to its market value. This is done by valuing the inventory at the lower-of-cost-or-market (LCM) in the period in which the price decline occurs. LCM is an example of the accounting **concept of conservatism**, which means that the best choice among accounting alternatives is the method that is least likely to overstate assets and net income.

Companies apply LCM to the items in inventory after they have used one of the cost flow methods (specific identification, FIFO, LIFO, or average cost) to determine cost. Under the LCM basis, market is defined as current replacement cost, not selling price. For a merchandising company, market is the cost of purchasing the same goods at the present time from the usual suppliers in the usual quantities. Current replacement cost is used because a decline in the replacement cost of an item usually leads to a decline in the selling price of the item.

To illustrate the application of LCM, assume that Ken Tuckie TV has the following lines of merchandise with costs and market values as indicated. LCM produces the results shown in Illustration 6-15. Note that the amounts shown in the final column are the lower-of-cost-or-market amounts for each item.

study objective 4

Explain the lower of cost or market basis of accounting for inventories.

International Note Under U.S. GAAP, companies cannot reverse inventory write-downs if inventory increases in value in subsequent periods. International accounting standards permit companies to reverse write-downs in some circumstances.

	Cost	Market	Lower-of-Cost-or-Market
Flat-panel TVs	$60,000	$55,000	$ 55,000
Satellite radios	45,000	52,000	45,000
DVD recorders	48,000	45,000	45,000
DVDs	15,000	14,000	14,000
Total inventory			$159,000

Illustration 6-15
Computation of inventory at lower-of-cost-or-market

Adherence to LCM is important. A Chinese manufacturer of silicon wafers for solar energy panels, LDK Solar Co., was accused of violating LCM. When the financial press reported accusations that two-thirds of its inventory of silicon was unsuitable for processing, the company's stock price fell by 40%.

before you go on...

LCM BASIS

Action Plan

- Determine whether cost or market value is lower for each inventory type.
- Sum the lowest value of each inventory type to determine the total value of inventory.

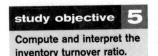

 Tracy Company sells three different types of home heating stoves (wood, gas, and pellet). The cost and market value of its inventory of stoves are as follows.

	Cost	Market
Gas	$ 84,000	$ 79,000
Wood	250,000	280,000
Pellet	112,000	101,000

Determine the value of the company's inventory under the lower-of-cost-or-market approach.

Solution

The lowest value for each inventory type is: gas $79,000, wood $250,000, and pellet $101,000. The total inventory value is the sum of these figures, $430,000.

Analysis of Inventory

For companies that sell goods, managing inventory levels can be one of the most critical tasks. Having too much inventory on hand costs the company money in storage costs, interest cost (on funds tied up in inventory), and costs associated with the obsolescence of technical goods (e.g., computer chips) or shifts in fashion (e.g., clothes). But having too little inventory on hand results in lost sales. In this section we discuss some issues related to evaluating inventory levels.

INVENTORY TURNOVER RATIO

Compute and interpret the inventory turnover ratio.

The inventory turnover ratio is calculated as cost of goods sold divided by average inventory. It indicates how quickly a company sells its goods—the number of times the average inventory "turns over" (is sold) during the year. Inventory turnover can be divided into 365 days to compute days in inventory, which indicates the average number of days inventory is held.

High inventory turnover (low days in inventory) indicates the company has minimal funds tied up in inventory—that it has a minimal amount of inventory on hand at any one time. Although minimizing the funds tied up in inventory is efficient, too high an inventory turnover ratio may indicate that the company is losing sales opportunities because of inventory shortages. For example, investment analysts at one time suggested that Office Depot had gone too far in reducing its inventory—they said they were seeing too many empty shelves. Thus, management should closely monitor this ratio to achieve the best balance between too much and too little inventory.

In Chapter 5 we discussed the increasingly competitive environment of retailers like Wal-Mart and Target. Wal-Mart has implemented **just-in-time inventory procedures** as well as many technological innovations to improve the efficiency of its inventory management. The following data are available for Wal-Mart.

(in millions)	2007	2006	2005
Ending inventory	$ 33,685	$ 31,910	$29,419
Cost of goods sold	264,152	237,649	

Illustration 6-16 presents the inventory turnover ratios and days in inventory for Wal-Mart and Target, using data from the financial statements of those corporations for 2007 and 2006.

Illustration 6-16 Inventory turnover ratio and days in inventory

Inventory Turnover Ratio $=\dfrac{\text{Cost of Goods Sold}}{\text{Average Inventory}}$			
Days in Inventory $=\dfrac{365}{\text{Inventory Turnover Ratio}}$			
		2007	**2006**
Wal-Mart ($ in millions)	Inventory turnover ratio	$\dfrac{\$264{,}152}{(\$33{,}685 + \$31{,}910)/2} = 8.1$ times	$\dfrac{\$237{,}649}{(\$31{,}910 + \$29{,}419)/2} = 7.7$ times
	Days in inventory	$\dfrac{365 \text{ days}}{8.1} = 45.1$ days	$\dfrac{365 \text{ days}}{7.7} = 47.4$ days
Target	Inventory turnover ratio	6.5 times	6.2 times
	Days in inventory	56.2 days	58.9 days

The calculations in Illustration 6-16 show that Wal-Mart turns its inventory more frequently than Target (8.1 times for Wal-Mart versus 6.5 times for Target). Consequently, the average time an item spends on a Wal-Mart shelf is shorter (45.1 days for Wal-Mart versus 56.2 days for Target). This suggests that Wal-Mart is more efficient than Target in its inventory management.

Note also that Wal-Mart's inventory turnover, which was already better than Target's in 2006, improved slightly in 2007. Wal-Mart's sophisticated inventory tracking and distribution system allows it to keep minimum amounts of inventory on hand, while still keeping the shelves full of what customers are looking for.

Accounting Across the Organization

Wal-Mart improved its inventory control with the introduction of radio frequency identification (RFID). Much like bar codes, which tell a retailer the number of boxes of a specific product it has, RFID goes a step farther, helping to distinguish one box of a specific product from another. RFID uses technology similar to that used by keyless remotes that unlock car doors.

Companies currently use RFID to track shipments from supplier to distribution center to store. Other potential uses include monitoring product expiration dates and acting quickly on product recalls. Wal-Mart also anticipates faster returns and warranty processing using RFID. This technology will further assist Wal-Mart managers in their efforts to ensure that their store has just the right type of inventory, in just the right amount, in just the right place. Other companies are also interested in RFID. Best Buy has spent millions researching possible applications in its stores.

? Why is inventory control important to managers such as those at Wal-Mart and Best Buy?

the navigator

DECISION TOOLKIT

DECISION CHECKPOINTS	INFO NEEDED FOR DECISION	TOOL TO USE FOR DECISION	HOW TO EVALUATE RESULTS
How long is an item in inventory?	Cost of goods sold; beginning and ending inventory	$\text{Inventory turnover ratio} = \dfrac{\text{Cost of goods sold}}{\text{Average inventory}}$ $\text{Days in inventory} = \dfrac{365 \text{ days}}{\text{Inventory turnover ratio}}$	A higher inventory turnover ratio or lower average days in inventory suggests that management is reducing the amount of inventory on hand, relative to cost of goods sold.

---

before you go on...

INVENTORY TURNOVER

Do it! Early in 2010 Westmoreland Company switched to a just-in-time inventory system. Its sales, cost of goods sold, and inventory amounts for 2009 and 2010 are shown below.

	2009	2010
Sales	$2,000,000	$1,800,000
Cost of goods sold	1,000,000	910,000
Beginning inventory	290,000	210,000
Ending inventory	210,000	50,000

Determine the inventory turnover and days in inventory for 2009 and 2010. Discuss the changes in the amount of inventory, the inventory turnover and days in inventory, and the amount of sales across the two years.

Action Plan

• To find the inventory turnover ratio, divide cost of goods sold by average inventory.

• To determine days in inventory, divide 365 days by the inventory turnover ratio.

• Just-in-time inventory reduces the amount of inventory on hand, which reduces carrying costs. Reducing inventory levels by too much has potential negative implications for sales.

Solution

	2009	2010
Inventory turnover ratio	$\dfrac{\$1,000,000}{(\$290,000 + \$210,000)/2} = 4$	$\dfrac{\$910,000}{(\$210,000 + \$50,000)/2} = 7$
Days in inventory	$365 \div 4 = 91.3$ days	$365 \div 7 = 52.1$ days

The company experienced a very significant decline in its ending inventory as a result of the just-in-time inventory. This decline improved its inventory turnover ratio and its days in inventory. However, its sales declined by 10%. It is possible that this decline was caused by the dramatic reduction in the amount of inventory that was on hand, which increased the likelihood of "stock-outs." To determine the optimal inventory level, management must weigh the benefits of reduced inventory against the potential lost sales caused by stock-outs.

ANALYSTS' ADJUSTMENTS FOR LIFO RESERVE

study objective 6

Describe the LIFO reserve and explain its importance for comparing results of different companies.

Earlier we noted that using LIFO rather than FIFO can result in significant differences in the results reported in the balance sheet and the income statement. With increasing prices, FIFO will result in higher income than LIFO. On the balance sheet, FIFO will result in higher reported inventory. The financial statement differences from using LIFO normally increase the longer a company uses LIFO.

Use of different inventory cost flow assumptions complicates analysts' attempts to compare companies' results. Fortunately, companies using LIFO are required to report the difference between inventory reported using LIFO and inventory using FIFO. This amount is referred to as the LIFO reserve. Reporting the LIFO reserve enables analysts to make adjustments to compare companies that use different cost flow methods.

Illustration 6-17 presents an excerpt from the notes to Caterpillar's 2007 financial statements that discloses and discusses Caterpillar's LIFO reserve.

CATERPILLAR INC.
Notes to the Financial Statements

Inventories: Inventories are stated at the lower of cost or market. Cost is principally determined using the last-in, first-out (LIFO) method . . . . If the FIFO (first-in, first-out) method had been in use, inventories would have been $2,617, $2,403, and $2,345 million higher than reported at December 31, 2007, 2006, and 2005, respectively.

Illustration 6-17
Caterpillar LIFO reserve

Caterpillar has used LIFO for over 50 years. Thus, the cumulative difference between LIFO and FIFO reflected in the inventory account is very large. In fact, the 2007 LIFO reserve of $2,617 million is 36 percent of the 2007 LIFO inventory of $7,204 million. Such a huge difference would clearly distort any comparisons you might try to make with one of Caterpillar's competitors that used FIFO.

To adjust Caterpillar's inventory balance we add the LIFO reserve to reported inventory, as shown in Illustration 6-18. That is, if Caterpillar had used FIFO all along, its inventory would be $9,821 million, rather than $7,204 million.

	(in millions)
2007 inventory using LIFO	$ 7,204
2007 LIFO reserve	2,617
2007 inventory assuming FIFO	**$9,821**

Illustration 6-18
Conversion of inventory from LIFO to FIFO

The LIFO reserve can have a significant effect on ratios that analysts commonly use. Using the LIFO reserve adjustment, Illustration 6-19 calculates the value of the current ratio (current assets ÷ current liabilities) for Caterpillar under both the LIFO and FIFO cost flow assumptions.

($ in millions)	LIFO	FIFO
Current ratio	$\dfrac{\$25,477}{\$22,245} = 1.15{:}1$	$\dfrac{\$25,477 + \$2,617}{\$22,245} = 1.26{:}1$

Illustration 6-19 Impact of LIFO reserve on ratios

As Illustration 6-19 shows, if Caterpillar used FIFO, its current ratio would be 1.26:1 rather than 1.15:1 under LIFO. Thus, Caterpillar's liquidity appears stronger if a FIFO assumption were used in valuing inventories. If a similar adjustment is made for the inventory turnover ratio, Caterpillar's inventory turnover actually would look worse under FIFO than under LIFO, dropping from 4.8 times for LIFO to 3.5 times for FIFO.[2] The reason: LIFO reports low inventory amounts, which cause inventory turnover to be higher.

---

[2]The LIFO reserve also affects cost of goods sold, although typically by a much less material amount. The cost of goods sold adjustment is discussed in more advanced financial statement analysis texts.

CNH Global, a competitor of Caterpillar, uses FIFO to account for its inventory. Comparing Caterpillar to CNH without converting Caterpillar's inventory to FIFO would lead to distortions and potentially erroneous decisions.

DECISION TOOLKIT

DECISION CHECKPOINTS	INFO NEEDED FOR DECISION	TOOL TO USE FOR DECISION	HOW TO EVALUATE RESULTS
What is the impact of LIFO on the company's reported inventory?	LIFO reserve, cost of goods sold, ending inventory, current assets, current liabilities	$\dfrac{\text{LIFO}}{\text{inventory}} + \dfrac{\text{LIFO}}{\text{reserve}} = \dfrac{\text{FIFO}}{\text{inventory}}$	If these adjustments are material, they can significantly affect such measures as the current ratio and the inventory turnover ratio.

USING THE DECISION TOOLKIT

The Manitowoc Company is located in Manitowoc, Wisconsin. In recent years it has made a series of strategic acquisitions to grow and enhance its market-leading positions in each of its three business segments. These include: cranes and related products (crawler cranes, tower cranes, and boom trucks); food service equipment (commercial ice-cube machines, ice-beverage dispensers, and commercial refrigeration equipment); and marine operations (shipbuilding and ship-repair services). The company reported inventory of $597.7 million for 2007 and of $492.4 million for 2006. Here is the inventory note taken from the 2007 financial statements.

THE MANITOWOC COMPANY
Notes to the Financial Statements

Inventories: The components of inventories are summarized at December 31 as follows (in millions).

	2007	2006
Inventories—gross		
Raw materials	$254.6	$198.3
Work-in-process	220.9	174.2
Finished goods	188.5	187.2
Total	664.0	559.7
Less: Excess and obsolete inventory reserve	(42.6)	(44.4)
Net inventories at FIFO cost	621.4	515.3
Less: Excess of FIFO costs over LIFO value	(23.7)	(22.9)
Inventories—net	$597.7	$492.4

Manitowoc carries inventory at the lower-of-cost-or-market using the first-in, first-out (FIFO) method for 88% and 85% of total inventory for 2007 and 2006, respectively. The remainder of the inventory is costed using the last-in, first-out (LIFO) method.

Additional facts:

2007 Current liabilities	$1,074.6
2007 Current assets (as reported)	1,575.6
2007 Cost of goods sold	3,093.4

Instructions

Answer the following questions.
1. Why does the company report its inventory in three components?
2. Why might the company use two methods (LIFO and FIFO) to account for its inventory?
3. Perform each of the following.
   (a) Calculate the inventory turnover ratio and days in inventory using the LIFO inventory.
   (b) Show the conversion of the 2007 and 2006 LIFO inventory values to FIFO values.
   (c) Calculate the 2007 current ratio using LIFO and the current ratio using FIFO. Discuss the difference.

Solution

1. The Manitowoc Company is a manufacturer, so it purchases raw materials and makes them into finished products. At the end of each period, it has some goods that have been started but are not yet complete (work in process).

   By reporting all three components of inventory, a company reveals important information about its inventory position. For example, if amounts of raw materials have increased significantly compared to the previous year, we might assume the company is planning to step up production. On the other hand, if levels of finished goods have increased relative to last year and raw materials have declined, we might conclude that sales are slowing down—that the company has too much inventory on hand and is cutting back production.
2. Companies are free to choose different cost flow assumptions for different types of inventory. A company might choose to use FIFO for a product that is expected to decrease in price over time. One common reason for choosing a method other than LIFO is that many foreign countries do not allow LIFO; thus, the company cannot use LIFO for its foreign operations.
3. (a) $\text{Inventory turnover ratio} = \dfrac{\text{Cost of goods sold}}{\text{Average inventory}} = \dfrac{\$3,093,4}{(\$597.7 + \$492.4)/2} = 5.7$

   $\text{Days in inventory} = \dfrac{365}{\text{Inventory turnover ratio}} = \dfrac{365}{5.7} = 64.0 \text{ days}$

   (b) Conversion from LIFO to FIFO values

	2004	2003
LIFO inventory	$597.7	$492.4
LIFO reserve	23.7	22.9
FIFO inventory	$621.4	$515.3

   (c) Current ratio

LIFO	FIFO
$\dfrac{\text{Current assets}}{\text{Current liabilities}} = \dfrac{\$1,575.6}{\$1,074.6} = 1.47{:}1$	$\dfrac{\$1,575.6 + \$23.7}{\$1,074.6} = 1.49{:}1$

   This represents a 1.4% increase in the current ratio $(1.49 - 1.47)/1.47$.

Summary of Study Objectives

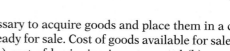

1 **Describe the steps in determining inventory quantities.** The steps are (1) take a physical inventory of goods on hand and (2) determine the ownership of goods in transit or on consignment.

2 **Explain the basis of accounting for inventories and apply the inventory cost flow methods under a periodic inventory system.** The primary basis of accounting for inventories is cost. Cost includes all expenditures nec-

essary to acquire goods and place them in a condition ready for sale. Cost of goods available for sale includes (a) cost of beginning inventory and (b) cost of goods purchased. The inventory cost flow methods are: specific identification and three assumed cost flow methods—FIFO, LIFO, and average cost.

3 **Explain the financial statement and tax effects of each of the inventory cost flow assumptions.** The cost of goods available for sale may be allocated to cost of goods sold and ending inventory by specific identification or by a method based on an assumed cost flow. When prices are rising, the first-in, first-out (FIFO) method results in lower cost of goods sold and higher net income than the average cost and the last-in, first-out (LIFO) methods. The reverse is true when prices are falling. In the balance sheet, FIFO results in an ending inventory that is closest to current value, whereas the inventory under LIFO is the farthest from current value. LIFO results in the lowest income taxes (because of lower taxable income).

4 **Explain the lower-of-cost-or-market basis of accounting for inventories.** Companies use the lower-of-cost-or-market (LCM) basis when the current replacement cost (market) is less than cost. Under LCM, companies recognize the loss in the period in which the price decline occurs.

5 **Compute and interpret the inventory turnover ratio.** The inventory turnover ratio is calculated as cost of goods sold divided by average inventory. It can be converted to average days in inventory by dividing 365 days by the inventory turnover ratio. A higher turnover ratio or lower average days in inventory suggests that management is trying to keep inventory levels low relative to its sales level.

6 **Describe the LIFO reserve and explain its importance for comparing results of different companies.** The LIFO reserve represents the difference between ending inventory using LIFO and ending inventory if FIFO were employed instead. For some companies this difference can be significant, and ignoring it can lead to inappropriate conclusions when using the current ratio or inventory turnover ratio.

✔ the navigator

DECISION TOOLKIT A SUMMARY

DECISION CHECKPOINTS	INFO NEEDED FOR DECISION	TOOL TO USE FOR DECISION	HOW TO EVALUATE RESULTS
Which inventory costing method should be used?	Are prices increasing, or are they decreasing?	Income statement, balance sheet, and tax effects	Depends on objective. In a period of rising prices, income and inventory are higher and cash flow is lower under FIFO. LIFO provides opposite results. Average cost can moderate the impact of changing prices.
How long is an item in inventory?	Cost of goods sold; beginning and ending inventory	$\text{Inventory turnover ratio} = \dfrac{\text{Cost of goods sold}}{\text{Average inventory}}$ $\text{Days in inventory} = \dfrac{365 \text{ days}}{\text{Inventory turnover ratio}}$	A higher inventory turnover ratio or lower average days in inventory suggests that management is reducing the amount of inventory on hand, relative to cost of goods sold.
What is the impact of LIFO on the company's reported inventory?	LIFO reserve, cost of goods sold, ending inventory, current assets, current liabilities	$\text{LIFO inventory} + \text{LIFO reserve} = \text{FIFO inventory}$	If these adjustments are material, they can significantly affect such measures as the current ratio and the inventory turnover ratio.

---

appendix 6A

Inventory Cost Flow Methods in Perpetual Inventory Systems

study objective 7

Apply the inventory cost flow methods to perpetual inventory records.

Each of the inventory cost flow methods described in the chapter for a periodic inventory system may be used in a perpetual inventory system. To illustrate the application of the three assumed cost flow methods (FIFO, LIFO, and average cost), we will use the data shown in Illustration 6A-1 (next page) and in this chapter for Houston Electronics' Astro condensers.

HOUSTON ELECTRONICS
Astro Condensers

Date	Explanation	Units	Unit Cost	Total Cost	Balance in Units
1/1	Beginning inventory	100	$10	$ 1,000	100
4/15	Purchase	200	11	2,200	300
8/24	Purchase	300	12	3,600	600
9/10	Sale	550			50
11/27	Purchase	400	13	5,200	450
				$12,000	

Illustration 6A-1
Inventoriable units and costs

FIRST-IN, FIRST-OUT (FIFO)

Under FIFO, the cost of the earliest goods on hand **prior to each sale** is charged to cost of goods sold. Therefore, the cost of goods sold on September 10 consists of the units on hand January 1 and the units purchased April 15 and August 24. Illustration 6A-2 shows the inventory under a FIFO method perpetual system.

Date	Purchases	Cost of Goods Sold	Balance
Jan. 1			(100 @ $10) $1,000
Apr. 15	(200 @ $11) $2,200		(100 @ $10)⎱ $3,200 (200 @ $11)⎰
Aug. 24	(300 @ $12) $3,600		(100 @ $10)⎱ (200 @ $11)⎬ $6,800 (300 @ $12)⎰
Sept. 10		(100 @ $10) (200 @ $11) (250 @ $12) $6,200	(50 @ $12) $ 600
Nov. 27	(400 @ $13) $5,200		(50 @ $12)⎱ $5,800 (400 @ $13)⎰

Illustration 6A-2
Perpetual system–FIFO

The ending inventory in this situation is $5,800, and the cost of goods sold is $6,200 [(100 @ $10) + (200 @ $11) + (250 @ $12)].

The results under FIFO in a perpetual system are the **same as in a periodic system**. (See Illustration 6-5 on page 282 where, similarly, the ending inventory is $5,800 and cost of goods sold is $6,200.) Regardless of the system, the first costs in are the costs assigned to cost of goods sold.

LAST-IN, FIRST-OUT (LIFO)

Under the LIFO method using a perpetual system, the cost of the most recent purchase prior to sale is allocated to the units sold. Therefore, the cost of the goods sold on September 10 consists of all the units from the August 24 and April 15 purchases plus 50 of the units in beginning inventory. The ending inventory under the LIFO method is computed in Illustration 6A-3 (next page).

The use of LIFO in a perpetual system will usually produce cost allocations that differ from use of LIFO in a periodic system. In a perpetual system, the latest units purchased *prior to each sale* are allocated to cost of goods sold. In contrast, in a periodic system, the latest units purchased *during the period* are

Illustration 6A-3
Perpetual system—LIFO

Date	Purchases	Cost of Goods Sold	Balance
Jan. 1			(100 @ $10) $1,000
Apr. 15	(200 @ $11) $2,200		(100 @ $10)⎫ (200 @ $11)⎭ $3,200
Aug. 24	(300 @ $12) $3,600		(100 @ $10)⎫ (200 @ $11)⎬ $6,800 (300 @ $12)⎭
Sept. 10		(300 @ $12) (200 @ $11) (50 @ $10) —————— **$6,300**	(50 @ $10) $ 500
Nov. 27	(400 @ $13) $5,200		(50 @ $10)⎫ **$5,700** (400 @ $13)⎭

allocated to cost of goods sold. Thus, when a purchase is made after the last sale, the LIFO periodic system will apply this purchase to the previous sale. See Illustration 6-8 (on page 284) where the proof shows the 400 units at $13 purchased on November 27 applied to the sale of 550 units on September 10.

As shown above, under the LIFO perpetual system the 400 units at $13 purchased on November 27 are all applied to the ending inventory.

The ending inventory in this LIFO perpetual illustration is $5,700 and cost of goods sold is $6,300. Compare this to the LIFO periodic illustration (Illustration 6-7 on page 283) where the ending inventory is $5,000 and cost of goods sold is $7,000.

AVERAGE COST

The average-cost method in a perpetual inventory system is called the **moving-average method**. Under this method the company computes a new average **after each purchase**. The average cost is computed by dividing the cost of goods available for sale by the units on hand. The average cost is then applied to: (1) the units sold, to determine the cost of goods sold, and (2) the remaining units on hand, to determine the ending inventory amount. Illustration 6A-4 shows the application of the average-cost method by Houston Electronics.

Illustration 6A-4
Perpetual system—average-cost method

Date	Purchases	Cost of Goods Sold	Balance
Jan. 1			(100 @ $10) $ 1,000
Apr. 15	(200 @ $11) $2,200		(300 @ $10.667) $ 3,200
Aug. 24	(300 @ $12) $3,600		(600 @ $11.333) $ 6,800
Sept. 10		(550 @ $11.333) **$6,233**	(50 @ $11.333) $ 567
Nov. 27	(400 @ $13) $5,200		(450 @ $12.816) **$5,767**

As indicated above, the company computes **a new average each time it makes a purchase**. On April 15, after 200 units are purchased for $2,200, a total of 300 units costing $3,200 ($1,000 + $2,200) are on hand. The average unit cost is $10.667 ($3,200 ÷ 300). On August 24, after 300 units are purchased for $3,600, a total of 600 units costing $6,800 ($1,000 + $2,200 + $3,600) are on hand at an average cost per unit of $11.333 ($6,800 ÷ 600). Houston Electronics uses this unit cost of $11.333 in costing sales until another purchase is made, when the company computes a new unit cost. Accordingly, the unit cost of the 550 units sold on September 10 is $11.333, and the total cost of goods sold is $6,233. On November 27, following the purchase of 400 units for $5,200, there are 450 units on hand costing $5,767 ($567 + $5,200) with a new average cost of $12.816 ($5,767 ÷ 450).

Compare this moving-average cost under the perpetual inventory system to Illustration 6-10 (on page 284) showing the weighted-average method under a periodic inventory system.

Summary of Study Objective for Appendix 6A

7 **Apply the inventory cost flow methods to perpetual inventory records.** Under FIFO, the cost of the earliest goods on hand prior to each sale is charged to cost of goods sold. Under LIFO, the cost of the most recent purchase prior to sale is charged to cost of goods sold. Under the average-cost method, a new average cost is computed after each purchase.

appendix 6B

Inventory Errors

Unfortunately, errors occasionally occur in accounting for inventory. In some cases, errors are caused by failure to count or price the inventory correctly. In other cases, errors occur because companies do not properly recognize the transfer of legal title to goods that are in transit. When inventory errors occur, they affect both the income statement and the balance sheet.

> **study objective 8**
>
> Indicate the effects of inventory errors on the financial statements.

INCOME STATEMENT EFFECTS

Under a periodic inventory system, both the beginning and ending inventories appear in the income statement. The ending inventory of one period automatically becomes the beginning inventory of the next period. Thus, inventory errors affect the computation of cost of goods sold and net income in two periods.

The effects on cost of goods sold can be computed by entering incorrect data in the formula in Illustration 6B-1 and then substituting the correct data.

Beginning Inventory	+	Cost of Goods Purchased	−	Ending Inventory	=	Cost of Goods Sold

Illustration 6B-1
Formula for cost of goods sold

If *beginning* inventory is understated, cost of goods sold will be understated. If *ending* inventory is understated, cost of goods sold will be overstated. Illustration 6B-2 shows the effects of inventory errors on the current year's income statement.

Inventory Error	Cost of Goods Sold	Net Income
Beginning inventory understated	Understated	Overstated
Beginning inventory overstated	Overstated	Understated
Ending inventory understated	Overstated	Understated
Ending inventory overstated	Understated	Overstated

Illustration 6B-2 Effects of inventory errors on current year's income statement

Ethics Note Inventory fraud increases during recessions. Such fraud includes pricing inventory at amounts in excess of its actual value, or claiming to have inventory when no inventory exists. Inventory fraud is usually done to overstate ending inventory, thereby understating cost of goods sold and creating higher income.

An error in the ending inventory of the current period will have a **reverse effect on net income of the next accounting period**. This is shown in Illustration 6B-3 (page 300). Note that the understatement of ending inventory in 2009 results in an understatement of beginning inventory in 2010 and an overstatement of net income in 2010.

Over the two years, total net income is correct because the errors offset each other. Notice that total income using incorrect data is $35,000 ($22,000 + $13,000), which is the same as the total income of $35,000 ($25,000 + $10,000) using correct data. Also note in this example that an error in the beginning inventory does not result in a corresponding error in the ending inventory for that period. The correctness of the ending inventory depends entirely on the accuracy of taking and costing the inventory at the balance sheet date under the periodic inventory system.

Illustration 6B-3 Effects of inventory errors on two years' income statements

SAMPLE COMPANY
Condensed Income Statements

	2009 Incorrect	2009 Correct	2010 Incorrect	2010 Correct
Sales	$80,000	$80,000	$90,000	$90,000
Beginning inventory	$20,000	$20,000	$12,000	$15,000
Cost of goods purchased	40,000	40,000	68,000	68,000
Cost of goods available for sale	60,000	60,000	80,000	83,000
Ending inventory	12,000	15,000	23,000	23,000
Cost of goods sold	48,000	45,000	57,000	60,000
Gross profit	32,000	35,000	33,000	30,000
Operating expenses	10,000	10,000	20,000	20,000
Net income	$22,000	$25,000	$13,000	$10,000

$(3,000)
Net income
understated

$3,000
Net income
overstated

The errors cancel. Thus the combined total income for the 2-year period is correct.

BALANCE SHEET EFFECTS

The effect of ending inventory errors on the balance sheet can be determined by using the basic accounting equation: Assets = Liabilities + Stockholders' equity. Errors in the ending inventory have the effects shown in Illustration 6B-4.

Illustration 6B-4 Effects of ending inventory errors on balance sheet

Ending Inventory Error	Assets	Liabilities	Stockholders' Equity
Overstated	Overstated	No effect	Overstated
Understated	Understated	No effect	Understated

The effect of an error in ending inventory on the subsequent period was shown in Illustration 6B-3. Recall that if the error is not corrected, the combined total net income for the two periods would be correct. Thus, total stockholders' equity reported on the balance sheet at the end of 2010 will also be correct.

Summary of Study Objective for Appendix 6B

8 Indicate the effects of inventory errors on the financial statements. In the income statement of the current year: (a) An error in beginning inventory will have a reverse effect on net income (e.g., overstatement of inventory results in understatement of net income, and vice versa). (b) An error in ending inventory will have a similar effect on net income (e.g., overstatement of inventory results in overstatement of net income). If ending inventory errors are not corrected in the following period, their effect on net income for that period is reversed, and total net income for the two years will be correct.

In the balance sheet: Ending inventory errors will have the same effect on total assets and total stockholders' equity and no effect on liabilities.

Glossary

Average-cost method *(p. 284)* An inventory costing method that uses the weighted average unit cost to allocate the cost of goods available for sale to ending inventory and cost of goods sold.

Consigned goods *(p. 278)* Goods held for sale by one party although ownership of the goods is retained by another party.

Current replacement cost *(p. 289)* The cost of purchasing the same goods at the present time from the usual suppliers in the usual quantities.

Days in inventory *(p. 290)* Measure of the average number of days inventory is held; calculated as 365 divided by inventory turnover ratio.

Finished goods inventory *(p. 276)* Manufactured items that are completed and ready for sale.

First-in, first-out (FIFO) method *(p. 281)* An inventory costing method that assumes that the earliest goods purchased are the first to be sold.

FOB destination *(p. 278)* Freight terms indicating that ownership of goods remains with the seller until the goods reach the buyer.

FOB shipping point *(p. 278)* Freight terms indicating that ownership of goods passes to the buyer when the public carrier accepts the goods from the seller.

Inventory turnover ratio *(p. 290)* A ratio that measures the liquidity of inventory by measuring the number of times average inventory sold during the period; computed by dividing cost of goods sold by the average inventory during the period.

Just-in-time (JIT) inventory *(p. 277)* Inventory system in which companies manufacture or purchase goods just in time for use.

Last-in, first-out (LIFO) method *(p. 282)* An inventory costing method that assumes that the latest units purchased are the first to be sold.

LIFO reserve *(p. 292)* For a company using LIFO, the difference between inventory reported using LIFO and inventory using FIFO.

Lower-of-cost-or-market (LCM) *(p. 289)* A basis whereby inventory is stated at the lower of either its cost or its market value as determined by current replacement cost.

Raw materials *(p. 276)* Basic goods that will be used in production but have not yet been placed in production.

Specific identification method *(p. 280)* An actual physical flow costing method in which items sold and items still in inventory are specifically costed to arrive at cost of goods sold and ending inventory.

Weighted average unit cost *(p. 284)* Average cost that is weighted by the number of units purchased at each unit cost.

Work in process *(p. 276)* That portion of manufactured inventory that has begun the production process but is not yet complete.

Comprehensive

Englehart Company has the following inventory, purchases, and sales data for the month of March.

Inventory, March 1	200 units @ $4.00	$ 800
Purchases		
March 10	500 units @ $4.50	2,250
March 20	400 units @ $4.75	1,900
March 30	300 units @ $5.00	1,500
Sales		
March 15	500 units	
March 25	400 units	

The physical inventory count on March 31 shows 500 units on hand.

Instructions

Under a **periodic inventory system**, determine the cost of inventory on hand at March 31 and the cost of goods sold for March under (a) the first-in, first-out (FIFO) method; (b) the last-in, first-out (LIFO) method; and (c) the average-cost method. (For average cost, carry cost per unit to three decimal places.)

Action Plan

- For FIFO, allocate the latest costs to inventory.
- For LIFO, allocate the earliest costs to inventory.
- For average cost, use a weighted average.
- Remember, the costs allocated to cost of goods sold can be proved.
- Total purchases are the same under all three cost flow assumptions.

Solution to Comprehensive Do it!

The cost of goods available for sale is $6,450:

Inventory Purchases		
	200 units @ $4.00	$ 800
March 10	500 units @ $4.50	2,250
March 20	400 units @ $4.75	1,900
March 30	300 units @ $5.00	1,500
Total cost of goods available for sale		$6,450

(a)   **FIFO Method**

Ending inventory:

Date	Units	Unit Cost	Total Cost	
Mar. 30	300	$5.00	$1,500	
Mar. 20	200	4.75	950	$2,450

Cost of goods sold: $6,450 − $2,450 = $4,000

(b)   **LIFO Method**

Ending inventory:

Date	Units	Unit Cost	Total Cost	
Mar. 1	200	$4.00	$ 800	
Mar. 10	300	4.50	1,350	$2,150

Cost of goods sold: $6,450 − $2,150 = $4,300

(c)   **Weighted Average-Cost Method**

Weighted average unit cost: $6,450 ÷ 1,400 = $4.607
Ending inventory: 500 × $4.607 = $2,303.50
Cost of goods sold: $6,450 − $2,303.50 = $4,146.50

Note: All Questions, Exercises, and Problems marked with an asterisk relate to material in the appendices to the chapter.

Self-Study Questions

Answers are at the end of the chapter.

(SO 1)   **1.** When is a physical inventory usually taken?
     (a) When the company has its greatest amount of inventory.
     (b) When a limited number of goods are being sold or received.
     (c) At the end of the company's fiscal year.
     (d) Both (b) and (c).

(SO 1)   **2.** Which of the following should *not* be included in the physical inventory of a company?
     (a) Goods held on consignment from another company.

     (b) Goods shipped on consignment to another company.
     (c) Goods in transit from another company shipped FOB shipping point.
     (d) All of the above should be included.

3. As a result of a thorough physical inventory, Railway (SO 1) Company determined that it had inventory worth $180,000 at December 31, 2010. This count did not take into consideration the following facts: Rogers Consignment store currently has goods worth $35,000 on its sales floor that belong to Railway but

are being sold on consignment by Rogers. The selling price of these goods is $50,000. Railway purchased $13,000 of goods that were shipped on December 27, FOB destination, that will be received by Railway on January 3. Determine the correct amount of inventory that Railway should report.
(a) $230,000.
(b) $215,000.
(c) $228,000.
(d) $193,000.

(SO 2) **4.** Kam Company has the following units and costs.

	Units	Unit Cost
Inventory, Jan. 1	8,000	$11
Purchase, June 19	13,000	12
Purchase, Nov. 8	5,000	13

If 9,000 units are on hand at December 31, what is the cost of the ending inventory under FIFO?
(a) $99,000.   (c) $113,000.
(b) $108,000.   (d) $117,000.

(SO 2) **5.** From the data in question 4, what is the cost of the ending inventory under LIFO?
(a) $113,000.   (c) $99,000.
(b) $108,000.   (d) $100,000.

(SO 2) **6.** Davidson Electronics has the following:

	Units	Unit Cost
Inventory, Jan. 1	5,000	$ 8
Purchase, April 2	15,000	10
Purchase, Aug. 28	20,000	12

If Davidson has 7,000 units on hand at December 31, the cost of ending inventory under the average-cost method is:
(a) $84,000.   (c) $56,000.
(b) $70,000.   (d) $75,250.

(SO 3) **7.** In periods of rising prices, LIFO will produce:
(a) higher net income than FIFO.
(b) the same net income as FIFO.
(c) lower net income than FIFO.
(d) higher net income than average costing.

(SO 3) **8.** Considerations that affect the selection of an inventory costing method do *not* include:
(a) tax effects.
(b) balance sheet effects.
(c) income statement effects.
(d) perpetual versus periodic inventory system.

(SO 4) **9.** The lower-of-cost-or-market rule for inventory is an example of the application of:
(a) the conservatism constraint.
(b) the historical cost principle.
(c) the materiality constraint.
(d) the economic entity assumption.

(SO 5) **10.** Which of these would cause the inventory turnover ratio to increase the most?
(a) Increasing the amount of inventory on hand.

(b) Keeping the amount of inventory on hand constant but increasing sales.
(c) Keeping the amount of inventory on hand constant but decreasing sales.
(d) Decreasing the amount of inventory on hand and increasing sales.

11. Carlos Company had beginning inventory of $80,000, (SO 5) ending inventory of $110,000, cost of goods sold of $285,000, and sales of $475,000. Carlos's days in inventory is:
(a) 73 days.
(b) 121.7 days.
(c) 102.5 days.
(d) 84.5 days.

12. The LIFO reserve is: (SO 6)
(a) the difference between the value of the inventory under LIFO and the value under FIFO.
(b) an amount used to adjust inventory to the lower-of-cost-or-market.
(c) the difference between the value of the inventory under LIFO and the value under average cost.
(d) an amount used to adjust inventory to historical cost.

*13. In a perpetual inventory system, (SO 7)
(a) LIFO cost of goods sold will be the same as in a periodic inventory system.
(b) average costs are based entirely on unit-cost simple averages.
(c) a new average is computed under the average cost method after each sale.
(d) FIFO cost of goods sold will be the same as in a periodic inventory system.

*14. Fran Company's ending inventory is understated by (SO 8) $4,000. The effects of this error on the current year's cost of goods sold and net income, respectively, are:
(a) understated and overstated.
(b) overstated and understated.
(c) overstated and overstated.
(d) understated and understated.

*15. Harold Company overstated its inventory by $15,000 (SO 4) at December 31, 2010. It did not correct the error in 2010 or 2011. As a result, Harold's owner's equity was:
(a) overstated at December 31, 2010, and understated at December 31, 2011.
(b) overstated at December 31, 2010, and properly stated at December 31, 2011.
(c) understated at December 31, 2010, and understated at December 31, 2011.
(d) overstated at December 31, 2010, and overstated at December 31, 2011.

Go to the book's companion website, **www. wiley.com/college/kimmel**, to access additional Self-Study Questions.

Questions

1. "The key to successful business operations is effective inventory management." Do you agree? Explain.

2. An item must possess two characteristics to be classified as inventory. What are these two characteristics?

3. ⬅ What is just-in-time inventory management? What are its potential advantages?

4. Your friend Diane Helbert has been hired to help take the physical inventory in Mozena's Hardware Store. Explain to Diane what this job will entail.

5. (a) Bradshaw Company ships merchandise to Ecklund Corporation on December 30. The merchandise reaches the buyer on January 5. Indicate the terms of sale that will result in the goods being included in (1) Bradshaw's December 31 inventory and (2) Ecklund's December 31 inventory.
   (b) Under what circumstances should Bradshaw Company include consigned goods in its inventory?

6. Redd Hat Shop received a shipment of hats for which it paid the wholesaler $2,940. The price of the hats was $3,000, but Redd was given a $60 cash discount and required to pay freight charges of $75. In addition, Redd paid $100 to cover the travel expenses of an employee who negotiated the purchase of the hats. What amount should Redd include in inventory? Why?

7. What is the primary basis of accounting for inventories? What is the major objective in accounting for inventories?

8. Ben Winslow believes that the allocation of cost of goods available for sale should be based on the actual physical flow of the goods. Explain to Ben why this may be both impractical and inappropriate.

9. What are the major advantage and major disadvantage of the specific identification method of inventory costing?

10. ⬅ "The selection of an inventory cost flow method is a decision made by accountants." Do you agree? Explain. Once a method has been selected, what accounting requirement applies?

11. Which assumed inventory cost flow method:
   (a) usually parallels the actual physical flow of merchandise?
   (b) assumes that goods available for sale during an accounting period are similar in nature?
   (c) assumes that the latest units purchased are the first to be sold?

12. In a period of rising prices, the inventory reported in Knott Company's balance sheet is close to the current cost of the inventory, whereas Quirk Company's inventory is considerably below its current cost. Identify the inventory cost flow method used by each company. Which company probably has been reporting the higher gross profit?

13. Andover Corporation has been using the FIFO cost flow method during a prolonged period of inflation. During the same time period, Andover has been paying out all of its net income as dividends. What adverse effects may result from this policy?

14. Jason Hatfield, a mid-level product manager for Stella's Shoes, thinks his company should switch from LIFO to FIFO. He says, "My bonus is based on net income. If we switch it will increase net income and increase my bonus. The company would be better off and so would I." Is he correct? Explain.

15. Discuss the impact the use of LIFO has on taxes paid, cash flows, and the quality of earnings ratio relative to the impact of FIFO when prices are increasing.

16. ▨ What inventory cost flow method does Tootsie Roll Industries use for U.S. inventories? What method does it use for foreign inventories? (*Hint:* You will need to examine the notes for Tootsie Roll's financial statements.) Why does it use a different method for foreign inventories?

17. Andrea Davies is studying for the next accounting midterm examination. What should Andrea know about (a) departing from the cost basis of accounting for inventories and (b) the meaning of "market" in the lower-of-cost-or-market method?

18. Capaldo Music Center has five CD players on hand at the balance sheet date that cost $400 each. The current replacement cost is $350 per unit. Under the lower-of-cost-or-market basis of accounting for inventories, what value should Capaldo report for the CD players on the balance sheet? Why?

19. ⊙━━C What cost flow assumption may be used under the lower-of-cost-or-market basis of accounting for inventories?

20. Why is it inappropriate for a company to include freight-out expense in the Cost of Goods Sold account?

21. Beckett Company's balance sheet shows Inventories $162,800. What additional disclosures should be made?

22. ⬅ ⊙━━C Under what circumstances might the inventory turnover ratio be too high—that is, what possible negative consequences might occur?

23. ⊙━━C What is the LIFO reserve? What are the consequences of ignoring a large LIFO reserve when analyzing a company?

*24. "When perpetual inventory records are kept, the results under the FIFO and LIFO methods are the same as they would be in a periodic inventory system." Do you agree? Explain.

*25. How does the average method of inventory costing differ between a perpetual inventory system and a periodic inventory system?

*26. Nele Company discovers in 2010 that its ending inventory at December 31, 2009, was $5,000 understated. What effect will this error have on (a) 2009 net income, (b) 2010 net income, and (c) the combined net income for the 2 years?

Brief Exercises

BE6-1 Jack Penny Company identifies the following items for possible inclusion in the physical inventory. Indicate whether each item should be included or excluded from the inventory taking.
(a) Goods shipped on consignment by Penny to another company.
(b) Goods in transit from a supplier shipped FOB destination.
(c) Goods sold but being held for customer pickup.
(d) Goods held on consignment from another company.

Identify items to be included in taking a physical inventory.
(SO 1)

BE6-2 In its first month of operations, Ceretti Company made three purchases of merchandise in the following sequence: (1) 300 units at $6, (2) 400 units at $8, and (3) 500 units at $9. Assuming there are 300 units on hand, compute the cost of the ending inventory under (a) the FIFO method and (b) the LIFO method. Ceretti uses a periodic inventory system.

Compute ending inventory using FIFO and LIFO.
(SO 2)

BE6-3 Data for Ceretti Company are presented in BE6-2. Compute the cost of the ending inventory under the average-cost method, assuming there are 300 units on hand. (Round the cost per unit to three decimal places.)

Compute the ending inventory using average cost.
(SO 2)

BE6-4 The management of Eckel Corp. is considering the effects of various inventory-costing methods on its financial statements and its income tax expense. Assuming that the price the company pays for inventory is increasing, which method will:
(a) provide the highest net income?
(b) provide the highest ending inventory? FIFO
(c) result in the lowest income tax expense? LIFO
(d) result in the most stable earnings over a number of years? Average Cost

Explain the financial statement effect of inventory cost flow assumptions.
(SO 3)

BE6-5 In its first month of operation, Maze Company purchased 100 units of inventory for $6, then 200 units for $7, and finally 150 units for $8. At the end of the month, 180 units remained. Compute the amount of phantom profit that would result if the company used FIFO rather than LIFO. Explain why this amount is referred to as phantom profit. The company uses the periodic method.

Explain the financial statement effect of inventory cost flow assumptions.
(SO 3)

BE6-6 For each of the following cases, state whether the statement is true for LIFO or for FIFO. Assume that prices are rising.
(a) Results in a higher quality of earnings ratio.
(b) Results in higher phantom profits.
(c) Results in higher net income.
(d) Results in lower taxes.
(e) Results in lower net cash provided by operating activities.

Identify the impact of LIFO versus FIFO.
(SO 3)

BE6-7 O'Connor Video Center accumulates the following cost and market data at December 31.

Determine the LCM valuation.
(SO 4)

Inventory Categories	Cost Data	Market Data
Cameras	$12,500	$13,400
Camcorders	9,000	9,500
DVDs	13,000	12,800

Compute the lower-of-cost-or-market valuation for O'Connor's inventory.

BE6-8 At December 31, 2006, the following information (in thousands) was available for sunglasses manufacturer Oakley, Inc.: ending inventory $155,377; beginning inventory $119,035; cost of goods sold $349,114; and sales revenue $761,865. Calculate the inventory turnover ratio and days in inventory for Oakley, Inc.

Compute inventory turnover ratio and days in inventory.
(SO 5)

BE6-9 Winnebago Industries, Inc. is a leading manufacturer of motor homes. Winnebago reported ending inventory at August 25, 2007, of $101,208,000 under the LIFO inventory method. In the notes to its financial statements, Winnebago reported a LIFO reserve of $32,705,000 at August 25, 2007. What would Winnebago Industries' ending inventory have been if it had used FIFO?

Determine ending inventory and cost of goods sold using LIFO reserve.
(SO 6)

*BE6-10 Dakin's Department Store uses a perpetual inventory system. Data for product E2-D2 include the purchases shown on page 306.

Apply cost flow methods to perpetual inventory records.
(SO 7)

Date	Number of Units	Unit Price
May 7	50	$10
July 28	30	15

On June 1 Dakin sold 30 units, and on August 27, 33 more units. Compute the cost of goods sold using (1) FIFO, (2) LIFO, and (3) average cost.

Determine correct financial statement amount.
(SO 8)

*BE6-11 Ringler Company reports net income of $89,000 in 2010. However, ending inventory was understated by $7,000. What is the correct net income for 2010? What effect, if any, will this error have on total assets as reported in the balance sheet at December 31, 2010?

Do it! Review

Apply rules of ownership to determine inventory cost.
(SO 1)

Do it! 6-1 Neverwas Company just took its physical inventory. The count of inventory items on hand at the company's business locations resulted in a total inventory cost of $300,000. In reviewing the details of the count and related inventory transactions, you have discovered the following items that had not been considered.

1. Neverwas has sent inventory costing $26,000 on consignment to Niagara Company. All of this inventory was at Niagara's showrooms on December 31.
2. The company did not include in the count inventory (cost, $20,000) that was sold on December 28, terms FOB shipping point. The goods were in transit on December 31.
3. The company did not include in the count inventory (cost, $17,000) that was purchased with terms of FOB shipping point. The goods were in transit on December 31.

Compute the correct December 31 inventory.

Compute cost of goods sold under different cost flow methods.
(SO 2)

Do it! 6-2 The accounting records of Oats Electronics show the following data.

Beginning inventory	3,000 units at $5
Purchases	8,000 units at $7
Sales	9,200 units at $10

Determine cost of goods sold during the period under a periodic inventory system using (a) the FIFO method, (b) the LIFO method, and (c) the average-cost method. (Round unit cost to nearest tenth of a cent.)

Compute inventory value under LCM.
(SO 4)

Do it! 6-3 Blank Company sells three different categories of tools (small, medium and large). The cost and market value of its inventory of tools are as follows.

	Cost	Market
Small	$ 64,000	$ 73,000
Medium	290,000	260,000
Large	152,000	171,000

Determine the value of the company's inventory under the lower-of-cost-or-market approach.

Compute inventory turnover ratio and assess inventory level.
(SO 5)

Do it! 6-4 Early in 2010 Aragon Company switched to a just-in-time inventory system. Its sales and inventory amounts for 2009 and 2010 are shown below.

	2009	2010
Sales	$3,120,000	$3,713,000
Cost of goods sold	1,200,000	1,425,000
Beginning inventory	180,000	220,000
Ending inventory	220,000	80,000

Determine the inventory turnover and days in inventory for 2009 and 2010. Discuss the changes in the amount of inventory, the inventory turnover and days in inventory, and the amount of sales across the two years.

Exercises

E6-1 Leavenworth Bank and Trust is considering giving Mabry Company a loan. Before doing so, they decide that further discussions with Mabry's accountant may be desirable. One area of particular concern is the inventory account, which has a year-end balance of $275,000. Discussions with the accountant reveal the following.

Determine the correct inventory amount.
(SO 1)

1. Mabry sold goods costing $55,000 to Ace Company FOB shipping point on December 28. The goods are not expected to reach Ace until January 12. The goods were not included in the physical inventory because they were not in the warehouse.   — subtract

2. The physical count of the inventory did not include goods costing $95,000 that were shipped to Mabry FOB destination on December 27 and were still in transit at year-end.   — dont Add

3. Mabry received goods costing $25,000 on January 2. The goods were shipped FOB shipping point on December 26 by Lenny Co. The goods were not included in the physical count.   — Add

4. Mabry sold goods costing $51,000 to Flanders of Canada FOB destination on December 30. The goods were received in Canada on January 8. They were not included in Mabry's physical inventory.   — ~~dont~~ add

5. Mabry received goods costing $37,000 on January 2 that were shipped FOB destination on December 29. The shipment was a rush order that was supposed to arrive December 31. This purchase was included in the ending inventory of $275,000.   — dont add

Instructions
Determine the correct inventory amount on December 31.   *December 31st 245,000*

E6-2 Gary Kifer, an auditor with Neely CPAs, is performing a review of Dudley Company's inventory account. Dudley did not have a good year, and top management is under pressure to boost reported income. According to its records, the inventory balance at year-end was $740,000. However, the following information was not considered when determining that amount.

Determine the correct inventory amount.
(SO 1)

1. Included in the company's count were goods with a cost of $250,000 that the company is holding on consignment. The goods belong to Anya Corporation.

2. The physical count did not include goods purchased by Dudley with a cost of $40,000 that were shipped FOB shipping point on December 28 and did not arrive at Dudley's warehouse until January 3.

3. Included in the inventory account was $17,000 of office supplies that were stored in the warehouse and were to be used by the company's supervisors and managers during the coming year.

4. The company received an order on December 29 that was boxed and was sitting on the loading dock awaiting pick-up on December 31. The shipper picked up the goods on January 1 and delivered them on January 6. The shipping terms were FOB shipping point. The goods had a selling price of $40,000 and a cost of $25,000. The goods were not included in the count because they were sitting on the dock.

5. On December 29 Dudley shipped goods with a selling price of $80,000 and a cost of $50,000 to Shawnee Sales Corporation FOB shipping point. The goods arrived on January 3. Shawnee Sales had only ordered goods with a selling price of $10,000 and a cost of $6,000. However, a sales manager at Dudley had authorized the shipment and said that if Shawnee wanted to ship the goods back next week, it could.

6. Included in the count was $50,000 of goods that were parts for a machine that the company no longer made. Given the high-tech nature of Dudley's products, it was unlikely that these obsolete parts had any other use. However, management would prefer to keep them on the books at cost, "since that is what we paid for them, after all."

Instructions
Prepare a schedule to determine the correct inventory amount. Provide explanations for each item above, saying why you did or did not make an adjustment for each item.

E6-3 Guardado Inc. had the following inventory situations to consider at January 31, its year end.

Identify items in inventory.
(SO 1)

(a) Goods held on consignment for MailBoxes Corp. since December 12.
(b) Goods shipped on consignment to Rinehart Holdings Inc. on January 5.
(c) Goods shipped to a customer, FOB destination, on January 29 that are still in transit.
(d) Goods shipped to a customer, FOB shipping point, on January 29 that are still in transit.

(e) Goods purchased FOB destination from a supplier on January 25, that are still in transit.
(f) Goods purchased FOB shipping point from a supplier on January 25, that are still in transit.
(g) Office supplies on hand at January 31.

Instructions
Identify which of the preceding items should be included in inventory. If the item should not be included in inventory, state in what account, if any, it should have been recorded.

Compute inventory and cost of goods sold using periodic FIFO and LIFO.
(SO 2)

E6-4 Snoslope sells a snowboard, Xpert, that is popular with snowboard enthusiasts. Below is information relating to Snoslope's purchases of Xpert snowboards during September. During the same month, 118 Xpert snowboards were sold. Snoslope uses a periodic inventory system.

Date	Explanation	Units	Unit Cost	Total Cost
Sept. 1	Inventory	14	$100	$ 1,400
Sept. 12	Purchases	45	102	4,590
Sept. 19	Purchases	20	104	2,080
Sept. 26	Purchases	50	105	5,250
	Totals	129		$13,320

Instructions
(a) Compute the ending inventory at September 30 using the FIFO and LIFO methods. Prove the amount allocated to cost of goods sold under each method.
(b) For both FIFO and LIFO, calculate the sum of ending inventory and cost of goods sold. What do you notice about the answers you found for each method?

Calculate inventory and cost of goods sold using FIFO, average, and LIFO in a periodic inventory system.
(SO 2)

E6-5 Naab Inc. uses a periodic inventory system. Its records show the following for the month of May, in which 78 units were sold.

Date	Explanation	Units	Unit Cost	Total Cost
May 1	Inventory	30	$ 9	$270
15	Purchase	25	10	250
24	Purchase	40	11	440
	Total	95		$960

Instructions
Calculate the ending inventory at May 31 using the (a) FIFO, (b) average-cost, and (c) LIFO methods. (For average cost, round the average unit cost to three decimal places.) Prove the amount allocated to cost of goods sold under each method.

Calculate cost of goods sold using specific identification and FIFO periodic.
(SO 2, 3)

E6-6 On December 1, Discount Electronics has three DVD players left in stock. All are identical, all are priced to sell at $85. One of the three DVD players left in stock, with serial #1012, was purchased on June 1 at a cost of $52. Another, with serial #1045, was purchased on November 1 for $48. The last player, serial #1056, was purchased on November 30 for $43.

Instructions
(a) Calculate the cost of goods sold using the FIFO periodic inventory method assuming that two of the three players were sold by the end of December, Discount Electronic's year-end.
(b) If Discount Electronics used the specific identification method instead of the FIFO method, how might it alter its earnings by "selectively choosing" which particular players to sell to the two customers? What would Discount's cost of goods sold be if the company wished to minimize earnings? Maximize earnings?
(c) Which inventory method, FIFO or specific identification, do you recommend that Discount use? Explain why.

E6-7 Kiser Company reports the following for the month of June.

Compute inventory and cost of goods sold using periodic FIFO, LIFO, and average cost.
(SO 2, 3)

Date	Explanation	Units	Unit Cost	Total Cost
June 1	Inventory	125	$5	$ 625
12	Purchase	375	6	2,250
23	Purchase	500	7	3,500
30	Inventory	200		

Instructions
(a) Compute the cost of the ending inventory and the cost of goods sold under (1) FIFO, (2) LIFO, and (3) average cost.
(b) Which costing method gives the highest ending inventory? The highest cost of goods sold? Why?
(c) How do the average-cost values for ending inventory and cost of goods sold relate to ending inventory and cost of goods sold for FIFO and LIFO?
(d) Explain why the average cost is not $6.

E6-8 The following comparative information is available for Public Company for 2010.

Evaluate impact of LIFO and FIFO on cash flows and earnings quality.
(SO 3)

	LIFO	FIFO
Sales	$83,000	$83,000
Cost of goods sold	38,000	29,000
Operating expenses		
(including depreciation)	27,000	27,000
Depreciation	10,000	10,000
Cash paid for inventory purchases	34,000	34,000

Instructions
(a) Determine net income under each approach. Assume a 30% tax rate.
(b) Determine net cash provided by operating activities under each approach. Assume that all sales were on a cash basis and that income taxes and operating expenses, other than depreciation, were on a cash basis.
(c) Calculate the quality of earnings ratio under each approach and explain your findings.

E6-9 Lebo Camera Shop Inc. uses the lower-of-cost-or-market basis for its inventory. The following data are available at December 31.

Determine LCM valuation.
(SO 4)

	Units	Cost/Unit	Market Value/Unit
Cameras			
Minolta	5	$175	$160
Canon	7	145	152
Light Meters			
Vivitar	12	125	119
Kodak	10	120	135

Instructions
What amount should be reported on Lebo Camera Shop's financial statements, assuming the lower-of-cost-or-market rule is applied?

E6-10 This information is available for PepsiCo, Inc. for 2004, 2005, and 2006.

Compute inventory turnover ratio, days in inventory, and gross profit rate.
(SO 5)

(in millions)	2004	2005	2006
Beginning inventory	$ 1,412	$ 1,541	$ 1,693
Ending inventory	1,541	1,693	1,926
Cost of goods sold	12,674	14,176	15,762
Sales	29,261	32,562	35,137

Instructions

Calculate the inventory turnover ratio, days in inventory, and gross profit rate for PepsiCo., Inc. for 2004, 2005, and 2006. Comment on any trends.

Determine the effect of the LIFO reserve on current ratio.
(SO 5, 6)

E6-11 Deere & Company is a global manufacturer and distributor of agricultural, construction, and forestry equipment. It reported the following information in its 2006 annual report.

(in millions)	**2006**	**2005**
Inventories (LIFO)	$ 1,957	2,135
Current assets	26,838	
Current liabilities	12,788	
LIFO reserve	1,140	
Cost of goods sold	15,362	

Instructions

(a) Compute Deere's inventory turnover ratio and days in inventory for 2006.
(b) Compute Deere's current ratio using the 2006 data as presented, and then again after adjusting for the LIFO reserve.
(c) Comment on how ignoring the LIFO reserve might affect your evaluation of Deere's liquidity.

Calculate inventory and cost of goods sold using three cost flow methods in a perpetual inventory system.
(SO 7)

*E6-12 Inventory data for Kiser Company are presented in E6-7.

Instructions

(a) Calculate the cost of the ending inventory and the cost of goods sold for each cost flow assumption, using a perpetual inventory system. Assume a sale of 430 units occurred on June 15 for a selling price of $8 and a sale of 370 units on June 27 for $9. (*Note:* For the average-cost method, round unit cost to three decimal places.)
(b) How do the results differ from E6-7?
(c) Why is the average unit cost not $6 [($5 + $6 + $7) ÷ 3 = $6]?

Apply cost flow methods to perpetual records.
(SO 7)

*E6-13 Information about Snoslope is presented in E6-4. Additional data regarding the company's sales of Xpert snowboards are provided below. Assume that Snoslope uses a perpetual inventory system.

Date		Units
Sept. 5	Sale	8
Sept. 16	Sale	48
Sept. 29	Sale	62
	Totals	118

Instructions

(a) Compute ending inventory at September 30 using FIFO, LIFO, and average cost. (*Note:* For average cost, round unit cost to three decimal places.)
(b) Compare ending inventory for FIFO and LIFO using a perpetual inventory system to ending inventory using a periodic inventory system (from E6-4).
(c) Which inventory cost flow method (FIFO, LIFO) gives the same ending inventory value under both periodic and perpetual? Which method gives different ending inventory values?

Determine effects of inventory errors.
(SO 8)

*E6-14 Boles Hardware reported cost of goods sold as follows.

	2010	**2009**
Beginning inventory	$ 30,000	$ 20,000
Cost of goods purchased	175,000	164,000
Cost of goods available for sale	205,000	184,000
Ending inventory	37,000	30,000
Cost of goods sold	$168,000	$154,000

Boles made two errors:
1. 2009 ending inventory was overstated by $6,000.
2. 2010 ending inventory was understated by $3,000.

Instructions

Compute the correct cost of goods sold for each year.

*E6-15   Notson Company reported these income statement data for a 2-year period.

Prepare correct income statements.
(SO 8)

	2010	2009
Sales	$250,000	$210,000
Beginning inventory	40,000	34,000
Cost of goods purchased	202,000	173,000
Cost of goods available for sale	242,000	207,000
Ending inventory	55,000	40,000
Cost of goods sold	187,000	167,000
Gross profit	$ 63,000	$ 43,000

Notson Company uses a periodic inventory system. The inventories at January 1, 2009, and December 31, 2010, are correct. However, the ending inventory at December 31, 2009, is overstated by $10,000.

Instructions
(a) Prepare correct income statement data for the 2 years.
(b) What is the cumulative effect of the inventory error on total gross profit for the 2 years?
(c) Explain in a letter to the president of Notson Company what has happened—that is, the nature of the error and its effect on the financial statements.

Exercises: Set B

Visit the book's companion website, at **www.wiley.com/college/kimmel**, and choose the Student Companion site, to access Exercise Set B.

Problems: Set A

P6-1A   Kitselman Limited is trying to determine the value of its ending inventory as of February 28, 2010, the company's year-end. The accountant counted everything that was in the warehouse, as of February 28, which resulted in an ending inventory valuation of $48,000. However, she didn't know how to treat the following transactions so she didn't record them.

Determine items and amounts to be recorded in inventory.
(SO 1)

(a) On February 26, Kitselman shipped to a customer goods costing $800. The goods were shipped FOB shipping point, and the receiving report indicates that the customer received the goods on March 2.
(b) On February 26, Seller Inc. shipped goods to Kitselman FOB destination. The invoice price was $350 plus $25 for freight. The receiving report indicates that the goods were received by Kitselman on March 2.
(c) Kitselman had $500 of inventory at a customer's warehouse "on approval." The customer was going to let Kitselman know whether it wanted the merchandise by the end of the week, March 4.
(d) Kitselman also had $400 of inventory at a Balena craft shop, on consignment from Kitselman.
(e) On February 26, Kitselman ordered goods costing $750. The goods were shipped FOB shipping point on February 27. Kitselman received the goods on March 1.
(f) On February 28, Kitselman packaged goods and had them ready for shipping to a customer FOB destination. The invoice price was $350 plus $25 for freight; the cost of the items was $280. The receiving report indicates that the goods were received by the customer on March 2.

(g) Kitselman had damaged goods set aside in the warehouse because they are no longer saleable. These goods originally cost $400 and, originally, Kitselman expected to sell these items for $600.

Instructions
For each of the above transactions, specify whether the item in question should be included in ending inventory, and if so, at what amount. For each item that is not included in ending inventory, indicate who owns it and what account, if any, it should have been recorded in.

Determine cost of goods sold and ending inventory using FIFO, LIFO, and average cost, with analysis.
(SO 2, 3)

P6-2A Laramie Distribution markets CDs of numerous performing artists. At the beginning of March, Laramie had in beginning inventory 2,500 CDs with a unit cost of $7. During March Laramie made the following purchases of CDs.

March 5	2,000 @ $8 +1500	March 21	4,000 @ $10 1000 × 10
March 13	5,500 @ $9	March 26	2,000 @ $11 2000 × 11

During March 13,000 units were sold. Laramie uses a periodic inventory system.

Cost of goods sold:
FIFO $113,000
LIFO $123,500
Average $117,811

Instructions
(a) Determine the cost of goods available for sale.
(b) Determine (1) the ending inventory and (2) the cost of goods sold under each of the assumed cost flow methods (FIFO, LIFO, and average cost). Prove the accuracy of the cost of goods sold under the FIFO and LIFO methods. (*Note:* For average cost, round cost per unit to three decimal places.)
(c) Which cost flow method results in (1) the highest inventory amount for the balance sheet and (2) the highest cost of goods sold for the income statement?

Determine cost of goods sold and ending inventory using FIFO, LIFO, and average cost in a periodic inventory system, and assess financial statement effects.
(SO 2, 3)

P6-3A Reeble Company Inc. had a beginning inventory of 200 units of Product MLN at a cost of $8 per unit. During the year, purchases were:

Feb. 20	700 units at $ 9	Aug. 12	400 units at $11
May 5	500 units at $10	Dec. 8	100 units at $12

Reeble Company uses a periodic inventory system. Sales totalled 1,400 units.

Cost of goods sold:
FIFO $12,900
LIFO $14,200
Average $13,632

Instructions
(a) Determine the cost of goods available for sale.
(b) Determine the ending inventory and the cost of goods sold under each of the assumed cost flow methods (FIFO, LIFO, and average cost). Prove the accuracy of the cost of goods sold under the FIFO and LIFO methods. (Round average unit cost to three decimal places.)
(c) Which cost flow method results in the lowest inventory amount for the balance sheet? The lowest cost of goods sold for the income statement?

Compute ending inventory, prepare income statements, and answer questions using FIFO and LIFO.
(SO 2, 3)

P6-4A The management of Kirchner Inc. asks your help in determining the comparative effects of the FIFO and LIFO inventory cost flow methods. For 2010 the accounting records show these data.

Inventory, January 1 (10,000 units)	$ 35,000
Cost of 120,000 units purchased	471,000
Selling price of 95,000 units sold	730,000
Operating expenses	120,000

Units purchased consisted of 35,000 units at $3.70 on May 10; 60,000 units at $3.90 on August 15; and 25,000 units at $4.30 on November 20. Income taxes are 28%.

Gross profit:
FIFO $370,500
LIFO $351,500

Instructions
(a) Prepare comparative condensed income statements for 2010 under FIFO and LIFO. (Show computations of ending inventory.)
(b) Answer the following questions for management in the form of a business letter.
   (1) Which inventory cost flow method produces the most meaningful inventory amount for the balance sheet? Why?
   (2) Which inventory cost flow method produces the most meaningful net income? Why?

(3) Which inventory cost flow method is most likely to approximate the actual physical flow of the goods? Why?

(4) How much more cash will be available under LIFO than under FIFO? Why?

(5) How much of the gross profit under FIFO is illusionary in comparison with the gross profit under LIFO?

P6-5A You have the following information for McHugh Inc. for the month ended October 31, 2010. McHugh uses a periodic method for inventory.

Calculate ending inventory, cost of goods sold, gross profit, and gross profit rate under periodic method; compare results.

(SO 2, 3)

Date	Description	Units	Unit Cost or Selling Price
Oct. 1	Beginning inventory	60	$25
Oct. 9	Purchase	120	26
Oct. 11	Sale	100	35
Oct. 17	Purchase	90	27
Oct. 22	Sale	60	40
Oct. 25	Purchase	80	29
Oct. 29	Sale	110	40

Instructions

(a) Calculate (i) ending inventory, (ii) cost of goods sold, (iii) gross profit, and (iv) gross profit rate under each of the following methods.

(1) LIFO.

(2) FIFO.

(3) Average cost. (Round cost per unit to three decimal places.)

(b) Compare results for the three cost flow assumptions.

Gross profit:
LIFO	$2,950
FIFO	$3,250
Average	$3,072

P6-6A You have the following information for Gold Nugget Gems. Gold Nugget uses the periodic method of accounting for its inventory transactions. Gold Nugget only carries one brand and size of diamonds—all are identical. Each batch of diamonds purchased is carefully coded and marked with its purchase cost.

Compare specific identification, FIFO, and LIFO under periodic method; use cost flow assumption to influence earnings.

(SO 2, 3)

March 1	Beginning inventory 150 diamonds at a cost of $300 per diamond.
March 3	Purchased 200 diamonds at a cost of $350 each.
March 5	Sold 180 diamonds for $600 each.
March 10	Purchased 350 diamonds at a cost of $375 each.
March 25	Sold 400 diamonds for $650 each.

Instructions

(a) Assume that Gold Nugget Gems uses the specific identification cost flow method.

(1) Demonstrate how Gold Nugget could maximize its gross profit for the month by specifically selecting which diamonds to sell on March 5 and March 25.

(2) Demonstrate how Gold Nugget could minimize its gross profit for the month by selecting which diamonds to sell on March 5 and March 25.

(b) Assume that Gold Nugget uses the FIFO cost flow assumption. Calculate cost of goods sold. How much gross profit would Gold Nugget report under this cost flow assumption?

(c) Assume that Gold Nugget uses the LIFO cost flow assumption. Calculate cost of goods sold. How much gross profit would the company report under this cost flow assumption?

(d) Which cost flow method should Gold Nugget Gems select? Explain.

Gross profit:
Maximum	$166,750
Minimum	$157,750

P6-7A This information is available for the Automotive and Other Operations Divisions of General Motors Corporation for 2006. General Motors uses the LIFO inventory method.

Compute inventory turnover ratio and days in inventory; compute current ratio based on LIFO and after adjusting for LIFO reserve.

(SO 5, 6)

(in millions)	**2006**
Beginning inventory	$ 13,862
Ending inventory	13,921
LIFO reserve	1,508
Current assets	64,131
Current liabilities	67,822
Cost of goods sold	164,682
Sales	172,927

Instructions
(a) Calculate the inventory turnover ratio and days in inventory.
(b) Calculate the current ratio based on inventory as reported using LIFO.
(c) Calculate the current ratio after adjusting for the LIFO reserve.
(d) Comment on any difference between parts (b) and (c).

Calculate cost of goods sold, ending inventory, and gross profit for LIFO, FIFO, and average cost under the perpetual system; compare results.

(SO 3, 7)

*P6-8A   Selbe Inc. is a retailer operating in Edmonton, Alberta. Selbe uses the perpetual inventory method. All sales returns from customers result in the goods being returned to inventory. (Assume that the inventory is not damaged.) Assume that there are no credit transactions; all amounts are settled in cash. You are provided with the following information for Selbe Inc. for the month of January 2010.

Date	Description	Quantity	Unit Cost or Selling Price
Dec. 31	Ending inventory	160	$20
Jan. 2	Purchase	100	22
Jan. 6	Sale	180	40
Jan. 9	Sale return	10	40
Jan. 9	Purchase	75	24
Jan. 10	Purchase return	15	24
Jan. 10	Sale	50	45
Jan. 23	Purchase	100	26
Jan. 30	Sale	120	50

Gross profit:
LIFO $7,210
FIFO $7,690
Average $7,533

Instructions
(a) For each of the following cost flow assumptions, calculate (i) cost of goods sold, (ii) ending inventory, and (iii) gross profit.
  (1) LIFO. (Assume sales returns had a cost of $20 and purchase returns had a cost of $24.)
  (2) FIFO. (Assume sales returns had a cost of $20 and purchase returns had a cost of $24.)
  (3) Moving-average. (Round cost per unit to three decimal places.)
(b) Compare results for the three cost flow assumptions.

Determine ending inventory under a perpetual inventory system.

(SO 3, 7)

*P6-9A   Quality Center began operations on July 1. It uses a perpetual inventory system. During July the company had the following purchases and sales.

Date	Purchases Units	Unit Cost	Sales Units
July 1	7	$62	
July 6			3
July 11	4	$66	
July 14			3
July 21	3	$71	
July 27			5

FIFO $213
Average $200
LIFO $186

Instructions
(a) Determine the ending inventory under a perpetual inventory system using (1) FIFO, (2) average cost (round unit cost to three decimal places), and (3) LIFO.
(b) Which costing method produces the highest ending inventory valuation?

Problems: Set B

Determine items and amounts to be recorded in inventory.

(SO 1)

P6-1B   Ewing Limited is trying to determine the value of its ending inventory as of February 28, 2010, the company's year-end. The following transactions occurred, and the accountant asked your help in determining whether they should be recorded or not.
(a) On February 26, Ewing shipped goods costing $800 to a customer and charged the customer $1,000. The goods were shipped with terms FOB destination and the receiving report indicates that the customer received the goods on March 2.

(b) On February 26, Seller Inc. shipped goods to Ewing under terms FOB shipping point. The invoice price was $300 plus $25 for freight. The receiving report indicates that the goods were received by Ewing on March 2.

(c) Ewing had $500 of inventory isolated in the warehouse. The inventory is designated for a customer who has requested that the goods be shipped on March 10.

(d) Also included in Ewing's warehouse is $400 of inventory that Meredith Producers shipped to Ewing on consignment.

(e) On February 26, Ewing issued a purchase order to acquire goods costing $750. The goods were shipped with terms FOB destination on February 27. Ewing received the goods on March 2.

(f) On February 26, Ewing shipped goods to a customer under terms FOB shipping point. The invoice price was $350 plus $25 for freight; the cost of the items was $280. The receiving report indicates that the goods were received by the customer on March 2.

Instructions

For each of the above transactions, specify whether the item in question should be included in ending inventory, and if so, at what amount.

P6-2B Strom Distribution markets CDs of the performing artist Little Sister. At the beginning of October, Strom had in beginning inventory 1,500 Sister's CDs with a unit cost of $5. During October Strom made the following purchases of Sister's CDs.

Oct. 3	4,000 @ $6	Oct. 19	2,000 @ $8
Oct. 9	3,000 @ $7	Oct. 25	2,500 @ $9

During October 9,000 units were sold. Strom uses a periodic inventory system.

Instructions

(a) Determine the cost of goods available for sale.

(b) Determine (1) the ending inventory and (2) the cost of goods sold under each of the assumed cost flow methods (FIFO, LIFO, and average cost). Prove the accuracy of the cost of goods sold under the FIFO and LIFO methods.

(c) Which cost flow method results in (1) the highest inventory amount for the balance sheet and (2) the highest cost of goods sold for the income statement?

Determine cost of goods sold and ending inventory using FIFO, LIFO, and average cost with analysis.

(SO 2, 3)

Cost of goods sold:	
FIFO	$56,500
LIFO	$68,500
Average	$63,000

P6-3B Timmons Company had a beginning inventory on January 1 of 100 units of Product SXL at a cost of $20 per unit. During the year, purchases were:

Mar. 15	300 units at $23	Sept. 4	350 units at $28
July 20	250 units at $25	Dec. 2	100 units at $30

Timmons Company sold 800 units, and it uses a periodic inventory system.

Instructions

(a) Determine the cost of goods available for sale.

(b) Determine the ending inventory and the cost of goods sold under each of the assumed cost flow methods (FIFO, LIFO, and average cost). Prove the accuracy of the cost of goods sold under each method. (Round cost per unit to three decimal places.)

(c) Which cost flow method results in the highest inventory amount for the balance sheet? The highest cost of goods sold for the income statement?

Determine cost of goods sold and ending inventory using FIFO, LIFO, and average cost in a periodic inventory system and assess financial statement effects.

(SO 2, 3)

Cost of goods sold:	
FIFO	$19,350
LIFO	$21,350
Average	$20,327

P6-4B The management of Hadaway is reevaluating the appropriateness of using its present inventory cost flow method, which is average cost. The company requests your help in determining the results of operations for 2010 if either the FIFO or the LIFO method had been used. For 2010 the accounting records show these data:

Compute ending inventory, prepare income statements, and answer questions using FIFO and LIFO.

(SO 2, 3)

Inventories		Purchases and Sales	
Beginning (10,000 units)	$22,800	Total net sales (220,000 units)	$862,000
Ending (20,000 units)		Total cost of goods purchased	
		(230,000 units)	576,000

Purchases were made quarterly as follows.

Quarter	Units	Unit Cost	Total Cost
1	60,000	$2.30	$138,000
2	50,000	2.50	125,000
3	50,000	2.55	127,500
4	70,000	2.65	185,500
	230,000		$576,000

Operating expenses were $147,000, and the company's income tax rate is 32%.

Gross profit:
FIFO $316,200
LIFO $309,000

Instructions

(a) Prepare comparative condensed income statements for 2010 under FIFO and LIFO. (Show computations of ending inventory.)
(b) Answer the following questions for management in business-letter form.
  (1) Which cost flow method (FIFO or LIFO) produces the more meaningful inventory amount for the balance sheet? Why?
  (2) Which cost flow method (FIFO or LIFO) produces the more meaningful net income? Why?
  (3) Which cost flow method (FIFO or LIFO) is more likely to approximate the actual physical flow of goods? Why?
  (4) How much more cash will be available for management under LIFO than under FIFO? Why?
  (5) Will gross profit under the average cost method be higher or lower than FIFO? Than LIFO? (*Note:* It is not necessary to quantify your answer.)

Calculate ending inventory, cost of goods sold, gross profit, and gross profit rate under periodic method; compare results.

(SO 2, 3)

P6-5B You have the following information for Waner Inc. for the month ended June 30, 2010. Waner uses the periodic method for inventory.

Date	Description	Quantity	Unit Cost or Selling Price
June 1	Beginning inventory	25	$60
June 4	Purchase	85	64
June 10	Sale	70	90
June 11	Sale return	5	90
June 18	Purchase	35	68
June 18	Purchase return	15	68
June 25	Sale	55	95
June 28	Purchase	20	70

Instructions

Gross profit:
LIFO $3,195
FIFO $3,455
Average $3,315

(a) Calculate (i) ending inventory, (ii) cost of goods sold, (iii) gross profit, and (iv) gross profit rate under each of the following methods.
  (1) LIFO.
  (2) FIFO.
  (3) Average cost. (Round cost per unit to three decimal places.)
(b) Compare results for the three cost flow assumptions.

Compare specific identification, FIFO, and LIFO under periodic method; use cost flow assumption to justify price increase.

(SO 2, 3)

P6-6B You have the following information for Gas Saver Plus. Gas Saver Plus uses the periodic method of accounting for its inventory transactions.

March 1   Beginning inventory 1,500 litres at a cost of 40¢ per litre.
March 3   Purchased 2,000 litres at a cost of 45¢ per litre.
March 5   Sold 1,800 litres for 60¢ per litre.
March 10   Purchased 3,500 litres at a cost of 49¢ per litre.
March 20   Purchased 2,000 litres at a cost of 55¢ per litre.
March 30   Sold 5,000 litres for 70¢ per litre.

Gross profit:
Specific
identification $1,331
FIFO $1,463
LIFO $1,180

Instructions

(a) Prepare partial income statements through gross profit, and calculate the value of ending inventory that would be reported on the balance sheet, under each of the following cost flow assumptions.

(1) Specific identification method assuming:
  (i) the March 5 sale consisted of 900 litres from the March 1 beginning inventory and 900 litres from the March 3 purchase; and
  (ii) the March 30 sale consisted of the following number of units sold from each purchase: 400 litres from March 1; 500 litres from March 3; 2,600 litres from March 10; 1,500 litres from March 20.
(2) FIFO.
(3) LIFO.
(b) How can companies use a cost flow method to justify price increases? Which cost flow method would best support an argument to increase prices?

P6-7B Gehl Company manufactures a full line of construction and agriculture equipment. The following information is available for Gehl for 2006. The company uses the LIFO inventory method.

Compute inventory turnover ratio and days in inventory; compute current ratio based on LIFO and after adjusting for LIFO reserve.

(SO 5, 6)

(in thousands)	**2006**
Beginning inventory	$ 39,121
Ending inventory	48,649
LIFO reserve	29,652
Current assets	291,033
Current liabilities	89,504
Cost of goods sold	381,813
Sales	486,217

Instructions
(a) Calculate the inventory turnover ratio and days in inventory.
(b) Calculate the current ratio based on LIFO inventory.
(c) After adjusting for the LIFO reserve, calculate the current ratio.
(d) Comment on any difference between parts (b) and (c).

*P6-8B Mavity Inc. is a retail company that uses the perpetual inventory method. All sales returns from customers result in the goods being returned to inventory. (Assume that the inventory is not damaged.) Assume that there are no credit transactions; all amounts are settled in cash. You have the following information for Mavity Inc. for the month of January 2010.

Calculate cost of goods sold, ending inventory, and gross profit under LIFO, FIFO, and average cost under the perpetual system; compare results.

(SO 3, 7)

Date	Description	Quantity	Unit Cost or Selling Price
January 1	Beginning inventory	40	$14
January 5	Purchase	100	16
January 8	Sale	75	25
January 10	Sale return	10	25
January 15	Purchase	30	18
January 16	Purchase return	5	18
January 20	Sale	80	25
January 25	Purchase	20	20

Gross profit:
LIFO	$1,295
FIFO	$1,375
Average	$1,336

Instructions
(a) For each of the following cost flow assumptions, calculate (i) cost of goods sold, (ii) ending inventory, and (iii) gross profit.
  (1) LIFO. (Assume sales returns had a cost of $16 and purchase returns had a cost of $18.)
  (2) FIFO. (Assume sales returns had a cost of $16 and purchase returns had a cost of $18.)
  (3) Moving-average cost. (Round cost per unit to three decimal places.)
(b) Compare results for the three cost flow assumptions.

Determine ending inventory under a perpetual inventory system.

(SO 3, 7)

*P6-9B U-Save-More Center began operations on July 1. It uses a perpetual inventory system. During July the company had the following purchases and sales.

Date	Purchases Units	Unit Cost	Sales Units
July 1	6	$47	
July 6			4
July 11	5	$51	
July 14			3
July 21	3	$54	
July 27			2

Instructions

(a) Determine the ending inventory under a perpetual inventory system using (1) FIFO, (2) average cost, and (3) LIFO. (*Note:* For average cost, round cost per unit to three decimal places.)

(b) Which costing method produces the highest ending inventory valuation?

FIFO $264
Average $258
LIFO $250

Problems: Set C

Visit the book's companion website at **www.wiley.com/college/kimmel** and choose the Student Companion site to access Problem Set C.

Comprehensive Problem

CP6 On December 1, 2010, Gonzalez Company had the account balances shown below.

	Debits		Credits
Cash	$ 4,800	Accumulated Depreciation—Equipment	$ 1,500
Accounts Receivable	3,900	Accounts Payable	3,000
Merchandise Inventory	1,800*	Common Stock	10,000
Equipment	21,000	Retained Earnings	17,000
	$31,500		$31,500

*(3,000 × $0.60)

The following transactions occurred during December.

Dec. 3 Purchased 4,000 units on account at a cost of $0.75 per unit.
      5 Sold 4,500 units on account for $0.90 per unit. (It sold 3,000 of the $0.60 units and 1,500 of the $0.75)
      7 Granted the December 5 customer $180 credit for 200 units returned costing $150. These units were returned to inventory.
      17 Purchased 2,400 units for cash at $0.80 each.
      22 Sold 2,000 units on account for $0.95 per unit. (It sold 2,000 of the $0.75 units).

Adjustment data:

1. Accrued salaries payable $400.
2. Depreciation $200 per month.
3. Income tax expense was $175, to be paid next year.

Instructions

(a) Journalize the December transactions and adjusting entries assuming Gonzalez uses the perpetual inventory method.

(b) Enter the December 1 balances in the ledger T accounts and post the December transactions. In addition to the accounts mentioned above use the following additional accounts: Cost of Goods Sold, Depreciation Expense, Salaries Expense, Salaries Payable, Sales, Sales Returns and Allowances Income Tax Expense and Income Tax Payable.

(c) Prepare an adjusted trial balance as of December 31, 2010.

(d) Prepare an income statement for December 2010 and a classified balance sheet at December 31, 2010.

(e) Compute ending inventory and cost of goods sold under FIFO assuming Gonzalez Company uses the periodic inventory system.

(f) Compute ending inventory and cost of goods sold under LIFO assuming Gonzalez Company uses the periodic inventory system.

Continuing Cookie Chronicle

(*Note:* This is a continuation of the Cookie Chronicle from Chapters 1 through 5.)

CCC6 Natalie is busy establishing both divisions of her business (cookie classes and mixer sales) and completing her business degree. Her goals for the next 11 months are to sell one mixer per month and to give two to three classes per week. Natalie has decided to use a periodic inventory system and now must choose a cost flow assumption for her mixer inventory.

Go to the book's companion website, **www.wiley.com/college/kimmel**, to find the completion of this problem.

broadening your perspective

Financial Reporting and Analysis

FINANCIAL REPORTING PROBLEM: *Tootsie Roll, Industries Inc.*

BYP6-1 The notes that accompany a company's financial statements provide informative details that would clutter the amounts and descriptions presented in the statements. Refer to the financial statements of Tootsie Roll and the accompanying Notes to Consolidated Financial Statements in Appendix A.

Instructions
Answer the following questions. (Give the amounts in thousands of dollars, as shown in Tootsie Roll's annual report.)

(a) What did Tootsie Roll report for the amount of inventories in its Consolidated Balance Sheet at December 31, 2007? At December 31, 2006?

(b) Compute the dollar amount of change and the percentage change in inventories between 2006 and 2007. Compute inventory as a percentage of current assets for 2007.

(c) What are the (product) cost of goods sold reported by Tootsie Roll for 2007, 2006, and 2005? Compute the ratio of (product) cost of goods sold to net (product) sales in 2007.

COMPARATIVE ANALYSIS PROBLEM: *Tootsie Roll vs. Hershey Foods*

BYP6-2 The financial statements of Hershey Foods appear in Appendix B, following the financial statements for Tootsie Roll in Appendix A.

Instructions
(a) Based on the information in the financial statements, compute these 2007 values for each company. (Do not adjust for the LIFO reserve.)
   (1) Inventory turnover ratio. (Use product cost of goods sold.)
   (2) Days in inventory.
(b) What conclusions concerning the management of the inventory can you draw from these data?

RESEARCH CASE

BYP6-3 The February 9, 2007, issue of the *Wall Street Journal* contains an article by Neal E. Boudette titled "Lots of Vehicles: Big Dealer to Detroit: Fix How You Make Cars."

Instructions

Read the article and answer the following questions.
(a) Explain what the article identifies as the biggest problem with U.S. auto manufacturers. How does the article's author think they can solve the problem?
(b) At the time of the article, Toyota had 15.4% of the U.S. market and General Motors (GM) had 24.6%. How did the total inventory of the two companies compare? How did the inventory per 1% of market share compare? What are some possible implications of this difference?
(c) How did days in inventory of AutoNation's Toyota and Honda stores compare to its GM, Ford, and Chrysler stores at the time of the article?

INTERPRETING FINANCIAL STATEMENTS

BYP6-4 The following information is from the 2007 annual report of American Greetings Corporation (all dollars in thousands).

	Feb. 28, 2007	Feb. 28, 2006
Inventories		
Finished goods	$207,676	$235,657
Work in process	11,315	15,399
Raw materials and supplies	42,772	41,456
	261,763	292,512
Less: LIFO reserve	79,145	79,403
Total (as reported)	$182,618	$213,109
Cost of goods sold	$826,791	$846,958
Current assets (as reported)	$799,281	$1,165,845
Current liabilities	$373,000	$559,082

The following information comes from the notes to the company's financial statements.

Finished products, work in process, and raw material inventories are carried at the lower-of-cost-or-market. The last-in, first-out (LIFO) cost method is used for approximately 65% of the domestic inventories in 2007 and approximately 55% in 2006. The foreign subsidiaries principally use the first-in, first-out method. Display material and factory supplies are carried at average cost.

Instructions

(a) Define each of the following: finished goods, work in process, and raw materials.
(b) What might be a possible explanation for why the company uses FIFO for its non-domestic inventories?
(c) Calculate the company's inventory turnover ratio and days in inventory for 2006 and 2007. (2005 inventory was $218,711.) Discuss the implications of any change in the ratios.
(d) What percentage of total inventory does the 2007 LIFO reserve represent? If the company used FIFO in 2007, what would be the value of its inventory? Do you consider this difference a "material" amount from the perspective of an analyst? Which value accurately represents the value of the company's inventory?
(e) Calculate the company's 2007 current ratio with the numbers as reported, then recalculate after adjusting for the LIFO reserve.

FINANCIAL ANALYSIS ON THE WEB

BYP6-5 *Purpose:* Use SEC filings to learn about a company's inventory accounting practices.

Address: **http://biz.yahoo.com/p/_capgds-bldmch.html**,
or go to **www.wiley.com/college/kimmel**

Steps

1. Go to this site and click on the name of an equipment manufacturer other than those discussed in the chapter.
2. Click on **SEC filings**.
3. Under "Recent filings" choose **Form 10K** (annual report) and click on **Full Filing at Edgar Online**.
4. Choose option "3," **Online HTML Version**.

If the 10K is not listed among the recent filings then click on **View All Filings on EDGAR Online**.

Instructions
Review the 10K to answer the following questions.

(a) What is the name of the company?
(b) How has its inventory changed from the previous year?
(c) What is the amount of raw materials, work in process, and finished goods inventory?
(d) What inventory method does the company use?
(e) Calculate the inventory turnover ratio and days in inventory for the current year.
(f) If the company uses LIFO, what was the amount of its LIFO reserve?

Critical Thinking

DECISION MAKING ACROSS THE ORGANIZATION

BYP6-6 Gentry Electronics has enjoyed tremendous sales growth during the last 10 years. However, even though sales have steadily increased, the company's CEO, Erica Harding, is concerned about certain aspects of its performance. She has called a meeting with the corporate controller and the vice presidents of finance, operations, sales, and marketing to discuss the company's performance. Erica begins the meeting by making the following observations:

> We have been forced to take significant write-downs on inventory during each of the last three years because of obsolescence. In addition, inventory storage costs have soared. We rent four additional warehouses to store our increasingly diverse inventory. Five years ago inventory represented only 20% of the value of our total assets. It now exceeds 35%. Yet, even with all of this inventory, "stockouts" (measured by complaints by customers that the desired product is not available) have increased by 40% during the last three years. And worse yet, it seems that we constantly must discount merchandise that we have too much of.

Erica asks the group to review the following data and make suggestions as to how the company's performance might be improved.

(in millions)	2010	2009	2008	2007
Inventory				
Raw materials	$242	$198	$155	$128
Work in process	116	77	49	33
Finished goods	567	482	398	257
Total inventory	$925	$757	$602	$418
Current assets	$1,800	$1,423	$1,183	$841
Total assets	$2,643	$2,523	$2,408	$2,090
Current liabilities	$600	$590	$525	$420
Sales	$9,428	$8,674	$7,536	$6,840
Cost of goods sold	$6,328	$5,474	$4,445	$3,557
Net income	$754	$987	$979	$958

Instructions

Using the information provided, answer the following questions.

(a) Compute the current ratio, gross profit rate, profit margin ratio, inventory turnover ratio, and days in inventory for 2008, 2009, and 2010.

(b) Discuss the trends and potential causes of the changes in the ratios in part (a).

(c) Discuss potential remedies to any problems discussed in part (b).

(d) What concerns might be raised by some members of management with regard to your suggestions in part (c)?

COMMUNICATION ACTIVITIES

BYP6-7 In a discussion of dramatic increases in coffee bean prices, a *Wall Street Journal* article noted the following fact about Starbucks.

> Before this year's bean-price hike, Starbucks added several defenses that analysts say could help it maintain earnings and revenue. The company last year began accounting for its coffee-bean purchases by taking the average price of all beans in inventory.
>
> *Source:* Aaron Lucchetti, "Crowded Coffee Market May Keep a Lid on Starbucks After Price Rise Hurt Stock," *Wall Street Journal* (June 4, 1997), p. C1.

Prior to this change the company was using FIFO.

Instructions

Your client, the CEO of Hot Cup Coffee, Inc., read this article and sent you an e-mail message requesting that you explain why Starbucks might have taken this action. Your response should explain what impact this change in accounting method has on earnings, why the company might want to do this, and any possible disadvantages of such a change.

*BYP6-8 You are the controller of Blue Jays Inc. B. J. Dell, the president, recently mentioned to you that she found an error in the 2009 financial statements which she believes has corrected itself. She determined, in discussions with the purchasing department, that 2009 ending inventory was overstated by $1 million. B. J. says that the 2010 ending inventory is correct, and she assumes that 2010 income is correct. B. J. says to you, "What happened has happened—there's no point in worrying about it anymore."

Instructions

You conclude that B. J. is incorrect. Write a brief, tactful memo to her, clarifying the situation.

ETHICS CASE

BYP6-9 Heinen Wholesale Corp. uses the LIFO cost flow method. In the current year, profit at Heinen is running unusually high. The corporate tax rate is also high this year, but it is scheduled to decline significantly next year. In an effort to lower the current year's net income and to take advantage of the changing income tax rate, the president of Heinen Wholesale instructs the plant accountant to recommend to the purchasing department a large purchase of inventory for delivery 3 days before the end of the year. The price of the inventory to be purchased has doubled during the year, and the purchase will represent a major portion of the ending inventory value.

Instructions

(a) What is the effect of this transaction on this year's and next year's income statement and income tax expense? Why?

(b) If Heinen Wholesale had been using the FIFO method of inventory costing, would the president give the same directive?

(c) Should the plant accountant order the inventory purchase to lower income? What are the ethical implications of this order?

"ALL ABOUT YOU" ACTIVITY

BYP6-10 Some of the largest business frauds ever perpetrated have involved the misstatement of inventory. Two classics were at Leslie Fay Cos, and McKesson Corporation.

Instructions

There is considerable information regarding inventory frauds available on the Internet. Search for information about one of the two cases mentioned above, or inventory fraud at any other company, and prepare a short explanation of the nature of the inventory fraud.

Answers to Insight and Accounting Across the Organization Questions

p. 277

Q: What steps might the companies take to avoid such a serious disruption in the future?

A: The manufacturer of the piston rings should spread its manufacturing facilities across a few locations that are far enough apart that they would not all be at risk at once. In addition, the automakers might consider becoming less dependent on a single supplier.

p. 278

Q: What effect does an overstatement of inventory have on a company's financial statements?

A: The balance sheet looks stronger because inventory and retained earnings are overstated. The income statement looks better because cost of goods sold is understated and income is overstated.

p. 287

Q: What are the arguments for and against the use of LIFO?

A: Proponents of LIFO argue that it is conceptually superior because it matches the most recent cost with the most recent selling price. Critics contend that it artificially understates the company's net income and consequently reduces tax payments. Also, because most foreign companies are not allowed to use LIFO, its use by U.S. companies reduces the ability of investors to compare U.S. companies with foreign companies.

p. 291

Q: Why is inventory control important to managers such as those at Wal-Mart and Best Buy?

A: In the very competitive environment of discount retailing, where Wal-Mart and Best Buy are the major players, small differences in price matter to the customer. Wal-Mart sells a high volume of inventory at a low gross profit rate. When operating in a high-volume, low-margin environment, small cost savings can mean the difference between being profitable or going out of business.

Answers to Self-Study Questions

1. d   2. a   3. b   4. c   5. d   6. d   7. c   8. d   9. a   10. d   11. b   12. a   *13. d   14. b   15. b

 Remember to go back to the navigator box on the chapter-opening page and check off your completed work.

chapter 7

Fraud, Internal Control, and Cash

✔ the navigator

- Scan **Study Objectives** ○
- Read **Feature Story** ○
- Scan **Preview** ○
- Read **Text and Answer** **Do it!** ○
  p. 336 ○   p. 340 ○   p. 349 ○   p. 354 ○
- Work **Using the Decision Toolkit** ○
- Review **Summary of Study Objectives** ○
- Work **Comprehensive** **Do it!** p. 360 ○
- Answer **Self-Study Questions** ○
- Complete **Assignments** ○

study objectives

After studying this chapter, you should be able to:

1 Define fraud and internal control.

2 Identify the principles of internal control activities.

3 Explain the applications of internal control principles to cash receipts.

4 Explain the applications of internal control principles to cash disbursements.

5 Prepare a bank reconciliation.

6 Explain the reporting of cash.

7 Discuss the basic principles of cash management.

8 Identify the primary elements of a cash budget.

Minding the Money in Moose Jaw

If you're ever looking for a cappuccino in Moose Jaw, Saskatchewan, stop by Stephanie's Gourmet Coffee and More, located on Main Street. Staff there serve, on average, 650 cups of coffee a day, including both regular and specialty coffees, not to mention soups, Italian sandwiches, and a wide assortment of gourmet cheesecakes.

"We've got high school students who come here, and students from the community college," says owner/manager Stephanie Mintenko, who has run the place since opening it in 1995. "We have customers who are retired, and others who are working people and have only 30 minutes for lunch. We have to be pretty quick."

That means that the cashiers have to be efficient. Like most businesses where purchases are low-cost and high-volume, cash control has to be simple.

"We have an electronic cash register, but it's not the fancy new kind where you just punch in the item," explains Ms. Mintenko. "You have to punch in the prices." The machine does keep track of sales in several categories, however. Cashiers punch a button to indicate whether each item is a beverage, a meal, or a charge for the cafe's Internet connections. An internal tape in the machine keeps a record of all transactions; the customer receives a receipt only upon request.

There is only one cash register. "Up to three of us might operate it on any given shift, including myself," says Ms. Mintenko.

She and her staff do two "cashouts" each day—one with the shift change at 5:00 p.m. and one when the shop closes at 10:00 p.m. At each cashout, they count the cash in the register drawer. That amount, minus the cash change carried forward (the float), should match the shift total on the register tape. If there's a discrepancy, they do another count. Then, if necessary, "we go through the whole tape to find the mistake," she explains. "It usually turns out to be someone who punched in $18 instead of $1.80, or something like that."

Ms. Mintenko sends all the cash tapes and float totals to a bookkeeper, who double-checks everything and provides regular reports. "We try to keep the accounting simple, so we can concentrate on making great coffee and food."

As the story about recording cash sales at Stephanie's Gourmet Coffee and More indicates, control of cash is important to ensure that fraud does not occur. Companies also need controls to safeguard other types of assets. For example, Stephanie's undoubtedly has controls to prevent the theft of food and supplies, and controls to prevent the theft of tableware and dishes from its kitchen.

In this chapter, we explain the essential features of an internal control system and how it prevents fraud. We also describe how those controls apply to a specific asset–cash. The applications include some controls with which you may be already familiar, such as the use of a bank.

The content and organization of Chapter 7 are as follows.

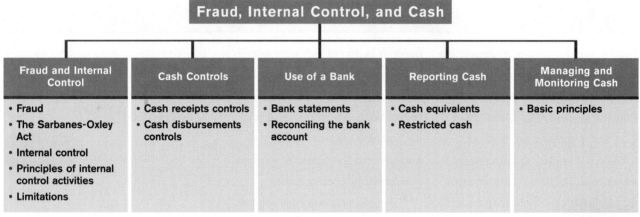

Fraud, Internal Control, and Cash				
Fraud and Internal Control	**Cash Controls**	**Use of a Bank**	**Reporting Cash**	**Managing and Monitoring Cash**
• Fraud • The Sarbanes-Oxley Act • Internal control • Principles of internal control activities • Limitations	• Cash receipts controls • Cash disbursements controls	• Bank statements • Reconciling the bank account	• Cash equivalents • Restricted cash	• Basic principles

the navigator

Fraud and Internal Control

study objective 1

Define fraud and internal control.

The Feature Story describes many of the internal control procedures used by Stephanie's Gourmet Coffee and More. These procedures are necessary to discourage employees from fraudulent activities.

FRAUD

A fraud is a dishonest act by an employee that results in personal benefit to the employee at a cost to the employer. Examples of fraud reported in the financial press include:

*   A bookkeeper in a small company diverted $750,000 of bill payments to a personal bank account over a three-year period.

*   A shipping clerk with 28 years of service shipped $125,000 of merchandise to himself.

*   A computer operator embezzled $21 million from Wells Fargo Bank over a two-year period.

*   A church treasurer "borrowed" $150,000 of church funds to finance a friend's business dealings.

Why does fraud occur? The three main factors that contribute to fraudulent activity are depicted by the fraud triangle in Illustration 7-1 (next page).

The most important element of the fraud triangle is **opportunity**. For an employee to commit fraud, the workplace environment must provide opportunities that an employee can exploit. Opportunities occur when the workplace lacks sufficient controls to deter and detect fraud. For example, inadequate

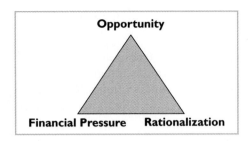

Illustration 7-1 Fraud triangle

monitoring of employee actions can create opportunities for theft and can embolden employees because they believe they will not be caught.

A second factor that contributes to fraud is **financial pressure**. Employees sometimes commit fraud because of personal financial problems caused by too much debt. Or they might commit fraud because they want to lead a lifestyle that they cannot afford on their current salary.

The third factor that contributes to fraud is **rationalization**. In order to justify their fraud, employees rationalize their dishonest actions. For example, employees sometimes justify fraud because they believe they are underpaid while the employer is making lots of money. These employees feel justified in stealing because they believe they deserve to be paid more.

THE SARBANES-OXLEY ACT

What can be done to prevent or to detect fraud? After numerous corporate scandals came to light in the early 2000s, Congress addressed this issue by passing the Sarbanes-Oxley Act of 2002 (SOX). Under SOX, all publicly traded U.S. corporations are required to maintain an adequate system of internal control. Corporate executives and boards of directors must ensure that these controls are reliable and effective. In addition, independent outside auditors must attest to the adequacy of the internal control system. Companies that fail to comply are subject to fines, and company officers can be imprisoned. SOX also created the Public Company Accounting Oversight Board (PCAOB), to establish auditing standards and regulate auditor activity.

One poll found that 60% of investors believe that SOX helps safeguard their stock investments. Many say they would be unlikely to invest in a company that fails to follow SOX requirements. Although some corporate executives have criticized the time and expense involved in following the SOX requirements, SOX appears to be working well. For example, the chief accounting officer of Eli Lily noted that SOX triggered a comprehensive review of how the company documents controls. This review uncovered redundancies and pointed out controls that needed to be added. In short, it added up to time and money well spent. And the finance chief at General Electric noted, "We have seen value in SOX. It helps build investors' trust and gives them more confidence."[1]

INTERNAL CONTROL

Internal control consists of all the related methods and measures adopted within an organization to safeguard its assets, enhance the reliability of its accounting records, increase efficiency of operations, and ensure compliance with

---

[1]"Corporate Regulation Must Be Working—There's a Backlash," *Wall Street Journal,* June 16, 2004, p. C1; and Judith Burns, "Is Sarbanes-Oxley Working?" *Wall Street Journal,* June 21, 2004, pp. R8–R9.

laws and regulations. Internal control systems have five primary components as listed below.[2]

- **A control environment.** It is the responsibility of top management to make it clear that the organization values integrity and that unethical activity will not be tolerated. This component is often referred to as the "tone at the top."
- **Risk assessment.** Companies must identify and analyze the various factors that create risk for the business and must determine how to manage these risks.
- **Control activities.** To reduce the occurrence of fraud, management must design policies and procedures to address the specific risks faced by the company.
- **Information and communication.** The internal control system must capture and communicate all pertinent information both down and up the organization, as well as communicate information to appropriate external parties.
- **Monitoring.** Internal control systems must be monitored periodically for their adequacy. Significant deficiencies need to be reported to top management and/or the board of directors.

PRINCIPLES OF INTERNAL CONTROL ACTIVITIES

study objective 2

Identify the principles of internal control activities.

Each of the five components of an internal control system is important. Here, we will focus on one component, the control activities. The reason? These activities are the backbone of the company's efforts to address the risks it faces, such as fraud. The specific control activities used by a company will vary, depending on management's assessment of the risks faced. This assessment is heavily influenced by the size and nature of the company.

The six principles of control activities are as follows.

- Establishment of responsibility
- Segregation of duties
- Documentation procedures
- Physical controls
- Independent internal verification
- Human resource controls

We explain these principles in the following sections. You should recognize that they apply to most companies and are relevant to both manual and computerized accounting systems.

In the explanations that follow, we have added "Anatomy of a Fraud" stories that describe some recent real-world frauds. At the end of each story, we discuss the missing control activity that, had it been in place, is likely to have prevented or uncovered the fraud.[3]

Establishment of Responsibility

An essential principle of internal control is to assign responsibility to specific employees. **Control is most effective when only one person is responsible for a given task.**

---

[2]The Committee of Sponsoring Organizations of the Treadway Commission, "Internal Control—Integrated Framework," *www.coso.org/publications/executive_summary_integrated_framework.htm* (accessed March 2008).
[3]The "Anatomy of a Fraud" stories on pages 329–335 are adapted from *Fraud Casebook: Lessons from the Bad Side of Business*, edited by Joseph T. Wells (Hoboken, NJ: John Wiley & Sons, Inc., 2007). Used by permission. The names of some of the people and organizations in the stories are fictitious, but the facts in the stories are true.

To illustrate, assume that the cash on hand at the end of the day in a Safeway supermarket is $10 short of the cash rung up on the cash register. If only one person has operated the register, the shift manager can quickly determine responsibility for the shortage. If two or more individuals have worked the register, it may be impossible to determine who is responsible for the error. In the Feature Story, the principle of establishing responsibility does not appear to be strictly applied by Stephanie's, since three people operate the cash register on any given shift.

Establishing responsibility often requires limiting access only to authorized personnel, and then identifying those personnel. For example, the automated systems used by many companies have mechanisms such as identifying passcodes that keep track of who made a journal entry, who rang up a sale, or who entered an inventory storeroom at a particular time. Use of identifying passcodes enables the company to establish responsibility by identifying the particular employee who carried out the activity.

It's your shift now. I'm turning in my cash drawer and heading home.

Transfer of cash drawers

ANATOMY OF A FRAUD

Maureen Frugali was a training supervisor for claims processing at Colossal Healthcare. As a standard part of the claims processing training program, Maureen created fictitious claims for use by trainees. These fictitious claims were then sent to Accounts Payable. After the training claims had been processed, she was to notify the accounts payable department of all fictitious claims, so that they would not be paid. However, she did not inform Accounts Payable about every fictitious claim. She created some fictitious claims for entities that she controlled (that is, she would receive the payment), and she let Accounts Payable pay her.

Total take: $11 million

THE MISSING CONTROL

Establishment of responsibility. The healthcare company did not adequately restrict the responsibility for authoring and approving claims transactions. The training supervisor should not have been authorized to create claims in the company's "live" system.

Source: Adapted from Wells, *Fraud Casebook* (2007), pp. 61–70.

Segregation of Duties

Segregation of duties is indispensable in an internal control system. There are two common applications of this principle:

1. Different individuals should be responsible for related activities.
2. The responsibility for record-keeping for an asset should be separate from the physical custody of that asset.

The rationale for segregation of duties is this: **The work of one employee should, without a duplication of effort, provide a reliable basis for evaluating the work of another employee.** For example, the personnel that design and program computerized systems should not be assigned duties related to day-to-day use of the system. Otherwise, they could design the system to benefit them personally and conceal the fraud through day-to-day use.

SEGREGATION OF RELATED ACTIVITIES. Making one individual responsible for related activities increases the potential for errors and irregularities.

For example, companies should assign related *purchasing activities* to different individuals. Related purchasing activities include ordering merchandise, order approval, receiving goods, authorizing payment, and paying for goods or services. Various frauds are possible when one person handles related purchasing activities. For example:

- If a purchasing agent can order goods without supervisory approval, the likelihood of the agent receiving kickbacks from suppliers increases.
- If an employee who orders goods also handles receipt of the goods (and invoice) as well as payment authorization, he or she might authorize payment for a fictitious invoice.

These abuses are less likely to occur when companies divide the purchasing tasks.

Similarly, companies should assign related *sales activities* to different individuals. Related selling activities include making a sale, shipping (or delivering) the goods to the customer, billing the customer, and receiving payment. Various frauds are possible when one person handles related sales transactions. For example:

- If a salesperson can make a sale without obtaining supervisory approval, he or she might make sales at unauthorized prices to increase sales commissions.
- A shipping clerk who also has access to accounting records could ship goods to himself.
- A billing clerk who handles billing and cash receipts could understate the amount billed for sales made to friends and relatives.

These abuses are less likely to occur when companies divide the sales tasks: the salespeople make the sale; the shipping department ships the goods on the basis of the sales order; and the billing department prepares the sales invoice after comparing the sales order with the report of goods shipped.

ANATOMY OF A FRAUD

Lawrence Fairbanks, the assistant vice-chancellor of communications at Aesop University was allowed to make purchases for his department of under $2,500 without external approval. Unfortunately, he also sometimes bought items for himself, such as expensive antiques and other collectibles. How did he do it? He replaced the vendor invoices he received with fake vendor invoices that he created. The fake invoices had descriptions that were more consistent with the communications department's operations. He submitted these fake invoices to the accounting department as the basis for their journal entries and to Accounts Payable as the basis for payment.

Total take: $475,000

THE MISSING CONTROL

Segregation of duties. The university had not properly segregated related purchasing activities. Lawrence was ordering items, receiving the items, and receiving the invoice. By receiving the invoice, he had control over the documents that were used to account for the purchase and thus was able to substitute a fake invoice.

Source: Adapted from Wells, *Fraud Casebook* (2007), pp. 3–15.

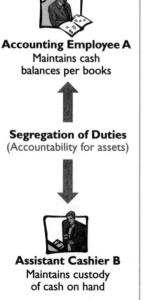

Accounting Employee A
Maintains cash
balances per books

Segregation of Duties
(Accountability for assets)

Assistant Cashier B
Maintains custody
of cash on hand

SEGREGATION OF RECORD-KEEPING FROM PHYSICAL CUSTODY. The accountant should have neither physical custody of the asset nor access to it. Likewise, the custodian of the asset should not maintain or have access to the accounting records. **The custodian of the asset is not likely to convert the asset to personal use when one employee maintains the record of the asset, and a different employee has physical custody of the asset.** The separation of accounting responsibility from the custody of assets is especially important for cash and inventories because these assets are very vulnerable to fraud.

Documentation Procedures

Documents provide evidence that transactions and events have occurred. At Stephanie's Gourmet Coffee and More, the cash register tape is the restaurant's documentation for the sale and the amount of cash received. Similarly, a shipping document indicates that the goods have been shipped, and a sales invoice indicates that the company has billed the customer for the goods. By requiring signatures (or initials) on the documents, the company can identify the individual(s) responsible for the transaction or event. Companies should document transactions when the transaction occurs.

Companies should establish procedures for documents. First, whenever possible, companies should use **prenumbered documents, and all documents should be accounted for**. Prenumbering helps to prevent a transaction from being recorded more than once, or conversely, from not being recorded at all. Second, the control system should require that employees **promptly forward source documents for accounting entries to the accounting department. This control measure helps to ensure timely recording of the transaction** and contributes directly to the accuracy and reliability of the accounting records.

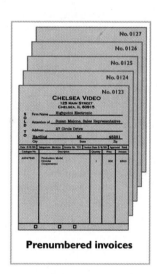

Prenumbered invoices

THE MISSING CONTROL

Documentation procedures. Mod Fashions should require the original, detailed receipt. It should not accept photocopies, and it should not accept credit card statements. In addition, documentation procedures could be further improved by requiring the use of a corporate credit card (rather than personal credit card) for all business expenses.

Source: Adapted from Wells, *Fraud Casebook* (2007), pp. 79–90.

Physical Controls

Use of physical controls is essential. *Physical controls* relate to the safeguarding of assets and enhance the accuracy and reliability of the accounting records. Illustration 7-2 shows examples of these controls.

Illustration 7-2 Physical controls

Physical Controls

Safes, vaults, and safety deposit boxes for cash and business papers

Locked warehouses and storage cabinets for inventories and records

Computer facilities with pass key access or fingerprint or eyeball scans

Alarms to prevent break-ins

Television monitors and garment sensors to deter theft

Time clocks for recording time worked

ANATOMY OF A FRAUD

At Centerstone Health, a large insurance company, the mailroom each day received insurance applications from prospective customers. Mailroom employees scanned the applications into electronic documents before the applications were processed. Once the applications are scanned they can be accessed online by authorized employees.

Insurance agents at Centerstone Health earn commissions based upon successful applications. The sales agent's name is listed on the application. However, roughly 15% of the applications are from customers who did not work with a sales agent. Two friends—Alex, an employee in record keeping, and Parviz, a sales agent—thought up a way to perpetrate a fraud. Alex identified scanned applications that did not list a sales agent. After business hours, he entered the mailroom and found the hardcopy applications that did not show a sales agent. He wrote in Parviz's name as the sales agent and then rescanned the application for processing. Parviz received the commission, which the friends then split.

Total take: $240,000

THE MISSING CONTROL

Physical controls. Centerstone Health lacked two basic physical controls that could have prevented this fraud. First, the mailroom should have been locked during nonbusiness hours, and access during business hours should have been tightly controlled. Second, the scanned applications supposedly could be accessed only by authorized employees using their password. However, the password for each employee was the same as the employee's user ID. Since employee user ID numbers were available to all other employees, all employees knew all other employees' passwords. Thus, Alex could enter the system using another employee's password and access the scanned applications.

Source: Adapted from Wells, *Fraud Casebook* (2007), pp. 316–326.

Independent Internal Verification

Most internal control systems provide for **independent internal verification**. This principle involves the review of data prepared by employees. To obtain maximum benefit from independent internal verification:

1. Companies should verify records periodically or on a surprise basis.

2. An employee who is independent of the personnel responsible for the information should make the verification.

3. Discrepancies and exceptions should be reported to a management level that can take appropriate corrective action.

Independent internal verification is especially useful in comparing recorded transactions with existing assets. The reconciliation of the cash register tape with the cash in the register at Stephanie's Gourmet Coffee and More is an example of this internal control principle. Another common example is the reconciliation of a company's cash balance per books with the cash balance per bank and the verification of the perpetual inventory records through a count of physical inventory. Illustration 7-3 shows the relationship between this principle and the segregation of duties principle.

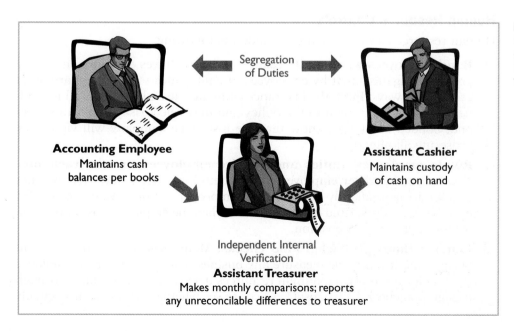

Accounting Employee
Maintains cash balances per books

Segregation of Duties

Assistant Cashier
Maintains custody of cash on hand

Independent Internal Verification
Assistant Treasurer
Makes monthly comparisons; reports any unreconcilable differences to treasurer

Illustration 7-3
Comparison of segregation of duties principle with independent internal verification principle

Large companies often assign independent internal verification to internal auditors. **Internal auditors** are company employees who continuously evaluate the effectiveness of the company's internal control systems. They review the activities of departments and individuals to determine whether prescribed internal controls are being followed. They also recommend improvements when needed. In fact, most fraud is discovered by the company through internal mechanisms such as existing internal controls and internal audits. For example, the fraud at WorldCom, involving billions of dollars, was uncovered by an internal auditor.

ANATOMY OF A FRAUD

Bobbi Jean Donnelly, the office manager for Mod Fashions Corporation's design center, was responsible for preparing the design center budget and reviewing expense reports submitted by design center employees. Her desire to upgrade her wardrobe got the better of her, and she enacted a fraud that involved filing expense-reimbursement requests for her own personal clothing purchases. She was able to conceal the fraud because she was responsible for reviewing all expense reports, including her own. In addition, she sometimes was given ultimate responsibility for signing off on the expense reports when her boss was "too busy." Also, because she controlled the budget, when she submitted her expenses, she coded them to budget items that she knew were running under budget, so that they would not catch anyone's attention.

Total take: $275,000

THE MISSING CONTROL

Independent internal verification. Bobbi Jean's boss should have verified her expense reports. When asked what he thought her expenses for a year were, the boss said about $10,000. At $115,000 per year, her actual expenses were more than ten times what would have been expected. However, because he was "too busy" to verify her expense reports or to review the budget, he never noticed.

Source: Adapted from Wells, *Fraud Casebook* (2007), pp. 79–90.

Human Resource Controls

Human resource control activities include the following.

1. **Bond employees who handle cash. Bonding** involves obtaining insurance protection against theft by employees. It contributes to the safeguarding of cash in two ways: First, the insurance company carefully screens all individuals before adding them to the policy and may reject risky applicants. Second, bonded employees know that the insurance company will vigorously prosecute all offenders.

2. **Rotate employees' duties and require employees to take vacations.** These measures deter employees from attempting thefts since they will not be able to permanently conceal their improper actions. Many banks, for example, have discovered employee thefts when the employee was on vacation or assigned to a new position.

3. **Conduct thorough background checks.** Many believe that the most important and inexpensive measure any business can take to reduce employee theft and fraud is for the human resources department to conduct thorough background checks. Two tips: (1) Check to see whether job applicants actually

graduated from the schools they list. (2) Never use the telephone numbers for previous employers given on the reference sheet; always look them up yourself.

ANATOMY OF A FRAUD

Ellen Lowry was the desk manager and Josephine Rodriquez was the head of housekeeping at the Excelsior Inn, a luxury hotel. The two best friends were so dedicated to their jobs that they never took vacations, and they frequently filled in for other employees. In fact, Ms. Rodriquez, whose job as head of housekeeping did not include cleaning rooms, often cleaned rooms herself, "just to help the staff keep up." These two "dedicated" employees, working as a team, found a way to earn a little more cash. Ellen, the desk manager, provided significant discounts to guests who paid with cash. She kept the cash and did not register the guest in the hotel's computerized system. Instead, she took the room out of circulation "due to routine maintenance." Because the room did not show up as being used, it did not receive a normal housekeeping assignment. Instead, Josephine, the head of housekeeping, cleaned the rooms during the guests' stay.

Total take: $95,000

THE MISSING CONTROL

Human resource controls. Ellen, the desk manager, had been fired by a previous employer after being accused of fraud. If the Excelsior Inn had conducted a thorough background check, it would not have hired her. The hotel fraud was detected when Ellen missed work for a few days due to illness. A system of mandatory vacations and rotating days off would have increased the chances of detecting the fraud before it became so large.

Source: Adapted from Wells, *Fraud Casebook* (2007), pp. 145–155.

 ## Accounting Across the Organization

Under SOX, a company needs to keep track of employees' degrees and certifications to ensure that employees continue to meet the specified requirements of a job. Also, to ensure proper employee supervision and proper separation of duties, companies must develop and monitor an organizational chart. When one corporation went through this exercise it found that out of 17,000 employees, there were 400 people who did not report to anyone, and they had 35 people who reported to each other. In addition, if an employee complains of an unfair firing and mentions financial issues at the company, HR must refer the case to the company audit committee and possibly to its legal counsel.

 Why would unsupervised employees or employees who report to each other represent potential internal control threats?

LIMITATIONS OF INTERNAL CONTROL

Companies generally design their systems of internal control to provide **reasonable assurance** of proper safeguarding of assets and reliability of the accounting records. The concept of reasonable assurance rests on the premise that the costs of establishing control procedures should not exceed their expected benefit.

To illustrate, consider shoplifting losses in retail stores. Stores could eliminate such losses by having a security guard stop and search customers as they leave the store. But store managers have concluded that the negative effects of such a procedure cannot be justified. Instead, stores have attempted to control shoplifting losses by less costly procedures: They post signs saying, "We reserve the right to inspect all packages" and "All shoplifters will be prosecuted." They use hidden TV cameras and store detectives to monitor customer activity, and they install sensor equipment at exits.

The **human element** is an important factor in every system of internal control. A good system can become ineffective as a result of employee fatigue, carelessness, or indifference. For example, a receiving clerk may not bother to count goods received and may just "fudge" the counts. Occasionally, two or more individuals may work together to get around prescribed controls. Such **collusion** can significantly reduce the effectiveness of a system, eliminating the protection offered by segregation of duties. No system of internal control is perfect.

The size of the business also may impose limitations on internal control. A small company, for example, may find it difficult to segregate duties or to provide for independent internal verification.

Ethics Insight

A study by the Association of Certified Fraud Examiners indicates that businesses with fewer than 100 employees are most at risk for employee theft. Nearly 46% of frauds occurred at companies with fewer than 100 employees. The average loss at small companies was $98,000, which was only slightly less than the average fraud at companies with more than 10,000 employees. A $100,000 loss can threaten the very existence of a small company.

Source: 2004 Report to the Nation on Occupational Fraud and Abuse, Association of Certified Fraud Examiners, *http://www.cfenet.com/pdfs/2004RttN.pdf*, p. 6.

 Why are small companies more susceptible to employee theft?

DECISION TOOLKIT

DECISION CHECKPOINTS	INFO NEEDED FOR DECISION	TOOL TO USE FOR DECISION	HOW TO EVALUATE RESULTS
Are the company's financial statements supported by adequate internal controls?	Auditor's report, management discussion and analysis, articles in financial press	The principles of internal control activities are (1) establishment of responsibility, (2) segregation of duties, (3) documentation procedures, (4) physical controls, (5) independent internal verification, and (6) human resource controls.	If any indication is given that these or other controls are lacking, use the financial statements with caution.

before you go on...

CONTROL ACTIVITIES   **Do it!**   Identify which control activity is violated in each of the following situations, and explain how the situation creates an opportunity for a fraud.

   1. The person with primary responsibility for reconciling the bank account is also the company's accountant and makes all bank deposits.

2. Wellstone Company's treasurer received an award for distinguished service because he had not taken a vacation in 30 years.

3. In order to save money on order slips, and to reduce time spent keeping track of order slips, a local bar/restaurant does not buy prenumbered order slips.

Action Plan

• Familiarize yourself with each of the control activities listed on page 328.

• Understand the nature of the frauds that each control activity is intended to address.

Solution

1. Violates the control activity of segregation of duties. Record-keeping should be separate from physical custody. As a consequence, the employee could embezzle cash and make journal entries to hide the theft.

2. Violates the control activity of human resource controls. Key employees, such as a treasurer, should be required to take vacations. The treasurer, who manages the company's cash, might embezzle cash and use his position to conceal the theft.

3. Violates the control activity of documentation procedures. If pre-numbered documents are not used, then it is virtually impossible to account for the documents. As a consequence, an employee could write up a dinner sale, receive the cash from the customer, and then throw away the order slip and keep the cash.

Cash Controls

Cash is the one asset that is readily convertible into any other type of asset. It also is easily concealed and transported, and is highly desired. Because of these characteristics, **cash is the asset most susceptible to fraudulent activities**. In addition, because of the large volume of cash transactions, numerous errors may occur in executing and recording them. To safeguard cash and to ensure the accuracy of the accounting records for cash, effective internal control over cash is critical.

CASH RECEIPTS CONTROLS

Illustration 7-4 (page 338) shows how the internal control principles explained earlier apply to cash receipts transactions. As you might expect, companies vary considerably in how they apply these principles. To illustrate internal control over cash receipts, we will examine control activities for a retail store with both over-the-counter and mail receipts.

study objective 3

Explain the applications of internal control principles to cash receipts.

Over-the-Counter Receipts

In retail businesses, control of over-the-counter receipts centers on cash registers that are visible to customers. A cash sale is rung-up on a cash register with the amount clearly visible to the customer. This activity prevents the cashier from ringing up a lower amount and pocketing the difference. The customer receives an itemized cash register receipt slip and is expected to count the change received. The cash register's tape is locked in the register until a supervisor removes it. This tape accumulates the daily transactions and totals.

At the end of the clerk's shift, the clerk counts the cash and sends the cash and the count to the cashier. The cashier counts the cash, prepares a deposit slip, and deposits the cash at the bank. The cashier also sends a duplicate of the deposit slip to the accounting department to indicate cash received. The supervisor removes the cash register tape and sends it to the accounting department as the basis for a journal entry to record the cash received. The tape is compared to the deposit slip for any discrepancies. Illustration 7-5 (page 339) summarizes this process.

Cash Receipts Controls

Establishment of Responsibility

Only designated personnel are authorized to handle cash receipts (cashiers)

Physical Controls

Store cash in safes and bank vaults; limit access to storage areas; use cash registers

Segregation of Duties

Different individuals receive cash, record cash receipts, and hold the cash

Independent Internal Verification

Supervisors count cash receipts daily; treasurer compares total receipts to bank deposits daily

Documentation Procedures

Use remittance advice (mail receipts), cash register tapes, and deposit slips

Human Resource Controls

Bond personnel who handle cash; require employees to take vacations; conduct background checks

Illustration 7-4
Application of internal control principles to cash receipts

This system for handling cash receipts uses an important internal control principle—segregation of record-keeping from physical custody. The supervisor has access to the cash register tape, but **not** to the cash. The clerk and the cashier have access to the cash, but **not** to the register tape. In addition, the cash register tape provides documentation and enables independent internal verification with the deposit slip. Use of these three principles of internal control (segregation of record-keeping from physical custody, documentation, and independent internal verification) provides an effective system of internal control. Any attempt at fraudulent activity should be detected unless there is collusion among the employees.

In some instances, the amount deposited at the bank will not agree with the cash recorded in the accounting records based on the cash register tape. These differences often result because the clerk hands incorrect change back to the retail customer. In this case, the difference between the actual cash and the amount reported on the cash register tape is reported in a Cash Over and Short account. For example, suppose that the cash register tape indicated sales of $6,956.20 but

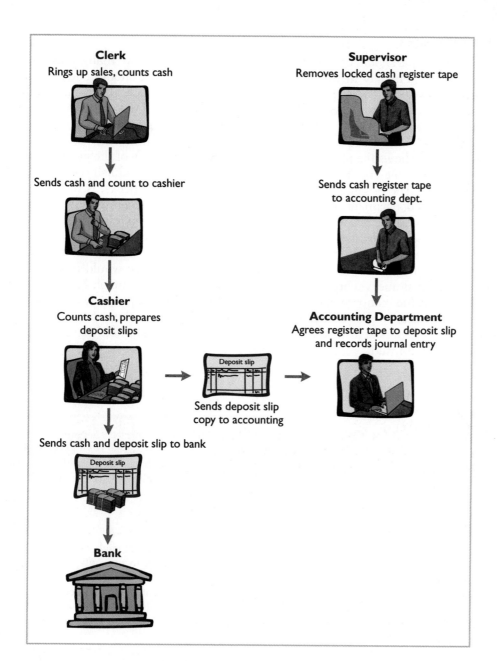

Illustration 7-5 Control of over-the-counter receipts

Helpful Hint Flowcharts such as this one enhance the understanding of the flow of documents, the processing steps, and the internal control procedures.

the amount of cash was only $6,946.10. A cash shortfall of $10.10 exists. To account for this cash shortfall and related cash, the company makes the following entry.

Cash	6,946.10	
Cash Over and Short	10.10	
Sales Revenue		6,956.20
(To record cash shortfall)		

A	=	L	+	SE
+6,946.10				
				−10.10
				+6,956.20

Cash Flows
+6,946.10

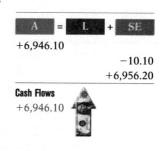

Cash Over and Short is an income statement item. It is reported as miscellaneous expense when there is a cash shortfall, and as miscellaneous revenue when there is an overage. Clearly, the amount should be small. Any material amounts in this account should be investigated.

Mail Receipts

All mail receipts should be opened in the presence of at least two mail clerks. These receipts are generally in the form of checks. A mail clerk should endorse each check "For Deposit Only." This restrictive endorsement reduces the likelihood that someone could divert the check to personal use. Banks will not give an individual cash when presented with a check that has this type of endorsement.

The mail-receipt clerks prepare, in triplicate, a list of the checks received each day. This list shows the name of the check issuer, the purpose of the payment, and the amount of the check. Each mail clerk signs the list to establish responsibility for the data. The original copy of the list, along with the checks, is then sent to the cashier's department. A copy of the list is sent to the accounting department for recording in the accounting records. The clerks also keep a copy.

This process provides excellent internal control for the company. By employing two clerks, the chance of fraud is reduced; each clerk knows he or she is being observed by the other clerk(s). To engage in fraud, they would have to collude. The customers who submit payments also provide control, because they will contact the company with a complaint if they are not properly credited for payment. Because the cashier has access to cash but not the records, and the accounting department has access to records but not cash, neither can engage in undetected fraud.

---

before you go on...

CONTROL OVER CASH RECEIPTS

Action Plan

- Differentiate among the internal control principles of (1) establishment of responsibility, (2) physical controls, and (3) independent internal verification.
- Design an effective system of internal control over cash receipts.

Do it! L. R. Cortez is concerned about the control over cash receipts in his fast-food restaurant, Big Cheese. The restaurant has two cash registers. At no time do more than two employees take customer orders and ring up sales. Work shifts for employees range from 4 to 8 hours. Cortez asks your help in installing a good system of internal control over cash receipts.

Solution

Cortez should assign a cash register to each employee at the start of each work shift, with register totals set at zero. Each employee should be instructed to use only the assigned register and to ring up all sales. Each customer should be given a receipt. At the end of the shift, the employee should do a cash count. A separate employee should compare the cash count with the register tape, to be sure they agree. In addition, Cortez should install an automated system that would enable the company to compare orders rung up on the register to orders processed by the kitchen.

CASH DISBURSEMENTS CONTROLS

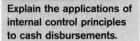

study objective **4**

Explain the applications of internal control principles to cash disbursements.

Companies disburse cash for a variety of reasons, such as to pay expenses and liabilities or to purchase assets. **Generally, internal control over cash disbursements is more effective when companies pay by check, rather than by cash.** One exception is **for incidental amounts that are paid out of petty cash.**[4]

Companies generally issue checks only after following specified control procedures. Illustration 7-6 shows how principles of internal control apply to cash disbursements.

---

[4]We explain the operation of a petty cash fund in the appendix to this chapter on pages 357–359.

Cash Disbursements Controls

Establishment of Responsibility

Only designated personnel are authorized to sign checks (treasurer) and approve vendors

Physical Controls

Store blank checks in safes, with limited access; print check amounts by machine in indelible ink

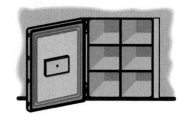

Segregation of Duties

Different individuals approve and make payments; check signers do not record disbursements

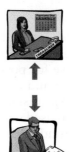
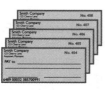

Independent Internal Verification

Compare checks to invoices; reconcile bank statement monthly

Documentation Procedures

Use prenumbered checks and account for them in sequence; each check must have an approved invoice; require employees to use corporate credit cards for reimbursable expenses; stamp invoices "paid."

Human Resource Controls

Bond personnel who handle cash; require employees to take vacations; conduct background checks

Illustration 7-6
Application of internal control principles to cash disbursements

Voucher System Controls

Most medium and large companies use vouchers as part of their internal control over cash disbursements. A **voucher system** is a network of approvals by authorized individuals, acting independently, to ensure that all disbursements by check are proper.

The system begins with the authorization to incur a cost or expense. It ends with the issuance of a check for the liability incurred. A **voucher** is an authorization form prepared for each expenditure in a voucher system. Companies require vouchers for all types of cash disbursements except those from petty cash.

The starting point in preparing a voucher is to fill in the appropriate information about the liability on the face of the voucher. The vendor's invoice provides most of the needed information. Then, an employee in accounts payable records the voucher (in a journal called a **voucher register**) and files it according to the date on which it is to be paid. The company issues and sends a check on that date, and stamps the voucher "paid." The paid voucher is sent to the accounting department for recording (in a journal called the **check register**). A voucher system involves two journal entries, one to issue the voucher and a second to pay the voucher.

The use of a voucher system improves internal control over cash disbursements. First, the authorization process inherent in a voucher system establishes responsibility. Each individual has responsibility to review the underlying documentation to ensure that it is correct. In addition, the voucher system keeps track of the documents that back up each transaction. By keeping these documents in one place, a supervisor can independently verify the authenticity of each transaction. Consider, for example, the case of Aesop University presented on page 330. Aesop did not use a voucher system for transactions under $2,500. As a consequence, there was no independent verification of the documents, which enabled the employee to submit fake invoices to hide his unauthorized purchases.

Petty Cash Fund

Ethics Note Internal control over a petty cash fund is strengthened by: (1) having a supervisor make surprise counts of the fund to confirm whether the paid vouchers and fund cash equal the imprest amount, and (2) canceling or mutilating the paid vouchers so they cannot be resubmitted for reimbursement.

As you learned earlier in the chapter, better internal control over cash disbursements is possible when companies make payments by check. However, using checks to pay such small amounts as those for postage due, employee working lunches, and taxi fares is both impractical and a nuisance. A common way of handling such payments, while maintaining satisfactory control, is to use a petty cash fund. A **petty cash fund** is a cash fund used to pay relatively small amounts. We explain the operation of a petty cash fund in the appendix at the end of this chapter.

Ethics Insight

A recent study by the Association of Certified Fraud Examiners found that two-thirds of all employee thefts involved a fraudulent disbursement by an employee. The most common form (28.3% of cases) was fraudulent billing schemes. In these, the employee causes the company to issue a payment to the employee by submitting a bill for nonexistent goods or services, purchases of personal goods by the employee, or inflated invoices. The following graph shows various types of fraudulent disbursements and the median loss from each.

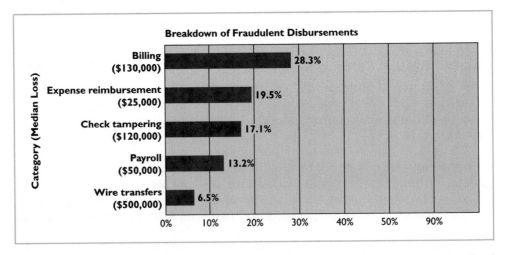

Source: 2006 Report to the Nation on Occupational Fraud and Abuse, Association of Certified Fraud Examiners, *www.acfe.com/documents/2006_rttn.pdf*, p. 14.

 How can companies reduce the likelihood of fraudulent disbursements?

Control Features: Use of a Bank

The use of a bank contributes significantly to good internal control over cash. A company can safeguard its cash by using a bank as a depository and clearinghouse for checks received and checks written. The use of a bank minimizes the amount of currency that must be kept on hand. It also facilitates control of cash because a double record is maintained of all bank transactions—one by the business and the other by the bank. The asset account Cash maintained by the company is the "flip-side" of the bank's liability account for that company. A bank reconciliation is the process of comparing the bank's balance with the company's balance, and explaining the differences to make them agree.

Many companies have more than one bank account. For efficiency of operations and better control, national retailers like Wal-Mart and Target often have regional bank accounts. Similarly, a company such as ExxonMobil with more than 100,000 employees may have a payroll bank account as well as one or more general bank accounts. In addition, a company may maintain several bank accounts in order to have more than one source for short-term loans.

BANK STATEMENTS

Each month, the company receives from the bank a bank statement showing its bank transactions and balances.[5] For example, the statement for Laird Company in Illustration 7-7 (on page 344) shows the following: (1) checks paid and other debits that reduce the balance in the depositor's account, (2) deposits and other credits that increase the balance in the depositor's account, and (3) the account balance after each day's transactions.

Remember that bank statements are prepared from the *bank's* perspective. For example, every deposit the bank receives is an increase in the bank's liabilities (an account payable to the depositor). Therefore, in Illustration 7-7, National Bank and Trust *credits* to Laird Company every deposit it received from Laird. The reverse occurs when the bank "pays" a check issued by Laird Company on its checking account balance: Payment reduces the bank's liability and is therefore *debited* to Laird's account with the bank.

The bank statement lists in numerical sequence all paid checks along with the date the check was paid and its amount. Upon paying a check, the bank stamps the check "paid"; a paid check is sometimes referred to as a **canceled** check. In addition, the bank includes with the bank statement memoranda explaining other debits and credits it made to the depositor's account.

A check that is not paid by a bank because of insufficient funds in a bank account is called an NSF check (not sufficient funds). The bank uses a debit memorandum when a previously deposited customer's check "bounces" because of insufficient funds. In such a case, the customer's bank marks the check NSF (not sufficient funds) and returns it to the depositor's bank. The bank then debits (decreases) the depositor's account, as shown by the symbol NSF in Illustration 7-7, and sends the NSF check and debit memorandum to the depositor as notification of the charge. The NSF check creates an account receivable for the depositor and reduces cash in the bank account.

Helpful Hint Essentially, the bank statement is a copy of the bank's records sent to the customer for periodic review.

---

[5]Our presentation assumes that a company makes all adjustments at the end of the month. In practice, a company may also make journal entries during the month as it receives information from the bank regarding its account.

Illustration 7-7 Bank statement

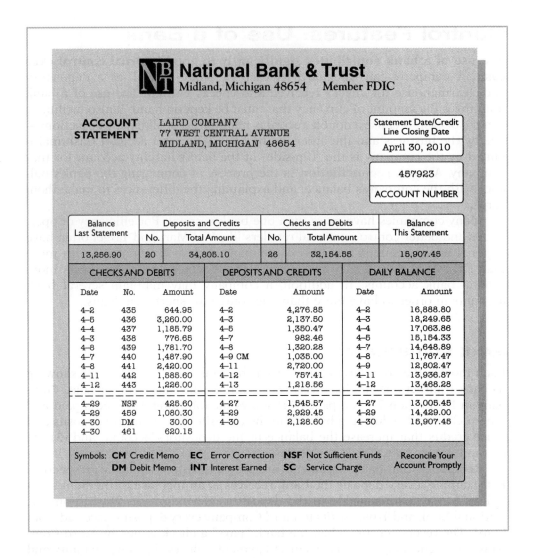

RECONCILING THE BANK ACCOUNT

study objective 5

Prepare a bank reconciliation.

Because the bank and the company maintain independent records of the company's checking account, you might assume that the respective balances will always agree. In fact, the two balances are seldom the same at any given time. Therefore it is necessary to make the balance per books agree with the balance per bank—a process called **reconciling the bank account**. The lack of agreement between the balances has two causes:

1. **Time lags** that prevent one of the parties from recording the transaction in the same period.

2. **Errors** by either party in recording transactions.

Time lags occur frequently. For example, several days may elapse between the time a company pays by check and the date the bank pays the check. Similarly, when a company uses the bank's night depository to make its deposits, there will be a difference of one day between the time the company records the receipts and the time the bank does so. A time lag also occurs whenever the bank mails a debit or credit memorandum to the company.

The incidence of errors depends on the effectiveness of the internal controls maintained by the company and the bank. Bank errors are infrequent. However, either party could accidentally record a $450 check as $45 or $540. In addition, the bank might mistakenly charge a check drawn by C. D. Berg to the account of C. D. Burg.

Reconciliation Procedure

In reconciling the bank account, it is customary to reconcile the balance per books and balance per bank to their adjusted (correct or true) cash balances. **To obtain maximum benefit from a bank reconciliation, an employee who has no other responsibilities related to cash should prepare the reconciliation.** When companies do not follow the internal control principle of independent internal verification in preparing the reconciliation, cash embezzlements may escape unnoticed. For example, in the Anatomy of a Fraud box at the top of page 331, a bank reconciliation by someone other than Angela Bauer might have exposed her embezzlement.

Illustration 7-8 shows the reconciliation process. The starting point in preparing the reconciliation is to enter the balance per bank statement and balance per books on a schedule. The following steps should reveal all the reconciling items that cause the difference between the two balances.

Helpful Hint Deposits in transit and outstanding checks are reconciling items because of time lags.

Illustration 7-8 Bank reconciliation adjustments

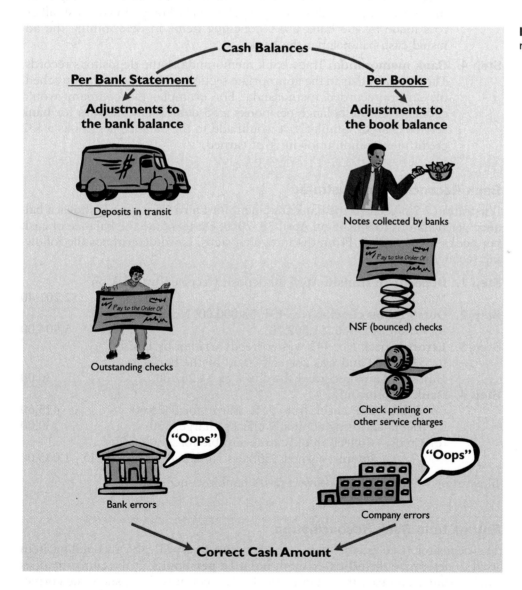

Step 1. Deposits in transit. Compare the individual deposits on the bank statement with the deposits in transit from the preceding bank reconciliation and with the deposits per company records or copies of duplicate deposit slips. Deposits recorded by the depositor that have not been

recorded by the bank represent **deposits in transit**. Add these deposits to the balance per bank.

Step 2. **Outstanding checks.** Compare the paid checks shown on the bank statement or the paid checks returned with the bank statement with (a) checks outstanding from the preceding bank reconciliation, and (b) checks issued by the company as recorded in the cash payments journal. Issued checks recorded by the company that have not been paid by the bank represent **outstanding checks**. Deduct outstanding checks from the balance per the bank.

Step 3. **Errors.** Note any errors discovered in the previous steps and list them in the appropriate section of the reconciliation schedule. For example, if the company mistakenly recorded as $159 a paid check correctly written for $195, the company would deduct the error of $36 from the balance per books. All errors made by the depositor are reconciling items in determining the adjusted cash balance per books. In contrast, all errors made by the bank are reconciling items in determining the adjusted cash balance per the bank.

Step 4. **Bank memoranda.** Trace bank memoranda to the depositor's records. The company lists in the appropriate section of the reconciliation schedule any unrecorded memoranda. For example, the company would deduct from the balance per books a $5 debit memorandum for bank service charges. Similarly, it would add to the balance per books a $32 credit memorandum for interest earned.

Bank Reconciliation Illustrated

Helpful Hint Note in the bank statement that the bank has paid checks No. 459 and 461, but check No. 460 is not listed. Thus, this check is outstanding. If a complete bank statement were provided, checks No. 453 and 457 also would not be listed. Laird obtains the amounts for these three checks from its cash payments records.

Illustration 7-7 presented the bank statement for Laird Company. It shows a balance per bank of $15,907.45 on April 30, 2010. On this date the balance of cash per books is $11,589.45. From the foregoing steps, Laird determines the following reconciling items.

Step 1. **Deposits in transit:** April 30 deposit (received by bank on May 1). $2,201.40

Step 2. **Outstanding checks:** No. 453, $3,000.00; No. 457, $1,401.30; No. 460, $1,502.70.   5,904.00

Step 3. **Errors:** Check No. 443 was correctly written by Laird for $1,226.00 and was correctly paid by the bank. However, Laird recorded the check as $1,262.00.   36.00

Step 4. **Bank memoranda:**
(a) Debit—NSF check from J. R. Baron for $425.60   425.60
(b) Debit—Printing company checks charge, $30   30.00
(c) Credit—Collection of note receivable for $1,000 plus interest earned $50, less bank collection fee $15   1,035.00

Illustration 7-9 (next page) shows Laird's bank reconciliation.

Entries from Bank Reconciliation

Helpful Hint These entries are adjusting entries. In prior chapters, we considered Cash an account that did not require adjustment because we had not yet explained a bank reconciliation.

The depositor (that is, the company) next must record each reconciling item used to determine the **adjusted cash balance per books**. If the company does not journalize and post these items, the Cash account will not show the correct balance. The adjusting entries for the Laird Company bank reconciliation on April 30 are as follows.

COLLECTION OF NOTE RECEIVABLE. This entry involves four accounts. Assuming that the interest of $50 has not been recorded and the collection fee is charged

LAIRD COMPANY
Bank Reconciliation
April 30, 2010

Cash balance per bank statement		$ 15,907.45
Add: Deposits in transit		2,201.40
		18,108.85
Less: Outstanding checks		
No. 453	$3,000.00	
No. 457	1,401.30	
No. 460	1,502.70	5,904.00
Adjusted cash balance per bank		**$12,204.85**
Cash balance per books		$ 11,589.45
Add: Collection of note receivable for $1,000 plus interest earned $50, less collection fee $15	$1,035.00	
Error in recording check No. 443	36.00	1,071.00
		12,660.45
Less: NSF check	425.60	
Bank service charge	30.00	455.60
Adjusted cash balance per books		**$12,204.85**

Illustration 7-9 Bank reconciliation

Alternative Terminology The terms *adjusted cash balance, true cash balance,* and *correct cash balance* are used interchangeably.

to Miscellaneous Expense, the entry is:

Apr. 30	Cash		1,035	
	Miscellaneous Expense		15	
	Notes Receivable			1,000
	Interest Revenue			50
	(To record collection of note receivable by bank)			

A = L + SE
+1,035
−15 Exp
−1,000
+50 Rev
Cash Flows
+1,035

BOOK ERROR. An examination of the cash disbursements journal shows that check No. 443 was a payment on account to Andrea Company, a supplier. The correcting entry is:

Apr. 30	Cash		36	
	Accounts Payable—Andrea Company			36
	(To correct error in recording check No. 443)			

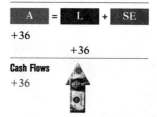

A = L + SE
+36
+36
Cash Flows
+36

NSF CHECK. As indicated earlier, an NSF check becomes an accounts receivable to the depositor. The entry is:

Apr. 30	Accounts Receivable—J. R. Baron		425.60	
	Cash			425.60
	(To record NSF check)			

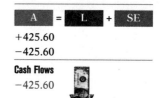

A = L + SE
+425.60
−425.60
Cash Flows
−425.60

BANK SERVICE CHARGES. Companies typically debit to Miscellaneous Expense the check printing charges (DM) and other bank service charges (SC) because

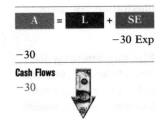

A = L + SE

−30 Exp

−30

Cash Flows
−30

they are usually small in amount. Laird's entry is:

Apr. 30	Miscellaneous Expense	30	
	Cash		30
	(To record charge for printing company checks)		

The foregoing entries could also be combined into one compound entry.

After Laird posts the entries, the Cash account will appear as in Illustration 7-10. The adjusted cash balance in the ledger should agree with the adjusted cash balance per books in the bank reconciliation in Illustration 7-9.

Illustration 7-10
Adjusted balance in cash account

Cash					
Apr. 30	Bal.	11,589.45	Apr. 30	425.60	
30		1,035.00	30	30.00	
30		36.00			
Apr. 30	Bal.	12,204.85			

What entries does the bank make? If the company discovers any bank errors in preparing the reconciliation, it should notify the bank so the bank can make the necessary corrections on its records. The bank does not make any entries for deposits in transit or outstanding checks. Only when these items reach the bank will the bank record these items.

Electronic Funds Transfer (EFT) System

It is not surprising that companies and banks have developed approaches to transfer funds among parties without the use of paper (deposit tickets, checks, etc.). Such procedures, called **electronic funds transfers (EFTs)**, are disbursement systems that use wire, telephone, or computers to transfer cash balances from one location to another. Use of EFT is quite common. For example, many employees receive no formal payroll checks from their employers. Instead, employers send electronic payroll data to the appropriate banks. Also, individuals now frequently make regular payments such as those for house, car, and utilities by EFT.

EFT transfers normally result in better internal control since no cash or checks are handled by company employees. This does not mean that opportunities for fraud are eliminated. In fact, the same basic principles related to internal control apply to EFT transfers. For example, without proper segregation of duties and authorizations, an employee might be able to redirect electronic payments into a personal bank account and conceal the theft with fraudulent accounting entries.

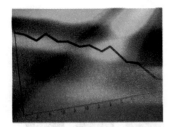

Investor Insight

Poor internal controls can cost a company money even if no theft occurs. For example, Eastman Kodak Co., SunTrust Banks Inc., and Toys "R" Us Inc. all recently reported material weaknesses in internal controls. When a company announces that it has deficiencies in its internal controls, its stock price often falls.

Under the Sarbanes-Oxley Act companies must evaluate their internal controls systems and report on any deficiencies. Some analysts estimate that as many as 10% of all publicly traded companies will report weaknesses in their internal controls. The estimate for smaller companies is even higher.

Source: William M. Bulkeley and Robert Tomsho, "Kodak to Get Auditors Adverse View," *Wall Street Journal Online* (January 27, 2005).

 Why would a company's stock price fall if it reports deficiencies in its internal controls?

Do it! Sally Kist owns Linen Kist Fabrics. Sally asks you to explain how she should treat the following reconciling items when reconciling the company's bank account: (1) a debit memorandum for an NSF check, (2) a credit memorandum for a note collected by the bank, (3) outstanding checks, and (4) a deposit in transit.

Solution

Sally should treat the reconciling items as follows.

(1) NSF check: Deduct from balance per books.
(2) Collection of note: Add to balance per books.
(3) Outstanding checks: Deduct from balance per bank.
(4) Deposit in transit: Add to balance per bank.

BANK RECONCILIATION

Action Plan

• Understand the purpose of a bank reconciliation.

• Identify time lags and explain how they cause reconciling items.

 the navigator

Reporting Cash

Cash consists of coins, currency (paper money), check, money orders, and money on hand or on deposit in a bank or similar depository. Companies report cash in two different statements: the balance sheet and the statement of cash flows. The balance sheet reports the amount of cash available at a given point in time. The statement of cash flows shows the sources and uses of cash during a period of time. The cash flow statement was introduced in Chapters 1 and 2 and will be discussed in much detail in Chapter 12. In this section we discuss some important points regarding the presentation of cash in the balance sheet.

When presented in a balance sheet, cash on hand, cash in banks, and petty cash are often combined and reported simply as **Cash**. Because it is the most liquid asset owned by the company, cash is listed first in the current assets section of the balance sheet.

study objective 6

Explain the reporting of cash.

CASH EQUIVALENTS

Many companies use the designation "Cash and cash equivalents" in reporting cash. (See Illustration 7-11 for an example.) Cash equivalents are short-term, highly liquid investments that are both:

1. Readily convertible to known amounts of cash, and

2. So near their maturity that their market value is relatively insensitive to changes in interest rates.

DELTA AIR LINES, INC.
Balance Sheet (partial)
December 31, 2007
(in millions)

Assets	
Current assets	
Cash and cash equivalents	$2,648
Short-term investments	138
Restricted cash	520
Accounts receivable, net	1,066
Parts inventories	262
Prepaid expenses and other	606
Total current assets	$5,240

Illustration 7-11 Balance sheet presentation of cash

Examples of cash equivalents are Treasury bills, commercial paper (short-term corporate notes), and money market funds. All typically are purchased with cash that is in excess of immediate needs.

Occasionally a company will have a net negative balance in its bank account. In this case, the company should report the negative balance among current liabilities. For example, farm equipment manufacturer Ag-Chem recently reported "Checks outstanding in excess of cash balances" of $2,145,000 among its current liabilities.

RESTRICTED CASH

A company may have restricted cash, cash that is not available for general use but rather is restricted for a special purpose. For example, landfill companies are often required to maintain a fund of restricted cash to ensure they will have adequate resources to cover closing and clean-up costs at the end of a landfill site's useful life. McKessor Corp. recently reported restricted cash of $962 million to be paid out as the result of investor lawsuits.

Cash restricted in use should be reported separately on the balance sheet as restricted cash. If the company expects to use the restricted cash within the next year, it reports the amount as a current asset. When this is not the case, it reports the restricted funds as a noncurrent asset.

Illustration 7-11 shows restricted cash reported in the financial statements of Delta Air Lines. The company is required to maintain restricted cash as collateral to support insurance obligations related to workers' compensation claims. Delta does not have access to these funds for general use, and so it must report them separately, rather than as part of cash and cash equivalents.

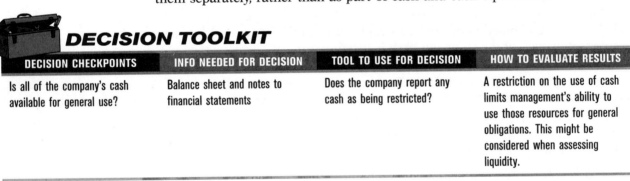

DECISION TOOLKIT

DECISION CHECKPOINTS	INFO NEEDED FOR DECISION	TOOL TO USE FOR DECISION	HOW TO EVALUATE RESULTS
Is all of the company's cash available for general use?	Balance sheet and notes to financial statements	Does the company report any cash as being restricted?	A restriction on the use of cash limits management's ability to use those resources for general obligations. This might be considered when assessing liquidity.

Managing and Monitoring Cash

Many companies struggle, not because they fail to generate sales, but because they can't manage their cash. A real-life example of this is a clothing manufacturing company owned by Sharon McCollick. McCollick gave up a stable, high-paying marketing job with Intel Corporation to start her own company. Soon she had more orders from stores such as JC Penney and Dayton Hudson (now Target) than she could fill. Yet she found herself on the brink of financial disaster, owing three mortgage payments on her house and $2,000 to the IRS. Her company could generate sales, but it was not collecting cash fast enough to support its operations. The bottom line is that a business must have cash.[6]

A merchandising company's operating cycle is generally shorter than that of a manufacturing company. Illustration 7-12 shows the cash to cash operating cycle of a merchandising operation.

---

[6]Adapted from T. Petzinger, Jr., "The Front Lines—Sharon McCollick Got Mad and Tore Down a Bank's Barriers," *Wall Street Journal* (May 19, 1995), p. B1.

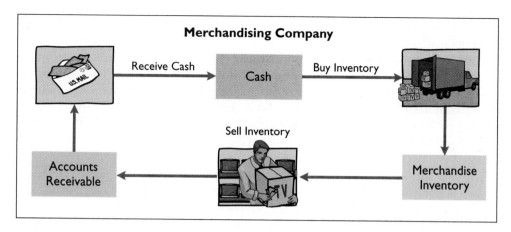

Illustration 7-12
Operating cycle of a
merchandising company

To understand cash management, consider the operating cycle of Sharon McCollick's clothing manufacturing company. First, it purchases cloth. Let's assume that it purchases the cloth on credit provided by the supplier, so the company owes its supplier money. Next, employees convert the cloth to clothing. Now the company also owes its employees money. Next, it sells the clothing to retailers, on credit. McCollick's company will have no money to repay suppliers or employees until it receives payments from customers. In a manufacturing operation there may be a significant lag between the original purchase of raw materials and the ultimate receipt of cash from customers.

Managing the often-precarious balance created by the ebb and flow of cash during the operating cycle is one of a company's greatest challenges. The objective is to ensure that a company has sufficient cash to meet payments as they come due, yet minimize the amount of non-revenue-generating cash on hand.

BASIC PRINCIPLES OF CASH MANAGEMENT

Management of cash is the responsibility of the company treasurer. Any company can improve its chances of having adequate cash by following five basic principles of cash management.

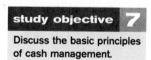

study objective 7

Discuss the basic principles of cash management.

1. **Increase the speed of receivables collection.** Money owed Sharon McCollick by her customers is money that she can't use. The more quickly customers pay her, the more quickly she can use those funds. Thus, rather than have an average collection period of 30 days, she may want an average collection period of 15 days. However, she must carefully weigh any attempt to force her customers to pay earlier against the possibility that she may anger or alienate customers. Perhaps her competitors are willing to provide a 30-day grace period. As noted in Chapter 5, one common way to encourage customers to pay more quickly is to offer cash discounts for early payment under such terms as 2/10, n/30.

2. **Keep inventory levels low.** Maintaining a large inventory of cloth and finished clothing is costly. It ties up large amounts of cash, as well as warehouse space. Increasingly, companies are using techniques to reduce the inventory on hand, thus conserving their cash. Of course, if Sharon McCollick has inadequate inventory, she will lose sales. The proper level of inventory is an important decision.

3. **Delay payment of liabilities.** By keeping track of when her bills are due, Sharon McCollick's company can avoid paying bills too early. Let's say her supplier allows 30 days for payment. If she pays in 10 days, she has lost the use of that cash for 20 days. Therefore, she should use the full payment period. But she should not "stretch" payment past the point that could damage her credit rating (and future borrowing ability). Sharon McCollick's

company also should conserve cash by taking cash discounts offered by suppliers, when possible.

4. **Plan the timing of major expenditures.** To maintain operations or to grow, all companies must make major expenditures, which normally require some form of outside financing. In order to increase the likelihood of obtaining outside financing, McCollick should carefully consider the timing of major expenditures in light of her company's operating cycle. If at all possible, she should make any major expenditure when the company normally has excess cash—usually during the off-season.

5. **Invest idle cash.** Cash on hand earns nothing. An important part of the treasurer's job is to ensure that the company invests any excess cash, even if it is only overnight. Many businesses, such as Sharon McCollick's clothing company, are seasonal. During her slow season, when she has excess cash, she should invest it.

To avoid a cash crisis, however, it is very important that investments of idle cash be highly liquid and risk-free. A *liquid investment* is one with a market in which someone is always willing to buy or sell the investment. A *risk-free investment* means there is no concern that the party will default on its promise to pay its principal and interest. For example, using excess cash to purchase stock in a small company because you heard that it was probably going to increase in value in the near term is totally inappropriate. First, the stock of small companies is often illiquid. Second, if the stock suddenly decreases in value, you might be forced to sell the stock at a loss in order to pay your bills as they come due. The most common form of liquid investments is interest-paying U.S. government securities.

Illustration 7-13 summarizes these five principles of cash management.

International Note International sales complicate cash management. For example, if Nike must repay a Japanese supplier 30 days from today in Japanese yen, Nike will be concerned about how the exchange rate of U.S. dollars for yen might change during those 30 days. Often corporate treasurers make investments known as *hedges* to lock in an exchange rate to reduce the company's exposure to exchange-rate fluctuation.

Illustration 7-13 Five principles of sound cash management

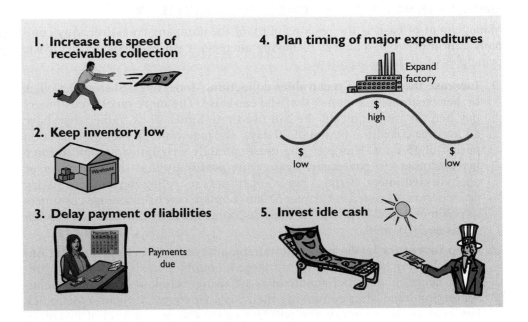

1. **Increase the speed of receivables collection**

2. **Keep inventory low**

3. **Delay payment of liabilities**
   Payments due

4. **Plan timing of major expenditures**
   Expand factory
   $ high
   $ low $ low

5. **Invest idle cash**

KEEPING AN EYE ON CASH

Because cash is so vital to a company, **planning the company's cash needs** is a key business activity. It enables the company to plan ahead to cover possible cash shortfalls and to make investments of idle funds. The cash budget shows anticipated cash flows, usually over a one- to two-year period. In this section we introduce the basics of cash budgeting. More advanced discussion of cash budgets and budgets in general is provided in managerial accounting texts.

study objective **8**

Identify the primary elements of a cash budget.

As shown below, the cash budget contains three sections—cash receipts, cash disbursements, and financing—and the beginning and ending cash balances.

ANY COMPANY Cash Budget	
Beginning cash balance	$X,XXX
Add: **Cash receipts** (itemized)	X,XXX
Total available cash	X,XXX
Less: **Cash disbursements** (itemized)	X,XXX
Excess (deficiency) of available cash over cash disbursements	X,XXX
Financing needed	X,XXX
Ending cash balance	$X,XXX

The **Cash receipts** section includes expected receipts from the company's principal source(s) of cash, such as cash sales and collections from customers on credit sales. This section also shows anticipated receipts of interest and dividends, and proceeds from planned sales of investments, plant assets, and the company's capital stock.

The **Cash disbursements** section shows expected payments for inventory, labor, overhead, and selling and administrative expenses. This section also includes projected payments for income taxes, dividends, investments, and plant assets.

The **Financing** section shows expected borrowings and the repayment of the borrowed funds plus interest. The financing entry is needed when there is a cash deficiency or when the cash balance is less than management's minimum required balance.

Companies must prepare the data in the cash budget in sequence because the ending cash balance of one period becomes the beginning cash balance for the next period. They obtain data for preparing the cash budget from other budgets and from information provided by management. In practice, companies often prepare cash budgets for the next 12 months on a monthly basis.

To minimize detail, we will assume that Hayes Company prepares an annual cash budget by quarters. Preparing a cash budget requires making some assumptions. For example, Hayes makes assumptions regarding collection of accounts receivable, sales of securities, payments for materials and salaries, and purchases of property, plant, and equipment. The accuracy of the cash budget is very dependent on the accuracy of these assumptions.

On the next page, we present the cash budget for Hayes Company. The budget indicates that the company will need $3,000 of financing in the second quarter to maintain a minimum cash balance of $15,000. Since there is an excess of available cash over disbursements of $22,500 at the end of the third quarter, Hayes will repay the borrowing, plus $100 interest, in that quarter.

A cash budget contributes to more effective cash management. For example, it can show when a company will need additional financing, well before the actual need arises. Conversely, it can indicate when the company will have excess cash available for investments or other purposes.

HAYES COMPANY
Cash Budget
For the Year Ending December 31, 2010

	Quarter			
	1	**2**	**3**	**4**
Beginning cash balance	$ 38,000	$ 25,500	$ 15,000	$ 19,400
Add: **Cash receipts**				
Collections from customers	168,000	198,000	228,000	258,000
Sale of securities	2,000	0	0	0
Total receipts	170,000	198,000	228,000	258,000
Total available cash	208,000	223,500	243,000	277,400
Less: **Cash disbursements**				
Inventory	23,200	27,200	31,200	35,200
Salaries	62,000	72,000	82,000	92,000
Selling and administrative expenses (excluding depreciation)	94,300	99,300	104,300	109,300
Purchase of truck	0	10,000	0	0
Income tax expense	3,000	3,000	3,000	3,000
Total disbursements	182,500	211,500	220,500	239,500
Excess (deficiency) of available cash over disbursements	25,500	12,000	22,500	37,900
Financing				
Borrowings	0	3,000	0	0
Repayments—plus $100 interest	0	0	3,100	0
Ending cash balance	$ 25,500	$ 15,000	$ 19,400	$ 37,900

DECISION TOOLKIT

DECISION CHECKPOINTS	INFO NEEDED FOR DECISION	TOOL TO USE FOR DECISION	HOW TO EVALUATE RESULTS
Will the company be able to meet its projected cash needs?	Cash budget (typically available only to management)	The cash budget shows projected sources and uses of cash. If cash uses exceed internal cash sources, then the company must look for outside sources.	Two issues: (1) Are management's projections reasonable? (2) If outside sources are needed, are they available?

before you go on...

CASH BUDGET   **Do it!**   Martian Company's management wants to maintain a minimum monthly cash balance of $15,000. At the beginning of March the cash balance is $16,500; expected cash receipts for March are $210,000; and cash disbursements are expected to be $220,000. How much cash, if any, must Martian borrow to maintain the desired minimum monthly balance?

Solution

Beginning cash balance	$ 16,500
Add: Cash receipts for March	210,000
Total available cash	226,500
Less: Cash disbursements for March	220,000
Excess of available cash over cash disbursements	6,500
Financing	**8,500**
Ending cash balance	$ 15,000

To maintain the desired minimum cash balance of $15,000, Martian Company must borrow $8,500 of cash.

Action Plan

• Add the beginning cash balance to receipts to determine total available cash.

• Subtract disbursements to determine excess or deficiency.

• Compare excess or deficiency with desired minimum cash to determine borrowing needs.

USING THE DECISION TOOLKIT

Presented below is hypothetical financial information for Mattel Corporation. Included in this information is financial statement data from the year ended December 31, 2009, which should be used to evaluate Mattel's cash position.

Selected Financial Information
Year Ended December 31, 2009
(in millions)

Net cash provided by operations	$325
Capital expenditures	162
Dividends paid	80
Total expenses	680
Depreciation expense	40
Cash balance	206

Also provided are projected data which are management's best estimate of its sources and uses of cash during 2010. This information should be used to prepare a cash budget for 2010.

Projected Sources and Uses of Cash
(in millions)

Beginning cash balance	$206
Cash receipts from sales of product	355
Cash receipts from sale of short-term investments	20
Cash payments for inventory	357
Cash payments for selling and administrative expense	201
Cash payments for property, plant, and equipment	45
Cash payments for taxes	17

Mattel Corporation's management believes it should maintain a balance of $200 million cash.

Instructions

(a) Using the hypothetical projected sources and uses of cash information presented above, prepare a cash budget for 2010 for Mattel Corporation.

(b) Comment on the company's cash adequacy, and discuss steps that might be taken to improve its cash position.

Solution

(a)

MATTEL CORPORATION
Cash Budget
For the Year 2010
(in millions)

Beginning cash balance		$206
Add: Cash receipts		
From sales of product	$355	
From sale of short-term investments	20	375
Total available cash		581
Less: Cash disbursements		
Payments for inventory	357	
Payments for selling and administrative costs	201	
Payments for property, plant, and equipment	45	
Payments for taxes	17	
Total disbursements		620
Excess (deficiency) of available cash over disbursements		(39)
Financing needed		**239**
Ending cash balance		$200

(b) Using these hypothetical data, Mattel's cash position appears adequate. For 2010 Mattel is projecting a cash shortfall. This is not necessarily of concern, but it should be investigated. Given that its primary line of business is toys, and that most toys are sold during December, we would expect Mattel's cash position to vary significantly during the course of the year. After the holiday season it probably has a lot of excess cash. Earlier in the year, when it is making and selling its product but has not yet been paid, it may need to borrow to meet any temporary cash shortfalls.

   If Mattel's management is concerned with its cash position, it could take the following steps: (1) Offer its customers cash discounts for early payment, such as 2/10, n/30. (2) Implement inventory management techniques to reduce the need for large inventories of such things as the plastics used to make its toys. (3) Carefully time payments to suppliers by keeping track of when payments are due, so as not to pay too early. (4) If it has plans for major expenditures, time those expenditures to coincide with its seasonal period of excess cash.

Summary of Study Objectives

1 **Define fraud and internal control.** A fraud is a dishonest act by an employee that results in personal benefit to the employee at a cost to the employer. The fraud triangle refers to the three factors that contribute to fraudulent activity by employees: opportunity, financial pressure, and rationalization. Internal control consists of all the related methods and measures adopted within an organization to safeguard its assets, enhance the reliability of its accounting records, increase efficiency of operations, and ensure compliance with laws and regulations.

2 **Identify the principles of internal control activities.** The principles of internal control are: establishment of responsibility; segregation of duties; documentation procedures; physical controls; independent internal verification; and human resource controls.

3 **Explain the applications of internal control principles to cash receipts.** Internal controls over cash receipts include: (a) designating only personnel such as cashiers to handle cash; (b) assigning the duties of receiving cash, recording cash, and having custody of cash to different individuals; (c) obtaining remittance advices for mail receipts, cash register tapes for over-the-counter receipts, and deposit slips for bank deposits; (d) using company safes and bank vaults to store cash with access limited to authorized personnel, and using cash registers in executing over-the-counter receipts; (e) making independent daily counts of register receipts and daily comparisons of total receipts with total deposits; and (f) bonding personnel who handle cash and requiring them to take vacations.

4 **Explain the applications of internal control to cash disbursements.** Internal controls over cash disbursements include: (a) having only specified individuals such as the treasurer authorized to sign checks; (b) assigning the duties of approving items for payment, paying the items, and recording the payment to different individuals; (c) using prenumbered checks and accounting for all checks, with each check supported by an approved invoice; after payment, stamping each approved invoice "paid"; (d) storing blank checks in a safe or vault with access restricted to authorized personnel, and using a machine with indelible ink to imprint amounts on checks; (e) comparing each check with the approved invoice before issuing the check, and making monthly reconciliations of bank and book balances; and (f) bonding personnel who handle cash, requiring employees to take vacations, and conducting background checks.

5 **Prepare a bank reconciliation.** In reconciling the bank account, it is customary to reconcile the balance per books and the balance per bank to their adjusted balance. The steps reconciling the cash account are to determine deposits in transit, outstanding checks, errors by the depositor or the bank, and unrecorded bank memoranda.

6 **Explain the reporting of cash.** Cash is listed first in the current assets section of the balance sheet. Companies often report cash together with cash equivalents. Cash restricted for a special purpose is reported separately as a current asset or as a noncurrent asset, depending on when the company expects to use the cash.

7 **Discuss the basic principles of cash management.** The basic principles of cash management include: (a) increase the speed of receivables collection, (b) keep inventory levels low, (c) delay payment of liabilities, (d) plan timing of major expenditures, and (e) invest idle cash.

8 **Identify the primary elements of a cash budget.** The three main elements of a cash budget are the cash receipts section, cash disbursements section, and financing section.

✔ the navigator

DECISION TOOLKIT A SUMMARY

DECISION CHECKPOINTS	INFO NEEDED FOR DECISION	TOOL TO USE FOR DECISION	HOW TO EVALUATE RESULTS
Are the company's financial statements supported by adequate internal controls?	Auditor's report, management discussion and analysis, articles in financial press	The principles of internal control activities are (1) establishment of responsibility, (2) segregation of duties, (3) documentation procedures, (4) physical controls, (5) independent internal verification, and (6) human resource controls.	If any indication is given that these or other controls are lacking, use the financial statements with caution.
Is all of the company's cash available for general use?	Balance sheet and notes to financial statements	Does the company report any cash as being restricted?	A restriction on the use of cash limits management's ability to use those resources for general obligations. This might be considered when assessing liquidity.
Will the company be able to meet its projected cash needs?	Cash budget (typically available only to management)	The cash budget shows projected sources and uses of cash. If cash uses exceed internal cash sources, then the company must look for outside sources.	Two issues: (1) Are management's projections reasonable? (2) If outside sources are needed, are they available?

appendix

Operation of the Petty Cash Fund

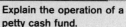

study objective **9**

Explain the operation of a petty cash fund.

The operation of a petty cash fund involves (1) establishing the fund, (2) making payments from the fund, and (3) replenishing the fund.

ESTABLISHING THE PETTY CASH FUND

Two essential steps in establishing a petty cash fund are: (1) appointing a petty cash custodian who will be responsible for the fund, and (2) determining the size of the fund. Ordinarily, a company expects the amount in the fund to cover anticipated disbursements for a three- to four-week period.

When the company establishes the petty cash fund, it issues a check payable to the petty cash custodian for the stipulated amount. If Laird Company decides to establish a $100 fund on March 1, the entry in general journal form is:

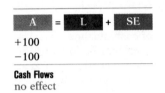

Cash Flows
no effect

Mar.	1	Petty Cash	100	
		Cash		100
		(To establish a petty cash fund)		

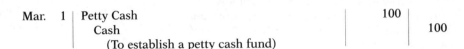

Ethics Note Petty cash funds are authorized and legitimate. In contrast, "slush" funds are unauthorized and hidden (under the table).

The fund custodian cashes the check and places the proceeds in a locked petty cash box or drawer. Most petty cash funds are established on a fixed-amount basis. Moreover, the company will make no additional entries to the Petty Cash account unless the stipulated amount of the fund is changed. For example, if Laird Company decides on July 1 to increase the size of the fund to $250, it would debit Petty Cash $150 and credit Cash $150.

MAKING PAYMENTS FROM PETTY CASH

The custodian of the petty cash fund has the authority to make payments from the fund that conform to prescribed management policies. Usually management limits the size of expenditures that come from petty cash and does not permit use of the fund for certain types of transactions (such as making short-term loans to employees).

Helpful Hint From the standpoint of internal control, the receipt satisfies two principles: (1) establishing responsibility (signature of custodian), and (2) documentation procedures.

Each payment from the fund must be documented on a prenumbered petty cash receipt (or petty cash voucher). The signatures of both the custodian and the individual receiving payment are required on the receipt. If other supporting documents such as a freight bill or invoice are available, they should be attached to the petty cash receipt.

The custodian keeps the receipts in the petty cash box until the fund is replenished. As a result, the sum of the petty cash receipts and money in the fund should equal the established total at all times. This means that management can make surprise counts at any time by an independent person, such as an internal auditor, to determine the correctness of the fund.

The company does not make an accounting entry to record a payment at the time it is taken from petty cash. It is considered both inexpedient and unnecessary to do so. Instead, the company recognizes the accounting effects of each payment when the fund is replenished.

REPLENISHING THE PETTY CASH FUND

When the money in the petty cash fund reaches a minimum level, the company replenishes the fund. The petty cash custodian initiates a request for reimbursement. This individual prepares a schedule (or summary) of the payments that have been made and sends the schedule, supported by petty cash receipts and other documentation, to the treasurer's office. The receipts and supporting documents are examined in the treasurer's office to verify that they were proper payments from the fund. The treasurer then approves the request, and a check is prepared to restore the fund to its established amount. At the same time, all supporting documentation is stamped "paid" so that it cannot be submitted again for payment.

Helpful Hint Replenishing involves three internal control procedures: segregation of duties, documentation procedures, and independent internal verification.

To illustrate, assume that on March 15 the petty cash custodian requests a check for $87. The fund contains $13 cash and petty cash receipts for postage

$44, supplies $38, and miscellaneous expenses $5. The entry, in general journal form, to record the check is:

Mar. 15	Postage Expense	44	
	Supplies	38	
	Miscellaneous Expense	5	
	Cash		87
	(To replenish petty cash fund)		

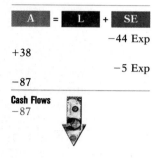

Note that the reimbursement entry does not affect the Petty Cash account. Replenishment changes the composition of the fund by replacing the petty cash receipts with cash, but it does not change the balance in the fund.

Occasionally, in replenishing a petty cash fund the company may need to recognize a cash shortage or overage. To illustrate, assume in the preceding example that the custodian had only $12 in cash in the fund plus the receipts as listed. The request for reimbursement would therefore be for $88, and the following entry would be made.

Mar. 15	Postage Expense	44	
	Supplies	38	
	Miscellaneous Expense	5	
	Cash Over and Short	1	
	Cash		88
	(To replenish petty cash fund)		

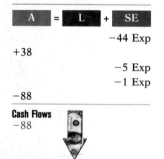

Conversely, if the custodian had $14 in cash, the reimbursement request would be for $86, and Cash Over and Short would be credited for $1. A debit balance in Cash Over and Short is reported in the income statement as miscellaneous expense; a credit balance is reported as miscellaneous revenue. The company closes Cash Over and Short to Income Summary at the end of the year.

Companies should replenish a petty cash fund **at the end of the accounting period, regardless of the cash in the fund**. Replenishment at this time is necessary in order to recognize the effects of the petty cash payments on the financial statements.

Internal control over a petty cash fund is strengthened by (1) having a supervisor make surprise counts of the fund to ascertain whether the paid vouchers and fund cash equal the designated amount, and (2) canceling or mutilating the paid vouchers so they cannot be resubmitted for reimbursement.

Summary of Study Objective for Appendix

9 **Explain the operation of a petty cash fund.** In operating a petty cash fund, a company establishes the fund by appointing a custodian and determining the size of the fund. The custodian makes payments from the fund for documented expenditures. The company replenishes the fund as needed, and at the end of each accounting period. Accounting entries to record payments are made each time the fund is replenished.

Glossary

Bank reconciliation (p. 343) The process of comparing the bank's account balance with the company's balance, and explaining the differences to make them agree.

Bank statement (p. 343) A statement received monthly from the bank that shows the depositor's bank transactions and balances.

Bonding (p. 334) Obtaining insurance protection against theft by employees.

Cash (p. 349) Resources that consist of coins, currency, checks, money orders, and money on hand or on deposit in a bank or similar depository.

Cash budget (p. 352) A projection of anticipated cash flows, usually over a one- to two-year period.

Cash equivalents (p. 349) Short-term, highly liquid investments that can be converted to a specific amount of cash.

Deposits in transit (p. 346) Deposits recorded by the depositor that have not been recorded by the bank.

Electronic funds transfer (EFT) (p. 348) A disbursement system that uses wire, telephone, or computer to transfer cash from one location to another.

Fraud *(p. 326)* A dishonest act by an employee that results in personal benefit to the employee at a cost to the employer.

Fraud triangle *(p. 326)* The three factors that contribute to fraudulent activity by employees: opportunity, financial pressure, and rationalization.

Internal auditors *(p. 334)* Company employees who continuously evaluate the effectiveness of the company's internal control systems.

Internal control *(p. 327)* All the related methods and measures adopted within an organization to safeguard its assets and enhance the reliability of its accounting records, increase efficiency of operation, and ensure compliance with laws and regulations.

NSF check *(p. 343)* A check that is not paid by a bank because of insufficient funds in a bank account.

Outstanding checks *(p. 346)* Checks issued and recorded by a company that have not been paid by the bank.

Petty cash fund *(p. 342)* A cash fund used to pay relatively small amounts.

Restricted cash *(p. 350)* Cash that is not available for general use, but instead is restricted for a particular purpose.

Sarbanes-Oxley Act of 2002 (SOX) *(p. 327)* Law that requires companies to maintain adequate systems of internal control.

Treasurer *(p. 351)* Employee responsible for the management of a company's cash.

Voucher *(p. 341)* An authorization form prepared for each expenditure in a voucher system.

Voucher system *(p. 341)* A network of approvals by authorized individuals acting independently to ensure that all disbursements by check are proper.

Comprehensive *Do it!*

Trillo Company's bank statement for May 2010 shows these data.

Balance May 1	$12,650	Balance May 31	$14,280
Debit memorandum:		Credit memorandum:	
NSF check	175	Collection of note receivable	505

The cash balance per books at May 31 is $13,319. Your review of the data reveals the following.

1. The NSF check was from Hup Co., a customer.
2. The note collected by the bank was a $500, 3-month, 12% note. The bank charged a $10 collection fee. No interest has been previously accrued.
3. Outstanding checks at May 31 total $2,410.
4. Deposits in transit at May 31 total $1,752.
5. A Trillo Company check for $352 dated May 10 cleared the bank on May 25. This check, which was a payment on account, was journalized for $325.

Instructions

(a) Prepare a bank reconciliation at May 31.
(b) Journalize the entries required by the reconciliation.

Action Plan

• Follow the four steps used in reconciling items (p. 345–346).

• Work carefully to minimize mathematical errors in the reconciliation.

• Prepare entries based on reconciling items per books.

• Make sure the cash ledger balance after posting the reconciling entries agrees with the adjusted cash balance per books.

Solution to Comprehensive *Do it!*

(a)

Cash balance per bank statement		$14,280
Add: Deposits in transit		1,752
		16,032
Less: Outstanding checks		2,410
Adjusted cash balance per bank		$13,622
Cash balance per books		$13,319
Add: Collection of note receivable $500,		
plus $15 interest less collection fee $10		505
		13,824
Less: NSF check	$175	
Error in recording check	27	202
Adjusted cash balance per books		$13,622

(b)

May 31	Cash		505	
	Miscellaneous Expense		10	
	Notes Receivable			500
	Interest Revenue			15
	(To record collection of note by bank)			
31	Accounts Receivable—Hup Co.		175	
	Cash			175
	(To record NSF check from Hup Co.)			
31	Accounts Payable		27	
	Cash			27
	(To correct error in recording check)			

Note: All Questions, Exercises, and Problems marked with an asterisk relate to material in the appendix to the chapter.

Self-Study Questions

Answers are at the end of the chapter.

(SO 1)   **1.** Which of the following is *not* an element of the fraud triangle?
(a) Rationalization.
(b) Financial pressure.
(c) Segregation of duties.
(d) Opportunity.

(SO 1)   **2.** Internal control is used in a business to enhance the accuracy and reliability of its accounting records and to:
(a) safeguard its assets.
(b) create fraud.
(c) analyze financial statements.
(d) determine employee bonuses.

(SO 2)   **3.**  The principles of internal control do *not* include:
(a) establishment of responsibility.
(b) documentation procedures.
(c) financial performance measures.
(d) independent internal verification.

(SO 2)   **4.** Physical controls do *not* include:
(a) safes and vaults to store cash.
(b) independent bank reconciliations.
(c) locked warehouses for inventories.
(d) bank safety deposit boxes for important papers.

(SO 1)   **5.** Which of the following was *not* a result of the Sarbanes-Oxley Act?
(a) Companies must file financial statements with the Internal Revenue Service.
(b) All publicly traded companies must maintain adequate internal controls.
(c) The Public Company Accounting Oversight Board was created to establish auditing standards and regulate auditor activity.
(d) Corporate executives and board of directors must ensure that controls are reliable and effective, and they can be fined or imprisoned for failure to do so.

(SO 3)   **6.** Permitting only designated personnel such as cashiers to handle cash receipts is an application of the principle of:
(a) documentation procedures.
(b) establishment of responsibility.
(c) independent internal verification.
(d) other controls.

(SO 4)   **7.** The use of prenumbered checks in disbursing cash is an application of the principle of:
(a) establishment of responsibility.
(b) segregation of duties.
(c) physical controls.
(d) documentation procedures.

(SO 4)   **8.** The control features of a bank account do *not* include:
(a) having bank auditors verify the correctness of the bank balance per books.
(b) minimizing the amount of cash that must be kept on hand.
(c) providing a double record of all bank transactions.
(d) safeguarding cash by using a bank as a depository.

(SO 2)   **9.** Which of the following control activities is *not* relevant to when a company uses a computerized (rather than manual) accounting system?
(a) Establishment of responsibility.
(b) Segregation of duties.
(c) Independent internal verification.
(d) All of these control activities are relevant to a computerized system.

(SO 5)   **10.** In a bank reconciliation, deposits in transit are:
(a) deducted from the book balance.
(b) added to the book balance.
(c) added to the bank balance.
(d) deducted from the bank balance.

(SO 6) **11.** Which of the following items in a cash drawer at November 30 is *not* cash?
(a) Money orders.
(b) Coins and currency.
(c) A customer check dated December 1.
(d) A customer check dated November 28.

(SO 6) **12.** Which statement correctly describes the reporting of cash?
(a) Cash cannot be combined with cash equivalents.
(b) Restricted cash funds may be combined with Cash.
(c) Cash is listed first in the current assets section.
(d) Restricted cash funds cannot be reported as a current asset.

(SO 7) **13.** Which of the following would *not* be an example of good cash management?
(a) Provide discounts to customers to encourage early payment.
(b) Invest temporary excess cash in stock of a small company.
(c) Carefully monitor payments so that payments are not made early.

(d) Employ just-in-time inventory methods to keep inventory low.

14. Which of the following is *not* one of the sections of a cash budget? (SO 8)
(a) Cash receipts section.
(b) Cash disbursements section.
(c) Financing section.
(d) Cash from operations section.

*****15.** A check is written to replenish a $100 petty cash fund when the fund contains receipts of $94 and $2 in cash. In recording the check: (SO 9)
(a) Cash Over and Short should be debited for $4.
(b) Petty Cash should be debited for $94.
(c) Cash should be credited for $94.
(d) Petty Cash should be credited for $4.

Go to the book's companion website, **www.wiley.com/college/kimmel**, to access additional Self-Study Questions.

Questions

1. A local bank reported that it lost $150,000 as the result of an employee fraud. Randal Smith is not clear on what is meant by an "employee fraud." Explain the meaning of fraud to Randal and give an example of frauds that might occur at a bank.

2. Fraud experts often say that there are three primary factors that contribute to employee fraud. Identify the three factors and explain what is meant by each.

3. Identify and describe the five components of a good internal control system.

4. "Internal control is concerned only with enhancing the accuracy of the accounting records." Do you agree? Explain.

5. Discuss how the Sarbanes-Oxley Act has increased the importance of internal control to all employees in a company.

6. What principles of internal control apply to most business enterprises?

7. In the corner grocery store, all sales clerks make change out of one cash register drawer. Is this a violation of internal control? Why?

8. Gloria Modine is reviewing the principle of segregation of duties. What are the two common applications of this principle?

9. How do documentation procedures contribute to good internal control?

10. What internal control objectives are met by physical controls?

11. (a) Explain the control principle of independent internal verification.
(b) What practices are important in applying this principle?

12. As the company accountant, explain the following ideas to the management of Keane Company.
(a) The concept of reasonable assurance in internal control.
(b) The importance of the human factor in internal control.

13. Discuss the human resources department's involvement in internal controls.

14. Commerford Inc. owns the following assets at the balance sheet date.

Cash in bank—savings account	$ 8,000
Cash on hand	1,100
Cash refund due from the IRS	1,000
Checking account balance	12,000
Postdated checks	500

What amount should be reported as Cash in the balance sheet?

15. What principle(s) of internal control is (are) involved in making daily cash counts of over-the-counter receipts?

16. Assume that Kohl's Department Stores installed new electronic cash registers in its stores. How do cash registers improve internal control over cash receipts?

17. At Unruh Wholesale Company two mail clerks open all mail receipts. How does this strengthen internal control?

18. "To have maximum effective internal control over cash disbursements, all payments should be made by check." Is this true? Explain.

19. Rondelli Company's internal controls over cash disbursements provide for the treasurer to sign checks imprinted by a checkwriter after comparing the check with the approved invoice. Identify the internal control principles that are present in these controls.

20. How do these principles apply to cash disbursements:
    (a) Physical controls?
    (b) Documentation controls?

21. What is the essential feature of an electronic funds transfer (EFT) procedure?

22. "The use of a bank contributes significantly to good internal control over cash." Is this true? Why?

23. Stanley Delong is confused about the lack of agreement between the cash balance per books and the balance per bank. Explain the causes for the lack of agreement to Stanley, and give an example of each cause.

24. Describe the basic principles of cash management.

25. Julie Ellis asks your help concerning an NSF check. Explain to Julie (a) what an NSF check is, (b) how it

is treated in a bank reconciliation, and (c) whether it will require an adjusting entry on the company's books.

26.
    (a) "Cash equivalents are the same as cash." Do you agree? Explain.
    (b) How should restricted cash funds be reported on the balance sheet?

27. [Tootsie Roll] What was Tootsie Roll's balance in cash and cash equivalents at December 31, 2007? Did it report any restricted cash? How did Tootsie Roll define cash equivalents?

*28. (a) Identify the three activities that pertain to a petty cash fund, and indicate an internal control principle that is applicable to each activity.
    (b) When are journal entries required in the operation of a petty cash fund?

Brief Exercises

BE7-1 Match each situation with the fraud triangle factor (opportunity, financial pressure, or rationalization) that best describes it.
(a) An employee's monthly credit card payments are nearly 75% of their monthly earnings.
(b) An employee earns minimum wage at a firm that has reported record earnings for each of the last five years.
(c) An employee has an expensive gambling habit.
(d) An employee has check writing and signing responsibilities for a small company, and is also responsible for reconciling the bank account.

Identify fraud-triangle concepts.
(SO 1)

BE7-2 Deb Baden is the new owner of Birk Co. She has heard about internal control but is not clear about its importance for her business. Explain to Deb the four purposes of internal control, and give her one application of each purpose for Birk Co.

Explain the importance of internal control.
(SO 1)

BE7-3 The internal control procedures in Payton Company make the following provisions. Identify the principles of internal control that are being followed in each case.
(a) Employees who have physical custody of assets do not have access to the accounting records.
(b) Each month the assets on hand are compared to the accounting records by an internal auditor.
(c) A prenumbered shipping document is prepared for each shipment of goods to customers.

Identify internal control principles.
(SO 2)

BE7-4 Beaty Company has the following internal control procedures over cash receipts. Identify the internal control principle that is applicable to each procedure.
(a) All over-the-counter receipts are registered on cash registers.
(b) All cashiers are bonded.
(c) Daily cash counts are made by cashier department supervisors.
(d) The duties of receiving cash, recording cash, and having custody of cash are assigned to different individuals.
(e) Only cashiers may operate cash registers.

Identify the internal control principles applicable to cash receipts.
(SO 3)

BE7-5 While examining cash receipts information, the accounting department determined the following information: opening cash balance $150, cash on hand $1,125.74, and cash sales per register tape $990.83. Prepare the required journal entry based upon the cash count sheet.

Make journal entry using cash count sheet.
(SO 3)

BE7-6 Newell Company has the following internal control procedures over cash disbursements. Identify the internal control principle that is applicable to each procedure.
(a) Company checks are prenumbered.
(b) The bank statement is reconciled monthly by an internal auditor.

Identify the internal control principles applicable to cash disbursements.
(SO 4)

(c) Blank checks are stored in a safe in the treasurer's office.
(d) Only the treasurer or assistant treasurer may sign checks.
(e) Check signers are not allowed to record cash disbursement transactions.

Identify the control features of a bank account.
(SO 4)

BE7-7 Brent Bosch is uncertain about the control features of a bank account. Explain the control benefits of (a) a check and (b) a bank statement.

Indicate location of reconciling items in a bank reconciliation.
(SO 5)

BE7-8 The following reconciling items are applicable to the bank reconciliation for Gammill Co. Indicate how each item should be shown on a bank reconciliation.
(a) Outstanding checks.
(b) Bank debit memorandum for service charge.
(c) Bank credit memorandum for collecting a note for the depositor.
(d) Deposit in transit.

Identify reconciling items that require adjusting entries.
(SO 5)

BE7-9 Using the data in BE7-8, indicate (a) the items that will result in an adjustment to the depositor's records and (b) why the other items do not require adjustment.

Prepare partial bank reconciliation.
(SO 5)

BE7-10 At July 31 Eidman Company has this bank information: cash balance per bank $7,300; outstanding checks $762; deposits in transit $1,350; and a bank service charge $40. Determine the adjusted cash balance per bank at July 31.

Analyze outstanding checks.
(SO 5)

BE7-11 In the month of November, Hickox Company Inc. wrote checks in the amount of $9,750. In December, checks in the amount of $11,880 were written. In November, $8,800 of these checks were presented to the bank for payment, and $10,889 in December. What is the amount of outstanding checks at the end of November? At the end of December?

Explain the statement presentation of cash balances.
(SO 6)

BE7-12 Luzinski Company has these cash balances: cash in bank $12,742; payroll bank account $6,000; and plant expansion fund cash $25,000. Explain how each balance should be reported on the balance sheet.

Prepare a cash budget.
(SO 8)

BE7-13 The following information is available for Eusey Company for the month of January: expected cash receipts $62,000; expected cash disbursements $67,000; cash balance on January 1, $12,000. Management wishes to maintain a minimum cash balance of $8,000. Prepare a basic cash budget for the month of January.

Prepare entry to replenish a petty cash fund.
(SO 9)

*BE7-14 On March 20 Pineda's petty cash fund of $100 is replenished when the fund contains $19 in cash and receipts for postage $40, supplies $26, and travel expense $15. Prepare the journal entry to record the replenishment of the petty cash fund.

Do it! Review

WILEY
PLUS

Identify violations of control activities.
(SO 2)

Do it! 7-1 Identify which control activity is violated in each of the following situations, and explain how the situation creates an opportunity for fraud or inappropriate accounting practices.
1. Once a month the sales department sends sales invoices to the accounting department to be recorded.
2. Jay Margan orders merchandise for Rice Lake Company; he also receives merchandise and authorizes payment for merchandise.
3. Several clerks at Dick's Groceries use the same cash register drawer.

Design system of internal control over cash receipts.
(SO 3)

Do it! 7-2 Javier Vasquez is concerned with control over mail receipts at Javy's Sporting Goods. All mail receipts are opened by Nick Swisher. Nick sends the checks to the accounting department, where they are stamped "For Deposit Only." The accounting department records and deposits the mail receipts weekly. Javier asks your help in installing a good system of internal control over mail receipts.

Explain treatment of items in bank reconciliation.
(SO 5)

Do it! 7-3 Linus Hugt owns Linus Blankets. Linus asks you to explain how he should treat the following reconciling items when reconciling the company's bank account.
1. Outstanding checks
2. A deposit in transit
3. The bank charged to our account a check written by another company
4. A debit memorandum for a bank service charge

Do it! **7-4**   Rally Corporation's management wants to maintain a minimum monthly cash balance of $9,000. At the beginning of September the cash balance is $12,300; expected cash receipts for September are $97,200; cash disbursements are expected to be $115,000. How much cash, if any, must Rally borrow to maintain the desired minimum monthly balance? Determine your answer by using the basic form of the cash budget.

Prepare a cash budget.
(SO 8)

Exercises

E7-1   Bank employees use a system known as the "maker-checker" system. An employee will record an entry in the appropriate journal, and then a supervisor will verify and approve the entry. These days, as all of a bank's accounts are computerized, the employee first enters a batch of entries into the computer, and then the entries are posted automatically to the general ledger account after the supervisor approves them on the system.

Access to the computer system is password-protected and task-specific, which means that the computer system will not allow the employee to approve a transaction or the supervisor to record a transaction.

Identify the principles of internal control.
(SO 2)

Instructions
Identify the principles of internal control inherent in the "maker-checker" procedure used by banks.

E7-2   Gambino's Pizza operates strictly on a carryout basis. Customers pick up their orders at a counter where a clerk exchanges the pizza for cash. While at the counter, the customer can see other employees making the pizzas and the large ovens in which the pizzas are baked.

Identify the principles of internal control.
(SO 2)

Instructions
Identify the six principles of internal control and give an example of each principle that you might observe when picking up your pizza. (*Note:* It may not be possible to observe all the principles.)

E7-3   The following control procedures are used in Falk Company for over-the-counter cash receipts.
1. Cashiers are experienced; thus, they are not bonded.
2. All over-the-counter receipts are registered by three clerks who share a cash register with a single cash drawer.
3. To minimize the risk of robbery, cash in excess of $100 is stored in an unlocked attaché case in the stock room until it is deposited in the bank.
4. At the end of each day the total receipts are counted by the cashier on duty and reconciled to the cash register total.
5. The company accountant makes the bank deposit and then records the day's receipts.

List internal control weaknesses over cash receipts and suggest improvements.
(SO 2, 3)

Instructions
(a) For each procedure, explain the weakness in internal control and identify the control principle that is violated.
(b) For each weakness, suggest a change in the procedure that will result in good internal control.

E7-4   The following control procedures are used in Karina's Boutique Shoppe for cash disbursements.
1. Each week Karina leaves 100 company checks in an unmarked envelope on a shelf behind the cash register.
2. The store manager personally approves all payments before signing and issuing checks.
3. The company checks are unnumbered.
4. After payment, bills are "filed" in a paid invoice folder.
5. The company accountant prepares the bank reconciliation and reports any discrepancies to the owner.

List internal control weaknesses for cash disbursements and suggest improvements.
(SO 2, 4)

Instructions
(a) For each procedure, explain the weakness in internal control and identify the internal control principle that is violated.
(b) For each weakness, suggest a change in the procedure that will result in good internal control.

Identify internal control weaknesses for cash disbursements and suggest improvements.

(SO 2, 4)

E7-5 At Ratliff Company checks are not prenumbered because both the purchasing agent and the treasurer are authorized to issue checks. Each signer has access to unissued checks kept in an unlocked file cabinet. The purchasing agent pays all bills pertaining to goods purchased for resale. Prior to payment, the purchasing agent determines that the goods have been received and verifies the mathematical accuracy of the vendor's invoice. After payment, the invoice is filed by vendor and the purchasing agent records the payment in the cash disbursements journal. The treasurer pays all other bills following approval by authorized employees. After payment, the treasurer stamps all bills "paid," files them by payment date, and records the checks in the cash disbursements journal. Ratliff Company maintains one checking account that is reconciled by the treasurer.

Instructions
(a) List the weaknesses in internal control over cash disbursements.
(b) Identify improvements for correcting these weaknesses.

Prepare bank reconciliation and adjusting entries.

(SO 5)

E7-6 Juan Ortiz is unable to reconcile the bank balance at January 31. Juan's reconciliation is shown here.

Cash balance per bank	$3,660.20
Add: NSF check	470.00
Less: Bank service charge	25.00
Adjusted balance per bank	$4,105.20
Cash balance per books	$3,975.20
Less: Deposits in transit	590.00
Add: Outstanding checks	770.00
Adjusted balance per books	$4,155.20

Instructions
(a) What is the proper adjusted cash balance per bank?
(b) What is the proper adjusted cash balance per books?
(c) Prepare the adjusting journal entries necessary to determine the adjusted cash balance per books.

Determine outstanding checks.

(SO 5)

E7-7 At April 30 the bank reconciliation of Guardado Company shows three outstanding checks: No. 254 $650, No. 255 $700, and No. 257 $410. The May bank statement and the May cash payments journal are given here.

Bank Statement Checks Paid				Cash Payments Journal Checks Issued		
Date	**Check No.**	**Amount**		**Date**	**Check No.**	**Amount**
5-4	254	$650		5-2	258	$159
5-2	257	410		5-5	259	275
5-17	258	159		5-10	260	925
5-12	259	275		5-15	261	500
5-20	261	500		5-22	262	750
5-29	263	480		5-24	263	480
5-30	262	750		5-29	264	360

Instructions
Using step 2 in the reconciliation procedure (see page 346), list the outstanding checks at May 31.

Prepare bank reconciliation and adjusting entries.

(SO 5)

E7-8 The following information pertains to Gilmore Company.
1. Cash balance per bank, July 31, $7,328.
2. July bank service charge not recorded by the depositor $40.
3. Cash balance per books, July 31, $7,280.
4. Deposits in transit, July 31, $2,700.
5. Note for $2,000 collected for Gilmore in July by the bank, plus interest $36 less fee $20. The collection has not been recorded by Gilmore, and no interest has been accrued.
6. Outstanding checks, July 31, $772.

Instructions
(a) Prepare a bank reconciliation at July 31, 2010.
(b) Journalize the adjusting entries at July 31 on the books of Gilmore Company.

E7-9 This information relates to the Cash account in the ledger of Hadaway Company.

Prepare bank reconciliation and adjusting entries.

(SO 5)

Balance September 1—$16,400; Cash deposited—$64,000
Balance September 30—$17,600; Checks written—$62,800

The September bank statement shows a balance of $16,422 at September 30 and the following memoranda.

Credits		Debits	
Collection of $1,800 note plus interest $30	$1,830	NSF check: J. Hower	$560
Interest earned on checking account	45	Safety deposit box rent	50

At September 30 deposits in transit were $4,826 and outstanding checks totaled $2,383.

Instructions
(a) Prepare the bank reconciliation at September 30, 2010.
(b) Prepare the adjusting entries at September 30, assuming (1) the NSF check was from a customer on account, and (2) no interest had been accrued on the note.

E7-10 The cash records of Haig Company show the following.

Compute deposits in transit and outstanding checks for two bank reconciliations.

(SO 5)

For July:

1. The June 30 bank reconciliation indicated that deposits in transit total $750. During July the general ledger account Cash shows deposits of $16,900, but the bank statement indicates that only $15,600 in deposits were received during the month.
2. The June 30 bank reconciliation also reported outstanding checks of $940. During the month of July, Haig Company books show that $17,500 of checks were issued, yet the bank statement showed that $16,400 of checks cleared the bank in July.

For September:

3. In September deposits per bank statement totaled $25,900, deposits per books were $26,400, and deposits in transit at September 30 were $2,200.
4. In September cash disbursements per books were $23,700, checks clearing the bank were $24,000, and outstanding checks at September 30 were $2,100.

There were no bank debit or credit memoranda, and no errors were made by either the bank or Haig Company.

Instructions
Answer the following questions.
(a) In situation 1, what were the deposits in transit at July 31?
(b) In situation 2, what were the outstanding checks at July 31?
(c) In situation 3, what were the deposits in transit at August 31?
(d) In situation 4, what were the outstanding checks at August 31?

E7-11 Kane Inc.'s bank statement from Western Bank at August 31, 2010, gives the following information.

Prepare bank reconciliation and adjusting entries.

(SO 5)

Balance, August 1	$16,400	Bank debit memorandum:		
August deposits	73,000	Safety deposit box fee	$	25
Checks cleared in August	68,678	Service charge		50
Bank credit memorandum:		Balance, August 31		20,692
Interest earned	45			

A summary of the Cash account in the ledger for August shows the following: balance, August 1, $16,900; receipts $77,000; disbursements $73,570; and balance, August 31, $20,330. Analysis reveals that the only reconciling items on the July 31 bank reconciliation were a deposit in transit for $5,000 and outstanding checks of $4,500. In addition, you determine that there was an error involving a company check drawn in August: A check for $400 to a creditor on account that cleared the bank in August was journalized and posted for $40.

Instructions
(a) Determine deposits in transit.
(b) Determine outstanding checks. (*Hint:* You need to correct disbursements for the check error.)
(c) Prepare a bank reconciliation at August 31.
(d) Journalize the adjusting entry(ies) to be made by Kane Inc. at August 31.

E7-12 A new accountant at Nicholsen Inc. is trying to identify which of the amounts shown on page 368 should be reported as the current asset "Cash and cash equivalents" in the year-end balance sheet, as of April 30, 2010.

Identify reporting of cash.

(SO 6)

1. $60 of currency and coin in a locked box used for incidental cash transactions.
2. A $10,000 U.S. Treasury bill, due May 31, 2010.
3. $300 of April-dated checks that Nicholson has received from customers but not yet deposited.
4. An $85 check received from a customer in payment of its April account, but post-dated to May 1.
5. $2,500 in the company's checking account.
6. $4,500 in its savings account.
7. $75 of prepaid postage in its postage meter.
8. A $25 IOU from the company receptionist.

Instructions

(a) What balance should Nicholsen report as its "Cash and cash equivalents" balance at April 30, 2010?
(b) In what account(s) and in what financial statement(s) should the items not included in "Cash and cash equivalents" be reported?

Review cash management practices.

(SO 7)

E7-13 Adams, Loomis, and Vogt, three law students who have joined together to open a law practice, are struggling to manage their cash flow. They haven't yet built up sufficient clientele and revenues to support their legal practice's ongoing costs. Initial costs, such as advertising, renovations to their premises, and the like, all result in outgoing cash flow at a time when little is coming in. Adams, Loomis, and Vogt haven't had time to establish a billing system since most of their clients' cases haven't yet reached the courts, and the lawyers didn't think it would be right to bill them until "results were achieved."

Unfortunately, Adams, Loomis, and Vogt's suppliers don't feel the same way. Their suppliers expect them to pay their accounts payable within a few days of receiving their bills. So far, there hasn't even been enough money to pay the three lawyers, and they are not sure how long they can keep practicing law without getting some money into their pockets.

Instructions

Can you provide any suggestions for Adams, Loomis, and Vogt to improve their cash management practices?

Prepare a cash budget for two months.

(SO 8)

E7-14 Mayfield Company expects to have a cash balance of $46,000 on January 1, 2010. These are the relevant monthly budget data for the first two months of 2010.

1. Collections from customers: January $75,000, February $146,000.
2. Payments to suppliers: January $40,000, February $75,000.
3. Wages: January $30,000, February $40,000. Wages are paid in the month they are incurred.
4. Administrative expenses: January $21,000, February $31,000. These costs include depreciation of $1,000 per month. All other costs are paid as incurred.
5. Selling expenses: January $15,000, February $20,000. These costs are exclusive of depreciation. They are paid as incurred.
6. Sales of short-term investments in January are expected to realize $12,000 in cash. Mayfield has a line of credit at a local bank that enables it to borrow up to $25,000. The company wants to maintain a minimum monthly cash balance of $20,000.

Instructions

Prepare a cash budget for January and February.

Prepare journal entries for a petty cash fund.

(SO 9)

*E7-15 During October, Eastern Light Company experiences the following transactions in establishing a petty cash fund.

Oct. 1 A petty cash fund is established with a check for $100 issued to the petty cash custodian.

31 A count of the petty cash fund disclosed the following items:

Currency	$7.00
Coins	0.40
Expenditure receipts (vouchers):	
Office supplies	$26.10
Telephone, Internet, and fax	16.40
Postage	42.00
Freight-out	6.80

31 A check was written to reimburse the fund and increase the fund to $200.

Instructions

Journalize the entries in October that pertain to the petty cash fund.

*E7-16 Otto Company maintains a petty cash fund for small expenditures. These transactions occurred during the month of August.

Journalize and post petty cash fund transactions.
(SO 9)

Aug. 1 Established the petty cash fund by writing a check on Central Bank for $200.

     15 Replenished the petty cash fund by writing a check for $175. On this date, the fund consisted of $25 in cash and these petty cash receipts: freight-out $74.40, entertainment expense $41, postage expense $33.70 and miscellaneous expense $27.50.

     16 Increased the amount of the petty cash fund to $400 by writing a check for $200.

     31 Replenished the petty cash fund by writing a check for $283. On this date, the fund consisted of $117 in cash and these petty cash receipts: postage expense $145, entertainment expense $90.60, and freight-out $46.40.

Instructions

(a) Journalize the petty cash transactions.
(b) Post to the Petty Cash account.
(c) What internal control features exist in a petty cash fund?

Exercises: Set B

Visit the book's companion website, at **www.wiley.com/college/kimmel**, and choose the Student Companion site, to access Exercise Set B.

Problems: Set A

P7-1A Cherokee Theater is in the Federal Mall. A cashier's booth is located near the entrance to the theater. Two cashiers are employed. One works from 1:00 to 5:00 P.M., the other from 5:00 to 9:00 P.M. Each cashier is bonded. The cashiers receive cash from customers and operate a machine that ejects serially numbered tickets. The rolls of tickets are inserted and locked into the machine by the theater manager at the beginning of each cashier's shift.

Identify internal control weaknesses for cash receipts.
(SO 2, 3)

After purchasing a ticket, the customer takes the ticket to a doorperson stationed at the entrance of the theater lobby some 60 feet from the cashier's booth. The doorperson tears the ticket in half, admits the customer, and returns the ticket stub to the customer. The other half of the ticket is dropped into a locked box by the doorperson.

At the end of each cashier's shift, the theater manager removes the ticket rolls from the machine and makes a cash count. The cash count sheet is initialed by the cashier. At the end of the day, the manager deposits the receipts in total in a bank night deposit vault located in the mall. In addition, the manager sends copies of the deposit slip and the initialed cash count sheets to the theater company treasurer for verification and to the company's accounting department. Receipts from the first shift are stored in a safe located in the manager's office.

Instructions

(a) Identify the internal control principles and their application to the cash receipts transactions of Cherokee Theater.
(b) If the doorperson and cashier decided to collaborate to misappropriate cash, what actions might they take?

P7-2A Scottsdale Middle School wants to raise money for a new sound system for its auditorium. The primary fund-raising event is a dance at which the famous disc jockey Jay Dee will play classic and not-so-classic dance tunes. Steve Cerra, the music and theater

Identify internal control weaknesses in cash receipts and cash disbursements.
(SO 2, 3, 4)

instructor, has been given the responsibility for coordinating the fund-raising efforts. This is Steve's first experience with fund-raising. He decides to put the eighth-grade choir in charge of the event; he will be a relatively passive observer.

Steve had 500 unnumbered tickets printed for the dance. He left the tickets in a box on his desk and told the choir students to take as many tickets as they thought they could sell for $5 each. In order to ensure that no extra tickets would be floating around, he told them to dispose of any unsold tickets. When the students received payment for the tickets, they were to bring the cash back to Steve, and he would put it in a locked box in his desk drawer.

Some of the students were responsible for decorating the gymnasium for the dance. Steve gave each of them a key to the money box and told them that if they took money out to purchase materials, they should put a note in the box saying how much they took and what it was used for. After two weeks the money box appeared to be getting full, so Steve asked Emily Polzin to count the money, prepare a deposit slip, and deposit the money in a bank account Steve had opened.

The day of the dance, Steve wrote a check from the account to pay Jay Dee. The DJ said, however, that he accepted only cash and did not give receipts. So Steve took $200 out of the cash box and gave it to Jay. At the dance Steve had Lisa Depriest working at the entrance to the gymnasium, collecting tickets from students and selling tickets to those who had not pre-purchased them. Steve estimated that 400 students attended the dance.

The following day Steve closed out the bank account, which had $250 in it, and gave that amount plus the $180 in the cash box to Principal Skinner. Principal Skinner seemed surprised that, after generating roughly $2,000 in sales, the dance netted only $430 in cash. Steve did not know how to respond.

Instructions
Identify as many internal control weaknesses as you can in this scenario, and suggest how each could be addressed.

Prepare a bank reconciliation and adjusting entries.

(SO 5)

P7-3A On July 31, 2010, Fenton Company had a cash balance per books of $6,140. The statement from Jackson State Bank on that date showed a balance of $7,695.80. A comparison of the bank statement with the cash account revealed the following facts.

1. The bank service charge for July was $25.

2. The bank collected a note receivable of $1,500 for Fenton Company on July 15, plus $30 of interest. The bank made a $10 charge for the collection. Fenton has not accrued any interest on the note.

3. The July 31 receipts of $1,193.30 were not included in the bank deposits for July. These receipts were deposited by the company in a night deposit vault on July 31.

4. Company check No. 2480 issued to H. Coby, a creditor, for $384 that cleared the bank in July was incorrectly entered in the cash payments journal on July 10 for $348.

5. Checks outstanding on July 31 totaled $1,980.10.

6. On July 31 the bank statement showed an NSF charge of $690 for a check received by the company from P. Figura, a customer, on account.

Instructions

(a) Cash bal. $6,909.00

(a) Prepare the bank reconciliation as of July 31.
(b) Prepare the necessary adjusting entries at July 31.

Prepare a bank reconciliation and adjusting entries from detailed data.

(SO 5)

P7-4A The bank portion of the bank reconciliation for Hunsaker Company at October 31, 2010, is shown here and on the next page.

HUNSAKER COMPANY
Bank Reconciliation
October 31, 2010

Cash balance per bank	$12,367.90
Add: Deposits in transit	1,530.20
	13,898.10

Less: Outstanding checks

Check Number	Check Amount	
2451	$ 1,260.40	
2470	720.10	
2471	844.50	
2472	426.80	
2474	1,050.00	4,301.80
Adjusted cash balance per bank		$ 9,596.30

The adjusted cash balance per bank agreed with the cash balance per books at October 31. The November bank statement showed the following checks and deposits.

Bank Statement

	Checks			Deposits	
Date	Number	Amount	Date	Amount	
11-1	2470	$ 720.10	11-1	$ 1,530.20	
11-2	2471	844.50	11-4	1,211.60	
11-5	2474	1,050.00	11-8	990.10	
11-4	2475	1,640.70	11-13	2,575.00	
11-8	2476	2,830.00	11-18	1,472.70	
11-10	2477	600.00	11-21	2,945.00	
11-15	2479 error	1,750.00	11-25	2,567.30	
11-18	2480	1,330.00	11-28	1,650.00	
11-27	2481	695.40	11-30	1,186.00	
11-30	2483	575.50	Total	$16,127.90	
11-29	2486	900.00			
	Total	$12,936.20			

The cash records per books for November showed the following.

Cash Payments Journal

Date	Number	Amount	Date	Number	Amount
11-1	2475	$1,640.70	11-20	2483	$ 575.50
11-2	2476	2,830.00	11-22	2484	829.50
11-2	2477	600.00	11-23	2485	974.80
11-4	2478	538.20	11-24	2486	900.00
11-8	2479 error	1,705.00	11-29	2487	398.00
11-10	2480	1,330.00	11-30	2488	800.00
11-15	2481	695.40	Total		$14,429.10
11-18	2482	612.00			

Cash Receipts Journal

Date	Amount
11-3	$ 1,211.60
11-7	990.10
11-12	2,575.00
11-17	1,472.70
11-20	2,954.00
11-24	2,567.30
11-27	1,650.00
11-29	1,186.00
11-30	1,218.00
Total	$15,824.70

The bank statement contained two bank memoranda:

1. A credit of $2,242 for the collection of a $2,100 note for Hunsaker Company plus interest of $157 and less a collection fee of $15. Hunsaker Company has not accrued any interest on the note.

2. A debit for the printing of additional company checks $85.

At November 30 the cash balance per books was $10,991.90 and the cash balance per bank statement was $17,716.60. The bank did not make any errors, but **Hunsaker Company made two errors.**

Instructions

(a) Cash bal. $13,094.90

(a) Using the four steps in the reconciliation procedure described on pages 345–346, prepare a bank reconciliation at November 30, 2010.

(b) Prepare the adjusting entries based on the reconciliation. (*Note:* The correction of any errors pertaining to recording checks should be made to Accounts Payable. The correction of any errors relating to recording cash receipts should be made to Accounts Receivable.)

Prepare a bank reconciliation and adjusting entries.
(SO 5)

P7-5A Shellankamp Company of Canton, Iowa, spreads herbicides and applies liquid fertilizer for local farmers. On May 31, 2010, the company's cash account per its general ledger showed a balance of $6,738.90.

The bank statement from Canton State Bank on that date showed the following balance.

CANTON STATE BANK

Checks and Debits	Deposits and Credits	Daily Balance
XXX	XXX	5-31 7,112.00

A comparison of the details on the bank statement with the details in the cash account revealed the following facts.

1. The statement included a debit memo of $40 for the printing of additional company checks.

2. Cash sales of $833.15 on May 12 were deposited in the bank. The cash receipts journal entry and the deposit slip were incorrectly made for $839.15. The bank credited Shellankamp Company for the correct amount.

3. Outstanding checks at May 31 totaled $276.25, and deposits in transit were $1,880.15.

4. On May 18, the company issued check No. 1181 for $685 to R. Delzer, on account. The check, which cleared the bank in May, was incorrectly journalized and posted by Shellankamp Company for $658.

5. A $2,700 note receivable was collected by the bank for Shellankamp Company on May 31 plus $110 interest. The bank charged a collection fee of $20. No interest has been accrued on the note.

6. Included with the cancelled checks was a check issued by Shellman Company to P. Jonet for $360 that was incorrectly charged to Shellankamp Company by the bank.

7. On May 31, the bank statement showed an NSF charge of $380 for a check issued by Natalie Fong, a customer, to Shellankamp Company on account.

Instructions

(a) Cash bal. $9,075.90

(a) Prepare the bank reconciliation at May 31, 2010.

(b) Prepare the necessary adjusting entries for Shellankamp Company at May 31, 2010.

Prepare a cash budget.
(SO 8)

P7-6A You are provided with the following information taken from Weinberger Inc.'s March 31, 2010, balance sheet.

Cash	$ 8,000
Accounts receivable	20,000
Inventory	36,000
Property, plant, and equipment, net of depreciation	120,000
Accounts payable	22,400
Common stock	150,000
Retained earnings	11,600

Additional information concerning Weinberger Inc. is as follows.

1. Gross profit is 25% of sales.

2. Actual and budgeted sales data:

March (actual)	$50,000
April (budgeted)	70,000

3. Sales are both cash and credit. Cash collections expected in April are:

March	$20,000	(40% of $50,000)
April	42,000	(60% of $70,000)
	$62,000	

4. Half of a month's purchases are paid for in the month of purchase and half in the following month. Cash disbursements expected in April are:

Purchases March	$22,400
Purchases April	28,100
	$50,500

5. Cash operating costs are anticipated to be $11,700 for the month of April.

6. Equipment costing $2,500 will be purchased for cash in April.

7. The company wishes to maintain a minimum cash balance of $8,000. An open line of credit is available at the bank. All borrowing is done at the beginning of the month, and all repayments are made at the end of the month. The interest rate is 12% per year, and interest expense is accrued at the end of the month and paid in the following month.

Instructions

Prepare a cash budget for the month of April. Determine how much cash Weinberger Inc. must borrow, or can repay, in April.

Apr. borrowings $2,700

P7-7A   Fogelberg Corporation prepares monthly cash budgets. Here are relevant data from operating budgets for 2010.

Prepare a cash budget.
(SO 8)

	January	February
Sales	$360,000	$400,000
Purchases	120,000	130,000
Salaries	84,000	95,000
Administrative expenses	72,000	75,000
Selling expenses	79,000	88,000

All sales and purchases are on account. Budgeted collections and disbursement data are given below. All other expenses are paid in the month incurred except for administrative expenses, which include $1,000 of depreciation per month.

Other data.

1. Collections from customers: January $332,000; February $378,000.

2. Payments for purchases: January $110,000; February $125,000.

3. Other receipts: January: collection of December 31, 2009, notes receivable $15,000; February: proceeds from sale of securities $6,000

4. Other disbursements: February $12,000 cash dividend

The company's cash balance on January 1, 2010, is expected to be $52,000. The company wants to maintain a minimum cash balance of $50,000.

Instructions

Prepare a cash budget for January and February.

Jan. 31 cash bal. $ 55,000

P7-8A   Frederickson Company is a very profitable small business. It has not, however, given much consideration to internal control. For example, in an attempt to keep clerical and office expenses to a minimum, the company has combined the jobs of cashier and bookkeeper. As a result, Kenny Dillon handles all cash receipts, keeps the accounting records, and prepares the monthly bank reconciliations.

Prepare a comprehensive bank reconciliation with theft and internal control deficiencies.
(SO 2, 3, 4, 5)

The balance per the bank statement on October 31, 2010, was $18,380. Outstanding checks were: No. 62 for $126.75, No. 183 for $180, No. 284 for $253.25, No. 862 for $190.71, No. 863 for $226.80, and No. 864 for $165.28. Included with the statement was a credit memorandum of $200 indicating the collection of a note receivable for Frederickson Company by the bank on October 25. This memorandum has not been recorded by Frederickson.

The company's ledger showed one cash account with a balance of $21,892.72. The balance included undeposited cash on hand. Because of the lack of internal controls, Kenny took for personal use all of the undeposited receipts in excess of $3,795.51. He then prepared the following bank reconciliation in an effort to conceal his theft of cash.

Cash balance per books, October 31		$21,892.72
Add: Outstanding checks		
No. 862	$190.71	
No. 863	226.80	
No. 864	165.28	482.79
		22,375.51
Less: Undeposited receipts		3,795.51
Unadjusted balance per bank, October 31		18,580.00
Less: Bank credit memorandum		200.00
Cash balance per bank statement, October 31		$18,380.00

Instructions

(a) Cash bal. $21,032.72

(a) Prepare a correct bank reconciliation. (*Hint:* Deduct the amount of the theft from the adjusted balance per books.)

(b) Indicate the three ways that Kenny attempted to conceal the theft and the dollar amount involved in each method.

(c) What principles of internal control were violated in this case?

Problems: Set B

Identify internal control principles for cash disbursements.

(SO 2, 4)

P7-1B Celtic Company recently changed its system of internal control over cash disbursements. The system includes the following features.

1. Instead of being unnumbered and manually prepared, all checks must now be prenumbered and written by using the new checkwriter purchased by the company.

2. Before a check can be issued, each invoice must have the approval of Jane Bell, the purchasing agent, and Dick McRae, the receiving department supervisor.

3. Checks must be signed by either Frank Person, the treasurer, or Sara Goss, the assistant treasurer. Before signing a check, the signer is expected to compare the amounts of the check with the amounts on the invoice.

4. After signing a check, the signer stamps the invoice "paid" and inserts within the stamp, the date, check number, and amount of the check. The "paid" invoice is then sent to the accounting department for recording.

5. Blank checks are stored in a safe in the treasurer's office. The combination to the safe is known by only the treasurer and assistant treasurer.

6. Each month the bank statement is reconciled with the bank balance per books by the assistant chief accountant.

7. All employees who handle or account for cash are bonded.

Instructions

Identify the internal control principles and their application to cash disbursements of Celtic Company.

Identify internal control weaknesses in cash receipts.

(SO 2, 3)

P7-2B The board of trustees of a local church is concerned about the internal accounting controls pertaining to the offering collections made at weekly services. They ask you to serve on a three-person audit team with the internal auditor of the university and a CPA who has just joined the church. At a meeting of the audit team and the board of trustees you learn the following.

1. The church's board of trustees has delegated responsibility for the financial management and audit of the financial records to the finance committee. This group pre-

pares the annual budget and approves major disbursements but is not involved in collections or recordkeeping. No audit has been made in recent years because the same trusted employee has kept church records and served as financial secretary for 15 years. The church does not carry any fidelity insurance.

2. The collection at the weekly service is taken by a team of ushers who volunteer to serve for 1 month. The ushers take the collection plates to a basement office at the rear of the church. They hand their plates to the head usher and return to the church service. After all plates have been turned in, the head usher counts the cash received. The head usher then places the cash in the church safe along with a notation of the amount counted. The head usher volunteers to serve for 3 months.

3. The next morning the financial secretary opens the safe and recounts the collection. The secretary withholds $150–$200 in cash, depending on the cash expenditures expected for the week, and deposits the remainder of the collections in the bank. To facilitate the deposit, church members who contribute by check are asked to make their checks payable to "Cash."

4. Each month the financial secretary reconciles the bank statement and submits a copy of the reconciliation to the board of trustees. The reconciliations have rarely contained any bank errors and have never shown any errors per books.

Instructions
(a) Indicate the weaknesses in internal accounting control in the handling of collections.
(b) List the improvements in internal control procedures that you plan to make at the next meeting of the audit team for (1) the ushers, (2) the head usher, (3) the financial secretary, and (4) the finance committee.
(c) What church policies should be changed to improve internal control?

P7-3B On May 31, 2010, Lombard Company had a cash balance per books of $5,681.50. The bank statement from Community Bank on that date showed a balance of $7,964.60. A comparison of the statement with the cash account revealed the following facts.

Prepare a bank reconciliation and adjusting entries.
(SO 5)

1. The statement included a debit memo of $70 for the printing of additional company checks.

2. Cash sales of $786.15 on May 12 were deposited in the bank. The cash receipts journal entry and the deposit slip were incorrectly made for $796.15. The bank credited Lombard Company for the correct amount.

3. Outstanding checks at May 31 totaled $1,106.25, and deposits in transit were $836.15.

4. On May 18 the company issued check No. 1181 for $685 to N. Habben, on account. The check, which cleared the bank in May, was incorrectly journalized and posted by Lombard Company for $658.

5. A $2,500 note receivable was collected by the bank for Lombard Company on May 31 plus $80 interest. The bank charged a collection fee of $30. No interest has been accrued on the note.

6. Included with the cancelled checks was a check issued by Lonshek Company to C. Young for $290 that was incorrectly charged to Lombard Company by the bank.

7. On May 31 the bank statement showed an NSF charge of $140 for a check issued by K. Uzong, a customer, to Lombard Company on account.

Instructions
(a) Prepare the bank reconciliation as of May 31, 2010.
(b) Prepare the necessary adjusting entries at May 31, 2010.

(a) Cash bal. $7,984.50

P7-4B The bank portion of the bank reconciliation for Christiansen Company at November 30, 2010, is shown here and on the next page.

Prepare a bank reconciliation and adjusting entries from detailed data.
(SO 5)

CHRISTIANSEN COMPANY
Bank Reconciliation
November 30, 2010

Cash balance per bank	$14,367.90
Add: Deposits in transit	2,530.20
	16,898.10

Less: Outstanding checks

Check Number	Check Amount	
3451	$ 2,260.40	
3470	1,100.10	
3471	844.50	
3472	1,426.80	
3474	1,050.00	6,681.80
Adjusted cash balance per bank		$10,216.30

The adjusted cash balance per bank agreed with the cash balance per books at November 30. The December bank statement showed the following checks and deposits.

Bank Statement

	Checks			Deposits	
Date	Number	Amount	Date		Amount
12-1	3451	$ 2,260.40	12-1		$ 2,530.20
12-2	3470	1,100.10	12-4		1,211.60
12-7	3472	1,426.80	12-8		2,365.10
12-4	3475	1,640.70	12-16		2,672.70
12-8	3476	1,300.00	12-21		2,945.00
12-10	3477	2,130.00	12-26		2,567.30
12-15	3479	3,080.00	12-29		2,836.00
12-27	3480	600.00	12-30		1,025.00
12-30	3482	475.50	Total		$18,152.90
12-29	3484	764.00			
12-31	3485	540.80			
	Total	$15,318.30			

The cash records per books for December showed the following.

Cash Payments Journal

Date	Number	Amount	Date	Number	Amount
12-1	3475	$1,640.70	12-20	3482	$ 475.50
12-2	3476	1,300.00	12-22	3483	1,140.00
12-2	3477	2,130.00	12-23	3484	764.00
12-4	3478	538.20	12-24	3485	450.80
12-8	3479	3,080.00	12-30	3486	1,389.50
12-10	3480	600.00	Total		$14,316.10
12-17	3481	807.40			

Cash Receipts Journal

Date	Amount
12-3	$ 1,211.60
12-7	2,365.10
12-15	2,672.70
12-20	2,954.00
12-25	2,567.30
12-28	2,836.00
12-30	1,025.00
12-31	1,190.40
Total	$16,822.10

The bank statement contained two memoranda.

1. A credit of $2,645 for the collection of a $2,500 note for Christiansen Company plus interest of $160 and less a collection fee of $15. Christiansen Company has not accrued any interest on the note.

2. A debit of $819.10 for an NSF check written by J. Waller, a customer. At December 31 the check had not been redeposited in the bank.

At December 31 the cash balance per books was $12,722.30, and the cash balance per bank statement was $19,028.40. The bank did not make any errors, **but Christiansen Company made two errors.**

Instructions

(a) Using the four steps in the reconciliation procedure described on pages 345–346, prepare a bank reconciliation at December 31, 2010.

(b) Prepare the adjusting entries based on the reconciliation. [*Note:* The correction of any errors pertaining to recording checks should be made to Accounts Payable. The correction of any errors relating to recording cash receipts should be made to Accounts Receivable.]

(a) Cash bal. $14,449.20

P7-5B Greenwood Company of Omaha, Nebraska, provides liquid fertilizer and herbicides to regional farmers. On July 31, 2010, the company's cash account per its general ledger showed a balance of $5,909.70.

Prepare a bank reconciliation and adjusting entries.
(SO 5)

The bank statement from Tri-County Bank on that date showed the following balance.

TRI-COUNTY BANK

Checks and Debits	Deposits and Credits	Daily Balance
XXX	XXX	7-31 7,075.80

A comparison of the details on the bank statement with the details in the cash account revealed the following facts.

1. The bank service charge for July was $32.

2. The bank collected a note receivable of $900 for Greenwood Company on July 15, plus $48 of interest. The bank made a $10 charge for the collection. Greenwood has not accrued any interest on the note.

3. The July 31 receipts of $1,339 were not included in the bank deposits for July. These receipts were deposited by the company in a night deposit vault on July 31.

4. Company check No. 2480 issued to N. Teig, a creditor, for $492 that cleared the bank in July was incorrectly entered in the cash payments journal on July 10 for $429.

5. Checks outstanding on July 31 totaled $2,480.10.

6. On July 31, the bank statement showed an NSF charge of $818 for a check received by the company from N. O. Doe, a customer, on account.

Instructions

(a) Prepare the bank reconciliation as of July 31, 2010.
(b) Prepare the necessary adjusting entries at July 31, 2010.

(a) Cash bal. $5,934.70

P7-6B Polk Co. expects to have a cash balance of $26,000 on January 1, 2010. Relevant monthly budget data for the first two months of 2010 are as follows.

Prepare a cash budget.
(SO 8)

Collections from customers: January $70,000; February $160,000
Payments to suppliers: January $45,000; February $75,000
Salaries: January $35,000; February $40,000. Salaries are paid in the month they are incurred.
Selling and administrative expenses: January $27,000; February $35,000. These costs are exclusive of depreciation and are paid as incurred.
Sales of short-term investments in January are expected to realize $7,000 in cash.

Polk has a line of credit at a local bank that enables it to borrow up to $45,000. The company wants to maintain a minimum monthly cash balance of $25,000. Any excess cash above the $25,000 minimum is used to pay off the line of credit.

Instructions

(a) Prepare a cash budget for January and February.
(b) Explain how a cash budget contributes to effective management.

(a) Jan. cash bal. $25,000

Prepare a cash budget.
(SO 8)

P7-7B Ybarra Inc. prepares monthly cash budgets. Shown on page 378 are relevant data from operating budgets for 2010.

	January	February
Sales	$330,000	$400,000
Purchases	110,000	130,000
Salaries	80,000	95,000
Selling and administrative expenses	135,000	150,000

All sales and purchases are on account. Collections and disbursement data are given below. All other items above are paid in the month incurred. Depreciation has been excluded from selling and administrative expenses.

Other data.

1. Collections from customers: January $297,000; February $358,000.

2. Payments for purchases: January $98,000; February $118,000.

3. Other receipts: January: collection of December 31, 2009, interest receivable $2,000; February: proceeds from sale of short-term investments $8,000

4. Other disbursements: February payment of $20,000 for land

The company's cash balance on January 1, 2010, is expected to be $60,000. The company wants to maintain a minimum cash balance of $40,000.

Instructions

Prepare a cash budget for January and February.

Jan. 31 cash bal. $46,000

Prepare a comprehensive bank reconciliation with theft and internal control deficiencies.
(SO 2, 3, 4, 5)

P7-8B McNally Company is a very profitable small business. It has not, however, given much consideration to internal control. For example, in an attempt to keep clerical and office expenses to a minimum, the company has combined the jobs of cashier and book-keeper. As a result, M. Mordica handles all cash receipts, keeps the accounting records, and prepares the monthly bank reconciliations.

The balance per the bank statement on October 31, 2010, was $13,600. Outstanding checks were: No. 62 for $126.75, No. 183 for $180, No. 284 for $253.25, No. 862 for $190.71, No. 863 for $226.80, and No. 864 for $165.28. Included with the statement was a credit memorandum of $490 indicating the collection of a note receivable for McNally Company by the bank on October 25. This memorandum has not been recorded by McNally Company.

The company's ledger showed one cash account with a balance of $15,847.21. The balance included undeposited cash on hand. Because of the lack of internal controls, Mordica took for personal use all of the undeposited receipts in excess of $2,240. He then prepared the following bank reconciliation in an effort to conceal his theft of cash.

Cash balance per books, October 31		$15,847.21
Add: Outstanding checks		
No. 862	$190.71	
No. 863	226.80	
No. 864	165.28	482.79
		16,330.00
Less: Undeposited receipts		2,240.00
Unadjusted balance per bank, October 31		14,090.00
Less: Bank credit memorandum		490.00
Cash balance per bank statement, October 31		$13,600.00

Instructions

(a) Cash bal. $14,697.21

(a) Prepare a correct bank reconciliation. (*Hint:* Deduct the amount of the theft from the adjusted balance per books.)

(b) Indicate the three ways that Mordica attempted to conceal the theft and the dollar amount pertaining to each method.

(c) What principles of internal control were violated in this case?

Problems: Set C

Visit the book's companion website at **www.wiley.com/college/kimmel** and choose the Student Companion site to access Problem Set C.

Comprehensive Problem

CP7 On December 1, 2010, Moreland Company had the following account balances.

Debits		**Credits**	
Cash	$18,200	Accumulated Depreciation	$ 3,000
Notes Receivable	2,500	Accounts Payable	6,100
Accounts Receivable	7,500	Common Stock	20,000
Merchandise Inventory	16,000	Retained Earnings	44,700
Prepaid Insurance	1,600		$73,800
Equipment	28,000		
	$73,800		

During December the company completed the following transactions.

Dec. 7 Received $3,200 cash from customers in payment of account (no discount allowed).
12 Purchased merchandise on account from King Co. $12,000, terms 2/10, n/30.
17 Sold merchandise on account $15,000, terms 1/10, n/30. The cost of the merchandise sold was $10,000.
19 Paid salaries $2,500.
22 Paid King Co. in full, less discount.
26 Received collections in full, less discounts, from customers billed on December 17.

Adjustment data:

1. Depreciation $200 per month.
2. Insurance expired $400.
3. Income tax expense was $425. It was unpaid at December 31.

Instructions
(a) Journalize the December transactions. (Assume a perpetual inventory system.)
(b) Enter the December 1 balances in the ledger T accounts and post the December transactions. Use Cost of Goods Sold, Depreciation Expense, Insurance Expense, Salaries Expense, Sales, Sales Discounts, Income Tax Payable, and Income Tax Expense.
(c) The statement from Lyon County Bank on December 31 showed a balance of $22,164. A comparison of the bank statement with the cash account revealed the following facts.
  1. The bank collected a note receivable of $2,500 for Moreland Company on December 15.
  2. The December 31 receipts of $2,736 were not included in the bank deposits for December. The company deposited these receipts in a night deposit vault on December 31.
  3. Checks outstanding on December 31 totaled $1,210.
  4. On December 31 the bank statement showed a NSF charge of $800 for a check received by the company from C. Park, a customer, on account.

  Prepare a bank reconciliation as of December 31 based on the available information. (*Hint:* The cash balance per books is $21,990. This can be proven by finding the balance in the Cash account from parts (a) and (b).)
(d) Journalize the adjusting entries resulting from the bank reconciliation and adjustment data.
(e) Post the adjusting entries to the ledger T accounts.
(f) Prepare an adjusted trial balance.
(g) Prepare an income statement for December and a classified balance sheet at December 31.

(f) Totals $89,425
(g) Net income $ 1,325
Total assets $72,550

Continuing Cookie Chronicle

(*Note:* This is a continuation of the Cookie Chronicle from Chapters 1 through 6.)

CCC7 **Part 1** Natalie is struggling to keep up with the recording of her accounting transactions. She is spending a lot of time marketing and selling mixers and giving her cookie classes. Her friend John is an accounting student who runs his own accounting service. He has asked Natalie if she would like to have him do her accounting. John and Natalie meet and discuss her business.

Part 2 Natalie decides that she cannot afford to hire John to do her accounting. One way that she can ensure that her cash account does not have any errors and is accurate and up-to-date is to prepare a bank reconciliation at the end of each month. Natalie would like you to help her.

 Go to the book's companion website, **www.wiley.com/college/kimmel**, to see the completion of this problem.

broadening your perspective

Financial Reporting and Analysis

FINANCIAL REPORTING PROBLEM: *Tootsie Roll Industries Inc.*

BYP7-1 The financial statements of Tootsie Roll are presented in Appendix A of this book, together with an auditor's report—Report of Independent Auditors.

Instructions
Using the financial statements and reports, answer these questions about Tootsie Roll's internal controls and cash.
(a) What comments, if any, are made about cash in the report of the independent auditors?
(b) What data about cash and cash equivalents are shown in the consolidated balance sheet (statement of financial condition)?
(c) What activities are identified in the consolidated statement of cash flows as being responsible for the changes in cash during 2007?
(d) How are cash equivalents defined in the Notes to Consolidated Financial Statements?
(e) Read the section of the report titled "Management's Report on Internal Control Over Financial Reporting." Summarize the statements made in that section of the report.

COMPARATIVE ANALYSIS PROBLEM: *Tootsie Roll vs. Hershey Foods*

BYP7-2 The financial statements of Hershey Foods are presented in Appendix B, following the financial statements for Tootsie Roll in Appendix A.

Instructions
Answer the following questions for each company.
(a) What is the balance in cash and cash equivalents at December 31, 2007?
(b) What percentage of total assets does cash represent for each company over the last two years? Has it changed significantly for either company?
(c) How much cash was provided by operating activities during 2007?
(d) Comment on your findings in parts (a) through (c).

RESEARCH CASE

BYP7-3 The May 13, 2008, issue of the *Wall Street Journal* contains an article by Jeffrey McCracken entitled "Economy Puts Tight Squeeze on RV Makers."

Instructions
Read the article and answer the following questions.
(a) What are the factors that have caused RV sales to decline?
(b) What did Coachmen Industries do to address its cash shortfall? What other steps does the article suggest that the company might take to address its cash shortfall?

(c) What did Fleetwood Enterprises Inc. do to address its cash shortfall? What event does the company have in the near-term that will require significant cash? What other steps is the company considering to address its cash shortfall?

INTERPRETING FINANCIAL STATEMENTS

BYP7-4   The international accounting firm Ernst and Young recently performed a global survey. The results of that survey are summarized in a report titled "Fraud Risk in Emerging Markets." You can find this report at: **http://www.ey.com/Global/assets.nsf/International/FIDS_-_9th_Global_Fraud_Survey_2006/$file/EY_Fraud_Survey_June2006.pdf,** or do an Internet search for "9th Global Fraud Survey—Fraud Risk in Emerging Markets."

Instructions
Read the Executive Summary section, and then skim the remainder of the report to answer the following questions.
(a) What did survey respondents consider to be the top three factors to prevent fraud?
(b) What type of fraud poses the greatest threat in developed markets? What type of fraud poses the greatest threat in emerging markets?
(c) In what three regions are anti-fraud measures most likely to be considered when deciding whether to begin doing business in that region?

FINANCIAL ANALYSIS ON THE WEB

BYP7-5   The Financial Accounting Standards Board (FASB) is a private organization established to improve accounting standards and financial reporting. The FASB conducts extensive research before issuing a "Statement of Financial Accounting Standards," which represents an authoritative expression of generally accepted accounting principles.

Address: **www.fasb.org**, or go to
www.wiley.com/college/kimmel

Steps:
Choose **Facts about FASB**.

Instructions
Answer the following questions.
(a) What is the mission of the FASB?
(b) How are topics added to the FASB technical agenda?
(c) What characteristics make the FASB's procedures an "open" decision-making process?

BYP7-6   The Public Company Accounting Oversight Board (PCAOB) was created as a result of the Sarbanes-Oxley Act. It has oversight and enforcement responsibilities over accounting firms in the U.S.

Address: **http://www.pcaobus.org/,**
        or go to **www.wiley.com/college/kimmel**

Instructions
Answer the following questions.
(a) What is the mission of the PCAOB?
(b) Briefly summarize its responsibilities related to inspections.
(c) Briefly summarize its responsibilities related to enforcement.

Critical Thinking

DECISION MAKING ACROSS THE ORGANIZATION

BYP7-7   Alternative Distributor Corp., a distributor of groceries and related products, is headquartered in Medford, Massachusetts.
  During a recent audit, Alternative Distributor Corp. was advised that existing internal controls necessary for the company to develop reliable financial statements were inadequate. The audit report stated that the current system of accounting for sales, receivables, and cash receipts constituted a material weakness. Among other items, the report focused on nontimely deposit of cash receipts, exposing Alternative Distributor to potential loss or

misappropriation, excessive past due accounts receivable due to lack of collection efforts, disregard of advantages offered by vendors for prompt payment of invoices, absence of appropriate segregation of duties by personnel consistent with appropriate control objectives, inadequate procedures for applying accounting principles, lack of qualified management personnel, lack of supervision by an outside board of directors, and overall poor recordkeeping.

Instructions
(a) Identify the principles of internal control violated by Alternative Distributor Corporation.
(b) Explain why managers of various functional areas in the company should be concerned about internal controls.

COMMUNICATION ACTIVITY

BYP7-8 As a new auditor for the CPA firm of Ticke and Tie, you have been assigned to review the internal controls over mail cash receipts of Proehl Company. Your review reveals that checks are promptly endorsed "For Deposit Only," but no list of the checks is prepared by the person opening the mail. The mail is opened either by the cashier or by the employee who maintains the accounts receivable records. Mail receipts are deposited in the bank weekly by the cashier.

Instructions
Write a letter to S.A. Dykstra, owner of the Proehl Company, explaining the weaknesses in internal control and your recommendations for improving the system.

ETHICS CASES

BYP7-9 As noted in the chapter, banks charge fees of up to $30 for "bounced" checks—that is, checks that exceed the balance in the account. It has been estimated that processing bounced checks costs a bank roughly $1.50 per check. Thus, the profit margin on bounced checks is very high. Recognizing this, some banks have started to process checks from largest to smallest. By doing this, they maximize the number of checks that bounce if a customer overdraws an account. For example, NationsBank (now Bank of America) projected a $14 million increase in fee revenue as a result of processing largest checks first. In response to criticism, banks have responded that their customers prefer to have large checks processed first, because those tend to be the most important. At the other extreme, some banks will cover their customers' bounced checks, effectively extending them an interest-free loan while their account is overdrawn.

Instructions
Answer each of the following questions.
(a) William Preston had a balance of $1,500 in his checking account at First National Bank on a day when the bank received the following five checks for processing against his account.

Check Number	Amount	Check Number	Amount
3150	$ 35	3165	$ 550
3162	400	3166	1,510
		3169	180

Assuming a $30 fee assessed by the bank for each bounced check, how much fee revenue would the bank generate if it processed checks (1) from largest to smallest, (2) from smallest to largest, and (3) in order of check number?
(b) Do you think that processing checks from largest to smallest is an ethical business practice?
(c) In addition to ethical issues, what other issues must a bank consider in deciding whether to process checks from largest to smallest?
(d) If you were managing a bank, what policy would you adopt on bounced checks?

BYP7-10 Fraud Bureau is a free service, established to alert consumers and investors about prior complaints relating to online vendors, including sellers at online auctions,

and to provide consumers, investors, and users with information and news. One of the services it provides is a collection of online educational articles related to fraud.

Address: **www.fraudbureau.com/articles/**, or go to
www.wiley.com/college/kimmel

Instructions
Go to this site and choose an article of interest to you. Write a short summary of your findings.

"ALL ABOUT YOU" ACTIVITY

BYP7-11 The print and electronic media are full of stories about potential security risks that can arise from your personal computer. It is important to keep in mind, however, that there are also many ways that your identity can be stolen other than from your computer. The federal government provides many resources to help protect you from identity thieves.

Instructions
Go to **http://onguardonline.gov/idtheft.html**, and click on ID Theft Faceoff. Complete the quiz provided there.

Answers to Insight and Accounting Across the Organization Questions

p. 335
Q: Why would unsupervised employees or employees who report to each other represent potential internal control threats?
A. An unsupervised employee may have a fraudulent job (or may even be a fictitious person)—e.g., a person drawing a paycheck without working. Or, if two employees supervise each other, there is no real separation of duties, and they can conspire to defraud the company.

p. 336
Q. Why are small companies more susceptible to employee theft?
A. The high degree of trust often found in small companies makes them more vulnerable. Also, small companies tend to have less sophisticated systems of internal control, and they usually lack internal auditors. In addition, it is very hard to achieve some internal control features, such as segregation of duties, when you have very few employees.

p. 342
Q. How can companies reduce the likelihood of fraudulent disbursements?
A. To reduce the occurrence of fraudulent disbursements a company should follow the procedures discussed in this chapter. These include having only designated personnel sign checks; having different personnel approve payments and make payments; ensuring that check signers do not record disbursements; using prenumbered checks and matching each check to an approved invoice; storing blank checks securely; reconciling the bank statement; and stamping invoices PAID.

p. 348
Q. Why would a company's stock price fall if it reports deficiencies in its internal controls?
A. Internal controls protect against employee theft, but they also provide protection against manipulation of accounting numbers. If a company has poor internal controls, investors will have less confidence that its financial statements are accurate. As a consequence, its stock price will suffer.

Answers to Self-Study Questions

1. c 2. a 3. c 4. b 5. a 6. b 7. d 8. a 9. d 10. c 11. c 12. c 13. b 14. d
*15. a

✔ Remember to go back to the navigator box on the chapter-opening page and check off your completed work.

chapter 8

Reporting and Analyzing Receivables

✔ the navigator

- Scan **Study Objectives** ○
- Read **Feature Story** ○
- Scan **Preview** ○
- Read **Text and Answer** *Do it!*
  p. 394 ○ p. 398 ○ p. 403 ○ p. 407 ○
- Work **Using the Decision Toolkit** ○
- Review **Summary of Study Objectives** ○
- Work **Comprehensive** *Do it!* p. 410 ○
- Answer **Self-Study Questions** ○
- Complete **Assignments** ○

study objectives

After studying this chapter, you should be able to:

1 Identify the different types of receivables.

2 Explain how accounts receivable are recognized in the accounts.

3 Describe the methods used to account for bad debts.

4 Compute the interest on notes receivable.

5 Describe the entries to record the disposition of notes receivable.

6 Explain the statement presentation of receivables.

7 Describe the principles of sound accounts receivable management.

8 Identify ratios to analyze a company's receivables.

9 Describe methods to accelerate the receipt of cash from receivables.

Dose of Careful Management Keeps Receivables Healthy

"Sometimes you have to know when to be very tough, and sometimes you can give them a bit of a break," says Vivi Su. She's not talking about her children, but about the customers of a subsidiary of pharmaceutical company Whitehall-Robins, where she works as supervisor of credit and collections.

For example, while the company's regular terms are 1/15, n/30 (1% discount if paid within 15 days), a customer might ask for and receive a few days of grace and still get the discount. Or a customer might place orders above its credit limit, in which case, depending on its payment history and the circumstances, Ms. Su might authorize shipment of the goods anyway.

"It's not about drawing a line in the sand, and that's all," she explains. "You want a good relationship with your customers—but you also need to bring in the money."

"The money," in Whitehall-Robins's case amounts to some $170 million in sales a year. Nearly all of it comes in through the credit accounts Ms. Su manages. The process starts with the decision to grant a customer an account in the first place, Ms. Su explains. The sales rep gives the

customer a credit application. "My department reviews this application very carefully; a customer needs to supply three good references, and we also run a check with a credit firm like Equifax. If we accept them, then based on their size and history, we assign a credit limit."

Once accounts are established, the company supervises them very carefully. "I get an aging report every single day," says Ms. Su.

"The rule of thumb is that we should always have at least 85% of receivables current—meaning they were billed less than 30 days ago," she continues. "But we try to do even better than that—I like to see 90%." Similarly, her guideline is never to have more than 5% of receivables at over 90 days. But long before that figure is reached, "we jump on it," she says firmly.

At 15 days overdue, Whitehall-Robins phones the client. Often there's a reasonable explanation for the delay—an invoice may have gone astray, or the payables clerk is away. "But if a customer keeps on delaying, and tells us several times that it'll only be a few more days, we know there's a problem," says Ms. Su. After 45 days,

"I send a letter. Then a second notice is sent in writing. After the third and final notice, the client has 10 days to pay, and then I hand it over to a collection agency, and it's out of my hands."

Ms. Su's boss, Terry Norton, records an estimate for bad debts every year, based on a percentage of receivables. The percentage depends on the current aging history. He also calculates and monitors the company's receivables turnover ratio, which the company reports in its financial statements. "I think of it in terms of collection period of DSO—days of sales outstanding," he explains.

Ms. Su knows that she and Mr. Norton are crucial to the profitability of Whitehall-Robins. "Receivables are generally the second-largest asset of any company (after its capital assets)," she points out. "So it's no wonder we keep a very close eye on them."

On the World Wide Web
Whitehall-Robins Healthcare, Inc.
www.whitehall-robins.com

In this chapter we discuss some of the decisions related to reporting and analyzing receivables. As indicated in the Feature Story, receivables are a significant asset on the books of pharmaceutical company Whitehall-Robins. Receivables are significant to companies in other industries as well, because a significant portion of sales are made on credit in the United States. As a consequence, companies must pay close attention to their receivables balances and manage them carefully.

The organization and content of the chapter are as follows.

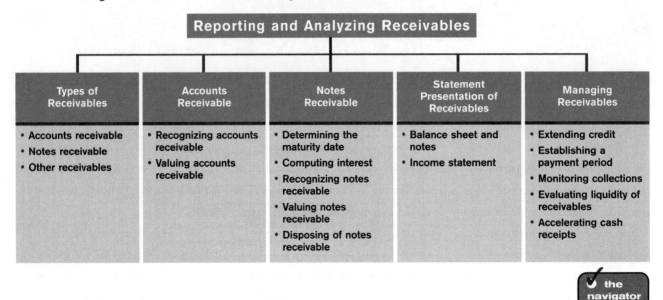

Types of Receivables

study objective 1

Identify the different types of receivables.

The term **receivables** refers to amounts due from individuals and companies. Receivables are claims that are expected to be collected in cash. The management of receivables is a very important activity for any company that sells goods or services on credit.

Receivables are important because they represent one of a company's most liquid assets. For many companies, receivables are also one of the largest assets. For example, receivables represented 11% of the current assets of pharmacy giant Rite Aid in 2007. Illustration 8-1 lists receivables as a percentage of total assets for five other well-known companies in a recent year.

Illustration 8-1
Receivables as a percentage of assets

Company	Receivables as a Percentage of Total Assets
General Electric	52%
Ford Motor Company	42%
Minnesota Mining and Manufacturing Company (3M)	14%
DuPont Co.	17%
Intel Corporation	5%

The relative significance of a company's receivables as a percentage of its assets depends on various factors: its industry, the time of year, whether it extends long-term financing, and its credit policies. To reflect important differences among receivables, they are frequently classified as (1) accounts receivable, (2) notes receivable, and (3) other receivables.

Accounts receivable are amounts customers owe on account. They result from the sale of goods and services. Companies generally expect to collect accounts receivable within 30 to 60 days. They are usually the most significant type of claim held by a company.

Notes receivable represent claims for which formal instruments of credit are issued as evidence of the debt. The credit instrument normally requires the debtor to pay interest and extends for time periods of 60–90 days or longer. Notes and accounts receivable that result from sales transactions are often called trade receivables.

Other receivables include non-trade receivables such as interest receivable, loans to company officers, advances to employees, and income taxes refundable. These do not generally result from the operations of the business. Therefore, they are generally classified and reported as separate items in the balance sheet.

Ethics Note Companies report receivables from employees separately in the financial statements. The reason: Sometimes those assets are not the result of an "arm's-length" transaction.

Accounts Receivable

Two accounting issues associated with accounts receivable are:

1. Recognizing accounts receivable.
2. Valuing accounts receivable.

A third issue, accelerating cash receipts from receivables, is discussed later in the chapter.

RECOGNIZING ACCOUNTS RECEIVABLE

Initial recognition of accounts receivable is relatively straightforward. A service organization records a receivable when it provides service on account. A merchandiser records accounts receivable at the point of sale of merchandise on account. When a merchandiser sells goods, it increases both the Accounts Receivable and Sales accounts.

study objective 2

Explain how accounts receivable are recognized in the accounts.

The seller may offer terms that encourage early payment by providing a discount. For example, terms of 2/10, n/30 provide the buyer with a 2% discount if it pays within 10 days. If the buyer chooses to pay within the discount period, the seller reduces its accounts receivable by the sum of cash received and the discount taken.

Sales returns also reduce receivables. The buyer might find some of the goods unacceptable and choose to return the unwanted goods. For example, if the buyer returns merchandise with a selling price of $100, the seller reduces Accounts Receivable by $100 upon receipt of the returned merchandise.

Some retailers issue their own credit cards. When you use a retailer's credit card (JCPenney, for example), the retailer charges interest on the balance due if not paid within a specified period (usually 25–30 days).

To illustrate, assume that you use your JCPenney Company credit card to purchase clothing with a sales price of $300. JCPenney will increase (debit) Accounts Receivable for $300 and increase (credit) Sales for $300. Assuming that you owe $300 at the end of the month, and JCPenney charges 1.5% per month on the balance due, the adjusting entry to record interest revenue of $4.50 ($300 × 1.5%) is as follows.

Accounts Receivable	4.50	
Interest Revenue		4.50
(To record interest on amount due)		

A = L + SE

+4.50

+4.50 Rev

Cash Flows
no effect

Interest revenue is often substantial for many retailers.

VALUING ACCOUNTS RECEIVABLE

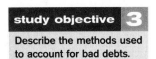

Describe the methods used to account for bad debts.

Once companies record receivables in the accounts, the next question is: How should they report receivables in the financial statements? Companies report accounts receivable on the balance sheet as an asset. Determining the **amount** to report is sometimes difficult because some receivables will become uncollectible.

Although each customer must satisfy the credit requirements of the seller before the credit sale is approved, inevitably some accounts receivable become uncollectible. For example, a corporate customer may not be able to pay because it experienced a sales decline due to an economic downturn. Similarly, individuals may be laid off from their jobs or be faced with unexpected hospital bills. The seller records these losses from extending credit as Bad Debts Expense. Such losses are a normal and necessary risk of doing business on a credit basis.

Alternative Terminology You will sometimes see *Bad Debts Expense* called *Uncollectible Accounts Expense.*

Recently when U.S. home prices fell, home foreclosures rose, and the economy in general slowed, lenders experienced huge increases in their bad debts expense. For example, during a recent quarter Wachovia, the fourth largest U.S. bank, increased bad debts expense from $108 million to $408 million. Similarly, American Express increased its bad debt expense by 70%.

The accounting profession uses two methods for uncollectible accounts: (1) the direct write-off method, and (2) the allowance method. We explain each of these methods in the following sections.

Direct Write-off Method for Uncollectible Accounts

Under the direct write-off method, when a company determines receivables from a particular company to be uncollectible, it charges the loss to Bad Debts Expense. Assume, for example, that Warden Co. writes off M. E. Doran's $200 balance as uncollectible on December 12. Warden's entry is:

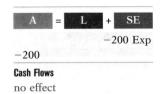

−200

Cash Flows
no effect

Dec. 12	Bad Debts Expense	200	
	Accounts Receivable — M. E. Doran		200
	(To record write-off of M. E. Doran account)		

Under this method, bad debts expense will show only **actual losses** from uncollectibles. The company will report accounts receivable at its gross amount.

Use of the direct write-off method can reduce the usefulness of both the income statement and balance sheet. Consider the following example. In 2010, Quick Buck Computer Company decided it could increase its revenues by offering computers to college students without requiring any money down, and with no credit-approval process. It went on campuses across the country and sold one million computers at a selling price of $800 each. This promotion increased Quick Buck's revenues and receivables by $800,000,000. It was a huge success: The 2010 balance sheet and income statement looked wonderful. Unfortunately, during 2011, nearly 40% of the college student customers defaulted on their loans. The 2011 income statement and balance sheet looked terrible. Illustration 8-2 shows

Illustration 8-2 Effects of direct write-off method

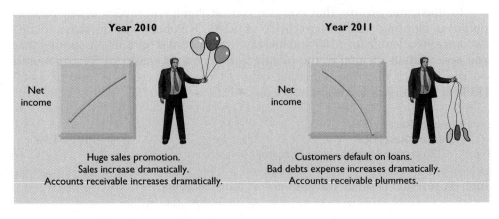

the effect of these events on the financial statements using the direct write-off method.

Under the direct write-off method, companies often record bad debts expense in a period different from the period in which they recorded the revenue. Thus, no attempt is made to match bad debts expense to sales revenues in the income statement. Nor does the company try to show accounts receivable in the balance sheet at the amount actually expected to be received. **Consequently, unless a company expects bad debts losses to be insignificant, the direct write-off method is not acceptable for financial reporting purposes.**

Allowance Method for Uncollectible Accounts

The allowance method of accounting for bad debts involves estimating uncollectible accounts at the end of each period. This provides better matching of expenses with revenues on the income statement. It also ensures that receivables are stated at their cash (net) realizable value on the balance sheet. Cash (net) realizable value is the net amount a company expects to receive in cash from receivables. It excludes amounts that the company estimates it will not collect. Estimated uncollectible receivables therefore reduce receivables on the balance sheet through use of the allowance method.

Companies must use the allowance method for financial reporting purposes when bad debts are material in amount. It has three essential features:

1. Companies **estimate** uncollectible accounts receivable and **match them against revenues** in the same accounting period in which the revenues are recorded.

2. Companies record estimated uncollectibles as an increase (a debit) to Bad Debts Expense and an increase (a credit) to Allowance for Doubtful Accounts through an adjusting entry at the end of each period. Allowance for Doubtful Accounts is a contra account to Accounts Receivable.

3. Companies debit actual uncollectibles to Allowance for Doubtful Accounts and credit them to Accounts Receivable at the time the specific account is written off as uncollectible.

RECORDING ESTIMATED UNCOLLECTIBLES. To illustrate the allowance method, assume that Hampson Furniture has credit sales of $1,200,000 in 2010, of which $200,000 remains uncollected at December 31. The credit manager estimates that $12,000 of these sales will prove uncollectible. The adjusting entry to record the estimated uncollectibles increases (debits) Bad Debts Expense and increases (credits) Allowance for Doubtful Accounts, as follows.

Dec. 31	Bad Debts Expense	12,000	
	Allowance for Doubtful Accounts		12,000
	(To record estimate of uncollectible accounts)		

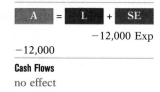

A = L + SE
−12,000 Exp
−12,000

Cash Flows
no effect

Companies report Bad Debts Expense in the income statement as an operating expense (usually as a selling expense). Thus, Hampson matches the estimated uncollectibles with sales in 2010 because the expense is recorded in the same year the company makes the sales.

Allowance for Doubtful Accounts shows the estimated amount of claims on customers that companies expect will become uncollectible in the future. Companies use a contra account instead of a direct credit to Accounts Receivable because they do not know *which* customers will not pay. The credit balance in the allowance account will absorb the specific write-offs when they occur. The company deducts the allowance account from Accounts Receivable in the current assets section of the balance sheet as shown in Illustration 8-3 (page 390).

Illustration 8-3
Presentation of allowance for doubtful accounts

HAMPSON FURNITURE		
Balance Sheet (partial)		
Current assets		
Cash		$ 14,800
Accounts receivable	$200,000	
Less: Allowance for doubtful accounts	12,000	188,000
Merchandise inventory		310,000
Prepaid expense		25,000
Total current assets		$537,800

The amount of $188,000 in Illustration 8-3 represents the expected **cash realizable value** of the accounts receivable at the statement date. **Companies do not close Allowance for Doubtful Accounts at the end of the fiscal year.**

RECORDING THE WRITE-OFF OF AN UNCOLLECTIBLE ACCOUNT. Companies use various methods of collecting past-due accounts, as discussed in the Feature Story. When a company has exhausted all means of collecting a past-due account and collection appears unlikely, the company should write off the account. In the credit card industry it is standard practice to write off accounts that are 210 days past due. To prevent premature or unauthorized write-offs, authorized management personnel should formally approve each write-off. To maintain good internal control, companies should not authorize someone to write off accounts who also has daily responsibilities related to cash or receivables.

To illustrate a receivables write-off, assume that the vice-president of finance of Hampson Furniture on March 1, 2011, authorizes a write-off of the $500 balance owed by R. A. Ware. The entry to record the write-off is:

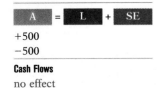

+500
−500

Cash Flows
no effect

Mar. 1	Allowance for Doubtful Accounts	500	
	Accounts Receivable — R. A. Ware		500
	(Write-off of R. A. Ware account)		

The company does not increase Bad Debts Expense when the write-off occurs. **Under the allowance method, a company debits every bad debt write-off to the allowance account and not to Bad Debts Expense.** A debit to Bad Debts Expense would be incorrect because the company has already recognized the expense when it made the adjusting entry for estimated bad debts. Instead, the entry to record the write-off of an uncollectible account reduces both Accounts Receivable and the Allowance for Doubtful Accounts. After posting, the general ledger accounts will appear as in Illustration 8-4.

Illustration 8-4 General ledger balances after write-off

Accounts Receivable		Allowance for Doubtful Accounts	
Jan. 1 Bal. 200,000	Mar. 1 **500**	Mar. 1 **500**	Jan. 1 Bal. 12,000
Mar. 1 Bal. 199,500			Mar. 1 Bal. 11,500

A write-off affects only balance sheet accounts. Cash realizable value in the balance sheet, therefore, remains the same, as shown in Illustration 8-5.

	Before Write-off	After Write-off
Accounts receivable	$ 200,000	$ 199,500
Allowance for doubtful accounts	12,000	11,500
Cash realizable value	**$188,000**	**$188,000**

Illustration 8-5 Cash realizable value comparison

RECOVERY OF AN UNCOLLECTIBLE ACCOUNT. Occasionally, a company collects from a customer after the account has been written off as uncollectible. The company must make two entries to record the recovery of a bad debt: (1) It reverses the entry made in writing off the account. This reinstates the customer's account. (2) It journalizes the collection in the usual manner.

To illustrate, assume that on July 1, R. A. Ware pays the $500 amount that Hampson Furniture had written off on March 1. Hampson makes these entries:

		(1)		
July	1	Accounts Receivable — R. A. Ware	500	
		Allowance for Doubtful Accounts		500
		(To reverse write-off of R. A. Ware		
		account)		

A = L + SE
+500
−500

Cash Flows
no effect

		(2)		
	1	Cash	500	
		Accounts Receivable — R. A. Ware		500
		(To record collection from R. A. Ware)		

A = L + SE
+500
−500

Cash Flows
+500

Note that the recovery of a bad debt, like the write-off of a bad debt, affects only balance sheet accounts. The net effect of the two entries is an increase in Cash and an increase in Allowance for Doubtful Accounts for $500. Accounts Receivable and the Allowance for Doubtful Accounts both increase in entry (1) for two reasons: First, the company made an error in judgment when it wrote off the account receivable. Second, R. A. Ware did pay, and therefore the Accounts Receivable account should show this reinstatement and collection for possible future credit purposes.

Helpful Hint Like the write-off, a recovery does not involve the income statement.

ESTIMATING THE ALLOWANCE. For Hampson Furniture in Illustration 8-3, the amount of the expected uncollectibles was given. However, in "real life," companies must estimate the amount of expected uncollectible accounts if they use the allowance method. Frequently they estimate the allowance as a percentage of the outstanding receivables.

Under the percentage of receivables basis, management establishes a percentage relationship between the amount of receivables and expected losses from uncollectible accounts. The company prepares a schedule, called aging the accounts receivable, in which it classifies customer balances by the length of time they have been unpaid. Because of its emphasis on time, this schedule is often called an **aging schedule**.

After the company arranges the accounts by age, it determines the expected bad debt losses by applying percentages, based on past experience, to the totals of each category. The longer a receivable is past due, the less likely it is to be collected. As a result, the estimated percentage of uncollectible debts increases as the number of days past due increases. Illustration 8-6 (page 392) shows an aging schedule for Dart Company. Note the increasing uncollectible percentages from 2% to 40%.

Illustration 8-6 Aging schedule

Customer	Total	Not Yet Due	Number of Days Past Due			
			1–30	31–60	61–90	Over 90
T. E. Adert	$ 600		$ 300		$ 200	$ 100
R. C. Bortz	300	$ 300				
B. A. Carl	450		200	$ 250		
O. L. Diker	700	500			200	
T. O. Ebbet	600			300		300
Others	36,950	26,200	5,200	2,450	1,600	1,500
	$39,600	$27,000	$5,700	$3,000	$2,000	$1,900
Estimated percentage uncollectible		2%	4%	10%	20%	40%
Total estimated uncollectible accounts	**$ 2,228**	$ 540	$ 228	$ 300	$ 400	$ 760

Total estimated uncollectible accounts for Dart Company ($2,228) represent the existing customer claims expected to become uncollectible in the future. Thus, this amount represents the **required balance** in Allowance for Doubtful Accounts at the balance sheet date. Accordingly, **the amount of the bad debts expense adjusting entry is the difference between the required balance and the existing balance in the allowance account**. The existing, unadjusted balance is the net result of the beginning balance (a normal credit balance) less the write-offs of specific accounts during the year (debits to the account).

For example, if the unadjusted trial balance shows Allowance for Doubtful Accounts with a credit balance of $528, then an adjusting entry for $1,700 ($2,228 − $528) is necessary:

A = L + SE
−1,700 Exp
−1,700
Cash Flows
no effect

Dec. 31	Bad Debts Expense	1,700	
	Allowance for Doubtful Accounts		1,700
	(To adjust allowance account to total estimated uncollectibles)		

After Dart posts the adjusting entry, its accounts will appear as in Illustration 8-7.

Illustration 8-7 Bad debts accounts after posting

Bad Debts Expense		Allowance for Doubtful Accounts	
Dec. 31 Adj. **1,700**			Jan. 1 Bal. 528
			Dec. 31 Adj. **1,700**
			Dec. 31 Bal. 2,228

An important aspect of accounts receivable management is simply maintaining a close watch on the accounts. Studies have shown that accounts more than 60 days past due lose approximately 50% of their value if no payment activity occurs within the next 30 days. For each additional 30 days that pass, the collectible value halves once again. As noted in our Feature Story, Vivi Su of Whitehall-Robins monitors accounts receivable closely, using an aging schedule to set the percentage of bad debts and computing the company's receivables turnover.

Occasionally the allowance account will have a **debit balance** prior to adjustment. This occurs because the debits to the allowance account from write-offs during the year **exceeded** the beginning balance in the account which was based on previous estimates for bad debts. In such a case, the company **adds the debit balance to the required balance** when it makes the adjusting entry.

Thus, if there had been a $500 debit balance in the allowance account before adjustment, the adjusting entry would have been for $2,728 ($2,228 + $500) in order to arrive at a credit balance of $2,228.

The percentage of receivables basis provides an estimate of the cash realizable value of the receivables. It also provides a reasonable matching of expense to revenue.

DECISION TOOLKIT

DECISION CHECKPOINTS	INFO NEEDED FOR DECISION	TOOL TO USE FOR DECISION	HOW TO EVALUATE RESULTS
Is the amount of past due accounts increasing? Which accounts require management's attention?	List of outstanding receivables and their due dates	Prepare an aging schedule showing the receivables in various stages: outstanding 0–30 days, 31–60 days, 61–90 days, and over 90 days.	Accounts in the older categories require follow-up: letters, phone calls, and possible renegotiation of terms.

The following note regarding accounts receivable comes from the annual report of healthcare company McKesson Corp.

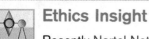

McKESSON CORP.
Notes to the Financial Statements

Illustration 8-8 Note disclosure of accounts receivable

Receivables, net

	March 31,	
(In millions)	**2007**	**2006**
Customer accounts	$5,753	$5,684
Other	953	694
Total	6,706	6,378
Allowances	(140)	(131)
Net	$6,566	$6,247

The allowances are primarily for uncollectible accounts and sales returns.

Ethics Insight

Recently Nortel Networks announced that half of its previous year's earnings were "fake." Should investors have seen this coming? Well, there were issues in its annual report that should have caused investors to ask questions. The company had cut its allowance for doubtful accounts on all receivables from $1,253 million to $544 million, even though its total balance of receivables remained relatively unchanged.

This reduction in bad debt expense was responsible for a very large part of the company's earnings that year. At the time it was unclear whether Nortel might have set the reserves too high originally and needed to reduce them, or whether it slashed the allowance to artificially boost earnings. But one thing is certain—when a company makes an accounting change of this magnitude, investors need to ask questions.

Source: Jonathan Weil, "Outside Audit: At Nortel, Warning Signs Existed Months Ago," *Wall Street Journal* (May 18, 2004), p. C3.

 When would it be appropriate for a company to lower its allowance for doubtful accounts as a percentage of its receivables?

before you go on...

BAD DEBTS EXPENSE
Action Plan

- Report receivables at their cash (net) realizable value—that is, the amount the company expects to collect in cash.

- Estimate the amount the company does not expect to collect.

- Consider the existing balance in the allowance account when using the percentage of receivables basis.

Do it!

Brule Corporation has been in business for 5 years. The ledger at the end of the current year shows: Accounts Receivable $30,000; Sales $180,000; and Allowance for Doubtful Accounts with a debit balance of $2,000. Brule estimates bad debts to be 10% of accounts receivable. Prepare the entry necessary to adjust the Allowance for Doubtful Accounts.

Solution

Brule should make the following entry to bring the debit balance in the Allowance for Doubtful Accounts up to a normal, credit balance of $3,000 (.1 × $30,000):

Bad Debts Expense	5,000	
Allowance for Doubtful Accounts		5,000
(To record estimate of		
uncollectible accounts)		

✔ the navigator

Notes Receivable

Companies also may grant credit in exchange for a formal credit instrument known as a promissory note. A **promissory note** is a written promise to pay a specified amount of money on demand or at a definite time. Promissory notes may be used (1) when individuals and companies lend or borrow money, (2) when the amount of the transaction and the credit period exceed normal limits, and (3) in settlement of accounts receivable.

In a promissory note, the party making the promise to pay is called the **maker**. The party to whom payment is to be made is called the **payee**. The promissory note may specifically identify the payee by name or may designate the payee simply as the bearer of the note.

In the note shown in Illustration 8-9, Brent Company is the maker, and Wilma Company is the payee. To Wilma Company, the promissory note is a note receivable; to Brent Company, the note is a note payable.

Illustration 8-9
Promissory note

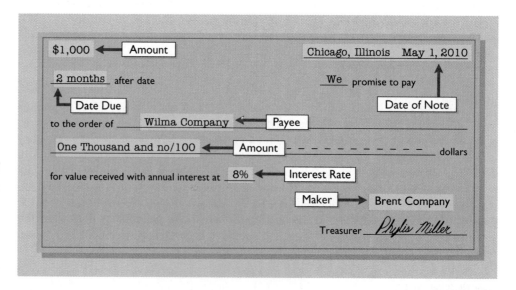

Helpful Hint Who are the two key parties to a note? What entry does each party make when the note is issued?
Answer:
1. The maker, Brent Company, credits Notes Payable.
2. The payee, Wilma Company, debits Notes Receivable.

Notes receivable give the holder a stronger legal claim to assets than do accounts receivable. Like accounts receivable, notes receivable can be readily sold to another party. Promissory notes are negotiable instruments (as are checks), which means that, when sold, the seller can transfer them to another party by endorsement.

Companies frequently accept notes receivable from customers who need to extend the payment of an outstanding account receivable, and they often require them from high-risk customers. In some industries (e.g., the pleasure and sport boat industry) all credit sales are supported by notes. The majority of notes, however, originate from lending transactions.

There are three basic issues in accounting for notes receivable:

1. **Recognizing** notes receivable.
2. **Valuing** notes receivable.
3. **Disposing** of notes receivable.

We will look at each of these issues, but first we need to consider an issue that did not apply to accounts receivable: computing interest.

DETERMINING THE MATURITY DATE

When the life of a note is expressed in terms of months, you find the date when it matures by counting the months from the date of issue. For example, the maturity date of a three-month note dated May 1 is August 1. A note drawn on the last day of a month matures on the last day of a subsequent month. That is, a July 31 note due in two months matures on September 30.

When the due date is stated in terms of days, you need to count the exact number of days to determine the maturity date. In counting, **omit the date the note is issued but include the due date**.

COMPUTING INTEREST

Illustration 8-10 gives the basic formula for computing interest on an interest-bearing note.

study objective 4
Compute the interest on notes receivable.

$$\text{Face Value of Note} \times \text{Annual Interest Rate} \times \text{Time in Terms of One Year} = \text{Interest}$$

Illustration 8-10 Formula for computing interest

The interest rate specified on the note is an **annual** rate of interest. The time factor in the computation expresses the fraction of a year that the note is outstanding. When the maturity date is stated in days, the time factor is frequently the number of days divided by 360. When counting days, omit the date the note is issued, but include the due date. When the due date is stated in months, the time factor is the number of months divided by 12. Illustration 8-11 shows computation of interest for various time periods.

Terms of Note	Interest Computation
	Face × Rate × Time = Interest
$ 730, 12%, 120 days	$ 730 × 12% × 120/360 = $ 29.20
$1,000, 9%, 6 months	$1,000 × 9% × 6/12 = $ 45.00
$2,000, 6%, 1 year	$2,000 × 6% × 1/1 = $120.00

Illustration 8-11 Computation of interest

There are different ways to calculate interest. For example, the computation in Illustration 8-11 assumed 360 days for the year. Most financial institutions use 365 days to compute interest. (*For homework problems, assume 360 days to simplify computations.*)

RECOGNIZING NOTES RECEIVABLE

To illustrate the basic entry for notes receivable, we will use Brent Company's $1,000, two-month, 8% promissory note dated May 1. Assuming that Brent Company wrote the note to settle an open account, Wilma Company makes the following entry for the receipt of the note.

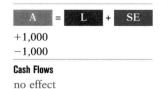

A = L + SE
+1,000
−1,000

Cash Flows
no effect

May 1	Notes Receivable	1,000	
	Accounts Receivable — Brent Company		1,000
	(To record acceptance of Brent Company note)		

The company records the note receivable at its **face value**, the value shown on the face of the note. No interest revenue is reported when the company accepts the note because the revenue recognition principle does not recognize revenue until earned. Interest is earned (accrued) as time passes.

If a company exchanges a note for cash, the entry is a debit to Notes Receivable and a credit to Cash in the amount of the loan.

VALUING NOTES RECEIVABLE

Like accounts receivable, companies report short-term notes receivable at their **cash (net) realizable value**. The notes receivable allowance account is Allowance for Doubtful Accounts. Valuing short-term notes receivable is the same as valuing accounts receivable. The computations and estimations involved in determining cash realizable value and in recording the proper amount of bad debts expense and related allowance are similar.

Long-term notes receivable, however, pose additional estimation problems. As an example, we need only look at the problems large U.S. banks sometimes have in collecting their receivables. Loans to less-developed countries are particularly worrisome. Developing countries need loans for development but often find repayment difficult. U.S. loans (notes) to less-developed countries at one time totaled approximately $135 billion. In Brazil alone, **Citigroup** at one time had loans equivalent to 80% of its stockholders' equity. In some cases, developed nations have intervened to provide financial assistance to the financially troubled borrowers so as to minimize the political and economic turmoil to the borrower and to ensure the survival of the lender.

 ## Accounting Across the Organization

Management must decide to whom it will grant credit. This is one of the hardest, and most critical, decisions that it makes. Consider the case of Mitsubishi Motors. It had been floundering, reporting large losses for a number of years in a row. Then management came up with what appeared to be a great plan. It began a marketing campaign aimed at giving Mitsubishi a hip image (think flashy ads with loud music), thus making its vehicles attractive to single people in their early twenties. The company combined this campaign with easy credit terms—so called "zero-zero-zero" deals. This meant no down-payment, no payments for the first six months, and 0% financing.

The plan worked great—sort of. Sales took off. But then the twenty-somethings started defaulting on their loans. Soon Mitsubishi's losses were even bigger than before. It has since refocused its ads and credit terms. It now focuses on people who are "young at heart" (as opposed to just young)—and "economically safer."

Source: Todd Zaun, "Bad Loans Bump Mitsubishi Motors Off Road to Recovery," *Wall Street Journal Online* (November 12, 2003).

 How would reported net income likely differ during the first year of this promotion if Mitsubishi used the direct write-off method versus the allowance method?

DISPOSING OF NOTES RECEIVABLE

Notes may be held to their maturity date, at which time the face value plus accrued interest is due. In some situations, the maker of the note defaults, and the payee must make an appropriate adjustment. In other situations, similar to accounts receivable, the holder of the note speeds up the conversion to cash by selling the receivables as described later in this chapter.

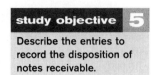

study objective **5**

Describe the entries to record the disposition of notes receivable.

Honor of Notes Receivable

A note is **honored** when its maker pays in full at its maturity date. For each interest-bearing note, the **amount due at maturity** is the face value of the note plus interest for the length of time specified on the note.

To illustrate, assume that Wolder Co. lends Higley Inc. $10,000 on June 1, accepting a five-month, 9% interest note. In this situation, interest is $375 ($10,000 $\times$ 9% $\times \frac{5}{12}$). The amount due, the maturity value, is $10,375 ($10,000 + $375). To obtain payment, Wolder (the payee) must present the note either to Higley Inc. (the maker) or to the maker's agent, such as a bank. If Wolder presents the note to Higley Inc. on November 1, the maturity date, Wolder's entry to record the collection is:

Helpful Hint How many days of interest should be accrued at September 30 for a 90-day note issued on August 16? *Answer:* 45 days (15 days in August plus 30 days in September).

Nov. 1	Cash	10,375	
	Notes Receivable		10,000
	Interest Revenue ($10,000 $\times$ 9% $\times \frac{5}{12}$)		375
	(To record collection of Higley Inc. note and interest)		

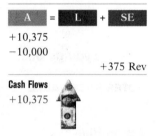

A = L + SE
+10,375
−10,000
+375 Rev

Cash Flows
+10,375

Accrual of Interest Receivable

Suppose instead that Wolder Co. prepares financial statements as of September 30. The following timeline presents this situation.

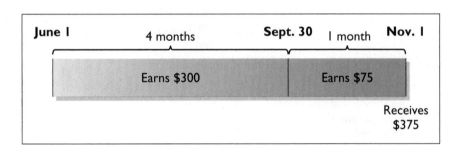

June 1   4 months   **Sept. 30**   1 month   **Nov. 1**

Earns $300   Earns $75

Receives $375

To reflect interest earned but not yet received, Wolder must accrue interest on September 30. In this case, the adjusting entry by Wolder is for four months of interest, or $300, as shown below.

Sept. 30	Interest Receivable ($10,000 $\times$ 9% $\times \frac{4}{12}$)	300	
	Interest Revenue		300
	(To accrue 4 months' interest on Higley note)		

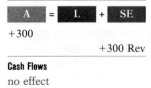

A = L + SE
+300
+300 Rev

Cash Flows
no effect

At the note's maturity on November 1, Wolder receives $10,375. This amount represents repayment of the $10,000 note as well as five months of interest, or $375, as shown on the next page. The $375 is comprised of the $300 Interest

Receivable accrued on September 30 plus $75 earned during October. Wolder's entry to record the honoring of the Higley note on November 1 is:

A	=	L	+	SE
+10,375				
−10,000				
−300				
				+75 Rev

Cash Flows
+10,375

Nov. 1	Cash [$10,000 + ($10,000 × 9% × $\frac{5}{12}$)]		10,375	
	Notes Receivable			10,000
	Interest Receivable			300
	Interest Revenue ($10,000 × 9% × $\frac{1}{12}$)			75
	(To record collection of Higley Inc. note and interest)			

In this case, Wolder credits Interest Receivable because the receivable was established in the adjusting entry on September 30.

Dishonor of Notes Receivable

A **dishonored note** is a note that is not paid in full at maturity. A dishonored note receivable is no longer negotiable; however, the payee still has a claim against the maker of the note for both the note and the interest. If the lender expects that it eventually will be able to collect, the two parties negotiate new terms to make it easier for the borrower to repay the debt. If there is no hope of collection, the payee should write off the face value of the note.

before you go on...

NOTES RECEIVABLE

Action Plan

- Determine whether interest was accrued.
- Compute the accrued interest.
- Prepare the entry for payment of the note and the interest. The entry to record interest at maturity in this solution assumes that no interest has been previously accrued on this note.

Do it!

Gambit Stores accepts from Leonard Co. a $3,400, 90-day, 6% note dated May 10 in settlement of Leonard's overdue open account. The note matures on August 8. What entry does Gambit make at the maturity date, assuming Leonard pays the note and interest in full at that time?

Solution

The interest payable at maturity date is $51, computed as follows.

$$\text{Face} \times \text{Rate} \times \text{Time} = \text{Interest}$$
$$\$3,400 \times 6\% \times \frac{90}{360} = \$51$$

Gambit Stores records this entry at the maturity date:

Cash		3,451	
Notes Receivable			3,400
Interest Revenue			51
(To record collection of Leonard note and interest)			

Financial Statement Presentation of Receivables

study objective 6

Explain the statement presentation of receivables.

Companies should identify in the balance sheet or in the notes to the financial statements each of the major types of receivables. Short-term receivables are reported in the current assets section of the balance sheet, below short-term investments. Short-term investments appear before short-term receivables because these investments are nearer to cash. Companies report both the gross amount of receivables and the allowance for doubtful accounts.

Illustration 8-12 shows a presentation of receivables for Deere & Company from its 2007 balance sheet and notes.

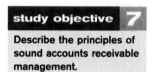

DEERE & COMPANY
Balance Sheet (partial)
(in millions)

Receivables		
Receivables from unconsolidated subsidiaries	$	29.6
Trade accounts and notes receivable		3,055.0
Financing receivables		18,092.2
Other receivables		596.3
Total receivables		21,773.1
Less: Allowance for doubtful trade receivables		172.0
Net receivables		$21,601.1

Illustration 8-12 Balance sheet presentation of receivables

In the income statement, companies report bad debts expense under "Selling expenses" in the operating expenses section. They show interest revenue under "Other revenues and gains" in the nonoperating section of the income statement.

If a company has significant risk of uncollectible accounts or other problems with its receivables, it is required to discuss this possibility in the notes to the financial statements.

Managing Receivables

Managing accounts receivable involves five steps:

1. Determine to whom to extend credit.
2. Establish a payment period.
3. Monitor collections.
4. Evaluate the liquidity of receivables.
5. Accelerate cash receipts from receivables when necessary.

study objective 7

Describe the principles of sound accounts receivable management.

EXTENDING CREDIT

A critical part of managing receivables is determining who should be extended credit and who should not. Many companies increase sales by being generous with their credit policy, but, like Mitsubishi in the *Accounting across the Organization* story, they may end up extending credit to risky customers who do not pay. If the credit policy is too tight, you will lose sales. If it is too loose, you may sell to "deadbeats" who will pay either very late or not at all. One CEO noted that prior to getting his credit and collection department in order, his salespeople had 300 square feet of office space **per person**, while the people in credit and collections had six people crammed into a single 300-square-foot space. Although this focus on sales boosted sales, it had very expensive consequences in bad debts expense.

Companies can take certain steps to help minimize losses if they relax credit standards. They might require risky customers to provide letters of credit or bank guarantees. Then if the customer does not pay, the bank that provided the guarantee will do so. Particularly risky customers might be required to pay cash on delivery. For example, retailer Linens 'n Things, Inc. recently reported that it was paying its largest vendors cash before it had even received the goods. The vendors had cut off shipments because the company had been slow in paying. Kmart's suppliers also required it to pay cash in advance when it was financially troubled.

In addition, companies should ask potential customers for references from banks and suppliers, to determine their payment history. It is important to check these references on potential new customers as well as periodically to check the financial health of continuing customers. Many resources are available for investigating customers. For example, *The Dun & Bradstreet Reference Book of American Business* (*www.dnb.com*) lists millions of companies and provides credit ratings for many of them.

Accounting Across the Organization

Many factors have contributed to the recent credit crisis. One significant factor that resulted in many bad loans was a failure by lenders to investigate loan customers sufficiently. For example, Countrywide Financial Corporation wrote many loans under its "Fast and Easy" loan program. That program required borrowers to provide little or no documentation for their income or their assets. Other lenders had similar programs, which earned the nickname "liars' loans." One study found that in these situations 60% of applicants overstated their incomes by more than 50% in order to qualify for a loan. Critics of the banking industry say that because loan officers were compensated for loan volume, and because banks were selling the loans to investors rather than holding them, the lenders had little incentive to investigate the borrowers' creditworthiness.

Source: Glenn R. Simpson and James R. Hagerty, "Countrywide Loss Focuses Attention on Underwriting," *Wall Street Journal* (April 30, 2008), p. B1; and Michael Corkery, "Fraud Seen as Driver in Wave of Foreclosures, *Wall Street Journal* (December 21, 2007), p. A1.

 What steps should the banks have taken to ensure the accuracy of financial information provided on loan applications?

ESTABLISHING A PAYMENT PERIOD

Companies that extend credit should determine a required payment period and communicate that policy to their customers. It is important that the payment period is consistent with that of competitors. For example, if you decide to require payment within 15 days, but your competitors require payment within 45 days, you may lose sales to your competitors. However, to match competitors' terms yet still encourage prompt payment of accounts, you might allow up to 45 days to pay but offer a sales discount for people paying within 15 days.

MONITORING COLLECTIONS

We discussed preparation of the accounts receivable aging schedule earlier in the chapter (pages 391–392). Companies should prepare an accounts receivable aging schedule at least monthly. In addition to estimating the allowance for doubtful accounts, the aging schedule has other uses: It helps managers estimate the timing of future cash inflows, which is very important to the treasurer's efforts to prepare a cash budget. It provides information about the overall collection experience of the company and identifies problem accounts. For example, as discussed in the Feature Story about Whitehall-Robins, management would compute and compare the percentage of receivables that are over 90 days past due.

The aging schedule identifies problem accounts that the company needs to pursue with phone calls, letters, and occasionally legal action. Sometimes special arrangements must be made with problem accounts. For example, it was reported that Intel Corporation (a major manufacturer of computer chips) required that Packard Bell (at one time one of the largest U.S. sellers of personal computers) exchange its past-due account receivable for an interest-bearing note receivable. This caused concern within the investment community. The move suggested that Packard Bell was in trouble, which worried Intel investors concerned about Intel's accounts receivable.

DECISION TOOLKIT

DECISION CHECKPOINTS	INFO NEEDED FOR DECISION	TOOL TO USE FOR DECISION	HOW TO EVALUATE RESULTS
Is the company's credit risk increasing?	Customer account balances and due dates	Accounts receivable aging schedule	Compute and compare the percentage of receivables over 90 days old.

If a company has significant concentrations of credit risk, it must discuss this risk in the notes to its financial statements. A concentration of credit risk is a threat of nonpayment from a single large customer or class of customers that could adversely affect the financial health of the company. Illustration 8-13 shows an excerpt from the credit risk note from the 2007 annual report of McKesson Corp. McKesson reports that its ten largest customers account for 48% of its total revenues and receivables.

McKESSON CORP.
Notes to the Financial Statements

Illustration 8-13 Excerpt from note on concentration of credit risk

Concentrations of Credit Risk: Trade receivables subject us to a concentration of credit risk with customers primarily in our Pharmaceutical Solutions segment. A significant proportion of our revenue growth has been with a limited number of large customers and as a result, our credit concentration has increased. Accordingly, any defaults in payment by or a reduction in purchases from these large customers could have a significant negative impact on our financial condition, results of operations and liquidity. At March 31, 2007, revenues and accounts receivable from our ten largest customers accounted for approximately 48% of total consolidated revenues and accounts receivable. Fiscal 2007 revenues and March 31, 2007 receivables from our largest customer, Caremark RX, Inc., represented approximately 11% of total consolidated revenues and 12% of accounts receivable. We have also provided financing arrangements to certain of our customers within our Pharmaceutical Solutions segment, some of which are on a revolving basis. At March 31, 2007, these customer financing arrangements totaled approximately $122 million.

This note to McKesson Corp.'s financial statements indicates it has a high level of credit concentration. A default by any of these large customers could have a significant negative impact on its financial performance.

DECISION TOOLKIT

DECISION CHECKPOINTS	INFO NEEDED FOR DECISION	TOOL TO USE FOR DECISION	HOW TO EVALUATE RESULTS
Does the company have significant concentrations of credit risk?	Note to the financial statements on concentrations of credit risk.	If risky credit customers are identified, the financial health of those customers should be evaluated to gain an independent assessment of the potential for a material credit loss.	If a material loss appears likely, the potential negative impact of that loss on the company should be carefully evaluated, along with the adequacy of the allowance for doubtful accounts.

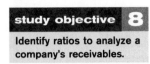

Identify ratios to analyze a company's receivables.

EVALUATING LIQUIDITY OF RECEIVABLES

Investors and managers keep a watchful eye on the relationship among sales, accounts receivable, and cash collections. If sales increase, then accounts receivable are also expected to increase. But a disproportionate increase in accounts receivable might signal trouble. Perhaps the company increased its sales by loosening its credit policy, and these receivables may be difficult or impossible to collect. Such receivables are considered less liquid. Recall that liquidity is measured by how quickly certain assets can be converted to cash.

The ratio that analysts use to assess the liquidity of receivables is the receivables turnover ratio, computed by dividing net credit sales (net sales less cash sales) by the average net accounts receivable during the year. This ratio measures the number of times, on average, a company collects receivables during the period. Unless seasonal factors are significant, **average** accounts receivable outstanding can be computed from the beginning and ending balances of the net receivables.[1]

A popular variant of the receivables turnover ratio is the average collection period, which measures the average amount of time that a receivable is outstanding. This is done by dividing the receivables turnover ratio into 365 days. Companies use the average collection period to assess the effectiveness of a company's credit and collection policies. The average collection period should not greatly exceed the credit term period (i.e., the time allowed for payment).

The following data (in millions) are available for McKesson Corp.

	For the year ended March 31,	
	2007	**2006**
Sales	$92,977	$86,983
Accounts receivable (net)	6,566	6,247

Illustration 8-14 shows the receivables turnover ratio and average collection period for McKesson Corp., along with comparative industry data. These calculations assume that all sales were credit sales.

Illustration 8-14
Receivables turnover and average collection period

$$\text{Receivables Turnover Ratio} = \frac{\text{Net Credit Sales}}{\text{Average Net Receivables}}$$

$$\text{Average Collection Period} = \frac{365}{\text{Receivables Turnover Ratio}}$$

($ in millions)		2007	2006
McKesson	Receivables turnover	$\dfrac{\$92,977}{(\$6,566 + \$6,247)/2} = 14.5$ times	$\dfrac{\$86,983}{(\$6,247 + \$5,732)/2*} = 14.5$ times
	Average collection period	$\dfrac{365}{14.5} = 25.2$ days	$\dfrac{365}{14.5} = 25.2$ days
Industry average	Receivables turnover	8.38 times	
	Average collection period	43.6 days	

*The receivables balance at March 31, 2005, was $5,732 million.

[1] If seasonal factors are significant, the company might determine the average accounts receivable balance by using monthly or quarterly amounts.

McKesson's receivables turnover was 14.5 times in 2007, with a corresponding average collection period of 25.2 days. This was the same as its 2006 collection period. It compares favorably with the industry average collection period of 43.6 days. What this means is that McKesson is able to turn its receivables into cash more quickly than most of its competitors. Therefore, it has a better likelihood of paying its current obligations than a company with a slower receivables turnover.

DECISION TOOLKIT

DECISION CHECKPOINTS	INFO NEEDED FOR DECISION	TOOL TO USE FOR DECISION	HOW TO EVALUATE RESULTS
Are collections being made in a timely fashion?	Net credit sales and average net receivables balance	$$\text{Receivables turnover ratio} = \frac{\text{Net credit sales}}{\text{Average net receivables}}$$ $$\text{Average collection period} = \frac{365 \text{ days}}{\text{Receivables turnover ratio}}$$	Average collection period should be consistent with corporate credit policy. An increase may suggest a decline in financial health of customers.

In some cases, receivables turnover may be misleading. Some large retail chains that issue their own credit cards encourage customers to use these cards for purchases. If customers pay slowly, the stores earn a healthy return on the outstanding receivables in the form of interest at rates of 18% to 22%. On the other hand, companies that sell (factor) their receivables on a consistent basis will have a faster turnover than those that do not. Thus, to interpret receivables turnover, you must know how a company manages its receivables. In general, the faster the turnover, the greater the reliability of the current ratio for assessing liquidity.

before you go on...

Do it!

In 2010, Lebron James Company had net credit sales of $923,795 for the year. It had a beginning accounts receivable (net) balance of $38,275 and an ending accounts receivable (net) balance of $35,988. Compute Lebron James Company's (a) accounts receivable turnover and (b) average collection period in days.

Solution

(a)

Net credit sales	÷	Average net accounts receivable	=	Accounts receivable turnover
$923,795	÷	$\dfrac{\$38,275 + \$35,988}{2}$	=	24.9 times

(b)

Days in year	÷	Accounts receivable turnover	=	Average collection period in days
365	÷	24.9 times	=	14.7 days

ANALYSIS OF RECEIVABLES

Action Plan

- Review the formula to compute the accounts receivable turnover.
- Make sure that both the beginning and ending accounts receivable are considered in the computation.
- Review the formula to compute the average collection period in days.

the navigator

ACCELERATING CASH RECEIPTS

In the normal course of events, companies collect accounts receivable in cash and remove them from the books. However, as credit sales and receivables have grown in size and significance, the "normal course of events" has changed. Two common expressions apply to the collection of receivables: (1) "Time is money"—that is, waiting for the normal collection process costs money. (2) "A bird in the hand is worth two in the bush"—that is, getting the cash now is better than getting it later or not at all. Therefore, in order to accelerate the receipt of cash from receivables, companies frequently sell their receivables to another company for cash, thereby shortening the cash-to-cash operating cycle.

There are three reasons for the sale of receivables. The first is their **size**. In recent years, for competitive reasons, sellers (retailers, wholesalers, and manufacturers) often have provided financing to purchasers of their goods. For example, many major companies in the automobile, truck, industrial and farm equipment, computer, and appliance industries have created companies that accept responsibility for accounts receivable financing. General Motors has General Motors Acceptance Corp. (GMAC), General Electric has GE Capital, and Ford has Ford Motor Credit Corp. (FMCC). These companies are referred to as **captive finance companies** because they are owned by the company selling the product. The purpose of captive finance companies is to encourage the sale of the company's products by assuring financing to buyers. However, the parent companies involved do not necessarily want to hold large amounts of receivables, so they may sell them.

Second, **companies may sell receivables because they may be the only reasonable source of cash**. When credit is tight, companies may not be able to borrow money in the usual credit markets. Even if credit is available, the cost of borrowing may be prohibitive.

A final reason for selling receivables is that **billing and collection are often time-consuming and costly**. As a result, it is often easier for a retailer to sell the receivables to another party that has expertise in billing and collection matters. Credit card companies such as MasterCard, Visa, American Express, and Discover specialize in billing and collecting accounts receivable.

National Credit Card Sales

Approximately one billion credit cards were in use recently—more than three credit cards for every man, woman, and child in this country. A common type of credit card is a national credit card such as Visa and MasterCard. Three parties are involved when national credit cards are used in making retail sales: (1) the credit card issuer, who is independent of the retailer, (2) the retailer, and (3) the customer. **A retailer's acceptance of a national credit card is another form of selling—factoring—the receivable by the retailer.**

The use of national credit cards translates to more sales and zero bad debts for the retailer. Both are powerful reasons for a retailer to accept such cards. Illustration 8-15 (next page) shows the major advantages of national credit cards to the retailer. In exchange for these advantages, the retailer pays the credit card issuer a fee of 2% to 4% of the invoice price for its services.

The retailer considers sales resulting from the use of Visa and MasterCard as **cash sales**. Upon notification of a credit card charge from a retailer, the bank that issued the card immediately adds the amount to the seller's bank balance. Companies therefore record these credit card charges in the same manner as checks deposited from a cash sale. The banks that issue national credit cards generally charge retailers a fee of 2% to 4% of the credit card sales slips for this service.

To illustrate, Morgan Marie purchases $1,000 of compact discs for her restaurant from Sondgeroth Music Co., and she charges this amount on her Visa First

Illustration 8-15
Advantages of credit cards
to the retailer

Bank Card. The service fee that First Bank charges Sondgeroth Music is 3%.
Sondgeroth Music's entry to record this transaction is:

Cash	970	
Service Charge Expense	30	
Sales		1,000
(To record Visa credit card sales)		

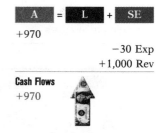

A = L + SE
+970
 −30 Exp
+1,000 Rev

Cash Flows
+970

Sale of Receivables to a Factor

A common way to accelerate receivables collection is a sale to a factor. A **factor**
is a finance company or bank that buys receivables from businesses for a fee
and then collects the payments directly from the customers.

Factoring was traditionally associated with the textiles, apparel, footwear,
furniture, and home furnishing industries. It has now spread to other types of
businesses and is a multibillion dollar industry. For example, Sears, Roebuck &
Co. (now Sears Holdings) once sold $14.8 billion of customer accounts receivable.
McKesson has a pre-arranged agreement allowing it to sell up to $700 million of
its receivables. McKesson's sale of receivables may explain why its receivables
turnover ratio exceeds the industry average.

Factoring arrangements vary widely, but typically the factor charges a
commission. It ranges from 1% to 3% of the amount of receivables purchased.
To illustrate, assume that Hendredon Furniture factors $600,000 of receivables
to Federal Factors, Inc. Federal Factors assesses a service charge of 2% of the
amount of receivables sold. The following journal entry records Hendredon's sale
of receivables.

International Note GAAP
has less stringent requirements
regarding the sale of receivables.
Thus, GAAP companies can more
easily use factoring transactions
as a form of financing without
showing a related liability on their
books. Some argue that this type
of so-called "off balance sheet"
financing would be more difficult
to achieve under IFRS.

Cash	588,000	
Service Charge Expense (2% × $600,000)	12,000	
Accounts Receivable		600,000
(To record the sale of accounts		
receivable)		

If the company usually sells its receivables, it records the service charge expense as a selling expense. If the company sells receivables infrequently, it may report this amount under "Other expenses and losses" in the income statement.

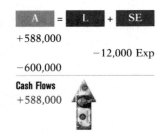

Accounting Across the Organization

In the past, smaller companies primarily factored receivables. Today, businesses of all sizes and types factor their receivables. For example, Wal-Mart's suppliers, many of them large companies, need their cash more quickly than Wal-Mart wants to pay, so many of them factor their receivables. Also, some businesses have found it economical to outsource their whole billing and collection function to factors. One factor, CDS Capital, will provide all billing and collecting, as well as a record of clients' daily cash position, cash received, bills paid, and receivables still outstanding.

Source: Martin Mayer, "Taking the Fear Out of Factoring," *Inc. Magazine* (December 2003), pp. 90–97.

? What issues should management consider in deciding whether to factor its receivables?

Illustration 8-16 summarizes the basic principles of managing accounts receivable.

Illustration 8-16
Managing receivables

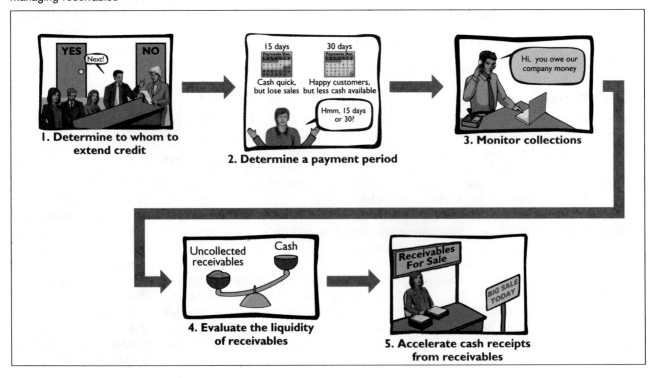

Do it!   Peter M. Kell Wholesalers Co. needs to raise $120,000 in cash to safely cover next Friday's employee payroll. Kell has reached its debt ceiling. Kell's present balance of outstanding receivables totals $750,000. What might Kell do to alleviate this cash crunch? Record the entry that Kell would make when it raises the needed cash. (Assume a 1% service charge.)

FACTORING

Action Plan

• Consider sale of receivables to a factor.

• Weigh cost of factoring against benefit of having cash in hand.

Solution

If Kell Co. factors $125,000 of its accounts receivable at a 1% service charge, it would make this entry:

Cash	123,750	
Service Charge Expense	1,250	
Accounts Receivable		125,000
(To record sale of receivables to factor)		

A lot of companies report strong sales growth but have cash flow problems. How can this be? The reason for the difference is timing: Sales revenue is recorded when goods are delivered, even if cash is not received until later. For example, McKesson Corp. had sales of $92,977 million during 2007. Does that mean it received cash of $92,977 million from its customers? Most likely not. So how do we determine the amount of cash related to sales revenue that is actually received from customers? We analyze the changes that take place in Accounts Receivable.

To illustrate, suppose Bestor Corporation started the year with $10,000 in accounts receivable. During the year it had sales of $100,000. At the end of the year the balance in accounts receivable was $25,000. As a result, accounts receivable increased $15,000 during the year. How much cash did Bestor collect from customers during the year? Using the following T account we can determine that collections were $85,000.

KEEPING AN EYE ON CASH

Accounts Receivable			
Beginning balance	10,000	85,000	Collections
Sales	100,000		
Ending balance	25,000		

As shown, the difference between sales and cash collections is explained by the change in Accounts Receivable. Accounts Receivable increased by $15,000. Therefore, since sales were $100,000, cash collections were only $85,000.

To illustrate another situation, let's use McKesson Corporation (see page 402). Recall that it had sales of $92,977 million. Its ending receivable balance was $6,566 million, and its beginning receivables balance was $6,247 million—an increase of $319 million. Given this change, we can determine that the cash collected from customers during the year was $92,658 million ($92,977 − $319). This is shown in the following T account.

Accounts Receivable			
Beginning balance	6,247	92,658	Collections
Sales	92,977		
Ending balance	6,566		

USING THE DECISION TOOLKIT

The information below was taken from the September 30, 2007, financial statements of Amerisource Bergen Corp., Inc. Similar to McKesson Corp., Amerisource Bergen distributes drugs and related services to pharmaceutical manufacturers and health-care providers in the United States and Puerto Rico.

Instructions

Comment on Amerisource Bergen's accounts receivable management and liquidity relative to that of McKesson, using (1) the current ratio and (2) the receivables turnover ratio and average collection period. McKesson's current ratio was 1.16:1. The other ratio values for McKesson were calculated earlier in the chapter.

AMERISOURCE BERGEN CORP., INC.
Selected Financial Information
(in millions)

	2007	**2006**
Sales	$66,074	$61,203
Current assets		
Cash and cash equivalents	$ 640	$ 1,261
Short-term investment securities	467	68
Accounts receivable (net)	3,472	3,427
Merchandise inventories	4,102	4,422
Prepaid expenses and other	33	32
Total current assets	$ 8,714	$ 9,210
Total current liabilities	$ 7,857	$ 7,459

Solution

1. Here is the current ratio (Current assets ÷ Current liabilities) for each company.

McKesson	**Amerisource Bergen**
1.16:1	$\dfrac{\$8,714}{\$7,857} = 1.11{:}1$

This suggests that McKesson and Amerisource Bergen have similar liquidity. Both have relatively low current ratios.

2. The receivables turnover ratio and average collection period for each company are:

	McKesson	**Amerisource Bergen**
Receivables turnover ratio	14.5 times	$\dfrac{\$66,074}{(\$3,472 + \$3,427)/2} = 19.2$ times
Average collection period	25.2 days	$\dfrac{365}{19.2} = 19.0$ days

Amerisource Bergen's receivables turnover ratio of 19.2 compared to McKesson's 14.5, and its average collection days of 19 days versus McKesson's 25.2 days, suggest that Amerisource Bergen is able to collect from its customers much more rapidly. The high receivables turnover ratios of both companies help to compensate for their relatively low current ratios when evaluating their liquidity.

Summary of Study Objectives

1 **Identify the different types of receivables.** Receivables are frequently classified as accounts, notes, and other. Accounts receivable are amounts customers owe on account. Notes receivable represent claims that are evidenced by formal instruments of credit. Other receivables include nontrade receivables such as interest receivable, loans to company officers, advances to employees, and income taxes refundable.

2 **Explain how accounts receivable are recognized in the accounts.** Accounts receivable are recorded at invoice price. They are reduced by sales returns and allowances. Cash discounts reduce the amount received on accounts receivable.

3 **Describe the methods used to account for bad debts.** The two methods of accounting for uncollectible accounts are the allowance method and the direct write-off method. Under the allowance method, companies estimate uncollectible accounts as a percentage of receivables. It emphasizes the cash realizable value of the accounts receivable. An aging schedule is frequently used with this approach.

4 **Compute the interest on notes receivable.** The formula for computing interest is: Face value × Interest rate × Time.

5 **Describe the entries to record the disposition of notes receivable.** Notes can be held to maturity, at which time the borrower (maker) pays the face value plus accrued interest and the payee removes the note from the accounts. In many cases, however, similar to accounts receivable, the holder of the note speeds up the conversion by selling the receivable to another party. In some situations, the maker of the note dishonors the note (defaults), and the note is written off.

6 **Explain the statement presentation of receivables.** Companies should identify each major type of receivable in the balance sheet or in the notes to the financial statements. Short-term receivables are considered current assets. Companies report the gross amount of receivables and allowance for doubtful accounts. They report bad debts and service charge expenses in the income statement as operating (selling) expenses, and interest revenue as other revenues and gains in the nonoperating section of the statement.

7 **Describe the principles of sound accounts receivable management.** To properly manage receivables, management must (a) determine to whom to extend credit, (b) establish a payment period, (c) monitor

(Summary continues on next page)

DECISION TOOLKIT A SUMMARY

DECISION CHECKPOINTS	INFO NEEDED FOR DECISION	TOOL TO USE FOR DECISION	HOW TO EVALUATE RESULTS
Is the amount of past due accounts increasing? Which accounts require management's attention?	List of outstanding receivables and their due dates	Prepare an aging schedule showing the receivables in various stages: outstanding 0–30 days, 31–60 days, 61–90 days, and over 90 days.	Accounts in the older categories require follow-up: letters, phone calls, and possible renegotiation of terms.
Is the company's credit risk increasing?	Customer account balances and due dates	Accounts receivable aging schedule	Compute and compare the percentage of receivables over 90 days old.
Does the company have significant concentrations of credit risk?	Note to the financial statements on concentrations of credit risk	If risky credit customers are identified, the financial health of those customers should be evaluated to gain an independent assessment of the potential for a material credit loss.	If a material loss appears likely, the potential negative impact of that loss on the company should be carefully evaluated, along with the adequacy of the allowance for doubtful accounts.
Are collections being made in a timely fashion?	Net credit sales and average net receivables balance	$$\text{Receivables turnover ratio} = \frac{\text{Net credit sales}}{\text{Average net receivables}}$$ $$\text{Average collection period} = \frac{365 \text{ days}}{\text{Receivables turnover ratio}}$$	Average collection period should be consistent with corporate credit policy. An increase may suggest a decline in financial health of customers.

collections, (d) evaluate the liquidity of receivables, and (e) accelerate cash receipts from receivables when necessary.

8 Identify ratios to analyze a company's receivables. The receivables turnover ratio and the average collection period both are useful in analyzing management's effectiveness in managing receivables. The accounts receivable aging schedule also provides useful information.

9 Describe methods to accelerate the receipt of cash from receivables. If the company needs additional cash, management can accelerate the collection of cash from receivables by selling (factoring) its receivables or by allowing customers to pay with bank credit cards.

Glossary

Accounts receivable *(p. 387)* Amounts customers owe on account.

Aging the accounts receivable *(p. 391)* A schedule of customer balances classified by the length of time they have been unpaid.

Allowance method *(p. 389)* A method of accounting for bad debts that involves estimating uncollectible accounts at the end of each period.

Average collection period *(p. 402)* The average amount of time that a receivable is outstanding, calculated by dividing 365 days by the receivables turnover ratio.

Bad debts expense *(p. 389)* An expense account to record losses from extending credit.

Cash (net) realizable value *(p. 389)* The net amount a company expects to receive in cash from receivables.

Concentration of credit risk *(p. 401)* The threat of nonpayment from a single large customer or class of customers that could adversely affect the financial health of the company.

Direct write-off method *(p. 388)* A method of accounting for bad debts that involves expensing receivable accounts at the time receivables from a particular company are determined to be uncollectible.

Dishonored note *(p. 398)* A note that is not paid in full at maturity.

Factor *(p. 405)* A finance company or bank that buys receivables from businesses for a fee and then collects the payments directly from the customers.

Maker *(p. 394)* The party in a promissory note who is making the promise to pay.

Notes receivable *(p. 387)* Claims for which formal instruments of credit are issued as evidence of the debt.

Payee *(p. 394)* The party to whom payment of a promissory note is to be made.

Percentage of receivables basis *(p. 391)* A method of estimating the amount of bad debt expense whereby management establishes a percentage relationship between the amount of receivables and the expected losses from uncollectible accounts.

Promissory note *(p. 394)* A written promise to pay a specified amount of money on demand or at a definite time.

Receivables *(p. 386)* Amounts due from individuals and companies that are expected to be collected in cash.

Receivables turnover ratio *(p. 402)* A measure of the liquidity of receivables, computed by dividing net credit sales by average net receivables.

Trade receivables *(p. 387)* Notes and accounts receivable that result from sales transactions.

Comprehensive **Do it!**

made a note

Presented here are selected transactions related to B. Dylan Corp.

Mar. 1 Sold $20,000 of merchandise to Potter Company, terms 2/10, n/30.

11 Received payment in full from Potter Company for balance due.

12 Accepted Juno Company's $20,000, 6-month, 12% note for balance due on outstanding account receivable.

13 Made B. Dylan Corp. credit card sales for $13,200.

15 Made Visa credit sales totaling $6,700. A 5% service fee is charged by Visa.

Apr. 11 Sold accounts receivable of $8,000 to Harcot Factor. Harcot Factor assesses a service charge of 2% of the amount of receivables sold.

13 Received collections of $8,200 on B. Dylan Corp. credit card sales.

May 10 Wrote off as uncollectible $16,000 of accounts receivable. (B. Dylan Corp. uses the percentage of receivables basis to estimate bad debts.)

June 30 The balance in accounts receivable at the end of the first 6 months is $200,000 and the bad debt percentage is 10%. At June 30 the credit balance in the allowance account prior to adjustment is $3,500. Recorded bad debt expense.

July 16 One of the accounts receivable written off in May pays the amount due, $4,000, in full.

Instructions

Prepare the journal entries for the transactions.

Solution to Comprehensive Do it!

Mar.	1	Accounts Receivable—Potter Company	20,000	
		Sales		20,000
		(To record sales on account)		
	11	Cash	19,600	
		Sales Discounts (2% × $20,000)	400	
		Accounts Receivable—Potter Company		20,000
		(To record collection of accounts		
		receivable)		
	12	Notes Receivable	20,000	
		Accounts Receivable—Juno Company		20,000
		(To record acceptance of Juno		
		Company note)		
	13	Accounts Receivable	13,200	
		Sales		13,200
		(To record company credit card sales)		
	15	Cash	6,365	
		Service Charge Expense (5% × $6,700)	335	
		Sales		6,700
		(To record credit card sales)		
Apr.	11	Cash	7,840	
		Service Charge Expense (2% × $8,000)	160	
		Accounts Receivable		8,000
		(To record sale of receivables to factor)		
	13	Cash	8,200	
		Accounts Receivable		8,200
		(To record collection of accounts		
		receivable)		
May	10	Allowance for Doubtful Accounts	16,000	
		Accounts Receivable		16,000
		(To record write-off of accounts		
		receivable)		
June	30	Bad Debts Expense	16,500	
		Allowance for Doubtful Accounts		16,500
		[($200,000 × 10%) − $3,500]		
		(To record estimate of uncollectible		
		accounts)		
July	16	Accounts Receivable	4,000	
		Allowance for Doubtful Accounts		4,000
		(To reverse write-off of accounts		
		receivable)		
		Cash	4,000	
		Accounts Receivable		4,000
		(To record collection of accounts		
		receivable)		

Action Plan

- Generally, record accounts receivable at invoice price.
- Recognize that sales returns and allowances and cash discounts reduce the amount received on accounts receivable.
- Record a service charge expense on the seller's books when accounts receivable are sold.
- Prepare an adjusting entry for bad debts expense.
- Recognize the balance in the allowance account under the percentage of receivables basis.
- Record write-offs of accounts receivable only in balance sheet accounts.

the navigator

Self-Study Questions

Answers are at the end of the chapter.

(SO 1) **1.** A receivable that is evidenced by a formal instrument and that normally requires the payment of interest is:
(a) an account receivable.
(b) a trade receivable.
(c) a note receivable.
(d) a classified receivable.

(SO 2) **2.** Kersee Company on June 15 sells merchandise on account to Soo Eng Co. for $1,000, terms 2/10, n/30. On June 20 Eng Co. returns merchandise worth $300 to Kersee Company. On June 24 payment is received from Eng Co. for the balance due. What is the amount of cash received?
(a) $700.   (c) $686.
(b) $680.   (d) None of the above.

(SO 3, 6) **3.** Accounts and notes receivable are reported in the current assets section of the balance sheet at:
(a) Cash (net) realizable value.
(b) net book value.
(c) lower-of-cost-or-market value.
(d) invoice cost.

(SO 3) **4.** Net credit sales for the month are $800,000. The accounts receivable balance is $160,000. The allowance is calculated as 7.5% of the receivables balance using the percentage of receivables basis. If the Allowance for Doubtful Accounts has a credit balance of $5,000 before adjustment, what is the balance after adjustment?
(a) $12,000.   (c) $17,000.
(b) $7,000.   (d) $31,000.

(SO 3) **5.** In 2010 Patterson Wholesale Company had net credit sales of $750,000. On January 1, 2010, Allowance for Doubtful Accounts had a credit balance of $18,000. During 2010, $30,000 of uncollectible accounts receivable were written off. Past experience indicates that the allowance should be 10% of the balance in receivables (percentage of receivables basis). If the accounts receivable balance at December 31 was $200,000, what is the required adjustment to the Allowance for Doubtful Accounts at December 31, 2010?
(a) $20,000.   (c) $32,000.
(b) $75,000.   (d) $30,000.

(SO 3) **6.** An analysis and aging of the accounts receivable of Raja Company at December 31 reveal these data:

Accounts receivable	$800,000
Allowance for doubtful accounts per books before adjustment (credit)	50,000
Amounts expected to become uncollectible	65,000

What is the cash realizable value of the accounts receivable at December 31, after adjustment?
(a) $685,000.   (c) $800,000.
(b) $750,000.   (d) $735,000.

(SO 4) **7.** Which of these statements about promissory notes is *incorrect?*
(a) The party making the promise to pay is called the maker.
(b) The party to whom payment is to be made is called the payee.
(c) A promissory note is not a negotiable instrument.
(d) A promissory note is more liquid than an account receivable.

(SO 4) **8.** Michael Co. accepts a $1,000, 3-month, 12% promissory note in settlement of an account with Tani Co. The entry to record this transaction is:

(a) Notes Receivable	1,030	
Accounts Receivable		1,030
(b) Notes Receivable	1,000	
Accounts Receivable		1,000
(c) Notes Receivable	1,000	
Sales		1,000
(d) Notes Receivable	1,020	
Accounts Receivable		1,020

(SO 5) **9.** Schleis Co. holds Murphy Inc.'s $10,000, 120-day, 9% note. The entry made by Schleis Co. when the note is collected, assuming no interest has previously been accrued, is:

(a) Cash	10,300	
Notes Receivable		10,300
(b) Cash	10,000	
Notes Receivable		10,000
(c) Accounts Receivable	10,300	
Notes Receivable		10,000
Interest Revenue		300
(d) Cash	10,300	
Notes Receivable		10,000
Interest Revenue		300

(SO 7) **10.** If a company is concerned about lending money to a risky customer, it could do any of the following *except:*
(a) require the customer to pay cash in advance.
(b) require the customer to provide a letter of credit or a bank guarantee.
(c) contact references provided by the customer, such as banks and other suppliers.
(d) provide the customer a lengthy payment period to increase the chance of paying.

(SO 8) **11.** Eddy Corporation had net credit sales during the year of $800,000 and cost of goods sold of $500,000. The balance in receivables at the beginning of the year was $100,000 and at the end of the year was $150,000. What was the receivables turnover ratio?
(a) 6.4   (b) 8.0   (c) 5.3   (d) 4.0

(SO 8) **12.** Prall Corporation sells its goods on terms of 2/10, n/30. It has a receivables turnover ratio of 7. What is its average collection period (days)?
(a) 2,555   (b) 30   (c) 52   (d) 210

(SO 9) **13.** Which of these statements about Visa credit card sales is *incorrect*?
  (a) The credit card issuer conducts the credit investigation of the customer.
  (b) The retailer is not involved in the collection process.
  (c) The retailer must wait to receive payment from the issuer.
  (d) The retailer receives cash more quickly than it would from individual customers.

(SO 9) **14.** Good Stuff Retailers accepted $50,000 of Citibank Visa credit card charges for merchandise sold on July 1. Citibank charges 4% for its credit card use. The entry to record this transaction by Good Stuff Retailers will include a credit to Sales of $50,000 and a debit(s) to:
  (a) Cash $48,000 and Service Charge Expense $2,000.
  (b) Accounts Receivable $48,000 and Service Charge Expense $2,000.
  (c) Cash $50,000.
  (d) Accounts Receivable $50,000.

(SO 9) **15.** A company can accelerate its cash receipts by all of the following *except*:
  (a) offering discounts for early payment.
  (b) accepting national credit cards for customer purchases.
  (c) selling receivables to a factor.
  (d) writing off receivables.

Go to the book's companion website, **www.wiley.com/college/kimmel**, to access additional Self-Study Questions.

Questions

1. What is the difference between an account receivable and a note receivable?

2. What are some common types of receivables other than accounts receivable or notes receivable?

3. What are the essential features of the allowance method of accounting for bad debts?

4. Kristi Bolinger cannot understand why the cash realizable value does not decrease when an uncollectible account is written off under the allowance method. Clarify this point for Kristi.

5. Criss Company has a credit balance of $2,200 in Allowance for Doubtful Accounts before adjustment. The estimated uncollectibles under the percentage of receivables basis is $5,800. Prepare the adjusting entry.

6. What types of receivables does Tootsie Roll report on its balance sheet? Does it use the allowance method or the direct write-off method to account for uncollectibles?

7. How are bad debts accounted for under the direct write-off method? What are the disadvantages of this method?

8. Alice Hamm, the vice president of sales for Holiday Pools and Spas, wants the company's credit department to be less restrictive in granting credit. "How can we sell anything when you guys won't approve anybody?" she asks. Discuss the pros and cons of "easy credit." What are the accounting implications?

9. Your roommate is uncertain about the advantages of a promissory note. Compare the advantages of a note receivable with those of an account receivable.

10. How may the maturity date of a promissory note be stated?

11. Compute the missing amounts for each of the following notes.

Principal	Annual Interest Rate	Time	Total Interest
(a)	9%	90 days	$ 270
$30,000	8%	3 years	(d)
$60,000	(b)	5 months	$2,500
$50,000	11%	(c)	$2,750

12. Dotson Company dishonors a note at maturity. What are the options available to the lender?

13. General Motors Company has accounts receivable and notes receivable. How should the receivables be reported on the balance sheet?

14. What are the steps to good receivables management?

15. How might a company monitor the risk related to its accounts receivable?

16. What is meant by a concentration of credit risk?

17. The President of Grider Inc. proudly announces her company's improved liquidity since its current ratio has increased substantially from one year to the next. Does an increase in the current ratio always indicate improved liquidity? What other ratio or ratios might you review to determine whether or not the increase in the current ratio is an improvement in financial health?

18. Since hiring a new sales director, Percy Inc. has enjoyed a 50% increase in sales. The CEO has also noticed, however, that the company's average collection period has increased from 17 days to 38 days. What might be the cause of this increase? What are the implications to management of this increase?

19. The Coca-Cola Company's receivables turnover ratio was 9.90 in 2006, and its average amount of net receivables during the period was

$2,434 million. What is the amount of its net credit sales for the period? What is the average collection period in days?

20. ⬅ ◉━━━━◖ JCPenney Company accepts both its own credit cards and national credit cards. What are the advantages of accepting both types of cards?

21. ⬅ ◉━━━━◖ An article in the *Wall Street Journal* indicated that companies are selling their receivables at a record rate. Why do companies sell their receivables?

22. Calico Corners decides to sell $430,000 of its accounts receivable to First Central Factors Inc. First Central Factors assesses a service charge of 3% of the amount of receivables sold. Prepare the journal entry that Calico Corners makes to record this sale.

23. Ranier Corp. has experienced tremendous sales growth this year, but it is always short of cash. What is one explanation for this occurrence?

24. How can the amount of collections from customers be determined?

Brief Exercises

WILEY
PLUS

Identify different types of receivables.

(SO 1)

BE8-1 Presented below are three receivables transactions. Indicate whether these receivables are reported as accounts receivable, notes receivable, or other receivables on a balance sheet.

(a) Advanced $10,000 to an employee.

(b) Received a promissory note of $34,000 for services performed.

(c) Sold merchandise on account for $60,000 to a customer.

Record basic accounts receivable transactions.

(SO 2)

BE8-2 Record the following transactions on the books of Kenney Co.

(a) On July 1 Kenney Co. sold merchandise on account to Fife Inc. for $19,000, terms 2/10, n/30.

(b) On July 8 Fife Inc. returned merchandise worth $2,400 to Kenney Co.

(c) On July 11 Fife Inc. paid for the merchandise.

Prepare entry for write-off, and determine cash realizable value.

(SO 3)

BE8-3 At the end of 2009, Tatum Co. has accounts receivable of $700,000 and an allowance for doubtful accounts of $28,000. On January 24, 2010, it is learned that the company's receivable from Novinger Inc. is not collectible and therefore management authorizes a write-off of $2,000.

(a) Prepare the journal entry to record the write-off.

(b) What is the cash realizable value of the accounts receivable (1) before the write-off and (2) after the write-off?

Prepare entries for collection of bad debt write-off.

(SO 3)

BE8-4 Assume the same information as BE8-3 and that on March 4, 2010, Tatum Co. receives payment of $2,000 in full from Novinger Inc. Prepare the journal entries to record this transaction.

Prepare entry using percentage of receivables method.

(SO 3)

BE8-5 Lang Co. uses the percentage of receivables basis to record bad debts expense and concludes that 2% of accounts receivable will become uncollectible. Accounts receivable are $400,000 at the end of the year, and the allowance for doubtful accounts has a credit balance of $1,500.

(a) Prepare the adjusting journal entry to record bad debts expense for the year.

(b) If the allowance for doubtful accounts had a debit balance of $600 instead of a credit balance of $1,500, prepare the adjusting journal entry for bad debts expense.

Compute interest rate and interest on note.

(SO 4)

BE8-6 Presented below are three promissory notes. Determine the missing amounts.

Date of Note	Terms	Principal	Annual Interest Rate	Total Interest
April 1	2 years	$700,000	8%	(a)
July 2	30 days	79,000	(b)	$592.50
March 7	6 months	60,000	11%	(c)

Prepare entry for note receivable exchanged for accounts receivable.

(SO 4)

BE8-7 On January 10, 2010, Gonzalez Co. sold merchandise on account to Ernst for $6,000, terms n/30. On February 9 Ernst gave Gonzalez Co. a 7% promissory note in settlement of this account. Prepare the journal entry to record the sale and the settlement of the accounts receivable.

Prepare entry for estimated uncollectibles and classifications, and compute ratios.

(SO 3, 6, 7, 8)

BE8-8 During its first year of operations, Morales Company had credit sales of $3,000,000, of which $600,000 remained uncollected at year-end. The credit manager estimates that $18,000 of these receivables will become uncollectible.

(a) Prepare the journal entry to record the estimated uncollectibles. (Assume an unadjusted balance of zero in Allowance for Doubtful Accounts.)

◉━━━━◖

(b) Prepare the current assets section of the balance sheet for Morales Company, assuming that in addition to the receivables it has cash of $90,000, merchandise inventory of $180,000, and prepaid expenses of $13,000.

(c) Calculate the receivables turnover ratio and average collection period. Assume that average net receivables were $300,000. Explain what these measures tell us.

BE8-9 The 2006 financial statements of 3M Company report net sales of $22.9 billion. Accounts receivable (net) are $2.8 billion at the beginning of the year and $3.1 billion at the end of the year. Compute 3M's receivables turnover ratio. Compute 3M's average collection period for accounts receivable in days.

Analyze accounts receivable.
(SO 8)

BE8-10 Consider these transactions:

(a) Espinosa Restaurant accepted a Visa card in payment of a $100 lunch bill. The bank charges a 3% fee. What entry should Espinosa make?

(b) Guthrie Company sold its accounts receivable of $65,000. What entry should Guthrie make, given a service charge of 3% on the amount of receivables sold?

Prepare entries for credit card sale and sale of accounts receivable.
(SO 9)

BE8-11 Ranger Corp. had a beginning balance in accounts receivable of $70,000 and an ending balance of $91,000. Sales during the period were $483,000. Determine cash collections.

Determine cash collections.
(SO 9)

Do it! Review

Do it! 8-1 Etienne Company has been in business several years. At the end of the current year, the ledger shows:

Accounts Receivable	$ 310,000 Dr.
Sales	2,200,000 Cr.
Allowance for Doubtful Accounts	6,100 Cr.

Bad debts are estimated to be 7% of receivables. Prepare the entry to adjust the Allowance for Doubtful Accounts.

Prepare entry for uncollectible accounts.
(SO 3)

Do it! 8-2 Galen Wholesalers accepts from Picard Stores a $6,200, 4-month, 12% note dated May 31 in settlement of Picard's overdue account. The maturity date of the note is September 30. What entry does Galen make at the maturity date, assuming Picard pays the note and interest in full at that time?

Prepare entries for notes receivable.
(SO 4, 5)

Do it! 8-3 In 2010, Drew Gooden Company has net credit sales of $1,600,000 for the year. It had a beginning accounts receivable (net) balance of $101,000 and an ending accounts receivable (net) balance of $107,000. Compute Drew Gooden Company's (a) accounts receivable turnover and (b) average collection period in days.

Compute ratios for receivables.
(SO 8)

Do it! 8-4 Ronald Distributors is a growing company whose ability to raise capital has not been growing as quickly as its expanding assets and sales. Ronald's local banker has indicated that the company cannot increase its borrowing for the foreseeable future. Ronald's suppliers are demanding payment for goods acquired within 30 days of the invoice date, but Ronald's customers are slow in paying for their purchases (60–90 days). As a result, Ronald has a cash flow problem.

Prepare entry for factored accounts.
(SO 9)

Ronald needs $160,000 to cover next Friday's payroll. Its balance of outstanding accounts receivable totals $1,000,000. What might Ronald do to alleviate this cash crunch? Record the entry that Ronald would make when it raises the needed cash. (Assume a 2% service charge.)

Exercises

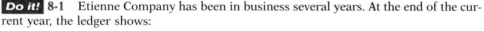

E8-1 On January 6 Gramke Co. sells merchandise on account to Colt Inc. for $8,000, terms 1/10, n/30. On January 16 Colt pays the amount due.

Prepare entries for recognizing accounts receivable.
(SO 2)

Instructions
Prepare the entries on Gramke Co.'s books to record the sale and related collection.

E8-2 On January 10 Bette Eaton uses her Stage Co. credit card to purchase merchandise from Stage Co. for $1,400. On February 10 Eaton is billed for the amount due of $1,400. On

Prepare entries for recognizing accounts receivable.
(SO 2)

February 12 Eaton pays $1,100 on the balance due. On March 10 Eaton is billed for the amount due, including interest at 1% per month on the unpaid balance as of February 12.

Instructions
Prepare the entries on Stage Co.'s books related to the transactions that occurred on January 10, February 12, and March 10.

Journalize receivables transactions.
(SO 2, 3)

E8-3 At the beginning of the current period, Emler Corp. had balances in Accounts Receivable of $200,000 and in Allowance for Doubtful Accounts of $9,000 (credit). During the period, it had net credit sales of $800,000 and collections of $763,000. It wrote off as uncollectible accounts receivable of $7,000. However, a $3,000 account previously written off as uncollectible was recovered before the end of the current period. Uncollectible accounts are estimated to total $25,000 at the end of the period.

Instructions
(a) Prepare the entries to record sales and collections during the period.
(b) Prepare the entry to record the write-off of uncollectible accounts during the period.
(c) Prepare the entries to record the recovery of the uncollectible account during the period.
(d) Prepare the entry to record bad debts expense for the period.
(e) Determine the ending balances in Accounts Receivable and Allowance for Doubtful Accounts.
(f) What is the net realizable value of the receivables at the end of the period?

Prepare entries to record allowance for doubtful accounts.
(SO 3)

E8-4 The ledger of Molina Company at the end of the current year shows Accounts Receivable $86,000; Credit Sales $780,000; and Sales Returns and Allowances $40,000.

Instructions
(a) If Molina uses the direct write-off method to account for uncollectible accounts, journalize the adjusting entry at December 31, assuming Molina determines that Banner's $900 balance is uncollectible.
(b) If Allowance for Doubtful Accounts has a credit balance of $1,100 in the trial balance, journalize the adjusting entry at December 31, assuming bad debts are expected to be 10% of accounts receivable.
(c) If Allowance for Doubtful Accounts has a debit balance of $500 in the trial balance, journalize the adjusting entry at December 31, assuming bad debts are expected to be 8% of accounts receivable.

Determine bad debt expense, and prepare the adjusting entry.
(SO 3)

E8-5 Proehl Company has accounts receivable of $95,100 at March 31, 2010. An analysis of the accounts shows these amounts.

| | **Balance, March 31** | |
Month of Sale	**2010**	**2009**
March	$65,000	$75,000
February	12,600	8,000
December and January	10,100	2,400
November and October	7,400	1,100
	$95,100	$86,500

Credit terms are 2/10, n/30. At March 31, 2010, there is a $2,400 credit balance in Allowance for Doubtful Accounts prior to adjustment. The company uses the percentage of receivables basis for estimating uncollectible accounts. The company's estimates of bad debts are as shown below.

Age of Accounts	**Estimated Percentage Uncollectible**
Current	2%
1–30 days past due	5
31–90 days past due	30
Over 90 days past due	50

Instructions
(a) Determine the total estimated uncollectibles.
(b) Prepare the adjusting entry at March 31, 2010, to record bad debts expense.
(c) Discuss the implications of the changes in the aging schedule from 2009 to 2010.

E8-6 On December 31, 2009, when its Allowance for Doubtful Accounts had a debit balance of $1,000, Brite Star Co. estimates that 9% of its accounts receivable balance of $90,000 will become uncollectible and records the necessary adjustment to the Allowance for Doubtful Accounts. On May 11, 2010, Brite Star Co. determined that J. Reno's account was uncollectible and wrote off $1,500. On June 12, 2010, Reno paid the amount previously written off.

Prepare entry for estimated uncollectibles, write-off, and recovery.
(SO 3)

Instructions
Prepare the journal entries on December 31, 2009, May 11, 2010, and June 12, 2010.

E8-7 Green Plains Supply Co. has the following transactions related to notes receivable during the last 2 months of the year.

Prepare entries for notes receivable transactions.
(SO 4, 5)

Nov.	1	Loaned $60,000 cash to B. Younger on a 1-year, 8% note.
Dec.	11	Sold goods to R. P. Meier, Inc., receiving a $3,600, 90-day, 7% note.
	16	Received a $12,000, 6-month, 9% note to settle an open account from M. Chen.
	31	Accrued interest revenue on all notes receivable.

Instructions
Journalize the transactions for Green Plains Supply Co.

E8-8 These transactions took place for Ralston Co.

Journalize notes receivable transactions.
(SO 4, 5)

2009

May	1	Received a $6,000, 1-year, 9% note in exchange for an outstanding account receivable from S. Dolan.
Dec.	31	Accrued interest revenue on the S. Dolan note.

2010

May	1	Received principal plus interest on the S. Dolan note. (No interest has been accrued since December 31, 2009.)

Instructions
Record the transactions in the general journal.

E8-9 Kiner Corp. had the following balances in receivable accounts at October 31, 2010 (in thousands): Allowance for Doubtful Accounts $56; Accounts Receivable $2,870; Other Receivables $189; Notes Receivable $1,353.

Prepare a balance sheet presentation of receivables.
(SO 6)

Instructions
Prepare the balance sheet presentation of Kiner Corp.'s receivables in good form.

E8-10 The following is a list of activities that companies perform in relation to their receivables.

Identify the principles of receivables management.
(SO 7)

1. Selling receivables to a factor.
2. Reviewing company ratings in *The Dun and Bradstreet Reference Book of American Business*.
3. Collecting information on competitors' payment period policies.
4. Preparing monthly accounts receivable aging schedule and investigating problem accounts.
5. Calculating the receivables turnover ratio and average collection period.

Instructions
Match each of the activities listed above with a purpose of the activity listed below.
(a) Determine to whom to extend credit.
(b) Establish a payment period.
(c) Monitor collections.
(d) Evaluate the liquidity of receivables.
(e) Accelerate cash receipts from receivables when necessary.

E8-11 The following information was taken from the 2007 financial statements of FedEx Corporation, a major global transportation/delivery company.

Compute ratios to evaluate a company's receivables balance.
(SO 7, 8)

(in millions)	2007	2006
Accounts receivable (gross)	$ 4,078	$ 3,660
Accounts receivable (net)	3,942	3,516
Allowance for doubtful accounts	136	144
Sales	35,214	32,294
Total current assets	6,629	6,464

Instructions

Answer each of the following questions.

(a) Calculate the receivables turnover ratio and the average collection period for 2007 for FedEx.

(b) Is accounts receivable a material component of the company's total current assets?

(c) Evaluate the balance in FedEx's allowance for uncollectible accounts.

Evaluate liquidity.

(SO 7, 8, 9)

E8-12 The following ratios are available for Garcia Inc.

	2010	2009
Current ratio	1.3:1	1.5:1
Receivables turnover	12 times	10 times
Inventory turnover	11 times	9 times

Instructions

(a) Is Garcia's short-term liquidity improving or deteriorating in 2010? Be specific in your answer, referring to relevant ratios.

(b) Do changes in turnover ratios affect profitability? Explain.

(c) Identify any steps Garcia might have taken, or might wish to take, to improve its management of its receivables and inventory turnover.

Prepare entry for sale of accounts receivable.

(SO 9)

E8-13 On March 3 Pride Appliances sells $710,000 of its receivables to American Factors Inc. American Factors Inc. assesses a service charge of 5% of the amount of receivables sold.

Instructions

Prepare the entry on Pride Appliances' books to record the sale of the receivables.

Identify reason for sale of receivables.

(SO 9)

E8-14 In a recent annual report, Office Depot, Inc. notes that the company entered into an agreement to sell all of its credit card program receivables to financial service companies.

Instructions

Explain why Office Depot, a financially stable company with positive cash flow, would choose to sell its receivables.

Prepare entry for credit card sale.

(SO 9)

E8-15 On May 10 Ritz Company sold merchandise for $6,000 and accepted the customer's First Business Bank MasterCard. At the end of the day, the First Business Bank MasterCard receipts were deposited in the company's bank account. First Business Bank charges a 3.5% service charge for credit card sales.

Instructions

Prepare the entry on Ritz Company's books to record the sale of merchandise.

Prepare entry for credit card sale.

(SO 9)

E8-16 On July 4 Linda's Restaurant accepts a Visa card for a $200 dinner bill. Visa charges a 3% service fee.

Instructions

Prepare the entry on Linda's books related to the transaction.

Determine cash flows and evaluate quality of earnings.

(SO 9)

E8-17 Rapid Corp. significantly reduced its requirements for credit sales. As a result, sales during the current year increased dramatically. It had receivables at the beginning of the year of $35,000 and ending receivables of $195,000. Sales were $380,000.

Instructions

(a) Determine cash collections during the period.

(b) Discuss how your findings in part (a) would affect Rapid Corp.'s quality of earnings ratio. (Do not compute.)

(c) What concerns might you have regarding Rapid's accounting?

Exercises: Set B

Visit the book's companion website, at **www.wiley.com/college/kimmel**, and choose the Student Companion site, to access Exercise Set B.

Problems: Set A

P8-1A   Kwikdeal.com uses the allowance method to estimate uncollectible accounts receivable. The company produced the following aging of the accounts receivable at year end.

Journalize transactions related to bad debts.
(SO 2, 3)

		Number of Days Outstanding				
	Total	**0–30**	**31–60**	**61–90**	**91–120**	**Over 120**
Accounts receivable	$375,000	$222,000	$90,000	$38,000	$10,000	$15,000
% uncollectible		1%	4%	5%	6%	10%
Estimated bad debts						

Instructions
(a) Calculate the total estimated bad debts based on the above information.
(b) Prepare the year-end adjusting journal entry to record the bad debts using the aged uncollectible accounts receivable determined in (a). Assume the unadjusted balance in Allowance for Doubtful Accounts is a $4,000 debit.
(c) Of the above accounts, $5,000 is determined to be specifically uncollectible. Prepare the journal entry to write off the uncollectible account.
(d) The company collects $5,000 subsequently on a specific account that had previously been determined to be uncollectible in (c). Prepare the journal entry(ies) necessary to restore the account and record the cash collection.
(e) Comment on how your answers to (a)–(d) would change if Kwikdeal.com used 3% of total accounts receivable, rather than aging the accounts receivable. What are the advantages to the company of aging the accounts receivable rather than applying a percentage to total accounts receivable?

(a) Tot. est.
bad debts $9,820

P8-2A   At December 31, 2009, Kelso Imports reported this information on its balance sheet.

Prepare journal entries related to bad debt expense, and compute ratios.
(SO 2, 3, 8)

Accounts receivable	$600,000
Less: Allowance for doubtful accounts	40,000

During 2010 the company had the following transactions related to receivables.

1. Sales on account	$2,500,000
2. Sales returns and allowances	40,000
3. Collections of accounts receivable	2,200,000
4. Write-offs of accounts receivable deemed uncollectible	45,000
5. Recovery of bad debts previously written off as uncollectible	15,000

Instructions
(a) Prepare the journal entries to record each of these five transactions. Assume that no cash discounts were taken on the collections of accounts receivable.
(b) Enter the January 1, 2010, balances in Accounts Receivable and Allowance for Doubtful Accounts, post the entries to the two accounts (use T accounts), and determine the balances.
(c) Prepare the journal entry to record bad debts expense for 2010, assuming that aging the accounts receivable indicates that estimated bad debts are $46,000.
(d) Compute the receivables turnover ratio and average collection period.

(b) A/R bal. $815,000

Journalize transactions related to bad debts.

(SO 2, 3)

P8-3A Presented below is an aging schedule for Galena Company.

| Customer | Total | Not Yet Due | Number of Days Past Due | | | |
			1–30	31–60	61–90	Over 90
Aber	$ 20,000		$ 9,000	$11,000		
Bloom	30,000	$ 30,000				
Cheng	50,000	5,000	5,000		$40,000	
Dahl	38,000					$38,000
Others	120,000	72,000	35,000	13,000		
	$258,000	$107,000	$49,000	$24,000	$40,000	$38,000
Estimated percentage uncollectible		3%	7%	12%	24%	50%
Total estimated bad debts	$ 38,120	$ 3,210	$ 3,430	$ 2,880	$ 9,600	$19,000

At December 31, 2009, the unadjusted balance in Allowance for Doubtful Accounts is a credit of $8,000.

Instructions
(a) Journalize and post the adjusting entry for bad debts at December 31, 2009. (Use T accounts.)
(b) Journalize and post to the allowance account these 2010 events and transactions:
  1. March 1, a $600 customer balance originating in 2009 is judged uncollectible.
  2. May 1, a check for $600 is received from the customer whose account was written off as uncollectible on March 1.
(c) Journalize the adjusting entry for bad debts at December 31, 2010, assuming that the unadjusted balance in Allowance for Doubtful Accounts is a debit of $1,100 and the aging schedule indicates that total estimated bad debts will be $36,700.

Compute bad debt amounts.

(SO 3)

P8-4A Here is information related to Schellhamer Company for 2010.

Total credit sales	$1,500,000
Accounts receivable at December 31	840,000
Bad debts written off	41,000

Instructions
(a) What amount of bad debts expense will Schellhamer Company report if it uses the direct write-off method of accounting for bad debts?
(b) Assume that Schellhamer Company decides to estimate its bad debts expense based on 3% of accounts receivable. What amount of bad debts expense will the company record if Allowance for Doubtful Accounts has a credit balance of $3,000?
(c) Assume the same facts as in part (b), except that there is a $1,000 debit balance in Allowance for Doubtful Accounts. What amount of bad debts expense will Schellhamer record?
(d) What is a weakness of the direct write-off method of reporting bad debts expense?

Journalize entries to record transactions related to bad debts.

(SO 2, 3)

P8-5A At December 31, 2010, the trial balance of Olpe Company contained the following amounts before adjustment.

	Debits	Credits
Accounts Receivable	$200,000	
Allowance for Doubtful Accounts		$ 1,500
Sales		875,000

Instructions
(a) Prepare the adjusting entry at December 31, 2010, to record bad debts expense assuming that the aging schedule indicates that $10,800 of accounts receivable will be uncollectible.

(b) Repeat part (a) assuming that instead of a credit balance there is a $1,500 debit balance in the Allowance for Doubtful Accounts.

(c) During the next month, January 2011, a $2,700 account receivable is written off as uncollectible. Prepare the journal entry to record the write-off.

(d) Repeat part (c) assuming that Olpe Company uses the direct write-off method instead of the allowance method in accounting for uncollectible accounts receivable.

(e) ▰▰▰▷ What are the advantages of using an aging schedule and the allowance method in accounting for uncollectible accounts as compared to the direct write-off method?

P8-6A   On January 1, 2010, Sands Company had Accounts Receivable of $54,200 and Allowance for Doubtful Accounts of $3,700. Sands Company prepares financial statements annually and uses a perpetual inventory system. During the year the following selected transactions occurred.

Journalize various receivables transactions.
(SO 1, 2, 4, 5)

Jan.	5	Sold $7,000 of merchandise to Norris Company, terms n/30. Cost of the merchandise sold was $4,000.
Feb.	2	Accepted a $7,000, 4-month, 9% promissory note from Norris Company for balance due.
	12	Sold $9,000 of merchandise costing $5,000 to Loflin Company and accepted Loflin's $9,000, 2-month, 10% note for the balance due.
	26	Sold $5,200 of merchandise costing $3,300 to Hossfeld Co., terms n/10.
Apr.	5	Accepted a $5,200, 3-month, 8% note from Hossfeld Co. for balance due.
	12	Collected Loflin Company note in full.
June	2	Collected Norris Company note in full.
	15	Sold $2,000 of merchandise costing $1,500 to Madrid Inc. and accepted a $2,000, 6-month, 12% note for the amount due.

Instructions
Journalize the transactions.

P8-7A   The president of Space Enterprises asks if you could indicate the impact certain transactions have on the following ratios.

Explain the impact of transactions on ratios.
(SO 8)

Transaction	Current Ratio (2:1)	Receivables Turnover (10X)	Average Collection Period (36.5 days)
1. Received $3,000 on cash sale. The cost of the goods sold was $1,800.			
2. Recorded bad debts expense of $500 using allowance method.			
3. Wrote off a $100 account receivable as uncollectible (Uses allowance method.)			
4. Recorded $2,500 sales on account. The cost of the goods sold was $1,500.			

Instructions
Complete the table, indicating whether each transaction will increase (I), decrease (D), or have no effect (NE) on the specific ratios provided for Space Enterprises.

P8-8A   Lorenz Company closes its books on July 31. On June 30 the Notes Receivable account balance is $23,800. Notes Receivable include the following.

Prepare entries for various credit card and notes receivable transactions.
(SO 2, 4, 5, 6, 9)

Date	Maker	Face Value	Term	Maturity Date	Interest Rate
May 21	Agler Inc.	$ 6,000	60 days	July 20	8%
May 25	Girard Co.	7,800	60 days	July 24	10%
June 30	LSU Corp.	10,000	6 months	December 31	9%

During July the following transactions were completed.

July 5 Made sales of $5,100 on Lorenz credit cards.
 14 Made sales of $600 on Visa credit cards. The credit card service charge is 3%.
 20 Received payment in full from Agler Inc. on the amount due.
 24 Received payment in full from Girard Co. on the amount due.

Instructions
(a) Journalize the July transactions and the July 31 adjusting entry for accrued interest receivable. (Interest is computed using 360 days.)

(b) A/R bal. $ 5,100

(b) Enter the balances at July 1 in the receivable accounts and post the entries to all of the receivable accounts. (Use T accounts.)

(c) Tot. receivables $15,175

(c) Show the balance sheet presentation of the receivable accounts at July 31.

Calculate and interpret various ratios.
(SO 7, 8)

P8-9A Presented here is basic financial information (in millions) from the 2006 annual reports of Nike and Adidas.

	Nike	Adidas
Sales	$16,325.9	$10,084
Allowance for doubtful accounts, Jan. 1	67.6	81
Allowance for doubtful accounts, Dec. 31	71.5	112
Accounts receivable balance (gross), Jan. 1	2,450.5	1,046
Accounts receivable balance (gross), Dec. 31	2,566.2	1,527

Instructions
Calculate the receivables turnover ratio and average collection period for both companies. Comment on the difference in their collection experiences.

Problems: Set B

Journalize transactions related to bad debts.
(SO 2, 3)

P8-1B The following represents selected information taken from a company's aging schedule to estimate uncollectible accounts receivable at year end.

	Total	Number of Days Outstanding				
		0–30	31–60	61–90	91–120	Over 120
Accounts receivable	$285,000	$107,000	$60,000	$50,000	$38,000	$30,000
% uncollectible		1%	5%	7.5%	10%	12%
Estimated bad debts						

Instructions
(a) Calculate the total estimated bad debts based on the above information.

(a) Tot. est. bad debts $15,220

(b) Prepare the year-end adjusting journal entry to record the bad debts using the allowance method and the aged uncollectible accounts receivable determined in (a). Assume the unadjusted balance in the Allowance for Doubtful Accounts account is a $10,000 credit.
(c) Of the above accounts, $2,600 is determined to be specifically uncollectible. Prepare the journal entry to write off the uncollectible accounts.
(d) The company subsequently collects $1,000 on a specific account that had previously been determined to be uncollectible in (c). Prepare the journal entry(ies) necessary to restore the account and record the cash collection.
(e) Explain how establishing an allowance account satisfies the matching principle.

P8-2B At December 31, 2009, Longbine Company reported this information on its balance sheet.

Accounts receivable	$960,000
Less: Allowance for doubtful accounts	84,000

Prepare journal entries related to bad debt expense, and compute ratios.
(SO 2, 3, 8)

During 2010 the company had the following transactions related to receivables.

1. Sales on account $3,600,000
2. Sales returns and allowances 50,000
3. Collections of accounts receivable 3,000,000
4. Write-offs of accounts receivable deemed uncollectible 92,000
5. Recovery of bad debts previously written off as uncollectible 30,000

Instructions
(a) Prepare the journal entries to record each of these five transactions. Assume that no cash discounts were taken on the collections of accounts receivable.
(b) Enter the January 1, 2010, balances in Accounts Receivable and Allowance for Doubtful Accounts, post the entries to the two accounts (use T accounts), and determine the balances.
(c) Prepare the journal entry to record bad debts expense for 2010, assuming that aging the accounts receivable indicates that expected bad debts are $113,000.
(d) Compute the receivables turnover ratio and average collection period.

(b) A/R bal. $1,418,000

P8-3B Presented here is an aging schedule for Zimmerman Company.

Journalize transactions related to bad debts.
(SO 2, 3)

Customer	Total	Not Yet Due	Number of Days Past Due			
			1–30	31–60	61–90	Over 90
Aaron	$ 22,000		$12,000	$10,000		
Barry	40,000	$ 40,000				
Cara	60,000	16,000	6,000		$38,000	
Donald	28,000					$28,000
Others	126,000	96,000	16,000	14,000		
	$276,000	$152,000	$34,000	$24,000	$38,000	$28,000
Estimated percentage uncollectible		4%	9%	13%	25%	50%
Total estimated bad debts	$ 35,760	$ 6,080	$ 3,060	$ 3,120	$ 9,500	$14,000

At December 31, 2009, the unadjusted balance in Allowance for Doubtful Accounts is a credit of $11,700.

Instructions
(a) Journalize and post the adjusting entry for bad debts at December 31, 2009. (Use T accounts.)
(b) Journalize and post to the allowance account these 2010 events and transactions:
   1. March 31, a $500 customer balance originating in 2009 is judged uncollectible.
   2. May 31, a check for $500 is received from the customer whose account was written off as uncollectible on March 31.
(c) Journalize the adjusting entry for bad debts on December 31, 2010, assuming that the unadjusted balance in Allowance for Doubtful Accounts is a debit of $800 and the aging schedule indicates that total estimated bad debts will be $33,800.

P8-4B Here is information related to Younger Company for 2010.

Compute bad debt amounts.
(SO 3)

Total credit sales	$2,000,000
Accounts receivable at December 31	700,000
Bad debts written off	26,000

Instructions

(a) What amount of bad debts expense will Younger Company report if it uses the direct write-off method of accounting for bad debts?

(b) Assume that Younger Company decides to estimate its bad debts expense based on 4% of accounts receivable. What amount of bad debts expense will the company record if it has an Allowance for Doubtful Accounts credit balance of $4,000?

(c) Assume the same facts as in part (b), except that there is a $2,000 debit balance in Allowance for Doubtful Accounts. What amount of bad debts expense will Younger record?

(d) What is the weakness of the direct write-off method of reporting bad debts expense?

Journalize entries to record transactions related to bad debts.

(SO 2, 3)

P8-5B At December 31, 2010, the trial balance of Stine Company contained the following amounts before adjustment.

	Debits	Credits
Accounts Receivable	$500,000	
Allowance for Doubtful Accounts		$ 4,800
Sales		2,200,000

Instructions

(a) Based on the information given, which method of accounting for bad debts is Stine Company using—the direct write-off method or the allowance method? How can you tell?

(b) Prepare the adjusting entry at December 31, 2010, for bad debts expense assuming that the aging schedule indicates that $21,000 of accounts receivable will be uncollectible.

(c) Repeat part (b) assuming that instead of a credit balance there is a $4,800 debit balance in the Allowance for Doubtful Accounts.

(d) During the next month, January 2011, a $5,000 account receivable is written off as uncollectible. Prepare the journal entry to record the write-off.

(e) Repeat part (d) assuming that Stine uses the direct write-off method instead of the allowance method in accounting for uncollectible accounts receivable.

(f) ▐▐▌▌▌▌➤ What type of account is the allowance for doubtful accounts? How does it affect how accounts receivable is reported on the balance sheet at the end of the accounting period?

Journalize various receivables transactions.

(SO 1, 2, 4, 5)

P8-6B On January 1, 2010, Moxley Company had Accounts Receivable $154,000; Notes Receivable of $11,000; and Allowance for Doubtful Accounts of $13,200. The note receivable is from Hoelter Company. It is a 4-month, 9% note dated December 31, 2009. Moxley Company prepares financial statements annually. During the year the following selected transactions occurred. (Moxley Company uses a periodic inventory system.)

Jan. 5 Sold $10,000 of merchandise to Frizell Company, terms n/15.

20 Accepted Frizell Company's $10,000, 3-month, 9% note for balance due.

Feb. 18 Sold $4,000 of merchandise to Zheng Company and accepted Zheng's $4,000, 6-month, 10% note for the amount due.

Apr. 20 Collected Frizell Company note in full.

30 Received payment in full from Hoelter Company on the amount due.

May 25 Accepted Ardan Inc.'s $9,000, 6-month, 8% note in settlement of a past-due balance on account.

Aug. 18 Received payment in full from Zheng Company on note due.

Sept. 1 Sold $8,000 of merchandise to Charles Company and accepted an $8,000, 6-month, 10% note for the amount due.

Explain the impact of transactions on ratios: discuss acceleration of receipt of cash from receivables.

(SO 8, 9)

Instructions

Journalize the transactions.

P8-7B The president of Ferman Enterprises Ltd., Angela Ferman, is considering the impact that certain transactions have on the company's receivables turnover and average collection period ratios. Prior to the following transactions, Ferman's receivables turnover was 6 times, and its average collection period was 61 days.

Transaction	Receivables Turnover (6×)	Average Collection Period (61 days)
1. Recorded sales on account $100,000.		
2. Collected $25,000 owing from customers.		
3. Wrote off a $2,500 account from a customer as uncollectible (Uses allowance method.)		
4. Recorded sales returns of $1,500 and credited the customers' accounts.		
5. Recorded bad debts expense for the year $7,500, using the allowance method.		

Instructions
(a) Complete the table, indicating whether each transaction will increase (I), decrease (D), or have no effect (NE) on the ratios.
(b) Angela was reading through the financial statements for some publicly traded companies and noticed that they had recorded a loss on sale of receivables. She would like you to explain why companies sell their receivables.

P8-8B Brown Company closes its books on October 31. On September 30 the Notes Receivable account balance is $20,200. Notes Receivable include the following.

Prepare entries for various credit card and notes receivable transactions.
(SO 2, 4, 5, 6, 9)
GLS

Date	Maker	Face Value	Term	Maturity Date	Interest Rate
Aug. 16	Foran Inc.	$ 7,000	60 days	Oct. 15	9%
Aug. 25	Marsh Co.	3,000	2 months	Oct. 25	7%
Sept. 30	Flagg Corp.	10,200	6 months	Mar. 30	8%

Interest is computed using a 360-day year. During October the following transactions were completed.

Oct. 7 Made sales of $4,600 on Brown credit cards.
    12 Made sales of $600 on Visa credit cards. The credit card service charge is 3%.
    15 Received payment in full from Foran Inc. on the amount due.
    25 Received payment in full from Marsh Co. on amount due.

Instructions
(a) Journalize the October transactions and the October 31 adjusting entry for accrued interest receivable.
(b) Enter the balances at October 1 in the receivable accounts and post the entries to all of the receivable accounts. (Use T accounts.)
(c) Show the balance sheet presentation of the receivable accounts at October 31.

(b) A/R bal. $ 4,600

(c) Tot. receivables $14,868

P8-9B Presented here is basic financial information from the 2006 annual reports of Intel and Advanced Micro Devices (AMD), the two primary manufacturers of silicon chips for personal computers.

Calculate and interpret various ratios.
(SO 7, 8)

(in millions)	Intel	AMD
Sales	$35,382	$5,649
Allowance for doubtful accounts, Jan. 1	64	13
Allowance for doubtful accounts, Dec. 31	32	13
Accounts receivable balance (gross), Jan. 1	3,978	818
Accounts receivable balance (gross), Dec. 31	2,741	1,153

Instructions
Calculate the receivables turnover ratio and average collection period for both companies. Comment on the difference in their collection experiences.

Problems: Set C

Visit the book's companion website at **www.wiley.com/college/kimmel** and choose the Student Companion site to access Problem Set C.

Comprehensive Problem

CP8 Posada Corporation's balance sheet at December 31, 2009, is presented below.

POSADA CORPORATION
Balance Sheet
December 31, 2009

Cash	$13,100	Accounts payable	$ 8,750
Accounts receivable	19,780	Common stock	20,000
Allowance for doubtful accounts	(1,000)	Retained earnings	12,530
Merchandise inventory	9,400		$41,280
	$41,280		

During January 2010, the following transactions occurred. Posada uses the perpetual inventory method.

Jan. 1   Posada accepted a 4-month, 12% note from Alien Company in payment of Alien's $1,000 account.

3   Posada wrote off as uncollectible the accounts of Ex Corporation ($450) and Files Company ($230).

8   Posada purchased $17,200 of inventory on account.

11   Posada sold for $25,000 on account inventory that cost $17,500.

15   Posada sold inventory that cost $700 to Ben Borke for $1,000. Borke charged this amount on his Visa First Bank card. The service fee charged Posada by First Bank is 3%.

17   Posada collected $22,900 from customers on account.

21   Posada paid $16,300 on accounts payable.

24   Posada received payment in full ($230) from Files Company on the account written off on January 3.

27   Posada purchased advertising supplies for $1,400 cash.

31   Posada paid other operating expenses, $3,218.

Adjustment data:

1. Interest is recorded for the month on the note from January 1.
2. Bad debts are expected to be 6% of the January 31, 2010, accounts receivable.
3. A count of advertising supplies on January 31, 2010, reveals that $560 remains unused.
4. The income tax rate is 30%. (*Hint:* Prepare the income statement up to "Income before taxes" and multiply by 30% to compute the amount.)

Instructions

(You may want to set up T accounts to determine ending balances.)

(a) Prepare journal entries for the transactions listed above and adjusting entries.

(b) Prepare an adjusted trial balance at January 31, 2010.

(c) Prepare an income statement and a retained earnings statement for the month ending January 31, 2010, and a classified balance sheet as of January 31, 2010.

Continuing Cookie Chronicle

(*Note:* This is a Continuation of the Cookie Chronicle from Chapters 1 through 7.)

CCC8   One of Natalie's friends, Curtis Lesperance, runs a coffee shop where he sells specialty coffees and prepares and sells muffins and cookies. He is eager to buy one of Natalie's fine European mixers, which would enable him to make larger batches of muffins and cookies. However, Curtis cannot afford to pay for the mixer for at least 30 days. He asks Natalie if she would be willing to sell him the mixer on credit. Natalie comes to you for advice.

Go to the book's companion website, **www.wiley.com/college/kimme**l, to see the completion of this problem.

broadening your perspective

Financial Reporting and Analysis

FINANCIAL REPORTING PROBLEM: *Tootsie Roll Industries*

BYP8-1   Refer to the financial statements of Tootsie Roll Industries and the accompanying notes to its financial statements in Appendix A.

Instructions
(a) Calculate the receivables turnover ratio and average collection period for 2007. (Use "Net Product Sales." Assume all sales were credit sales.)
(b) Did Tootsie Roll have any potentially significant credit risks in 2007? (*Hint:* Review Note 1 under Revenue recognition and Note 9 to the financial statements.)
(c) What conclusions can you draw from the information in parts (a) and (b)?

COMPARATIVE ANALYSIS PROBLEM: *Tootsie Roll vs. Hershey Foods*

BYP8-2   The financial statements of Hershey Foods are presented in Appendix B, following the financial statements for Tootsie Roll in Appendix A.

Instructions
(a) Based on the information contained in these financial statements, compute the following 2007 values for each company.
  (1) Receivables turnover ratio. (For Tootsie Roll use "Net product sales." Assume all sales were credit sales.)
  (2) Average collection period for receivables.
(b) What conclusions concerning the management of accounts receivable can be drawn from these data?

RESEARCH CASE

BYP8-3   The September 24, 2007, issue of the *Wall Street Journal* includes an article by Simona Covel titled "Small Business Link: Three Approaches to Reining in Customer Debt."

Instructions
Read the article and answer the following questions.
(a) Describe the steps taken by Slack & Co. Contracting Inc., and discuss the pros and cons of it approach.
(b) Describe the steps taken by Nicholas & Co., and discuss the pros and cons of its approach.
(c) Describe the steps taken by KTM Auto Inc., and discuss the pros and cons of its approach.

INTERPRETING FINANCIAL STATEMENTS

BYP8-4 The information below is from the 2006 financial statements and accompanying notes of The Scotts Company, a major manufacturer of lawn-care products.

(in millions)	2006	2005
Accounts receivable	$ 380.4	$ 323.3
Allowance for uncollectible accounts	11.3	11.4
Sales	2,697.1	2,369.3
Total current assets	942.0	787.8

THE SCOTTS COMPANY
Notes to the Financial Statements

Note 17. Concentrations of Credit Risk

Financial instruments which potentially subject the Company to concentration of credit risk consist principally of trade accounts receivable. The Company sells its consumer products to a wide variety of retailers, including mass merchandisers, home centers, independent hardware stores, nurseries, garden outlets, warehouse clubs and local and regional chains. Professional products are sold to commercial nurseries, greenhouses, landscape services, and growers of specialty agriculture crops.

At September 30, 2006, 76% of the Company's accounts receivable were due from customers geographically located in North America. Approximately 79% of these receivables were generated from the consumer business with the remaining 21% due from customers of Scotts LawnService®, the professional businesses (primarily distributors), Smith & Hawken®, and Morning Song®. Our top 3 customers within the consumer business accounted for 53% of total consumer accounts receivable.

At September 30, 2005, 76% of the Company's accounts receivable were due from customers geographically located in North America. Approximately 83% of these receivable were generated from the Company's consumer business with the remaining 17% generated from customers of Scotts LawnService® and the professional businesses (primarily distributors). Our top 3 customers within the consumer business accounted for 80% of total consumer accounts receivable.

The remainder of the Company's accounts receivable at September 30, 2006 and 2005, were generated from customers located outside of North America, primarily retailers, distributors, nurseries and growers in Europe. No concentrations of customers or individual customers within this group account for more than 10% of the Company's accounts receivable at either balance sheet date.

The Company's three largest customers accounted for the following percentage of net sales in each respective period:

	Largest Customer	2nd Largest Customer	3rd Largest Customer
2006	21.5%	11.2%	10.5%
2005	23.5%	11.9%	9.7%
2004	25.0%	12.9%	9.4%

Sales to the Company's three largest customers are reported within the Company's North America segment. No other customers accounted for more than 10% of fiscal 2006, fiscal 2005 or fiscal 2004 net sales.

Instructions
Answer each of the following questions.
(a) Calculate the receivables turnover ratio and average collection period for 2006 for the company.
(b) Is accounts receivable a material component of the company's total current assets?
(c) Scotts sells seasonal products. How might this affect the accuracy of your answer to part (a)?

(d) Evaluate the credit risk of Scotts' concentrated receivables.

(e) Comment on the informational value of Scotts' Note 17 on concentrations of credit risk.

BYP8-5 Art World Industries, Inc., was incorporated in 1986 in Delaware, although it is located in Los Angeles. The company prints, publishes, and sells limited-edition graphics and reproductive prints in the wholesale market.

The company's balance sheet at the end of a recent year showed an allowance for doubtful accounts of $175,477. The allowance was set up against certain Japanese accounts receivable that average more than one year in age. The Japanese acknowledge the amount due, but with the slow economy in Japan, they lack the resources to pay at this time.

Instructions

(a) Which method of accounting for uncollectible accounts does Art World Industries use?

(b) Explain the difference between the direct write-off and percentage of receivables methods. Based on Art World's disclosure above, what important factor would you have to consider in arriving at appropriate percentages to apply for the percentage of receivables method?

(c) What are the implications for a company's receivables management of selling its products internationally?

FINANCIAL ANALYSIS ON THE WEB

BYP8-6 *Purpose:* To learn more about factoring from websites that provide factoring services.

Address: **www.ccapital.net**,
or go to **www.wiley.com/college/kimmel**

Instructions

Go to the website, click on Invoice Factoring, and answer the following questions.

(a) What are some of the benefits of factoring?

(b) What is the range of the percentages of the typical discount rate?

(c) If a company factors its receivables, what percentage of the value of the receivables can it expect to receive from the factor in the form of cash, and how quickly will it receive the cash?

Critical Thinking

DECISION MAKING ACROSS THE ORGANIZATION

BYP8-7 Sue and Sam Fielder own Club Fab. From its inception Club Fab has sold merchandise on either a cash or credit basis, but no credit cards have been accepted. During the past several months, the Fielders have begun to question their credit-sales policies. First, they have lost some sales because of their refusal to accept credit cards. Second, representatives of two metropolitan banks have convinced them to accept their national credit cards. One bank, City National Bank, has stated that (1) its credit card fee is 4% and (2) it pays the retailer 96 cents on each $1 of sales within 3 days of receiving the credit card billings.

The Fielders decide that they should determine the cost of carrying their own credit sales. From the accounting records of the past 3 years they accumulate these data:

	2010	2009	2008
Net credit sales	$500,000	$600,000	$400,000
Collection agency fees for slow-paying customers	2,900	2,600	1,600
Salary of part-time accounts receivable clerk	4,400	4,400	4,400

Credit and collection expenses as a percentage of net credit sales are as follows: uncollectible accounts 1.6%, billing and mailing costs .5%, and credit investigation fee on new customers .2%.

Sue and Sam also determine that the average accounts receivable balance outstanding during the year is 5% of net credit sales. The Fielders estimate that they could earn an average of 10% annually on cash invested in other business opportunities.

Instructions

With the class divided into groups, answer the following.

(a) Prepare a tabulation for each year showing total credit and collection expenses in dollars and as a percentage of net credit sales.

(b) Determine the net credit and collection expenses in dollars and as a percentage of sales after considering the revenue not earned from other investment opportunities. (*Note:* The income lost on the cash held by the bank for 3 days is considered to be immaterial.)

(c) Discuss both the financial and nonfinancial factors that are relevant to the decision.

COMMUNICATION ACTIVITY

BYP8-8   Messtopper Corporation is a recently formed business selling the "World's Best Doormat." The corporation is selling doormats faster than Messtopper can make them. It has been selling the product on a credit basis, telling customers to "pay when they can." Oddly, even though sales are tremendous, the company is having trouble paying its bills.

Instructions

Write a memo to the president of Messtopper Corporation discussing these questions:

(a) What steps should be taken to improve the company's ability to pay its bills?

(b) What accounting steps should be taken to measure its success in improving collections and in recording its collection success?

(c) If the corporation is still unable to pay its bills, what additional steps can be taken with its receivables to ease its liquidity problems?

ETHICS CASE

BYP8-9   The controller of Gomez Corporation believes that the company's yearly allowance for doubtful accounts should be 2% of net credit sales. The president of Gomez Corporation, nervous that the stockholders might expect the company to sustain its 10% growth rate, suggests that the controller increase the allowance for doubtful accounts to 4%. The president thinks that the lower net income, which reflects a 6% growth rate, will be a more sustainable rate for Gomez Corporation.

Instructions

(a) Who are the stakeholders in this case?

(b) Does the president's request pose an ethical dilemma for the controller?

(c) Should the controller be concerned with Gomez Corporation's growth rate in estimating the allowance? Explain your answer.

"ALL ABOUT YOU" ACTIVITY

BYP8-10   Credit card usage in the United States is substantial. Many startup companies use credit cards as a way to help meet short-term financial needs. The most common forms of debt for startups are use of credit cards and loans from relatives.

Suppose that you start up Brothers Sandwich Shop. You invested your savings of $20,000 and borrowed $70,000 from your relatives. Although sales in the first few months are good, you see that you may not have sufficient cash to pay expenses and maintain your inventory at acceptable levels, at least in the short term. You decide you may need to use one or more credit cards to fund the possible cash shortfall.

Instructions

(a) Go to the Web and find two sources that provide insight into how to compare credit card terms.

(b) Develop a list, in descending order of importance, as to what features are most important to you in selecting a credit card for your business.

(c) Examine the features of your present credit card. (If you do not have a credit card, select a likely one online for this exercise.) Given your analysis above, what are the three major disadvantages of your present credit card?

Answers to Insight and Accounting Across the Organization Questions

p. 393

Q: When would it be appropriate for a company to lower its allowance for doubtful accounts as a percentage of its receivables?

A: It would be appropriate for a company to lower its allowance for doubtful accounts as a percentage of receivables if the company's collection experience had improved, or was expected to improve, and therefore the company expected lower defaults as a percentage of receivables.

p. 396

Q: How would reported net income likely differ during the first year of this promotion if Mitsubishi used the direct write-off method versus the allowance method?

A: Under the direct write-off method, Mitsubishi would not record bad debt expense until a customer actually defaulted on a loan. Under the allowance method, Mitsubishi would estimate how many of its loans would default rather than waiting until they actually default. For Mitsubishi, the direct write-off method would have resulted in higher net income during the first year of the promotion.

p. 400

Q: What steps should the banks have taken to ensure the accuracy of financial information provided on loan applications?

A: At a minimum, the bank should have requested copies of recent income tax forms and contacted the supposed employer to verify income. To verify ownership and value of assets, it should have examined bank statements, investment statements, and title documents and should have employed appraisers.

p. 406

Q: What issues should management consider in deciding whether to factor its receivables?

A: Management must prepare a cash budget and evaluate its projected cash needs. If it projects a cash deficiency, it should first pursue more traditional bank financing, since it tends to be less expensive than factoring. If traditional bank financing is not available, management could pursue factoring. If carefully structured, a factoring arrangement can be quite cost-effective since it can enable the company to outsource much of its billing and collection activities.

Answers to Self-Study Questions

1. c   2. c   3. a   4. a   5. c   6. d   7. c   8. b   9. d   10. d   11. a   12. c   13. c   14. a
15. d

Reporting and Analyzing Long-Lived Assets

study objectives

After studying this chapter, you should be able to:

1 Describe how the cost principle applies to plant assets.

2 Explain the concept of depreciation.

3 Compute periodic depreciation using the straight-line method, and contrast its expense pattern with those of other methods.

4 Describe the procedure for revising periodic depreciation.

5 Explain how to account for the disposal of plant assets.

6 Describe methods for evaluating the use of plant assets.

7 Identify the basic issues related to reporting intangible assets.

8 Indicate how long-lived assets are reported in the financial statements.

✓ the navigator

A Tale of Two Airlines

So, you're interested in starting a new business. Have you thought about the airline industry? Your only experience with airlines is as a passenger? Don't let that stop you. Today the most profitable airlines in the industry are not well-known majors like American Airlines and United. In fact, most giant, old airlines are either bankrupt or on the verge of bankruptcy. In a recent year, five major airlines representing 24% of total U.S. capacity were operating under bankruptcy protection.

Not all airlines are hurting. The growth and profitability in the airline industry today is found at relative newcomers like Southwest Airlines and JetBlue. These and other new airlines compete primarily on ticket prices. During a recent five-year period, the low-fare airline market share increased by 47%; the low-fare airlines now have over 22% of U.S. airline capacity.

Southwest was the first upstart to make it big. It did so by taking a different approach. It bought small, new, fuel-efficient planes. Also, instead of the "hub-and-spoke" approach used by the majors, it opted for direct, short hop, no frills flights. It was all about controlling costs—getting the most out of its efficient new planes.

Other upstarts, such as Valujet, chose a different approach. They bought planes that were 20 to 30 years old (known in the industry as *zombies*). By buying used planes Valujet was able to add one or two planes a month to its fleet—an unheard of expansion. Valujet started with a $3.4 million investment and grew to be worth $630 million in its first three years.

But a terrible crash of a Valujet aircraft focused the spotlight on its strategy of using old planes. Although the cause of the crash appears to have been unrelated to the age of its planes, in the aftermath of the crash Valujet struggled to survive under the weight of government scrutiny and lack of customer confidence. In the face of continuing financial problems and customer skepticism, Valujet merged with AirWays Corp. and took the name of its airline, AirTran Airways. Today AirTran is one of the most profitable airlines in the industry.

But with fuel costs at record high levels, AirTran is no longer in the market for old planes. Nobody is. In fact, the old Boeing 727, which until very recently was a mainstay of nearly every airline, is no longer used for passenger flights because it couldn't be operated efficiently. Today success in the airline business comes from owning the newest and most efficient equipment, and knowing how to get the most out of it.

On the World Wide Web
Southwest Airlines:
www.southwest.com
AirTran Airways: www.airtran.com
JetBlue Airways: www.jetblue.com

Was Valujet's approach to buying equipment really the "right formula," or was it a recipe for disaster? For airlines and many other companies, making the right decisions regarding long-lived assets is critical because these assets represent huge investments. Management must make many ongoing decisions about long-lived assets—what assets to acquire and when, how to finance them, how to account for them, and when to dispose of them.

In this chapter we address these and other issues surrounding long-lived assets. The discussion is in two parts: plant assets and intangible assets. *Plant assets* are the property, plant, and equipment (physical assets) that commonly come to mind when we think of what a company owns. Companies also have many important *intangible assets*. These assets, such as copyrights and patents, lack physical substance but can be extremely valuable and vital to a company's success.

The content and organization of this chapter are as follows.

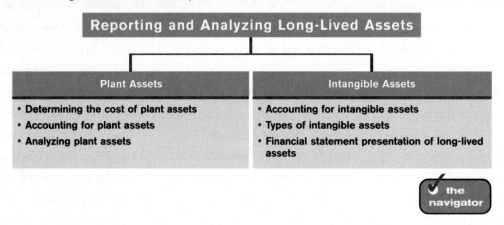

Reporting and Analyzing Long-Lived Assets	
Plant Assets	**Intangible Assets**
• Determining the cost of plant assets • Accounting for plant assets • Analyzing plant assets	• Accounting for intangible assets • Types of intangible assets • Financial statement presentation of long-lived assets

✔ the navigator

section one

Plant Assets

Plant assets are resources that have physical substance (a definite size and shape), are used in the operations of a business, and are not intended for sale to customers. They are called various names—*property, plant, and equipment; plant and equipment;* and *fixed assets.* By whatever name, these assets are expected to provide service to the company for a number of years. Except for land, plant assets decline in service potential (value) over their useful lives.

Plant assets are critical to a company's success because they determine the company's capacity and therefore its ability to satisfy customers. With too few planes, for example, AirTran and Southwest Airlines would lose customers to their competitors. But with too many planes, they would be flying with empty seats. Management must constantly monitor its needs and acquire assets accordingly. Failure to do so results in lost business opportunities or inefficient use of existing assets and is likely to show up eventually in poor financial results.

It is important for a company to (1) keep assets in good operating condition, (2) replace worn-out or outdated assets, and (3) expand its productive assets as needed. The decline of rail travel in the United States can be traced in part to the failure of railroad companies to maintain and update their assets. Conversely, the growth of air travel in this country can be attributed in part to the general willingness of airline companies to follow these essential guidelines.

For many companies, investments in plant assets are substantial. Illustration 9-1 shows the percentages of plant assets in relation to total assets in various companies.

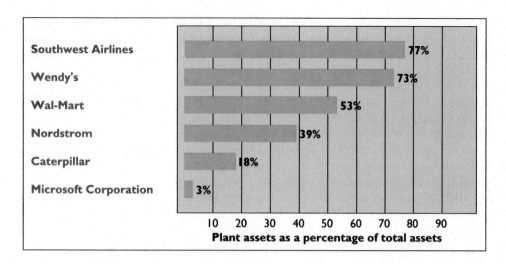

Illustration 9-1
Percentages of plant
assets in relation to
total assets

Determining the Cost of Plant Assets

The **cost principle** requires that companies record plant assets at cost. Thus, AirTran and Southwest Airlines record their planes at cost. **Cost consists of all expenditures necessary to acquire an asset and make it ready for its intended use.** For example, the purchase price, freight costs paid by the purchaser, and installation costs are all part of the cost of factory machinery.

> **study objective** **1**
> Describe how the cost principle applies to plant assets.

Determining which costs to include in a plant asset account and which costs not to include is very important. If a cost is not included in a plant asset account, then it must be expensed immediately. Such costs are referred to as revenue expenditures. On the other hand, costs that are not expensed immediately but are instead included in a plant asset account are referred to as capital expenditures.

> **International Note** IFRS is flexible regarding asset valuation. Companies revalue to fair value when they believe this information is more relevant.

This distinction is important; it has immediate, and often material, implications for the income statement. Some companies, in order to boost current income, have **improperly capitalized expenditures** that they should have expensed. For example, suppose that a company improperly capitalizes to a building account $1,000 of maintenance costs incurred at the end of the year. (That is, the costs are included in the asset account Buildings rather than being expensed immediately.) If the company is allocating the cost of the building as an expense (depreciating it) over a 40-year life, then the maintenance cost of $1,000 will be incorrectly spread across 40 years instead of being expensed in the current year. As a result, the company will understate current-year expenses by $1,000, and will overstate current-year income by $1,000. Thus, determining which costs to capitalize and which to expense is very important.

Cost is measured by the cash paid in a cash transaction or by the **cash equivalent price** paid when companies use noncash assets in payment. **The cash equivalent price is equal to the fair market value of the asset given up or the fair market value of the asset received, whichever is more clearly determinable.** Once cost is established, it becomes the basis of accounting for the plant asset over its useful life. Current market value is not used to increase the recorded cost after acquisition. We explain the application of the cost principle to each of the major classes of plant assets in the following sections.

LAND

Companies often use land as a building site for a manufacturing plant or office site. The cost of land includes (1) the cash purchase price, (2) closing costs such as title and attorney's fees, (3) real estate brokers' commissions, and (4) accrued property taxes and other liens on the land assumed by the purchaser. For example, if the cash price is $50,000 and the purchaser agrees to pay accrued taxes of $5,000, the cost of the land is $55,000.

All necessary costs incurred in making land **ready for its intended use** increase (debit) the Land account. When a company acquires vacant land, its cost includes expenditures for clearing, draining, filling, and grading. If the land has a building on it that must be removed to make the site suitable for construction of a new building, the company includes all demolition and removal costs, less any proceeds from salvaged materials, in the Land account.

To illustrate, assume that Hayes Manufacturing Company acquires real estate at a cash cost of $100,000. The property contains an old warehouse that is razed at a net cost of $6,000 ($7,500 in costs less $1,500 proceeds from salvaged materials). Additional expenditures are for the attorney's fee $1,000 and the real estate broker's commission $8,000. Given these factors, the cost of the land is $115,000, computed as shown in Illustration 9-2.

Illustration 9-2
Computation of cost of land

Land	
Cash price of property	$ 100,000
Net removal cost of warehouse	6,000
Attorney's fee	1,000
Real estate broker's commission	8,000
Cost of land	**$115,000**

When Hayes records the acquisition, it debits Land and credits Cash for $115,000.

LAND IMPROVEMENTS

Land improvements are structural additions made to land, such as driveways, parking lots, fences, landscaping, and underground sprinklers. The cost of land improvements includes all expenditures necessary to make the improvements ready for their intended use. For example, the cost of a new company parking lot includes the amount paid for paving, fencing, and lighting. Thus the company would debit the total of all of these costs to Land Improvements.

Land improvements have limited useful lives, and their maintenance and replacement are the responsibility of the company. Because of their limited useful life, companies expense (depreciate) the cost of land improvements over their useful lives.

BUILDINGS

Buildings are facilities used in operations, such as stores, offices, factories, warehouses, and airplane hangers. Companies charge to the Buildings account all necessary expenditures relating to the purchase or construction of a building. When a building is **purchased**, such costs include the purchase price, closing costs (attorney's fees, title insurance, etc.), and real estate broker's commission. Costs to make the building ready for its intended use consist of expenditures for remodeling rooms and offices and replacing or repairing the roof, floors, electrical wiring, and plumbing. When a new building is **constructed**, its cost consists of the contract price plus payments made by the owner for architects' fees, building permits, and excavation costs.

In addition, companies add certain interest costs to the cost of a building: Interest costs incurred to finance a construction project are included in the cost of the asset when a significant period of time is required to get the asset ready for use. In these circumstances, interest costs are considered as necessary as materials and labor. However, the inclusion of interest costs in the cost of a constructed building is **limited to interest costs incurred during the construction period**. When construction has been completed, subsequent interest payments on funds borrowed to finance the construction are recorded as increases (debits) to Interest Expense.

EQUIPMENT

Equipment includes assets used in operations, such as store check-out counters, office furniture, factory machinery, delivery trucks, and airplanes. The cost of equipment consists of the cash purchase price, sales taxes, freight charges, and insurance during transit paid by the purchaser. It also includes expenditures required in assembling, installing, and testing the unit. However, companies treat as expenses the costs of motor vehicle licenses and accident insurance on company trucks and cars. Such items are **annual recurring expenditures and do not benefit future periods**. Two criteria apply in determining the cost of equipment: (1) the frequency of the cost—one time or recurring, and (2) the benefit period—the life of the asset or one year.

To illustrate, assume that Lenard Company purchases a delivery truck at a cash price of $22,000. Related expenditures are sales taxes $1,320, painting and lettering $500, motor vehicle license $80, and a three-year accident insurance policy $1,600. The cost of the delivery truck is $23,820, computed as shown in Illustration 9-3.

Delivery Truck	
Cash price	$ 22,000
Sales taxes	1,320
Painting and lettering	500
Cost of delivery truck	**$23,820**

Illustration 9-3
Computation of cost of delivery truck

Lenard treats the cost of a motor vehicle license as an expense and the cost of an insurance policy as a prepaid asset. Thus, the company records the purchase of the truck and related expenditures as follows.

Delivery Truck	23,820	
License Expense	80	
Prepaid Insurance	1,600	
Cash		25,500
(To record purchase of delivery truck and related expenditures)		

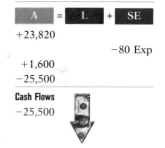

A = L + SE
+23,820
        −80 Exp
+1,600
−25,500

Cash Flows
−25,500

For another example, assume Merten Company purchases factory machinery at a cash price of $50,000. Related expenditures are sales taxes $3,000, insurance during shipping $500, and installation and testing $1,000. The cost of the factory machinery is $54,500, computed as in Illustration 9-4.

Factory Machinery	
Cash price	$ 50,000
Sales taxes	3,000
Insurance during shipping	500
Installation and testing	1,000
Cost of factory machinery	**$54,500**

Illustration 9-4
Computation of cost of factory machinery

Thus, Merten records the purchase and related expenditures as follows.

Factory Machinery	54,500	
Cash		54,500
(To record purchase of factory machinery and related expenditures)		

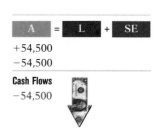

A = L + SE
+54,500
−54,500

Cash Flows
−54,500

TO BUY OR LEASE?

In this chapter we focus on purchased assets, but we want to expose you briefly to an alternative—leasing. A lease is a contractual agreement in which the owner of an asset (the **lessor**) allows another party (the **lessee**) to use the asset for a period of time at an agreed price. In many industries leasing is quite common. For example, one-third of heavy-duty commercial trucks are leased.

Some advantages of leasing an asset versus purchasing it are:

1. **Reduced risk of obsolescence.** Frequently, lease terms allow the party using the asset (the lessee) to exchange the asset for a more modern one if it becomes outdated. This is much easier than trying to sell an obsolete asset.

2. **Little or no down payment.** To purchase an asset, most companies must borrow money, which usually requires a down payment of at least 20%. Leasing an asset requires little or no down payment.

3. **Shared tax advantages.** Startup companies typically do not make much money in their early years, and so they have little need for the tax deductions available from owning an asset. In a lease, the lessor gets the tax advantage because it owns the asset. It often will pass these tax savings on to the lessee in the form of lower lease payments.

4. **Assets and liabilities not reported.** Many companies prefer to keep assets and especially liabilities off their books. Reporting lower assets improves the return on assets ratio (discussed later in this chapter). Reporting fewer liabilities makes the company look less risky. Certain types of leases, called **operating leases**, allow the lessee to account for the transaction as a rental, with neither an asset nor a liability recorded.

Airlines often choose to lease many of their airplanes in long-term lease agreements. In recent financial statements, Southwest Airlines stated that it leased 88 of its 417 planes under operating leases. Because operating leases are accounted for as rentals, these 88 planes did not show up on its balance sheet.

Under another type of lease, a **capital lease**, lessees show both the asset and the liability on the balance sheet. The lessee accounts for capital lease agreements in a way that is very similar to purchases: The lessee shows the leased item as an asset on its balance sheet, and the obligation owed to the lessor as a liability. The lessee depreciates the leased asset in a manner similar to purchased assets. Capital leases represent only about 0.5% of Southwest Airlines' property, plant, and equipment. We discuss leasing further in Chapter 10 on liabilities.

Accounting Across the Organization

Leasing is big business for U.S. companies. For example, in a recent year leasing accounted for about 31% of all business investment ($218 billion).

Who does the most leasing? Interestingly major banks, such as Continental Bank, J.P. Morgan Leasing, and US Bancorp Equipment Finance, are the major lessors. Also, many companies have established separate leasing companies, such as Boeing Capital Corporation, Dell Financial Services, and John Deere Capital Corporation. And, as an excellent example of the magnitude of leasing, leased planes account for nearly 40% of the U.S. fleet of commercial airlines. Lease Finance Corporation in Los Angeles owns more planes than any airline in the world.

In addition, leasing is becoming increasingly common in the hotel industry. Marriott, Hilton, and InterContinental are increasingly choosing to lease hotels that are owned by someone else.

 Why might airline managers choose to lease rather than purchase their planes?

Do it! Assume that Drummond Corp. purchases a delivery truck for $15,000 cash plus sales taxes of $900 and delivery costs of $500. The buyer also pays $200 for painting and lettering, $600 for an annual insurance policy, and $80 for a motor vehicle license. Explain how the company should account for each of these costs.

Solution

The first four payments ($15,000 purchase price, $900 sales taxes, $500 delivery, and $200 painting and lettering) are expenditures necessary to make the truck ready for its intended use. Thus, the cost of the truck is $16,600. The payments for insurance and the license are operating expenses incurred during the useful life of the asset.

COST OF PLANT ASSETS

Action Plan

- Identify expenditures made in order to get delivery equipment ready for its intended use.
- Expense operating costs incurred during the useful life of the equipment.

Accounting for Plant Assets

DEPRECIATION

As explained in Chapter 4, depreciation **is the process of allocating to expense the cost of a plant asset over its useful (service) life in a rational and systematic manner**. Such cost allocation is designed to properly match expenses with revenues. (See Illustration 9-5.)

study objective **2**

Explain the concept of depreciation.

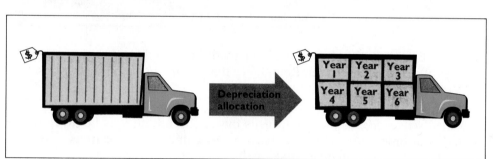

Illustration 9-5
Depreciation as a cost allocation concept

Depreciation Tutorial

Depreciation affects the balance sheet through accumulated depreciation, which companies report as a deduction from plant assets. It affects the income statement through depreciation expense.

It is important to understand that **depreciation is a cost allocation process, not an asset valuation process**. No attempt is made to measure the change in an asset's market value during ownership. Thus, the **book value**—cost less accumulated depreciation—of a plant asset may differ significantly from its **market value**. In fact, if an asset is fully depreciated, it can have zero book value but still have a significant market value.

Depreciation applies to **three classes of plant assets**: land improvements, buildings, and equipment. Each of these classes is considered to be a **depreciable asset** because the usefulness to the company and the revenue-producing ability of each class decline over the asset's useful life. Depreciation **does not apply to land** because its usefulness and revenue-producing ability generally remain intact as long as the land is owned. In fact, in many cases, the usefulness of land increases over time because of the scarcity of good sites. Thus, **land is not a depreciable asset**.

During a depreciable asset's useful life its revenue-producing ability declines because of wear and tear. A delivery truck that has been driven 100,000 miles will be less useful to a company than one driven only 800 miles.

A decline in revenue-producing ability may also occur because of obsolescence. **Obsolescence** is the process by which an asset becomes out of date before it physically wears out. The rerouting of major airlines from Chicago's

Helpful Hint Remember that depreciation is the process of *allocating cost* over the useful life of an asset. It is not a measure of value.

Helpful Hint Land does not depreciate because it does not wear out.

Ethics Note When a business is acquired, proper allocation of the purchase price to various asset classes is important, since different depreciation treatment can materially affect income. For example, buildings are depreciated, but land is not.

Midway Airport to Chicago-O'Hare International Airport because Midway's runways were too short for giant jets is an example. Similarly, many companies replace their computers long before they originally planned to do so because improvements in new computers make their old computers obsolete.

Recognizing depreciation for an asset does not result in the accumulation of cash for replacement of the asset. The balance in Accumulated Depreciation represents the total amount of the asset's cost that the company has charged to expense to date; **it is not a cash fund**.

FACTORS IN COMPUTING DEPRECIATION

Three factors affect the computation of depreciation, as shown in Illustration 9-6.

Illustration 9-6 Three factors in computing depreciation

Helpful Hint Depreciation expense is reported on the income statement. Accumulated depreciation is reported on the balance sheet as a deduction from plant assets.

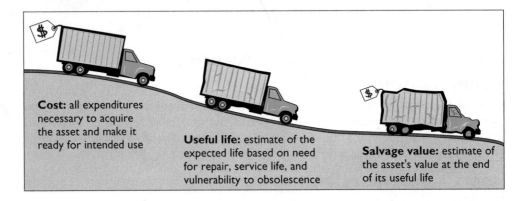

Cost: all expenditures necessary to acquire the asset and make it ready for intended use

Useful life: estimate of the expected life based on need for repair, service life, and vulnerability to obsolescence

Salvage value: estimate of the asset's value at the end of its useful life

1. **Cost.** Earlier in the chapter we explained the considerations that affect the cost of a depreciable asset. Remember that companies record plant assets at cost, in accordance with the cost principle.

2. **Useful life.** Useful life is an estimate of the expected productive life, also called *service life*, of the asset for its owner. Useful life may be expressed in terms of time, units of activity (such as machine hours), or units of output. Useful life is an estimate. In making the estimate, management considers such factors as the intended use of the asset, repair and maintenance policies, and vulnerability of the asset to obsolescence. The company's past experience with similar assets is often helpful in deciding on expected useful life.

3. **Salvage value.** Salvage value is an estimate of the asset's value at the end of its useful life for its owner. Companies may base the value on the asset's worth as scrap or on its expected trade-in value. Like useful life, salvage value is an estimate. In making the estimate, management considers how it plans to dispose of the asset and its experience with similar assets.

Depreciation Methods

study objective 3

Compute periodic depreciation using the straight-line method, and contrast its expense pattern with those of other methods.

Although a number of methods exist, depreciation is generally computed using one of three methods:

1. Straight-line
2. Declining-balance
3. Units-of-activity

Like the alternative inventory methods discussed in Chapter 6, each of these depreciation methods is acceptable under generally accepted accounting principles. Management selects the method it believes best measures an asset's contribution to revenue over its useful life. Once a company chooses a method, it should apply that method consistently over the useful life of the asset. Consistency enhances the ability to analyze financial statements over multiple years.

Illustration 9-7 shows the distribution of the *primary* depreciation methods in 600 of the largest U.S. companies. Clearly, straight-line depreciation is the most widely used approach. In fact, because some companies use more than one method, **straight-line depreciation is used for some or all of the depreciation taken by more than 95% of U.S. companies**. For this reason, we illustrate procedures for straight-line depreciation and discuss the alternative depreciation approaches only at a conceptual level. This coverage introduces you to the basic idea of depreciation as an allocation concept without entangling you in too much procedural detail. (Also, note that many hand-held calculators are preprogrammed to perform the basic depreciation methods.) Details on the alternative approaches are presented in the appendix to this chapter (pages 460–463).

Our illustration of depreciation methods, both here and in the appendix, is based on the following data relating to a small delivery truck purchased by Bill's Pizzas on January 1, 2010.

Cost	$13,000
Expected salvage value	$1,000
Estimated useful life (in years)	5
Estimated useful life (in miles)	100,000

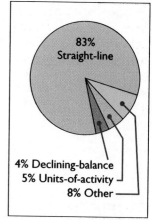

Illustration 9-7 Use of depreciation methods in major U.S. companies

STRAIGHT-LINE. Under the straight-line method, companies expense an equal amount of depreciation each year of the asset's useful life. Management must choose the useful life of an asset based on its own expectations and experience.

To compute the annual depreciation expense, we divide depreciable cost by the estimated useful life. Depreciable cost represents the total amount subject to depreciation; it is calculated as the cost of the plant asset less its salvage value. Illustration 9-8 shows the computation of depreciation expense in the first year for Bill's Pizzas' delivery truck.

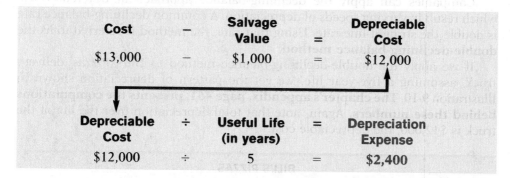

Illustration 9-8 Formula for straight-line method

Alternatively, we can compute an annual *rate* at which the company depreciates the delivery truck. In this case, the rate is 20% (100% ÷ 5 years). When an annual rate is used under the straight-line method, the company applies the percentage rate to the depreciable cost of the asset, as shown in the **depreciation schedule** in Illustration 9-9.

Illustration 9-9 Straight-line depreciation schedule

BILL'S PIZZAS

	Computation			End of Year	
Year	Depreciable Cost	× Depreciation Rate	= Annual Depreciation Expense	Accumulated Depreciation	Book Value
2010	$12,000	20%	$ 2,400	$ 2,400	$10,600*
2011	12,000	20	2,400	4,800	8,200
2012	12,000	20	2,400	7,200	5,800
2013	12,000	20	2,400	9,600	3,400
2014	12,000	20	2,400	12,000	1,000
			Total $12,000		

*$13,000 − $2,400

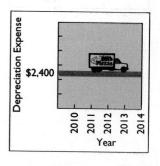

Note that the depreciation expense of $2,400 is the same each year. The book value at the end of the useful life is equal to the estimated $1,000 salvage value.

What happens when an asset is purchased **during** the year, rather than on January 1 as in our example? In that case, it is necessary to **prorate the annual depreciation** for the portion of a year used. If Bill's Pizzas had purchased the delivery truck on April 1, 2010, the company would use the truck for 9 months in 2010. The depreciation for 2010 would be $1,800 ($12,000 × 20% × $\frac{9}{12}$ of a year).

As indicated earlier, the straight-line method predominates in practice. For example, such large companies as Campbell Soup, Marriott, and General Mills use the straight-line method. It is simple to apply, and it matches expenses with revenues appropriately when the use of the asset is reasonably uniform throughout the service life. The types of assets that give equal benefits over useful life generally are those for which daily use does not affect productivity. Examples are office furniture and fixtures, buildings, warehouses, and garages for motor vehicles.

DECLINING-BALANCE. The declining-balance method computes periodic depreciation using a declining book value. This method is called an accelerated-depreciation method because it results in higher depreciation in the early years of an asset's life than does the straight-line approach. However, because the total amount of depreciation (the depreciable cost) taken over an asset's life is the same **no matter what approach** is used, the declining-balance method produces a decreasing annual depreciation expense over the asset's useful life. In early years declining-balance depreciation expense will exceed straight-line, but in later years it will be less than straight-line. Managers might choose an accelerated approach if they think that an asset's utility will decline quickly.

Companies can apply the declining-balance approach at different rates, which result in varying speeds of depreciation. A common declining-balance rate is double the straight-line rate. Using that rate, the method is referred to as the **double-declining-balance method**.

If we apply the double-declining-balance method to Bill's Pizzas' delivery truck, assuming a five-year life, we get the pattern of depreciation shown in Illustration 9-10. **The chapter's appendix, page 461, presents the computations behind these numbers.** Again, note that total depreciation over the life of the truck is $12,000, the depreciable cost.

Illustration 9-10
Declining-balance depreciation schedule

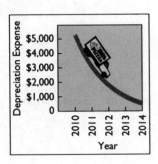

			BILL'S PIZZAS	
	Annual		End of Year	
Year	Depreciation Expense		Accumulated Depreciation	Book Value
2010	$ 5,200		$ 5,200	$7,800
2011	3,120		8,320	4,680
2012	1,872		10,192	2,808
2013	1,123		11,315	1,685
2014	685		12,000	1,000
Total	$12,000			

UNITS-OF-ACTIVITY. As indicated earlier, useful life can be expressed in ways other than a time period. Under the units-of-activity method, useful life is expressed in terms of the total units of production or the use expected from the asset. The units-of-activity method is ideally suited to factory machinery: Companies can measure production in terms of units of output or in terms of machine hours used in operating the machinery. It is also possible to use the method for such items as delivery equipment (miles driven) and airplanes (hours in use). The units-of-activity method is generally not suitable for such assets as buildings or furniture because activity levels are difficult to measure for these assets.

Applying the units-of-activity method to the delivery truck owned by Bill's Pizzas, we first must know some basic information. Bill's expects to be able to drive the truck a total of 100,000 miles. Illustration 9-11 shows depreciation over the five-year life based on an assumed mileage pattern. **The chapter's appendix, pages 462–463, presents the computations used to arrive at these results.**

			End of Year	
BILL'S PIZZAS				
Year	**Units of Activity (miles)**	**Annual Depreciation Expense**	**Accumulated Depreciation**	**Book Value**
2010	15,000	$ 1,800	$ 1,800	$11,200
2011	30,000	3,600	5,400	7,600
2012	20,000	2,400	7,800	5,200
2013	25,000	3,000	10,800	2,200
2014	10,000	1,200	12,000	1,000
Total	100,000	$12,000		

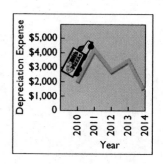

Illustration 9-11 Units-of-activity depreciation schedule

As the name implies, under units-of-activity depreciation, the amount of depreciation is proportional to the activity that took place during that period. For example, the delivery truck was driven twice as many miles in 2011 as in 2010, and depreciation was exactly twice as much in 2011 as it was in 2010.

Management's Choice: Comparison of Methods

Illustration 9-12 compares annual and total depreciation expense for Bill's Pizzas under the three methods.

Year	**Straight-Line**	**Declining-Balance**	**Units-of-Activity**
2010	$ 2,400	$ 5,200	$ 1,800
2011	2,400	3,120	3,600
2012	2,400	1,872	2,400
2013	2,400	1,123	3,000
2014	2,400	685	1,200
	$12,000	$12,000	$12,000

Illustration 9-12
Comparison of depreciation methods

Periodic depreciation varies considerably among the methods, but **total depreciation is the same for the five-year period**. Each method is acceptable in accounting because each recognizes the decline in service potential of the asset in a rational and systematic manner. Illustration 9-13 graphs the depreciation expense pattern under each method.

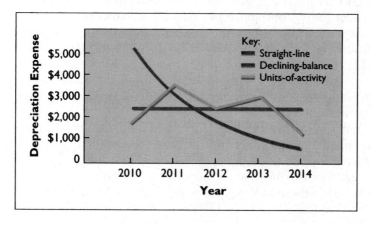

Illustration 9-13 Patterns of depreciation

Depreciation and Income Taxes

Helpful Hint Depreciation per financial statements is usually different from depreciation per tax returns.

The Internal Revenue Service (IRS) allows corporate taxpayers to deduct depreciation expense when computing taxable income. However, the tax regulations of the IRS do not require the taxpayer to use the same depreciation method on the tax return that it uses in preparing financial statements.

Consequently, many large corporations use straight-line depreciation in their financial statements in order to maximize net income; at the same time they use a special accelerated-depreciation method on their tax returns in order to minimize their income taxes. For tax purposes, taxpayers must use on their tax returns either the straight-line method or a special accelerated-depreciation method called the **Modified Accelerated Cost Recovery System** (MACRS).

Depreciation Disclosure in the Notes

Companies must disclose the choice of depreciation method in their financial statements or in related notes that accompany the statements. Illustration 9-14 shows the "Property and equipment" notes from the financial statements of Southwest Airlines.

Illustration 9-14
Disclosure of depreciation policies

SOUTHWEST AIRLINES
Notes to the Financial Statements

Property and equipment Depreciation is provided by the straight-line method to estimated residual values over periods ranging from 20 to 25 years for flight equipment and 5 to 30 years for ground property and equipment once the asset is placed in service. Amortization of property under capital leases is on a straight-line basis over the lease term and is included in depreciation expense.

From this note we learn that Southwest Airlines uses the straight-line method to depreciate its planes over periods of 20 to 25 years.

Revising Periodic Depreciation

study objective 4

Describe the procedure for revising periodic depreciation.

Management should periodically review annual depreciation expense. If wear and tear or obsolescence indicates that annual depreciation is either inadequate or excessive, the company should change the depreciation expense amount.

When a change in an estimate is required, the company makes the change in **current and future years but not to prior periods**. Thus, when making the change, the company (1) does not correct previously recorded depreciation expense, but (2) revises depreciation expense for current and future years. The rationale for this treatment is that continual restatement of prior periods would adversely affect users' confidence in financial statements.

Companies must disclose in the financial statements significant changes in estimates. Although a company may have a legitimate reason for changing an estimated life, financial statement users should be aware that some companies might change an estimate simply to achieve financial statement goals. For example, extending an asset's estimated life reduces depreciation expense and increases current period income.

In a recent year, AirTran Airways increased the estimated useful lives of some of its planes from 25 to 30 years and increased the estimated lives of related aircraft parts from 5 years to 30 years. It disclosed that the change in estimate decreased its net loss for the year by approximately $0.6 million, or about $0.01 per share. Whether these changes were appropriate depends on how reasonable it is to assume that planes will continue to be used for a long time. Our Feature Story suggests that although in the past many planes lasted a long time, it is also clear that because of high fuel costs, airlines are now scrapping many of their old, inefficient planes.

before you go on...

Do it! On January 1, 2010, Iron Mountain Ski Corporation purchased a new snow grooming machine for $50,000. The machine is estimated to have a 10-year life with a $2,000 salvage value. What journal entry would Iron Mountain Ski Corporation make at December 31, 2010, if it uses the straight-line method of depreciation?

STRAIGHT-LINE DEPRECIATION

Action Plan

- Calculate depreciable cost (Cost − Salvage value).
- Divide the depreciable cost by the asset's estimated useful life.

Solution

$$\text{Depreciation expense} = \frac{\text{Cost} - \text{Salvage value}}{\text{Useful life}} = \frac{\$50,000 - \$2,000}{10} = \$4,800$$

Iron Mountain would record the first year's depreciation as follows:

Dec. 31	Depreciation Expense	4,800	
	Accumulated Depreciation—Machinery		4,800
	(To record annual depreciation on snow grooming machine)		

EXPENDITURES DURING USEFUL LIFE

During the useful life of a plant asset, a company may incur costs for ordinary repairs, additions, and improvements. Ordinary repairs are expenditures to maintain the operating efficiency and expected productive life of the unit. They usually are fairly small amounts that occur frequently throughout the service life. Examples are motor tune-ups and oil changes, the painting of buildings, and the replacing of worn-out gears on factory machinery. Ordinary repairs are debited to Repair (or Maintenance) Expense as incurred.

In contrast, additions and improvements are costs incurred to **increase** the operating efficiency, productive capacity, or expected useful life of the plant asset. These expenditures are usually material in amount and occur infrequently during the period of ownership. Expenditures for additions and improvements increase the company's investment in productive facilities and are generally debited to the plant asset affected. Thus, they are **capital expenditures**. The accounting for capital expenditures varies depending on the nature of the expenditure.

Northwest Airlines at one time spent $120 million to spruce up 40 DC9-30 jets. The improvements were designed to extend the lives of the planes, meet stricter government noise limits, and save money. The capital expenditure was expected to extend the life of the jets by 10 to 15 years and save about $560 million compared to the cost of buying new planes. The DC9 jets were, on average, 24 years old.

IMPAIRMENTS

As noted earlier, the book value of plant assets is rarely the same as the market value. In instances where the value of a plant asset declines substantially, its market value might fall materially below book value. This may happen because a machine has become obsolete, or the market for the product made by the machine has dried up or has become very competitive. A **permanent decline** in the market value of an asset is referred to as an impairment. So as not to overstate the asset on the books, the company writes the asset down to its new

Ethics Note WorldCom perpetrated the largest accounting fraud in history by treating $7 billion of "line costs" as capital expenditures. *Line costs* are rental payments to access other companies' networks. Like any other rental payment, they should have been expensed as incurred. Instead, capitalization delayed expense recognition to future periods and thus boosted current-period profits.

market value during the year in which the decline in value occurs. For example, AirTran recently announced a $28 million impairment loss on its DC9s and a $10.8 million impairment loss on its B737s. AirTran used appraisals and considered recent transactions and market trends involving similar aircraft in determining the fair market values.

In the past, some companies **improperly** delayed recording losses on impairments until a year when it was "convenient" to do so—when the impact on the company's reported results was minimized. For example, if a company has record profits in one year, it can then afford to write down some of its bad assets without hurting its reported results too much. As discussed in Chapter 4, the practice of timing the recognition of gains and losses to achieve certain income results is known as **earnings management**. Earnings management reduces earnings quality. Immediate recognition of these write-downs is now required.

Write-downs can create problems for users of financial statements. Critics of write-downs note that after a company writes down assets, its depreciation expense will be lower in all subsequent periods. Some companies improperly inflate asset write-downs in bad years, when they are going to report poor results anyway. Then in subsequent years, when the company recovers, its results will look even better because of lower depreciation expense.

PLANT ASSET DISPOSALS

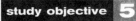

study objective 5

Explain how to account for the disposal of plant assets.

Companies dispose of plant assets that are no longer useful to them. Illustration 9-15 shows the three ways in which companies make plant asset disposals.

Whatever the disposal method, the company must determine the book value of the plant asset at the time of disposal in order to determine the gain or loss. Recall that the book value is the difference between the cost of the plant asset and the accumulated depreciation to date. If the disposal occurs at any time during the year, the company must record depreciation for the fraction of the year to the date of disposal. The company then eliminates the book value by reducing (debiting) Accumulated Depreciation for the total depreciation associated with that asset to the date of disposal and reducing (crediting) the asset account for the cost of the asset.

Illustration 9-15
Methods of plant asset disposal

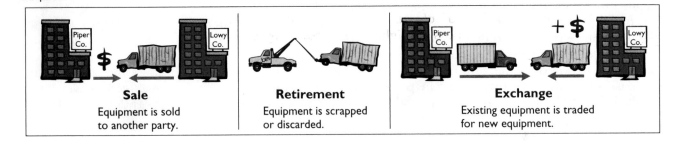

Sale	**Retirement**	**Exchange**
Equipment is sold to another party.	Equipment is scrapped or discarded.	Existing equipment is traded for new equipment.

Sale of Plant Assets

In a disposal by sale, the company compares the book value of the asset with the proceeds received from the sale. If the proceeds from the sale **exceed** the book value of the plant asset, a **gain on disposal** occurs. If the proceeds from the sale **are less than** the book value of the plant asset sold, a **loss on disposal** occurs.

Only by coincidence will the book value and the fair market value of the asset be the same at the time the asset is sold. Gains and losses on sales of plant assets are therefore quite common. As an example, Delta Air Lines reported a $94,343,000 gain on the sale of five Boeing B-727-200 aircraft and five Lockheed L-1011-1 aircraft.

GAIN ON SALE. To illustrate a gain on sale of plant assets, assume that on July 1, 2010, Wright Company sells office furniture for $16,000 cash. The office furniture originally cost $60,000 and as of January 1, 2010, had accumulated depreciation of $41,000. Depreciation for the first six months of 2010 is $8,000. Wright records depreciation expense and updates accumulated depreciation to July 1 as follows.

49,000

July	1	Depreciation Expense	8,000	
		Accumulated Depreciation—Office Furniture		8,000
		(To record depreciation expense for the		
		first 6 months of 2010)		

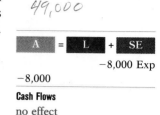

A = L + SE
−8,000 Exp
−8,000
Cash Flows
no effect

After the accumulated depreciation balance is updated, the company computes the gain or loss as the difference between the proceeds from sale and the book value at the date of disposal. Wright Company has a gain on disposal of $5,000, as computed in Illustration 9-16.

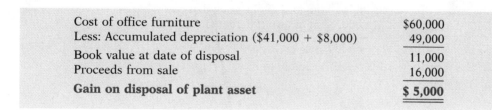

Cost of office furniture	$60,000
Less: Accumulated depreciation ($41,000 + $8,000)	49,000
Book value at date of disposal	11,000
Proceeds from sale	16,000
Gain on disposal of plant asset	**$ 5,000**

Illustration 9-16
Computation of gain on disposal

Wright records the sale and the gain on sale of the plant asset as follows.

July	1	Cash	16,000	
		Accumulated Depreciation—Office Furniture	49,000	
		Office Furniture		60,000
		Gain on Disposal		5,000
		(To record sale of office furniture		
		at a gain)		

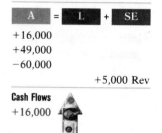

A = L + SE
+16,000
+49,000
−60,000
+5,000 Rev
Cash Flows
+16,000

Companies report a gain on disposal of plant assets in the "Other revenues and gains" section of the income statement.

LOSS ON SALE. Assume that instead of selling the office furniture for $16,000, Wright sells it for $9,000. In this case, Wright experiences a loss of $2,000, as computed in Illustration 9-17.

Cost of office furniture	$60,000
Less: Accumulated depreciation	49,000
Book value at date of disposal	11,000
Proceeds from sale	9,000
Loss on disposal of plant asset	**$ 2,000**

Illustration 9-17
Computation of loss on disposal

Wright records the sale and the loss on sale of the plant asset as follows.

July	1	Cash	9,000	
		Accumulated Depreciation—Office Furniture	49,000	
		Loss on Disposal	2,000	
		Office Furniture		60,000
		(To record sale of office furniture at a		
		loss)		

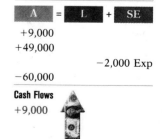

A = L + SE
+9,000
+49,000
−2,000 Exp
−60,000
Cash Flows
+9,000

Companies report a loss on disposal of the plant asset in the "Other expenses and losses" section of the income statement.

Retirement of Plant Assets

Companies simply retire, rather than sell, some assets at the end of their useful life. For example, some productive assets used in manufacturing may have very specific uses, and they consequently have no ready market when the company no longer needs them. In such a case the asset is simply retired.

Companies record retirement of an asset as a special case of a disposal where no cash is received. They decrease (debit) Accumulated Depreciation for the full amount of depreciation taken over the life of the asset and decrease (credit) the asset account for the original cost of the asset. The loss (a gain is not possible on a retirement) is equal to the asset's book value on the date of retirement.[1]

---

before you go on...

PLANT ASSET DISPOSALS

Action Plan

• Compare the asset's book value and its fair value to determine whether a gain or loss has occurred.

• Make sure that both the Truck account and Accumulated Depreciation–Truck are reduced upon disposal.

Do it!

Overland Trucking has an old truck that cost $30,000 and has accumulated depreciation of $16,000. Assume two different situations:

1. The company sells the old truck for $17,000 cash.
2. The truck is worthless, so the company simply retires it.

What entry should Overland use to record each scenario?

Solution

1. Sale of truck for cash:

Cash	17,000	
Accumulated Depreciation—Truck	16,000	
Truck		30,000
Gain on Disposal [$17,000 − ($30,000 − $16,000)]		3,000
(To record sale of truck at a gain)		

2. Retirement of truck:

Accumulated Depreciation—Truck	16,000	
Loss on Disposal	14,000	
Truck		30,000
(To record retirement of truck at a loss)		

---

study objective **6**

Describe methods for evaluating the use of plant assets.

Analyzing Plant Assets

The presentation of financial statement information about plant assets enables decision makers to analyze the company's use of its plant assets. We will use two measures to analyze plant assets: return on assets ratio, and asset turnover ratio.

RETURN ON ASSETS RATIO

An overall measure of profitability is the **return on assets ratio**. This ratio is computed by dividing net income by average assets. (Average assets are commonly calculated by adding the beginning and ending values of assets and dividing by 2.) The return on assets ratio indicates the amount of net income generated by each dollar of assets. Thus, the higher the return on assets, the more profitable the company.

---

[1]More advanced courses discuss the accounting for exchanges, the third method of plant asset disposal.

Information is provided below related to AirTran and Southwest Airlines.

	AirTran (in millions)	Southwest Airlines (in millions)
Net income, 2007	$ 53	$ 645
Net income, 2006	15	499
Total assets, 12/31/07	2,049	16,772
Total assets, 12/31/06	1,604	13,460
Total assets, 12/31/05	1,162	14,003
Net sales, 2007	2,310	9,861
Net sales, 2006	1,892	9,086

Illustration 9-18 presents the 2007 and 2006 return on assets of AirTran, Southwest Airlines, and industry averages.

Illustration 9-18 Return on assets ratio

$$\text{Return on Assets Ratio} = \frac{\text{Net Income}}{\text{Average Total Assets}}$$

	2007	2006
AirTran ($ in millions)	$\dfrac{\$53}{(\$2,049 + \$1,604)/2*} = 2.9\%$	$\dfrac{\$15}{(\$1,604 + \$1,162)/2} = 1.1\%$
Southwest Airlines ($ in millions)	$\dfrac{\$645}{(\$16,772 + \$13,460)/2} = 4.3\%$	$\dfrac{\$499}{(\$13,460 + \$14,003)/2} = 3.6\%$
Industry average	0.42%	

*Amounts in the ratio calculations have been rounded.

Southwest Airlines' return on assets was better than that of AirTran and the airline industry in both years. The airline industry has experienced financial difficulties in recent years as it attempted to cover high labor, fuel, and security costs while offering fares low enough to attract customers. Such difficulties are reflected in the very low industry average for return on assets and in the volatility of this ratio between years for a single airline.

Accounting Across the Organization

Marketing executives now are using the basic finance concept underlying return on assets to determine "marketing return on investment (ROI)." They calculate *marketing ROI* as the profit generated by a marketing initiative divided by the investment in that initiative.

It can be tricky to determine what to include in the "investment" amount and how to attribute profit to a particular marketing initiative. However, many firms feel that measuring marketing ROI is worth the effort because it allows managers to evaluate the relative effectiveness of various programs. In addition, it helps quantify the benefits that marketing provides to the organization. In periods of tight budgets, the marketing ROI number can provide particularly valuable evidence to help a marketing manager avoid budget cuts.

Source: James O. Mitchel, "Marketing ROI," *LIMRA's MarketFacts Quarterly* (Summer 2004), p. 15.

? How does measuring marketing ROI support the overall efforts of the organization?

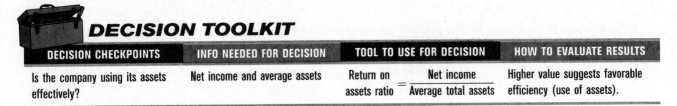

DECISION CHECKPOINTS	INFO NEEDED FOR DECISION	TOOL TO USE FOR DECISION	HOW TO EVALUATE RESULTS
Is the company using its assets effectively?	Net income and average assets	$\text{Return on assets ratio} = \dfrac{\text{Net income}}{\text{Average total assets}}$	Higher value suggests favorable efficiency (use of assets).

ASSET TURNOVER RATIO

The asset turnover ratio indicates how efficiently a company uses its assets to generate sales—that is, how many dollars of sales a company generates for each dollar invested in assets. It is calculated by dividing net sales by average total assets. When we compare two companies in the same industry, the one with the higher asset turnover ratio is operating more *efficiently:* It is generating more sales per dollar invested in assets. Illustration 9-19 presents the asset turnover ratios for AirTran and Southwest Airlines for 2007.

Illustration 9-19 Asset turnover ratio for AirTran and Southwest Airlines

$\text{Asset Turnover Ratio} = \dfrac{\text{Net Sales}}{\text{Average Total Assets}}$	
AirTran ($ in millions)	**Southwest Airlines** ($ in millions)
$\dfrac{\$2,310}{(\$2,049 + \$1,604)/2} = 1.26 \text{ times}$	$\dfrac{\$9,861}{(\$16,772 + \$13,460)/2} = .65 \text{ times}$

These asset turnover ratios tell us that for each dollar of assets, AirTran generates sales of $1.26 and Southwest $0.65. AirTran is more successful in generating sales per dollar invested in assets, perhaps due in part to its decision to purchase older planes. The average asset turnover ratio for the airline industry is .63 times, more in line with Southwest's asset turnover.

Asset turnover ratios vary considerably across industries. The average asset turnover for electric utility companies is .34; the grocery industry has an average asset turnover of 2.89. Asset turnover ratios, therefore, are only comparable within—not between—industries.

PROFIT MARGIN RATIO REVISITED

In Chapter 5 you learned about the profit margin ratio. That ratio is calculated by dividing net income by net sales. It tells how effective a company is in turning its sales into income—that is, how much income each dollar of sales provides. Illustration 9-20 shows that the return on assets ratio can be computed from the profit margin ratio and the asset turnover ratio.

Illustration 9-20 Composition of return on assets ratio

Profit Margin	×	Asset Turnover	=	Return on Assets
$\dfrac{\text{Net Income}}{\text{Net Sales}}$	×	$\dfrac{\text{Net Sales}}{\text{Average Total Assets}}$	=	$\dfrac{\text{Net Income}}{\text{Average Total Assets}}$

This relationship has very important strategic implications for management. From Illustration 9-20 we can see that if a company wants to increase its return on assets, it can do so in two ways: (1) by increasing the margin it generates from each dollar of goods that it sells (the profit margin ratio), or (2) by increasing the volume of goods that it sells (the asset turnover). For example, most grocery stores have very low profit margins, often in the range of 1 or 2 cents for every dollar of goods sold. Grocery stores, therefore, focus on asset turnover: They rely on high turnover to increase their return on assets. Alternatively, a store selling luxury goods, such as expensive jewelry, doesn't generally have a high turnover. Consequently, a seller of luxury goods focuses on having a high profit margin. Recently Apple decided to offer a less expensive version of its popular iPod. This new product would provide a lower margin, but higher volume, than Apple's more expensive version.

Let's evaluate the return on assets ratio of Southwest Airlines for 2007 by evaluating its components—the profit margin ratio and the asset turnover ratio. See Illustration 9-21.

	Profit Margin	×	Asset Turnover	=	Return on Assets
Southwest Airlines	6.5%	×	.65 times	=	4.2%

Illustration 9-21
Components of Southwest Airlines' rate of return

Southwest Airlines has a profit margin ratio of 6.5% ($645 ÷ $9,861). Compared to the industry average of 0.69%, this suggests that Southwest has better control of its costs than most in the industry. As noted previously, Southwest's asset turnover is about equal to the industry average. Therefore, it would appear that if Southwest can increase its asset turnover by increasing the amount of sales it generates per dollar invested in planes, it will increase its reputation even further as one of the most profitable companies in the industry.

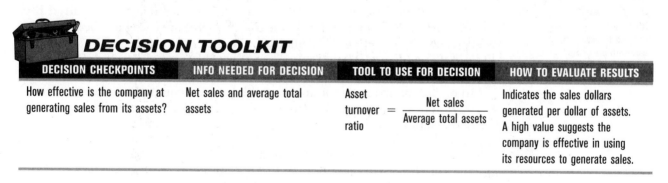

DECISION TOOLKIT

DECISION CHECKPOINTS	INFO NEEDED FOR DECISION	TOOL TO USE FOR DECISION	HOW TO EVALUATE RESULTS
How effective is the company at generating sales from its assets?	Net sales and average total assets	Asset turnover ratio = $\dfrac{\text{Net sales}}{\text{Average total assets}}$	Indicates the sales dollars generated per dollar of assets. A high value suggests the company is effective in using its resources to generate sales.

section two

Intangible Assets

Intangible assets are rights, privileges, and competitive advantages that result from ownership of long-lived assets that do not possess physical substance. Many companies' most valuable assets are intangible. Some widely known intangibles are Microsoft's patents, McDonalds's franchises, the trade name iPod, and Nike's trademark "swoosh."

Analysts estimated that in the early 1980s the market value of intangible assets to total assets was close to 40%. By 2000, the percentage was over 80%—quite a difference. What has happened is that research and development (e.g., hi-tech and bio-tech) has grown substantially. At the same time, many companies (e.g., Nike and Gatorade) have developed brand power which enables them to maintain their market position.

As you will learn in this section, financial statements do report numerous intangibles. Yet, many other financially significant intangibles are not reported. To give an example, according to its 2007 financial statements, Google had total stockholders' equity of $22.7 billion. But its *market* value—the total market price of all its shares on that same date—was roughly $178.5 billion. Thus, its actual market value was about $155.8 billion greater than the amount reported for stockholders' equity on the balance sheet. It is not uncommon for a company's reported book value to differ from its market value, because balance sheets are reported at historical cost. But such an extreme difference seriously diminishes the usefulness of the balance sheet to decision makers. In the case of Google, the difference is due to unrecorded intangibles. For many high-tech or so-called intellectual-property companies, most of their value is from intangibles, many of which are not reported under current accounting rules.

Intangibles may be evidenced by contracts, licenses, and other documents. Intangibles may arise from the following sources:

1. Government grants such as patents, copyrights, franchises, trademarks, and trade names.

2. Acquisition of another business in which the purchase price includes a payment for goodwill.

3. Private monopolistic arrangements arising from contractual agreements, such as franchises and leases.

Accounting for Intangible Assets

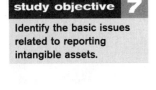

study objective 7

Identify the basic issues related to reporting intangible assets.

Companies record intangible assets at cost. Intangibles are categorized as having either a limited life or an indefinite life. If an intangible has a **limited life**, the company allocates its cost over the asset's useful life using a process similar to depreciation. The process of allocating to expense the cost of intangibles is referred to as amortization. The cost of intangible assets with **indefinite lives should not be amortized**.

To record amortization of an intangible asset, a company increases (debits) Amortization Expense, and decreases (credits) the specific intangible asset. (Unlike depreciation, no contra account, such as Accumulated Amortization, is usually used.)

Intangible assets are typically amortized on a straight-line basis. For example, the legal life of a patent is 20 years. Companies **amortize the cost of a patent over its 20-year life or its useful life, whichever is shorter.** To illustrate the computation of patent amortization, assume that National Labs purchases a patent at a cost of $60,000 on June 30. If National estimates the useful life of the patent to be eight years, the annual amortization expense is $7,500 ($60,000 ÷ 8) per year. National records $3,750 ($7,500 × $\frac{6}{12}$) of amortization for the six-month period ended December 31 as follows.

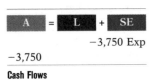

A = L + SE
                    −3,750 Exp
−3,750
Cash Flows
no effect

Dec. 31	Amortization Expense—Patent	3,750	
	Patent		3,750
	(To record patent amortization)		

When a company has significant intangibles, analysts should evaluate the reasonableness of the useful life estimates. In determining useful life, the company should consider obsolescence, inadequacy, and other factors. These may cause a patent or other intangible to become economically ineffective before the end of its legal life.

For example, suppose Intel obtained a patent on a new computer chip it had developed. The legal life of the patent is 20 years. From experience, however, we know that the useful life of a computer chip patent is rarely more than five years. Because new superior chips are developed so rapidly, existing chips become obsolete. Consequently, we would question the amortization expense of Intel if it amortized its patent on a computer chip for a life significantly longer than a five-year period. Amortizing an intangible over a period that is too long will understate amortization expense, overstate Intel's net income, and overstate its assets.

DECISION TOOLKIT

DECISION CHECKPOINTS	INFO NEEDED FOR DECISION	TOOL TO USE FOR DECISION	HOW TO EVALUATE RESULTS
Is the company's amortization of intangibles reasonable?	Estimated useful life of intangibles from notes to financial statements of this company and its competitors	If the company's estimated useful life significantly exceeds that of competitors or does not seem reasonable in light of the circumstances, the reason for the difference should be investigated.	Too high an estimated useful life will result in understating amortization expense and overstating net income.

Types of Intangible Assets

PATENTS

A **patent** is an exclusive right issued by the United States Patent Office that enables the recipient to manufacture, sell, or otherwise control an invention for a period of 20 years from the date of the grant. **The initial cost of a patent is the cash or cash equivalent price paid to acquire the patent.**

The saying "A patent is only as good as the money you're prepared to spend defending it" is very true. Most patents are subject to some type of litigation by competitors. A well-known example is the patent infringement suit brought by Amazon.com against Barnes & Noble.com regarding its online shopping software. If the owner incurs legal costs in successfully defending the patent in an infringement suit, such costs are considered necessary to establish the validity of the patent. Thus, **the owner adds those costs to the Patent account and amortizes them over the remaining life of the patent**.

RESEARCH AND DEVELOPMENT COSTS

Research and development costs are expenditures that may lead to patents, copyrights, new processes, and new products. Many companies spend considerable sums of money on research and development (R&D) in an ongoing effort to develop new products or processes. For example, in a recent year IBM spent over $5.1 billion on research and development. There are uncertainties in identifying the extent and timing of the future benefits of these expenditures. As a result, companies usually record research and development costs **as an expense when incurred**, whether the R&D is successful or not.

Helpful Hint Research and development costs are not intangible costs, but because these expenditures may lead to patents and copyrights, we discuss them in this section.

International Note IFRS allows capitalization of some development costs. This may contribute to differences in R&D expenditures across nations.

To illustrate, assume that Laser Scanner Company spent $3 million on research and development that resulted in two highly successful patents. It spent $20,000 on legal fees for the patents. It can include the legal fees in the cost of the patents, but cannot include the R&D costs in the cost of the patents. Instead, Laser Scanner records the R&D costs as an expense when incurred.

Many disagree with this accounting approach. They argue that to expense these costs leads to understated assets and net income. Others argue that capitalizing these costs would lead to highly speculative assets on the balance sheet. Who is right is difficult to determine.

COPYRIGHTS

The federal government grants copyrights, which give the owner the exclusive right to reproduce and sell an artistic or published work. Copyrights last for the life of the creator plus 70 years. The cost of the copyright consists of the **cost of acquiring and defending it**. The cost may be only the small fee paid to the U.S. Copyright Office, or it may amount to a great deal more if a copyright infringement suit is involved. The useful life of a copyright generally is significantly shorter than its legal life.

TRADEMARKS AND TRADE NAMES

A trademark or trade name is a word, phrase, jingle, or symbol that distinguishes or identifies a particular enterprise or product. Trade names like Wheaties, Monopoly, Sunkist, Kleenex, Coca-Cola, Big Mac, and Jeep create immediate product identification and generally enhance the sale of the product. The creator or original user may obtain the exclusive legal right to the trademark or trade name by registering it with the U.S. Patent Office. Such registration provides 20 years' protection and may be renewed indefinitely as long as the trademark or trade name is in use.

If a company purchases the trademark or trade name, the cost is the purchase price. If the company develops the trademark or trade name itself, the cost includes attorney's fees, registration fees, design costs, successful legal defense costs, and other expenditures directly related to securing it. Because trademarks and trade names have indefinite lives, they are not amortized.

FRANCHISES AND LICENSES

When you drive down the street in your RAV4 purchased from a Toyota dealer, fill up your tank at the corner Shell station, eat lunch at Subway, or make plans to vacation at a Marriott resort, you are dealing with franchises. A franchise is a contractual arrangement under which the franchisor grants the franchisee the right to sell certain products, to provide specific services, or to use certain trademarks or trade names, usually within a designated geographic area.

Another type of franchise, granted by a governmental body, permits the business to use public property in performing its services. Examples are the use of city streets for a bus line or taxi service; the use of public land for telephone, electric, and cable television lines; and the use of airwaves for radio or TV broadcasting. Such operating rights are referred to as licenses.

Franchises and licenses may be granted for a definite period of time, an indefinite period, or perpetual. **When a company can identify costs with the acquisition of the franchise or license, it should recognize an intangible asset.** Companies record as **operating expenses** annual payments made under a franchise agreement in the period in which they are incurred. In the case of a limited life, a company amortizes the cost of a franchise (or license) as operating expense over the useful life. If the life is indefinite or perpetual, the cost is not amortized.

Accounting Across the Organization

What is a well-known franchise worth? Recently ESPN outbid its rivals for the right to broadcast Monday Night Football. At a price of $1.1 billion per year—nearly twice what rival ABC paid in previous years—it isn't clear who won and who lost.

When bidding for a unique franchise like Monday Night Football, management must consider many factors to determine a price. As part of the deal, ESPN also got wireless rights and Spanish-language telecasts. By its estimation, ESPN will generate a profit of $200 million per year from Monday Night Football. ABC was losing $150 million per year.

Another factor in the decision was ESPN management's concern that if ESPN didn't win the bid, a buyer would emerge that would use Monday Night Football as a launching pad for a new sports network. ESPN doesn't want any more competitors than it already has. It is hard to put a price tag on the value of keeping the competition to a minimum.

Source: Ronald Grover and Tom Lowry, "A Ball ESPN Couldn't Afford to Drop," *BusinessWeek* (May 2, 2005), p. 42.

 How should ESPN account for the $1.1 billion per year franchise fee?

GOODWILL

Usually the largest intangible asset that appears on a company's balance sheet is goodwill. Goodwill represents the value of all favorable attributes that relate to a company that are not attributable to any other specific asset. These include exceptional management, desirable location, good customer relations, skilled employees, high-quality products, fair pricing policies, and harmonious relations with labor unions. Goodwill is unique because unlike other assets such as investments, plant assets, and even other intangibles, which can be sold *individually* in the marketplace, goodwill can be identified only with the business *as a whole.*

If goodwill can be identified only with the business as a whole, how can it be determined? Certainly, many business enterprises have many of the factors cited above (exceptional management, desirable location, and so on). However, to determine the amount of goodwill in these situations would be difficult and very subjective. In other words, to recognize goodwill without an exchange transaction that puts a value on the goodwill would lead to subjective valuations that do not contribute to the reliability of financial statements. **Therefore, companies record goodwill only when there is an exchange transaction that involves the purchase of an entire business. When an entire business is purchased, goodwill is the excess of cost over the fair market value of the net assets (assets less liabilities) acquired.**

In recording the purchase of a business, a company debits the identifiable acquired assets and credits liabilities at their fair market values, credits cash for the purchase price, and records the difference as the cost of goodwill. Goodwill is not amortized because it is considered to have an indefinite life. However, it must be written down if a company determines the value of goodwill has been permanently impaired.

 International Insight

Softbank Corp. is Japan's biggest Internet company. It recently boosted the profit margin of its mobile-phone unit from 3.2% to 11.2% through what appeared to some as accounting tricks. What did it do? It wrote down the value of its mobile-phone-unit assets by half. This would normally result in a huge loss. But rather than take a loss, the company wrote up goodwill by the same amount. How did this move increase earnings? The assets were being depreciated over 10 years, but the company amortizes goodwill over 20 years. While the new treatment did not break any rules, the company was criticized by investors for not providing sufficient justification or a detailed explanation for the sudden shift in policy.

Source: Andrew Morse and Yukari Iwatani Kane, "Softbank's Accounting Shift Raises Eyebrows," *Wall Street Journal* (August 28, 2007), p. C1.

? Do you think that this treatment would be allowed under U.S. GAAP?

---

before you go on...

CLASSIFICATION CONCEPTS

Action Plan

• Know that the accounting for intangibles often depends on whether the item has a finite or indefinite life.

• Recognize the many similarities and differences between the accounting for plant assets and intangible assets.

Do it! Match the statement with the term most directly associated with it.

Copyright	Amortization
Intangible assets	Franchise
Research and development costs	

1. _____ The allocation to expense of the cost of an intangible asset over the asset's useful life.

2. _____ Rights, privileges, and competitive advantages that result from the ownership of long-lived assets that do not possess physical substance.

3. _____ An exclusive right granted by the federal government to reproduce and sell an artistic or published work.

4. _____ A right to sell certain products or services or to use certain trademarks or trade names within a designated geographic area.

5. _____ Costs incurred by a company that often lead to patents or new products. These costs must be expensed as incurred.

Solution

1. Amortization	4. Franchise
2. Intangible assets	5. Research and development costs
3. Copyright	

Financial Statement Presentation of Long-Lived Assets

study objective 8

Indicate how long-lived assets are reported in the financial statements.

Usually companies show plant assets in the financial statements under "Property, plant, and equipment," and they show intangibles separately under "Intangible assets." Illustration 9-22 shows a typical balance sheet presentation of long-lived assets, adapted from The Coca-Cola Company's 2007 balance sheet.

Intangibles do not usually use a contra asset account like the contra asset account Accumulated Depreciation used for plant assets. Instead, companies record amortization of intangibles as a direct decrease (credit) to the asset account.

The Coca-Cola Company

THE COCA-COLA COMPANY
Balance Sheet (partial)
(in millions)

Property, plant, and equipment		
Land	$ 731	
Buildings and improvements	3,539	
Machinery and equipment	8,924	
Containers and other	1,250	
	14,444	
Less: Accumulated depreciation	5,951	
	8,493	
Intangible assets		
Trademarks with indefinite lives	5,153	
Goodwill	4,256	
Other intangible assets	2,810	
	$12,219	

Illustration 9-22
Presentation of property, plant, and equipment and intangible assets

Either within the balance sheet or in the notes, companies should disclose the balances of the major classes of assets, such as land, buildings, and equipment, and of accumulated depreciation by major classes or in total. In addition, they should describe the depreciation and amortization methods used and disclose the amount of depreciation and amortization expense for the period.

One of the most significant differences between accrual-accounting net income and net cash provided by operating activities is caused by depreciation and amortization expense. Depreciation and amortization reduce net income, but they do not use up any cash. Therefore, to determine net cash provided by operating activities, companies add depreciation and amortization back to net income. For example, if a company reported net income of $175,000 during the year and had depreciation expense of $40,000, net cash provided by operating activities would be $215,000 (assuming no other accrual accounting differences). The operating activities section of Coca-Cola's statement of cash flows reports the following adjustment for depreciation and amortization.

KEEPING AN EYE ON CASH

The Coca-Cola Company

THE COCA-COLA COMPANY
Statement of Cash Flows (partial)
(in millions)

Cash flow from operating activities	
Net income	$5,981
Plus: Depreciation and amortization	1,163

The adjustment for depreciation and amortization was more than twice as big as any other adjustment required to convert net income to net cash provided by operating activities.

It is also interesting to examine the statement of cash flows to determine the amount of property, plant, and equipment a company purchased and the cash it received from property, plant, and equipment sold in a given year. For example, the investing activities section of Coca-Cola reports the following.

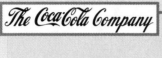

THE COCA-COLA COMPANY
Statement of Cash Flows (partial)
(in millions)

Cash flow from investing activities	
Acquisitions and investments	$(5,653)
Purchases of property, plant, and equipment	(1,648)
Proceeds from disposals of property, plant, and equipment	239

As indicated, Coca-Cola made significant purchases and sales of property, plant, and equipment. The level of purchases suggests that Coca-Cola believes that it can earn a reasonable rate of return on these assets.

USING THE DECISION TOOLKIT

JetBlue Airways Corporation is a low-cost airline operating primarily out of New York. It operates hundreds of flights to 51 destinations daily. Although it has operated for only eight years, it is now the tenth largest U.S. airline based on total passenger miles. It currently operates 104 planes.

Instructions

Review the excerpts from the company's 2007 annual report that follow and then answer the following questions.

1. What method does the company use to depreciate its aircraft? Over what period is the company depreciating these aircraft?

2. What type of intangible assets does the company have, and how are they being accounted for?

3. Compute the company's return on assets ratio, asset turnover ratio, and profit margin ratio for 2006 and 2007. Comment on your results.

(in millions)	**2007**	**2006**
Net income (loss)	$ 18	$ (1)
Net sales	2,842	2,363
Beginning total assets	4,843	3,892
Ending total assets	5,598	4,843

JETBLUE AIRWAYS CORPORATION
Notes to the Financial Statements

Property and Equipment: We record our property and equipment at cost and depreciate these assets on a straight-line basis to their estimated residual values over their estimated useful lives. Additions, modifications that enhance the operating performance of our assets, and interest related to predelivery deposits to acquire new aircraft and for the construction of facilities are capitalized.

Estimated useful lives and residual values for our property and equipment are as follows:

	Estimated Useful Life	**Residual Value**
Aircraft	25 years	20%
In-flight entertainment systems	12 years	0%
Aircraft parts	Fleet life	10%
Flight equipment leasehold improvements	Lease term	0%
Ground property and equipment	3–10 years	0%
Leasehold improvements	15 years or lease term	0%

We record impairment losses on long-lived assets used in operations when events and circumstances indicate that the assets may be impaired and the undiscounted future cash flows estimated to be generated by these assets are less than the assets' net book value. If impairment occurs, the loss is measured by comparing the fair value of the asset to its carrying amount.

Note 5—LiveTV Purchased technology, which is an intangible asset related to our September 2002 acquisition of the membership interests of LiveTV, is being amortized over seven years based on the average number of aircraft expected to be in service as of the date of acquisition. Projected amortization expense is $13 million and $8 million in 2008 and 2009, respectively.

Solution

1. The company depreciates property and equipment using the straight-line approach. It depreciates aircraft over a 25-year life.

2. The company has an intangible asset called "purchased technology" related to its purchase of membership interests in "LiveTV." It amortizes this intangible asset based on the company's estimate of the average number of aircraft expected to be in service over a seven-year period.

3.

	2007	**2006**
Return on assets	$\dfrac{\$18}{(\$5,598+\$4,843)/2}=0.3\%$	$\dfrac{\$(1)}{(\$4,843+\$3,892)/2}=0.0\%$
Asset turnover	$\dfrac{\$2,842}{(\$5,598+\$4,843)/2}=0.54 \text{ times}$	$\dfrac{\$2,363}{(\$4,843+\$3,892)/2}=.54 \text{ times}$
Profit margin	$\dfrac{\$18}{\$2,842}=0.06\%$	$\dfrac{(1)}{\$2,363}=0.00\%$

JetBlue's return on assets ratio increased slightly from 2006 to 2007. While its profit margin was very low in both years, JetBlue was not able to increase its asset turnover. This suggests that its ability to generate sales from its planes remained constant, while its ability to generate profits from sales remained very low.

Summary of Study Objectives

1 **Describe how the cost principle applies to plant assets.** The cost of plant assets includes all expenditures necessary to acquire the asset and make it ready for its intended use. Cost is measured by the cash or cash equivalent price paid.

2 **Explain the concept of depreciation.** Depreciation is the process of allocating to expense the cost of a plant asset over its useful (service) life in a rational and

systematic manner. Depreciation is not a process of valuation, and it is not a process that results in an accumulation of cash. Depreciation reflects an asset's decreasing usefulness and revenue-producing ability, resulting from wear and tear and from obsolescence.

3 **Compute periodic depreciation using the straight-line method, and contrast its expense pattern with those of**

other methods. The formula for straight-line depreciation is:

$$\frac{\text{Cost} - \text{Salvage value}}{\text{Useful life (in years)}}$$

The expense patterns of the three depreciation methods are as follows.

Method	Annual Depreciation Pattern
Straight-line	Constant amount
Declining-balance	Decreasing amount
Units-of-activity	Varying amount

4 **Describe the procedure for revising periodic depreciation.** Companies make revisions of periodic depreciation in present and future periods, not retroactively.

5 **Explain how to account for the disposal of plant assets.** The procedure for accounting for the disposal of a plant asset through sale or retirement is: (a) Eliminate the book value of the plant asset at the date of disposal. (b) Record cash proceeds, if any. (c) Account for the difference between the book value and the cash proceeds as a gain or a loss on disposal.

6 **Describe methods for evaluating the use of plant assets.** Plant assets may be analyzed using the return on assets ratio and the asset turnover ratio. The return

on assets ratio consists of two components: the asset turnover ratio and the profit margin ratio.

7 **Identify the basic issues related to reporting intangible assets.** Companies report intangible assets at their cost less any amounts amortized. If an intangible asset has a limited life, its cost should be allocated (amortized) over its useful life. Intangible assets with indefinite lives should not be amortized.

8 **Indicate how long-lived assets are reported in the financial statements.** Companies usually show plant assets under "Property, plant, and equipment"; they show intangibles separately under "Intangible assets." Either within the balance sheet or in the notes, companies disclose the balances of the major classes of assets, such as land, buildings, and equipment, and accumulated depreciation by major classes or in total. They describe the depreciation and amortization methods used, and disclose the amount of depreciation and amortization expense for the period. In the statement of cash flows, depreciation and amortization expense are added back to net income to determine net cash provided by operating activities. The investing section reports cash paid or received to purchase or sell property, plant, and equipment.

✔ the navigator

DECISION TOOLKIT   A SUMMARY

DECISION CHECKPOINTS	INFO NEEDED FOR DECISION	TOOL TO USE FOR DECISION	HOW TO EVALUATE RESULTS
Is the company using its assets effectively?	Net income and average assets	$\text{Return on assets ratio} = \dfrac{\text{Net income}}{\text{Average total assets}}$	Higher value suggests favorable efficiency (use of assets).
How effective is the company at generating sales from its assets?	Net sales and average total assets	$\text{Assets turnover ratio} = \dfrac{\text{Net sales}}{\text{Average total assets}}$	Indicates the sales dollars generated per dollar of assets. A high value suggests the company is effective in using its resources to generate sales.
Is the company's amortization of intangibles reasonable?	Estimated useful life of intangibles from notes to financial statements of this company and its competitors	If the company's estimated useful life significantly exceeds that of competitors or does not seem reasonable in light of the circumstances, the reason for the difference should be investigated.	Too high an estimated useful life will result in understating amortization expense and overstating net income.

appendix

study objective	9

Compute periodic depreciation using the declining-balance method and the units-of-activity method.

Calculation of Depreciation Using Other Methods

In this appendix we show the calculations of the depreciation expense amounts that we used in the chapter for the declining-balance and units-of-activity methods.

DECLINING-BALANCE

The declining-balance method produces a decreasing annual depreciation expense over the useful life of the asset. The method is so named because the computation of periodic depreciation is based on a **declining book value** (cost less accumulated depreciation) of the asset. Annual depreciation expense is computed by multiplying the book value at the beginning of the year by the declining-balance depreciation rate. **The depreciation rate remains constant from year to year, but the book value to which the rate is applied declines each year.**

Book value for the first year is the cost of the asset because the balance in accumulated depreciation at the beginning of the asset's useful life is zero. In subsequent years, book value is the difference between cost and accumulated depreciation at the beginning of the year. **Unlike other depreciation methods, the declining-balance method ignores salvage value in determining the amount to which the declining-balance rate is applied.** Salvage value, however, does limit the total depreciation that can be taken. Depreciation stops when the asset's book value equals its expected salvage value.

As noted in the chapter, a common declining-balance rate is double the straight-line rate—the **double-declining-balance method**. If Bill's Pizzas uses the double-declining-balance method, the depreciation rate is 40% (2 × the straight-line rate of 20%). Illustration 9A-1 presents the formula and computation of depreciation for the first year on the delivery truck.

Helpful Hint The straight-line rate is approximated as 1 ÷ Estimated life. In this case it is 1 ÷ 5 = 20%.

Illustration 9A-1
Formula for declining-balance method

Book Value at Beginning of Year	×	Declining-Balance Rate	=	Depreciation Expense
$13,000	×	40%	=	$5,200

Illustration 9A-2 presents the depreciation schedule under this method.

Illustration 9A-2
Double-declining-balance depreciation schedule

BILL'S PIZZAS

	Computation			Annual	End of Year	
Year	Book Value Beginning of Year	× Depreciation Rate	=	Depreciation Expense	Accumulated Depreciation	Book Value
2010	$13,000	40%		$5,200	$ 5,200	$ 7,800*
2011	7,800	40		3,120	8,320	4,680
2012	4,680	40		1,872	10,192	2,808
2013	2,808	40		1,123	11,315	1,685
2014	1,685	40		685**	12,000	1,000

*$13,000 − $5,200
**Computation of $674 ($1,685 × 40%) is adjusted to $685 in order for book value to equal salvage value.

Helpful Hint Depreciation stops when the asset's book value equals its expected salvage value.

The delivery equipment is 69% depreciated ($8,320 ÷ $12,000) at the end of the second year. Under the straight-line method it would be depreciated 40% ($4,800 ÷ $12,000) at that time. Because the declining-balance method produces higher depreciation expense in the early years than in the later years, it is considered an **accelerated-depreciation method**.

The declining-balance method is compatible with the matching principle. It matches the higher depreciation expense in early years with the higher benefits received in these years. Conversely, it recognizes lower depreciation expense in later years when the asset's contribution to revenue is less. Also, some assets lose their usefulness rapidly because of obsolescence. In these cases, the declining-balance method provides a more appropriate depreciation amount.

When an asset is purchased during the year, it is necessary to prorate the declining-balance depreciation in the first year on a time basis. For example, if Bill's Pizzas had purchased the delivery equipment on April 1, 2010, depreciation for 2010 would be $3,900 ($13,000 × 40% × $\frac{9}{12}$). The book value for computing depreciation in 2011 then becomes $9,100 ($13,000 − $3,900), and the 2011 depreciation is $3,640 ($9,100 × 40%).

UNITS-OF-ACTIVITY

Alternative Terminology Another term often used is the *units-of-production method*.

Under the **units-of-activity method**, useful life is expressed in terms of the total units of production or use expected from the asset. The units-of-activity method is ideally suited to equipment whose activity can be measured in units of output, miles driven, or hours in use. The units-of-activity method is generally not suitable for assets for which depreciation is a function more of time than of use.

To use this method, a company estimates the total units of activity for the entire useful life and divides that amount into the depreciable cost to determine the depreciation cost per unit. It then multiplies the depreciation cost per unit by the units of activity during the year to find the annual depreciation for that year.

To illustrate, assume that Bill's Pizzas estimates it will drive its new delivery truck 15,000 miles in the first year. Illustration 9A-3 presents the formula and computation of depreciation expense in the first year.

Illustration 9A-3
Formula for units-of-activity method

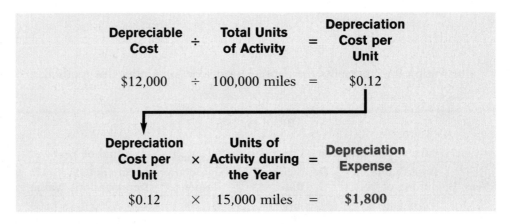

Illustration 9A-4 shows the depreciation schedule, using assumed mileage data.

Illustration 9A-4 Units-of-activity depreciation schedule

			BILL'S PIZZAS			
	Computation			**Annual**	**End of Year**	
Year	**Units of Activity**	×	**Depreciation Cost/Unit** =	**Depreciation Expense**	**Accumulated Depreciation**	**Book Value**
2010	15,000		$0.12	$1,800	$ 1,800	$11,200*
2011	30,000		0.12	3,600	5,400	7,600
2012	20,000		0.12	2,400	7,800	5,200
2013	25,000		0.12	3,000	10,800	2,200
2014	10,000		0.12	1,200	12,000	1,000

*$13,000 − $1,800

Helpful Hint Depreciation stops when the asset's book value equals its expected salvage value.

The units-of-activity method is not nearly as popular as the straight-line method, primarily because it is often difficult to make a reasonable estimate of total activity. However, this method is used by some very large companies, such as Standard Oil Company of California and Boise Cascade Corporation. When the productivity of the asset varies significantly from one period to another, the units-of-activity method results in the best matching of expenses with revenues.

This method is easy to apply when assets are purchased during the year. In such a case, companies use the productivity of the asset for the partial year in computing the depreciation.

Summary of Study Objective for Appendix

9 **Compute periodic depreciation using the declining-balance method and the units-of-activity method.** The depreciation expense calculation for each of these methods is:

Declining-balance:

$$\begin{matrix}\text{Book value at} \\ \text{beginning of year}\end{matrix} \times \begin{matrix}\text{Declining-balance} \\ \text{rate}\end{matrix} = \begin{matrix}\text{Depreciation} \\ \text{expense}\end{matrix}$$

Units-of-activity:

$$\begin{matrix}\text{Depreciable} \\ \text{cost}\end{matrix} \div \begin{matrix}\text{Total units} \\ \text{of activity}\end{matrix} = \begin{matrix}\text{Depreciation} \\ \text{cost per unit}\end{matrix}$$

$$\begin{matrix}\text{Depreciation cost} \\ \text{per unit}\end{matrix} \times \begin{matrix}\text{Units of activity} \\ \text{during year}\end{matrix} = \begin{matrix}\text{Depreciation} \\ \text{expense}\end{matrix}$$

Glossary

Accelerated-depreciation method *(p. 442)* A depreciation method that produces higher depreciation expense in the early years than the straight-line approach.

Additions and improvements *(p. 445)* Costs incurred to increase the operating efficiency, productive capacity, or expected useful life of a plant asset.

Amortization *(p. 452)* The process of allocating to expense the cost of an intangible asset.

Asset turnover ratio *(p. 450)* Indicates how efficiently a company uses its assets to generate sales; calculated as net sales divided by average total assets.

Capital expenditures *(p. 435)* Expenditures that increase the company's investment in plant assets.

Capital lease *(p. 438)* A contractual agreement allowing one party (the lessee) to use another party's asset (the lessor); accounted for like a debt-financed purchase by the lessee.

Cash equivalent price *(p. 435)* An amount equal to the fair market value of the asset given up or the fair market value of the asset received, whichever is more clearly determinable.

Copyright *(p. 454)* An exclusive right granted by the federal government allowing the owner to reproduce and sell an artistic or published work.

Declining-balance method *(pp. 442, 461)* A depreciation method that applies a constant rate to the declining book value of the asset and produces a decreasing annual depreciation expense over the asset's useful life.

Depreciable cost *(p. 441)* The cost of a plant asset less its salvage value.

Depreciation *(p. 439)* The process of allocating to expense the cost of a plant asset over its useful life in a rational and systematic manner.

Franchise *(p. 454)* A contractual arrangement under which the franchisor grants the franchisee the right to sell certain products, to provide specific services, or to use certain trademarks or trade names, usually within a designated geographic area.

Goodwill *(p. 455)* The value of all favorable attributes that relate to a company that are not attributable to any other specific asset.

Impairment *(p. 445)* A permanent decline in the market value of an asset.

Intangible assets *(p. 451)* Rights, privileges, and competitive advantages that result from the ownership of long-lived assets that do not possess physical substance.

Lessee *(p. 438)* A party that has made contractual arrangements to use another party's asset for a period at an agreed price.

Lessor *(p. 438)* A party that has agreed contractually to let another party use its asset for a period at an agreed price.

Licenses *(p. 454)* Operating rights to use public property, granted by a governmental agency to a business.

Operating lease *(p. 438)* A contractual agreement allowing one party (the lessee) to use the asset of another party (the lessor); accounted for as a rental by the lessee.

Ordinary repairs *(p. 445)* Expenditures to maintain the operating efficiency and expected productive life of the asset.

Patent (p. 453) An exclusive right issued by the U.S. Patent Office that enables the recipient to manufacture, sell, or otherwise control an invention for a period of 20 years from the date of the grant.

Plant assets (p. 434) Tangible resources that have physical substance, are used in the operations of the business, and are not intended for sale to customers.

Research and development costs (p. 453) Expenditures that may lead to patents, copyrights, new processes, and new products; must be expensed as incurred.

Return on assets ratio (p. 448) A profitability measure that indicates the amount of net income generated by each dollar of assets; computed as net income divided by average assets.

Revenue expenditures (p. 435) Expenditures that are immediately charged against revenues as an expense.

Straight-line method (p. 441) A method in which companies expense an equal amount of depreciation for each year of the asset's useful life.

Trademark (trade name) (p. 454) A word, phrase, jingle, or symbol that distinguishes or identifies a particular enterprise or product.

Units-of-activity method (pp. 442, 462) A depreciation method in which useful life is expressed in terms of the total units of production or use expected from the asset.

Comprehensive 1

DuPage Company purchased a factory machine at a cost of $18,000 on January 1, 2010. DuPage expected the machine to have a salvage value of $2,000 at the end of its 4-year useful life.

Instructions

Prepare a depreciation schedule using the straight-line method.

Action Plan

- Under the straight-line method, apply the depreciation rate to depreciable cost.

Solution to Comprehensive **1**

DUPAGE COMPANY
Depreciation Schedule—Straight-Line Method

| | Computation | | | Annual | End of Year | |
| | Depreciable | × | Depreciation | Depreciation | Accumulated | Book |
Year	Cost (a)		Rate (b) =	Expense	Depreciation	Value (c)
2010	$16,000		25%	$4,000	$ 4,000	$14,000
2011	16,000		25	4,000	8,000	10,000
2012	16,000		25	4,000	12,000	6,000
2013	16,000		25	4,000	16,000	2,000

(a) $18,000 − $2,000   (b) $\frac{1}{4}$ = 25%   (c) Cost less accumulated depreciation.

Comprehensive 2

On January 1, 2007, Skyline Limousine Co. purchased a limousine at an acquisition cost of $28,000. Skyline depreciated the vehicle by the straight-line method using a 4-year service life and a $4,000 salvage value. The company's fiscal year ends on December 31.

Instructions

Prepare the journal entry or entries to record the disposal of the limousine assuming that it was:
(a) Retired and scrapped with no salvage value on January 1, 2011.
(b) Sold for $5,000 on July 1, 2010.

Solution to Comprehensive `Do it!` **2**

(a) Jan. 1, 2011	Accumulated Depreciation—Limousine	24,000	
	Loss on Disposal	4,000	
	Limousine		28,000
	(To record retirement of limousine)		
(b) July 1, 2010	Depreciation Expense	3,000	
	Accumulated Depreciation—Limousine		3,000
	(To record depreciation to date of disposal)		
	Cash	5,000	
	Accumulated Depreciation—Limousine	21,000	
	Loss on Disposal	2,000	
	Limousine		28,000
	(To record sale of limousine)		

Action Plan

• Calculate accumulated depreciation (depreciation expense per year × years in use).

• At the time of disposal, determine the book value of the asset.

• Recognize any gain or loss from disposal of the asset.

Note: All Questions, Exercises, and Problems marked with an asterisk relate to material in the appendix to the chapter.

Self-Study Questions

Answers are at the end of the chapter.

(SO 1) **1.** Corrieten Company purchased equipment and incurred these costs:

Cash price	$24,000
Sales taxes	1,200
Insurance during transit	200
Installation and testing	400
Total costs	$25,800

What amount should be recorded as the cost of the equipment?
(a) $24,000. (c) $25,400.
(b) $25,200. (d) $25,800.

(SO 1) **2.** 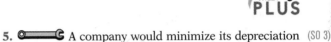 Harrington Corporation recently leased a number of trucks from Andre Corporation. In inspecting the books of Harrington Corporation, you notice that the trucks have not been recorded as assets on its balance sheet. From this you can conclude that Harrington is accounting for this transaction as a/an:
(a) operating lease. (c) purchase.
(b) capital lease. (d) None of the above.

(SO 2) **3.** Depreciation is a process of:
(a) valuation. (c) cash accumulation.
(b) cost allocation. (d) appraisal.

(SO 3) **4.** Cuso Company purchased equipment on January 1, 2009, at a total invoice cost of $400,000. The equipment has an estimated salvage value of $10,000 and an estimated useful life of 5 years. What is the amount of accumulated depreciation at December 31, 2010, if the straight-line method of depreciation is used?
(a) $80,000. (c) $78,000.
(b) $160,000. (d) $156,000.

5. 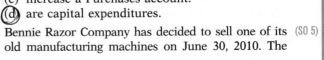 A company would minimize its depreciation (SO 3) expense in the first year of owning an asset if it used:
(a) a high estimated life, a high salvage value, and declining-balance depreciation.
(b) a low estimated life, a high salvage value, and straight-line depreciation.
(c) a high estimated life, a high salvage value, and straight-line depreciation.
(d) a low estimated life, a low salvage value, and declining-balance depreciation.

6. When there is a change in estimated depreciation: (SO 4)
(a) previous depreciation should be corrected.
(b) current and future years' depreciation should be revised.
(c) only future years' depreciation should be revised.
(d) None of the above.

7. Able Towing Company purchased a tow truck for (SO 4) $60,000 on January 1, 2010. It was originally depreciated on a straight-line basis over 10 years with an assumed salvage value of $12,000. On December 31, 2012, before adjusting entries had been made, the company decided to change the remaining estimated life to 4 years (including 2012) and the salvage value to $2,000. What was the depreciation expense for 2012?
(a) $6,000. (c) $15,000.
(b) $4,800. (d) $12,100.

8. Additions to plant assets: (SO 4)
(a) decrease liabilities.
(b) increase a Repair Expense account.
(c) increase a Purchases account.
(d) are capital expenditures.

9. Bennie Razor Company has decided to sell one of its (SO 5) old manufacturing machines on June 30, 2010. The

machine was purchased for $80,000 on January 1, 2006, and was depreciated on a straight-line basis for 10 years assuming no salvage value. If the machine was sold for $26,000, what was the amount of the gain or loss recorded at the time of the sale?
(a) $18,000.   (c) $22,000.
(b) $54,000.   (d) $46,000.

(SO 6) **10.** Which of the following measures provides an indication of how efficient a company is in employing its assets?
(a) Current ratio.
(b) Profit margin ratio.
(c) Debt to total assets ratio.
(d) Asset turnover ratio.

(SO 6) **11.** Lake Coffee Company reported net sales of $180,000, net income of $54,000, beginning total assets of $200,000, and ending total assets of $300,000. What was the company's asset turnover ratio?
(a) 0.90   (c) 0.72
(b) 0.20   (d) 1.39

(SO 7) **12.** Pierce Company incurred $150,000 of research and development costs in its laboratory to develop a new product. It spent $20,000 in legal fees for a patent granted on January 2, 2010. On July 31, 2010, Pierce paid $15,000 for legal fees in a successful defense of the patent. What is the total amount that should be debited to Patents through July 31, 2010?
(a) $150,000.   (c) $185,000.
(b) $35,000.   (d) Some other amount.

(SO 7, **13.** Indicate which one of these statements is *true*.
(a) Since intangible assets lack physical substance, they need to be disclosed only in the notes to the financial statements.
(b) Goodwill should be reported as a contra account in the stockholders' equity section.
(c) Totals of major classes of assets can be shown in the balance sheet, with asset details disclosed in the notes to the financial statements.
(d) Intangible assets are typically combined with plant assets and inventory and then shown in the property, plant, and equipment section.

14. If a company reports goodwill as an intangible asset (SO 7) on its books, what is the one thing you know with certainty?
(a) The company is a valuable company worth investing in.
(b) The company has a well-established brand name.
(c) The company purchased another company.
(d) The goodwill will generate a lot of positive business for the company for many years to come.

15. Which of the following statements is *false*? (SO 7)
(a) If an intangible asset has a finite life, it should be amortized.
(b) The amortization period of an intangible asset can exceed 20 years.
(c) Goodwill is recorded only when a business is purchased.
(d) Research and development costs are expensed when incurred, except when the research and development expenditures result in a successful patent.

*****16.** Kant Enterprises purchased a truck for $11,000 on (SO 9) January 1, 2009. The truck will have an estimated salvage value of $1,000 at the end of 5 years. If you use the units-of-activity method, the balance in accumulated depreciation at December 31, 2010, can be computed by the following formula:
(a) ($11,000 ÷ Total estimated activity) × Units of activity for 2010.
(b) ($10,000 ÷ Total estimated activity) × Units of activity for 2010.
(c) ($11,000 ÷ Total estimated activity) × Units of activity for 2009 and 2010.
(d) ($10,000 ÷ Total estimated activity) × Units of activity for 2009 and 2010.

Go to the book's companion website, **www.wiley.com/college/kimmel**, to access additional Self-Study Questions.

Questions

1. Mrs. Vangundy is uncertain about how the cost principle applies to plant assets. Explain the principle to Mrs. Vangundy.

2. How is the cost for a plant asset measured in a cash transaction? In a noncash transaction?

3. What are the primary advantages of leasing?

4. Jasper Company acquires the land and building owned by Benz Company. What types of costs may be incurred to make the asset ready for its intended use if Jasper Company wants to use only the land? If it wants to use both the land and the building?

5. Pickert Inc. needs to upgrade its diagnostic equipment. At the time of purchase, Pickert had expected the equipment to last 8 years. Unfortunately, it was obsolete after only 4 years. Chuck Kellum, CFO of Pickert Inc., is considering leasing new equipment rather than buying it. What are the potential benefits of leasing?

6. In a recent newspaper release, the president of Fraley Company asserted that something has to be done about depreciation. The president said, "Depreciation does not come close to accumulating the cash needed to replace the asset at the end of its useful life." What is your response to the president?

7. Megan is studying for the next accounting examination. She asks your help on two questions: (a) What is salvage value? (b) How is salvage value used in determining depreciable cost under the straight-line method? Answer Megan's questions.

8. Contrast the straight-line method and the units-of-activity method in relation to (a) useful life and (b) the pattern of periodic depreciation over useful life.

9. Contrast the effects of the three depreciation methods on annual depreciation expense.

10. In the fourth year of an asset's 5-year useful life, the company decides that the asset will have a 6-year service life. How should the revision of depreciation be recorded? Why?

11. Distinguish between ordinary repairs and capital expenditures during an asset's useful life.

12. How is a gain or a loss on the sale of a plant asset computed?

13. Kingery Corporation owns a machine that is fully depreciated but is still being used. How should Kingery account for this asset and report it in the financial statements?

14. What does Tootsie Roll use as the estimated useful life on its buildings? On its machinery and equipment?

15. What are the similarities and differences between depreciation and amortization?

16. During a recent management meeting, Ralph Dale, director of marketing, proposed that the company begin capitalizing its marketing expenditures as goodwill. In his words, "Marketing expenditures create goodwill for the company which benefits the company for multiple periods. Therefore it doesn't make good sense to have to expense it as it is incurred. Besides, if we capitalize it as goodwill we won't have to amortize it, and this will boost reported income." Discuss the merits of Ralph's proposal.

17. Alpha Company hires an accounting intern who says that intangible assets should always be amortized over their legal lives. Is the intern correct? Explain.

18. Goodwill has been defined as the value of all favorable attributes that relate to a business enterprise. What types of attributes could result in goodwill?

19. Jane Farr, a business major, is working on a case problem for one of her classes. In this case problem, the company needs to raise cash to market a new product it developed. Lenny Gaston, an engineering major, takes one look at the company's balance sheet and says, "This company has an awful lot of good-will. Why don't you recommend that they sell some of it to raise cash?" How should Jane respond to Lenny?

20. Under what conditions is goodwill recorded? What is the proper accounting treatment for amortizing goodwill?

21. Often research and development costs provide companies with benefits that last a number of years. (For example, these costs can lead to the development of a patent that will increase the company's income for many years.) However, generally accepted accounting principles require that such costs be recorded as an expense when incurred. Why?

22. In 2007 Campbell Soup Company reported average total assets of $3,095 million, net sales of $7,867 million, and net income of $854 million. What was Campbell Soup's return on assets ratio?

23. Andrea Reeble, a marketing executive for Fresh Views Inc., has proposed expanding its product line of framed graphic art by producing a line of lower-quality products. These would require less processing by the company and would provide a lower profit margin. Steve Hillmon, the company's CFO, is concerned that this new product line would reduce the company's return on assets. Discuss the potential effect on return on assets that this product might have.

24. Give an example of an industry that would be characterized by (a) a high asset turnover ratio and a low profit margin ratio, and (b) a low asset turnover ratio and a high profit margin ratio.

25. Aldrich Corporation and Benjamin Corporation operate in the same industry. Aldrich uses the straight-line method to account for depreciation, whereas Benjamin uses an accelerated method. Explain what complications might arise in trying to compare the results of these two companies.

26. Garza Corporation uses straight-line depreciation for financial reporting purposes but an accelerated method for tax purposes. Is it acceptable to use different methods for the two purposes? What is Garza Corporation's motivation for doing this?

27. You are comparing two companies in the same industry. You have determined that Mane Corp. depreciates its plant assets over a 40-year life, whereas Nienstedt Corp. depreciates its plant assets over a 20-year life. Discuss the implications this has for comparing the results of the two companies.

28. Explain how plant assets and intangibles are reported in the statement of cash flows.

Brief Exercises

BE9-1 These expenditures were incurred by Sanler Company in purchasing land: cash price $60,000; accrued taxes $5,000; attorney's fees $2,100; real estate broker's commission $2,800; and clearing and grading $3,500. What is the cost of the land?

Determine the cost of land.
(SO 1)

Determine the cost of a truck.
(SO 1)

BE9-2 Denney Company incurs these expenditures in purchasing a truck: cash price $24,000; accident insurance (during use) $2,000; sales taxes $1,080; motor vehicle license $300; and painting and lettering $1,200. What is the cost of the truck?

Compute straight-line depreciation.
(SO 3)

BE9-3 Apex Chemicals Company acquires a delivery truck at a cost of $31,000 on January 1, 2010. The truck is expected to have a salvage value of $4,000 at the end of its 5-year useful life. Compute annual depreciation for the first and second years using the straight-line method.

Compute depreciation and evaluate treatment.
(SO 3)

BE9-4 Ecklund Company purchased land and a building on January 1, 2010. Management's best estimate of the value of the land was $100,000 and of the building $200,000. However, management told the accounting department to record the land at $220,000 and the building at $80,000. The building is being depreciated on a straight-line basis over 20 years with no salvage value. Why do you suppose management requested this accounting treatment? Is it ethical?

Compute revised depreciation.
(SO 4)

BE9-5 On January 1, 2010, the Ewing Company ledger shows Equipment $36,000 and Accumulated Depreciation $14,000. The depreciation resulted from using the straight-line method with a useful life of 10 years and a salvage value of $2,000. On this date the company concludes that the equipment has a remaining useful life of only 2 years with the same salvage value. Compute the revised annual depreciation.

Prepare entries for delivery truck costs.
(SO 4)

BE9-6 Firefly Company had the following two transactions related to its delivery truck.
1. Paid $45 for an oil change.
2. Paid $400 to install special shelving units, which increase the operating efficiency of the truck.

Prepare Firefly's journal entries to record these two transactions.

Journalize entries for disposal of plant assets.
(SO 5)

BE9-7 Prepare journal entries to record these transactions: (a) Blaska Company retires its delivery equipment, which cost $41,000. Accumulated depreciation is also $41,000 on this delivery equipment. No salvage value is received. (b) Assume the same information as in part (a), except that accumulated depreciation for the equipment is $38,800 instead of $41,000.

Journalize entries for sale of plant assets.
(SO 5)

BE9-8 Carlton Company sells office equipment on September 30, 2010, for $21,000 cash. The office equipment originally cost $72,000 and as of January 1, 2010, had accumulated depreciation of $42,000. Depreciation for the first 9 months of 2010 is $6,000. Prepare the journal entries to (a) update depreciation to September 30, 2010, and (b) record the sale of the equipment.

Compute return on assets ratio and asset turnover ratio.
(SO 6)

BE9-9 In its 2006 annual report, McDonald's Corporation reports beginning total assets of $30.0 billion; ending total assets of $29.0 billion; net sales of $21.6 billion, and net income of $3.5 billion.
(a) Compute McDonald's return on assets ratio.
(b) Compute McDonald's asset turnover ratio.

Account for intangibles— patents.
(SO 7)

BE9-10 Jazz Company purchases a patent for $150,000 on January 2, 2010. Its estimated useful life is 5 years.
(a) Prepare the journal entry to record amortization expense for the first year.
(b) Show how this patent is reported on the balance sheet at the end of the first year.

Classification of long-lived assets on balance sheet.
(SO 8)

BE9-11 Nike, Inc. reported the following plant assets and intangible assets for the year ended May 31, 2007 (in millions): other plant assets $767.2; land $193.8; patents and trademarks (at cost) $115.5; machinery and equipment $1,817.2; buildings $840.9; goodwill (at cost) $130.8; accumulated amortization $47.1; accumulated depreciation $1,940.8. Prepare a partial balance sheet for Nike for these items.

Determine net cash provided by operating activities.
(SO 8)

BE9-12 Nichols Company reported net income of $157,000. It reported depreciation expense of $12,000 and accumulated depreciation of $47,000. Amortization expense was $6,000. Nichols purchased new equipment during the year for $50,000. Show how this information would be used to determine net cash provided by operating activities.

Compute declining-balance depreciation.
(SO 9)

*BE9-13 Depreciation information for Apex Chemicals Company is given in BE9-3. Assuming the declining-balance depreciation rate is double the straight-line rate, compute annual depreciation for the first and second years under the declining-balance method.

Compute depreciation using units-of-activity method.
(SO 9)

*BE9-14 Pack in Taxi Service uses the units-of-activity method in computing depreciation on its taxicabs. Each cab is expected to be driven 150,000 miles. Taxi 10 cost $27,500 and is expected to have a salvage value of $500. Taxi 10 was driven 28,000 miles in 2009 and 30,000 miles in 2010. Compute the depreciation for each year.

Do it! Review

Do it! 9-1 African Lakes Company purchased a delivery truck. The total cash payment was $27,900, including the following items.

Negotiated purchase price	$24,000
Installation of special shelving	1,100
Painting and lettering	900
Motor vehicle license	100
Annual insurance policy	500
Sales tax	1,300
Total paid	$27,900

Explain how each of these costs would be accounted for.

Explain accounting for cost of plant assets
(SO 1)

Do it! 9-2 On January 1, 2010, Pine Grove Country Club purchased a new riding mower for $15,000. The mower is expected to have an 8-year life with a $1,000 salvage value. What journal entry would Pine Grove make at December 31, 2010, if it uses straight-line depreciation?

Calculate depreciation expense and make journal entry.
(SO 2)

Do it! 9-3 Ritenour Manufacturing has an old factory machine that cost $50,000. The machine has accumulated depreciation of $28,000. Ritenour has decided to sell the machine.
(a) What entry would Ritenour make to record the sale of the machine for $26,000 cash?
(b) What entry would Ritenour make to record the sale of the machine for $15,000 cash?

Make journal entries to record plant asset disposal.
(SO 5)

Do it! 9-4 Match the statement with the term most directly associated with it.

Goodwill	Amortization
Intangible assets	Franchise
Research and development costs	

Match intangible assets with concepts.
(SO 7, 8)

1. _____ Rights, privileges, and competitive advantages that result from the ownership of long-lived assets that do not possess physical substance.
2. _____ The allocation of the cost of an intangible asset to expense in a rational and systematic manner.
3. _____ A right to sell certain products or services, or use certain trademarks or trade names within a designated geographic area.
4. _____ Costs incurred by a company that often lead to patents or new products. These costs must be expensed as incurred.
5. _____ The excess of the cost of a company over the fair market value of the net assets required.

Exercises

E9-1 The following expenditures relating to plant assets were made by Bel Air Company during the first 2 months of 2010.
1. Paid $7,000 of accrued taxes at the time the plant site was acquired. ~~debit land~~
2. Paid $200 insurance to cover a possible accident loss on new factory machinery while the machinery was in transit. ~~Debit to factory machinery~~
3. Paid $850 sales taxes on a new delivery truck. ~~Debit delivery truck~~
4. Paid $21,000 for parking lots and driveways on the new plant site. ~~Debit land improvements~~
5. Paid $250 to have the company name and slogan painted on the new delivery truck. ~~Delivery truck~~
6. Paid $8,000 for installation of new factory machinery. ~~debit delivery truck factory machinery~~
7. Paid $900 for a 1-year accident insurance policy on the new delivery truck.
8. Paid $75 motor vehicle license fee on the new truck. ~~license expense~~

Determine cost of plant acquisitions.
(SO 1)

Instructions
(a) Explain the application of the cost principle in determining the acquisition cost of plant assets.
(b) List the numbers of the transactions, and opposite each indicate the account title to which each expenditure should be debited.

Determine property, plant, and equipment costs.

(SO 1)

E9-2 Trudy Company incurred the following costs.

1. Sales tax on factory machinery purchased	$ 5,000
2. Painting of and lettering on truck immediately upon purchase	700
3. Installation and testing of factory machinery	2,000
4. Real estate broker's commission on land purchased	3,500
5. Insurance premium paid for first year's insurance on new truck	880
6. Cost of landscaping on property purchased	7,200
7. Cost of paving parking lot for new building constructed	17,900
8. Cost of clearing, draining, and filling land	13,300
9. Architect's fees on self-constructed building	10,000

Instructions

Indicate to which account Trudy would debit each of the costs.

Determine acquisition costs of land.

(SO 1)

E9-3 On March 1, 2010, Edington Company acquired real estate, on which it planned to construct a small office building, by paying $80,000 in cash. An old warehouse on the property was demolished at a cost of $8,200; the salvaged materials were sold for $1,700. Additional expenditures before construction began included $1,500 attorney's fee for work concerning the land purchase, $5,000 real estate broker's fee, $9,100 architect's fee, and $14,000 to put in driveways and a parking lot.

Instructions

(a) Determine the amount to be reported as the cost of the land.

(b) For each cost not used in part (a), indicate the account to be debited.

Understand depreciation concepts.

(SO 2)

E9-4 Chris Rock has prepared the following list of statements about depreciation.

1. Depreciation is a process of asset valuation, not cost allocation.
2. Depreciation provides for the proper matching of expenses with revenues.
3. The book value of a plant asset should approximate its market value.
4. Depreciation applies to three classes of plant assets: land, buildings, and equipment.
5. Depreciation does not apply to a building because its usefulness and revenue-producing ability generally remain intact over time.
6. The revenue-producing ability of a depreciable asset will decline due to wear and tear and to obsolescence.
7. Recognizing depreciation on an asset results in an accumulation of cash for replacement of the asset.
8. The balance in accumulated depreciation represents the total cost that has been charged to expense.
9. Depreciation expense and accumulated depreciation are reported on the income statement.
10. Four factors affect the computation of depreciation: cost, useful life, salvage value, and residual value.

Instructions

Identify each statement as true or false. If false, indicate how to correct the statement.

Determine straight-line depreciation for partial period.

(SO 3)

E9-5 Downing Company purchased a new machine on September 1, 2010, at a cost of $90,000. The company estimated that the machine has a salvage value of $6,000. The machine is expected to be used for 70,000 working hours during its 8-year life.

Instructions

Compute the depreciation expense under the straight-line method for 2010 and 2011, assuming a December 31 year-end.

Compute revised annual depreciation.

(SO 3,4)

E9-6 Jack Reese, the new controller of Muckenthaler Company, has reviewed the expected useful lives and salvage values of selected depreciable assets at the beginning of 2010. Here are his findings:

Type of Asset	Date Acquired	Cost	Accumulated Depreciation, Jan. 1, 2010	Useful Life (in years) Old	Useful Life (in years) Proposed	Salvage Value Old	Salvage Value Proposed
Building	Jan. 1, 2002	$900,000	$172,000	40	50	$40,000	$35,000
Warehouse	Jan. 1, 2005	120,000	23,000	25	20	5,000	3,600

All assets are depreciated by the straight-line method. Muckenthaler Company uses a calendar year in preparing annual financial statements. After discussion, management has agreed to accept Jack's proposed changes. (The "Proposed" useful life is total life, not remaining life.)

Instructions
(a) Compute the revised annual depreciation on each asset in 2010. (Show computations.)
(b) Prepare the entry (or entries) to record depreciation on the building in 2010.

E9-7 Kobel Co. has delivery equipment that cost $50,000 and has been depreciated $20,000.

Journalize transactions related to disposals of plant assets.
(SO 5)

Instructions
Record entries for the disposal under the following assumptions.
(a) It was scrapped as having no value.
(b) It was sold for $37,000.
(c) It was sold for $18,000.

E9-8 Here are selected 2010 transactions of Falk Corporation.

Record disposal of equipment.
(SO 5)

Jan.	1	Retired a piece of machinery that was purchased on January 1, 2000. The machine cost $62,000 and had a useful life of 10 years with no salvage value.
June	30	Sold a computer that was purchased on January 1, 2008. The computer cost $39,000 and had a useful life of 3 years with no salvage value. The computer was sold for $5,000 cash.
Dec.	31	Sold a delivery truck for $9,000 cash. The truck cost $25,000 when it was purchased on January 1, 2007, and was depreciated based on a 5-year useful life with a $3,000 salvage value.

Instructions
Journalize all entries required on the above dates, including entries to update depreciation on assets disposed of, where applicable. Falk Corporation uses straight-line depreciation.

E9-9 The following situations are independent of one another:
1. An accounting student recently employed by a small company doesn't understand why the company is only depreciating its buildings and equipment, but not its land. The student prepared journal entries to depreciate all the company's property, plant, and equipment for the current year-end.
2. The same student also thinks the company's amortization policy on its intangible assets is wrong. The company is currently amortizing its patents but not its goodwill. The student fixed that for the current year-end by adding goodwill to her adjusting entry for amortization. She told a fellow employee that she felt she had improved the consistency of the company's accounting policies by making these changes.
3. The same company has a building still in use that has a zero book value but a substantial market value. The student felt that this practice didn't benefit the company's users—especially the bank—and wrote the building up to its market value. After all, she reasoned, you can write down assets if market values are lower. Writing them up if market value is higher is yet another example of the improved consistency that she has brought to the company's accounting practices.

Apply accounting concepts.
(SO 1, 2, 6, 7)

Instructions
Explain whether or not the accounting treatment in each of the above situations is in accordance with generally accepted accounting principles. Explain what accounting principle or assumption, if any, has been violated and what the appropriate accounting treatment should be.

E9-10 During 2007 Federal Express reported the following information (in millions): net sales of $35,214 and net income of $2,016. Its balance sheet also showed total assets at the beginning of the year of $22,690 and total assets at the end of the year of $24,000.

Calculate asset turnover ratio and return on assets ratio.
(SO 6)

Instructions
Calculate the (a) asset turnover ratio and (b) return on assets ratio.

E9-11 Myler International is considering a significant expansion to its product line. The sales force is excited about the opportunities that the new products will bring. The new products are a significant step up in quality above the company's current offerings, but offer a complementary fit to its existing product line. Frank Peralta, senior production department manager, is very excited about the high-tech new equipment that will have

Calculate and interpret ratios.
(SO 6)

to be acquired to produce the new products. Carol Herbert, the company's CFO, has provided the following projections based on results with and without the new products.

	Without New Products	With New Products
Sales	$10,000,000	$18,000,000
Net income	$600,000	$1,350,000
Average total assets	$5,000,000	$15,000,000

Instructions

(a) Compute the company's return on assets ratio, profit margin ratio, and asset turnover ratio, both with and without the new product line.

(b) Discuss the implications that your findings in part (a) have for the company's decision.

Calculate and interpret ratios.
(SO 6)

E9-12 Hopson Company reports the following information (in millions) during a recent year: net sales, $11,408.5; net earnings, $244.9; total assets, ending, $4,312.6; and total assets, beginning, $4,254.3.

Instructions

(a) Calculate the (1) return on assets, (2) asset turnover, and (3) profit margin ratios.

(b) Prove mathematically how the profit margin and asset turnover ratios work together to explain return on assets, by showing the appropriate calculation.

(c) Hopson Company owns Villas (grocery), Hopson Theaters, Lawton Drugstores, and Urbin (heavy equipment), and manages commercial real estate, among other activities. Does this diversity of activities affect your ability to interpret the ratios you calculated in (a)? Explain.

Prepare adjusting entries for amortization.
(SO 7)

E9-13 These are selected 2010 transactions for Hammon Corporation:

Jan.   1   Purchased a copyright for $120,000. The copyright has a useful life of 8 years and a remaining legal life of 30 years.

May   1   Purchased a patent with an estimated useful life of 4 years and a legal life of 20 years for $54,000.

Sept.   1   Purchased a small company and recorded goodwill of $150,000. Its useful life is indefinite.

Instructions

Prepare all adjusting entries at December 31 to record amortization required by the events.

Prepare entries to set up appropriate accounts for different intangibles; calculate amortization.
(SO 7)

E9-14 Gladow Company, organized in 2010, has these transactions related to intangible assets in that year:

Jan.   2   Purchased a patent (5-year life) $300,000.

Apr.   1   Goodwill purchased (indefinite life) $360,000.

July   1   Acquired a 9-year franchise; expiration date July 1, 2019, $540,000.

Sept.   1   Research and development costs $185,000.

Instructions

(a) Prepare the necessary entries to record these intangibles. All costs incurred were for cash.

(b) Make the entries as of December 31, 2010, recording any necessary amortization.

(c) Indicate what the balances should be on December 31, 2010.

Discuss implications of amortization period.
(SO 7)

E9-15 Alliance Atlantis Communications Inc. changed its accounting policy to amortize broadcast rights over the contracted exhibition period, which is based on the estimated useful life of the program. Previously, the company amortized broadcast rights over the lesser of 2 years or the contracted exhibition period.

Instructions

▭▬▬▶ Write a short memo to your client explaining the implications this has for the analysis of Alliance Atlantis's results. Also, discuss whether this change in amortization period appears reasonable.

Answer questions on depreciation and intangibles.
(SO 2, 7)

E9-16 The questions listed below are independent of one another.

Instructions

Provide a brief answer to each question.

(a) Why should a company depreciate its buildings?

(b) How can a company have a building that has a zero reported book value but substantial market value?

(c) What are some examples of intangibles that you might find on your college campus?

(d) Give some examples of company or product trademarks or trade names. Are trade names and trademarks reported on a company's balance sheet?

E9-17   Raintree Corporation reported net income of $62,000. Depreciation expense for the year was $134,000. The company calculates depreciation expense using the straight-line method, with an average useful life of 10 years. Top management would like to switch to a 15-year useful life because depreciation expense would be reduced to $88,000. The CEO says, "Increasing the useful life would increase net income and net cash provided by operating activities."

Determine net cash provided by operating activities.
(SO 8)

Instructions
Provide a comparative analysis showing net income and net cash provided by operating activities (ignoring other accrual adjustments) using a 10-year and a 15-year useful life. (Ignore income taxes.) Evaluate the CEO's suggestion.

*E9-18   Jayhawk Bus Lines uses the units-of-activity method in depreciating its buses. One bus was purchased on January 1, 2010, at a cost of $136,000. Over its 4-year useful life, the bus is expected to be driven 160,000 miles. Salvage value is expected to be $8,000.

Compute depreciation under units-of-activity method.
(SO 9)

Instructions
(a) Compute the depreciation cost per unit.
(b) Prepare a depreciation schedule assuming actual mileage was: 2010, 40,000; 2011, 52,000; 2012, 41,000; and 2013, 27,000.

*E9-19   Basic information relating to a new machine purchased by Downing Company is presented in E9-5.

Compute declining-balance and units-of-activity depreciation.
(SO 9)

Instructions
Using the facts presented in E9-5, compute depreciation using the following methods in the year indicated.
(a) Declining-balance using double the straight-line rate for 2010 and 2011.
(b) Units-of-activity for 2010, assuming machine usage was 2,900 hours. (Round depreciation per unit to the nearest cent.)

Exercises: Set B

Visit the book's companion website, at **www.wiley.com/college/kimmel**, and choose the Student Companion site, to access Exercise Set B.

Problems: Set A

P9-1A   Elbert Company was organized on January 1. During the first year of operations, the following plant asset expenditures and receipts were recorded in random order.

Determine acquisition costs of land and building.
(SO 1)

Debits	
1. Cost of real estate purchased as a plant site (land $255,000 and building $25,000)	$ 280,000
2. Installation cost of fences around property	6,800
3. Cost of demolishing building to make land suitable for construction of new building	24,000
4. Excavation costs for new building	23,000
5. Accrued real estate taxes paid at time of purchase of real estate	2,179
6. Cost of parking lots and driveways	29,000
7. Architect's fees on building plans	33,000
8. Real estate taxes paid for the current year on land	5,800
9. Full payment to building contractor	640,000
	$1,043,779

Credits	
10. Proceeds from salvage of demolished building	$ 8,000

Instructions
Analyze the transactions using the following table column headings. Enter the number of each transaction in the Item column, and enter the amounts in the appropriate columns. For amounts in the Other Accounts column, also indicate the account title.

Land $298,179

Item	Land	Building	Other Accounts

Journalize equipment transactions related to purchase, sale, retirement, and depreciation.

(SO 3, 5, 8)

P9-2A At December 31, 2010, Rijo Corporation reported the following plant assets.

Land		$ 3,000,000
Buildings	$26,500,000	
Less: Accumulated depreciation—buildings	12,100,000	14,400,000
Equipment	40,000,000	
Less: Accumulated depreciation—equipment	5,000,000	35,000,000
Total plant assets		$52,400,000

During 2011, the following selected cash transactions occurred.

Apr. 1 Purchased land for $2,200,000.
May 1 Sold equipment that cost $600,000 when purchased on January 1, 2004. The equipment was sold for $170,000.
June 1 Sold land for $1,800,000. The land cost $1,000,000.
July 1 Purchased equipment for $1,300,000.
Dec. 31 Retired equipment that cost $500,000 when purchased on December 31, 2001. No salvage value was received.

Instructions
(a) Journalize the transactions. (*Hint:* You may wish to set up T accounts, post beginning balances, and then post 2011 transactions.) Rijo uses straight-line depreciation for buildings and equipment. The buildings are estimated to have a 40-year useful life and no salvage value; the equipment is estimated to have a 10-year useful life and no salvage value. Update depreciation on assets disposed of at the time of sale or retirement.
(b) Record adjusting entries for depreciation for 2011.

(c) Tot. plant assets $50,052,500

(c) Prepare the plant assets section of Rijo's balance sheet at December 31, 2011.

Journalize entries for disposal of plant assets.

(SO 5)

P9-3A Presented here are selected transactions for Sager Company for 2010.

Jan. 1 Retired a piece of machinery that was purchased on January 1, 2000. The machine cost $71,000 on that date and had a useful life of 10 years with no salvage value.
June 30 Sold a computer that was purchased on January 1, 2007. The computer cost $30,000 and had a useful life of 5 years with no salvage value. The computer was sold for $10,000.
Dec. 31 Discarded a delivery truck that was purchased on January 1, 2005. The truck cost $31,000 and was depreciated based on an 8-year useful life with a $3,000 salvage value.

Instructions
Journalize all entries required on the above dates, including entries to update depreciation, where applicable, on assets disposed of. Sager Company uses straight-line depreciation. (Assume depreciation is up to date as of December 31, 2009.)

Prepare entries to record transactions related to acquisition and amortization of intangibles; prepare the intangible assets section and note.

(SO 7, 8)

P9-4A The intangible assets section of Salmiento Corporation's balance sheet at December 31, 2010, is presented here.

Patents ($60,000 cost less $6,000 amortization)	$54,000
Copyrights ($36,000 cost less $25,200 amortization)	10,800
Total	$64,800

The patent was acquired in January 2010 and has a useful life of 10 years. The copyright was acquired in January 2004 and also has a useful life of 10 years. The following cash transactions may have affected intangible assets during 2011.

Jan. 2 Paid $45,000 legal costs to successfully defend the patent against infringement by another company.
Jan.–June Developed a new product, incurring $210,000 in research and development costs. A patent was granted for the product on July 1, and its useful life is equal to its legal life. Legal and other costs for the patent were $20,000.

Sept. 1 Paid $40,000 to a quarterback to appear in commercials advertising the company's products. The commercials will air in September and October.

Oct. 1 Acquired a copyright for $200,000. The copyright has a useful life and legal life of 50 years.

Instructions

(a) Prepare journal entries to record the transactions.

(b) Prepare journal entries to record the 2011 amortization expense for intangible assets.

(c) Prepare the intangible assets section of the balance sheet at December 31, 2011.

(d) Prepare the note to the financial statements on Salmiento Corporation's intangible assets as of December 31, 2011.

(c) Tot. intangibles $313,700

P9-5A Due to rapid employee turnover in the accounting department, the following transactions involving intangible assets were improperly recorded by Garcia Corporation in 2010.

1. Garcia developed a new manufacturing process, incurring research and development costs of $150,000. The company also purchased a patent for $40,000. In early January Garcia capitalized $190,000 as the cost of the patents. Patent amortization expense of $9,500 was recorded based on a 20-year useful life.

2. On July 1, 2010, Garcia purchased a small company and as a result acquired goodwill of $80,000. Garcia recorded a half-year's amortization in 2010, based on a 40-year life ($1,000 amortization). The goodwill has an indefinite life.

Prepare entries to correct errors in recording and amortizing intangible assets.
(SO 7)

Instructions

Prepare all journal entries necessary to correct any errors made during 2010. Assume the books have not yet been closed for 2010.

P9-6A Titus Corporation and Vane Corporation, two companies of roughly the same size, are both involved in the manufacture of shoe-tracing devices. Each company depreciates its plant assets using the straight-line approach. An investigation of their financial statements reveals the information shown below.

Calculate and comment on return on assets, profit margin, and asset turnover ratio.
(SO 6)

	Titus Corp.	Vane Corp.
Net income	$ 240,000	$ 300,000
Sales	1,250,000	1,200,000
Total assets (average)	3,300,000	3,000,000
Plant assets (average)	2,400,000	1,800,000
Intangible assets (goodwill)	300,000	0

Instructions

(a) For each company, calculate these values:
 (1) Return on assets ratio.
 (2) Profit margin.
 (3) Asset turnover ratio.

(b) Based on your calculations in part (a), comment on the relative effectiveness of the two companies in using their assets to generate sales. What factors complicate your ability to compare the two companies?

*P9-7A In recent years Wang Company has purchased three machines. Because of frequent employee turnover in the accounting department, a different accountant was in charge of selecting the depreciation method for each machine, and various methods have been used. Information concerning the machines is summarized in the table below.

Compute depreciation under different methods.
(SO 3, 9)

Machine	Acquired	Cost	Salvage Value	Useful Life (in years)	Depreciation Method
1	Jan. 1, 2008	$96,000	$ 12,000	6	Straight-line
2	July 1, 2009	85,000	10,000	5	Declining-balance
3	Nov. 1, 2009	66,000	6,000	6	Units-of-activity

For the declining-balance method, Wang Company uses the double-declining rate. For the units-of-activity method, total machine hours are expected to be 24,000. Actual hours of use in the first 3 years were: 2009, 400; 2010, 4,500; and 2011, 5,000.

Instructions

(a) Compute the amount of accumulated depreciation on each machine at December 31, 2011.

(a) Machine 2 $60,520

(b) If machine 2 was purchased on October 1 instead of July 1, what would be the depreciation expense for this machine in 2009? In 2010?

Compute depreciation under different methods.
(SO 3, 9)

*P9-8A Roblez Corporation purchased machinery on January 1, 2010, at a cost of $250,000. The estimated useful life of the machinery is 4 years, with an estimated residual value at the end of that period of $10,000. The company is considering different depreciation methods that could be used for financial reporting purposes.

Instructions

(a) Double-declining-balance expense 2012 $26,250

(a) Prepare separate depreciation schedules for the machinery using the straight-line method, and the declining-balance method using double the straight-line rate. Round to the nearest dollar.

(b) Which method would result in the higher reported 2010 income? In the highest total reported income over the 4-year period?

(c) Which method would result in the lower reported 2010 income? In the lowest total reported income over the 4-year period?

Problems: Set B

Determine acquisition costs of land and building.
(SO 1)

P9-1B Fitch Company was organized on January 1. During the first year of operations, the following plant asset expenditures and receipts were recorded in random order.

Debits

1. Cost of real estate purchased as a plant site (land $180,000 and building $70,000)	$ 250,000
2. Accrued real estate taxes paid at time of purchase of real estate	6,000
3. Cost of demolishing building to make land suitable for construction of new building	32,000
4. Cost of filling and grading the land	7,100
5. Excavation costs for new building	21,900
6. Architect's fees on building plans	40,000
7. Full payment to building contractor	629,500
8. Cost of parking lots and driveways	36,000
9. Real estate taxes paid for the current year on land	7,300
	$1,029,800

Credits

10. Proceeds for salvage of demolished building	$ 12,700

Instructions
Analyze the transactions using the table column headings provided here. Enter the number of each transaction in the Item column, and enter the amounts in the appropriate columns. For amounts in the Other Accounts column, also indicate the account titles.

Land $282,400

Item	Land	Building	Other Accounts

Journalize equipment transactions related to purchase, sale, retirement, and depreciation.
(SO 3, 5, 8)

P9-2B At December 31, 2010, Kretsinger Corporation reported these plant assets.

Land		$ 4,000,000
Buildings	$28,500,000	
Less: Accumulated depreciation—buildings	12,100,000	16,400,000
Equipment	48,000,000	
Less: Accumulated depreciation—equipment	5,000,000	43,000,000
Total plant assets		$63,400,000

During 2011, the following selected cash transactions occurred.

Apr.	1	Purchased land for $2,630,000.
May	1	Sold equipment that cost $750,000 when purchased on January 1, 2006. The equipment was sold for $370,000.
June	1	Sold land purchased on June 1, 1998, for $1,800,000. The land cost $800,000.
July	1	Purchased equipment for $800,000.
Dec.	31	Retired fully depreciated equipment that cost $470,000 when purchased on December 31, 2001. No salvage value was received.

Instructions

(a) Journalize the transactions. (*Hint:* You may wish to set up T accounts, post beginning balances, and then post 2011 transactions.) Kretsinger uses straight-line depreciation for buildings and equipment. The buildings are estimated to have a 40-year life and no salvage value; the equipment is estimated to have a 10-year useful life and no salvage value. Update depreciation on assets disposed of at the time of sale or retirement.

(b) Record adjusting entries for depreciation for 2011. (*Note:* The only assets that are fully depreciated are those that were retired on December 31.)

(c) Prepare the plant assets section of Kretsinger's balance sheet at December 31, 2011.

(c) Tot. plant assets $60,177,500

Journalize entries for disposal of plant assets.
(SO 5)

P9-3B   Here are selected transactions for Cagle Corporation for 2010.

Jan.   1   Retired a piece of machinery that was purchased on January 1, 2000. The machine cost $52,000 and had a useful life of 10 years with no salvage value.

June   30   Sold a computer that was purchased on January 1, 2007. The computer cost $42,000 and had a useful life of 7 years with no salvage value. The computer was sold for $23,000.

Dec.   31   Discarded a delivery truck that was purchased on January 1, 2007. The truck cost $30,000 and was depreciated based on a 6-year useful life with a $3,000 salvage value.

Instructions

Journalize all entries required on the above dates, including entries to update depreciation on assets disposed of, where applicable. Cagle Corporation uses straight-line depreciation.

P9-4B   The intangible assets section of the balance sheet for Gore Company at December 31, 2010, is presented here.

Patents ($70,000 cost less $7,000 amortization)	$63,000
Copyrights ($48,000 cost less $18,000 amortization)	30,000
Total	$93,000

Prepare entries to record transactions related to acquisition and amortization of intangibles; prepare the intangible assets section and note.
(SO 7, 8)

The patent was acquired in January 2010 and has a useful life of 10 years. The copyright was acquired in January 2008 and also has a useful life of 8 years. The following cash transactions may have affected intangible assets during 2011.

Jan.   2   Paid $27,000 legal costs to successfully defend the patent against infringement by another company.

Jan.–June   Developed a new product, incurring $220,000 in research and development costs. A patent was granted for the product on July 1, and its useful life is equal to its legal life. Legal and other costs for the patent were $12,000.

Sept.   1   Paid $110,000 to an extremely large defensive lineman to appear in commercials advertising the company's products. The commercials will air in September and October.

Oct.   1   Acquired a copyright for $120,000. The copyright has a useful life and legal life of 50 years.

Instructions

(a) Prepare journal entries to record the transactions.
(b) Prepare journal entries to record the 2011 amortization expense.
(c) Prepare the intangible assets section of the balance sheet at December 31, 2011.

(c) Tot. intangibles $235,100

(d) Prepare the note to the financial statements on Gore Company's intangible assets as of December 31, 2011.

P9-5B   Due to rapid employee turnover in the accounting department, the following transactions involving intangible assets were improperly recorded by the Hamlin Company in 2010.

Prepare entries to correct errors in recording and amortizing intangible assets.
(SO 7)

1. Hamlin developed a new manufacturing process, incurring research and development costs of $120,000. The company also purchased a patent for $96,000. In early January Hamlin capitalized $216,000 as the cost of the patents. Patent amortization expense of $18,000 was recorded based on a 12-year useful life.

2. On July 1, 2010, Hamlin purchased a small company and as a result acquired goodwill of $40,000. Hamlin recorded a half-year's amortization in 2010 based on a 40-year life ($500 amortization). The goodwill has an indefinite life.

Calculate and comment on return on assets, profit margin, and asset turnover ratio.

(SO 6)

Instructions

Prepare all journal entries necessary to correct any errors made during 2010. Assume the books have not yet been closed for 2010.

P9-6B Riverton Corporation and Salina Corporation, two corporations of roughly the same size, are both involved in the manufacture of umbrellas. Each company depreciates its plant assets using the straight-line approach. An investigation of their financial statements reveals the following information.

	Riverton Corp.	Salina Corp.
Net income	$ 800,000	$ 900,000
Sales	2,400,000	2,500,000
Total assets (average)	3,000,000	2,700,000
Plant assets (average)	1,400,000	1,200,000
Intangible assets (goodwill)	450,000	0

Instructions

(a) For each company, calculate these values:
   (1) Return on assets ratio.
   (2) Profit margin.
   (3) Asset turnover ratio.
(b) ▭▭▭▭▷ Based on your calculations in part (a), comment on the relative effectiveness of the two companies in using their assets to generate sales. What factors complicate your ability to compare the two companies?

Compute depreciation under different methods.

(SO 3, 9)

*P9-7B In recent years Dobbs Transportation purchased three used buses. Because of frequent employee turnover in the accounting department, a different accountant selected the depreciation method for each bus, and various methods have been used. Information concerning the buses is summarized in the table below.

Bus	Acquired	Cost	Salvage Value	Useful Life (in years)	Depreciation Method
1	Jan. 1, 2009	$ 96,000	$ 6,000	4	Straight-line
2	Jan. 1, 2009	135,000	10,000	4	Declining-balance
3	Jan. 1, 2009	100,000	9,000	5	Units-of-activity

For the declining-balance method, Dobbs Transportation uses the double-declining rate. For the units-of-activity method, total miles are expected to be 140,000. Actual miles of use in the first 3 years were: 2009, 26,000; 2010, 34,000; and 2011, 30,000.

(a) Bus 1 $67,500

Instructions

(a) Compute the amount of accumulated depreciation on each bus at December 31, 2011.
(b) If Bus 2 was purchased on March 1 instead of January 1, what would be the depreciation expense for this bus in 2009? In 2010?

Compute depreciation under different methods.

(SO 3, 9)

*P9-8B Navarro Corporation purchased machinery on January 1, 2010, at a cost of $330,000. The estimated useful life of the machinery is 5 years, with an estimated salvage value at the end of that period of $30,000. The company is considering different depreciation methods that could be used for financial reporting purposes.

(a) Double-declining-balance exp. 2011 $79,200

Instructions

(a) Prepare separate depreciation schedules for the machinery using the straight-line method, and the declining-balance method using double the straight-line rate.
(b) Which method would result in the higher reported 2010 income? In the higher total reported income over the 5-year period?
(c) Which method would result in the lower reported 2010 income? In the lower total reported income over the 5-year period?

Problems: Set C

Visit the book's companion website at **www.wiley.com/college/kimmel** and choose the Student Companion site to access Problem Set C.

Comprehensive Problem

CP9 Pinkerton Corporation's trial balance at December 31, 2010, is presented below. All 2010 transactions have been recorded except for the items described after the trial balance.

	Debit	Credit
Cash	$ 28,000	
Accounts Receivable	36,800	
Notes Receivable	10,000	
Interest Receivable	–0–	
Merchandise Inventory	36,200	
Prepaid Insurance	3,600	
Land	20,000	
Building	150,000	
Equipment	60,000	
Patent	9,000	
Allowance for Doubtful Accounts		$ 500
Accumulated Depreciation—Building		50,000
Accumulated Depreciation—Equipment		24,000
Accounts Payable		27,300
Salaries Payable		–0–
Unearned Rent		6,000
Notes Payable (short-term)		11,000
Interest Payable		–0–
Notes Payable (long-term)		35,000
Common Stock		50,000
Retained Earnings		63,600
Dividends	12,000	
Sales		900,000
Interest Revenue		–0–
Rent Revenue		–0–
Gain on Disposal		–0–
Bad Debts Expense	–0–	
Cost of Goods Sold	630,000	
Depreciation Expense—Buildings	–0–	
Depreciation Expense—Equipment	–0–	
Insurance Expense	–0–	
Interest Expense	–0–	
Other Operating Expenses	61,800	
Amortization Expense—Patents	–0–	
Salaries Expense	110,000	
Total	$1,167,400	$1,167,400

Unrecorded transactions

1. On May 1, 2010, Pinkerton purchased equipment for $16,000 plus sales taxes of $800 (all paid in cash).
2. On July 1, 2010, Pinkerton sold for $3,500 equipment which originally cost $5,000. Accumulated depreciation on this equipment at January 1, 2010, was $1,800; 2010 depreciation prior to the sale of equipment was $450.
3. On December 31, 2010, Pinkerton sold for $5,000 on account inventory that cost $3,500.
4. Pinkerton estimates that uncollectible accounts receivable at year-end are $4,000.
5. The note receivable is a one-year, 8% note dated April 1, 2010. No interest has been recorded.
6. The balance in prepaid insurance represents payment of a $3,600, 6-month premium on September 1, 2010.
7. The building is being depreciated using the straight-line method over 30 years. The salvage value is $30,000.
8. The equipment owned prior to this year is being depreciated using the straight-line method over 5 years. The salvage value is 10% of cost.

9. The equipment purchased on May 1, 2010, is being depreciated using the straight-line method over 5 years, with a salvage value of $1,800.
10. The patent was acquired on January 1, 2010, and has a useful life of 9 years from that date.
11. Unpaid salaries at December 31, 2010, total $2,200.
12. The unearned rent of $6,000 was received on December 1, 2010, for 3 months rent.
13. Both the short-term and long-term notes payable are dated January 1, 2010, and carry a 10% interest rate. All interest is payable in the next 12 months.
14. Income tax expense was $15,000. It was unpaid at December 31.

Instructions
(a) Prepare journal entries for the transactions listed above.
(b) Prepare an updated December 31, 2010, trial balance.
(c) Prepare a 2010 income statement and a 2010 retained earnings statement.
(d) Prepare a December 31, 2010, balance sheet.

(b) Totals $1,213,150
(c) Net income $58,000
(d) Total assets $258,700

Continuing Cookie Chronicle

(*Note:* This is a continuation of the Cookie Chronicle from Chapters 1 through 8.)

CCC9

Part 1   Now that she is selling mixers and her customers can use credit cards to pay for them, Natalie is thinking of upgrading her website so that she can sell mixers online, to broaden her range of customers. She will need to known how to account for the costs of upgrading the site.

Part 2   Natalie is also thinking of buying a van that will be used only for business. Natalie is concerned about the impact of the van's cost on her income statement and balance sheet. She has come to you advice on calculating the van's depreciation.

Go to the book's companion website. **www.wiley.com/college/kimmel**, to see the completion of this problem.

broadening your perspective

Financial Reporting and Analysis

FINANCIAL REPORTING PROBLEM: *Tootsie Roll Industries, Inc.*

BYP9-1   Refer to the financial statements and the Notes to Consolidated Financial Statements of Tootsie Roll Industries in Appendix A.

Instructions
Answer the following questions.
(a) What were the total cost and book value of property, plant, and equipment at December 31, 2007?
(b) What method or methods of depreciation are used by Tootsie Roll for financial reporting purposes?
(c) What was the amount of depreciation and amortization expense for each of the 3 years 2005–2007? (Hint: Use statement of cash flows.)
(d) Using the statement of cash flows, what are the amounts of property, plant, and equipment purchased (capital expenditures) in 2007 and 2006?
(e) Explain how Tootsie Roll accounted for its intangible assets in 2007.

COMPARATIVE ANALYSIS PROBLEM: *Tootsie Roll vs. Hershey Foods*

BYP9-2   The financial statements of Hershey Foods are presented in Appendix B, following the financial statements for Tootsie Roll Industries in Appendix A.

Instructions
(a) Based on the information in these financial statements and the accompanying notes and schedules, compute the following values for each company in 2007.
   (1) Return on assets ratio.
   (2) Profit margin.
   (3) Asset turnover ratio.
(b) What conclusions concerning the management of plant assets can be drawn from these data?

RESEARCH CASE

BYP9-3   The September 9, 2007, issue of the *New York Times* includes an article by Denise Caruso titled "When Balance Sheets Collide with the New Economy."

Instructions
Read the article and answer the following questions.
(a) What are some examples of "valuable assets" that the article says currently do not have a home on the balance sheet?
(b) What examples does the company give of the value of reputation and how it can affect a stock price?
(c) What justification does the article give for having companies report on their environmental and social responsibility, and their strategy for dealing with disasters?
(d) Are any initiatives currently being used that try to account for intangible assets that do not currently show up on the balance sheet?

INTERPRETING FINANCIAL STATEMENTS

BYP9-4   Bob Evans Farms, Inc. operates 579 restaurants in 18 states and produces fresh and fully cooked sausage products, fresh salads, and related products distributed to grocery stores in the Midwest, Southwest, and Southeast. For a recent 3-year period Bob Evans Farms reported the following selected income statement data (in millions of dollars).

	2007	2006	2005
Sales	$1,654.5	$1,584.8	$1,460.2
Cost of goods sold	482.1	469.7	443.2
Net income	60.5	54.8	37.0
Total assets	1,197.0	1,185.1	1,150.9

Instructions
(a) Compute the percentage change in sales and in net income from 2005 to 2007.
(b) What contribution, if any, did the company's gross profit rate make to the decline in earnings?
(c) What was Bob Evans's profit margin ratio in each of the 3 years? Comment on any trend in this percentage.
(d) The chief executive officer's letter stated that the company continued to invest prudently in restaurants, opening 10 new restaurants in 2007, compared to 20 openings in 2006. What effect would you expect this change to have on return on assets? Calculate the company's return on assets for 2006 and 2007 to see if it reflects the increase in number of stores.

BYP9-5   The accounting for goodwill differs in countries around the world. The discussion of a change in goodwill accounting practices shown below was taken from the notes to the financial statements of J Sainsbury Plc, one of the world's leading retailers. Headquartered in the United Kingdom, it serves 11 million customers a week.

J SAINSBURY PLC
Notes to the Financial Statements

Accounting Policies   Goodwill arising in connection with the acquisition of shares in subsidiaries and associated undertakings is calculated as the excess of the purchase price over the fair value of the net tangible assets acquired. In prior years goodwill has been deducted from reserves in the period of acquisition. FRS 10 is applicable in the current financial year, and in accordance with the standard acquired goodwill is now shown as an asset on the Group's Balance Sheet. As permitted by FRS 10, goodwill written off to reserves in prior periods has not been restated as an asset.

  Goodwill is treated as having an indefinite economic life where it is considered that the acquired business has strong customer loyalty built up over a long period of time, based on advantageous store locations and a commitment to maintain the marketing advantage of the retail brand. The carrying value of the goodwill will be reviewed annually for impairment and adjusted to its recoverable amount if required. Where goodwill is considered to have a finite life, amortisation will be applied over that period.

  For amounts stated as goodwill which are considered to have indefinite life, no amortisation is charged to the Profit and Loss Account.

Instructions
Answer the following questions.
(a) How does the initial determination and recording of goodwill compare with that in the United States? That is, is goodwill initially recorded in the same circumstances, and is the calculation of the amount the same in both the United Kingdom and the United States?
(b) Prior to adoption of the new accounting standard (*FRS 10*), how did the company account for goodwill? What were the implications for the income statement?
(c) Under the new accounting standard, how does the company account for its goodwill? Is it possible, under the new standard, for a company to avoid charging goodwill amortization to net income?
(d) In what ways is the new standard similar to U.S. standards, and in what ways is it different?

FINANCIAL ANALYSIS ON THE WEB

BYP9-6   *Purpose:* Use an annual report to identify a company's plant assets and the depreciation method used.

Address: **www.annualreports.com**, or go to **www.wiley.com/college/kimmel**

Steps
  1. Select a particular company.
  2. Search by company name.
  3. Follow instructions below.

Instructions
Answer the following questions.
(a) What is the name of the company?
(b) What is the Internet address of the annual report?
(c) At fiscal year-end, what is the net amount of its plant assets?
(d) What is the accumulated depreciation?
(e) Which method of depreciation does the company use?

Critical Thinking

DECISION MAKING ACROSS THE ORGANIZATION

BYP9-7 Percival Furniture Corp. is nationally recognized for making high-quality products. Management is concerned that it is not fully exploiting its brand power. Percival's production managers are also concerned because their plants are not operating at anywhere near full capacity. Management is currently considering a proposal to offer a new line of affordable furniture.

Those in favor of the proposal (including the vice president of production) believe that, by offering these new products, the company could attract a clientele that it is not currently servicing. Also, it could operate its plants at full capacity, thus taking better advantage of its assets.

The vice president of marketing, however, believes that the lower-priced (and lower-margin) product would have a negative impact on the sales of existing products. The vice president believes that $10,000,000 of the sales of the new product will be from customers that would have purchased the more expensive product, but switched to the lower-margin product because it was available. (This is often referred to as cannibalization of existing sales). Top management feels, however, that even with cannibalization, the company's sales will increase and the company will be better off.

The following data are available.

(in thousands)	Current results	Proposed results without cannibalization	Proposed results with cannibalization
Sales	$45,000	$60,000	$50,000
Net income	$12,000	$13,500	$12,000
Average total assets	$100,000	$100,000	$100,000

Instructions

(a) Compute Percival's return on assets ratio, profit margin ratio, and asset turnover ratio, both with and without the new product line.
(b) Discuss the implications that your findings in part (a) have for Percival's decision.
(c) Are there any other options that Percival should consider? What impact would each of these have on the above ratios?

COMMUNICATION ACTIVITY

BYP9-8 The chapter presented some concerns regarding the current accounting standards for research and development expenditures.

Instructions

Assume that you are either (a) the president of a company that is very dependent on ongoing research and development, writing a memo to the FASB complaining about the current accounting standards regarding research and development, or (b) the FASB member defending the current standards regarding research and development. Your memo should address the questions shown below.
1. By requiring expensing of R&D, do you think companies will spend less on R&D? Why or why not? What are the possible implications for the competitiveness of U.S. companies?
2. If a company makes a commitment to spend money for R&D, it must believe it has future benefits. Shouldn't these costs therefore be capitalized just like the purchase of any long-lived asset that you believe will have future benefits?

ETHICS CASE

BYP9-9 Clean Air Anti-Pollution Company is suffering declining sales of its principal product, nonbiodegradable plastic cartons. The president, Danny Fort, instructs his controller, Steve Penny, to lengthen asset lives to reduce depreciation expense. A processing line of automated plastic extruding equipment, purchased for $3.5 million in January 2009, was originally estimated to have a useful life of 8 years and a salvage value of $400,000. Depreciation has been recorded for 2 years on that basis. Danny wants the estimated life changed to 12 years total and the straight-line method continued. Steve is hesitant to make the change, believing it is unethical to increase net income in this manner. Danny says, "Hey, the life is only an estimate, and I've heard that our competition uses a 12-year life on their production equipment."

Instructions

(a) Who are the stakeholders in this situation?

(b) Is the proposed change in asset life unethical, or is it simply a good business practice by an astute president?

(c) What is the effect of Danny's proposed change on income before taxes in the year of change?

"ALL ABOUT YOU" ACTIVITY

BYP9-10   A company's tradename is a very important asset to the company, as it creates immediate product identification. Companies invest substantial sums to ensure that their product is well-known to the consumer. Test your knowledge of who owns some famous brands and their impact on the financial statements.

Instructions

(a) Provide an answer to the five multiple-choice questions below.

   (1) Which company owns both Taco Bell and Pizza Hut?
       (a) McDonald's.
       (b) CKE.
       (c) Yum Brands.
       (d) Wendy's.
   (2) Dairy Queen belongs to:
       (a) Breyer.
       (b) Berkshire Hathaway.
       (c) GE.
       (d) The Coca-Cola Company.
   (3) Phillip Morris, the cigarette maker, is owned by:
       (a) Altria.
       (b) GE.
       (c) Boeing.
       (d) ExxonMobil.
   (4) AOL, a major Internet provider, belongs to:
       (a) Microsoft.
       (b) Cisco.
       (c) NBC.
       (d) Time Warner.
   (5) ESPN, the sports broadcasting network, is owned by:
       (a) Procter & Gamble.
       (b) Altria.
       (c) Walt Disney.
       (d) The Coca-Cola Company.

(b) How do you think the value of these brands is reported on the appropriate company's balance sheet?

? *Answers to Insight and Accounting Across the Organization Questions*

p. 438

Q: Why might airline managers choose to lease rather than purchase their planes?

A: The reasons for leasing include favorable tax treatment, better financing options, increased flexibility, reduced risk of obsolescence, and low airline income.

p. 449

Q: How does measuring marketing ROI support the overall efforts of the organization?

A: Top management is ultimately concerned about maximizing the company's return on assets. Holding marketing managers accountable for the marketing ROI will contribute to the company's overall goal of maximizing return on assets.

p. 455

Q: How should ESPN account for the $1.1 billion per year franchise fee?

A: Since this is an annual franchise fee, ESPN should expense it each year, rather than capitalizing and amortizing it.

p. 456

Q: Do you think that this treatment would be allowed under U.S. GAAP?

A: The write-down of assets would have been allowed if it could be shown that the assets had declined in value (an impairment). However, the creation of goodwill to offset the write-down would not have been allowed. Goodwill can be recorded only when it results from the acquisition of a business. It cannot be recorded as the result of being created internally.

Answers to Self-Study Questions

1. d 2. a 3. b 4. d 5. c 6. b 7. d 8. d 9. a 10. d 11. c 12. b 13. c 14. c 15. d *16. d

✔ Remember to go back to the navigator box on the chapter-opening page and check off your completed work.

Reporting and Analyzing Liabilities

study objectives

After studying this chapter, you should be able to:

1 Explain a current liability and identify the major types of current liabilities.

2 Describe the accounting for notes payable.

3 Explain the accounting for other current liabilities.

4 Identify the types of bonds.

5 Prepare the entries for the issuance of bonds and interest expense.

6 Describe the entries when bonds are redeemed.

7 Identify the requirements for the financial statement presentation and analysis of liabilities.

And Then There Were Two

Debt can help a company acquire the things it needs to grow, but it is often the very thing that kills a company. A brief history of Maxwell Car Company illustrates the role of debt in the U.S. auto industry. In 1920 Maxwell Car Company was on the brink of financial ruin. Because it was axle-deep in debt and unable to pay its bills, its creditors stepped in and took over. They hired a former General Motors executive named Walter Chrysler to reorganize the company. By 1925 he had taken over the company and renamed it Chrysler. By 1933 Chrysler was booming, with sales surpassing even those of Ford.

But the next few decades saw Chrysler make a series of blunders. During the 1940s, while its competitors were making yearly design changes to boost customer interest, Chrysler made no changes. During the 1960s, when customers wanted large cars, Chrysler produced small cars. During the 1970s, when customers wanted small cars, Chrysler offered big "boats." By 1980, with its creditors pounding at the gates, Chrysler was again on the brink of financial ruin.

At that point Chrysler brought in a former Ford executive named Lee Iacocca to save the company. Iacocca, considered by many as good a politician as a businessman, argued that the United States could not afford to let Chrysler fail because of the loss of jobs. He convinced the federal government to grant loan guarantees—promises that if Chrysler failed to pay its creditors, the government would pay them. Iacocca then streamlined operations and brought out some profitable products. Chrysler repaid all of its government-guaranteed loans by 1983, seven years ahead of the scheduled final payment.

What has happened since? In the 1990s Chrysler knew both feast and famine: In 1991 it operated in the red, with Iacocca leaving the company under pressure in 1992. By 1995 Chrysler was the most profitable U.S.-based car manufacturer and the envy of the entire industry.

However, to compete in today's global vehicle market, you must be big—really big. So in 1998 Chrysler merged with German automaker Daimler-Benz, to form DaimlerChrysler.

For a time this left just two U.S.-based auto manufacturers—General Motors and Ford. But in 2007 DaimlerChrysler sold 81% of Chrysler to Cerberus, an investment group. In the previous year, GM had sold 51% of its finance division, GMAC, to Cerberus. These transactions were done to provide much-needed cash infusions to the automakers. Whether it was enough to solve the companies' financial problems remains to be seen.

These companies are giants. General Motors and Ford typically rank among the top five U.S. firms in total assets. But General Motors and Ford have accumulated a truckload of debt on their way to getting this big. Combined, they have approximately $460 billion in total outstanding liabilities. Although debt has made it possible to get so big, the Chrysler story makes it clear that debt can also threaten a company's survival.

On the World Wide Web
Chrysler: www.chrysler.com
Ford: www.ford.com
General Motors: www.gm.com

The Feature Story suggests that General Motors and Ford have tremendous amounts of debt. It is unlikely that they could have grown so large without this debt, but at times the debt threatens their very existence. Given this risk, why do companies borrow money? Why do they sometimes borrow short-term and other times long-term? Besides bank borrowings, what other kinds of debts do companies incur? In this chapter we address these issues.

The content and organization of the chapter are as follows.

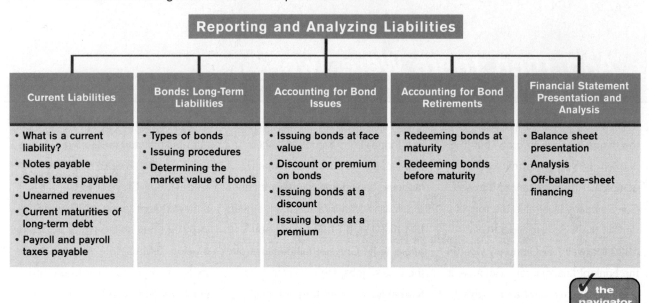

Reporting and Analyzing Liabilities				
Current Liabilities	**Bonds: Long-Term Liabilities**	**Accounting for Bond Issues**	**Accounting for Bond Retirements**	**Financial Statement Presentation and Analysis**
• What is a current liability? • Notes payable • Sales taxes payable • Unearned revenues • Current maturities of long-term debt • Payroll and payroll taxes payable	• Types of bonds • Issuing procedures • Determining the market value of bonds	• Issuing bonds at face value • Discount or premium on bonds • Issuing bonds at a discount • Issuing bonds at a premium	• Redeeming bonds at maturity • Redeeming bonds before maturity	• Balance sheet presentation • Analysis • Off-balance-sheet financing

the navigator

Current Liabilities

WHAT IS A CURRENT LIABILITY?

study objective 1

Explain a current liability and identify the major types of current liabilities.

You have learned that liabilities are defined as "creditors' claims on total assets" and as "existing debts and obligations." Companies must settle or pay these claims, debts, and obligations at some time in the future by transferring assets or services. The future date on which they are due or payable (the maturity date) is a significant feature of liabilities.

As explained in Chapter 2, a **current liability** is a debt that a company reasonably expects to pay (1) from existing current assets or through the creation of other current liabilities, and (2) within one year or the operating cycle, whichever is longer. Debts that do not meet both criteria are **long-term liabilities**.

Financial statement users want to know whether a company's obligations are current or long-term. A company that has more current liabilities than current assets often lacks liquidity, or short-term debt-paying ability. In addition, users want to know the types of liabilities a company has. If a company declares bankruptcy, a specific, predetermined order of payment to creditors exists. Thus, the amount and type of liabilities are of critical importance.

Helpful Hint In previous chapters we explained the entries for accounts payable and the adjusting entries for some current liabilities.

The different types of current liabilities include notes payable, accounts payable, unearned revenues, and accrued liabilities such as taxes, salaries and wages, and interest. In the sections that follow, we discuss a few of the common and more important types of current liabilities.

NOTES PAYABLE

study objective 2

Describe the accounting for notes payable.

Companies record obligations in the form of written notes as **notes payable**. They often use notes payable instead of accounts payable because notes payable give the lender written documentation of the obligation in case legal remedies are needed to collect the debt. Companies frequently issue notes payable to meet short-term financing needs. Notes payable usually require the borrower to pay interest.

Notes are issued for varying periods of time. **Those due for payment within one year of the balance sheet date are usually classified as current liabilities.** Most notes are interest-bearing.

To illustrate the accounting for notes payable, assume that First National Bank agrees to lend $100,000 on September 1, 2010, if Cole Williams Co. signs a $100,000, 12%, four-month note maturing on January 1. When a company issues an interest-bearing note, the amount of assets it receives generally equals the note's face value. Cole Williams Co. therefore will receive $100,000 cash and will make the following journal entry.

Sept. 1	Cash	100,000	
	Notes Payable		100,000
	(To record issuance of 12%, 4-month note to First National Bank)		

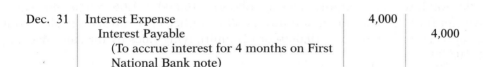

Interest accrues over the life of the note, and the issuer must periodically record that accrual. (You may find it helpful to review the discussion of interest computations that was provided in Chapter 8, page 395, with regard to notes receivable.) If Cole Williams Co. prepares financial statements annually, it makes an adjusting entry at December 31 to recognize four months of interest expense and interest payable of $4,000 ($100,000 × 12% × $\frac{4}{12}$):

Dec. 31	Interest Expense	4,000	
	Interest Payable		4,000
	(To accrue interest for 4 months on First National Bank note)		

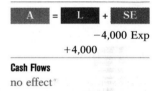

In the December 31 financial statements, the current liabilities section of the balance sheet will show notes payable $100,000 and interest payable $4,000. In addition, the company will report interest expense of $4,000 under "Other expenses and losses" in the income statement.

At maturity (January 1), Cole Williams Co. must pay the face value of the note ($100,000) plus $4,000 interest ($100,000 × 12% × $\frac{4}{12}$). It records payment of the note and accrued interest as follows.

Jan. 1	Notes Payable	100,000	
	Interest Payable	4,000	
	Cash		104,000
	(To record payment of First National Bank interest-bearing note and accrued interest at maturity)		

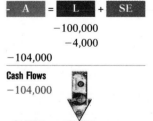

Appendix 10C at the end of this chapter discusses the accounting for long-term installment notes payable.

SALES TAXES PAYABLE

Many of the products we purchase at retail stores are subject to sales taxes. Many states are now implementing sales taxes on purchases made on the Internet as

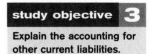

study objective 3

Explain the accounting for other current liabilities.

well. Sales taxes are expressed as a percentage of the sales price. The selling company collects the tax from the customer when the sale occurs and periodically (usually monthly) remits the collections to the state's department of revenue.

Under most state laws, the selling company must ring up separately on the cash register the amount of the sale and the amount of the sales tax collected. (Gasoline sales are a major exception.) The company then uses the cash register readings to credit Sales and Sales Taxes Payable. For example, if the March 25 cash register readings for Cooley Grocery show sales of $10,000 and sales taxes of $600 (sales tax rate of 6%), the journal entry is:

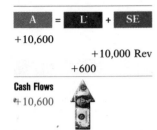

+10,600

   +10,000 Rev
  +600

Cash Flows
+10,600

Mar. 25	Cash	10,600	
	Sales		10,000
	Sales Taxes Payable		600
	(To record daily sales and sales taxes)		

When the company remits the taxes to the taxing agency, it decreases (debits) Sales Taxes Payable and decreases (credits) Cash. The company does not report sales taxes as an expense; it simply forwards to the government the amount paid by the customer. Thus, Cooley Grocery serves only as a **collection agent** for the taxing authority.

Sometimes companies do not ring up sales taxes separately on the cash register. To determine the amount of sales in such cases, divide total receipts by 100% plus the sales tax percentage. For example, assume that Cooley Grocery rings up total receipts of $10,600. Because the amount received from the sale is equal to the sales price 100% plus 6% of sales, or 1.06 times the sales total, we can compute sales as follows: $10,600 ÷ 1.06 = $10,000. Thus, we can find the sales tax amount of $600 by either (1) subtracting sales from total receipts ($10,600 − $10,000) or (2) multiplying sales by the sales tax rate ($10,000 × 6%).

UNEARNED REVENUES

A magazine publisher such as Sports Illustrated may receive a customer's check when magazines are ordered. An airline company such as American Airlines often receives cash when it sells tickets for future flights. Season tickets for concerts, sporting events, and theatre programs are also paid for in advance. How do companies account for unearned revenues that are received before goods are delivered or services are provided?

1. When the company receives an advance, it increases (debits) Cash and also increases (credits) a current liability account identifying the source of the unearned revenue.

2. When the company earns the revenue, it decreases (debits) the unearned revenue account and increases (credits) an earned revenue account.

To illustrate, assume that Superior University sells 10,000 season football tickets at $50 each for its five-game home schedule. The entry is:

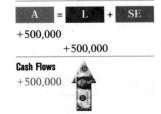

+500,000
  +500,000

Cash Flows
+500,000

Aug. 6	Cash	500,000	
	Unearned Football Ticket Revenue		500,000
	(To record sale of 10,000 season tickets)		

As each game is completed, Superior records the earning of revenue with the following entry.

Helpful Hint Watch how sales are rung up at local retailers to see whether the sales tax is computed separately.

Sept. 7	Unearned Football Ticket Revenue	100,000		
	Football Ticket Revenue		100,000	
	(To record football ticket revenues earned)			

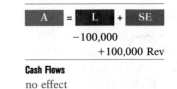

A = L + SE

−100,000

+100,000 Rev

Cash Flows
no effect

The account Unearned Football Ticket Revenue represents unearned revenue, and the university would report it as a current liability. As the school earns the revenue, it reclassifies the amount from unearned revenue to earned revenue. Unearned revenue is material for some companies: In the airline industry, tickets sold for future flights represent almost 50% of total current liabilities. At United Airlines, unearned ticket revenue recently was the largest current liability, amounting to more than $1 billion.

Illustration 10-1 shows specific unearned and earned revenue accounts used in selected types of businesses.

Type of Business	Account Title	
	Unearned Revenue	**Earned Revenue**
Airline	Unearned Passenger Ticket Revenue	Passenger Ticket Revenue
Magazine publisher	Unearned Subscription Revenue	Subscription Revenue
Hotel	Unearned Rental Revenue	Rental Revenue

Illustration 10-1
Unearned and earned revenue accounts

CURRENT MATURITIES OF LONG-TERM DEBT

Companies often have a portion of long-term debt that comes due in the current year. As an example, assume that Wendy Construction issues a five-year, interest-bearing $25,000 note on January 1, 2009. This note specifies that each January 1, starting January 1, 2010, Wendy should pay $5,000 of the note. When the company prepares financial statements on December 31, 2009, it should report $5,000 as a current liability and $20,000 as a long-term liability. Companies often identify current maturities of long-term debt on the balance sheet as **long-term debt due within one year**. At December 31, 2007, General Motors had $1,893 million of such debt.

It is not necessary to prepare an adjusting entry to recognize the current maturity of long-term debt. At the balance sheet date, all obligations due within one year are classified as current, and all other obligations are classified as long-term.

before you go on...

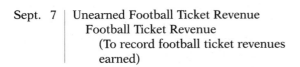 You and several classmates are studying for the next accounting examination. They ask you to answer the following questions.

1. If cash is borrowed on a $50,000, 6-month, 12% note on September 1, how much interest expense would be incurred by December 31?
2. How is the sales tax amount determined when the cash register total includes sales taxes?
3. If $15,000 is collected in advance on November 1 for 3-months' rent, what amount of rent revenue is earned by December 31?

CURRENT LIABILITIES

Action Plan

• Use the interest formula: Face value of note × Annual interest rate × Time in terms of one year.

Action Plan (cont.)	Solution
• Divide total receipts by 100% plus the tax rate to determine sales; then subtract sales from the total receipts. • Determine what fraction of the total unearned rent was earned this year.	1. $\$50,000 \times 12\% \times 4/12 = \$2,000$ 2. First, divide the total cash register receipts by 100% plus the sales tax percentage to find the sales amount. Second, subtract the sales amount from the total cash register receipts to determine the sales taxes. 3. $\$15,000 \times 2/3 = \$10,000$

PAYROLL AND PAYROLL TAXES PAYABLE

Assume that Susan Alena works 40 hours this week for Pepitone Inc., earning a wage of $10 per hour. Will Susan receive a $400 check at the end of the week? Not likely. The reason: Pepitone is required to withhold amounts from her wages to pay various governmental authorities. For example, Pepitone will withhold amounts for Social Security taxes[1] and for federal and state income taxes. If these withholdings total $100, Susan will receive a check for only $300. Illustration 10-2 summarizes the types of payroll deductions that normally occur for most companies.

Illustration 10-2 Payroll deductions

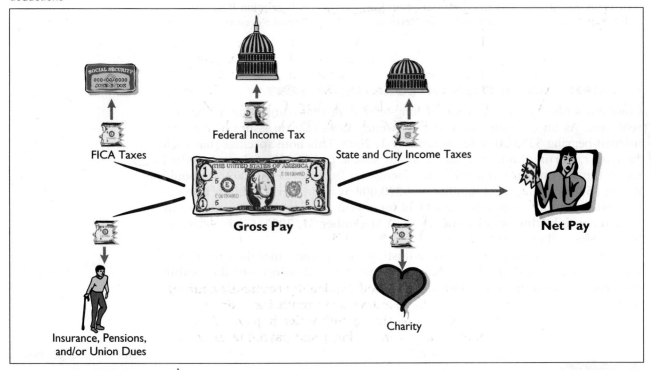

As a result of these deductions, companies withhold from employee paychecks amounts that must be paid to other parties. Pepitone therefore has

---

[1]Social Security taxes are commonly called FICA taxes. In 1937 Congress enacted the Federal Insurance Contribution Act (FICA). As can be seen in this journal entry and the payroll tax journal entry, the employee and employer must make equal contributions to Social Security. The Social Security rate in 2008 was 7.65% for each.

incurred a liability to pay these third parties, and must report this liability in its balance sheet.

As a second illustration, assume that Cargo Corporation records its payroll for the week of March 7 with the journal entry shown below.

Mar. 7	Salaries and Wages Expense	100,000		
	FICA Taxes Payable[1]		7,650	
	Federal Income Taxes Payable		21,864	
	State Income Taxes Payable		2,922	
	Salaries and Wages Payable		67,564	
	(To record payroll and withholding taxes for the week ending March 7)			

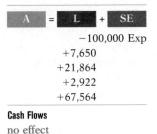

A = L + SE

−100,000 Exp
+7,650
+21,864
+2,922
+67,564

Cash Flows
no effect

Cargo then records payment of this payroll on March 7 as follows.

Mar. 7	Salaries and Wages Payable	67,564	
	Cash		67,564
	(To record payment of the March 7 payroll)		

A = L + SE

−67,564
−67,564

Cash Flows
−67,564

In this case Cargo reports $100,000 in wages and salaries expense. In addition, it reports liabilities for the wages payable as well as liabilities to governmental agencies. Rather than pay the employees $100,000, Cargo instead must withhold the taxes and make the tax payments directly. In summary, Cargo is essentially serving as a tax collector.

In addition to the liabilities incurred as a result of withholdings, employers also incur a second type of payroll-related liability. With every payroll, the employer incurs liabilities to pay various **payroll taxes** levied upon the employer. These payroll taxes include the *employer's share* of Social Security (FICA) taxes and state and federal unemployment taxes. Based on Cargo Corp.'s $100,000 payroll, the company would record the employer's expense and liability for these payroll taxes as follows.

Mar. 7	Payroll Tax Expense	13,850	
	FICA Taxes Payable		7,650
	Federal Unemployment Taxes Payable		800
	State Unemployment Taxes Payable		5,400
	(To record employer's payroll taxes on March 7 payroll)		

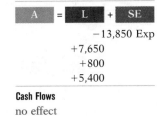

A = L + SE

−13,850 Exp
+7,650
+800
+5,400

Cash Flows
no effect

Companies classify the payroll and payroll tax liability accounts as current liabilities because they must be paid to employees or remitted to taxing authorities periodically and in the near term. Taxing authorities impose substantial fines and penalties on employers if the withholding and payroll taxes are not computed correctly and paid on time.

before you go on...

Do it!   During the month of September, Lake Corporation's employees earned wages of $60,000. Withholdings related to these wages were $3,500 for Social Security (FICA), $6,500 for federal income tax, and $2,000 for state income tax. Costs incurred for unemployment taxes were $90 for federal and $150 for state.

Prepare the September 30 journal entries for (a) wages expense and wages payable assuming that all September wages will be paid in October and (b) the company's payroll tax expense.

WAGES AND PAYROLL TAXES

Action Plan

- Remember that wages earned are an expense to the company, but withholdings reduce the amount due to be paid to the employee.
- Payroll taxes are taxes the company incurs related to its employees.

Solution

(a) To determine wages payable, reduce wages expense by the withholdings for FICA, federal income tax, and state income tax.

Sept. 30	Wages Expense	60,000	
	FICA Taxes Payable		3,500
	Federal Income Taxes Payable		6,500
	State Income Taxes Payable		2,000
	Wages Payable		48,000

(b) Payroll taxes would be for the company's share of FICA, as well as for federal and state unemployment tax.

Sept. 30	Payroll Tax Expense	3,740	
	FICA Taxes Payable		3,500
	Federal Unemployment Taxes Payable		90
	State Unemployment Taxes Payable		150

Bonds: Long-Term Liabilities

Long-term liabilities are obligations that a company expects to pay more than one year in the future. In this section we explain the accounting for the principal types of obligations reported in the long-term liabilities section of the balance sheet. These obligations often are in the form of bonds or long-term notes.

Bonds are a form of interest-bearing note payable issued by corporations, universities, and governmental agencies. Bonds, like common stock, are sold in small denominations (usually $1,000 or multiples of $1,000). As a result, bonds attract many investors.

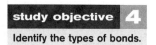

TYPES OF BONDS

Bonds may have different features. In the following sections we describe some commonly issued types of bonds.

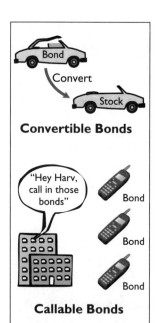

Secured and Unsecured Bonds

Secured bonds have specific assets of the issuer pledged as collateral for the bonds. **Unsecured bonds** are issued against the general credit of the borrower. Large corporations with good credit ratings use unsecured bonds extensively. For example, in a recent annual report, Dupont reported more than $2 billion of unsecured bonds outstanding.

Convertible and Callable Bonds

Bonds that can be converted into common stock at the bondholder's option are **convertible bonds**. Bonds that the issuing company can retire at a stated dollar amount prior to maturity are **callable bonds**. Convertible bonds have features that are attractive both to bondholders and to the issuer. The conversion often gives bondholders an opportunity to benefit if the market price of the common stock increases substantially. Furthermore, until conversion, the bondholder receives interest on the bond. For the issuer, the bonds sell at a higher price and pay a lower rate of interest than comparable debt securities that do not have a conversion option. Many corporations, such as USAir, United States Steel Corp., and General Motors Corporation, have convertible bonds outstanding.

Accounting Across the Organization

During the boom times of the late 1990s, many rapidly growing companies issued large quantities of convertible bonds. Investors found the convertible bonds attractive because they paid regular interest but also had the upside potential of being converted to stock if the stock price increased. At the time, stock prices were increasing rapidly, so many investors viewed convertible bonds as a cheap and safe way to buy stock.

As a consequence, companies were able to pay much lower interest rates on convertible bonds than on standard bonds. When the bonds were issued, company managers assumed that the bonds would be converted. Thus the company would never have to repay the debt with cash. It seemed too good to be true—and it was.

When stock prices plummeted in the early 2000s, investors no longer had an incentive to convert, since the market price was below the conversion price. When many of these massive bonds came due, companies were forced either to pay them off or to issue new debt at much higher rates.

The drop in stock prices did not change the debt to total assets ratios of these companies. Discuss how the perception of a high debt to total assets ratio changed before and after the fall in stock prices.

ISSUING PROCEDURES

A **bond certificate** is issued to the investor to provide evidence of the investor's claim against the company. As Illustration 10-3 (page 496) shows, the bond certificate provides information such as the name of the company that issued the bonds, the face value of the bonds, the maturity date of the bonds, and the contractual interest rate. The **face value** is the amount of principal due at the maturity date. The **maturity date** is the date that the final payment is due to the investor from the issuing company. The **contractual interest rate** is the rate used to determine the amount of cash interest the borrower pays and the investor receives. Usually the contractual rate is stated as an annual rate, and interest is generally paid semiannually.

Alternative Terminology The contractual rate is often referred to as the *stated rate*.

DETERMINING THE MARKET VALUE OF BONDS

If you were an investor wanting to purchase a bond, how would you determine how much to pay? To be more specific, assume that Coronet, Inc. issues a zero-interest (pays no interest) bond with a face value of $1,000,000 due in 20 years. For this bond, the only cash you receive is $1 million at the end of 20 years. Would you pay $1 million for this bond?

We hope not, because $1 million received 20 years from now is not the same as $1 million received today. The term **time value of money** is used to indicate the relationship between time and money—that a dollar received today is worth more than a dollar promised at some time in the future. If you had $1 million today, you would invest it and earn interest so that at the end of 20 years, your investment would be worth much more than $1 million. Thus, if someone is going to pay you $1 million 20 years from now, you would want to find its equivalent today, or its **present value**. In other words, you would want to determine the value today of the amount to be received in the future after taking into account current interest rates.

Same dollars at different times are not equal.

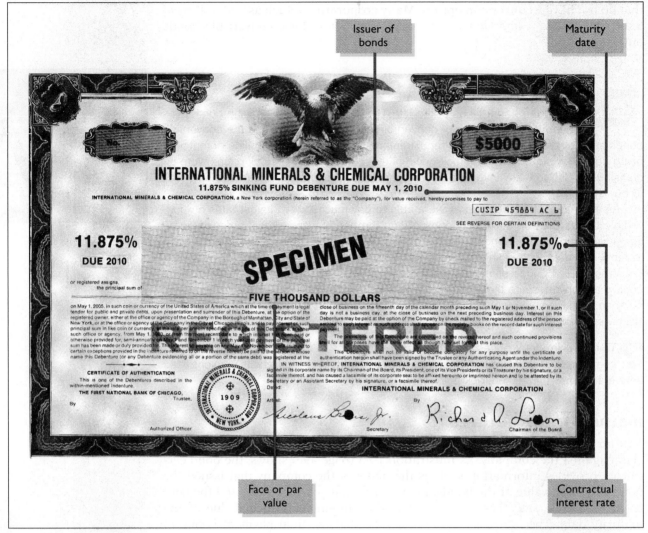

Illustration 10-3 Bond certificate

The current market value (present value) of a bond is therefore a function of three factors: (1) the dollar amounts to be received, (2) the length of time until the amounts are received, and (3) the market interest rate. The **market interest rate** is the rate investors demand for loaning funds. The process of finding the present value is referred to as **discounting** the future amounts.

To illustrate, assume that Acropolis Company on January 1, 2010, issues $100,000 of 9% bonds, due in five years, with interest payable annually at year-end. The purchaser of the bonds would receive the following two types of cash payments: (1) **principal** of $100,000 to be paid at maturity, and (2) five $9,000 **interest payments** ($100,000 × 9%) over the term of the bonds. Illustration 10-4 shows a time diagram depicting both cash flows.

Illustration 10-4 Time diagram depicting cash flows

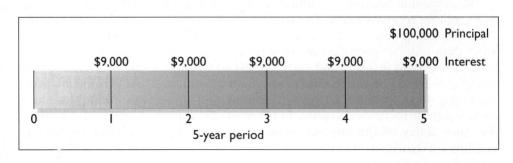

The current market value of a bond is equal to the present value of all the future cash payments promised by the bond. Illustration 10-5 lists and totals the present values of these amounts, assuming the market rate of interest is 9%.

Present value of $100,000 received in 5 years	$ 64,993
Present value of $9,000 received annually for 5 years	35,007
Market price of bonds	**$100,000**

Illustration 10-5
Computing the market price of bonds

Tables are available to provide the present value numbers to be used, or these values can be determined mathematically.[2] Appendix C, near the end of the book, provides further discussion of the concepts and the mechanics of the time value of money computations.

before you go on...

Do it!

State whether each of the following statements is true or false.

BOND TERMINOLOGY

_____ 1. Secured bonds have specific assets of the issuer pledged as collateral.

_____ 2. Callable bonds can be retired by the issuing company at a stated dollar amount prior to maturity.

_____ 3. The contractual rate is the rate investors demand for loaning funds.

_____ 4. The face value is the amount of principal the issuing company must pay at the maturity date.

_____ 5. The market value of a bond is equal to its maturity value.

Solution

1. True.

2. True.

3. False. The contractual interest rate is used to determine the amount of cash interest the borrower pays.

4. True.

5. False. The market value of a bond is equal to the present value of all the future cash payments promised by the bond.

Action Plan

• Review the types of bonds and the basic terms associated with bonds.

Accounting for Bond Issues

A corporation records bond transactions when it issues or retires (buys back) bonds and when bondholders convert bonds into common stock. If bondholders sell their bond investments to other investors, the issuing firm receives no further money on the transaction, **nor does the issuing corporation journalize the transaction** (although it does keep records of the names of bondholders in some cases).

Bonds may be issued at face value, below face value (discount), or above face value (premium). Bond prices for both new issues and existing bonds are

[2]For those knowledgeable in the use of present value tables, the computations in this example are: $100,000 × .64993 = $64,993 and $9,000 × 3.88965 = $35,007 (rounded).

quoted as **a percentage of the face value of the bond. Face value is usually $1,000.** Thus, a $1,000 bond with a quoted price of 97 means that the selling price of the bond is 97% of face value, or $970.

ISSUING BONDS AT FACE VALUE

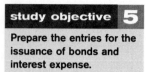

To illustrate the accounting for bonds issued at face value, assume that Devor Corporation issues 100, five-year, 10%, $1,000 bonds dated January 1, 2010, at 100 (100% of face value). The entry to record the sale is:

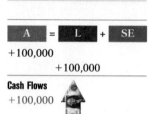

A = L + SE
+100,000
+100,000

Cash Flows
+100,000

Jan.	1	Cash	100,000	
		Bonds Payable		100,000
		(To record sale of bonds at face value)		

Devor reports bonds payable in the long-term liabilities section of the balance sheet because the maturity date is January 1, 2015 (more than one year away).

Over the term (life) of the bonds, companies make entries to record bond interest. Interest on bonds payable is computed in the same manner as interest on notes payable, as explained earlier. If we assume that interest is payable annually on January 1 on the bonds described above, Devor accrues interest of $10,000 ($100,000 × 10% × $\frac{12}{12}$) on December 31.

At December 31 Devor recognizes the $10,000 of interest expense incurred with the following adjusting entry.

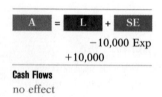

A = L + SE
−10,000 Exp
+10,000

Cash Flows
no effect

Dec. 31	Bond Interest Expense	10,000	
	Bond Interest Payable		10,000
	(To accrue bond interest)		

The company classifies **bond interest payable as a current liability** because it is scheduled for payment within the next year. When Devor pays the interest on January 1, 2011, it decreases (debits) Bond Interest Payable and decreases (credits) Cash for $10,000.

Devor records the payment on January 1 as follows.

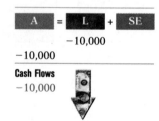

A = L + SE
−10,000
−10,000

Cash Flows
−10,000

Jan.	1	Bond Interest Payable	10,000	
		Cash		10,000
		(To record payment of bond interest)		

DISCOUNT OR PREMIUM ON BONDS

The previous illustrations assumed that the contractual (stated) interest rate and the market (effective) interest rate paid on bonds were the same. Recall that the **contractual interest rate** is the rate applied to the face (par) value to arrive at the interest paid in a year. The **market interest rate** is the rate investors demand for loaning funds to the corporation. When the contractual interest rate and the market interest rate are the same, **bonds sell at face value.**

However, market interest rates change daily. The type of bond issued, the state of the economy, current industry conditions, and the company's individual performance all affect market interest rates. As a result, the contractual and market interest rates often differ. To make bonds salable when the two rates differ, bonds sell below or above face value.

To illustrate, suppose that a company issues 10% bonds at a time when other bonds of similar risk are paying 12%. Investors will not be interested in buying the 10% bonds, so their value will fall below their face value. When a bond is sold for less than its face value, the difference between the face value of a bond and its selling price is called a discount. As a result of the decline in the bonds' selling price, the actual interest rate incurred by the company increases to the level of the current market interest rate.

Conversely, if the market rate of interest is **lower than** the contractual interest rate, investors will have to pay more than face value for the bonds. That is, if the market rate of interest is 8% but the contractual interest rate on the bonds is 10%, the price on the bonds will be bid up. When a bond is sold for more than its face value, the difference between the face value and its selling price is called a premium. Illustration 10-6 shows these relationships graphically.

Helpful Hint Bond prices *vary inversely* with changes in the market interest rate: As market interest rates decline, bond prices will increase. When a bond is issued, if the market interest rate is below the contractual rate, the price will be higher than the face value.

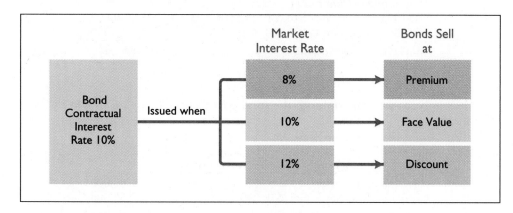

Illustration 10-6 Interest rates and bond prices

Issuance of bonds at an amount different from face value is quite common. By the time a company prints the bond certificates and markets the bonds, it will be a coincidence if the market rate and the contractual rate are the same. Thus, the issuance of bonds at a discount does not mean that the financial strength of the issuer is suspect. Conversely, the sale of bonds at a premium does not indicate that the financial strength of the issuer is exceptional.

Helpful Hint Some bonds are sold at a discount by design. "Zero-coupon" bonds, which pay no interest, sell at a deep discount to face value.

ISSUING BONDS AT A DISCOUNT

To illustrate the issuance of bonds at a discount, assume that on January 1, 2010, Candlestick Inc. sells $100,000, five-year, 10% bonds at 98 (98% of face value) with interest payable on January 1. The entry to record the issuance is:

Jan.	1	Cash	98,000	
		Discount on Bonds Payable	2,000	
		Bonds Payable		100,000
		(To record sale of bonds at a discount)		

A	=	L	+	SE
+98,000				
		−2,000		
		+100,000		

Cash Flows
+98,000

Although Discount on Bonds Payable has a debit balance, **it is not an asset.** Rather it is a **contra account,** which is **deducted from bonds payable** on the balance sheet as shown in Illustration 10-7.

Illustration 10-7 Statement presentation of discount on bonds payable

CANDLESTICK INC. Balance Sheet (partial)		
Long-term liabilities		
Bonds payable	$100,000	
Less: Discount on bonds payable	2,000	$98,000

Helpful Hint The carrying value (book value) of bonds issued at a discount is determined by subtracting the balance of the discount account from the balance of the Bonds Payable account.

The $98,000 represents the **carrying (or book) value** of the bonds. On the date of issue this amount equals the market price of the bonds.

The issuance of bonds below face value causes the total cost of borrowing to differ from the bond interest paid. That is, the issuing corporation not only must pay the contractual interest rate over the term of the bonds but also must pay the face value (rather than the issuance price) at maturity. Therefore, the difference between the issuance price and the face value of the bonds—the discount—is an **additional cost of borrowing**. The company records this cost as **bond interest expense** over the life of the bonds. The total cost of borrowing $98,000 for Candlestick Inc. is $52,000, computed as shown in Illustration 10-8.

Illustration 10-8
Computation of total cost of borrowing–bonds issued at discount

Bonds Issued at a Discount	
Annual interest payments	
($100,000 × 10% = $10,000; $10,000 × 5)	$ 50,000
Add: Bond discount ($100,000 − $98,000)	2,000
Total cost of borrowing	**$52,000**

Alternatively, we can compute the total cost of borrowing as shown in Illustration 10-9.

Illustration 10-9
Alternative computation of total cost of borrowing–bonds issued at discount

Bonds Issued at a Discount	
Principal at maturity	$100,000
Annual interest payments ($10,000 × 5)	50,000
Cash to be paid to bondholders	150,000
Cash received from bondholders	98,000
Total cost of borrowing	**$ 52,000**

To follow the matching principle, companies allocate bond discount to expense in each period in which the bonds are outstanding. This is referred to as **amortizing the discount**. Amortization of the discount **increases** the amount of interest expense reported each period. That is, after the company amortizes the discount, the amount of interest expense it reports in a period will exceed the contractual amount. As shown in Illustration 10-8, for the bonds issued by Candlestick Inc., total interest expense will exceed the contractual interest by $2,000 over the life of the bonds.

As the discount is amortized, its balance declines. As a consequence, the carrying value of the bonds will increase, until at maturity the carrying value of the bonds equals their face amount. This is shown in Illustration 10-10.

Illustration 10-10
Amortization of bond discount

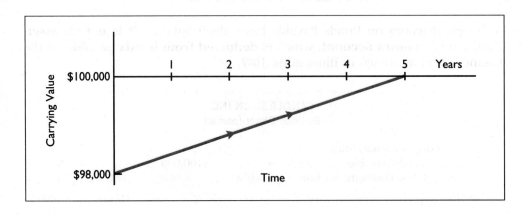

Appendix 10A and Appendix 10B at the end of this chapter discuss procedures for amortizing bond discount.

ISSUING BONDS AT A PREMIUM

We can illustrate the issuance of bonds at a premium by now assuming the Candlestick Inc. bonds described above sell at 102 (102% of face value) rather than at 98. The entry to record the sale is:

Jan. 1	Cash		102,000	
	Bonds Payable			100,000
	Premium on Bonds Payable			2,000
	(To record sale of bonds at a premium)			

Candlestick adds the premium on bonds payable **to the bonds payable** amount on the balance sheet, as shown in Illustration 10-11.

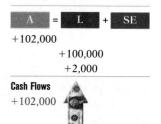

A = L + SE
+102,000
+100,000
+2,000

Cash Flows
+102,000

CANDLESTICK INC.
Balance Sheet (partial)

Long-term liabilities		
Bonds payable	$100,000	
Add: Premium on bonds payable	2,000	$102,000

Illustration 10-11
Statement presentation of bond premium

The sale of bonds above face value causes the total cost of borrowing to be **less than the bond interest paid** because the borrower is not required to pay the bond premium at the maturity date of the bonds. Thus, the premium is considered to be **a reduction in the cost of borrowing** that reduces bond interest expense over the life of the bonds. The total cost of borrowing $102,000 for Candlestick Inc. is $48,000, computed as in Illustration 10-12.

Bonds Issued at a Premium

Annual interest payments	
($100,000 × 10% = $10,000; $10,000 × 5)	$ 50,000
Less: Bond premium ($102,000 − $100,000)	2,000
Total cost of borrowing	**$48,000**

Illustration 10-12
Computation of total cost of borrowing–bonds issued at a premium

Alternatively, we can compute the cost of borrowing as shown in Illustration 10-13.

Bonds Issued at a Premium

Principal at maturity	$100,000
Annual interest payments ($10,000 × 5)	50,000
Cash to be paid to bondholders	150,000
Cash received from bondholders	102,000
Total cost of borrowing	**$ 48,000**

Illustration 10-13
Alternative computation of total cost of borrowing–bonds issued at a premium

Similar to bond discount, companies allocate bond premium to expense in each period in which the bonds are outstanding. This is referred to as **amortizing the premium**. Amortization of the premium **decreases** the amount of interest expense reported each period. That is, after the company amortizes the premium, the amount of interest expense it reports in a period will be less than the contractual amount. As shown in Illustration 10-12, for the bonds issued by Candlestick Inc., contractual interest will exceed the interest expense by $2,000 over the life of the bonds.

As the premium is amortized, its balance declines. As a consequence, the carrying value of the bonds will decrease, until at maturity the carrying value of the bonds equals their face amount. This is shown in Illustration 10-14. Appendix 10A and Appendix 10B at the end of this chapter discuss procedures for amortizing bond premium.

Illustration 10-14
Amortization of bond premium

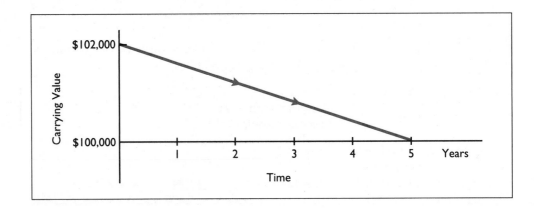

before you go on...

BOND ISSUANCE

Action Plan

• Record cash received, bonds payable at face value, and the difference as a discount or premium.

• Report discount as a deduction from bonds payable and premium as an addition to bonds payable.

Do it! Giant Corporation issues $200,000 of bonds for $189,000. (a) Prepare the journal entry to record the issuance of the bonds, and (b) show how the bonds would be reported on the balance sheet at the date of issuance.

Solution

(a)

Cash	189,000	
Discount on Bonds Payable	11,000	
Bonds Payable		200,000
(To record sale of bonds at a discount)		

(b)

Long-term liabilities		
Bonds payable	$200,000	
Less: Discount on bonds payable	(11,000)	$189,000

✔ the navigator

Accounting for Bond Retirements

study objective 6

Describe the entries when bonds are redeemed.

Bonds are retired when the issuing corporation purchases (redeems) them. The appropriate entries for these transactions are explained next.

REDEEMING BONDS AT MATURITY

Regardless of the issue price of bonds, the book value of the bonds at maturity will equal their face value. Assuming that the company pays and records separately the interest for the last interest period, Candlestick records the redemption of its bonds at maturity as:

Bonds Payable	100,000	
Cash		100,000
(To record redemption of bonds at maturity)		

REDEEMING BONDS BEFORE MATURITY

Bonds may be redeemed before maturity. A company may decide to retire bonds before maturity in order to reduce interest cost and remove debt from its balance sheet. A company should retire debt early only if it has sufficient cash resources.

When bonds are retired before maturity, it is necessary to: (1) eliminate the carrying value of the bonds at the redemption date, (2) record the cash paid, and (3) recognize the gain or loss on redemption. The **carrying value** of the bonds is the face value of the bonds less unamortized bond discount or plus unamortized bond premium at the redemption date.

To illustrate, assume at the end of the fourth period, Candlestick Inc., having sold its bonds at a premium, retires the bonds at 103 after paying the annual interest. Assume that the carrying value of the bonds at the redemption date is $100,400 (principal $100,000 and premium $400). Candlestick records the redemption at the end of the fourth interest period (January 1, 2014) as:

Jan. 1	Bonds Payable	100,000	
	Premium on Bonds Payable	400	
	Loss on Bond Redemption	2,600	
	Cash		103,000
	(To record redemption of bonds at 103)		

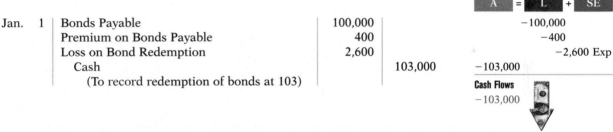

Note that the loss of $2,600 is the difference between the $103,000 cash paid and the $100,400 carrying value of the bonds.

Do it! R & B Inc. issued $500,000, 10-year bonds at a premium. Prior to maturity, when the carrying value of the bonds is $508,000, the company retires the bonds at 102. Prepare the entry to record the redemption of the bonds.

Solution

There is a loss on redemption: The cash paid, $510,000 ($500,000 × 102%), is greater than the carrying value of $508,000. The entry is:

Bonds Payable	500,000	
Premium on Bonds Payable	8,000	
Loss on Bond Redemption	2,000	
Cash ($500,000 × 1.02)		510,000
(To record redemption of bonds at 102)		

before you go on...

BOND REDEMPTION

Action Plan

- Determine and eliminate the carrying value of the bonds.
- Record the cash paid.
- Compute and record the gain or loss (the difference between the first two items).

Financial Statement Presentation and Analysis

BALANCE SHEET PRESENTATION

Current liabilities are the first category under "Liabilities" on the balance sheet. Companies list each of the principal types of current liabilities separately within the category.

Within the current liabilities section, companies usually list notes payable first, followed by accounts payable. Other items sometimes are listed in the order of their magnitude. *In your homework, you should present notes payable first, followed by accounts payable, and then other liabilities in order of magnitude.*

Companies report long-term liabilities in a separate section of the balance sheet immediately following "Current liabilities." Illustration 10-15 shows an example.

Illustration 10-15
Balance sheet presentation of liabilities

MARAIS COMPANY		
Balance Sheet (partial)		
Liabilities		
Current liabilities		
Notes payable	$ 250,000	
Accounts payable	125,000	
Current maturities of long-term debt	300,000	
Accrued liabilities	75,000	
Total current liabilities		$ 750,000
Long-term liabilities		
Bonds payable	1,000,000	
Less: Discount on bonds payable	80,000	920,000
Notes payable, secured by plant assets		540,000
Lease liability		500,000
Total long-term liabilities		1,960,000
Total liabilities		$2,710,000

Disclosure of debt is very important. Failures at Enron, WorldCom, and Global Crossing have made investors very concerned about companies' debt obligations. Summary data regarding debts may be presented in the balance sheet with detailed data (such as interest rates, maturity dates, conversion privileges, and assets pledged as collateral) shown in a supporting schedule in the notes. Companies should report current maturities of long-term debt as a current liability.

KEEPING AN EYE ON CASH

The balance sheet presents the balances of a company's debts at a point in time. The statement of cash flows also presents information about a company's debts. Information regarding cash inflows and outflows during the year that resulted from the principal portion of debt transactions appears in the "Financing activities" section of the statement of cash flows. Interest expense is reported in the "Operating activities" section, even though it resulted from debt transactions.

The statement of cash flows shown below presents the cash flows from financing activities for Toyota Motor Corporation. From this we learn that the company issued new long-term debt of $24,481 million and repaid long-term debt of $14,628 million.

TOYOTA MOTOR CORPORATION
Statement of Cash Flows (partial)
2007
(in millions)

Cash flows from financing activities	
Purchase of common stock	$ (2,505)
Proceeds from issuance of long-term debt	24,481
Payments of long-term debt	(14,628)
Increase in short-term borrowings	2,994
Dividends paid	(2,873)
Net cash provided by financing activities	$ 7,469

ANALYSIS

Careful examination of debt obligations helps you assess a company's ability to pay its current and long-term obligations. It also helps you determine whether a company can obtain debt financing in order to grow. We will use the following information from the financial statements of Toyota Motor Corporation to illustrate the analysis of a company's liquidity and solvency.

TOYOTA MOTOR CORPORATION
Balance Sheets
December 31, 2007 and 2006
(in millions)

Assets	2007	2006
Total current assets	$ 99,823	$ 91,387
Noncurrent assets	176,118	153,200
Total assets	$275,941	244,587
Liabilities and Stockholders' Equity		
Total current liabilities	$ 99,680	$ 85,373
Noncurrent liabilities	75,998	69,315
Total liabilities	175,678	154,688
Total stockholders' equity	100,263	89,899
Total liabilities and stockholders' equity	$275,941	$244,587

Illustration 10-16
Simplified balance sheets for Toyota Motor Corporation

Liquidity

Liquidity ratios measure the short-term ability of a company to pay its maturing obligations and to meet unexpected needs for cash. A commonly used measure of liquidity is the current ratio (presented in Chapter 2). The current ratio is calculated as current assets divided by current liabilities. Illustration 10-17 presents the current ratio for Toyota along with the industry average.

Illustration 10-17
Current ratio

($ in millions)	Toyota		Industry Average
	2007	2006	2007
Current Ratio	$\frac{\$99,823}{\$99,680} = 1.0:1$	$\frac{\$91,387}{\$85,373} = 1.07:1$	1.08:1

Toyota's current assets are approximately equal to its current liabilities. Therefore its current ratio is about 1 in both 2006 and 2007. The industry average current ratio for manufacturers of autos and trucks is 1.08:1. Thus, Toyota's current ratio, like the industry average, is quite low.

Many companies today minimize their liquid assets (such as accounts receivable, and inventory) in order to improve profitability measures, such as return on assets. This is particularly true of large companies such as GM and Toyota. Companies that keep fewer liquid assets on hand must rely on other sources of liquidity. One such source is a **bank line of credit**. A line of credit is a prearranged agreement between a company and a lender that permits the company, should it be necessary, to borrow up to an agreed-upon amount. For example, the disclosure regarding debt in General Motors' financial statements states that it has $3.3 billion of unused lines of credit. This represents a substantial amount of available cash. In addition, the Management Discussion and Analysis section of GM's annual report provides an extensive discussion of the company's liquidity. In it, GM notes that even though its credit rating was downgraded during the year, its "access to the capital markets remained sufficient to meet the Corporation's capital needs." Thus, even though General Motors has a low current ratio, its available lines of credit as well as other sources of financing appear adequate to meet any short-term cash deficiency it might experience.

DECISION TOOLKIT

DECISION CHECKPOINTS	INFO NEEDED FOR DECISION	TOOL TO USE FOR DECISION	HOW TO EVALUATE RESULTS
Can the company obtain short-term financing when necessary?	Available lines of credit, from notes to the financial statements.	Compare available lines of credit to current liabilities. Also, evaluate liquidity ratios.	If liquidity ratios are low, then lines of credit should be high to compensate.

Solvency

Solvency ratios measure the ability of a company to survive over a long period of time. The Feature Story in this chapter mentioned that although there once were many U.S. automobile manufacturers, only three U.S.-based companies remain today. Many of the others went bankrupt. This highlights the fact that when making a long-term loan or purchasing a company's stock, you must give consideration to a company's solvency.

To reduce the risks associated with having a large amount of debt during an economic downturn, some U.S. automobile manufacturers took two precautionary steps while they enjoyed strong profits. First, they built up large balances of cash and cash equivalents to avoid a cash crisis. Second, they were reluctant to build new plants or hire new workers to meet their production needs. Instead, they asked workers to put in overtime, or they "outsourced" work to other companies. In this way, when the economic downturn occurred, they hoped to avoid having to make debt payments on idle production plants and to minimize layoffs. As a result, in the middle of 2008 Ford still had cash of $29 billion, about double the amount of cash it would expect to use over a two-year period.

In Chapter 2 you learned that one measure of a company's solvency is the debt to total assets ratio. This is calculated as total liabilities divided by total assets. This ratio indicates the extent to which a company's assets are financed with debt.

Another useful solvency measure is the **times interest earned ratio**. It provides an indication of a company's ability to meet interest payments as they come due. It is computed by dividing income before interest expense and income taxes by interest expense. It uses income before interest expense and taxes because this number best represents the amount available to pay interest.

We can use the balance sheet information presented on page 505 and the additional information below to calculate solvency ratios for Toyota.

($ in millions)	2007	2006
Net income	$13,927	11,681
Interest expense	418	184
Tax expense	7,609	6,769

The debt to total assets ratios and times interest earned ratios for Toyota and averages for the industry are shown in Illustration 10-18.

Illustration 10-18
Solvency ratios

$$\text{Debt to Total Assets Ratio} = \frac{\text{Total Liabilities}}{\text{Total Assets}}$$

$$\text{Times Interest Earned Ratio} = \frac{\text{Net Income} + \text{Interest Expense} + \text{Tax Expense}}{\text{Interest Expense}}$$

($ in millions)	Toyota 2007	Toyota 2006	Industry Average 2007
Debt to Total Assets Ratio	$\frac{\$175,678}{\$275,941} = 64\%$	$\frac{\$154,688}{\$244,587} = 63\%$	65.0%
Times Interest Earned Ratio	$\frac{\$13,927 + \$418 + \$7,609}{\$418}$ $= 52.5 \text{ times}$	$\frac{\$11,681 + \$184 + \$6,769}{\$184}$ $= 101.3 \text{ times}$	3.0 times

Toyota's debt to total assets ratio was 64%. The industry average for manufacturers of autos and trucks is 65%. Thus Toyota is approximately as reliant on debt financing as the average firm in the auto and truck industry.

Toyota's times interest earned ratio declined from 101.3 times in 2006 to 52.5 in 2007. This means that in 2007 Toyota had earnings before interest and taxes that were more than 50 times the amount needed to pay interest. The higher the multiple, the lower the likelihood that the company will default on interest payments. Because many of the companies in this industry had huge losses in 2007, the industry average was only 3.0. This suggests that while Toyota's ability to meet interest payments was extremely high, the average company in the industry had a much lower ability to meet interest payments.

Investor Insight

The Williams Companies recently faced the prospect of a credit-rating downgrade by Moody's Investors Service Inc. Lenders are heavily influenced by these ratings, so a downgrade would make it harder for the company to borrow funds, as well as make borrowing more expensive. The company quickly announced plans to improve its liquidity and solvency. It said it would sell assets of $1.5 to $3.0 billion, issue common stock of $1 to $1.5 billion, and cut annual costs by $100 million. It also said it would continue to evaluate the size of its dividend payment on common stock. It said it would use the funds generated by these actions to pay down existing debt and to increase its liquidity.

Source: "Williams Unveils Measures to Bolster its Balance Sheet," *Wall Street Journal Online* (May 28, 2002).

? Explain how the sale of plant assets could improve the company's solvency.

DECISION TOOLKIT

DECISION CHECKPOINTS	INFO NEEDED FOR DECISION	TOOL TO USE FOR DECISION	HOW TO EVALUATE RESULTS
Can the company meet its obligations in the long term?	Interest expense and net income before interest and taxes	Times interest earned ratio $= \dfrac{\text{Net Income} + \text{Interest expense} + \text{Tax expense}}{\text{Interest expense}}$	High ratio indicates ability to meet interest payments as scheduled.

OFF-BALANCE-SHEET FINANCING

A concern for analysts when they evaluate a company's liquidity and solvency is whether that company has properly recorded all of its obligations. The bankruptcy of Enron Corporation, one of the largest bankruptcies in U.S. history, demonstrated how much damage can result when a company does not properly record or disclose all of its debts. Many would say Enron was practicing off-balance-sheet financing. Off-balance-sheet financing is an intentional effort by a company to structure its financing arrangements so as to avoid showing liabilities on its balance sheet. Two common types of off-balance-sheet financing result from unreported contingencies and lease transactions.

Contingencies

One reason a company's balance sheet might not fully reflect its potential obligations is due to contingencies. Contingencies are events with uncertain outcomes that may represent potential liabilities. A common type of contingency is lawsuits. Suppose, for example, that you were analyzing the financial statements of a cigarette manufacturer and did not consider the possible negative implications of existing unsettled lawsuits. Your analysis of the company's financial position would certainly be misleading. Other common types of contingencies are product warranties and environmental clean-up obligations. For example, in a recent year Novartis AG began offering a money-back guarantee on its blood-pressure medications. This guarantee would necessitate an accrual for the estimated claims that will result from returns.

Accounting rules require that companies disclose contingencies in the notes; in some cases they must accrue them as liabilities. For example, suppose that Waterbury Inc. is sued by a customer for $1 million due to an injury sustained by a defective product. If at the company's year-end, the lawsuit had not yet been resolved, how should Waterbury account for this event? If the company can determine **a reasonable estimate** of the expected loss and if it is **probable** it will lose the suit, then the company should accrue for the loss. It records the loss by increasing (debiting) a loss account and increasing (crediting) a liability such as Lawsuit Liability. If *both* of these conditions are not met, then the company discloses the basic facts regarding this suit in the notes to its financial statements.

Leasing

One common type of off-balance-sheet financing results from leasing. Most lessees do not like to report leases on their balance sheets because the lease increases the company's total liabilities. Recall from Chapter 9 that operating leases are treated like rentals—no asset or liabilities show on the books. Capital leases are treated like a debt-financed purchase—increasing both assets and liabilities. **As a result, many companies structure their lease agreements to avoid meeting the criteria of a capital lease.**

Recall from Chapter 9 that many U.S. airlines lease a large portion of their planes without showing any debt related to them on their balance sheets. For example, the total increase in assets and liabilities that would result if Southwest Airlines recorded on the balance sheet its off-balance-sheet **"operating" leases** would be approximately $2.3 billion. Illustration 10-19 presents Southwest Airlines' debt to total assets ratio using the numbers presented in its balance sheet and also shows the ratio after adjusting for the off-balance-sheet leases. After those adjustments, Southwest has a ratio of 64% versus 59% before. This means that of every dollar of assets, 64 cents was funded by debt. This would be of interest to analysts evaluating Southwest's solvency.

Ethics Note Accounting standard setters are attempting to rewrite rules on lease accounting because of concerns that abuse of the current standards is reducing the usefulness of financial statements.

	Using numbers as presented on balance sheet	Adjusted for off-balance-sheet leases
Debt to total assets ratio	$\dfrac{\$9,831}{\$16,772} = 59\%$	$\dfrac{\$9,831 + \$2,339}{\$16,772 + \$2,339} = 64\%$

Illustration 10-19
Debt to total assets ratio adjusted for leases

International Note GAAP accounting for leases is more "rules-based" than IFRS. GAAP relies on precisely defined cut-offs to determine whether an item is treated as a capital or operating lease. This rules-based approach may enable companies to structure leases "around the rules." Creating a jointly prepared leasing standard is a top priority for the IASB and FASB.

Critics of off-balance-sheet financing contend that many leases represent unavoidable obligations that meet the definition of a liability, and therefore companies should report them as liabilities on the balance sheet. To reduce these concerns, companies are required to report their operating lease obligations for subsequent years in a note. This allows analysts and other financial statement users to adjust a company's financial statements by adding leased assets and lease liabilities if they feel that this treatment is more appropriate.

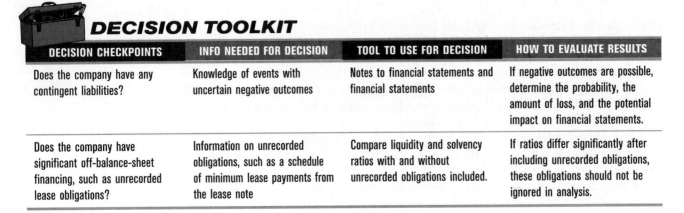

DECISION TOOLKIT

DECISION CHECKPOINTS	INFO NEEDED FOR DECISION	TOOL TO USE FOR DECISION	HOW TO EVALUATE RESULTS
Does the company have any contingent liabilities?	Knowledge of events with uncertain negative outcomes	Notes to financial statements and financial statements	If negative outcomes are possible, determine the probability, the amount of loss, and the potential impact on financial statements.
Does the company have significant off-balance-sheet financing, such as unrecorded lease obligations?	Information on unrecorded obligations, such as a schedule of minimum lease payments from the lease note	Compare liquidity and solvency ratios with and without unrecorded obligations included.	If ratios differ significantly after including unrecorded obligations, these obligations should not be ignored in analysis.

Investor Insight

In many corporate loans and bond issuances the lending agreement specifies *debt covenants*. These covenants typically are specific financial measures, such as minimum levels of retained earnings, cash flows, times interest earned ratios, or other measures that a company must maintain during the life of the loan. If the company violates a covenant, it is considered to have violated the loan agreement; the creditors can demand immediate repayment, or they can renegotiate the loan's terms. Covenants protect lenders because they enable lenders to step in and try to get their money back before the borrower gets too deep into trouble.

During the 1990s most traditional loans specified between three to six covenants or "triggers." In more recent years, however, when there was lots of cash available, lenders began reducing or completely eliminating covenants from loan agreements in order to be more competitive with other lenders. In a weaker economy these lenders will be more likely to lose big money when companies default.

Source: Cynthia Koons, "Risky Business: Growth of 'Covenant-Lite' Debt," *Wall Street Journal*, June 18, 2007, p. C2.

How can financial ratios such as those covered in this chapter provide protection for creditors?

 ## USING THE DECISION TOOLKIT

Ford Motor Company has enjoyed some tremendous successes, including its popular Taurus and Explorer vehicles. Yet observers are looking for the next big hit. Development of a new vehicle costs billions. A flop is financially devastating, and the financial effect is magnified if the company has large amounts of outstanding debt.

The balance sheets below provide financial information for the Automotive Division of Ford Motor Company as of December 31, 2007 and 2006. We have chosen to analyze only the Automotive Division rather than the total corporation, which includes Ford's giant financing division. In an actual analysis you would want to analyze the major divisions individually as well as the combined corporation as a whole.

Instructions

1. Evaluate Ford's liquidity using appropriate ratios, and compare to those of Toyota and to industry averages.

2. Evaluate Ford's solvency using appropriate ratios, and compare to those of Toyota and to industry averages.

3. Comment on Ford's available lines of credit.

FORD MOTOR COMPANY—
AUTOMOTIVE DIVISION
Balance Sheets
December 31, 2007 and 2006
(in millions)

Assets	2007	2006
Current assets	$ 54,243	$ 54,953
Noncurrent assets	64,246	67,681
Total assets	$118,489	$ 122,634
Liabilities and Shareholders' Equity		
Current liabilities	$ 50,218	$ 51,690
Noncurrent liabilities	73,317	83,725
Total liabilities	123,535	135,415
Total shareholders' equity	(5,046)	(12,781)
Total liabilities and shareholders' equity	$118,489	$ 122,634
Other Information		
Net income (loss)	$ (4,970)	$(17,040)
Tax expense (refund)	(1,541)	(5,282)
Interest expense	2,252	995
Available lines of credit (Automotive Division)	10,900	

Solution

1. Ford's liquidity can be measured using the current ratio:

	2007	2006
Current ratio	$\dfrac{\$54,243}{\$50,218} = 1.08{:}1$	$\dfrac{\$54,953}{\$51,690} = 1.06{:}1$

Ford's current ratio is approximately the same as the industry average of 1.08:1 and roughly the same as Toyota's. These are increasingly common levels for large companies that have reduced the amount of inventory and receivables they hold. As noted earlier, these low current ratios are not necessarily cause for concern, but they do require more careful monitoring. Ford must also make sure to have other short-term financing options available, such as lines of credit.

2. Ford's solvency can be measured with the debt to total assets ratio and the times interest earned ratio:

	2007	2006
Debt to total assets ratio	$\dfrac{\$123,535}{\$118,489} = 104\%$	$\dfrac{\$135,415}{\$122,634} = 110\%$
Times interest earned ratio	$\dfrac{\$(4,970) + \$2,252 - \$1,541}{\$2,252}$	$\dfrac{\$(17,040) + \$995 - \$5,282}{\$995}$
	= 0 times	= 0 times

The debt to total assets ratio suggests that Ford relies very heavily on debt financing. The ratio decreased from 2006 to 2007, indicating that the company's solvency improved slightly. But in both years it exceeded 100%. This is possible because we have calculated the ratio for the Automotive Division only, rather than the whole company. The debt to total assets ratio for the entire company is 94.5%. This is extremely high.

The times interest earned ratio is zero in both years. The ratio is zero because, even after adding back interest and taxes, the company's income was negative. This is well below the industry average of 3.0 times. It is likely that the company's solvency was a concern to investors and creditors and would be closely monitored. Note that because Ford reported net losses, it had tax refunds rather than tax expense. Since tax expense is added in the numerator, tax refunds are subtracted.

3. Ford has available lines of credit of $10.9 billion. These financing sources significantly improve its liquidity and help reduce the concerns of its short-term creditors.

Summary of Study Objectives

1 **Explain a current liability and identify the major types of current liabilities.** A current liability is a debt that a company can reasonably expect to pay (a) from existing current assets or through the creation of other current liabilities, and (b) within one year or the operating cycle, whichever is longer. The major types of current liabilities are notes payable, accounts payable, sales taxes payable, unearned revenues, and accrued liabilities such as taxes, salaries and wages, and interest payable.

2 **Describe the accounting for notes payable.** When a promissory note is interest-bearing, the amount of assets received upon the issuance of the note is generally equal to the face value of the note, and interest expense is accrued over the life of the note. At maturity, the amount paid is equal to the face value of the note plus accrued interest.

3 **Explain the accounting for other current liabilities.** Companies record sales taxes payable at the time the related sales occur. The company serves as a collection agent for the taxing authority. Sales taxes are not an expense to the company. Companies hold employee withholding taxes, and credit them to appropriate liability accounts, until they remit these taxes to the governmental taxing authorities. Unearned revenues are initially recorded in an unearned revenue account. As the company earns the revenue, a transfer from unearned revenue to earned revenue occurs. Companies should report the current maturities of long-term debt as a current liability in the balance sheet.

4 **Identify the types of bonds.** The following different types of bonds may be issued: secured and unsecured bonds, and convertible and callable bonds.

5 **Prepare the entries for the issuance of bonds and interest expense.** When companies issue bonds, they debit Cash for the cash proceeds and credit Bonds Payable for the face value of the bonds. In addition, they use the accounts Premium on Bonds Payable and Discount on Bonds Payable to show the bond premium and bond discount, respectively. Bond discount and bond premium are amortized over the life of the bond, which increases or decreases interest expense, respectively.

6 **Describe the entries when bonds are redeemed.** When companies redeem bonds at maturity, they credit Cash and debit Bonds Payable for the face value of the bonds. When companies redeem bonds before maturity, they (a) eliminate the carrying value of the bonds at the redemption date, (b) record the cash paid, and (c) recognize the gain or loss on redemption.

7 **Identify the requirements for the financial statement presentation and analysis of liabilities.** Current liabilities appear first on the balance sheet, followed by long-term liabilities. Companies should report the nature and amount of each liability in the balance sheet or in schedules in the notes accompanying the statements. They report inflows and outflows of cash related to the principal portion of long-term debt in the financing section of the statement of cash flows.

The liquidity of a company may be analyzed by computing the current ratio. The long-run solvency of a company may be analyzed by computing the debt to total assets ratio and the times interest earned ratio. Other factors to consider are contingent liabilities and lease obligations.

DECISION TOOLKIT   A SUMMARY

DECISION CHECKPOINTS	INFO NEEDED FOR DECISION	TOOL TO USE FOR DECISION	HOW TO EVALUATE RESULTS
Can the company obtain short-term financing when necessary?	Available lines of credit, from notes to the financial statements	Compare available lines of credit to current liabilities. Also, evaluate liquidity ratios.	If liquidity ratios are low, then lines of credit should be high to compensate.
Can the company meet its obligations in the long term?	Interest expense and net income before interest and taxes	$$\text{Times interest earned ratio} = \frac{\text{Net income} + \text{Interest expense} + \text{Tax expense}}{\text{Interest expense}}$$	High ratio indicates ability to meet interest payments as scheduled.
Does the company have any contingent liabilities?	Knowledge of events with uncertain negative outcomes	Notes to financial statements and financial statements	If negative outcomes are possible, determine the probability, the amount of loss, and the potential impact on financial statements.

(continued)

| Does the company have significant off-balance-sheet financing, such as unrecorded lease obligations? | Information on unrecorded obligations, such as a schedule of minimum lease payments from the lease note | Compare liquidity and solvency ratios with and without unrecorded obligations included. | If ratios differ significantly after including unrecorded obligations, these obligations should not be ignored in analysis. |

appendix 10A

Straight-Line Amortization

AMORTIZING BOND DISCOUNT

To follow the matching principle, companies allocate bond discount to expense in each period in which the bonds are outstanding. The straight-line method of amortization allocates the same amount to interest expense in each interest period. The calculation is presented in Illustration 10A-1.

study objective 8

Apply the straight-line method of amortizing bond discount and bond premium.

| Bond Discount | ÷ | Number of Interest Periods | = | Bond Discount Amortization |

Illustration 10A-1
Formula for straight-line method of bond discount amortization

In the Candlestick Inc. example (page 499), the company sold $100,000, five-year, 10% bonds on January 1, 2010, for $98,000. This resulted in a $2,000 bond discount ($100,000 − $98,000). The bond discount amortization is $400 ($2,000 ÷ 5) for each of the five amortization periods. Candlestick records the first accrual of bond interest and the amortization of bond discount on December 31 as follows.

Dec. 31	Bond Interest Expense		10,400	
	Discount on Bonds Payable			400
	Bond Interest Payable			10,000
	(To record accrued bond interest and amortization of bond discount)			

A	=	L	+	SE
				−10,400 Exp
		+400		
		+10,000		

Cash Flows
no effect

Over the term of the bonds, the balance in Discount on Bonds Payable will decrease annually by the same amount until it has a zero balance at the maturity date of the bonds. Thus, the carrying value of the bonds at maturity will be equal to the face value of the bonds.

Preparing a bond discount amortization schedule, as shown in Illustration 10A-2 (page 514), is useful to determine interest expense, discount amortization, and the carrying value of the bond. As indicated, the interest expense recorded each period is $10,400. Also note that the carrying value of the bond increases $400 each period until it reaches its face value of $100,000 at the end of period 5.

Alternative Terminology The amount in the Discount on Bonds Payable account is often referred to as *Unamortized Discount on Bonds Payable*.

BOND DISCOUNT AMORTIZATION SCHEDULE
Straight-Line Method–Annual Interest Payments
$100,000 of 10%, 5-Year Bonds

Interest Periods	(A) Interest To Be Paid (10% × $100,000)	(B) Interest Expense To Be Recorded (A) + (C)	(C) Discount Amortization ($2,000 ÷ 5)	(D) Unamortized Discount (D) − (C)	(E) Bond Carrying Value ($100,000 − D)
Issue date				$2,000	$ 98,000
1	$10,000	$10,400	$ 400	1,600	98,400
2	10,000	10,400	400	1,200	98,800
3	10,000	10,400	400	800	99,200
4	10,000	10,400	400	400	99,600
5	10,000	10,400	400	0	100,000
	$50,000	$52,000	$2,000		

Column **(A)** remains constant because the face value of the bonds ($100,000) is multiplied by the annual contractual interest rate (10%) each period.
Column **(B)** is computed as the interest paid (Column A) plus the discount amortization (Column C).
Column **(C)** indicates the discount amortization each period.
Column **(D)** decreases each period by the same amount until it reaches zero at maturity.
Column **(E)** increases each period by the amount of discount amortization until it equals the face value at maturity.

Illustration 10A-2 Bond discount amortization schedule

AMORTIZING BOND PREMIUM

The amortization of bond premium parallels that of bond discount. Illustration 10A-3 presents the formula for determining bond premium amortization under the straight-line method.

Illustration 10A-3
Formula for straight-line method of bond premium amortization

Bond Premium	÷	Number of Interest Periods	=	Bond Premium Amortization

Continuing our example, assume Candlestick Inc., sells the bonds described above for $102,000, rather than $98,000. This results in a bond premium of $2,000 ($102,000 − $100,000). The premium amortization for each interest period is $400 ($2,000 ÷ 5). Candlestick records the first accrual of interest on December 31 as follows.

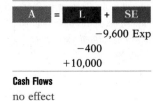

A	=	L	+	SE

−9,600 Exp
−400
+10,000

Cash Flows
no effect

Dec. 31	Bond Interest Expense	9,600	
	Premium on Bonds Payable	400	
	Bond Interest Payable		10,000
	(To record accrued bond interest and amortization of bond premium)		

Over the term of the bonds, the balance in Premium on Bonds Payable will decrease annually by the same amount until it has a zero balance at maturity.

A bond premium amortization schedule, as shown in Illustration 10A-4, is useful to determine interest expense, premium amortization, and the carrying value of the bond. As indicated, the interest expense Candlestick records each period is $9,600. Note that the carrying value of the bond decreases $400 each period until it reaches its face value of $100,000 at the end of period 5.

Illustration 10A-4   Bond premium amortization schedule

	(A) Interest To Be Paid (10% × $100,000)	(B) Interest Expense To Be Recorded (A) – (C)	(C) Premium Amortization ($2,000 ÷ 5)	(D) Unamortized Premium (D) – (C)	(E) Bond Carrying Value ($100,000 + D)
Interest Periods					
Issue date				$2,000	$ 102,000
1	$10,000	$ 9,600	$ 400	1,600	101,600
2	10,000	9,600	400	1,200	101,200
3	10,000	9,600	400	800	100,800
4	10,000	9,600	400	400	100,400
5	10,000	9,600	400	0	100,000
	$50,000	$48,000	$2,000		

BOND PREMIUM AMORTIZATION SCHEDULE
Straight-Line Method–Annual Interest Payments
$100,000 of 10%, 5-Year Bonds

Column **(A)** remains constant because the face value of the bonds ($100,000) is multiplied by the annual contractual interest rate (10%) each period.
Column **(B)** is computed as the interest paid (Column A) less the premium amortization (Column C).
Column **(C)** indicates the premium amortization each period.
Column **(D)** decreases each period by the same amount until it reaches zero at maturity.
Column **(E)** decreases each period by the amount of premium amortization until it equals the face value at maturity.

Summary of Study Objective for Appendix 10A

8 **Apply the straight-line method of amortizing bond discount and bond premium.** The straight-line method of amortization results in a constant amount of amortization and interest expense per period.

appendix 10B

Effective-Interest Amortization

study objective **9**

Apply the effective-interest method of amortizing bond discount and bond premium.

To follow the matching principle, companies allocate bond discount to expense in each period in which the bonds are outstanding. However, to completely comply with the matching principle, interest expense as a percentage of carrying value should not change over the life of the bonds. This percentage, referred to as the effective-interest rate, is established when the bonds are issued and remains constant in each interest period. Unlike the straight-line method, the effective-interest method of amortization accomplishes this result.

Under the effective-interest method, the amortization of bond discount or bond premium results in periodic interest expense equal to a constant percentage of the carrying value of the bonds. The effective-interest method results in **varying amounts** of amortization and interest expense per period but a **constant percentage rate.** In contrast, the straight-line method results in constant amounts of amortization and interest expense per period but a varying percentage rate.

Companies follow three steps under the effective-interest method:

1. Compute the **bond interest expense** by multiplying the carrying value of the bonds at the beginning of the interest period by the effective-interest rate.

2. Compute the **bond interest paid** (or accrued) by multiplying the face value of the bonds by the contractual interest rate.

3. Compute the **amortization amount** by determining the difference between the amounts computed in steps (1) and (2).

Illustration 10B-1 depicts these steps.

Illustration 10B-1
Computation of amortization using effective-interest method

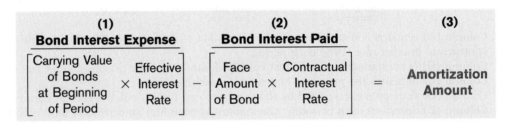

Both the straight-line and effective-interest methods of amortization result in the same total amount of interest expense over the term of the bonds. Furthermore, interest expense each interest period is generally comparable in amount. However, **when the amounts are materially different, generally accepted accounting principles (GAAP) require use of the effective-interest method.**

Helpful Hint Note that the amount of periodic interest expense increases over the life of the bonds when the effective-interest method is used for bonds issued at a discount. The reason is that a constant percentage is applied to an increasing bond carrying value to compute interest expense. The carrying value is increasing because of the amortization of the discount.

AMORTIZING BOND DISCOUNT

In the Candlestick Inc. example (page 499), the company sold $100,000, five-year, 10% bonds on January 1, 2010, for $98,000. This resulted in a $2,000 bond discount ($100,000 – $98,000). This discount results in an effective-interest rate of approximately 10.53%. (The effective-interest rate can be computed using the techniques shown in Appendix C at the end of this book.)

Preparing a bond discount amortization schedule as shown in Illustration 10B-2 facilitates the recording of interest expense and the discount amortization. Note that interest expense as a percentage of carrying value remains constant at 10.53%.

	(A) Interest to Be Paid (10% × $100,000)	(B) Interest Expense to Be Recorded (10.53% × Preceding Bond Carrying Value)		(C) Discount Amortization (B) − (A)	(D) Unamortized Discount (D) − (C)	(E) Bond Carrying Value ($100,000 − D)
Interest Periods						
Issue date					$2,000	$ 98,000
1	$10,000	$10,319	(10.53% × $98,000)	$319	1,681	98,319
2	10,000	10,353	(10.53% × $ 98,319)	353	1,328	98,672
3	10,000	10,390	(10.53% × $ 98,672)	390	938	96,062
4	10,000	10,431	(10.53% × $ 99,062)	431	507	99,493
5	10,000	10,507*	(10.53% × $ 99,493)	507*	–0–	100,000
	$ 50,000	$ 52,000		$ 2,000		

CANDLESTICK INC.
Bond Discount Amortization
Effective-Interest Method–Annual Interest Payments
10% Bonds Issued at 10.53%

Column (A) remains constant because the face value of the bonds ($100,000) is multiplied by the annual contractual interest rate (10%) each period.
Column (B) is computed as the preceding bond carrying value times the annual effective-interest rate (10.53%).
Column (C) indicates the discount amortization each period.
Column (D) decreases each period until it reaches zero at maturity.
Column (E) increases each period until it equals face value at maturity.

*Rounded to eliminate remaining discount resulting from rounding the effective rate.

Illustration 10B-2 Bond discount amortization schedule

For the first interest period, the computations of bond interest expense and the bond discount amortization are as follows.

Bond interest expense ($98,000 × 10.53%)	$10,319
Bond interest paid ($100,000 × 10%)	10,000
Bond discount amortization	$ 319

Illustration 10B-3
Computation of bond discount amortization

As a result, Candlestick Inc. records the accrual of interest and amortization of bond discount on December 31, as follows.

	A	=	L	+	SE

Dec. 31	Bond Interest Expense	10,319		−10,319 Exp
	Discount on Bonds Payable		319	+319
	Bond Interest Payable		10,000	+10,000
	(To record accrued interest and amortization of bond discount)			

Cash Flows
no effect

For the second interest period, bond interest expense will be $10,353 ($98,319 × 10.53%), and the discount amortization will be $353. At December 31, Candlestick makes the following adjusting entry.

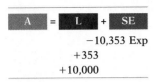

		Dec. 31	Bond Interest Expense	10,353	
			Discount on Bonds Payable		353
−10,353 Exp			Bond Interest Payable		10,000
+353			(To record accrued interest and		
+10,000			amortization of bond discount)		

Cash Flows
no effect

AMORTIZING BOND PREMIUM

Continuing our example, assume Candlestick Inc. sells the bonds described above for $102,000 rather than $98,000. This would result in a bond premium of $2,000 ($102,000 − $100,000). This premium results in an effective-interest rate of approximately 9.48%. (The effective-interest rate can be solved for using the techniques shown in Appendix C at the end of this book.) Illustration 10B-4 shows the bond premium amortization schedule.

CANDLESTICK INC.
Bond Premium Amortization
Effective-Interest Method—Annual Interest Payments
10% Bonds Issued at 9.48%

Interest Periods	(A) Interest to Be Paid (10% × $100,000)	(B) Interest Expense to Be Recorded (9.48% × Preceding Bond Carrying Value)	(C) Premium Amortization (A) − (B)	(D) Unamortized Premium (D) − (C)	(E) Bond Carrying Value ($100,000 + D)
Issue date				$2,000	$102,000
1	$10,000	$9,670 (9.48% × $102,000)	$330	1,670	101,670
2	10,000	9,638 (9.48% × $ 101,670)	362	1,308	101,308
3	10,000	9,604 (9.48% × $ 101,308)	396	912	100,912
4	10,000	9,566 (9.48% × $ 100,912)	434	478	100,478
5	10,000	9,522* (9.48% × $ 100,478)	478*	−0−	100,000
	$ 50,000	$ 48,000	$ 2,000		

Column **(A)** remains constant because the face value of the bonds ($100,000) is multiplied by the contractual interest rate (10%) each period.
Column **(B)** is computed as the carrying value of the bonds times the annual effective-interest rate (9.48%).
Column **(C)** indicates the premium amortization each period.
Column **(D)** decreases each period until it reaches zero at maturity.
Column **(E)** decreases each period until it equals face value at maturity.

*Rounded to eliminate remaining discount resulting from rounding the effective rate.

Illustration 10B-4 Bond premium amortization schedule

For the first interest period, the computations of bond interest expense and the bond premium amortization are:

Illustration 10B-5
Computation of bond premium amortization

Bond interest paid ($100,000 × 10%)	$10,000
Bond interest expense ($102,000 × 9.48%)	9,670
Bond premium amortization	$ 330

The entry Candlestick makes on December 31 is:

Dec. 31	Bond Interest Expense	9,670	
	Premium on Bonds Payable	330	
	Bond Interest Payable		10,000
	(To record accrued interest and		
	amortization of bond premium)		

A	=	L	+	SE
				−9,670 Exp
		−330		
		+10,000		

Cash Flows
no effect

For the second interest period, interest expense will be $9,638, and the premium amortization will be $362. Note that the amount of periodic interest expense decreases over the life of the bond when companies apply the effective-interest method to bonds issued at a premium. The reason is that a constant percentage is applied to a decreasing bond carrying value to compute interest expense. The carrying value is decreasing because of the amortization of the premium.

Summary of Study Objective for Appendix 10B

9 **Apply the effective-interest method of amortizing bond discount and bond premium.** The effective-interest method results in varying amounts of amortization and interest expense per period but a constant percentage rate of interest. When the difference between the straight-line and effective-interest method is material, GAAP requires use of the effective-interest method.

appendix 10C

Accounting for Long-Term Notes Payable

The use of notes payable in long-term debt financing is quite common. Long-term notes payable are similar to short-term interest-bearing notes payable except that the terms of the notes exceed one year. In periods of unstable interest rates, lenders may tie the interest rate on long-term notes to changes in the market rate for comparable loans. Examples are the 8.03% adjustable rate notes issued by General Motors and the floating-rate notes issued by American Express Company.

A long-term note may be secured by a document called a **mortgage** that pledges title to specific assets as security for a loan. Individuals widely use mortgage notes payable to purchase homes, as do many small and some large companies to acquire plant assets. For example, at one time approximately 18% of McDonald's long-term debt related to mortgage notes on land, buildings, and improvements.

Like other long-term notes payable, the mortgage loan terms may stipulate either a fixed or an adjustable interest rate. Typically, the terms require the borrower to make equal installment payments over the term of the loan. Each payment consists of (1) interest on the unpaid balance of the loan and (2) a reduction of loan principal. While the total amount paid remains constant, the interest decreases each period and the portion applied to the loan principal increases.

study objective 10

Describe the accounting for long-term notes payable.

Helpful Hint Electronic spreadsheet programs can create a schedule of installment loan payments. This allows you to put in the data for your own mortgage loan and get an illustration that really hits home.

Companies initially record mortgage notes payable at face value, and subsequently make entries for each installment payment. To illustrate, assume that Porter Technology Inc. issues a $500,000, 12%, 20-year mortgage note on December 31, 2010, to obtain needed financing for the construction of a new research laboratory. The terms provide for semiannual installment payments of $33,231 (not including real estate taxes and insurance). The installment payment schedule for the first two years is as follows.

Illustration 10C-1
Mortgage installment payment schedule

Semiannual Interest Period	(A) Cash Payment	(B) Interest Expense (D) × 6%	(C) Reduction of Principal (A) − (B)	(D) Principal Balance (D) − (C)
Issue date				$500,000
1	$33,231	$30,000	$3,231	496,769
2	33,231	29,806	3,425	493,344
3	33,231	29,601	3,630	489,714
4	33,231	29,383	3,848	485,866

Porter Technology records the mortgage loan and first installment payment as follows.

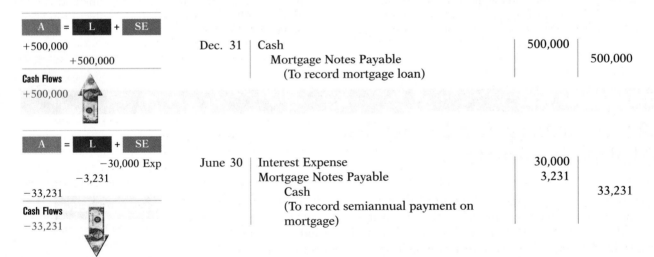

Dec. 31	Cash	500,000	
	Mortgage Notes Payable		500,000
	(To record mortgage loan)		

A = L + SE
+500,000
+500,000
Cash Flows
+500,000

A = L + SE
−30,000 Exp
−3,231
−33,231
Cash Flows
−33,231

June 30	Interest Expense	30,000	
	Mortgage Notes Payable	3,231	
	Cash		33,231
	(To record semiannual payment on		
	mortgage)		

In the balance sheet, the company reports the reduction in principal for the next year as a current liability, and classifies the remaining unpaid principal balance as a long-term liability. At December 31, 2011 (the end of semiannual period 2), the total liability is $493,344, of which $7,478 ($3,630 + $3,848) is current and $485,866 ($493,344 − $7,478) is long-term.

Summary of Study Objective for Appendix 10C

10 **Describe the accounting for long-term notes payable.**
Each payment consists of (1) interest on the unpaid balance of the loan, and (2) a reduction of loan principal. The interest decreases each period, while the portion applied to the loan principal increases each period.

Glossary

Bond certificate *(p. 495)* A legal document that indicates the name of the issuer, the face value of the bonds, and such other data as the contractual interest rate and the maturity date of the bonds.

Bonds *(p. 494)* A form of interest-bearing notes payable issued by corporations, universities, and governmental entities.

Callable bonds *(p. 494)* Bonds that are the issuing company can retire at a stated dollar amount prior to maturity.

Capital lease *(p. 509)* A contractual agreement allowing one party (the lessee) to use the assets of another party (the lessor); accounted for like a debt-financed purchase by the lessee.

Contingencies *(p. 508)* Events with uncertain outcomes that may represent potential liabilities.

Contractual (stated) interest rate *(p. 495)* Rate used to determine the amount of interest the borrower pays and the investor receives.

Convertible bonds *(p. 494)* Bonds that can be converted into common stock at the bondholder's option.

Current liability *(p. 488)* A debt that a company reasonably expects to pay (1) from existing current assets or through the creation of other current liabilities, and (2) within one year or the operating cycle, whichever is longer.

Discount (on a bond) *(p. 499)* The difference between the face value of a bond and its selling price, when a bond is sold for less than its face value.

Effective-interest method of amortization *(p. 516)* A method of amortizing bond discount or bond premium that results in periodic interest expense equal to a constant percentage of the carrying value of the bonds.

Effective-interest rate *(p. 516)* Rate established when bonds are issued that remains constant in each interest period.

Face value *(p. 495)* Amount of principal due at the maturity date of the bond.

Long-term liabilities *(p. 494)* Obligations that a company expects to pay more than one year in the future.

Market interest rate *(p. 496)* The rate investors demand for loaning funds to the corporation.

Maturity date *(p. 495)* The date on which the final payment on a bond is due from the bond issuer to the investor.

Mortgage note payable *(p. 519)* A long-term note secured by a mortgage that pledges title to specific assets as security for the loan.

Notes payable *(p. 488)* An obligation in the form of a written note.

Off-balance-sheet financing *(p. 508)* The intentional effort by a company to structure its financing arrangements so as to avoid showing liabilities on its balance sheet.

Operating lease *(p. 509)* A contractual agreement allowing one party (the lessee) to use the asset of another party (the lessor); accounted for as a rental.

Premium (on a bond) *(p. 499)* The difference between the selling price and the face value of a bond when a bond is sold for more than its face value.

Present value *(p. 495)* The value today of an amount to be received at some date in the future after taking into account current interest rates.

Secured bonds *(p. 494)* Bonds that have specific assets of the issuer pledged as collateral.

Straight-line method of amortization *(p. 513)* A method of amortizing bond discount or bond premium that allocates the same amount to interest expense in each interest period.

Time value of money *(p. 495)* The relationship between time and money. A dollar received today is worth more than a dollar promised at some time in the future.

Times interest earned ratio *(p. 507)* A measure of a company's solvency, calculated by dividing income before interest expense and taxes by interest expense.

Unsecured bonds *(p. 494)* Bonds issued against the general credit of the borrower.

Comprehensive Do it!

Snyder Software Inc. successfully developed a new spreadsheet program. However, to produce and market the program, the company needed $2.0 million of additional financing. On January 1, 2009, Snyder borrowed money as follows.

1. Snyder issued $500,000, 11%, 10-year bonds. The bonds sold at face value and pay interest on January 1.

2. Snyder issued $1.0 million, 10%, 10-year bonds for $886,996. Interest is payable on January 1. Snyder uses the straight-line method of amortization.

Instructions

(a) For the 11% bonds, prepare journal entries for the following items.
  (1) The issuance of the bonds on January 1, 2009.
  (2) Accrue interest expense on December 31, 2009.
  (3) The payment of interest on January 1, 2010.

(b) For the 10-year, 10% bonds:
  (1) Journalize the issuance of the bonds on January 1, 2009.
  (2) Prepare the entry for the redemption of the bonds at 101 on January 1, 2012, after paying the interest due on this date. The carrying value of the bonds at the redemption date was $920,897.

Action Plan

- Record the discount on bonds issued as a contra liability account.
- Compute the loss on bond redemption as the excess of the cash paid over the carrying value of the redeemed bonds.

Solution to Comprehensive Do it!

(a) (1) 2009			
Jan. 1	Cash	500,000	
	Bonds Payable		500,000
	(To record issue of 11%, 10-year bonds at face value)		
(2) 2009			
Dec. 31	Bond Interest Expense	55,000	
	Bond Interest Payable		55,000
	(To record accrual of bond interest)		
(3) 2010			
Jan. 1	Bond Interest Payable	55,000	
	Cash		55,000
	(To record payment of accrued interest)		
(b) (1) 2009			
Jan. 1	Cash	886,996	
	Discount on Bonds Payable	113,004	
	Bonds Payable		1,000,000
	(To record issuance of bonds at a discount)		
(2) 2012			
Jan. 1	Bonds Payable	1,000,000	
	Loss on Bond Redemption	89,103*	
	Discount on Bonds Payable		79,103
	Cash		1,010,000
	(To record redemption of bonds at 101)		
	*($1,010,000 − $920,897)		

Note: All Questions, Exercises, and Problems marked with an asterisk relate to material in the appendixes to the chapter.

Self-Study Questions

Answers are at the end of the chapter.

(SO 1) **1.** The time period for classifying a liability as current is one year or the operating cycle, whichever is:
  (a) longer.
  (b) shorter.
  (c) probable.
  (d) possible.

2. To be classified as a current liability, a debt must be (SO 1) expected to be paid:
  (a) out of existing current assets.
  (b) by creating other current liabilities.
  (c) within 2 years.
  (d) Either (a) or (b)

(SO 2) **3.** Corricten Company borrows $88,500 on September 1, 2010, from Harrington State Bank by signing an $88,500, 12%, one-year note. What is the accrued interest at December 31, 2010?
(a) $2,655.   (c) $4,425.
(b) $3,540.   (d) $10,620.

(SO 2) **4.** RS Company borrowed $70,000 on December 1 on a 6-month, 12% note. At December 31:
(a) neither the note payable nor the interest payable is a current liability.
(b) the note payable is a current liability, but the interest payable is not.
(c) the interest payable is a current liability but the note payable is not.
(d) both the note payable and the interest payable are current liabilities.

(SO 3) **5.** Andre Company has total proceeds from sales of $4,515. If the proceeds include sales taxes of 5%, what is the amount to be credited to Sales?
(a) $4,000.
(b) $4,300.
(c) $4,289.25.
(d) The correct answer is not given.

(SO 3) **6.** When recording payroll:
(a) gross earnings are recorded as salaries and wages payable.
(b) net pay is recorded as salaries and wages expense.
(c) payroll deductions are recorded as liabilities.
(d) More than one of the above.

(SO 3) **7.** Sensible Insurance Company collected a premium of $18,000 for a 1-year insurance policy on April 1. What amount should Sensible report as a current liability for Unearned Insurance Premiums at December 31?
(a) $0.   (c) $13,500.
(b) $4,500.   (d) $18,000.

(SO 4) **8.** What term is used for bonds that have specific assets pledged as collateral?
(a) Callable bonds.
(b) Convertible bonds.
(c) Secured bonds.
(d) Discount bonds.

(SO 4) **9.** The market interest rate:
(a) is the contractual interest rate used to determine the amount of cash interest paid by the borrower.
(b) is listed in the bond indenture.
(c) is the rate investors demand for loaning funds.
(d) More than one of the above is true.

(SO 5) **10.** Cuso Inc. issues 10-year bonds with a maturity value of $200,000. If the bonds are issued at a premium, this indicates that:
(a) the contractual interest rate exceeds the market interest rate.
(b) the market interest rate exceeds the contractual interest rate.

(c) the contractual interest rate and the market interest rate are the same.
(d) no relationship exists between the two rates.

(SO 5) **11.** On January 1, 2010, Scissors Corp. issues $200,000, 5-year, 7% bonds at face value. The entry to record the issuance of the bonds would include a:
(a) debit to cash for $14,000.
(b) debit to bonds payable for $200,000.
(c) credit to bonds payable for $200,000.
(d) credit to bond interest expense of $14,000.

(SO 5) **12.** Four-Nine Corporation issued bonds that pay interest every July 1 and January 1. The entry to accrue bond interest at December 31 includes a:
(a) debit to Interest Payable.
(b) credit to Cash.
(c) credit to Interest Expense.
(d) credit to Interest Payable.

(SO 6) **13.** Kant Corporation retires its $100,000 face value bonds at 105 on January 1, following the payment of interest. The carrying value of the bonds at the redemption date is $103,745. The entry to record the redemption will include a:
(a) credit of $3,745 to Loss on Bond Redemption.
(b) debit of $3,745 to Premium on Bonds Payable.
(c) credit of $1,255 to Gain on Bond Redemption.
(d) debit of $5,000 to Premium on Bonds Payable.

(SO 7) **14.** ▭━━▭ In a recent year Day Corporation had net income of $150,000, interest expense of $30,000, and tax expense of $20,000. What was Day Corporation's times interest earned ratio for the year?
(a) 5.00.   (c) 6.67.
(b) 4.00.   (d) 7.50.

(SO 7) **15.** ▭━━▭ Which of the following is *not* a measure of liquidity?
(a) Debt to total assets ratio.
(b) Working capital.
(c) Current ratio.
(d) Current cash debt coverage.

(SO 8) ***16.** On January 1 Pierce Corporation issues $500,000, 5-year, 12% bonds at 96 with interest payable on January 1. The entry on December 31 to record accrued bond interest and the amortization of bond discount using the straight-line method will include a:
(a) debit to Interest Expense, $57,600.
(b) debit to Interest Expense, $60,000.
(c) credit to Discount on Bonds Payable, $4,000.
(d) credit to Discount on Bonds Payable, $2,000.

(SO 8) ***17.** For the bonds issued in question 16, what is the carrying value of the bonds at the end of the third interest period?
(a) $492,000.
(b) $488,000.
(c) $472,000.
(d) $464,000.

(SO 9) ***18.** On January 1, Daisey Duke Inc. issued $1,000,000, 10-year, 9% bonds for $938,554. The market rate of interest for these bonds is 10%. Interest is payable

annually on December 31. Daisey Duke uses the effective-interest method of amortizing bond discount. At the end of the first year, Daisey Duke should report unamortized bond discount of:
(a) $54,900.   (c) $51,610.
(b) $57,590.   (d) $51,000.

(SO 9) *19. On January 1, Anthony Corporation issued $1,000,000, 14%, 5-year bonds with interest payable on December 31. The bonds sold for $1,072,096. The market rate of interest for these bonds was 12%. On the first interest date, using the effective-interest

method, the debit entry to Bond Interest Expense is for:
(a) $120,000.
(b) $125,581.
(c) $128,652.
(d) $140,000.

Go to the book's companion website, **www.wiley.com/college/kimmel**, to access additional Self-Study Questions.

Questions

1. Deborah Helkamp believes a current liability is a debt that can be expected to be paid in one year. Is Deborah correct? Explain.

2. McFarland Company obtains $20,000 in cash by signing a 9%, 6-month, $20,000 note payable to First Bank on July 1. McFarland's fiscal year ends on September 30. What information should be reported for the note payable in the annual financial statements?

3. (a) Your roommate says, "Sales taxes are reported as an expense in the income statement." Do you agree? Explain.
   (b) Brenda's Cafe has cash proceeds from sales of $8,550. This amount includes $550 of sales taxes. Give the entry to record the proceeds.

4. Troy University sold 9,000 season football tickets at $90 each for its five-game home schedule. What entries should be made (a) when the tickets are sold and (b) after each game?

5. Identify three taxes commonly withheld by the employer from an employee's gross pay.

6. (a) Identify three taxes commonly paid by employers on employees' salaries and wages.
   (b) Where in the financial statements does the employer report taxes withheld from employees' pay?

7. [Tootsie Roll] Identify the liabilities classified by Tootsie Roll as current.

8. (a) What are long-term liabilities? Give two examples.
   (b) What is a bond?

9. Contrast these types of bonds:
   (a) Secured and unsecured.
   (b) Convertible and callable.

10. Explain each of these important terms in issuing bonds:
    (a) Face value.
    (b) Contractual interest rate.
    (c) Bond certificate.

11. (a) What is a convertible bond?
    (b) Discuss the advantages of a convertible bond from the standpoint of the bondholders and of the issuing corporation.

12. Describe the two major obligations incurred by a company when bonds are issued.

13. Assume that Neer Inc. sold bonds with a face value of $100,000 for $104,000. Was the market interest rate equal to, less than, or greater than the bonds' contractual interest rate? Explain.

14. Oprah and Ellen are discussing how the market price of a bond is determined. Oprah believes that the market price of a bond is solely a function of the amount of the principal payment at the end of the term of a bond. Is she right? Discuss.

15. If a 6%, 10-year, $800,000 bond is issued at face and interest is paid annually, what is the amount of the interest payment at the end of the first period?

16. If the Bonds Payable account has a balance of $700,000 and the Discount on Bonds Payable account has a balance of $36,000, what is the carrying value of the bonds?

17. Which accounts are debited and which are credited if a bond issue originally sold at a premium is redeemed before maturity at 97 immediately following the payment of interest?

18. Elizabeth Falcone, the chief financial officer of Hangers Inc., is considering the options available to her for financing the company's new plant. Short-term interest rates right now are 6%, and long-term rates are 8%. The company's current ratio is 2.2:1. If she finances the new plant with short-term debt, the current ratio will fall to 1.5:1. Briefly discuss the issues that Elizabeth should consider.

19.
(a) In general, what are the requirements for the financial statement presentation of long-term liabilities?
(b) What ratios may be computed to evaluate a company's liquidity and solvency?

20. William Ventura says that liquidity and solvency are the same thing. Is he correct? If not, how do they differ?

21. The management of North Vehicle Corporation is concerned because survey data suggest that many potential customers do not buy vehicles due to quality concerns. It is considering taking the bold step

of increasing the length of its warranty from the industry standard of 3 years up to an unprecedented 10 years in an effort to increase confidence in its quality. Discuss the business as well as accounting implications of this move.

22. Julio Velasquez needs a few new trucks for his business. He is considering buying the trucks but is concerned that the additional debt he will need to borrow will make his liquidity and solvency ratios look bad. What options does he have other than purchasing the trucks, and how will these options affect his financial statements?

23. Melton Corporation has a current ratio of 1.1. Sam has always been told that a corporation's current ratio should exceed 2.0. Melton argues that its ratio is low because it has a minimal amount of inventory on hand so as to reduce operating costs. Melton also points out that it has significant available lines of credit. Is Sam still correct? What do some companies do to compensate for having fewer liquid assets?

24. What are the implications for analysis if a company has significant operating leases?

25. What criteria must be met before a contingency must be recorded as a liability? How should the contingency be disclosed if the criteria are not met?

*26. Explain the straight-line method of amortizing discount and premium on bonds payable.

*27. Menza Corporation issues $200,000 of 6%, 5-year bonds on January 1, 2010, at 103. Assuming that the straight-line method is used to amortize the premium, what is the total amount of interest expense for 2010?

*28. Lucia Ranos is discussing the advantages of the effective-interest method of bond amortization with her accounting staff. What do you think Lucia is saying?

*29. Peavler Corporation issues $400,000 of 9%, 5-year bonds on January 1, 2010, at 104. If Peavler uses the effective-interest method in amortizing the premium, will the annual interest expense increase or decrease over the life of the bonds? Explain.

Brief Exercises

WILEY
PLUS

BE10-1 Howland Company has these obligations at December 31: (a) a note payable for $100,000 due in 2 years, (b) a 10-year mortgage payable of $200,000 payable in ten $20,000 annual payments, (c) interest payable of $15,000 on the mortgage, and (d) accounts payable of $60,000. For each obligation, indicate whether it should be classified as a current liability.

Identify whether obligations are current liabilities.
(SO 1)

BE10-2 Kile Company borrows $90,000 on July 1 from the bank by signing a $90,000, 8%, 1-year note payable. Prepare the journal entries to record (a) the proceeds of the note and (b) accrued interest at December 31, assuming adjusting entries are made only at the end of the year.

Prepare entries for an interest-bearing note payable.
(SO 2)

BE10-3 Farm Supply does not segregate sales and sales taxes at the time of sale. The register total for March 16 is $11,395. All sales are subject to a 6% sales tax. Compute sales taxes payable and make the entry to record sales taxes payable and sales.

Compute and record sales taxes payable.
(SO 3)

BE10-4 Hilman University sells 3,800 season basketball tickets at $80 each for its 10-game home schedule. Give the entry to record (a) the sale of the season tickets and (b) the revenue earned by playing the first home game.

Prepare entries for unearned revenues.
(SO 3)

BE10-5 Burden Inc. is considering these two alternatives to finance its construction of a new $2 million plant:
(a) Issuance of 200,000 shares of common stock at the market price of $10 per share.
(b) Issuance of $2 million, 6% bonds at face value.

Compare bond financing to stock financing.
(SO 4)

Complete the table and indicate which alternative is preferable.

	Issue Stock	Issue Bond
Income before interest and taxes	$1,500,000	$1,500,000
Interest expense from bonds	_____	_____
Income before income taxes		
Income tax expense (30%)	_____	_____
Net income	$ _____	$ _____
Outstanding shares		700,000
Earnings per share	$ _____	$ _____

Prepare journal entries for bonds issued at face value.
(SO 5)

BE10-6 Mahon Corporation issued 2,000 7%, 5-year, $1,000 bonds dated January 1, 2010, at face value. Interest is paid each January 1.
(a) Prepare the journal entry to record the sale of these bonds on January 1, 2010.
(b) Prepare the adjusting journal entry on December 31, 2010, to record interest expense.
(c) Prepare the journal entry on January 1, 2011, to record interest paid.

Prepare journal entry for redemption of bonds.
(SO 6)

BE10-7 The balance sheet for Reading Company reports the following information on July 1, 2010.

READING COMPANY
Balance Sheet (partial)

Long-term liabilities		
Bonds payable	$2,000,000	
Less: Discount on bonds payable	30,000	$1,970,000

Reading decides to redeem these bonds at 102 after paying annual interest. Prepare the journal entry to record the redemption on July 1, 2010.

Prepare statement presentation of long-term liabilities.
(SO 7)

BE10-8 Presented here are long-term liability items for Felkner Inc. at December 31, 2010. Prepare the long-term liabilities section of the balance sheet for Felkner Inc.

Bonds payable, due 2014	$700,000
Notes payable, due 2012	80,000
Discount on bonds payable	21,000

Prepare liabilities section of balance sheet.
(SO 7)

BE10-9 Presented here are liability items for Sheely Inc. at December 31, 2010. Prepare the liabilities section of Sheely's balance sheet.

Accounts payable	$155,000	Employee benefits payable	$ 7,800
Bank note payable (due May 1, 2011)	20,000	Interest payable	40,000
Bonds payable, due 2014	900,000	Notes payable, due 2012	80,000
Current portion of long-term debt	240,000	Property tax payable	3,500
Discount on bonds payable	45,000	Sales taxes payable	1,400

Analyze solvency.
(SO 7)

BE10-10 The 2006 Adidas financial statements contain the following selected data (in millions).

Current assets	$3,925	Interest expense	$197
Total assets	8,379	Income taxes	227
Current liabilities	2,192	Net income	496
Total liabilities	5,543		
Cash	311		

Compute the following values and provide a brief interpretation of each.
(a) Working capital.   (c) Debt to total assets ratio.
(b) Current ratio.   (d) Times interest earned ratio.

Analyze solvency.
(SO 7)

BE10-11 The Canadian National Railway Company's (CN) total assets in a recent year were $24,004 million and its total liabilities were $14,180 million. That year, CN reported operating lease commitments for its locomotives, freight cars, and equipment totalling $740 million. If these assets had been recorded as capital leases, assume that assets and liabilities would have risen by approximately $740 million.
(a) Calculate CN's debt to total assets ratio, first using the figures reported, and then after increasing assets and liabilities for the unrecorded operating leases.
(b) Discuss the potential effect of these operating leases on your assessment of CN's solvency.

Prepare journal entries for bonds issued at a discount.
(SO 8)

*BE10-12** Upton Company issues $3 million, 10-year, 6% bonds at 99, with interest payable on December 31. The straight-line method is used to amortize bond discount.
(a) Prepare the journal entry to record the sale of these bonds on January 1, 2010.
(b) Prepare the journal entry to record interest expense and bond discount amortization on December 31, 2010, assuming no previous accrual of interest.

Prepare journal entries for bonds issued at a premium.
(SO 8)

*BE10-13** Paine Inc. issues $4 million, 5-year, 8% bonds at 103, with interest payable on January 1. The straight-line method is used to amortize bond premium.
(a) Prepare the journal entry to record the sale of these bonds on January 1, 2010.
(b) Prepare the journal entry to record interest expense and bond premium amortization on December 31, 2010, assuming no previous accrual of interest.

***BE10-14** Presented below is the partial bond discount amortization schedule for Osaki Corp., which uses the effective-interest method of amortization.

Use effective-interest method of bond amortization.
(SO 9)

Interest Periods	Interest to Be Paid	Interest Expense to Be Recorded	Discount Amortization	Unamortized Discount	Bond Carrying Value
Issue date				$62,311	$937,689
1	$45,000	$46,884	$1,884	60,427	939,573
2	45,000	46,979	1,979	58,448	941,552

Instructions
(a) Prepare the journal entry to record the payment of interest and the discount amortization at the end of period 1.
(b) Explain why interest expense is greater than interest paid.
(c) Explain why interest expense will increase each period.

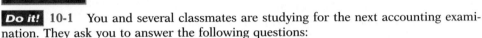 Review

Do it! 10-1 You and several classmates are studying for the next accounting examination. They ask you to answer the following questions:
1. If cash is borrowed on a $70,000, 9-month, 12% note on August 1, how much interest expense would be incurred by December 31?
2. The cash register total including sales taxes is $42,000, and the sales tax rate is 5%. What is the sales taxes payable?
3. If $42,000 is collected in advance on November 1 for 6-month magazine subscriptions, what amount of subscription revenue is earned by December 31?

Answer questions about current liabilities.
(SO 2, 3)

Do it! 10-2 During the month of February, Western Corporation's employees earned wages of $74,000. Withholdings related to these wages were $4,200 for Social Security (FICA), $7,300 for federal income tax, and $1,800 for state income tax. Costs incurred for unemployment taxes were $110 for federal and $160 for state.
Prepare the February 28 journal entries for (a) wages expense and wages payable assuming that all February wages will be paid in March and (b) the company's payroll tax expense.

Prepare entries for payroll and payroll taxes.
(SO 3)

Do it! 10-3 State whether each of the following statements is true or false.
_____ 1. Mortgage bonds and sinking fund bonds are both examples of debenture bonds.
_____ 2. Convertible bonds are also known as callable bonds.
_____ 3. The market rate is the rate investors demand for loaning funds.
_____ 4. Semiannual interest on bonds is equal to the face value times the stated rate times 6/12.
_____ 5. The present value of a bond is the value at which it should sell in the market.

Evaluate statements about bonds.
(SO 4)

Do it! 10-4 Goliath Corporation issues $300,000 of bonds for $312,000. (a) Prepare the journal entry to record the issuance of the bonds, and (b) show how the bonds would be reported on the balance sheet at the date of issuance.

Prepare journal entry for bond issuance and show balance sheet presentation.
(SO 5)

Do it! 10-5 Hucklebuckers Corporation issued $400,000 of 10-year bonds at a discount. Prior to maturity, when the carrying value of the bonds was $390,000, the company retired the bonds at 99. Prepare the entry to record the redemption of the bonds.

Prepare entry for bond redemption.
(SO 6)

Exercises

E10-1 Melissa Hoadley and Kelly Quayle borrowed $16,000 on a 7-month, 9% note from Gopher State Bank to open their business, MK's Coffee House. The money was borrowed on June 1, 2010, and the note matures January 1, 2011.

Prepare entries for interest-bearing notes.
(SO 2)

Instructions
(a) Prepare the entry to record the receipt of the funds from the loan.
(b) Prepare the entry to accrue the interest on June 30.

(c) Assuming adjusting entries are made at the end of each month, determine the balance in the interest payable account at December 31, 2010.

(d) Prepare the entry required on January 1, 2011, when the loan is paid back.

Prepare entries for interest-bearing notes.

(SO 2)

E10-2 On May 15, Gott's Outback Clothiers borrowed some money on a 4-month note to provide cash during the slow season of the year. The interest rate on the note was 8%. At the time the note was due, the amount of interest owed was $400.

Instructions

(a) Determine the amount borrowed by Gott's.

(b) Assume the amount borrowed was $18,500. What was the interest rate if the amount of interest owed was $555?

(c) Prepare the entry for the initial borrowing and the repayment for the facts in part (a).

Prepare entries for interest-bearing notes.

(SO 2)

E10-3 On June 1, Coble Company Ltd. borrows $40,000 from First Bank on a 6-month, $40,000, 9% note. The note matures on December 1.

Instructions

(a) Prepare the entry on June 1.

(b) Prepare the adjusting entry on June 30.

(c) Prepare the entry at maturity (December 1), assuming monthly adjusting entries have been made through November 30.

(d) What was the total financing cost (interest expense)?

Journalize sales and related taxes.

(SO 3)

E10-4 In providing accounting services to small businesses, you encounter the following situations pertaining to cash sales.

1. Grainger Company rings up sales and sales taxes separately on its cash register. On April 10 the register totals are sales $25,000 and sales taxes $1,750.

2. Darby Company does not segregate sales and sales taxes. Its register total for April 15 is $13,780, which includes a 6% sales tax.

Instructions

Prepare the entries to record the sales transactions and related taxes for (a) Grainger Company and (b) Darby Company.

Journalize payroll entries.

(SO 3)

E10-5 During the month of March, Neufeld Company's employees earned wages of $60,000. Withholdings related to these wages were $4,590 for Social Security (FICA), $7,500 for federal income tax, $3,100 for state income tax, and $400 for union dues. The company incurred no cost related to these earnings for federal unemployment tax, but incurred $700 for state unemployment tax.

Instructions

(a) Prepare the necessary March 31 journal entry to record wages expense and wages payable. Assume that wages earned during March will be paid during April.

(b) Prepare the entry to record the company's payroll tax expense.

Journalize unearned revenue transactions.

(SO 3)

E10-6 Season tickets for the Longhorns are priced at $230 and include 20 games. Revenue is recognized after each game is played. When the season began, the amount credited to Unearned Season Ticket Revenue was $1,265,000. By the end of October, $759,000 of the Unearned Season Ticket Revenue had been recorded as earned.

Instructions

(a) How many season tickets did the Longhorns sell?

(b) How many home games had the Longhorns played by the end of October?

(c) Prepare the entry for the initial recording of the Unearned Season Ticket Revenue.

(d) Prepare the entry to recognize the revenue after the first home game had been played.

Journalize unearned subscription revenue.

(SO 3)

E10-7 Teeter Company Ltd. publishes a monthly sports magazine, *Fishing Preview*. Subscriptions to the magazine cost $26 per year. During November 2010, Teeter sells 6,000 subscriptions for cash, beginning with the December issue. Teeter prepares financial statements quarterly and recognizes subscription revenue earned at the end of the quarter. The company uses the accounts Unearned Subscription Revenue and Subscription Revenue. The company has a December 31 year-end.

Instructions

(a) Prepare the entry in November for the receipt of the subscriptions.

(b) Prepare the adjusting entry at December 31, 2010, to record subscription revenue earned in December 2010.

(c) Prepare the adjusting entry at March 31, 2011, to record subscription revenue earned in the first quarter of 2011.

E10-8 On September 1, 2010, Elmdale Corporation issued $600,000, 8%, 10-year bonds at face value. Interest is payable annually on September 1. Elmdale's year-end is December 31.

Prepare journal entries for issuance of bonds and payment and accrual of interest.
(SO 5)

Instructions
Prepare journal entries to record the following events.
(a) The issuance of the bonds.
(b) The accrual of interest on December 31, 2010.
(c) The payment of interest on September 1, 2011.

E10-9 On January 1 Kreitzer Company issued $300,000, 7%, 10-year bonds at face value. Interest is payable annually on January 1.

Prepare journal entries for issuance of bonds and payment and accrual of interest.
(SO 5)

Instructions
Prepare journal entries to record the following events.
(a) The issuance of the bonds.
(b) The accrual of interest on December 31.
(c) The payment of interest on January 1.

E10-10 Assume that the following are independent situations recently reported in the *Wall Street Journal*.
1. General Electric (GE) 7% bonds, maturing January 28, 2013, were issued at 111.12.
2. Boeing 7% bonds, maturing September 24, 2027, were issued at 99.08.

Prepare entries for issue of bonds.
(SO 5)

Instructions
(a) Were GE and Boeing bonds issued at a premium or a discount?
(b) Explain how bonds, both paying the same contractual interest rate, could be issued at different prices.
(c) Prepare the journal entry to record the issue of each of these two bonds, assuming each company issued $800,000 of bonds in total.

E10-11 Didde Company issued $400,000 of 8%, 20-year bonds on January 1, 2010, at face value. Interest is payable annually on January 1.

Prepare journal entries to record issuance of bonds, payment of interest, and redemption at maturity.
(SO 5, 6)

Instructions
Prepare the journal entries to record the following events.
(a) The issuance of the bonds.
(b) The accrual of interest on December 31, 2010.
(c) The payment of interest on January 1, 2011.
(d) The redemption of the bonds at maturity, assuming interest for the last interest period has been paid and recorded.

E10-12 The situations presented here are independent of each other.

Prepare journal entries for redemption of bonds.
(SO 6)

Instructions
For each situation prepare the appropriate journal entry for the redemption of the bonds.
(a) Garland Corporation retired $140,000 face value, 12% bonds on June 30, 2010, at 102. The carrying value of the bonds at the redemption date was $122,500. The bonds pay annual interest, and the interest payment due on June 30, 2010, has been made and recorded.
(b) Hutchison, Inc., retired $170,000 face value, 12.5% bonds on June 30, 2010, at 98. The carrying value of the bonds at the redemption date was $184,000. The bonds pay annual interest, and the interest payment due on June 30, 2010, has been made and recorded.

E10-13 Edmonds, Inc. reports the following liabilities (in thousands) on its January 31, 2010, balance sheet and notes to the financial statements.

Prepare liabilities section of balance sheet.
(SO 7)

Accounts payable	$4,263.9	Notes payable—long-term	$6,746.7
Accrued pension liability	1,215.2	Operating leases	1,641.7
Accrued liabilities	1,258.1	Loans payable—long-term	335.6
Bonds payable	1,961.2	Payroll-related liabilities	558.1
Current portion of		Short-term borrowings	2,563.6
long-term debt	1,992.2	Unused operating line of credit	3,337.6
Income taxes payable	235.2	Warranty liability—current	1,417.3

Instructions
(a) Identify which of the above liabilities are likely current and which are likely long-term. Say if an item fits in neither category. Explain the reasoning for your selection.
(b) Prepare the liabilities section of Edmonds's balance sheet as at January 31, 2010.

Calculate liquidity and solvency ratios; discuss impact of unrecorded obligations on liquidity and solvency.
(SO 7)

E10-14 McDonald's 2006 financial statements contain the following selected data (in millions).

Current assets	$ 3,625.3	Interest expense	$ 402.0
Total assets	29,023.8	Income taxes	1,293.4
Current liabilities	3,008.1	Net income	3,544.2
Total liabilities	13,565.5		

Instructions
(a) Compute the following values and provide a brief interpretation of each.
(1) Working capital. (3) Debt to total assets ratio.
(2) Current ratio. (4) Times interest earned ratio.
(b) The notes to McDonald's financial statements show that subsequent to 2006 the company will have future minimum lease payments under operating leases of $11,119.8 million. If these assets had been purchased with debt, assets and liabilities would rise by approximately $9,900 million. Recompute the debt to total assets ratio after adjusting for this. Discuss your result.

Calculate current ratio before and after paying accounts payable.
(SO 7)

E10-15 3M Company reported the following financial data for 2006 and 2005 ($ in millions).

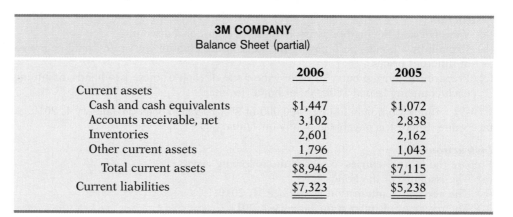

3M COMPANY
Balance Sheet (partial)

	2006	2005
Current assets		
Cash and cash equivalents	$1,447	$1,072
Accounts receivable, net	3,102	2,838
Inventories	2,601	2,162
Other current assets	1,796	1,043
Total current assets	$8,946	$7,115
Current liabilities	$7,323	$5,238

Instructions
(a) Calculate the current ratio for 3M for 2006 and 2005.
(b) Suppose that at the end of 2006 3M management used $300 million cash to pay off $300 million of accounts payable. How would its current ratio change?

Calculate current ratio before and after paying accounts payable.
(SO 7)

E10-16 Lancer Boutique reported the following financial data for 2010 and 2009.

LANCER BOUTIQUE
Balance Sheet (partial)
September 30 (in thousands)

	2010	2009
Current assets		
Cash and short-term deposits	$2,574	$1,021
Accounts receivable	2,347	1,575
Inventories	1,201	1,010
Other current assets	322	192
Total current assets	$6,444	$3,798
Current liabilities	$4,803	$3,508

Instructions
(a) Calculate the current ratio for Lancer Boutique for 2010 and 2009.
(b) Suppose that at the end of 2010, Lancer Boutique used $1.5 million cash to pay off $1.5 million of accounts payable. How would its current ratio change?

(c) At September 30, Lancer Boutique has an undrawn operating line of credit of $12.5 million. Would this affect any assessment that you might make of Lancer Boutique's short-term liquidity? Explain.

E10-17 Wal-Mart was sued nearly 5,000 times in a recent year—about once every two hours every day of the year. Wal-Mart has been sued for everything imaginable—ranging from falls on icy parking lots to injuries sustained in shoppers' stampedes to a murder with a rifle purchased at Wal-Mart.

Discuss contingent liabilities.

(SO 7)

Wal-Mart does not adhere to the legal strategy many businesses use of "Settle quickly and cut your losses." Instead, Wal-Mart aggressively fights lawsuits, even when it would be cheaper to settle. The company reported the following in the notes to its financial statements:

> The Company and its subsidiaries are involved from time to time in claims, proceedings, and litigation arising from the operation of its business. The Company does not believe that any such claim, proceeding, or litigation, either alone or in the aggregate, will have a material adverse effect on the Company's financial position or results of its operations.

Instructions
(a) Explain why Wal-Mart does not have to record these contingent liabilities.
(b) Comment on any implications for analysis of the financial statements.

*E10-18 Ellison Company issued $500,000, 7%, 20-year bonds on January 1, 2010, at 103. Interest is payable annually on January 1. Ellison uses straight-line amortization for bond premium or discount.

Prepare journal entries to record issuance of bonds, payment of interest, amortization of premium using straight-line, and redemption at maturity.

(SO 5, 6, 8)

Instructions
Prepare the journal entries to record the following events.
(a) The issuance of the bonds.
(b) The accrual of interest and the premium amortization on December 31, 2010.
(c) The payment of interest on January 1, 2011.
(d) The redemption of the bonds at maturity, assuming interest for the last interest period has been paid and recorded.

*E10-19 Rooney Company issued $300,000, 8%, 10-year bonds on December 31, 2009, for $290,000. Interest is payable annually on December 31. Rooney uses the straight-line method to amortize bond premium or discount.

Prepare journal entries to record issuance of bonds, payment of interest, amortization of discount using straight-line, and redemption at maturity.

(SO 5, 6, 8)

Instructions
Prepare the journal entries to record the following events.
(a) The issuance of the bonds.
(b) The payment of interest and the discount amortization on December 31, 2010.
(c) The redemption of the bonds at maturity, assuming interest for the last interest period has been paid and recorded.

*E10-20 Osage Corporation issued $600,000, 7%, 10-year bonds on January 1, 2010, for $559,740. This price resulted in an effective-interest rate of 8% on the bonds. Interest is payable annually on January 1. Osage uses the effective-interest method to amortize bond premium or discount.

Prepare journal entries for issuance of bonds, payment of interest, and amortization of discount using effective-interest method.

(SO 5, 9)

Instructions
Prepare the journal entries to record (round to the nearest dollar):
(a) The issuance of the bonds.
(b) The accrual of interest and the discount amortization on December 31, 2010.
(c) The payment of interest on January 1, 2011.

*E10-21 Pedigo Company issued $450,000, 7%, 10-year bonds on January 1, 2010, for $483,120. This price resulted in an effective-interest rate of 6% on the bonds. Interest is payable annually on January 1. Pedigo uses the effective-interest method to amortize bond premium or discount.

Prepare journal entries for issuance of bonds, payment of interest, and amortization of premium using effective-interest method.

(SO 5, 9)

Instructions
Prepare the journal entries (rounded to the nearest dollar) to record:
(a) The issuance of the bonds.
(b) The accrual of interest and the premium amortization on December 31, 2010.
(c) The payment of interest on January 1, 2011.

Prepare journal entries to record mortgage note and installment payments.
(SO 10)

*E10-22 Kelso Co. receives $330,000 when it issues a $330,000, 8%, mortgage note payable to finance the construction of a building at December 31, 2010. The terms provide for semiannual installment payments of $21,123 on June 30 and December 31.

Instructions
Prepare the journal entries to record the mortgage loan and the first two installment payments.

Exercises: Set B

Visit the book's companion website, at **www.wiley.com/college/kimmel**, and choose the Student Companion site, to access Exercise Set B.

Problems: Set A

Prepare current liability entries, adjusting entries, and current liabilities section.
(SO 1, 2, 3, 7)

P10-1A On January 1, 2010, the ledger of Glennon Company contained these liability accounts.

Accounts Payable	$42,500
Sales Taxes Payable	6,600
Unearned Service Revenue	19,000

During January the following selected transactions occurred.

Jan. 1 Borrowed $15,000 in cash from Midland Bank on a 4-month, 8%, $15,000 note.

5 Sold merchandise for cash totaling $6,510, which includes 5% sales taxes.

12 Provided services for customers who had made advance payments of $10,000. (Credit Service Revenue.)

14 Paid state treasurer's department for sales taxes collected in December 2009, $6,600.

20 Sold 500 units of a new product on credit at $48 per unit, plus 5% sales tax.

During January the company's employees earned wages of $70,000. Withholdings related to these wages were $5,355 for Social Security (FICA), $5,000 for federal income tax, and $1,500 for state income tax. The company owed no money related to these earnings for federal or state unemployment tax. Assume that wages earned during January will be paid during February. No entry had been recorded for wages or payroll tax expense as of January 31.

Instructions
(a) Journalize the January transactions.
(b) Journalize the adjusting entries at January 31 for the outstanding note payable and for wages expense and payroll tax expense.

(c) Tot. current liabilities $143,465

(c) Prepare the current liabilities section of the balance sheet at January 31, 2010. Assume no change in Accounts Payable.

Journalize and post note transactions; show balance sheet presentation.
(SO 2, 7)

P10-2A McCullough Corporation sells rock-climbing products and also operates an indoor climbing facility for climbing enthusiasts. During the last part of 2010, McCullough had the following transactions related to notes payable.

Sept. 1 Issued a $12,000 note to Jernigan to purchase inventory. The 3-month note payable bears interest of 8% and is due December 1.

Sept. 30 Recorded accrued interest for the Jernigan note.

Oct. 1 Issued a $16,000, 9%, 4-month note to Lebo Bank to finance the purchase of a new climbing wall for advanced climbers. The note is due February 1.

Oct. 31 Recorded accrued interest for the Jernigan note and the Lebo Bank note.

Nov.	1	Issued a $25,000 note and paid $8,000 cash to purchase a vehicle to transport clients to nearby climbing sites as part of a new series of climbing classes. This note bears interest of 6% and matures in 12 months.
Nov.	30	Recorded accrued interest for the Jernigan note, the Lebo Bank note, and the vehicle note.
Dec.	1	Paid principal and interest on the Jernigan note.
Dec.	31	Recorded accrued interest for the Lebo Bank note and the vehicle note.

Instructions
(a) Prepare journal entries for the transactions noted above.
(b) Post the above entries to the Notes Payable, Interest Payable, and Interest Expense accounts. (Use T accounts.)
(c) Show the balance sheet presentation of notes payable and interest payable at December 31.
(d) How much interest expense relating to notes payable did McCullough incur during the year?

(b) Interest Payable $610

P10-3A The following section is taken from Pickeril balance sheet at December 31, 2009.

Prepare journal entries to record interest payments and redemption of bonds.
(SO 5, 6)

Current liabilities	
Bond interest payable	$ 40,000
Long-term liabilities	
Bonds payable, 8%, due January 1, 2013	500,000

Interest is payable annually on January 1. The bonds are callable on any annual interest date.

Instructions
(a) Journalize the payment of the bond interest on January 1, 2010.
(b) Assume that on January 1, 2010, after paying interest, Pickeril calls bonds having a face value of $100,000. The call price is 104. Record the redemption of the bonds.
(c) Prepare the adjusting entry on December 31, 2010, to accrue the interest on the remaining bonds.

(b) Loss $4,000

P10-4A On October 1, 2009, Havenhill Corp. issued $700,000, 7%, 10-year bonds at face value. The bonds were dated October 1, 2009, and pay interest annually on October 1. Financial statements are prepared annually on December 31.

Prepare journal entries to record issuance of bonds, interest, balance sheet presentation, and bond redemption.
(SO 5, 6, 7)

Instructions
(a) Prepare the journal entry to record the issuance of the bonds.
(b) Prepare the adjusting entry to record the accrual of interest on December 31, 2009.
(c) Show the balance sheet presentation of bonds payable and bond interest payable on December 31, 2009.
(d) Prepare the journal entry to record the payment of interest on October 1, 2010.
(e) Prepare the adjusting entry to record the accrual of interest on December 31, 2010.
(f) Assume that on January 1, 2011, Havenhill pays the accrued bond interest and calls the bonds. The call price is 102. Record the payment of interest and redemption of the bonds.

(f) Loss $14,000

P10-5A Pettigrew Company sold $6,000,000, 8%, 20-year bonds on January 1, 2010. The bonds were dated January 1, 2010, and pay interest on December 31. The bonds were sold at 98.

Prepare journal entries to record issuance of bonds, show balance sheet presentation, and record bond redemption.
(SO 5, 6, 7)

Instructions
(a) Prepare the journal entry to record the issuance of the bonds on January 1, 2010.
(b) At December 31, 2010, $6,000 of the bond discount had been amortized. Show the balance sheet presentation of the bond liability at December 31, 2010. (Assume that interest has been paid.)
(c) At December 31, 2011, when the carrying value of the bonds was $5,892,000, the company redeemed the bonds at 102. Record the redemption of the bonds assuming that interest for the year had already been paid.

(c) Loss $228,000

P10-6A You have been presented with the selected information taken from the financial statements of Southwest Airlines Co. shown on the next page.

Calculate and comment on ratios.
(SO 7)

SOUTHWEST AIRLINES CO.
Balance Sheet (partial)
December 31
(in millions)

	2006	2005
Total current assets	$ 2,601	$ 3,620
Noncurrent assets	10,859	10,383
Total assets	$13,460	$14,003
Current liabilities	$ 2,887	$ 3,848
Long-term liabilities	4,124	3,480
Total liabilities	7,011	7,328
Shareholders' equity	6,449	6,675
Total liabilities and shareholders' equity	$13,460	$14,003

Other information:

	2006	2005
Net income (loss)	$ 499	$ 484
Income tax expense	291	295
Interest expense	128	122
Cash provided by operations	1,406	2,118
Capital expenditures	1,399	1,146
Cash dividends	14	14

Note 8. Leases
The majority of the Company's terminal operations space, as well as 84 aircraft, were under operating leases at December 31, 2006. Future minimum lease payments under noncancelable operating leases are as follows: 2007, $360,000; 2008, $318,000; 2009, $280,000; 2010, $250,000; 2011, $203,000; after 2011, $1,000,000.

Instructions
(a) Calculate each of the following ratios for 2006 and 2005.
  (1) Current ratio.
  (2) Free cash flow.
  (3) Debt to total assets.
  (4) Times interest earned ratio.
(b) Comment on the trend in ratios.
(c) Read the company's note on leases. If the operating leases had instead been accounted for like a purchase, assets and liabilities would increase by approximately $1,500 million. Recalculate the debt to total assets ratio for 2006 in light of this information, and discuss the implictions for analysis.

Prepare journal entries to record interest payments, straight-line discount amortization, and redemption of bonds.
(SO 5, 6, 8)

*P10-7A The following information is taken from Kuehn Corp.'s balance sheet at December 31, 2009.

Current liabilities		
Bond interest payable		$ 168,000
Long-term liabilities		
Bonds payable, 7%, due January 1, 2020	$2,400,000	
Less: Discount on bonds payable	42,000	2,358,000

Interest is payable annually on January 1. The bonds are callable on any annual interest date. Kuehn uses straight-line amortization for any bond premium or discount. From December 31, 2009, the bonds will be outstanding for an additional 10 years (120 months).

Instructions
(Round all computations to the nearest dollar.)
(a) Journalize the payment of bond interest on January 1, 2010.
(b) Prepare the entry to amortize bond discount and to accrue the interest on December 31, 2010.

(c) Assume on January 1, 2011, after paying interest, that Kuehn Corp. calls bonds having a face value of $400,000. The call price is 103. Record the redemption of the bonds.

(d) Prepare the adjusting entry at December 31, 2011, to amortize bond discount and to accrue interest on the remaining bonds.

(c) Loss $18,300

*P10-8A   Lore Corporation sold $2,000,000, 6%, 10-year bonds on January 1, 2010. The bonds were dated January 1, 2010, and pay interest on January 1. Lore Corporation uses the straight-line method to amortize bond premium or discount.

Prepare journal entries to record issuance of bonds, interest, and straight-line amortization, and balance sheet presentation.
(SO 5, 7, 8)

Instructions

(a) Prepare all the necessary journal entries to record the issuance of the bonds and bond interest expense for 2010, assuming that the bonds sold at 103.

(b) Prepare journal entries as in part (a) assuming that the bonds sold at 98.

(c) Show the balance sheet presentation for the bond issue at December 31, 2010, using (1) the 103 selling price, and then (2) the 98 selling price.

*P10-9A   Kinzie Co. sold $3,000,000, 9%, 5-year bonds on January 1, 2010. The bonds were dated January 1, 2010, and pay interest on January 1. The company uses straight-line amortization on bond premiums and discounts. Financial statements are prepared annually.

Prepare journal entries to record issuance of bonds, interest, and straight-line amortization, and balance sheet presentation.
(SO 5, 6, 8)

Instructions

(a) Prepare the journal entries to record the issuance of the bonds assuming they sold at:
    (1) 101.
    (2) 97.

(b) Prepare amortization tables for both assumed sales for the first three interest payments.

(c) Prepare the journal entries to record interest expense for 2010 under both assumed sales.

(c) (2) 12/31/10 Interest Expense $288,000

(d) Show the balance sheet presentation for both assumed sales at December 31, 2010.

*P10-10A   On January 1, 2010, Irik Corporation issued $1,800,000 face value, 7%, 10-year bonds at $1,679,219. This price resulted in an effective-interest rate of 8% on the bonds. Irik uses the effective-interest method to amortize bond premium or discount. The bonds pay annual interest January 1.

Prepare journal entries to record issuance of bonds, payment of interest, and amortization of bond discount using effective-interest method.
(SO 5, 9)

Instructions

(Round all computations to the nearest dollar.)

(a) Prepare the journal entry to record the issuance of the bonds on January 1, 2010.

(b) Prepare an amortization table through December 31, 2012 (three interest periods) for this bond issue.

(c) Prepare the journal entry to record the accrual of interest and the amortization of the discount on December 31, 2010.

(c) Interest Expense $134,338

(d) Prepare the journal entry to record the payment of interest on January 1, 2011.

(e) Prepare the journal entry to record the accrual of interest and the amortization of the discount on December 31, 2011.

*P10-11A   On January 1, 2010, Fair Company issued $3,000,000 face value, 8%, 10-year bonds at $3,441,605. This price resulted in a 6% effective-interest rate on the bonds. Fair uses the effective-interest method to amortize bond premium or discount. The bonds pay annual interest on each January 1.

Prepare journal entries to record issuance of bonds, payment of interest, and effective-interest amortization, and balance sheet presentation.
(SO 5, 7, 9)

Instructions

(a) Prepare the journal entries to record the following transactions.
    (1) The issuance of the bonds on January 1, 2010.
    (2) Accrual of interest and amortization of the premium on December 31, 2010.
    (3) The payment of interest on January 1, 2011.
    (4) Accrual of interest and amortization of the premium on December 31, 2011.

(a) (4) Interest Expense $204,486

(b) Show the proper balance sheet presentation for the liability for bonds payable on the December 31, 2011, balance sheet.

(c) Provide the answers to the following questions in narrative form.
    (1) What amount of interest expense is reported for 2011?
    (2) Would the bond interest expense reported in 2011 be the same as, greater than, or less than the amount that would be reported if the straight-line method of amortization were used?

Prepare installment payments schedule, journal entries, and balance sheet presentation for a mortgage note payable.
(SO 7, 10)

*P10-12A Dambro purchased a new piece of equipment to be used in its new facility. The $350,000 piece of equipment was purchased with a $50,000 down payment and with cash received through the issuance of a $300,000, 8%, 4-year mortgage note payable issued on October 1, 2010. The terms provide for quarterly installment payments of $22,095 on December 31, March 31, June 30, and September 30.

Instructions

(Round all computations to the nearest dollar.)

(a) Prepare an installment payments schedule for the first five payments of the notes payable.

(b) Prepare all journal entries related to the notes payable for December 31, 2010.

(c) Current portion $67,664

(c) Show the balance sheet presentation for this obligation for December 31, 2010. (*Hint:* Be sure to distinguish between the current and long-term portions of the note.)

Prepare journal entries to record payments for long-term note payable, and balance sheet presentation.
(SO 7, 10)

*P10-13A Stacy Button has just approached a venture capitalist for financing for her new business venture, the development of a local ski hill. On July 1, 2009, Stacy was loaned $120,000 at an annual interest rate of 7%. The loan is repayable over 5 years in annual installments of $29,267, principal and interest, due each June 30. The first payment is due June 30, 2010. Stacy uses the effective-interest method for amortizing debt. Her ski hill company's year-end will be June 30.

Instructions

(a) Prepare an amortization schedule for the 5 years, 2009–2014. Round all calculations to the nearest dollar.

(b) 6/30/10 Interest Expense $8,400

(b) Prepare all journal entries for Stacy Button for the first 2 fiscal years ended June 30, 2010, and June 30, 2011. Round all calculations to the nearest dollar.

(c) Show the balance sheet presentation of the note payable as of June 30, 2011. (*Hint:* Be sure to distinguish between the current and long-term portions of the note.)

Problems: Set B

Prepare current liability entries, adjusting entries, and current liabilities section.
(SO 1, 2, 3, 7)

GLS

P10-1B On January 1, 2010, the ledger of Euler Company contained the following liability accounts.

Accounts Payable	$52,000
Sales Taxes Payable	8,500
Unearned Service Revenue	11,000

During January the following selected transactions occurred.

Jan. 1 Borrowed $18,000 from TriCounty Bank on a 3-month, 7%, $18,000 note.

5 Sold merchandise for cash totaling $18,550, which includes 6% sales taxes.

12 Provided services for customers who had made advance payments of $8,000. (Credit Service Revenue.)

14 Paid state revenue department for sales taxes collected in December 2009 ($8,500).

20 Sold 500 units of a new product on credit at $50 per unit, plus 6% sales tax.

During January the company's employees earned wages of $50,000. Withholdings related to these wages were $3,825 for Social Security (FICA), $3,800 for federal income tax, and $1,100 for state income tax. The company owed no money related to these earnings for federal or state unemployment tax. Assume that wages earned during January will be paid during February. No entry had been recorded for wages or payroll tax expense as of January 31.

Instructions

(a) Journalize the January transactions.

(b) Journalize the adjusting entries at January 31 for the outstanding notes payable and for wages expense and payroll tax expense.

(c) Tot. current liabilities $129,480

(c) Prepare the current liabilities section of the balance sheet at January 31, 2010. Assume no change in accounts payable.

P10-2B Rockie Mountain Bikes markets mountain-bike tours to clients vacationing in various locations in the mountains of Colorado. In preparation for the upcoming summer biking season, Rockie entered into the following transactions related to notes payable.

Journalize and post note transactions; show balance sheet presentation.
(SO 2, 7)

Mar.	1	Purchased Puma bikes for use as rentals by issuing a $10,000, 3-month, 6% note payable that is due June 1.
Mar.	31	Recorded accrued interest for the Puma note.
Apr.	1	Issued a $30,000 9-month note for the purchase of mountain property on which to build bike trails. The note bears 8% interest and is due January 1.
Apr.	30	Recorded accrued interest for the Puma note and the land note.
May	1	Issued a 4-month note to Paola National Bank for $15,000 at 6%. The funds will be used for working capital for the beginning of the season; the note is due September 1.
May	31	Recorded accrued interest for all three notes.
June	1	Paid principal and interest on the Puma note.
June	30	Recorded accrued interest for the land note and the Paola Bank note.

Instructions
(a) Prepare journal entries for the transactions noted above.
(b) Post the above entries to the Notes Payable, Interest Payable, and Interest Expense accounts. (Use T accounts.)
(c) Assuming that Rockie's year-end is June 30, show the balance sheet presentation of notes payable and interest payable at that date.
(d) How much interest expense relating to notes payable did Rockie incur during the year?

(b) Interest Payable $750

P10-3B The following section is taken from Dorothy Corp.'s balance sheet at December 31, 2009.

Prepare journal entries to record interest payments and redemption of bonds.
(SO 5, 6)

Current liabilities	
Bond interest payable	$ 96,000
Long-term liabilities	
Bonds payable, 8%, due January 1, 2014	1,200,000

Interest is payable annually on January 1. The bonds are callable on any annual interest date.

Instructions
(a) Journalize the payment of the bond interest on January 1, 2010.
(b) Assume that on January 1, 2010, after paying interest, Dorothy Corp. calls bonds having a face value of $300,000. The call price is 105. Record the redemption of the bonds.
(c) Prepare the adjusting entry on December 31, 2010, to accrue the interest on the remaining bonds.

(b) Loss $15,000

P10-4B On April 1, 2009, LRF Corp. issued $600,000, 7%, 5-year bonds at face value. The bonds were dated April 1, 2009, and pay interest annually on April 1. Financial statements are prepared annually on December 31.

Prepare journal entries to record issuance of bonds, interest, balance sheet presentation, and bond redemption.
(SO 5, 6, 7)

Instructions
(a) Prepare the journal entry to record the issuance of the bonds.
(b) Prepare the adjusting entry to record the accrual of interest on December 31, 2009.
(c) Show the balance sheet presentation of bonds payable and bond interest payable on December 31, 2009.
(d) Prepare the journal entry to record the payment of interest on April 1, 2010.
(e) Prepare the adjusting entry to record the accrual of interest on December 31, 2010.
(f) Assume that on January 1, 2011, LRF pays the accrued bond interest and calls the bonds. The call price is 102. Record the payment of interest and redemption of the bonds.

(f) Loss   12,000

P10-5B Star Electric sold $5,000,000, 9%, 20-year bonds on January 1, 2010. The bonds were dated January 1 and pay interest on January 1. The bonds were sold at 103.

Prepare journal entries to record issuance of bonds, show balance sheet presentation, and record bond redemption.
(SO 5, 6, 7)

Instructions
(a) Prepare the journal entry to record the issuance of the bonds on January 1, 2010.
(b) At December 31, 2010, $7,500 of the bond premium had been amortized. Show the balance sheet presentation of the bond liability at December 31, 2010. (Assume that interest has been paid.)

(c) Loss $65,000

(c) At December 31, 2011, when the carrying value of the bonds was $5,135,000, the company redeemed the bonds at 104. Record the redemption of the bonds assuming that interest for the year had already been paid.

Calculate and comment on ratios.

(SO 7)

P10-6B The following selected information was taken from the financial statements of Krispy Kreme Doughnuts, Inc.

KRISPY KREME DOUGHNUTS, INC. Balance Sheet (partial) (in thousands)		
	Jan. 28, 2007	**Jan. 29, 2006**
Total current assets	$131,818	$147,025
Capital assets and other long-term assets	217,674	263,830
	$349,492	$410,855
Current liabilities	$134,870	$153,919
Long-term liabilities	135,660	148,265
Total liabilities	270,530	302,184
Shareholders' equity	78,962	108,671
Total liabilities and shareholders' equity	$349,492	$410,855

Other information:

	2007	**2006**
Interest expense	$ 20,334	$ 20,211
Tax expense (benefit)	1,211	(776)
Net loss	(42,236)	(135,760)
Cash provided by operations	22,108	1,865
Capital expenditures	4,005	10,381
Cash dividends	-0-	-0-

Note 10. Lease Commitments

The Company conducts some of its operations from leased facilities and, additionally, leases certain equipment under operating leases. Generally, these have initial terms of 3 to 20 years and contain provisions for renewal options of 5 to 10 years.

At January 28, 2007, future minimum annual rental commitments, gross, under non-cancelable operating leases, including lease commitments on consolidated joint ventures, are as follows:

Fiscal Year Ending in	Amount (in thousands)
2008	$ 11,436
2009	10,137
2010	9,767
2011	9,752
2012	9,676
Thereafter	138,725
	$189,493

Rent expense, net of rental income, totaled $24.2 million in fiscal 2005, $23.5 million in fiscal 2006 and $17.7 million in fiscal 2007.

Instructions

(a) Calculate each of the following ratios for 2007 and 2006.
  (1) Current ratio.
  (2) Free cash flow.
  (3) Debt to total assets ratio.
(b) Comment on Krispy Kreme's liquidity and solvency.

(c) Read the company's note on leases (Note 10). If the operating leases had instead been accounted for like a purchase, assets and liabilities would have increased by approximately $135,000,000. Recalculate the debt to total assets ratio for 2007 and discuss the implications for analysis.

*P10-7B   The following section is taken from Fanestill Oil Company's balance sheet at December 31, 2009.

Current liabilities		
Bond interest payable		$ 324,000
Long-term liabilities		
Bonds payable, 9% due January 1, 2020	$3,600,000	
Add: Premium on bonds payable	400,000	4,000,000

Interest is payable annually on January 1. The bonds are callable on any annual interest date. Fanestill uses straight-line amortization for any bond premium or discount. From December 31, 2009, the bonds will be outstanding for an additional 10 years (120 months).

Instructions
(Round all computations to the nearest dollar.)
(a) Journalize the payment of bond interest on January 1, 2010.
(b) Prepare the entry to amortize bond premium and to accrue interest due on December 31, 2010.
(c) Assume on January 1, 2011, after paying interest, that Fanestill Company calls bonds having a face value of $1,800,000. The call price is 102. Record the redemption of the bonds.
(d) Prepare the adjusting entry at December 31, 2011, to amortize bond premium and to accrue interest on the remaining bonds.

Prepare journal entries to record interest payments, straight-line premium amortization, and redemption of bonds
(SO 5, 6, 8)

(c) Gain $144,000

*P10-8B   Lester Company sold $2,500,000, 10%, 10-year bonds on January 1, 2010. The bonds were dated January 1, 2010, and pay interest on January 1. Lester Company uses the straight-line method to amortize bond premium or discount.

Instructions
(a) Prepare all the necessary journal entries to record the issuance of the bonds and bond interest expense for 2010, assuming that the bonds sold at 102.
(b) Prepare journal entries as in part (a) assuming that the bonds sold at 96.
(c) Show the balance sheet presentation for the bond issue at December 31, 2010, using (1) the 102 selling price, and then (2) the 96 selling price.

Prepare journal entries to record issuance of bonds, interest, and straight-line amortization, and balance sheet presentation.
(SO 5, 7, 8)

*P10-9B   Wylie Corporation sold $2,500,000, 7%, 20-year bonds on December 31, 2009. The bonds were dated December 31, 2009, and pay interest on December 31. The company uses straight-line amortization for premiums and discounts. Financial statements are prepared annually.

Instructions
(a) Prepare the journal entry to record the issuance of the bonds assuming they sold at:
   (1) 98.
   (2) 104.
(b) Prepare amortization tables for both of the assumed sales for the first three interest payments.
(c) Prepare the journal entries to record interest expense for the first two interest payments under both assumed sales.
(d) Show the balance sheet presentation for both assumed sales at December 31, 2010.

Prepare journal entries to record issuance of bonds, interest, and straight-line amortization, and balance sheet presentation.
(SO 5, 7, 8)

(c) (2) 12/31/10 Interest Expense $170,000

*P10-10B   On January 1, 2010, Vineyard Corporation issued $2,000,000 face value, 12%, 10-year bonds at $2,245,783. This price resulted in an effective-interest rate of 10% on the bonds. Vineyard uses the effective-interest method to amortize bond premium or discount. The bonds pay annual interest January 1.

Instructions
(Round all computations to the nearest dollar.)
(a) Prepare the journal entry to record the issuance of the bonds on January 1, 2010.
(b) Prepare an amortization table through December 31, 2012 (three interest periods) for this bond issue.

Prepare journal entries to record issuance of bonds, payment of interest, and amortization of bond premium using effective-interest method.
(SO 5, 9)

(c) Interest
    Expense $224,578

(c) Prepare the journal entry to record the accrual of interest and the amortization of the premium on December 31, 2010.
(d) Prepare the journal entry to record the payment of interest on January 1, 2011.
(e) Prepare the journal entry to record the accrual of interest and the amortization of the premium on December 31, 2011.

Prepare journal entries to record issuance of bonds, payment of interest, and effective-interest amortization, and balance sheet presentation.
(SO 5, 7, 9)

*P10-11B On January 1, 2010, Jagard Company issued $4,000,000 face value, 10%, 15-year bonds at $3,455,131. This price resulted in an effective-interest rate of 12% on the bonds. Jagard uses the effective-interest method to amortize bond premium or discount. The bonds pay annual interest January 1.

Instructions
(a) Prepare the journal entries to record the following transactions.
    (1) The issuance of the bonds on January 1, 2010.
    (2) The accrual of interest and the amortization of the discount on December 31, 2010.
    (3) The payment of interest on January 1, 2011.
    (4) The accrual of interest and the amortization of the discount on December 31, 2011.
(b) Show the proper balance sheet presentation for the liability for bonds payable on the December 31, 2011, balance sheet.

(c) (1) $416,370

(c) Provide the answers to the following questions in narrative form.
    (1) What amount of interest expense is reported for 2011?
    (2) Would the bond interest expense reported in 2011 be the same as, greater than, or less than the amount that would be reported if the straight-line method of amortization were used?
    (3) Determine the total cost of borrowing over the life of the bond.
    (4) Would the total bond interest expense be greater than, the same as, or less than the total interest expense that would be reported if the straight-line method of amortization were used?

Prepare installment payments schedule, journal entries for a mortgage note payable, and balance sheet presentation.
(SO 7, 10)

*P10-12B Donald Corporation purchased a new piece of equipment to be used in its new facility. The $450,000 piece of equipment was purchased with a $50,000 down payment and with cash received through the issuance of a $400,000, 8%, 4-year mortgage note payable issued on October 1, 2010. The terms provide for quarterly installment payments of $29,460 on December 31, March 31, June 30, and September 30.

Instructions
(Round all computations to the nearest dollar.)
(a) Prepare an installment payments schedule for the first five payments of the notes payable.

(b) Interest Expense $8,000

(b) Prepare all necessary journal entries related to the notes payable for December 31, 2010.
(c) Show the balance sheet presentation for these obligations for December 31, 2010. (*Hint:* Be sure to distinguish between the current and long-term portions of the note.)

Prepare journal entries to record payments for long-term note payable.
(SO 10)

*P10-13B Keith Pryor has just approached a venture capitalist for financing for his sailing school. The venture capitalist is willing to loan Keith $90,000 at a high-risk annual interest rate of 24%. The loan is payable over 3 years in monthly installments of $3,531. Each payment includes principal and interest, calculated using the effective-interest method for amortizing debt. Keith receives the loan on May 1, 2010, which is the first day of his fiscal year. Keith makes the first payment on May 31, 2010.

Instructions
(a) Prepare an amortization schedule for the period from May 1, 2010, to August 31, 2010. Round all calculations to the nearest dollar.

(b) 6/30 Interest
    Expense $1,765

(b) Prepare all journal entries for Keith Pryor for the period beginning May 1, 2010, and ending July 31, 2010. Round all calculations to the nearest dollar.

Problems: Set C

Visit the book's companion website at **www.wiley.com/college/kimmel** and choose the Student Companion site to access Problem Set C.

Comprehensive Problem

CP10   Aber Corporation's balance sheet at December 31, 2009, is presented below.

ABER CORPORATION
Balance Sheet
December 31, 2009

Cash	$30,500	Accounts payable	$13,750
Inventory	25,750	Bond interest payable	3,000
Prepaid insurance	5,600	Bonds payable	50,000
Equipment	38,000	Common stock	20,000
	$99,850	Retained earnings	$13,100
			$99,850

During 2010, the following transactions occurred.
1. Aber paid $3,000 interest on the bonds on January 1, 2010.
2. Aber purchased $241,100 of inventory on account.
3. Aber sold for $450,000 cash inventory which cost $250,000. Aber also collected $27,000 sales taxes.
4. Aber paid $230,000 on accounts payable.
5. Aber paid $3,000 interest on the bonds on July 1, 2010.
6. The prepaid insurance ($5,600) expired on July 31.
7. On August 1, Aber paid $10,200 for insurance coverage from August 1, 2010, through July 31, 2011.
8. Aber paid $17,000 sales taxes to the state.
9. Paid other operating expenses, $91,000.
10. Retired the bonds on December 31, 2010, by paying $48,000 plus $3,000 interest.
11. Issued $90,000 of 8% bonds on December 31, 2010, at 104. The bonds pay interest every June 30 and December 31.

Adjustment data:
1. Recorded the insurance expired from item 7.
2. The equipment was acquired on December 31, 2009, and will be depreciated on a straight-line basis over 5 years with a $3,000 salvage value.
3. The income tax rate is 30%. (*Hint:* Prepare the income statement up to income before taxes and multiply by 30% to compute the amount.)

Instructions
(You may want to set up T accounts to determine ending balances.)
(a) Prepare journal entries for the transactions listed above and adjusting entries.
(b) Prepare an adjusted trial balance at December 31, 2010.
(c) Prepare an income statement and a retained earnings statement for the year ending December 31, 2010, and a classified balance sheet as of December 31, 2010.

(b) Totals $646,995
(c) N.I. $61,705

Continuing Cookie Chronicle

(*Note:* This is a continuation of the Cookie Chronicle from Chapters 1 through 9.)

CCC10   Recall that Cookie Creations borrowed $2,000 from Natalie's grandmother. Natalie now is thinking of repaying all amounts outstanding on that loan. She needs to know the amounts of interest payable and interest expense and needs to make the correct journal entries for repayment of the loan.

Go to the book's companion website, **www.wiley.com/college/kimmel**, to find the completion of this problem.

Financial Reporting and Analysis

FINANCIAL REPORTING PROBLEM: *Tootsie Roll Industries*

BYP10-1 Refer to the financial statements of Tootsie Roll Industries and the Notes to Consolidated Financial Statements in Appendix A.

Instructions
Answer the following questions.
(a) What were Tootsie Roll's total current liabilities at December 31, 2007? What was the increase/decrease in Tootsie Roll's total current liabilities from the prior year?
(b) How much were the accounts payable at December 31, 2007?
(c) What were the components of total current liabilities on December 31, 2007 (other than accounts payable already discussed above)?

COMPARATIVE ANALYSIS PROBLEM: *Tootsie Roll vs. Hershey Foods*

BYP10-2 The financial statements of Hershey Foods are presented in Appendix B, following the financial statements for Tootsie Roll Industries in Appendix A.

Instructions
(a) Based on the information contained in these financial statements, compute the current ratio for 2007 for each company.

What conclusions concerning the companies' liquidity can be drawn from these ratios?
(b) Based on the information contained in these financial statements, compute the following 2007 ratios for each company.
(1) Debt to total assets.
(2) Times interest earned. (Hershey's total interest expense for 2007 was $121,066,000. See Tootsie Roll's Note 6 for its interest expense.)

What conclusions about the companies' long-run solvency can be drawn from the ratios?

RESEARCH CASE

BYP10-3 The May 8, 2008, edition of the *Wall Street Journal* contains an article by Heather Won Tesoriero titled "Oil Firms Settle Claims in MTBE Leak Cases."

Instructions
Read the article and answer the following questions.
(a) In addition to paying $423 million in cash, the oil companies agreed to pay cleanup costs that arise in the next 30 years. What accounting issues arise for the oil companies from the promise to pay in the future?
(b) Discuss the accounting criteria that the oil companies must apply toward their promise to pay future costs.
(c) What accounting challenges do the companies face in trying to apply the accounting criteria to the promise to pay in the future? What challenges are faced by investors who are analyzing the oil companies?
(d) Exxon Mobil Corp. chose to not settle. Instead it will go to court to dispute the charges. Discuss the implications of this decision for Exxon Mobil's accounting versus that of the companies that chose to settle the case.

INTERPRETING FINANCIAL STATEMENTS

BYP10-4 Hechinger Co. and Home Depot are two home improvement retailers. Compared to Hechinger, founded in the early 1900s, Home Depot is a relative newcomer. But, in recent years, while Home Depot was reporting large increases in net income, Hechinger was reporting increasingly large net losses. Finally, largely due to competition from Home Depot, Hechinger was forced to file for bankruptcy. Here are financial data for both companies (in millions).

	Hechinger	Home Depot
Cash	$ 21	$ 62
Receivables	0	469
Total current assets	1,153	4,933
Beginning total assets	1,668	11,229
Ending total assets	1,577	13,465
Beginning current liabilities	935	2,456
Ending current liabilities	938	2,857
Beginning total liabilities	1,392	4,015
Ending total liabilities	1,339	4,716
Interest expense	67	37
Income tax expense	3	1,040
Cash provided (used) by operations	(257)	1,917
Net income	(93)	1,614
Net sales	3,444	30,219

Instructions

Using the data provided, perform the following analysis.

(a) Calculate working capital and the current ratio for each company. Discuss their relative liquidity.

(b) Calculate the debt to total assets ratio and times interest earned for each company. Discuss their relative solvency.

(c) Calculate the return on assets ratio and profit margin ratio for each company. Comment on their relative profitability.

(d) The notes to Home Depot's financial statements indicate that it leases many of its facilities using operating leases. If these assets had instead been purchased with debt, assets and liabilities would have increased by approximately $2,347 million. Calculate the company's debt to total assets ratio employing this adjustment. Discuss the implications.

BYP10-5 Many multinational companies find it beneficial to have their shares listed on stock exchanges in foreign countries. In order to do this, they must comply with the securities laws of those countries. Some of these laws relate to the form of financial disclosure the company must provide, including disclosures related to contingent liabilities. This exercise investigates the Tokyo Stock Exchange, the largest stock exchange in Japan.

Address: **www.tse.or.jp/english/** or go to **www.wiley.com/college/kimmel**

Steps:

1. Choose **About TSE**.
2. Choose **History of TSE**. Answer questions (a) and (b).
3. Choose **Listed Company information**.
4. Choose **Disclosure**. Answer questions (c) and (d).

Instructions

Answer the following questions.

(a) When was the first stock exchange opened in Japan? How many exchanges does Japan have today?

(b) What event caused trading to stop for a period of time in Japan?

(c) What are four examples of decisions by corporations that must be disclosed at the time of their occurrence?

(d) What are four examples of "occurrence of material fact" that must be disclosed at the time of their occurrence?

FINANCIAL ANALYSIS ON THE WEB

BYP10-6 *Purpose:* Bond or debt securities pay a stated rate of interest. This rate of interest is dependent on the risk associated with the investment. Moody's Investment Service provides ratings for companies that issue debt securities.

Address: **www.moodys.com**,or go to **www.wiley.com/college/kimmel**

Steps: From Moody's homepage, choose **About Moody's**.

Instructions

Answer the following questions.

(a) In what year did Moody's introduce the first bond rating? (See **Moody's History**.)

(b) What is the total amount of debt securities that Moody's analysts "track"? (See **An Introduction**.)

(c) What characteristics must debt ratings have in order to be useful to the capital markets? (See **Understand Risk: The Truth About Credit Ratings**.)

BYP10-7 *Purpose:* To illustrate the usefulness of financial calculators on the Web.

Address: **www.centura.com/tools**, or go to **www.wiley.com/college/kimmel**

Steps: Go to the site shown above.

Instructions

Choose one of the many financial decisions listed at the site. Fill in inputs based on two different sets of assumptions. Print out your results, and then write up a short description of the decision model for your instructor. Describe the inputs and assumptions the model uses. Also try to identify the strengths and weaknesses of the site.

Critical Thinking

DECISION MAKING ACROSS THE ORGANIZATION

BYP10-8 On January 1, 2008, Colt Corporation issued $3,000,000 of 5-year, 8% bonds at 97. The bonds pay interest annually on January 1. By January 1, 2010, the market rate of interest for bonds of risk similar to those of Colt Corporation had risen. As a result the market value of these bonds was $2,500,000 on January 1, 2010—below their carrying value of $2,946,000.

Rich Heyman, president of the company, suggests repurchasing all of these bonds in the open market at the $2,500,000 price. But to do so the company will have to issue $2,500,000 (face value) of new 10-year, 12% bonds at par. The president asks you, as controller, "What is the feasibility of my proposed repurchase plan?"

Instructions

With the class divided into groups, answer the following.

(a) Prepare the journal entry to retire the 5-year bonds on January 1, 2010. Prepare the journal entry to issue the new 10-year bonds.

(b) Prepare a short memo to the president in response to his request for advice. List the economic factors that you believe should be considered for his repurchase proposal.

COMMUNICATION ACTIVITY

BYP10-9 Leon Housten, president of Kosko, Inc., is considering the issuance of bonds to finance an expansion of his business. He has asked you to do the following: (1) discuss the advantages of bonds over common stock financing, (2) indicate the types of bonds he might issue, and (3) explain the issuing procedures used in bond transactions.

Instructions

Write a memorandum to the president, answering his request.

ETHICS CASE

BYP10-10 The July 1998 issue of *Inc.* magazine includes an article by Jeffrey L. Seglin entitled "Would You Lie to Save Your Company?" It recounts the following true situation:

"A Chief Executive Officer (CEO) of a $20-million company that repairs aircraft engines received notice from a number of its customers that engines that it had recently repaired had failed, and that the company's parts were to blame. The CEO had not yet determined whether his company's parts were, in fact, the cause of the problem. The Federal Aviation Administration (FAA) had been notified and was investigating the matter.

What complicated the situation was that the company was in the midst of its year-end audit. As part of the audit, the CEO was required to sign a letter saying that he was not aware of any significant outstanding circumstances that could negatively impact the company—in accounting terms, of any contingent liabilities. The auditor was not aware of the customer complaints or the FAA investigation.

The company relied heavily on short-term loans from eight banks. The CEO feared that if these lenders learned of the situation, they would pull their loans. The loss of these loans would force the company into bankruptcy, leaving hundreds of people without jobs. Prior to this problem, the company had a stellar performance record."

Instructions
Answer the following questions.
(a) Who are the stakeholders in this situation?
(b) What are the CEO's possible courses of action? What are the potential results of each course of action? (Take into account the two alternative outcomes: the FAA determines the company (1) was not at fault, and (2) was at fault.)
(c) What would you do, and why?
(d) Suppose the CEO decides to conceal the situation, and that during the next year the company is found to be at fault and is forced into bankruptcy. What losses are incurred by the stakeholders in this situation? Do you think the CEO should suffer legal consequences if he decides to conceal the situation?

BYP10-11 During the summer of 2002 the financial press reported that Citigroup was being investigated for allegations that it had arranged transactions for Enron so as to intentionally misrepresent the nature of the transactions and consequently achieve favorable balance sheet treatment. Essentially, the deals were structured to make it appear that money was coming into Enron from trading activities, rather than from loans.

A July 23, 2002, *New York Times* article by Richard Oppel and Kurt Eichenwald entitled "Citigroup Said to Mold Deal to Help Enron Skirt Rules" suggested that Citigroup intentionally kept certain parts of a secret oral agreement out of the written record for fear that it would change the accounting treatment. Critics contend that this had the effect of significantly understating Enron's liabilities, thus misleading investors and creditors. Citigroup maintains that, as a lender, it has no obligation to ensure that its clients account for transactions properly. The proper accounting, Citigroup insists, is the responsibility of the client and its auditor.

Instructions
Answer the following questions.
(a) Who are the stakeholders in this situation?
(b) Do you think that a lender, in general, in arranging so called "structured financing" has a responsibility to ensure that its clients account for the financing in an appropriate fashion, or is this the responsibility of the client and its auditor?
(c) What effect did the fact that the written record did not disclose all characteristics of the transaction probably have on the auditor's ability to evaluate the accounting treatment of this transaction?
(d) The *New York Times* article noted that in one presentation made to sell this kind of deal to Enron and other energy companies, Citigroup stated that using such an arrangement "eliminates the need for capital markets disclosure, keeping structure mechanics private." Why might a company wish to conceal the terms of a financing arrangement from the capital markets (investors and creditors)? Is this appropriate? Do you think it is ethical for a lender to market deals in this way?
(e) Why was this deal more potentially harmful to shareholders than other off-balance-sheet transactions (for example, lease financing)?

"ALL ABOUT YOU" ACTIVITY

BYP10-12 For most U.S. families, medical costs are substantial and rising. But will medical costs be your most substantial expense over your lifetime? Not likely. Will it be housing or food? Again, not likely. The answer: Taxes are likely to be your biggest expense. On average, Americans work 74 days to afford their federal taxes. Companies, too, have large tax burdens. They look very hard at tax issues in deciding where to build their plants and where to locate their administrative headquarters.

Instructions

(a) Determine what your state income taxes are if your taxable income is $60,000 and you file as a single taxpayer in the state in which you live.

(b) Assume that you own a home worth $200,000 in your community and the tax rate is 2.1%. Compute the property taxes you would pay.

(c) Assume that the total gasoline bill for your automobile is $1,200 a year (300 gallons at $4 per gallon).What are the amounts of state and federal taxes that you pay on the $1,200?

(d) Assume that your purchases for the year total $9,000. Of this amount, $5,000 was for food and prescription drugs.What is the amount of sales tax you would pay on these purchases?
(Note that many states do not have a sales tax for food or prescription drug purchases. Does yours?).

(e) Determine what your Social Security taxes are if your income is $60,000.

(f) Determine what your federal income taxes are if your taxable income is $60,000 and you file as a single taxpayer.

(g) Determine your *total* taxes paid based on the above calculations, and determine the percentage of income that you would pay in taxes based on the following formula:
Total taxes paid ÷ Total income.

Answers to Business Insight and Accounting Across the Organization Questions

p. 495

Q: The drop in stock prices did not change the debt to total assets ratios of these companies. Discuss how the perception of a high debt to total assets ratio changed before and after the fall in stock prices.

A. When stock prices fell, the debt to total assets of these companies was unchanged: The debt was outstanding before the fall, and it was outstanding after the fall. However, before the fall, many investors did not worry if a company had a high debt to total assets ratio; they assumed that the debt would be converted to stock and so would never have to be repaid with cash. After the fall it became clear that the debt would not be converted to stock; suddenly, a high debt to total assets ratio was a real concern.

p. 508

Q: Explain how the sale of plant assets could improve the company's solvency.

A. A common measure of solvency is the debt to total assets ratio. By selling some of its fixed assets and using the cash to pay off debt, the company would reduce its reliance on debt financing and improve its debt to assets ratio.

p. 510

Q: How can financial ratios such as those covered in this chapter provide protection for creditors?

A. Financial ratios such as the current ratio, debt to total assets ratio, and the times interest earned ratio provide indications of a company's liquidity and solvency. By specifying minimum levels of liquidity and solvency, as measured by these ratios, a creditor creates triggers that enable it to step in before a company's financial situation becomes too dire.

Answers to Self-Study Questions

1. a 2. d 3. b 4. d 5. b 6. c 7. b 8. c 9. c 10. a 11. c 12. d 13. b 14. c 15. a *16. c *17. a *18. b *19. c

✔ Remember to go back to the navigator box on the chapter-opening page and check off your completed work.

chapter 11

Reporting and Analyzing Stockholders' Equity

✔ the navigator

- Scan **Study Objectives** ○
- Read **Feature Story** ○
- Scan **Preview** ○
- Read **Text and Answer** *Do it!*
  - p. 557 ○ p. 559 ○ p. 561 ○
  - p. 563 ○ p. 568 ○ p. 572 ○
- Work **Using the Decision Toolkit** ○
- Review **Summary of Study Objectives** ○
- Work **Comprehensive** *Do it!* p. 579 ○
- Answer **Self-Study Questions** ○
- Complete **Assignments** ○

study objectives

After studying this chapter, you should be able to:

1 Identify and discuss the major characteristics of a corporation.

2 Record the issuance of common stock.

3 Explain the accounting for the purchase of treasury stock.

4 Differentiate preferred stock from common stock.

5 Prepare the entries for cash dividends and understand the effect of stock dividends and stock splits.

6 Identify the items that affect retained earnings.

7 Prepare a comprehensive stockholders' equity section.

8 Evaluate a corporation's dividend and earnings performance from a stockholder's perspective.

What's Cooking?

What major U.S. corporation got its start 38 years ago with a waffle iron? Hint: It doesn't sell food. Another hint: Swoosh. Another hint: "Just do it." That's right, Nike. In 1971 Nike cofounder Bill Bowerman put a piece of rubber into a kitchen waffle iron, and the trademark waffle sole was born. It seems fair to say that at Nike, "They don't make 'em like they used to."

Nike was co-founded by Bowerman and Phil Knight, a member of Bowerman's University of Oregon track team. Each began in the shoe business independently during the early 1960s. Bowerman got his start by making hand-crafted running shoes for his University of Oregon track team. Knight, after completing graduate school, started a small business importing low-cost, high-quality shoes from Japan. In 1964 the two joined forces, each contributing $500, and formed Blue Ribbon Sports, a partnership, marketing Japanese shoes.

It wasn't until 1971 that the company began manufacturing its own line of shoes. With the new shoes came a new corporate name— Nike—the Greek goddess of victory.

It is hard to imagine that the company that now boasts a stable full of world-class athletes as promoters at one time had part-time employees selling shoes out of car trunks at track meets. Nike has achieved its success through relentless innovation combined with unbridled promotion.

By 1980 Nike was sufficiently established that it was able to issue its first stock to the public. In that same year it also created a stock ownership program for its employees, allowing them to share in the company's success. Since then Nike has enjoyed phenomenal growth, with 2007 sales reaching $16.3 billion and total dividends paid of $300 million.

Nike is not alone in its quest for the top of the sport shoe world. Reebok used to be Nike's arch rival (get it? "arch"), but then Reebok was acquired by the German company Adidas. Now Adidas pushes Nike every step of the way.

The shoe market is fickle, with new styles becoming popular almost daily and vast international markets still lying untapped. Whether one of these two giants does eventually take control of the pedi-planet remains to be seen. Meanwhile the shareholders sit anxiously in the stands as this Olympic-size drama unfolds.

On the World Wide Web
Nike: www.nike.com
Adidas: www.adidas.com

Corporations like Nike and Adidas have substantial resources at their disposal. In fact, the corporation is the dominant form of business organization in the United States in terms of sales, earnings, and number of employees. All of the 500 largest U.S. companies are corporations. In this chapter we look at the essential features of a corporation and explain the accounting for a corporation's capital stock transactions.

The content and organization of the chapter are as follows.

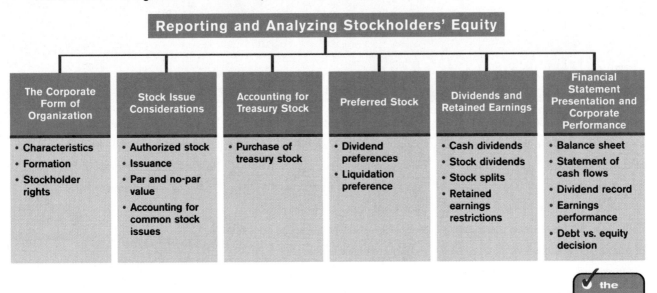

The Corporate Form of Organization

A corporation is created by law. As a legal entity, a corporation has most of the rights and privileges of a person. The major exceptions relate to privileges that can be exercised only by a living person, such as the right to vote or to hold public office. Similarly, a corporation is subject to the same duties and responsibilities as a person. For example, it must abide by the law and it must pay taxes.

We can classify corporations in a variety of ways. Two common classifications are **by purpose** and **by ownership**. A corporation may be organized for the purpose of making a profit (such as Nike or General Motors), or it may be a nonprofit charitable, medical, or educational corporation (such as the Salvation Army or the American Cancer Society).

Classification by ownership differentiates publicly held and privately held corporations. A publicly held corporation may have thousands of stockholders, and its stock is traded on a national securities market such as the New York Stock Exchange. Examples are IBM, Caterpillar, and General Electric. In contrast, a privately held corporation, often referred to as a closely held corporation, usually has only a few stockholders and does not offer its stock for sale to the general public. Privately held companies are generally much smaller than publicly held companies, although some notable exceptions exist. Cargill Inc., a private corporation that trades in grain and other commodities, is one of the largest companies in the United States. This chapter deals primarily with issues related to publicly held companies.

Identify and discuss the major characteristics of a corporation.

CHARACTERISTICS OF A CORPORATION

In 1964, when Nike's founders, Knight and Bowerman, were just getting started in the running shoe business, they formed their original organization as a partnership. In 1968 they reorganized the company as a corporation. A number of characteristics distinguish a corporation from sole proprietorships and partnerships. The most important of these characteristics are explained below.

Separate Legal Existence

As an entity separate and distinct from its owners, the corporation acts under its own name rather than in the name of its stockholders. Nike, for example, may buy, own, and sell property, borrow money, and enter into legally binding contracts in its own name. It may also sue or be sued. It pays taxes as a separate entity.

In contrast to a partnership, in which the acts of the owners (partners) bind the partnership, the acts of the owners (stockholders) do not bind the corporation unless such owners are agents of the corporation. For example, if you owned shares of Nike stock, you would not have the right to purchase inventory for the company unless you were designated as an agent of the corporation.

Legal existence separate from owners

Limited Liability of Stockholders

Since a corporation is a separate legal entity, creditors ordinarily have recourse only to corporate assets to satisfy their claims. The liability of stockholders is normally limited to their investment in the corporation. Creditors have no legal claim on the personal assets of the stockholders unless fraud has occurred. Thus, even in the event of bankruptcy of the corporation, stockholders' losses are generally limited to the amount of capital they have invested in the corporation.

Limited liability of stockholders

Transferable Ownership Rights

Ownership of a corporation is held in shares of capital stock, which are transferable units. Stockholders may dispose of part or all of their interest in a corporation simply by selling their stock. The transfer of an ownership interest in a partnership requires the consent of each partner. In contrast, the transfer of stock is entirely at the discretion of the stockholder. It does not require the approval of either the corporation or other stockholders.

The transfer of ownership rights among stockholders normally has no effect on the operating activities of the corporation. Nor does it affect the corporation's assets, liabilities, and total stockholders' equity. The transfer of ownership rights is a transaction between individual owners. The company does not participate in the transfer of these ownership rights after the original sale of the capital stock.

Transferable ownership rights

Ability to Acquire Capital

It is relatively easy for a corporation to obtain capital through the issuance of stock. Buying stock in a corporation is often attractive to an investor because a stockholder has limited liability and shares of stock are readily transferable. Also, numerous individuals can become stockholders by investing small amounts of money.

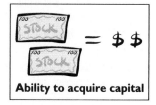

Ability to acquire capital

Continuous Life

The life of a corporation is stated in its charter. The life may be perpetual or it may be limited to a specific number of years. If it is limited, the company can extend the period of existence through renewal of the charter. Since a corporation is a separate legal entity, its continuance as a going concern is not affected by the withdrawal, death, or incapacity of a stockholder, employee, or officer. As a result, a successful corporation can have a continuous and perpetual life.

Continuous life

Corporation Management

Although stockholders legally own the corporation, they manage it indirectly through a board of directors they elect. Philip Knight is the chairman of Nike's board of directors. The board, in turn, formulates the operating policies for the company. The board also selects officers, such as a president and one or more vice-presidents, to execute policy and to perform daily management functions. As a result of the Sarbanes-Oxley Act, the board is now required to monitor management's actions more closely. Many feel that the failures at Enron and World-Com could have been avoided by more diligent boards.

Illustration 11-1 depicts a typical organization chart showing the delegation of responsibility.

Illustration 11-1
Corporation organization chart

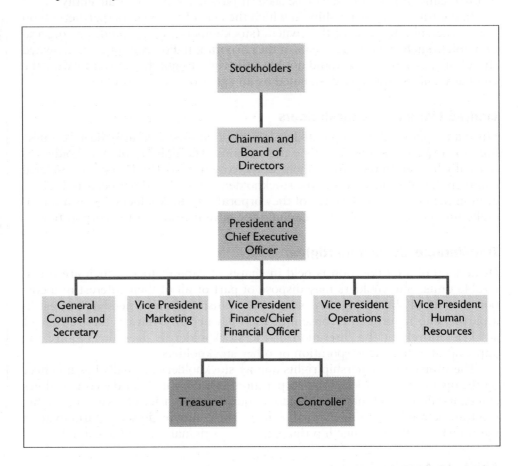

Ethics Note Managers who are not owners are often compensated based on the performance of the company. They thus may be tempted to exaggerate company performance by inflating income figures.

The chief executive officer (CEO) has overall responsibility for managing the business. As the organization chart shows, the CEO delegates responsibility to other officers. The chief accounting officer is the **controller**. The controller's responsibilities are to (1) maintain the accounting records, (2) maintain an adequate system of internal control and (3) prepare financial statements, tax returns, and internal reports. The **treasurer** has custody of the corporation's funds and is responsible for maintaining the company's cash position.

The organizational structure of a corporation enables a company to hire professional managers to run the business. On the other hand, the separation of ownership and management often reduces an owner's ability to actively manage the company.

Government Regulations

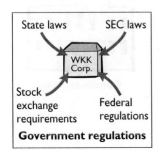

A corporation is subject to numerous state and federal regulations. For example, state laws usually prescribe the requirements for issuing stock, the distributions of earnings permitted to stockholders, and acceptable methods for retiring stock. Federal securities laws govern the sale of capital stock to the general public. Also, most publicly held corporations are required to make extensive disclosure of their financial affairs to the Securities and Exchange Commission (SEC) through quarterly and annual reports. The Sarbanes-Oxley Act increased the company's responsibility for the accuracy of these reports. In addition, when a corporate stock is listed and traded on organized securities exchanges, the corporation must comply with the reporting requirements of these exchanges.

 ## Accounting Across the Organization

During the hot stock market of the late 1990s, the dream of nearly every entrepreneur was to "take the company public." But times have changed, and now top managers at small- to medium-sized companies are reevaluating the costs versus the benefits of being a publicly traded company.

In 2004 and 2005 a record number of publicly traded companies repurchased all of their shares and took their companies private. Most cited the increased regulatory costs associated with Sarbanes-Oxley as the reason for going private. Estimates of these costs were about $2.3 million per year—roughly ten times what they were a few years earlier. In about two-thirds of the deals it was the managers themselves who bought the company's shares.

Source: Emily Thorton, "A Little Privacy Please," *Business Week* (May 24, 2004), pp. 74–75.

? In addition to regulatory cost, what is another reason why some owners choose not to take their companies public?

Additional Taxes

Owners of proprietorships and partnerships report their share of earnings on their personal income tax returns. The individual owner then pays taxes on this amount. Corporations, on the other hand, must pay federal and state income taxes as a separate legal entity. These taxes are substantial: They can amount to as much as 40% of taxable income.

In addition, stockholders are required to pay taxes on cash dividends. Thus, many argue that corporate income is **taxed twice (double taxation)**—once at the corporate level and again at the individual level.

Illustration 11-2 shows the advantages and disadvantages of a corporation compared to a sole proprietorship and partnership.

Additional taxes

Advantages	Disadvantages
• Separate legal existence	• Corporation management—separation of ownership and management
• Limited liability of stockholders	• Government regulations
• Transferable ownership rights	• Additional taxes
• Ability to acquire capital	
• Continuous life	
• Corporation management—professional managers	

Illustration 11-2
Advantages and disadvantages of a corporation

Other Forms of Business Organization

A variety of "hybrid" organizational forms—forms that combine different attributes of partnerships and corporations—now exist. For example, one type of corporate form, called an **S corporation**, allows for legal treatment as a corporation but tax treatment as a partnership—that is, no double taxation. Because of changes to the S corporation's rules, more small- and medium-sized businesses now may choose S corporation treatment. One of the primary criteria is that the company cannot have more than 75 shareholders. Other forms of organization include limited partnerships, limited liability partnerships (LLPs), and limited liability companies (LLCs).

DECISION TOOLKIT   A SUMMARY

DECISION CHECKPOINTS	INFO NEEDED FOR DECISION	TOOL TO USE FOR DECISION	HOW TO EVALUATE RESULTS
Should the company incorporate?	Capital needs, growth expectations, type of business, tax status	Corporations have limited liability, easier capital raising ability, and professional managers; but they suffer from additional taxes, government regulations, and separation of ownership from management.	Must carefully weigh the costs and benefits in light of the particular circumstances.

FORMING A CORPORATION

A corporation is formed by grant of a state charter. The charter is a document that describes the name and purpose of the corporation; the types and number of shares of stock that are authorized to be issued; the names of the individuals that formed the company; and the number of shares that these individuals agreed to purchase. Regardless of the number of states in which a corporation has operating divisions, it is incorporated in only one state. It is to the company's advantage to incorporate in a state whose laws are favorable to the corporate form of business organization. For example, although General Motors has its headquarters in Michigan, it is incorporated in New Jersey. In fact, more and more corporations have been incorporating in states with rules that favor existing management. For example, Gulf Oil changed its state of incorporation to Delaware to thwart possible unfriendly takeovers. There, certain defensive tactics against takeovers can be approved by the board of directors alone, without a vote by shareholders.

Upon receipt of its charter from the state of incorporation, the corporation establishes **by-laws**. The by-laws establish the internal rules and procedures for conducting the affairs of the corporation. Corporations engaged in interstate commerce must also obtain a **license** from each state in which they do business. The license subjects the corporation's operating activities to the general corporation laws of the state.

STOCKHOLDER RIGHTS

When chartered, the corporation may begin selling shares of stock. When a corporation has only one class of stock, it is identified as **common stock**. Each share of common stock gives the stockholder the ownership rights pictured in Illustration 11-3 (next page). The articles of incorporation or the by-laws state the ownership rights of a share of stock.

Proof of stock ownership is evidenced by a printed or engraved form known as a **stock certificate**. As shown in Illustration 11-4 (page 556), the face of the certificate shows the name of the corporation, the stockholder's name, the class and special features of the stock, the number of shares owned, and the signatures of authorized corporate officials. Certificates are prenumbered to ensure proper control over their use; they may be issued for any quantity of shares.

Stockholders have the right to:

1. Vote in election of board of directors at annual meeting and vote on actions that require stockholder approval.

2. Share the corporate earnings through receipt of dividends.

3. Keep the same percentage ownership when new shares of stock are issued (**preemptive right**[1]).

4. Share in assets upon liquidation in proportion to their holdings. This is called a **residual claim** because owners are paid with assets that remain after all other claims have been paid.

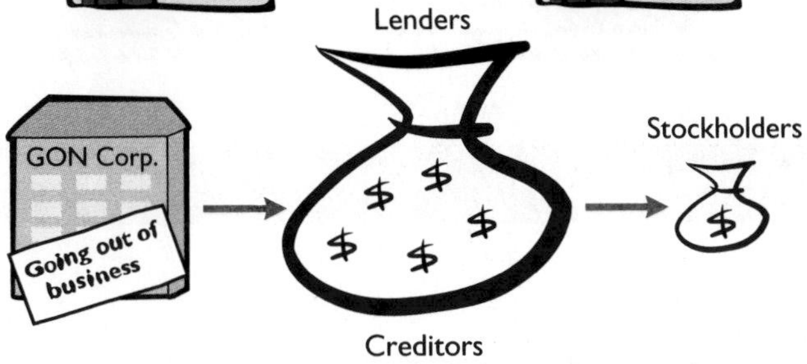

Illustration 11-3
Ownership rights of stockholders

Stock Issue Considerations

Although Nike incorporated in 1968, it did not sell stock to the public until 1980. At that time Nike evidently decided it would benefit from the infusion of cash that a public sale of its shares would bring. When a corporation decides to issue stock, it must resolve a number of basic questions: How many shares should it authorize for sale? How should it issue the stock? What value should it assign to the stock? We address these questions in the following sections.

AUTHORIZED STOCK

Authorized stock is the amount of stock that a corporation is authorized to sell as indicated in its charter. If the corporation has sold all of its authorized stock, then it must obtain permission from the state to change its charter before it can issue additional shares.

The authorization of common stock does not result in a formal accounting entry. The reason is that the event has no immediate effect on either corporate assets or stockholders' equity. However, the corporation must disclose in the stockholders' equity section of the balance sheet the number of shares authorized.

---

[1]A number of companies have eliminated the preemptive right because they believe it places an unnecessary and cumbersome demand on management. For example, IBM, by stockholder approval, has dropped its preemptive right for stockholders.

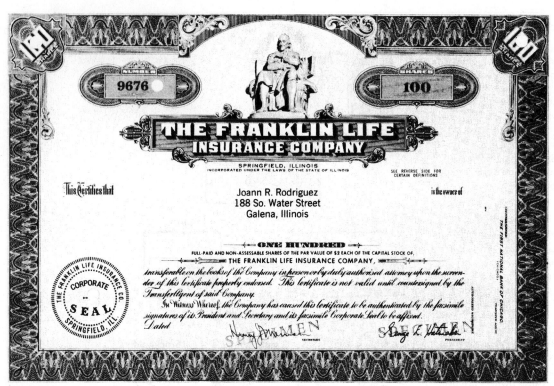

Illustration 11-4 A stock certificate

International Note U.S. and U.K. corporations raise most of their capital through millions of outside shareholders and bondholders. In contrast, companies in Germany, France, and Japan acquire financing mostly from large banks or other financial institutions. Consequently, in the latter environment, shareholders are less important, and external reporting and auditing receive less emphasis.

ISSUANCE OF STOCK

A corporation can issue common stock **directly** to investors. Alternatively, it can issue common stock **indirectly** through an investment banking firm that specializes in bringing securities to the attention of prospective investors. Direct issue is typical in closely held companies. Indirect issue is customary for a publicly held corporation.

New issues of stock may be offered for sale to the public through various organized U.S. securities exchanges: the New York Stock Exchange, the American Stock Exchange, and 13 regional exchanges. Stock may also be traded on the NASDAQ national market.

PAR AND NO-PAR VALUE STOCKS

Par value stock is capital stock that has been assigned a value per share in the corporate charter. Years ago, par value was used to determine the legal capital that must be retained in the business for the protection of corporate creditors. That amount is not available for withdrawal by stockholders. Thus, in the past, most states required the corporation to sell its shares at par or above.

However, the usefulness of par value as a protective device to creditors was questionable because par value was often immaterial relative to the value of the company's stock in the securities markets—even at the time of issue. For example, Loews Corporation's par value is $0.01 per share, yet a new issue in 2008 would have sold at a **market value** in the $49 per share range. Thus, par has no relationship with market value and in the vast majority of cases is an immaterial amount. As a consequence, today many states do not require a par value. Instead, they use other means to determine legal capital to protect creditors.

No-par value stock is capital stock that has not been assigned a value in the corporate charter. No-par value stock is quite common today. For example, Nike, Procter & Gamble, and North American Van Lines all have no-par stock. In many states the board of directors assigns a stated value to the no-par shares.

before you go on...

Do it!

Indicate whether each of the following statements is true or false.

_____ 1. Similar to partners in a partnership, stockholders of a corporation have unlimited liability.

_____ 2. It is relatively easy for a corporation to obtain capital through the issuance of stock.

_____ 3. The separation of ownership and management is an advantage of the corporate form of business.

_____ 4. The journal entry to record the authorization of capital stock includes a credit to the appropriate capital stock account.

_____ 5. All states require a par value per share for capital stock.

Solution

1. False. The liability of stockholders is normally limited to their investment in the corporation.

2. True.

3. False. The separation of ownership and management is a disadvantage of the corporate form of business.

4. False. The authorization of capital stock does not result in a formal accounting entry.

5. False. Many states do not require a par value.

CORPORATE ORGANIZATION

Action Plan

• Review the characteristics of a corporation and understand which are advantages and which are disadvantages.

• Understand that corporations raise capital through the issuance of stock, which can be par or no-par.

the navigator

ACCOUNTING FOR COMMON STOCK ISSUES

The stockholders' equity section of a corporation's balance sheet includes: (1) **paid-in (contributed) capital** and (2) **retained earnings (earned capital)**. The distinction between paid-in capital and retained earnings is important from both a legal and an economic point of view. Paid-in capital is the amount stockholders paid to the corporation in exchange for shares of ownership. **Retained earnings** is earned capital held for future use in the business. In this section we discuss the accounting for paid-in capital. In a later section we discuss retained earnings.

Let's now look at how to account for new issues of common stock. The primary objectives in accounting for the issuance of common stock are: (1) to identify the specific sources of paid-in capital and (2) to maintain the distinction between paid-in capital and retained earnings. As shown below, **the issuance of common stock affects only paid-in capital accounts**.

As discussed earlier, par value does not indicate a stock's market value. The cash proceeds from issuing par value stock may be equal to, greater than, or less than par value. When a company records the issuance of common stock for cash, it credits the par value of the shares to Common Stock, and records in a separate paid-in capital account the portion of the proceeds that is above or below par value.

To illustrate, assume that Hydro-Slide, Inc. issues 1,000 shares of $1 par value common stock at par for cash. The entry to record this transaction is:

study objective 2
Record the issuance of common stock.

Helpful Hint Stock is sometimes issued in exchange for services (payment to attorneys or consultants, for example) or other noncash assets (land or buildings). The value recorded for the shares issued is determined by either the market value of the shares, or the value of the good or service received depending upon which value the company can more readily determine.

			A = L + SE
Cash	1,000		+1,000
Common Stock		1,000	+1,000 CS
(To record issuance of 1,000 shares of $1 par common stock at par)			**Cash Flows** +1,000

Now assume Hydro-Slide, Inc. issues an additional 1,000 shares of the $1 par value common stock for cash at $5 per share. The amount received above the par value, in this case $4 ($5 − $1), would be credited to Paid-in Capital in Excess of Par Value. The entry is:

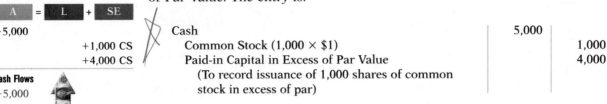

Cash	5,000	
Common Stock (1,000 × $1)		1,000
Paid-in Capital in Excess of Par Value		4,000
(To record issuance of 1,000 shares of common stock in excess of par)		

The total paid-in capital from these two transactions is $6,000. If Hydro-Slide, Inc. has retained earnings of $27,000, the stockholders' equity section of the balance sheet is as shown in Illustration 11-5.

Illustration 11-5
Stockholders' equity—paid-in capital in excess of par value

HYDRO-SLIDE, INC.
Balance Sheet (partial)

Stockholders' equity	
Paid-in capital	
Common stock	$ 2,000
Paid-in capital in excess of par value	**4,000**
Total paid-in capital	6,000
Retained earnings	27,000
Total stockholders' equity	$33,000

Some companies issue no-par stock with a stated value. For accounting purposes, companies treat the stated value in the same way as the par value. For example, if in our Hydro-Slide example the stock was no-par stock with a stated value of $1, the entries would be the same as those presented for the par stock except the term "Par Value" would be replaced with "Stated Value." If a company issues no-par stock that does not have a stated value, then it credits to the Common Stock account the full amount received. In such a case, there is no need for the Paid-in Capital in Excess of Stated Value account.

Investor Insight

Organized exchanges trade the stock of publicly held companies at dollar prices per share established by the interaction between buyers and sellers. For each listed security the financial press reports the high and low prices of the stock during the year, the total volume of stock traded on a given day, the high and low prices for the day, and the closing market price, with the net change for the day. Nike is listed on the New York Stock Exchange. Here is a recent listing for Nike:

	52 Weeks						
Stock	High	Low	Volume	High	Low	Close	Net Change
Nike	71.58	51.08	3,204,946	69.58	67.93	67.93	−2.14

These numbers indicate the following: The high and low market prices for the last 52 weeks have been $71.58 and $51.08. The trading volume for the day was 3,204,946 shares. The high, low, and closing prices for that date were $69.58, $67.93, and $67.93, respectively. The net change for the day was a decrease of $2.14 per share.

? For stocks traded on organized exchanges, how are the dollar prices per share established? What factors might influence the price of shares in the marketplace?

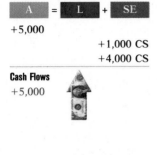

Cash Flows
+5,000

Do it!   Cayman Corporation begins operations on March 1 by issuing 100,000 shares of $10 par value common stock for cash at $12 per share. Journalize the issuance of the shares.

ISSUANCE OF STOCK

Action Plan

- In issuing shares for cash, credit Common Stock for par value per share.
- Credit any additional proceeds in excess of par value to a separate paid-in capital account.

Solution

Mar. 1	Cash		1,200,000	
	Common Stock			1,000,000
	Paid-in Capital in Excess of Par Value			200,000
	(To record issuance of 100,000 shares at $12 per share)			

Accounting for Treasury Stock

Treasury stock is a corporation's own stock that has been reacquired by the corporation and is being held for future use. A corporation may acquire treasury stock for various reasons:

1. To reissue the shares to officers and employees under bonus and stock compensation plans.
2. To increase trading of the company's stock in the securities market. Companies expect that buying their own stock will signal that management believes the stock is underpriced, which they hope will enhance its market value.
3. To have additional shares available for use in acquiring other companies.
4. To reduce the number of shares outstanding and thereby increase earnings per share.

study objective 3

Explain the accounting for the purchase of treasury stock.

Another infrequent reason for purchasing treasury shares is that management may want to eliminate hostile shareholders by buying them out.

Many corporations have treasury stock. For example, in the United States approximately 68% of companies have treasury stock.[2] In the first quarter of 2007, companies in the Standard & Poor's 500-stock index spent a record of about $118 billion to buy treasury stock. In a recent year, Nike purchased more than 6 million treasury shares. Stock repurchases have been so substantial that a recent study by two Federal Reserve economists suggested that a sharp reduction in corporate purchases of treasury shares might result in a sharp drop in the value of the U.S. stock market.

PURCHASE OF TREASURY STOCK

The purchase of treasury stock is generally accounted for by the **cost method**. This method derives its name from the fact that the Treasury Stock account is maintained at the cost of shares purchased. Under the cost method, **companies increase (debit) Treasury Stock by the price paid to reacquire the shares. Treasury Stock decreases by the same amount when the company later sells the shares.**

To illustrate, assume that on January 1, 2010, the stockholders' equity section for Mead, Inc. has 100,000 shares of $5 par value common stock outstanding (all issued at par value) and Retained Earnings of $200,000. Illustration 11-6

---

[2]*Accounting Trends & Techniques—2007* (New York: American Institute of Certified Public Accountants).

shows the stockholders' equity section of the balance sheet before purchase of treasury stock.

Illustration 11-6
Stockholders' equity with no treasury stock

MEAD, INC. Balance Sheet (partial)	
Stockholders' equity	
Paid-in capital	
Common stock, $5 par value, 400,000 shares authorized,	
100,000 shares issued and outstanding	$500,000
Retained earnings	200,000
Total stockholders' equity	$700,000

On February 1, 2010, Mead acquires 4,000 shares of its stock at $8 per share. The entry is:

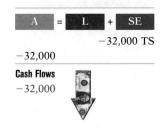

−32,000

Cash Flows
−32,000

Feb.	1	Treasury Stock	32,000	
		Cash		32,000
		(To record purchase of 4,000 shares of treasury stock at $8 per share)		

Ethics Note The purchase of treasury stock reduces the cushion for creditors. To protect creditors, a restriction for the cost of treasury stock purchased is often required. The restriction is usually applied to retained earnings.

The Treasury Stock account would increase by the cost of the shares purchased ($32,000). The original paid-in capital account, Common Stock, would not be affected because **the number of issued shares does not change**.

Companies show treasury stock as a deduction from total paid-in capital and retained earnings in the stockholders' equity section of the balance sheet. Illustration 11-7 shows this presentation for Mead, Inc. Thus, the acquisition of treasury stock reduces stockholders' equity.

Illustration 11-7
Stockholders' equity with treasury stock

MEAD, INC. Balance Sheet (partial)	
Stockholders' equity	
Paid-in capital	
Common stock, $5 par value, 400,000 shares authorized,	
100,000 shares issued and 96,000 shares outstanding	$500,000
Retained earnings	200,000
Total paid-in capital and retained earnings	700,000
Less: Treasury stock (4,000 shares)	**32,000**
Total stockholders' equity	$668,000

Helpful Hint Treasury Stock is a contra stockholders' equity account.

Companies disclose in the balance sheet both the number of shares issued (100,000) and the number in the treasury (4,000). The difference is the number of shares of stock outstanding (96,000). The term *outstanding stock* means the number of shares of issued stock that are being held by stockholders.

Accounting Across the Organization

In a bold (and some would say risky) move, Reebok at one time bought back nearly a *third* of its shares. This repurchase of shares dramatically reduced Reebok's available cash. In fact, the company borrowed significant funds to accomplish the repurchase. In a press release, management stated that it was repurchasing the shares because it believed that the stock was severely underpriced. The repurchase of so many shares was meant to signal management's belief in good future earnings.

Skeptics, however, suggested that Reebok's management was repurchasing shares to make it less likely that the company would be acquired by another company (in which case Reebok's top managers would likely lose their jobs). Acquiring companies like to purchase companies with large cash reserves so they can pay off debt used in the acquisition. By depleting its cash, Reebok became a less likely acquisition target.

? What signal might a large stock repurchase send to investors regarding management's belief about the company's growth opportunities?

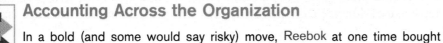 **Do it!** Santa Anita Inc. purchases 3,000 shares of its $50 par value common stock for $180,000 cash on July 1. It expects to hold the shares in the treasury until resold. Journalize the treasury stock transaction.

Solution

July	1	Treasury Stock	180,000	
		Cash		180,000
		(To record the purchase of 3,000 shares at $60 per share)		

before you go on...

TREASURY STOCK

Action Plan
* Record the purchase of treasury stock at cost.
* Report treasury stock as a deduction from stockholders' equity (contra account) at the bottom of the stockholders' equity section.

Preferred Stock

To appeal to a larger segment of potential investors, a corporation may issue an additional class of stock, called preferred stock. Preferred stock has contractual provisions that give it preference or priority over common stock in certain areas. Typically, preferred stockholders have a priority in relation to (1) dividends and (2) assets in the event of liquidation. However, they sometimes do not have voting rights. Adidas has no outstanding preferred stock, whereas Nike has a very minor amount outstanding. Approximately 18% of U.S. companies have one or more classes of preferred stock.[3]

Like common stock, companies may issue preferred stock for cash or for noncash consideration. The entries for these transactions are similar to the entries for common stock. When a corporation has more than one class of stock, each paid-in capital account title should identify the stock to which it relates (e.g., Preferred Stock, Common Stock, Paid-in Capital in Excess of Par Value—Preferred Stock, and Paid-in Capital in Excess of Par Value—Common Stock).

study objective 4
Differentiate preferred stock from common stock.

[3]*Accounting Trends & Techniques—2007* (New York: American Institute of Certified Public Accountants).

Assume that Stine Corporation issues 10,000 shares of $10 par value preferred stock for $12 cash per share. The entry to record the issuance is:

A = L + SE			
+120,000	Cash	120,000	
+100,000 PS	Preferred Stock		100,000
+20,000 PS	Paid-in Capital in Excess of Par Value—Preferred Stock		20,000
Cash Flows	(To record the issuance of 10,000 shares of $10 par		
+120,000	value preferred stock)		

Preferred stock may have either a par value or no-par value. In the stockholders' equity section of the balance sheet, companies show preferred stock first because of its dividend and liquidation preferences over common stock.

DIVIDEND PREFERENCES

As indicated above, **preferred stockholders have the right to share in the distribution of corporate income before common stockholders**. For example, if the dividend rate on preferred stock is $5 per share, common shareholders will not receive any dividends in the current year until preferred stockholders have received $5 per share. The first claim to dividends does not, however, **guarantee** dividends. Dividends depend on many factors, such as adequate retained earnings and availability of cash.

For preferred stock, companies state the per share dividend amount as a percentage of the par value of the stock or as a specified amount. For example, EarthLink specifies a 3% dividend, whereas Nike pays 10 cents per share on its $1 par preferred stock.

Cumulative Dividend

Preferred stock contracts often contain a cumulative dividend feature. This right means that preferred stockholders must be paid both current-year dividends and any unpaid prior-year dividends before common stockholders receive dividends. When preferred stock is cumulative, preferred dividends not declared in a given period are called dividends in arrears.

To illustrate, assume that Scientific Leasing has 5,000 shares of 7%, $100 par value cumulative preferred stock outstanding. Each $100 share pays a $7 dividend (.07 × $100). The annual dividend is $35,000 (5,000 × $7 per share). If dividends are two years in arrears, preferred stockholders are entitled to receive in the current year the dividends as shown in Illustration 11-8.

Illustration 11-8
Computation of total dividends to preferred stock

Dividends in arrears ($35,000 × 2)	$ 70,000
Current-year dividends	35,000
Total preferred dividends	**$105,000**

No distribution can be made to common stockholders until Scientific Leasing pays this entire preferred dividend. In other words, companies cannot pay dividends to common stockholders while any preferred stock dividend is in arrears.

Dividends in arrears are not considered a liability. No obligation exists until the board of directors formally "declares" that the corporation will pay a dividend. However, companies should disclose in the notes to the financial statements the amount of dividends in arrears. Doing so enables investors to assess the potential impact of this commitment on the corporation's financial position.

The investment community does not look favorably upon companies that are unable to meet their dividend obligations. As a financial officer noted in discussing one company's failure to pay its cumulative preferred dividend for a period of time, "Not meeting your obligations on something like that is a major black mark on your record."

LIQUIDATION PREFERENCE

Most preferred stocks have a preference on corporate assets if the corporation fails. This feature provides security for the preferred stockholder. The preference to assets may be for the par value of the shares or for a specified liquidating value. For example, Commonwealth Edison issued preferred stock that entitles the holders to receive $31.80 per share, plus accrued and unpaid dividends, in the event of involuntary liquidation. The liquidation preference is used in litigation pertaining to bankruptcy lawsuits involving the respective claims of creditors and preferred stockholders.

before you go on...

Do it! MasterMind Corporation has 2,000 shares of 6%, $100 par value preferred stock outstanding at December 31, 2010. At December 31, 2010, the company declared a $60,000 cash dividend. Determine the dividend paid to preferred stockholders and common stockholders under each of the following scenarios.

1. The preferred stock is noncumulative, and the company has not missed any dividends in previous years.
2. The preferred stock is noncumulative, and the company did not pay a dividend in each of the two previous years.
3. The preferred stock is cumulative, and the company did not pay a dividend in each of the two previous years.

Solution

1. The company has not missed past dividends and the preferred stock is noncumulative; thus, the preferred stockholders are paid only this year's dividends. The dividend paid to preferred stockholders would be $12,000 (2,000 ×.06 × $100). The dividend paid to common stockholders would be $48,000 ($60,000 − $12,000).

2. The preferred stock is noncumulative; thus, past unpaid dividends do not have to be paid. The dividend paid to preferred stockholders would be $12,000 (2,000 ×.06 × $100). The dividend paid to common stockholders would be $48,000 ($60,000 − $12,000).

3. The preferred stock is cumulative; thus, dividends that have been missed (dividends in arrears) must be paid. The dividend paid to preferred stockholders would be $36,000 (3 × 2,000 ×.06 × $100). The dividend paid to common stockholders would be $24,000 ($60,000 − $36,000).

PREFERRED STOCK DIVIDENDS

Action Plan
• Determine dividends on preferred shares by multiplying the dividend rate times the par value of the stock times the number of preferred shares.
• Understand the cumulative feature: If preferred stock is cumulative, then any missed dividends (dividends in arrears) and the current year's dividend must be paid to preferred stockholders before dividends are paid to common stockholders.

 the navigator

Dividends

As noted earlier, a dividend **is a distribution by a corporation to its stockholders on a pro rata** (proportional to ownership) **basis**. *Pro rata* means that if you own, say, 10% of the common shares, you will receive 10% of the dividend. Dividends can take four forms: cash, property, scrip (promissory note to pay cash), or stock. Cash dividends, which predominate in practice, and stock dividends, which are declared with some frequency, are the focus of our discussion.

Investors are very interested in a company's dividend practices. In the financial press, **dividends are generally reported quarterly as a dollar amount per share**. (Sometimes they are reported on an annual basis.) For example,

study objective 5

Prepare the entries for cash dividends and understand the effect of stock dividends and stock splits.

Nike's **quarterly** dividend rate in the fourth quarter of 2006 was 15.5 cents per share; the dividend rate for the fourth quarter of 2007 for GE was 31 cents, and for ConAgra Foods it was 18 cents.

CASH DIVIDENDS

A cash dividend is a pro rata (proportional to ownership) distribution of cash to stockholders. For a corporation to pay a cash dividend, it must have the following.

1. **Retained earnings.** Many states prohibit payment of dividends from legal capital. However, payment of dividends from paid-in capital in excess of par is legal in some states. **Payment of dividends from retained earnings is legal in all states.** In addition, loan agreements frequently constrain companies to pay dividends only from retained earnings.

2. **Adequate cash.** Recently Nike had a balance in retained earnings of $3,983 million but a cash balance of only $828 million. If it had wanted to pay a dividend equal to its retained earnings, Nike would have had to raise $3,155 million more in cash. It would have been unlikely to do this because it would not be able to pay this much in dividends in future years. In addition, such a dividend would completely deplete Nike's balance in retained earnings, so it would not be able to pay a dividend in the next year unless it had positive net income.

3. **Declared dividends.** The board of directors has full authority to determine the amount of income to distribute in the form of dividends and the amount to retain in the business. Dividends do not accrue like interest on a note payable, and they are not a liability until they are declared.

   In order to remain in business, companies must honor their interest payments to creditors, bankers, and bondholders. But the payment of dividends to stockholders is another matter. Many companies can survive, and even thrive, without such payouts. "Why give money to those strangers?" was the response of one company president.

The amount and timing of a dividend are important issues for management to consider. The payment of a large cash dividend could lead to liquidity problems for the company. Conversely, a small dividend or a missed dividend may cause unhappiness among stockholders who expect to receive a reasonable cash payment from the company on a periodic basis. Many companies declare and pay cash dividends quarterly. On the other hand, a number of high-growth companies pay no dividends, preferring to conserve cash to finance future capital expenditures.

Investors must keep an eye on the company's dividend policy and understand what it may mean. For most companies, for example, regular dividend boosts in the face of irregular earnings can be a warning signal. Companies with high dividends and rising debt may be borrowing money to pay shareholders. On the other hand, low dividends may not be a negative sign because it may mean the company is reinvesting in itself, which may result in high returns through increases in the stock price. Presumably, investors seeking regular dividends buy stock in companies that pay periodic dividends, and those seeking growth in the stock price (capital gains) buy stock in companies that retain their earnings rather than pay dividends.

Entries for Cash Dividends

Three dates are important in connection with dividends: (1) the declaration date, (2) the record date, and (3) the payment date. Companies make accounting entries on the declaration date and the payment date.

On the declaration date, the board of directors formally authorizes the cash dividend and announces it to stockholders. The declaration of a cash dividend **commits the corporation to a binding legal obligation.** Thus, the company must make an entry to recognize the increase in Cash Dividends and the increase in the liability Dividends Payable.

To illustrate, assume that on December 1, 2010, the directors of Media General declare a $0.50 per share cash dividend on 100,000 shares of $10 par value common stock. The dividend is $50,000 (100,000 × $0.50). The entry to record the declaration is:

Declaration Date

Dec. 1	Cash Dividends	50,000	
	Dividends Payable		50,000
	(To record declaration of cash dividend)		

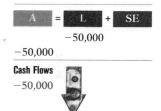

−50,000 Div
+50,000

Cash Flows
no effect

In Chapter 3 we used an account called Dividends to record a cash dividend. Here, we use the more specific title Cash Dividends to differentiate from other types of dividends, such as stock dividends. Dividends Payable is a current liability: It will normally be paid within the next several months.

At the record date, the company determines ownership of the outstanding shares for dividend purposes. The stockholders' records maintained by the corporation supply this information.

For Media General, the record date is December 22. No entry is required on the record date.

Helpful Hint The record date is important in determining the dividend to be paid to each stockholder but not the total dividend.

Record Date

| Dec. 22 | No entry necessary | | |

On the payment date, the company makes cash dividend payments to the stockholders on record as of December 22, and it also records the payment of the dividend. If January 20 is the payment date for Media General, the entry on that date is:

Payment Date

Jan. 20	Dividends Payable	50,000	
	Cash		50,000
	(To record payment of cash dividend)		

−50,000

−50,000

Cash Flows
−50,000

Note that payment of the dividend on the payment date reduces both current assets and current liabilities, but it has no effect on stockholders' equity. The cumulative effect of the **declaration and payment** of a cash dividend on a company's financial statements is to **decrease both stockholders' equity and total assets**.

Accounting Across the Organization

The decision whether to pay a cash dividend, and how much, is a very important management decision. In recent years, many companies have substantially increased their dividends, and total dividends paid by U.S. companies hit record levels.

One explanation for the increase is that Congress lowered, from 39% to 15%, the tax rate paid by investors on dividends received, making dividends more attractive to investors. Another driving force for the dividend increases was that companies were sitting on record amounts of cash. Because they did not see a lot of good expansion opportunities, companies decided to return the cash to shareholders.

Bigger dividends are still possible in the future. Large companies paid out 32% of their earnings as dividends in 2007—well below the historical average payout of 54% of earnings.

Source: Alan Levinsohn, "Divine Dividends," *Strategic Finance* (May 2005), pp. 59–60.

 What factors must management consider in deciding how large a dividend to pay?

STOCK DIVIDENDS

A stock dividend is a pro rata (proportional to ownership) distribution of the corporation's own stock to stockholders. Whereas a cash dividend is paid in cash, a stock dividend is paid in stock. **A stock dividend results in a decrease in retained earnings and an increase in paid-in capital.** Unlike a cash dividend, a stock dividend does not decrease total stockholders' equity or total assets.

Because a stock dividend does not result in a distribution of assets, many view it as nothing more than a publicity gesture. Stock dividends are often issued by companies that do not have adequate cash to issue a cash dividend. These companies may not want to announce that they are not going to be issuing a cash dividend at their normal time to do so. By issuing a stock dividend they "save face" by giving the appearance of distributing a dividend. Note that since a stock dividend neither increases nor decreases the assets in the company, investors are not receiving anything they didn't already own. In a sense it is like asking for two pieces of pie and having your host take one piece of pie and cut it into two smaller pieces. You are not better off, but you got your two pieces of pie.

To illustrate a stock dividend, assume that you have a 2% ownership interest in Cetus Inc.; you own 20 of its 1,000 shares of common stock. If Cetus declares a 10% stock dividend, it would issue 100 shares (1,000 × 10%) of stock. You would receive two shares (2% × 100), but your ownership interest would remain at 2% (22 ÷ 1,100). **You now own more shares of stock, but your ownership interest has not changed.** Moreover, the company disburses no cash, and assumes no liabilities.

What, then, are the purposes and benefits of a stock dividend? Corporations generally issue stock dividends for one of the following reasons.

> **Helpful Hint** Because of its effects, a stock dividend is also referred to as *capitalizing retained earnings.*

1. To satisfy stockholders' dividend expectations without spending cash.
2. To increase the marketability of the stock by increasing the number of shares outstanding and thereby decreasing the market price per share. Decreasing the market price of the stock makes it easier for smaller investors to purchase the shares.
3. To emphasize that the company has permanently reinvested in the business a portion of stockholders' equity, which therefore is unavailable for cash dividends.

When the dividend is declared, the board of directors determines the size of the stock dividend and the value per share to use to record the transaction. In order to meet legal requirements, the per share amount must be at least equal to the par or stated value.

The accounting profession distinguishes between a **small stock dividend** (less than 20%–25% of the corporation's issued stock) and a **large stock dividend** (greater than 20%–25%). It recommends that the company use the **fair market value per share** to record small stock dividends. The recommendation is based on the assumption that a small stock dividend will have little effect on the market price of the shares previously outstanding. Thus, many stockholders consider small stock dividends to be distributions of earnings equal to the fair market value of the shares distributed. The accounting profession does not specify the value to use to record a large stock dividend. However, companies normally use **par or stated value per share**. Small stock dividends predominate in practice. In the appendix at the end of the chapter, we illustrate the journal entries for small stock dividends.

Effects of Stock Dividends

How do stock dividends affect stockholders' equity? They **change the composition of stockholders' equity** because they result in a transfer of a portion of retained earnings to paid-in capital. However, **total stockholders' equity remains the same.** Stock dividends also have no effect on the par or stated value per share, but the number of shares outstanding increases.

To illustrate, assume that Medland Corp. declares a 10% stock dividend on its $10 par common stock when 50,000 shares were outstanding. The market price was $15 per share.

Illustration 11-9 Stock dividend effects

	Before Dividend	Change	After Dividend
Stockholders' equity			
Paid-in capital			
Common stock, $10 par	$ 500,000		$ 550,000
Paid-in capital in excess of par value	—		25,000
Total paid-in capital	500,000	+$75,000	575,000
Retained earnings	300,000	− 75,000	225,000
Total stockholders' equity	$800,000	$ 0	$800,000
Outstanding shares	50,000		55,000

In this example, total paid-in capital increased by $75,000 (50,000 shares × 10% × $15), and retained earnings decreased by the same amount. Note also that total stockholders' equity remains unchanged at $800,000.

STOCK SPLITS

A stock split, like a stock dividend, involves the issuance of additional shares of stock to stockholders according to their percentage ownership. However, **a stock split results in a reduction in the par or stated value per share**. The purpose of a stock split is to increase the marketability of the stock by lowering its market value per share. This, in turn, makes it easier for the corporation to issue additional stock. After hitting a peak of 114 stock splits in 1986, the number of splits in the United States has fallen to about 30 per year. Nike was one of the few firms to split in 2007. It justified the action by noting that its stock price had increased by 70% during the previous five years.

Like a stock dividend, a stock split increases the number of shares owned by a shareholder, but it does not change the percentage of the total company that the shareholder owns. These effects are shown in Illustration 11-10.

Helpful Hint A stock split changes the par value per share but does not affect any balances in stockholders' equity.

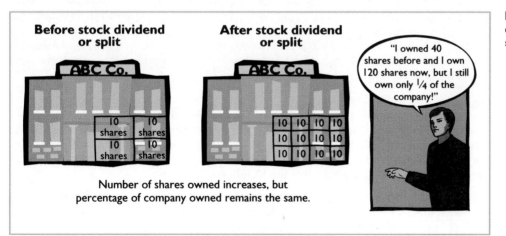

Illustration 11-10 Effect of stock dividend or stock split for stockholders

The effect of a split on market value is generally **inversely proportional** to the size of the split. For example, after a recent 2-for-1 stock split, the market value of Nike's stock fell from $111 to approximately $55.

In a stock split, the company increases the number of shares in the same proportion that it decreases the par or stated value per share. For example, in a 2-for-1 split, the company exchanges one share of $10 par value stock for two shares of $5 par value stock. **A stock split does not have any effect on paid-in capital, retained earnings, and total stockholders' equity.** However, the number of shares outstanding increases. These effects are shown in Illustration 11-11, assuming that instead of issuing a 10% stock dividend, Medland splits its 50,000 shares of common stock on a 2-for-1 basis.

Illustration 11-11 Stock split effects

	Before Stock Split	After Stock Split
Stockholders' equity		
Paid-in capital		
Common stock (Before: 50,000 $10 par shares; after: 100,000 $5 par shares)	$ 500,000	$ 500,000
Paid-in capital in excess of par value	0	0
Total paid-in capital	500,000	500,000
Retained earnings	300,000	300,000
Total stockholders' equity	$800,000	$800,000
Outstanding shares	50,000	100,000

Because a stock split does not affect the balances in any stockholders' equity accounts, a company **does not need to journalize a stock split**. However, a memorandum entry explaining the effect of the split is typically made.

The differences between the effects of stock dividends and stock splits are shown in Illustration 11-12.

Illustration 11-12 Effects of stock splits and stock dividends differentiated

Item	Stock Dividend	Stock Split
Total paid-in capital	Increase	No change
Total retained earnings	Decrease	No change
Total par value (common stock)	Increase	No change
Par value per share	No change	Decrease

before you go on...

STOCK DIVIDENDS; STOCK SPLITS

Action Plan

• Calculate the stock dividend's effect on retained earnings by multiplying the number of new shares times the market price of the stock (or par value for a large stock dividend).

• Recall that a stock dividend increases the number of shares without affecting total equity.

• Recall that a stock split only increases the number of shares outstanding and decreases the par value per share without affecting total equity.

Do it!   Due to five years of record earnings at Sing CD Corporation, the market price of its 500,000 shares of $2 par value common stock tripled from $15 per share to $45. During this period, paid-in capital remained the same at $2,000,000. Retained earnings increased from $1,500,000 to $10,000,000. President Joan Elbert is considering either a 10% stock dividend or a 2-for-1 stock split. She asks you to show the before and after effects of each option on retained earnings.

Solution

The stock dividend amount is $2,250,000 [(500,000 × 10%) × $45]. The new balance in retained earnings is $7,750,000 ($10,000,000 − $2,250,000). The retained earnings balance after the stock split is the same as it was before the split: $10,000,000. The effects on the stockholders' equity accounts are as follows.

	Original Balances	After Dividend	After Split
Paid-in capital	$ 2,000,000	$ 4,250,000	$ 2,000,000
Retained earnings	10,000,000	7,750,000	10,000,000
Total stockholders' equity	$12,000,000	$12,000,000	$12,000,000
Shares outstanding	500,000	550,000	1,000,000

Retained Earnings

Retained earnings is net income that a company retains in the business. The balance in retained earnings is part of the stockholders' claim on the total assets of the corporation. It does not, however, represent a claim on any specific asset. Nor can the amount of retained earnings be associated with the balance of any asset account. For example, a $100,000 balance in retained earnings does not mean that there should be $100,000 in cash. The reason is that the company may have used the cash resulting from the excess of revenues over expenses to purchase buildings, equipment, and other assets. Illustration 11-13 shows recent amounts of retained earnings and cash in selected companies.

study objective 6

Identify the items that affect retained earnings.

Company	(in millions) Retained Earnings	Cash
Circuit City Stores, Inc.	$ 981	$ 296
Nike, Inc.	4,885	1,855
Starbucks Coffee Company	2,189	281
Amazon.com	(1,375)	2,539

Illustration 11-13
Retained earnings and cash balances

When expenses exceed revenues, a **net loss** results. In contrast to net income, a net loss decreases retained earnings. In closing entries a company debits a net loss to the Retained Earnings account. **It does not debit net losses to paid-in capital accounts.** To do so would destroy the distinction between paid-in and earned capital. If cumulative losses exceed cumulative income over a company's life, a debit balance in Retained Earnings results. A debit balance in retained earnings, such as that of Amazon.com in 2007, is a deficit. A company reports a deficit as a deduction in the stockholders' equity section of the balance sheet, as shown in Illustration 11-14.

Illustration 11-14
Stockholders' equity with deficit

AMAZON.COM
Balance Sheet (partial)
December 31, 2007
(in millions)

Stockholders' equity	
Paid-in capital	
Common stock	$ 4
Paid-in capital in excess of par value	3,068
Total paid-in capital	3,072
Accumulated deficit	**(1,375)**
Total paid-in capital and retained earnings	1,697
Less: Treasury stock	500
Total stockholders' equity	$1,197

RETAINED EARNINGS RESTRICTIONS

The balance in retained earnings is generally available for dividend declarations. Some companies state this fact. In some circumstances, however, there may be retained earnings restrictions. These make a portion of the balance currently unavailable for dividends. Restrictions result from one or more of these causes: legal, contractual, or voluntary.

Companies generally disclose retained earnings restrictions in the notes to the financial statements. For example, Tektronix Inc., a manufacturer of electronic measurement devices, recently had total retained earnings of $774 million, but the unrestricted portion was only $223.8 million.

Illustration 11-15
Disclosure of unrestricted retained earnings

TEKTRONIX INC.
Notes to the Financial Statements

Certain of the Company's debt agreements require compliance with debt covenants. The Company had unrestricted retained earnings of $223.8 million after meeting those requirements.

Financial Statement Presentation of Stockholders' Equity

BALANCE SHEET PRESENTATION

study objective 7

Prepare a comprehensive stockholders' equity section.

In the stockholders' equity section of the balance sheet, companies report paid-in capital and retained earnings and identify the specific sources of paid-in capital. Within paid-in capital, two classifications are recognized:

1. **Capital stock**, which consists of preferred and common stock. Companies show preferred stock before common stock because of its preferential rights. They report information about the par value, shares authorized, shares issued, and shares outstanding for each class of stock.

2. **Additional paid-in capital**, which includes the excess of amounts paid in over par or stated value.

Illustration 11-16 presents the stockholders' equity section of the balance sheet of Graber Inc. The company discloses a retained earnings restriction in the notes. The stockholders' equity section for Graber Inc. includes most of the accounts discussed in this chapter. The disclosures pertaining to Graber's common stock indicate that 400,000 shares are issued; 100,000 shares are unissued (500,000

Illustration 11-16
Comprehensive stockholders' equity section

International Note Like GAAP, under IFRS companies typically disclose separate categories of capital on the balance sheet. However, because of varying accounting treatments of certain transactions (such as treasury stock or asset revaluations), some categories used under IFRS vary from those under GAAP.

GRABER INC. Balance Sheet (partial)		
Stockholders' equity		
Paid-in capital		
Capital stock		
9% preferred stock, $100 par value, cumulative, 10,000 shares authorized, 6,000 shares issued and outstanding		$ 600,000
Common stock, no par, $5 stated value, 500,000 shares authorized, 400,000 shares issued, and 390,000 outstanding		2,000,000
Total capital stock		2,600,000
Additional paid-in capital		
In excess of par value—preferred stock	$ 30,000	
In excess of stated value—common stock	1,050,000	
Total additional paid-in capital		1,080,000
Total paid-in capital		3,680,000
Retained earnings (see Note R)		1,160,000
Total paid-in capital and retained earnings		4,840,000
Less: Treasury stock—common (10,000 shares)		(80,000)
Total stockholders' equity		$4,760,000

Note R: Retained earnings is restricted for the cost of treasury stock, $80,000.

authorized less 400,000 issued); and 390,000 shares are outstanding (400,000 issued less 10,000 shares in treasury).

In published annual reports, companies seldom present subclassifications within the stockholders' equity section. Moreover, they often combine and report as a single amount the individual sources of additional paid-in capital. Notes often provide additional detail. Illustration 11-17 is an excerpt from Procter & Gamble Company's 2007 balance sheet.

PROCTER & GAMBLE COMPANY
Balance Sheet (partial)
December 31, 2007
(in millions)

Shareholders' equity	
Convertible Class A preferred stock, stated value	
$1 per share (600 shares authorized)	$ 1,406
Non-voting Class B preferred stock, stated value	
$1 per share (200 shares authorized)	–
Common stock, stated value $1 per share	
(10,000 shares authorized; issued: 2007—3,989.7, 2006—3,975.8)	3,990
Additional paid-in capital	59,030
Total paid-in capital	64,426
Reserve for ESOP debt retirement	(1,308)
Retained earnings	41,797
Total paid-in capital and retained earnings	104,915
Accumulated other comprehensive income	617
Treasury stock, at cost (shares held: 2007—857.8, 2006—797.0)	(38,772)
Total shareholders' equity	$ 66,760

Illustration 11-17
Stockholders' equity section

The balance sheet presents the balances of a company's stockholders' equity accounts at a point in time. Companies report in the "Financing Activities" section of the statement of cash flows information regarding cash inflows and outflows during the year that resulted from equity transactions. The excerpt below presents the cash flows from financing activities from the statement of cash flows of Sara Lee Corporation. From this information we learn that the company's purchases of treasury stock during the period far exceeded its issuances of new common stock, and its financing activities resulted in a net reduction in its cash balance.

KEEPING AN EYE ON CASH

SARA LEE CORPORATION
Statement of Cash Flows (partial)
For the Year Ended June 30, 2007
(in millions)

Cash flows from financing activities	
Issuances of common stock	$ 38
Purchases of common stock	(686)
Payments of dividends	(374)
Borrowings of long-term debt	2,895
Repayments of long-term debt	(416)
Short-term (repayments) borrowings, net	(1,720)
Net cash used in financing activities	$ (263)

before you go on...

STOCKHOLDERS' EQUITY SECTION

Action Plan

- Present capital stock first; list preferred stock before common stock.
- Present additional paid-in capital after capital stock.
- Report retained earnings after capital stock and additional paid-in capital.
- Deduct treasury stock from total paid-in capital and retained earnings.

Do it! Jennifer Corporation has issued 300,000 shares of $3 par value common stock. It is authorized to issue 600,000 shares. The paid-in capital in excess of par value on the common stock is $380,000. The corporation has reacquired 15,000 shares at a cost of $50,000 and is currently holding those shares.

The corporation also has 4,000 shares issued and outstanding of 8%, $100 par value preferred stock. It is authorized to issue 10,000 shares. The paid-in capital in excess of par value on the preferred stock is $97,000. Retained earnings is $610,000.

Prepare the stockholders' equity section of the balance sheet.

Solution

JENNIFER CORPORATION
Balance Sheet (partial)

Stockholders' equity		
Paid-in capital		
Capital stock		
8% preferred stock, $100 par value, 10,000 shares authorized, 4,000 shares issued and outstanding		$ 400,000
Common stock, $3 par value, 600,000 shares authorized, 300,000 shares issued, and 285,000 shares outstanding		900,000
Total capital stock		1,300,000
Additional paid-in capital		
In excess of par value—preferred stock	$ 97,000	
In excess of par value—common stock	380,000	
Total additional paid-in capital		477,000
Total paid-in capital		1,777,000
Retained earnings		610,000
Total paid-in capital and retained earnings		2,387,000
Less: Treasury stock—common (15,000 shares) (at cost)		(50,000)
Total stockholders' equity		$2,337,000

Measuring Corporate Performance

Investors are interested in both a company's dividend record and its earnings performance. Although those two measures are often parallel, that is not always the case. Thus, investors should investigate each one separately.

DIVIDEND RECORD

study objective 8

Evaluate a corporation's dividend and earnings performance from a stockholder's perspective.

One way that companies reward stock investors for their investment is to pay them dividends. The payout ratio measures the percentage of earnings a company distributes in the form of cash dividends to common stockholders. It is computed by **dividing total cash dividends declared to common shareholders by net income**. Using the information shown below, the payout ratio for Nike in 2007 and 2006 is calculated in Illustration 11-18.

	2007	2006
Dividends (in millions)	$ 357.2	$ 304.9
Net income (in millions)	1,491.5	1,392.0

Payout Ratio =	Cash Dividends Declared on Common Stock	
	Net Income	
($ in millions)	**2007**	**2006**
Payout Ratio	$\dfrac{\$357.2}{\$1,491.5} = 24\%$	$\dfrac{\$304.9}{\$1,392.0} = 22\%$

Illustration 11-18 Nike's payout ratio

Companies that have high growth rates are characterized by low payout ratios because they reinvest most of their net income in the business. Thus, a low payout ratio is not necessarily bad news. Companies that believe they have many good opportunities for growth, such as Nike, will reinvest those funds in the company rather than pay high dividends. However, low dividend payments, or a cut in dividend payments, might signal that a company has liquidity or solvency problems and is trying to conserve cash by not paying dividends. Thus, investors and analysts should investigate the reason for low dividend payments.

Illustration 11-19 lists recent payout ratios of four well-known companies.

Company	Payout Ratio
Microsoft	24.5%
Kellogg	43.3%
Google	0%
Wal-Mart	49.0%

Illustration 11-19
Payout ratios of companies

DECISION TOOLKIT

DECISION CHECKPOINTS	INFO NEEDED FOR DECISION	TOOL TO USE FOR DECISION	HOW TO EVALUATE RESULTS
What portion of its earnings does the company pay out in dividends?	Net income and total cash dividends on common stock	$\text{Payout ratio} = \dfrac{\text{Cash dividends declared on common stock}}{\text{Net income}}$	A low ratio may suggest that the company is retaining its earnings for investment in future growth.

EARNINGS PERFORMANCE

Another way to measure corporate performance is through profitability. A widely used ratio that measures profitability from the common stockholders' viewpoint is return on common stockholders' equity. This ratio shows how many dollars of net income a company earned for each dollar of common stockholders' equity. It is computed by dividing net income available to common stockholders (Net income − Preferred stock dividends) by average common stockholders' equity.

Using the information on the previous page and the additional information presented below, Illustration 11-20 (next page) shows Nike's return on common stockholders' equity ratios, calculated for 2007 and 2006.

(in millions)	2007	2006	2005
Preferred stock dividends	$ 0	$ 0	$ 0
Common stockholders' equity	7,025.4	6,285.2	5,644.2

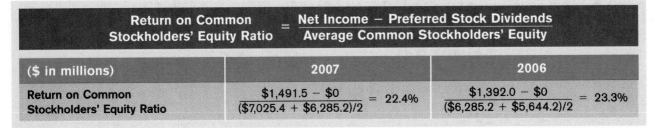

Return on Common Stockholders' Equity Ratio	= Net Income − Preferred Stock Dividends / Average Common Stockholders' Equity	
($ in millions)	**2007**	**2006**
Return on Common Stockholders' Equity Ratio	$\dfrac{\$1,491.5 - \$0}{(\$7,025.4 + \$6,285.2)/2} = 22.4\%$	$\dfrac{\$1,392.0 - \$0}{(\$6,285.2 + \$5,644.2)/2} = 23.3\%$

Illustration 11-20 Nike's return on common stockholders' equity

From 2006 to 2007, Nike's return on common shareholders' equity decreased. As a company grows larger, it becomes increasingly hard to sustain a high return. In Nike's case, since many believe the U.S. market for expensive sports shoes is saturated, it will need to grow either along new product lines, such as hiking shoes and golf equipment, or in new markets, such as Europe and Asia.

DEBT VERSUS EQUITY DECISION

When obtaining long-term capital, corporate managers must decide whether to issue bonds or to sell common stock. Bonds have three primary advantages relative to common stock, as shown in Illustration 11-21.

Illustration 11-21
Advantages of bond financing over common stock

Bond Financing	Advantages
	1. **Stockholder control is not affected.** Bondholders do not have voting rights, so current owners (stockholders) retain full control of the company.
	2. **Tax savings result.** Bond interest is deductible for tax purposes; dividends on stock are not.
	3. **Return on common stockholders' equity may be higher.** Although bond interest expense reduces net income, return on common stockholders' equity often is higher under bond financing because no additional shares of common stock are issued.

How does the debt versus equity decision affect the return on common stockholders' equity ratio? Illustration 11-22 shows that the return on common stockholders' equity is affected by the return on assets ratio and the amount of leverage a company uses—that is, by the company's reliance on debt (often measured

Illustration 11-22
Components of the return on common stockholders' equity

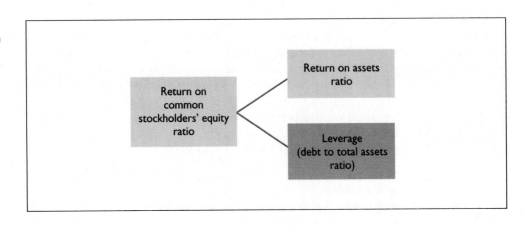

by the debt to total assets ratio). **If a company wants to increase its return on common stockholders' equity, it can either increase its return on assets or increase its reliance on debt financing.**

To illustrate the potential effect of debt financing on the return on common stockholders' equity, assume that Microsystems Inc. currently has 100,000 shares of common stock outstanding issued at $25 per share and no debt. It is considering two alternatives for raising an additional $5 million: Plan A involves issuing 200,000 shares of common stock at the current market price of $25 per share. Plan B involves issuing $5 million of 12% bonds at face value. Income before interest and taxes will be $1.5 million; income taxes are expected to be 30%. The alternative effects on the return on common stockholders' equity are shown in Illustration 11-23.

	Plan A: Issue stock	Plan B: Issue bonds	
Income before interest and taxes	$1,500,000	$1,500,000	**Illustration 11-23**
Interest (12% × $5,000,000)	—	600,000	Effects on return on common stockholders'
Income before income taxes	1,500,000	900,000	equity of issuing debt
Income tax expense (30%)	450,000	270,000	
Net income	$1,050,000	$ 630,000	
Common stockholders' equity	$7,500,000	$2,500,000	
Return on common stockholders' equity	14%	25.2%	

Note that with long-term debt financing (bonds), net income is $420,000 ($1,050,000 − $630,000) less. However, the return on common stockholders' equity increases from 14% to 25.2% with the use of debt financing because net income is spread over a smaller amount of common stockholders' equity. **In general, as long as the return on assets rate exceeds the rate paid on debt, a company will increase the return on common stockholders' equity by the use of debt.**

After seeing this illustration, one might ask, why don't companies rely almost exclusively on debt financing, rather than equity? Debt has one major disadvantage: **Debt reduces solvency. The company locks in fixed payments that it must make in good times and bad. The company must pay interest on a periodic basis, and must pay the principal (face value) of the bonds at maturity.** A company with fluctuating earnings and a relatively weak cash position may experience great difficulty in meeting interest requirements in periods of low earnings. In the extreme, this can result in bankruptcy. With common stock financing, on the other hand, the company can decide to pay low (or no) dividends if earnings are low.

DECISION TOOLKIT

DECISION CHECKPOINTS	INFO NEEDED FOR DECISION	TOOL TO USE FOR DECISION	HOW TO EVALUATE RESULTS
What is the company's return on common stockholders' investment?	Earnings available to common stockholders and average common stockholders' equity	Return on common stockholders' equity ratio $= \dfrac{\text{Net income} - \text{Preferred stock dividends}}{\text{Average common stockholders' equity}}$	A high measure suggests strong earnings performance from common stockholders' perspective.

USING THE DECISION TOOLKIT

Adidas is one of Nike's fiercest competitors. In such a competitive and rapidly changing environment, one wrong step can spell financial disaster.

Instructions

The following facts are available for Adidas. Using this information, evaluate its (1) dividend record and (2) earnings performance, and contrast them with those for Nike for 2006 and 2007. Nike's earnings per share were $2.96 in 2007 and $2.69 in 2006.

(in millions)*	2006	2005	2004
Dividends declared	$66	$60	$50
Net income	$496	$390	$321
Preferred stock dividends	0	0	0
Shares outstanding at end of year	203	203	199
Common stockholders' equity	$2,836	$2,712	$1,564

Adjusted for 4-for-1 stock split

*Nike has a year-end of May 31, 2007. For comparative purpose, we used Adidas's December 31, 2006, data since that represents the closest year-end.

Solution

1. *Dividend record:* A measure to evaluate dividend record is the payout ratio. For Adidas, this measure in 2006 and 2005 is calculated as shown below.

	2006	2005
Payout ratio	$\dfrac{\$66}{\$496} = 13.3\%$	$\dfrac{\$60}{\$390} = 15.4\%$

Nike's payout ratio was 24%. Adidas's payout ratio decreased from 2005 to 2006 and was only 55% of Nike's ratio.

2. *Earnings performance:* There are many measures of earnings performance. Some of those presented thus far in the book were earnings per share (page 55) and the return on common stockholders' equity ratio (this chapter). These measures for Adidas in 2006 and 2005 are calculated as shown here.

	2006	2005
Earnings per share	$\dfrac{\$496 - 0}{(203 + 203)/2} = \$2.44$	$\dfrac{\$390 - 0}{(203 + 199)/2} = \$1.94$
Return on common stockholders' equity ratio	$\dfrac{\$496 - 0}{(\$2,836 + \$2,712)/2} = 17.9\%$	$\dfrac{\$390 - 0}{(\$2,712 + \$1,564)/2} = 18.2\%$

From 2005 to 2006, Adidas's net income improved 27% and its earnings per share increased 26%. Earnings per share should not be compared across companies because the number of shares varies considerably. Thus we should not compare Adidas's earnings per share with Nike's.

Adidas's return on common stockholders' equity decreased slightly from 18.2% to 17.9%. While this represents a healthy return, it is still less than Nike's.

✓ the navigator

Summary of Study Objectives

1 Identify and discuss the major characteristics of a corporation. The major characteristics of a corporation are separate legal existence, limited liability of stockholders, transferable ownership rights, ability to acquire capital, continuous life, corporation management, government regulations, and additional taxes.

2 Record the issuance of common stock. When a company records issuance of common stock for cash, it credits the par value of the shares to Common Stock; it records in a separate paid-in capital account the portion of the proceeds that is above par value. When no-par common stock has a stated value, the entries are similar to those for par value stock. When no-par common stock does not have a stated value, the entire proceeds from the issue are credited to Common Stock.

3 Explain the accounting for the purchase of treasury stock. Companies generally use the cost method in accounting for treasury stock. Under this approach, a company debits Treasury Stock at the price paid to reacquire the shares.

4 Differentiate preferred stock from common stock. Preferred stock has contractual provisions that give it priority over common stock in certain areas. Typically, preferred stockholders have a preference as to (1) dividends and (2) assets in the event of liquidation. However, they often do not have voting rights.

5 Prepare the entries for cash dividends and understand the effect of stock dividends and stock splits. Companies make entries for dividends at the declaration date and the payment date. At the declaration date the entries for a cash dividend are: debit Cash Dividends and credit Dividends Payable. The effects of stock dividends and splits: Small *stock dividends* transfer an amount equal to the fair market value of the shares issued from retained earnings to the paid-in capital accounts. *Stock splits* reduce the par value per share of the common stock while increasing the number of shares so that the balance in the Common Stock account remains the same.

6 Identify the items that affect retained earnings. Additions to retained earnings consist of net income. Deductions consist of net loss and cash and stock dividends. In some instances, portions of retained earnings are restricted, making that portion unavailable for the payment of dividends.

7 Prepare a comprehensive stockholders' equity section. In the stockholders' equity section of the balance sheet, companies report paid-in capital and retained earnings and identify specific sources of paid-in capital. Within paid-in capital, companies show two classifications: capital stock and additional paid-in capital. If a corporation has treasury stock, it deducts the cost of treasury stock from total paid-in capital and retained earnings to determine total stockholders' equity.

8 Evaluate a corporation's dividend and earnings performance from a stockholder's perspective. A company's dividend record can be evaluated by looking at what percentage of net income it chooses to pay out in dividends, as measured by the dividend payout ratio (dividends divided by net income). Earnings performance is measured with the return on common stockholders' equity ratio (income available to common stockholders divided by average common stockholders' equity).

DECISION TOOLKIT   A SUMMARY

DECISION CHECKPOINTS	INFO NEEDED FOR DECISION	TOOL TO USE FOR DECISION	HOW TO EVALUATE RESULTS
Should the company incorporate?	Capital needs, growth expectations, type of business, tax status	Corporations have limited liability, easier capital raising ability, and professional managers; but they suffer from additional taxes, government regulations, and separation of ownership from management.	Must carefully weigh the costs and benefits in light of the particular circumstances.
What portion of its earnings does the company pay out in dividends?	Net income and total cash dividends on common stock	$\text{Payout ratio} = \dfrac{\text{Cash dividends declared on common stock}}{\text{Net income}}$	A low ratio may suggest that the company is retaining its earnings for investment in future growth.
What is the company's return on common stockholders' investment?	Earnings available to common stockholders and average common stockholders' equity	$\text{Return on common stockholders' equity ratio} = \dfrac{\text{Net income} - \text{Preferred stock dividends}}{\text{Average common stockholders' equity}}$	A high measure suggests strong earnings performance from common stockholders' perspective.

Entries for Stock Dividends

study objective 9

Prepare entries for stock dividends.

To illustrate the accounting for stock dividends, assume that Medland Corporation has a balance of $300,000 in retained earnings and declares a 10% stock dividend on its 50,000 shares of $10 par value common stock. The current fair market value of its stock is $15 per share. The number of shares to be issued is 5,000 (10% × 50,000), and the total amount to be debited to Retained Earnings is $75,000 (5,000 × $15). The entry to record this transaction at the declaration date is:

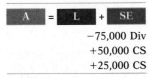

A = L + SE

−75,000 Div
+50,000 CS
+25,000 CS

Cash Flows
no effect

Stock Dividends	75,000	
Common Stock Dividends Distributable		50,000
Paid-in Capital in Excess of Par Value		25,000
(To record declaration of 10% stock dividend)		

At the declaration date Medland increases (debits) Stock Dividends for the fair market value of the stock issued; increases (credits) Common Stock Dividends Distributable for the par value of the dividend shares (5,000 × $10); and increases (credits) the excess over par (5,000 × $5) to an additional paid-in capital account.

Common Stock Dividends Distributable is a stockholders' equity account; it is not a liability because assets will not be used to pay the dividend. If Medland prepares a balance sheet before it issues the dividend shares, it reports the distributable account in paid-in capital as an addition to common stock issued, as shown in Illustration 11A-1.

Illustration 11A-1
Statement presentation of common stock dividends distributable

MEDLAND CORPORATION		
Balance Sheet (partial)		
Paid-in capital		
Common stock	$500,000	
Common stock dividends distributable	50,000	$550,000

Helpful Hint Note that the dividend account title is *distributable*, not *payable*.

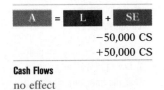

A = L + SE

−50,000 CS
+50,000 CS

Cash Flows
no effect

When Medland issues the dividend shares, it decreases Common Stock Dividends Distributable and increases Common Stock as follows.

Common Stock Dividends Distributable	50,000	
Common Stock		50,000
(To record issuance of 5,000 shares in a stock dividend)		

Summary of Study Objective for Appendix

9 Prepare entries for stock dividends. To record the declaration of a small stock dividend (less than 20%), debit Stock Dividends for an amount equal to the fair value of the shares issued. Record a credit to a temporary stockholders' equity account—Common Stock Dividends Distributable—for the par value of the shares, and credit the balance to Paid-in Capital in Excess of Par Value. When the shares are issued, debit Common Stock Dividends Distributable and credit Common Stock.

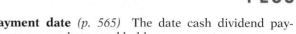

Glossary

Authorized stock *(p. 555)* The amount of stock that a corporation is authorized to sell as indicated in its charter.

Cash dividend *(p. 564)* A pro rata (proportional to ownership) distribution of cash to stockholders.

Charter *(p. 554)* A document that describes a corporation's name and purpose; types of stock and number of shares authorized; names of individuals involved in the formation; and number of shares each individual has agreed to purchase.

Corporation *(p. 550)* A company organized as a separate legal entity, with most of the rights and privileges of a person.

Cumulative dividend *(p. 562)* A feature of preferred stock entitling the stockholder to receive current and unpaid prior-year dividends before common stockholders receive any dividends.

Declaration date *(p. 564)* The date the board of directors formally authorizes the dividend and announces it to stockholders.

Deficit *(p. 569)* A debit balance in retained earnings.

Dividend *(p. 563)* A distribution by a corporation to its stockholders on a pro rata (proportional to ownership) basis.

Dividends in arrears *(p. 562)* Preferred dividends that were supposed to be declared but were not declared during a given period.

Legal capital *(p. 556)* The amount of capital that must be retained in the business for the protection of corporate creditors.

No-par value stock *(p. 556)* Capital stock that has not been assigned a value in the corporate charter.

Outstanding stock *(p. 560)* Capital stock that has been issued and is being held by stockholders.

Paid-in capital *(p. 557)* The amount stockholders paid in to the corporation in exchange for shares of ownership.

Par value stock *(p. 556)* Capital stock that has been assigned a value per share in the corporate charter.

Payment date *(p. 565)* The date cash dividend payments are made to stockholders.

Payout ratio *(p. 572)* A measure of the percentage of earnings a company distributes in the form of cash dividends to common stockholders.

Preferred stock *(p. 561)* Capital stock that has contractual preferences over common stock in certain areas.

Privately held corporation *(p. 550)* A corporation that has only a few stockholders and whose stock is not available for sale to the general public.

Publicly held corporation *(p. 550)* A corporation that may have thousands of stockholders and whose stock is traded on a national securities market.

Record date *(p. 565)* The date when the company determines ownership of outstanding shares for dividend purposes.

Retained earnings *(p. 569)* Net income that a company retains in the business.

Retained earnings restrictions *(p. 569)* Circumstances that make a portion of retained earnings currently unavailable for dividends.

Return on common stockholders' equity ratio *(p. 573)* A measure of profitability from the stockholders' point of view; computed by dividing net income minus preferred stock dividends by average common stockholders' equity.

Stated value *(p. 556)* The amount per share assigned by the board of directors to no-par stock.

Stock dividend *(p. 566)* A pro rata (proportional to ownership) distribution of the corporation's own stock to stockholders.

Stock split *(p. 567)* The issuance of additional shares of stock to stockholders accompanied by a reduction in the par or stated value per share.

Treasury stock *(p. 559)* A corporation's own stock that has been reacquired by the corporation and is being held for future use.

Comprehensive

Rolman Corporation is authorized to issue 1,000,000 shares of $5 par value common stock. In its first year the company has the following stock transactions.

Jan.   10   Issued 400,000 shares of stock at $8 per share.
Sept.   1   Purchased 10,000 shares of common stock for the treasury at $9 per share.
Dec.   24   Declared a cash dividend of 10 cents per share on common stock outstanding.

Instructions

(a) Journalize the transactions.
(b) Prepare the stockholders' equity section of the balance sheet assuming the company had retained earnings of $150,600 at December 31.

Action Plan

- When common stock has a par value, credit Common Stock for par value and Paid-in Capital in Excess of Par Value for the amount above par value.

- Debit the Treasury Stock account at cost.

Solution to Comprehensive Do it!

(a) Jan. 10	Cash	3,200,000	
	Common Stock		2,000,000
	Paid-in Capital in Excess of Par Value		1,200,000
	(To record issuance of 400,000 shares of $5 par value stock)		
Sept. 1	Treasury Stock	90,000	
	Cash		90,000
	(To record purchase of 10,000 shares of treasury stock at cost)		
Dec. 24	Cash Dividends	39,000	
	Dividends Payable		39,000
	(To record declaration of 10 cents per share cash dividend)		

(b)
ROLMAN CORPORATION
Balance Sheet (partial)

Stockholders' equity
  Paid-in capital
    Capital stock

Common stock, $5 par value, 1,000,000 shares authorized, 400,000 shares issued, 390,000 outstanding	$2,000,000
Additional paid-in capital	
In excess of par value—common stock	1,200,000
Total paid-in capital	3,200,000
Retained earnings	150,600
Total paid-in capital and retained earnings	3,350,600
Less: Treasury stock (10,000 shares)	90,000
Total stockholders' equity	$3,260,600

 the navigator

Note: All Questions, Exercises, and Problems marked with an asterisk relate to material in the appendix to the chapter.

Self-Study Questions

 WILEY PLUS

Answers are at the end of the chapter.

(SO 1) **1.** Which of these is *not* a major advantage of a corporation?
  (a) Separate legal existence.
  (b) Continuous life.
  (c) Government regulations.
  (d) Transferable ownership rights.

(SO 1) **2.** A major disadvantage of a corporation is:
  (a) limited liability of stockholders.
  (b) additional taxes.
  (c) transferable ownership rights.
  (d) None of the above.

(SO 1) **3.** Which of these statements is *false?*
  (a) Ownership of common stock gives the owner a voting right.

  (b) The stockholders' equity section begins with paid-in capital.
  (c) The authorization of capital stock does not result in a formal accounting entry.
  (d) Legal capital is intended to protect stockholders.

4. ABC Corp. issues 1,000 shares of $10 par value common stock at $12 per share. When the transaction is recorded, credits are made to: (SO 2)
  (a) Common Stock $10,000 and Paid-in Capital in Excess of Stated Value $2,000.
  (b) Common Stock $12,000.
  (c) Common Stock $10,000 and Paid-in Capital in Excess of Par Value $2,000.
  (d) Common Stock $10,000 and Retained Earnings $2,000.

(SO 3) 5. Treasury stock may be repurchased:
    (a) to reissue the shares to officers and employees under bonus and stock compensation plans.
    (b) to signal to the stock market that management believes the stock is underpriced.
    (c) to have additional shares available for use in the acquisition of other companies.
    (d) more than one of the above.

(SO 4) 6. Preferred stock may have which of the following features?
    (a) dividend preference.
    (b) preference to assets in the event of liquidation.
    (c) cumulative dividends.
    (d) all of the above.

(SO 4) 7. M-Bot Corporation has 10,000 shares of 8%, $100 par value, cumulative preferred stock outstanding at December 31, 2010. No dividends were declared in 2008 or 2009. If M-Bot wants to pay $375,000 of dividends in 2010, common stockholders will receive:
    (a) $0.   (c) $215,000.
    (b) $295,000.   (d) $135,000.

(SO 5) 8. Entries for cash dividends are required on the:
    (a) declaration date and the record date.
    (b) record date and the payment date.
    (c) declaration date, record date, and payment date.
    (d) declaration date and the payment date.

(SO 5) 9. Which of these statements about stock dividends is *true?*
    (a) Stock dividends reduce a company's cash balance.
    (b) A stock dividend has no effect on total stockholders' equity.
    (c) A stock dividend decreases total stockholders' equity.
    (d) A stock dividend ordinarily will increase total stockholders' equity.

(SO 5) 10. Raptor Inc. has retained earnings of $500,000 and total stockholders' equity of $2,000,000. It has 100,000 shares of $8 par value common stock outstanding, which is currently selling for $30 per share. If Raptor declares a 10% stock dividend on its common stock:
    (a) net income will decrease by $80,000.
    (b) retained earnings will decrease by $80,000 and total stockholders' equity will increase by $80,000.
    (c) retained earnings will decrease by $300,000 and total stockholders' equity will increase by $300,000.
    (d) retained earnings will decrease by $300,000 and total paid-in capital will increase by $300,000.

11. In the stockholders' equity section of the balance sheet, common stock: (SO 7)
    (a) is listed before preferred stock.
    (b) is listed after retained earnings.
    (c) is part of paid-in capital.
    (d) is subtracted from treasury stock.

12. In the stockholders' equity section, the cost of treasury stock is deducted from: (SO 7)
    (a) total paid-in capital and retained earnings.
    (b) retained earnings.
    (c) total stockholders' equity.
    (d) common stock in paid-in capital.

13. The return on common stockholders' equity is usually increased by all of the following, *except*: (SO 8)
    (a) an increase in the return on assets ratio.
    (b) an increase in the use of debt financing.
    (c) an increase in the company's stock price.
    (d) an increase in the company's net income.

14. Roger is nearing retirement and would like to invest in a stock that will provide a good steady income. Roger should choose a stock with a: (SO 8)
    (a) high current ratio.
    (b) high dividend payout.
    (c) high earnings per share.
    (d) high price-earnings ratio.

15. Katie Inc. reported net income of $186,000 during 2010 and paid dividends of $26,000 on common stock. It also paid dividend on its 10,000 shares of 6%, $100 par value, noncumulative preferred stock. Common stockholders' equity was $1,200,000 on January 1, 2010, and $1,600,000 on December 31, 2010. The company's return on common stockholders' equity for 2010 is: (SO 8)
    (a) 10.0%.   (c) 7.1%.
    (b) 9.0%.   (d) 13.3%.

16. If everything else is held constant, earnings per share is increased by: (SO 8)
    (a) the payment of a cash dividend to common shareholders.
    (b) the payment of a cash dividend to preferred shareholders.
    (c) the issuance of new shares of common stock.
    (d) the purchase of treasury stock.

Go to the book's companion website, **www.wiley.com/college/kimmel**, to access additional Self-Study Questions.

Questions

1. Thomas, a student, asks your help in understanding some characteristics of a corporation. Explain each of these to Thomas.
    (a) Separate legal existence.
    (b) Limited liability of stockholders.
    (c) Transferable ownership rights.

2. (a) Your friend N. J. Golde cannot understand how the characteristic of corporate management is both an advantage and a disadvantage. Clarify this problem for N. J.
    (b) Identify and explain two other disadvantages of a corporation.

3. Kim Brown believes a corporation must be incorporated in the state in which its headquarters office is located. Is Kim correct? Explain.

4. What are the basic ownership rights of common stockholders in the absence of restrictive provisions?

5. A corporation has been defined as an entity separate and distinct from its owners. In what ways is a corporation a separate legal entity?

6. What are the two principal components of stockholders' equity?

7. The corporate charter of Earl Corporation allows the issuance of a maximum of 100,000 shares of common stock. During its first 2 years of operation, Earl sold 70,000 shares to shareholders and reacquired 4,000 of these shares. After these transactions, how many shares are authorized, issued, and outstanding?

8. Which is the better investment—common stock with a par value of $5 per share or common stock with a par value of $20 per share?

9. For what reasons might a company like **IBM** repurchase some of its stock (treasury stock)?

10. Geitz, Inc. purchases 1,000 shares of its own previously issued $5 par common stock for $11,000. Assuming the shares are held in the treasury, what effect does this transaction have on (a) net income, (b) total assets, (c) total paid-in capital, and (d) total stockholders' equity?

11. (a) What are the principal differences between common stock and preferred stock?
    (b) Preferred stock may be cumulative. Discuss this feature.
    (c) How are dividends in arrears presented in the financial statements?

12. Identify the events that result in credits and debits to retained earnings.

13. Indicate how each of these accounts should be classified in the stockholders' equity section of the balance sheet.
    (a) Common Stock.
    (b) Paid-in Capital in Excess of Par Value.
    (c) Retained Earnings.
    (d) Treasury Stock.
    (e) Paid-in Capital in Excess of Stated Value.
    (f) Preferred Stock.

14. What three conditions must be met before a cash dividend is paid?

15. Three dates associated with Copp Company's cash dividend are May 1, May 15, and May 31. Discuss the significance of each date and give the entry at each date.

16. Contrast the effects of a cash dividend and a stock dividend on a corporation's balance sheet.

17. Diane Barone asks, "Since stock dividends don't change anything, why declare them?" What is your answer to Diane?

18. Henke Corporation has 10,000 shares of $15 par value common stock outstanding when it announces a 3-for-1 split. Before the split, the stock had a market price of $120 per share. After the split, how many shares of stock will be outstanding, and what will be the approximate market price per share?

19. The board of directors is considering a stock split or a stock dividend. They understand that total stockholders' equity will remain the same under either action. However, they are not sure of the different effects of the two actions on other aspects of stockholders' equity. Explain the differences to the directors.

20. What was the total cost of Tootsie Roll's treasury stock at December 31, 2007? What was the amount of the 2007 cash dividend? What was the total charge to Retained Earnings for the 2007 stock dividend?

21. (a) What is the purpose of a retained earnings restriction?
    (b) Identify the possible causes of retained earnings restrictions.

22. Fry Inc.'s common stock has a par value of $1 and a current market value of $15. Explain why these amounts are different.

23. What is the formula for the payout ratio? What does it indicate?

24. Explain the circumstances under which debt financing will increase the return on common stockholders' equity ratio.

25. Under what circumstances will the return on assets ratio and the return on common stockholders' equity ratio be equal?

26. Emig Corp. has a return on assets ratio of 12%. It plans to issue bonds at 8% and use the cash to repurchase stock. What effect will this have on its debt to total assets ratio and on its return on common stockholders' equity?

Brief Exercises

Cite advantages and disadvantages of a corporation.
(SO 1)

BE11-1 Rita Valdez is planning to start a business. Identify for Rita the advantages and disadvantages of the corporate form of business organization.

Journalize issuance of par value common stock.
(SO 2)

BE11-2 On May 10 Troyer Corporation issues 2,000 shares of $5 par value common stock for cash at $13 per share. Journalize the issuance of the stock.

Journalize issuance of no-par common stock.
(SO 2)

BE11-3 On June 1 Penner Inc. issues 3,000 shares of no-par common stock at a cash price of $6 per share. Journalize the issuance of the shares.

BE11-4   Farris Inc. issues 8,000 shares of $100 par value preferred stock for cash at $108 per share. Journalize the issuance of the preferred stock.

Journalize issuance of preferred stock.
(SO 4)

BE11-5   Longacre Corporation has 5,000 shares of common stock outstanding. It declares a $1 per share cash dividend on November 1 to stockholders of record on December 1. The dividend is paid on December 31. Prepare the entries on the appropriate dates to record the declaration and payment of the cash dividend.

Prepare entries for a cash dividend.
(SO 5)

BE11-6   The stockholders' equity section of Platt Corporation's balance sheet consists of common stock ($10 par) $1,000,000 and retained earnings $300,000. A 10% stock dividend (10,000 shares) is declared when the market value per share is $19. Show the before and after effects of the dividend on (a) the components of stockholders' equity and (b) the shares outstanding.

Show before and after effects of a stock dividend.
(SO 5)

BE11-7   Indicate whether each of the following transactions would increase (+), decrease (−), or not affect (N/A) total assets, total liabilities, and total stockholders' equity.

Compare impact of cash dividend, stock dividend, and stock split.
(SO 5)

Transaction	Assets	Liabilities	Stockholders' Equity
(a) Declared cash dividend.			
(b) Paid cash dividend declared in (a).			
(c) Declared stock dividend.			
(d) Distributed stock dividend declared in (c).			
(e) Split stock 3-for-1.			

BE11-8   Moran Corporation has these accounts at December 31: Common Stock, $10 par, 5,000 shares issued, $50,000; Paid-in Capital in Excess of Par Value $18,000; Retained Earnings $42,000; and Treasury Stock—Common, 500 shares, $12,000. Prepare the stockholders' equity section of the balance sheet.

Prepare a stockholders' equity section.
(SO 7)

BE11-9   Matt Kifer, president of Kifer Corporation, believes that it is a good practice for a company to maintain a constant payout of dividends relative to its earnings. Last year net income was $600,000, and the corporation paid $120,000 in dividends. This year, due to some unusual circumstances, the corporation had income of $1,500,000. Matt expects next year's net income to be about $700,000. What was Kifer Corporation's payout ratio last year? If it is to maintain the same payout ratio, what amount of dividends would it pay this year? Is this necessarily a good idea—that is, what are the pros and cons of maintaining a constant payout ratio in this scenario?

Evaluate a company's dividend record.
(SO 8)

BE11-10   SUPERVALU, one of the largest grocery retailers in the United States, is headquartered in Minneapolis. The following financial information (in millions) was taken from the company's 2007 annual report. Net sales $37,406; net income $452; beginning stockholders' equity $2,619; ending stockholders' equity $5,306. Compute the return on common stockholders' equity ratio. Provide a brief interpretation of your findings.

Calculate the return on stockholders' equity.
(SO 8)

*BE11-11   Leiker Corporation has 200,000 shares of $10 par value common stock outstanding. It declares a 10% stock dividend on December 1 when the market value per share is $17. The dividend shares are issued on December 31. Prepare the entries for the declaration and distribution of the stock dividend.

Prepare entries for a stock dividend.
(SO 9)

Do it! Review

Do it! **11-1**   Indicate whether each of the following statements in true or false.

1. The corporation is an entity separate and distinct from its owners.
2. The liability of stockholders is normally limited to their investment in the corporation.
3. The relative lack of government regulation is an advantage of the corporate form of business.
4. There is no journal entry to record the authorization of capital stock.
5. No-par value stock is quite rare today.

Analyze statements about corporate organization.
(SO 1)

Journalize issuance of stock.
(SO 2)

Do it! 11-2 Caribbean Corporation began operations on April 1 by issuing 60,000 shares of $5 par value common stock for cash at $13 per share. Journalize the issuance.

Journalize treasury stock transaction.
(SO 3)

Do it! 11-3 Chiapas Corporation purchased 2,000 shares of its $10 par value common stock for $120,000 on August 1. It will hold these in the treasury until resold. Journalize the treasury stock transaction.

Determine dividends paid to preferred and common stockholders.
(SO 4)

Do it! 11-4 Mensa Corporation has 3,000 shares of 7%, $100 par value preferred stock outstanding at December 31, 2010. At December 31, 2010, the company declared a $105,000 cash dividend. Determine the dividend paid to preferred stockholders and common stockholders under each of the following scenarios.

1. The preferred stock is noncumulative, and the company has not missed any dividends in previous years.
2. The preferred stock is noncumulative, and the company did not pay a dividend in each of the two previous years.
3. The preferred stock is cumulative, and the company did not pay a dividend in each of the two previous years.

Determine effects of stock dividend and stock split.
(SO 5)

Do it! 11-5 Riff CD Company has had 4 years of record earnings. Due to this success, the market price of its 400,000 shares of $3 par value common stock has increased from $12 per share to $51. During this period, paid-in capital remained the same at $2,400,000. Retained earnings increased from $1,800,000 to $12,000,000. CEO Josh Borke is considering either (1) a 15% stock dividend or (2) a 2-for-1 stock split. He asks you to show the before-and-after effects of each option on (a) retained earnings and (b) total stockholders' equity.

Prepare stockholders' equity section.
(SO 7)

Do it! 11-6 Connolly Corporation has issued 100,000 shares of $5 par value common stock. It was authorized 500,000 shares. The paid-in capital in excess of par value on the common stock is $287,000. The corporation has reacquired 7,000 shares at a cost of $46,000 and is currently holding those shares.

The corporation also has 2,000 shares issued and outstanding of 7%, $100 par-value preferred stock. It authorized 10,000 shares. The paid-in capital in excess of par value on the preferred stock is $23,000.

Retained earnings is $372,000.

Prepare the stockholders' equity section of the balance sheet.

Exercises

WILEY
PLUS

Journalize issuance of common stock.
(SO 2)

E11-1 During its first year of operations, Privat Corporation had these transactions pertaining to its common stock.

Jan. 10 Issued 70,000 shares for cash at $5 per share.
July   1 Issued 40,000 shares for cash at $7 per share.

Instructions
(a) Journalize the transactions, assuming that the common stock has a par value of $5 per share.
(b) Journalize the transactions, assuming that the common stock is no-par with a stated value of $1 per share.

Journalize issuance of common stock and preferred stock and purchase of treasury stock.
(SO 2, 3, 4)

E11-2 Noble Co. had these transactions during the current period.

June 12 Issued 80,000 shares of $1 par value common stock for cash of $300,000.
July 11 Issued 3,000 shares of $100 par value preferred stock for cash at $104 per share.
Nov. 28 Purchased 2,000 shares of treasury stock for $11,000.

Instructions
Prepare the journal entries for the transactions shown on page 584.

E11-3   Tovar Corporation is authorized to issue both preferred and common stock. The par value of the preferred is $50. During the first year of operations, the company had the following events and transactions pertaining to its preferred stock.

Journalize preferred stock transactions and indicate statement presentation.
(SO 4, 7)

Feb. 1   Issued 60,000 shares for cash at $51 per share.
July   1   Issued 30,000 shares for cash at $56 per share.

Instructions
(a) Journalize the transactions.
(b) Post to the stockholders' equity accounts. (Use T accounts.)
(c) Discuss the statement presentation of the accounts.

E11-4   The stockholders' equity section of Sundberg Corporation's balance sheet at December 31 is presented here.

Answer questions about stockholders' equity section.
(SO 2, 3, 4, 7)

SUNDBERG CORPORATION
Balance Sheet (partial)

Stockholders' equity	
Paid-in capital	
Preferred stock, cumulative, 10,000 shares authorized,	
6,000 shares issued and outstanding	$ 600,000
Common stock, no par, 750,000 shares authorized,	
600,000 shares issued	2,100,000
Total paid-in capital	2,700,000
Retained earnings	1,158,000
Total paid-in capital and retained earnings	3,858,000
Less: Treasury stock (8,000 common shares)	(32,000)
Total stockholders' equity	$3,826,000

300,000
312,000

Instructions
From a review of the stockholders' equity section, answer the following questions.
(a) How many shares of common stock are outstanding?
(b) Assuming there is a stated value, what is the stated value of the common stock?
(c) What is the par value of the preferred stock?
(d) If the annual dividend on preferred stock is $36,000, what is the dividend rate on preferred stock?
(e) If dividends of $72,000 were in arrears on preferred stock, what would be the balance reported for retained earnings?

E11-5   Zerbe Corporation recently hired a new accountant with extensive experience in accounting for partnerships. Because of the pressure of the new job, the accountant was unable to review what he had learned earlier about corporation accounting. During the first month, he made the following entries for the corporation's capital stock.

Prepare correct entries for capital stock transactions.
(SO 2, 3, 4)

May 2	Cash	120,000	
	Capital Stock		120,000
	(Issued 10,000 shares of $10 par value		
	common stock at $12 per share)		
10	Cash	530,000	
	Capital Stock		530,000
	(Issued 10,000 shares of $20 par value		
	preferred stock at $53 per share)		
15	Capital Stock	7,200	
	Cash		7,200
	(Purchased 600 shares of common stock		
	for the treasury at $12 per share)		

Instructions
On the basis of the explanation for each entry, prepare the entries that should have been made for the capital stock transactions.

[handwritten: $300,000 : TV   60,000 @ 5 per share value]

[handwritten: 1.50 × 68,000]

*[handwritten: 1.78 * 126,000]*

E11-6   On January 1 Trear Corporation had 60,000 shares of no-par common stock issued and outstanding. The stock has a stated value of $5 per share. During the year, the following transactions occurred.

Apr.	1	Issued 8,000 additional shares of common stock for $11 per share.
June	15	Declared a cash dividend of $1.50 per share to stockholders of record on June 30.
July	10	Paid the $1.50 cash dividend. *[handwritten: − 48,000]*
Dec.	1	Issued 4,000 additional shares of common stock for $12 per share.
	15	Declared a cash dividend on outstanding shares of $1.75 per share to stockholders of record on December 31.

Instructions
(a) Prepare the entries, if any, on each of the three dates that involved dividends.
(b) How are dividends and dividends payable reported in the financial statements prepared at December 31?

E11-7   On October 31 the stockholders' equity section of Lynch Company's balance sheet consists of common stock $648,000 and retained earnings $400,000. Lynch is considering the following two courses of action: (1) declaring a 5% stock dividend on the 81,000 $8 par value shares outstanding or (2) effecting a 2-for-1 stock split that will reduce par value to $4 per share. The current market price is $14 per share.

Instructions
Prepare a tabular summary of the effects of the alternative actions on the company's stockholders' equity and outstanding shares. Use these column headings: **Before Action**, **After Stock Dividend**, and **After Stock Split**.

E11-8   **Wells Fargo & Company**, headquartered in San Francisco, is one of the nation's largest financial institutions. It reported the following selected accounts (in millions) as of December 31, 2006.

Retained earnings	$35,277
Preferred stock	384
Common stock—$1⅔ par value, authorized 6,000,000,000 shares;	
issued 3,472,762,050 shares	5,788
Treasury stock—95,612,189 shares	(3,203)
Additional paid-in capital—common stock	7,739

Instructions
Prepare the stockholders' equity section of the balance sheet for Wells Fargo as of December 31, 2006.

E11-9   The following stockholders' equity accounts, arranged alphabetically, are in the ledger of Kenton Corporation at December 31, 2010.

Common Stock ($5 stated value)	$2,000,000
Paid-in Capital in Excess of Par Value—Preferred Stock	45,000
Paid-in Capital in Excess of Stated Value—Common Stock	1,050,000
Preferred Stock (8%, $100 par, noncumulative)	500,000
Retained Earnings	1,334,000
Treasury Stock—Common (8,000 shares)	78,000

Instructions
Prepare the stockholders' equity section of the balance sheet at December 31, 2010.

E11-10   The following accounts appear in the ledger of Rosswell Inc. after the books are closed at December 31, 2010.

Common Stock (no-par, $1 stated value, 400,000 shares authorized, 250,000 shares issued)	$ 250,000
Paid-in Capital in Excess of Stated Value—Common Stock	1,200,000
Preferred Stock ($50 par value, 8%, 40,000 shares authorized, 12,000 shares issued)	600,000
Retained Earnings	700,000
Treasury Stock (10,000 common shares)	64,000
Paid-in Capital in Excess of Par Value—Preferred Stock	24,000

Instructions
Prepare the stockholders' equity section at December 31, assuming $100,000 of retained earnings is restricted for plant expansion. (Use Note R.)

E11-11 The following financial information is available for **Sara Lee Corporation.**

Calculate ratios to evaluate dividend and earnings performance.
(SO 8)

(in millions)	2007	2006
Average common stockholders' equity	$2,532	$2,591
Dividends declared for common stockholders	298	611
Dividends declared for preferred stockholders	0	0
Net income	504	555

Instructions
Calculate the payout ratio and return on common stockholders' equity ratio for 2007 and 2006. Comment on your findings.

E11-12 The following financial information is available for **Walgreen Company.**

Calculate ratios to evaluate dividend and earnings performance.
(SO 8)

(in millions)	2007	2006
Average common stockholders' equity	$10,610.1	$9,502.8
Dividends declared for common stockholders	326.2	275.2
Dividends declared for preferred stockholders	0	0
Net income	2,041.3	1,750.6

Instructions
Calculate the payout ratio and return on common stockholders' equity ratio for 2007 and 2006. Comment on your findings.

E11-13 Oslo Corporation decided to issue common stock and used the $300,000 proceeds to retire all of its outstanding bonds on January 1, 2010. The following information is available for the company for 2009 and 2010.

Calculate ratios to evaluate profitability and solvency.
(SO 8)

	2010	2009
Net income	$ 182,000	$ 150,000
Average stockholders' equity	1,000,000	700,000
Total assets	1,200,000	1,200,000
Current liabilities	100,000	100,000
Total liabilities	200,000	500,000

Instructions
(a) Compute the return on stockholder's equity ratio for both years.
(b) Explain how it is possible that net income increased, but the return on common stockholders' equity decreased.
(c) Compute the debt to total assets ratio for both years, and comment on the implications of this change in the company's solvency.

E11-14 Flypaper Airlines is considering these two alternatives for financing the purchase of a fleet of airplanes:

Compare issuance of stock financing to issuance of bond financing.
(SO 8)

1. Issue 60,000 shares of common stock at $45 per share. (Cash dividends have not been paid nor is the payment of any contemplated.)
2. Issue 13%, 10-year bonds at face value for $2,700,000.

It is estimated that the company will earn $800,000 before interest and taxes as a result of this purchase. The company has an estimated tax rate of 30% and has 90,000 shares of common stock outstanding prior to the new financing.

Instructions
Determine the effect on net income and earnings per share for (a) issuing stock and (b) issuing bonds. Assume the new shares or new bonds will be outstanding for the entire year.

E11-15 Alexander Company has $1,000,000 in assets and $1,000,000 in stockholders' equity, with 50,000 shares outstanding the entire year. It has a return on assets ratio of 10%. In the past year it had net income of $100,000. On January 1, 2010, it issued $500,000 in debt at 5% and immediately repurchased 25,000 shares for $500,000. Management expected that, had it not issued the debt, it would have again had net income of $100,000.

Compute ratios and interpret.
(SO 8)

Instructions

(a) Determine the company's net income and earnings per share for 2009 and 2010. (Ignore taxes in your computations.)
(b) Compute the company's return on common stockholders' equity for 2009 and 2010.
(c) Compute the company's debt to assets ratio for 2009 and 2010.
(d) Discuss the impact that the borrowing had on the company's profitability and solvency. Was it a good idea to borrow the money to buy the treasury stock?

Journalize stock dividends.
(SO 5, 9)

*E11-16 On January 1, 2010, Gant Corporation had $1,500,000 of common stock outstanding that was issued at par and retained earnings of $750,000. The company issued 30,000 shares of common stock at par on July 1 and earned net income of $400,000 for the year.

Instructions

Journalize the declaration of a 15% stock dividend on December 10, 2010, for the following two independent assumptions.
(a) Par value is $10 and market value is $15.
(b) Par value is $5 and market value is $8.

Exercises: Set B

Visit the book's companion website, at **www.wiley.com/college/kimmel,** and choose the Student Companion site, to access Exercise Set B.

Problems: Set A

Journalize stock transactions, post, and prepare paid-in capital section.
(SO 2, 4, 7)

P11-1A Pinson Corporation was organized on January 1, 2010. It is authorized to issue 20,000 shares of 6%, $50 par value preferred stock and 500,000 shares of no-par common stock with a stated value of $1 per share. The following stock transactions were completed during the first year.

Jan.	10	Issued 80,000 shares of common stock for cash at $4 per share.
Mar.	1	Issued 12,000 shares of preferred stock for cash at $54 per share.
May	1	Issued 120,000 shares of common stock for cash at $5 per share.
Sept.	1	Issued 5,000 shares of common stock for cash at $6 per share.
Nov.	1	Issued 3,000 shares of preferred stock for cash at $56 per share.

Instructions

(a) Journalize the transactions.
(b) Post to the stockholders' equity accounts. (Use T accounts.)

(c) Tot. paid-in capital $1,766,000

(c) Prepare the paid-in capital portion of the stockholders' equity section at December 31, 2010.

Journalize transactions, post, and prepare a stockholders' equity section; calculate ratios.
(SO 2, 3, 5, 7, 8)

P11-2A The stockholders' equity accounts of Sigma Corporation on January 1, 2010, were as follows.

Preferred Stock (8%, $100 par noncumulative, 5,000 shares authorized)	$ 300,000
Common Stock ($5 stated value, 300,000 shares authorized)	1,000,000
Paid-in Capital in Excess of Par Value—Preferred Stock	15,000
Paid-in Capital in Excess of Stated Value—Common Stock	480,000
Retained Earnings	688,000
Treasury Stock—Common (5,000 shares)	40,000

During 2010 the corporation had the following transactions and events pertaining to its stockholders' equity.

Feb.	1	Issued 5,000 shares of common stock for $30,000.
Mar.	20	Purchased 1,000 additional shares of common treasury stock at $7 per share.
Oct.	1	Declared an 8% cash dividend on preferred stock, payable November 1.
Nov.	1	Paid the dividend declared on October 1.

Dec.   1   Declared a $0.50 per share cash dividend to common stockholders of record on December 15, payable December 31, 2010.

31   Determined that net income for the year was $280,000. Paid the dividend declared on December 1.

Instructions

(a) Journalize the transactions. (Include entries to close net income and dividends to Retained Earnings.)

(b) Enter the beginning balances in the accounts and post the journal entries to the stockholders' equity accounts. (Use T accounts.)

(c) Prepare the stockholders' equity section of the balance sheet at December 31, 2010.

(d) Calculate the payout ratio, earnings per share, and return on common stockholders' equity ratio. (*Note:* Use the common shares outstanding on January 1 and December 31 to determine the average shares outstanding.)

(c) Tot. paid-in capital $1,825,000

P11-3A   On December 31, 2009, Milo Company had 1,300,000 shares of $5 par common stock issued and outstanding. The stockholders' equity accounts at December 31, 2009, had the balances listed here.

Prepare a stockholders' equity section.
(SO 7)

Common Stock	$6,500,000
Additional Paid-in Capital	1,800,000
Retained Earnings	1,200,000

Transactions during 2010 and other information related to stockholders' equity accounts were as follows.

1. On January 10, 2010, issued at $109 per share 120,000 shares of $100 par value, 8% cumulative preferred stock.

2. On February 8, 2010, reacquired 20,000 shares of its common stock for $11 per share.

3. On June 8, 2010, declared a cash dividend of $1.20 per share on the common stock outstanding, payable on July 10, 2010, to stockholders of record on July 1, 2010.

4. On December 9, 2010, declared the yearly cash dividend on preferred stock, payable January 10, 2011, to stockholders of record on December 15, 2010.

5. Net income for the year was $3,600,000.

Instructions

Prepare the stockholders' equity section of Milo's balance sheet at December 31, 2010.

Tot. stockholders' equity $23,464,000

P11-4A   The ledger of Gamma Corporation at December 31, 2010, after the books have been closed, contains the following stockholders' equity accounts.

Reproduce retained earnings account, and prepare a stockholders' equity section.
(SO 5, 6, 7)

Preferred Stock (10,000 shares issued)	$1,000,000
Common Stock (400,000 shares issued)	2,000,000
Paid-in Capital in Excess of Par Value—Preferred Stock	200,000
Paid-in Capital in Excess of Stated Value—Common Stock	1,600,000
Retained Earnings	2,860,000

A review of the accounting records reveals this information:

1. Preferred stock is 7%, $100 par value, noncumulative. Since January 1, 2009, 10,000 shares have been outstanding; 20,000 shares are authorized.

2. Common stock is no-par with a stated value of $5 per share; 600,000 shares are authorized.

3. The January 1, 2010, balance in Retained Earnings was $2,380,000.

4. On October 1, 60,000 shares of common stock were sold for cash at $8 per share.

5. A cash dividend of $400,000 was declared and properly allocated to preferred and common stock on November 1. No dividends were paid to preferred stockholders in 2009.

6. Net income for the year was $880,000.

7. On December 31, 2010, the directors authorized disclosure of a $130,000 restriction of retained earnings for plant expansion. (Use Note A.)

Instructions

(a) Reproduce the retained earnings account (T account) for the year.

(b) Prepare the stockholders' equity section of the balance sheet at December 31.

(b) Tot. paid-in capital $4,800,000

Prepare entries for stock transactions, and prepare a stockholders' equity section.
(SO 2, 3, 4, 7)

P11-5A   Bodley Corporation has been authorized to issue 20,000 shares of $100 par value, 10%, noncumulative preferred stock and 1,000,000 shares of no-par common stock.

The corporation assigned a $5 stated value to the common stock. At December 31, 2010, the ledger contained the following balances pertaining to stockholders' equity.

Preferred Stock	$ 150,000
Paid-in Capital in Excess of Par Value—Preferred Stock	20,000
Common Stock	2,000,000
Paid-in Capital in Excess of Stated Value—Common Stock	1,650,000
Treasury Stock—Common (5,000 shares)	55,000
Retained Earnings	82,000

The preferred stock was issued for $170,000 cash. All common stock issued was for cash. In November 5,000 shares of common stock were purchased for the treasury at a per share cost of $11. No dividends were declared in 2010.

Instructions
(a) Prepare the journal entries for the following.
  (1) Issuance of preferred stock for cash.
  (2) Issuance of common stock for cash.
  (3) Purchase of common treasury stock for cash.

(b) Tot. stockholders' equity
$3,847,000

(b) Prepare the stockholders' equity section of the balance sheet at December 31, 2010.

Prepare a stockholders'
equity section.
(SO 7)

P11-6A On January 1, 2010, Sampson Inc. had these stockholders' equity balances.

Common Stock, $1 par (2,000,000 shares authorized,	
800,000 shares issued and outstanding)	$ 800,000
Paid-in Capital in Excess of Par Value	1,500,000
Retained Earnings	600,000

During 2010, the following transactions and events occurred.

1. Issued 50,000 shares of $1 par value common stock for $3 per share.
2. Issued 60,000 shares of common stock for cash at $4 per share.
3. Purchased 20,000 shares of common stock for the treasury at $3.50 per share.
4. Declared and paid a cash dividend of $115,000.
5. Earned net income of $350,000.

Instructions

Tot. stockholders' equity $3,455,000

Prepare the stockholders' equity section of the balance sheet at December 31, 2010.

Evaluate a company's
profitability and solvency.
(SO 8)

P11-7A Parcells Company manufactures backpacks. During 2010 Parcells issued bonds at 10% interest and used the cash proceeds to purchase treasury stock. The following financial information is available for Parcells Company for the years 2010 and 2009.

	2010	**2009**
Sales	$ 9,000,000	$ 9,000,000
Net income	2,240,000	2,600,000
Interest expense	500,000	140,000
Tax expense	670,000	780,000
Dividends paid	890,000	1,026,000
Total assets (year-end)	14,500,000	16,875,000
Average total assets	14,937,500	17,647,000
Total liabilities (year-end)	6,000,000	3,000,000
Aver. total common stockholders' equity	9,400,000	14,100,000

Instructions
(a) Use the information above to calculate the following ratios for both years: (i) return on assets ratio, (ii) return on common stockholders' equity ratio, (iii) payout ratio, (iv) debt to total assets ratio, (v) times interest earned ratio.
(b) Referring to your findings in part (a), discuss the changes in the company's profitability from 2009 to 2010.
(c) Referring to your findings in part (a), discuss the changes in the company's solvency from 2009 to 2010.
(d) Based on your findings in (b), was the decision to issue debt to purchase common stock a wise one?

*P11-8A   On January 1, 2010, Werth Corporation had these stockholders' equity accounts.

Common Stock ($10 par value, 80,000 shares issued and outstanding) $800,000
Paid-in Capital in Excess of Par Value   500,000
Retained Earnings   620,000

During the year, the following transactions occurred.

Jan.	15	Declared a $0.50 cash dividend per share to stockholders of record on January 31, payable February 15.
Feb.	15	Paid the dividend declared in January.
Apr.	15	Declared a 10% stock dividend to stockholders of record on April 30, distributable May 15. On April 15 the market price of the stock was $14 per share.
May	15	Issued the shares for the stock dividend.
Dec.	1	Declared a $0.55 per share cash dividend to stockholders of record on December 15, payable January 10, 2011.
	31	Determined that net income for the year was $400,000.

Instructions
(a) Journalize the transactions. (Include entries to close net income and dividends to Retained Earnings.)
(b) Enter the beginning balances and post the entries to the stockholders' equity T accounts. (*Note:* Open additional stockholders' equity accounts as needed.)
(c) Prepare the stockholders' equity section of the balance sheet at December 31.
(d) Calculate the payout ratio and return on common stockholders' equity ratio.

Prepare dividend entries, prepare a stockholders' equity section, and calculate ratios.
(SO 5, 7, 8, 9)

(c) Tot. stockholders' equity
$2,231,600

Problems: Set B

P11-1B   Cates Corporation was organized on January 1, 2010. It is authorized to issue 10,000 shares of 8%, $100 par value preferred stock and 500,000 shares of no-par common stock with a stated value of $2 per share. The following stock transactions were completed during the first year.

Jan.	10	Issued 60,000 shares of common stock for cash at $3.50 per share.
Mar.	1	Issued 5,000 shares of preferred stock for cash at $102 per share.
May	1	Issued 90,000 shares of common stock for cash at $4 per share.
Sept.	1	Issued 10,000 shares of common stock for cash at $5 per share.
Nov.	1	Issued 4,000 shares of preferred stock for cash at $104 per share.

Instructions
(a) Journalize the transactions.
(b) Post to the stockholders' equity accounts. (Use T accounts.)
(c) Prepare the paid-in capital section of stockholders' equity at December 31, 2010.

Journalize stock transactions, post, and prepare paid-in capital section.
(SO 2, 4, 7)

(c) Tot. paid-in capital $1,546,000

P11-2B   The stockholders' equity accounts of Mota Corporation on January 1, 2010, were as follows.

Preferred Stock (7%, $50 par cumulative, 10,000 shares authorized) $ 300,000
Common Stock ($1 stated value, 2,000,000 shares authorized)   1,000,000
Paid-in Capital in Excess of Par Value—Preferred Stock   80,000
Paid-in Capital in Excess of Stated Value—Common Stock   1,400,000
Retained Earnings   1,716,000
Treasury Stock—Common (10,000 shares)   30,000

During 2010 the corporation had these transactions and events pertaining to its stockholders' equity.

Feb.	1	Issued 20,000 shares of common stock for $60,000.
Nov.	10	Purchased 4,000 shares of common stock for the treasury at a cost of $18,000.
Nov.	15	Declared a 7% cash dividend on preferred stock, payable December 15.
Dec.	1	Declared a $0.30 per share cash dividend to stockholders of record on December 15, payable December 31, 2010.

Journalize transactions, post, and prepare a stockholders' equity section; calculate ratios.
(SO 2, 3, 5, 7, 8)

Dec. 15 Paid the dividend declared on November 15.
31 Determined that net income for the year was $408,000. The market price of the common stock on this date was $5 per share. Paid the dividend declared on December 1.

Instructions
(a) Journalize the transactions. (Include entries to close net income and dividends to Retained Earnings.)
(b) Enter the beginning balances in the accounts, and post the journal entries to the stockholders' equity accounts. (Use T accounts.)

(c) Tot. paid-in capital $2,840,000

(c) Prepare the stockholders' equity section of the balance sheet at December 31, 2010.
(d) Calculate the payout ratio, earnings per share, and return on common stockholders' equity ratio. (*Hint:* Use the common shares outstanding on January 1 and December 31 to determine average shares outstanding.)

Prepare a stockholders' equity section.
(SO 7)

P11-3B On December 31, 2009, Brant Company had 1,000,000 shares of $1 par common stock issued and outstanding. The stockholders' equity accounts at December 31, 2009, had the balances listed here.

Common Stock	$1,000,000
Additional Paid-in Capital	100,000
(Credit) Retained Earnings	800,000

Transactions during 2010 and other information related to stockholders' equity accounts were as follows.

1. On January 9, 2010, issued at $8 per share 120,000 shares of $5 par value, 9% cumulative preferred stock.
2. On February 8, 2010, reacquired 15,000 shares of its common stock for $9 per share.
3. On June 10, 2010, declared a cash dividend of $1 per share on the common stock outstanding, payable on July 10, 2010, to stockholders of record on July 1, 2010.
4. On December 15, 2010, declared the yearly cash dividend on preferred stock, payable December 28, 2010, to stockholders of record on December 15, 2010.
5. Net income for the year is $2,400,000. At December 31, 2010, the market price of the common stock was $12 per share.

Instructions

Tot. stockholders' equity $4,086,000

Prepare the stockholders' equity section of Brant Company's balance sheet at December 31, 2010.

Reproduce retained earnings account, and prepare a stockholders' equity section.
(SO 5, 6, 7)

P11-4B The post-closing trial balance of Fernetti Corporation at December 31, 2010, contains these stockholders' equity accounts.

Preferred Stock (8,000 shares issued)	$400,000
Common Stock (350,000 shares issued)	3,500,000
Paid-in Capital in Excess of Par Value—Preferred Stock	250,000
Paid-in Capital in Excess of Par Value—Common Stock	700,000
Retained Earnings	915,000

A review of the accounting records reveals this information:

1. Preferred stock is $50 par, 10%, and cumulative; 8,000 shares have been outstanding since January 1, 2009.
2. Authorized stock is 20,000 shares of preferred and 500,000 shares of common with a $10 par value.
3. The January 1, 2010, balance in Retained Earnings was $660,000.
4. On July 1, 20,000 shares of common stock were sold for cash at $16 per share.
5. A cash dividend of $220,000 was declared and properly allocated to preferred and common stock on October 1. No dividends were paid to preferred stockholders in 2009.
6. Net income for the year was $475,000.
7. On December 31, 2010, the directors authorized disclosure of a $150,000 restriction of retained earnings for plant expansion. (Use Note X.)

Instructions
(a) Reproduce the retained earnings account for the year.

(b) Tot. paid-in capital $4,850,000

(b) Prepare the stockholders' equity section of the balance sheet at December 31.

P11-5B   The following stockholders' equity accounts, arranged alphabetically, are in the ledger of Selig Corporation at December 31, 2010.

Prepare a stockholders' equity section.

(SO 7)

Common Stock ($5 stated value, 800,000 shares authorized)	$2,900,000
Paid-in Capital in Excess of Par Value—Preferred Stock	158,000
Paid-in Capital in Excess of Stated Value—Common Stock	1,500,000
Preferred Stock (8%, $50 par, noncumulative, 50,000 shares authorized)	900,000
Retained Earnings	1,958,000
Treasury Stock—Common (20,000 shares)	200,000

Instructions

Prepare the stockholders' equity section of the balance sheet at December 31, 2010.

Tot. stockholders' equity $7,216,000

P11-6B   On January 1, 2010, Leyland Inc. had these stockholder equity balances.

Prepare a stockholders' equity section.

(SO 7)

Common Stock, $1 par (1,000,000 shares authorized; 500,000 shares issued and outstanding)	$ 500,000
Paid-in Capital in Excess of Par Value	1,000,000
Retained Earnings	600,000

During 2010, the following transactions and events occurred.

1. Issued 50,000 shares of $1 par common stock for $125,000.
2. Issued 40,000 common shares for cash at $4 per share.
3. Purchased 15,000 shares of common stock for the treasury at $4 per share.
4. Declared and paid a cash dividend of $160,000.
5. Reported net income of $450,000.

Instructions

Prepare the stockholders' equity section of the balance sheet at December 31, 2010.

Tot. stockholders' equity $2,615,000

P11-7B   Willingham Company manufactures raingear. During 2010 Willingham Company decided to issue bonds at 8% interest and then used the cash to purchase a significant amount of treasury stock. The following information is available for Willingham Company.

Evaluate a company's profitability and solvency.

(SO 8)

	2010	2009
Sales	$3,000,000	$3,000,000
Net income	780,000	850,000
Interest expense	120,000	50,000
Tax expense	166,000	200,000
Total assets	5,000,000	5,625,000
Average total assets	5,312,500	6,250,000
Total liabilities	2,000,000	1,200,000
Average total stockholders' equity	3,312,500	5,250,000
Dividends	270,000	300,000

Instructions

(a) Use the information above to calculate the following ratios for both years: (i) return on assets ratio, (ii) return on common stockholders' equity ratio, (iii) payout ratio, (iv) debt to total assets ratio, (v) times interest earned ratio.
(b) Referring to your findings in part (a), discuss the changes in the company's profitability from 2009 to 2010.
(c) Referring to your findings in part (a), discuss the changes in the company's solvency from 2009 to 2010.
(d) Based on your findings in (b), was the decision to issue debt to purchase common stock a wise one?

*P11-8B   On January 1, 2010, Dolen Corporation had these stockholders' equity accounts.

Prepare dividend entries, prepare a stockholders' equity section, and calculate ratios

(SO 5, 7, 8, 9)

Common Stock ($20 par value, 90,000 shares issued and outstanding)	$1,800,000
Paid-in Capital in Excess of Par Value	240,000
Retained Earnings	750,000

During the year, the following transactions occurred.

Feb. 1 Declared a $0.50 cash dividend per share to stockholders of record on February 15, payable March 1.

Mar. 1 Paid the dividend declared in February.

July 1 Declared a 10% stock dividend to stockholders of record on July 15, distributable July 31. On July 1 the market price of the stock was $26 per share.

31 Issued the shares for the stock dividend.

Dec. 1 Declared a $1 per share dividend to stockholders of record on December 15, payable January 5, 2011.

31 Determined that net income for the year was $500,000. The market price of the common stock on this date was $32.

Instructions

(a) Journalize the transactions. (Include entries to close net income and dividends to Retained Earnings.)

(b) Enter the beginning balances and post the entries to the stockholders' equity T accounts. (*Note:* Open additional stockholders' equity accounts as needed.)

(c) Tot. stockholders' equity $3,146,000

(c) Prepare the stockholders' equity section of the balance sheet at December 31.

(d) Calculate the payout ratio and return on common stockholders' equity ratio.

Problems: Set C

Visit the book's companion website at **www.wiley.com/college/kimmel** and choose the Student Companion site to access Problem Set C.

Comprehensive Problem

CP11 Hiatt Corporation's balance sheet at December 31, 2009, is presented below.

HIATT CORPORATION
Balance Sheet
December 31, 2009

Cash	$ 24,600	Accounts payable	$ 25,600
Accounts receivable	45,500	Common stock ($10 par)	80,000
Allowance for doubtful		Retained earnings	127,400
accounts	(1,500)		$233,000
Supplies	4,400		
Land	40,000		
Building	142,000		
Accumulated depreciation-			
building	(22,000)		
	$233,000		

During 2010, the following transactions occurred.

1. On January 1, 2010, Hiatt issued 1,500 shares of $20 par, 7% preferred stock for $33,000.
2. On January 1, 2010, Hiatt also issued 900 shares of the $10 par value common stock for $21,000.
3. Hiatt performed services for $280,000 on account.
4. On April 1, 2010, Hiatt collected fees of $36,000 in advance for services to be performed from April 1, 2010, to March 31, 2011.
5. Hiatt collected $267,000 from customers on account.
6. Hiatt bought $35,100 of supplies on account.
7. Hiatt paid $32,200 on accounts payable.
8. Hiatt reacquired 400 shares of its common stock on June 1, 2010, for $38 per share.
9. Paid other operating expenses of $188,200.

10. On December 31, 2010, Hiatt declared the annual preferred stock dividend and a $1.20 per share dividend on the outstanding common stock, all payable on January 15, 2011.
11. An account receivable of $1,300 which originated in 2009 is written off as uncollectible.

Adjustment data:

1. A count of supplies indicates that $5,900 of supplies remain unused at year-end.
2. Recorded revenue earned from item 4 above.
3. The allowance for doubtful accounts should have a balance of $3,500 at year end.
4. Depreciation is recorded on the building on a straight-line basis based on a 30-year life and a salvage value of $10,000.
5. The income tax rate is 30%. (*Hint:* Prepare the income statement up to income before taxes and multiply by 30% to compute the amount.)

Instructions
(You may want to set up T accounts to determine ending balances.)
(a) Prepare journal entries for the transactions listed above and adjusting entries.
(b) Prepare an adjusted trial balance at December 31, 2010.
(c) Prepare an income statement and a retained earnings statement for the year ending December 31, 2010, and a classified balance sheet as of December 31, 2010.

(b) Totals $671,350
(c) Net income $54,250
Tot. assets $361,200

Continuing Cookie Chronicle

(*Note:* This is a continuation of the Cookie Chronicle from Chapters 1 through 10.)

CCC11

Part 1 Because Natalie has been so successful with Cookie Creations and her friend Curtis Lesperance has been just as successful with his coffee shop, they conclude that they could benefit from each other's business expertise. Curtis and Natalie next evaluate the different types of business organization and because of the advantage of limited personal liability, they decide to form a corporation.

Natalie and Curtis are very excited about this new business venture. They come to you with information they have gathered about their companies and with a number of questions.

Part 2 After establishing their company's fiscal year to be October 31, Natalie and Curtis began operating Cookie & Coffee Creations Inc. on November 1, 2010. On that date they issued both preferred and common stock. Natalie and Curtis now want to prepare financial information for the first year of operations.

Go to the book's companion website, **www.wiley.com/college/kimmel**, to find the completion of this problem.

broadening your perspective

Financial Reporting and Analysis

FINANCIAL REPORTING PROBLEM: *Tootsie Roll Industries, Inc.*

BYP11-1 The stockholders' equity section of Tootsie Roll Industries' balance sheet is shown in the Consolidated Statement of Financial Position in Appendix A. You will also find data relative to this problem on other pages of Appendix A. (Note that Tootsie Roll has two classes of common stock. To answer the following questions, add the two classes of stock together.)

Instructions
Answer the following questions.
(a) What is the par or stated value per share of Tootsie Roll's common stock?
(b) What percentage of Tootsie Roll's authorized common stock was issued at December 31, 2007? (Round to the nearest full percent.)

(c) How many shares of common stock were outstanding at December 31, 2006, and at December 31, 2007?

(d) Calculate the payout ratio, earnings per share, and return on common stockholders' equity ratio for 2007.

COMPARATIVE ANALYSIS PROBLEM: *Tootsie Roll vs. Hershey Foods*

BYP11-2   The financial statements of Hershey Foods are presented in Appendix B, following the financial statements for Tootsie Roll in Appendix A.

Instructions

(a) Based on the information in these financial statements, compute the 2007 return on common stockholders' equity, debt to total assets ratio, and return on assets ratio for each company.

(b) What conclusions concerning the companies' profitability can be drawn from these ratios? Which company relies more on debt to boost its return to common shareholders?

(c) Compute the payout ratio for each company. Which pays out a higher percentage of its earnings?

RESEARCH CASE

BYP11-3   The March 27, 2007, edition of the *Wall Street Journal* has an article by Serena Ng and Karen Richardson titled "How Borrowing Yields Dividends at Many Firms."

Instructions

Read the article and answer the following questions.

(a) According to the authors of the article, what factors led Scotts Miracle-Gro to decide to take on more debt?

(b) Describe the steps that Scotts took to increase its reliance on debt.

(c) What are the potential benefits of increasing leverage, as discussed in the chapter and in this article?

(d) What are the potential pitfalls of increasing reliance on debt?

(e) What other motivation might a company's management have for taking on additional debt?

INTERPRETING FINANCIAL STATEMENTS

BYP11-4   Marriott Corporation split into two companies: Host Marriott Corporation and Marriott International. Host Marriott retained ownership of the corporation's vast hotel and other properties, while Marriott International, rather than owning hotels, managed them. The purpose of this split was to free Marriott International from the "baggage" associated with Host Marriott, thus allowing it to be more aggressive in its pursuit of growth. The following information (in millions) is provided for each corporation for their first full year operating as independent companies.

	Host Marriott	**Marriott International**
Sales	$1,501	$8,415
Net income	(25)	200
Total assets	3,822	3,207
Total liabilities	3,112	2,440
Common stockholders' equity	710	767

Instructions

(a) The two companies were split by the issuance of shares of Marriott International to all shareholders of the previous combined company. Discuss the nature of this transaction.

(b) Calculate the debt to total assets ratio for each company.

(c) Calculate the return on assets and return on common stockholders' equity ratios for each company.

(d) The company's debtholders were fiercely opposed to the original plan to split the two companies because the original plan had Host Marriott absorbing the majority of the company's debt. They relented only when Marriott International agreed to absorb a larger share of the debt. Discuss the possible reasons the debtholders were opposed to the plan to split the company.

BYP11-5 The January 25, 2005, edition of the *Wall Street Journal* has an article by Mary Kissel (on p. C1) titled "Known for Growth, Asian Firms Answer Call of the Dividend."

Instructions
Read the article and answer the following questions.
(a) What is the "dividend yield"? How does the dividend yield of Asian companies compare to that of companies in other regions?
(b) What has happened to Asian company debt levels in recent years? What implications has this had for return on equity? Explain why this would be the case.
(c) What measure is used to determine whether a company is paying out a high percentage of its earnings in the form of dividends? What percentage of their earnings are Asian firms paying out? According to the article, how have the stock prices of dividend-paying companies performed relative to non-dividend-paying companies? What explanations are given for this?

FINANCIAL ANALYSIS ON THE WEB

BYP11-6   *Purpose:* Use the stockholders' equity section of an annual report and identify the major components.

Address: **www.annualreports.com**, or go to **www.wiley.com/college/kimmel**

Steps

1. Select a particular company.
2. Search by company name.
3. Follow instructions below.

Instructions
Answer the following questions.
(a) What is the company's name?
(b) What classes of capital stock has the company issued?
(c) For each class of stock:
 (1) How many shares are authorized, issued, and/or outstanding?
 (2) What is the par value?
(d) What are the company's retained earnings?
(e) Has the company acquired treasury stock? How many shares?

Critical Thinking

DECISION MAKING ACROSS THE ORGANIZATION

BYP11-7   In recent years the fast-food chain Wendy's International has purchased many treasury shares. From December 28, 2003, to December 31, 2006, the number of shares outstanding has fallen from 115 million to 96 million. The following information was drawn from the company's financial statements (in millions).

	Year ended	
	Dec. 31, 2006	**Dec. 28, 2003**
Net income	$ 94.3	$ 236.0
Total assets	2,060.3	3,164.0
Average total assets	2,750.3	2,943.7
Total common stockholders' equity	1,011.7	1,758.6
Average common stockholders' equity	1,535.1	1,603.6
Total liabilities	1,048.7	1,405.4
Average total liabilities	1,215.2	1,340.1
Interest expense	35.7	45.8
Income taxes	5.4	141.6
Cash provided by operations	271.4	430.2
Cash dividends paid on common stock	69.7	27.3
Preferred stock dividends	0	0
Average number of common shares outstanding	114.2	113.9

Instructions

Use the information provided to answer the following questions.

(a) Compute earnings per share, return on common stockholders' equity, and return on assets for both years. Discuss the change in the company's profitability over this period.

(b) Compute the dividend payout ratio. Also compute the average cash dividend paid per share of common stock (dividends paid divided by the average number of common shares outstanding). Discuss any change in these ratios during this period and the implications for the company's dividend policy.

(c) Compute the debt to total assets ratio and times interest earned. Discuss the change in the company's solvency.

(d) Based on your findings in (a) and (c), discuss to what extent any change in the return on common stockholders' equity was the result of increased reliance on debt.

COMMUNICATION ACTIVITY

BYP11-8   Frank DeMotte, your uncle, is an inventor who has decided to incorporate. Uncle Frank knows that you are an accounting major at U.N.O. In a recent letter to you, he ends with the question, "I'm filling out a state incorporation application. Can you tell me the difference among the following terms: (1) authorized stock, (2) issued stock, (3) outstanding stock, and (4) preferred stock?"

Instructions

In a brief note, differentiate for Uncle Frank the four different stock terms. Write the letter to be friendly, yet professional.

ETHICS CASES

BYP11-9   The R&D division of Nanco Corp. has just developed a chemical for steriliz-ing the vicious Brazilian "killer bees" which are invading Mexico and the southern United States. The president of Nanco is anxious to get the chemical on the market because Nanco profits need a boost—and his job is in jeopardy because of decreasing sales and profits. Nanco has an opportunity to sell this chemical in Central American countries, where the laws are much more relaxed than in the United States.

   The director of Nanco's R&D division strongly recommends further research in the laboratory to test the side effects of this chemical on other insects, birds, animals, plants, and even humans. He cautions the president, "We could be sued from all sides if the chemical has tragic side effects that we didn't even test for in the lab." The president an-swers, "We can't wait an additional year for your lab tests. We can avoid losses from such lawsuits by establishing a separate wholly owned corporation to shield Nanco Corp. from such lawsuits. We can't lose any more than our investment in the new corporation, and we'll invest just the patent covering this chemical. We'll reap the benefits if the chemical works and is safe, and avoid the losses from lawsuits if it's a disaster." The following week Nanco creates a new wholly owned corporation called Zimmerman Inc., sells the chem-ical patent to it for $10, and watches the spraying begin.

Instructions

(a) Who are the stakeholders in this situation?

(b) Are the president's motives and actions ethical?

(c) Can Nanco shield itself against losses of Zimmerman Inc.?

BYP11-10   Tomlinson Corporation has paid 60 consecutive quarterly cash dividends (15 years). The last 6 months have been a real cash drain on the company, however, as profit margins have been greatly narrowed by increasing competition. With a cash balance suf-ficient to meet only day-to-day operating needs, the president, Sam Ripken, has decided that a stock dividend instead of a cash dividend should be declared. He tells Tomlinson's financial vice-president, Angie Baden, to issue a press release stating that the company is extending its consecutive dividend record with the issuance of a 5% stock dividend. "Write the press release convincing the stockholders that the stock dividend is just as good as a cash dividend," he orders. "Just watch our stock rise when we announce the stock dividend; it must be a good thing if that happens."

Instructions

(a) Who are the stakeholders in this situation?

(b) Is there anything unethical about president Ripken's intentions or actions?

(c) What is the effect of a stock dividend on a corporation's stockholders' equity accounts? Which would you rather receive as a stockholder—a cash dividend or a stock dividend? Why?

"ALL ABOUT YOU" ACTIVITY

BYP11-11 In response to the Sarbanes-Oxley Act, many companies have implemented formal ethics codes. Many other organizations also have ethics codes.

Instructions

Obtain the ethics code from an organization that you belong to (e.g., student organization, business school, employer, or a volunteer organization). Evaluate the ethics code based on how clearly it identifies proper and improper behaviour. Discuss its strengths, and how it might be improved.

Answers to Insight and Accounting Across the Organization Questions

p. 553

Q: In addition to regulatory cost, what is another reason why some owners choose not to take their companies public?

A: One reason for being a private company is that managers then have more control over the company's future. For example, they can make decisions that they feel might be best for the company over the long-term, and not have to worry about the short-term stock price implications.

p. 558

Q: For stocks traded on organized stock exchanges, how are the dollar prices per share established? What factors might influence the price of shares in the marketplace?

A: The dollar prices per share are established by the interaction between buyers and sellers of the shares. The prices of shares are influenced by a company's earnings and dividends as well as by factors beyond a company's control, such as changes in interest rates, labor strikes, scarcity of supplies or resources, and politics. The number of willing buyers and sellers (demand and supply) also plays a part in the price of shares.

p. 561

Q: What signal might a large stock repurchase send to investors regarding management's belief about the company's growth opportunities?

A: When a company has many growth opportunities it will normally conserve its cash in order to be better able to fund expansion. A large use of cash to buy back stock (and essentially shrink the company) would suggest that management was not optimistic about its growth opportunities.

p. 565

Q: What factors must management consider in deciding how large a dividend to pay?

A: Management must consider the size of its retained earnings balance, the amount of available cash, its expected near-term cash needs, its growth opportunities, and what level of dividend it will be able to sustain based upon its expected future earnings.

Answers to Self-Study Questions

1. c 2. b 3. d 4. c 5. d 6. d 7. d 8. d 9. b 10. d 11. c 12. a 13. c 14. b 15. b 16. d

 Remember to go back to the navigator box on the chapter-opening page and check off your completed work.

12

Statement of Cash Flows

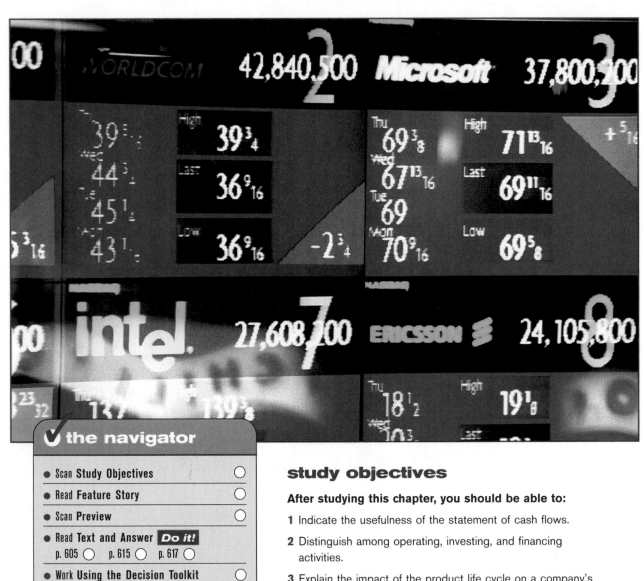

✔ the navigator

- Scan **Study Objectives** ○
- Read **Feature Story** ○
- Scan **Preview** ○
- Read **Text and Answer** *Do it!*
  p. 605 ○   p. 615 ○   p. 617 ○
- Work **Using the Decision Toolkit** ○
- Review **Summary of Study Objectives** ○
- Work **Comprehensive** *Do it!* p. 633 ○
- Answer **Self-Study Questions** ○
- Complete **Assignments** ○

study objectives

After studying this chapter, you should be able to:

1 Indicate the usefulness of the statement of cash flows.

2 Distinguish among operating, investing, and financing activities.

3 Explain the impact of the product life cycle on a company's cash flows.

4 Prepare a statement of cash flows using the indirect method.

5 Use the statement of cash flows to evaluate a company.

Got Cash?

In today's environment, companies must be ready to respond to changes quickly in order to survive and thrive. They need to produce new products and expand into new markets continually. To do this takes cash—lots and lots of cash. Keeping lots of cash available is a real challenge for a young company. It requires careful cash management and attention to cash flow.

One company that managed cash successfully in its early years was Microsoft. During those years the company paid much of its payroll with stock options (rights to purchase company stock in the future at a given price) instead of cash. This strategy conserved cash, and turned more than a thousand of its employees into millionaires during the company's first 20 years of business.

In recent years Microsoft has had a different kind of cash problem. Now that it has reached a more "mature" stage in life, it generates so much cash—roughly $1 billion per month—that it cannot always figure out what to do with it. By 2004 Microsoft had accumulated $60 billion.

The company said it was accumulating cash to invest in new opportunities, buy other companies, and pay off pending lawsuits. But for many years, the federal government blocked attempts by Microsoft to buy anything other than small firms because it feared that purchase of a large firm would only increase Microsoft's monopolistic position.

Microsoft's stockholders have complained for years that holding all this cash was putting a drag on the company's profitability. Why? Because Microsoft had the cash invested in very low-yielding government securities. Stockholders felt that the company either should find new investment projects that would bring higher returns, or return some of the cash to stockholders.

Finally, in July 2004 Microsoft announced a plan to return cash to stockholders, by paying a special one-time $32 billion dividend in December 2004. This special dividend was so large that, according to the U.S. Commerce Department, it caused total personal income in the United States to rise by 3.7% in

one month—the largest increase ever recorded by the agency. (It also made the holiday season brighter, especially for retailers in the Seattle area.) Microsoft also doubled its regular annual dividend to $3.50 per share. Further, it announced that it would spend another $30 billion over the next four years buying treasury stock. In addition, in 2008 Microsoft offered to buy Yahoo for $44.6 billion (Yahoo declined the offer). These actions will help to deplete some of its massive cash horde, but as you will see in this chapter, for a cash-generating machine like Microsoft, the company will be anything but cash-starved.

Source: "Business: An End to Growth? Microsoft's Cash Bonanza," *The Economist* (July 23, 2005), p. 61.

On the World Wide Web
Microsoft: www.microsoft.com

The balance sheet, income statement, and retained earnings statement do not always show the whole picture of the financial condition of a company or institution. In fact, looking at the financial statements of some well-known companies, a thoughtful investor might ask questions like these: How did Eastman Kodak finance cash dividends of $649 million in a year in which it earned only $17 million? How could United Airlines purchase new planes that cost $1.9 billion in a year in which it reported a net loss of over $2 billion? How did the companies that spent a combined fantastic $3.4 trillion on mergers and acquisitions in a recent year finance those deals? Answers to these and similar questions can be found in this chapter, which presents the statement of cash flows.

The content and organization of this chapter are as follows.

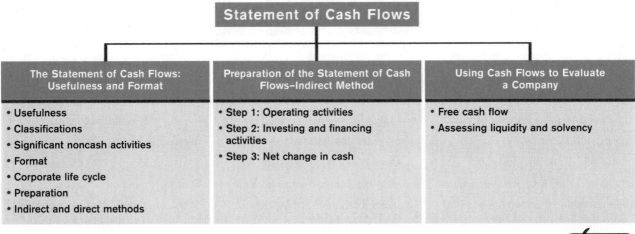

Statement of Cash Flows

The Statement of Cash Flows: Usefulness and Format	Preparation of the Statement of Cash Flows–Indirect Method	Using Cash Flows to Evaluate a Company
• Usefulness • Classifications • Significant noncash activities • Format • Corporate life cycle • Preparation • Indirect and direct methods	• Step 1: Operating activities • Step 2: Investing and financing activities • Step 3: Net change in cash	• Free cash flow • Assessing liquidity and solvency

the navigator

The Statement of Cash Flows: Usefulness and Format

The balance sheet, income statement, and retained earnings statement provide only limited information about a company's cash flows (cash receipts and cash payments). For example, comparative balance sheets show the increase in property, plant, and equipment during the year. But they do not show how the additions were financed or paid for. The income statement shows net income. But it does not indicate the amount of cash generated by operating activities. The retained earnings statement shows cash dividends declared but not the cash dividends paid during the year. None of these statements presents a detailed summary of where cash came from and how it was used.

USEFULNESS OF THE STATEMENT OF CASH FLOWS

study objective 1

Indicate the usefulness of the statement of cash flows.

The statement of cash flows reports the cash receipts and cash payments from operating, investing, and financing activities during a period, in a format that reconciles the beginning and ending cash balances. The information in a statement of cash flows helps investors, creditors, and others assess:

1. **The entity's ability to generate future cash flows.** By examining relationships between items in the statement of cash flows, investors make predictions of the amounts, timing, and uncertainty of future cash flows better than they can from accrual basis data.

2. **The entity's ability to pay dividends and meet obligations.** If a company does not have adequate cash, it cannot pay employees, settle debts, or pay dividends. Employees, creditors, and stockholders should be particularly interested in this statement, because it alone shows the flows of cash in a business.

3. **The reasons for the difference between net income and net cash provided (used) by operating activities.** Net income provides information on the success or failure of a business enterprise. However, some financial statement users are critical of accrual-basis net income because it requires many estimates. As a result, users often challenge the reliability of the number. Such is not the case with cash. Many readers of the statement of cash flows want to know the reasons for the difference between net income and net cash provided by operating activities. Then they can assess for themselves the reliability of the income number.

4. **The cash investing and financing transactions during the period.** By examining a company's investing and financing transactions, a financial statement reader can better understand why assets and liabilities changed during the period.

Ethics Note Though we would discourage reliance on cash flows to the exclusion of accrual accounting, comparing cash from operations to net income can reveal important information about the "quality" of reported net income. Such a comparison can reveal the extent to which net income provides a good measure of actual performance.

CLASSIFICATION OF CASH FLOWS

The statement of cash flows classifies cash receipts and cash payments as operating, investing, and financing activities. Transactions and other events characteristic of each kind of activity are as follows.

study objective 2
Distinguish among operating, investing, and financing activities.

1. **Operating activities** include the cash effects of transactions that create revenues and expenses. They thus enter into the determination of net income.

2. **Investing activities** include (a) acquiring and disposing of investments and property, plant, and equipment, and (b) lending money and collecting the loans.

3. **Financing activities** include (a) obtaining cash from issuing debt and repaying the amounts borrowed, and (b) obtaining cash from stockholders, repurchasing shares, and paying dividends.

The operating activities category is the most important. It shows the cash provided by company operations. This source of cash is generally considered to be the best measure of a company's ability to generate sufficient cash to continue as a going concern.

Illustration 12-1 (next page) lists typical cash receipts and cash payments within each of the three classifications. **Study the list carefully.** It will be very useful in solving homework exercises and problems.

Note the following general guidelines:

1. Operating activities involve income statement items.

2. Investing activities involve cash flows resulting from changes in investments and long-term asset items.

3. Financing activities involve cash flows resulting from changes in long-term liability and stockholders' equity items.

Companies classify as operating activities some cash flows related to investing or financing activities. For example, receipts of investment revenue (interest and dividends) are classified as operating activities. So are payments of interest to lenders. Why are these considered operating activities? **Because companies report these items in the income statement, where results of operations are shown.**

SIGNIFICANT NONCASH ACTIVITIES

Not all of a company's significant activities involve cash. Examples of significant noncash activities are:

1. Direct issuance of common stock to purchase assets.

2. Conversion of bonds into common stock.

3. Direct issuance of debt to purchase assets.

4. Exchanges of plant assets.

International Note The statement of cash flows is very similar under GAAP and IFRS. One difference is that, under IFRS, noncash investing and financing activities are not reported in the statement of cash flows but instead are reported in the notes to the financial statements.

Illustration 12-1 Typical receipt and payment classifications

Operating activities

Investing activities

Financing activities

Types of Cash Inflows and Outflows

Operating activities—Income statement items

Cash inflows:

From sale of goods or services.

From interest received and dividends received.

Cash outflows:

To suppliers for inventory.

To employees for services.

To government for taxes.

To lenders for interest.

To others for expenses.

Investing activities—Changes in investments and long-term assets

Cash inflows:

From sale of property, plant, and equipment.

From sale of investments in debt or equity securities of other entities.

From collection of principal on loans to other entities.

Cash outflows:

To purchase property, plant, and equipment.

To purchase investments in debt or equity securities of other entities.

To make loans to other entities.

Financing activities—Changes in long-term liabilities and stockholders' equity

Cash inflows:

From sale of common stock.

From issuance of debt (bonds and notes).

Cash outflows:

To stockholders as dividends.

To redeem long-term debt or reacquire capital stock (treasury stock).

Companies do not report in the body of the statement of cash flows significant financing and investing activities that do not affect cash. Instead, they report these activities in either a **separate schedule** at the bottom of the statement of cash flows or in a **separate note or supplementary schedule** to the financial statements. The reporting of these noncash activities in a separate schedule satisfies the **full disclosure principle**.

In solving homework assignments you should present significant noncash investing and financing activities in a separate schedule at the bottom of the statement of cash flows. (See the last entry in Illustration 12-2 for an example.)

Helpful Hint Do not include **noncash** investing and financing activities in the body of the statement of cash flows. Report this information in a separate schedule below the statement of cash flows.

Accounting Across the Organization

Net income is not the same as net cash provided by operations. The differences are illustrated by the following results from annual reports for 2007 ($ in millions). Note the wide disparity among these companies that all engaged in retail merchandising.

Company	Net Income	Net Cash Provided by Operations
Kohl's Corporation	$ 1,083	$ 1,234
Wal-Mart Stores, Inc.	11,284	20,169
JCPenney Company, Inc.	1,153	1,255
Costco Wholesale Corp.	1,082	2,076
Target Corporation	2,849	4,125

? In general, why do differences exist between net income and net cash provided by operating activities?

FORMAT OF THE STATEMENT OF CASH FLOWS

The general format of the statement of cash flows presents the results of the three activities discussed previously—operating, investing, and financing—plus the significant noncash investing and financing activities. Illustration 12–2 shows a widely used form of the statement of cash flows.

Illustration 12-2 Format of statement of cash flows

COMPANY NAME		
Statement of Cash Flows		
Period Covered		
Cash flows from operating activities		
(List of individual items)	XX	
Net cash provided (used) by operating activities		XXX
Cash flows from investing activities		
(List of individual inflows and outflows)	XX	
Net cash provided (used) by investing activities		XXX
Cash flows from financing activities		
(List of individual inflows and outflows)	XX	
Net cash provided (used) by financing activities		XXX
Net increase (decrease) in cash		XXX
Cash at beginning of period		XXX
Cash at end of period		XXX
Noncash investing and financing activities		
(List of individual noncash transactions)		XXX

The sum of the operating, investing, and financing sections equals the net increase or decrease in cash for the period. This amount is added to the beginning cash balance to arrive at the ending cash balance—the same amount reported on the balance sheet.

before you go on...

Do it! During its first week, Duffy & Stevenson Company had these transactions.

1. Issued 100,000 shares of $5 par value common stock for $800,000 cash.
2. Borrowed $200,000 from Castle Bank, signing a 5-year note bearing 8% interest.
3. Purchased two semi-trailer trucks for $170,000 cash.
4. Paid employees $12,000 for salaries and wages.
5. Collected $20,000 cash for services provided.

Classify each of these transactions by type of cash flow activity.

Solution

1. Financing activity
2. Financing activity
3. Investing activity
4. Operating activity
5. Operating activity

CASH FLOW ACTIVITIES

Action Plan

- Identify the three types of activities used to report all cash inflows and outflows.
- Report as operating activities the cash effects of transactions that create revenues and expenses and enter into the determination of net income.
- Report as investing activities transactions that (a) acquire and dispose of investments and productive long-lived assets and (b) lend money and collect loans.
- Report as financing activities transactions that (a) obtain cash from issuing debt and repay the amounts borrowed and (b) obtain cash from stockholders and pay them dividends.

THE CORPORATE LIFE CYCLE

study objective **3**

Explain the impact of the product life cycle on a company's cash flows.

All products go through a series of phases called the product life cycle. The phases (in order of their occurrence) are: **introductory phase**, **growth phase**, **maturity phase**, and **decline phase**. The introductory phase occurs at the beginning of a company's life, when it is purchasing fixed assets and beginning to produce and sell products. During the growth phase, the company is striving to expand its production and sales. In the maturity phase, sales and production level off. During the decline phase, sales of the product fall due to a weakening in consumer demand.

If a company had only one product and that product was nearing the end of its salable life, we could easily say that the company was in the decline phase. Companies generally have more than one product, however, and not all of a company's products are in the same phase of the product life cycle at the same time. Still, we can characterize a company as being in one of the four phases, because the majority of its products are in a particular phase.

Illustration 12-3 shows that the phase a company is in affects its cash flows. In the **introductory phase**, we expect that the company will not be generating positive cash from operations. That is, cash used in operations will exceed cash generated by operations in the introductory phase. Also, the company will be spending considerable amounts to purchase productive assets such as buildings and equipment. To support its asset purchases the company will have to issue stock or debt. Thus, during the introductory phase we expect cash from operations to be negative, cash from investing to be negative, and cash from financing to be positive.

Illustration 12-3 Impact of product life cycle on cash flows

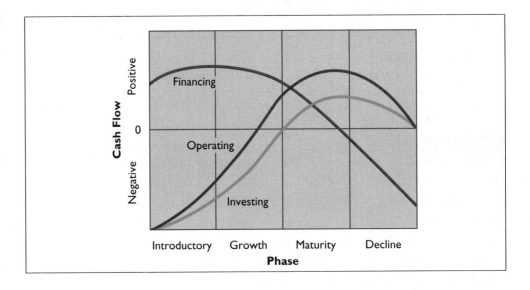

During the **growth phase**, we expect to see the company start to generate small amounts of cash from operations. During this phase, cash from operations on the statement of cash flows will be less than net income on the income statement. One reason income will exceed cash flow from operations during this period is explained by the difference between the cash paid for inventory and the amount expensed as cost of goods sold. Since the company projects increasing sales, the size of inventory purchases must increase. Thus, in the growth phase the company will expense less inventory on an accrual basis than it purchases on a cash basis. Also, collections on accounts receivable will lag behind sales, and accrual sales during a period will exceed cash collections during that period. Cash needed for asset acquisitions will continue to exceed cash provided by operations, requiring that the company make up the deficiency by issuing new stock or debt. Thus, in the growth phase, the company continues to show negative cash from investing and positive cash from financing.

During the **maturity phase**, cash from operations and net income are approximately the same. Cash generated from operations exceeds investing needs. Thus, in the maturity phase the company can actually start to pay dividends, retire debt, or buy back stock.

Finally, during the **decline phase**, cash from operations decreases. Cash from investing might actually become positive as the company sells off excess assets. Cash from financing may be negative as the company buys back stock and retires debt.

Consider Microsoft: During its early years it had significant product development costs and little revenue. Microsoft was lucky in that its agreement with IBM to provide the operating system for IBM PCs gave it an early steady source of cash to support growth. As noted in the Feature Story, one way Microsoft conserved cash was to pay employees with stock options rather than cash. Today Microsoft could best be characterized as being in the maturity phase. It continues to spend considerable amounts on research and development and investment in new assets. For the last three years, though its cash from operations has exceeded its net income. Also, cash from operations over this period exceeded cash used for investing, and common stock repurchased exceeded common stock issued. For Microsoft, as for any large company, the challenge is to maintain its growth. In the software industry, where products become obsolete very quickly, the challenge is particularly great.

 Investor Insight

Listed here are recent amounts of net income and cash provided (used) by operations, investing, and financing for a variety of companies. The final column suggests their likely phase in the life cycle based on these figures.

Company ($ in millions)	Net Income	Cash Provided (Used) by Operations	Cash Provided (Used) by Investing	Cash Provided (Used) by Financing	Likely Phase in Life Cycle
Amazon.com	$ 476	$1,405	$ (42)	$ (50)	Early maturity
LDK Solar	(144)	(81)	(329)	462	Introductory/ early growth
United States Steel	879	1,745	(4,675)	(1,891)	Maturity
Kellogg	1,103	1,503	(601)	(788)	Early decline
Southwest Airlines	645	2,845	(1,529)	493	Maturity
Starbucks	673	1,331	(1,202)	(172)	Maturity

 Why do companies have negative cash from operations during the introductory phase?

PREPARING THE STATEMENT OF CASH FLOWS

Companies prepare the statement of cash flows differently from the three other basic financial statements. First, it is not prepared from an adjusted trial balance. It requires detailed information concerning the changes in account balances that occurred between two points in time. An adjusted trial balance will not provide the necessary data. Second, the statement of cash flows deals with cash receipts and payments. As a result, the company **must adjust** the effects of the use of accrual accounting **to determine cash flows**.

The information to prepare this statement usually comes from three sources:

• **Comparative balance sheets.** Information in the comparative balance sheets indicates the amount of the changes in assets, liabilities, and stockholders' equities from the beginning to the end of the period.

- **Current income statement.** Information in this statement helps determine the amount of cash provided or used by operations during the period.
- **Additional information.** Such information includes transaction data that are needed to determine how cash was provided or used during the period.

Preparing the statement of cash flows from these data sources involves three major steps, explained in Illustration 12-4 below.

Illustration 12-4 Three major steps in preparing the statement of cash flows

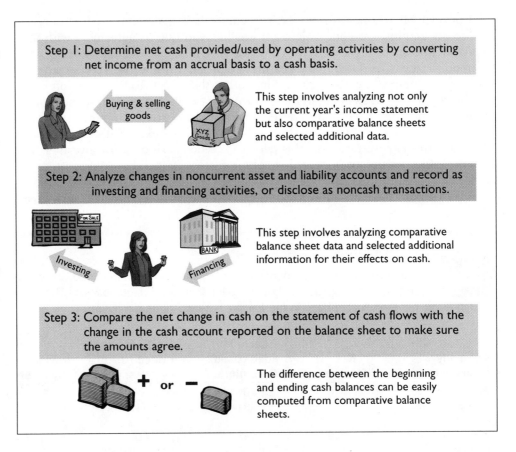

Step 1: Determine net cash provided/used by operating activities by converting net income from an accrual basis to a cash basis.

Buying & selling goods

This step involves analyzing not only the current year's income statement but also comparative balance sheets and selected additional data.

Step 2: Analyze changes in noncurrent asset and liability accounts and record as investing and financing activities, or disclose as noncash transactions.

Investing   Financing

This step involves analyzing comparative balance sheet data and selected additional information for their effects on cash.

Step 3: Compare the net change in cash on the statement of cash flows with the change in the cash account reported on the balance sheet to make sure the amounts agree.

+ or −

The difference between the beginning and ending cash balances can be easily computed from comparative balance sheets.

INDIRECT AND DIRECT METHODS

In order to perform step 1, a company **must convert net income from an accrual basis to a cash basis**. This conversion may be done by either of two methods: (1) the indirect method or (2) the direct method. **Both methods arrive at the same total amount** for "Net cash provided by operating activities." They differ in **how** they arrive at the amount.

The indirect method adjusts net income for items that do not affect cash to determine net cash provided by operating activities. A great majority of companies (99%) use this method, as shown in the nearby chart.[1] Companies favor the indirect method for two reasons: (1) It is easier and less costly to prepare, and (2) it focuses on the differences between net income and net cash flow from operating activities.

The direct method shows operating cash receipts and payments. It is prepared by adjusting each item in the income statement from the accrual basis to the cash basis. The FASB has expressed a preference for the direct method, but allows the use of either method.

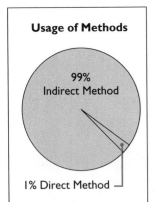

Usage of Methods

99% Indirect Method

1% Direct Method

---

[1]*Accounting Trends and Techniques—2007* (New York: American Institute of Certified Public Accountants, 2007).

The next section illustrates the more popular indirect method. The appendix to this chapter illustrates the direct method.

Preparation of the Statement of Cash Flows—Indirect Method

To explain how to prepare a statement of cash flows using the indirect method, we use financial information from Computer Services Company. Illustration 12-5 presents Computer Services' current and previous-year balance sheets, its current-year income statement, and related financial information.

study objective 4

Prepare a statement of cash flows using the indirect method.

Illustration 12-5
Comparative balance sheets, income statement, and additional information for Computer Services Company

COMPUTER SERVICES COMPANY
Comparative Balance Sheets
December 31

Assets	2010	2009	Change in Account Balance Increase/Decrease
Current assets			
Cash	$ 55,000	$ 33,000	$ 22,000 Increase
Accounts receivable	20,000	30,000	10,000 Decrease
Merchandise inventory	15,000	10,000	5,000 Increase
Prepaid expenses	5,000	1,000	4,000 Increase
Property, plant, and equipment			
Land	130,000	20,000	110,000 Increase
Building	160,000	40,000	120,000 Increase
Accumulated depreciation—building	(11,000)	(5,000)	6,000 Increase
Equipment	27,000	10,000	17,000 Increase
Accumulated depreciation—equipment	(3,000)	(1,000)	2,000 Increase
Total assets	$398,000	$138,000	
Liabilities and Stockholders' Equity			
Current liabilities			
Accounts payable	$ 28,000	$ 12,000	$ 16,000 Increase
Income tax payable	6,000	8,000	2,000 Decrease
Long-term liabilities			
Bonds payable	130,000	20,000	110,000 Increase
Stockholders' equity			
Common stock	70,000	50,000	20,000 Increase
Retained earnings	164,000	48,000	116,000 Increase
Total liabilities and stockholders' equity	$398,000	$138,000	

COMPUTER SERVICES COMPANY
Income Statement
For the Year Ended December 31, 2010

Revenues		$507,000
Cost of goods sold	$150,000	
Operating expenses (excluding depreciation)	111,000	
Depreciation expense	9,000	
Loss on sale of equipment	3,000	
Interest expense	42,000	315,000
Income before income tax		192,000
Income tax expense		47,000
Net income		$145,000

Illustration 12-5
(continued) Additional
information for Computer
Services Company

Additional information for 2010:
1. The company declared and paid a $29,000 cash dividend.
2. Issued $110,000 of long-term bonds in direct exchange for land.
3. A building costing $120,000 was purchased for cash. Equipment costing $25,000 was also purchased for cash.
4. The company sold equipment with a book value of $7,000 (cost $8,000, less accumulated depreciation $1,000) for $4,000 cash.
5. Issued common stock for $20,000 cash.
6. Depreciation expense was comprised of $6,000 for building and $3,000 for equipment.

We will now apply the three steps to the information provided for Computer Services Company.

STEP 1: OPERATING ACTIVITIES

DETERMINE NET CASH PROVIDED/USED BY OPERATING ACTIVITIES BY CONVERTING NET INCOME FROM AN ACCRUAL BASIS TO A CASH BASIS

To determine net cash provided by operating activities under the indirect method, companies **adjust net income in numerous ways**. A useful starting point is to understand **why** net income must be converted to net cash provided by operating activities.

Under generally accepted accounting principles, most companies use the accrual basis of accounting. As you have learned, this basis requires that companies record revenue when earned and record expenses when incurred. Earned revenues may include credit sales for which the company has not yet collected cash. Expenses incurred may include some items that it has not yet paid in cash. Thus, under the accrual basis of accounting, net income is not the same as net cash provided by operating activities.

Therefore, under the **indirect method**, companies must adjust net income to convert certain items to the cash basis. The indirect method (or reconciliation method) starts with net income and converts it to net cash provided by operating activities. Illustration 12-6 lists the three types of adjustments.

Illustration 12-6 Three types of adjustments to convert net income to net cash provided by operating activities

Net Income +/−	Adjustments	=	Net Cash Provided/ Used by Operating Activities
	• **Add back noncash expenses**, such as depreciation expense, amortization, or depletion.		
	• **Deduct gains and add losses** that resulted from investing and financing activities.		
	• **Analyze changes** to noncash current asset and current liability accounts.		

Helpful Hint Depreciation is similar to any other expense in that it reduces net income. It differs in that it does not involve a current cash outflow; that is why it must be *added back* to net income to arrive at cash provided by operations.

We explain the three types of adjustments in the next three sections.

Depreciation Expense

Computer Services' income statement reports depreciation expense of $9,000. Although depreciation expense reduces net income, it does not reduce cash. In other words, depreciation expense is a noncash charge. The company must add it back to net income to arrive at net cash provided by operating activities.

Computer Services reports depreciation expense as follows in the statement of cash flows.

Illustration 12-7
Adjustment for depreciation

Cash flows from operating activities	
Net income	$145,000
Adjustments to reconcile net income to net cash provided by operating activities:	
Depreciation expense	9,000
Net cash provided by operating activities	$154,000

As the first adjustment to net income in the statement of cash flows, companies frequently list depreciation and similar noncash charges such as amortization of intangible assets, depletion expense, and bad debt expense.

Loss on Sale of Equipment

Illustration 12-1 states that the investing activities section should report cash received from the sale of plant assets. Because of this, **companies must eliminate from net income all gains and losses resulting from investing activities, to arrive at cash provided by operating activities**.

In our example, Computer Services' income statement reports a $3,000 loss on the sale of equipment (book value $7,000, less cash received from sale of equipment $4,000). The company's loss of $3,000 should be eliminated in the operating activities section of the statement of cash flows. Illustration 12-8 shows that the $3,000 loss is eliminated by adding $3,000 back to net income to arrive at net cash provided by operating activities.

Illustration 12-8
Adjustment for loss on sale
of equipment

Cash flows from operating activities		
Net income		$145,000
Adjustments to reconcile net income to net cash provided by operating activities:		
Depreciation expense	$9,000	
Loss on sale of equipment	3,000	12,000
Net cash provided by operating activities		$157,000

If a gain on sale occurs, the company deducts the gain from its net income in order to determine net cash provided by operating activities. **In the case of either a gain or a loss, companies report the actual amount of cash received from the sale as a source of cash in the investing activities section of the statement of cash flows.**

Changes to Noncash Current Asset and Current Liability Accounts

A final adjustment in reconciling net income to net cash provided by operating activities involves examining all changes in current asset and current liability accounts. The accrual accounting process records revenues in the period earned and expenses in the period incurred. For example, companies use Accounts Receivable to record amounts owed to the company for sales that have been made but for which cash collections have not yet been received. They use the Prepaid Insurance account to reflect insurance that has been paid for, but which has not yet expired, and therefore has not been expensed. Similarly, the Salaries Payable account reflects salaries expense that has been incurred by the company but has not been paid.

As a result, we need to adjust net income for these accruals and prepayments to determine net cash provided by operating activities. Thus we must analyze the change in each current asset and current liability account to determine its impact on net income and cash.

CHANGES IN NONCASH CURRENT ASSETS. The adjustments required for changes in noncash current asset accounts are as follows: **Deduct from net income increases in current asset accounts, and add to net income decreases in current asset accounts, to arrive at net cash provided by operating activities.** We can observe these relationships by analyzing the accounts of Computer Services Company.

DECREASE IN ACCOUNTS RECEIVABLE. Computer Services Company's accounts receivable decreased by $10,000 (from $30,000 to $20,000) during the period. For Computer Services this means that cash receipts were $10,000 higher than revenues. The Accounts Receivable account in Illustration 12-9 shows that Computer Services Company had $507,000 in revenues (as reported on the income statement), but it collected $517,000 in cash. As shown in Illustration 12-10, to adjust net income to net cash provided by operating activities, the company adds to net income the decrease of $10,000 in accounts receivable.

Illustration 12-9 Analysis of accounts receivable

Accounts Receivable			
1/1/10	Balance	30,000	**Receipts from customers** 517,000
	Revenues	**507,000**	
12/31/10	Balance	20,000	

When the Accounts Receivable balance increases, cash receipts are lower than revenue earned under the accrual basis. Therefore, the company deducts from net income the amount of the increase in accounts receivable, to arrive at net cash provided by operating activities.

INCREASE IN MERCHANDISE INVENTORY. Computer Services Company's Merchandise Inventory balance increased $5,000 (from $10,000 to $15,000) during the period. The change in the Merchandise Inventory account reflects the difference between the amount of inventory purchased and the amount sold. For Computer Services this means that the cost of merchandise purchased exceeded the cost of goods sold by $5,000. As a result, cost of goods sold does not reflect $5,000 of cash payments made for merchandise. The company deducts from net income this inventory increase of $5,000 during the period, to arrive at net cash provided by operating activities (see Illustration 12-10). If inventory decreases, the company adds to net income the amount of the change, to arrive at net cash provided by operating activities.

INCREASE IN PREPAID EXPENSES. Computer Services' prepaid expenses increased during the period by $4,000. This means that cash paid for expenses is higher than expenses reported on an accrual basis. In other words, the company has made cash payments in the current period, but will not charge expenses to income until future periods (as charges to the income statement). To adjust net income to net cash provided by operating activities, the company deducts from net income the $4,000 increase in prepaid expenses (see Illustration 12-10).

If prepaid expenses decrease, reported expenses are higher than the expenses paid. Therefore, the company adds to net income the decrease in prepaid expense, to arrive at net cash provided by operating activities.

CHANGES IN CURRENT LIABILITIES. The adjustments required for changes in current liability accounts are as follows: **Add to net income increases in current liability accounts, and deduct from net income decreases in current liability accounts, to arrive at net cash provided by operating activities.**

Illustration 12-10
Adjustments for changes in current asset accounts

Cash flows from operating activities		
Net income		$145,000
Adjustments to reconcile net income to net cash		
provided by operating activities:		
Depreciation expense	$ 9,000	
Loss on sale of equipment	3,000	
Decrease in accounts receivable	**10,000**	
Increase in merchandise inventory	**(5,000)**	
Increase in prepaid expenses	**(4,000)**	13,000
Net cash provided by operating activities		$158,000

INCREASE IN ACCOUNTS PAYABLE. For Computer Services Company, Accounts Payable increased by $16,000 (from $12,000 to $28,000) during the period. That means the company received $16,000 more in goods than it actually paid for. As shown in Illustration 12-11 (below), to adjust net income to determine net cash provided by operating activities, the company adds to net income the $16,000 increase in Accounts Payable.

DECREASE IN INCOME TAXES PAYABLE. When a company incurs income tax expense but has not yet paid its taxes, it records income tax payable. A change in the Income Tax Payable account reflects the difference between income tax expense incurred and income tax actually paid. Computer Services' Income Tax Payable account decreased by $2,000. That means the $47,000 of income tax expense reported on the income statement was $2,000 less than the amount of taxes paid during the period of $49,000. As shown in Illustration 12-11, to adjust net income to a cash basis, the company must reduce net income by $2,000.

Illustration 12-11
Adjustments for changes in current liability accounts

Cash flows from operating activities		
Net income		$145,000
Adjustments to reconcile net income to net cash		
provided by operating activities:		
Depreciation expense	$ 9,000	
Loss on sale of equipment	3,000	
Decrease in accounts receivable	10,000	
Increase in merchandise inventory	(5,000)	
Increase in prepaid expenses	(4,000)	
Increase in accounts payable	**16,000**	
Decrease in income tax payable	**(2,000)**	27,000
Net cash provided by operating activities		$172,000

Illustration 12-11 shows that, after starting with net income of $145,000, the sum of all of the adjustments to net income was $27,000. This resulted in net cash provided by operating activities of $172,000.

SUMMARY OF CONVERSION TO NET CASH PROVIDED BY OPERATING ACTIVITIES—INDIRECT METHOD

As shown in the previous illustrations, the statement of cash flows prepared by the indirect method starts with net income. It then adds or deducts items to arrive at net cash provided by operating activities. The required adjustments are of three types:

1. Noncash charges such as depreciation, amortization, and depletion.
2. Gains and losses on the sale of plant assets.
3. Changes in noncash current asset and current liability accounts.

Illustration 12-12 provides a summary of these changes.

Illustration 12-12
Adjustments required to convert net income to net cash provided by operating activities

		Adjustment Required to Convert Net Income to Net Cash Provided by Operating Activities
Noncash charges	Depreciation expense	Add
	Patent amortization expense	Add
Gains and losses	Loss on sale of plant asset	Add
	Gain on sale of plant asset	Deduct
Changes in current assets and current liabilities	Increase in current asset account	Deduct
	Decrease in current asset account	Add
	Increase in current liability account	Add
	Decrease in current liability account	Deduct

Accounting Across the Organization

Market share matters—and it shows up in the accounting numbers. Just ask General Motors (GM). In recent years GM has seen its market share erode until, at 25.6% of the market, the company reached the point where it actually consumes more cash than it generates. It isn't time to panic yet—GM has billions in cash on hand—but it is time to come up with a plan.

To address immediate cash needs, GM management may be forced to quit paying its $1.1 billion annual dividend, and it may sell off some assets and businesses. But in the long term, GM must either increase its market share or shrink its operations to fit its sales figures. The following table shows net income and cash provided by operating activities at various market-share levels.

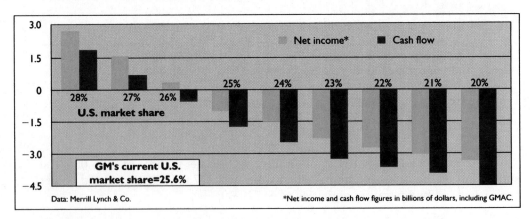

Data: Merrill Lynch & Co.   *Net income and cash flow figures in billions of dollars, including GMAC.

Assumes overall North American car sales hold steady at a 16.9 million vehicle annual rate.

Source: David Welch and Dan Beucke, "Why GM's Plan Won't Work," *Business Week* (May 9, 2005), pp. 85–93.

? Why does GM's cash provided by operating activities drop so precipitously when the company's sales figures decline?

Do it!

Josh's PhotoPlus reported net income of $73,000 for 2010. Included in the income statement were depreciation expense of $7,000 and a gain on sale of equipment of $2,500. Josh's comparative balance sheets show the following balances.

	12/31/10	12/31/09	
Accounts Receivable	$21,000	$17,000	4000
Accounts Payable	2,200	6,000	(3800)

Calculate net cash provided by operating activities for Josh's PhotoPlus.

Solution

Cash flows from operating activities		
Net income		$73,000
Adjustments to reconcile net income to net cash provided by operating activities:		
Depreciation expense	$ 7,000	
Gain on sale of equipment	(2,500)	
Increase in accounts receivable	(4,000)	
Decrease in accounts payable	(3,800)	(3,300)
Net cash provided by operating activities		$69,700

NET CASH FROM OPERATING ACTIVITIES

Action Plan

- Add noncash charges such as depreciation back to net income to compute net cash provided by operating activities.
- Deduct gains and add back losses from the sale of plant assets to compute net cash provided by operating activities.
- Use changes in noncash current asset and current liability accounts to compute net cash provided by operating activities.

STEP 2: INVESTING AND FINANCING ACTIVITIES

ANALYZE CHANGES IN NONCURRENT ASSET AND LIABILITY ACCOUNTS AND RECORD AS INVESTING AND FINANCING ACTIVITIES, OR DISCLOSE AS NONCASH TRANSACTIONS

INCREASE IN LAND. As indicated from the change in the Land account and the additional information, the company purchased land of $110,000 by directly exchanging bonds for land. The exchange of bonds payable for land has no effect on cash. But it is a significant noncash investing and financing activity that merits disclosure in a separate schedule. (See Illustration 12–14 on next page.)

INCREASE IN BUILDING. As the additional data indicate, Computer Services Company acquired an office building for $120,000 cash. This is a cash outflow reported in the investing section. (See Illustration 12–14 on next page.)

INCREASE IN EQUIPMENT. The Equipment account increased $17,000. The additional information explains that this was a net increase that resulted from two transactions: (1) a purchase of equipment of $25,000, and (2) the sale for $4,000 of equipment costing $8,000. These transactions are both investing activities. The company should report each transaction separately. Thus it reports the purchase of equipment as an outflow of cash for $25,000. It reports the sale as an inflow of cash for $4,000. The T account below shows the reasons for the change in this account during the year.

Helpful Hint The investing and financing activities are measured and reported the same under both the direct and indirect methods.

Ethics Note Because investors and management bonus contracts often focus on cash flow from operations, some managers have taken unethical actions to artificially increase cash flow from operations. For example, Dynegy restated its statement of cash flows because it had improperly included in operating activities $300 million that should have been reported as financing activities. This increased cash from operating activities by 37%.

Equipment			
1/1/10 Balance	10,000	Cost of equipment sold	8,000
Purchase of equipment	25,000		
12/31/10 Balance	27,000		

Illustration 12-13
Analysis of equipment

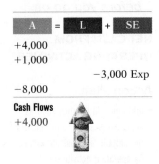

A	=	L	+	SE
+4,000				
+1,000				
				−3,000 Exp
−8,000				

Cash Flows
+4,000

Helpful Hint When companies issue stocks or bonds for cash, the actual proceeds will appear in the statement of cash flows as a financing inflow (rather than the par value of the stocks or face value of bonds).

The following entry shows the details of the equipment sale transaction.

Cash	4,000	
Accumulated Depreciation	1,000	
Loss on Sale of Equipment	3,000	
Equipment		8,000

INCREASE IN BONDS PAYABLE. The Bonds Payable account increased $110,000. As indicated in the additional information, the company acquired land by directly exchanging bonds for land. It reports this noncash transaction in a separate schedule at the bottom of the statement.

INCREASE IN COMMON STOCK. The balance sheet reports an increase in Common Stock of $20,000. The additional information section notes that this increase resulted from the issuance of new shares of stock. This is a cash inflow reported in the financing section.

INCREASE IN RETAINED EARNINGS. Retained earnings increased $116,000 during the year. This increase can be explained by two factors: (1) Net income of $145,000 increased retained earnings. (2) Dividends of $29,000 decreased retained earnings. The company adjusts net income to net cash provided by operating activities in the operating activities section. Payment of the dividends (not the declaration) is **a cash outflow that the company reports as a financing activity**.

Statement of Cash Flows–2010

Using the previous information, we can now prepare a statement of cash flows for 2010 for Computer Services Company as shown in Illustration 12-14.

Illustration 12-14
Statement of cash flows, 2010–indirect method

Helpful Hint Note that in the investing and financing activities sections, positive numbers indicate cash inflows (receipts), and negative numbers indicate cash outflows (payments).

COMPUTER SERVICES COMPANY
Statement of Cash Flows–Indirect Method
For the Year Ended December 31, 2010

Cash flows from operating activities		
Net income		$ 145,000
Adjustments to reconcile net income to net cash		
provided by operating activities:		
Depreciation expense	$ 9,000	
Loss on sale of equipment	3,000	
Increase in accounts payable	16,000	
Decrease in accounts receivable	10,000	
Increase in merchandise inventory	(5,000)	
Increase in prepaid expenses	(4,000)	
Decrease in income tax payable	(2,000)	27,000
Net cash provided by operating activities		172,000
Cash flows from investing activities		
Sale of equipment	4,000	
Purchase of building	(120,000)	
Purchase of equipment	(25,000)	
Net cash used by investing activities		(141,000)
Cash flows from financing activities		
Issuance of common stock	20,000	
Payment of cash dividends	(29,000)	
Net cash used by financing activities		(9,000)
Net increase in cash		22,000
Cash at beginning of period		33,000
Cash at end of period		$ 55,000
Noncash investing and financing activities		
Issuance of bonds payable to purchase land		$ 110,000

STEP 3: NET CHANGE IN CASH

COMPARE THE NET CHANGE IN CASH ON THE STATEMENT OF CASH FLOWS WITH THE CHANGE IN THE CASH ACCOUNT REPORTED ON THE BALANCE SHEET TO MAKE SURE THE AMOUNTS AGREE

Illustration 12-14 indicates that the net change in cash during the period was an increase of $22,000. This agrees with the change in Cash account reported on the balance sheet in Illustration 12-5 (page 609).

before you go on...

Do it! Presented below is information related to Reynolds Company. Use it to prepare a statement of cash flows using the indirect method.

INDIRECT METHOD

REYNOLDS COMPANY
Comparative Balance Sheets
December 31

Assets	2010	2009	Change Increase/Decrease
Cash	$ 54,000	$ 37,000	$ 17,000 Increase
Accounts receivable	68,000	26,000	42,000 Increase
Inventories	54,000	–0–	54,000 Increase
Prepaid expenses	4,000	6,000	2,000 Decrease
Land	45,000	70,000	25,000 Decrease
Buildings	200,000	200,000	–0–
Accumulated depreciation—buildings	(21,000)	(11,000)	10,000 Increase
Equipment	193,000	68,000	125,000 Increase
Accumulated depreciation—equipment	(28,000)	(10,000)	18,000 Increase
Totals	$569,000	$386,000	

Liabilities and Stockholders' Equity			
Accounts payable	$ 23,000	$ 40,000	$ 17,000 Decrease
Accrued expenses payable	10,000	–0–	10,000 Increase
Bonds payable	110,000	150,000	40,000 Decrease
Common stock ($1 par)	220,000	60,000	160,000 Increase
Retained earnings	206,000	136,000	70,000 Increase
Totals	$569,000	$386,000	

REYNOLDS COMPANY
Income Statement
For the Year Ended December 31, 2010

Revenues		$890,000
Cost of goods sold	$465,000	
Operating expenses	221,000	
Interest expense	12,000	
Loss on sale of equipment	2,000	700,000
Income before income taxes		190,000
Income tax expense		65,000
Net income		$125,000

Additional information:
1. Operating expenses include depreciation expense of $33,000 and charges from prepaid expenses of $2,000.
2. Land was sold at its book value for cash.
3. Cash dividends of $55,000 were declared and paid in 2010.
4. Interest expense of $12,000 was paid in cash.
5. Equipment with a cost of $166,000 was purchased for cash. Equipment with a cost of $41,000 and a book value of $36,000 was sold for $34,000 cash.
6. Bonds of $10,000 were redeemed at their book value for cash. Bonds of $30,000 were converted into common stock.
7. Common stock ($1 par) of $130,000 was issued for cash.
8. Accounts payable pertain to merchandise suppliers.

Action Plan

• Determine net cash provided/used by operating activities by adjusting net income for items that did not affect cash.

• Determine net cash provided/used by investing activities and financing activities.

• Determine the net increase/decrease in cash.

Solution

REYNOLDS COMPANY
Statement of Cash Flows–Indirect Method
For the Year Ended December 31, 2010

Cash flows from operating activities		
Net income		$ 125,000
Adjustments to reconcile net income to net cash provided by operating activities:		
Depreciation expense	$ 33,000	
Loss on sale of equipment	2,000	
Increase in accrued expenses payable	10,000	
Decrease in prepaid expenses	2,000	
Increase in inventories	(54,000)	
Increase in accounts receivable	(42,000)	
Decrease in accounts payable	(17,000)	(66,000)
Net cash provided by operating activities		59,000
Cash flows from investing activities		
Sale of equipment	34,000	
Sale of land	25,000	
Purchase of equipment	(166,000)	
Net cash used by investing activities		(107,000)
Cash flows from financing activities		
Sale of common stock	130,000	
Payment of dividends	(55,000)	
Redemption of bonds	(10,000)	
Net cash provided by financing activities		65,000
Net increase in cash		17,000
Cash at beginning of period		37,000
Cash at end of period		$ 54,000
Noncash investing and financing activities		
Conversion of bonds into common stock		$ 30,000

Using Cash Flows to Evaluate a Company

study objective 5

Use the statement of cash flows to evaluate a company.

Traditionally, investors and creditors have most commonly used ratios based on accrual accounting. These days, cash-based ratios are gaining increased acceptance among analysts. In this section we review free cash flow and introduce two new measures.

FREE CASH FLOW

In the statement of cash flows, cash provided by operating activities is intended to indicate the cash-generating capability of the company. Analysts have noted, however, that **cash provided by operating activities fails to take into account that a company must invest in new fixed assets** just to maintain its current level of operations. Companies also must at least **maintain dividends at current levels** to satisfy investors. As we discussed in Chapter 2, the measurement of free cash flow provides additional insight regarding a company's cash-generating ability. Free cash flow describes the cash remaining from operations after adjustment for capital expenditures and dividends.

Consider the following example: Suppose that MPC produced and sold 10,000 personal computers this year. It reported $100,000 cash provided by operating activities. In order to maintain production at 10,000 computers, MPC invested $15,000 in equipment. It chose to pay $5,000 in dividends. Its free cash flow was $80,000 ($100,000 − $15,000 − $5,000). The company could use this $80,000 either to purchase new assets, to pay off debt, or to pay an $80,000 dividend. In practice, free cash flow is often calculated with the formula in Illustration 12-15. Alternative definitions also exist.

Free Cash Flow	=	Cash Provided by Operations	−	Capital Expenditures	−	Cash Dividends

Illustration 12-15 Free cash flow

Illustration 12-16 provides basic information excerpted from the 2007 statement of cash flows of Microsoft Corporation.

MICROSOFT CORPORATION
Statement of Cash Flows (partial)
2007

Cash provided by operations		$17,796
Cash flows from investing activities		
Additions to property and equipment	$ (2,264)	
Purchases of investments	(36,308)	
Sales of investments	41,451	
Acquisitions of companies	(1,150)	
Maturities of investments	4,736	
Securities lending payable	(376)	
Cash provided by investing activities		6,089
Cash paid for dividends		(3,805)

Illustration 12-16
Microsoft cash flow information ($ in millions)

Microsoft's free cash flow is calculated as shown in Illustration 12-17.

Cash provided by operating activities	$17,796
Less: Expenditures on property, plant, and equipment	2,264
Dividends paid	3,805
Free cash flow	$11,727

Illustration 12-17
Calculation of Microsoft's free cash flow ($ in millions)

This is a tremendous amount of cash generated in a single year. It is available for the acquisition of new assets, the retirement of stock or debt, or the payment of dividends.

Also note that Microsoft's cash from operations exceeds its 2007 net income of $14,065 million. This lends additional credibility to Microsoft's income number as an indicator of potential future performance. If anything, Microsoft's net income might understate its actual performance.

Oracle Corporation is one of the world's largest sellers of database software and information management services. Like Microsoft, its success depends on continuing to improve its existing products while developing new products to keep pace with rapid changes in technology. Oracle's free cash flow for 2007 was $5,201 million. This is impressive, but significantly less than Microsoft's amazing ability to generate cash.

DECISION TOOLKIT

DECISION CHECKPOINTS	INFO NEEDED FOR DECISION	TOOL TO USE FOR DECISION	HOW TO EVALUATE RESULTS
How much cash did the company generate to either expand operations or pay dividends?	Cash provided by operating activities, cash spent on fixed assets, and cash dividends	$\text{Free cash flow} = \text{Cash provided by operations} - \text{Capital expenditures} - \text{Cash dividends}$	Significant free cash flow indicates greater potential to finance new investment and pay additional dividends.

KEEPING AN EYE ON CASH

Free cash flow is closely monitored by analysts and investors for many reasons and in a variety of ways. One measure that is gaining increased attention is "price to free cash flow." This is a variant of the price to earnings (P-E) ratio, which has been a staple of analysts for a long time. The difference is that rather than divide the company's stock price by its earnings per share (an accrual-accounting–based number), the price to free cash flow ratio divides the company's stock price by its free cash flow per share. A high measure suggests that the stock price is high relative to the company's ability to generate cash. A low measure indicates that the company's stock might be a bargain.

The average price to free cash flow ratio for companies in the Standard and Poor's 500-stock index was recently 22. At the same time, the following companies reported measures way below the average. While you should not use this measure as the sole factor in choosing a stock, it can serve as a useful screen by which to identify companies that merit further investigation.

Company	Price/Free Cash Flow	Price/EPS
CACI International	12	18
Getty Images	15	20
Global Industries	11	19
Heico	9	30
Humana	6	15
ManTech International	8	18
Multi-Color	12	20
Perini	12	27

Source: Jack Hough, "Smartmoney Stock Screen: Free Cash Flow," *Wall Street Journal*, July 26, 2007, p. D6.

ASSESSING LIQUIDITY AND SOLVENCY USING CASH FLOWS

Previous chapters have presented ratios used to analyze a company's liquidity and solvency. Many of those ratios used accrual-based numbers from the income statement and balance sheet. In this section we focus on ratios that are *cash-based* rather than accrual-based. That is, instead of using numbers from the income statement, these ratios use numbers from the statement of cash flows.

As discussed earlier, many analysts are critical of accrual-based numbers because they feel that the adjustment process allows too much management discretion. These analysts like to supplement accrual-based analysis with measures that use the cash flow statement. One disadvantage of these cash-based measures is that, unlike the more commonly employed accrual-based measures, there are no readily available industry averages for comparison. In the following discussion we use cash flow-based ratios to analyze Microsoft. In addition to the cash flow information provided in Illustration 12-16 (page 619), we need the following information related to Microsoft.

($ in millions)	2007	2006
Current liabilities	$23,754	$22,442
Total liabilities	32,074	29,493

Liquidity

Liquidity is the ability to pay obligations expected to become due within the next year. In Chapter 2 you learned that one measure of liquidity is the *current ratio*: current assets divided by current liabilities. A disadvantage of the current ratio is that it uses year-end balances of current asset and current liability accounts. These year-end balances may not be representative of the company's position during most of the year.

A ratio that partially corrects this problem is the current cash debt coverage ratio. It is computed as cash provided by operating activities divided by average current liabilities. Because cash provided by operating activities involves the entire year rather than a balance at one point in time, this ratio is often considered a better representation of liquidity on the average day. In general, a value below .40 times is cause for additional investigation of a company's liquidity. Illustration 12-18 shows the current cash debt coverage ratio for Microsoft, with comparative numbers for Oracle. For comparative purposes, we have also provided each company's current ratio.

Illustration 12-18
Current cash debt coverage ratio

Current Cash Debt Coverage Ratio	=	Cash Provided by Operations / Average Current Liabilities	

	Current cash debt coverage ratio	Current ratio
Microsoft ($ in millions)	$\dfrac{\$17,796}{(\$23,754 + \$22,442)/2} = .77$ times	1.69:1
Oracle	.76 times	1.81:1

Microsoft's net cash provided by operating activities is .77 times its average current liabilities. Oracle's ratio of .76 times is approximately the same as that of Microsoft. Both companies far exceed the threshold of .40 times. Keep in mind that Microsoft's cash position is extraordinary. For example, many large companies now have current ratios in the range of 1.0. By this standard, Oracle's current ratio of 1.81:1 and Microsoft's current ratio of 1.69:1 are both strong.

DECISION TOOLKIT

DECISION CHECKPOINTS	INFO NEEDED FOR DECISION	TOOL TO USE FOR DECISION	HOW TO EVALUATE RESULTS
Is the company generating sufficient cash provided by operating activities to meet its current obligations?	Cash provided by operating activities and average current liabilities	Current cash debt coverage ratio $= \dfrac{\text{Cash provided by operations}}{\text{Average current liabilities}}$	A high value suggests good liquidity. Since the numerator contains a "flow" measure, it provides a good supplement to the current ratio.

Solvency

Solvency is the ability of a company to survive over the long term. A measure of solvency that uses cash figures is the cash debt coverage ratio. It is computed as the ratio of cash provided by operating activities to total debt as represented by average total liabilities. This ratio indicates a company's ability to repay its liabilities from cash generated from operations—that is, without having to liquidate productive assets such as property, plant, and equipment. A general rule of thumb is that a cash debt coverage ratio below .20 times is cause for additional investigation.

Illustration 12-19 shows the cash debt coverage ratios for Microsoft and Oracle for 2007. For comparative purposes, we have also provided the debt to total assets ratios for each company.

Illustration 12-19 Cash debt coverage ratio

$$\text{Cash Debt Coverage Ratio} = \frac{\text{Cash Provided by Operations}}{\text{Average Total Liabilities}}$$

	Cash debt coverage ratio	Debt to total assets ratio
Microsoft ($ in millions)	$\dfrac{\$17{,}796}{(\$32{,}074 + \$29{,}493)/2} = .58$ times	51%
Oracle	.35 times	51%

Because Microsoft has long-term obligations, its cash debt coverage ratio is lower than its current cash debt coverage ratio. Obviously, Microsoft is very solvent. Oracle's cash debt coverage ratio of .35 times is not as strong as Microsoft's but still far exceeds the .20 threshold. Neither the cash nor accrual measures suggest any cause for concern regarding the solvency of either company.

DECISION TOOLKIT

DECISION CHECKPOINTS	INFO NEEDED FOR DECISION	TOOL TO USE FOR DECISION	HOW TO EVALUATE RESULTS
Is the company generating sufficient cash provided by operating activities to meet its long-term obligations?	Cash provided by operating activities and average total liabilities	Cash debt coverage ratio $= \dfrac{\text{Cash provided by operations}}{\text{Average total liabilities}}$	A high value suggests the company is solvent; that is, it will meet its obligations in the long term.

USING THE DECISION TOOLKIT

Intel Corporation is the leading producer of computer chips for personal computers. Its primary competitor is AMD. The two are vicious competitors, with frequent lawsuits filed between them. Financial statement data for Intel are provided below.

Instructions

Calculate the following cash-based measures for Intel, and compare them with the comparative data for AMD provided on page 624.

1. Free cash flow.
2. Current cash debt coverage ratio.
3. Cash debt coverage ratio.

INTEL CORPORATION
Balance Sheets
December 31, 2007 and 2006
(in millions)

Assets	2007	2006
Current assets	$23,885	$18,280
Noncurrent assets	31,766	30,088
Total assets	$55,651	$48,368
Liabilities and Stockholders' Equity		
Current liabilities	$ 8,571	$ 8,514
Long-term liabilities	4,318	3,102
Total liabilities	12,889	11,616
Stockholders' equity	42,762	36,752
Total liabilities and stockholders' equity	$55,651	$48,368

INTEL CORPORATION
Income Statements
For the Years Ended December 31, 2007 and 2006
(in millions)

	2007	2006
Net revenues	$38,334	$35,382
Expenses	31,358	30,338
Net income	$ 6,976	$ 5,044

INTEL CORPORATION
Statements of Cash Flows
For the Years Ended December 31, 2007 and 2006
(in millions)

	2007	2006
Net cash provided by operating activities	$12,625	$10,632
Net cash used for investing activities	(9,926)	(4,988)
Net cash used for financing activities	(1,990)	(6,370)
Net increase (decrease) in cash and cash equivalents	$ 709	$ (726)

Note. Cash spent on property, plant, and equipment in 2007 was $5,000. Cash paid for dividends was $2,618.

Comparative data for AMD:

1. Free cash flow   −$1,995 million
2. Current cash debt coverage ratio   −.11 times
3. Cash debt coverage ratio   −.39 times

Solution

1. Intel's free cash flow is $5,007 million ($12,625 − $5,000 − $2,618). AMD's is actually a negative $1,995 million. This gives Intel a huge advantage in the ability to move quickly to invest in new projects.

2. The current cash debt coverage ratio for Intel is calculated as follows.

$$\frac{\$12,625}{(\$8,571 + \$8,514)/2} = 1.48 \text{ times}$$

Compared to AMD's value of −.11 times, Intel is significantly more liquid.

3. The cash debt coverage ratio for Intel is calculated as follows.

$$\frac{\$12,625}{(\$12,889 + \$11,616)/2} = 1.03 \text{ times}$$

Compared to AMD's value of −.39 times, Intel appears to be significantly more solvent.

Summary of Study Objectives

1 **Indicate the usefulness of the statement of cash flows.** The statement of cash flows provides information about the cash receipts, cash payments, and net change in cash resulting from the operating, investing, and financing activities of a company during the period.

2 **Distinguish among operating, investing, and financing activities.** Operating activities include the cash effects of transactions that enter into the determination of net income. Investing activities involve cash flows resulting from changes in investments and long-term asset items. Financing activities involve cash flows resulting from changes in long-term liability and stockholders' equity items.

3 **Explain the impact of the product life cycle on a company's cash flows.** During the introductory stage, cash provided by operating activities and cash from investing are negative, and cash from financing is positive.

During the growth stage, cash provided by operating activities becomes positive but is still not sufficient to meet investing needs. During the maturity stage, cash provided by operating activities exceeds investing needs, so the company begins to retire debt. During the decline stage, cash provided by operating activities is reduced, cash from investing becomes positive (from selling off assets), and cash from financing becomes more negative.

4 **Prepare a statement of cash flows using the indirect method.** The preparation of a statement of cash flows involves three major steps: (1) Determine net cash provided/used by operating activities by converting net income from an accrual basis to a cash basis. (2) Analyze changes in noncurrent asset and liability accounts and record as investing and financing activities, or disclose as noncash transactions. (3) Compare the net change in cash on the statement of cash flows with the change in the cash account reported on the balance sheet to make sure the amounts agree.

5 **Use the statement of cash flows to evaluate a company.** A number of measures can be derived by using information from the statement of cash flows as well as the other required financial statements. Free cash flow indicates the amount of cash a company generated during the current year that is available for the payment of dividends or for expansion. Liquidity can be measured with the current cash debt coverage ratio (cash provided by operating activities divided by average current liabilities). Solvency can be measured by the cash debt coverage ratio (cash provided by operating activities divided by average total liabilities).

DECISION TOOLKIT   A SUMMARY

DECISION CHECKPOINTS	INFO NEEDED FOR DECISION	TOOL TO USE FOR DECISION	HOW TO EVALUATE RESULTS
How much cash did the company generate to either expand operations or pay dividends?	Cash provided by operating activities, cash spent on fixed assets, and cash dividends	$\text{Free cash flow} = \text{Cash provided by operations} - \text{Capital expenditures} - \text{Cash dividends}$	Significant free cash flow indicates greater potential to finance new investment and pay additional dividends.
Is the company generating sufficient cash provided by operating activities to meet its current obligations?	Cash provided by operating activities and average current liabilities	$\text{Current cash debt coverage ratio} = \dfrac{\text{Cash provided by operations}}{\text{Average current liabilities}}$	A high value suggests good liquidity. Since the numerator contains a "flow" measure, it provides a good supplement to the current ratio.
Is the company generating sufficient cash provided by operating activities to meet its long-term obligations?	Cash provided by operating activities and average total liabilities	$\text{Cash debt coverage ratio} = \dfrac{\text{Cash provided by operations}}{\text{Average total liabilities}}$	A high value suggests the company is solvent; that is, it will meet its obligations in the long term.

appendix

Statement of Cash Flows—Direct Method

To explain and illustrate the direct method, we will use the transactions of Computer Services Company for 2010, to prepare a statement of cash flows. Illustration 12A-1 (page 626) presents information related to 2010 for Computer Services Company.

study objective **6**

Prepare a statement of cash flows using the direct method.

Illustration 12A-1
Comparative balance
sheets, income statement,
and additional information
for Computer Services
Company

COMPUTER SERVICES COMPANY
Comparative Balance Sheets
December 31

Assets	2010	2009	Change in Account Balance Increase/Decrease
Current assets			
Cash	$ 55,000	$ 33,000	$ 22,000 Increase
Accounts receivable	20,000	30,000	10,000 Decrease
Merchandise inventory	15,000	10,000	5,000 Increase
Prepaid expenses	5,000	1,000	4,000 Increase
Property, plant, and equipment			
Land	130,000	20,000	110,000 Increase
Building	160,000	40,000	120,000 Increase
Accumulated depreciation—building	(11,000)	(5,000)	6,000 Increase
Equipment	27,000	10,000	17,000 Increase
Accumulated depreciation—equipment	(3,000)	(1,000)	2,000 Increase
Total assets	$398,000	$138,000	

Liabilities and Stockholders' Equity	2010	2009	
Current liabilities			
Accounts payable	$ 28,000	$ 12,000	$ 16,000 Increase
Income tax payable	6,000	8,000	2,000 Decrease
Long-term liabilities			
Bonds payable	130,000	20,000	110,000 Increase
Stockholders' equity			
Common stock	70,000	50,000	20,000 Increase
Retained earnings	164,000	48,000	116,000 Increase
Total liabilities and stockholders' equity	$398,000	$138,000	

COMPUTER SERVICES COMPANY
Income Statement
For the Year Ended December 31, 2010

Revenues		$507,000
Cost of goods sold	$150,000	
Operating expenses (excluding depreciation)	111,000	
Depreciation expense	9,000	
Loss on sale of equipment	3,000	
Interest expense	42,000	315,000
Income before income tax		192,000
Income tax expense		47,000
Net income		$145,000

Additional information for 2010:
1. The company declared and paid a $29,000 cash dividend.
2. Issued $110,000 of long-term bonds in direct exchange for land.
3. A building costing $120,000 was purchased for cash. Equipment costing $25,000 was also purchased for cash.
4. The company sold equipment with a book value of $7,000 (cost $8,000, less accumulated depreciation $1,000) for $4,000 cash.
5. Issued common stock for $20,000 cash.
6. Depreciation expense was comprised of $6,000 for building and $3,000 for equipment.

To prepare a statement of cash flows under the direct approach, we will apply the three steps outlined in Illustration 12-4 (page 608).

STEP 1: OPERATING ACTIVITIES

DETERMINE NET CASH PROVIDED/USED BY OPERATING ACTIVITIES BY CONVERTING NET INCOME FROM AN ACCRUAL BASIS TO A CASH BASIS

Under the **direct method**, companies compute net cash provided by operating activities by **adjusting each item in the income statement** from the accrual basis to the cash basis. To simplify and condense the operating activities section, companies **report only major classes of operating cash receipts and cash payments**. For these major classes, the difference between cash receipts and cash payments is the net cash provided by operating activities. These relationships are as shown in Illustration 12A-2.

Illustration 12A-2 Major classes of cash receipts and payments

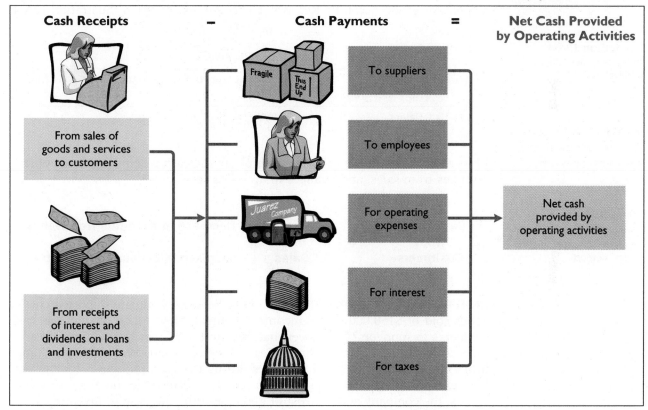

An efficient way to apply the direct method is to analyze the items reported in the income statement in the order in which they are listed. We then determine cash receipts and cash payments related to these revenues and expenses. The following pages present the adjustments required to prepare a statement of cash flows for Computer Services Company using the direct approach.

CASH RECEIPTS FROM CUSTOMERS. The income statement for Computer Services Company reported revenues from customers of $507,000. How much of that was cash receipts? To answer that, companies need to consider the change in accounts receivable during the year. When accounts receivable increase during the year, revenues on an accrual basis are higher than cash receipts from customers. Operations led to revenues, but not all of these revenues resulted in cash receipts.

To determine the amount of cash receipts, the company deducts from sales revenues the increase in accounts receivable. On the other hand, there may be a decrease in accounts receivable. That would occur if cash receipts from customers exceeded sales revenues. In that case, the company adds to sales revenues the decrease in accounts receivable. For Computer Services Company, accounts receivable decreased $10,000. Thus, cash receipts from customers were $517,000, computed as shown in Illustration 12A-3.

Illustration 12A-3
Computation of cash receipts from customers

Revenues from sales	$ 507,000
Add: Decrease in accounts receivable	10,000
Cash receipts from customers	**$517,000**

Computer Services can also determine cash receipts from customers from an analysis of the Accounts Receivable account, as shown in Illustration 12A-4.

Illustration 12A-4
Analysis of accounts receivable

Accounts Receivable			
1/1/10 Balance	30,000	**Receipts from customers**	**517,000**
Revenues from sales	507,000		
12/31/10 Balance	20,000		

Helpful Hint The T account shows that revenue plus decrease in receivables equals cash receipts.

Illustration 12A-5 shows the relationships among cash receipts from customers, revenues from sales, and changes in accounts receivable.

Illustration 12A-5
Formula to compute cash receipts from customers–direct method

Cash Receipts from Customers	=	Revenues from Sales	{ + Decrease in Accounts Receivable
			or
			− Increase in Accounts Receivable

CASH PAYMENTS TO SUPPLIERS. Computer Services Company reported cost of goods sold of $150,000 on its income statement. How much of that was cash payments to suppliers? To answer that, it is first necessary to find purchases for the year. To find purchases, companies adjust cost of goods sold for the change in inventory. When inventory increases during the year, purchases for the year have exceeded cost of goods sold. As a result, to determine the amount of purchases, the company adds to cost of goods sold the increase in inventory.

In 2010, Computer Services Company's inventory increased $5,000. It computes purchases as follows.

Illustration 12A-6
Computation of purchases

Cost of goods sold	$ 150,000
Add: Increase in inventory	5,000
Purchases	**$155,000**

After computing purchases, a company can determine cash payments to suppliers. This is done by adjusting purchases for the change in accounts payable. When accounts payable increase during the year, purchases on an accrual basis are higher than they are on a cash basis. As a result, to determine cash payments to suppliers, a company deducts from purchases the increase in accounts payable. On the other hand, if cash payments to suppliers exceed purchases, there may be a decrease in accounts payable. In that case, a company adds to purchases the decrease in accounts payable. For Computer Services Company, cash payments to suppliers were $139,000, computed as follows.

Purchases	$ 155,000
Deduct: Increase in accounts payable	16,000
Cash payments to suppliers	**$139,000**

Illustration 12A-7
Computation of cash payments to suppliers

Computer Services also can determine cash payments to suppliers from an analysis of the Accounts Payable account, as shown in Illustration 12A-8.

Accounts Payable				
Payments to suppliers	139,000	1/1/10 Balance		12,000
		Purchases		155,000
		12/31/10 Balance		28,000

Illustration 12A-8
Analysis of accounts payable

Helpful Hint The T account shows that purchases less increase in accounts payable equals payments to suppliers.

Illustration 12A-9 shows the relationships among cash payments to suppliers, cost of goods sold, changes in inventory, and changes in accounts payable.

Illustration 12A-9
Formula to compute cash payments to suppliers—direct method

$$\begin{matrix} \text{Cash} \\ \text{Payments} \\ \text{to} \\ \text{Suppliers} \end{matrix} = \begin{matrix} \text{Cost} \\ \text{of} \\ \text{Goods} \\ \text{Sold} \end{matrix} \left\{ \begin{matrix} \text{+ Increase in Inventory} \\ \text{or} \\ \text{− Decrease in Inventory} \end{matrix} \right. \left\{ \begin{matrix} \text{+ Decrease in} \\ \text{Accounts Payable} \\ \text{or} \\ \text{− Increase in} \\ \text{Accounts Payable} \end{matrix} \right.$$

CASH PAYMENTS FOR OPERATING EXPENSES. Computer Services reported on its income statement operating expenses of $111,000. How much of that amount was cash paid for operating expenses? To answer that, we need to adjust this amount for any changes in prepaid expenses and accrued expenses payable. For example, if prepaid expenses increased during the year, cash paid for operating expenses is higher than operating expenses reported on the income statement. To convert operating expenses to cash payments for operating expenses, a company adds the increase in prepaid expenses to operating expenses. On the other hand, if prepaid expenses decrease during the year, it deducts the decrease from operating expenses.

Companies must also adjust operating expenses for changes in accrued expenses payable. When accrued expenses payable increase during the year, operating expenses on an accrual basis are higher than they are in a cash basis. As a result, to determine cash payments for operating expenses, a company deducts from operating expenses an increase in accrued expenses payable. On the other hand, a company adds to operating expenses a decrease in accrued expenses payable because cash payments exceed operating expenses.

Computer Services Company's cash payments for operating expenses were $115,000, computed as follows.

Operating expenses	$ 111,000
Add: Increase in prepaid expenses	4,000
Cash payments for operating expenses	**$115,000**

Illustration 12A-10
Computation of cash payments for operating expenses

Illustration 12A-11 (page 630) shows the relationships among cash payments for operating expenses, changes in prepaid expenses, and changes in accrued expenses payable.

Illustration 12A-11
Formula to compute cash payments for operating expenses–direct method

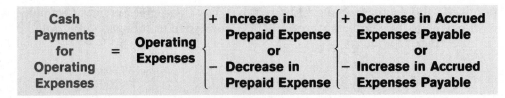

DEPRECIATION EXPENSE AND LOSS ON SALE OF EQUIPMENT. Computer Services' depreciation expense in 2010 was $9,000. Depreciation expense is not shown on a statement of cash flows under the direct method because it is a noncash charge. If the amount for operating expenses includes depreciation expense, operating expenses must be reduced by the amount of depreciation to determine cash payments for operating expenses.

The loss on sale of equipment of $3,000 is also a noncash charge. The loss on sale of equipment reduces net income, but it does not reduce cash. Thus, the loss on sale of equipment is not shown on the statement of cash flows under the direct method.

Other charges to expense that do not require the use of cash, such as the amortization of intangible assets, depletion expense, and bad debt expense, are treated in the same manner as depreciation.

CASH PAYMENTS FOR INTEREST. Computer Services reported on the income statement interest expense of $42,000. Since the balance sheet did not include an accrual for interest payable for 2009 or 2010, the amount reported as expense is the same as the amount of interest paid.

CASH PAYMENTS FOR INCOME TAXES. Computer Services reported income tax expense of $47,000 on the income statement. Income taxes payable, however, decreased $2,000. This decrease means that income taxes paid were more than income taxes reported in the income statement. Cash payments for income taxes were, therefore, $49,000 as shown below.

Illustration 12A-12
Computation of cash payments for income taxes

Income tax expense	$ 47,000
Add: Decrease in income taxes payable	2,000
Cash payments for income taxes	**$ 49,000**

Illustration 12A-13 shows the relationships among cash payments for income taxes, income tax expense, and changes in income taxes payable.

Illustration 12A-13
Formula to compute cash payments for income taxes–direct method

Cash Payments for Income Taxes	=	Income Tax Expense	+ Decrease in Income Taxes Payable or − Increase in Income Taxes Payable

The operating activities section of the statement of cash flows of Computer Services Company is shown in Illustration 12A-14.

Illustration 12A-14
Operating activities section of the statement of cash flows

Cash flows from operating activities		
Cash receipts from customers		$517,000
Less: Cash payments:		
To suppliers	$139,000	
For operating expenses	115,000	
For interest expense	42,000	
For income taxes	49,000	345,000
Net cash provided by operating activities		$172,000

When a company uses the direct method, it must also provide in a **separate schedule** (not shown here) the net cash flows from operating activities as computed under the indirect method.

STEP 2: INVESTING AND FINANCING ACTIVITIES

ANALYZE CHANGES IN NONCURRENT ASSET AND LIABILITY ACCOUNTS AND RECORD AS INVESTING AND FINANCING ACTIVITIES, OR DISCLOSE AS NONCASH TRANSACTIONS

INCREASE IN LAND. As indicated from the change in the Land account and the additional information, the company purchased land of $110,000 by directly exchanging bonds for land. The exchange of bonds payable for land has no effect on cash. But it is a significant noncash investing and financing activity that merits disclosure in a separate schedule. (See Illustration 12A-16 on page 632.)

> **Helpful Hint** The investing and financing activities are measured and reported the same under both the direct and indirect methods.

INCREASE IN BUILDING. As the additional data indicate, Computer Services Company acquired an office building for $120,000 cash. This is a cash outflow reported in the investing section. (See Illustration 12A-16 on page 632.)

INCREASE IN EQUIPMENT. The Equipment account increased $17,000. The additional information explains that this was a net increase that resulted from two transactions: (1) a purchase of equipment of $25,000, and (2) the sale for $4,000 of equipment costing $8,000. These transactions are investing activities. The company should report each transaction separately. The statement in Illustration 12A-16 (page 632) reports the purchase of equipment as an outflow of cash for $25,000. It reports the sale as an inflow of cash for $4,000. The T account below shows the reasons for the change in this account during the year.

Equipment			
1/1/10 Balance	10,000	Cost of equipment sold	8,000
Purchase of equipment	**25,000**		
12/31/10 Balance	27,000		

> **Illustration 12A-15**
> Analysis of equipment

The following entry shows the details of the equipment sale transaction.

Cash	4,000	
Accumulated Depreciation	1,000	
Loss on Sale of Equipment	3,000	
Equipment		8,000

A	=	L	+	SE
+4,000				
+1,000				
				−3,000 Exp
−8,000				

Cash Flows
+4,000

INCREASE IN BONDS PAYABLE. The Bonds Payable account increased $110,000. As indicated in the additional information, the company acquired land by directly exchanging bonds for land. Illustration 12A-16 (page 632) reports this noncash transaction in a separate schedule at the bottom of the statement.

INCREASE IN COMMON STOCK. The balance sheet reports an increase in Common Stock of $20,000. The additional information section notes that this increase resulted from the issuance of new shares of stock. This is a cash inflow reported in the financing section in Illustration 12A-16 (page 632).

> **Helpful Hint** When companies issue stocks or bonds for cash, the actual proceeds will appear in the statement of cash flows as a financing inflow (rather than the par value of the stocks or face value of bonds).

INCREASE IN RETAINED EARNINGS. Retained earnings increased $116,000 during the year. This increase can be explained by two factors: (1) Net income of

$145,000 increased retained earnings. (2) Dividends of $29,000 decreased retained earnings. The company adjusts net income to net cash provided by operating activities in the operating activities section. **Payment** of the dividends (not the declaration) is a **cash outflow that the company reports as a financing activity in Illustration 12A-16.**

Statement of Cash Flows–2007

Illustration 12A-16 shows the statement of cash flows for Computer Services Company.

Illustration 12A-16
Statement of cash flows, 2010–direct method

COMPUTER SERVICES COMPANY
Statement of Cash Flows–Direct Method
For the Year Ended December 31, 2010

Cash flows from operating activities		
Cash receipts from customers		$ 517,000
Less: Cash payments:		
To suppliers	$ 139,000	
For operating expenses	115,000	
For income taxes	49,000	
For interest expense	42,000	345,000
Net cash provided by operating activities		172,000
Cash flows from investing activities		
Sale of equipment	4,000	
Purchase of building	(120,000)	
Purchase of equipment	(25,000)	
Net cash used by investing activities		(141,000)
Cash flows from financing activities		
Issuance of common stock	20,000	
Payment of cash dividends	(29,000)	
Net cash used by financing activities		(9,000)
Net increase in cash		22,000
Cash at beginning of period		33,000
Cash at end of period		$ 55,000
Noncash investing and financing activities		
Issuance of bonds payable to purchase land		$ 110,000

STEP 3: NET CHANGE IN CASH

COMPARE THE NET CHANGE IN CASH ON THE STATEMENT OF CASH FLOWS WITH THE CHANGE IN THE CASH ACCOUNT REPORTED ON THE BALANCE SHEET TO MAKE SURE THE AMOUNTS AGREE

Illustration 12A-16 indicates that the net change in cash during the period was an increase of $22,000. This agrees with the change in balances in the cash account reported on the balance sheets in Illustration 12A-1 (page 626).

Summary of Study Objective for Appendix

6 Prepare a statement of cash flows using the direct method. The preparation of the statement of cash flows involves three major steps: (1) Determine net cash provided/used by operating activities by converting net income from an accrual basis to a cash basis. (2) Analyze changes in noncurrent asset and liability accounts and record as investing and financing activities, or disclose as noncash transactions. (3) Compare the net change in cash on the statement of cash flows with the change in the cash account reported on the balance sheet to make sure the amounts agree. The direct method reports cash receipts less cash payments to arrive at net cash provided by operating activities.

Glossary

Cash debt coverage ratio *(p. 622)*   A cash-basis ratio used to evaluate solvency, calculated as cash provided by operating activities divided by average total liabilities.

Current cash debt coverage ratio *(p. 621)*   A cash-basis ratio used to evaluate liquidity, calculated as cash provided by operating activities divided by average current liabilities.

Direct method *(p. 608)*   A method of determining net cash provided by operating activities by adjusting each item in the income statement from the accrual basis to the cash basis. The direct method shows operating cash receipts and payments.

Financing activities *(p. 603)*   Cash flow activities that include (a) obtaining cash from issuing debt and repaying the amounts borrowed and (b) obtaining cash from stockholders, repurchasing shares, and paying dividends.

Free cash flow *(p. 619)*   Cash remaining from operating activities after adjusting for capital expenditures and dividends paid.

Indirect method *(p. 608)*   A method of preparing a statement of cash flows in which net income is adjusted for items that do not affect cash, to determine net cash provided by operating activities.

Investing activities *(p. 603)*   Cash flow activities that include (a) purchasing and disposing of investments and property, plant, and equipment using cash and (b) lending money and collecting the loans.

Operating activities *(p. 603)*   Cash flow activities that include the cash effects of transactions that create revenues and expenses and thus enter into the determination of net income.

Product life cycle *(p. 606)*   A series of phases in a product's sales and cash flows over time; these phases, in order of occurrence, are introductory, growth, maturity, and decline.

Statement of cash flow *(p. 602)*   A basic financial statement that provides information about the cash receipts and cash payments of an entity during a period, classified as operating, investing, and financing activities, in a format that reconciles the beginning and ending cash balances.

Comprehensive

The income statement for Kosinski Manufacturing Company contains the following condensed information.

KOSINSKI MANUFACTURING COMPANY
Income Statement
For the Year Ended December 31, 2010

Revenues		$6,583,000
Operating expenses, excluding depreciation	$4,920,000	
Depreciation expense	880,000	5,800,000
Income before income taxes		783,000
Income tax expense		353,000
Net income		$ 430,000

Included in operating expenses is a $24,000 loss resulting from the sale of machinery for $270,000 cash. Machinery was purchased at a cost of $750,000. The following balances are reported on Kosinski's comparative balance sheet at December 31.

	2010	2009
Cash	$672,000	$130,000
Accounts receivable	775,000	610,000
Inventories	834,000	867,000
Accounts payable	521,000	501,000

Income tax expense of $353,000 represents the amount paid in 2010. Dividends declared and paid in 2010 totaled $200,000.

Instructions

(a) Prepare the statement of cash flows using the indirect method.
*(b) Prepare the statement of cash flows using the direct method.

Action Plan

- Apply the same data to the preparation of a statement of cash flows under both the indirect and direct methods.

- Note the similarities of the two methods: Both methods report the same information in the investing and financing sections.

- Note the differences between the two methods: The cash flows from operating activities sections report different information, but the amount of net cash provided by operating activities is the same for both methods.

Solution to Comprehensive Do it!

(a)

KOSINSKI MANUFACTURING COMPANY
Statement of Cash Flows—Indirect Method
For the Year Ended December 31, 2010

Cash flows from operating activities		
Net income		$ 430,000
Adjustments to reconcile net income to net cash provided by operating activities:		
Depreciation expense	$ 880,000	
Loss on sale of machinery	24,000	
Increase in accounts receivable	(165,000)	
Decrease in inventories	33,000	
Increase in accounts payable	20,000	792,000
Net cash provided by operating activities		1,222,000
Cash flows from investing activities		
Sale of machinery	270,000	
Purchase of machinery	(750,000)	
Net cash used by investing activities		(480,000)
Cash flows from financing activities		
Payment of cash dividends	(200,000)	
Net cash used by financing activities		(200,000)
Net increase in cash		542,000
Cash at beginning of period		130,000
Cash at end of period		$ 672,000

*(b)

KOSINSKI MANUFACTURING COMPANY
Statement of Cash Flows—Direct Method
For the Year Ended December 31, 2010

Cash flows from operating activities		
Cash collections from customers		$6,418,000*
Cash payments:		
For operating expenses	$4,843,000**	
For income taxes	353,000	5,196,000
Net cash provided by operating activities		1,222,000
Cash flows from investing activities		
Sale of machinery	270,000	
Purchase of machinery	(750,000)	
Net cash used by investing activities		(480,000)
Cash flows from financing activities		
Payment of cash dividends	(200,000)	
Net cash used by financing activities		(200,000)
Net increase in cash		542,000
Cash at beginning of period		130,000
Cash at end of period		$ 672,000

Direct-Method Computations:

*Computation of cash collections from customers:	
Revenues per the income statement	$6,583,000
Deduct: Increase in accounts receivable	(165,000)
Cash collections from customers	$6,418,000
**Computation of cash payments for operating expenses:	
Operating expenses per the income statement	$4,920,000
Deduct: Loss from sale of machinery	(24,000)
Deduct: Decrease in inventories	(33,000)
Deduct: Increase in accounts payable	(20,000)
Cash payments for operating expenses	$4,843,000

the navigator

Note: All Questions, Exercises, and Problems marked with an asterisk relate to material in the appendix to the chapter.

Self-Study Questions

Answers are at the end of the chapter.

(SO 1) **1.** Which of the following is *incorrect* about the statement of cash flows?
   (a) It is a fourth basic financial statement.
   (b) It provides information about cash receipts and cash payments of an entity during a period.
   (c) It reconciles the ending cash account balance to the balance per the bank statement.
   (d) It provides information about the operating, investing, and financing activities of the business.

(SO 1, 2) **2.** Which of the following will *not* be reported in the statement of cash flows?
   (a) The net change in plant assets during the year.
   (b) Cash payments for plant assets during the year.
   (c) Cash receipts from sales of plant assets during the year.
   (d) Sources of financing during the period.

(SO 2) **3.** The statement of cash flows classifies cash receipts and cash payments by these activities:
   (a) operating and nonoperating.
   (b) operating, investing, and financing.
   (c) financing, operating, and nonoperating.
   (d) investing, financing, and nonoperating.

(SO 2) **4.** Which is an example of a cash flow from an operating activity?
   (a) Payment of cash to lenders for interest.
   (b) Receipt of cash from the sale of capital stock.
   (c) Payment of cash dividends to the company's stockholders.
   (d) None of the above.

(SO 2) **5.** Which is an example of a cash flow from an investing activity?
   (a) Receipt of cash from the issuance of bonds payable.
   (b) Payment of cash to repurchase outstanding capital stock.
   (c) Receipt of cash from the sale of equipment.
   (d) Payment of cash to suppliers for inventory.

(SO 2) **6.** Cash dividends paid to stockholders are classified on the statement of cash flows as:
   (a) operating activities.
   (b) investing activities.
   (c) a combination of (a) and (b).
   (d) financing activities.

(SO 2) **7.** Which is an example of a cash flow from a financing activity?
   (a) Receipt of cash from sale of land.
   (b) Issuance of debt for cash.
   (c) Purchase of equipment for cash.
   (d) None of the above

(SO 2) **8.** Which of the following is *incorrect* about the statement of cash flows?
   (a) The direct method may be used to report cash provided by operating activities.

   (b) The statement shows the cash provided (used) for three categories of activity.
   (c) The operating section is the last section of the statement.
   (d) The indirect method may be used to report cash provided by operations.

(SO 3) **9.** During the introductory phase of a company's life cycle, one would normally expect to see:
   (a) negative cash from operations, negative cash from investing, and positive cash from financing.
   (b) negative cash from operations, positive cash from investing, and positive cash from financing.
   (c) positive cash from operations, negative cash from investing, and negative cash from financing.
   (d) positive cash from operations, negative cash from investing, and positive cash from financing.

Questions 10 through 12 apply only to the indirect method.

(SO 4) **10.** Net income is $132,000, accounts payable increased $10,000 during the year, inventory decreased $6,000 during the year, and accounts receivable increased $12,000 during the year. Under the indirect method, what is net cash provided by operations?
   (a) $102,000.   (c) $124,000.
   (b) $112,000.   (d) $136,000.

(SO 4) **11.** Items that are added back to net income in determining cash provided by operations under the indirect method do *not* include:
   (a) depreciation expense.
   (b) an increase in inventory.
   (c) amortization expense.
   (d) loss on sale of equipment.

(SO 4) **12.** The following data are available for Allen Clapp Corporation.

Net income	$200,000
Depreciation expense	40,000
Dividends paid	60,000
Gain on sale of land	10,000
Decrease in accounts receivable	20,000
Decrease in accounts payable	30,000

Net cash provided by operating activities is:
   (a) $160,000.   (c) $240,000.
   (b) $220,000.   (d) $280,000.

(SO 4, 6) **13.** The following are data concerning cash received or paid from various transactions for Orange Peels Corporation.

Sale of land	$100,000
Sale of equipment	50,000
Issuance of common stock	70,000
Purchase of equipment	30,000
Payment of cash dividends	60,000

Net cash provided by investing activities is:
(a) $120,000.   (c) $150,000.
(b) $130,000.   (d) $190,000.

(SO 4, 6) **14.** The following data are available for Something Strange!

Increase in bonds payable	$100,000
Sale of investment	50,000
Issuance of common stock	60,000
Payment of cash dividends	30,000

Net cash provided by financing activities is:
(a) $90,000.   (c) $160,000.
(b) $130,000.   (d) $170,000.

(SO 5) **15.** The cash debt coverage ratio is:
(a) a measure of liquidity.
(b) a measure of profitability.
(c) net income divided by average total liabilities.
(d) a measure of solvency.

(SO 5) **16.** Free cash flow provides an indication of a company's ability to:
(a) generate net income.
(b) generate cash to pay dividends.
(c) generate cash to invest in new capital expenditures.
(d) both (b) and (c).

Questions 17 and 18 apply only to the direct method.

(SO 6) ***17.** The beginning balance in accounts receivable is $44,000, the ending balance is $42,000, and sales during the period are $129,000. What are cash receipts from customers?
(a) $127,000.   (c) $131,000.
(b) $129,000.   (d) $141,000.

(SO 6) ***18.** Which of the following items is reported on a cash flow statement prepared by the direct method?
(a) Loss on sale of building.
(b) Increase in accounts receivable.
(c) Depreciation expense.
(d) Cash payments to suppliers.

Go to the book's companion website, **www.wiley.com/college/kimmel**, to access additional Self-Study Questions.

Questions

1. (a) What is a statement of cash flows?
(b) Kyle Towers maintains that the statement of cash flows is an optional financial statement. Do you agree? Explain.

2. What questions about cash are answered by the statement of cash flows?

3. Distinguish among the three activities reported in the statement of cash flows.

4. (a) What are the major sources (inflows) of cash in a statement of cash flows?
(b) What are the major uses (outflows) of cash?

5. Why is it important to disclose certain noncash transactions? How should they be disclosed?

6. Wilma Flintstone and Barny Rublestone were discussing the format of the statement of cash flows of Fine Candy Co. At the bottom of Fine Candy's statement of cash flows was a separate section entitled "Noncash investing and financing activities." Give three examples of significant noncash transactions that would be reported in this section.

7. Why is it necessary to use comparative balance sheets, a current income statement, and certain transaction data in preparing a statement of cash flows?

8. (a) What are the phases of the corporate life cycle?
(b) What effect does each phase have on the numbers reported in a statement of cash flows?

9. Based on its statement of cash flows, in what stage of the product life cycle is Tootsie Roll Industries?

10. Contrast the advantages and disadvantages of the direct and indirect methods of preparing the statement of cash flows. Are both methods acceptable? Which method is preferred by the FASB? Which method is more popular?

11. When the total cash inflows exceed the total cash outflows in the statement of cash flows, how and where is this excess identified?

12. Describe the indirect method for determining net cash provided (used) by operating activities.

13. Why is it necessary to convert accrual-based net income to cash-basis income when preparing a statement of cash flows?

14. The president of Sherwin Company is puzzled. During the last year, the company experienced a net loss of $800,000, yet its cash increased $300,000 during the same period of time. Explain to the president how this could occur.

15. Identify five items that are adjustments to convert net income to net cash provided by operating activities under the indirect method.

16. Why and how is depreciation expense reported in a statement prepared using the indirect method?

17. Why is the statement of cash flows useful?

18. During 2010 Rusmussen Company converted $1,700,000 of its total $2,000,000 of bonds payable into common stock. Indicate how the transaction would be reported on a statement of cash flows, if at all.

19. Give examples of accrual-based and cash-based ratios to measure each of these characteristics of a company:
(a) Liquidity.
(b) Solvency.

***20.** Describe the direct method for determining net cash provided by operating activities.

***21.** Give the formulas under the direct method for computing (a) cash receipts from customers and (b) cash payments to suppliers.

***22.** Molina Inc. reported sales of $2 million for 2010. Accounts receivable decreased $100,000 and accounts payable increased $300,000. Compute cash receipts from customers, assuming that the receivable and payable transactions related to operations.

***23.** In the direct method, why is depreciation expense not reported in the cash flows from operating activities section?

Brief Exercises

BE12-1 Each of these items must be considered in preparing a statement of cash flows for Mauer Co. for the year ended December 31, 2010. For each item, state how it should be shown in the statement of cash flows for 2010.
(a) Issued bonds for $200,000 cash.
(b) Purchased equipment for $150,000 cash.
(c) Sold land costing $20,000 for $20,000 cash.
(d) Declared and paid a $50,000 cash dividend.

Indicate statement presentation of selected transactions.
(SO 2)

BE12-2 Classify each item as an operating, investing, or financing activity. Assume all items involve cash unless there is information to the contrary.
(a) Purchase of equipment.
(b) Sale of building.
(c) Redemption of bonds.
(d) Depreciation.
(e) Payment of dividends.
(f) Issuance of capital stock.

Classify items by activities.
(SO 2)

BE12-3 The following T account is a summary of the cash account of Crowley Company.

Identify financing activity transactions.
(SO 2)

Cash (Summary Form)

Balance, Jan. 1	8,000		
Receipts from customers	364,000	Payments for goods	200,000
Dividends on stock investments	6,000	Payments for operating expenses	140,000
Proceeds from sale of equipment	36,000	Interest paid	10,000
Proceeds from issuance of		Taxes paid	8,000
bonds payable	300,000	Dividends paid	70,000
Balance, Dec. 31	286,000		

What amount of net cash provided (used) by financing activities should be reported in the statement of cash flows?

BE12-4
(a) Why is cash from operations likely to be lower than reported net income during the growth phase?
(b) Why is cash from investing often positive during the late maturity phase and during the decline phase?

Answer questions related to the phases of product life cycle.
(SO 3)

BE12-5 Gonzalez, Inc. reported net income of $2.5 million in 2010. Depreciation for the year was $110,000, accounts receivable decreased $350,000, and accounts payable decreased $280,000. Compute net cash provided by operating activities using the indirect approach.

Compute cash provided by operating activities—indirect method.
(SO 4)

BE12-6 The net income for Dodson Co. for 2010 was $280,000. For 2010 depreciation on plant assets was $70,000, and the company incurred a loss on sale of plant assets of $22,000. Compute net cash provided by operating activities under the indirect method.

Compute cash provided by operating activities—indirect method.
(SO 4)

BE12-7 The comparative balance sheets for Layton Company show these changes in noncash current asset accounts: accounts receivable decrease $80,000, prepaid expenses increase $28,000, and inventories increase $40,000. Compute net cash provided by operating activities using the indirect method assuming that net income is $200,000.

Compute net cash provided by operating activities—indirect method.
(SO 4)

Determine cash received from sale of equipment.
(SO 4)

BE12-8 The T accounts for Equipment and the related Accumulated Depreciation for Kimberlain Company at the end of 2010 are shown here.

Equipment				Accumulated Depreciation			
Beg. bal.	80,000	Disposals	22,000	Disposals	5,500	Beg. bal.	44,500
Acquisitions	41,600					Depr. exp.	12,000
End. bal.	99,600					End. bal.	51,000

In addition, Kimberlain Company's income statement reported a loss on the sale of equipment of $3,500. What amount was reported on the statement of cash flows as "cash flow from sale of equipment"?

Calculate cash-based ratios.
(SO 5)

BE12-9 During 2006 Cypress Semiconductor Corporation reported cash provided by operations of $127,260,000 cash used in investing of $207,175,000, and cash from financing of $272,245,000. In addition, cash spent for fixed assets during the period was $221,160,000. Average current liabilities were $243,668,000, and average total liabilities were $928,464,500. No dividends were paid. Calculate these values:
(a) Free cash flow.
(b) Current cash debt coverage ratio.
(c) Cash debt coverage ratio.

Calculate cash-based ratios.
(SO 5)

BE12-10 Fort Corporation reported cash provided by operating activities of $405,000, cash used by investing activities of $250,000, and cash provided by financing activities of $70,000. In addition, cash spent for capital assets during the period was $200,000. Average current liabilities were $150,000, and average total liabilities were $225,000. No dividends were paid. Calculate these values:
(a) Free cash flow.
(b) Current cash debt coverage ratio.
(c) Cash debt coverage ratio.

Calculate cash-based ratios.
(SO 5)

BE12-11 Alliance Atlantis Communications Inc. reported cash provided by operating activities of $123,100,000 and revenues of $1,175,400,000 during 2006. Cash spent on plant asset additions during the year was $20,800,000. Calculate free cash flow.

Calculate and analyze free cash flow.
(SO 5)

BE12-12 The management of Payne Inc. is trying to decide whether it can increase its dividend. During the current year it reported net income of $875,000. It had cash provided by operating activities of $734,000, paid cash dividends of $90,000, and had capital expenditures of $280,000. Compute the company's free cash flow, and discuss whether an increase in the dividend appears warranted. What other factors should be considered?

Compute receipts from customers—direct method.
(SO 6)

BE12-13 Columbia Sportswear Company had accounts receivable of $284,029,000 at January 1, 2006, and $285,942,000 at December 31, 2006. Sales revenues were $1,287,672,000 for the year 2006. What is the amount of cash receipts from customers in 2006?

Compute cash payments for income taxes—direct method.
(SO 6)

BE12-14 Oakes Corporation reported income taxes of $370,000,000 on its 2010 income statement and income taxes payable of $277,000,000 at December 31, 2009, and $522,000,000 at December 31, 2010. What amount of cash payments were made for income taxes during 2010?

Compute cash payments for operating expenses—direct method.
(SO 6)

BE12-15 Locey Corporation reports operating expenses of $90,000 excluding depreciation expense of $15,000 for 2010. During the year prepaid expenses decreased $6,600 and accrued expenses payable increased $4,400. Compute the cash payments for operating expenses in 2010.

Do it! Review

Classify transactions by type of cash flow activity.
(SO 2)

Do it! 12-1 Rapture Corporation had the following transactions.
1. Issued $200,000 of bonds payable. F
2. Paid utilities expense. O
3. Issued 500 shares of preferred stock for $45,000. F
4. Sold land and a building for $250,000. I
5. Lent $30,000 to Dead End Corporation, receiving Dead End's 1-year, 12% note. I

Classify each of these transactions by type of cash flow activity (operating, investing, or financing).

Do it! 12-2 JMB Photography reported net income of $100,000 for 2010. Included in the income statement were depreciation expense of $6,000, patent amortization expense of $2,000, and a gain on sale of equipment of $3,600. JMB's comparative balance sheets show the following balances.

Calculate net cash from operating activities.
(SO 3)

	12/31/10	**12/31/09**
Accounts receivable	$21,000	$27,000
Accounts payable	9,200	6,000

D(6,000)
I(3,200)

Calculate net cash provided by operating activities for JMB Photography.

Do it! 12-3 Grinders Corporation issued the following statement of cash flows for 2010.

Compute and discuss free cash flow.
(SO 5)

GRINDERS CORPORATION
Statement of Cash Flows—Indirect Method
For the Year Ended December 31, 2010

Cash flows from operating activities		
Net income	$59,000	
Adjustments to reconcile net income to net cash provided by operating activities:		
Depreciation expense	9,100	
Decrease in accounts receivable	9,500	
Increase in inventory	(5,000)	
Decrease in accounts payable	(2,200)	
Loss on sale of equipment	3,300	
Net cash provided by operating activities		$73,700
Cash flows from investing activities		
Sale of investments	3,100	
Purchase of equipment	(27,000)	
Net cash used by investing activities		(23,900)
Cash flows from financing activities		
Issuance of stock	20,000	
Payment on long-term note payable	(10,000)	
Payment for dividends	(15,000)	
Net cash used by financing activities		(5,000)
Net increase in cash		44,800
Cash at beginning of year		13,000
Cash at end of year		$57,800

(a) Compute free cash flow for Grinders Corporation.
(b) Explain why free cash flow often provides better information than "Net cash provided by operating activities."

Exercises

E12-1 Rensing Corporation had these transactions during 2010.
(a) Purchased a machine for $30,000, giving a long-term note in exchange. NonCash
(b) Issued $50,000 par value common stock for cash. F
(c) Issued $200,000 par value common stock upon conversion of bonds having a face value of $200,000. Non Cash
(d) Declared and paid a cash dividend of $18,000. F
(e) Sold a long-term investment with a cost of $15,000 for $15,000 cash. I
(f) Collected $16,000 of accounts receivable. O
(g) Paid $18,000 on accounts payable. O

Classify transactions by type of activity.
(SO 2)

Instructions
Analyze the transactions and indicate whether each transaction resulted in a cash flow from operating activities, investing activities, financing activities, or noncash investing and financing activities.

Classify transactions by type of activity.
(SO 2)

E12-2 An analysis of comparative balance sheets, the current year's income statement, and the general ledger accounts of Kingsley Corp. uncovered the following items. Assume all items involve cash unless there is information to the contrary.

(a) Payment of interest on notes payable.
(b) Exchange of land for patent.
(c) Sale of building at book value.
(d) Payment of dividends.
(e) Depreciation.
(f) Conversion of bonds into common stock.
(g) Receipt of interest on notes receivable.
(h) Issuance of capital stock.
(i) Amortization of patent.
(j) Issuance of bonds for land.
(k) Purchase of land.
(l) Receipt of dividends on investment in stock.
(m) Loss on sale of land.
(n) Retirement of bonds.

Instructions
Indicate how each item should be classified in the statement of cash flows using these four major classifications: operating activity (indirect method), investing activity, financing activity, and significant noncash investing and financing activity.

Identify phases of product life cycle.
(SO 3)

E12-3 The information in the table is from the statement of cash flows for a company at four different points in time (A, B, C, and D). Negative values are presented in parentheses.

	Point in Time			
	A	**B**	**C**	**D**
Cash provided by operations	$ (60,000)	$ 30,000	$120,000	$(10,000)
Cash provided by investing	(100,000)	25,000	30,000	(40,000)
Cash provided by financing	70,000	(110,000)	(50,000)	120,000
Net income	(40,000)	10,000	100,000	(5,000)

Instructions
For each point in time, state whether the company is most likely in the introductory phase, growth phase, maturity phase, or decline phase. In each case explain your choice.

Prepare the operating activities section—indirect method.
(SO 4)

E12-4 Jerez Company reported net income of $190,000 for 2010. Jerez also reported depreciation expense of $35,000 and a loss of $5,000 on the sale of equipment. The comparative balance sheet shows a decrease in accounts receivable of $15,000 for the year, a $17,000 increase in accounts payable, and a $4,000 decrease in prepaid expenses.

Instructions
Prepare the operating activities section of the statement of cash flows for 2010. Use the indirect method.

Prepare the operating activities section—indirect method.
(SO 4)

E12-5 The current sections of Kitselton Inc.'s balance sheets at December 31, 2009 and 2010, are presented here.

Kitselton's net income for 2010 was $153,000. Depreciation expense was $34,000.

	2010	**2009**	
Current assets			
Cash	$105,000	$ 99,000	in 6000
Accounts receivable	100,000	89,000	in 11,000
Inventory	168,000	172,000	dec 4000
Prepaid expenses	27,000	22,000	in 5000
Total current assets	$400,000	$382,000	
Current liabilities			
Accrued expenses payable	$ 15,000	$ 5,000	in 10,000
Accounts payable	85,000	92,000	dec 7000
Total current liabilities	$100,000	$ 97,000	

Instructions
Prepare the net cash provided by operating activities section of the company's statement of cash flows for the year ended December 31, 2010, using the indirect method.

E12-6 The following information is available for Felix Corporation for the year ended December 31, 2010.

Prepare statement of cash flows—indirect method.

(SO 4)

Beginning cash balance	$ 45,000
Accounts payable decrease	3,700 *O (−)*
~~Depreciation expense~~	~~187,000~~ *O*
Accounts receivable increase	8,200 *O (−)*
Inventory increase	11,000 *O (−)*
Net income	284,100
Cash received for sale of land at book value	35,000 *I*
Sales	~~747,000~~
Cash dividends paid	12,000 *F*
Income tax payable increase	~~4,700~~ *O (+)*
Cash used to purchase building	129,000 *I*
Cash used to purchase treasury stock	32,000 *F*
Cash received from issuing bonds	200,000 *F*

Instructions

Prepare a statement of cash flows using the indirect method.

E12-7 The three accounts shown below appear in the general ledger of Tovar Corp. during 2010.

Prepare partial statement of cash flows—indirect method.

(SO 4)

Equipment

Date		Debit	Credit	Balance
Jan. 1	Balance			160,000
July 31	Purchase of equipment	70,000		230,000
Sept. 2	Cost of equipment constructed	53,000		283,000
Nov. 10	Cost of equipment sold		49,000	234,000

Accumulated Depreciation—Equipment

Date		Debit	Credit	Balance
Jan. 1	Balance			71,000
Nov. 10	Accumulated depreciation on equipment sold	30,000		41,000
Dec. 31	Depreciation for year		28,000	69,000

Retained Earnings

Date		Debit	Credit	Balance
Jan. 1	Balance			105,000
Aug. 23	Dividends (cash)	19,000		86,000
Dec. 31	Net income		72,000	158,000

Instructions

From the postings in the accounts, indicate how the information is reported on a statement of cash flows using the indirect method. The loss on sale of equipment was $8,000. (*Hint:* Cost of equipment constructed is reported in the investing activities section as a decrease in cash of $53,000.)

E12-8 Shown below and on the next page are comparative balance sheets for Matsui Company.

Prepare a statement of cash flows—indirect method, and compute cash-based ratios.

(SO 4, 5)

MATSUI COMPANY
Comparative Balance Sheets
December 31

Assets	2010	2009	
Cash	$ 68,000	$ 22,000	+ 46,000
Accounts receivable	85,000	76,000	− 9000
Inventories	170,000	189,000	− (19,000)
Land	80,000	100,000	− (20,000)
Equipment	260,000	200,000	+ 60,000
Accumulated depreciation	(66,000)	(32,000)	+ 60,000
Total	$597,000	$555,000	+ 34,000

Liabilities and Stockholders' Equity	2010	2009
Accounts payable	$ 39,000	$ 47,000
Bonds payable	150,000	200,000
Common stock ($1 par)	216,000	174,000
Retained earnings	192,000	134,000
Total	$597,000	$555,000

Additional information:

1. Net income for 2010 was $93,000.
2. Cash dividends of $35,000 were declared and paid.
3. Bonds payable amounting to $50,000 were redeemed for cash $50,000.
4. Common stock was issued for $42,000 cash.
5. No equipment was sold during 2010.

Instructions

(a) Prepare a statement of cash flows for 2010 using the indirect method.
(b) Compute these cash-basis ratios:

    (1) Current cash debt coverage.
    (2) Cash debt coverage.

Compare two companies by using cash-based ratios.

(SO 5)

E12-9 Presented below is 2006 information for PepsiCo, Inc. and The Coca-Cola Company.

($ in millions)	PepsiCo	Coca-Cola
Cash provided by operations	$ 6,084	$ 5,957
Average current liabilities	8,133	9,363
Average total liabilities	16,019	13,058
Net income	5,642	5,080
Sales	35,137	24,088
Capital expenditures	2,068	1,407
Dividends paid	1,854	2,911

Instructions

Using the cash-based measures presented in this chapter, compare the (a) liquidity and (b) solvency of the two companies.

Compare two companies by using cash-based ratios.

(SO 5)

E12-10 Information for two companies in the same industry, Hoyt Corporation and Rex Corporation, is presented here.

	Hoyt Corporation	Rex Corporation
Cash provided by operating activities	$100,000	$100,000
Average current liabilities	50,000	100,000
Average total liabilities	200,000	250,000
Net earnings	200,000	200,000
Capital expenditures	40,000	70,000
Dividends paid	5,000	10,000

Instructions

Using the cash-based measures presented in this chapter, compare the (a) liquidity and (b) solvency of the two companies.

Compute cash provided by operating activities—direct method.

(SO 6)

*E12-11 Grainger Company completed its first year of operations on December 31, 2010. Its initial income statement showed that Grainger had revenues of $192,000 and operating expenses of $83,000. Accounts receivable and accounts payable at year-end were $70,000 and $23,000, respectively. Assume that accounts payable related to operating expenses. Ignore income taxes.

Instructions
Compute net cash provided by operating activities using the direct method.

*E12-12 The 2006 income statement for McDonald's Corporation shows cost of goods sold $5,349.7 million and operating expenses (including depreciation expense of $1,249.9 million) $11,791.6 million. The comparative balance sheet for the year shows that inventory increased $4.7 million, prepaid expenses decreased $204.5 million, accounts payable (merchandise suppliers) increased $156.1 million, and accrued expenses payable increased $37 million.

Compute cash payments—direct method.
(SO 6)

Instructions
Using the direct method, compute (a) cash payments to suppliers and (b) cash payments for operating expenses.

*E12-13 The 2010 accounting records of Spaulding Transport reveal these transactions and events.

Compute cash flow from operating activities—direct method.
(SO 6)

Payment of interest	$ 10,000	Payment of salaries and wages	53,000
Cash sales	48,000	Depreciation expense	16,000
Receipt of dividend revenue	18,000	Proceeds from sale of vehicles	812,000
Payment of income taxes	12,000	Purchase of equipment for cash	22,000
Net income	38,000	Loss on sale of vehicles	3,000
Payment for merchandise	105,000	Payment of dividends	14,000
Payment for land	74,000	Payment of operating expenses	28,000
Collection of accounts receivable	192,000		

Instructions
Prepare the cash flows from operating activities section using the direct method. (Not all of the items will be used.)

*E12-14 The following information is available for Mosquito Hollow Corp. for 2010.

Prepare statement of cash flows—direct method.
(SO 6)

Cash used to purchase treasury stock	$ 57,300
Cash dividends paid	21,800
Cash paid for interest	22,400
Net income	464,300
Sales	802,000
Cash paid for taxes	93,000
Cash received from customers	566,100
Cash received from sale of building (at book value)	202,400
Cash paid for operating expenses	77,000
Beginning cash balance	11,000
Cash paid for goods and services	279,100
Cash received from issuing common stock	355,000
Cash paid to redeem bonds at maturity	200,000
Cash paid to purchase equipment	113,200

Instructions
Prepare a statement of cash flows using the direct method.

*E12-15 The following information is taken from the 2010 general ledger of Luzinski Company.

Calculate cash flows—direct method.
(SO 6)

Rent	Rent expense	$ 30,000
	Prepaid rent, January 1	5,900
	Prepaid rent, December 31	9,000
Salaries	Salaries expense	$ 54,000
	Salaries payable, January 1	10,000
	Salaries payable, December 31	8,000
Sales	Revenue from sales	$160,000
	Accounts receivable, January 1	16,000
	Accounts receivable, December 31	7,000

Instructions

In each case, compute the amount that should be reported in the operating activities section of the statement of cash flows under the direct method.

Exercises: Set B

Visit the book's companion website, at **www.wiley.com/college/kimmel,** and choose the Student Companion site, to access Exercise Set B.

Problems: Set A

Distinguish among operating, investing, and financing activities.
(SO 2)

P12-1A You are provided with the following transactions that took place during a recent fiscal year.

Transaction	Where Reported on Statement	Cash Inflow, Outflow, or No Effect?
(a) Recorded depreciation expense on the plant assets.		
(b) Recorded and paid interest expense.		
(c) Recorded cash proceeds from a sale of plant assets.		
(d) Acquired land by issuing common stock.		
(e) Paid a cash dividend to preferred stockholders.		
(f) Distributed a stock dividend to common stockholders.		
(g) Recorded cash sales.		
(h) Recorded sales on account.		
(i) Purchased inventory for cash.		
(j) Purchased inventory on account.		

Instructions

Complete the table indicating whether each item (1) should be reported as an operating (O) activity, investing (I) activity, financing (F) activity, or as a noncash (NC) transaction reported in a separate schedule, and (2) represents a cash inflow or cash outflow or has no cash flow effect. Assume use of the indirect approach.

Determine cash flow effects of changes in equity accounts.
(SO 4)

P12-2A The following account balances relate to the stockholders' equity accounts of Espy Corp. at year-end.

	2010	2009
Common stock, 10,500 and 10,000 shares, respectively, for 2010 and 2009	$165,000	$140,000
Preferred stock, 5,000 shares	125,000	125,000
Retained earnings	300,000	270,000

A small stock dividend was declared and issued in 2010. The market value of the shares was $10,500. Cash dividends were $20,000 in both 2010 and 2009. The common stock has no par or stated value.

Instructions

(a) Net income $60,500

(a) What was the amount of net income reported by Espy Corp. in 2010?

(b) Determine the amounts of any cash inflows or outflows related to the common stock and dividend accounts in 2010.

(c) Indicate where each of the cash inflows or outflows identified in (b) would be classified on the statement of cash flows.

P12-3A   The income statement of Grider Company is presented here.

Prepare the operating activities section—indirect method.
(SO 4)

GRIDER COMPANY
Income Statement
For the Year Ended November 30, 2010

Sales		$7,700,000
Cost of goods sold		
Beginning inventory	$1,900,000	
Purchases	4,400,000	
Goods available for sale	6,300,000	
Ending inventory	1,400,000	
Total cost of goods sold		4,900,000
Gross profit		2,800,000
Operating expenses		
Selling expenses	450,000	
Administrative expenses	700,000	1,150,000
Net income		$1,650,000

Additional information:

1. Accounts receivable increased $300,000 during the year, and inventory decreased $500,000.
2. Prepaid expenses increased $150,000 during the year.
3. Accounts payable to suppliers of merchandise decreased $350,000 during the year.
4. Accrued expenses payable decreased $100,000 during the year.
5. Administrative expenses include depreciation expense of $80,000.

Instructions
Prepare the operating activities section of the statement of cash flows for the year ended November 30, 2010, for Grider Company, using the indirect method.

Cash from operations
$1,330,000

*P12-4A   Data for Grider Company are presented in P12-3A.

Prepare the operating activities section—direct method.
(SO 6)

Instructions
Prepare the operating activities section of the statement of cash flows using the direct method.

Cash from operations
$1,330,000

P12-5A   Jantzen Company's income statement contained the condensed information below.

Prepare the operating activities section—indirect method.
(SO 4)

JANTZEN COMPANY
Income Statement
For the Year Ended December 31, 2010

Revenues		$970,000
Operating expenses, excluding depreciation	$614,000	
Depreciation expense	70,000	
Loss on sale of equipment	16,000	700,000
Income before income taxes		270,000
Income tax expense		40,000
Net income		$230,000

Jantzen's balance sheet contained the comparative data at December 31.

	2010	2009
Accounts receivable	$70,000	$60,000
Accounts payable	41,000	28,000
Income taxes payable	13,000	7,000

Accounts payable pertain to operating expenses.

Instructions
Prepare the operating activities section of the statement of cash flows using the indirect method.

Cash from operations
$325,000

Prepare the operating activities section—direct method.

(SO 6)

Cash from operations
$325,000

Prepare a statement of cash flows—indirect method, and compute cash-based ratios.

(SO 4, 5)

*P12-6A Data for Jantzen Company are presented in P12-5A.

Instructions

Prepare the operating activities section of the statement of cash flows using the direct method.

P12-7A Presented below are the financial statements of Trahan Company.

TRAHAN COMPANY
Comparative Balance Sheets
December 31

Assets	2010	2009
Cash	$ 38,000	$ 20,000
Accounts receivable	33,000	14,000
Merchandise inventory	27,000	20,000
Property, plant, and equipment	60,000	78,000
Accumulated depreciation	(32,000)	(24,000)
Total	$126,000	$ 108,000

Liabilities and Stockholders' Equity	2010	2009
Accounts payable	$ 24,000	$ 15,000
Income taxes payable	7,000	8,000
Bonds payable	27,000	33,000
Common stock	18,000	14,000
Retained earnings	50,000	38,000
Total	$126,000	$ 108,000

TRAHAN COMPANY
Income Statement
For the Year Ended December 31, 2010

Sales		$242,000
Cost of goods sold		175,000
Gross profit		67,000
Selling expenses	$18,000	
Administrative expenses	6,000	24,000
Income from operations		43,000
Interest expense		3,000
Income before income taxes		40,000
Income tax expense		8,000
Net income		$ 32,000

Additional data:

1. Dividends declared and paid were $20,000.
2. During the year equipment was sold for $8,500 cash. This equipment cost $18,000 originally and had a book value of $8,500 at the time of sale.
3. All depreciation expense is in the selling expense category.
4. All sales and purchases are on account.

Instructions

(a) Cash from operations
$31,500

(a) Prepare a statement of cash flows using the indirect method.
(b) Compute these cash-basis measures:
   (1) Current cash debt coverage ratio.
   (2) Cash debt coverage ratio.
   (3) Free cash flow.

Prepare a statement of cash flows—direct method, and compute cash-based ratios.

(SO 5, 6)

*P12-8A Data for Trahan Company are presented in P12-7A. Further analysis reveals the following.

1. Accounts payable pertain to merchandise suppliers.
2. All operating expenses except for depreciation were paid in cash.

Instructions

(a) Prepare a statement of cash flows for Trahan Company using the direct method.

(b) Compute these cash-basis measures:
   (1) Current cash debt coverage ratio.
   (2) Cash debt coverage ratio.
   (3) Free cash flow.

(a) Cash from operations
$31,500

P12-9A   Condensed financial data of Cipra Inc. follow.

Prepare a statement of cash flows—indirect method.
(SO 4)

CIPRA INC.
Comparative Balance Sheets
December 31

Assets	2010	2009
Cash	$ 80,800	$ 48,400
Accounts receivable	87,800	33,000
Inventories	112,500	102,850
Prepaid expenses	28,400	26,000
Investments	138,000	114,000
Plant assets	285,000	242,500
Accumulated depreciation	(50,000)	(52,000)
Total	$682,500	$514,750

Liabilities and Stockholders' Equity		
Accounts payable	$102,000	$ 67,300
Accrued expenses payable	16,500	17,000
Bonds payable	110,000	150,000
Common stock	220,000	175,000
Retained earnings	234,000	105,450
Total	$682,500	$514,750

CIPRA INC.
Income Statement Data
For the Year Ended December 31, 2010

Sales		$392,780
Less:		
Cost of goods sold	$135,460	
Operating expenses, excluding depreciation	12,410	
Depreciation expense	46,500	
Income taxes	27,280	
Interest expense	4,730	
Loss on sale of plant assets	7,500	233,880
Net income		$158,900

Additional information:

1. New plant assets costing $100,000 were purchased for cash during the year.
2. Old plant assets having an original cost of $57,500 were sold for $1,500 cash.
3. Bonds matured and were paid off at face value for cash.
4. A cash dividend of $30,350 was declared and paid during the year.

Instructions

Prepare a statement of cash flows using the indirect method.

Cash from operations
$180,250

*P12-10A   Data for Cipra Inc. are presented in P12-9A. Further analysis reveals that accounts payable pertain to merchandise creditors.

Prepare a statement of cash flows—direct method.
(SO 6)

Instructions

Prepare a statement of cash flows for Cipra Inc. using the direct method.

Cash from operations
$180,250

Prepare a statement of cash flows—indirect method.
(SO 4)

P12-11A The comparative balance sheets for Mercado Company as of December 31 are presented below.

MERCADO COMPANY
Comparative Balance Sheets
December 31

Assets	2010	2009
Cash	$ 65,000	$ 45,000
Accounts receivable	50,000	62,000
Inventory	151,450	142,000
Prepaid expenses	15,280	21,000
Land	105,000	130,000
Equipment	228,000	155,000
Accumulated depreciation—equipment	(45,000)	(35,000)
Building	200,000	200,000
Accumulated depreciation—building	(60,000)	(40,000)
Total	$709,730	$680,000

Liabilities and Stockholders' Equity		
Accounts payable	$ 44,730	$ 40,000
Bonds payable	260,000	300,000
Common stock, $1 par	200,000	160,000
Retained earnings	205,000	180,000
Total	$709,730	$680,000

Additional information:

1. Operating expenses include depreciation expense of $42,000 and charges from prepaid expenses of $5,720.
2. Land was sold for cash at book value.
3. Cash dividends of $12,000 were paid.
4. Net income for 2010 was $37,000.
5. Equipment was purchased for $95,000 cash. In addition, equipment costing $22,000 with a book value of $10,000 was sold for $8,000 cash.
6. Bonds were converted at face value by issuing 40,000 shares of $1 par value common stock.

Instructions

Cash from operations
$94,000

Prepare a statement of cash flows for the year ended December 31, 2010, using the indirect method.

Identify the impact of transactions on ratios.
(SO 5)

P12-12A You are provided with the following transactions that took place during the year.

Transactions	Free Cash Flow ($125,000)	Current Cash Debt Coverage Ratio (0.5 times)	Cash Debt Coverage Ratio (0.3 times)
(a) Recorded credit sales $2,500.			
(b) Collected $1,500 owing from customers.			
(c) Paid amount owing to suppliers $2,750.			
(d) Recorded sales returns of $500 and credited the customer's account.			
(e) Purchased new equipment $5,000; signed a long-term note payable for the cost of the equipment.			
(f) Purchased a patent and paid $15,000 cash for the asset.			

Instructions

For each transaction listed above, indicate whether it will increase (I), decrease (D), or have no effect (NE) on the ratios.

Problems: Set B

P12-1B   You are provided with the following transactions that took place during a recent fiscal year.

Distinguish among operating, investing, and financing activities.
(SO 2)

Transaction	Where Reported on Statement	Cash Inflow, Outflow, or No Effect?
(a) Recorded depreciation expense on the plant assets.		
(b) Incurred a loss on disposal of plant assets.		
(c) Acquired a building by paying cash.		
(d) Made principal repayments on a mortgage.		
(e) Issued common stock.		
(f) Purchased shares of another company to be held as a long-term equity investment.		
(g) Paid dividends to common stockholders.		
(h) Sold inventory on credit. The company uses a perpetual inventory system.		
(i) Purchased inventory on credit.		
(j) Paid wages to employees.		

Instructions
Complete the table indicating whether each item (1) should be reported as an operating (O) activity, investing (I) activity, financing (F) activity, or as a noncash (NC) transaction reported in a separate schedule, and (2) represents a cash inflow or cash outflow or has no cash flow effect. Assume use of the indirect approach.

P12-2B   The following selected account balances relate to the plant asset accounts of Venable Inc. at year-end.

Determine cash flow effects of changes in plant asset accounts.
(SO 4)

	2010	2009
Accumulated depreciation—buildings	$337,500	$300,000
Accumulated depreciation—equipment	144,000	96,000
Buildings	750,000	750,000
Depreciation expense	101,500	85,500
Equipment	300,000	240,000
Land	100,000	70,000
Loss on sale of equipment	6,000	0

Additional information:

1. Venable purchased $90,000 of equipment and $30,000 of land for cash in 2010.
2. Venable also sold equipment in 2010.
3. Depreciation expense in 2010 was $37,500 on building and $64,000 on equipment.

Instructions
(a) Determine the amounts of any cash inflows or outflows related to the plant asset accounts in 2010.
(b) Indicate where each of the cash inflows or outflows identified in (a) would be classified on the statement of cash flows.

(a) Cash proceeds $8,000

P12-3B   The income statement of Percival Company is presented on page 650.

Additional information:

Prepare the operating activities section—indirect method.
(SO 4)

1. Accounts receivable decreased $320,000 during the year, and inventory increased $140,000.
2. Prepaid expenses increased $175,000 during the year.
3. Accounts payable to merchandise suppliers increased $60,000 during the year.
4. Accrued expenses payable increased $145,000 during the year.

PERCIVAL COMPANY
Income Statement
For the Year Ended December 31, 2010

Sales		$5,400,000
Cost of goods sold		
Beginning inventory	$1,780,000	
Purchases	3,430,000	
Goods available for sale	5,210,000	
Ending inventory	1,920,000	
Total cost of goods sold		3,290,000
Gross profit		2,110,000
Operating expenses		
Selling expenses	420,000	
Administrative expense	525,000	
Depreciation expense	105,000	
Amortization expense	20,000	1,070,000
Net income		$1,040,000

Cash from operations
$1,375,000

Instructions

Prepare the operating activities section of the statement of cash flows for the year ended December 31, 2010, for Percival Company, using the indirect method.

Prepare the operating activities section—direct method.

(SO 6)

Cash from operations
$1,375,000

*P12-4B   Data for Percival Company are presented in P12-3B.

Instructions

Prepare the operating activities section of the statement of cash flows using the direct method.

Prepare the operating activities section—indirect method.

(SO 4)

P12-5B   The income statement of Belini Inc. reported the following condensed information.

BELINI INC.
Income Statement
For the Year Ended December 31, 2010

Revenues	$545,000
Operating expenses	400,000
Income from operations	145,000
Income tax expense	47,000
Net income	$ 98,000

Belini's balance sheet contained these comparative data at December 31.

	2010	2009
Accounts receivable	$60,000	$75,000
Accounts payable	35,000	51,000
Income taxes payable	10,000	6,000

Belini has no depreciable assets. Accounts payable pertain to operating expenses.

Cash from operations
$101,000

Instructions

Prepare the operating activities section of the statement of cash flows using the indirect method.

Prepare the operating activities section—direct method.

(SO 6)   Cash from operations
$101,000

*P12-6B   Data for Belini Inc. are presented in P12-5B.

Instructions

Prepare the operating activities section of the statement of cash flows using the direct method.

P12-7B   Shown on page 651 are the financial statements of Rivera Company.

RIVERA COMPANY
Comparative Balance Sheets
December 31

Assets	2010		2009	
Cash		$ 25,000		$ 33,000
Accounts receivable		23,000		14,000
Merchandise inventory		41,000		25,000
Property, plant, and equipment	$ 73,000		$ 78,000	
Less: Accumulated depreciation	(27,000)	46,000	(24,000)	54,000
Total		$135,000		$126,000
Liabilities and Stockholders' Equity				
Accounts payable		$ 23,000		$ 43,000
Income taxes payable		26,000		20,000
Bonds payable		20,000		10,000
Common stock		25,000		25,000
Retained earnings		41,000		28,000
Total		$135,000		$126,000

RIVERA COMPANY
Income Statement
For the Year Ended December 31, 2010

Sales		$286,000
Cost of goods sold		194,000
Gross profit		92,000
Selling expenses	$28,000	
Administrative expenses	9,000	37,000
Income from operations		55,000
Interest expense		7,000
Income before income taxes		48,000
Income tax expense		10,000
Net income		$ 38,000

Additional data:

1. Dividends of $25,000 were declared and paid.
2. During the year equipment was sold for $10,000 cash. This equipment cost $13,000 originally and had a book value of $10,000 at the time of sale.
3. All depreciation expense, $6,000, is in the selling expense category.
4. All sales and purchases are on account.
5. Additional equipment was purchased for $8,000 cash.

Instructions
(a) Prepare a statement of cash flows using the indirect method.
(b) Compute these cash-basis measures:
  (1) Current cash debt coverage ratio.
  (2) Cash debt coverage ratio.
  (3) Free cash flow.

*P12-8B   Data for Rivera Company are presented in P12-7B. Further analysis reveals the following.

1. Accounts payable pertains to merchandise creditors.
2. All operating expenses except for depreciation are paid in cash.

Instructions
(a) Prepare a statement of cash flows using the direct method.
(b) Compute these cash-basis measures:
  (1) Current cash debt coverage ratio.
  (2) Cash debt coverage ratio.
  (3) Free cash flow.

Prepare a statement of cash flows—indirect method.
(SO 4)

P12-9B Condensed financial data of Ulrich Company are shown below.

ULRICH COMPANY
Comparative Balance Sheets
December 31

Assets	2010	2009
Cash	$ 82,700	$ 33,400
Accounts receivable	75,800	37,000
Inventories	121,900	102,650
Investments	89,500	107,000
Plant assets	320,000	205,000
Accumulated depreciation	(49,500)	(40,000)
Total	$640,400	$445,050

Liabilities and Stockholders' Equity		
Accounts payable	$ 52,700	$ 48,280
Accrued expenses payable	15,100	18,830
Bonds payable	140,000	70,000
Common stock	250,000	200,000
Retained earnings	182,600	107,940
Total	$640,400	$445,050

ULRICH COMPANY
Income Statement Data
For the Year Ended December 31, 2010

Sales		$297,500
Gain on sale of plant assets		5,000
		302,500
Less:		
Cost of goods sold	$99,460	
Operating expenses, excluding depreciation expense	14,670	
Depreciation expense	35,500	
Income taxes	27,270	
Interest expense	2,940	179,840
Net income		$122,660

Additional information:

1. New plant assets costing $151,000 were purchased for cash during the year.
2. Investments were sold at cost.
3. Plant assets costing $36,000 were sold for $15,000, resulting in a gain of $5,000.
4. A cash dividend of $48,000 was declared and paid during the year.

Cash from operations
$95,800

Instructions
Prepare a statement of cash flows using the indirect method.

Prepare a statement of cash flows—direct method.
(SO 6)

*P12-10B** Data for Ulrich Company are presented in P12-9B. Further analysis reveals that accounts payable pertain to merchandise creditors.

Cash from operations
$95,800

Instructions
Prepare a statement of cash flows for Ulrich Company using the direct method.

Prepare a statement of cash flows—indirect method.
(SO 4)

P12-11B Presented on the next page are the comparative balance sheets for Nunez Company at December 31.

NUNEZ COMPANY
Comparative Balance Sheets
December 31

Assets	2010	2009
Cash	$ 41,000	$ 57,000
Accounts receivable	77,000	64,000
Inventory	192,000	140,000
Prepaid expenses	12,140	16,540
Land	100,000	150,000
Equipment	205,000	175,000
Accumulated depreciation—equipment	(70,000)	(42,000)
Building	250,000	250,000
Accumulated depreciation—building	(70,000)	(50,000)
Total	$737,140	$760,540

Liabilities and Stockholders' Equity	2010	2009
Accounts payable	$ 48,000	$ 45,000
Bonds payable	235,000	265,000
Common stock, $1 par	280,000	250,000
Retained earnings	174,140	200,540
Total	$737,140	$760,540

Additional information:

1. Operating expenses include depreciation expense $65,000 and charges from prepaid expenses of $4,400.
2. Land was sold for cash at cost.
3. Cash dividends of $59,290 were paid.
4. Net income for 2010 was $32,890.
5. Equipment was purchased for $70,000 cash. In addition, equipment costing $40,000 with a book value of $23,000 was sold for $25,000 cash.
6. Bonds were converted at face value by issuing 30,000 shares of $1 par value common stock.

Instructions
Prepare a statement of cash flows for 2010 using the indirect method.

Cash from operations
$38,290

Problems: Set C

Visit the book's companion website at **www.wiley.com/college/kimmel** and choose the Student Companion site to access Problem Set C.

Continuing Cookie Chronicle

(*Note:* This is a continuation of the Cookie Chronicle from Chapters 1 through 11.)

Natalie has prepared the balance sheet and income statement of Cookie & Coffee Creations Inc. and would like you to prepare the cash flow statement.

Go to the book's companion website, **www.wiley.com/college/kimmel**, to find the completion of this problem.

broadening your perspective

Financial Reporting and Analysis

FINANCIAL REPORTING PROBLEM: *Tootsie Roll Industries, Inc.*

BYP12-1   The financial statements of Tootsie Roll Industries are presented in Appendix A.

Instructions
Answer the following questions.
(a) What was the amount of net cash provided by operating activities for 2007? For 2006? What were some causes of any significant changes in cash from operations between 2006 and 2007?
(b) What was the amount of increase or decrease in cash and cash equivalents for the year ended December 31, 2007?
(c) Which method of computing net cash provided by operating activities does Tootsie Roll use?
(d) From your analysis of the 2007 statement of cash flows, was the change in accounts receivable a decrease or an increase? Was the change in inventories a decrease or an increase? Was the change in accounts payable a decrease or an increase?
(e) What was the net cash used by investing activities for 2007?
(f) What was the amount of interest paid in 2007? What was the amount of income taxes paid in 2007?

COMPARATIVE ANALYSIS PROBLEM: *Tootsie Roll vs. Hershey Foods*

BYP12-2   The financial statements of Hershey Foods are presented in Appendix B, following the financial statements for Tootsie Roll Industries in Appendix A.

Instructions
(a) Based on the information in these financial statements, compute these 2007 ratios for each company:
    (1) Current cash debt coverage.
    (2) Cash debt coverage.
(b) What conclusions about the management of cash can you draw from these data?

RESEARCH CASE

BYP12-3   The February 8, 2008, edition of the *Wall Street Journal* contains an article by Peter Eavis titled "Worries Ring Up at Sears."

Instructions
Read the article and answer the following questions.
(a) What does the article's author say are the primary reasons investors might be concerned about declining cash flows at Sears?
(b) Given that the company had not reported its cash flow number yet, what sparked concern among investors that cash flows might be declining?
(c) How did Sears's defenders respond to the suggestion that cash flows might be declining?
(d) If, in fact, Sears's cash flow is declining, why does the article say that it is a particularly bad time of year for cash flow to be declining?

INTERPRETING FINANCIAL STATEMENTS

BYP12-4   The incredible growth of Amazon.com has put fear into the hearts of traditional retailers. Its stock price has soared to amazing levels. However, in 2001 many investors were very concerned about whether Amazon would survive since it had never earned a profit, and it was burning through cash. Some investors sold, but others decided to hold on to their investment in the company's stock. The following information is taken from the 2001 and 2004 financial statements of Amazon.com.

($ in millions)	2001	2004
Current assets	$1,207.9	$2,539.4
Total assets	1,637.5	3,248.5
Current liabilities	921.4	1,620.4
Total liabilities	3,077.5	5,096.1
Cash provided by operations	(119.8)	566.6
Capital expenditures	50.3	89.1
Dividends paid	0	0
Net income (loss)	(567.3)	588.5
Average current liabilities	948.2	1,436.6
Average total liabilities	3,090.0	4,773.4

Instructions

(a) Calculate the current ratio and current cash debt coverage ratio for Amazon.com for 2001 and 2004, and discuss its comparative liquidity.

(b) Calculate the cash debt coverage ratio and the debt to total assets ratio for Amazon.com for 2001 and 2004, and discuss its comparative solvency.

(c) Amazon.com has avoided purchasing large warehouses. Instead, it has used those of others. In order to increase customer satisfaction Amazon may have to build its own warehouses. Calculate free cash flow for Amazon.com for 2001 and 2004, and discuss its ability to purchase warehouses and to finance expansion from internally generated cash.

(d) Based on your findings in parts (a) through (c), can you conclude whether or not Amazon.com's amazing stock price is justified?

FINANCIAL ANALYSIS ON THE WEB

BYP12-5 *Purpose:* Use the Internet to view SEC filings.

Address: **biz.yahoo.com/i**, or go to **www.wiley.com/college/kimmel**

Steps

1. Enter a company's name.
2. Choose **Quote**. Answer questions (a) and (b).
3. Choose **Profile**; then choose **SEC**. Answer questions (c) and (d).

Instructions

Answer the following questions.

(a) What company did you select?

(b) What is its stock symbol? What is its selling price?

(c) What recent SEC filings are available for your viewing?

(d) Which filing is the most recent? What is the date?

Critical Thinking

DECISION MAKING ACROSS THE ORGANIZATION

BYP12-6 Dan Pine and Jill Alton are examining the following statement of cash flows for Devito Company for the year ended January 31, 2010.

DEVITO COMPANY
Statement of Cash Flows
For the Year Ended January 31, 2010

Sources of cash	
From sales of merchandise	$385,000
From sale of capital stock	405,000
From sale of investment (purchased below)	80,000
From depreciation	55,000
From issuance of note for truck	20,000
From interest on investments	6,000
Total sources of cash	951,000

(continues on next page)

Uses of cash		
For purchase of fixtures and equipment	320,000	
For merchandise purchased for resale	258,000	
For operating expenses (including depreciation)	170,000	
For purchase of investment	75,000	
For purchase of truck by issuance of note	20,000	
For purchase of treasury stock	10,000	
For interest on note payable	3,000	
Total uses of cash	856,000	
Net increase in cash	$ 95,000	

Dan claims that Devito's statement of cash flows is an excellent portrayal of a superb first year with cash increasing $95,000. Jill replies that it was not a superb first year. Rather, she says, the year **was** an operating failure, that the statement is presented incorrectly, and that $95,000 is not the actual increase in cash. The cash balance at the beginning of the year was $140,000.

Instructions
With the class divided into groups, answer the following.
(a) Using the data provided, prepare a statement of cash flows in proper form using the indirect method. The only noncash items in the income statement are depreciation and the gain from the sale of the investment.
(b) With whom do you agree, Dan or Jill? Explain your position.

COMMUNICATION ACTIVITY

BYP12-7 Rick Darman, the owner-president of Computer Services, is unfamiliar with the statement of cash flows that you, as his accountant, prepared. He asks for further explanation.

Instructions
Write him a brief memo explaining the form and content of the statement of cash flows as shown in Illustration 12-14 (page 616).

ETHICS CASE

BYP12-8 Christy Automotive Corp. is a medium-sized wholesaler of automotive parts. It has 10 stockholders who have been paid a total of $1 million in cash dividends for 8 consecutive years. The board's policy requires that, for this dividend to be declared, net cash provided by operating activities as reported in Christy Automotive's current year's statement of cash flows must exceed $1 million. President and CEO Albert Roland's job is secure so long as he produces annual operating cash flows to support the usual dividend.

At the end of the current year, controller George Ellerby presents president Albert Roland with some disappointing news: The net cash provided by operating activities is calculated by the indirect method to be only $970,000. The president says to George, "We must get that amount above $1 million. Isn't there some way to increase operating cash flow by another $30,000?" George answers, "These figures were prepared by my assistant. I'll go back to my office and see what I can do." The president replies, "I know you won't let me down, George."

Upon close scrutiny of the statement of cash flows, George concludes that he can get the operating cash flows above $1 million by reclassifying a $60,000, 2-year note payable listed in the financing activities section as "Proceeds from bank loan—$60,000." He will report the note instead as "Increase in payables—$60,000" and treat it as an adjustment of net income in the operating activities section. He returns to the president, saying, "You can tell the board to declare their usual dividend. Our net cash flow provided by operating activities is $1,030,000." "Good man, George! I knew I could count on you," exults the president.

Instructions
(a) Who are the stakeholders in this situation?
(b) Was there anything unethical about the president's actions? Was there anything unethical about the controller's actions?
(c) Are the board members or anyone else likely to discover the misclassification?

"ALL ABOUT YOU" ACTIVITY

BYP12-9 In this chapter you learned that companies prepare a statement of cash flows in order to keep track of their sources and uses of cash and to help them plan for their future cash needs. Planning for your own short- and long-term cash needs is every bit as important as it is for a company.

Instructions
Read the article "Financial 'Uh-oh'? No Problem," at **www.fool.com/savings/shortterm/ 02.htm**, and answer the following questions.
(a) Describe the three factors that determine how much money you should set aside for short term needs.
(b) How many months of living expenses does the article suggest to set aside?
(c) Estimate how much you should set aside based upon your current situation. Are you closer to Cliff's scenario or to Prudence's?

Answers to Insight and Accounting Across the Organization Questions

p. 604
Q: In general, why do differences exist between net income and net cash provided by operating activities?
A: The differences are explained by differences in the timing of the reporting of revenues and expenses under accrual accounting versus cash. Under accrual accounting, companies report revenues when earned, even if cash hasn't been received, and they report expenses when incurred, even if cash hasn't been paid.

p. 607
Q: Why do companies have negative cash from operations during the introductory phase?
A: During the introductory phase companies usually spend more on inventory than the amount expensed for cost of goods sold because they are building up inventory, and their cash collections frequently lag the amount reported for sales. Therefore, even if they are reporting positive net income, they frequently report negative cash from operations.

p. 614
Q: Why does GM's cash provided by operating activities drop so precipitously when the company's sales figures decline?
A: GM's cash inflow is directly related to how many cars it sells. But many of its cash outflows are not tied to sales—they are "fixed." For example, many of its employee payroll costs are very rigid due to labor contracts. Therefore, even though sales (and therefore cash inflows) fall, these cash outflows don't decline.

Answers to Self-Study Questions

1. c 2. a 3. b 4. a 5. c 6. d 7. b 8. c 9. a 10. d 11. b 12. b 13. a 14. b 15. d 16. d *17. c *18. d

✔ Remember to go back to the navigator box on the chapter-opening page and check off your completed work.

chapter 13

Financial Analysis:
The Big Picture

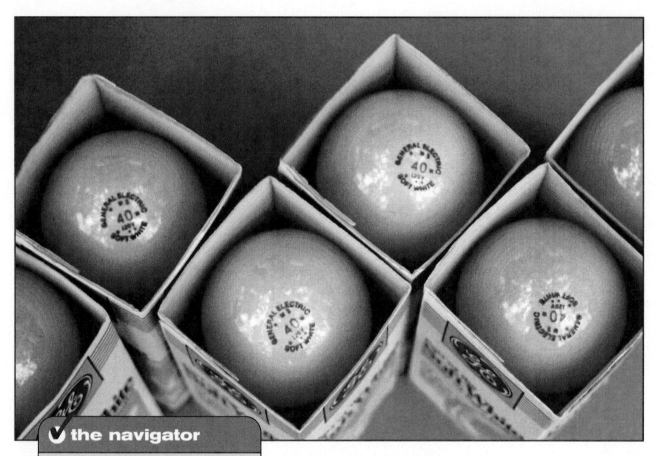

✔ the navigator

- Scan Study Objectives ○
- Read Feature Story ○
- Scan Preview ○
- Read Text and Answer **Do it!**
  p. 666 ○   p. 670 ○   p. 677 ○
- Work Using the Decision Toolkit ○
- Review Summary of Study Objectives ○
- Work Comprehensive **Do it!** p. 694 ○
- Answer Self-Study Questions ○
- Complete Assignments ○

study objectives

After studying this chapter, you should be able to:

1 Understand the concept of sustainable income.

2 Indicate how irregular items are presented.

3 Explain the concept of comprehensive income.

4 Describe and apply horizontal analysis.

5 Describe and apply vertical analysis.

6 Identify and compute ratios used in analyzing a company's liquidity, solvency, and profitability.

7 Understand the concept of quality of earnings.

✔ **the navigator**

Making the Numbers

There it is again, perched near the top of *Fortune*'s "Most Admired Companies" list. But when the people who run General Electric go out in public these days, they don't exactly get to bask in adulation. Instead, they have to explain how their company is *not* like Enron, or Global Crossing, or Tyco.

At one level, that's a pretty easy argument to make. GE is not about to collapse or to break up. It has tons of cash, and its businesses generate upwards of a billion dollars every month. It is one of only a handful of companies with a triple-A credit rating. It makes real things like turbines and refrigerators that people spend real money to buy.

GE also has an enviable record of pleasing Wall Street. Quarter after quarter, year after year, GE's earnings come gushing in, usually at least 10% higher than the year before, and almost invariably in line with analysts' estimates.

This used to be seen as a good thing. "Making the numbers" became the most watched measure of corporate performance. By missing only once during a 10-year period (by a penny, in the fourth quarter of 1997), GE ensured itself a hallowed place in the corporate hall of fame.

But as one analyst noted, "Smoking used to be chic and fashionable and cool; now it's not. The companies that reliably deliver 15% earnings growth year after year are the new smokers." All of which means that GE's chief executive, Jeffrey Immelt, now finds himself having to tell interviewer after interviewer that no, he's not an earnings cheat.

"Would a miss be more honest?" Immelt asks, with exasperation in his voice. "I think that's terrible. That's where the world has gotten totally turned on its head, where somewhere I'd walk up to a podium and get a Nobel Peace Prize for saying 'I missed my numbers—aren't you proud of me?'"

In the spring of 2008, GE did miss its earnings target. In the words of one writer, GE missed it "by a country mile." Rather than winning a prize, Mr. Immelt watched GE's value fall by $47 billion. It was the second largest one-day loss by any company in history.

Source: Adapted from Justin Fox, "What's So Great About GE?" *Fortune* (March 4, 2002), pp. 65–66.

On the World Wide Web
General Electric: www.ge.com

As indicated in our Feature Story, even the most admired companies in the United States are under attack for their earnings and disclosure practices. A climate of skepticism has caused many companies to lose billions of dollars in market value if there is even the slightest hint that the company is involved in some form of creative accounting. The purpose of this chapter is to explain the importance of **performance measurement** and to highlight the difficulties of developing **high-quality earnings numbers**, given the complexities of modern business transactions.

The content and organization of this chapter are as follows.

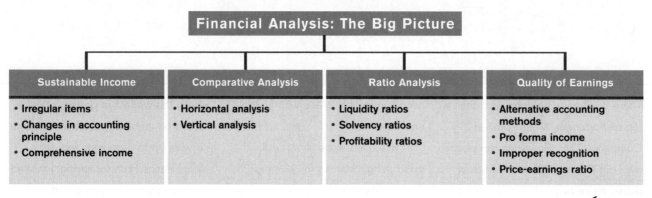

Financial Analysis: The Big Picture

Sustainable Income	Comparative Analysis	Ratio Analysis	Quality of Earnings
• Irregular items • Changes in accounting principle • Comprehensive income	• Horizontal analysis • Vertical analysis	• Liquidity ratios • Solvency ratios • Profitability ratios	• Alternative accounting methods • Pro forma income • Improper recognition • Price-earnings ratio

Sustainable Income

study objective 1

Understand the concept of sustainable income.

Ultimately, the value of a company is a function of its future cash flows. When analysts use this year's net income to estimate future cash flows, they must make sure that this year's net income does not include irregular (i.e., out of the ordinary) revenues, expenses, gains, or losses. Net income adjusted for irregular items is referred to as sustainable income. **Sustainable income is the most likely level of income to be obtained in the future.** Sustainable income differs from actual net income by the amount of irregular revenues, expenses, gains, and losses included in this year's net income.

Users are interested in sustainable income because it helps them derive an estimate of future earnings without the "noise" of irregular items. For example, suppose Rye Corporation reports that this year's net income is $500,000 but included in that amount is a once-in-a-lifetime gain of $400,000. In estimating next year's net income for Rye Corporation, we would likely ignore this $400,000 gain and estimate that next year's net income will be in the neighborhood of $100,000. That is, based on this year's results, the company's sustainable income is roughly $100,000. Therefore, identifying irregular items is important if you are going to use reported earnings to estimate a company's value.

In earlier chapters you learned how to prepare and use a basic multiple-step income statement. In this chapter we will explain additional components of the income statement as well as a broader measure of performance called *comprehensive income*. Illustration 13-1 presents the components of the income statement and comprehensive income; new items are presented in red. When estimating future cash flows, analysts must consider the implications that each of these components has for future cash flows.

IRREGULAR ITEMS

study objective 2

Indicate how irregular items are presented.

As an aid in determining sustainable income, we identify irregular items by type on the income statement. There, companies report two types of irregular items:

1. Discontinued operations
2. Extraordinary items

Illustration 13-1
Components of the income statement

Income Statement

Sales	$XX
Cost of goods sold	XX
Gross profit	XX
Operating expenses	XX
Income from operations	XX
Other revenues (expenses) and gains (losses)	XX
Income before income taxes	XX
Income tax expense	XX
Income before irregular items	XX
Discontinued operations (net of tax)	XX
Extraordinary items (net of tax)	XX
Net income	XX
Other comprehensive income items (net of tax)	XX
Comprehensive income	$XX

Irregular items are reported net of income taxes. That is, a company first calculates income tax expense for the income before irregular items. Then it calculates income tax expense for each individual irregular item. The general concept is, "Let the tax follow the income or loss."

Discontinued Operations

To downsize its operations, General Dynamics Corp. sold its missile business to Hughes Aircraft Co. for $450 million. In its income statement, General Dynamics reported the sale in a separate section entitled "Discontinued operations." Discontinued operations refers to the disposal of a significant component of a business, such as the elimination of a major class of customers or an entire activity. When the disposal of a significant component occurs, the income statement should report the gain (or loss) from discontinued operations, net of tax.

To illustrate, assume that Rozek Inc. has revenues of $2.5 million and expenses of $1.7 million from continuing operations in 2010. The company therefore has income before income taxes of $800,000. During 2010 the company discontinued and sold its unprofitable chemical division. The loss on disposal of the chemical division (net of $90,000 tax savings) was $210,000. Illustration 13-2 shows the income statement presentation, assuming a 30% tax rate on income before income taxes.

Illustration 13-2
Statement presentation of discontinued operations

ROZEK INC.
Income Statement (partial)
For the Year Ended December 31, 2010

Income before income taxes	$ 800,000
Income tax expense	240,000
Income before irregular items	560,000
Discontinued operations	
Loss from disposal of chemical division, net of $90,000 income tax savings	(210,000)
Net income	$ 350,000

This presentation clearly indicates the separate effects of continuing operations and discontinued operations on net income.

DECISION TOOLKIT

DECISION CHECKPOINTS	INFO NEEDED FOR DECISION	TOOL TO USE FOR DECISION	HOW TO EVALUATE RESULTS
Has the company sold any major components of its business?	Discontinued operations section of income statement	Anything reported in this section indicates that the company has discontinued a major component of its business.	If a major component has been discontinued, its results during the current period should not be included in estimates of future net income.

Extraordinary Items

Extraordinary items are events and transactions that meet two conditions: They are **unusual in nature** and **infrequent in occurrence**. To be considered *unusual*, the item should be abnormal and only incidentally related to the customary activities of the entity. To be regarded as *infrequent*, the event or transaction should not be reasonably expected to recur in the foreseeable future.

A company must evaluate both criteria in terms of the environment in which it operates. Thus, Weyerhaeuser Co. reported the $36 million in damages to its timberland caused by the eruption of Mount St. Helens as an extraordinary item because the event was both unusual and infrequent. In contrast, Florida Citrus Company does not report frost damage to its citrus crop as an extraordinary item because frost damage is not viewed as infrequent.

Helpful Hint Ordinary gains and losses are reported at pretax amounts in arriving at income before income taxes.

Companies report extraordinary items net of taxes in a separate section of the income statement, immediately below discontinued operations. To illustrate, assume that in 2010 a revolutionary foreign government expropriated property held as an investment by Rozek Inc. If the loss is $70,000 before applicable income tax savings of $21,000, the income statement presentation will show a deduction of $49,000, as in Illustration 13-3.

Illustration 13-3
Statement presentation of extraordinary items

ROZEK INC. Income Statement (partial) For the Year Ended December 31, 2010	
Income before income taxes	$ 800,000
Income tax expense	240,000
Income before irregular items	560,000
Discontinued operations: Loss from disposal of chemical division, net of $90,000 income tax savings	(210,000)
Extraordinary item: Expropriation of investment, net of $21,000 income tax savings	(49,000)
Net income	$ 301,000

If a transaction or event meets one but not both of the criteria for an extraordinary item, a company should report it in a separate line item in the upper portion of the income statement, rather than in the bottom portion as an extraordinary item. Usually companies report these items under either "Other revenues and gains" or "Other expenses and losses" at their gross amount (not net of tax). This is true, for example, of gains (losses) resulting from the sale of property, plant, and equipment, as explained in Chapter 9. Illustration 13-4 shows the appropriate classification of extraordinary and ordinary items.

Illustration 13-4
Classification of extraordinary and ordinary items

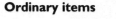

Extraordinary items   **Ordinary items**

1. Effects of major natural casualties, if rare in the area.

I. Effects of major natural casualties, not uncommon in the area.

2. Expropriation (takeover) of property by a foreign government.

2. Write-down of inventories or write-off of receivables.
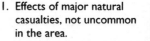

3. Effects of a newly enacted law or regulation, such as a condemnation action.
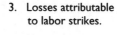

3. Losses attributable to labor strikes.
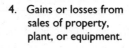

4. Gains or losses from sales of property, plant, or equipment.

   In summary, in evaluating a company, it generally makes sense to eliminate all irregular items in estimating future sustainable income.

Investor Insight

Many companies incur restructuring charges as they attempt to reduce costs. They often label these items in the income statement as "non-recurring" charges, to suggest that they are isolated events, unlikely to occur in future periods. The question for analysts is, are these costs really one-time, "non-recurring events," or do they reflect problems that the company will be facing for many periods in the future? If they are one-time events, then they can be largely ignored when trying to predict future earnings.

   But some companies report "one-time" restructuring charges over and over again. For example, Procter and Gamble Co. reported a restructuring charge in 12 consecutive quarters, and Motorola had "special" charges in 14 consecutive quarters. On the other hand, other companies have a restructuring charge only once in a five- or ten-year period. There appears to be no substitute for careful analysis of the numbers that comprise net income.

 If a company takes a large restructuring charge, what is the effect on the company's current income statements versus future ones?

DECISION TOOLKIT

DECISION CHECKPOINTS	INFO NEEDED FOR DECISION	TOOL TO USE FOR DECISION	HOW TO EVALUATE RESULTS
Has the company experienced any extraordinary events or transactions?	Extraordinary item section of income statement	Anything reported in this section indicates that the company experienced an event that was both unusual and infrequent.	These items should usually be ignored in estimating future net income.

CHANGES IN ACCOUNTING PRINCIPLE

Ethics Note Changes in accounting principle should result in financial statements that are more informative for statement users. They should not be used to artificially improve the reported performance or financial position of the corporation.

For ease of comparison, users of financial statements expect companies to prepare such statements on a basis **consistent** with the preceding period. A change in accounting principle occurs when the principle used in the current year is different from the one used in the preceding year. An example is a change in inventory costing methods (such as FIFO to average cost). Accounting rules permit a change when management can show that the new principle is preferable to the old principle.

Companies report most changes in accounting principle retroactively.[1] That is, they report both the current period and previous periods using the new principle. As a result the same principle applies in all periods. This treatment improves the ability to compare results across years.

DECISION TOOLKIT

DECISION CHECKPOINTS	INFO NEEDED FOR DECISION	TOOL TO USE FOR DECISION	HOW TO EVALUATE RESULTS
Has the company changed any of its accounting principles?	Effect of change in accounting principle on current and prior periods.	Management indicates that the new principle is preferable to the old principle.	Examine current and prior years reported income, using new-principle basis to assess trends for estimating future income.

COMPREHENSIVE INCOME

study objective 3

Explain the concept of comprehensive income.

Most revenues, expenses, gains, and losses are included in net income. However, certain gains and losses bypass net income. Instead, companies record these items as direct adjustments to stockholders' equity. Many analysts have expressed concern about this practice because they believe it reduces the usefulness of the income statement. To address this concern, the FASB requires companies to report not only net income, but also comprehensive income. Comprehensive income includes all changes in stockholders' equity during a period except those changes resulting from investments by stockholders and distributions to stockholders.

Illustration of Comprehensive Income

Accounting standards require that companies adjust most investments in stocks and bonds up or down to their market value at the end of each accounting period. For example, assume that during 2010 Stassi Company purchased IBM stock for $10,000 as an investment. At the end of 2010 Stassi was still holding the investment, but the stock's market value was now $8,000. In this case, Stassi is required to reduce the recorded value of its IBM investment by $2,000. The $2,000 difference is an unrealized loss.

---

[1]An exception to the general rule is a change in depreciation methods. The effects of this change are reported in current and future periods. Discussion of this approach is left for more advanced courses.

Should Stassi include this $2,000 unrealized loss in net income? It depends on whether Stassi classifies the IBM stock as a trading security or an available-for-sale security. A trading security is bought and held primarily for sale in the near term to generate income on short-term price differences. Companies report unrealized losses on trading securities in the "Other expenses and losses" section of the income statement. The rationale: It is likely that the company will realize the unrealized loss (or an unrealized gain), so the company should report the loss (gain) as part of net income.

If Stassi did not purchase the investment for trading purposes, it is classified as available-for-sale. Available-for-sale securities are held with the intent of selling them sometime in the future. Companies do not include unrealized gains or losses on available-for-sale securities in net income. Instead, they report them as part of "Other comprehensive income." Other comprehensive income is not included in net income. It bypasses net income and is recorded as a direct adjustment to stockholders' equity.

Format

One format for reporting comprehensive income is to report a combined statement of income and comprehensive income.[2] For example, assuming that Stassi Company has a net income of $300,000, the unrealized loss would be reported below net income as follows.

STASSI CORPORATION Combined Statement of Income and Comprehensive Income (partial)	
Net income	$300,000
Unrealized loss on available-for-sale securities	2,000
Comprehensive income	$298,000

Illustration 13-5 Lower portion of combined statement of income and comprehensive income

Companies also report the unrealized loss on available-for-sale securities as a separate component of stockholders' equity. To illustrate, assume Stassi Corporation has common stock of $3,000,000, retained earnings of $1,500,000, and an unrealized loss on available-for-sale securities of $2,000. Illustration 13-6 shows the balance sheet presentation of the unrealized loss.

STASSI CORPORATION Balance Sheet (partial)	
Stockholders' equity	
Common stock	$3,000,000
Retained earnings	1,500,000
Total paid-in capital and retained earnings	4,500,000
Less: Unrealized loss on available-for-sale securities	(2,000)
Total stockholders' equity	$4,498,000

Illustration 13-6 Unrealized loss in stockholders' equity section

---

[2]Computation of comprehensive income is sometimes shown in a separate statement of comprehensive income or as a section in the stockholders' equity statement.

Note that the presentation of the loss is similar to the presentation of the cost of treasury stock in the stockholders' equity section. (An unrealized gain would be added in this section of the balance sheet.) Reporting the unrealized gain or loss in the stockholders' equity section serves two important purposes: (1) It reduces the volatility of net income due to fluctuations in fair value, and (2) it informs the financial statement user of the gain or loss that would occur if the company sold the securities at fair value.

Complete Income Statement

The income statement for Pace Corporation in Illustration 13-7 presents the types of items found on this statement, such as net sales, cost of goods sold, operating expenses, and income taxes. In addition, it shows how companies report irregular items and comprehensive income (highlighted in red).

Illustration 13-7
Complete income statement

PACE CORPORATION Income Statement and Statement of Comprehensive Income For the Year Ended December 31, 2010		
Net sales		$440,000
Cost of goods sold		260,000
Gross profit		180,000
Operating expenses		110,000
Income from operations		70,000
Other revenues and gains	$ 5,600	
Other expenses and losses	(9,600)	(4,000)
Income before income taxes		66,000
Income tax expense ($66,000 × 30%)		19,800
Income before irregular items		46,200
Discontinued operations: Gain on disposal of		
Plastics Division, net of $15,000 income taxes		
($50,000 × 30%)		35,000
Extraordinary item: Tornado loss, net of income		
tax savings $18,000 ($60,000 × 30%)		(42,000)
Net income		39,200
Add: Unrealized gain on available-for-sale securities		10,000
Comprehensive income		$ 49,200

CONCLUDING REMARKS

We have shown that the computation of the correct net income number can be elusive. In assessing the future prospects of a company, some investors focus on income from operations and therefore ignore all irregular and other items. Others use measures such as net income, comprehensive income, or some modified version of one of these amounts.

before you go on...

IRREGULAR ITEMS

Do it! In its draft 2010 income statement, AIR Corporation reports income before income taxes $400,000, extraordinary loss due to earthquake $100,000, income taxes $120,000 (not including irregular items), and loss on disposal of discontinued flower division $140,000. The income tax rate is 30%. Prepare a correct income statement, beginning with income before income taxes.

Solution

AIR CORPORATION **Income Statement (partial)**	
Income before income taxes	$400,000
Income tax expense	120,000
Income before irregular items	280,000
Discontinued operations	
Loss on disposal of discontinued flower division, net of $42,000 tax saving	98,000
Extraordinary earthquake loss net of $30,000 tax saving	70,000
Net income	$112,000

- Recall that a loss is extraordinary if it is both unusual and infrequent.
- Disclose the income tax effect of each component of income, beginning with income before any irregular items.
- Show discontinued operations before extraordinary items.

✓ **the navigator**

Comparative Analysis

As indicated, in assessing the financial performance of a company, investors are interested in the core or sustainable earnings of a company. In addition, investors are interested in making comparisons from period to period. Throughout this book, we have relied on three types of comparisons to improve the decision usefulness of financial information.

1. **Intracompany basis.** Comparisons within a company are often useful to detect changes in financial relationships and significant trends. For example, a comparison of Kellogg's current year's cash amount with the prior year's cash amount shows either an increase or a decrease. Likewise, a comparison of Kellogg's year-end cash amount with the amount of its total assets at year-end shows the proportion of total assets in the form of cash.

2. **Intercompany basis.** Comparisons with other companies provide insight into a company's competitive position. For example, investors can compare Kellogg's total sales for the year with the total sales of its competitors in the breakfast cereal area, such as General Mills.

3. **Industry averages.** Comparisons with industry averages provide information about a company's relative position within the industry. For example, financial statement readers can compare Kellogg's financial data with the averages for its industry compiled by financial ratings organizations such as Dun & Bradstreet, Moody's, and Standard & Poor's, or with information provided on the Internet by organizations such as Yahoo on its financial site.

International Note As more countries adopt international accounting standards, the ability of analysts to compare companies from different countries should improve. However, international standards are open to widely varying interpretations. In addition, some countries adopt international standards "with modifications." As a consequence, most cross-country comparisons are still not as transparent as within-country comparisons.

We use three basic tools in financial statement analysis to highlight the significance of financial statement data:

1. Horizontal analysis
2. Vertical analysis
3. Ratio analysis

In previous chapters we relied primarily on ratio analysis, supplemented with some basic horizontal and vertical analysis. In the remainder of this section, we introduce more formal forms of horizontal and vertical analysis. In the next section we review ratio analysis in some detail.

HORIZONTAL ANALYSIS

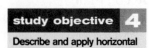

study objective **4**

Describe and apply horizontal analysis.

Horizontal analysis, also known as trend analysis, is a technique for evaluating a series of financial statement data over a period of time. Its purpose is to determine the increase or decrease that has taken place, expressed as either an amount or a percentage. For example, here are recent net sales figures (in millions) of Kellogg Company:

2007	2006	2005	2004	2003
$11,776	$10,907	$10,177	$9,614	$8,812

If we assume that 2003 is the base year, we can measure all percentage increases or decreases relative to this base-period amount with the formula shown in Illustration 13-8.

Illustration 13-8
Horizontal analysis–
Computation of changes since base period

$$\text{Change Since Base Period} = \frac{\text{Current-Year Amount} - \text{Base-Year Amount}}{\text{Base-Year Amount}}$$

For example, we can determine that net sales for Kellogg Company increased approximately 9.1% [($9,614 − $8,812) ÷ $8,812] from 2003 to 2004. Similarly, we can also determine that net sales increased by 33.6% [($11,776 − $8,812) ÷ $8,812] from 2003 to 2007.

Alternatively, we can express current-year sales as a percentage of the base period. To do so, we would divide the current-year amount by the base-year amount, as shown in Illustration 13-9.

Illustration 13-9
Horizontal analysis–
Computation of current year in relation to base year

$$\text{Current Results in Relation to Base Period} = \frac{\text{Current-Year Amount}}{\text{Base-Year Amount}}$$

Current-period sales expressed as a percentage of the base period for each of the five years, using 2003 as the base period, are shown in Illustration 13-10.

Illustration 13-10
Horizontal analysis of net sales

KELLOGG COMPANY
Net Sales (in millions)
Base Period 2003

2007	2006	2005	2004	2003
$11,776	$10,907	$10,177	$9,614	$8,812
133.64%	123.77%	115.49%	109.10%	100%

The large increase in net sales during 2004 would raise questions regarding possible reasons for such a significant change. Kellogg's 2004 notes to the financial statements explain that "the Company completed its acquisition of Keebler Foods Company" during 2004. This major acquisition would help explain the increase in sales highlighted by horizontal analysis.

To further illustrate horizontal analysis, we use the financial statements of Kellogg Company. Its two-year condensed balance sheets for 2007 and 2006, showing dollar and percentage changes, are presented in Illustration 13-11.

KELLOGG COMPANY, INC. Condensed Balance Sheets December 31 (in millions)				
			Increase (Decrease) during 2007	
Assets	**2007**	**2006**	**Amount**	**Percent**
Current assets	$ 2,717	$ 2,427	$ 290	11.9
Property assets (net)	2,990	2,816	174	6.2
Other assets	5,690	5,471	219	4.0
Total assets	$11,397	$10,714	$ 683	6.4
Liabilities and Stockholders' Equity				
Current liabilities	$ 4,044	$ 4,020	$ 24	.6
Long-term liabilities	4,827	4,625	202	4.4
Total liabilities	8,871	8,645	226	2.6
Stockholders' equity				
Common stock	493	397	96	24.2
Retained earnings	3,390	2,584	806	31.2
Treasury stock (cost)	(1,357)	(912)	(445)	48.8
Total stockholders' equity	2,526	2,069	457	22.1
Total liabilities and stockholders' equity	$11,397	$10,714	$ 683	6.4

Illustration 13-11
Horizontal analysis of a balance sheet

The comparative balance sheet shows that a number of changes occurred in Kellogg's financial position from 2006 to 2007. In the assets section, current assets increased $290 million, or 11.9% ($290 ÷ $2,427), and property assets (net) increased $174 million, or 6.2%. Other assets increased $219 million, or 4.0%. In the liabilities section, current liabilities increased $24 million, or 0.6%, while long-term liabilities increased $202 million, or 4.4%. In the stockholders' equity section, we find that retained earnings increased $806 million, or 31.2%.

Illustration 13-12 presents a two-year comparative income statement of Kellogg Company for 2007 and 2006, showing dollar and percentage changes.

Helpful Hint When using horizontal analysis, be sure to examine both dollar amount changes and percentage changes. It is not necessarily bad if a company's earnings are growing at a declining rate. The **amount** of increase may be the same as or more than the base year, but the **percentage** change may be less because the base is greater each year.

KELLOGG COMPANY, INC. Condensed Income Statements For the Years Ended December 31 (in millions)				
			Increase (Decrease) during 2007	
	2007	**2006**	**Amount**	**Percent**
Net sales	$11,776	$10,907	$869	8.0
Cost of goods sold	6,597	6,082	515	8.5
Gross profit	5,179	4,825	354	7.3
Selling and administrative expenses	3,311	3,059	252	8.2
Income from operations	1,868	1,766	102	5.8
Interest expense	319	307	12	3.9
Other income (expense), net	(2)	13	(15)	(115.4)
Income before income taxes	1,547	1,472	75	5.1
Income tax expense	444	468	(24)	(5.1)
Net income	$ 1,103	$ 1,004	$ 99	9.9

Illustration 13-12
Horizontal analysis of an income statement

Helpful Hint Note that, in a horizontal analysis, while the amount column is additive (the total is $99 million), the percentage column is not additive (9.9% is **not a total**).

Horizontal analysis of the income statements shows the following changes: Net sales increased $869 million, or 8.0% ($869 ÷ $10,907). Cost of goods sold increased $515 million, or 8.5% ($515 ÷ $6,082). Selling and administrative expenses increased $252 million, or 8.2% ($252 ÷ $3,059). Overall, gross profit increased 7.3% and net income increased 9.9%. The increase in net income can be attributed to the increase in net sales and a decrease in income tax expense.

The measurement of changes from period to period in percentages is relatively straightforward and quite useful. However, complications can result in making the computations. If an item has no value in a base year or preceding year and a value in the next year, no percentage change can be computed. Likewise, no percentage change can be computed if a negative amount appears in the base or preceding period and a positive amount exists the following year.

DECISION TOOLKIT

DECISION CHECKPOINTS	INFO NEEDED FOR DECISION	TOOL TO USE FOR DECISION	HOW TO EVALUATE RESULTS
How do the company's financial position and operating results compare with those of the previous period?	Income statement and balance sheet	Comparative financial statements should be prepared over at least two years, with the first year reported being the base year. Changes in each line item relative to the base year should be presented both by amount and by percentage. This is called horizontal analysis.	Significant changes should be investigated to determine the reason for the change.

before you go on...

HORIZONTAL ANALYSIS

Summary financial information for Rosepatch Company is as follows.

	December 31, 2010	December 31, 2009
Current assets	$234,000	$180,000
Plant assets (net)	756,000	420,000
Total assets	$990,000	$600,000

Compute the amount and percentage changes in 2010 using horizontal analysis, assuming 2009 is the base year.

Action Plan

• Find the percentage change by dividing the amount of the increase by the 2009 amount (base year).

Solution

	Increase in 2010	
	Amount	Percent
Current assets	$ 54,000	30% [($234,000 − $180,000) ÷ $180,000]
Plant assets (net)	336,000	80% [($756,000 − $420,000) ÷ $420,000]
Total assets	$390,000	65% [($990,000 − $600,000) ÷ $600,000]

VERTICAL ANALYSIS

study objective 5
Describe and apply vertical analysis.

Vertical analysis, also called common-size analysis, is a technique for evaluating financial statement data that expresses each item in a financial statement as a **percent of a base amount**. For example, on a balance sheet we might say that current assets are 22% of total assets (total assets being the base amount). Or on an income statement we might say that selling expenses are 16% of net sales (net sales being the base amount).

Presented in Illustration 13-13 is the comparative balance sheet of Kellogg for 2007 and 2006, analyzed vertically. The base for the asset items is **total assets**, and the base for the liability and stockholders' equity items is **total liabilities and stockholders' equity**.

Illustration 13-13
Vertical analysis of a balance sheet

KELLOGG COMPANY, INC.
Condensed Balance Sheets
December 31 (in millions)

	2007		2006	
Assets	**Amount**	**Percent***	**Amount**	**Percent***
Current assets	$ 2,717	23.8	$ 2,427	22.6
Property assets (net)	2,990	26.2	2,816	26.3
Other assets	5,690	50.0	5,471	51.1
Total assets	$11,397	100.0	$10,714	100.0
Liabilities and Stockholders' Equity				
Current liabilities	$ 4,044	35.5	$ 4,020	37.5
Long-term liabilities	4,827	42.4	4,625	43.2
Total liabilities	8,871	77.9	8,645	80.7
Stockholders' equity				
Common stock	493	4.3	397	3.7
Retained earnings	3,390	29.7	2,584	24.1
Treasury stock (cost)	(1,357)	(11.9)	(912)	(8.5)
Total stockholders' equity	2,526	22.1	2,069	19.3
Total liabilities and stockholders' equity	$11,397	100.0	$10,714	100.0

*Numbers have been rounded to total 100%.

In addition to showing the relative size of each category on the balance sheet, vertical analysis may show the percentage change in the individual asset, liability, and stockholders' equity items. In this case, current assets increased $290 million from 2006 to 2007, and they increased from 22.6% to 23.8% of total assets. Property assets (net) decreased from 26.3% to 26.2% of total assets. Other assets decreased from 51.1% to 50.0% of total assets. Also, retained earnings increased by $806 million from 2006 to 2007, and total stockholders' equity increased from 19.3% to 22.1% of total liabilities and stockholders' equity. This switch to a higher percentage of equity financing has two causes: First, while total liabilities increased by $226 million, the percentage of liabilities declined from 80.7% to 77.9% of total liabilities and stockholders' equity. Second, retained earnings increased by $806 million, going from 24.1% to 29.7% of total liabilities and stockholders' equity. Thus, the company shifted toward equity financing by relying less on debt and by increasing the amount of retained earnings.

Vertical analysis of the comparative income statements of Kellogg, shown in Illustration 13-14 (page 672), reveals that cost of goods sold **as a percentage of net sales** increased from 55.8% to 56.0%, and selling and administrative expenses increased from 28.0% to 28.1%. Net income as a percent of net sales increased from 9.1% to 9.4%. Kellogg's increase in net income as a percentage of sales is due primarily to the decrease in interest expense and income tax expense as a percent of sales.

Illustration 13-14
Vertical analysis of an
income statement

KELLOGG COMPANY, INC.
Condensed Income Statements
For the Years Ended December 31 (in millions)

	2007		2006	
	Amount	Percent*	Amount	Percent*
Net sales	$11,776	100.0	$10,907	100.0
Cost of goods sold	6,597	56.0	6,082	55.8
Gross profit	5,179	44.0	4,825	44.2
Selling and administrative expenses	3,311	28.1	3,059	28.0
Income from operations	1,868	15.9	1,766	16.2
Interest expense	319	2.7	307	2.8
Other income (expense), net	(2)	.0	13	.0
Income before income taxes	1,547	13.2	1,472	13.4
Income tax expense	444	3.8	468	4.3
Net income	$ 1,103	9.4	$ 1,004	9.1

*Numbers have been rounded to total 100%.

Vertical analysis also enables you to compare companies of different sizes. For example, one of Kellogg's main competitors is General Mills. Using vertical analysis, we can more meaningfully compare the condensed income statements of Kellogg and General Mills, as shown in Illustration 13-15.

Illustration 13-15
Intercompany comparison
by vertical analysis

CONDENSED INCOME STATEMENTS
For the Year Ended December 31, 2007
(in millions)

	Kellogg Company, Inc.		General Mills, Inc.	
	Amount	Percent*	Amount	Percent*
Net sales	$11,776	100.0	$12,442	100.0
Cost of goods sold	6,597	56.0	7,955	63.9
Gross profit	5,179	44.0	4,487	36.1
Selling and administrative expenses	3,311	28.1	2,390	19.2
Nonrecurring charges	0	—	39	.3
Income from operations	1,868	15.9	2,058	16.6
Other expenses and revenues (including income taxes)	765	6.5	914	7.4
Net income	$ 1,103	9.4	$ 1,144	9.2

*Numbers have been rounded to total 100%.

Although Kellogg's net sales are less than those of General Mills, vertical analysis eliminates the impact of this size difference for our analysis. Kellogg has a higher gross profit percentage 44.0%, compared to 36.1% for General Mills, but Kellogg's selling and administrative expenses are 28.1% of net sales, while those of General Mills are 19.2% of net sales. Looking at net income, we see that the companies report similar percentages: Kellogg's net income as a percentage of net sales is 9.4%, compared to 9.2% for General Mills.

DECISION TOOLKIT

DECISION CHECKPOINTS	INFO NEEDED FOR DECISION	TOOL TO USE FOR DECISION	HOW TO EVALUATE RESULTS
How do the relationships between items in this year's financial statements compare with those of last year or those of competitors?	Income statement and balance sheet	Each line item on the income statement should be presented as a percentage of net sales, and each line item on the balance sheet should be presented as a percentage of total assets or total liabilities and stockholders' equity. These percentages should be investigated for differences either across years in the same company or in the same year across different companies. This is called vertical analysis.	Any significant differences either across years or between companies should be investigated to determine the cause.

Ratio Analysis

In previous chapters we presented many ratios used for evaluating the financial health and performance of a company. Here we provide a summary listing of those ratios. (Page references to prior discussions are provided if you feel you need to review any individual ratios.) The appendix to this chapter provides an example of a comprehensive financial analysis employing these ratios.

> **study objective 6**
>
> Identify and compute ratios used in analyzing a company's liquidity, solvency, and profitability.

LIQUIDITY RATIOS

Liquidity ratios (Illustration 13-16) measure the short-term ability of the company to pay its maturing obligations and to meet unexpected needs for cash. Short-term creditors such as bankers and suppliers are particularly interested in assessing liquidity.

Illustration 13-16
Summary of liquidity ratios

Liquidity Ratios		
Working capital	Current assets − Current liabilities	p. 59
Current ratio	$\dfrac{\text{Current assets}}{\text{Current liabilities}}$	p. 59
Current cash debt coverage ratio	$\dfrac{\text{Cash provided by operations}}{\text{Average current liabilities}}$	p. 621
Inventory turnover ratio	$\dfrac{\text{Cost of goods sold}}{\text{Average inventory}}$	p. 290
Days in inventory	$\dfrac{\text{365 days}}{\text{Inventory turnover ratio}}$	p. 290
Receivables turnover ratio	$\dfrac{\text{Net credit sales}}{\text{Average net receivables}}$	p. 402
Average collection period	$\dfrac{\text{365 days}}{\text{Receivables turnover ratio}}$	p. 402

SOLVENCY RATIOS

Solvency ratios (Illustration 13-17) measure the ability of the company to survive over a long period of time. Long-term creditors and stockholders are interested in a company's long-run solvency, particularly its ability to pay interest as it comes due and to repay the balance of debt at its maturity.

Illustration 13-17
Summary of solvency ratios

Solvency Ratios		
Debt to total assets ratio	$\dfrac{\text{Total liabilities}}{\text{Total assets}}$	p. 60
Cash debt coverage ratio	$\dfrac{\text{Cash provided by operations}}{\text{Average total liabilities}}$	p. 622
Times interest earned ratio	$\dfrac{\text{Net income + Interest expense + Tax expense}}{\text{Interest expense}}$	p. 507
Free cash flow	$\dfrac{\text{Cash provided by}}{\text{operations}} - \dfrac{\text{Capital}}{\text{expenditures}} - \dfrac{\text{Cash}}{\text{dividends}}$	p. 62

PROFITABILITY RATIOS

Profitability ratios (Illustration 13-18) measure the income or operating success of a company for a given period of time. A company's income, or lack of it, affects its ability to obtain debt and equity financing, its liquidity position,

Illustration 13-18
Summary of profitability ratios

Profitability Ratios		
Earnings per share	$\dfrac{\text{Net income} - \text{Preferred stock dividends}}{\text{Average common shares outstanding}}$	p. 55
Price-earnings ratio	$\dfrac{\text{Stock price per share}}{\text{Earnings per share}}$	p. 676
Gross profit rate	$\dfrac{\text{Gross profit}}{\text{Net sales}}$	p. 241
Profit margin ratio	$\dfrac{\text{Net income}}{\text{Net sales}}$	p. 243
Return on assets ratio	$\dfrac{\text{Net income}}{\text{Average total assets}}$	p. 448
Asset turnover ratio	$\dfrac{\text{Net sales}}{\text{Average total assets}}$	p. 450
Payout ratio	$\dfrac{\text{Cash dividends declared on common stock}}{\text{Net income}}$	p. 572
Return on common stockholders' equity ratio	$\dfrac{\text{Net income} - \text{Preferred stock dividends}}{\text{Average common stockholders' equity}}$	p. 573

 Investor Insight

The apparent simplicity of the current ratio can have real-world limitations because adding equal amounts to both the numerator and the denominator causes the ratio to decrease.

Assume, for example, that a company has $2,000,000 of current assets and $1,000,000 of current liabilities; its current ratio is 2:1. If it purchases $1,000,000 of inventory on account, it will have $3,000,000 of current assets and $2,000,000 of current liabilities; its current ratio decreases to 1.5:1. If, instead, the company pays off $500,000 of its current liabilities, it will have $1,500,000 of current assets and $500,000 of current liabilities; its current ratio increases to 3:1. Thus, any trend analysis should be done with care because the ratio is susceptible to quick changes and is easily influenced by management.

 How might management influence a company's current ratio?

and its ability to grow. As a consequence, creditors and investors alike are interested in evaluating profitability. Profitability is frequently used as the ultimate test of management's operating effectiveness.

Quality of Earnings

In evaluating the financial performance of a company, the quality of a company's earnings is of extreme importance to analysts. A company that has a high quality of earnings provides full and transparent information that will not confuse or mislead users of the financial statements.

study objective **7**
Understand the concept of quality of earnings.

The issue of quality of earnings has taken on increasing importance because recent accounting scandals suggest that some companies are spending too much time managing their income and not enough time managing their business. Here are some of the factors affecting quality of earnings.

ALTERNATIVE ACCOUNTING METHODS

Variations among companies in the application of generally accepted accounting principles may hamper comparability and reduce quality of earnings. For example, one company may use the FIFO method of inventory costing, while another company in the same industry may use LIFO. If inventory is a significant asset to both companies, it is unlikely that their current ratios are comparable. For example, if General Motors Corporation had used FIFO instead of LIFO for inventory valuation, its inventories in a recent year would have been 26% higher, which significantly affects the current ratio (and other ratios as well).

In addition to differences in inventory costing methods, differences also exist in reporting such items as depreciation, and amortization. Although these differences in accounting methods might be detectable from reading the notes to the financial statements, adjusting the financial data to compensate for the different methods is often difficult, if not impossible.

PRO FORMA INCOME

Companies whose stock is publicly traded are required to present their income statement following generally accepted accounting principles (GAAP). In recent years, many companies have been also reporting a second measure of income, called pro forma income. Pro forma income usually excludes items that the company thinks are unusual or nonrecurring. For example, in a recent year, Cisco Systems (a high-tech company) reported a quarterly net loss under GAAP of $2.7 billion. Cisco reported pro forma income for the same quarter as a profit of $230 million. This large difference in profits between GAAP income numbers and pro forma income is not unusual these days. For example, during one recent 9-month period the 100 largest companies on the Nasdaq stock exchange reported a total pro forma income of $19.1 billion, but a total loss as measured by GAAP of $82.3 billion—a difference of about $100 billion!

To compute pro forma income, companies generally can exclude any items they deem inappropriate for measuring their performance. Many analysts and investors are critical of the practice of using pro forma income because these numbers often make companies look better than they really are. As the financial press noted, pro forma numbers might be called "earnings before bad stuff." Companies, on the other hand, argue that pro forma numbers more clearly indicate sustainable income because they exclude unusual and nonrecurring expenses. "Cisco's technique gives readers of financial statements a clear picture of Cisco's normal business activities," the company said in a statement issued in response to questions about its pro forma income accounting.

Recently, the SEC provided some guidance on how companies should present pro forma information. Stay tuned: Everyone seems to agree that pro forma numbers can be useful if they provide insights into determining a company's sustainable income. However, many companies have abused the flexibility that pro forma numbers allow and have used the measure as a way to put their companies in a more favorable light.

IMPROPER RECOGNITION

Because some managers have felt pressure from Wall Street to continually increase earnings, they have manipulated the earnings numbers to meet these expectations. The most common abuse is the improper recognition of revenue. One practice that companies are using is *channel stuffing*: Offering deep discounts on their products to customers, companies encourage their customers to buy early (stuff the channel) rather than later. This lets the company report good earnings in the current period, but it often leads to a disaster in subsequent periods because customers have no need for additional goods. To illustrate, Bristol-Myers Squibb recently indicated that it used sales incentives to encourage wholesalers to buy more drugs than needed to meet patients' demands. As a result, the company had to issue revised financial statements showing corrected revenues and income.

Another practice is the improper capitalization of operating expenses. The classic case is WorldCom. It capitalized over $7 billion of operating expenses so that it would report positive net income. In other situations, companies fail to report all their liabilities. Enron had promised to make payments on certain contracts if financial difficulty developed, but these guarantees were not reported as liabilities. In addition, disclosure was so lacking in transparency that it was impossible to understand what was happening at the company.

PRICE-EARNINGS RATIO

Earnings per share is net income available to common stockholders divided by the average number of common shares outstanding. The market value of a company's stock changes based on investors' expectations about a company's future earnings per share. In order to make a meaningful comparison of market values and earnings across firms, investors calculate the price-earnings (P-E) ratio. The P-E ratio divides the market price of a share of common stock by earnings per share.

Illustration 13-19
Formula for price-earnings (P-E) ratio

$$\text{Price-Earnings (P-E) Ratio} = \frac{\text{Stock Price per Share}}{\text{Earnings per Share}}$$

The P-E ratio reflects investors' assessment of a company's future earnings. The ratio of price to earnings will be higher if investors think that earnings will increase substantially in the future and therefore are willing to pay more per share of stock. A low price-earnings ratio often signifies that investors think the company's future earnings will not be strong. In addition, sometimes a low P-E ratio reflects the market's belief that a company has poor-quality earnings.

To illustrate, assume that two identical companies each have earnings per share of $5, but that one of the companies manipulated its accounting numbers to achieve the $5 figure. If investors perceive that one firm has lower-quality earnings, this perception will be reflected in a lower stock price, and consequently, a lower P-E.

Illustration 13-20 shows earnings per share and P-E ratios for five companies for 2007. Note the difference in the P-E ratio of General Electric versus Google Inc.

Illustration 13-20
Earnings per share and P-E ratios of various companies

Company	Earnings Per Share	Price-Earnings Ratio
Southwest Airlines	$ 0.44	18.6
Google Inc.	13.30	30.8
General Electric	2.17	13.2
Merck	1.49	14.6
Nike	3.70	15.9

Accounting Across the Organization

Many company managers preparing their annual reports are piling on the paper in order to ease Enron-type worries on the part of investors. Natural-gas producer Williams Companies, Inc. turned out an eye-glazing annual report 1,234 pages in length. Nortel Networks Corporation added an extra two dozen pages to its annual report. Other companies have followed suit.

The trend to fuller disclosure has been a long time coming, observers say. But they caution that more paper does not necessarily mean more information that the average investor will understand. In addition, it is important to remember that annual reports are just one piece of the puzzle as to how companies present information to decision-makers.

Source: Elizabeth Church, "No Item Too Small as Firms Cave to Enron Disclosure Craze," *The (Toronto) Globe and Mail* (April 1, 2002), p. B1.

 Why might adding extra pages to the annual report not be beneficial to investors and analysts? What should be management's overriding objective in financial reporting?

---

before you go on...

Do it!

Match each of the following terms with the phrase that it best matches.

Comprehensive income   Vertical analysis
Quality of earnings   Pro forma income
Solvency ratio   Extraordinary items

QUALITY OF EARNINGS, FINANCIAL STATEMENT ANALYSIS

1. Measures the ability of the company to survive over a long period of time.
2. Usually excludes items that a company thinks are unusual or non-recurring.
3. Includes all changes in stockholders' equity during a period except those resulting from investments by stockholders and distributions to stockholders.
4. Indicates the level of full and transparent information provided to users of the financial statements.
5. Describes events and transactions that are unusual in nature and infrequent in occurrence.
6. Expresses each item within a financial statement as a percent of a base amount.

Solution

1. Solvency ratio: Measures the ability of the company to survive over a long period of time.
2. Pro forma income: Usually excludes items that a company thinks are unusual or non-recurring.
3. Comprehensive income: Includes all changes in stockholders' equity during a period except those resulting from investments by stockholders and distributions to stockholders.
4. Quality of earnings: Indicates the level of full and transparent information provided to users of the financial statements.
5. Extraordinary items: Describes events and transactions that are unusual in nature and infrequent in occurrence.
6. Vertical analysis: Expresses each item within a financial statement as a percent of a base amount.

Action Plan

• Develop a sound understanding of basic methods used for financial reporting.
• Understand the use of fundamental analysis techniques.

the navigator

USING THE DECISION TOOLKIT

In analyzing a company, you should always investigate an extended period of time in order to determine whether the condition and performance of the company are changing. The condensed financial statements of Kellogg Company for 2005 and 2004 are presented here. (The appendix to this chapter provides a complete analysis of Kellogg's 2007 and 2006 financial statements.)

KELLOGG COMPANY, INC.
Balance Sheets
December 31 (in millions)

Assets	2005	2004
Current assets		
Cash and short-term investments	$ 219.1	$ 417.4
Accounts receivable (net)	879.1	776.4
Inventories	717.0	681.0
Other current assets	381.3	247.0
Total current assets	2,196.5	2,121.8
Property (net)	2,648.4	2,715.1
Other assets	5,729.6	5,725.0
Total assets	$10,574.5	$10,561.9
Liabilities and Stockholders' Equity		
Current liabilities	$ 3,162.8	$ 2,846.0
Long-term liabilities	5,128.0	5,458.7
Stockholders' equity—common	2,283.7	2,257.2
Total liabilities and stockholders' equity	$10,574.5	$10,561.9

KELLOGG COMPANY, INC.
Condensed Income Statements
For the Years Ended December 31
(in millions)

	2005	2004
Net sales	$10,177.2	$9,613.9
Cost of goods sold	5,611.6	5,298.7
Gross profit	4,565.6	4,315.2
Selling and administrative expenses	2,815.3	2,634.1
Income from operations	1,750.3	1,681.1
Interest expense	300.3	308.6
Other income (expense), net	(24.9)	(6.6)
Income before income taxes	1,425.1	1,365.9
Income tax expense	444.7	475.3
Net income	$ 980.4	$ 890.6

Instructions

Compute the following ratios for Kellogg for 2005 and 2004 and discuss your findings.

1. Liquidity:
   (a) Current ratio.
   (b) Inventory turnover ratio. (Inventory on December 31, 2003, was $649.8 million.)

2. Solvency:
   (a) Debt to total assets ratio.
   (b) Times interest earned ratio.

3. Profitability:
   (a) Return on common stockholders' equity ratio. (Stockholders' equity on December 31, 2003, was $1,443.2 million.)
   (b) Return on assets ratio. (Assets on December 31, 2003, were $10,142.7 million.)
   (c) Profit margin ratio.

Solution

1. Liquidity
   (a) Current ratio:

   $$2005: \frac{\$2,196.5}{\$3,162.8} = .69:1 \qquad 2004: \frac{\$2,121.8}{\$2,846} = .75:1$$

   (b) Inventory turnover ratio:

   $$2005: \frac{\$5,611.6}{(\$717.0 + \$681.0)/2} = 8.0 \text{ times}$$

   $$2004: \frac{\$5,298.7}{(\$681.0 + \$649.8)/2} = 8.0 \text{ times}$$

We see that between 2004 and 2005 the current ratio decreased. The inventory turnover ratio was constant. The current ratio indicates that the company was less liquid in 2005.

2. Solvency
   (a) Debt to total assets ratio:

   $$2005: \frac{\$8,290.8}{\$10,574.5} = 78\% \qquad 2004: \frac{\$8,304.7}{\$10,561.9} = 79\%$$

   (b) Times interest earned ratio:

   $$2005: \frac{\$980.4 + \$444.7 + \$300.3}{\$300.3} = 5.7 \text{ times}$$

   $$2004: \frac{\$890.6 + \$475.3 + \$308.6}{\$308.6} = 5.4 \text{ times}$$

Kellogg's solvency as measured by the debt to total assets ratio improved slightly in 2005. We also can see that the times interest earned ratio increased.

3. Profitability
   (a) Return on common stockholders' equity ratio:

   $$2005: \frac{\$980.4}{(\$2,283.7 + \$2,257.2)/2} = 43\%$$

   $$2004: \frac{\$890.6}{(\$2,257.2 + \$1,443.2)/2} = 48\%$$

   (b) Return on assets ratio:

   $$2005: \frac{\$980.4}{(\$10,574.5 + \$10,561.9)/2} = 9.3\%$$

   $$2004: \frac{\$890.6}{(\$10,561.9 + \$10,142.7)/2} = 8.6\%$$

   (c) Profit margin ratio:

   $$2005: \frac{\$980.4}{\$10,177.2} = 9.6\% \qquad 2004: \frac{\$890.6}{\$9,613.9} = 9.3\%$$

Kellogg's return on common stockholders' equity ratio decreased even though there was an increase in both its return on assets and its profit margin ratios.

Summary of Study Objectives

1 **Understand the concept of sustainable income.** Sustainable income refers to a company's ability to sustain its profits from operations.

2 **Indicate how irregular items are presented.** Irregular items—discontinued operations and extraordinary items—are presented on the income statement net of tax below "Income before irregular items" to highlight their unusual nature. Changes in accounting principle are reported retroactively.

3 **Explain the concept of comprehensive income.** Comprehensive income includes all changes in stockholders' equity during a period except those resulting from investments by stockholders and distributions to stockholders. "Other comprehensive income" is added to net income to arrive at comprehensive income.

4 **Describe and apply horizontal analysis.** Horizontal analysis is a technique for evaluating a series of data over a period of time to determine the increase or decrease that has taken place, expressed as either an amount or a percentage.

5 **Describe and apply vertical analysis.** Vertical analysis is a technique that expresses each item in a financial statement as a percentage of a relevant total or a base amount.

6 **Identify and compute ratios used in analyzing a company's liquidity, solvency, and profitability.** Financial ratios are provided in Illustration 13-16 (liquidity), Illustration 13-17 (solvency), and Illustration 13-18 (profitability).

7 **Understand the concept of quality of earnings.** A high quality of earnings provides full and transparent information that will not confuse or mislead users of the financial statements. Issues related to quality of earnings are (1) alternative accounting methods, (2) pro forma income, and (3) improper recognition. The price-earnings (P-E) ratio reflects investors' assessment of a company's future earnings potential.

DECISION TOOLKIT   A SUMMARY

DECISION CHECKPOINTS	INFO NEEDED FOR DECISION	TOOL TO USE FOR DECISION	HOW TO EVALUATE RESULTS
Has the company sold any major components of its business?	Discontinued operations section of income statement	Anything reported in this section indicates that the company has discontinued a major component of its business.	If a major component has been discontinued, its results during the current period should not be included in estimates of future net income.
Has the company experienced any extraordinary events or transactions?	Extraordinary item section of income statement	Anything reported in this section indicates that the company experienced an event that was both unusual and infrequent.	These items should usually be ignored in estimating future net income.
Has the company changed any of its accounting principles?	Effect of change in accounting principle on current and prior periods.	Management indicates that the new principle is preferable to the old principle.	Examine current and prior years reported income, using new-principle basis to assess trends for estimating future income.
How do the company's financial position and operating results compare with those of the previous period?	Income statement and balance sheet	Comparative financial statements should be prepared over at least two years, with the first year reported being the base year. Changes in each line item relative to the base year should be presented both by amount and by percentage. This is called horizontal analysis.	Significant changes should be investigated to determine the reason for the change.

DECISION CHECKPOINTS	INFO NEEDED FOR DECISION	TOOL TO USE FOR DECISION	HOW TO EVALUATE RESULTS
How do the relationships between items in this year's financial statements compare with those of last year or those of competitors?	Income statement and balance sheet	Each line item on the income statement should be presented as a percentage of net sales, and each line item on the balance sheet should be presented as a percentage of total assets or total liabilities and stockholders' equity. These percentages should be investigated for differences either across years in the same company or in the same year across different companies. This is called vertical analysis.	Any significant differences either across years or between companies should be investigated to determine the cause.

appendix

Comprehensive Illustration of Ratio Analysis

In previous chapters we presented many ratios used for evaluating the financial health and performance of a company. In this appendix we provide a comprehensive review of those ratios and discuss some important relationships among them. Since earlier chapters demonstrated the calculation of each of these ratios, in this chapter we instead focus on their interpretation. Page references to prior discussions point you to any individual ratios you feel you need to review.

We used the financial information in Illustrations 13A-1 through 13A-4 to calculate Kellogg's 2007 ratios. You can use these data to review the computations.

KELLOGG COMPANY, INC.
Balance Sheets
December 31 (in millions)

Illustration 13A-1
Kellogg Company's balance sheet

Assets	2007	2006
Current assets		
Cash and short-term investments	$ 524	$ 411
Accounts receivable	1,026	945
Inventories	924	824
Prepaid expenses and other current assets	243	247
Total current assets	2,717	2,427
Property assets (net)	2,990	2,816
Intangibles and other assets	5,690	5,471
Total assets	$11,397	$10,714
Liabilities and Stockholders' Equity		
Current liabilities	$ 4,044	$ 4,020
Long-term liabilities	4,827	4,625
Stockholders' equity—common	2,526	2,069
Total liabilities and stockholders' equity	$11,397	$10,714

Illustration 13A-2
Kellogg Company's income statement

KELLOGG COMPANY, INC.
Condensed Income Statements
For the Years Ended December 31 (in millions)

	2007	2006
Net sales	$11,776	$10,907
Cost of goods sold	6,597	6,082
Gross profit	5,179	4,825
Selling and administrative expenses	3,311	3,059
Income from operations	1,868	1,766
Interest expense	319	307
Other income (expense), net	(2)	13
Income before income taxes	1,547	1,472
Income tax expense	444	468
Net income	$ 1,103	$ 1,004

Illustration 13A-3
Kellogg Company's statement of cash flows

KELLOGG COMPANY, INC.
Condensed Statements of Cash Flows
For the Years Ended December 31 (in millions)

	2007	2006
Cash flows from operating activities		
Cash receipts from operating activities	$ 11,695	$10,841
Cash payments for operating activities	10,192	9,431
Net cash provided by operating activities	1,503	1,410
Cash flows from investing activities		
Purchases of property, plant, and equipment	(472)	(453)
Other investing activities	(129)	8
Net cash used in investing activities	(601)	(445)
Cash flows from financing activities		
Issuance of common stock	163	218
Issuance of debt	2,179	721
Reductions of debt	(2,011)	(650)
Payment of dividends	(475)	(450)
Repurchase of common stock and other items	(644)	(628)
Net cash provided (used) by financing activities	(788)	(789)
Other	(1)	16
Increase (decrease) in cash and cash equivalents	113	192
Cash and cash equivalents at beginning of year	411	219
Cash and cash equivalents at end of year	$ 524	$ 411

Illustration 13A-4
Additional information for Kellogg Company

Additional information

	2007	2006
Average number of shares (millions)	418.7	418.5
Stock price at year-end	$52.92	$50.06

As indicated in the chapter, we can classify ratios into three types for analysis of the primary financial statements.

1. **Liquidity ratios:** Measures of the short-term ability of the company to pay its maturing obligations and to meet unexpected needs for cash.

2. **Solvency ratios:** Measures of the ability of the company to survive over a long period of time.

3. **Profitability ratios:** Measures of the income or operating success of a company for a given period of time.

As a tool of analysis, ratios can provide clues to underlying conditions that may not be apparent from an inspection of the individual components of a particular ratio. But a single ratio by itself is not very meaningful. Accordingly, in this discussion we use the three comparisons listed below.

1. **Intracompany comparisons** covering two years for Kellogg Company (using comparative financial information from Illustrations 13A-1 through 13A-4).

2. **Intercompany comparisons** using General Mills as one of Kellogg's principal competitors.

3. **Industry average comparisons** based on Reuters.com's median ratios for manufacturers of flour and other grain mill products and comparisons with other sources. For some of the ratios that we use, industry comparisons are not available. (These are denoted "na.")

LIQUIDITY RATIOS

Liquidity ratios measure the short-term ability of the enterprise to pay its maturing obligations and to meet unexpected needs for cash. Short-term creditors such as bankers and suppliers are particularly interested in assessing liquidity. The measures used to determine the enterprise's short-term debt-paying ability are the current ratio, the current cash debt coverage ratio, the receivables turnover ratio, the average collection period, the inventory turnover ratio, and average days in inventory.

1. **Current ratio.** The current ratio expresses the relationship of current assets to current liabilities, computed by dividing current assets by current liabilities. It is widely used for evaluating a company's liquidity and short-term debt-paying ability. The 2007 and 2006 current ratios for Kellogg and comparative data are shown in Illustration 13A-5.

Illustration 13A-5
Current ratio

Ratio	Formula	Indicates:	Kellogg 2007	Kellogg 2006	General Mills 2007	Industry 2007	Page in book
Current ratio	Current assets / Current liabilities	Short-term debt-paying ability	.67	.60	.52	1.41	59

What do the measures tell us? Kellogg's 2007 current ratio of .67 means that for every dollar of current liabilities, Kellogg has $0.67 of current assets. We sometimes state such ratios as .67:1 to reinforce this interpretation. Kellogg's current ratio—and therefore its liquidity—increased significantly in 2007. It is well below the industry average but above that of General Mills.

2. **Current cash debt coverage ratio.** A disadvantage of the current ratio is that it uses year-end balances of current asset and current liability accounts. These year-end balances may not represent the company's current position during most of the year. The current cash debt coverage ratio partially

corrects for this problem. It is the ratio of cash provided by operating activities to average current liabilities. Because it uses cash provided by operating activities rather than a balance at one point in time, it may provide a better representation of liquidity. Kellogg's current cash debt coverage ratio is shown in Illustration 13A-6.

Illustration 13A-6
Current cash debt coverage ratio

Ratio	Formula	Indicates:	Kellogg 2007	Kellogg 2006	General Mills 2007	Industry 2007	Page in book
Current cash debt coverage ratio	Cash provided by operations / Average current liabilities	Short-term debt-paying ability (cash basis)	.37	.39	.29	na	621

This ratio decreased slightly in 2007 for Kellogg. Is the coverage adequate? Probably so. Kellogg's operating cash flow coverage of average current liabilities is better than that of General Mills, and it approximates a commonly accepted threshold of .40. No industry comparison is available.

3. **Receivables turnover ratio.** Analysts can measure liquidity by how quickly a company converts certain assets to cash. Low values of the previous ratios can sometimes be compensated for if some of the company's current assets are highly liquid.

How liquid, for example, are the receivables? The ratio used to assess the liquidity of the receivables is the **receivables turnover ratio**, which measures the number of times, on average, a company collects receivables during the period. The receivables turnover ratio is computed by dividing net credit sales (net sales less cash sales) by average net receivables during the year. The receivables turnover ratio for Kellogg is shown in Illustration 13A-7.

Illustration 13A-7
Receivables turnover ratio

Ratio	Formula	Indicates:	Kellogg 2007	Kellogg 2006	General Mills 2007	Industry 2007	Page in book
Receivables turnover ratio	Net credit sales / Average net receivables	Liquidity of receivables	11.9	12.0	13.3	11.5	402

We have assumed that all Kellogg's sales are credit sales. The receivables turnover ratio for Kellogg declined slightly in 2007. The turnover of 11.9 times compares favorably with the industry average of 11.5 times, but is lower than General Mills's turnover of 13.3 times.

4. **Average collection period.** A popular variant of the receivables turnover ratio converts it into an **average collection period** in days. This is done by dividing the receivables turnover ratio into 365 days. The average collection period for Kellogg is shown in Illustration 13A-8.

Illustration 13A-8
Average collection period

Ratio	Formula	Indicates:	Kellogg 2007	Kellogg 2006	General Mills 2007	Industry 2007	Page in book
Average collection period	365 days / Receivables turnover ratio	Liquidity of receivables and collection success	30.7	30.4	27.4	31.7	402

Kellogg's 2007 receivables turnover of 11.9 times is divided into 365 days to obtain approximately 31 days. This means that the average collection period for receivables is about 31 days.

Analysts frequently use the average collection period to assess the effectiveness of a company's credit and collection policies. The general rule is that the collection period should not greatly exceed the credit term period (i.e., the time allowed for payment). Kellogg's average collection period is similar to those of General Mills and the industry.

5. **Inventory turnover ratio.** The inventory turnover ratio measures the number of times average inventory was sold during the period. Its purpose is to measure the liquidity of the inventory. A high measure indicates that inventory is being sold and replenished frequently. The inventory turnover ratio is computed by dividing the cost of goods sold by the average inventory during the period. Unless seasonal factors are significant, average inventory can be computed from the beginning and ending inventory balances. Kellogg's inventory turnover ratio is shown in Illustration 13A-9.

Illustration 13A-9
Inventory turnover ratio

Ratio	Formula	Indicates:	Kellogg 2007	Kellogg 2006	General Mills 2007	Industry 2007	Page in book
Inventory turnover ratio	Cost of goods sold / Average inventory	Liquidity of inventory	7.5	7.9	7.1	6.6	290

Kellogg's inventory turnover ratio decreased slightly in 2007. The turnover ratio of 7.5 times is higher than the industry average of 6.6 times and better than General Mills's 7.1 times. Generally, the faster the inventory turnover, the less cash is tied up in inventory and the less the chance of inventory becoming obsolete. Of course, a downside of high inventory turnover is that the company can run out of inventory when it is needed.

6. **Days in inventory.** A variant of the inventory turnover ratio is the days in inventory, which measures the average number of days inventory is held. The days in inventory for Kellogg is shown in Illustration 13A-10.

Illustration 13A-10
Days in inventory

Ratio	Formula	Indicates:	Kellogg 2007	Kellogg 2006	General Mills 2007	Industry 2007	Page in book
Days in inventory	365 days / Inventory turnover ratio	Liquidity of inventory and inventory management	48.7	46.2	51.4	55.3	290

Kellogg's 2007 inventory turnover ratio of 7.5 divided into 365 is approximately 49 days. An average selling time of 49 days is faster than the industry average and faster than that of General Mills. Some of this difference might be explained by differences in product lines across the two companies, although in many ways the types of products of these two companies are quite similar.

Inventory turnover ratios vary considerably among industries. For example, grocery store chains have a turnover of 10 times and an average selling period of 37 days. In contrast, jewelry stores have an average turnover of 1.3 times and an average selling period of 281 days. Within a company there may even be significant differences in inventory turnover among different types of products. Thus, in a grocery store the turnover of perishable items such as produce, meats, and dairy products is faster than the turnover of soaps and detergents.

To conclude, nearly all of these liquidity measures suggest that Kellogg's liquidity changed little during 2007. Its liquidity appears acceptable when compared to the industry as a whole and when compared to General Mills.

SOLVENCY RATIOS

Solvency ratios measure the ability of the enterprise to survive over a long period of time. Long-term creditors and stockholders are interested in a company's long-run solvency, particularly its ability to pay interest as it comes due and to repay the face value of debt at maturity. The debt to total assets ratio, the times interest earned ratio, and the cash debt coverage ratio provide information about debt-paying ability. In addition, free cash flow provides information about the company's solvency and its ability to pay additional dividends or invest in new projects.

7. **Debt to total assets ratio.** The debt to total assets ratio measures the percentage of total financing provided by creditors. It is computed by dividing total debt (both current and long-term) by total assets. This ratio indicates the degree of financial leveraging. It also provides some indication of the company's ability to withstand losses without impairing the interests of its creditors. The higher the percentage of debt to total assets, the greater the risk that the company may be unable to meet its maturing obligations. The lower the ratio, the more equity "buffer" is available to creditors if the company becomes insolvent. Thus, from the creditors' point of view, a low ratio of debt to total assets is desirable. Kellogg's debt to total assets ratio is shown in Illustration 13A-11.

Illustration 13A-11
Debt to total assets ratio

Ratio	Formula	Indicates:	Kellogg 2007	Kellogg 2006	General Mills 2007	Industry 2007	Page in book
Debt to total assets ratio	Total liabilities / Total assets	Percentage of total assets provided by creditors	78%	81%	64%	48%	60

Kellogg's 2007 ratio of 78% means that creditors have provided financing sufficient to cover 78% of the company's total assets. Alternatively, it says that Kellogg would have to liquidate 78% of its assets at their book value in order to pay off all of its debts. Kellogg's 78% is above the industry average of 48% as well as the 64% ratio of General Mills. Kellogg's solvency improved slightly during the year.

The adequacy of this ratio is often judged in light of the company's earnings. Generally, companies with relatively stable earnings, such as public utilities, have higher debt to total assets ratios than cyclical companies with widely fluctuating earnings, such as many high-tech companies.

Another ratio with a similar meaning is the **debt to equity ratio**. It shows the relative use of borrowed funds (total liabilities) compared with resources invested by the owners. Because this ratio can be computed in several ways, be careful when making comparisons with it. Debt may be defined to include only the noncurrent portion of liabilities, and intangible assets may be excluded from stockholders' equity (which would equal tangible net worth). If debt and assets are defined as above (all liabilities and all assets), then when the debt to total assets ratio equals 50%, the debt to equity ratio is 1:1.

8. **Times interest earned ratio.** The times interest earned ratio (also called interest coverage) indicates the company's ability to meet interest payments as they come due. It is computed by dividing income before interest expense and income taxes by interest expense. Note that this ratio uses income before interest expense and income taxes because this amount represents what is available to cover interest. Kellogg's times interest earned ratio is shown in Illustration 13A-12.

Illustration 13A-12
Times interest earned ratio

Ratio	Formula	Indicates:	Kellogg 2007	Kellogg 2006	General Mills 2007	Industry 2007	Page in book
Times interest earned ratio	$\dfrac{\text{Net Income} + \text{Interest expense} + \text{Tax expense}}{\text{Interest expense}}$	Ability to meet interest payments as they come due	5.8	5.8	5.0	5.9	507

For Kellogg the 2007 interest coverage was 5.8, which indicates that income before interest and taxes was 5.8 times the amount needed for interest expense. This exceeds the rate for General Mills, but it is slightly less than the average rate for the industry. The debt to total assets ratio decreased for Kellogg during 2007, and its times interest earned ratio held constant. These ratios indicate that Kellogg is better able to service its debt.

9. **Cash debt coverage ratio.** The ratio of cash provided by operating activities to average total liabilities, called the cash debt coverage ratio, is a cash-basis measure of solvency. This ratio indicates a company's ability to repay its liabilities from cash generated from operating activities without having to liquidate the assets used in its operations. Illustration 13A-13 shows Kellogg's cash debt coverage ratio.

Illustration 13A-13
Cash debt coverage ratio

Ratio	Formula	Indicates:	Kellogg 2007	Kellogg 2006	General Mills 2007	Industry 2007	Page in book
Cash debt coverage ratio	$\dfrac{\text{Cash provided by operations}}{\text{Average total liabilities}}$	Long-term debt-paying ability (cash basis)	.17	.17	.15	na	622

An industry average for this measure is not available. Kellogg's .17 is higher than General Mills's .15, and it remained unchanged from 2006. One way of interpreting this ratio is to say that net cash generated from one year of operations would be sufficient to pay off 17% of Kellogg's total liabilities. If 17% of this year's liabilities were retired each year, it would take approximately 6 years to retire all of its debt. It would take General Mills approximately 6.7 years to do so. A general rule of thumb is that a cash debt coverage ratio above .20 is acceptable.

10. **Free cash flow.** One indication of a company's solvency, as well as of its ability to pay dividends or expand operations, is the amount of excess cash it generated after investing in capital expenditures and paying dividends. This amount is referred to as *free cash flow*. For example, if you generate $100,000 of cash from operations but you spend $30,000 on capital expenditures and pay $10,000 in dividends, you have $60,000 ($100,000 − $30,000 − $10,000) to use either to expand operations, pay additional dividends, or pay down debt. Kellogg's free cash flow is shown in Illustration 13A-14.

Illustration 13A-14
Free cash flow

Ratio	Formula				Indicates:	Kellogg 2007	Kellogg 2006	General Mills 2007	Industry 2007	Page in book
Free cash flow	Cash provided by operations	−	Capital expenditures	− Cash dividends	Cash available for paying dividends or expanding operations	$556 (in millions)	$507	$799 (in millions)	na	62

Kellogg's free cash flow increased slightly from 2006 to 2007. During both years, the cash provided by operations was more than enough to allow Kellogg to acquire additional productive assets and maintain dividend payments. Kellogg could have used the remaining cash to reduce debt if necessary.

PROFITABILITY RATIOS

Profitability ratios measure the income or operating success of an enterprise for a given period of time. A company's income, or the lack of it, affects its ability to obtain debt and equity financing, its liquidity position, and its ability to grow. As a consequence, creditors and investors alike are interested in evaluating profitability. Analysts frequently use profitability as the ultimate test of management's operating effectiveness.

Throughout this book we have introduced numerous measures of profitability. The relationships among measures of profitability are very important. Understanding them can help management determine where to focus its efforts to improve profitability. Illustration 13A-15 diagrams these relationships. Our discussion of Kellogg's profitability is structured around this diagram.

Illustration 13A-15
Relationships among profitability measures

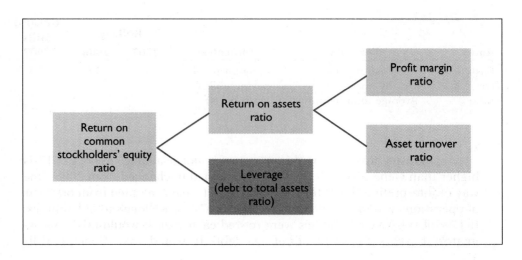

11. **Return on common stockholders' equity ratio.** A widely used measure of profitability from the common stockholder's viewpoint is the return on common stockholders' equity ratio. This ratio shows how many dollars of net income the company earned for each dollar invested by the owners. It is computed by dividing net income minus any preferred stock dividends—that is, income available to common stockholders—by average common stockholders' equity. The return on common stockholders' equity for Kellogg is shown in Illustration 13A-16.

Illustration 13A-16
Return on common stockholders' equity ratio

Ratio	Formula	Indicates:	Kellogg 2007	Kellogg 2006	General Mills 2007	Industry 2007	Page in book
Return on common stockholders' equity ratio	Net income − Preferred stock dividends / Average common stockholders' equity	Profitability of common stockholders' investment	48%	46%	21%	23%	573

Kellogg's 2007 rate of return on common stockholders' equity is unusually high at 48%, considering an industry average of 23% and General Mills's return of 21%. In the subsequent sections we investigate the causes of this high return.

12. **Return on assets ratio.** The return on common stockholders' equity ratio is affected by two factors: the return on assets ratio and the degree of leverage. The return on assets ratio measures the overall profitability of assets in terms of the income earned on each dollar invested in assets. It is computed by dividing net income by average total assets. Kellogg's return on assets ratio is shown in Illustration 13A-17.

Illustration 13A-17
Return on assets ratio

Ratio	Formula	Indicates:	Kellogg 2007	Kellogg 2006	General Mills 2007	Industry 2007	Page in book
Return on assets ratio	Net income / Average total assets	Overall profitability of assets	10.0%	9.4%	6.3%	7%	448

Kellogg had a 10.0% return on assets in 2007. This rate is significantly higher than that of General Mills and the industry average.

Note that Kellogg's rate of return on common stockholders' equity (48%) is substantially higher than its rate of return on assets (10%). The reason is that Kellogg has made effective use of **leverage**. Leveraging or trading on the equity at a gain means that the company has borrowed money at a lower rate of interest than the rate of return it earns on the assets it purchased with the borrowed funds. Leverage enables management to use money supplied by nonowners to increase the return to owners.

A comparison of the rate of return on assets with the rate of interest paid for borrowed money indicates the profitability of trading on the equity. If you borrow money at 8% and your rate of return on assets is 11%, you are trading on the equity at a gain. Note, however, that trading on the equity is a two-way street: For example, if you borrow money at 11% and earn only 8% on it, you are trading on the equity at a loss.

Kellogg earns more on its borrowed funds than it has to pay in interest. Thus, the return to stockholders exceeds the return on the assets because of the positive benefit of leverage. Recall from our earlier discussion that Kellogg's percentage of debt financing as measured by the ratio of debt to total assets (or debt to equity) was higher than General Mills's and the industry average. It appears that Kellogg's high return on common stockholders' equity is due in part to its use of leverage.

13. **Profit margin ratio.** The return on assets ratio is affected by two factors, the first of which is the profit margin ratio. The profit margin ratio, or rate of return on sales, is a measure of the percentage of each dollar of sales that results in net income. It is computed by dividing net income by net sales for the period. Kellogg's profit margin ratio is shown in Illustration 13A-18.

Illustration 13A-18
Profit margin ratio

Ratio	Formula	Indicates:	Kellogg 2007	Kellogg 2006	General Mills 2007	Industry 2007	Page in book
Profit margin ratio	Net income / Net sales	Net income generated by each dollar of sales	9.4%	9.2%	9.2%	7%	243

Kellogg experienced a slight increase in its profit margin ratio from 2006 to 2007 of 9.2% to 9.4%. Its profit margin ratio was greater than the industry average of 7% and slightly higher than General Mills's 9.2%.

High-volume (high inventory turnover) businesses such as grocery stores and pharmacy chains generally have low profit margins. Low-volume businesses such as jewelry stores and airplane manufacturers have high profit margins.

14. **Asset turnover ratio.** The other factor that affects the return on assets ratio is the asset turnover ratio. The asset turnover ratio measures how efficiently a company uses its assets to generate sales. It is determined by dividing net sales by average total assets for the period. The resulting number shows the dollars of sales produced by each dollar invested in assets. Illustration 13A-19 shows the asset turnover ratio for Kellogg.

Illustration 13A-19
Asset turnover ratio

Ratio	Formula	Indicates:	Kellogg 2007	Kellogg 2006	General Mills 2007	Industry 2007	Page in book
Asset turnover ratio	Net sales / Average total assets	How efficiently assets are used to generate sales	1.07	1.02	.69	1.17	450

The asset turnover ratio shows that in 2007 Kellogg generated sales of $1.07 for each dollar it had invested in assets. The ratio rose from 2006 to 2007. Kellogg's asset turnover ratio is below the industry average of 1.17 times but well above General Mills's ratio of .69.

Asset turnover ratios vary considerably among industries. The average asset turnover for utility companies is .45, for example, while the grocery store industry has an average asset turnover of 3.49.

In summary, Kellogg's return on assets ratio increased from 9.4% in 2006 to 10.1% in 2007. Underlying this increase was an increased profitability on each dollar of sales (as measured by the profit margin ratio) and a rise in the sales-generating efficiency of its assets (as measured by the asset turnover ratio). We can analyze the combined effects of profit margin and asset turnover on return on assets for Kellogg as shown in Illustration 13A-20.

Illustration 13A-20
Composition of return on assets ratio

	Profit Margin	×	Asset Turnover	=	Return on Assets
Ratios:	Net Income / Net Sales	×	Net Sales / Average Total Assets	=	Net Income / Average Total Assets
Kellogg					
2007	9.4%	×	1.07 times	=	10.1%
2006	9.2%	×	1.02 times	=	9.4%

15. **Gross profit rate.** Two factors strongly influence the profit margin ratio. One is the gross profit rate. The gross profit rate is determined by dividing gross profit (net sales less cost of goods sold) by net sales. This rate indicates a company's ability to maintain an adequate selling price above its cost of goods sold.

As an industry becomes more competitive, this ratio declines. For example, in the early years of the personal computer industry, gross profit rates were quite high. Today, because of increased competition and a belief that most brands of personal computers are similar in quality, gross profit rates have become thin. Analysts should closely monitor gross profit rates over time. Illustration 13A-21 shows Kellogg's gross profit rate.

Illustration 13A-21
Gross profit rate

Ratio	Formula	Indicates:	Kellogg 2007	Kellogg 2006	General Mills 2007	Industry 2007	Page in book
Gross profit rate	Gross profit / Net sales	Margin between selling price and cost of goods sold	44%	44%	36%	32%	241

Kellogg's gross profit rate remained constant from 2006 to 2007.

16. **Earnings per share (EPS).** Stockholders usually think in terms of the number of shares they own or plan to buy or sell. Expressing net income earned on a per share basis provides a useful perspective for determining profitability. Earnings per share is a measure of the net income earned on each share of common stock. It is computed by dividing net income by the average number of common shares outstanding during the year.

The terms "net income per share" or "earnings per share" refer to the amount of net income applicable to each share of *common stock*. Therefore, when we compute earnings per share, if there are preferred dividends declared for the period, we must deduct them from net income to arrive at income available to the common stockholders. Kellogg's earnings per share is shown in Illustration 13A-22.

Illustration 13A-22
Earnings per share

Ratio	Formula	Indicates:	Kellogg 2007	Kellogg 2006	General Mills 2007	Industry 2007	Page in book
Earnings per share (EPS)	Net income − Preferred stock dividends / Average common shares outstanding	Net income earned on each share of common stock	$2.63	$2.40	$3.30	na	55

Note that no industry average is presented in Illustration 13A-22. Industry data for earnings per share are not reported, and in fact the Kellogg and General Mills ratios should not be compared. Such comparisons are not meaningful because of the wide variations in the number of shares of outstanding stock among companies. Kellogg's earnings per share increased 23 cents per share in 2007. This represents a 9.6% increase from the 2006 EPS of $2.40.

17. **Price-earnings ratio.** The price-earnings ratio is an oft-quoted statistic that measures the ratio of the market price of each share of common stock to the earnings per share. The price-earnings (P-E) ratio reflects investors' assessments of a company's future earnings. It is computed by dividing the market price per share of the stock by earnings per share. Kellogg's price-earnings ratio is shown in Illustration 13A-23.

Illustration 13A-23
Price-earnings ratio

Ratio	Formula	Indicates:	Kellogg 2007	Kellogg 2006	General Mills 2007	Industry 2007	Page in book
Price-earnings ratio	Stock price per share / Earnings per share	Relationship between market price per share and earnings per share	20.1	20.9	17.5	19.9	676

At the end of 2007 and 2006 the market price of Kellogg's stock was $52.92 and $50.06, respectively. General Mills's stock was selling for $57.84 at the end of 2007.

In 2007 each share of Kellogg's stock sold for 20.1 times the amount that was earned on each share. Kellogg's price-earnings ratio is higher than General Mills's ratio of 17.5 but lower than the industry average of 19.9 times. Its higher P-E ratio suggests that the market is more optimistic about Kellogg than about General Mills. However, it might also signal that its stock is overpriced. That is a matter for the analyst to determine.

18. **Payout ratio.** The payout ratio measures the percentage of earnings distributed in the form of cash dividends. It is computed by dividing cash dividends declared on common stock by net income. Companies that have high growth rates are characterized by low payout ratios because they reinvest most of their net income in the business. The payout ratio for Kellogg is shown in Illustration 13A-24.

Ratio	Formula	Indicates:	Kellogg 2007	Kellogg 2006	General Mills 2007	Industry 2007	Page in book
Payout ratio	Cash dividends declared on common stock / Net income	Percentage of earnings distributed in the form of cash dividends	43%	45%	44%	37%	572

Illustration 13A-24
Payout ratio

The 2007 and 2006 payout ratios for Kellogg are about the same as that of General Mills (44%) but higher than the industry average (37%).

Management has some control over the amount of dividends paid each year, and companies are generally reluctant to reduce a dividend below the amount paid in a previous year. Therefore, the payout ratio will actually increase if a company's net income declines but the company keeps its total dividend payment the same. Of course, unless the company returns to its previous level of profitability, maintaining this higher dividend payout ratio is probably not possible over the long run.

Before drawing any conclusions regarding Kellogg's dividend payout ratio, we should calculate this ratio over a longer period of time to evaluate any trends, and also try to find out whether management's philosophy regarding dividends has changed recently. The "Selected Financial Data" section of Kellogg's Management Discussion and Analysis shows that over a 5-year period earnings per share rose 45%, while dividends per share grew only 19%.

In terms of the types of financial information available and the ratios used by various industries, what can be practically covered in this textbook gives you only the "Titanic approach": That is, you are seeing only the tip of the iceberg compared to the vast databases and types of ratio analysis that are available on computers. The availability of information is not a problem. The real trick is to be discriminating enough to perform relevant analysis and select pertinent comparative data.

Glossary

Asset turnover ratio *(p. 690)* A measure of how efficiently a company uses its assets to generate sales; computed as net sales divided by average total assets.

Available-for-sale securities *(p. 665)* Securities that are held with the intent of selling them sometime in the future.

Average collection period *(p. 684)* The average number of days that receivables are outstanding; calculated as receivables turnover divided into 365 days.

Cash debt coverage ratio *(p. 687)* A cash-basis measure used to evaluate solvency, computed as cash from operations divided by average total liabilities.

Change in accounting principle *(p. 664)* Use of an accounting principle in the current year different from the one used in the preceding year.

Comprehensive income *(p. 664)* A measure of income that includes all changes in stockholders' equity during a period except those resulting from investments by stockholders and distributions to stockholders.

Current cash debt coverage ratio *(p. 683)* A cash-basis measure of liquidity; computed as cash provided by operations divided by average current liabilities.

Current ratio *(p. 683)* A measure used to evaluate a company's liquidity and short-term debt-paying ability; calculated as current assets divided by current liabilities.

Days in inventory *(p. 685)* A measure of the average number of days inventory is held; computed as inventory turnover divided into 365 days.

Debt to total assets ratio *(p. 686)* A measure of the percentage of total financing provided by creditors; computed as total debt divided by total assets.

Discontinued operations *(p. 661)* The disposal of a significant component of a business.

Earnings per share *(p. 691)* The net income earned by each share of common stock; computed as net income less dividends on preferred stock divided by the average common shares outstanding.

Extraordinary items *(p. 662)* Events and transactions that meet two conditions: (1) unusual in nature and (2) infrequent in occurrence.

Free cash flow *(p. 688)* A measure of solvency. Cash remaining from operating activities after adjusting for capital expenditures and dividends paid.

Gross profit rate *(p. 691)* Gross profit expressed as a percentage; computed as gross profit divided by net sales.

Horizontal analysis *(p. 668)* A technique for evaluating a series of financial statement data over a period of time to determine the increase (decrease) that has taken place, expressed as either an amount or a percentage.

Inventory turnover ratio *(p. 685)* A measure of the liquidity of inventory. Measures the number of times average inventory was sold during the period; computed as cost of goods sold divided by average inventory.

Leveraging *(p. 689)* Borrowing money at a lower rate of interest than can be earned by using the borrowed money; also referred to as trading on the equity.

Liquidity ratios *(p. 673)* Measures of the short-term ability of the company to pay its maturing obligations and to meet unexpected needs for cash.

Payout ratio *(p. 692)* A measure of the percentage of earnings distributed in the form of cash dividends; calculated as cash dividends declared on common stock divided by net income.

Price-earnings (P-E) ratio *(pp. 676, 692)* A comparison of the market price of each share of common stock to the earnings per share; computed as the market price of the stock divided by earnings per share.

Pro forma income *(p. 675)* A measure of income that usually excludes items that a company thinks are unusual or nonrecurring.

Profit margin ratio *(p. 690)* A measure of the net income generated by each dollar of sales; computed as net income divided by net sales.

Profitability ratios *(p. 674)* Measures of the income or operating success of a company for a given period of time.

Quality of earnings *(p. 675)* Indicates the level of full and transparent information that is provided to users of the financial statements.

Receivables turnover ratio *(p. 684)* A measure of the liquidity of receivables; computed as net credit sales divided by average net receivables.

Return on assets ratio *(p. 689)* A profitability measure that indicates the amount of net income generated by each dollar of assets; calculated as net income divided by average total assets.

Return on common stockholders' equity ratio *(p. 689)* A measure of the dollars of net income earned for each dollar invested by the owners; computed as income available to common stockholders divided by average common stockholders' equity.

Solvency ratios *(p. 673)* The ability of a company to pay interest as it comes due and to repay the balance of debt at its maturity.

Sustainable income *(p. 660)* The most likely level of income to be obtained in the future; calculated as net income adjusted for irregular items.

Times interest earned ratio *(p. 687)* A measure of a company's solvency and ability to meet interest payments as they come due; calculated as income before interest expense and income taxes divided by interest expense.

Trading on the equity *(p. 689)* Same as leveraging.

Trading securities *(p. 665)* Securities bought and held primarily for sale in the near term to generate income on short-term price differences.

Vertical analysis *(p. 670)* A technique for evaluating financial statement data that expresses each item in a financial statement as a percent of a base amount.

Comprehensive Do it!

The events and transactions of Dever Corporation for the year ending December 31, 2010, resulted in these data.

Cost of goods sold	$2,600,000
Net sales	4,400,000
Other expenses and losses	9,600
Other revenues and gains	5,600
Selling and administrative expenses	1,100,000
Gain from discontinued division	570,000
Loss from tornado disaster (extraordinary loss)	600,000

Analysis reveals the following.

1. All items are before the applicable income tax rate of 30%.
2. The plastics division was sold on July 1.

Instructions

Prepare an income statement for the year.

Solution to Comprehensive **Do it!**

DEVER CORPORATION
Income Statement
For the Year Ended December 31, 2010

Net sales		$ 4,400,000
Cost of goods sold		2,600,000
Gross profit		1,800,000
Selling and administrative expenses		1,100,000
Income from operations		700,000
Other revenues and gains	$ 5,600	
Other expenses and losses	(9,600)	(4,000)
Income before income taxes		696,000
Income tax expense ($696,000 × 30%)		208,800
Income before irregular items		487,200
Discontinued operations: Gain from discontinued division, net of taxes of $171,000 ($570,000 × 30%)		399,000
Extraordinary item: Tornado loss, net of income tax savings $180,000 ($600,000 × 30%)		(420,000)
Net income		$ 466,200

Action Plan

• Remember that material items not typical of operations are reported in separate sections net of taxes.

• Associate income taxes with the item that affects the taxes.

• On a corporation income statement, report income tax expense when there is income before income tax.

Self-Study Questions

Answers are at the end of the chapter.

All of the Self-Study Questions in this chapter employ decision tools.

(SO 2) **1.** In reporting discontinued operations, the income statement should show in a special section:
  (a) gains on the disposal of the discontinued component.
  (b) losses on the disposal of the discontinued component.
  (c) Neither (a) nor (b).
  (d) Both (a) and (b).

(SO 2) **2.** Cool Stools Corporation has income before taxes of $400,000 and an extraordinary loss of $100,000. If the income tax rate is 25% on all items, the income statement should show income before irregular items and an extraordinary loss, respectively, of
  (a) $325,000 and $100,000.
  (b) $325,000 and $75,000.
  (c) $300,000 and $100,000.
  (d) $300,000 and $75,000.

(SO 3) **3.** Which of the following would be considered an "Other comprehensive income" item?
  (a) gain on disposal of discontinued operations.
  (b) unrealized loss on available-for-sale securities.
  (c) extraordinary loss related to flood.
  (d) net income.

(SO 4) **4.** In horizontal analysis, each item is expressed as a percentage of the:
  (a) net income amount.
  (b) stockholders' equity amount.

  (c) total assets amount.
  (d) base-year amount.

(SO 4) **5.** Adams Corporation reported net sales of $300,000, $330,000, and $360,000 in the years 2008, 2009, and 2010, respectively. If 2008 is the base year, what percentage do 2010 sales represent of the base?
  (a) 77%.   (c) 120%.
  (b) 108%.   (d) 130%.

(SO 5) **6.** The following schedule is a display of what type of analysis?

	Amount	Percent
Current assets	$200,000	25%
Property, plant, and equipment	600,000	75%
Total assets	$800,000	

  (a) Horizontal analysis.
  (b) Differential analysis.
  (c) Vertical analysis.
  (d) Ratio analysis.

(SO 5) **7.** In vertical analysis, the base amount for depreciation expense is generally:
  (a) net sales.
  (b) depreciation expense in a previous year.
  (c) gross profit.
  (d) fixed assets.

(SO 6) **8.** Which measure is an evaluation of a company's ability to pay current liabilities?
  (a) Current cash debt coverage ratio.
  (b) Current ratio.

(c) Both (a) and (b).

(d) None of the above.

(SO 6)   **9.** Which measure is useful in evaluating the efficiency in managing inventories?

(a) Inventory turnover ratio.

(b) Days in inventory.

(c) Both (a) and (b).

(d) None of the above.

(SO 6)   **10.** Which of these is *not* a liquidity ratio?

(a) Current ratio.

(b) Asset turnover ratio.

(c) Inventory turnover ratio.

(d) Receivables turnover ratio.

(SO 6)   **11.** Plano Corporation reported net income $24,000; net sales $400,000; and average assets $600,000 for 2010. What is the 2010 profit margin ratio?

(a) 6%. (c) 40%.

(b) 12%. (d) 200%.

Use the following financial statement information as of the end of each year to answer Self-Study Questions 12–16.

	2010	2009
Inventory	$ 54,000	$ 48,000
Current assets	81,000	106,000
Total assets	382,000	326,000
Current liabilities	27,000	36,000
Total liabilities	102,000	88,000
Stockholders' equity	280,000	238,000
Net sales	784,000	697,000
Cost of goods sold	306,000	277,000
Net income	134,000	90,000
Tax expense	22,000	18,000
Interest expense	12,000	12,000
Dividends paid to preferred stockholders	20,000	20,000
Dividends paid to common stockholders	15,000	10,000

12. Compute the days in inventory for 2010.   (SO 6)

(a) 64.4 days.

(b) 60.8 days.

(c) 6 days.

(d) 24 days.

13. Compute the current ratio for 2010.   (SO 6)

(a) 1.26:1.

(b) 3.0:1.

(c) 0.80:1.

(d) 3.75:1.

14. Compute the profit margin ratio for 2010.   (SO 6)

(a) 17.1%.

(b) 18.1%.

(c) 37.9%.

(d) 5.9%.

15. Compute the return on common stockholders' equity   (SO 6) for 2010.

(a) 47.9%.

(b) 51.7%.

(c) 40.7%.

(d) 44.0%.

16. Compute the times interest earned for 2010.   (SO 6)

(a) 11.2 times.

(b) 65.3 times.

(c) 14.0 times.

(d) 13.0 times.

17. Which situation below might indicate a company has   (SO 7) a low quality of earnings?

(a) The same accounting principles are used each year.

(b) Revenue is recognized when earned.

(c) Maintenance costs are capitalized and then depreciated.

(d) The company's P-E ratio is high relative to competitors.

Go to the book's companion website, **www.wiley.com/college/kimmel**, to access additional Self-Study Questions.

Questions

All of the Questions in this chapter employ decision tools.

1. Explain sustainable income. What relationship does this concept have to the treatment of irregular items on the income statement?

2. Indicate which of the following items would be reported as an extraordinary item on Denison Corporation's income statement.

(a) Loss from damages caused by a volcano eruption.

(b) Loss from the sale of short-term investments.

(c) Loss attributable to a labor strike.

(d) Loss caused when the Food and Drug Administration prohibited the manufacture and sale of a product line.

(e) Loss of inventory from flood damage because a warehouse is located on a flood plain that floods every 5 to 10 years.

(f) Loss on the write-down of outdated inventory.

(g) Loss from a foreign government's expropriation of a production facility.

(h) Loss from damage to a warehouse in southern California from a minor earthquake.

3. McDonnell Inc. reported 2009 earnings per share of $3.26 and had no extraordinary items. In 2010 earnings per share on income before extraordinary items was $2.99, and earnings per share on net income was $3.49. Do you consider this trend to be favorable? Why or why not?

4. Bullock Inc. has been in operation for 3 years. and uses the FIFO method of pricing inventory. During the fourth year, Bullock changes to the average cost method for all its inventory. How will Bullock report this change?

5. What amount did Tootsie Roll Industries report as "Other comprehensive earnings" in 2007? By what percentage did Tootsie Roll's "Comprehensive earnings" differ from its "Net earnings"?

6. (a) Andrea Monee believes that the analysis of financial statements is directed at two characteristics of a company: liquidity and profitability. Is Andrea correct? Explain.
   (b) Are short-term creditors, long-term creditors, and stockholders interested in primarily the same characteristics of a company? Explain.

7. (a) Distinguish among the following bases of comparison: intracompany, intercompany and industry averages.
   (b) Give the principal value of using each of the three bases of comparison.

8. Two popular methods of financial statement analysis are horizontal analysis and vertical analysis. Explain the difference between these two methods.

9. (a) If Fassi Company had net income of $300,000 in 2009 and it experienced a 24.5% increase in net income for 2010, what is its net income for 2010?
   (b) If 6 cents of every dollar of Fassi's revenue is net income in 2009, what is the dollar amount of 2009 revenue?

10. Name the major ratios useful in assessing (a) liquidity and (b) solvency.

11. Ralph Massey is puzzled. His company had a profit margin of 10% in 2010. He feels that this is an indication that the company is doing well. Joan Douglas, his accountant, says that more information is needed to determine the company's financial well-being. Who is correct? Why?

12. What does each type of ratio measure?
   (a) Liquidity ratios.
   (b) Solvency ratios.
   (c) Profitability ratios.

13. What is the difference between the current ratio and working capital?

14. Kwik Mart, a retail store, has a receivables turnover ratio of 4.5 times. The industry average is 12.5 times. Does Kwik Mart have a collection problem with its receivables?

15. Which ratios should be used to help answer each of these questions?
   (a) How efficient is a company in using its assets to produce sales?
   (b) How near to sale is the inventory on hand?

(c) How many dollars of net income were earned for each dollar invested by the owners?
(d) How able is a company to meet interest charges as they fall due?

16. At year end, the price-earnings ratio of General Motors was 11.3, and the price-earnings ratio of Microsoft was 28.14. Which company did the stock market favor? Explain.

17. What is the formula for computing the payout ratio? Do you expect this ratio to be high or low for a growth company?

18. Holding all other factors constant, indicate whether each of the following changes generally signals good or bad news about a company.
   (a) Increase in profit margin ratio.
   (b) Decrease in inventory turnover ratio.
   (c) Increase in current ratio.
   (d) Decrease in earnings per share.
   (e) Increase in price-earnings ratio.
   (f) Increase in debt to total assets ratio.
   (g) Decrease in times interest earned ratio.

19. The return on assets for Boitano Corporation is 7.6%. During the same year Boitano's return on common stockholders' equity is 12.8%. What is the explanation for the difference in the two rates?

20. Which two ratios do you think should be of greatest interest in each of the following cases?
   (a) A pension fund considering the purchase of 20-year bonds.
   (b) A bank contemplating a short-term loan.
   (c) A common stockholder.

21. Comaneci Inc. has net income of $200,000, average shares of common stock outstanding of 50,000, and preferred dividends for the period of $20,000. What is Comaneci's earnings per share of common stock? Sid Brey, the president of Comaneci, believes that the computed EPS of the company is high. Comment.

22. Identify and explain factors that affect quality of earnings.

23. Explain how the choice of one of the following accounting methods over the other raises or lowers a company's net income during a period of continuing inflation.
   (a) Use of FIFO instead of LIFO for inventory costing.
   (b) Use of a 6-year life for machinery instead of a 9-year life.
   (c) Use of straight-line depreciation instead of accelerated declining-balance depreciation.

Brief Exercises

WILEY
PLUS

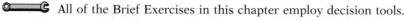 All of the Brief Exercises in this chapter employ decision tools.

BE13-1 On June 30 Gomez Corporation discontinued its operations in Mexico. On September 1 Gomez disposed of the Mexico facility at a pretax loss of $680,000. The applicable tax rate is 25%. Show the discontinued operations section of Gomez's income statement.

Prepare a discontinued operations section of an income statement.

(SO 2)

Prepare a corrected income statement with an extraordinary item.
(SO 2)

BE13-2 An inexperienced accountant for Osborn Corporation showed the following in Osborn's 2010 income statement: Income before income taxes $300,000; Income tax expense $72,000; Extraordinary loss from flood (before taxes) $60,000; and Net income $168,000. The extraordinary loss and taxable income are both subject to a 30% tax rate. Prepare a corrected income statement beginning with "Income before income taxes."

Indicate how a change in accounting principles is reported.
(SO 2)

BE13-3 On January 1, 2010, Robins Inc. changed from the LIFO method of inventory pricing to the FIFO method. Explain how this change in accounting principle should be treated in the company's financial statements.

Prepare horizontal analysis.
(SO 4)

BE13-4 Using these data from the comparative balance sheet of Patillo Company, perform horizontal analysis.

	December 31, 2010	December 31, 2009
Accounts receivable	$ 560,000	$ 400,000
Inventory	780,000	650,000
Total assets	3,220,000	2,800,000

Prepare vertical analysis.
(SO 5)

BE13-5 Using the data presented in BE13-4 for Patillo Company, perform vertical analysis.

Calculate percentage of change.
(SO 4)

BE13-6 Net income was $500,000 in 2008, $480,000 in 2009, and $518,400 in 2010. What is the percentage of change from (a) 2008 to 2009, and (b) from 2009 to 2010? Is the change an increase or a decrease?

Calculate net income.
(SO 4)

BE13-7 If Underwood Company had net income of $561,600 in 2010 and it experienced a 17% increase in net income over 2009, what was its 2009 net income?

Analyze change in net income.
(SO 5)

BE13-8 Vertical analysis (common-size) percentages for Waubons Company's sales, cost of goods sold, and expenses are listed here.

Vertical Analysis	2010	2009	2008
Sales	100.0%	100.0%	100.0%
Cost of goods sold	60.5	62.4	64.5
Expenses	26.0	26.6	28.5

Did Waubons's net income as a percent of sales increase, decrease, or remain unchanged over the 3-year period? Provide numerical support for your answer.

Analyze change in net income.
(SO 4)

BE13-9 Horizontal analysis (trend analysis) percentages for Olympic Company's sales, cost of goods sold, and expenses are listed here.

Horizontal Analysis	2010	2009	2008
Sales	96.2%	104.8%	100.0%
Cost of goods sold	102.0	97.0	100.0
Expenses	105.6	95.4	100.0

Explain whether Olympic's net income increased, decreased, or remained unchanged over the 3-year period.

Calculate current ratio.
(SO 6)

BE13-10 These selected condensed data are taken from recent balance sheets of Bob Evans Farms (in thousands).

	2007	2006
Cash	$ 29,287	$ 16,727
Accounts receivable	20,515	16,131
Inventories	28,673	28,058
Other current assets	23,989	21,486
Total current assets	$102,464	$ 82,402
Total current liabilities	$201,183	$159,485

Compute the current ratio for each year and comment on your results.

BE13-11 The following data are taken from the financial statements of Fleetwood Company.

Evaluate collection of accounts receivable.
(SO 6)

	2010	2009
Accounts receivable (net), end of year	$ 560,000	$ 540,000
Net sales on account	4,400,000	4,000,000
Terms for all sales are 1/10, n/45.		

Compute for each year (a) the receivables turnover ratio and (b) the average collection period. What conclusions about the management of accounts receivable can be drawn from these data? At the end of 2008, accounts receivable was $500,000.

BE13-12 The following data were taken from the income statements of Bordeaux Company.

Evaluate management of inventory.
(SO 6)

	2010	2009
Sales revenue	$6,420,000	$6,240,000
Beginning inventory	970,000	837,000
Purchases	4,840,000	4,661,000
Ending inventory	1,020,000	970,000

Compute for each year (a) the inventory turnover ratio and (b) days in inventory. What conclusions concerning the management of the inventory can be drawn from these data?

BE13-13 Staples, Inc. is one of the largest suppliers of office products in the United States. It had net income of $995.7 million and sales of $19,372.7 million in 2007. Its total assets were $8,397.3 million at the beginning of the year and $9,036.3 million at the end of the year. What is Staples, Inc.'s (a) asset turnover ratio and (b) profit margin ratio? (Round to two decimals.) Provide a brief interpretation of your results.

Calculate profitability ratios.
(SO 6)

BE13-14 McCormick Company has stockholders' equity of $400,000 and net income of $72,000. It has a payout ratio of 25% and a return on assets ratio of 16%. How much did McCormick pay in cash dividends, and what were its average total assets?

Calculate profitability ratios.
(SO 6)

BE13-15 Selected data taken from the 2006 financial statements of trading card company Topps Company, Inc. are as follows (in millions).

Calculate cash-basis liquidity and solvency ratios.
(SO 6)

	2006
Net sales for 2006	$326.7
Current liabilities, February 25, 2006	41.1
Current liabilities, March 3, 2007	62.4
Net cash provided by operating activities	10.4
Total liabilities, February 25, 2006	65.2
Total liabilities, March 3, 2007	73.2
Capital expenditures	3.7
Cash dividends	6.2

Compute these ratios at March 3, 2007: (a) current cash debt coverage ratio (b) cash debt coverage ratio, and (c) free cash flow. Provide a brief interpretation of your results.

Do it! Review

WILEY
PLUS

Do it! 13-1 In its draft 2010 income statement, Supply Corporation reports income before income taxes $500,000, extraordinary loss due to earthquake $150,000, income taxes $200,000 (not including irregular items), loss on disposal of discontinued music division $20,000. The income tax rate is 40%. Prepare a correct income statement, beginning with income before income taxes.

Prepare income statement, including irregular items.
(SO 2)

Do it! 13-2 Summary financial information for Holland Company is as follows.

Prepare horizontal analysis.
(SO 3)

	Dec. 31, 2011	Dec. 31, 2010
Current assets	$ 199,000	$ 220,000
Plant assets	821,000	780,000
Total assets	$1,020,000	$1,000,000

Compute the amount and percentage changes in 2011 using horizontal analysis, assuming 2010 is the base year.

Compute ratios.
(SO 5)

Do it! **13-3** The condensed financial statements of Eau Fraîche Company for the years 2009 and 2010 are presented below.

EAU FRAÎCHE COMPANY
Balance Sheets
December 31 (in thousands)

	2010	2009
Current assets		
Cash and cash equivalents	$ 330	$ 360
Accounts receivable (net)	470	400
Inventories	460	390
Prepaid expenses	120	160
Total current assets	1,380	1,310
Property, plant, and equipment	420	380
Investments	10	10
Intangibles and other assets	530	510
Total assets	$2,340	$2,210
Current liabilities	$ 900	$ 790
Long-term liabilities	410	380
Stockholders' equity—common	1,030	1,040
Total liabilities and stockholders' equity	$2,340	$2,210

EAU FRAÎCHE COMPANY
Income Statements
For the Year Ended December 31 (in thousands)

	2010	2009
Revenues	$3,800	$3,460
Costs and expenses		
Cost of goods sold	970	890
Selling & administrative expenses	2,400	2,330
Interest expense	10	20
Total costs and expenses	3,380	3,240
Income before income taxes	420	220
Income tax expense	168	132
Net income	$ 252	$ 88

Compute the following ratios for 2010 and 2009.
(a) Current ratio.
(b) Inventory turnover. (Inventory on December 31, 2008, was $340.)
(c) Profit margin ratio.
(d) Return on assets. (Assets on December 31, 2008, were $1,900.)
(e) Return on common stockholders' equity. (Equity on December 31, 2008, was $900.)
(f) Debt to total assets ratio.
(g) Times interest earned.

Match terms relating to
quality of earnings and
financial statement analysis.
(SO 3, 4, 5, 6, 7)

Do it! **13-4** Match each of the following terms with the phrase that best describes it.

Quality of earnings	Pro forma income
Current ratio	Discontinued operations
Horizontal analysis	Comprehensive income

1. A measure used to evaluate a company's liquidity.
2. Usually excludes items that a company thinks are unusual or non-recurring.
3. Indicates the level of full and transparent information provided to users of the financial statements.
4. The disposal of a significant segment of a business.
5. Determines increases or decreases in a series of financial statement data.
6. Includes all changes in stockholders' equity during a period except those resulting from investments by stockholders and distributions to stockholders.

Exercises

All of the Exercises in this chapter employ decision tools.

E13-1   Oklahoma Company has income before irregular items of $290,000 for the year ended December 31, 2010. It also has the following items (before considering income taxes): (1) an extraordinary fire loss of $50,000 and (2) a gain of $30,000 from the disposal of a division. Assume all items are subject to income taxes at a 30% tax rate.

Prepare irregular items portion of an income statement.
(SO 2)

Instructions
Prepare Oklahoma Company's income statement for 2010, beginning with "Income before irregular items."

E13-2   The *Wall Street Journal* routinely publishes summaries of corporate quarterly and annual earnings reports in a feature called the "Earnings Digest." A typical "digest" report takes the following form.

Evaluate the effects of unusual or irregular items.
(SO 1, 2, 6)

ENERGY ENTERPRISES (A)

	Quarter ending July 31	
	2010	**2009**
Revenues	$2,049,000,000	$1,754,000,000
Net income	97,000,000	(a) 68,750,000
EPS: Net income	1.31	0.93

	9 months ending July 31	
	2010	**2009**
Revenues	$5,578,500,000	$5,065,300,000
Extraordinary item	(b) 1,900,000	
Net income	102,700,000	(a) 33,250,000
EPS: Net income	1.39	0.48

(a) Includes a net charge of $26,000,000 from loss on the sale of electrical
   equipment
(b) Extraordinary gain on Middle East property expropriation

The letter in parentheses following the company name indicates the exchange on which Energy Enterprises' stock is traded—in this case, the American Stock Exchange.

Instructions
Answer the following questions.
(a) How was the loss on the electrical equipment reported on the income statement? Was it reported in the third quarter of 2009? How can you tell?
(b) Why did the *Wall Street Journal* list the extraordinary item separately?
(c) What is the extraordinary item? Was it included in income for the third quarter? How can you tell?
(d) Did Energy Enterprises have an operating loss in any quarter of 2009? Of 2010? How do you know?
(e) Approximately how many shares of stock were outstanding in 2010? Did the number of outstanding shares change from July 31, 2009 to July 31, 2010?
(f) As an investor, what numbers should you use to determine Energy Enterprises' profit margin ratio? Calculate the 9-month profit margin ratio for 2009 and 2010 that you consider most useful. Explain your decision.

E13-3   Here is financial information for Galenti Inc.

Prepare horizontal analysis.
(SO 4)

	December 31, 2010	December 31, 2009
Current assets	$106,000	$ 80,000
Plant assets (net)	400,000	360,000
Current liabilities	91,000	65,000
Long-term liabilities	122,000	90,000
Common stock, $1 par	138,000	115,000
Retained earnings	155,000	170,000

Instructions
Prepare a schedule showing a horizontal analysis for 2010 using 2009 as the base year.

Prepare vertical analysis.
(SO 5)

E13-4 Operating data for Robinson Corporation are presented below.

	2010	2009
Sales	$800,000	$600,000
Cost of goods sold	520,000	408,000
Selling expenses	120,000	72,000
Administrative expenses	72,000	48,000
Income tax expense	32,000	21,600
Net income	56,000	50,400

Instructions
Prepare a schedule showing a vertical analysis for 2010 and 2009.

Prepare horizontal and vertical analyses.
(SO 4, 5)

E13-5 The comparative balance sheets of Nike, Inc. are presented here.

NIKE, INC.
Comparative Balance Sheets
May 31
($ in millions)

Assets	2007	2006
Current assets	$ 8,076	$7,346
Property, plant, and equipment (net)	1,678	1,658
Other assets	934	866
Total assets	$10,688	$9,870

Liabilities and Stockholders' Equity		
Current liabilities	$ 2,584	$2,612
Long-term liabilities	1,079	973
Stockholders' equity	7,025	6,285
Total liabilities and stockholders' equity	$10,688	$9,870

Instructions
(a) Prepare a horizontal analysis of the balance sheet data for Nike using 2006 as a base. (Show the amount of increase or decrease as well.)
(b) Prepare a vertical analysis of the balance sheet data for Nike for 2007.

Prepare horizontal and vertical analyses.
(SO 4, 5)

E13-6 Here are the comparative income statements of Winfrey Corporation.

WINFREY CORPORATION
Comparative Income Statements
For the Years Ended December 31

	2010	2009
Net sales	$598,000	$520,000
Cost of goods sold	477,000	450,000
Gross profit	$121,000	$ 70,000
Operating expenses	80,000	45,000
Net income	$ 41,000	$ 25,000

Instructions
(a) Prepare a horizontal analysis of the income statement data for Winfrey Corporation using 2009 as a base. (Show the amounts of increase or decrease.)
(b) Prepare a vertical analysis of the income statement data for Winfrey Corporation for both years.

Compute liquidity ratios.
(SO 6)

E13-7 Nordstrom, Inc. operates department stores in numerous states. Selected financial statement data (in millions) for 2007 are presented below.

	End of Year	Beginning of Year
Cash and cash equivalents	$ 358	$ 403
Receivables (net)	1,788	684
Merchandise inventory	956	997
Other current assets	259	658
Total current assets	$3,361	$2,742
Total current liabilities	$1,635	$1,433

For the year, net credit sales were $8,828 million, cost of goods sold was $5,526 million, and cash from operations was $161 million.

Instructions
Compute the current ratio, current cash debt coverage ratio, receivables turnover ratio, average collection period, inventory turnover ratio, and days in inventory at the end of the current year.

E13-8 Talley Incorporated had the following transactions involving current assets and current liabilities during February 2010.

Perform current ratio analysis.
(SO 6)

Feb.	3	Collected accounts receivable of $15,000.
	7	Purchased equipment for $20,000 cash.
	11	Paid $3,000 for a 3-year insurance policy.
	14	Paid accounts payable of $12,000.
	18	Declared cash dividends, $6,000.

Additional information:
As of February 1, 2010, current assets were $110,000 and current liabilities were $40,000.

Instructions
Compute the current ratio as of the beginning of the month and after each transaction.

E13-9 Armada Company has these comparative balance sheet data:

Compute selected ratios.
(SO 6)

ARMADA COMPANY
Balance Sheets
December 31

	2010	2009
Cash	$ 25,000	$ 30,000
Receivables (net)	65,000	60,000
Inventories	60,000	50,000
Plant assets (net)	200,000	180,000
	$350,000	$320,000
Accounts payable	$ 50,000	$ 60,000
Mortgage payable (15%)	100,000	100,000
Common stock, $10 par	140,000	120,000
Retained earnings	60,000	40,000
	$350,000	$320,000

Additional information for 2010:
1. Net income was $25,000.
2. Sales on account were $375,000. Sales returns and allowances amounted to $25,000.
3. Cost of goods sold was $198,000.
4. Net cash provided by operating activities was $48,000.
5. Capital expenditures were $25,000, and cash dividends were $18,000.

Instructions
Compute the following ratios at December 31, 2010.
(a) Current.
(b) Receivables turnover.
(c) Average collection period.
(d) Inventory turnover.
(e) Days in inventory.
(f) Cash debt coverage.
(g) Current cash debt coverage.
(h) Free cash flow.

E13-10 Selected comparative statement data for the giant bookseller Barnes & Noble are presented here. All balance sheet data are as of the end of the fiscal year (in millions).

Compute selected ratios.
(SO 6)

	2006	2005
Net sales	$5,261.3	$5,103.0
Cost of goods sold	3,623.0	3,535.8
Net income	150.5	146.7
Accounts receivable	100.5	99.1
Inventory	1,354.6	1,314.0
Total assets	3,196.8	3,156.3
Total common stockholders' equity	1,164.9	1,115.8

Instructions

Compute the following ratios for 2006:

(a) Profit margin.

(b) Asset turnover.

(c) Return on assets.

(d) Return on common stockholders' equity.

(e) Gross profit rate.

Compute selected ratios.
(SO 6)

E13-11 Here is the income statement for Swayze, Inc.

SWAYZE, INC.
Income Statement
For the Year Ended December 31, 2010

Sales	$400,000
Cost of goods sold	230,000
Gross profit	170,000
Expenses (including $16,000 interest and $24,000 income taxes)	90,000
Net income	$ 80,000

Additional information:

1. Common stock outstanding January 1, 2010, was 30,000 shares, and 40,000 shares were outstanding at December 31, 2010.
2. The market price of Swayze, Inc., stock was $17.60 in 2010.
3. Cash dividends of $21,000 were paid, $10,000 of which were to preferred stockholders.

Instructions

Compute the following measures for 2010.

(a) Earnings per share.

(b) Price-earnings ratio.

(c) Payout ratio.

(d) Times interest earned ratio.

Compute amounts from
ratios.
(SO 6)

E13-12 Garcia Corporation experienced a fire on December 31, 2010, in which its financial records were partially destroyed. It has been able to salvage some of the records and has ascertained the following balances.

	December 31, 2010	December 31, 2009
Cash	$ 30,000	$ 10,000
Receivables (net)	72,500	126,000
Inventory	200,000	180,000
Accounts payable	50,000	10,000
Notes payable	30,000	20,000
Common stock, $100 par	400,000	400,000
Retained earnings	113,500	101,000

Additional information:

1. The inventory turnover is 4.4 times.
2. The return on common stockholders' equity is 18%. The company had no additional paid-in capital.
3. The receivables turnover is 11.2 times.
4. The return on assets is 16%.
5. Total assets at December 31, 2009, were $605,000.

Instructions

Compute the following for Garcia Corporation.

(a) Cost of goods sold for 2010.

(b) Net credit sales for 2010.

(c) Net income for 2010.

(d) Total assets at December 31, 2010.

Exercises: Set B

Visit the book's companion website, at **www.wiley.com/college/kimmel**, and choose the Student Companion site, to access Exercise Set B.

Problems: Set A

P13-1A Here are comparative statement data for Blue Company and Gray Company, two competitors. All balance sheet data are as of December 31, 2010, and December 31, 2009.

Prepare vertical analysis and comment on profitability.
(SO 5, 6)

	Blue Company		Gray Company	
	2010	**2009**	**2010**	**2009**
Net sales	$1,849,035		$546,000	
Cost of goods sold	1,080,490		278,000	
Operating expenses	250,000		82,000	
Interest expense	6,800		1,600	
Income tax expense	62,030		31,000	
Current assets	325,975	$312,410	83,336	$ 79,467
Plant assets (net)	526,800	500,000	139,728	125,812
Current liabilities	66,325	75,815	35,348	30,281
Long-term liabilities	113,990	90,000	29,620	25,000
Common stock, $10 par	500,000	500,000	120,000	120,000
Retained earnings	172,460	146,595	38,096	29,998

Instructions
(a) Prepare a vertical analysis of the 2010 income statement data for Blue Company and Gray Company.
(b) Comment on the relative profitability of the companies by computing the 2010 return on assets and the return on common stockholders' equity ratios for both companies.

P13-2A The comparative statements of McGillis Company are presented here.

Compute ratios from balance sheet and income statement.
(SO 6)

McGILLIS COMPANY
Income Statements
For the Years Ended December 31

	2010	**2009**
Net sales	$1,890,540	$1,750,500
Cost of goods sold	1,058,540	996,000
Gross profit	832,000	754,500
Selling and administrative expenses	506,000	479,000
Income from operations	326,000	275,500
Other expenses and losses		
Interest expense	25,000	19,000
Income before income taxes	301,000	256,500
Income tax expense	90,000	77,000
Net income	$ 211,000	$ 179,500

McGILLIS COMPANY
Balance Sheets
December 31

Assets	**2010**	**2009**
Current assets		
Cash	$ 60,100	$ 64,200
Short-term investments	74,000	50,000
Accounts receivable	117,800	102,800
Inventory	123,000	115,500
Total current assets	374,900	332,500
Plant assets (net)	615,300	520,300
Total assets	$990,200	$852,800

Liabilities and Stockholders' Equity	2010	2009
Current liabilities		
Accounts payable	$160,000	$145,400
Income taxes payable	43,500	42,000
Total current liabilities	203,500	187,400
Bonds payable	210,000	200,000
Total liabilities	413,500	387,400
Stockholders' equity		
Common stock ($5 par)	290,000	300,000
Retained earnings	286,700	165,400
Total stockholders' equity	576,700	465,400
Total liabilities and stockholders' equity	$990,200	$852,800

All sales were on account. Net cash provided by operating activities for 2010 was $220,000. Capital expenditures were $120,000, and cash dividends were $80,000.

Instructions
Compute the following ratios for 2010.

(a) Earnings per share.
(b) Return on common stockholders' equity.
(c) Return on assets.
(d) Current ratio.
(e) Receivables turnover.
(f) Average collection period.
(g) Inventory turnover.

(h) Days in inventory.
(i) Times interest earned.
(j) Asset turnover.
(k) Debt to total assets.
(l) Current cash debt coverage.
(m) Cash debt coverage.
(n) Free cash flow.

Perform ratio analysis, and discuss change in financial position and operating results.

(SO 6)

P13-3A Condensed balance sheet and income statement data for Breckenridge Corporation are presented here.

BRECKENRIDGE CORPORATION
Balance Sheets
December 31

	2010	2009	2008
Cash	$ 30,000	$ 20,000	$ 18,000
Receivables (net)	50,000	45,000	48,000
Other current assets	90,000	85,000	64,000
Investments	55,000	70,000	45,000
Plant and equipment (net)	500,000	370,000	258,000
	$725,000	$590,000	$433,000
Current liabilities	$ 85,000	$ 80,000	$ 30,000
Long-term debt	185,000	85,000	20,000
Common stock, $10 par	320,000	300,000	300,000
Retained earnings	135,000	125,000	83,000
	$725,000	$590,000	$433,000

BRECKENRIDGE CORPORATION
Income Statements
For the Years Ended December 31

	2010	2009
Sales	$640,000	$500,000
Less: Sales returns and allowances	40,000	30,000
Net sales	600,000	470,000
Cost of goods sold	425,000	300,000
Gross profit	175,000	170,000
Operating expenses (including income taxes)	110,000	99,000
Net income	$ 65,000	$ 71,000

Additional information:

1. The market price of Breckenridge's common stock was $6.00, $9.00, and $7.00 for 2008, 2009, and 2010, respectively.
2. You must compute dividends paid. All dividends were paid in cash.

Instructions

(a) Compute the following ratios for 2009 and 2010.
   (1) Profit margin.
   (2) Gross profit.
   (3) Asset turnover.
   (4) Earnings per share.
   (5) Price-earnings.
   (6) Payout.
   (7) Debt to total assets.
(b) Based on the ratios calculated, discuss briefly the improvement or lack thereof in the financial position and operating results from 2009 to 2010 of Breckenridge Corporation.

P13-4A   The following financial information is for Vail Company.

Compute ratios; comment on overall liquidity and profitability.
(SO 6)

VAIL COMPANY
Balance Sheets
December 31

Assets	2010	2009
Cash	$ 70,000	$ 65,000
Short-term investments	55,000	40,000
Receivables	104,000	80,000
Inventories	230,000	135,000
Prepaid expenses	25,000	23,000
Land	130,000	130,000
Building and equipment (net)	260,000	175,000
Total assets	$874,000	$648,000

Liabilities and Stockholders' Equity	2010	2009
Notes payable	$170,000	$100,000
Accounts payable	65,000	42,000
Accrued liabilities	40,000	40,000
Bonds payable, due 2009	250,000	150,000
Common stock, $10 par	200,000	200,000
Retained earnings	149,000	116,000
Total liabilities and stockholders' equity	$874,000	$648,000

VAIL COMPANY
Income Statements
For the Years Ended December 31

	2010	2009
Sales	$880,000	$790,000
Cost of goods sold	640,000	575,000
Gross profit	240,000	215,000
Operating expenses	190,000	167,000
Net income	$ 50,000	$ 48,000

Additional information:

1. Inventory at the beginning of 2009 was $115,000.
2. Receivables (net) at the beginning of 2009 were $88,000.
3. Total assets at the beginning of 2009 were $630,000.
4. No common stock transactions occurred during 2009 or 2010.
5. All sales were on account.

Instructions

(a) Indicate, by using ratios, the change in liquidity and profitability of Vail Company from 2009 to 2010. (*Note:* Not all profitability ratios can be computed nor can cash-basis ratios be computed.)

(b) Given below are three independent situations and a ratio that may be affected. For each situation, compute the affected ratio (1) as of December 31, 2010, and (2) as of December 31, 2011, after giving effect to the situation. Net income for 2011 was $40,000. Total assets on December 31, 2011, were $900,000.

Situation	Ratio
1. 18,000 shares of common stock were sold at par on July 1, 2011.	Return on common stockholders' equity
2. All of the notes payable were paid in 2011.	Debt to total assets
3. The market price of common stock was $9 and $12 on December 31, 2010 and 2011, respectively.	Price-earnings

Compute selected ratios, and compare liquidity, profitability, and solvency for two companies.
(SO 6)

P13-5A Selected financial data of Target and Wal-Mart for 2006 are presented here (in millions).

	Target Corporation	Wal-Mart Stores, Inc.
	Income Statement Data for Year	
Net sales	$57,878	$348,650
Cost of goods sold	39,399	264,152
Selling and administrative expenses	14,315	64,001
Interest expense	572	1,809
Other income (expense)	905	(1,039)
Income tax expense	1,710	6,365
Net income	$ 2,787	$ 11,284
	Balance Sheet Data (End of Year)	
Current assets	$14,706	$ 46,588
Noncurrent assets	22,643	104,605
Total assets	$37,349	$151,193
Current liabilities	$11,117	$ 51,754
Long-term debt	10,599	37,866
Total stockholders' equity	15,633	61,573
Total liabilities and stockholders' equity	$37,349	$151,193
	Beginning-of-Year Balances	
Total assets	$34,995	$138,187
Total stockholders' equity	14,205	53,171
Current liabilities	9,588	48,825
Total liabilities	20,790	85,016
	Other Data	
Average net receivables	$ 5,930	$ 2,707
Average inventory	6,046	32,797
Net cash provided by operating activities	4,862	20,209
Capital expenditures	3,928	15,666
Dividends	380	2,802

Instructions

(a) For each company, compute the following ratios.

(1) Current.	(8) Return on assets.
(2) Receivables turnover.	(9) Return on common stockholders' equity.
(3) Average collection period.	(10) Debt to total assets.
(4) Inventory turnover.	(11) Times interest earned.
(5) Days in inventory.	(12) Current cash debt coverage.
(6) Profit margin.	(13) Cash debt coverage.
(7) Asset turnover.	(14) Free cash flow.

(b) Compare the liquidity, solvency, and profitability of the two companies.

Problems: Set B

⊙━━━⊂ All of the Problems in this chapter employ decision tools.

P13-1B Here are comparative statement data for Clark Company and Kent Company, two competitors. All balance sheet data are as of December 31, 2010, and December 31, 2009.

Prepare vertical analysis and comment on profitability.
(SO 5, 6)

	Clark Company		Kent Company	
	2010	**2009**	**2010**	**2009**
Net sales	$350,000		$1,200,000	
Cost of goods sold	180,000		624,000	
Operating expenses	66,000		266,000	
Interest expense	3,000		10,000	
Income tax expense	17,000		54,000	
Current assets	130,000	$100,000	700,000	$650,000
Plant assets (net)	400,000	270,000	1,000,000	750,000
Current liabilities	60,000	52,000	250,000	275,000
Long-term liabilities	50,000	68,000	200,000	150,000
Common stock	360,000	210,000	950,000	700,000
Retained earnings	60,000	40,000	300,000	275,000

Instructions
(a) Prepare a vertical analysis of the 2010 income statement data for Clark Company and Kent Company.
(b) Comment on the relative profitability of the companies by computing the return on assets and the return on common stockholders' equity ratios for both companies.

P13-2B The comparative statements of Flintstone Company are shown below.

Compute ratios from balance sheet and income statement.
(SO 6)

FLINTSTONE COMPANY
Income Statements
For the Years Ended December 31

	2010	**2009**
Net sales	$780,000	$624,000
Cost of goods sold	440,000	405,600
Gross profit	340,000	218,400
Selling and administrative expense	146,880	149,760
Income from operations	193,120	68,640
Other expenses and losses		
Interest expense	9,920	7,200
Income before income taxes	183,200	61,440
Income tax expense	42,000	14,000
Net income	$141,200	$ 47,440

FLINTSTONE COMPANY
Balance Sheets
December 31

Assets	**2010**	**2009**
Current assets		
Cash	$ 23,100	$ 21,600
Short-term investments	44,800	33,000
Accounts receivable	106,200	83,800
Inventory	116,400	74,000
Total current assets	290,500	212,400
Plant assets (net)	485,300	439,600
Total assets	$775,800	$652,000

Liabilities and Stockholders' Equity	2010	2009
Current liabilities		
Accounts payable	$148,200	$132,000
Income taxes payable	25,300	24,000
Total current liabilities	173,500	156,000
Bonds payable	132,000	120,000
Total liabilities	305,500	276,000
Stockholders' equity		
Common stock ($10 par)	140,000	130,000
Retained earnings	330,300	246,000
Total stockholders' equity	470,300	376,000
Total liabilities and stockholders' equity	$775,800	$652,000

All sales were on account. Net cash provided by operating activities was $114,000. Capital expenditures were $47,000, and cash dividends were $55,000.

Instructions

Compute the following ratios for 2010.

(a) Earnings per share.
(b) Return on common stockholders' equity.
(c) Return on assets.
(d) Current.
(e) Receivables turnover.
(f) Average collection period.
(g) Inventory turnover.

(h) Days in inventory.
(i) Times interest earned.
(j) Asset turnover.
(k) Debt to total assets.
(l) Current cash debt coverage.
(m) Cash debt coverage.
(n) Free cash flow.

Perform ratio analysis, and discuss change in financial position and operating results.

(SO 6)

P13-3B The condensed balance sheet and income statement data for Cardinal Corporation are presented below.

CARDINAL CORPORATION
Balance Sheets
December 31

	2010	2009	2008
Cash	$ 30,000	$ 24,000	$ 20,000
Receivables (net)	110,000	48,000	48,000
Other current assets	80,000	78,000	62,000
Investments	90,000	70,000	50,000
Plant and equipment (net)	603,000	400,000	360,000
	$913,000	$620,000	$540,000
Current liabilities	$ 98,000	$ 75,000	$ 70,000
Long-term debt	230,000	75,000	65,000
Common stock, $10 par	400,000	340,000	300,000
Retained earnings	185,000	130,000	105,000
	$913,000	$620,000	$540,000

CARDINAL CORPORATION
Income Statements
For the Years Ended December 31

	2010	2009
Sales	$800,000	$750,000
Less: Sales returns and allowances	40,000	50,000
Net sales	760,000	700,000
Cost of goods sold	420,000	400,000
Gross profit	340,000	300,000
Operating expenses (including income taxes)	220,000	210,000
Net income	$120,000	$ 90,000

Additional information:

1. The market price of Cardinal common stock was $5.00, $3.50, and $2.30 for 2008, 2009, and 2010, respectively.
2. You must compute dividends paid. All dividends were paid in cash.

Instructions

(a) Compute the following ratios for 2009 and 2010.

    (1) Profit margin.   (5) Price-earnings.

    (2) Gross profit rate.   (6) Payout.

    (3) Asset turnover.   (7) Debt to total assets.

    (4) Earnings per share.

(b) Based on the ratios calculated, discuss briefly the improvement or lack thereof in the financial position and operating results from 2009 to 2010 of Cardinal Corporation.

P13-4B   Financial information for Hi-Tech Company is presented here.

Compute ratios; comment on overall liquidity and profitability.
(SO 6)

HI-TECH COMPANY
Balance Sheets
December 31

Assets	2010	2009
Cash	$ 50,000	$ 42,000
Short-term investments	80,000	50,000
Receivables	100,000	77,000
Inventories	410,000	310,000
Prepaid expenses	30,000	31,000
Land	75,000	75,000
Building and equipment (net)	570,000	400,000
Total assets	$1,315,000	$985,000

Liabilities and Stockholders' Equity		
Notes payable	$ 120,000	$ 25,000
Accounts payable	160,000	90,000
Accrued liabilities	50,000	50,000
Bonds payable, due 2012	180,000	100,000
Common stock, $5 par	500,000	500,000
Retained earnings	305,000	220,000
Total liabilities and stockholders' equity	$1,315,000	$985,000

HI-TECH COMPANY
Income Statements
For the Years Ended December 31

	2010	2009
Sales	$1,000,000	$940,000
Cost of goods sold	655,000	635,000
Gross profit	345,000	305,000
Operating expenses	230,000	215,000
Net income	$ 115,000	$ 90,000

Additional information:

1. Inventory at the beginning of 2009 was $350,000.
2. Receivables at the beginning of 2009 were $80,000.
3. Total assets at the beginning of 2009 were $1,175,000.
4. No common stock transactions occurred during 2009 or 2010.
5. All sales were on account.

Instructions

(a) Indicate, by using ratios, the change in liquidity and profitability of the company from 2009 to 2010. (*Note:* Not all profitability ratios can be computed nor can cash basis ratios be computed.)

(b) Given below are three independent situations and a ratio that may be affected. For each situation, compute the affected ratio (1) as of December 31, 2010, and (2) as of December 31, 2011, after giving effect to the situation. Net income for 2011 was $125,000. Total assets on December 31, 2011, were $1,450,000.

Situation	Ratio
1. 50,000 shares of common stock were sold at par on July 1, 2011.	Return on common stockholders' equity
2. All of the notes payable were paid in 2011.	Debt to total assets
3. The market price of common stock on December 31, 2011, was $6.25. The market price on December 31, 2010, was $5.	Price-earnings

Compute selected ratios, and compare liquidity, profitability, and solvency for two companies.
(SO 6)

P13-5B Selected financial data for Black & Decker and Snap-On Tools for 2007 are presented here (in millions).

	Black & Decker	Snap-On Tools
Income Statement Data for Year		
Net sales	$6,563.2	$2,841.2
Cost of goods sold	4,336.2	1,574.6
Selling and administrative expenses	1,644.8	964.2
Interest expense	102.1	46.1
Other income	17.5	17.4
Income tax expense (benefit)	(20.5)	92.5
Net income (before irregular items)	$ 518.1	$ 181.2
Balance Sheet Data (End of Year)		
Current assets	$2,839.5	$1,187.4
Property, plant, and equipment (net)	596.2	304.8
Other assets	1,975.2	1,272.9
Total assets	$5,410.9	$2,765.1
Current liabilities	$1,880.8	$ 639.2
Long-term debt	2,071.4	845.8
Total stockholders' equity	1,458.7	1,280.1
Total liabilities and stockholders' equity	$5,410.9	$2,765.1
Beginning-of-Year Balances		
Total assets	$5,247.7	$2,654.5
Total stockholders' equity	1,163.6	1,076.3
Current liabilities	1,779.6	682.0
Total liabilities	4,084.1	1,578.2
Other Data		
Average receivables (net)	$1,129.5	$ 573.1
Average inventory	1,104.7	322.7
Net cash provided by operating activities	725.9	231.1
Capital expenditures	116.4	61.9
Cash dividends	108.6	64.8

Instructions

(a) For each company, compute the following ratios.

(1) Current ratio.	(8) Return on assets.
(2) Receivables turnover.	(9) Return on common stockholders' equity.
(3) Average collection period.	(10) Debt to total assets.
(4) Inventory turnover.	(11) Times interest earned.
(5) Days in inventory.	(12) Current cash debt coverage.
(6) Profit margin.	(13) Cash debt coverage.
(7) Asset turnover.	(14) Free cash flow.

(b) Compare the liquidity, solvency, and profitability of the two companies.

Problems: Set C

Visit the book's companion website at **www.wiley.com/college/kimmel** and choose the Student Companion site to access Problem Set C.

Continuing Cookie Chronicle

(*Note:* This is a continuation of the Cookie Chronicle from Chapters 1 through 12.)

CCC13   Natalie and Curtis have comparative balance sheets and income statements for Cookie & Coffee Creations Inc. They have been told that they can use these financial statements to prepare horizontal and vertical analyses, and to calculate financial ratios, to analyze how their business is doing and to make some decisions they have been considering.

Go to the book's companion website, **www.wiley.com/college/kimmel**, to find the completion of this problem.

broadening your perspective

Financial Reporting and Analysis

FINANCIAL REPORTING PROBLEM: *Tootsie Roll Industries, Inc.*

BYP13-1   Your parents are considering investing in Tootsie Roll Industries common stock. They ask you, as an accounting expert, to make an analysis of the company for them. Fortunately, excerpts from a recent annual report of Tootsie Roll are presented in Appendix A of this textbook.

Instructions
(a) Make a 5-year trend analysis, using 2003 as the base year, of (1) net sales and (2) net earnings. Comment on the significance of the trend results.
(b) Compute for 2007 and 2006 the (1) debt to total assets ratio and (2) times interest earned ratio. (See note 6 for interest expense.) How would you evaluate Tootsie Roll's long-term solvency?
(c) Compute for 2007 and 2006 the (1) profit margin ratio, (2) asset turnover ratio, (3) return on assets ratio, and (4) return on common stockholders' equity ratio. How would you evaluate Tootsie Roll's profitability? Total assets at December 31, 2005, were $813,696,000, and total stockholders' equity at December 31, 2005, was $617,405,000.
(d) What information outside the annual report may also be useful to your parents in making a decision about Tootsie Roll?

COMPARATIVE ANALYSIS PROBLEM: *Tootsie Roll vs. Hershey Foods*

BYP13-2   The financial statements of Hershey Foods are presented in Appendix B, following the financial statements for Tootsie Roll Industries in Appendix A.

Instructions
(a) Based on the information in the financial statements, determine each of the following for each company:
  (1) The percentage increase (i) in net sales and (ii) in net income from 2006 to 2007.
  (2) The percentage increase (i) in total assets and (ii) in total stockholders' equity from 2006 to 2007.
  (3) The earnings per share for 2007.
(b) What conclusions concerning the two companies can be drawn from these data?

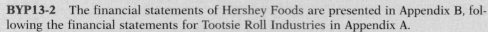

RESEARCH CASE

BYP13-3 The August 15, 2007, issue of the *New York Times* included an article by David Leonhardt titled "Remembering a Classic Investing Theory."

Instructions
Read the article and answer the following questions.
(a) At the time of the article, what was the average P-E ratio for the Standard & Poor's 500-stock index? How did this compare with the average P-E ratio since World War II?
(b) What criticism did Graham and Dodd have of the way the P-E is usually measured today?
(c) Using the Graham and Dodd approach to measuring the P-E ratio, what was the P-E at the time the article was written, and how did it compare with its value in previous years?
(d) What does the article's author say the Graham and Dodd P-E tells us about the stock market at the time the article was written?

INTERPRETING FINANCIAL STATEMENTS

BYP13-4 The Coca-Cola Company and PepsiCo, Inc. provide refreshments to every corner of the world. Selected data from the 2007 consolidated financial statements for The Coca-Cola Company and for PepsiCo, Inc., are presented here (in millions).

	Coca-Cola	PepsiCo
Total current assets	$12,105	$10,151
Total current liabilities	13,225	7,753
Net sales	28,857	39,474
Cost of goods sold	10,406	18,038
Net income	5,981	5,658
Average (net) receivables for the year	2,952	4,057
Average inventories for the year	1,931	2,108
Average total assets	36,616	32,279
Average common stockholders' equity	19,332	16,386
Average current liabilities	11,058	7,307
Average total liabilities	17,284	15,978
Total assets	43,269	32,279
Total liabilities	21,525	17,394
Income taxes	1,892	1,973
Interest expense	456	224
Cash provided by operating activities	7,150	6,934
Capital expenditures	1,648	2,430
Cash dividends	3,149	2,204

Instructions
(a) Compute the following liquidity ratios for 2007 for Coca-Cola and for PepsiCo and comment on the relative liquidity of the two competitors.
  (1) Current ratio.   (4) Inventory turnover.
  (2) Receivables turnover.   (5) Days in inventory.
  (3) Average collection period.   (6) Current cash debt coverage.
(b) Compute the following solvency ratios for the two companies and comment on the relative solvency of the two competitors.
  (1) Debt to total assets ratio.
  (2) Times interest earned.
  (3) Cash debt coverage ratio.
  (4) Free cash flow.
(c) Compute the following profitability ratios for the two companies and comment on the relative profitability of the two competitors.
  (1) Profit margin.
  (2) Asset turnover.
  (3) Return on assets.
  (4) Return on common stockholders' equity.

FINANCIAL ANALYSIS ON THE WEB

BYP13-5 *Purpose:* To employ comparative data and industry data to evaluate a company's performance and financial position.

Address: **http://www.reuters.com/finance/stocks**, or go to **www.wiley.com/college/kimmel**

Steps

(1) Identify two competing companies.
(2) Go to the above address.
(3) Type in the first company's stock symbol. (Use "symbol look-up.").
(4) Choose **Ratios**.
(5) Print out the results.
(6) Repeat steps 3–5 for the competitor.

Instructions

(a) Evaluate the company's liquidity relative to the industry averages and to the competitor that you chose.
(b) Evaluate the company's solvency relative to the industry averages and to the competitor that you chose.
(c) Evaluate the company's profitability relative to the industry averages and to the competitor that you chose.

Critical Thinking

DECISION MAKING ACROSS THE ORGANIZATION

BYP13-6 You are a loan officer for Lakeland Bank of Port Washington. Dennis Schwartz, president of D. Schwartz Corporation, has just left your office. He is interested in an 8-year loan to expand the company's operations. The borrowed funds would be used to purchase new equipment. As evidence of the company's debt-worthiness, Schwartz provided you with the following facts.

	2010	2009
Current ratio	3.1	2.1
Asset turnover ratio	2.8	2.2
Cash debt coverage ratio	.1	.2
Net income	Up 32%	Down 8%
Earnings per share	$3.30	$2.50

Schwartz is a very insistent (some would say pushy) man. When you told him that you would need additional information before making your decision, he acted offended, and said, "What more could you possibly want to know?" You responded that, at a minimum, you would need complete, audited financial statements.

Instructions

With the class divided into groups, answer the following.

(a) Explain why you would want the financial statements to be audited.
(b) Discuss the implications of the ratios provided for the lending decision you are to make. That is, does the information paint a favorable picture? Are these ratios relevant to the decision?
(c) List three other ratios that you would want to calculate for this company, and explain why you would use each.

COMMUNICATION ACTIVITY

BYP13-7 Sam Mead is the chief executive officer of Alemeda Electronics. Mead is an expert engineer but a novice in accounting. Mead asks you, as an accounting major, to explain (a) the bases for comparison in analyzing Alemeda financial statements and (b) the limitations, if any, in financial statement analysis.

Instructions

Write a memo to Sam Mead that explains the basis for comparison and the factors affecting quality of earnings.

ETHICS CASE

BYP13-8 Glenda Shumway, president of RF Industries, wishes to issue a press release to bolster her company's image and maybe even its stock price, which has been gradually falling. As controller, you have been asked to provide a list of 20 financial ratios and other operating statistics for RF Industries' first-quarter financials and operations.

Two days after you provide the data requested, Regina Tarow, the public relations director of RF, asks you to prove the accuracy of the financial and operating data contained in the press release written by the president and edited by Regina. In the news release, the president highlights the sales increase of 25% over last year's first quarter and the positive change in the current ratio from 1.5:1 last year to 3:1 this year. She also emphasizes that production was up 50% over the prior year's first quarter.

You note that the release contains only positive or improved ratios and none of the negative or deteriorated ratios. For instance, no mention is made that the debt to total assets ratio has increased from 35% to 55%, that inventories are up 89%, and that although the current ratio improved, the current cash debt coverage ratio fell from .15 to .05. Nor is there any mention that the reported profit for the quarter would have been a loss had not the estimated lives of RF plant and machinery been increased by 30%. Regina emphasized, "The Pres wants this release by early this afternoon."

Instructions
(a) Who are the stakeholders in this situation?
(b) Is there anything unethical in the president's actions?
(c) Should you as controller remain silent? Does Regina have any responsibility?

"ALL ABOUT YOU" ACTIVITY

BYP13-9 In this chapter you learned how to use many tools for performing a financial analysis of a company. When making personal investments, however, it is most likely that you won't be buying stocks and bonds in individual companies. Instead, when most people want to invest in stock, they buy mutual funds. By investing in a mutual fund, you reduce your risk because the fund diversifies by buying the stock of a variety of different companies, bonds, and other investments, depending on the stated goals of the fund.

Before you invest in a fund, you will need to decide what type of fund you want. For example, do you want a fund that has the potential of high growth (but also high risk), or are you looking for lower risk and a steady steam of income? Do you want a fund that invests only in U.S. companies, or do you want one that invests globally? Many resources are available to help you with these types of decisions.

Instructions
Go to **http://web.archive.org/web/20050210200843/http://www.cnb1.com/invallocmdl. htm** and complete the investment allocation questionnaire. Add up your total points to determine the type of investment fund that would be appropriate for you.

Answers to Insight and Accounting Across the Organization Questions

p. 663

Q: If a company takes a large restructuring charge, what is the effect on the company's current income statements versus future ones?

A: The current period's net income can be greatly diminished by a large restructuring charge. The net incomes in future periods can be enhanced because they are relieved of costs (i.e., depreciation and labor expenses) that would have been charged to them.

p. 674

Q: How might management influence a company's current ratio?

A: Management can affect the current ratio by speeding up or withholding payments on accounts payable just before the balance sheet date. Management can alter the cash balance by increasing or decreasing long-term assets or long-term debt, or by issuing or purchasing common stock.

p. 677

Q: Why might adding extra pages to the annual report not be beneficial to investors and analysts? What should be management's overriding objective in financial reporting?

A: When given too much information, investors may suffer from "information overload"— they may have a hard time sorting out what is important from what is not. Management's overriding financial reporting objective should be to provide an accurate depiction of the company's financial position and operating results in a clear and concise fashion. It should provide as much detail as is necessary to accomplish that.

Answers to Self-Study Questions

1. d   2. d   3. b   4. d   5. c   6. c   7. a   8. c   9. c   10. b   11. a   12. b   13. b   14. a   15. d   16. c   17. c

✔ Remember to go back to the navigator box on the chapter-opening page and check off your completed work.

Specimen Financial Statements: Tootsie Roll Industries, Inc.

The Annual Report

Once each year a corporation communicates to its stockholders and other interested parties by issuing a complete set of audited financial statements. The **annual report**, as this communication is called, summarizes the financial results of the company's operations for the year and its plans for the future. Many annual reports are attractive, multicolored, glossy public relations pieces, containing pictures of corporate officers and directors as well as photos and descriptions of new products and new buildings. Yet the basic function of every annual report is to report financial information, almost all of which is a product of the corporation's accounting system.

Tootsie Roll Annual Report Walkthrough

    The content and organization of corporate annual reports have become fairly standardized. Excluding the public relations part of the report (pictures, products, and propaganda), the following items are the traditional financial portions of the annual report:

Financial Highlights
Letter to the Stockholders
Management's Discussion and Analysis
Financial Statements
Notes to the Financial Statements
Management's Report on Internal Control
Management Certification of Financial Statements
Auditor's Report
Supplementary Financial Information

    In this appendix we illustrate current financial reporting with a comprehensive set of corporate financial statements that are prepared in accordance with generally accepted accounting principles and audited by an international independent certified public accounting firm. We are grateful for permission to use the actual financial statements and other accompanying financial information from the annual report of a large, publicly held company, Tootsie Roll Industries, Inc.

Financial Highlights

Companies usually present the financial highlights section inside the front cover of the annual report or on its first two pages. This section generally reports the total or per share amounts for five to ten financial items for the current year and one or more previous years.

The financial information herein is reprinted with permission from the Tootsie Roll Industries, Inc. 2007 Annual Report. The complete financial statements for Tootsie Roll Industries are also available on the book's companion website.

Corporate Profile

Tootsie Roll Industries, Inc. has been engaged in the manufacture and sale of confectionery products for 111 years. Our products are primarily sold under the familiar brand names: Tootsie Roll, Tootsie Roll Pops, Caramel Apple Pops, Child's Play, Charms, Blow Pop, Blue Razz, Cella's chocolate covered cherries, Mason Dots, Mason Crows, Junior Mints, Junior Caramels, Charleston Chew, Sugar Daddy, Sugar Babies, Andes, Fluffy Stuff cotton candy, Dubble Bubble, Razzles, Cry Baby, Nik-L-Nip and El Bubble.

Melvin J. Gordon, Chairman and Chief Executive Officer and Ellen R. Gordon, President and Chief Operating Officer.

Corporate Principles

We believe that the differences among companies are attributable to the caliber of their people, and therefore we strive to attract and retain superior people for each job.

We believe that an open family atmosphere at work combined with professional management fosters cooperation and enables each individual to maximize his or her contribution to the Company and realize the corresponding rewards.

We do not jeopardize long-term growth for immediate, short-term results.

We maintain a conservative financial posture in the deployment and management of our assets.

We run a trim operation and continually strive to eliminate waste, minimize cost and implement performance improvements.

We invest in the latest and most productive equipment to deliver the best quality product to our customers at the lowest cost.

We seek to outsource functions where appropriate and to vertically integrate operations where it is financially advantageous to do so.

We view our well known brands as prized assets to be aggressively advertised and promoted to each new generation of consumers.

We conduct business with the highest ethical standards and integrity which are codified in the Company's "Code of Business Conduct and Ethics."

Financial items from the income statement and the balance sheet that typically are presented are sales, income from continuing operations, net income, net income per share, dividends per common share, and the amount of capital expenditures. The financial highlights section from **Tootsie Roll Industries' Annual Report** is shown on page A-3. Above, we have also included Tootsie Roll's discussion of its corporate principles and corporate profile.

Letter to the Stockholders

Nearly every annual report contains a letter to the stockholders from the chairman of the board or the president, or both. This letter typically discusses the company's accomplishments during the past year and highlights significant events such as mergers and acquisitions, new products, operating achievements, business philosophy, changes in officers or directors, financing commitments, expansion plans, and future prospects. The letter to the stockholders signed by Melvin J. Gordon, Chairman of the Board and Chief Executive Officer, and Ellen R. Gordon, President and Chief Operating Officer, of Tootsie Roll Industries is shown on the next pages.

To Our Shareholders

To Our Shareholders:

Product sales in 2007 were $493 million compared with 2006 sales of $496 million. Sales increased in many of our core products and we had a strong Halloween selling season. These gains were offset by the conclusion of a contract to manufacture product under a private label for a third party and a non-recurring sale of certain inventory to a foreign distributor in 2006.

Net earnings in 2007 were $52 million compared to 2006 net earnings of $66 million. On a per share basis, earnings were $.94 in 2007 and $1.18 in 2006. Average shares outstanding declined as a result of share repurchases in 2007. As discussed in more detail later in this letter, the food industry has experienced extreme cost increases in many key ingredients. This was our experience as well. Substantially all of our principal ingredients as well as packaging and energy costs were significantly higher in 2007. In addition, the weakened U.S. dollar translated into higher costs in our Canadian manufacturing plants. All of these factors adversely impacted our margins and profitability.

At Tootsie Roll we have always maintained a bottom line focus and continually review all facets of our operations in order to increase efficiencies and eliminate waste. As a result of significantly higher input costs, we have also adjusted selling prices or package weights on some items and will continue to take other steps to increase profitability. We do, however, take a long-term view of the business and are mindful not to let our reactions to current market conditions jeopardize the Company's future prospects.

We are a value-oriented branded confectioner and deem it essential to be the low cost producer in each of our major product lines. To that end we continue to implement production technologies that are state-of-the-art, or even better. Accordingly, in 2007 $15 million of capital was invested in operations.

We ended the year with cash and investments of $157 million in excess of interest bearing debt. This strong financial position enables us to continue to distribute dividends, repurchase stock, support our brands in the marketplace, develop new products, invest in operating assets, and consider business acquisition opportunities.

During 2007, we paid cash dividends of 32 cents per share and again distributed a 3% stock dividend. This was the sixty-fifth consecutive year in which cash dividends have been paid and the forty-third consecutive year in which a 3% stock dividend has been distributed. Our record of paying dividends once again earned us the distinction of being named a Mergent "Dividend Achiever," an honor shared with only 3% of U.S. listed dividend paying companies.

During the year we also repurchased $27 million of our common stock in the open market.

Sales and Marketing

During 2007, we once again used targeted consumer and trade promotions to emphasize the high quality and attractive values that our well known brands provide. Carefully executed promotions of this kind move our product into distribution and, with high sell-through, subsequently move them off the retailer's shelf to the consumer.

Our portfolio of highly recognized brands remains popular across all classes of trade. We offer something for virtually all major consumer demographics and continually add new items or introduce new packs in response to changing consumer preferences in the highly competitive confectionery market.

Halloween continues to be our largest selling period. Through product offerings such as large bags of mixed product assortments and merchandising presentations such as pallet packs and display-ready cases we continue to enjoy high sales volume in our Halloween packaged goods line. We see

Financial Highlights

	December 31,	
	2007	2006
	(in thousands except per share data)	
Net Product Sales	$492,742	$495,990
Net Earnings	51,625	65,919
Working Capital	141,754	128,706
Net Property, Plant and Equipment	201,401	202,898
Shareholders' Equity	638,230	630,681
Average Shares Outstanding*	54,980	55,800
Per Share Items*		
Net Earnings	$0.94	$1.18
Cash Dividends Paid	.32	.32

*Adjusted for stock dividends.

good results in major trade classes including grocery, mass merchandisers, warehouse clubs, dollar stores and drug chains.

We also see continued consumer acceptance of our theater and home video box line in the super market, dollar store, mass merchandiser and drug store trade classes. Based on sales data tracked by Information Resources, Inc. in 2007 we had ten of the fifty top selling theater and home video box products, including Junior Mints and Dots, the #1 and #2 best selling items in this area.

Our theater and home video box line was expanded in 2007 to include DUBBLE BUBBLE. This iconic brand is offered in both the traditional pink "chunk" format and in colorful gumballs.

New Theater Boxes of DUBBLE BUBBLE

Seasonal offerings were also added in the theater box format. These included Peppermint Crunch Junior Mints, a dual-mint combination of real Junior Mints sprinkled with the refreshing crunch of peppermint candies.

Peppermint Crunch Junior Mints

Another new seasonal theater box item was Holiday Tootsie Mini Chews. These are mini Tootsie Rolls enrobed in a delicious white chocolaty coating and packed in boxes that feature red and green Christmas graphics. Both of these items are perfect for snacking on the go or for holiday gift bowls to share with friends.

Holiday Tootsie Mini Chews

Trick or treaters enjoyed frightfully fun Ghost Dots which were introduced for Halloween 2007. The five assorted flavor remain a mystery—masked behind a ghostly green translucent color!

Ghost Dots

Caramel Apple Sugar Babies were another seasonal addition to the theater box line. These are luscious caramel Sugar Babies with a tart green apple candy shell that are perfect for snacking!

Caramel Apple Sugar Babies

Two additions to our gift box line were introduced in 2007—Cella's Dark and Junior Mint Deluxe. Both items capitalize on the market trend with dark chocolate shells. Cella's Dark are filled with a maraschino cherry bathed in our unique 100% liquid center. Junior Mint Deluxe are filled with a creamy smooth mint fondant. These top shelf items make perfect gifts for any occasion.

Cella's Dark and Junior Mint Deluxe

We also introduced new items in the Andes line during 2007. Sugar free Andes is a traditional three layer mint thin made without sugar to appeal to consumers who must restrict their sugar intake.

Andes Sugar Free and Andes Trio

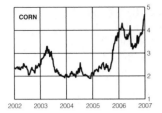

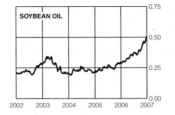

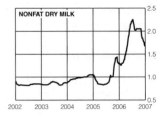

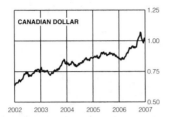

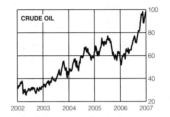

Advertising and Public Relations

Andes Trio is a gusseted bag filled with three popular Andes flavors—traditional Crème de Menthe, refreshing Peppermint Crunch and coffee flavor Mocha Mint—that is targeted to the warehouse club class of trade.

We again promoted our longstanding "How Many Licks" Tootsie Pop theme through campaigns on several children's channels on cable television. Also on cable, several of our products received extensive exposure through showings of popular special interest features including segments on the Food Network's *Unwrapped* program, a segment exploring "snack food technology" on The History Channel's *Modern Marvels,* and John Ratzenberger's *Made in America* show on the Travel Channel.

The Company's listing by KLD on the Domini 400 Social Index was affirmed in recognition of our leadership in the areas of corporate and social responsibility.

Purchasing

While 2007 was another year of generally modest consumer price inflation as measured by the Consumer Price Index, food producers experienced extreme increases in many of the commodities that we buy.

The accompanying charts depict the prices of three key commodities, oil and the Canadian dollar over the past five years. Corn is, of course, the key ingredient in corn syrup which is one of our highest volume commodities. Milk and soybean oil are also important ingredients used in Tootsie Rolls and other products that we manufacture.

Oil is used for fuel in transportation of both inbound and outbound shipments. Our Canadian operations are sensitive to the exchange rate between the U.S. and Canadian dollar for all labor, fringe benefits, and certain other factors of production.

The accompanying charts do not precisely mirror our actual costs of these commodities due to hedging and other programs that insulate the Company from short term fluctuations in market prices. Still, these techniques are limited in their ability to overcome significant cost trends over the long-term and our operating results reflect the impact of these higher costs.

We continue to use competitive bidding, volume purchases and other means to mitigate commodity and other cost increases to the fullest extent possible just as we strive to make operating improvements, increase our selling prices and take other actions to restore and improve profitability.

Supply Chain

We continue to invest capital and resources in projects and processes that keep our production and distribution facilities as efficient as possible, support growing product lines and changing distribution patterns and improve the quality of our products. Further, as technology continues to evolve, we have continued to realize benefits through automation.

During 2007, we embarked on a company wide upgrade of our ERP software. This multi-year project is consistent with our Corporate Principle to invest in our operations. We continue to examine every opportunity to search for operational improvements.

International

All of our international businesses grew profitably during 2007. Mexico had another strong sales year and higher profits. Our Canadian division experienced sales growth, improved distribution and increased profitability. Additionally, our export division, which reaches more than 50 countries in Europe, Asia, and

South and Central America, had higher sales and profits.

In Appreciation

We wish to thank our many loyal employees, customers, suppliers, sales brokers and domestic as well as foreign distributors for their contributions during 2007. We also thank our fellow shareholders for their support over the years. Excellence and

dedication is required at every level of the organization in order to meet the challenges of today's business environment and we are committed to both.

Melvin J. Gordon

Melvin J. Gordon
Chairman of the Board and
Chief Executive Officer

Ellen R. Gordon

Ellen R. Gordon
President and
Chief Operating Officer

Management Discussion and Analysis

The management discussion and analysis (MD&A) section covers three financial aspects of a company: its results of operations, its ability to pay near-term obligations, and its ability to fund operations and expansion. Management must highlight favorable or unfavorable trends and identify significant events and uncertainties that affect these three factors. This discussion obviously involves a number of subjective estimates and opinions. The MD&A section of Tootsie Roll's annual report is presented below.

Management's Discussion and Analysis of Financial Condition and Results of Operations

(in thousands except per share, percentage and ratio figures)

FINANCIAL REVIEW

This financial review discusses the Company's financial condition, results of operations, liquidity and capital resources, significant accounting policies and estimates, new accounting pronouncements, market risks and other matters. It should be read in conjunction with the Consolidated Financial Statements and related footnotes that follow this discussion.

FINANCIAL CONDITION

The Company's overall financial position was further strengthened by its 2007 net earnings and related cash flows provided by operating activities.

During 2007, the Company's cash flows from operating activities aggregated $90,064. The Company used these cash flows to pay cash dividends of $17,542, repurchase and retire $27,300 of its outstanding shares, and make capital expenditures of $14,767.

The Company's net working capital increased from $128,706 at December 31, 2006 to $141,754 at December 31, 2007, an increase of $13,048.

As of December 31, 2007, the Company's aggregate cash, cash equivalents and investments, including all long-term investments in marketable securities, was $164,906, compared to $130,841

at December 31, 2006, an increase of $34,065. These amounts include approximately $32,800 and $30,800 of trading securities as of December 31, 2007 and 2006, respectively, in which the Company has invested to hedge its deferred compensation liabilities, as further discussed in Note 7 to the financial statements.

Shareholders' equity increased from $630,681 at December 31, 2006 to $638,230 as of December 31, 2007, principally reflecting 2007 net earnings of $51,625 less cash dividends and share repurchases of $17,542 and $27,300, respectively.

The Company has a relatively straight-forward financial structure and has historically maintained a conservative financial position. Except for an immaterial amount of operating leases, the Company has no special financing arrangements or "off-balance sheet" special purpose entities. Cash flows from operations plus maturities of short term investments are expected to be adequate to meet the Company's overall financing needs, including capital expenditures, in 2008. The Company considers possible appropriate acquisitions on an ongoing basis, and if the Company were to pursue and complete such an acquisition, that could result in bank borrowings.

Results of Operations

2007 vs. 2006

Net product sales were $492,742 in 2007 compared to $495,990 in 2006, a decrease of $3,248 or 1%. This decline principally reflects the conclusion of a contract to manufacture product under a private label for a third party, which accounted for approximately $2,200 in net product sales in 2006, and a non-recurring sale of certain inventory in the amount of approximately $1,000 to a new foreign distributor in the first quarter of 2006.

Product cost of goods sold as a percentage of net sales increased from 62.8% in 2006 to 66.5% in 2007. This increase principally reflects significant cost increases in major ingredients, as well as increases in packaging materials, and labor and fringe benefits, including health insurance. In 2007, increases in ingredient and packaging costs approximated $10,500 and $1,500, respectively. The Company generally experienced significant cost increases in substantially all of its major ingredients, including corn syrup, vegetable oils, sugar,

dextrose, milk products, and gum base inputs. In addition, the adverse effects of foreign currency exchange on products manufactured in Canada is estimated to have been $1,800 in 2007.

Due to the seasonal nature of the Company's business and corresponding variations in product mix, gross margins have historically been lower in the second half of the year, and second half 2007 and 2006 were consistent with this trend.

Selling, marketing and administrative expenses were $97,821 in 2007 compared to $101,032 in 2006, a decrease of $3,211 or 3%. This decrease principally reflects the Company's cost reduction efforts as well as lower expenses that directly relate to the 1% sales decline. In addition, prior year 2006 operating expenses reflect approximately $1,500 of additional marketing expenses associated with the transition to new pack sizes and government mandated labeling changes. Additionally, higher freight, delivery and warehousing expenses, principally relating to higher energy and fuel costs, adversely impacted 2007 operating expenses compared to 2006.

Selling, marketing and administrative expenses as a percent of net product sales favorably decreased from 20.4% of net product sales in 2006 to 19.9% of product sales in 2007. These expenses include $41,775 and $40,353 of freight, warehousing and distribution expenses in 2007 and 2006, respectively. Freight, warehousing and distribution expenses increased from 8.1% of net product sales in 2006 to 8.5% of net product sales in 2007, primarily reflecting higher energy input costs and increased warehousing expenses in 2007.

Reported earnings from operations were $70,852 in 2007 compared to $87,529 in 2006, a decrease of $16,677 or 19.1%. This decrease principally reflects the decrease in gross profit resulting from higher input costs, principally ingredients, as discussed above.

The Company performs its annual impairment testing of its intangible assets, trademarks and goodwill, during the fourth quarter of each year. The Company believes that the carrying values of its trademarks and goodwill have indefinite lives as they are expected to generate cash flows indefinitely. There were no impairments in 2006 or 2007.

Other income, net, was $6,315 in 2007 compared to $7,186 in 2006, a decrease of $871. This is due to a decline in income from the Company's 50% interest in a joint venture, accounted for under the equity method, from $921 in 2006 to $182 in 2007.

The consolidated effective tax rate was 33.1% and 30.7% in 2007 and 2006, respectively. This increase in the effective tax rate principally reflects higher foreign income tax expense in 2007. During 2007 and 2006, the Company recorded $3,145 and $3,481 of valuation allowances, respectively, relating to foreign subsidiary tax loss carry-forwards to reduce the future income tax benefits to amounts expected to be realized. In addition, the 2007 effective tax rate was adversely impacted by $1,040 relating to the adoption of FASB Interpretation No. 48, "Accounting for Uncertainty in Income Taxes—an Interpretation of FASB Statement No. 109" (FIN 48) (see also section entitled New Accounting Pronouncements).

Net earnings were $51,625 in 2007 compared to $65,919 in 2006, and earnings per share were $.94 and $1.18 in 2007 and 2006, respectively. Twelve months 2007 results were adversely affected by lower sales and higher input costs, primarily relating to ingredients, as discussed above. Earnings per share did benefit from a reduction in average shares outstanding resulting from common stock purchases in the open market by the Company. Average shares outstanding decreased from 55,800 in 2006 to 54,980 in 2007.

The Company has taken actions and implemented programs, including selected price increases as well as cost reduction programs, with the objective of recovering some of these higher input costs. However these actions have not allowed the Company to recover all of these increases in ingredient and other input costs in 2007.

2006 vs. 2005

Net product sales were $495,990 in 2006, a new record, compared to $487,739 in 2005, reflecting an increase of $8,251 or 2%. Although this sales increase includes some selective price increases, the Company achieved record "back to school" and pre-Halloween product sales in third quarter 2006.

Product cost of goods sold as a percentage of net sales increased from 61.4% in 2005 to 62.8% in 2006. This increase reflects significant cost increases in major ingredients, as well as increases in packaging materials, labor and fringe benefits, and overall plant overhead. In 2006, increases in ingredient and packaging costs approximated $4,882 and $730, respectively. In addition, the adverse effect of foreign exchange on products manufactured in Canada is estimated to have been $2,200 in 2006.

Selling, marketing and administrative expenses were $101,032 in 2006 compared to $97,595 in 2005, an increase of $3,437 or 3.5%. This increase

principally reflects significantly higher freight and delivery expenses due to higher energy costs. In addition, marketing expenses associated with the transition to new pack sizes and government mandated labeling changes also added approximately $1,500 to these expenses. Selling, marketing and administrative expenses as a percent of net product sales increased slightly from 20.0% of sales in 2005 to 20.4% of sales in 2006. These expenses include $40,353 and $37,836 of freight, warehousing and distribution expenses in 2006 and 2005, respectively. The amount for 2006 reflects higher fuel surcharges due to higher energy input costs.

Reported earnings from operations were $87,529 in 2006, compared to $110,232 in 2005. Prior year 2005 operating earnings benefited from a $21,840 pre-tax gain on the sale of surplus real estate partially offset by a $4,743 pre-tax charge relating to the impairment of a minor trademark and related goodwill. There were no impairments in 2006. Excluding the nonrecurring net benefit in 2005 described above, earnings from operations were $87,529 in 2006 compared to $93,135 in 2005, a decrease of $5,606 or 6%. This decrease principally reflects the decrease in gross profit margin and higher freight and delivery expenses as discussed above.

Other income, net was $7,186 in 2006 compared to $3,420 in 2005, an increase of $3,766. This net increase principally reflects $1,524 of increased investment income and $1,811 of decreased interest expense due to the pay down of bank debt.

The consolidated effective tax rate was 30.7% and 32.3% in 2006 and 2005, respectively. The

decrease in the effective tax rate principally reflects the effects of additional taxes in 2005 relating to the repatriation of foreign dividends as allowed by the American Jobs Creation Act of 2004, as well as a minor reduction in rates relating to increased investment income from tax-exempt municipal bonds and lower state taxes. During 2006, the Company also recorded a $3,481 valuation allowance relating to foreign subsidiary tax loss carry-forwards to reduce the future income tax benefits to amounts expected to be realized.

Net earnings were $65,919 in 2006 compared to $77,227 in 2005, and earnings per share were $1.18 and $1.36 in 2006 and 2005, respectively, a decrease of $.18 per share or 13%. Both fourth quarter and twelve months 2005 periods benefited from a nonrecurring net after-tax gain $10,053 or $.18 per share relating to the sale of surplus real estate, net of the $4,743 write-off of a minor trademark and related goodwill and additional income taxes relating to repatriated foreign dividends. Earnings per share also benefits from a reduction in average shares outstanding resulting from common stock purchases in the open market by the Company. Average shares outstanding decreased from 56,732 in 2005 to 55,800 in 2006.

LIQUIDITY AND CAPITAL RESOURCES

Cash flows from operating activities were $90,064, $55,656, and $82,524 in 2007, 2006 and 2005, respectively. The $34,408 increase in 2007 from 2006 reflects changes in certain operating assets and liabilities. 2007 cash provided by operating activities principally benefited from a $13,481 increase in taxes payable and deferred, $6,506 decrease in inventories, and $2,591 decrease in accounts receivable. However, a $3,234 decrease in accounts payable and accrued liabilities negatively impacted 2007 cash flows from operating activities compared to 2006.

Cash flows from investing activities reflect capital expenditures of $14,767, $39,207 and $14,690 in 2007, 2006 and 2005 respectively, including $25,241 relating to investment of the proceeds of a sale of surplus real estate in like-kind real estate in 2006. 2005 cash flows also included $22,559 relating to the proceeds of such sale of surplus real estate. Cash flows from investing activities also reflect the 2005 recovery of $6,755 for a minimum working capital deficiency adjustment relating to the purchase of Concord Confections Inc. and certain of its affiliates in 2004.

Cash flows from financing activities reflect the repayment of various bank loans of $32,001 and $98,400 in 2006 and 2005, respectively, and bank borrowing of $38,401 in 2005. The Company had no bank borrowing or repayments in 2007, and has no outstanding bank borrowings as of December 31, 2007.

Financing activities also include common stock repurchases and retirements of $27,300, $30,694, and $17,248 in 2007, 2006 and 2005, respectively. Cash dividends of $17,542, $17,264, and $15,132 were paid in 2007, 2006 and 2005, respectively.

SIGNIFICANT ACCOUNTING POLICIES AND ESTIMATES

Preparation of the Company's financial statements involves judgments and estimates due to uncertainties affecting the application of accounting policies, and the likelihood that different amounts would be reported under different conditions or using different assumptions. The Company bases its estimates on historical experience and other assumptions, as discussed herein, that it believes are reasonable. If actual amounts are ultimately different from previous estimates, the revisions are included in the Company's results of operations for the period in which the actual amounts become known. The Company's significant accounting policies are discussed in Note 1 to the financial statements.

Following is a summary and discussion of the more significant accounting policies which management believes to have a significant impact on the Company's operating results, financial position, cash flows and footnote disclosure.

Revenue recognition

Revenue, net of applicable provisions for discounts, returns, allowances, and certain advertising and promotional costs, is recognized when products are delivered to customers based on a customer purchase order, and collectibility is reasonably assured. The accounting for such promotional programs is discussed below.

Provisions for bad debts are recorded as selling, marketing and administrative expenses. Such provisions have generally not exceeded 0.2% of net sales for 2007, 2006 and 2005 and, accordingly, have not been significant to the Company's financial position or results of operations.

Intangible assets

The Company's intangible assets consist primarily of acquired trademarks and related goodwill. In accordance with SFAS No. 142, goodwill and other indefinite lived assets are not amortized, but are instead subjected to annual testing for impairment. The Company performs its annual impairment testing in the fourth quarter of each year.

This determination is made by comparing the carrying value of the asset with its estimated fair value, which is calculated using estimates including discounted projected future cash flows. These projected future cash flows are dependent on a number of factors including the execution of business plans, achievement of projected sales, including but not limited to future price increases, projected operating margins, and projected capital expenditures. Such operating results are also dependent upon future ingredient and packaging material costs, exchange rates for products manufactured in foreign countries, operational efficiencies, cost savings initiatives, and competitive factors. Although the majority of the Company's trademarks relate to well established brands with a long history of consumer acceptance, projected cash flows are inherently uncertain. A change in the assumptions underlying the impairment analysis, including but not limited to a reduction in projected cash flows, the use of a different discount rate to discount future cash flows or a different royalty rate applied to the Company's trademarks, could cause impairment in the future. No impairments were recorded in 2007 or 2006, however, the Company recorded a pre-tax impairment charge of $4,743 during 2005 with respect to a minor trademark and related goodwill.

Customer incentive programs, advertising and marketing

Advertising and marketing costs are recorded in the period to which such costs relate. The Company does not defer the recognition of any amounts on its consolidated balance sheet with respect to such costs. Customer incentives and other promotional costs are recorded at the time of sale based upon incentive program terms and historical utilization statistics, which are generally consistent from year to year.

The liabilities associated with these programs are reviewed quarterly and adjusted if utilization rates differ from management's original estimates. Such adjustments have not historically been material to the Company's operating results.

Split dollar officer life insurance

The Company provides split dollar insurance benefits to certain executive officers and records an asset equal to the cumulative premiums paid on the related policies, as the Company will fully recover these premiums under the terms of the plan. The Company retains a collateral assignment of the cash surrender values and policy death benefits payable to insure recovery of these premiums.

Valuation of long-lived assets

Long-lived assets, primarily property, plant and equipment, are reviewed for impairment as events or changes in business circumstances occur indicating that the carrying value of the asset may not be recoverable. The estimated cash flows produced by the asset or asset groups are compared to the asset carrying value to determine whether impairment exists. Such estimates involve considerable management judgment and are based upon assumptions about expected future operating performance. As a result, actual cash flows could differ from management's estimates due to changes in business conditions, operating performance, and economic conditions. The

Company has recorded no such impairments in the years presented.

Income taxes

Deferred income taxes are recognized for future tax effects of temporary differences between financial and income tax reporting using tax rates in effect for the years in which the differences are expected to reverse. The Company records valuation allowances in situations where the realization of deferred tax assets is not likely. The Company, along with third-party tax advisors, periodically reviews assumptions and estimates of the Company's probable tax obligations using informed judgment and historical experience.

Other matters

In the opinion of management, other than contracts for raw materials, including commodity hedges and outstanding purchase orders for packaging, ingredients supplies, and operational services, all entered into in the ordinary course of business, the Company does not have any significant contractual obligations or future commitments. The Company's outstanding contractual commitments as of December 31, 2007, all of which are normal and recurring in nature, are summarized in the chart on page 10 (textbook page A-12).

RECENT ACCOUNTING PRONOUNCEMENTS

FASB Interpretation No. 48 "Accounting for Uncertainty in Income Taxes—an interpretation of FASB Statement 109." (FIN 48)

In July 2006, the FASB issued FIN 48 which prescribes a comprehensive model for recognizing, measuring, presenting and disclosing in the financial statements tax positions taken by the Company on its tax returns. Although the adoption of FIN 48 on January 1, 2007 had no impact on the Company's

retained earnings, it did result in the recognition of $14,987 of unrecognized tax benefits which was consistent with those recorded in current income taxes payable at December 31, 2006. This includes $7,802 of unrecognized tax benefits the Company recorded with a corresponding increase in the amount of deferred income tax assets. As of January 1, 2007, the Company's liability for uncertain tax positions included $3,382 of accrued interest relating to its uncertain tax positions.

During 2007, the Company recorded approximately $1,040 of additional income tax expense, including $577 of additional accrued interest and penalties, relating to uncertain tax positions. The Company is not currently subject to a U.S. federal or foreign income tax examination, however, the Company is currently subject to various state tax examinations. Although the Company is unable to determine the ultimate outcome of these examinations, the Company believes that its liability for uncertain tax positions relating to these tax jurisdictions for such years is adequate.

SFAS No. 157, "Fair Value Measurements" (SFAS No. 157)

In September 2006, the FASB issued SFAS No. 157 which establishes a common definition for fair value to be applied to U.S. GAAP guidance requiring use of fair value, establishes a framework for measuring fair value, and expands disclosure about such fair value measurements. SFAS No. 157 is effective for fiscal years beginning after November 15, 2007. The Company is currently assessing the impact of SFAS No. 157 and has not yet made any determination as to the effects, if any, that it may have on the Company's financial position and results of operations.

SFAS No. 159, "The Fair Value Option for Financial Assets and Financial Liabilities-including an amendment to FSAB Statement No. 115," (SFAS No. 159)

In February 2007, the FASB issued SFAS No. 159 which permits entities to choose to measure many financial instruments and certain other items at fair value that are not currently required to be measured at fair value. SFAS No. 159 is effective for fiscal years beginning after November 15, 2007. The Company is currently assessing the impact of SFAS No. 159 and has not yet made any determination as to the effects, if any, that it may have on the Company's financial position and results of operations.

MARKET RISKS

The Company is exposed to market risks related to commodity prices, interest rates, investments in marketable securities, equity prices and foreign exchange.

Commodities

Commodity price risks relate to ingredients, primarily sugar, cocoa, chocolate, corn syrup, dextrose, vegetable oils, milk, whey and gum base ingredients. The Company believes its competitors face similar risks, and the industry has historically adjusted prices to compensate for adverse fluctuations in commodity costs. The Company, as well as competitors in the confectionery industry, have taken actions, including price increases and selective product weight declines (indirect price increases) to mitigate rising input costs for ingredients, transportation, fuel and energy. Although management seeks to substantially recover cost increases over the long term, there is risk that price increases

and weight declines cannot be fully passed on to customers and, to the extent they are passed on, they could adversely affect customer and consumer acceptance and resulting sales volume.

The Company utilizes commodity futures contracts as well as annual supply agreements to hedge anticipated purchases of certain ingredients, including sugar, in order to mitigate commodity cost fluctuations. Such commodity future contracts are cash flow hedges and are effective as hedges as defined by Statement of Financial Accounting Standards (SFAS) 133, "Accounting for Derivative Instruments and Hedging Activities." The unrealized gains and losses on such contracts are deferred as a component of accumulated other comprehensive earnings (loss) and are recognized as a component of product cost of goods sold when the related inventory is sold.

The potential change in fair value of commodity derivative instruments (primarily sugar futures contracts) held by the Company, assuming a 10% change in the underlying commodity price, was $535. This analysis only includes commodity derivative instruments and, therefore, does not consider the offsetting effect of changes in the price of the underlying commodity. This amount is not significant compared with the net earnings and shareholders' equity of the Company.

Interest rates

Interest rate risks primarily relate to the Company's investments in tax exempt marketable securities, including auction rate securities (ARS), with maturities or auction dates of generally up to three years. Auction dates, generally every 35 days, are similar to

maturity dates in that the interest rate of the ARS is then reset based on current market conditions or, conversely, the holder of the security also can redeem the ARS at face value.

The majority of the Company's investments have historically been held to maturity or to auction date, which limits the Company's exposure to interest rate fluctuations. The accompanying chart summarizes the maturities or auction dates of the Company's investments in debt securities at December 31, 2007.

Less than 1 year	$41,245
1–2 years	19,939
2–3 years	12,685
Over 3 years	525
Total	$74,394

The Company had no outstanding debt at December 31, 2007 other than $7,500 in an IRB note in which interest rates reset each week based on the current market rate. Therefore, the Company does not believe that it has significant interest rate risk with respect to its interest bearing debt.

Investment in marketable securities

As stated above, the Company invests primarily in tax exempt marketable securities, including ARS, with maturities or auction dates generally up to three years. The Company utilizes professional money managers and maintains investment policy guidelines which emphasize quality and liquidity in order to minimize the potential loss exposures that could result in the event of a default or other adverse event, including failed auctions.

The Company believes that it has taken adequate measures to prevent a loss or impairment in the market value of such securities. However, given recent events in the municipal bond and ARS markets, including failed auctions, the Company continues to monitor these investments and markets, as well as investment policies.

As of December 31, 2007, the Company had $27,250 of ARS included in short-tem Investments. Subsequently, $13,700 of these ARS were redeemed at auction at face value. However, $13,550 of such ARS at December 31, 2007 have experienced a successful auction followed by a failed auction subsequent to December 31, 2007.

The Company presently believes that its ARS will not become impaired, given their high investment quality. Nonetheless, due to illiquidity in the ARS market the Company may be forced to hold its ARS for a longer period than originally anticipated. Furthermore, the financial markets seem to be experiencing unprecedented events, and a favorable ultimate outcome cannot be assured.

Equity price

Equity price risk relates to the Company's investments in mutual funds which are principally used to fund and hedge the Company's deferred compensation liabilities. At December 31, 2007, the Company has investments in mutual funds, classified as trading securities, of $32,800. Any change in the fair value of these trading securities would be completely offset by a corresponding change in the respective hedged deferred compensation liability.

Foreign currency exchange

Foreign currency exchange risk principally relates to the Company's foreign operations in Canada and Mexico, as well as periodic purchase commitments of machinery and equipment from foreign sources.

Certain of the Company's Canadian manufacturing costs,

including local payroll and a portion of its packaging, ingredients and supplies are sourced in Canadian dollars. The Company uses its Canadian dollar collections on Canadian sales as a partial hedge of its overall Canadian manufacturing obligations sourced in Canadian dollars. The Company also periodically purchases Canadian dollars to facilitate the risk management of these currency changes.

From time to time the Company may use forward foreign exchange contracts and derivative instruments to mitigate its exposure to foreign exchange risk, as well as those related to firm commitments to purchase equipment from foreign vendors. As of December 31, 2007 the Company did not have any material outstanding foreign exchange contracts.

RISK FACTORS

The Company's operations and financial results are subject to a number of risks and uncertainties that could adversely affect the Company's operating results and financial condition. Significant risk

factors, without limitation, that could impact the Company are the following: (i) significant competitive activity, including advertising, promotional and price competition, and changes in consumer demand for the Company's products; (ii) fluctuations in the cost and availability of various ingredients and packaging materials; (iii) inherent risks in the marketplace, including uncertainties about trade and consumer acceptance and seasonal events such as Halloween; (iv) the effect of acquisitions on the Company's results of operations and financial condition; (v) the effect of changes in foreign currencies on the Company's foreign subsidiaries operating results, and the effect of the Canadian dollar on products manufactured in Canada and marketed and sold in the United States in U.S. dollars; (vi) the Company's reliance on third-party vendors for various goods and services; (vii) the Company's ability to successfully implement new production processes and lines; (viii) the effect of changes in assumptions, including discount rates, sales growth and profit

Open Contractual Commitments as of December 31, 2007					
Payable in	Total	Less than 1 year	1 to 3 Years	3 to 5 Years	More than 5 Years
Commodity hedges	$ 5,351	$ 5,351	$ —	$ —	$ —
Purchase obligations ...	35,309	35,309	—	—	—
Interest bearing debt	7,500	—	—	—	7,500
Operating leases	5,154	1,177	1,897	998	1,082
Total	$53,314	$41,837	$1,897	$998	$8,582

Note: the above amounts exclude deferred income tax liabilities of $35,940, liabilities for uncertain tax positions of $20,056, postretirement health care and life insurance benefits of $13,214 and deferred compensation and other liabilities of $39,813 because the timing of payments relating to these items cannot be reasonably determined.

margins, and the capability to pass along higher ingredient and other input costs through price increases, relating to the Company's impairment testing and analysis of its goodwill and trademarks; (ix) changes in the confectionery marketplace including actions taken by major retailers and customers; (x) customer and consumer response to marketing programs and price and product weight adjustments, and new products; (xi) dependence on significant customers, including the volume and timing of their purchases, and availability of shelf space; (xii) increases in energy costs, including freight and delivery, that cannot be passed along to customers through increased prices due to competitive reasons; (xiii) any significant labor stoppages, strikes or production interruptions; and (xiv) changes in governmental laws and regulations including taxes and tariffs.

The Company's results may be affected by general factors, such as economic conditions, financial and securities' market factors, political developments, currency exchange rates, interest and inflation rates, accounting standards, taxes, and laws and regulations affecting the Company in markets where it competes, and those factors described in Part 1, Item 1A "Risk Factors" and elsewhere in the Company's Annual Report on Form 10-K and in other Company filings, including quarterly reports on Form 10-Q, with the Securities and Exchange Commission.

Forward-looking statements

This discussion and certain other sections contain forward-looking statements that are based largely on the Company's current expectations and are made pursuant to the safe harbor provisions of the Private Securities Litigation Reform Act of 1995. Forward-looking statements can be identified by the use of words such as "anticipated," "believe," "expect," "intend," "estimate," "project," and other words of similar meaning in connection with a discussion of future operating or financial performance and are subject to certain factors, risks, trends and uncertainties that could cause actual results and achievements to differ materially from those expressed in the forward-looking statements. Such factors, risks, trends and uncertainties, which in some instances are beyond the Company's control, including the overall competitive environment in the Company's industry, changes in assumptions and judgments discussed above under the heading "Significant Accounting Policies and Estimates", and factors identified and referred to above under the heading "Risk Factors."

The risk factors identified and referred to above are believed to be significant factors, but not necessarily all of the significant factors that could cause actual results to differ from those expressed in any forward-looking statement. Readers are cautioned not to place undue reliance on such forward-looking statements, which are made only as of the date of this report. The Company undertakes no obligation to update such forward-looking statements.

Management's Report on Internal Control and Management Certifications of Financial Statements

The Sarbanes-Oxley Act of 2002, requires managers of publicly traded companies to establish and maintain systems of internal control on the company's financial reporting processes. In addition, the Act requires the company's top management to provide certifications regarding the accuracy of the financial statements. The reports of Tootsie Roll are shown below.

Management's Report on Internal Control Over Financial Reporting

The management of Tootsie Roll Industries, Inc. is responsible for establishing and maintaining adequate internal control over financial reporting, as such term is defined in the Securities Exchange Act of 1934 (SEC) Rule 13a-15(f). Our management conducted an evaluation of the effectiveness of the Company's internal control over financial reporting as of December 31, 2007 as required by SEC Rule 13a-15(c). In making this assessment, we used the criteria established in *Internal Control—Integrated Framework* issued by the Committee of Sponsoring Organizations of the Treadway Commission (the COSO criteria). Based on our evaluation under the COSO criteria, our management concluded that our internal control over financial reporting was effective as of December 31, 2007.

The effectiveness of the Company's internal control over financial reporting as of December 31, 2007 has been audited by PricewaterhouseCoopers LLP, an independent registered public accounting firm, as stated in their report which appears on page 22 (textbook pages A-27 to A-28).

Tootsie Roll Industries, Inc.

Chicago, Illinois
February 28, 2008

Required Certifications

In 2007, the Company's Chief Executive Officer submitted to the New York Stock Exchange the required Annual CEO Certification certifying that he was not aware of any violation by the Company of the exchange's corporate governance listing standards.

The Company filed with the Securities and Exchange Commission the certifications required of the Company's Chief Executive Officer and Chief Financial Officer under Section 302 of the Sarbanes-Oxley Act of 2002 as exhibits to the Form 10-K for the year ended December 31, 2007.

Financial Statements and Accompanying Notes

The standard set of financial statements consists of: (1) a comparative income statement for three years, (2) a comparative balance sheet for two years, (3) a comparative statement of cash flows for three years, (4) a statement of retained earnings (or stockholders' equity) for three years, and (5) a set of accompanying notes that are considered an integral part of the financial statements. The auditor's report, unless stated otherwise, covers the financial statements and the accompanying notes. The financial statements and accompanying notes plus some supplementary data and analyses for Tootsie Roll Industries follow.

CONSOLIDATED STATEMENT OF

Earnings, Comprehensive Earnings and Retained Earnings

TOOTSIE ROLL INDUSTRIES, INC. AND SUBSIDIARIES

(in thousands except per share data)

	For the year ended December 31,		
	2007	2006	2005
Net product sales	$492,742	$495,990	$487,739
Rental and royalty revenue	4,975	5,150	3,345
Total revenue	497,717	501,140	491,084
Product cost of goods sold	327,695	311,267	299,683
Rental and royalty cost	1,349	1,312	671
Total costs	329,044	312,579	300,354
Product gross margin	165,047	184,723	188,056
Rental and royalty gross margin	3,626	3,838	2,674
Total gross margin	168,673	188,561	190,730
Selling, marketing and administrative expenses	97,821	101,032	97,595
Impairment charges	—	—	4,743
Gain on sale of real estate	—	—	(21,840)
Earnings from operations	70,852	87,529	110,232
Other income, net	6,315	7,186	3,420
Earnings before income taxes	77,167	94,715	113,652
Provision for income taxes	25,542	28,796	36,425
Net earnings	$ 51,625	$ 65,919	$ 77,227
Net earnings	$ 51,625	$ 65,919	$ 77,227
Other comprehensive earnings (loss)	810	(3,697)	2,984
Comprehensive earnings	$ 52,435	$ 62,222	$ 80,211
Retained earnings at beginning of year	$169,233	$164,236	$149,055
Net earnings	51,625	65,919	77,227
Cash dividends ($.32, $.32 and $.29 per share, respectively)	(17,421)	(17,170)	(15,406)
Stock dividends	(46,685)	(43,694)	(46,640)
Cumulative effect of SAB 108	—	(58)	—
Retained earnings at end of year	$156,752	$169,233	$164,236
Earnings per share	$0.94	$ 1.18	$ 1.36
Average common and class B common shares outstanding	54,980	55,800	56,732

(The accompanying notes are an integral part of these statements.)

CONSOLIDATED STATEMENT OF

Financial Position

TOOTSIE ROLL INDUSTRIES, INC. AND SUBSIDIARIES   (in thousands)

Assets

December 31,

	2007	2006
CURRENT ASSETS:		
Cash and cash equivalents	$ 57,606	$ 55,729
Investments	41,307	23,531
Accounts receivable trade, less allowances of $2,287 and $2,322.	32,371	35,075
Other receivables.	2,913	3,932
Inventories:		
Finished goods and work-in-process	37,031	42,146
Raw materials and supplies.	20,371	21,811
Prepaid expenses	6,551	6,489
Deferred income taxes.	1,576	2,204
Total current assets	199,726	190,917
PROPERTY, PLANT AND EQUIPMENT, at cost:		
Land	19,398	19,402
Buildings.	88,225	87,273
Machinery and equipment.	270,070	259,049
	377,693	365,724
Less—Accumulated depreciation	176,292	162,826
Net property, plant and equipment	201,401	202,898
OTHER ASSETS:		
Goodwill	73,237	74,194
Trademarks.	189,024	189,024
Investments	65,993	51,581
Split dollar officer life insurance	74,944	73,357
Investment in joint venture.	8,400	9,668
Total other assets	411,598	397,824
Total assets.	$812,725	$791,639

(The accompanying notes are an integral part of these statements.)

(in thousands except per share data)

Liabilities and Shareholders' Equity   December 31,

	2007	2006
CURRENT LIABILITIES:		
Accounts payable	$ 11,572	$ 13,102
Dividends payable	4,344	4,300
Accrued liabilities	42,056	43,802
Income taxes payable	—	1,007
Total current liabilities	57,972	62,211
NONCURRENT LIABILITIES:		
Deferred income taxes	35,940	40,864
Postretirement health care and life insurance benefits	13,214	12,582
Industrial development bonds	7,500	7,500
Liability for uncertain tax positions	20,056	—
Deferred compensation and other liabilities	39,813	37,801
Total noncurrent liabilities	116,523	98,747
SHAREHOLDERS' EQUITY:		
Common stock, $.69-4/9 par value—		
120,000 shares authorized—		
35,404 and 35,364, respectively, issued	24,586	24,558
Class B common stock, $.69-4/9 par value—		
40,000 shares authorized—		
18,892 and 18,390, respectively, issued	13,120	12,771
Capital in excess of par value	457,491	438,648
Retained earnings, per accompanying statement	156,752	169,233
Accumulated other comprehensive loss	(11,727)	(12,537)
Treasury stock (at cost)—		
63 shares and 62 shares, respectively	(1,992)	(1,992)
Total shareholders' equity	638,230	630,681
Total liabilities and shareholders' equity	$812,725	$791,639

CONSOLIDATED STATEMENT OF

Cash Flows

TOOTSIE ROLL INDUSTRIES, INC. AND SUBSIDIARIES   (in thousands)

	For the year ended December 31,		
	2007	2006	2005
CASH FLOWS FROM OPERATING ACTIVITIES:			
Net earnings	$ 51,625	$ 65,919	$ 77,227
Adjustments to reconcile net earnings to net cash provided by operating activities:			
Depreciation	15,859	15,816	14,687
Gain on sale of real estate	—	—	(21,840)
Impairment charges	—	—	4,743
Excess of earnings from joint venture over dividends received	—	(921)	(267)
Return on investment in joint venture	1,419	—	—
Amortization of marketable securities	521	909	1,680
Purchase of trading securities	(84)	(749)	(1,141)
Changes in operating assets and liabilities:			
Accounts receivable	2,591	(4,368)	(1,846)
Other receivables	7	(4,125)	1,519
Inventories	6,506	(8,451)	3,947
Prepaid expenses and other assets	283	(1,912)	(4,357)
Accounts payable and accrued liabilities	(3,234)	(3,688)	(1,868)
Income taxes payable and deferred	13,481	(3,984)	8,423
Postretirement health care and life insurance benefits	1,272	971	708
Deferred compensation and other liabilities	(12)	382	1,251
Other	(170)	(143)	(342)
Net cash provided by operating activities	90,064	55,656	82,524
CASH FLOWS FROM INVESTING ACTIVITIES:			
Working capital adjustment from acquisition	—	—	6,755
Proceeds from sale of real estate and other assets	434	1,343	22,559
(Increase) decrease in restricted cash	—	22,330	(22,330)
Return of investment in joint venture	1,206	—	—
Capital expenditures	(14,767)	(39,207)	(14,690)
Purchase of available for sale securities	(59,132)	(35,663)	(16,772)
Sale and maturity of available for sale securities	28,914	62,223	46,350
Net cash provided by (used in) investing activities	(43,345)	11,026	21,872
CASH FLOWS FROM FINANCING ACTIVITIES:			
Proceeds from bank loan	—	—	38,401
Repayment of bank loan	—	(32,001)	(98,400)
Shares repurchased and retired	(27,300)	(30,694)	(17,248)
Dividends paid in cash	(17,542)	(17,264)	(15,132)
Net cash used in financing activities	(44,842)	(79,959)	(92,379)
Increase (decrease) in cash and cash equivalents	1,877	(13,277)	12,017
Cash and cash equivalents at beginning of year	55,729	69,006	56,989
Cash and cash equivalents at end of year	$ 57,606	$ 55,729	$ 69,006
Supplemental cash flow information:			
Income taxes paid	$ 11,343	$ 29,780	$ 26,947
Interest paid	$ 537	$ 733	$ 2,537
Stock dividend issued	$ 46,520	$ 43,563	$ 46,310

(The accompanying notes are an integral part of these statements.)

Notes to Consolidated Financial Statements

TOOTSIE ROLL INDUSTRIES, INC. AND SUBSIDIARIES   *($ in thousands except per share data)*

NOTE 1—SIGNIFICANT ACCOUNTING POLICIES:

Basis of consolidation:

The consolidated financial statements include the accounts of Tootsie Roll Industries, Inc. and its wholly-owned subsidiaries (the Company), which are primarily engaged in the manufacture and sale of candy products. All significant intercompany transactions have been eliminated.

The preparation of financial statements in conformity with generally accepted accounting principles in the United States of America requires management to make estimates and assumptions that affect the reported amounts of assets and liabilities and disclosure of contingent assets and liabilities at the date of the financial statements and the reported amounts of revenues and expenses during the reporting period. Actual results could differ from those estimates.

Certain reclassifications have been made to the prior year financial statements to conform to the current year presentation.

Revenue recognition:

Products are sold to customers based on accepted purchase orders which include quantity, sales price and other relevant terms of sale. Revenue, net of applicable provisions for discounts, returns, allowances, and certain advertising and promotional costs, is recognized when products are delivered to customers and collectibility is reasonably assured. Shipping and handling costs of $41,775, $40,353 and $37,836 in 2007, 2006 and 2005, respectively, are included in selling, marketing and administrative expenses. Accounts receivable are unsecured. Revenues from a major customer aggregated approximately 22.4%, 23.7% and 24.0% of net product sales during the years ended December 31, 2007, 2006 and 2005, respectively.

Cash and cash equivalents:

The Company considers temporary cash investments with an original maturity of three months or less to be cash equivalents.

Restricted cash represents the net proceeds received from the sale of surplus real estate in 2005 which was held by a third party intermediary and earmarked for reinvestment in like-kind real estate as provided under U.S. Internal Revenue Code Section 1031. During 2006, the Company reinvested such restricted cash in like-kind real estate.

Investments:

Investments consist of various marketable securities with maturities of generally up to four years. The Company classifies debt and equity securities as either available for sale or trading. Available for sale are not actively traded and are carried at fair value. Unrealized gains and losses on these securities are excluded from earnings and are reported as a separate component of shareholders' equity, net of applicable taxes, until realized. Trading securities relate to deferred compensation arrangements and are carried at fair value. The Company invests in trading securities to hedge changes in its deferred compensation liabilities.

Hedging activities:

From time to time, the Company enters into commodities futures contracts that are intended and effective as hedges of market price risks associated with the anticipated purchase of certain raw materials (primarily sugar). To qualify as a hedge, the Company evaluates a variety of characteristics of these transactions, including the probability that the anticipated transaction will occur. If the anticipated transaction were not to occur, the gain or loss would then be recognized in current earnings. The Company does not engage in trading or other speculative use of derivative instruments. The Company does assume the risk that counter parties may not be able to meet the terms of their contracts. The Company does not expect any losses as a result of counter party defaults.

The Company's commodities futures contracts are being accounted for as cash flow hedges and are recorded on the balance sheet at fair value. Changes therein are recorded in other comprehensive earnings and are reclassified to earnings in the periods in which earnings are affected by the hedged item. Substantially all amounts reported in accumulated other comprehensive earnings (loss) are expected to be reclassified to cost of goods sold.

Inventories:

Inventories are stated at cost, not to exceed market. The cost of substantially all of the Company's inventories ($54,367 and $61,092 at December 31, 2007 and 2006, respectively) has been determined by the last-in, first-out (LIFO) method. The excess of current cost over LIFO cost of inventories approximates $11,284 and $7,350 at December 31, 2007 and 2006, respectively. The cost of certain foreign inventories ($3,036 and $2,865 at December 31, 2007 and 2006, respectively) has been determined by the first-in, first-out (FIFO) method. Rebates, discounts and other cash consideration received from a vendor related to inventory purchases is reflected as a reduction in the cost of the related inventory item, and is therefore reflected in cost of sales when the related inventory item is sold.

Property, plant and equipment:

Depreciation is computed for financial reporting purposes by use of the straight-line method based on useful lives of 20 to 35 years for buildings and 5 to 20 years for machinery and equipment. Depreciation expense was $15,859, $15,816, and $14,687 in 2007, 2006 and 2005, respectively.

Carrying value of long-lived assets:

The Company reviews long-lived assets to determine if there are events or circumstances indicating that the amount of the asset reflected in the Company's balance sheet may not be recoverable. When such indicators are present, the Company compares the carrying value of the long-lived asset, or asset group, to the future undiscounted cash flows of the underlying assets to determine if an impairment exists. If applicable, an impairment charge would be recorded to write down the carrying value to its fair value. The determination of fair value involves the use of estimates of future cash flows that involve considerable management judgment and are based upon assumptions about expected future operating performance. The actual cash flows could differ from management's estimates due to changes in business conditions, operating performance, and economic conditions. No impairment charges were recorded by the Company during 2007, 2006 or 2005.

Postretirement health care and life insurance benefits:

The Company provides certain postretirement health care and life insurance benefits. The cost of these postretirement benefits is accrued during employees' working careers. The Company also provides split dollar life insurance benefits to certain executive officers. The Company records an asset equal to the cumulative insurance premiums that will be recovered upon the death of a covered employee(s) or earlier under the terms of the plan. Split dollar premiums paid were $1,586, $3,002, and $3,678 in 2007, 2006 and 2005, respectively.

Goodwill and intangible assets:

The Company accounts for intangible assets in accordance with SFAS No. 142, "Goodwill and Other Intangible Assets." In accordance with this statement, goodwill and intangible assets with indefinite lives are not amortized, but rather tested for impairment at least annually. All trademarks have been assessed by management to have indefinite lives because they are expected to generate cash flows indefinitely. The Company has completed its annual impair-

ment testing of its goodwill and trademarks during the fourth quarter of each of the years presented, and recorded an impairment of $4,743 in the fourth quarter of 2005 relating to a minor trademark and related goodwill. No impairments were recorded in either 2007 or 2006.

Income taxes:

Deferred income taxes are recorded and recognized for future tax effects of temporary differences between financial and income tax reporting. The Company records valuation allowances in situations where the realization of deferred tax assets is not likely. Federal income taxes are provided on the portion of income of foreign subsidiaries that is expected to be remitted to the U.S. and become taxable, but not on the portion that is considered to be permanently invested in the foreign subsidiary.

Foreign currency translation:

The Company has determined the functional currency for each foreign subsidiary. The U.S. dollar is used as the functional currency where a substantial portion of the subsidiary's business is indexed to the U.S. dollar or where its manufactured products are principally sold in the U.S. All other foreign subsidiaries use the local currency as their functional currency. Where the U.S. dollar is used as the functional currency, foreign currency translation adjustments are recorded as a charge or credit to other income in the statement of earnings. Where the foreign currency is used as the functional currency, translation adjustments are recorded as a separate component of comprehensive earnings (loss).

Joint venture:

The Company's 50% interest in two companies is accounted for using the equity method. The Company records an increase in its investment in the joint venture to the extent of its share of the joint venture's earnings, and reduces its investment to the extent of dividends received. Dividends of $861, $1,946 and $651 were paid in 2007, 2006 and 2005, respectively, by the joint venture. The $1,946 dividend declared in 2006 was not received by the Company until after December 31, 2006; this amount is included in other receivables at December 31, 2006.

Comprehensive earnings:

Comprehensive earnings includes net earnings, foreign currency translation adjustments and unrealized gains/losses on commodity hedging contracts, available for sale securities and certain postretirement benefit obligations.

Earnings per share:

A dual presentation of basic and diluted earnings per share is not required due to the lack of potentially dilutive securities under the Company's simple capital structure. Therefore, all earnings per share amounts represent basic earnings per share.

The Class B Common Stock has essentially the same rights as Common Stock, except that each share of Class B Common Stock has ten votes per share (compared to one vote per share of Common Stock), is not traded on any exchange, is restricted as to transfer and is convertible on a share-for-share basis, at any time and at no cost to the holders, into shares of Common Stock which are traded on the New York Stock Exchange.

Recent accounting pronouncements:

In September 2006, the FASB issued SFAS No. 157, "Fair Value Measurements" (SFAS 157), SFAS 157 establishes a common definition for fair value to be applied to U.S. GAAP guidance requiring use of fair value, establishes a framework for measuring fair value, and expands disclosure about such fair value measurements. SFAS 157 is effective for fiscal years beginning after November 15, 2007. The Company is currently assessing the impact of SFAS 157 and has not yet made any determination as to the effects, if any, that they may have on the Company's financial position and results of operations.

In February 2007, the FASB issued SFAS No. 159. "The Fair Value Option for Financial Assets and Financial Liabilities— including an amendment to FASB Statement No. 115" (SFAS No. 159), which permits entities to choose to measure many financial instruments and certain other items at fair value that are not currently required to be measured at fair value SFAS No. 159 is effective for fiscal years beginning after November 15, 2007. The Company is currently assessing the impact of SFAS No. 159 and has not yet made any determination as to the effects, if any, that it may have on the Company's financial position and results of operations.

NOTE 2—ACCRUED LIABILITIES:

Accrued liabilities are comprised of the following:

	December 31,	
	2007	2006
Compensation	$12,072	$12,923
Other employee benefits	2,843	5,631
Taxes, other than income	1,802	1,781
Advertising and promotions	17,808	17,854
Other	7,531	5,613
	$42,056	$43,802

NOTE 3—BANK LOAN AND INDUSTRIAL DEVELOPMENT BONDS:

Industrial development bonds are due in 2027. The average floating interest rate was 3.8% and 3.6% in 2007 and 2006, respectively.

NOTE 4—INCOME TAXES:

The domestic and foreign components of pretax income are as follows:

	2007	2006	2005
Domestic	$69,250	$81,514	$103,725
Foreign	7,917	13,201	9,927
	$77,167	$94,715	$113,652

The provision for income taxes is comprised of the following:

	2007	2006	2005
Current:			
Federal	$21,785	$14,358	$33,036
Foreign	(702)	944	1,151
State	737	1,050	1,990
	21,820	16,352	36,177
Deferred:			
Federal	2,671	10,962	1,038
Foreign	918	1,196	(849)
State	133	286	59
	3,722	12,444	248
	$25,542	$28,796	$36,425

Significant components of the Company's net deferred tax liability at year end were as follows:

	December 31,	
	2007	2006
Deferred tax assets:		
Accrued customer promotions	$ 4,765	$ —
Deferred compensation	9,993	10,644
Post retirement benefits	4,658	3,938
Reserve for uncollectible accounts	560	567
Other accrued expenses	7,275	3,008
Foreign subsidiary tax loss carry forward	5,922	5,172
Foreign tax credit carry forward	3,651	4,900
Marked to market on investments	—	573
Inventory reserves	2,154	—
Other	1,485	687
	40,463	29,489
Valuation reserve	(7,556)	(4,329)
Total deferred tax assets	$32,907	$25,160

	December 31,	
	2007	2006
Deferred tax liabilities:		
Depreciation	$23,143	$22,330
Deductible goodwill and trademarks	25,050	22,447
Accrued export company commissions	4,100	3,974
Employee benefit plans	777	897
Inventory reserves	4,262	2,591
Prepaid insurance	430	627
Accounts receivable	914	—
Deferred gain on sale of real estate	7,972	7,972
Other	624	2,982
Total deferred tax liabilities	$67,272	$63,820
Net deferred tax liability	$34,365	$38,660

At December 31, 2007, the tax benefits of foreign subsidiary tax loss carry forwards expiring by year are as follows: $1,287 in 2011, $3,150 in 2015 and $498 in 2026 and $987 in 2027. A valuation allowance has been established for these tax loss carry forwards to reduce the future income tax benefits to amounts expected to be realized.

Also at December 31, 2007, the amounts of the foreign subsidiary tax credit carry forwards expiring by year are as follows: $147 in 2008, $173 in 2009, $331 in 2010, $351 in 2011, $334 in 2012, $274 in 2013, $340 in 2014, $1,220 in 2015 and $481 in 2016. A valuation allowance has been established for these carry forward credits to reduce the future income tax benefits to amounts expected to be realized.

The effective income tax rate differs from the statutory rate as follows:

	2007	2006	2005
U.S. statutory rate	35.0%	35.0%	35.0%
State income taxes net	0.9	0.9	1.2
Exempt municipal bond interest	(1.4)	(0.8)	(0.6)
Foreign tax rates	(1.6)	(2.8)	(2.8)
Qualified domestic production activities deduction	(1.9)	(0.8)	(0.9)
Repatriation of accumulated foreign earnings	—	—	0.7
Reserve for uncertain tax benefits	1.3	—	—
Other, net	0.8	(0.8)	(0.3)
Effective income tax rate	33.1%	30.7%	32.3%

The Company has not provided for U.S. federal or foreign withholding taxes on $4,743 and $6,561 of foreign subsidiaries' undistributed earnings as of December 31, 2007 and December 31, 2006, respectively, because such earnings are considered to be permanently reinvested. It is not practicable to determine the amount of income taxes that would be payable upon remittance of the undistributed earnings.

American Jobs Creation Act of 2004 created a temporary incentive for U.S. corporations to repatriate accumulated income earned abroad by providing an 85% dividends received deduction for certain dividends from controlled foreign corporations. In 2005, the Company repatriated accumulated income earned abroad by its controlled foreign corporations in the amount of $21,200 and incurred a U.S. tax expense of $800 net of foreign tax credits.

The Company adopted the provisions of FASB Interpretation No. 48, "Accounting for Uncertainty in Income Taxes" (FIN 48) effective January 1, 2007. The adoption of FIN 48

is reflected in the accompanying financial statements. At January 1, 2007, the Company had unrecognized tax benefits of $14,987. Included in this balance is $7,160 of unrecognized tax benefits that, if recognized, would favorably affect the annual effective income tax rate. The Company recognizes interest and penalties related to unrecognized tax benefits in the provision for income taxes on the Consolidated Statement of Earnings. As of January 1, 2007, $3,382 of interest and penalties were included in the Liability for Uncertain Tax Positions.

At December 31, 2007, the Company had unrecognized tax benefits of $15,867. Included in this balance is $7,622 of unrecognized tax benefits that, if recognized, would favorably affect the annual effective income tax rate. As of December 31, 2007, $4,189 of interest and penalties were included in the Liability for Uncertain Tax Positions.

A reconciliation of the beginning and ending balances of the total amounts of unrecognized tax benefits is as follows:

Unrecognized tax benefits at January 1, 2007	$14,987
Increases in tax positions for the current year	1,895
Reductions in tax positions for lapse of statute of limitations	(1,015)
Unrecognized tax benefits at December 31, 2007	$15,867

The Company is subject to taxation in the U.S. and various state and foreign jurisdictions. The Company remains subject to examination by U.S. federal and state and foreign tax authorities for the years 2004 through 2006. With few exceptions, the Company is no longer subject to examinations by tax authorities for the year 2003 and prior.

The Company is not currently subject to a U.S. federal or foreign income tax examination, however, the Company is currently subject to various state tax examinations. Although the Company is unable to determine the ultimate outcome of these examinations, the Company believes that its liability for uncertain tax positions relating to these jurisdictions for such years is adequate.

Beginning in 2008, statutory income tax rates in Canada will be reduced five percentage points with the final rate adjustment coming in 2012. Accordingly, the Company's Canadian subsidiary has revalued its deferred tax assets and liabilities based on the rate in effect for the year the differences are expected to reverse.

NOTE 5—SHARE CAPITAL AND CAPITAL IN EXCESS OF PAR VALUE:

	Common Stock		Class B Common Stock		Treasury Stock		Capital in excess of par value
	Shares	Amount	Shares	Amount	Shares	Amount	
	(000's)		(000's)		(000's)		
Balance at January 1, 2005	34,760	$24,139	17,515	$12,163	(58)	$(1,992)	$397,745
Issuance of 3% stock dividend	1,033	717	524	364	(2)	—	45,229
Conversion of Class B common shares to common shares	39	27	(39)	(27)	—	—	—
Purchase and retirement of common shares	(577)	(400)	—	—	—	—	(16,849)
Balance at December 31, 2005	35,255	24,483	18,000	12,500	(60)	(1,992)	426,125
Issuance of 3% stock dividend	1,048	727	539	375	(2)	—	42,461
Conversion of Class B common shares to common shares	149	104	(149)	(104)	—	—	—
Purchase and retirement of common shares	(1,088)	(756)	—	—	—	—	(29,938)
Balance at December 31, 2006	35,364	24,558	18,390	12,771	(62)	(1,992)	438,648
Issuance of 3% stock dividend	1,056	733	550	383	(1)	—	45,404
Conversion of Class B common shares to common shares	48	34	(48)	(34)	—	—	—
Purchase and retirement of common shares	(1,064)	(739)	—	—	—	—	(26,561)
Balance at December 31, 2007	35,404	$24,586	18,892	$13,120	(63)	$(1,992)	$457,491

Average shares outstanding and all per share amounts included in the financial statements and notes thereto have been adjusted retroactively to reflect annual three percent stock dividends.

While the Company does not have a formal or publicly announced stock repurchase program, the Company's board of directors periodically authorizes a dollar amount for share repurchases.

Based upon this policy, shares were purchased and retired as follows:

Year	Total Number Of Shares Purchased	Average Price Paid Per Share
2007	1,064	$25.61
2006	1,088	$28.17
2005	577	$29.87

NOTE 6—OTHER INCOME, NET:

Other income (expense) is comprised of the following:

	2007	2006	2005
Interest and dividend income	$5,495	$5,155	$3,631
Interest expense	(535)	(726)	(2,537)
Joint venture income	182	921	918
Foreign exchange gains	656	453	852
Capital gains (losses)	228	678	166
Insurance recovery	128	300	326
Miscellaneous, net	161	405	64
	$6,315	$7,186	$3,420

NOTE 7—EMPLOYEE BENEFIT PLANS:

Pension plans:

The Company sponsors defined contribution pension plans covering certain nonunion employees with over one year of credited service. The Company's policy is to fund pension costs accrued based on compensation levels. Total pension expense for 2007, 2006 and 2005 was $3,589, $3,364 and $3,362, respectively. The Company also maintains certain profit sharing and retirement savings-investment plans. Company contributions in 2007, 2006 and 2005 to these plans were $873, $916 and $905, respectively.

The Company also contributes to a multi-employer defined benefit pension plan for its union employees in the U.S. Such contributions aggregated $1,257, $1,084 and $1,011 in 2007, 2006 and 2005, respectively. Although the Company has been advised that the plan is currently in an underfunded status, the relative position of each employer associated with the multi-employer plan with respect to the actuarial present value of benefits and net plan assets is not determinable by the Company.

Deferred compensation:

The Company sponsors three deferred compensation plans for selected executives and other employees: (i) the Excess Benefit Plan, which restores retirement benefits lost due to IRS limitations on contributions to tax-qualified plans, (ii) the Supplemental Savings Plan, which allows eligible employees to defer the receipt of eligible compensation until designated future dates and (iii) the Career Achievement Plan, which provides a deferred annual incentive award to selected executives. Participants in these plans earn a return on amounts due them based on several investment options, which mirror returns on underlying investments (primarily mutual funds). The Company hedges its obligations under the plans by investing in the actual underlying investments. These investments are classified as trading securities and are carried at fair value. At December 31, 2007 and 2006, these investments totaled $32,800 and $30,800, respectively. All gains and losses in these investments are equally offset by corresponding gains and losses in the Company's deferred compensation liabilities.

Postretirement health care and life insurance benefit plans:

The Company provides certain postretirement health care and life insurance benefits for corporate office and management employees. Employees become eligible for these benefits based upon their age and service and if they agree to contribute a portion of the cost. The Company has the right to modify or terminate these benefits. The Company does not fund postretirement health care and life insurance benefits in advance of payments for benefit claims.

Amounts recognized in accumulated other comprehensive loss (pre-tax) at December 31, 2007 are as follows:

Prior service credit	$(1,127)
Net actuarial loss	1,812
Net amount recognized in accumulated other comprehensive loss	$ 685

The estimated actuarial loss, prior service credit and transition obligation to be amortized from accumulated other comprehensive income into net periodic benefit cost during 2008 are $158, $(125) and $0, respectively.

The changes in the accumulated postretirement benefit obligation at December 31, 2007 and 2006 consist of the following:

	December 31,	
	2007	2006
Benefit obligation, beginning of year	$12,582	$ 9,924
Service cost	667	524
Interest cost	694	539
Actuarial (gain)/loss	(550)	2,101
Benefits paid	(179)	(506)
Benefit obligation, end of year	$13,214	$12,582

Net periodic postretirement benefit cost included the following components:

	2007	2006	2005
Service cost—benefits attributed to service during the period	$ 667	$524	$474
Interest cost on the accumulated postretirement benefit obligation	694	539	519
Net amortization	90	(84)	(74)
Net periodic postretirement benefit cost	$1,451	$979	$919

For measurement purposes, the 2007 annual rate of increase in the per capita cost of covered health care benefits was assumed to be 8.0% for pre-age 65 retirees, 9.5% for post-age 65 retirees and 11.0% for prescription drugs; these rates were assumed to decrease gradually to 5.0% for 2014 and remain at that level thereafter. The health care cost trend rate assumption has a significant effect on the amounts reported. The weighted-average discount rate used in determining the accumulated postretirement benefit obligation was 5.70% and 5.60% at December 31, 2007 and 2006, respectively.

Increasing or decreasing the health care trend rates by one percentage point in each year would have the following effect on:

	1% Increase	1% Decrease
Postretirement benefit obligation	$1,814	$(1,497)
Total of service and interest cost components	$ 236	$ (190)

The Company estimates future benefit payments will be $453, $483, $569, $598 and $677 in 2008 through 2012, respectively, and a total of $4,723 in 2013 through 2017. The future benefit payments are net of the annual Medicare Part D subsidy of approximately $1,095 beginning in 2008.

NOTE 8—COMMITMENTS:

Rental expense aggregated $1,090, $1,132 and $1,090 in 2007, 2006 and 2005, respectively.

Future operating lease commitments are not significant.

NOTE 9—SEGMENT AND GEOGRAPHIC INFORMATION:

The Company operates as a single reportable segment encompassing the manufacture and sale of confectionery products. Its principal manufacturing operations are located in the United States and Canada, and its principal market is the United States. The Company also manufactures and sells confectionery products in Mexico, and exports products to Canada as well as to over 50 countries worldwide.

The following geographic data include net sales summarized on the basis of the customer location and long-lived assets based on their physical location.

	2007	2006	2005
Net Product Sales:			
United States	$445,820	$450,591	$445,405
Foreign	46,922	45,399	42,334
	$492,742	$495,990	$487,739
Long-lived assets:			
United States	$296,277	$282,490	$246,721
Foreign	54,461	55,014	57,160
	$350,738	$337,504	$303,881

NOTE 10—DISCLOSURES ABOUT THE FAIR VALUE AND CARRYING AMOUNT OF FINANCIAL INSTRUMENTS:

The carrying amount approximates fair value of cash and cash equivalents because of the short maturity of those instruments. The fair values of investments are estimated based on quoted market prices. The fair value of the Company's industrial development bonds approximates their carrying value because they have a floating interest rate.

The carrying amount and estimated fair values of the Company's financial instruments are as follows:

	2007		2006	
	Carrying Amount	Fair Value	Carrying Amount	Fair Value
Cash and cash equivalents	$57,606	$57,606	$55,729	$55,729
Investments available for sale	74,456	74,456	44,351	44,351
Investments in trading securities	32,844	32,844	30,761	30,761
Bank loan and industrial development bonds	7,500	7,500	7,500	7,500

A summary of the aggregate fair value, gross unrealized gains, gross unrealized losses and amortized cost basis of the Company's investment portfolio by major security type is as follows:

	December 31, 2007			
			Unrealized	
	Amortized Cost	Fair Value	Gains	Losses
Available for sale:				
Municipal bonds	$74,228	$74,394	$166	$ —
Mutual funds	57	62	5	—
	$74,285	$74,456	$171	$ —

	December 31, 2006			
			Unrealised	
	Amortized Cost	Fair Value	Gains	Losses
Available for sale:				
Municipal bonds	$44,532	$44,293	$ —	$(239)
tual funMuds	57	58	1	—
	$44,589	$44,351	$ 1	$(239)

Investments available for sale included $27,250 and $0 of auction based municipal bonds as of year end 2007 and 2006, respectively. Subsequent to December 31, 2007, $13,700 of such bonds were redeemed at auction at face value. The remaining $13,550 experienced a successful auction followed by a failed auction, and the Company may be forced to hold them for a longer period than originally anticipated. There were no securities with maturities greater than four years. The sale of available for sale securities resulted in realized gains of $118 and $684 in 2007 and 2006, respectively.

NOTE 11—COMPREHENSIVE INCOME:

The following table sets forth information with respect to accumulated other comprehensive income (loss):

	Foreign Currency Translation Adjustment	Unrealized Gain (Loss) on		Postretirement and Pension Benefits	Accumulated Other Comprehensive Earnings (Loss)
		Investments	Derivatives		
Balance at January 1, 2005	$(11,964)	$ 209	$ 824	$ —	$(10,931)
Unrealized gains (losses)..........	1,036	(184)	4,186	—	5,038
(Gains) losses reclassified to net earnings	—	36	(946)	—	(910)
Tax effect	—	55	(1,199)	—	(1,144)
Net of tax amount................	1,036	(93)	2,041	—	2,984
Balance at December 31, 2005	(10,928)	116	2,865	—	(7,947)
Unrealized gains (losses)..........	(296)	263	880	—	847
(Gains) losses reclassified to net earnings	—	(684)	(5,856)	—	(6,540)
Tax effect	—	156	1,840	—	1,996
Net of tax amount................	(296)	(265)	(3,136)	—	(3,697)
Adoption of SFAS 158 (Note 7)	—	—	—	(893)	(893)
Balance at December 31,2006	(11,224)	(149)	(271)	(893)	(12,537)
Unrealized gains (losses)..........	(272)	469	(462)	588	323
(Gains) losses reclassified to net earnings	—	(61)	1,202	—	1,141
Tax effect	—	(151)	(273)	(230)	(654)
Net of tax amount................	(272)	257	467	358	810
Balance at December 31, 2007	$(11,496)	$ 108	$ 196	$(535)	$(11,727)

NOTE 12—GAIN ON SALE OF REAL ESTATE:

During 2005, the Company sold surplus real estate and realized a pre-tax gain of $21,840. During 2006, the Company invested the net proceeds of $22,330 in new real estate investments in compliance with U.S. Internal Revenue Code (IRC) Section 1031 resulting in the deferral of income tax payable on such gain.

NOTE 13—SEC STAFF ACCOUNTING BULLETIN NO. 108:

In September 2006, the SEC issued Staff Accounting Bulletin No. 108, "Considering the Effects of Prior Year Misstatements when Quantifying Misstatements in Current Year Financial Statements" (SAB 108). Traditionally, there have been two widely-recognized methods for quantifying the effects of financial statement misstatements: the "roll-over" method and the "iron curtain" method. Prior to its application of the guidance in SAB 108, the Company used the "roll-over" method for quantifying financial statement misstatements, which focused primarily on the impact of a misstatement on the income statement (and net earnings), including the reversing effects, if any, of prior year misstatements. SAB 108 permits companies to initially apply its provisions by recording the cumulative effect of any misstatements as adjustments to the carrying values of assets and liabilities as of January 1, 2006 with an offsetting adjustment recorded to the opening balance of retained earnings. The Company previously evaluated these items under the "roll-over" method and concluded they were quantitatively and qualitatively immaterial, individually and in the aggregate. The following table, and accompanying footnotes, summarizes the effects of applying the guidance in SAB 108:

| | Period in which the Misstatement Originated | | | Adjustment |
| | Cumulative Prior to January 1, 2004 | Year Ended December 31, | | Recorded as of January 1, 2006 |
		2004	2005	
Current assets (1)	$ 3,252	$ —	$ —	$ 3,252
Noncurrent assets (2)	2,184	(464)	1,446	3,166
Current liabilities (3)	(1,625)	(242)	—	(1,867)
Noncurrent liabilities (4)	(2,280)	—	(2,329)	(4,609)
Impact on net income (5)	$ 1,531	$(706)	$ (883)	
Net decrease to retained earnings (6)				$ (58)

(1) Primarily includes adjustments to (a) inventory relating to the calculation of a valuation reserve of $333 and (b) accounts receivable for the classification of estimated collectible accounts on the balance sheet which were previously classified as an offset to an accrued liability of $2,635.

(2) Primarily includes adjustments to (a) property, plant and equipment for a computational correction relating to depreciation expense over several prior years of $1,500, the timing of the recognition of a loss associated with the abandonment and disposal of certain machinery and equipment of ($464), and the timing of the recognition of a minor asset retirement obligation of $1,446 which is partially offset by the related liability discussed in Note 4 (c) below, and (b) other assets relating to the carrying value of cumulative split-dollar life insurance premiums paid by the Company of $587.

(3) Primarily includes adjustments to (a) accounts payable relating to certain estimated liabilities recorded during various acquisition purchase accounting transactions which were not subsequently adjusted for the lower actual amounts paid of $940. (b) accrued liabilities resulting from higher estimates which were not subsequently adjusted to lower actual amounts of $809, and the classification on the balance sheet of estimated collectible accounts of ($2,635) as described in Note 1(b) above, and (c) income taxes payable and deferred to reflect the income tax impact of recording the items described herein of ($981).

(4) Primarily includes adjustments to (a) employee benefit obligations relating to the unintentional misapplication of certain technical GAAP requirements surrounding the establishment of employee disability obligations of $1,575, and of the timing of the recognition of liabilities relating to employee severance obligations of ($1,982), each of which are substantially offsetting, (b) deferred income tax liabilities for computational differences relating to the calculation and reconciliation of deferred tax liabilities of ($2,059), and (c) other long term liabilities relating to the timing of the recognition of a minor asset retirement obligation of ($2,143).

(5) Represents the net after-tax effect for the indicated periods resulting from the above-described items.

(6) Represents the net after tax impact on retained earnings as of January 1, 2006 to record the initial application of SAB 108.

Auditor's Report

All publicly held corporations, as well as many other enterprises and organizations (both profit and not-for-profit, large and small) engage the services of independent certified public accountants for the purpose of obtaining an objective, expert report on their financial statements. Based on a comprehensive examination of the company's accounting system, accounting records, and the financial statements, the outside CPA issues the auditor's report.

The standard auditor's report consists of three sections: (1) an introduction, (2) a scope section, and (3) the opinion. In the **introduction,** the auditor identifies who and what was audited and indicates the responsibilities of management and the auditor relative to the financial statements. In the **scope section** the auditor states that the audit was conducted in accordance with generally accepted auditing standards and discusses the nature and limitations of the audit. In the **opinion,** the auditor expresses an informed opinion as to (1) the fairness of the financial statements and (2) their conformity with generally accepted accounting principles. The Report of PricewaterhouseCoopers LLP appearing in Tootsie Roll's Annual Report is shown here.

Report of Independent Registered Public Accounting Firm

To the Board of Directors and Shareholders of Tootsie Roll Industries, Inc.:

In our opinion, the accompanying consolidated balance sheets and the related consolidated statements of earnings, comprehensive earnings, retained earnings, and cash flows present fairly, in all material respects, the financial position of Tootsie Roll Industries, Inc. and its subsidiaries at December 31, 2007 and December 31, 2006, and the results of their operations and their cash flows for each of the three years in the period ended December 31, 2007 in conformity with accounting principles generally accepted in the United States of America. Also in our opinion, the Company maintained, in all material respects, effective internal control over financial reporting as of December 31, 2007, based on criteria established in *Internal Control—Integrated Framework* issued by the Committee of Sponsoring Organizations of the Treadway Commission (COSO). The Company's management is responsible for these financial statements, for maintaining effective internal control over financial reporting and for its assessment of the effectiveness of internal control over financial reporting, included in Management's Report on Internal Control Over Financial Reporting in the accompanying Annual Report. Our responsibility is to express opinions on these financial statements and on the Company's internal control over financial reporting based on our integrated audits. We conducted our audits in accordance with the standards of the Public Company Accounting Oversight Board (United States). Those standards require that we plan and perform the audits to obtain reasonable assurance about whether the financial statements are free of material misstatement and whether effective internal control over financial reporting was maintained in all material respects. Our audits of the financial statements included examining, on a test basis, evidence supporting the amounts and disclosures in the financial statements, assessing the accounting principles used and significant estimates made by management, and evaluating the overall financial statement presentation. Our audit of internal control over financial reporting included obtaining an understanding of internal control over financial reporting, assessing the risk that a material weakness exists, and testing and evaluating the design and operating effectiveness of internal control based on the assessed risk. Our audits also included performing such other procedures as we considered necessary in the circumstances. We believe that our audits provide a reasonable basis for our opinions.

As discussed in Note 4 to the consolidated financial statements, the Company changed its method of accounting for uncertainty in income taxes as of January 1, 2007.

A company's internal control over financial reporting is a process designed to provide reasonable assurance regarding the reliability of financial reporting and the preparation of financial statements for external purposes in accordance with generally accepted accounting principles. A company's internal control over financial reporting includes those policies and procedures that (i) pertain to the maintenance of records that, in reasonable detail, accurately and fairly reflect the transactions and dispositions of the assets of the company; (ii) provide reasonable assurance that transactions are recorded as necessary to permit preparation of financial statements in accordance with generally accepted accounting principles, and that receipts and expenditures of the company are being made only in accordance with authorizations of management and directors of the company; and (iii) provide reasonable assurance regarding prevention or timely detection of unauthorized acquisition, use, or disposition of the company's assets that could have a material effect on the financial statements.

Because of its inherent limitations, internal control over financial reporting may not prevent or detect misstatements. Also, projections of any evaluation of effectiveness to future periods are subject to the risk that controls may become inadequate because of changes in conditions, or that the degree of compliance with the policies or procedures may deteriorate.

PricewaterhouseCoopers LLP

Chicago, Illinois
February 28, 2008

Supplementary Financial Information

In addition to the financial statements and the accompanying notes, companies often present supplementary financial information. Tootsie Roll has provided stock performance information, quarterly financial data, and a five-year summary of earnings and financial highlights.

Performance Graph

The following performance graphs compare the Company's cumulative total shareholder return on the Company's Common Stock for a five-year period (December 31, 2002 to December 31, 2007) and a ten-year period (December 31, 1997 to December 31, 2007 with the cumulative total return of Standard & Poor's 500 Stock Index ("S&P 500") and the Dow Jones Industry Food Index ("Peer Group," which includes the Company), assuming (i) $100 invested on December 31 of the first year of the chart in each of the Company's Common Stock, S&P 500 and the Dow Jones Industry Food Index and (ii) the reinvestment of dividends.

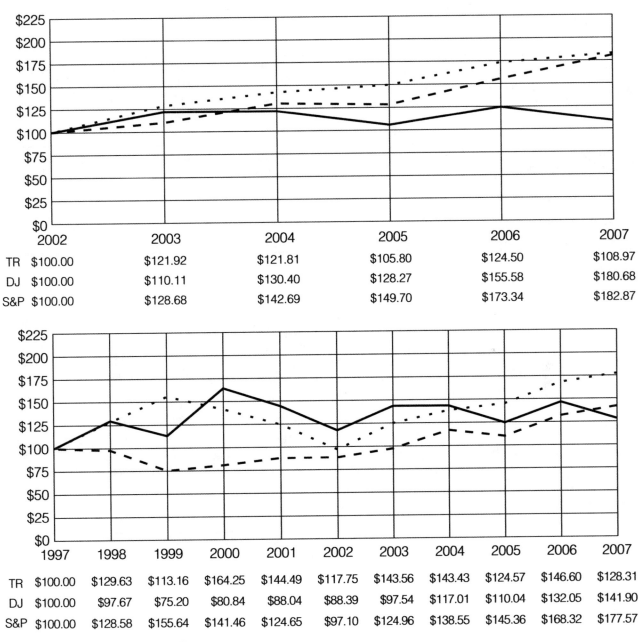

	2002	2003	2004	2005	2006	2007
TR	$100.00	$121.92	$121.81	$105.80	$124.50	$108.97
DJ	$100.00	$110.11	$130.40	$128.27	$155.58	$180.68
S&P	$100.00	$128.68	$142.69	$149.70	$173.34	$182.87

	1997	1998	1999	2000	2001	2002	2003	2004	2005	2006	2007
TR	$100.00	$129.63	$113.16	$164.25	$144.49	$117.75	$143.56	$143.43	$124.57	$146.60	$128.31
DJ	$100.00	$97.67	$75.20	$80.84	$88.04	$88.39	$97.54	$117.01	$110.04	$132.05	$141.90
S&P	$100.00	$128.58	$155.64	$141.46	$124.65	$97.10	$124.96	$138.55	$145.36	$168.32	$177.57

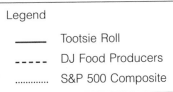

Legend

—————— Tootsie Roll

- - - - - DJ Food Producers

············ S&P 500 Composite

Quarterly Financial Data (Unaudited)

TOOTSIE ROLL INDUSTRIES, INC. AND SUBSIDIARIES

		(Thousands of dollars except per share data)			
2007	First	Second	Third	Fourth	Total
Net product sales......................	$92,914	$101,901	182,917	115,010	492,742
Gross product margin...................	33,178	34,425	60,659	36,785	165,047
Net earnings	9,811	10,226	23,432	8,156	51,625
Net earnings per share	.18	.19	.43	.15	.94
2006					
Net product sales......................	$103,822	$94,944	$186,403	$110,821	$495,990
Gross product margin...................	39,074	38,166	70,042	37,441	184,723
Net earnings	12,362	12,858	28,969	11,730	65,919
Net earnings per share	.22	.23	.52	.21	1.18
2005					
Net product sales......................	$97,925	$103,627	$173,692	$112,495	$487,739
Gross product margin...................	39,589	41,414	67,333	39,720	188,056
Net earnings	12,506	13,731	27,665	23,325	77,227
Net earnings per share	.22	.24	.49	.41	1.36

Net earnings per share is based upon average outstanding shares as adjusted for 3% stock dividends issued during the second quarter of each year. The sum of the per share amounts may not equal annual amounts due to rounding.

2007-2006 QUARTERLY SUMMARY OF TOOTSIE ROLL INDUSTRIES, INC. STOCK PRICE AND DIVIDENDS PER SHARE

STOCK PRICES*

....	2007		2006	
	High	Low	High	Low
1st Qtr.....	$32.69	$28.19	$29.71	$26.98
2nd Qtr	$30.50	$27.65	$31.42	$28.23
3rd Qtr.....	$30.85	$25.03	$29.75	$26.35
4th Qtr.....	$27.44	$23.55	$33.26	$29.08

*NYSE—Closing Price

Estimated Number of shareholders at February 2008:
Common Stock...................... 18,000
Class B Common Stock................ 5,000

DIVIDENDS

	2007	2006
1st Qtr.....	$.08	$.08
2nd Qtr	$.08	$.08
3rd Qtr.....	$.08	$.08
4th Qtr.....	$.08	$.08

NOTE: In addition to the above cash dividends, a 3% stock dividend was issued on April 12, 2007 and April 13, 2006. Cash dividends are not restated to reflect 3% stock dividends.

Five Year Summary of Earnings and Financial Highlights

TOOTSIE ROLL INDUSTRIES, INC. AND SUBSIDIARIES

(Thousands of dollars except per share, percentage and ratio figures)

(See Management's Comments starting on page 5 [textbook page A-6])

	2007	2006	2005	2004	2003
Sales and Earnings Data (2)					
Net product sales	$ 492,742	$495,990	$487,739	$420,110	$392,656
Gross product margin	165,047	184,723	188,056	174,539	168,833
Interest expense	535	726	2,537	912	172
Provision for income taxes	25,542	28,796	36,425	30,514	32,933
Net earnings	51,625	65,919	77,227	64,174	65,014
% of net product sales	10.5%	13.3%	15.8%	15.3%	16.6%
% of shareholders' equity	8.1%	10.5%	12.5%	11.3%	12.1%
Per Common Share Data (1)					
Net earnings	$ .94	$ 1.18	$ 1.36	$ 1.12	$ 1.12
Cash dividends declared	.32	.32	.29	.27	.25
Stock dividends	3%	3%	3%	3%	3%
Additional Financial Data					
Working capital	$ 141,754	$128,706	$132,940	$110,376	$180,818
Net cash provided by operating activities	90,064	55,656	82,524	76,228	83,466
Net cash provided by (used in) investing activities	(43,345)	11,026	21,872	(164,039)	(50,383)
Net cash provided by (used in) financing activities	(44,842)	(79,959)	(92,379)	60,716	(54,506)
Property, plant & equipment additions	14,767	39,207	14,690	17,948	12,150
Net property, plant & equipment	201,401	202,898	178,760	178,750	129,163
Total assets	812,725	791,639	813,696	811,753	665,297
Long term debt	7,500	7,500	7,500	93,167	7,500
Shareholders' equity	638,230	630,681	617,405	570,179	536,581
Average shares outstanding (1)	54,980	55,800	56,732	57,111	58,202

(1) Adjusted for annual 3% stock dividends.
(2) Certain reclassifications have been made to prior year numbers to conform to current year presentation.

Specimen Financial Statements: Hershey Foods Corporation

THE HERSHEY COMPANY

CONSOLIDATED STATEMENTS OF INCOME

For the years ended December 31, In thousands of dollars except per share amounts	2007	2006	2005
Net Sales	**$4,946,716**	$4,944,230	$4,819,827
Costs and Expenses:			
Cost of sales	**3,315,147**	3,076,718	2,956,682
Selling, marketing and administrative	**895,874**	860,378	912,986
Business realignment and impairment charges, net	**276,868**	14,576	96,537
Total costs and expenses	**4,487,889**	3,951,672	3,966,205
Income before Interest and Income Taxes	**458,827**	992,558	853,622
Interest expense, net	**118,585**	116,056	87,985
Income before Income Taxes	**340,242**	876,502	765,637
Provision for income taxes	**126,088**	317,441	277,090
Net Income	**$ 214,154**	$ 559,061	$ 488,547
Net Income Per Share—Basic—Class B Common Stock	**$ .87**	$ 2.19	$ 1.85
Net Income Per Share—Diluted—Class B Common Stock	**$ .87**	$ 2.17	$ 1.84
Net Income Per Share—Basic—Common Stock	**$ .96**	$ 2.44	$ 2.05
Net Income Per Share—Diluted—Common Stock	**$ .93**	$ 2.34	$ 1.97
Cash Dividends Paid Per Share:			
Common Stock	**$ 1.1350**	$ 1.030	$ .9300
Class B Common Stock	**1.0206**	.925	.8400

The notes to consolidated financial statements are an integral part of these statements.

THE HERSHEY COMPANY

CONSOLIDATED BALANCE SHEETS

December 31, In thousands of dollars	2007	2006
ASSETS		
Current Assets:		
Cash and cash equivalents	$ 129,198	$ 97,141
Accounts receivable—trade	487,285	522,673
Inventories	600,185	648,820
Deferred income taxes	83,668	61,360
Prepaid expenses and other	126,238	87,818
Total current assets	1,426,574	1,417,812
Property, Plant and Equipment, Net	1,539,715	1,651,300
Goodwill	584,713	501,955
Other Intangibles	155,862	140,314
Other Assets	540,249	446,184
Total assets	$ 4,247,113	$ 4,157,565
LIABILITIES, MINORITY INTEREST AND STOCKHOLDERS' EQUITY		
Current Liabilities:		
Accounts payable	$ 223,019	$ 155,517
Accrued liabilities	538,986	454,023
Accrued income taxes	373	—
Short-term debt	850,288	655,233
Current portion of long-term debt	6,104	188,765
Total current liabilities	1,618,770	1,453,538
Long-term Debt	1,279,965	1,248,128
Other Long-term Liabilities	544,016	486,473
Deferred Income Taxes	180,842	286,003
Total liabilities	3,623,593	3,474,142
Commitments and Contingencies	—	—
Minority Interest	30,598	—
Stockholders' Equity:		
Preferred Stock, shares issued: none in 2007 and 2006	—	—
Common Stock, shares issued: 299,095,417 in 2007 and 299,085,666 in 2006	299,095	299,085
Class B Common Stock, shares issued: 60,806,327 in 2007 and 60,816,078 in 2006	60,806	60,816
Additional paid-in capital	335,256	298,243
Retained earnings	3,927,306	3,965,415
Treasury—Common Stock shares, at cost: 132,851,893 in 2007 and 129,638,183 in 2006	(4,001,562)	(3,801,947)
Accumulated other comprehensive loss	(27,979)	(138,189)
Total stockholders' equity	592,922	683,423
Total liabilities, minority interest and stockholders' equity	$ 4,247,113	$ 4,157,565

The notes to consolidated financial statements are an integral part of these balance sheets.

THE HERSHEY COMPANY

CONSOLIDATED STATEMENTS OF CASH FLOWS

For the years ended December 31, In thousands of dollars	2007	2006	2005
Cash Flows Provided from (Used by) Operating Activities			
Net income	$ 214,154	$ 559,061	$ 488,547
Adjustments to reconcile net income to net cash provided from operations:			
Depreciation and amortization	310,925	199,911	218,032
Stock-based compensation expense, net of tax of $10,634, $14,524 and $19,716, respectively	18,987	25,598	34,449
Excess tax benefits from exercise of stock options	(9,461)	(9,275)	(20,186)
Deferred income taxes	(124,276)	4,173	71,038
Business realignment and impairment charges, net of tax of $144,928, $4,070, and $44,975, respectively	267,653	7,573	74,021
Contributions to pension plans	(15,836)	(23,570)	(277,492)
Changes in assets and liabilities, net of effects from business acquisitions and divestitures:			
Accounts receivable—trade	40,467	(14,919)	(130,663)
Inventories	45,348	(12,461)	(60,062)
Accounts payable	62,204	(13,173)	16,715
Other assets and liabilities	(31,329)	275	47,363
Net Cash Provided from Operating Activities	778,836	723,193	461,762
Cash Flows Provided from (Used by) Investing Activities			
Capital additions	(189,698)	(183,496)	(181,069)
Capitalized software additions	(14,194)	(15,016)	(13,236)
Business acquisitions	(100,461)	(17,000)	(47,074)
Proceeds from divestitures	—	—	2,713
Net Cash (Used by) Investing Activities	(304,353)	(215,512)	(238,666)
Cash Flows Provided from (Used by) Financing Activities			
Net change in short-term borrowings	195,055	(163,826)	475,582
Long-term borrowings	—	496,728	248,318
Repayment of long-term debt	(188,891)	(234)	(278,236)
Cash dividends paid	(252,263)	(235,129)	(221,235)
Exercise of stock options	50,497	37,111	81,632
Excess tax benefits from exercise of stock options	9,461	9,275	20,186
Repurchase of Common Stock	(256,285)	(621,648)	(536,997)
Net Cash (Used by) Financing Activities	(442,426)	(477,723)	(210,750)
Increase in Cash and Cash Equivalents	32,057	29,958	12,346
Cash and Cash Equivalents as of January 1	97,141	67,183	54,837
Cash and Cash Equivalents as of December 31	$ 129,198	$ 97,141	$ 67,183
Interest Paid	$ 126,450	$ 105,250	$ 88,077
Income Taxes Paid	253,977	325,451	206,704

The notes to consolidated financial statements are an integral part of these statements.

THE HERSHEY COMPANY
CONSOLIDATED STATEMENTS OF STOCKHOLDERS' EQUITY

In thousands of dollars

	Preferred Stock	Common Stock	Class B Common Stock	Additional Paid-in Capital	Unearned ESOP Compensation	Retained Earnings	Treasury Common Stock	Accumulated Other Comprehensive Income (Loss)	Total Stockholders' Equity
Balance as of January 1, 2005	$—	$299,060	$60,841	$171,413	$(6,387)	$3,374,171	$(2,762,304)	$ 309	$1,137,103
Net income						488,547			488,547
Other comprehensive (loss)								(9,631)	(9,631)
Comprehensive income									478,916
Dividends:									
Common Stock, $.93 per share						(170,147)			(170,147)
Class B Common Stock, $.84 per share						(51,088)			(51,088)
Conversion of Class B Common Stock into Common Stock		23	(23)						—
Incentive plan transactions				236			1,161		1,397
Stock-based compensation				35,764					35,764
Exercise of stock options				44,759			73,258		118,017
Employee stock ownership trust/benefits transactions				202	3,194		19		3,415
Repurchase of Common Stock							(536,997)		(536,997)
Balance as of December 31, 2005	—	299,083	60,818	252,374	(3,193)	3,641,483	(3,224,863)	(9,322)	1,016,380
Net income						559,061			559,061
Other comprehensive income								9,105	9,105
Comprehensive income									568,166
Adjustment to initially apply SFAS No. 158, net of tax								(137,972)	(137,972)
Dividends:									
Common Stock, $1.03 per share						(178,873)			(178,873)
Class B Common Stock, $.925 per share						(56,256)			(56,256)
Conversion of Class B Common Stock into Common Stock		2	(2)						
Incentive plan transactions				840			3,250		4,090
Stock-based compensation				34,374					34,374
Exercise of stock options				9,732			39,992		49,724
Employee stock ownership trust/benefits transactions				923	3,193		1,322		5,438
Repurchase of Common Stock							(621,648)		(621,648)
Balance as of December 31, 2006	—	299,085	60,816	298,243	—	3,965,415	(3,801,947)	(138,189)	683,423
Net income						214,154			214,154
Other comprehensive income								110,210	110,210
Comprehensive income									324,364
Dividends:									
Common Stock, $1.135 per share						(190,199)			(190,199)
Class B Common Stock, $1.0206 per share						(62,064)			(62,064)
Conversion of Class B Common Stock into Common Stock		10	(10)						—
Incentive plan transactions				1,426			2,082		3,508
Stock-based compensation				29,790					29,790
Exercise of stock options				5,797			54,588		60,385
Repurchase of Common Stock							(256,285)		(256,285)
Balance as of December 31, 2007	$—	$299,095	$60,806	$335,256	$ —	$3,927,306	$(4,001,562)	$ (27,979)	$ 592,922

The notes to consolidated financial statements are an integral part of these statements.

Time Value of Money

study objectives

After studying this appendix, you should be able to:

1 Distinguish between simple and compound interest.

2 Solve for future value of a single amount.

3 Solve for future value of an annuity.

4 Identify the variables fundamental to solving present value problems.

5 Solve for present value of a single amount.

6 Solve for present value of an annuity.

7 Compute the present value of notes and bonds.

8 Use a financial calculator to solve time value of money problems.

Would you rather receive $1,000 today or a year from now? You should prefer to receive the $1,000 today because you can invest the $1,000 and earn interest on it. As a result, you will have more than $1,000 a year from now. What this example illustrates is the concept of the **time value of money**. Everyone prefers to receive money today rather than in the future because of the interest factor.

Nature of Interest

Interest is payment for the use of another person's money. It is the difference between the amount borrowed or invested (called the **principal**) and the amount repaid or collected. The amount of interest to be paid or collected is usually stated as a rate over a specific period of time. The rate of interest is generally stated as an annual rate.

The amount of interest involved in any financing transaction is based on three elements:

1. **Principal (p):** The original amount borrowed or invested.
2. **Interest Rate (i):** An annual percentage of the principal.
3. **Time (n):** The number of years that the principal is borrowed or invested.

SIMPLE INTEREST

Simple interest is computed on the principal amount only. It is the return on the principal for one period. Simple interest is usually expressed as shown in Illustration C-1.

> **study objective** 1
>
> Distinguish between simple and compound interest.

Illustration C-1 Interest computation

Interest	=	Principal p	×	Rate i	×	Time n

For example, if you borrowed $5,000 for 2 years at a simple interest rate of 12% annually, you would pay $1,200 in total interest computed as follows:

$$\text{Interest} = p \times i \times n$$
$$= \$5,000 \times .12 \times 2$$
$$= \$1,200$$

COMPOUND INTEREST

Compound interest is computed on principal **and** on any interest earned that has not been paid or withdrawn. It is the return on (or growth of) the principal for two or more time periods. Compounding computes interest not only on the principal but also on the interest earned to date on that principal, assuming the interest is left on deposit.

To illustrate the difference between simple and compound interest, assume that you deposit $1,000 in Bank Two, where it will earn simple interest of 9% per year, and you deposit another $1,000 in Citizens Bank, where it will earn compound interest of 9% per year compounded annually. Also assume that in both cases you will not withdraw any cash until three years from the date of deposit. Illustration C-2 shows the computation of interest to be received and the accumulated year-end balances.

Illustration C-2 Simple versus compound interest

Bank Two				Citizens Bank		
Simple Interest Calculation	Simple Interest	Accumulated Year-end Balance		Compound Interest Calculation	Compound Interest	Accumulated Year-end Balance
Year 1 $1,000.00 × 9%	$ 90.00	$1,090.00		Year 1 $1,000.00 × 9%	$ 90.00	$1,090.00
Year 2 $1,000.00 × 9%	90.00	$1,180.00		Year 2 $1,090.00 × 9%	98.10	$1,188.10
Year 3 $1,000.00 × 9%	90.00	$1,270.00		Year 3 $1,188.10 × 9%	106.93	$1,295.03
	$ 270.00				$ 295.03	

$25.03 Difference

Note in Illustration C-2 that simple interest uses the initial principal of $1,000 to compute the interest in all three years. Compound interest uses the accumulated balance (principal plus interest to date) at each year-end to compute interest in the succeeding year—which explains why your compound interest account is larger.

Obviously, if you had a choice between investing your money at simple interest or at compound interest, you would choose compound interest, all other things—especially risk—being equal. In the example, compounding provides $25.03 of additional interest income. For practical purposes, compounding assumes that unpaid interest earned becomes a part of the principal, and the accumulated balance at the end of each year becomes the new principal on which interest is earned during the next year.

Illustration C-2 indicates that you should invest your money at a bank that compounds interest. Most business situations use compound interest. Simple interest is generally applicable only to short-term situations of one year or less.

section one

Future Value Concepts

Future Value of a Single Amount

study objective 2
Solve for future value of a single amount.

The **future value of a single amount** is the value at a future date of a given amount invested, assuming compound interest. For example, in Illustration C-2, $1,295.03 is the future value of the $1,000 investment earning 9% for three years. The $1,295.03 could be determined more easily by using the following formula:

$$FV = p \times (1 + i)^n$$

Illustration C-3   Formula for future value

where:

$$FV = \text{future value of a single amount}$$
$$p = \text{principal (or present value; the value today)}$$
$$i = \text{interest rate for one period}$$
$$n = \text{number of periods}$$

The $1,295.03 is computed as follows:

$$
\begin{aligned}
FV &= p \times (1 + i)^n \\
&= \$1{,}000 \times (1 + .09)^3 \\
&= \$1{,}000 \times 1.29503 \\
&= \$1{,}295.03
\end{aligned}
$$

The 1.29503 is computed by multiplying $(1.09 \times 1.09 \times 1.09)$. The amounts in this example can be depicted in the time diagram shown in Illustration C-4.

Illustration C-4   Time diagram

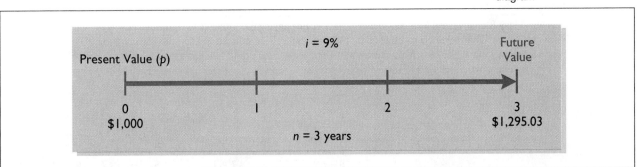

Another method used to compute the future value of a single amount involves a compound interest table. This table shows the future value of 1 for n periods. Table 1 on the next page is such a table.

In Table 1, n is the number of compounding periods, the percentages are the periodic interest rates, and the 5-digit decimal numbers in the respective columns are the future value of 1 factors. In using Table 1, you would multiply the principal amount by the future value factor for the specified number of periods and interest rate. For example, the future value factor for two periods at 9% is 1.18810. Multiplying this factor by $1,000 equals $1,188.10—which is the accumulated balance at the end of year 2 in the Citizens Bank example in Illustration C-2. The $1,295.03 accumulated balance at the end of the third year can be calculated from Table 1 by multiplying the future value factor for three periods (1.29503) by the $1,000.

The demonstration problem in Illustration C-5 (page C-4) shows how to use Table 1.

TABLE 1   Future Value of 1

(n) Periods	4%	5%	6%	8%	9%	10%	11%	12%	15%
0	1.00000	1.00000	1.00000	1.00000	1.00000	1.00000	1.00000	1.00000	1.00000
1	1.04000	1.05000	1.06000	1.08000	1.09000	1.10000	1.11000	1.12000	1.15000
2	1.08160	1.10250	1.12360	1.16640	1.18810	1.21000	1.23210	1.25440	1.32250
3	1.12486	1.15763	1.19102	1.25971	1.29503	1.33100	1.36763	1.40493	1.52088
4	1.16986	1.21551	1.26248	1.36049	1.41158	1.46410	1.51807	1.57352	1.74901
5	1.21665	1.27628	1.33823	1.46933	1.53862	1.61051	1.68506	1.76234	2.01136
6	1.26532	1.34010	1.41852	1.58687	1.67710	1.77156	1.87041	1.97382	2.31306
7	1.31593	1.40710	1.50363	1.71382	1.82804	1.94872	2.07616	2.21068	2.66002
8	1.36857	1.47746	1.59385	1.85093	1.99256	2.14359	2.30454	2.47596	3.05902
9	1.42331	1.55133	1.68948	1.99900	2.17189	2.35795	2.55803	2.77308	3.51788
10	1.48024	1.62889	1.79085	2.15892	2.36736	2.59374	2.83942	3.10585	4.04556
11	1.53945	1.71034	1.89830	2.33164	2.58043	2.85312	3.15176	3.47855	4.65239
12	1.60103	1.79586	2.01220	2.51817	2.81267	3.13843	3.49845	3.89598	5.35025
13	1.66507	1.88565	2.13293	2.71962	3.06581	3.45227	3.88328	4.36349	6.15279
14	1.73168	1.97993	2.26090	2.93719	3.34173	3.79750	4.31044	4.88711	7.07571
15	1.80094	2.07893	2.39656	3.17217	3.64248	4.17725	4.78459	5.47357	8.13706
16	1.87298	2.18287	2.54035	3.42594	3.97031	4.59497	5.31089	6.13039	9.35762
17	1.94790	2.29202	2.69277	3.70002	4.32763	5.05447	5.89509	6.86604	10.76126
18	2.02582	2.40662	2.85434	3.99602	4.71712	5.55992	6.54355	7.68997	12.37545
19	2.10685	2.52695	3.02560	4.31570	5.14166	6.11591	7.26334	8.61276	14.23177
20	2.19112	2.65330	3.20714	4.66096	5.60441	6.72750	8.06231	9.64629	16.36654

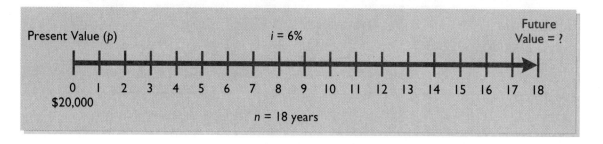

John and Mary Rich invested $20,000 in a savings account paying 6% interest at the time their son, Mike, was born. The money is to be used by Mike for his college education. On his 18th birthday, Mike withdraws the money from his savings account. How much did Mike withdraw from his account?

Present Value (p)   i = 6%   Future Value = ?

0   1   2   3   4   5   6   7   8   9   10   11   12   13   14   15   16   17   18
$20,000

n = 18 years

Answer: The future value factor from Table 1 is 2.85434 (18 periods at 6%). The future value of $20,000 earning 6% per year for 18 years is **$57,086.80** ($20,000 × 2.85434).

Illustration C-5
Demonstration problem–
Using Table 1 for FV of 1

Future Value of an Annuity

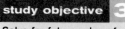

study objective 3

Solve for future value of an annuity.

The preceding discussion involved the accumulation of only a single principal sum. Individuals and businesses frequently encounter situations in which a **series** of equal dollar amounts are to be paid or received periodically, such as loans or lease (rental) contracts. Such payments or receipts of equal dollar amounts are referred to as **annuities**.

The **future value of an annuity** is the sum of all the payments (receipts) plus the accumulated compound interest on them. In computing the future value of an annuity, it is necessary to know (1) the interest rate, (2) the number of compounding periods, and (3) the amount of the periodic payments or receipts.

To illustrate the computation of the future value of an annuity, assume that you invest $2,000 at the end of each year for three years at 5% interest compounded annually. This situation is depicted in the time diagram in Illustration C-6.

Illustration C-6 Time diagram for a three-year annuity

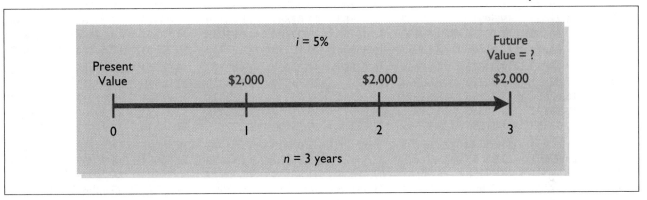

The $2,000 invested at the end of year 1 will earn interest for two years (years 2 and 3), and the $2,000 invested at the end of year 2 will earn interest for one year (year 3). However, the last $2,000 investment (made at the end of year 3) will not earn any interest. The future value of these periodic payments could be computed using the future value factors from Table 1, as shown in Illustration C-7.

Illustration C-7 Future value of periodic payment computation

Invested at End of Year	Number of Compounding Periods	Amount Invested	×	Future Value of 1 Factor at 5%	=	Future Value
1	2	$2,000	×	1.10250		$2,205
2	1	$2,000	×	1.05000		2,100
3	0	$2,000	×	1.00000		2,000
				3.15250		**$6,305**

The first $2,000 investment is multiplied by the future value factor for two periods (1.1025) because two years' interest will accumulate on it (in years 2 and 3). The second $2,000 investment will earn only one year's interest (in year 3) and therefore is multiplied by the future value factor for one year (1.0500). The final $2,000 investment is made at the end of the third year and will not earn any interest. Thus $n = 0$ and the future value factor is 1.00000. Consequently, the future value of the last $2,000 invested is only $2,000 since it does not accumulate any interest.

Calculating the future value of each individual cash flow is required when the periodic payments or receipts are not equal in each period. However, when the periodic payments (receipts) are **the same in each period**, the future value can be computed by using a future value of an annuity of 1 table. Table 2 (page C-6) is such a table.

TABLE 2 **Future Value of an Annuity of 1**

(n) Periods	4%	5%	6%	8%	9%	10%	11%	12%	15%
1	1.00000	1.00000	1.00000	1.00000	1.00000	1.00000	1.00000	1.00000	1.00000
2	2.04000	2.05000	2.06000	2.08000	2.09000	2.10000	2.11000	2.12000	2.15000
3	3.12160	3.15250	3.18360	3.24640	3.27810	3.31000	3.34210	3.37440	3.47250
4	4.24646	4.31013	4.37462	4.50611	4.57313	4.64100	4.70973	4.77933	4.99338
5	5.41632	5.52563	5.63709	5.86660	5.98471	6.10510	6.22780	6.35285	6.74238
6	6.63298	6.80191	6.97532	7.33592	7.52334	7.71561	7.91286	8.11519	8.75374
7	7.89829	8.14201	8.39384	8.92280	9.20044	9.48717	9.78327	10.08901	11.06680
8	9.21423	9.54911	9.89747	10.63663	11.02847	11.43589	11.85943	12.29969	13.72682
9	10.58280	11.02656	11.49132	12.48756	13.02104	13.57948	14.16397	14.77566	16.78584
10	12.00611	12.57789	13.18079	14.48656	15.19293	15.93743	16.72201	17.54874	20.30372
11	13.48635	14.20679	14.97164	16.64549	17.56029	18.53117	19.56143	20.65458	24.34928
12	15.02581	15.91713	16.86994	18.97713	20.14072	21.38428	22.71319	24.13313	29.00167
13	16.62684	17.71298	18.88214	21.49530	22.95339	24.52271	26.21164	28.02911	34.35192
14	18.29191	19.59863	21.01507	24.21492	26.01919	27.97498	30.09492	32.39260	40.50471
15	20.02359	21.57856	23.27597	27.15211	29.36092	31.77248	34.40536	37.27972	47.58041
16	21.82453	23.65749	25.67253	30.32428	33.00340	35.94973	39.18995	42.75328	55.71747
17	23.69751	25.84037	28.21288	33.75023	36.97351	40.54470	44.50084	48.88367	65.07509
18	25.64541	28.13238	30.90565	37.45024	41.30134	45.59917	50.39593	55.74972	75.83636
19	27.67123	30.53900	33.75999	41.44626	46.01846	51.15909	56.93949	63.43968	88.21181
20	29.77808	33.06595	36.78559	45.76196	51.16012	57.27500	64.20283	72.05244	102.44358

Table 2 shows the future value of 1 to be received periodically for a given number of periods. It assumes that each payment is made at the **end** of each period. We can see from Table 2 that the future value of an annuity of 1 factor for three periods at 5% is 3.15250. The future value factor is the total of the three individual future value factors was shown in Illustration C-7. Multiplying this amount by the annual investment of $2,000 produces a future value of $6,305. The demonstration problem in Illustration C-8 shows how to use Table 2.

Illustration C-8
Demonstration problem—Using Table 2 for *FV* of an annuity of 1

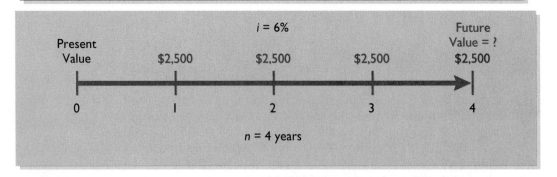

John and Char Lewis' daughter, Debra, has just started high school. They decide to start a college fund for her and will invest $2,500 in a savings account at the end of each year she is in high school (4 payments total). The account will earn 6% interest compounded annually. How much will be in the college fund at the time Debra graduates from high school?

Answer: The future value factor from Table 2 is 4.37462 (4 periods at 6%). The future value of $2,500 invested each year for 4 years at 6% interest is **$10,936.55** ($2,500 × 4.37462).

section two
Present Value Concepts

Present Value Variables

The **present value** is the value now of a given amount to be paid or received in the future, assuming compound interest. The present value, like the future value, is based on three variables: (1) the dollar amount to be received (future amount), (2) the length of time until the amount is received (number of periods), and (3) the interest rate (the discount rate). The process of determining the present value is referred to as **discounting the future amount**.

In this textbook, we use present value computations in measuring several items. For example, Chapter 10 computed the present value of the principal and interest payments to determine the market price of a bond. In addition, determining the amount to be reported for notes payable and lease liabilities involves present value computations.

study objective 4

Identify the variables fundamental to solving present value problems.

Present Value of a Single Amount

To illustrate present value, assume that you want to invest a sum of money today that will provide $1,000 at the end of one year. What amount would you need to invest today to have $1,000 one year from now? If you want a 10% rate of return, the investment or present value is $909.09 ($1,000 ÷ 1.10). The formula for calculating present value is shown in Illustration C-9.

study objective 5

Solve for present value of a single amount.

$$\text{Present Value} = \text{Future Value} \div (1 + i)^n$$

Illustration C-9 Formula for present value

The computation of $1,000 discounted at 10% for one year is as follows:

$$
\begin{aligned}
PV &= FV \div (1 + i)^n \\
&= \$1{,}000 \div (1 + .10)^1 \\
&= \$1{,}000 \div 1.10 \\
&= \$909.09
\end{aligned}
$$

The future amount ($1,000), the discount rate (10%), and the number of periods (1) are known. The variables in this situation can be depicted in the time diagram in Illustration C-10.

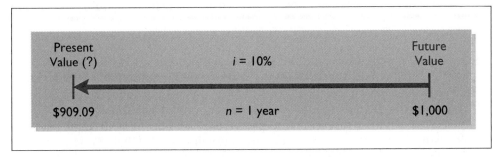

Illustration C-10
Finding present value if discounted for one period

If the single amount of $1,000 is to be received **in two years** and discounted at 10% [$PV = \$1{,}000 \div (1 + .10)^2$], its present value is $826.45 [($1,000 ÷ 1.21), depicted as shown in Illustration C-11 on the next page.

Illustration C-11
Finding present value if
discounted for two periods

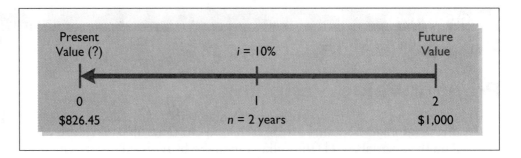

The present value of 1 may also be determined through tables that show the present value of 1 for n periods. In Table 3, n is the number of discounting periods involved. The percentages are the periodic interest rates or discount rates, and the 5-digit decimal numbers in the respective columns are the present value of 1 factors.

When using Table 3, the future value is multiplied by the present value factor specified at the intersection of the number of periods and the discount rate.

TABLE 3   Present Value of 1   *Principal*

(n) Periods	4%	5%	6%	8%	9%	10%	11%	12%	15%
1	.96154	.95238	.94340	.92593	.91743	.90909	.90090	.89286	.86957
2	.92456	.90703	.89000	.85734	.84168	.82645	.81162	.79719	.75614
3	.88900	.86384	.83962	.79383	.77218	.75132	.73119	.71178	.65752
4	.85480	.82270	.79209	.73503	.70843	.68301	.65873	.63552	.57175
5	.82193	.78353	.74726	.68058	.64993	.62092	.59345	.56743	.49718
6	.79031	.74622	.70496	.63017	.59627	.56447	.53464	.50663	.43233
7	.75992	.71068	.66506	.58349	.54703	.51316	.48166	.45235	.37594
8	.73069	.67684	.62741	.54027	.50187	.46651	.43393	.40388	.32690
9	.70259	.64461	.59190	.50025	.46043	.42410	.39092	.36061	.28426
10	.67556	.61391	.55839	.46319	.42241	.38554	.35218	.32197	.24719
11	.64958	.58468	.52679	.42888	.38753	.35049	.31728	.28748	.21494
12	.62460	.55684	.49697	.39711	.35554	.31863	.28584	.25668	.18691
13	.60057	.53032	.46884	.36770	.32618	.28966	.25751	.22917	.16253
14	.57748	.50507	.44230	.34046	.29925	.26333	.23199	.20462	.14133
15	.55526	.48102	.41727	.31524	.27454	.23939	.20900	.18270	.12289
16	.53391	.45811	.39365	.29189	.25187	.21763	.18829	.16312	.10687
17	.51337	.43630	.37136	.27027	.23107	.19785	.16963	.14564	.09293
18	.49363	.41552	.35034	.25025	.21199	.17986	.15282	.13004	.08081
19	.47464	.39573	.33051	.23171	.19449	.16351	.13768	.11611	.07027
20	.45639	.37689	.31180	.21455	.17843	.14864	.12403	.10367	.06110

For example, the present value factor for one period at a discount rate of 10% is .90909, which equals the $909.09 ($1,000 × .90909) computed in Illustration C-10. For two periods at a discount rate of 10%, the present value factor is .82645, which equals the $826.45 ($1,000 × .82645) computed previously.

Note that a higher discount rate produces a smaller present value. For example, using a 15% discount rate, the present value of $1,000 due one year from now is $869.57 versus $909.09 at 10%. Also note that the further removed from the present the future value is, the smaller the present value. For example, using the same discount rate of 10%, the present value of $1,000 due in **five years** is $620.92. The present value of $1,000 due in **one year** is $909.09, a difference of $288.17.

The following two demonstration problems (Illustrations C-12, C-13) illustrate how to use Table 3.

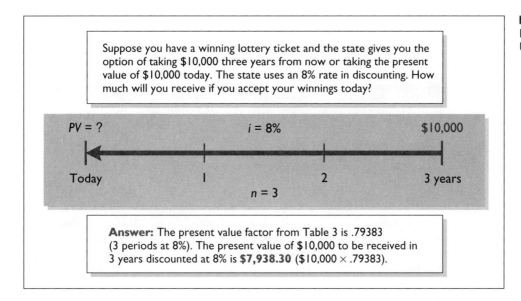

Illustration C-12
Demonstration problem—
Using Table 3 for *PV* of 1

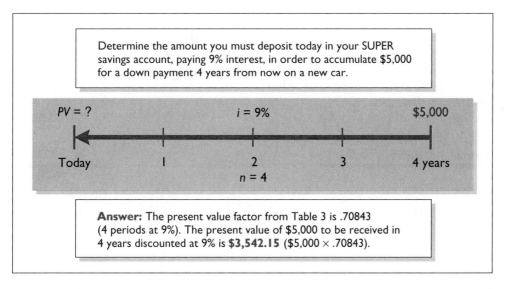

Illustration C-13
Demonstration problem—
Using Table 3 for *PV* of 1

Present Value of an Annuity

The preceding discussion involved the discounting of only a single future amount. Businesses and individuals frequently engage in transactions in which a series of equal dollar amounts are to be received or paid periodically. Examples of a series of periodic receipts or payments are loan agreements, installment sales, mortgage notes, lease (rental) contracts, and pension obligations. As discussed earlier, these periodic receipts or payments are **annuities**.

The **present value of an annuity** is the value now of a series of future receipts or payments, discounted assuming compound interest. In computing the present value of an annuity, it is necessary to know (1) the discount rate, (2) the number of discount periods, and (3) the amount of the periodic receipts or payments. To illustrate the computation of the present value of an annuity, assume

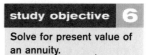

study objective 6

Solve for present value of an annuity.

that you will receive $1,000 cash annually for three years at a time when the discount rate is 10%. This situation is depicted in the time diagram in Illustration C-14. Illustration C-15 shows computation of the present value in this situation.

Illustration C-14 Time diagram for a three-year annuity

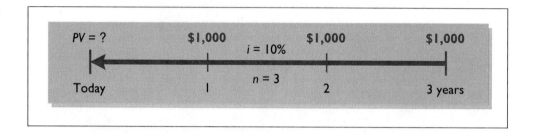

Illustration C-15
Present value of a series of future amounts computation

Future Amount	×	Present Value of 1 Factor at 10%	=	Present Value
$1,000 (one year away)		.90909		$ 909.09
1,000 (two years away)		.82645		826.45
1,000 (three years away)		.75132		751.32
		2.48686		**$2,486.86**

This method of calculation is required when the periodic cash flows are not uniform in each period. However, when the future receipts are the same in each period, an annuity table can be used. As illustrated in Table 4 below, an annuity table shows the present value of 1 to be received periodically for a given number of periods.

TABLE 4 Present Value of an Annuity of 1

(n) Periods	4%	5%	6%	8%	9%	10%	11%	12%	15%
1	.96154	.95238	.94340	.92593	.91743	.90909	.90090	.89286	.86957
2	1.88609	1.85941	1.83339	1.78326	1.75911	1.73554	1.71252	1.69005	1.62571
3	2.77509	2.72325	2.67301	2.57710	2.53130	2.48685	2.44371	2.40183	2.28323
4	3.62990	3.54595	3.46511	3.31213	3.23972	3.16986	3.10245	3.03735	2.85498
5	4.45182	4.32948	4.21236	3.99271	3.88965	3.79079	3.69590	3.60478	3.35216
6	5.24214	5.07569	4.91732	4.62288	4.48592	4.35526	4.23054	4.11141	3.78448
7	6.00205	5.78637	5.58238	5.20637	5.03295	4.86842	4.71220	4.56376	4.16042
8	6.73274	6.46321	6.20979	5.74664	5.53482	5.33493	5.14612	4.96764	4.48732
9	7.43533	7.10782	6.80169	6.24689	5.99525	5.75902	5.53705	5.32825	4.77158
10	8.11090	7.72173	7.36009	6.71008	6.41766	6.14457	5.88923	5.65022	5.01877
11	8.76048	8.30641	7.88687	7.13896	6.80519	6.49506	6.20652	5.93770	5.23371
12	9.38507	8.86325	8.38384	7.53608	7.16073	6.81369	6.49236	6.19437	5.42062
13	9.98565	9.39357	8.85268	7.90378	7.48690	7.10336	6.74987	6.42355	5.58315
14	10.56312	9.89864	9.29498	8.24424	7.78615	7.36669	6.98187	6.62817	5.72448
15	11.11839	10.37966	9.71225	8.55948	8.06069	7.60608	7.19087	6.81086	5.84737
16	11.65230	10.83777	10.10590	8.85137	8.31256	7.82371	7.37916	6.97399	5.95424
17	12.16567	11.27407	10.47726	9.12164	8.54363	8.02155	7.54879	7.11963	6.04716
18	12.65930	11.68959	10.82760	9.37189	8.75563	8.20141	7.70162	7.24967	6.12797
19	13.13394	12.08532	11.15812	9.60360	8.95012	8.36492	7.83929	7.36578	6.19823
20	13.59033	12.46221	11.46992	9.81815	9.12855	8.51356	7.96333	7.46944	6.25933

Table 4 shows that the present value of an annuity of 1 factor for three periods at 10% is 2.48685.[1] This present value factor is the total of the three individual present value factors, as shown in Illustration C-15. Applying this amount to the annual cash flow of $1,000 produces a present value of $2,486.85.

The following demonstration problem (Illustration C-16) illustrates how to use Table 4.

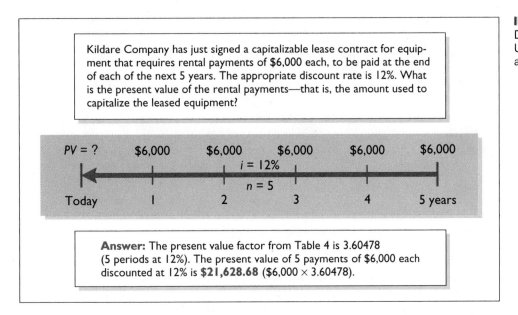

Illustration C-16
Demonstration problem—Using Table 4 for *PV* of an annuity of 1

Time Periods and Discounting

In the preceding calculations, the discounting was done on an annual basis using an annual interest rate. Discounting may also be done over shorter periods of time such as monthly, quarterly, or semiannually.

When the time frame is less than one year, it is necessary to convert the annual interest rate to the applicable time frame. Assume, for example, that the investor in Illustration C-14 received $500 **semiannually** for three years instead of $1,000 annually. In this case, the number of periods becomes six (3 × 2), the discount rate is 5% (10% ÷ 2), the present value factor from Table 4 is 5.07569 (6 periods at 5%), and the present value of the future cash flows is $2,537.85 (5.07569 × $500). This amount is slightly higher than the $2,486.86 computed in Illustration C-15 because interest is computed twice during the same year. That is, during the second half of the year, interest is earned on the first half-year's interest.

Computing the Present Value of a Long-Term Note or Bond

The present value (or market price) of a long-term note or bond is a function of three variables: (1) the payment amounts, (2) the length of time until the amounts are paid, and (3) the discount rate. Our illustration (on the next page) uses a five-year bond issue.

study objective 7

Compute the present value of notes and bonds.

---

[1]The difference of .00001 between 2.48686 and 2.48685 is due to rounding.

The first variable (dollars to be paid) is made up of two elements: (1) a series of interest payments (an annuity) and (2) the principal amount (a single sum). To compute the present value of the bond, both the interest payments and the principal amount must be discounted—two different computations. The time diagrams for a bond due in five years are shown in Illustration C-17.

Illustration C-17
Present value of a bond time diagram

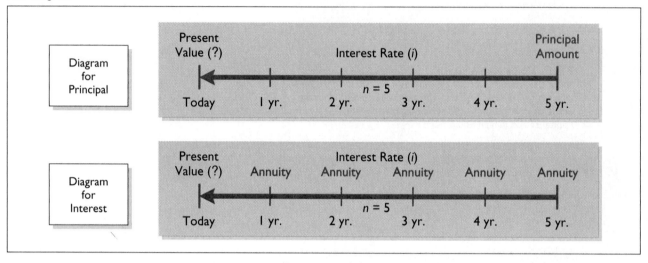

When the investor's market interest rate is equal to the bond's contractual interest rate, the present value of the bonds will equal the face value of the bonds. To illustrate, assume a bond issue of 10%, five-year bonds with a face value of $100,000 with interest payable **semiannually** on January 1 and July 1. If the discount rate is the same as the contractual rate, the bonds will sell at face value. In this case, the investor will receive (1) $100,000 at maturity and (2) a series of ten $5,000 interest payments [($100,000 × 10%) ÷ 2] over the term of the bonds. The length of time is expressed in terms of interest periods—in this case—10, and the discount rate per interest period, 5%. The following time diagram (Illustration C-18) depicts the variables involved in this discounting situation.

Illustration C-18
Time diagram for present value of a 10%, five-year bond paying interest semiannually

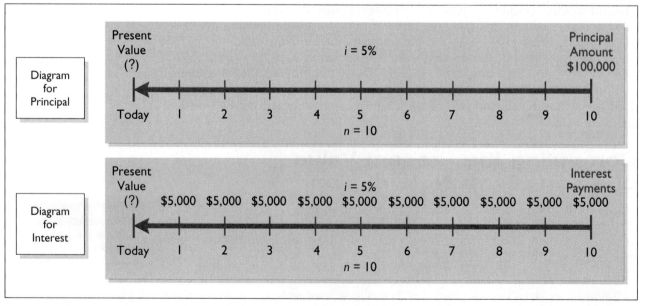

Illustration C-19 shows the computation of the present value of these bonds.

10% Contractual Rate—10% Discount Rate	
Present value of principal to be received at maturity	
$100,000 × *PV* of 1 due in 10 periods at 5%	
$100,000 × .61391 (Table 3)	$ 61,391
Present value of interest to be received periodically	
over the term of the bonds	
$5,000 × *PV* of 1 due periodically for 10 periods at 5%	
$5,000 × 7.72173 (Table 4)	38,609*
Present value of bonds	**$100,000**

*Rounded

Illustration C-19
Present value of principal and interest–face value

Now assume that the investor's required rate of return is 12%, not 10%. The future amounts are again $100,000 and $5,000, respectively, but now a discount rate of 6% (12% ÷ 2) must be used. The present value of the bonds is $92,639, as computed in Illustration C-20.

10% Contractual Rate—12% Discount Rate	
Present value of principal to be received at maturity	
$100,000 × .55839 (Table 3)	$ 55,839
Present value of interest to be received periodically	
over the term of the bonds	
$5,000 × 7.36009 (Table 4)	36,800
Present value of bonds	**$92,639**

Illustration C-20
Present value of principal and interest–discount

Conversely, if the discount rate is 8% and the contractual rate is 10%, the present value of the bonds is $108,111, computed as shown in Illustration C-21.

10% Contractual Rate—8% Discount Rate	
Present value of principal to be received at maturity	
$100,000 × .67556 (Table 3)	$ 67,556
Present value of interest to be received periodically	
over the term of the bonds	
$5,000 × 8.11090 (Table 4)	40,555
Present value of bonds	**$108,111**

Illustration C-21
Present value of principal and interest–premium

The above discussion relied on present value tables in solving present value problems. Electronic hand-held calculators may also be used to compute present values without the use of these tables. Many calculators, especially "financial" calculators, have present value (*PV*) functions that allow you to calculate present values by merely inputting the proper amount, discount rate, periods, and pressing the PV key. We discuss the use of financial calculators in the next section.

Using Financial Calculators

study objective **8**

Use a financial calculator to solve time value of money problems.

Business professionals, once they have mastered the underlying concepts in sections 1 and 2, often use a financial calculator to solve time value of money problems. In many cases, they must use calculators if interest rates or time periods do not correspond with the information provided in the compound interest tables.

To use financial calculators, you enter the time value of money variables into the calculator. Illustration C-22 shows the five most common keys used to solve time value of money problems.[2]

Illustration C-22
Financial calculator keys

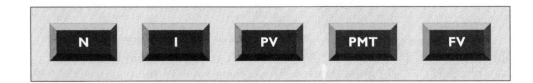

where

N = number of periods
I = interest rate per period (some calculators use I/YR or i)
PV = present value (occurs at the beginning of the first period)
PMT = payment (all payments are equal, and none are skipped)
FV = future value (occurs at the end of the last period)

In solving time value of money problems in this appendix, you will generally be given three of four variables and will have to solve for the remaining variable. The fifth key (the key not used) is given a value of zero to ensure that this variable is not used in the computation.

Present Value of A Single Sum

To illustrate how to solve a present value problem using a financial calculator, assume that you want to know the present value of $84,253 to be received in five years, discounted at 11% compounded annually. Illustration C-23 depicts this problem.

Illustration C-23
Calculator solution for present value of a single sum

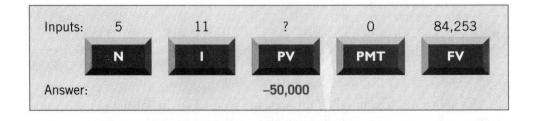

Inputs:	5	11	?	0	84,253
	N	I	PV	PMT	FV
Answer:			−50,000		

---

[2]On many calculators, these keys are actual buttons on the face of the calculator; on others they appear on the display after the user accesses a present value menu.

Illustration C-23 shows you the information (inputs) to enter into the calculator: N = 5, I = 11, PMT = 0, and FV = 84,253. You then press PV for the answer: −$50,000. As indicated, the PMT key was given a value of zero because a series of payments did not occur in this problem.

PLUS AND MINUS

The use of plus and minus signs in time value of money problems with a financial calculator can be confusing. Most financial calculators are programmed so that the positive and negative cash flows in any problem offset each other. In the present value problem above, we identified the $84,253 future value initial investment as a positive (inflow); the answer −$50,000 was shown as a negative amount, reflecting a cash outflow. If the 84,253 were entered as a negative, then the final answer would have been reported as a positive 50,000.

Hopefully, the sign convention will not cause confusion. If you understand what is required in a problem, you should be able to interpret a positive or negative amount in determining the solution to a problem.

COMPOUNDING PERIODS

In the problem above, we assumed that compounding occurs once a year. Some financial calculators have a default setting, which assumes that compounding occurs 12 times a year. You must determine what default period has been programmed into your calculator and change it as necessary to arrive at the proper compounding period.

ROUNDING

Most financial calculators store and calculate using 12 decimal places. As a result, because compound interest tables generally have factors only up to five decimal places, a slight difference in the final answer can result. In most time value of money problems, the final answer will not include more than two decimal places.

Present Value of an Annuity

To illustrate how to solve a present value of an annuity problem using a financial calculator, assume that you are asked to determine the present value of rental receipts of $6,000 each to be received at the end of each of the next five years, when discounted at 12%, as pictured in Illustration C-24.

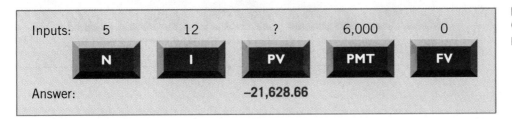

Illustration C-24
Calculator solution for present value of an annuity

In this case, you enter N = 5, I = 12, PMT = 6,000, FV = 0, and then press PV to arrive at the answer of −$21,628.66.

Useful Applications of the Financial Calculator

With a financial calculator you can solve for any interest rate or for any number of periods in a time value of money problem. Here are some examples of these applications.

AUTO LOAN

Assume you are financing a car with a three-year loan. The loan has a 9.5% stated annual interest rate, compounded monthly. The price of the car is $6,000, and you want to determine the monthly payments, assuming that the payments start one month after the purchase. This problem is pictured in Illustration C-25.

Illustration C-25
Calculator solution for auto loan payments

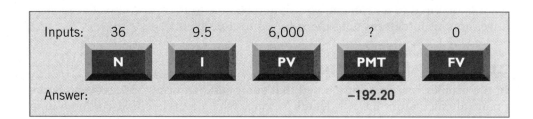

To solve this problem, you enter N = 36 (12 × 3), I = 9.5, PV = 6,000, FV = 0, and then press PMT. You will find that the monthly payments will be $192.20. Note that the payment key is usually programmed for 12 payments per year. Thus, you must change the default (compounding period) if the payments are other than monthly.

MORTGAGE LOAN AMOUNT

Let's say you are evaluating financing options for a loan on a house. You decide that the maximum mortgage payment you can afford is $700 per month. The annual interest rate is 8.4%. If you get a mortgage that requires you to make monthly payments over a 15-year period, what is the maximum home loan you can afford? Illustration C-26 depicts this problem.

Illustration C-26
Calculator solution for mortgage amount

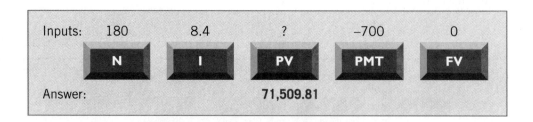

You enter N = 180 (12 × 15 years), I = 8.4, PMT = −700, FV = 0, and press PV. With the payments-per-year key set at 12, you find a present value of $71,509.81—the maximum home loan you can afford, given that you want to keep your mortgage payments at $700. Note that by changing any of the variables, you can quickly conduct "what-if" analyses for different situations.

Summary of Study Objectives

1 **Distinguish between simple and compound interest.** Simple interest is computed on the principal only, while compound interest is computed on the principal and any interest earned that has not been withdrawn.

2 **Solve for future value of a single amount.** Prepare a time diagram of the problem. Identify the principal amount, the number of compounding periods, and the interest rate. Using the future value of 1 table, multiply the principal amount by the future value factor specified at the intersection of the number of periods and the interest rate.

3 **Solve for future value of an annuity.** Prepare a time diagram of the problem. Identify the amount of the periodic payments, the number of compounding periods, and the interest rate. Using the future value of an annuity of 1 table, multiply the amount of the payments by the future value factor specified at the intersection of the number of periods and the interest rate.

4 **Identify the variables fundamental to solving present value problems.** The following three variables are fundamental to solving present value problems: (1) the future amount, (2) the number of periods, and (3) the interest rate (the discount rate).

5 **Solve for present value of a single amount.** Prepare a time diagram of the problem. Identify the future amount, the number of discounting periods, and the discount (interest) rate. Using the present value of a single amount table, multiply the future amount by the present value factor specified at the intersection of the number of periods and the discount rate.

6 **Solve for present value of an annuity.** Prepare a time diagram of the problem. Identify the amount of future periodic receipts or payment (annuities), the number of discounting periods, and the discount (interest) rate. Using the present value of an annuity of 1 table, multiply the amount of the annuity by the present value factor specified at the intersection of the number of periods and the interest rate.

7 **Compute the present value of notes and bonds.** Determine the present value of the principal amount: Multiply the principal amount (a single future amount) by the present value factor (from the present value of 1 table) intersecting at the number of periods (number of interest payments) and the discount rate. Determine the present value of the series of interest payments: Multiply the amount of the interest payment by the present value factor (from the present value of an annuity of 1 table) intersecting at the number of periods (number of interest payments) and the discount rate. Add the present value of the principal amount to the present value of the interest payments to arrive at the present value of the note or bond.

8 **Use a financial calculator to solve time value of money problems.** Financial calculators can be used to solve the same and additional problems as those solved with time value of money tables. One enters into the financial calculator the amounts for all of the known elements of a time value of money problem (periods, interest rate, payments, future or present value) and solves for the unknown element. Particularly useful situations involve interest rates and compounding periods not presented in the tables.

Glossary

Annuity *(p. C-4)* A series of equal dollar amounts to be paid or received periodically.

Compound interest *(p. C-2)* The interest computed on the principal and any interest earned that has not been paid or withdrawn.

Discounting the future amount(s) *(p. C-7)* The process of determining present value.

Future value of a single amount *(p. C-2)* The value at a future date of a given amount invested, assuming compound interest.

Future value of an annuity *(p. C-5)* The sum of all the payments or receipts plus the accumulated compound interest on them.

Interest *(p. C-1)* Payment for the use of another person's money.

Present value *(p. C-7)* The value now of a given amount to be paid or received in the future assuming compound interest.

Present value of an annuity *(p. C-9)* The value now of a series of future receipts or payments, discounted assuming compound interest.

Principal *(p. C-1)* The amount borrowed or invested.

Simple interest *(p. C-1)* The interest computed on the principal only.

Brief Exercises

(Use tables to solve exercises BEC-1 to BEC-23.)

BEC-1 Danny Reid invested $6,000 at 5% annual interest, and left the money invested without withdrawing any of the interest for 12 years. At the end of the 12 years, Danny withdrew the accumulated amount of money. (a) What amount did Danny withdraw, assuming the investment earns simple interest? (b) What amount did Danny withdraw, assuming the investment earns interest compounded annually?

Compute the future value of a single amount.

(SO 2)

Use future value tables.
(SO 2, 3)

BEC-2 For each of the following cases, indicate (a) to what interest rate columns and (b) to what number of periods you would refer in looking up the future value factor.

(1) In Table 1 (future value of 1):

	Annual Rate	Number of Years Invested	Compounded
Case A	6%	3	Annually
Case B	8%	4	Semiannually

(2) In Table 2 (future value of an annuity of 1):

	Annual Rate	Number of Years Invested	Compounded
Case A	5%	8	Annually
Case B	6%	6	Semiannually

Compute the future value of a single amount.
(SO 2)

BEC-3 Piper Company signed a lease for an office building for a period of 12 years. Under the lease agreement, a security deposit of $8,000 is made. The deposit will be returned at the expiration of the lease with interest compounded at 4% per year. What amount will Piper receive at the time the lease expires?

Compute the future value of an annuity.
(SO 3)

BEC-4 Weisman Company issued $1,000,000, 10-year bonds and agreed to make annual sinking fund deposits of $75,000. The deposits are made at the end of each year into an account paying 5% annual interest. What amount will be in the sinking fund at the end of 10 years?

Compute the future value of a single amount and of an annuity.
(SO 2, 3)

BEC-5 Jack and Susan Stine invested $5,000 in a savings account paying 4% annual interest when their daughter, Regina, was born. They also deposited $1,000 on each of her birthdays until she was 18 (including her 18th birthday). How much was in the savings account on her 18th birthday (after the last deposit)?

Compute the future value of a single amount.
(SO 2)

BEC-6 Kurt Heflin borrowed $30,000 on July 1, 2010. This amount plus accrued interest at 9% compounded annually is to be repaid on July 1, 2015. How much will Kurt have to repay on July 1, 2015?

Use present value tables.
(SO 5, 6)

BEC-7 For each of the following cases, indicate (a) to what interest rate columns and (b) to what number of periods you would refer in looking up the discount rate.

(1) In Table 3 (present value of 1):

	Annual Rate	Number of Years Involved	Discounts per Year
Case A	12%	6	Annually
Case B	10%	11	Annually
Case C	6%	9	Semiannually

(2) In Table 4 (present value of an annuity of 1):

	Annual Rate	Number of Years Involved	Number of Payments Involved	Frequency of Payments
Case A	12%	20	20	Annually
Case B	10%	5	5	Annually
Case C	8%	4	8	Semiannually

Determine present values.
(SO 5, 6)

BEC-8 (a) What is the present value of $30,000 due 9 periods from now, discounted at 10%?

(b) What is the present value of $30,000 to be received at the end of each of 6 periods, discounted at 9%?

BEC-9 Concord Company is considering an investment which will return a lump sum of $800,000 five years from now. What amount should Concord Company pay for this investment to earn a 9% return?

Compute the present value of a single amount investment.
(SO 5)

BEC-10 Cunningham Company earns 10% on an investment that will return $525,000 eight years from now. What is the amount Cunningham should invest now to earn this rate of return?

Compute the present value of a single amount investment.
(SO 5)

BEC-11 Shaw Company is considering investing in an annuity contract that will return $40,000 annually at the end of each year for 15 years. What amount should Shaw Company pay for this investment if it earns a 5% return?

Compute the present value of an annuity investment.
(SO 6)

BEC-12 Koehn Enterprises earns 8% on an investment that pays back $110,000 at the end of each of the next 6 years. What is the amount Koehn Enterprises invested to earn the 8% rate of return?

Compute the present value of an annuity investment.
(SO 6)

BEC-13 Agler Railroad Co. is about to issue $400,000 of 10-year bonds paying a 9% interest rate, with interest payable semiannually. The discount rate for such securities is 8%. How much can Agler expect to receive for the sale of these bonds?

Compute the present value of bonds.
(SO 5, 6, 7)

BEC-14 Assume the same information as BEC-13 except that the discount rate was 10% instead of 8%. In this case, how much can Agler expect to receive from the sale of these bonds?

Compute the present value of bonds.
(SO 5, 6, 7)

BEC-15 Molina Taco Company receives a $70,000, 6-year note bearing interest of 6% (paid annually) from a customer at a time when the discount rate is 8%. What is the present value of the note received by Molina?

Compute the present value of a note.
(SO 5, 6, 7)

BEC-16 Henderson Enterprises issued 9%, 8-year, $3,000,000 par value bonds that pay interest semiannually on October 1 and April 1. The bonds are dated April 1, 2010, and are issued on that date. The discount rate of interest for such bonds on April 1, 2010, is 10%. What cash proceeds did Henderson receive from issuance of the bonds?

Compute the present value of bonds.
(SO 5, 6, 7)

BEC-17 George Basler owns a garage and is contemplating purchasing a tire retreading machine for $16,100. After estimating costs and revenues, George projects a net cash flow from the retreading machine of $2,900 annually for 8 years. George hopes to earn a return of 10 percent on such investments. What is the present value of the retreading operation? Should George purchase the retreading machine?

Compute the present value of a machine for purposes of making a purchase decision.
(SO 6, 7)

BEC-18 Englehart Company issues an 8%, 5-year mortgage note on January 1, 2010, to obtain financing for new equipment. Land is used as collateral for the note. The terms provide for semiannual installment payments of $90,260. What were the cash proceeds received from the issuance of the note?

Compute the present value of a note.
(SO 6)

BEC-19 Popper Company is considering purchasing equipment. The equipment will produce the following cash flows: Year 1, $30,000; Year 2, $45,000; Year 3, $55,000. Popper requires a minimum rate of return of 10%. What is the maximum price Popper should pay for this equipment?

Compute the maximum price to pay for a machine.
(SO 6, 7)

BEC-20 If Andrea Costello invests $3,152.40 now and she will receive $10,000 at the end of 15 years, what annual rate of interest will Andrea earn on her investment? [*Hint:* Use Table 3.]

Compute the interest rate on a single amount.
(SO 5)

BEC-21 Robert Wilk has been offered the opportunity of investing $40,388 now. The investment will earn 12% per year and at the end of that time will return Robert $100,000. How many years must Robert wait to receive $100,000? [*Hint:* Use Table 3.]

Compute the number of periods of a single amount.
(SO 5)

BEC-22 Jane Duncan made an investment of $9,818.15. From this investment, she will receive $1,000 annually for the next 20 years starting one year from now. What rate of interest will Jane's investment be earning for her? [*Hint:* Use Table 4.]

Compute the interest rate on an annuity.
(SO 6)

BEC-23 Jessica Bakely invests $7,536.08 now for a series of $1,000 annual returns beginning one year from now. Jessica will earn a return of 8% on the initial investment. How many annual payments of $1,000 will Jessica receive? [*Hint:* Use Table 4.]

Compute the number of periods of an annuity.
(SO 6)

BEC-24 Reba McEntire wishes to invest $19,000 on July 1, 2010, and have it accumulate to $49,000 by July 1, 2020.

Determine interest rate.
(SO 8)

Instructions

Use a financial calculator to determine at what exact annual rate of interest Reba must invest the $19,000.

Determine interest rate.
(SO 8)

BEC-25 On July 17, 2010, Tim McGraw borrowed $42,000 from his grandfather to open a clothing store. Starting July 17, 2011, Tim has to make 10 equal annual payments of $6,500 each to repay the loan.

Instructions

Use a financial calculator to determine what interest rate Tim is paying.

Determine interest rate.
(SO 8)

BEC-26 As the purchaser of a new house, Patty Loveless has signed a mortgage note to pay the Memphis National Bank and Trust Co. $14,000 every 6 months for 20 years, at the end of which time she will own the house. At the date the mortgage is signed the purchase price was $198,000, and Loveless made a down payment of $20,000. The first payment will be made 6 months after the date the mortgage is signed.

Instructions

Using a financial calculator, compute the exact rate of interest earned on the mortgage by the bank.

Various time value of money situations.
(SO 8)

BEC-27 Using a financial calculator, solve for the unknowns in each of the following situations.

(a) On June 1, 2010, Shelley Long purchases lakefront property from her neighbor, Joey Brenner, and agrees to pay the purchase price in seven payments of $16,000 each, the first payment to be payable June 1, 2011. (Assume that interest compounded at an annual rate of 7.35% is implicit in the payments.) What is the purchase price of the property?

(b) On January 1, 2010, Cooke Corporation purchased 200 of the $1,000 face value, 8% coupon, 10-year bonds of Howe Inc. The bonds mature on January 1, 2018, and pay interest annually beginning January 1, 2011. Cooke purchased the bonds to yield 10.65%. How much did Cooke pay for the bonds?

Various time value of money situations.
(SO 8)

BEC-28 Using a financial calculator, provide a solution to each of the following situations.

(a) Bill Schroeder owes a debt of $35,000 from the purchase of his new sport utility vehicle. The debt bears annual interest of 9.1% compounded monthly. Bill wishes to pay the debt and interest in equal monthly payments over 8 years, beginning one month hence. What equal monthly payments will pay off the debt and interest?

(b) On January 1, 2010, Sammy Sosa offers to buy Mark Grace's used snowmobile for $8,000, payable in five equal annual installments, which are to include 8.25% interest on the unpaid balance and a portion of the principal. If the first payment is to be made on December 31, 2010, how much will each payment be?

Reporting and Analyzing Investments

study objectives

After studying this appendix, you should be able to:

1 Identify the reasons corporations invest in stocks and debt securities.

2 Explain the accounting for debt investments.

3 Explain the accounting for stock investments.

4 Describe the purpose and usefulness of consolidated financial statements.

5 Indicate how debt and stock investments are valued and reported in the financial statements.

6 Distinguish between short-term and long-term investments.

Why Corporations Invest

Corporations purchase investments in debt or equity securities generally for one of three reasons. First, a corporation may **have excess cash** that it does not need for the immediate purchase of operating assets. For example, many companies experience seasonal fluctuations in sales. A Cape Cod marina has more sales in the spring and summer than in the fall and winter. The reverse is true for an Aspen ski shop. Thus, at the end of an operating cycle, many companies may have cash on hand that is temporarily idle until the start of another operating cycle. These companies may invest the excess funds to earn—through interest and dividends—a greater return than they would get by just holding the funds in the bank. The role that such temporary investments play in the operating cycle is depicted in Illustration D-1.

study objective 1

Identify the reasons corporations invest in stocks and debt securities.

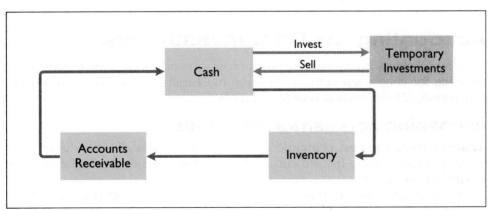

Illustration D-1
Temporary investments and the operating cycle

A second reason some companies such as banks purchase investments is to generate **earnings from investment income**. Although banks make most of their earnings by lending money, they also generate earnings by investing in debt and equity securities. Banks purchase investment securities because loan demand varies both seasonally and with changes in the economic climate. Thus, when loan demand is low, a bank must find other uses for its cash.

Pension funds and mutual funds are corporations that also regularly invest to generate earnings. However, they do so for *speculative reasons*. That is, they are speculating that the investment will increase in value and thus result in positive returns. Therefore, they invest primarily in the common stock of other corporations.

Third, companies also invest for **strategic reasons**. A company may purchase a noncontrolling interest in another company in a related industry in which it wishes to establish a presence. Alternatively, a company can exercise some influence over one of its customers or suppliers by purchasing a significant, but not controlling, interest in that company. Or, a corporation may choose to purchase a controlling interest in another company in order to enter a new industry without incurring the costs and risks associated with starting from scratch.

In summary, businesses invest in other companies for the reasons shown in Illustration D-2.

Illustration D-2 Why corporations invest

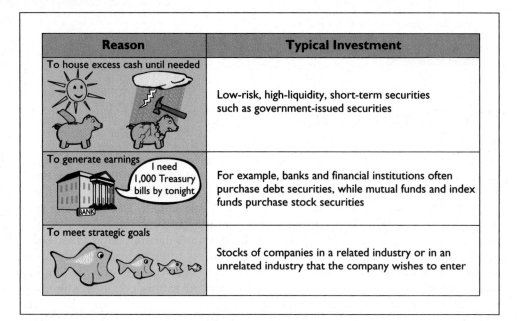

Reason	Typical Investment
To house excess cash until needed	Low-risk, high-liquidity, short-term securities such as government-issued securities
To generate earnings	For example, banks and financial institutions often purchase debt securities, while mutual funds and index funds purchase stock securities
To meet strategic goals	Stocks of companies in a related industry or in an unrelated industry that the company wishes to enter

Accounting for Debt Investments

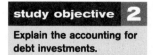
study objective 2
Explain the accounting for debt investments.

Debt investments are investments in government and corporation bonds. In accounting for debt investments, companies must make entries to record (1) the acquisition, (2) the interest revenue, and (3) the sale.

RECORDING ACQUISITION OF BONDS

At acquisition, the cost principle applies. Cost includes all expenditures necessary to acquire these investments, such as the price paid plus brokerage fees (commissions), if any.

For example, assume that Kuhl Corporation acquires 50 Doan Inc. 12%, 10-year, $1,000 bonds on January 1, 2010, for $54,000, including brokerage fees of $1,000. Kuhl records the investment as:

A	=	L	+	SE
+54,000				
−54,000				

Cash Flows
−$54,000

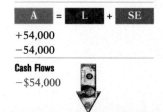

Jan. 1	Debt Investments	54,000	
	Cash		54,000
	(To record purchase of 50 Doan Inc. bonds)		

RECORDING BOND INTEREST

The Doan Inc. bonds pay interest of $3,000 semiannually on July 1 and January 1 ($50,000 $\times$ 12% $\times$ $\frac{1}{2}$). The entry for the receipt of interest on July 1 is:

July 1	Cash	3,000	
	Interest Revenue		3,000
	(To record receipt of interest on Doan		
	Inc. bonds)		

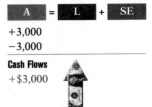

A = L + SE
+3,000
         +3,000 Rev

Cash Flows
+$3,000

If Kuhl Corporation's fiscal year ends on December 31, it accrues the interest of $3,000 earned since July 1. The adjusting entry is:

Dec. 31	Interest Receivable	3,000	
	Interest Revenue		3,000
	(To accrue interest on Doan Inc.		
	bonds)		

A = L + SE
+3,000
         +3,000 Rev

Cash Flows
no effect

Kuhl reports Interest Receivable as a current asset in the balance sheet. It reports Interest Revenue under "Other revenues and gains" in the income statement.
    Kuhl records receipt of the interest on January 1 as follows.

Jan. 1	Cash	3,000	
	Interest Receivable		3,000
	(To record receipt of accrued interest)		

A = L + SE
+3,000
−3,000

Cash Flows
+$3,000

A credit to Interest Revenue at this time would be incorrect. Why? Because the company earned and accrued the interest revenue in the preceding accounting period.

RECORDING SALE OF BONDS

When Kuhl sells the bond investments, it credits the investment account for the cost of the bonds. The company records as a gain or loss any difference between the net proceeds from the sale (sales price less brokerage fees) and the cost of the bonds.

    Assume, for example, that Kuhl Corporation receives net proceeds of $58,000 on the sale of the Doan Inc. bonds on January 1, 2011, after receiving the interest due. Since the securities cost $54,000, Kuhl has realized a gain of $4,000. It records the sale as follows.

Helpful Hint The accounting for short-term debt investments and long-term debt investments is similar. Any exceptions are discussed in more advanced courses.

Jan. 1	Cash	58,000	
	Debt Investments		54,000
	Gain on Sale of Debt Investments		4,000
	(To record sale of Doan Inc. bonds)		

A = L + SE
+58,000
−54,000
         +4,000 Rev

Cash Flows
+$58,000

Kuhl reports the gain on the sale of debt investments under "Other revenues and gains" in the income statement and reports losses under "Other expenses and losses."

Accounting for Stock Investments

study objective 3

Explain the accounting for stock investments.

Stock investments are investments in the capital stock of corporations. When a company holds stock (and/or debt) of several different corporations, the group of securities is an **investment portfolio**.

The accounting for investments in common stock depends on the extent of the investor's influence over the operating and financial affairs of the issuing corporation (the **investee**). Illustration D-3 shows the general guidelines.

Illustration D-3
Accounting guidelines for stock investments

Investor's Ownership Interest in Investee's Common Stock	Presumed Influence on Investee	Accounting Guidelines
Less than 20%	Insignificant	Cost method
Between 20% and 50%	Significant	Equity method
More than 50%	Controlling	Consolidated financial statements

Companies are required to use judgment instead of blindly following the guidelines.[1] We explain and illustrate the application of each guideline next.

HOLDINGS OF LESS THAN 20%

In the accounting for stock investments of less than 20%, companies use the cost method. Under the cost method, companies record the investment at cost, and recognize revenue only when cash dividends are received.

Recording Acquisition of Stock

At acquisition, the cost principle applies. Cost includes all expenditures necessary to acquire these investments, such as the price paid plus brokerage fees (commissions), if any.

Assume, for example, that on July 1, 2010, Sanchez Corporation acquires 1,000 shares (10% ownership) of Beal Corporation common stock at $40 per share plus brokerage fees of $500. The entry for the purchase is:

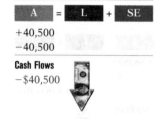

A = L + SE
+40,500
−40,500

Cash Flows
−$40,500

July 1	Stock Investments	40,500	
	Cash		40,500
	(To record purchase of 1,000 shares of Beal common stock)		

---

[1]Among the factors that companies should consider in determining an investor's influence are whether (1) the investor has representation on the investee's board of directors, (2) the investor participates in the investee's policy-making process, (3) there are material transactions between the investor and the investee, and (4) the common stock held by other stockholders is concentrated or dispersed.

Recording Dividends

During the time the company holds the stock, it makes entries for any cash dividends received. Thus, if Sanchez Corporation receives a $2 per share dividend on December 31, the entry is:

Dec. 31	Cash (1,000 × $2)	2,000	
	Dividend Revenue		2,000
	(To record receipt of a cash dividend)		

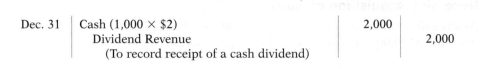

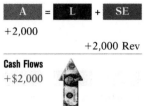

Sanchez reports Dividend Revenue under "Other revenues and gains" in the income statement.

Recording Sale of Stock

When a company sells a stock investment, it recognizes the difference between the net proceeds from the sale (sales price less brokerage fees) and the cost of the stock as a gain or a loss.

Assume, for instance, that Sanchez Corporation receives net proceeds of $39,500 on the sale of its Beal Corporation stock on February 10, 2011. Because the stock cost $40,500, Sanchez has incurred a loss of $1,000. It records the sale as:

Feb. 10	Cash	39,500	
	Loss on Sale of Stock Investments	1,000	
	Stock Investments		40,500
	(To record sale of Beal common stock)		

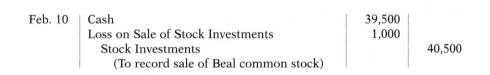

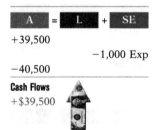

Sanchez reports the loss account under "Other expenses and losses" in the income statement, and would show a gain on sale under "Other revenues and gains."

HOLDINGS BETWEEN 20% AND 50%

When an investor company owns only a small portion of the shares of stock of another company, the investor cannot exercise control over the investee. But when an investor owns between 20% and 50% of the common stock of a corporation, it is presumed that the investor has significant influence over the financial and operating activities of the investee. The investor probably has a representative on the investee's board of directors. Through that representative, the investor begins to exercise some control over the investee—and the investee company in some sense becomes part of the investor company.

For example, even prior to purchasing all of Turner Broadcasting, Time Warner owned 20% of Turner. Because it exercised significant control over major decisions made by Turner, Time Warner used an approach called the equity method. Under the **equity method, the investor records its share of the net income of the investee in the year when it is earned**. An alternative might be to delay recognizing the investor's share of net income until a cash dividend is declared. But that approach would ignore the fact that the investor and investee are, in some sense, one company, making the investor better off by the investee's earned income.

Under the equity method, the company initially records the investment in common stock at cost. After that, it adjusts the investment account **annually** to show the investor's equity in the investee. Each year, the investor does the following: (1) It increases (debits) the investment account and increases (credits) revenue for its share of the investee's net income.[2] (2) The investor also decreases (credits) the investment account for the amount of dividends received. The investment account is reduced for dividends received because payment of a dividend decreases the net assets of the investee.

Recording Acquisition of Stock

Assume that Milar Corporation acquires 30% of the common stock of Beck Company for $120,000 on January 1, 2010. The entry to record this transaction is:

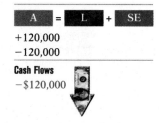

A = L + SE
+120,000
−120,000

Cash Flows
−$120,000

Jan. 1	Stock Investments		120,000	
	Cash			120,000
	(To record purchase of Beck common stock)			

Recording Revenue and Dividends

For 2010 Beck reports net income of $100,000. It declares and pays a $40,000 cash dividend. Milar must record (1) its share of Beck's income, $30,000 (30% × $100,000), and (2) the reduction in the investment account for the dividends received, $12,000 ($40,000 × 30%). The entries are:

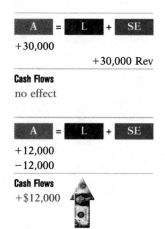

A = L + SE
+30,000
+30,000 Rev

Cash Flows
no effect

A = L + SE
+12,000
−12,000

Cash Flows
+$12,000

(1)

Dec. 31	Stock Investments		30,000	
	Revenue from Investment in Beck Company			30,000
	(To record 30% equity in Beck's 2010 net income)			

(2)

Dec. 31	Cash		12,000	
	Stock Investments			12,000
	(To record dividends received)			

After Milar posts the transactions for the year, the investment and revenue accounts are as shown in Illustration D-4.

Illustration D-4
Investment and revenue accounts after posting

Stock Investments				Revenue from Investment in Beck Company	
Jan. 1	120,000	Dec. 31	12,000		Dec. 31	30,000
Dec. 31	30,000				
Dec. 31 Bal.	138,000				

During the year, the investment account increased by $18,000. This $18,000 is Milar's 30% equity in the $60,000 increase in Beck's retained earnings ($100,000 − $40,000). In addition, Milar reports $30,000 of revenue from its investment, which is 30% of Beck's net income of $100,000.

---

[2]Conversely, the investor increases (debits) a loss account and decreases (credits) the investment account for its share of the investee's net loss.

Note that the difference between reported income under the cost method and reported revenue under the equity method can be significant. For example, Milar would report only $12,000 of dividend revenue (30% × $40,000) if it used the cost method.

HOLDINGS OF MORE THAN 50%

A company that owns more than 50% of the common stock of another entity is known as the parent company. The entity whose stock is owned by the parent company is called the subsidiary (affiliated) company. Because of its stock ownership, the parent company has a controlling interest in the subsidiary company.

When a company owns more than 50% of the common stock of another company, it usually prepares consolidated financial statements. Consolidated financial statements present the assets and liabilities controlled by the parent company. They also present the total revenues and expenses of the subsidiary companies. Companies prepare consolidated statements **in addition to** the financial statements for the individual parent and subsidiary companies.

> **study objective 4**
> Describe the purpose and usefulness of consolidated financial statements.

As noted earlier, prior to acquiring all of Turner Broadcasting, Time Warner accounted for its investment in Turner using the equity method. Time Warner's net investment in Turner was reported in a single line item—Other investments. After the merger, Time Warner instead consolidated Turner's results with its own. Under this approach, Time Warner included the individual assets and liabilities of Turner with its own assets. That is, Turner's plant and equipment were added to Time Warner's plant and equipment, its receivables were added to Time Warner's receivables, and so on. A similar sort of consolidation went on when AOL merged with Time Warner.

Consolidated statements are useful to the stockholders, board of directors, and management of the parent company. Consolidated statements indicate to creditors, prospective investors, and regulatory agencies the magnitude and scope of operations of the companies under common control. For example, regulators and the courts undoubtedly used the consolidated statements of AT&T to determine whether a breakup of AT&T was in the public interest. Listed here are three companies that prepare consolidated statements and some of the companies they have owned. Note that one, Disney, is Time Warner's arch rival.

> **Helpful Hint** If the parent (A) has three wholly owned subsidiaries (B, C, and D), there are four separate legal entities but only one economic entity from the viewpoint of the shareholders of the parent company.

PepsiCo	Cendant	The Walt Disney Company
Frito-Lay	Howard Johnson	Capital Cities/ABC, Inc.
Tropicana	Ramada Inn	Disneyland, Disney World
Quaker Oats	Century 21	Mighty Ducks
Pepsi-Cola	Coldwell Banker	Anaheim Angels
Gatorade	Avis	ESPN

Valuing and Reporting Investments

The value of debt and stock investments may fluctuate greatly during the time they are held. For example, in a 12-month period, the stock of Time Warner hit a high of $58\frac{1}{2}$ and a low of 9. In light of such price fluctuations, how should companies value investments at the balance sheet date? Valuation could be at cost, at fair value (market value), or at the lower-of-cost-or-market value.

> **study objective 5**
> Indicate how debt and stock investments are valued and reported in the financial statements.

Many people argue that fair value offers the best approach because it represents the expected cash realizable value of securities. Fair value is the amount for which a security could be sold in a normal market. Others counter that, unless a security is going to be sold soon, the fair value is not relevant because the price of the security will likely change again.

CATEGORIES OF SECURITIES

International Note A recent U.S. accounting standard gives companies the "option" of applying fair value accounting, rather than historical cost, to certain types of assets and liabilities. This makes U.S. accounting closer to international standards.

For purposes of valuation and reporting at a financial statement date, debt and stock investments are classified into three categories of securities:

1. Trading securities are bought and held primarily for sale in the near term to generate income on short-term price differences.

2. Available-for-sale securities are held with the intent of selling them sometime in the future.

3. Held-to-maturity securities are debt securities that the investor has the intent and ability to hold to maturity.[3]

Illustration D-5 shows the valuation guidelines for these securities. **These guidelines apply to all debt securities and all stock investments in which the holdings are less than 20%.**

Illustration D-5
Valuation guidelines

Trading	Available-for-sale	Held-to-maturity
"We'll sell within ten days."	"We'll hold the stock for a while to see how it performs."	"We intend to hold until maturity."
At fair value with changes reported in net income	At fair value with changes reported in the stockholders' equity section	At amortized cost

Trading Securities

Trading securities are held with the intention of selling them in a short period of time (generally less than a month). *Trading* means frequent buying and selling. As indicated in Illustration D-5, companies adjust trading securities to fair value at the end of each period (an approach referred to as mark-to-market accounting); they report changes from cost **as part of net income**. The changes are reported as **unrealized gains or losses** because the securities have not been sold. The unrealized gain or loss is the difference between the **total cost** of trading securities and their **total fair value**. Companies classify trading securities as a current asset.

As an example, Illustration D-6 shows the costs and fair values for investments classified as trading securities for Pace Corporation on December 31, 2010. Pace Corporation has an unrealized gain of $7,000 because total fair value ($147,000) is $7,000 greater than total cost ($140,000).

Illustration D-6
Valuation of trading securities

Trading Securities, December 31, 2010			
Investments	**Cost**	**Fair Value**	**Unrealized Gain (Loss)**
Yorkville Company bonds	$ 50,000	$ 48,000	$(2,000)
Kodak Company stock	90,000	99,000	9,000
Total	$140,000	$147,000	**$7,000**

---

[3]This category is provided for completeness. The accounting and valuation issues related to held-to-maturity securities are discussed in more advanced accounting courses.

The fact that trading securities are a short-term investment increases the likelihood that Pace will sell them at fair value for a gain. Pace records fair value and the unrealized gain through an adjusting entry at the time it prepares financial statements. In the entry, the company uses a valuation allowance account, Market Adjustment—Trading, to record the difference between the total cost and the total fair value of the securities. The adjusting entry for Pace Corporation is:

Helpful Hint Companies report an unrealized gain or loss in the income statement because of the likelihood that the securities will be sold at fair value since they are a short-term investment.

Dec. 31	Market Adjustment—Trading		7,000	
	Unrealized Gain—Income			7,000
	(To record unrealized gain on trading securities)			

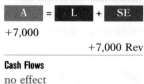

A = L + SE
+7,000
  +7,000 Rev

Cash Flows
no effect

The use of the Market Adjustment—Trading account enables the company to maintain a record of the investment cost. Actual cost is needed to determine the gain or loss realized when the securities are sold. The company adds the Market Adjustment—Trading balance to the cost of the investments to arrive at a fair value for the trading securities.

The fair value of the securities is the amount companies report on the balance sheet. They report the unrealized gain on the income statement under "Other revenues and gains." The term *income* in the account title indicates that the gain affects net income. If the total cost of the trading securities is greater than total fair value, an unrealized loss has occurred. In such a case, the adjusting entry is a debit to Unrealized Loss—Income and a credit to Market Adjustment—Trading. Companies report the unrealized loss under "Other expenses and losses" in the income statement.

The market adjustment account is carried forward into future accounting periods. No entries are made to this account during the period. At the end of each reporting period, a company adjusts the balance in the account to the difference between cost and fair value at that time. It closes the Unrealized Gain—Income account or Unrealized Loss—Income account at the end of the reporting period.

Available-for-Sale Securities

As indicated earlier, available-for-sale securities are held with the intent of selling them sometime in the future. If the intent is to sell the securities within the next year or operating cycle, a company classifies the securities as current assets in the balance sheet. Otherwise, it classifies them as long-term assets in the investments section of the balance sheet.

Companies also report available-for-sale securities at fair value. The procedure for determining fair value and unrealized gain or loss for these securities is the same as that for trading securities. To illustrate, assume that Elbert Corporation has two securities that are classified as available-for-sale. Illustration D-7 provides information on the cost, fair value, and amount of the unrealized gain or loss on December 31, 2010. There is an unrealized loss of $9,537 because total cost ($293,537) is $9,537 more than total fair value ($284,000).

Illustration D-7
Valuation of available-for-sale securities

Available-for-Sale Securities, December 31, 2010			
Investments	**Cost**	**Fair Value**	**Unrealized Gain (Loss)**
Campbell Soup Corporation			
8% bonds	$ 93,537	$103,600	$10,063
Hershey Foods stock	200,000	180,400	(19,600)
Total	$293,537	$284,000	$(9,537)

Both the adjusting entry and the reporting of the unrealized loss from Elbert's available-for-sale securities differ from those illustrated for trading securities. The differences result because these securities are not going to be sold in the near term. Thus, prior to actual sale it is much more likely that changes in fair value may reverse the unrealized loss. Therefore, Elbert does not report an unrealized loss in the income statement. Instead, it reports it as **a separate component of stockholders' equity**. In the adjusting entry, Elbert identifies the market adjustment account with available-for-sale securities, and identifies the unrealized gain or loss account with stockholders' equity. The adjusting entry for Elbert Corporation to record the unrealized loss of $9,537 is:

Helpful Hint The entry is the same regardless of whether the securities are considered short-term or long-term.

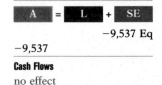

−9,537 Eq

−9,537

Cash Flows
no effect

Dec. 31	Unrealized Gain or Loss—Equity	9,537	
	Market Adjustment—Available-for-Sale		9,537
	(To record unrealized loss on		
	available-for-sale securities)		

Ethics Note Recently the SEC accused investment bank Morgan Stanley of overstating the value of certain bond investments by $75 million. The SEC stated that, in applying market value accounting, Morgan Stanley used its own more optimistic assumptions rather than relying on external pricing sources.

If total fair value exceeds total cost, Elbert would record the adjusting entry as an increase (debit) to Market Adjustment—Available-for-Sale and a credit to Unrealized Gain or Loss—Equity.

For available-for-sale securities, the company carries forward the Unrealized Gain or Loss—Equity account to future periods. At each future balance sheet date, the account is adjusted with the market adjustment account to show the difference between cost and fair value at that time.

BALANCE SHEET PRESENTATION

For balance sheet presentation, companies must classify investments as either short-term or long-term.

Short-Term Investments

study objective 6
Distinguish between short-term and long-term investments.

Short-term investments (also called **marketable securities**) are securities held by a company that are (1) **readily marketable** and (2) **intended to be converted into cash** within the next year or operating cycle, whichever is longer. Investments that do not meet **both criteria** are classified as long-term investments. In a recent survey of 600 large U.S. companies, 202 reported short-term investments.

Helpful Hint Trading securities are always classified as short-term. Available-for-sale securities can be either short-term or long-term.

READILY MARKETABLE. An investment is readily marketable when it can be sold easily whenever the need for cash arises. Short-term paper[4] meets this criterion because a company can readily sell it to other investors. Stocks and bonds traded on organized securities markets, such as the New York Stock Exchange, are readily marketable because they can be bought and sold daily. In contrast, there may be only a limited market for the securities issued by small corporations and no market for the securities of a privately held company.

INTENT TO CONVERT. Intent to convert means that management intends to sell the investment within the next year or operating cycle, whichever is longer. Generally, this criterion is satisfied when the investment is considered a resource that the company will use whenever the need for cash arises. For example, a ski resort may invest idle cash during the summer months with the intent to sell the securities to buy supplies and equipment shortly before the next winter season. This

---

[4]Short-term paper includes (1) certificates of deposits (CDs) issued by banks, (2) money market certificates issued by banks and savings and loan associations, (3) Treasury bills issued by the U.S. government, and (4) commercial paper issued by corporations with good credit ratings.

investment is considered short-term even if lack of snow cancels the next ski season and eliminates the need to convert the securities into cash as intended.

Because of their high liquidity, companies list short-term investments immediately below Cash in the current assets section of the balance sheet. Short-term investments are reported at fair value. For example, Weber Corporation would report its trading securities as shown in Illustration D-8.

<table>
<tr><td colspan="2">**WEBER CORPORATION**
Balance Sheet (partial)</td></tr>
<tr><td>Current assets</td><td></td></tr>
<tr><td>Cash</td><td>$21,000</td></tr>
<tr><td>**Short-term investments, at fair value**</td><td>**60,000**</td></tr>
</table>

Illustration D-8 Balance sheet presentation of short-term investments

Long-Term Investments

Companies generally report long-term investments in a separate section of the balance sheet immediately below "Current assets," as shown in Illustration D-9. Long-term investments in available-for-sale securities are reported at fair value. Investments in common stock accounted for under the equity method are reported at equity.

<table>
<tr><td colspan="3">**WEBER CORPORATION**
Balance Sheet (partial)</td></tr>
<tr><td>Investments</td><td></td><td></td></tr>
<tr><td>Bond sinking fund</td><td>$100,000</td><td></td></tr>
<tr><td>**Investments in stock of less than 20% owned
companies, at fair value**</td><td>**50,000**</td><td></td></tr>
<tr><td>**Investment in stock of 20%–50% owned
company, at equity**</td><td>**150,000**</td><td></td></tr>
<tr><td>Total investments</td><td></td><td>$300,000</td></tr>
</table>

Illustration D-9 Balance sheet presentation of long-term investments

PRESENTATION OF REALIZED AND UNREALIZED GAIN OR LOSS

Companies must present in the financial statements gains and losses on investments, whether realized or unrealized. In the income statement, companies report gains and losses, as well as interest and dividend revenue, in the nonoperating activities section under the categories listed in Illustration D-10.

Other Revenue and Gains	Other Expenses and Losses
Interest Revenue	Loss on Sale of Investments
Dividend Revenue	Unrealized Loss—Income
Gain on Sale of Investments	
Unrealized Gain—Income	

Illustration D-10 Nonoperating items related to investments

As indicated earlier, companies report an unrealized gain or loss on available-for-sale securities as a separate component of stockholders' equity. To illustrate, assume that Muzzillo Inc. has common stock of $3,000,000, retained earnings of $1,500,000, and an unrealized loss on available-for-sale securities of $100,000.

Illustration D-11 shows the financial statement presentation of the unrealized loss.

Illustration D-11
Unrealized loss in stockholders' equity section

MUZZILLO INC. Balance Sheet (partial)	
Stockholders' equity	
Common stock	$3,000,000
Retained earnings	1,500,000
Total paid-in capital and retained earnings	4,500,000
Less: **Unrealized loss on available-for-sale securities**	(100,000)
Total stockholders' equity	$4,400,000

Note that the presentation of the loss is similar to the presentation of the cost of treasury stock in the stockholders' equity section. (It decreases stockholders' equity.) An unrealized gain would be added in this section. Reporting the unrealized gain or loss in the stockholders' equity section serves two important purposes: (1) It reduces the volatility of net income due to fluctuations in fair value. (2) It informs the financial statement user of the gain or loss that would occur if the company sold the securities at fair value.

Companies must report, as part of a more inclusive measure called *comprehensive income*, items such as unrealized gains and losses on available-for-sale securities, which affect stockholders' equity but are not included in the calculation of net income. For example, Tootsie Roll reported other comprehensive income in 2007 of $810,000. Note 11 to Tootsie Roll's financial statements shows that one component of this amount was unrealized gains and losses on investment securities. Comprehensive income is discussed more fully in Chapter 13.

STATEMENT OF CASH FLOWS PRESENTATION

As shown previously in Illustrations D-8, 9, and 11, the balance sheet presents a company's investment accounts at a point in time. The "Investing activities" section of the statement of cash flows reports information on the cash inflows and outflows during the period that resulted from investment transactions.

Illustration D-12 presents the cash flows from investing activities from the 2007 statement of cash flows of The Walt Disney Company. From this information we learn that during the year 2007 Disney received $1,530 million from the sale or redemption of investments.

Illustration D-12
Statement of cash flows presentation of investment activities

THE WALT DISNEY COMPANY Statement of Cash Flows (partial) September 30, 2007 (in millions)	
Investing Activities	
Investments in parks, resorts and other property	$(1,566)
Acquisitions	(588)
Dispositions	—
Proceeds from sale of investments	**1,530**
Other	6
Cash used by investing activities	$ (618)

Summary of Study Objectives

1 Identify the reasons corporations invest in stocks and debt securities. Corporations invest for three common reasons: (a) They have excess cash. (b) They view investment income as a significant revenue source. (c) They have strategic goals such as gaining control of a competitor or supplier or moving into a new line of business.

2 Explain the accounting for debt investments. Entries for investments in debt securities are required when companies purchase bonds, receive or accrue interest, and sell bonds.

3 Explain the accounting for stock investments. Entries for investments in common stock are required when companies purchase stock, receive dividends, and sell stock. When ownership is less than 20%, the cost method is used—the investment is recorded at cost. When ownership is between 20% and 50%, the equity method should be used—the investor records its share of the net income of the investee in the year it is earned. When ownership is more than 50%, consolidated financial statements should be prepared.

4 Describe the purpose and usefulness of consolidated financial statements. When a company owns more than 50% of the common stock of another company, consolidated financial statements are usually prepared. These statements are especially useful to the stockholders, board of directors, and management of the parent company.

5 Indicate how debt and stock investments are valued and reported in the financial statements. Investments in debt and stock securities are classified as trading, available-for-sale, or held-to-maturity securities for valuation and reporting purposes. Trading securities are reported as current assets at fair value, with changes from cost reported in net income. Available-for-sale securities are also reported at fair value, with the changes from cost reported in stockholders' equity. Available-for-sale securities are classified as short-term or long-term depending on their expected realization.

6 Distinguish between short-term and long-term investments. Short-term investments are securities held by a company that are readily marketable and intended to be converted to cash within the next year or operating cycle, whichever is longer. Investments that do not meet both criteria are classified as long-term investments.

Glossary

Available-for-sale securities *(p. D-8)* Securities that are held with the intent of selling them sometime in the future.

Consolidated financial statements *(p. D-7)* Financial statements that present the assets and liabilities controlled by the parent company and the total revenues and expenses of the subsidiary companies.

Controlling interest *(p. D-7)* Ownership of more than 50% of the common stock of another entity.

Cost method *(p. D-4)* An accounting method in which the investment in common stock is recorded at cost and revenue is recognized only when cash dividends are received.

Debt investments *(p. D-2)* Investments in government and corporation bonds.

Equity method *(p. D-5)* An accounting method in which the investment in common stock is initially recorded at cost, and the investment account is then adjusted annually to show the investor's equity in the investee.

Fair value *(p. D-7)* Amount for which a security could be sold in a normal market.

Held-to-maturity securities *(p. D-8)* Debt securities that the investor has the intent and ability to hold to their maturity date.

Long-term investments *(p. D-10)* Investments that are not readily marketable or that management does not intend to convert into cash within the next year or operating cycle, whichever is longer.

Mark-to-market *(p. D-8)* A method of accounting for certain investments that requires that they be adjusted to their fair value at the end of each period.

Parent company *(p. D-7)* A company that owns more than 50% of the common stock of another entity.

Short-term investments (marketable securities) *(p. D-10)* Investments that are readily marketable and intended to be converted into cash within the next year or operating cycle, whichever is longer.

Stock investments *(p. D-4)* Investments in the capital stock of corporations.

Subsidiary (affiliated) company *(p. D-7)* A company in which more than 50% of its stock is owned by another company.

Trading securities *(p. D-8)* Securities bought and held primarily for sale in the near term to generate income on short-term price differences.

Self-Study Questions

Answers are at the end of the appendix.

(SO 1) **1.** Which of the following is *not* a primary reason why corporations invest in debt and equity securities?
(a) They wish to gain control of a competitor.
(b) They have excess cash.
(c) They wish to move into a new line of business.
(d) They are required to by law.

2. Debt investments are initially recorded at: (SO 2)
(a) cost.
(b) cost plus accrued interest.

(c) book value.

(d) None of the above

(SO 2) 3. Stan Free Company sells debt investments costing $26,000 for $28,000 plus accrued interest that has been recorded. In journalizing the sale, credits are:

(a) Debt Investments and Loss on Sale of Debt Investments.

(b) Debt Investments, Gain on Sale of Debt Investments, and Bond Interest Receivable.

(c) Stock Investments and Bond Interest Receivable.

(d) The correct answer is not given.

(SO 3) 4. Karen Duffy Company receives net proceeds of $42,000 on the sale of stock investments that cost $39,500. This transaction will result in reporting in the income statement a:

(a) loss of $2,500 under "Other expenses and losses."

(b) loss of $2,500 under "Operating expenses."

(c) gain of $2,500 under "Other revenues and gains."

(d) gain of $2,500 under "Operating revenues."

(SO 3) 5. The equity method of accounting for long-term investments in stock should be used when the investor has significant influence over an investee and owns:

(a) between 20% and 50% of the investee's common stock.

(b) 20% or more of the investee's bonds.

(c) more than 50% of the investee's common stock.

(d) less than 20% of the investee's common stock.

(SO 3) 6. Assume that Horicon Corp. acquired 25% of the common stock of Sheboygan Corp. on January 1, 2010, for $300,000. During 2010, Sheboygan Corp. reported net income of $160,000 and paid total dividends of $60,000. If Horicon uses the equity method to account for its investment, the balance in the investment account on December 31, 2010, will be;

(a) $300,000.

(b) $325,000.

(c) $400,000.

(d) $340,000.

(SO 3) 7. Using the information in the previous question, what entry would Horicon make to record the receipt of the dividend from Sheboygan?

(a) Debit cash and credit Revenue from Investment in Sheboygan Corp.

(b) Debit Dividends and credit Revenue from Investment in Sheboygan Corp.

(c) Debit cash and credit Stock Investment.

(d) Debit cash and credit Dividend Revenue.

(SO 3) 8. You have a controlling interest if:

(a) You own more than 20% of a company's stock.

(b) You are the president of the company.

(c) You use the equity method.

(d) You own more than 50% of a company's stock.

(SO 4) 9. Which of these statements is *not* true?

Consolidated financial statements are useful to:

(a) determine the profitability of specific subsidiaries.

(b) determine the aggregate profitability of enterprises under common control.

(c) determine the breadth of a parent company's operations.

(d) determine the full extent of aggregate obligations of enterprises under common control.

(SO 5) 10. At the end of the first year of operations, the total cost of the trading securities portfolio is $120,000 and the total fair value is $115,000. What should the financial statements show?

(a) A reduction of an asset of $5,000 and a realized loss of $5,000.

(b) A reduction of an asset of $5,000 and an unrealized loss of $5,000 in the stockholders' equity section.

(c) A reduction of an asset of $5,000 in the current assets section and an unrealized loss of $5,000 under "Other expenses and losses."

(d) A reduction of an asset of $5,000 in the current assets section and a realized loss of $5,000 under "Other expenses and losses."

(SO 5) 11. In the balance sheet, Unrealized Loss—Equity is reported as a:

(a) contra asset account.

(b) contra stockholders' equity account.

(c) loss in the income statement.

(d) loss in the retained earnings statement.

(SO 5) 12. If a company wants to increase its reported income by manipulating its investment accounts, which should it do?

(a) Sell its "winner" trading securities and hold its "loser" trading securities.

(b) Hold its "winner" trading securities and sell its "loser" trading securities.

(c) Sell its "winner" available-for-sale securities and hold its "loser" available-for-sale securities.

(d) Hold its "winner" available-for-sale securities and sell its "loser" available-for-sale securities.

(SO 5) 13. At December 31, 2010, the fair value of available-for-sale securities is $41,300 and the cost is $39,800. At January 1, 2010, there was a credit balance of $900 in the Market Adjustment-Available-for-Sale account. The required adjusting entry would be:

(a) Debit Market Adjustment—Available-for-Sale for $1,500, and credit Unrealized Gain or Loss—Equity for $1,500.

(b) Debit Market Adjustment—Available-for-Sale for $600, and credit Unrealized Gain or Loss—Equity for $600.

(c) Debit Market Adjustment—Available-for-Sale for $2,400, and credit Unrealized Gain or Loss—Equity for $2,400.

(d) Debit Unrealized Gain or Loss—Equity for $2,400, and credit Market Adjustment—Available-for-Sale for $2,400.

(SO 6) 14. To be classified as short-term investments, debt investments must be readily marketable and be expected to be sold within:

(a) 3 months from the date of purchase.

(b) the next year or operating cycle, whichever is shorter.

(c) the next year or operating cycle, whichever is longer.

(d) the operating cycle.

Questions

1. What are the reasons that corporations invest in securities?

2. (a) What is the cost of an investment in bonds?
   (b) When is interest on bonds recorded?

3. Judy Wooderson is confused about losses and gains on the sale of debt investments. Explain these issues to Judy:
   (a) How the gain or loss is computed.
   (b) The statement presentation of gains and losses.

4. Malone Company sells bonds that cost $40,000 for $45,000, including $1,000 of accrued interest. In recording the sale, Malone books a $5,000 gain. Is this correct? Explain.

5. What is the cost of an investment in stock?

6. To acquire Ingram Corporation stock, Batavia Co. pays $60,000 in cash plus $1,500 broker's fees. What entry should be made for this investment, assuming the stock is readily marketable?

7. (a) When should a long-term investment in common stock be accounted for by the equity method?
   (b) When is revenue recognized under the equity method?

8. Kirk Corporation uses the equity method to account for its ownership of 30% of the common stock of Saber Packing. During 2010 Saber reported a net income of $80,000 and declares and pays cash dividends of $10,000. What recognition should Kirk Corporation give to these events?

9. What constitutes "significant influence" when an investor's financial interest is less than 50%?

10. Distinguish between the cost and equity methods of accounting for investments in stocks.

11. What are consolidated financial statements?

12. What are the valuation guidelines for trading and available-for-sale investments at a balance sheet date?

13. Ashley Ranier is the controller of G-Products, Inc. At December 31 the company's investments in trading securities cost $74,000 and have a fair value of $70,000. Indicate how Ashley would report these data in the financial statements prepared on December 31.

14. Using the data in question 13, how would Ashley report the data if the investment were long-term and the securities were classified as available-for-sale?

15. Ankiel Company's investments in available-for-sale securities at December 31 show total cost of $202,000 and total fair value of $210,000. Prepare the adjusting entry.

16. Using the data in question 15, prepare the adjusting entry assuming the securities are classified as trading securities.

17. Where is Unrealized Gain or Loss—Equity reported on the balance sheet?

18. What purposes are served by reporting Unrealized Gains (Losses)—Equity in the stockholders' equity section?

19. Mather Wholesale Supply owns stock in Arnet Corporation, which it intends to hold indefinitely because of some negative tax consequences if sold. Should the investment in Arnet be classified as a short-term investment? Why?

Brief Exercises

WILEY PLUS

BED-1 Denali Corporation purchased debt investments for $43,500 on January 1, 2010. On July 1, 2010, Denali received cash interest of $1,660. Journalize the purchase and the receipt of interest. Assume no interest has been accrued.

Journalize entries for debt investments.
(SO 2)

BED-2 On August 1 Cutrell Company buys 1,000 shares of ABC common stock for $32,000 cash plus brokerage fees of $600. On December 1 the stock investments are sold for $38,000 in cash. Journalize the purchase and sale of the common stock.

Journalize entries for stock investments.
(SO 3)

BED-3 Fowler Company owns 25% of Mega Company. For the current year Mega reports net income of $150,000 and declares and pays a $50,000 cash dividend. Record Fowler's equity in Mega's net income and the receipt of dividends from Mega.

Journalize transactions under the equity method.
(SO 3)

BED-4 Cost and fair value data for the trading securities of Vanderpool Company at December 31, 2010, are $62,000 and $60,000, respectively. Prepare the adjusting entry to record the securities at fair value.

Prepare adjusting entry using fair value.
(SO 5)

BED-5 For the data presented in BED-4, show the financial statement presentation of the trading securities and related accounts.

Indicate statement presentation using fair value.
(SO 6)

BED-6 In its first year of operations Halloway Corporation purchased available-for-sale stock securities costing $72,000 as a long-term investment. At December 31, 2010, the fair value of the securities is $66,000. Prepare the adjusting entry to record the securities at fair value.

Prepare adjusting entry using fair value.
(SO 5)

Indicate statement presentation using fair value.
(SO 6)

BED-7 For the data presented in BED-6, show the financial statement presentation of the available-for-sale securities and related accounts. Assume the available-for-sale securities are noncurrent.

Prepare investments section of balance sheet.
(SO 6)

BED-8 Hagen Corporation has these long-term investments: common stock of Maley Co. (10% ownership) held as available-for-sale securities, cost $108,000, fair value $115,000; common stock of Kyle Inc. (30% ownership), cost $210,000, equity $230,000; and a bond sinking fund of $150,000. Prepare the investments section of the balance sheet.

Exercises

Journalize debt investment transactions, and accrue interest.
(SO 2)

ED-1 Hatteberg Corporation had these transactions pertaining to debt investments:

Jan. 1   Purchased 90 10%, $1,000 Drew Co. bonds for $90,000 cash plus brokerage fees of $900. Interest is payable semiannually on July 1 and January 1.
July 1   Received semiannual interest on Drew Co. bonds.
July 1   Sold 30 Drew Co. bonds for $32,000 less $400 brokerage fees.

Instructions
(a) Journalize the transactions.
(b) Prepare the adjusting entry for the accrual of interest at December 31.

Journalize stock investment transactions, and explain income statement presentation.
(SO 3)

ED-2 Ramirez Company had these transactions pertaining to stock investments:

Feb. 1   Purchased 1,200 shares of GET common stock (2% of outstanding shares) for $8,000 cash plus brokerage fees of $400.
July 1   Received cash dividends of $1 per share on GET common stock.
Sept. 1   Sold 500 shares of GET common stock for $5,500 less brokerage fees of $100.
Dec. 1   Received cash dividends of $1 per share on GET common stock.

Instructions
(a) Journalize the transactions.
(b) Explain how dividend revenue and the gain (loss) on sale should be reported in the income statement.

Journalize transactions for investments in stock.
(SO 3)

ED-3 Pedigo Inc. had these transactions pertaining to investments in common stock:

Jan. 1   Purchased 1,200 shares of Durler Corporation common stock (5% of outstanding shares) for $60,000 cash plus $1,200 broker's commission.
July 1   Received a cash dividend of $7 per share.
Dec. 1   Sold 900 shares of Durler Corporation common stock for $48,000 cash less $800 broker's commission.
    31   Received a cash dividend of $7 per share.

Instructions
Journalize the transactions.

Journalize and post transactions under the equity method.
(SO 3)

ED-4 On January 1 Swanson Corporation purchased a 25% equity investment in Westland Corporation for $150,000. At December 31 Westland declared and paid a $80,000 cash dividend and reported net income of $360,000.

Instructions
(a) Journalize the transactions.
(b) Determine the amount to be reported as an investment in Westland stock at December 31.

Journalize entries under cost and equity methods.
(SO 3)

ED-5 These are two independent situations:

1. Milton Cosmetics acquired 10% of the 300,000 shares of common stock of Fox Fashion at a total cost of $14 per share on March 18, 2010. On June 30 Fox declared and paid a $75,000 dividend. On December 31 Fox reported net income of $244,000 for the year. At December 31 the market price of Fox Fashion was $16 per share. The stock is classified as available-for-sale.

2. Isringhausen Inc. obtained significant influence over Garza Corporation by buying 25% of Garza's 30,000 outstanding shares of common stock at a total cost of $11 per share on January 1, 2010. On June 15 Garza declared and paid a cash dividend of $35,000. On December 31 Garza reported a net income of $120,000 for the year.

Instructions
Prepare all the necessary journal entries for 2010 for (a) Milton Cosmetics and (b) Isringhausen Inc.

ED-6   At December 31, 2010, the trading securities for Linger, Inc., are as follows.

Prepare adjusting entry to record fair value, and indicate statement presentation.
(SO 5, 6)

Security	Cost	Fair Value
A	$18,500	$16,000
B	12,500	14,000
C	23,000	18,000
Total	$54,000	$48,000

Instructions
(a) Prepare the adjusting entry at December 31, 2010, to report the securities at fair value.
(b) Show the balance sheet and income statement presentation at December 31, 2010, after adjustment to fair value.

ED-7   Data for investments in stock classified as trading securities are presented in ED-6. Assume instead that the investments are classified as available-for-sale securities with the same cost and fair value data. The securities are considered to be a long-term investment.

Prepare adjusting entry to record fair value, and indicate statement presentation.
(SO 5, 6)

Instructions
(a) Prepare the adjusting entry at December 31, 2010, to report the securities at fair value.
(b) Show the statement presentation at December 31, 2010, after adjustment to fair value.
(c) Megan Viola, a member of the board of directors, does not understand the reporting of the unrealized gains or losses on trading securities and available-for-sale securities. Write a letter to Mrs. Viola explaining the reporting and the purposes it serves.

ED-8   Jamison Company has these data at December 31, 2010:

Prepare adjusting entries for fair value, and indicate statement presentation for two classes of securities.
(SO 5, 6)

Securities	Cost	Fair Value
Trading	$110,000	$122,000
Available-for-sale	100,000	93,000

The available-for-sale securities are held as a long-term investment.

Instructions
(a) Prepare the adjusting entries to report each class of securities at fair value.
(b) Indicate the statement presentation of each class of securities and the related unrealized gain (loss) accounts.

Problems

PD-1   Schumaker Farms is a grower of hybrid seed corn for DeKalb Genetics Corporation. It has had two exceptionally good years and has elected to invest its excess funds in bonds. The following selected transactions relate to bonds acquired as an investment by Schumaker Farms, whose fiscal year ends on December 31.

Journalize debt investment transactions and show financial statement presentation.
(SO 2, 5, 6)

2010

Jan. 1   Purchased at par $800,000 of O'Malley Corporation 10-year, 8% bonds dated January 1, 2010, directly from the issuing corporation.
July 1   Received the semiannual interest on the O'Malley bonds.
Dec. 31   Accrual of interest at year-end on the O'Malley bonds.

Assume that all intervening transactions and adjustments have been properly recorded and the number of bonds owned has not changed from December 31, 2010, to December 31, 2012.

2013

Jan. 1 Received the semiannual interest on the O'Malley bonds.
Jan. 1 Sold $300,000 of O'Malley bonds at 110. The broker deducted $7,000 for commissions and fees on the sale.
July 1 Received the semiannual interest on the O'Malley bonds.
Dec. 31 Accrual of interest at year-end on the O'Malley bonds.

Instructions
(a) Journalize the listed transactions for the years 2010 and 2013.
(b) Assume that the fair value of the bonds at December 31, 2010, was $780,000. These bonds are classified as available-for-sale securities. Prepare the adjusting entry to record these bonds at fair value.
(c) Show the balance sheet presentation of the bonds and interest receivable at December 31, 2010. Assume the investments are considered long-term. Indicate where any unrealized gain or loss is reported in the financial statements.

Journalize investment transactions, prepare adjusting entry, and show financial statement presentation.

(SO 2, 3, 5, 6)

PD-2 In January 2010 the management of Wood Company concludes that it has sufficient cash to purchase some short-term investments in debt and stock securities. During the year, the following transactions occurred.

Feb. 1 Purchased 1,200 shares of NJF common stock for $50,600 plus brokerage fees of $1,000.
Mar. 1 Purchased 500 shares of SEK common stock for $20,000 plus brokerage fees of $500.
Apr. 1 Purchased 70 $1,000, 8% CRT bonds for $70,000 plus $1,200 brokerage fees. Interest is payable semiannually on April 1 and October 1.
July 1 Received a cash dividend of $0.60 per share on the NJF common stock.
Aug. 1 Sold 200 shares of NJF common stock at $42 per share less brokerage fees of $350.
Sept. 1 Received $2 per share cash dividend on the SEK common stock.
Oct. 1 Received the semiannual interest on the CRT bonds.
Oct. 1 Sold the CRT bonds for $77,000 less $1,000 brokerage fees.

At December 31 the fair values of the NJF and SEK common stocks were $39 and $30 per share, respectively.

Instructions
(a) Journalize the transactions and post to the accounts Debt Investments and Stock Investments. (Use the T account form.)
(b) Prepare the adjusting entry at December 31, 2010, to report the investments at fair value. All securities are considered to be trading securities.
(c) Show the balance sheet presentation of investment securities at December 31, 2010.
(d) Identify the income statement accounts and give the statement classification of each account.

Journalize transactions, prepare adjusting entry for stock investments, and show balance sheet presentation.

(SO 3, 5, 6)

PD-3 On December 31, 2009, Rich Associates owned the following securities that are held as long-term investments.

Common Stock	Shares	Cost
A Co.	1,000	$50,000
B Co.	5,000	36,000
C Co.	1,200	24,000

On this date the total fair value of the securities was equal to its cost. The securities are not held for influence or control over the investees. In 2010 the following transactions occurred.

July 1 Received $2.00 per share semiannual cash dividend on B Co. common stock.
Aug. 1 Received $0.50 per share cash dividend on A Co. common stock.
Sept. 1 Sold 500 shares of B Co. common stock for cash at $8 per share less brokerage fees of $100.
Oct. 1 Sold 300 shares of A Co. common stock for cash at $54 per share less brokerage fees of $600.
Nov. 1 Received $1 per share cash dividend on C Co. common stock.
Dec. 15 Received $0.50 per share cash dividend on A Co. common stock.
31 Received $2.00 per share semiannual cash dividend on B Co. common stock.

At December 31 the fair values per share of the common stocks were: A Co. $47, B Co. $7, and C Co. $24.

Instructions
(a) Journalize the 2010 transactions and post to the account Stock Investments. (Use the T account form.)
(b) Prepare the adjusting entry at December 31, 2010, to show the securities at fair value. The stock should be classified as available-for-sale securities.
(c) Show the balance sheet presentation of the investments and the unrealized gain (loss) at December 31, 2010. At this date Rich Associates has common stock $2,000,000 and retained earnings $1,200,000.

PD-4 Graf Company acquired 25% of the outstanding common stock of Sharp Inc. on January 1, 2010, by paying $1,700,000 for 60,000 shares. Sharp declared and paid a $0.50 per share cash dividend on June 30 and again on December 31, 2010. Sharp reported net income of $800,000 for the year.

Prepare entries under cost and equity methods, and prepare memorandum.
(SO 3)

Instructions
(a) Prepare the journal entries for Graf Company for 2010 assuming Graf cannot exercise significant influence over Sharp. (Use the cost method.)
(b) Prepare the journal entries for Graf Company for 2010 assuming Graf can exercise significant influence over Sharp. (Use the equity method.)
(c) The board of directors of Graf Company is confused about the differences between the cost and equity methods. Prepare a memorandum for the board that explains each method and shows in tabular form the account balances under each method at December 31, 2010.

PD-5 Here is Edmiston Company's portfolio of long-term available-for-sale securities at December 31, 2009:

Journalize stock transactions, and show balance sheet presentation.
(SO 3, 5, 6)

	Cost
1,000 shares of Ludwick Inc. common stock	$52,000
1,200 shares of B. Hunt Corporation common stock	84,000
800 shares of H. Kelso Corporation preferred stock	33,600

On December 31 the total cost of the portfolio equaled the total fair value. Edmiston had the following transactions related to the securities during 2010.

Jan. 20 Sold 1,000 shares of Ludwick Inc. common stock at $55 per share less brokerage fees of $600.
28 Purchased 400 shares of $10 par value common stock of M. McLain Corporation at $78 per share plus brokerage fees of $480.
30 Received a cash dividend of $1.15 per share on B. Hunt Corporation common stock.
Feb. 8 Received cash dividends of $0.40 per share on H. Kelso Corporation preferred stock.
18 Sold all 800 shares of H. Kelso preferred stock at $35 per share less brokerage fees of $360.
July 30 Received a cash dividend of $1 per share on B. Hunt Corporation common stock.
Sept. 6 Purchased an additional 600 shares of the $10 par value common stock of M. McLain Corporation at $82 per share plus brokerage fees of $800.
Dec. 1 Received a cash dividend of $1.50 per share on M. McLain Corporation common stock.

At December 31, 2010, the fair values of the securities were:

B. Hunt Corporation common stock	$64 per share
M. McLain Corporation common stock	$77 per share

Edmiston uses separate account titles for each investment, such as Investment in B. Corporation Common Stock.

Instructions
(a) Prepare journal entries to record the transactions.
(b) Post to the investment accounts. (Use separate T accounts for each investment.)

(c) Prepare the adjusting entry at December 31, 2010, to report the portfolio at fair value.

(d) Show the balance sheet presentation at December 31, 2010.

Prepare a balance sheet.
(SO 6)

PD-6 The following data, presented in alphabetical order, are taken from the records of Ritter Corporation.

Accounts payable	$ 150,000
Accounts receivable	90,000
Accumulated depreciation—building	180,000
Accumulated depreciation—equipment	52,000
Allowance for doubtful accounts	6,000
Bond investments	400,000
Bonds payable (10%, due 2021)	380,000
Buildings	900,000
Cash	82,000
Common stock ($5 par value; 500,000 shares authorized, 300,000 shares issued)	1,500,000
Discount on bonds payable	20,000
Dividends payable	50,000
Equipment	275,000
Goodwill	230,000
Income taxes payable	70,000
Investment in Jansen Inc. stock (30% ownership), at equity	240,000
Land	410,000
Merchandise inventory	170,000
Notes payable (due 2011)	70,000
Paid-in capital in excess of par value	200,000
Prepaid insurance	16,000
Retained earnings	310,000
Short-term stock investment, at fair value	135,000

Instructions

Prepare a balance sheet at December 31, 2010.

Answers to Self-Study Questions

1. d 2. a 3. b 4. c 5. a 6. b 7. c 8. d 9. a 10. c 11. b 12. c 13. c 14. c

photo credits

Chapter 1   Opener: Alex Wong/Getty Images. Page 7: Karen Roach/iStockphoto. Page 8: Petr Nad/iStockphoto. Page 9: Ed Wray/AP/Wide World Photos. Page 15: Lynn Goldsmith/Corbis Images.

Chapter 2   Opener: Jeanne Strongin. Page 51: Lowell Sannes/iStockphoto. Page 51: Denis Vorob'yev/iStockphoto. Page 52: Onur Dongel/iStockphoto, Nikki Ward/iStockphoto. Page 53: Vladislav Gurfinkel/iStockphoto. Page 55: Pixtal/ SUPERSTOCK. Page 57: Pixtal/ SUPERSTOCK. Page 60: PhotoDisc, Inc./Getty Images. Page 61: Wayne Ruston/iStockphoto. Page 62: Pixtal/SUPERSTOCK. Page 65: Toru Hanai/AP/Wide World Photos. Page 66: SUPERSTOCK.

Chapter 3   Opener: Mark Goldman/Icon SMI/NewsCom. Page 108: PhotoDisc, Inc./Getty Images. Page 114: Getty Images. Page 118: Koichi Kamoshida/AsiaPac/Getty Images.

Chapter 4   Opener: Witte Thomas E/Gamma-Presse, Inc. Page 165: Dan Chippendale/iStockphoto. Page 168: Robyn Beck/AFP/Getty Images. Page 172: Elle Wagner/Copyright John Wiley & Sons, Inc. Page 191: Curt Pickens/iStockphoto. Page 191: Curt Pickens/iStockphoto. Page 192: Curt Pickens/ iStockphoto.

Chapter 5   Opener: Stone/Getty Images. Page 227: Courtesy Morrow Snowboards Inc. Page 233: AP/Wide World Photos. Page 238: Dennis Galante/Stone/Getty Images. Page 244: Bonnie Kamin/PhotoEdit.

Chapter 6   Opener: VCG/FPG International/Getty Images. Page 291: Mario Ruiz/ZUMA/Corbis Images. Page 277: Alexey Dudoladov/iStockphoto. Page 278: iStockphoto. Page 287: Scott Olson/Getty Images. Page 289: PhotoDisc, Inc./Getty Images.

Chapter 7   Opener: Valerie Loiseleux/iStockphoto. Page 335: Terence John/Retna. Page 336: PhotoDisc, Inc./Getty Images. Page 348: Nick Koudis/PhotoDisc, Inc./Getty Images.

Chapter 8   Opener: Charles Orrico/SUPERSTOCK. Page 393: Ken Bank/Retna UK. Page 393: Joe Polillio/ Stone/Getty Images. Page 396: Brian Sullivan/iStockphoto. Page 399: Tomasz Szymanski/iStockphoto. Page 400: Andy Dean/iStockphoto. Page 401: Ken Bank/Retna UK. Page 406: Joe Sohm/Alamy Images. Page 408: Margreet De Groot/ iStockphoto.

Chapter 9   Opener: Teri Hanson/AP/Wide World Photos. Page 438: GoodShoot/Age Fotostock America, Inc. Page 449: Justin Sullivan/Getty Images. Page 455: Brandon Laufenberg/ iStockphoto. Page 456: iStockphoto.

Chapter 10   Opener: iStockphoto. Page 495: Christian Kober/Getty Images. Page 505: PhotoDisc, Inc./Getty Images. Page 505: PhotoDisc, Inc./Getty Images. Page 508: Neil Beer/PhotoDisc, Inc./Getty Images. Page 510: Geoffrey Hammond/iStockphoto. Page 511: Scott Mills/Alamy Images.

Chapter 11   Opener: Clive Brunskill/Getty Images/ NewsCom. Page 553: Eric Isselee/iStockphoto. Page 558: Courtesy Nike, Inc. Page 561: Alex Fevzer/Corbis Images. Page 565: Darren Robb/Stone/Getty Images. Page 569: Scott Leigh/iStockphoto. Page 571: Dane Steffes/iStockphoto.

Chapter 12   Opener: Rudi Von Briel/PhotoEdit. Page 604: Lisa Gee and Elle Wagner/John Wiley & Sons. Page 607: Neil Barclay/Retna. Page 619: PhotoDisc, Inc./Getty Images. Page 623: Justin Sullivan/Getty Images. Page 623: Justin Sullivan/Getty Images. Page 624: Justin Sullivan/Getty Images.

Chapter 13   Opener: Elle Wagner/Copyright John Wiley & Sons, Inc. Page 663: Steven Bronstein/The Image Bank/Getty Images. Page 674: SUPERSTOCK. Page 677: Steve Cole/ PhotoDisc, Inc./Getty Images.

Appendix D   Page: D-13: Digital Vision/Getty Images.

company index

subject index

TOOLS FOR ANALYSIS

Liquidity

Working capital	Current assets − Current liabilities	p. 59
Current ratio	$\dfrac{\text{Current assets}}{\text{Current liabilities}}$	p. 59
Current cash debt coverage ratio	$\dfrac{\text{Cash provided by operations}}{\text{Average current liabilities}}$	p. 607
Inventory turnover ratio	$\dfrac{\text{Cost of goods sold}}{\text{Average inventory}}$	p. 281
Days in inventory	$\dfrac{\text{365 days}}{\text{Inventory turnover ratio}}$	p. 281
Receivables turnover ratio	$\dfrac{\text{Net credit sales}}{\text{Average net receivables}}$	p. 388
Average collection period	$\dfrac{\text{365 days}}{\text{Receivables turnover ratio}}$	p. 388

Solvency

Debt to total assets ratio	$\dfrac{\text{Total liabilities}}{\text{Total assets}}$	p. 60
Cash debt coverage ratio	$\dfrac{\text{Cash provided by operations}}{\text{Average total liabilities}}$	p. 608
Times interest earned ratio	$\dfrac{\text{Net income + Interest expense + Tax expense}}{\text{Interest expense}}$	p. 493
Free cash flow	Cash provided by operations − Capital expenditures − Cash dividends	p. 63

Profitability

Earnings per share	$\dfrac{\text{Net income − Preferred stock dividends}}{\text{Average common shares outstanding}}$	p. 55
Price-earnings ratio	$\dfrac{\text{Stock price per share}}{\text{Earnings per share}}$	p. 662
Gross profit rate	$\dfrac{\text{Gross profit}}{\text{Net sales}}$	p. 234
Profit margin ratio	$\dfrac{\text{Net income}}{\text{Net sales}}$	p. 235
Return on assets ratio	$\dfrac{\text{Net income}}{\text{Average total assets}}$	p. 437
Asset turnover ratio	$\dfrac{\text{Net sales}}{\text{Average total assets}}$	p. 439
Payout ratio	$\dfrac{\text{Cash dividends declared on common stock}}{\text{Net income}}$	p. 556
Return on common stockholders' equity ratio	$\dfrac{\text{Net income − Preferred stock dividends}}{\text{Average common stockholders' equity}}$	p. 558

Understanding IFRS

Strong forces are in place to achieve a worldwide set of accounting standards in the not-too-distant future. Currently, many companies find it costly to comply with different reporting standards in different countries. Likewise, investors, attempting to diversify their holdings and manage their risks, have become very interested in investing in foreign companies. Having one common set of accounting rules will make it easier for international investors to compare the financial results of companies from different countries. In this summary, we provide additional insight into the movement toward one set of international accounting standards (International Financial Reporting Standards, IFRS) to be used by all companies.

Pathway Toward Global Standards

Most agree that there is a need for one set of globalized accounting standards. Consider that today's companies view the entire world as their market. Some of the best-known corporations, such as Coca-Cola, Intel, and McDonald's, generate more than 50 percent of their sales outside the United States. As a result, these organizations no longer think of themselves as simply U.S. companies. In addition, the mergers by such international giants as Budweiser and Vodafone/Mannesmann are creating massive corporations that bridge countries and cultures. Consumer behavior is changing as well. As communication barriers continue to drop, companies and individuals in different countries and markets are becoming comfortable buying and selling goods and services from one another. Most notably, investors no longer confine themselves to the markets of their home country. Whether it is currency, equity securities (stocks), or bonds, active markets throughout the world are trading these types of financial instruments.

For many years, foreign companies that listed on the U. S. exchanges were required to use U.S. GAAP or provide a reconciliation between IFRS and U.S. GAAP. Recently, this requirement was dropped. Currently, U.S. companies that list their shares on foreign exchanges do not have to convert to IFRS. However, it is possible that foreign exchanges may begin requiring U.S. firms to convert or reconcile their financial statements to IFRS to list on foreign exchanges. In addition, to attract foreign investors, U.S. companies may need to provide additional information regarding how IFRS would affect their financial statements. As investors gain a better understanding of IFRS, they may demand this additional information from U.S. companies.

REGULATORY INITIATIVES

In an effort to address this rapidly changing global environment, the SEC recently proposed a roadmap toward international accounting standards, whereby some large U.S. companies would have the option of reporting under IFRS as early as 2009. It is likely that all publicly traded U.S. companies would be required to report under IFRS no later than 2016. Many obstacles exist before these goals can be met, but it seems likely that given the potential benefits of switching to international standards, and the risks of not switching, U.S. regulators will make every effort to overcome the obstacles.

In recent years, the FASB and the international accounting standard setter, the International Accounting Standards Board (IASB) have worked diligently to narrow the differences between U.S. and international accounting standards. This effort is referred to as **convergence**. International accounting standards converge when differences between international and U.S. standards are eliminated. The elimination of differences between GAAP and IFRS that results from convergence will make an eventual switch to IFRS by U.S. companies that much easier.

DIFFERENCES BETWEEN IFRS AND GAAP

The differences between IFRS and GAAP may provide certain companies with a competitive advantage. For example, international standards that are more permissive for reporting the results of individual business segments of a company may lead to a presentation that is more favorable but in reality is misleading. Conversely, the U.S. standards may force a U.S. company to disclose more segment information. Understanding this difference may be important in judging the competing companies.

Here are two examples of such differences:

- IFRS permits companies to value property, plant, and equipment at fair value using appraisals. In the United States this practice is not allowed.
- IFRS prohibits use of LIFO costing for inventories. In the United States, a significant number of companies use LIFO to cost some, or their entire, inventory.

Other differences are highlighted in International Notes throughout this text. In addition, the summary table at the end of this section provides a comprehensive listing of key similarities and differences that are relevant to introductory financial accounting.

The fact that there are differences should not be surprising because standard setters worldwide have developed standards in response to different user needs. In some countries, the primary users of financial statements are private investors; in others, the primary users are tax authorities or central government planners. In the United States, capital market participants (investors and creditors) have driven accounting standard formulation.

STANDARD-SETTING ENVIRONMENT

As discussed in this text, the FASB has primary responsibility for establishing accounting standards in the United States. A governmental agency, the SEC, has the authority to delegate standard setting responsibility to the FASB, and to ensure that companies follow these standards appropriately. Both of these organizations have strongly supported the movement toward one set of international standards.

The primary organization involved in developing IFRS is the IASB. The IASB is a privately funded accounting standard setter based in London, United Kingdom. Its members currently come from nine countries. The IASB is committed to developing, in the public interest, a single set of high-quality, understandable, and enforceable global accounting standards. The IASB cooperates with national accounting standard setters to achieve convergence in accounting standards around the world. Because it is a private organization, the IASB has no regulatory mandate and therefore no enforcement mechanism in place. In other words, unlike the U.S.'s standard-setting procedures, there is no SEC to enforce the use of IASB standards. Use of IFRS is completely voluntary unless mandated by an authorized regulator. For example, effective January 1, 2005, the European Union (EU) required member country companies that list on EU securities exchanges to use IFRS.

As noted above, the FASB and the IASB are working together toward the goal of a single set of high-quality accounting standards that will be used both domestically and internationally. To achieve this goal, the FASB and IASB are undertaking several joint projects. One joint project is the development of a common conceptual framework for financial accounting and reporting. The goal of this project is to build a framework that both the FASB and the IASB can use when developing new and revised accounting standards. Other joint efforts involve developing new standards on major topics. Presently, the FASB and IASB are working on such major projects as leasing, revenue recognition, and reporting on financial performance.

The FASB and IASB have also eliminated or narrowed differences through short-term convergence projects. This approach has been quite successful so far. For example, the FASB has issued standards that mirror present IASB standards on such reporting issues as exchanges of nonmonetary assets and accounting changes. The goal of this collaboration is to select the better standard and move forward with it. As often stated, "the devil is in the details." Both groups are working hard to ensure that not only are the broad conceptual approaches the same, but also the methods of applying them. Thus, the FASB and IASB are not looking for mutual recognition of each other's standards. Rather, they want the same standards, interpretations, and language. Regarding the FASB and convergence, Bob Herz, present chair of the FASB, has taken a position he calls "killing three birds with one stone." That is, he hopes that new standards will (1) improve U.S. reporting, (2) simplify U.S. standards and standard setting, and (3) provide international convergence.

There are many challenges to convergence. Presently, domestic and international accounting parties are often starting from different places. Not only are the FASB and the IASB involved, but also numerous national standard setters are in the mix. There are significant cultural differences among countries and regions of the world. In the United States, the FASB is faced with a litigious society, and therefore is often encouraged to write detailed standards. In addition, there are often institutional or legal barriers to change. For example, any time a standard is issued that affects debt versus equity classifications, loan covenants may have to be changed. In some countries, changing loan covenants is very difficult.

Concluding Remarks

Financial statements prepared according to U.S. GAAP have been the standard for communicating financial information to the world. Regulators from around the world have readily accepted these financial statements when a company has chosen to list on an exchange. In 2005, however, the IASB standards have became the common financial statement language for over 7,000 listed companies in the European Union and in over 100 countries around the world. There are still many bumps in the road to the establishment of one set of worldwide standards, but the progress to date is remarkable. We are optimistic that the goal of worldwide standards can be achieved, which will be of value to all.

Summary Table of International Accounting Issues

Presented below are key similarities and differences between GAAP and international accounting standards (referred to hereafter as IFRS), as they relate to introductory financial accounting. As you will note, there are many similarities in the two systems. The Securities and Exchange Commission (SEC) has proposed a roadmap for publicly traded U.S. companies to adopt international accounting standards. While some smaller U.S. companies will not be required to switch until as late as 2016, some large companies will be allowed to adopt international standards (IFRS) as early as 2009. As they arise, additional international accounting developments that relate to introductory financial accounting are provided at the Student Companion portion of the book's website.

Topic	Similarities	Differences
Chapter 1: Introduction to Financial Statements		
Financial Statements	The primary types of financial statements required by international accounting standards (IFRS) and U.S. accounting standards (GAAP) are the same.	In practice, some format differences do exist in presentations commonly employed by IFRS companies compared to GAAP companies.
Chapter 2: A Further Look at Financial Statements		
Balance Sheet	GAAP and IFRS both require a balance sheet. The content and presentation of an IFRS balance sheet is similar to the one used for GAAP.	IFRS statements may report property, plant, and equipment first in the balance sheet. Some companies report the subtotal "net assets," which equals total assets minus total liabilities.
	Looking to the future: The IASB and the FASB are working on a project to converge their standards related to financial statement presentation. A key feature of the proposed framework for financial statement presentation is that each of the statements will be organized in the same format—to separate an entity's financing activities from its operating and other (investing) activities, and to further separate financing activities.	
Standard Setting Environment	IFRS includes the standards developed by the IASB. GAAP includes primarily FASB standards. The Boards have similar processes for creating new standards. In recent years they have worked closely together on reducing differences in existing standards and on creating new accounting standards jointly.	In many IFRS countries, the primary users of financial statements are private investors, tax authorities, or central government planners. In the United States, capital market participants (investors and creditors) have driven accounting standard formulation. IFRS tends to be simpler and less stringent (principle-based) in its accounting and disclosure requirements. GAAP is more detailed (rule-based).
	Looking to the future: The SEC eliminated a rule that required foreign companies that trade shares in U.S. markets to reconcile their accounting with GAAP. The SEC also is seeking comment on a proposal to allow some large U.S. companies to prepare financial statements using IFRS as early as 2009, and to require all publicly traded U.S. companies to use IFRS no later than 2016.	
Conceptual Framework	IASB and FASB frameworks are very similar: both frameworks are organized using the same concepts (objectives, elements, qualitative characteristics, etc.)	The IFRS conceptual framework puts more emphasis on accountability (referred to as stewardship) than does the GAAP conceptual framework.
	Looking to the future: The IASB and the FASB have a joint project to develop a common conceptual framework. This framework is based on the existing IASB framework and the FASB's conceptual framework.	
Chapter 3: The Accounting Information System		
Recording Process	Both IFRS and GAAP rely on the same double entry system to record transactions	GAAP is supported by much more detailed and stringent internal control rules that are designed to ensure the accuracy and reliability of the recording and reporting process.
Chapter 4: Accrual Accounting Concepts		
Revenue Recognition	The general concepts and principles used for revenue recognition are similar between GAAP and IFRS. A specific standard exists for revenue recognition under IFRS.	IFRS defines revenue to include both revenues and gains. GAAP provides separate definitions for revenues and gains. GAAP has a much more detailed collection of standards on revenue recognition than IFRS.
	Looking to the future: The FASB and IASB are working on a joint project to develop new revenue recognition standards.	
Chapter 5: Merchandising Operations and the Multiple-Step Income Statement		
Income Statement	The IFRS and GAAP accounting systems (perpetual and periodic) are essentially the same in recording sale transactions. GAAP and IFRS both require a statement of income. The content and presentation of an IFRS income statement is similar to the one used for GAAP.	Unlike GAAP, IFRS does not follow a single-step or multiple–step approach.
	Looking to the future: As indicated earlier, the IASB and FASB are working on a project that would rework the structure of the financial statements. This structure would use three categories mentioned earlier (operating, investing, and financing) consistently across the statements.	

Summary Table of International Accounting Issues (continued)

Topic	Similarities	Differences
Chapter 6: Reporting and Analyzing Inventory		
Inventories	Under IFRS and GAAP, who owns the goods—goods in transit, consigned goods—as well as the costs to include in inventory are essentially accounted for the same. FIFO and average-cost are the only two acceptable cost flow assumptions permitted under IFRS. Both sets of GAAP permit specific identification where appropriate.	GAAP permits the use of LIFO for inventory valuation. IFRS prohibits the use of LIFO. In the lower-of-cost-or-market test for inventory valuation, IFRS defines *market* in a different way than GAAP. In GAAP, if inventory is written down it cannot be written up if it subsequently increases in value. Under IFRS, the write-down may be reversed.

Looking to the future: One convergence issue that will be difficult to resolve relates to the use of the LIFO cost flow assumption. As indicated, IFRS specifically prohibits its use. Conversely, LIFO is widely used in the United States because of its favorable tax advantages. In addition, many argue that from a financial reporting point of view, LIFO provides a better matching of current costs against revenue and therefore enables companies to compute a more realistic income.

Topic	Similarities	Differences
Chapter 7: Fraud, Internal Control, and Cash		
Cash	The accounting and reporting related to cash is essentially the same under both IFRS and GAAP. In addition, the definition used for cash equivalents is essentially the same as well.	
Internal Control	All companies, whether preparing statements under GAAP or IFRS, need good internal controls.	Recently passed Sarbanes-Oxley (SOX) internal control standards apply only to large public companies listed on U.S. exchanges. There is continuing debate over whether foreign issuers should have to comply with this extra layer of regulation.

Looking to the future: Some critics of the SOX provisions attribute a decline in initial public offerings (IPOs) to the increased cost of complying with the internal control rules. Others argue that growth in non-U.S. markets is a natural consequence of general globalization of capital flows. In any event, the movement toward international accounting standards will necessitate increased international cooperation regarding internal control regulations and auditing standards.

Topic	Similarities	Differences
Chapter 8: Reporting and Analyzing Receivables		
Receivables	The basic accounting for receivables, such as the use of allowance accounts, how to record discounts, and factoring are essentially the same between IFRS and GAAP. Both IFRS and GAAP allow a so called "fair value option" which gives companies the choice of reporting certain financial instruments, such as receivables, at fair value.	IFRS and GAAP for the fair value option are similar but not identical. For example, there are differences in qualifying criteria and in the financial instruments covered.

Looking to the future: Both the IASB and the FASB have indicated that they believe that financial statements would be more useful if companies reported all financial instruments, such as receivables, at fair value. The fair value option for recording financial instruments is an important step in moving closer to fair value accounting.

Topic	Similarities	Differences
Chapter 9: Reporting and Analyzing Long-Lived Assets		
Property, Plant, and Equipment	IFRS views depreciation as an allocation of cost over an asset's life and permits the same depreciation methods (straight-line, accelerated, units-of-production) as GAAP.	IFRS permits in certain situations that property plant and equipment can be written up to fair value, which is not permitted by GAAP. IFRS allows "component depreciation" where significant parts of a fixed asset can be depreciated using different estimated lives.

Looking to the future: The IFRS provision allowing asset revaluations and the issues related to the use of fair value for the measurement of long-lived assets represent major obstacles to convergence.

Topic	Similarities	Differences
Intangible Assets	Under IFRS, as in GAAP, the costs associated with research and development are segregated into the two components. Costs in the research phase are always expensed under both IFRS and GAAP.	While both GAAP and IFRS require that research costs be expensed, under IFRS, costs in the development phase are capitalized once certain technical conditions are met. There are differences in how the amount of a loss due to the impairment of an asset is determined. IFRS allows reversal of impairment losses when there has been a change in economic conditions or in the expected use of the asset. Under GAAP, impairment losses cannot be reversed.

Looking to the future: IFRS permits more recognition of intangibles compared to GAAP. Thus, it will be challenging to develop converged standards for intangible assets, given the long-standing prohibition in GAAP on capitalizing development costs.